WHERE *to* SKI AND *SnoWboard* 2006

The 1,000 Best Winter Sports Resorts in Europe and North America

Edited by
Chris Gill
and
Dave Watts

NortonWood

Published in Great Britain by
NortonWood Publishing
The Old Forge
Norton St Philip
Bath BA2 7LW
United Kingdom

tel 01373 835208
e-mail w10@wtss.co.uk

Editors Chris Gill and Dave Watts
Assistant editors Mandy Crook,
Catherine Weakley, Leigh Thompson,
Henry Druce, Wendy-Jane King,
Sheila Reid
Australia/NZ editor Bronwen Gora
Contributors Chris Allan,
Alan Coulson, Nicky Holford,
James Hooke, Eric Jackson,
Tim Perry, Ian Porter, Adam Ruck,
Helena Wiesner, Fraser Wilkin
Research assistant Alex Gill

Advertising manager Sam Palmer
Advertising sales Sian Blackmar

Design by Val Fox
Production by Guide Editors
Contents photos generally
by Snowpix.com / Chris Gill
Production manager Ian Stratford
Proof-readers Sally Vince,
Robin Campbell
Printed and bound in Italy
by Officine Grafiche Calderini SpA

10 9 8 7 6 5 4 3 2 1

ISBN 0 9536371 7 4

A CIP catalogue entry for this book is
available from the British Library.

Book trade sales are handled by
Portfolio Books Ltd
Unit 5, Perivale Industrial Park
Horsenden Lane South
Greenford UB6 7RL

tel 020 8997 9000
fax 020 8997 9097
e-mail sales@portfoliobooks.com

**Individual copies of the book can be
bought by calling:
01373 835208**

This edition published 2005
Copyright (text and illustrations)
© Chris Gill and Dave Watts 2005

The right of Chris Gill and Dave Watts
to be identified as Authors of this
Work has been asserted by them in
accordance with the Copyright,
Design and Patents Act 1988.

Contents

Resort chapters

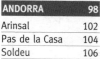

4

5

About this book

It's simply the best

Where to Ski and Snowboard is the best guide to winter sports resorts that you could buy. With this tenth edition, the gap between this and rival guides is opened wider than ever. Here's why:

- With every new edition we aim to take a step forward. This year, we have new chapters on areas in Austria, France and Bulgaria, and we have added 32 pages to the book – over the ten editions we have expanded it from 512 to 736 pages.

- By making the most of technology we are able to publish at the right time while going to press later and later – so we can include the late-breaking news that makes the book **up to date for the season ahead**. When we started in the early 1990s, we went to press in June; four years ago it was mid-July; this year, it's 5 August, only a month ahead of publication day. As late as 2 August we were able to include news that construction has started on America's highest chair-lift, to the top of Breckenridge's Peak 8.

- We work hard to make our information **reader-friendly**, with clearly structured text, comparative ratings and no-nonsense verdicts for the main aspects of each resort.

- We don't hesitate to express **critical views**. We learned our craft at Consumers' Association, where Chris became editor of *Holiday Which?* magazine and Dave became editor of *Which?* itself – so a consumerist attitude comes naturally to us.

- Our resort chapters give an **unrivalled level of detail** – including scale plans of each major resort and all the facts you need about them.

- We benefit enormously from the **reports that hundreds of readers send in on the resorts they visit**. (The 100 best reports are rewarded by a free copy of the book, and many of our best regular reporters get a free week's lift pass. Prove your worth by sending us useful reports, and you too could ski for free.)

- We use **colour printing** fully – this year more than ever. We include not only piste maps for every major resort but also scores of photographs, chosen not just to add colour but to allow you to see for yourself what the resorts are like.

Our ability to keep on improving *Where to Ski and Snowboard* is largely due to the support of our advertisers – many of whom have been with us since the first edition in 1994. We are grateful for that support, and hope our readers will in turn support our advertisers.

We are uncompromising in our commitment to helping you, our readers, to make an informed choice; we're confident that you'll find this edition the best yet. Enjoy your skiing and riding this season.

Chris Gill and Dave Watts
Norton St Philip, 5 August 2005

The editorial

This is the 10th edition of *Where to Ski and Snowboard*. We allowed ourselves a look back over the years in the last edition, which marked our 10th birthday (a discrepancy explained by the fact that we didn't publish annually in the early years) – so in this year's introduction to the book we're reverting to our traditional habit of sounding off about anything that catches the editorial eye. There is one difference, though: for the first time, we are making awards to certain resorts (and one tour operator who keeps us amused). Details on page 17.

FAST LIFTS RULE, OK?

We sometimes find ourselves in a resort with lots of slow old chair-lifts and drags, and inadvertently find ourselves grumbling within earshot of some local or, even worse, someone responsible for marketing the place. A little sermon follows, on the merits of riding up the mountain slowly, so as to appreciate the environment, and on the 'fact' that fast lifts create crowds on the pistes.

We're not very receptive to that line of thought. We appreciate the mountain environment as much as anyone, but we prefer to appreciate it from a sheltered restaurant terrace or a sun-baked rock, not from some freezing chair swinging in a blizzard. Broadly, crowds on pistes are confined to Europe and caused partly by resort authorities building (or permitting) too many beds at the foot of the mountains and partly by not building enough pistes to handle the numbers that the lifts can shift. In North America, the main culprits are Whistler and Vail, and there are plenty of uncrowded resorts with a higher proportion of fast lifts than either of those possesses – Beaver Creek, Keystone and Telluride, to name some US examples. (There's more on piste crowding later in the editorial.)

Modern fast lifts – gondolas, cable-cars, funiculars, detachable chairs – go at anything from three to six times the speed of drags and fixed-grip chair-lifts. It's only by riding fast lifts that you stand any chance of spending a significant proportion of the skiing day actually skiing. Isn't that what we go on holiday to do?

For years, we've marked fast lifts on the piste maps included in each of our main resort chapters – though in the case of chair-lifts we perhaps haven't made it sufficiently clear that it is *only* fast lifts that are marked with a chair symbol. Now, we are pleased to announce another way to avoid resorts where you will spend most of your day riding lifts: a fast lifts star rating. We've put it at the top of the list of ratings at the start of each chapter, where you can't miss it. And we've included it in our comparative table of ratings, just before the resorts section of the book.

The ratings are based on working out what percentage of lifts in each resort fall into the fast category. We've tried to weed out of the figures things like glacier lifts that are open only in summer, moving carpets on nursery slopes (a fast version might be quite amusing, but we doubt it), cable-cars that get you up to the slopes and remote cable-cars that run once an hour for the amusement of off-piste adventurers. The resulting percentages range from 0% in Ste-Foy – one of the few places where we're happy to ride slow lifts – to an amazing 62% in Ischgl.

The most striking thing about the results is how many Austrian resorts do well – and how few French ones. Three Austrian resorts get **✶✶✶✶✶**, but no French ones. The French showing is a bit better at the **✶✶✶✶** level. But then at the opposite extreme all but one of the resorts scoring **✶** are French. *Quelle surprise!*

Actually, the real surprise is that this bunch of under-investing resorts includes high-rent Megève. It does come at the top of the **✶** category, and we were tempted to massage it into our **✶✶** category, but our experience of skiing there twice last season did nothing to encourage that. It is definitely a resort that needs major investment in new lifts. Fast.

VIETATO FUMARE

We visited quite a few Italian resorts this year, and got something of a shock. No, it wasn't the affordable prices or the wonderfully good grooming – we're used to those. It was the crystal-clear atmosphere in the restaurants, the mountain restaurants and even the bars. The Italians have banned smoking in all public interior spaces, and they have made it work. Basically, smoking in such places has simply stopped. In Italy, of all places. Amazing.

Why can't the French do the same? We are reminded of a conversation with the Gauloise-smoking *patron* of a bar in the French Alps a few years back, shortly after introduction of the much less stringent rules there requiring separate spaces for smokers and non-smokers. When we pointed out in a jocular way that he seemed to be ignoring the law, he affected surprise, removed the fag from his lips and gestured along the bar to a sign, a good two metres away, saying 'éspace non-fumeur'. He took another drag, and shook his head. 'There is a law', he growled, 'but it is just ... on paper!'

OLYMPIC BLUES

It would not cross our minds to visit a ski resort during the Olympic Winter Games – even a World Cup race can seriously interfere with holidaymakers' access to lifts and runs. But post-2012-award euphoria might tempt some people to get in the Olympic habit early. Our advice would be to be wary, and to do some careful research into how the resorts will be operating during the Olympics. Security precautions will presumably be tighter than ever, following the terrorist atrocities of summer 2005. The resorts are Sestriere, Sansicario, Sauze d'Oulx and Bardonecchia. The dates are 10 to 26 February.

MAPPING OUT LUNCH

We are not ashamed to admit that we like a decent lunch when we're skiing. We know that views on this differ, and if you are of the 'pinch a bread roll and an apple from the breakfast buffet' persuasion, please accept our apologies for writing about mountain restaurants at such length. And skip the rest of this short item.

We want simply to applaud the growing tendency in Swiss resorts – Flims, St Moritz, Lenzerheide, for example – to include on the piste map a brief guide to the character of each mountain restaurant. In general, you get a little photo of the restaurant plus a short word-picture, which if you are lucky will be in English. Even if it's not, you can pick up clues about the style of each place.

We find these guides enormously helpful, and wish more resorts provided them. We thought we might get hold of 100 maps from Lenzerheide, for example, and send them to 100 other lift companies

GET YOUR MONEY BACK
when you book a holiday

You can reclaim the price of Where to Ski and Snowboard when you book a winter sports holiday for the 2005/06 or 2006/07 seasons. All you have to do is book the holiday through the specialist ski travel agency Ski Solutions.

Ski Solutions is Britain's original and leading ski travel agency. You can buy whatever kind of holiday you want through them.

Ski Solutions sells the package holidays offered by all the bonded tour operators in Britain (apart from the very few who are direct-sell only). And if that isn't enough choice, they can tailor-make a holiday, based on any form of travel and any kind of accommodation. No one is better placed to find you what you want than Ski Solutions.

Making a claim
Claiming your refund is easy. At the back of the book are two vouchers. When you make your definite booking, tell Ski Solutions that you want to take up this offer. Cut out the vouchers and send one to Ski Solutions and the other to Where to Ski and Snowboard (the addresses are on the vouchers).

Phone Ski Solutions on
020 7471 7700

Get next year's edition **free!**
by reporting on your holiday

There are too many resorts for us to visit them all every year, and too many hotels, bars and mountain restaurants for us to see. So we are very keen to encourage more readers to send in reports on their holiday experiences. As usual, we'll be giving 100 copies of the next edition to the writers of the best reports.

There are five main kinds of feedback we need:
- what you particularly **liked and disliked** about the resort
- what aspects of the resort came as a **surprise** to you
- your other suggestions for **changes to our evaluation** of the resort – changes we should make to the ratings, verdicts, descriptions etc
- your experience of **queues** and other weaknesses in the lift system, and the **ski school** and associated childcare arrangements
- your feedback on **individual facilities** in the resort – the hotels, bars, restaurants (including mountain restaurants), nightspots, equipment shops, sports facilities etc.

You can send your reports to us in three ways. In order of preference, they are:
- by e-mail to: reports@wtss.co.uk (don't forget to give us your postal address)
- word-processed and printed on paper

Consistently helpful reporters are invited to become 'resort observers', which means that when possible we'll arrange free lift passes in your holiday resorts, in exchange for detailed reports on those resorts.

Our postal address is:
Where to Ski and Snowboard, FREEPOST SN815,
The Old Forge, Norton St Philip, Bath BA2 7ZZ

to encourage them to do the same. If you are of the 'start early and finish late but make sure you get in a decent lunch along the way' persuasion, watch this space for a report on the response next year.

DO YOU REALLY WANT TO GO SKIING THIS AFTERNOON?
Serious though we are about lunch, we are not complete degenerates – we do like to ski in the afternoon. The pic on this page shows an arrangement apparently designed for people who have found themselves in a ski resort by mistake: sun-loungers that resemble hospital beds, but with the added convenience of built-in tables so that you can nibble at your rösti and slurp your weisswein in complete comfort.

   We encountered them in Arosa, Switzerland, a resort where if you are feeling really weak you can be ferried to many of the mountain restaurants by horse-drawn sleigh. Disgraceful.

THE IDEAL MAP
Talking about inclusion of restaurants on piste maps has led us on to some more general thoughts about them. Piste maps should:
• Be primarily designed to show each mountain face clearly – not to act as a marketing tool by showing a huge ski region in a single view
• Be big enough to be clear, but no bigger
• Be designed to fold instantly to a small size
• Be moderately resistant to mountain weather
• Not have acres of space devoted to lift pass prices or other stuff that should be in a separate brochure
• Specify operating times of key lifts
• Include relevant bus and train timetables, at least in outline
• If it's not otherwise clear, mark the direction in which each slope descends and each lift rises
• Include clear explanations of every kind of run marked on the map – particularly of 'ski routes' or 'ski runs' other than proper pistes
• Use the same lift/piste names/numbers that are used on the ground
• Include SOS phone numbers
• Clearly show which lifts are fast and which are not, and ideally show ride-times of key lifts
• Show forest areas accurately, so that you can predict which runs will be best in bad weather
• Include a guide to mountain restaurants (see above).

Who goes to Arosa to ski? →

We don't see much evidence that lift companies are generally getting closer to our notion of perfection, or indeed that they think very much about these issues at all. In Flims, for example, they have just stopped giving lift ride-times, which are a great aid to planning. In Les Arcs we have had complaints about 'self-ripping' piste maps. Cervinia and Zermatt have at last produced one shared map covering clearly both sides of their linked area and the interface between them – and Cervinia prints it on an excellent little Z-folded map of credit-card size. Zermatt, though, prints the same thing ten times bigger, on a sheet that takes two people to handle. Do these people ever go out in a wind and use their own maps? Silly question.

AFTER TEN EDITIONS: SIGNS OF PROGRESS

After ten editions of complaining about gross inadequacies of several otherwise world-class resorts, we at last feel we're getting somewhere. Last season Verbier finally replaced its awful on-mountain signposting; the new signs at least relate directly to the piste map (even if they still refuse to name or number pistes). And Val-d'Isère regraded two of its tricky runs back to the resort, one from blue to red and one from red to black. We look forward to their renaming the world's most difficult green down to La Daille (it's called Verte but is really Bleu or even Rouge).

BUT CHALLENGES REMAIN

We got very excited earlier this summer when we got wind of a major step forward in St Anton: construction of a new piste to relieve the dangerous overcrowding in the Steissbachtal, used by most people on the mountain to get back to the village. Sadly, the reports were exaggerated: we now understand that nothing more than improvements to the run below the Steissbachtal are planned.

We wonder whether the people who run St Anton, or other Alpine resorts with severely overcrowded pistes, ever go out on to the mountain to try their own product. The problem is getting more serious with every year that goes by – and we see no sign of any strategy to deal with it.

One of the reasons we always enjoy our annual outing to north America is that there is so much more space on the trails. It's like driving in remote parts of Continental Europe, which brings into sharp relief how crowded now are in the UK. But motoring isn't primarily about pleasure, whereas skiing primarily is. In the Alps in high season, the pleasure is often greatly diminished.

POND-CROSSING NEWS

If you are tempted to try north America (and there are many other reasons to think of doing so, apart from the lack of crowds), this might be a good year to do it. Sister companies Thomson and Crystal are operating twice-weekly charter flights direct to Denver. This means that British Airways' grip on direct flights to Colorado will be loosened, and may mean that it has to drop its fares to compete with the charter flights. It certainly should mean that package prices from the companies using the flights should be highly competitive.

READERS' FAVOURITES

Not for the first time, we have analysed readers' recent travels as indicated by the reports we receive. We seem to be seeing an interesting trend. A few years ago we would get countless reports on

Austria.
You've arrived!

www.austria.info/uk

Pinguin-Design © anaplus

the standard keen-skier destinations and lots on currently high-profile destinations such as Banff (which came top of the poll in 1997). This year, the spread seems to be much more even, and the resorts that have generated the most reports are not the ones you might expect (Val-d'Isère, Verbier and Méribel, for example). This could of course be a side-effect of our recent campaign to attract more reports on less popular resorts. But the list does not consist of really unusual resorts. Here is the top 12, in order of the number of reports we received:

1 St Anton	7 Zermatt
2 Les Arcs	8 Courchevel
3 Cervinia	9 Morzine
4 Val-Thorens	10 Chamonix
5 La Plagne	11 Lake Louise
6 Monterosa Ski	12 Tignes

We wonder whether the Vanoise Express link between Les Arcs and La Plagne has anything to do with the apparent popularity of those two. The popularity of Monterosa Ski could be the result of our evident enthusiasm for the place. Anyway, we thank all readers who sent in reports. Please keep them flowing, telling us about your travels in 2005/06 – see page 10.

PACKAGE FAVOURITES

The mega resorts do of course figure prominently in another regular bit of analysis we do, to establish how many operators go to each resort. We do this mainly to look at the bottom of the table – to see which resorts have doubled their tally from four to eight operators in the last year, for example – but of more general interest is the top twelve, which looks like this:

1 Méribel 67	7 Les Arcs 42
2 Val-d'Isère 65	8 La Plagne 42
3 Courchevel 59	9 Morzine 41
4 Chamonix 49	10 Verbier 41
5 Tignes 46	11 Whistler 40
6 St Anton 42	12 Alpe-d'Huez 35

A decade ago the list wouldn't have looked much different, except that Whistler came much higher and St Anton much lower – and that Morzine was nowhere in the list, its place occupied by Zermatt.

PICTURE THIS

You may notice one or two unfamiliar names in our picture credits this year. They are the names of readers who have kindly offered us the use of their holiday snaps. We're very grateful for their generosity – resort tourist offices are, with some conspicuous exceptions, not very good at providing informative, high-quality photographs for reproduction, so we are pleased to have alternative sources.

It's much easier to make use of readers' pictures now that digital cameras are commonly used. We don't have to worry about looking after and returning the originals, and there is very little work involved in preparing a picture for the page. If you'd like to see your photos in print, get in touch next season. We're planning some sort of prize for the best picture submitted.

TEN-YEAR AWARDS

After our first ten editions and many repeat visits to all these resorts, we make the following first decade awards:

BEST EUROPEAN RESORT – ZERMATT

Unbeatable combination of scenery, extensive high, snow-sure slopes, away-from-it-all runs, wonderful mountain restaurants and charming car-free resort

BEST NORTH AMERICAN RESORT – ASPEN

Four separate mountains that offer something for every ability level. Plus a lovely restored 19th-century gold-mining town

BEST SNOWMAKING OPERATION IN EUROPE – SELLA RONDA

The main runs can open on purely man-made snow, and reporters often tell of skiing strips of white between bare fields

MOST UNDERGRADED RUN – VERTE IN VAL-D'ISERE

This narrow green run to La Daille can be crowded and a mogul-field in parts by the afternoon. Many Italian resorts would proudly claim it as a black

MOST OUTDATED LIFT SYSTEM – MEGEVE

Only around one in seven lifts in Megève is high-speed, an astonishingly low number for such an upmarket resort

MOST UP-TO-DATE LIFT SYSTEM – ISCHGL

Over half the lifts (over 60% actually) in Ischgl are high-speed. The resort deserves to be better known on the British market

DECADE-LONG PROGRESS – VERBIER

After us banging on for 10 years, Verbier has at last redone its mountain signposting and linked it to its piste map so you can find your way around more easily. This is the latest in a series of welcome improvements, which include building major new lifts to cut queues and improving grooming, snowmaking and its ski schools. There's still a way to go (see the Verbier chapter), but we think Verbier's progress deserves recognition

BEST NO-BULLSHIT BROCHURE – YSE

Our only non-resort award goes to YSE, the specialist Val-d'Isère tour operator. John Yates-Smith has for many years written a no-bullshit brochure that amuses readers and tries to describe the bad points as well as the good points of YSE's chalets. We always look forward to receiving our copy

ANNUAL AWARDS

BEST NEW EUROPEAN RESORT DEVELOPMENT 2005 – KITZBUHEL

Last season Kitzbühel linked its two main ski areas with a new mountain-top gondola, which means you no longer have to ski down to the valley to get to the most snow-sure slopes above Pass Thurn (and no longer have to catch a bus back)

BEST NEW NORTH AMERICAN DEVELOPMENT 2005 – WHISTLER

For 2004/05 Whistler extended its terrain by 1,100 acres, which includes 700 acres of formerly out-of-bounds terrain in Flute Bowl and four new 1500m/ 4,920ft vertical runs from Whistler Peak to Creekside

BIGGEST LET-DOWN OF 2005 – MURREN

The cable-car out of one of our favourite Swiss resorts, Mürren, was closed from January till March for repairs, meaning that most of the runs (and all the best ones) were inaccessible. The annual Inferno race also had to be run on a dramatically shortened course. What happened to Swiss efficiency there?

What's new?

New lifts and other major developments in top resorts

In this chapter we summarise major developments in ski resorts last season and next. Each major resort chapter has a 'News' panel near the start; you'll find many more news items in those panels.

ANDORRA

LA MASSANA BECOMES A SKI RESORT

The long-awaited gondola from La Massana to Pal is now open, making the valley town quite a sensible base for skiers.

SOLDEU REPLACEMENTS

El Tarter, secondary base for the Soldeu slopes, is much more attractive now that it has a serious access lift in the shape of a 10-person gondola to Riba Escorxada. The high-altitude link to Canillo has been upgraded from a drag to a chair.

AUSTRIA

ALPBACH GETS MAJOR UPGRADES

The backwater hamlet of Inneralpbach will be a more practical base after access to Wiedersbergerhorn is transformed by a new eight-seat gondola replacing two successive slow double chairs. Inneralpbach will also see a quad chair replacing the Galtenberglift drag.

ISCHGL CONTINUES TO ERADICATE DRAG-LIFTS

Two six-packs with covers were installed last season in Ischgl, consolidating the resort's position at the top of our fast lifts league table. In Galtür there is a new eight-seat gondola to Alpkogel.

KITZBÜHEL'S AREA IS STRETCHED IN TWO DIRECTIONS

The 30-person jumbo-gondola at Kitzbühel, linking Pengelstein to Wurzhöhe above Jochberg, has created a much slicker link with the relatively snow-sure Resterhöhe sector above Pass Thurn. This season, the Westendorf ski area is to be extended to meet (more or less) the Kitzbühel area at Aschau, with an eight-seat gondola from there up to the Gampen sector of Westendorf. Meanwhile a new gondola will give access to Resterhöhe from near Mittersill, in the valley to the south, at the opposite extremity of the area.

MORE FAST LIFTS IN SAALBACH/HINTERGLEMM

Two old T-bars to Kohlmaiskopf and Bründlkopf above Saalbach will give way to fast six-seat chairs with covers and heated seats. And a new eight-seat gondola is due to replace the old double chair to Hochalm at the Lengau end of Hinterglemm's skiing. This brings the resort's gondola count to nine and fast chair count to 12, scoring highly on our new fast lifts rating.

WILDSCHÖNAU REPLACES DRAG-LIFTS

A second six-pack will replace the two top drag-lifts on Schatzberg, making the highest slopes in the area more easily accessible.

FRANCE

ALPE-D'HUEZ BEGINS UPGRADES

For 2005/06 a six-pack will supplant the three drag-lifts at Les Bergers. The Romains lift will be removed and a second tow added to the Rif Nel, improving access to the beginner slopes there.

First Choice

make the right choice
this winter

Chamonix link

Last season a new eight-person gondola opened at Vallorcine, linking the village to the slopes of Le Tour – so if you ski the long blue or off-piste runs down to Vallorcine you no longer have to catch the train and a bus to get back to a lift.

Six-pack for Courchevel

The lovely red runs at the far Courchevel 1650 end of the Three Valleys will now be skiable repeatedly using a new fast six-seat Chapelets chair instead of the slow Signal and Bel Air drags.

New link extends slopes of Megève

For 2004/05 the slopes of Le Jaillet were linked to the slopes of La Torraz above Le Plan, near La Giettaz. The link itself is rather hard work, but there are rewarding slopes at the end of it. An incidental benefit is the installation of a fast chair – one of the few in Megève – serving good intermediate runs at Le Christomet.

Pressure eased at Méribel

Last season a six-pack replaced the slow Plan de l'Homme quad from Méribel to halfway up Tougnète, which has taken pressure off the Tougnète gondola in the morning peak.

La Plagne links with Les Arcs improved both ways

The links to and from the Vanoise Express have been speeded up. For 2004/05 access from the cable-car towards La Plagne was improved by two new six-pack chairs. For 2005/06 the Arpette chair from Plagne-Bellecôte towards Montchavin and the Vanoise Express will be upgraded to an eight-seater, which should alleviate queues here.

Serre-Chevalier mid-mountain improvements

Two new six-seat chairs are being installed for 2005/06 in place of the Clos Gauthier chair above Fréjus and the Foret and Rouge drags above L'Aravet. Serre-Che still needs more lift investment, though.

New piste to La Tania

The attraction of the village for beginners and timid intermediates should be transformed this winter by a new green piste from Courchevel 1850 back through the trees into the village.

Tignes continues to catch up

The long overdue modernisation of lifts taking you up the western side of Tignes continues, with two six-packs replacing slow lifts for 2004/05 and another six-pack planned for 2005/06.

Yet another valley lift for Val-d'Isère

A new six-pack will go from the roadside at Le Laisinant up above the top of the cable-car from Le Fornet, so you no longer have to catch a bus if you ski one of the lovely runs down to Le Laisinant. It will also form an alternative way up the mountain in the morning.

ITALY

Bormio

The 2005 World Championships triggered worthwhile lift improvements on Bormio's upper slopes – for 2004/05 two fast quads with covers replaced four old lifts serving Cima Bianca.

Monterosa Ski continues its development

A new eight-seat gondola is planned above Champoluc to replace the two slow chairs up to Colle Sarezza. This should reduce queues and speed access to the upper slopes. For 2004/05 Alagna was linked to Gressoney properly: a cable-car opened between Pianalunga and Passo dei Salati, with a red piste back down.

Sauze d'Oulx, Sansicario and Sestriere reap Olympic benefits

The imminent Olympics have led to some major changes here. A fast quad is expected to replace the extremely antiquated chair between Sauze and Clotes this season – a much needed improvement. A two-stage gondola opened between the valley (near Cesana) and Sansicario for 2004/05. For 2005/06 a new eight-seat gondola is being built from Sestriere to Monte Fraiteve for access to Sansicario.

SWITZERLAND

Lagalb links at St Moritz

For last season a one-way link was created from the Diavolezza sector to the Lagalb sector, across the road. A new red piste leads to a short lift bringing you to the Lagalb base station. Since Diavolezza gets the morning sun and Lagalb gets the afternoon sun, the fact that it's one-way shouldn't matter much.

Verbier's 'chondola' makes life easier for early intermediates

For 2005/06 a major new lift – a 'chondola', which consists of gondola cabins and chairs on the same fast lift – is planned between Les Ruinettes and La Chaux via the ridge at Côte de Brunet. It will mean that early intermediates will be able to get to and from the gentle runs at La Chaux and then the glacier runs at Col des Gentianes by riding the lift, without having to tackle crowded, steep red runs.

And a 'chondola' for Zermatt too

For 2005/06 the old Sunnegga-Blauherd gondola, at the heart of Zermatt's busiest sector, is to be replaced by a 'chondola' with eight-seat cabins and six-seat chairs.

What's new?

23

SKI SOLUTIONS

Britain's original and largest specialist ski travel agency

- the first and only place you need to call to book your ski holiday

Call SKI SOLUTIONS first, rather than ringing round lots of tour operators - it's an instant short cut to your ideal ski holiday. Start the snowball rolling by giving us a rough idea of what you're looking for:

- *How many in your party?*
- *Are there any children? What ages?*
- *What levels of skier?*
- *Traditional or modern resort?*
- *Which departure airport?*
- *What standard of accommodation?*

Our experienced staff will gently "cross-examine" you to reveal any personal preferences. We will then research a shortlist of suitable holidays and will send this together with relevant brochures and other information. (If you're in a hurry, we can fax or e-mail these details to you.)

Or, if you are looking for the ideal chalet for your party, visit our chalet-search service at www.skisolutions.com. Here you will be able to browse through hundreds of chalets in Europe and North America, compile a shorlist and, if you like, e-mail this to your group. Once you've made your final selection, contact us by e-mail or phone.

We save you time, effort and money by costing each option exactly, taking into account all the various supplements and discounts. (We spend our lives immersed in brochures, so we are experts on the small print.) Without any obligation on your part, we can "hold" the holidays that interest you for a couple of days, while you make up your mind.

After further discussions with you we will then book the holiday of your choice. The price of the holiday will be exactly as in the brochure: our service is absolutely FREE.

Between us, the 25 staff of SKI SOLUTIONS have skied over 100 resorts on both sides of the Atlantic and we have a first-hand up-to-date knowledge of the hotels, chalets and apartments offered by most of the operators in these places.

We are a ski travel agency as opposed to a ski tour operator.
When you call us you immediately place at your disposal a choice
of thousands of holidays offered by a wide variety of different
reputable, fully bonded tour operator, both large and small.

We sell you the holiday you want,
not the holiday we need to sell

SKI
SOLUTIONS.com **020 7471 7700**

84 Pembroke Road, Kensington, London W8 6NX fax 020 7471 7701 www.skisolutions.com

CREDIT: OT Val Thorens / B. Boissiere

United States

Third fast chair at Alta

For 2004/05 the Collins fast quad from the Wildcat base replaced two old chairs, speeding the way up the mountain first thing in the morning and cutting out an uphill walk to the lift.

New terrain opened up at Aspen

A new triple chair called Deep Temerity will open at Aspen Highlands for 2005/06, serving new advanced and expert terrain below Highland Bowl and Steeplechase.

Breckenridge's record high to new terrain

Work started in August 2005 on a new high-speed quad called Imperial Express, which will run from the top of Chair 6 to just below the top of Peak 8. This will be North America's highest chairlift and will open up 400 acres of steep terrain previously accessible only by a 45-minute hike. When we went to press the resort was 'optimistic the new lift will be ready to ride this winter'.

All change at Jackson Hole

For 2005/06 a new triple chair-lift, Sweetwater, is planned between the upper beginner slopes and the Casper Bowl chair, giving direct access to the intermediate terrain there. This will also be the last season for Jackson's famous 'Tram', which has reached retirement age – so if you want one last ride, get there this season.

Canada

Stay up at Big White

For 2004/05 a two-person chair-lift opened to serve the steep Cliff area, so you don't have to go to the bottom after each run. A big new terrain-park was built above the village, served by a new two-person chair and by Big White's first snowmaking.

Village takes shape at Kicking Horse

The first phase of the new resort village opened last season and for 2005/06 there should be three small, friendly B&Bs and two bigger condo-hotels as well as self-catering lodging. But there are still very few bars and restaurants and you should expect very quiet evenings.

Keep warm at Lake Louise and scare yourself at Sunshine

Last season the Friendly Giant quad from the base area and the Eagle chair were replaced by the area's first gondola, the six-seat Grizzly Express, which will keep you warmer than the uncovered chairs. At nearby Sunshine Village a second very steep area called the Wild West opened on Goat's Eye.

More terrain at Whistler

For 2004/05 another 700 acres of formerly out-of-bounds terrain in Flute Bowl opened (you have to hike into and out of it). And four new runs with a vertical descent of over 1500m/4,920ft from the Peak down to Whistler Creekside were due to open, but poor snow conditions curtailed their use.

Bulgaria

Bansko improves

For 2004/05 two further fast quad chairs were put in, extending the slopes and improving access to the Shiligarnika lift base from the top of the gondola at Bunderishka. This consolidates Bansko's position as much the most impressive resort in Bulgaria.

The cost of skiing

Good news – holiday costs have fallen in real terms

by **Chris Allan**

Skiing can seriously damage your wealth – but not as much as it used to do. Taking account of inflation, the cost of holiday packages to many resorts has actually fallen over the last 10 years. Nowhere is this more apparent than in the once seriously money-guzzling Switzerland. The cost of a week in a 3-star hotel plus a lift-pass in the top Swiss resorts we looked at is around 20% cheaper in real terms than back in 1995.

We hope this information may be of some comfort when you hand over the plastic or cash this coming season. Skiing remains an expensive business, but you won't have to break the bank to go. Costs vary enormously and depend not only on your destination but also on the type of accommodation you choose and whether you go in high or low season. The differences become even more apparent when you add on the cost of a lift pass, equipment hire, ski school, meals, drink and nightlife.

We've checked the price of packages to the European and North American resorts that we looked at in our costs survey ten years ago. They represent a cross-section of popular destinations for Brits, from the plush peaks of the market such as Courchevel 1850 down to the bargain-basement Bulgarian resort of Borovets. We've also compared the costs of that other necessary item of expenditure for skiers and snowboarders – the lift pass.

EUROPEAN COSTS

We looked at the brochures of some of the major tour operators and worked out the typical costs of 3-star and 4-star hotels, chalets and studios (including flights, transfers and half-board in hotels and chalets) for two people sharing a room for a week in mid-season February. We list them on p28 in price order, based on the cost of 3-star packages.

Back in 1995, Courchevel 1850 was the runaway leader in the race to be crowned Europe's most expensive resort. Ten years later, there are still no serious challengers for the title. A week in a 3-star hotel can set you back around £1,060. That's £140 a week steeper than its nearest rival Val-d'Isère and over £300 more expensive than Serre-Chevalier in third place. The leap up the table by Serre-Chevalier from ninth spot 10 years ago to third place this year means that French resorts now occupy the first three positions in the expense league. After the French come the top Austrian resorts of St Anton and Obergurgl. The slide down the table by the Swiss resorts of Zermatt and Verbier from third and fourth positions to sixth and seventh provides the clearest indication of the shifting costs of skiing in Europe. The Italian destinations in our table occupy much the same positions they held ten years ago and are all much cheaper than the least expensive French resort we covered. Eastern Europe remains firmly rooted to the bottom of the table – a week in a 3-star hotel in Poiana Brasov or Borovets works out at around one-third of of the cost of a week in Courchevel 1850.

CHEAPER THAN 10 YEARS AGO

We did a similar price comparison 10 years ago and have compared today's prices with what you'd have paid if 1995 prices had risen in line with UK inflation. Below we list (in order of the % by which the cost has fallen in real terms) some examples of the cost now of a week's 3-star hotel and lift pass package (and in brackets the 1995 price adjusted for inflation). You can see that, for nearly all these resorts, the cost has actually fallen in real terms. Costs have stayed much the same for the two French resorts; but they have fallen by around 5% for the two Italian ones, by around 10% for the Austrian ones and by over 20% for the Swiss resorts.

Zermatt £831 (£1,079)
Verbier £793 (£1.018)
Wengen £721 (£907)
Borovets £425 (£507)
St Anton £851 (£960)
Obergurgl £824 (£904)
Söll £633 (£690)
Courmayeur £670 (£709)
Cervinia £701 (£738)
Soldeu £600 (£613)
Courchevel £1,206 (£1,248)
Val-d'Isère £1,054 (£1,041)

EUROPEAN PACKAGES				
	3* Hotel £	4* Hotel £	Chalet £	Studio £
Courchevel 1850	1060	1700	700	540
Val-d'Isère	920	1040	740	530
Serre-Chevalier	740	–	550	550
St Anton	720	890	620	–
Obergurgl	690	760	–	–
Zermatt	680	810	630	550
Verbier	650	750	590	410
Wengen	590	770	–	420
Cervinia	580	780	–	460
Courmayeur	540	780	450	520
Sauze d'Oulx	540	620	–	470
Söll	520	630	520	460
Soldeu	480	590	540	400
Poiana Brasov	380	420	–	–
Borovets	360	420	420	–

Notes: All prices are for mid-season February and are based on two people sharing a room. They include flights and transfers. Hotel and chalet prices are half-board. Not all types of accommodation were available in all resorts in the brochures we looked at.

Much the same pattern emerges with when it comes to the cost of staying in a 4-star hotel. The major exception is the move up the table of the top Italian resorts Cervinia and Courmayeur. But at around £780 a week they work out at less than half the cost of staying in Courchevel 1850. At around £1,700, Courchevel is in a league of its own – over 60% more expensive than its nearest rival Val-d'Isère. So, one week in Courchevel 1850 or four weeks in Borovets? Decisions, decisions.

Val-d'Isère takes over the top spot from Courchevel when it comes to the cost of a chalet holiday. The price of these is much more evenly spread, making the top resorts far more affordable. In those that we've covered, standard chalets (not the luxury kind we feature in the chapter starting on p39) work out cheaper than 3-star hotels – and that's before you add on your wine and bar bill and other extras to the hotel costs. Of course, there are plusher chalets than the ones we've looked at – these will, in all probability, cost you more. A studio can work out cheaper – particularly if you don't mind packing in the people. The brochure prices normally assume four people in a one-room studio, but for our comparisons we added on the small-print supplements to get the true prices for two living in relative comfort; but remember, there's no food included in these prices.

Next comes the cost of a six-day lift pass. And here there's some excellent news for skiers – the cost of a pass in some of the top Swiss and Austrian resorts has actually gone down since 1995 (see the table). For example, the price has fallen from £165 to £143 in Verbier and from £140 to £131 in St Anton (part of this is due to exchange rate changes; the Swiss franc and Austrian schilling were very strong against the pound ten years ago). But there's more good news to come – lift pass prices in most of the resorts that we've covered have lagged behind the rate of inflation over the last 10 years. So, in real terms you're paying less. The exceptions to this trend are the Italian resorts and Soldeu in Andorra, where prices have risen in real terms.

LIFT PASS PRICES		
	2005 £	1995 £
Zermatt	151	162
Courchevel 1850	146	132
Verbier	143	165
Obergurgl	134	137
Val-d'Isère	134	123
St Anton	131	140
Wengen	131	129
Courmayeur	130	87
Cervinia	121	89
Soldeu	120	83
Sauze d'Oulx	116	85
Serre-Chevalier	114	102
Söll	113	102
Borovets	65	61
Poiana Brasov	40	55

Ski school fees are more difficult to analyse simply because the numbers of hours and days of tuition vary from resort to resort. The most expensive school, at £171 for a week of group classes, is Courchevel, but you get 33 hours of tuition – that's an hourly rate of £5.70. Ski school in Verbier costs £91, but that's for just 12.5 hours. That works out to an hourly rate of £7.30, the most expensive of the resorts we looked at. At the other end of the price scale are Söll (20 hours, £4.40 an hour) and Borovets (24 hours, around £3 an hour).

THE TOTAL BILL
If you add up the cost the cost of staying in a 'glam' resort 3-star hotel, buying a lift pass and joining a ski school, the final figure may leave you needing to lie down in a dark room. A week in Courchevel 1850 will set you back by around £1380. A week in one of our mid-table resorts such as Cervinia will cost around £810. Going further down the league to Soldeu, the cost falls to around £660. And down in the bargain-basement of Borovets, a week will cost around £500.

The costs don't stop there, unless, of course, you lunch and rehydrate on tap water and Mars bars brought from home. Price studies by our reporters and ourselves on a variety of food and drink showed that, in general, French resorts are more expensive than average for ski resorts (especially for large beers and plats du jour), Swiss resorts are also more expensive than average (especially for wine and garnished meat dishes) but cheaper for large beers, Austrian resorts are generally cheaper than average except for wine (and especially cheap for meat dishes and beer), and Italian resorts are cheaper all round (especially for wine). We did not have enough reports on Andorra and Eastern Europe, but you can expect them to be cheap and very cheap respectively. So, the message seems to be that you'll spend a lot less (20% to 40%, say) on food and drink in Italy or Austria than in Switzerland or France. Thank you to everyone who took part in our price survey last season. We'd like many more people to do so this coming season; the idea would then be to do a resort-by-resort rather than just a country-by-country comparison. For the information we'd like you to collect, please send an email to reports@wtss.co.uk.

Vacation on highest

(Altitude 1.400 – 2.850 m)

Reschenpass in the Winter

Events Centre (600m2) with separate seminar room and in-house café • 90 kms of cross-country trails • 111 km prepared slopes • 30 modern lifts • 1 Halfpipe & ASA BoarderX • Nauderix-Mini club • 2 Ski & Snowboard schools • 111 cleared winter walks • 70 kms for snow-shoe walking • 3 ice rinks • 1 curling rink • Indoor swimming-pool with sauna and solarium • 5 toboggan runs (3 floodlit, one of which 8 km long) • Horse-drawn sleigh rides • Museums, galleries • 21 restaurants • 4 restaurants in the ski area • 5 bars & pubs • 7 après-ski bars • 1 disco • 4 cafés • 2 internet cafés • 4 sports shops • 2 department stores • 1 drugstore • 4 ski hut's • 4 mountain restaurants • 4 ski- & snowboard-hire shops • 1 sport- & adventure school • Library, and much, much more

RESCHENPASS

Urlaub auf höchster Ebene

Tourist office Nauders • Tel: 0043-5473-87220 • E-mail: nauders@reschenpass.info • **Tourist office Vinschgauer Oberland** • Tel: 0

www.reschenpass.info

vel...

NORTH AMERICAN COSTS

Like Europe, the real cost of staying in a North American 3-star hotel and buying a lift pass in the resorts we've looked at for our table (see below) has gone down over the past 10 years. Whistler leads the way – real prices there have fallen by nearly 25%.

At first glance, the prices we've listed below will look more expensive than those in the brochures. That's because we've worked out what it would cost for two people sharing a room – the brochure prices are often based on four. So, beware of the small print. When you compare prices with Europe, keep in mind that North American hotel costs exclude dinner, and in some cases breakfast, although you can eat out cheaply (or expensively if you like).

A 3-star hotel package to Vail is on a par with Val-d'Isère. Breckenridge works out about the same as Serre-Chevalier. The Canadian resorts of Whistler and Banff will cost around the same as Verbier and Cervinia for a week in a 3-star hotel. But at around £1,350 a week for a 4-star hotel, Vail leaves Val-d'Isère trailing. Whistler, Breckenridge and Banff, however, work out cheaper.

Unlike North American hotel packages, chalet packages include food. It's worth remembering that they are usually more luxurious than European chalets. They also work out more expensive than their European counterparts, particularly Vail and Breckenridge. At around £940 a week, Vail easily out-prices even Courchevel 1850 and Val-d'Isère. North American studios are also bigger and plusher than European ones, and the price difference between the two is even wider. Breckenridge, for example is around 50% pricier than Serre-Chevalier for a studio package, while Whistler works out at over 75% more expensive than Verbier. Given the air fare costs and the problems of jet lag, it makes sense to go for two weeks rather than one. Once again Vail is the most expensive, but a two week 3-star package in Banff is less expensive than one week in Courchevel 1850 or Val-d'Isère.

NORTH AMERICAN PACKAGES		3* Hotel	4* Hotel	Chalet	Studio
		£	£	£	£
Vail	1 wk	940	1350	940	–
	2 wks	1470	2240	1280	–
Breckenridge	1 wk	750	930	880	830
	2 wks	970	1330	1100	1180
Whistler	1 wk	650	810	680	730
	2 wks	970	1180	990	970
Banff/Louise	1 wk	580	700	550	660
	2 wks	740	1040	770	850

When it comes to the cost of a lift pass, North America is in a league of its own – megabucks ahead of the most expensive European resorts. A week's pass in Vail or Breckenridge will cost around £220 – and that's with the discount you get for buying your pass through a tour operator before you go. Without the discount the price is a staggering £270. The prices of passes in Whistler and Banff are cheaper, but at around £200 each they work out at around 33% more expensive than Zermatt – Europe's priciest pass. For eating and drinking in North America, US prices seem about average, with Canada coming out cheaper all round.

Seeking snow

A guide to where it falls, and why

by **Fraser Wilkin**

Nothing, but nothing, affects enjoyment of skiing and boarding like the quality of the snow you do it on. That's why snow reliability is one of the first things we deal with in the 'Mountains' section of each resort chapter, and why snow reliability has always come at the top of our ratings panels in each chapter (displaced this year by our new fast lifts rating, which we thought deserved the limelight for a while). You'll find our remarks and ratings a good guide to what to expect, but we thought readers would also welcome a more general discussion of this vital and interesting subject. We're focusing on the Alps, but there is more about other areas on our new website – see margin.

WEB WEATHER

A fuller version of this feature appears on our website at www.wtss.co.uk

If all goes according to plan, we'll also have medium-range snow forecast information on the site, so that you can plan last-minute trips to the areas most likely to have good snow.

THE SHORT-TERM: 2004/05 – AN UNUSUAL SEASON

In the Alps, a long period of good conditions in mid-season was the result of a sustained spell of extremely cold northerly winds; the snowfall was generally below average, but it was the southern alps where this led to an acute shortage of snow.

Despite a shaky start and real worries in early January, the season seemed quite a decent one in the northern alps, where from mid-January to mid-March northerly winds brought frequent snowfalls and relentless cold, giving many resorts two months of their best conditions in years, with the lower Austrian villages such as Söll, Saalbach and Kitzbühel faring particularly well. Many of the lower French and Swiss resorts such as Morzine, Megève, Wengen and Engelberg also did well. Yet snowfalls were generally below the long-term average, especially at altitude, affecting resorts as diverse as Val-d'Isère, Obergurgl, Verbier and Davos. With 340cm/135in, Arc 2000 even recorded its lowest snowfall total since records began – about half of what it would normally expect.

For most of the Southern Alps 2004/05 will be a season to forget. With northerly winds dominating the mid-season, little of the snow that hit the northern Alps got through to the south. Resorts such as Serre Chevalier, Risoul/Vars, Sestriere/Sauze d'Oulx had a lean season. The Dolomite resorts fared only slightly better, but in the low temperatures the extensive snowmaking worked well.

These wintry conditions came to an abrupt end in the second week of March with a rapid spring thaw that forced some resorts to close early. As is often the case, April saw a return to changeable conditions with some notably heavy snowfalls.

THE LONG VIEW: ARE THINGS CHANGING?

It is often suggested that snowfall in the Alps isn't what it used to be. Certainly the late 1970s and early '80s saw more than their fair share of bumper snow years and, at a time when skiing was fast becoming more accessible to the public, this may have served to raise expectations unduly.

This confidence was shattered by the infamous winters of 1988/89 and 1989/90, when severe snow shortages hit much of the Alps two years running – many resorts were barely able to function for the first half of each season. Although on both occasions the snow eventually arrived in February, the consequences were profound. The media inevitably stirred things up and, for the first time, the industry was forced to face the spectre of global warming head on.

As it turns out these disastrous seasons have not been repeated, but neither have we seen a return to the bounty years of the preceding decades. In fact, further mediocre years have only fuelled controversy over the future of skiing, with increasing evidence that Alpine seasons are getting shorter. Indeed it is widely accepted that what we now consider a 'normal' season would have been seen as unusually poor just 20 to 30 years ago.

Despite such concerns, in the last 15 years we have witnessed both the good and the bad. The 1993/94 and 1994/95 seasons, for example, were excellent for most resorts, especially in the north, while southern resorts were more favoured in 1995/96 and 1997/98.

The 1990s will also be remembered as a decade of extreme contrasts. The unusual winter of 1996/97 was probably the sunniest ever, with resorts relying almost entirely on heavy November falls to sustain them through an otherwise snowless season. Just two years later, the northern Alps witnessed exceptional snowfalls culminating in a series of tragic avalanches that destroyed large parts of the villages of Galtür in Austria and Montroc (near Chamonix) in France.

Despite two more poor snow years in 2000/01 and 2001/02, some consistency has been restored, with the last three seasons being largely successful.

So what does the future hold? Certainly most studies conclude that global warming will have a major effect on the European ski industry, especially in lower resorts. But when forming a view of trends, so much depends on exactly what data you look at. A 30-year study beginning in the early 1970s might conclude that winters are getting shorter. But make that study one covering 40 years from the early 1960s (which included a number of notably poor Alpine winters) and the trend is less obvious. Just what timescale should we be using? Should we be focusing on snowfall, or snow cover? And at what height? And if we can discern 'trends', are they really down to man-made global warming or just natural climatic variations?

UNDERSTANDING THE CLIMATE

The European Alps stretch in an arc from central Austria to the Mediterranean coast at the Franco-Italian border. Although the chain stretches a long way east to west, the differences in climate are more pronounced north to south. The influence of the Mediterranean is paramount in resorts on or near the southern side of this arc, including the southern French Alps, the Italian Alps and parts of southern Switzerland and Austria. However, many of the big-name resorts are closer to the northern side. Broadly speaking, these northern areas look to the north-west for much of their snow and resorts most exposed to this direction get the heaviest falls relative to their height. Areas on this 'front line' include the Arlberg in Austria (Lech, St Anton) and the Portes du Soleil in France (Morzine, Avoriaz). Avoriaz receives considerably more snow than Courchevel, Les Arcs or Val-d'Isère, all of which have similar altitudes but are set deeper in the Alps. Similarly, Lech (1450m/4,760ft) gets more snow than Obergurgl (1930m/6,330ft), which is more sheltered from the moisture-laden north-westerly winds.

Extremes of cold are rare in the Alps, due to the proximity of the Atlantic. Temperatures decrease slightly from west to east, explaining in part why many low Austrian resorts can operate at an altitude that would not be viable in France.

THE SNOW QUALITY EQUATION

Snowfall is only one one of several factors that contribute to good snow conditions in practice.

Average slope height It pays to consider at what altitude you will spend most of your time skiing – not only because altitude and snowfall are often related, but because snow lasts longer at high altitude. The slopes may be well above resort altitude, but they may also be below it. The resort in Europe with clearly the highest average slope height is Saas-Fee, in Switzerland, where you spend most of your time between 2500m/8,200ft and 3500m/11,480ft.

Orientation In the northern hemisphere, shady north-facing slopes hold their snow better than south-facing ones. Not so obvious perhaps is that west-facing slopes, which get direct sun in the afternoon when the air temperature is usually at its highest, are as vulnerable as south-facing ones.

Exposure/shelter Nothing is more damaging to snow cover than rain. The warm, wet weather that brings it usually comes from the west or south-west and so it is the western fringes of the Alps that tend to suffer most.

Terrain Some high ski areas such as Zermatt have rocky terrain and therefore need good cover to be able to operate. Lower resorts, including many in Austria, are more pastoral and can operate with minimal cover.

Crowds Heavy traffic on runs means that the snow gets heavily compacted and hard. Careful grooming overnight can restore an excellent skiing surface for the morning, but the cycle of heavy traffic and nightly grooming eventually produces snow that deteriorates more quickly during the skiing day. Good grooming makes a vital contribution to keeping pistes in operation, though.

Artificial snow North America has always led the way, with blanket coverage in many resorts. In Europe, use of snow-guns is more variable but has increased hugely in the last decade, with spectacular success in some areas – notably the Dolomites.

Seeking snow

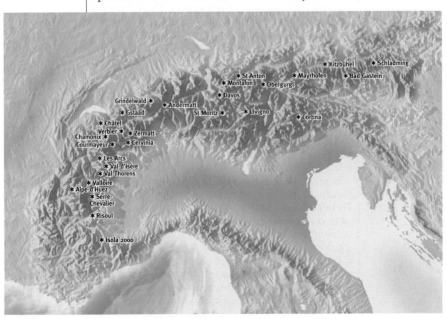

SOME AREAS WITH OUTSTANDING SNOWFALL OR SNOW COVER

Arlberg (Austria) Lech, Zürs and St Anton have long had a reputation for deep snow. With most storms arriving from between north and west, these mountains are among the first to be hit, and snowfalls are often heavier than in other Austrian areas of similar height. Snowiest of all is Zürs (1720m/5,640ft), with an exceptionally exposed position near the top of the Flexen pass. The average snowfall here is a massive 10.5m/415in a season, the most at resort level anywhere in the Alps. With more shelter and a lower altitude, nearby Lech (1450m/4,760ft) gets 'only' 7.5m/295 inches.

L'Espace Killy (France) Val-d'Isère and Tignes are one of the safest areas for snow in the Alps, but this isn't because of exceptional snowfall. The most important factor is average ski height – well over half of this huge ski area is over 2500m/8,200ft. Other factors are that many of the runs face north, and that the area is set deep into the Alps sheltered from mild south-westerly winds.

Le Tour (France) With 8.7m/345 inches of snow per year, little Le Tour (1450m/4,760ft) claims to be the snowiest village in France. Intriguingly, this is nearly three times the amount of snow received by Chamonix, just 11km/7 miles down the valley. Chamonix itself sits in an enclosed location, sheltered from westerlies by high mountains. Le Tour, however, sits at the head of the valley in a much less sheltered position. This allows it to benefit from the presence of Mt Blanc, forcing clouds to give up their moisture, with little of the rain shadow effect that afflicts Chamonix.

Andermatt (Switzerland) This small resort at 1445m/4,740ft is little known outside Switzerland but has an enviable snow record. It is one of the very few Alpine resorts that are susceptible to storms from most directions – north, west and, crucially, south. This is a handy insurance policy that means the resort is rarely short of snow.

Megève and **Les Contamines** (France) The comparison between these two adjacent resorts is interesting. At resort level, Megève gets more snow – an average of 4.25m/170 inches compared with 3.4m/135 inches in Les Contamines. The village of Les Contamines has a sheltered position at the bottom of a narrow valley protected by Mt Joly. Megève is much less enclosed. But look above resort height and the picture is reversed. Most of Les Contamines' slopes are higher than those of Megève, and crucially they are appreciably closer to Mt Blanc: the massif causes moisture-laden westerly or north-westerly winds to rise and produce precipitation.

La Rosière (France) This modern resort sits in an elevated position at the end of the long Tarentaise valley, which runs roughly SW–NE. Both the village and the ski area are open to storms from the west/south-west that are funnelled up the Tarentaise valley (though we saw few of these in 2004/05). La Rosière receives the full energy of these storms, and so gets more snow than, for example, nearby Val-d'Isère, at the same altitude but in a relatively enclosed position. La Rosière needs heavy snow, though: its slopes get an awful lot of sun.

Fieberbrunn (Austria) This little resort near Kitzbühel is an example of what the Austrians like to call a 'schneewinkl' – a 'snow-corner', which gets more snow than neighbouring areas. Is the reputation justified? Well, yes it is. According to records, on average it gets nearly twice as much snow as Kitzbühel. The explanation would appear to be that north-westerly storms get a relatively clear run at the slopes of Fieberbrunn, whereas Kitzbühel has more in the way of mountains to the north-west.

Heli-skiing

The ultimate Canadian high

by **Dave Watts**

BRAD WHITE

There's so much terrain you're always making fresh tracks. Once you've skied one valley, the chopper will whizz you off to another →

If you fancy the idea of run after run in untracked powder, day after day for a week, head for the snowy wilderness of western Canada. You might get some fresh tracks in places like Whistler, Big White and Kicking Horse but the only way to be sure of doing so run after run and day after day is to stay with a heli-skiing or snowcat operation. They have thousands of acres of terrain all to themselves. Last winter I had a week in the Cariboos with Canadian Mountain Holidays (CMH); 44 guests and four guides had almost 1500 square kilometres of virgin snow to themselves – that's 15 times as big as the Three Valleys. Everyone stays in a remote lodge on the slopes that in winter you can reach only by helicopter.

This was my second week with CMH. I had been to the Bugaboos with them a couple of years before. And I have to admit, I'm hooked on their set-up and addicted to the virgin white stuff they supply. You'll be in the company of lots of other addicts: two in my group had been coming regularly to the Cariboos most years since 1978, one of them two or three times a season. Once you have skied a million vertical feet with CMH, they give you a free ski suit; if you ski just the minimum vertical guaranteed in a week, you'll do 100,000 feet. So a million feet might take ten trips. One of these guys had done six million feet, another three million. So you can tell they have a severe addiction problem. Of the other nine in my group, only one was a CMH first-timer. That's pretty typical because 80% of guests are repeat clients. Try it once and you'll see why.

So what should you expect? First, great adventure skiing. You are picked up each morning by a chopper right outside the lodge. Just being in a helicopter, soaring over the mountains looking for the best place to land, is an adventure. Getting out with the noise of the blades whirling and snow being blown all over the place, huddling in a group and then seeing it fly off, leaving you in an eerie silence on top of a mountain in the middle of a snowy wilderness adds to

Early morning in the Cariboos, on a run called Crazy Horse near the Canoe Glacier, with a day of glorious powder to come →

DAVE WATTS

HELI-SKI TIPS

- Get fit for maximum enjoyment

- Go out early and stay in Banff to get in a couple of days on the slopes and get over the jet lag

- Use the powder skis that CMH supply free for the week

- Don't ski if you aren't enjoying it. You can be flown back to the lodge early

- Do go to the early morning stretching sessions. And have a massage or two during the week

- Don't worry about going on your own — there are lots of singles

- If you are not confident off-piste, go for one of their Powder Introduction weeks

- Don't go home early and miss the Saturday morning skiing (as many people do) – it was the best of the week on both my trips

UK Representative for CMH

Powder Skiing in North America
61 Doneraile Street
London SW6 6EW
t 020 7736 8191
info@psna.co.uk
www.cmhski.com

the adventure. Then there's the run: usually in untracked snow, maybe on a glacier, maybe through the trees, usually in good fresh powder near the top, sometimes in more difficult, cruddy conditions lower down. And always, at the end, there's a chopper waiting or on its way to pick you up and fly you to the top of another run. In a good day you'll get in 10 runs or so with an average vertical of 600m to 700m on each; I started counting the number of linked turns in untracked snow on each run and frequently hit 100.

Second, changeable weather. This is the one thing CMH cannot control. And on both my trips, the weather was constantly changing. Snow, flat light, high winds, glorious sunshine, we had it all at times. Sometimes it means you can't fly in the morning, sometimes you have to come in early, often you ski all day. That brings me to the third thing to expect: enormous care taken over your safety. Before you are allowed to go skiing you have several safety sessions, including videos, helicopter briefing and training in using avalanche transceivers. The guides meet twice daily to discuss avalanche conditions and the weather and to agree which runs are safe to ski and which not. If any guide has doubts about a run, it is closed. And if the heli-pilot has doubts about flying conditions, he can decide to fly everyone back to the lodge. All the guides are qualified mountain guides and there's always one extra to act as snow safety guide, check out any doubtful areas, dig snow-pits and trigger avalanches using bombs if necessary.

Differing ability levels among the skiers (and boarders) is another thing to expect. You don't have to be a great skier to go heli-skiing. The Volkl CMH skis they hand out are specially designed to make skiing deep snow easy, so that any confident intermediate can be sure of having a good time. The two guys who had skied millions of vertical feet weren't especially good skiers but they certainly enjoyed it, as did five guys from Utah who were brought up skiing the steep and deep and were also in my group. I had expected them to be bored waiting for me but not at all: everyone is free to go at their own pace (so long as you don't get in front of the guide) and you all have to wait for the chopper at the end of each run anyway.

A comfortable and relaxing lodge is another thing to expect. Rooms have en-suite facilities and most lodges have lots of single rooms for those who come on their own. The food is superb (rack of lamb, ahi tuna and fresh salmon are typical), the wine is reasonably priced, the bar is open once skiing has finished for the day, and the staff provide even better service than the usual excellent Canadian norm. The ambience is like that in a very comfortable large catered chalet, with everyone sharing tables and the guides helping serve and clear dishes.

And the skiing is awesome. Book up now and join the addicts.

Luxury chalets

The ultimate ski holiday?

by **Chris Gill**

The catered chalet goes from strength to strength. In compiling this annual review of the top of the market, we've found more choice than ever: more companies offering more chalets in more resorts – though there's no immediate threat to the ruling trio of Méribel, Val-d'Isère in France and Verbier in Switzerland.

You can find isolated luxury chalets in all sorts of places, from Austria to Aspen, but the breed in general is still not widespread: most are concentrated in the more upmarket French mega-resorts.

The greatest concentration is found in Méribel. Long-time local specialist Meriski, more than any other operator, illustrates the transformation of the chalet business. In the 1980s it was a run-of-the-mill operation, but then it successfully repositioned itself upmarket. It hasn't all been plain sailing for the company, which has changed hands a couple of times recently, but it still has a wide range of impressively comfortable chalets.

Descent International now has an enviable portfolio of properties in the secluded Brames area of the resort. The famously luxurious chalet Brames is the grandest property I have visited in Méribel, with a two-storey living room and a glorious view up the valley towards Mont Vallon. To this the company has added the equally desirable 10-bed chalets Aurore and Boréale, nearby, which share an outdoor heated pool – and more recently the chalet Génépi at Belvedere.

VIP has six impressive chalets, including Indiana Lodge – right on the slopes, with great views over town and an outdoor hot-tub – and Kublai Lodge – with Indonesian artefacts, steam room, gym and cinema. Sister company Snowline operates at a slightly more modest level but still has some very desirable properties. Their top chalet, Isba, has an outdoor hot-tub and a cinema.

Scott Dunn Ski has three properties here – in terms of luxury,

---

THE EVOLUTION OF THE CHALET HOLIDAY

The catered chalet holiday is a uniquely British idea. Tour operators install their own cooks and housekeepers in private chalets which they take over for the season. They package them with travel from the UK, normally offering half-board. Dinner is a no-choice affair at a communal table, including wine unlimited in quantity but often severely limited in quality. You can either book a whole chalet (the smallest typically sleep around six or eight) or book space in a larger chalet that you share with whoever else turns up.

In the early days of the chalet, in the 1960s and '70s, the catered chalet business didn't do luxury. Taking a chalet holiday meant roughing it in creaky old buildings, putting up with spartan furniture and paper-thin walls, and with six or more people sharing a bathroom. And the chalet girl – always a girl, back then – was often straight out of college or finishing school, and more intent on having a fun season on the slopes than preparing gourmet meals.

It was only in the late 1980s that one or two companies realised that people would pay a lot more for comfortable and stylish accommodation, good food and wine, and a little bit of personal service – just enough to make the customer feel the staff are there to do something other than have a good time. The new formula worked, probably better than anyone would have expected.

towards the lower end of this company's increasingly impressive range of properties. Lotus Supertravel has one 'superchalet', the 20-bed Cardamines. Several of Total's properties here deserve to be included in the luxury category, particularly Phoebe with its well-positioned outdoor hot-tub. Kaluma has the beautifully furnished Lodge, in the Belvedere suburb.

If you like the idea of luxury but want to keep the cost down, consider staying with Bonne Neige down in the old village of Les Allues. Les Allodis is a converted barn that makes a real change from the modern properties that dominate in Méribel – all beams and antique furniture, but with mod cons including outdoor hot-tub.

Courchevel is well established as the smartest resort in France, and at last has a growing number of smart chalets on the UK package market. The resort is at the heart of the Lotus Supertravel programme; they have 11 desirable properties here – some apartments but some proper chalets – of which the best (and a personal favourite of mine) is the 10-bed chalet Founets, which has a fine, high-ceilinged sitting/dining room and a great position. The company's Plein Sud looks impressive, too.

Kaluma is adding to its lovely chalet Vizelle a new fab-sounding property, chalet Totara. Flexiski has a rustic 10-bed chalet off the Bellecôte piste – Anemone, one of Courchevel's originals. But this is now rather eclipsed by the recently added Pralong – actually a luxury apartment, but with a very chalet-like atmosphere – and the cute little 8-bed chalet Chinchilla in the exclusive Hameau du Cospillot. The 10-bed Hermine, nearby, is now in the Descent portfolio. Scott Dunn Ski has nine properties in Courchevel, of which the undoubted gem is the swanky Aurea, costing twice as much as some of the company's more modest offerings.

Ski Link has a dozen more affordable properties down in Le Praz. La Tania, not far away towards Méribel, has developed quite a range of comfortable chalet properties, including the best of the Ski Amis range, the 14-bed Balkiss.

Val-d'Isère is the great rival to Méribel in the French chalet business. The local specialist, YSE, doesn't operate at the very top of the market, but the company's ancient Mountain Lodges are old favourites, offering no picture windows but atmospheric and comfortable living rooms, with stone walls and ample leather sofas.

Scott Dunn's impressive portfolio here is dominated by the 12-bed Eagle's Nest – an extraordinary place, complete with an indoor jet-stream pool, and all four floors linked by lift.

The grand enclave of four modern chalets at the southern extremity of the resort – Bergerie, Mistral, Lafitenia and Le Chardon – that once were operated by The Ski Company Ltd have passed through the hands of Scott Dunn into those of Le Chardon Mountain Lodges, apparently a sister company of Ski Activity. Descent has three properties including the extremely swanky Montana, with lovely pool, and the Valpierre – a renovated farmhouse done out in a highly distinctive style.

VIP has some very smart places, including 12 spacious, stylish chalet-apartments in their recently built Aspen Lodge on the main street – a novel concept in chalets, with a reception desk, lounge area and coffee bar. Their 200-year-old Farmhouse, by the church, is something else – a beautifully converted, er, farmhouse. Sister company Snowline has several properties, though the best are apartments. Lotus Supertravel has one luxury contender in the form of chalet Renard – a ground-floor apartment.

Luxury places in next-door Tignes are thin on the ground. Total has the best properties here, including one of the best in the company's portfolio – chalet Cairn, in an excellent position on the lake shore, with outdoor hot-tub.

Chamonix isn't known for luxury chalets, but Flexiski has a gem in the wood-built eight-bed chalet Bornian, with a particularly welcoming beamed living room. Locally based Collineige has secured an enviable range of very individual properties – chalet Valhalla is particularly striking, with its double-height living room.

Morzine is known mainly for cheap-and-cheerful properties, but Snowline has an impressive cluster of 'town house' properties right in the centre – while in the nearby backwater of Essert-Romand is the deeply comfortable Chalet Gueret, rebuilt with all mod cons a few years back after the all-wood original burned down. Up at Les Gets, Descent has the Ferme de Moudon, as seen on Channel 4's Grand Designs Abroad – a chic interior in a 17th century chalet.

In Switzerland, Verbier is the chalet capital. Chalet Goodwood is much the best I have visited here – fabulously comfortable and

---

stylish, in a central position. It is now run by Descent International, whose equally swanky Septième Ciel could scarcely be in a more different location – high on the Savoleyres side of Verbier. Ski Verbier's portfolio includes several glorious properties. At the top of the range are the recently built Attelas and Sorojasa, but a double-height living room makes chalet Danny equally compelling. The Kernow, still being completed during 2005, sounds like it will be irresistible, particularly if you can bag the master bedroom with cedar bath-tub. Flexiski's Bouvreuil is a richly furnished apartment.

Zermatt, curiously, has never been a great chalet resort. Scott Dunn has long been the main source, and went up a gear recently with the acquisition of two central, spacious and stylish 10-bed apartments that were briefly offered by the Ski Company – Saphir and Louise. I'm not convinced about the antique furnishings of Descent's chalet Zen, but its facilities and position are excellent. Total's handful of properties here includes the Génépy, stylishly created within a lovely old wooden building.

Elsewhere in Switzerland, Descent's chalet Eugenia in Klosters is a fabulous place – even the bathrooms are remarkable.

In Austria, luxury chalets are curiously rare. In St Anton Lotus Supertravel has the minimalist Chiara, plus a couple of more traditional places, and Flexiski and Total have properties, but there is nothing in the very top flight either here or in swanky Lech.

New gear for 2006

Skis give more fun, boots give more comfort

by **Dave Watts**

Skis just keep on getting shorter, wider and more fun – and high-performance women-specific models that help the ladies outperform the men are the big news for the coming season. Boots are becoming comfier and more responsive to help get the best performance out of the radical sidecuts of the latest skis. The market for helmets and protective gear is on the up and there's new gear around to help keep you safe in avalanches.

Skis have changed beyond recognition in the last ten years, with the changes being ushered in by the carving revolution which started in the early 1990s. The upshot of this is that we are now skiing on skis that are 20cm or more shorter than those we skied on in the old days, and which provide more stability, performance and confidence in return for less effort. Skis are not just shorter but also wider, meaning more surface area, and they have hourglass shapes to provide vastly improved carving power and quicker turns. The major benefits of these new skis are better edge grip, more floatation making off-piste attainable for a wider range of people, and skiing is now a lot less tiring. Last March I went on a week-long test of all the new skis for the 2006 season, organised by the Snowsports Industries of Great Britain (a trade body of UK equipment distributors and retailers). Out of over 500 skis from 15 different manufacturers in the test, there wasn't a poor ski to be seen.

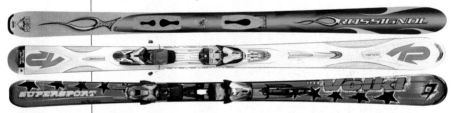

↑ Three of the best: Rossignol Bandit B3, K2 Apache Crossfire, Volkl Supersport 4 Star

GIRL POWER RULES

For years ski manufacturers have made skis aimed specifically at women. In the old days, many of these were simply lighter with 'girly' graphics and colours. But now nearly every manufacturer is taking the women's market very seriously and producing a range of skis designed specifically to help women ski better, taking account of their different physical make-up to men. In general, women tend to be lighter and less powerful than men and manufacturers adjust for this by giving their women's skis a softer flex and by using lighter materials. And often the flex pattern is changed by moving the binding mounting position further forward. All this makes for skis that are easier to turn.

Girl power – a selection of this season's women-specific skis:
K2 Burnin' Luv
K2 Phat Luv
K2 Lotta Luv
Rossignol Bandit B2W
Rossignol Saphir 300
Salomon Rush No 7
Salomon Siam No 10
Atomic
  Balanze 5:3 Girlie
Head Hot Thang
Volkl Attiva Queen
↓

In the ski test mentioned above we asked our women researchers to test several women-specific skis against their nearest unisex equivalent. Right the way through the scale from recreational to expert they (including one of Britain's top female ski instructors) preferred the performance of the women's skis in the majority of cases. So it seems like the manufacturers are getting it right.

Which isn't surprising considering the money they have invested in developing their women's ranges. K2, for example, has employed a team of top women skiers – including two-time World Extreme Skiing Champion Kim Reichhelm – to test and develop their skis. They describe their T:Nine series as 'designed specifically by women for women of all ability levels' and they are donating a portion of income from all T:Nine skis sold in 2005 to breast cancer charities. The seven skis in the range go from the First Luv (for first-time buyers wanting easy turns and stability) to Lotta Luv ('an all mountain ripper') and Phat Luv (for that heli-trip in Alaska). Our testers loved the Burnin' Luv all mountain ski that we put them on. K2 even has a women's twin-tip ski – the Missdemeanor.

Rossignol has a good range of women's skis under the Saphir and Zenith labels. And they even have women's versions of their fabulous Bandit free-ride skis. Salomon have their women-specific Rush skis for on-piste carving and the Siam range for all-mountain free-riding. Atomic have a range of women's skis including the Girlie, Lady, Diva and Puls. Head has its Thang range of women's skis from

↑
Head
  Monster IM77 CHIP
Rossignol
  Zenith Z9Ti Oversize
Salomon Crossmax
  V12 (pair showing
  piston graphic)
Salomon Crossmax V8
Salomon
  Streetracer 10
Atomic SX11
Atomic SX10
Volkl
  Supersport 5 star
Volkl Supersport
  Superspeed

Fine Thang and Cool Thang through to Hot Thang, Wild Thang and Fast Thang. Volkl has its Attiva range of on-piste skis for women.

Snow+Rock anticipates considerable growth in the women-specific ski market this coming season, given all the good skis now available.

STILL GETTING FATTER

The trend for skis to get wider is continuing for the coming season, with both free-ride and on-piste skis.

In the free-ride category two years ago the widest waisted ski was 75mm. Now pretty much all free-ride skis are 78mm or more and some are much wider – and that extra width makes a big difference to how much skiers of all abilities enjoy powder. Along with better floatation, the shorter lengths that these skis are now made in means easier manoeuverability and the whole package makes for great long turns (but slightly less lively short turns).

Rossignol has revamped its already market-leading Bandit series of skis. My personal favourite, the old B2, has been replaced as an expert free-ride ski by the new B3, which has become my new personal favourite. It is around 5mm wider at shovel, waist and tail (120/83/110) and skis like a dream – floating as if magically off-piste and carving with power and stability on-piste. The new B2 is another great ski, now aimed at advanced rather than expert free-riders and the new B1 has become a ski for those who want to stick to the piste. There's a new, giant-sized B4 for those lucky enough to be in places where there's just steep and deep to be enjoyed.

New gear

48

The Head Monster IM Chip has increased its waist this year from 75mm to 77mm and is one of the narrowest free-ride skis around (though you would not realise that if you skied it because its floatation is excellent, perhaps because of the built-in so-called Intelligence Chip). K2 has brought out a new super-wide Apache Outlaw ski for those who want to ski mainly off-piste all day – this measures 124/88/111. And Atomic's Sweet Daddy has an 80mm waist. If you can't ski off-piste on skis like these you know you should resign yourself to sticking to the piste.

And there are a lot of great high performance on-piste skis around too. The biggest trend here as well as getting fatter is the speed at which they have been getting shorter. Rossignol's Z9Ti Oversize came out well in our tests and comes in lengths starting at 154 cm and going up to a maximum of 176cm – a far cry from the 2m plus skis we were skiing on a decade ago. And the waist at 73mm is very wide for an on-piste ski, giving great stability, confidence and versatility. This is a full 7mm wider than one of its rivals – the Salomon Streetracer 10, which has a 66mm waist just like Salomon's highest-performance piste ski the Equipe SC. On-piste skiers looking for a trendier image might be attracted by the skiercross range of high-performance skis, with jazzier graphics than their standard on-piste rivals – examples include the Atomic SX, Dynastar Ski Cross, Head XRC, Salomon Crossmax and Volkl Supersport ranges.

↑
Rossignol
 Elite Bandit 2W
Tecnica
 Vento 10 Hiperfit
Nordica
 Speedmachine 10

GIVING DISCOMFORT THE BOOT

Ski boots are your most important purchase. Set aside enough time for a boot fitter to find the right pair for you and fit them properly. This will enhance your skiing pleasure and performance as well as comfort. The main development with boots in recent years has been to make them fit your feet better by all sorts of anatomical improvements. The use of different softer plastics in key areas of the boot gives a better fit and makes them easier to get into and get off again. Almost all boots today have heat mouldable liners to mirror image your foot for comfort as well as performance; and improvements in boot design have allowed these thermal liners to become thinner, giving greater power and control between foot and ski. However, for the ultimate performance try a personalised custom fit liner from Conform'able or Zipfit. Boots have also become much more dynamically flexible, making it easier to flex the boot and control your skis.

Boot makers have become more conscious of the cold feet problem that many (especially women) skiers have and are coming up with solutions such as fleece linings and built-in boot heaters. This season there will even be a Therm-ic bootwarmer available that has Bluetooth remote control technology.

Of the new models of boots on the market Snow+Rock recommend having a look at the Tecnica Vento and the women's Attiva version. These combine great performance with great comfort, exactly what the majority of keen UK skiers are looking for. The new Nordica range is also worth looking at, especially the Speedmachine 10 with its new anatomically improved design.

Snow+Rock offers the largest range of boots in Europe: 54 models from six manufacturers in UK adult size 2½ to 15½, and starting at children's size 7, so they should have the right boot for you no matter what size or shape your foot. Always use footbeds in your boots, especially custom-built footbeds made to the shape of your particular feet. These will support your foot and distribute pressure evenly under the whole foot, improving comfort and control and reducing muscle cramps and foot fatigue. Always wear a clean pair of technical ski socks when you are out on the mountain (and when you are trying out boots in a shop); I tried a couple of pairs of Falco socks towards the end of last season and loved their silky feel; Smartwool and Wigwam Ultimax are other great brands. It's important to dry your boots out thoroughly every night – consider investing in a pair of boot dryers.

↑ Dainese Wave Coat, Elbow Guard and Knee Guard

→ Head
 Stratum Pro Black
Head Pro J (back)
Giro Bad Lieutenant

New gear

49

↑ Suunto Observer
Suunto X6HR

Editor Dave Watts
quizzes a ski
technician at the ski
test, while Assistant
Editor Catherine
Weakley marks her
scorecards ↓

EXTRAS WORTH HAVING

Helmets are becoming more and more common on the slopes (one of the editors of this book now always wears one) and sales have been growing by 30 per cent a year for the last 4 years. Helmets are now becoming more aesthetically pleasing as well as being warmer on cold days and cooler on hot ones due to temperature regulating materials and vents being used. More and more are incorporating headphone technology so that you can use your phone or listen to music more easily. Head (new into the helmet market this year), Giro and Dainese are three of the strongest ranges. Dainese also provides an extensive range of protective clothing to safeguard your back, knees and the like from bumps and falls.

Watches that measure altitude and number of completed runs, act as compasses and even monitor your heart rate are becoming more and more popular – Suunto is the brand to look for here. With free-riding still on the increase, being properly prepared is essential – never venture off-piste without companions and ensure you are all equipped with a transceiver, backpack, shovel, probe, first-aid kit and thermal body bag to keep warm in. As an additional safety measure, you could wear an ABS pack, which incorporates a balloon that you can inflate if you are caught in an avalanche – the idea is that it (and you) float to the surface rather than lie buried. Snow+Rock is stocking these for the first time this season (on an exclusive basis).

WHY BUY IN THE UK

Prices within the UK are competitive with Europe and the range of choice available in the UK is far better. Shops in the mountains often tend to stock mainly local brands (eg French brands in France, Austrian or German in Austria). What's more, if you do find the product cheaper elsewhere in Europe Snow+Rock offers a price pledge on all products to give you the confidence to buy in the UK. It also offers a number of other exclusive guarantees to give you peace of mind to purchase in England, such as a comfort guarantee on all ski boots and a ski suitability and breakage guarantee.

Family holidays

Alphabetical reflections on ten years' parental joy

by **Chris Gill**

As you may have read elsewhere, this is the tenth edition of your favourite ski resort guide. This is not quite the tenth bulletin from the child-rearing front; a quick trip back to the early editions shows that it is in fact only the seventh. But it is roughly ten years since my children Alex and Laura really learned to ski, so I thought this year I might take stock, and look back over all the bulletins to distil the main lessons we have learned. I've included tips derived from the very valuable input from readers that formed the basis of last year's chapter. Here is an A to Z list.

AIRPORT TRANSFERS
Keep them short – preferably no more than two hours. If you have a fairly long transfer to the resort, try to travel in daylight so that the kids have something to look at. Bear in mind that transfers at peak periods can take much longer than the published times.

BOOKING
If you want to take advantage of the childcare and the tuition offered by UK operators and British-run schools, book early. This is, of course, particularly true of half-term holidays.

CLOTHES
There's no real alternative to buying/borrowing/renting salopettes, but they don't need to be very fancy or expensive. Jackets, on the other hand, can be general-purpose warm/waterproof items that are as useful at home as on the slopes.

DRY SLOPES
Familiarity with the mechanics of moving around on skis pays dividends when your precious week on real snow comes around, so dry slope lessons have to be a good idea. Some people even get to like dry slope skiing; not me: I've never been on one without damaging one thumb or the other (or both) in falls.

EXPECTATIONS
One of the main messages to emerge from last year's trawl for advice from readers was the crucial need to adjust your expectations of your holiday – to focus on enjoying the holiday as a whole, and not just the skiing/boarding.

FRIENDS
Chums for your kids should be arranged if possible – either by taking with you friends of similar age or by making it easy for them to make friends in the resort. The key to the latter is to travel with a specialist family operator. If you are going to a smallish chalet, ask about other children already booked, to maximise the chance of finding kids of the right specification.

GLOVES
Buy them by the dozen from your nearest Aldi, on the one day of the year when they have stock. You can't have too many.

HELMETS
The available evidence is that helmets reduce head injuries. I even wear a helmet myself, at least in wooded or rocky terrain.

INSTRUCTION

Unless your children are used to a harsh regime, avoid the ESF (the French national ski school) – and go instead for a British-run school staffed by native English-speakers and limiting class sizes to modest numbers. Prices are higher; and see 'Booking'.

JUMPS

Having come to skiing as a grown up, I've never really got into jumps; but it's clear that children love them. They don't have to be big, at first anyway – little bumpy trails slightly off-piste, preferably in woods, seem to generate great excitement.

KINDERGARTEN

Most resorts have them, these days even in Italy, traditionally the land of the non-skiing mamma. Research carefully how they are run and how universally English is spoken – or do what we always did, and go with a UK operator with its own crèche.

LODGINGS

OK, it should be 'Accommodation' – but I've used A for 'Airport transfers'. The question is: to cater, or not to cater? Or to put it another way, to stay in your own private apartment, or to share space with others in a catered chalet or hotel? Both have their merits, and we've enjoyed both. One neat formula was to go with another family and have two apartments in the same block.

MISSING THEM

When Alex was tiny Val and I left him at home for a week. By day four we were itching to get back home. We were in Norway, which didn't help, but my guess is we'd have felt the same in the Alps.

ESPRIT Ski

No.1 FOR FAMILY SKIING

17 Top resorts
in Switzerland, France, Austria and Italy

INCLUDING 3 NEW WORLD-CLASS RESORTS
★Saas Fee ★Val d'Isère ★Obergurgl

Huge range of guaranteed child care in every resort:
- ★ *Exclusive Esprit Nurseries – 1 nanny per 2 infants*
- ★ *Exclusive Esprit Ski Classes with maximum 6-8 children per class*
- ★ *Afternoon Activity Clubs* ★ *Free evening Cocoa Clubs* ★ *Free babysitting*

Flights nationwide – Gatwick, Stansted, Bristol, Manchester, Birmingham and Edinburgh

www.esprit-holidays.co.uk   Tel: 01252 618300

NANNIES AND GRANNIES

Taking your own childcare with you works well, especially if you're driving in a large car to a large apartment – you could take your regular nanny, or a friend's teenage daughter, or a granny.

OPERATORS, SPECIALIST

The UK operators who specialise in looking after children do a good job, and the reports we get on them are overwhelmingly positive. They offer other benefits, too – see 'Friends'.

PIZZA

In our family, we bless the day in 1830 when the first pizza saw the light of day in Naples. In France as well as Italy, a good proportion of restaurants do pizza alongside *entrecôte au poivre avec frites*, thus ensuring that we can all eat at one table.

QUEUES

Queues are no more popular with children than grown-ups; look for **** or ***** in our queues and fast lifts ratings.

RUNS

I know this is obvious, but: choose a mountain with suitably gentle runs – long, top-to-bottom runs, as well as nursery slopes. This doesn't mean you have to go without your moguls and off-piste.

SKI-IN, SKI-OUT

For grown-ups, ski-in, ski-out accommodation is about the convenience of getting to the lifts in the morning. With children, on-snow lodgings mean that it's easy to have lunch back at base, saving money and allowing a good rest, and that they can play safely in/on the snow in the early evening.

TOBOGGANS AND OTHER DIVERSIONS

Swimming pools and games rooms get the thumbs up from experienced skiing parents, of course. For many families, sledges are a key aid to holiday happiness, despite the considerable opportunities they offer for accidents. Accessible snow is a related key ingredient, of course – see 'Ski-in, ski-out'.

USA

If you think the little ones can put up with the flight, and if you can afford it, give it a try. It has everything else in its favour, from fun-oriented Anglophile instructors to abundant burgers. But check the costs carefully – childcare, instruction and lift passes are all pricey.

VILLAGE

Small, cosy and conveniently compact, or big and bursting with things to do off the slopes? Your call. We've had successful holidays in all kinds of places, from Montchavin to Chamonix.

Family holidays

55

WHEN TO GO

Going late in the season has lots of attractions – chief among them the ability to play out on the snow for hours after the lifts close, instead of retreating indoors. So Easter rather than half-term, or ideally sometime between the two, if the kids are not at some crucial stage of their education and you have a co-operative head-teacher.

XC SKIING

Haven't a clue how children get on at cross-country/langlauf/ski de fond, but we needed an entry for X.

YOUNG, YOUNGER, YOUNGEST

What age to start British kids on skis? Everyone's children are different, and I think the key thing is the child's resilience and persistence. They need the self-discipline to keep at it. Don't think that you have to start them at three or four so that they learn 'instinctively'; they'll still do that at seven or eight.

ZOOM LENS

A long lens is very handy for getting shots of the little ones in ski school without the need to go so close that they'll spot you and come hurtling down the nursery slope begging to be rescued from their misery. (Remember that, Laura?)

Buying property

Fancy a chalet or apartment on the slopes?

by **Dave Watts**

Buying a place in a ski resort has been many people's ambition for years. And now more and more of us are doing just that – the number of British people buying in the Alps has at least doubled in the last five years and lots of Brits are now buying places in North America, too. And the numbers are likely to increase over the next couple of years because of new rules that will allow us to buy residential property as part of our pension funds and receive up to 40% tax relief on the cost of the property. So where should you look, what can you expect to pay, what are the new pension tax rules and what are the pitfalls to beware of?

Most people see a place in the snow as a mixture of pleasure and investment. They hope to use their place themselves for a few weeks a year and let it out for the rest of the winter (and, perhaps, for part of the summer, too). Prices vary dramatically, depending on where you buy and the size of the property. While you can expect to pay well over £1 million for a decent chalet in top resorts such as Méribel and Megève, you can find decent-sized apartments in other resorts in France and Switzerland for £200,000 to £300,000, or less. And in Bulgaria, even £90,000 goes a long way.

So what should you look for when buying a home in the snow? First, you need to decide whether you want somewhere just for the skiing or a place in a resort that is lively and attractive in the summer as well. Many French resorts that were developed after the 1950s can be deadly dull in summer, whereas somewhere like Morzine or Chamonix is as busy in summer, or even busier. Second, if you want the place primarily for skiing and snowboarding, you will want

BUYING THROUGH YOUR PENSION FUND

From 6 April 2006 you will be allowed to buy residential property (including foreign property) through a Self-Invested Personal Pension Plan (SIPP). This has considerable UK tax advantages. You get income tax relief on the money you pay into a SIPP; so if you pay tax at the higher rate of 40%, a £10,000 payment will cost you only 6,000, and you will effectively be purchasing a property with a 40% subsidy paid for by the UK government. If you pay tax at the basic rate of 22%, a £10,000 SIPP payment will cost you only £7,800. From 6 April the rules will also be changed so that you will be allowed to contribute the full amount of your earnings, up to a maximum of £215,000 a year, into a SIPP and reduce your income tax bill to zero if you choose to (you can use other savings to make the payments, so you do not have to live on zero income!). An employer can also contribute to your fund. You can use money that has been built up in existing pension arrangements to buy a property by transferring it to your SIPP (but you will not get income tax relief again on any money you use in this way). More than one SIPP can be used to purchase a property, enabling a husband and wife to use their funds together, for example, and making syndication purchase possible. And your SIPP can borrow up to 50% of the value of the fund towards a property purchase. So if you have £200,000 in the SIPP, it can borrow up to £100,000. Any rental income has to be retained by the SIPP, and you have to pay the SIPP rent for any time you spend in the property. All income and capital gains made by the SIPP are free from UK tax but they may be liable to tax in the country in which the property is located.

A complication is that most Alpine countries do not allow trusts (which is what a SIPP is) to purchase property. There are various ways round this, such as setting up a company to purchase the property, with the shares in the company being held in the SIPP, or by assigning the property to the SIPP. It is essential to take good legal and financial advice on this and on other aspects of the purchase from specialist firms such as John Howell & Co (lawyers that specialise in foreign property law) and Progress Financial Planning (financial advisers that specialise in SIPPs and overseas property investment).

reliable snow. And with global warming likely to continue, that means going for somewhere with access to high, snow-sure slopes. Third, if you intend to use it yourself frequently, you will probably want somewhere within a couple of hours of an easily accessible airport such as Geneva, Zürich or Salzburg. Fourth, make sure you understand the legal and taxation aspects of what you are considering purchasing – buying and running costs, income, capital gains and inheritance tax and any resale restrictions. It is highly advisable to get professional advice on these. Fifth, if you are intending to rent out the property, don't overestimate the income you will get from it and the number of weeks it will be let.

You also need to decide whether you want to buy a new or a resale property. Building restrictions in many areas of the Alps have severely curtailed the number of new properties being built. But, as Simon Malster of Investors in Property points out, 'New apartments and chalets, especially in France, now tend to be of much higher quality and with more spacious rooms than was the case in the past.' More and more old buildings are now being converted into high-quality apartments, particularly in villages near the major ski resorts.

WHERE TO BUY?

Most British buyers still head for France. As the big resorts such as Méribel, Courchevel 1850 and Val-d'Isère have become more expensive, shrewd buyers have been opting to buy in less fashionable and more up-and-coming resorts such as Peisey-Nancroix and Montchavin-Les Coches (on either side of the cable-car that now links Les Arcs to La Plagne), Ste-Foy-Tarentaise (which has seen a fledgling village developed from scratch in the last few years) and Samoëns (a beautiful old mountain village now linked by gondola to the slopes of a ski area it shares with Flaine).

One of the most successful new developments in the last few years has been Arc 1950, a brand new ski,-in ski-out, traffic-free village in the Les Arcs ski area, designed and built by Canadian company Intrawest (see page 237). Joanna Yellowlees-Bound of Erna Low Property, which represents Intrawest in the UK, said, 'By the time this book is published Arc 1950 will have virtually sold out, as the final phase was launched for sale in June 2005. However, there may be a few apartments still available. We will also have another Intrawest development, in Flaine, for sale in 2006, as well as new developments at Snowmass near Aspen in Colorado and at Tremblant and Whistler in Canada. In addition, Erna Low Property has some smart new two- and four-bedroom chalet-apartments on the slopes of Les Houches, near Chamonix, with prices starting at £460,000 for 92 square metres. At Argentière, the other side of Chamonix, the old Globe hotel is being renovated, and another building in the same style is being built next to it; a two-bedroom 55-square-metre apartment will cost from around £360,000.'

Zigi Davenport of Alpine Apartments Agency (AAA) points out: 'The Chamonix area is getting expensive. For better value for money, we have new four-bedroom chalets with 150 square metres of living space in Châtel in the Portes du Soleil for only £400,000 or so. And in Sallanches, just off the motorway on the way to Megève, we have some apartments in the grounds of an old chateau with views of Mont Blanc for around £100,000 for one bedroom to £150,000 for two bedrooms. They are within easy driving distance of the slopes at resorts such as Megève, Flaine, the Portes du Soleil and Chamonix.'

THE ALPS
INVEST IN YOUR DREAMS

Simon Malster of Investors in Property says that Austria and Switzerland now offer much better value for money than France. But foreigners are allowed to buy property only in certain parts of both countries. Malster says, 'I'm delighted to be able to offer new three-bedroom chalets in the Dachstein-West region of Austria for around £145,000 to £175,000. These are available on a sale and leaseback arrangement, which saves buyers 20% of the purchase price as the developer can claim back the VAT that would otherwise be payable. The chalets will be let out through a Dutch tour operator, and give an income of around 5% of the purchase cost.' Many French properties are also sold on a sale and leaseback arrangement to save VAT and give an income, but Malster recommends looking at a one-to-three-year lease to a tour operator, as that can be more flexible and often more profitable than a 20-year leaseback deal.

Examples of good-value properties that Malster has in Switzerland are at Mayens de Riddes, a tiny hamlet linked with the Verbier ski area, where a five-bedroom chalet goes for around £350,000, and in the unspoiled resort of Grimentz to the east (see the resort directory). If you want a better-known resort, Malster is taking reservations for new chalets to be built in Saas-Fee at around £600,000 for a typical four-bedroom, four-bathroom chalet; there was a building moratorium in Saas-Fee when we wrote this, but Malster says, 'That should end in September 2005, or April 2006 at the latest.'

Pure International has properties available in Grimentz and Verbier, and on the shores of Lake Geneva within easy driving distance of several ski areas. But they also sell a lot of properties in Canada. Managing director Sean Collins told me: 'We have 100 log-built homes beautifully set around a lake 10 minutes' drive from Tremblant and costing from £270,000 for a 300-square-metre four-bedroom property in an acre of land.' They also have properties from £90,000 near Canmore (90 minutes from Calgary airport and not far from Banff's ski areas) and from £160,000 at Invermere (near Panorama ski resort).

If rock-bottom prices are your priority, Barrasford and Bird specialise in selling properties in Bulgaria and have apartments in Pamporovo and the outskirts of the capital Sofia (with direct lift access to the Vitosha ski area) for around £40,000 for a one-bedroom apartment and £90,000 for a two-floor duplex apartment. Robin Barrasford says, 'We expect property prices to soar in the run-up to Bulgaria joining the EU – scheduled for 2007. We say that if your property has not doubled in value in three years, we'll buy it back for the original price. We also have a deal with Balkan Holidays to rent out properties we sell – a typical yield is 6% after management fees.'

INVESTORS IN PROPERTY /
GRIMENTZ

Most people see their own place on the slopes as being a mixture of pleasure and investment →

All-inclusive holidays

Come home on-budget

by **Chris Gill**

For anyone who wants to keep control of their holiday spending, there's nothing to beat an all-inclusive holiday. Perhaps surprisingly, no one sells winter sports packages that include absolutely everything. But there are a couple of companies that come close.

Club Med is the big name in this game, with huge hotels (called 'villages') in around 20 resorts in the Alps. The great majority are in France (it's a French company), but Club Med has taken over a handful of old hotels in Swiss resorts and also has places elsewhere.

Holidays are available with or without flights and transfers. They all include insurance. But the key feature of the package is that it includes all meals, including beer and wine. Because this is a French operation, lunch is a serious meal. Usually, it's taken back at the village; most are in high resorts, where this is not difficult, but returning to base half-way through the day doesn't appeal to everyone. In a very few resorts Club Med has taken over a mountain restaurant, which is a better arrangement.

Generally, Club Med prices include your lift pass and tuition. Some do only half-day tuition, but most do a full day. Skiing or boarding equipment costs extra, but is usually available on-site.

Most villages have childcare facilities, and for many Club Med regulars these are at the heart of the formula – though how well they will work for English-speaking kids must be open to doubt.

Equity Ski's pricing is a lot simpler, as well as different. They don't include lunch, and they include drinks with dinner only in the case of catered chalet holidays. But all their holiday prices include your equipment hire, as well as lift pass, insurance and either tuition or guiding around the slopes (it depends on where you are staying).

The Equity programme falls roughly into two halves. They offer a moderate number of Austrian and French resorts, in which they generally run their own catered chalets or hotels, and sometimes offer other hotels too. Then, in a larger number of Italian resorts, they offer two or three standard hotels that may be shared with other companies' clients, in the conventional way.

Equity's 27 resorts are a mix of established big names – La Plagne, Mayrhofen, Bormio – and smaller, less well-known places such as St Michael and Le Corbier (part of Les Sybelles). It includes one or two interesting 'back-door' resorts attached to major ski areas – Claviere for the Milky Way, Folgarida for Madonna di Campiglio.

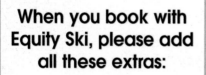

Corporate ski trips

A great way to motivate your staff and clients

Most companies choose to get groups of staff or clients together out of the office occasionally for a whole variety of reasons. Team building, rewarding performance, bonding with clients, problem solving, communicating key messages and planning future strategy are just a few. Getting together in another boring UK hotel can seem a bit tedious – but getting together in a splendid ski resort environment is most certainly not. That's why more and more firms are doing just that.

The mountain environment is one that has lots of advantages for corporate events. The perceived status of ski resorts is high – whoever you invite will be in no doubt that they are being given a treat (as will their friends and business colleagues). And the clear fresh air, the sun and the snowy, dramatic mountain scenery have a huge and immediate impact on people arriving from the European lowlands and their dreary winters. There is a great sense of fun and liberation, and people are happy to cast inhibitions aside and let their hair down. And a winter sports break need not appeal just to skiers. Helena Kania went on a team building weekend to Morzine organised by her company Cable & Wireless and told us, 'I didn't set foot on skis or board but just loved the fresh air, sunshine, views, walks and meeting up with the others in mountain restaurants. And we all got on much better when we got back to work after sharing a great experience.'

63

HOW LONG FOR AND WHAT'S THE COST?

The answer is that it depends on your goals. Corporate trips of a few days are the norm – Thursday to Sunday, say. But you can have two full, action-packed days in the Alps by leaving on Friday after work and returning late on Sunday night – arriving back at work on Monday morning refreshed, invigorated and remotivated. Some companies take over a cluster of chalets for a week or two and have different groups moving in and out, staying for a variety of durations. Others hire helicopters for airport transfers and just go for one night. The cost can be a lot less than you'd think and, indeed, less than some of the alternatives, because UK hotel and restaurant costs are relatively high.

HOW BIG A GROUP?

In principle, your group can be any size you like. A lot of groups are 30 to 50. But they can be smaller or much larger. When we were in Whistler a couple of years back, the whole of the 550-room Fairmont Chateau Whistler had been taken over by a medical conference. Someone with plenty of experience of handling large groups is Amin Momen of Momentum Travel, who for the last few years has organised the Swiss International City Ski Championships in Courmayeur, involving around 200 racers, plus lots of hangers-on. 'Such a large group is quite a challenge,' says Amin, 'but it helps enormously that we have such good local contacts in the resort. If strings need to be pulled to solve a problem, we know exactly which strings.' With really small groups, be aware that the social success is going to depend on how the individuals mesh.

WHERE TO GO AND WHAT KIND OF ACCOMMODATION?

How easy it is to settle on a resort for a corporate trip depends hugely on the nature of your project. If it's a group spread around the world that you want to get together, you could consider North American resorts as well as the Alps. But if they are UK or European based, the Alps would be best. Because corporate trips tend to be short, you'll want to keep the travel time to the minimum so that it doesn't dominate the proceedings. Transfer times from airports to resorts generally range from one to four hours, and you'll probably want to operate at the lower end of that range if you can. On the other hand, you may want your choice of resort to carry a message to your 'delegates'. Choosing Courchevel or St Moritz is effectively saying, 'No expense spared – nothing but the best for you.'

Whatever you do, choose a resort with a good snow record and/or extensive snowmaking. You don't want to invite people on a skiing break to find that there's no snow. Avoid early season for the same reason. A March trip to a high resort will mean good snow and it should mean strong sunshine, too. Don't get hung up on size – with only a couple of days to spend on the slopes, almost any resort has plenty of terrain, especially with good local guides to help you make the most of it. It's likely that not everyone in the group will want to go skiing or boarding, so you may want to choose a resort that has good walks available and maybe lots of other activities that can be organised, such as snow-shoeing, dog-sledding, snowmobiling, skating, curling, tobogganing, ballooning, flights in planes or helicopters or luxuriating in a spa enjoying treatments and massages.

As for accommodation, if it's a dozen people travelling out together for a relaxed couple of days, a swanky chalet might be good:

Corporate ski trips

65

see the 'Luxury Chalets' chapter on page 39 to get an idea of what's available.

If you are getting a large group together and need serious conference facilities, you're playing a different ball game. Finding the right resort and accommodation, meeting rooms and support services can be a real headache, and it's in dealing with this sort of challenge that the services of a tour operator or event management company will really pay off. If you put them in charge of the whole event, you can make them responsible for staying within budget, including on-the-spot costs, as well as the basic accommodation and travel costs.

ORGANISING THE DAYS AND EVENINGS

This is another area where the services of a tour operator or event management company will really pay off. You'll need to make sure everyone is equipped with suitable clothing, equipment and lift passes. You'll also want to organise tuition or guiding specially for your group. Make sure you have enough instructors/guides so that you can form groups of equal ability. You'll also want to ensure that activities for non-skiers are carefully choreographed, so that people do what they want to do and have their time filled (or have time off to relax if that's what they want).

↑ Sophie Keene of
Merrill Lynch at the
2005 City Ski
Championships
valiantly trying to
emulate former
Olympic downhiller
Graham Bell ↗

Lunch in a mountain restaurant can be an opportunity to get your group together, and if you choose one near the top of a lift that pedestrians can use, everyone will be able to get there easily. Another possibility, in good weather, is a swanky picnic, with plenty of champagne buried in the snow.

You might want to think about a race for delegates, though bear in mind that this won't appeal to the complete beginners in the group. Other forms of competition, such as on-snow treasure hunts, could be used to include non-skiers too. You might want to make make these team events (eg relay races) to build relationships.

Then there are the evenings to consider. They are a time when all the group can be brought together, so it's important to think about how you're going to use those opportunities to best effect. You can create social events that reinforce your message – perhaps taking over a whole bar or a mountain restaurant, for example. In the right resort, dinner in a mountain restaurant could be followed by dangerous descents on skis or toboggans.

Corporate ski trips

SWISS INTERNATIONAL CITY SKI CHAMPIONSHIPS

The City Ski Championships have been organised by weekend skiing specialist Momentum Ski and held annually in Courmayeur in Italy's Aosta valley since 2000. Among its attractions is the array of former skiing stars who turn up to set the pace. Former Olympic gold medallist Tommy Moe of the USA and Britain's downhill star of the 1980s Konrad Bartelski are regulars. Around 200 skiers from 40 City firms take part in the event. In 2005, the fastest genuine amateur was Richard Goodenough of FutureTec, with ex-pro racer Einar Johansen of Deutsche Bank, as usual, head to head with Tommy Moe and former Olympic downhiller Graham Bell after two runs on the World Cup-standard giant slalom course.

The Saturday GS race is the main event but only part of the attraction of this weekend. Three other races are held on the Friday: a team parallel slalom (a relay race with four in each team), the Volvo Radar Trap (speed skiing) and, new for 2006, the Crew Clothing boarder-cross. On the Friday evening, there's a welcome drinks party, dinner at various restaurants, late-night drinks in the Bar Roma; on the Saturday, there's a race-side buffet on the piste, champagne reception in the evening courtesy of Veuve Clicquot, followed by a gala presentation dinner and then ... clubbing till dawn. On Sunday the hard core either take advantage of Courmayeur's off-piste terrain on the Toula Glacier or heli-ski; others just enjoy Momentum's complimentary Bloody Marys at Christiania's on the slopes.

The 2006 event, from 16 to 19 March, promises to be even better than ever. Konrad Bartelski will again be running the Snow+Rock pre-race ski clinics, which are really popular with the competitors, and Graham Bell and Matt Chilton from the BBC will be doing the commentary. For more details contact Momentum on 020 7371 9111 or see www.cityskichampionships.com.

Corporate entertainment closer to home
Sailing in the Solent

- Entertain your most valued clients
- Reward your hard-working staff
- Weld your managers into a real team
- Get the attention of key journalists

Take them out for a day's sailing in the Solent on one (or more) of our imposing, powerful yachts, with lunch in a lively port or at anchor in a quiet creek. Your guests will find the day satisfying and memorable – quite unlike other, less involving forms of corporate entertainment. And you'll have an unrivalled opportunity to get to know them better.

Yacht Ventures

t 01373 835201
www.yachtventures.com
info@yachtventures.com

Weekend breaks

Three days on the slopes can feel as good as a week

A weekend away with just one day off work can give you three great days on the slopes, leaving you with the feeling of having been away for ages and returning to work feeling really refreshed. And it does not need to cost you an arm and a leg.

Short-break ski trips have become much more popular in the last few years, partly because of the growth of budget airlines. I was very sceptical of them before I tried them myself several years ago. But now I'm convinced they are a great idea. A quick fix of the white stuff really does seem almost as good as a week. I have had successful weekends all over the place. My first was in the classic weekend destination of Chamonix, which has local areas suitable for all types of weather and snow conditions. Next came Zell am See in Austria, with skiing on the glacier at Kaprun. Then a weekend in Val-d'Isère at the time of the Premier Neige race – great fun. Other good pre-Christmas weekends have been in Courchevel and Saas-Fee. A January weekend in Courmayeur, a February one in Aosta (skiing Cervinia, Monterosa and Pila on successive days) and March ones in Engelberg and Verbier have all been great.

And I've met many other weekend converts, including people who rent apartments for the season and go out every other weekend and others who book up 12 or so weekend flights well in advance and decide where to go when they know where the best snow is.

69

ARRANGING THE WEEKEND

The key to making the most of your time is to catch late flights each way (or a very early flight out, allowing you to be on the slopes by lunch time) – so it helps if you live near a suitable airport. With the growth of budget airlines, there's a big choice of regional and destination airports to use as well as the big ones favoured by longer-established airlines. I've had excellently timed Ryanair flights to and from Salzburg from Stansted as well as EasyJet to Geneva from Luton, for example. And a reader emailed us this summer delighted that Jet2 will now be flying from Manchester and Leeds-Bradford to Chambéry, with short transfers to lots of French resorts (they will fly to Geneva too).

We don't recommend flying to Munich if you are travelling out on a Friday or back on a Sunday – the queues on the motorway can be horrendous, as the whole of Munich seems to go weekend skiing and the airport is on the far side of the city from the Alps. Similarly, allow plenty of time if you are driving back to Lyon airport on a Sunday evening – we encountered very heavy traffic after leaving Courchevel in what we had thought was good time.

Booking a rental car or transfer in advance is usually cheaper than arranging one after you arrive. Taxis can be ridiculously expensive compared with the cost of renting a car. For example, you would expect to pay over £200 each way between Geneva airport and Courchevel by taxi if you book locally – but renting a small car for the weekend would be much less than the one-way taxi price. In our experience, train and bus times between airports and resorts are more suitable for week-long visitors than for weekenders looking for maximum time on the slopes. Airport transfer companies such as those listed in the reference section at the back of this book are

worth trying; but you might waste valuable time waiting around if you go for a shared transfer.

Using a weekend specialist, such as one of those advertising in this chapter, makes sense if you don't want the hassle of making your own arrangements. They know the best resorts to go to, can arrange transfers or car hire and have special deals with hotels that do them good room rates or that might not otherwise take weekend bookings. Some arrange special weekend courses (eg with off-piste guides or even heli-skiing) and can arrange groups of similar standard for you to ski with. And local tour operator reps and contacts can save you valuable time arranging lift passes (beware of big weekend queues on Saturday and Sunday mornings) and equipment hire, and advise on local restaurants and other facilities.

CHOOSING A RESORT

As for choosing a resort, there are various considerations. Many people think they should go for a resort within a short drive of their arrival airport. But by definition, resorts close to major airports are close to large numbers of people poised to hit the slopes on fine weekends, which can mean queues for the lifts, crowds on the slopes and competition for hotel beds. These days, most resorts are within striking distance of a major airport and an hour's extra transfer time

is not really that much if it gets you to quieter slopes.

Resorts close to Geneva include Chamonix, St-Gervais, Megève and Les Contamines (all in the Mont Blanc area and sharing an area lift pass), Flaine and La Clusaz in France, and Villars and Les Diablerets in Switzerland. All these are within an hour or so of Geneva by car. Verbier and Crans-Montana in Switzerland are a bit further, as are the Three Valleys and other Tarentaise resorts – Val-d'Isère can be reached in under three hours now – and Morzine and the Portes du Soleil resorts in France. EasyJet's Nice flight puts Isola 2000 within a 90km/56 mile drive.

Flying to Zürich opens up lots of other possibilities. Flims, Davos and Klosters are the nearest big resorts, and the less well-known resorts of Engelberg and Andermatt are within easy reach. St Anton and Lech in Austria are within striking distance, as are the resorts of the Montafon valley. Ryanair's Salzburg flights make most of the eastern Austrian resorts a short drive away.

In Italy, Courmayeur is a popular weekend destination and is easily accessible from Geneva through the Mont Blanc tunnel. Resorts such as Champoluc, Sauze d'Oulx and Sestriere are easily accessible from Milan or Turin. Ryanair's Verona flights put you very near the Sella Ronda resorts and Cortina d'Ampezzo.

Unless you are booking at short notice when you know the snow is good, we'd be tempted to avoid low resorts such as Megève and Villars – unless you have transport to get you to more snow-sure slopes. And because you don't want your whole weekend ruined by a white-out, we'd also be tempted to avoid very high resorts where the skiing is entirely above the tree line – this rules out places such as Tignes and Val-Thorens in France, Obergurgl in Austria and Cervinia in Italy. Another consideration is that hotels in big, popular winter resorts such as St Anton, Verbier and Val-d'Isère now often refuse to take weekend bookings except in very low season (eg early Jan or late March) because they can get more profitable week-long bookings. But more summer-oriented resorts, which generally have accommodation spare in winter, are worth considering – such as Chamonix, Morzine, Engelberg, Villars and Mürren.

WHAT ABOUT PRICE?

The cost can vary enormously. The flight and transfer are expensive fixed costs and obviously make a weekend proportionately more expensive than a full week. In general, through a good specialist tour operator you can expect to pay from around £350 a head for flights, car hire and a double room in a 3-star hotel on B&B for three nights, assuming two people sharing. With lift passes and meals you could be looking at around £500. For a 4-star hotel add another £100 or so.

MIDWEEK BREAKS

If you can get away midweek, there are many advantages. Flights (especially on budget airlines) should be cheaper, and possibly accommodation, too. And resorts that get busy at weekends, such as Verbier and Courmayeur, can be very quiet midweek in low season.

Flying to the snow

Competition means good deals for consumers

by **Chris Gill**

Most Brits going to the Alps go by plane; that's been the case since skiing became a mass-market activity in the 1960s. But most of us have traditionally travelled on one-week packages, using charter flights. What has changed in the last decade is that a growing number of us travel independently by air, often going for a period other than the standard seven nights that most package operators deal in. And we don't pay a fortune for the privilege. Here is our annual review of the options.

This change in our travelling habits has been brought about by budget airlines operating scheduled services, on which anyone can buy a seat, choosing flights to suit their own plans. The key player was and is EasyJet, which started cheap scheduled flights to the Alps in the mid-1990s; now, it operates about ten flights a day from the London area to Geneva, main gateway to the French and Swiss Alps. EasyJet and other major budget airlines have added more routes as well as more flights, while more minor airlines have entered the market. The budget flight business is clearly here to stay. Wherever you want to go, there's a budget flight to consider.

AIRLINES FOR THE ALPS
Budget airlines operate from most UK airports other than pricey Heathrow. When they have a choice, they use destination airports that are cheap, too, although they have to take account of possible demand for travel to Britain among people on the Continent. One of the cheapest ways to fly to Switzerland, for example, is with Helvetic, based in Zürich. The map below shows the arrival airports dotted around the Alps. There isn't so much scope here as in other parts of the Continent for budget airlines to use budget airports, but there are one or two unfamiliar names on the map. You can work out from the map which arrival airports are likely to work for your chosen resort. We're concentrating on the Alps, but budget airlines can also get you to the Pyrenees, the Massif Central and the Sierra Nevada.

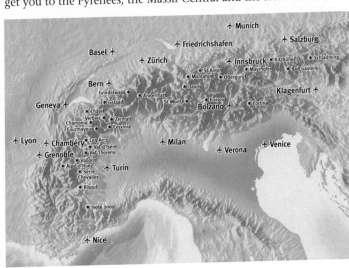

EasyJet still has by far the biggest range of flights to the key Alpine destination airport of Geneva – seven or eight departure airports around the UK. The airline also serves more Alpine airports – roughly seven from the London area. For those living south of London, the fact that it operates several routes from Gatwick will be important.

Ryanair has a lot of flights from Stansted and Luton to a number of convenient Alpine airports. Its baggage pricing policy (see below) is not designed to attract skiers and boarders.

Flybe serves several Alpine/Pyrenean airports from UK regional airports such as Exeter, Southampton and Norwich.

Bmibaby has flights from Cardiff, Manchester, Birmingham and East Midlands to Geneva and some other relevant airports.

Jet2.com is based at Manchester and Leeds/Bradford, offering flights to Geneva and Chambéry.

Helvetic is a Swiss budget airline, based in Zürich. It now uses Luton, offering two daily flight to Zürich. Fares start at 19 euros, and at the time of writing seats are available this winter at this price.

Thomsonfly goes to Lyon and Salzburg from Coventry, Bournemouth and Doncaster/Sheffield.

Don't overlook other national airlines, which fly between Heathrow (and sometimes major regional airports such as Birmingham and Manchester) and major home airports. They are increasingly competitive. **Air France** flies to Lyon, **Alitalia** to Milan, **Austrian** to Salzburg, **Lufthansa** to Munich. And **British Airways** goes to Geneva, Zürich, Munich, Milan, Venice and Verona from a variety of UK airports. You can also consider indirect routes via hubs in Germany, the Netherlands etc, if you have time.

Swiss International Air Lines operates several direct flights a day

from Heathrow, London City, Birmingham and Manchester to Zürich and shares British Airways flights from Heathrow to Geneva.

TRAVEL TIPS

How low can you go? Budget airline fares vary according to demand, and in general the cheapest are for midweek flights, early or late in the day, booked months in advance (or at the last minute). As a flight fills up, the fares go up; it it looks like the flight might not sell out, the fares go down again. You can pay less than £30 return if you time it right; while researching this article we booked tickets for a trip to Zürich in December for £27 return.

Flexibility Although the budget airlines won't normally give you a refund if you decide not to travel, most will now allow you to change the flight time or route, or the name of the passenger – but at a cost of perhaps £15 each way for each change. Check when you book, because the rules change.

Baggage Airline policies on baggage vary, and they are liable to change – so it's important to check. For example, EasyJet no longer carries skis free – they now cost an extra £10 per flight. EasyJet allows 20kg of hold baggage. Ryanair has a mean baggage allowance of 15kg; skis cost £17 per flight. Excess baggage is generally charged at £4/kg to £5/kg (for one flight) – the cost can mount up quickly. Major national airlines treat skis as part of your general baggage. Swiss carries one pair of skis or a snowboard free.

TRANSATLANTIC FLIGHTS

Lots of airlines serve the USA but most routes involve a change of plane along the way; make sure you allow several hours at your point of immigration to get through the controls. The main exceptions are flights to San Francisco or Los Angeles, for California resorts, and the daily British Airways direct flights to Denver, Colorado. Most airlines allow two pieces of hold luggage, each up to 32kg; skis or board count as one, so pack your boots in one of your main bags.

Zoom is a budget airline, launched in 2004, flying to Canada, with direct (but not necessarily non-stop) flights from Gatwick, Manchester and Glasgow to Vancouver (for Whistler), to Calgary (for the Rockies resorts), and to airports in the east, with economy and premium cabins. They allow 20kg of baggage plus skis or board.

DON'T FORGET CHARTER FLIGHTS

We've been concentrating here on scheduled services, which allow a wide choice of travel arrangements. Charter flights, where a tour operator (or group of operators) takes over a plane for package holiday purposes, are sometimes sold on a seat-only basis – and you can find out about these, as well as scheduled flight options, by spending hours on the internet. One new service that may be of particular interest this winter is a twice-weekly Thomson charter flight direct from Gatwick to Denver, Colorado. Charter flights can allow you to use airports not served by scheduled services – eg Bolzano, for resorts in the Dolomites.

Flying to the snow

75

Drive to the Alps

And ski where you please

by **Chris Allan**

More and more people from Britain are doing what the French, the Germans and the Dutch have done for years, and driving to their Alpine resorts. It has various advantages, even for those going on a pretty standard week in the Alps. For many people, it's just less hassle than checking in at dawn for a flight from Gatwick, and less tedious than sitting around waiting for a delayed charter plane that's stuck in Majorca. For families (especially those going self-catering), it simplifies the job of moving half the contents of your house to the Alps. If there are four or five people in your party, the cost can be lower than travelling by air.

If you fancy something a bit more adventurous, taking a car opens up the exciting possibility of touring around several resorts in one trip, and even making up your plans as you go.

Cross-Channel ferries are faster and more pleasant than ever, with the possibility of a seriously good lunch on P&O's short crossings as an alternative to the quicker shuttle-trains through the tunnel. And the motorway networks in north-eastern France and on the approaches to the Alps have improved immensely in the last decade. You can now get to most resorts easily in a day, if you're based in south-east England, in some cases using motorways virtually all the way.

For us, the freedom factor is the key. If the snow's bad in your resort, if the lift queues are horrendous, or if the resort you've plumped for turns out to be a let-down, you don't have to grin and bear it – if you have a car, you can try somewhere else (provided of course that you haven't already invested in a weekly lift pass).

Another plus-point is that you can extend the standard six-day holiday by two days by taking only one extra day off work – crossing the Channel early on a Friday morning and returning nine days later on the Sunday evening. On the outward journey, we often spend a day in a different resort before moving on to our final destination late on the Saturday. After a full day on the slopes on the final Saturday, driving for a few hours before stopping for the night means you won't find Sunday's journey too demanding, and you may even have time for a traditional French Sunday lunch.

AS YOU LIKE IT

If you fancy visiting several resorts, you can use one as a base and make day trips to others when it suits you. This way, you can still take advantage of package holiday prices.

The key to turning this kind of holiday into a success is to go for a base that offers easy road access to other resorts. Our suggestions for France are in a separate chapter. A good choice in Austria is the Tirol: the resorts east of Innsbruck offer many options. Söll is a convenient base for exploring resorts such as Alpbach and Kitzbühel. Further east in Salzburgerland there are lots of possibilities – and the Ski Amadé lift pass described in our Austrian introduction means you can exploit them conveniently and economically. Western Austria is not ideal for this sort of holiday – many resorts are tucked away at the head of long valleys – but from St Anton you could make day trips to Ischgl and Serfaus, as well as nearby Lech and Zürs.

AROUND THE ALPS IN SEVEN DAYS

If you want to see as much of the Alps as possible, consider making a Grand Tour by car, moving every day or two to a different resort and enjoying the complete freedom of going where you want, when you want. Out of high season there's no need to book accommodation before you go, so you can decide at the last minute which part of the Alps and which countries to visit – going where the snow is best, unless you have other special requirements.

A touring holiday doesn't mean you'll be spending more time on the road than on the piste – provided you plan your route carefully. An hour's drive after the lifts have shut is all it need take. It does eat into your après-ski time, of course; you have to be prepared to trade beers in the bar for fruit juice in the car.

Italy is far more suitable for tourers than day-trippers, provided you're prepared to put up with some slow drives on winding passes. For example, you could start in Livigno, drive to Bormio and then to the Dolomites, visiting Madonna di Campiglio and Selva, and finish your Italian expedition in Cortina. A tour of resorts off the Valle d'Aosta in the west of the Italian Alps doesn't involve passes, but some long drives up to places like Cervinia and Champoluc.

Eastern Switzerland also offers a very attractive touring holiday. You could start in Davos/Klosters, take in Lenzerheide and Arosa and end up in Flims. With a little extra driving, you could even include St Moritz. Or tack Disentis, Sedrun and snowy Andermatt on to the end, leaving a short drive to Zürich airport.

There's no need to confine yourself to one country. You could imitate the famous Haute-Route by starting in Argentière in France and ending up in Switzerland's Saas-Fee, taking in Verbier and Zermatt along the way– even diverting to Crans-Montana if time permits and the conditions (for once) look promising. The Valle d'Aosta tour mentioned above could start and finish with a day or two in Megève, or the Portes du Soleil.

The major thing that you have to watch out for with a touring holiday is the cost of accommodation. Checking into a resort hotel as an independent traveller for a night or two doesn't come cheap, and can be a bit of a rip-off. You can save money by staying down the valley – and you don't necessarily have to drive up to the slopes in the morning: some valley towns are linked by lifts. For example, you can take a funicular from Bourg-St-Maurice up to Les Arcs; a gondola links Brides-les-Bains to Méribel.

TYRES / CHAINS

For several seasons we have used winter tyres made by a specialist Dutch company, Vredestein. The editorial Audi Allroad is shown here wearing Wintrac 'V'-rated tyres, good for 149mph. We've found these (like the company's Snowtracs) excellent both on-snow and off. We leave them on year-round – they are no noisier than standard tyres.

So effective is the combination of 4WD and Wintracs that we haven't had a chance to evaluate Spikes Spiders. These are clever Swiss gadgets that you use instead of chains on cars (like the Audi) with wide wheels that can't take chains. You can hire or buy from the UK agents.

www.vredestein.com
t 01933 677770

www.spikesspider.com
t 01706 819365

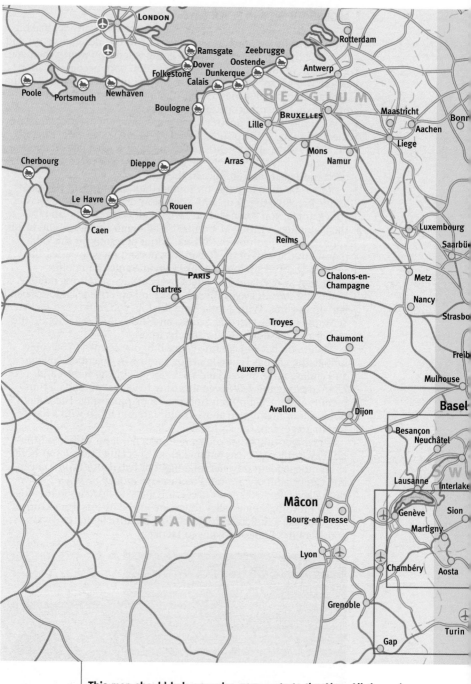

This map should help you plan your route to the Alps. All the main routes from the Channel and all the routes up into the mountains funnel through (or close to) three 'gateways', picked out on the map in larger type – Mâcon, Basel and Ulm. Decide which gateway suits your destination, and pick a route to it. Occasionally, using different Channel ports will lead you to use different gateways.

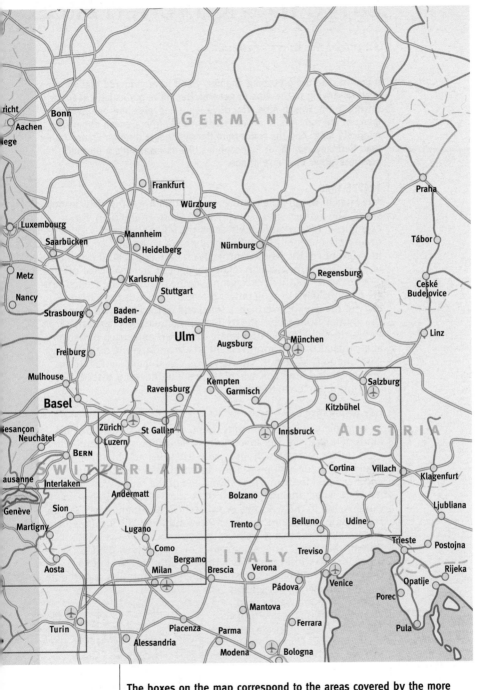

The boxes on the map correspond to the areas covered by the more
detailed maps at the start of the main country sections of the book:
Austria page 110
France page 218
Italy page 402
Switzerland page 462

Drive to the French Alps

To make the most of them

by **Chris Gill**

If you've read the preceding chapter, you'll have gathered that we are keen on driving to the Alps in general. But we're particularly keen on driving to the French Alps. The drive is a relatively short one, whereas many of the transfers to major French resorts from Geneva airport are relatively long. And the route from the Channel is through France rather than Germany, which for Francophiles like us means it's a pleasant prospect rather than a grim one.

TRAVEL TIME

The French Alps are the number-one destination for British car-borne skiers. The journey time is surprisingly short. From Calais, for example, you can comfortably cover the 900km/560 miles to Chamonix in about nine hours plus stops – with the exception of the final few miles, the whole journey is on motorways. And except on peak weekends the traffic is relatively light, if you steer clear of Paris.

With some southern exceptions, all the resorts of the French Alps are within a day's driving range, provided you cross the Channel early in the day (or overnight). Weekend traffic jams used to make the journey from Albertville to the Tarentaise resorts (from the Trois Vallées to Val-d'Isère) a nightmare for drivers and coach passengers alike; thanks to road improvements these are largely a thing of the past, but on peak-season Saturdays you can still encounter serious queues around Moûtiers, where there are traffic lights placed well away from the town, to minimise pollution.

DAY-TRIP BASES

As we explained in the previous chapter, a car opens up different kinds of holiday for the adventurous. Day-tripping, for example.

In the southern French Alps, Serre-Chevalier and Montgenèvre are ideal bases for day-tripping. They are within easy reach of one another, and Montgenèvre is at one end of the Milky Way lift network, which includes Sauze d'Oulx and Sestriere in Italy – you can drive on to these resorts, or reach them by lift and piste. On the French side of the border, a few miles south, Puy-St-Vincent is an underrated resort that is well worth a visit for a day – as is Risoul, a little further south. The major resorts of Alpe-d'Huez and Les Deux-Alpes are also within range, as is the cult off-piste resort of La Grave. Getting to them involves crossing a high pass, but it's a major route and is kept open pretty reliably.

The Chamonix valley is an ideal destination for day-trippers. The Mont-Blanc lift pass covers Chamonix, Les Contamines, Megève and others. Flaine and its satellites are fairly accessible – and so are Verbier in Switzerland, if the intervening passes are open, and Courmayeur in Italy, via the Mont Blanc tunnel. You could stay in a valley town such as Cluses, to escape resort prices.

80

MOVING ON

A look at the map over the page shows that a different approach will pay dividends in the Tarentaise region of France. Practically all the resorts here – from Valmorel to Val-d'Isère – are found at the end of long winding roads up from the main valley. You could visit them all from a base such as Aime, but it would be hard work. If instead you stayed in a different resort each night, moving on from one to the next in the early evening, you could have the trip of a lifetime.

GETTING THERE

Whatever route you prefer across the Channel, the gateway to the French Alps is Mâcon – though if you're taking a short crossing to Calais, this may be only roughly true. Your route south is via Reims, Troyes and Dijon; but if you are heading for Geneva, to get to the northern French Alps, you no longer have to tangle with the busy A6 from Paris via Beaune to Mâcon and Lyon. The relatively new A39 autoroute south from Dijon means you can head for Bourg-en-Bresse, well east of Mâcon. North of Dijon, there are plenty of characterful towns for an overnight stop – Arras, St-Quentin, Laon, Troyes, Reims.

From the more westerly Channel ports of Le Havre or Caen your route to Mâcon sounds dead simple: the A13 to Paris then the A6 south. But you have to get through or around Paris in the process. The most direct way around the city is the notorious périphérique – a hectic, multi-lane urban motorway close to the centre, with exits every few hundred yards and traffic that is either worryingly fast-moving or jammed solid. If the périphérique is jammed it takes ages. The more reliable alternative is to take a series of motorways and dual carriageways through the south-west fringes of Greater Paris.

Drive to the French Alps

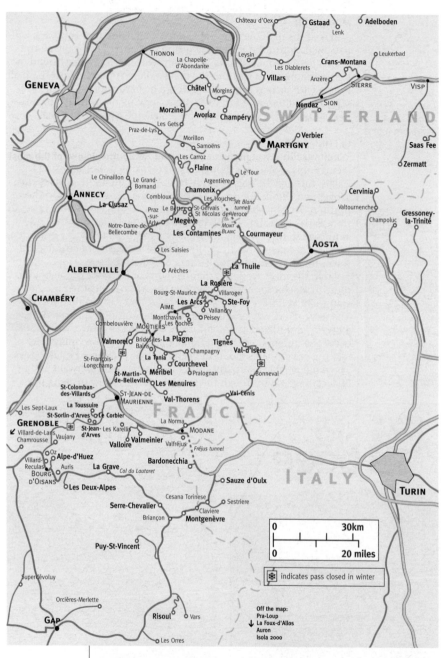

Pick the right gateway – Geneva, Chambéry or Grenoble – and you can hardly go wrong. The approach to Serre-Chevalier and Montgenèvre involves the 2060m/6,760ft Col du Lauteret; but the road is a major one and is kept clear of snow or reopened quickly after a fall. Crossing the French-Swiss border between Chamonix and Verbier involves two closure-prone passes – the Montets and the Forclaz. When necessary, one-way traffic runs beside the tracks through the rail tunnel beneath the passes.

Travelling by rail

Let the train take the strain

by **Dave Watts**

Taking the train to the Alps can be a great way to get more time on the slopes without taking more time off work. You can leave on Friday night, arriving in your resort on Saturday morning, and return on the following Saturday night, arriving back home on the Sunday – eight days' skiing for five days out of the office. Even if you opt for a different service that doesn't deliver the eight-day week, travelling by train is one of the most restful (and environmentally friendly) ways to get to the Alps.

The most popular train destination, with several different direct and indirect services, is the Tarentaise valley in France. You can step off the train in Bourg-St-Maurice and on to a funicular straight up to Arc 1600 in seven minutes, and there are quick bus transfers to the other famous mega-resorts of this region – including Val-d'Isère, Tignes, La Plagne, Courchevel, Méribel, Les Menuires and Val-Thorens.

But you can travel by train to many other resorts. And many traditional resorts, especially in Switzerland, are on the rail network and therefore reachable without resorting to buses. How many times you'll have to change trains is another matter.

DIRECT TRAIN SERVICES TO THE FRENCH ALPS

Since 1997, Eurostar has offered a truly direct service to the Alps – you board the train at London Waterloo or Ashford in Kent and disembark at Moûtiers, Bourg-St-Maurice or Aime (between Moûtiers and Bourg-St-Maurice) in the Tarentaise valley, without changing trains en route. The special winter services will run from 23/24 December through to Easter weekend on 14/15 April (with the last trains returning the following weekend). Standard return tickets cost from £179 (£269 for Leisure Select, which includes a bigger seat pitch, meals, and drinks with meals). Seats can also be booked as part of a package holiday. There's an overnight service that, for most of the season, allows you two extra days' skiing or boarding – it leaves on Friday night, arriving early on Saturday morning, and returns late Saturday evening, arriving back on Sunday morning. The service uses standard Eurostar carriages with no special sleeping arrangements – you just doze (or not) in your seat. The daytime service gives you no more than the standard six days on the slopes: both outward and return services leave on Saturday morning, arriving late afternoon. The return service doesn't stop at Aime (because the station does not have the security screening facilities necessary for passengers boarding a Eurostar train to leave France). In 2006, extra trains will be laid on for the peak February period – for three weekends starting on 11 February an extra train will go out on Saturday night (arriving Sunday morning), returning as a Sunday daytime service.

All the other train services to the Alps involve a change somewhere along the line, but they can still be fairly convenient and also allow for extra time on the slopes. Unlike Eurostar, many of the other services are equipped with sleeping facilities.

The Snowtrain is another weekly overnight service to the Tarentaise giving an eight-day week on the slopes, but it starts from Calais. It runs from 30 December until 17 March, normally leaving Calais on Friday night and arriving in the Alps the following morning. For the return journey you leave the Alps on Saturday evening, arriving back Sunday morning. You cross the Channel on a coach through the Eurotunnel from Folkestone (that route is new for 2005/06). Booking independently costs from £169 return. The train can also be booked through UK tour operators who have allocated spaces on each service. Overnight amenities include on-board couchettes (six drop-down berths to a compartment) and a disco/bar. It is possible (for an extra charge) to book a compartment for the exclusive use of four or five people on both legs of the journey.

There is a similar Friday night sleeper service to the Tarentaise starting from Paris. It runs from 23 December until 31 March. You take the Eurostar to Paris from London Waterloo and change trains at Paris Gare du Nord for an overnight service to the Alps. The return journey leaves the Alps on Saturday evening, arriving in Paris early on Sunday morning. It costs from £205 return including couchettes.

There are a number of indirect services available on the French railway throughout the week, but most mean crossing Paris from the Gare du Nord to the Gare de Lyon or Gare d'Austerlitz – the change of station is not difficult, though, with a direct metro, regular buses and plenty of taxis at your disposal. Indirect services to many Alpine destinations via Brussels or Lille also run and involve only a change of platform.

Note that, unlike on most budget airline services, there is no extra charge for taking skis or a snowboard on a train service.

For more details of French rail services contact Rail Europe on 08701 244 646 for overnight ski trains or 08705 848 848 for Eurostar trains. Or visit www.raileurope.co.uk or www.eurostar.com.

RAIL EUROPE

The Snowtrain's disco/bar gets much more crowded than this after dark ↓

Choosing your resort

Get it right first time

Most people get to go skiing or boarding only once or twice a year – and then only for a week at a time. So choosing the right resort is crucially important. Here is some advice on how to use our information to best effect, for the benefit of readers with relatively narrow experience of different resorts. Chamonix, Châtel and Courchevel are all French resorts, but they are as similar as chalk and Camembert. Start to consider resorts in other countries – Alpbach in Austria, say, or Zermatt in Switzerland – and the differences become even more pronounced.

Each resort chapter is organised in the same way, to help you choose the right resort. This short introduction takes you through the structure and what you will find under each heading we use.

GETTING A FEEL FOR THE PLACE

Our Costs ratings, ranging from ①②③④⑤⑥ to ①②③④⑤⑥, reflect the total cost of a week's holiday from Britain, including a typical package of flights plus half-board accommodation, a lift pass and meals and drinks on the spot. Three coins means on the low side of average, four means on the high side. Then, in the Ratings section, we rate each resort from 12 points of view – the more stars the better.

For major resorts, the next things to look at are our lists of the main good and bad points about the resort and its slopes, picked out with ➕ and ➖. These lists are followed by a summary in **bold type**, in which we've aimed to weigh up the pros and cons, coming off the fence and giving our view of who might like the resort.

You'll know by now whether this is, for example, a high, hideous, convenient, purpose-built resort with superb, snow-sure, challenging slopes but absolutely no nightlife, or a pretty, traditional village with gentle wooded slopes, ideal for beginners if only it had some snow.

THE RESORT

Resorts vary enormously in character and charm. At the extremes of the range are the handful of really hideous modern apartment-block resorts thrown up in France in the 1960s and the captivating old traffic-free mountain villages of which Switzerland has an unfair number. But it isn't simply a question of old versus new. Some purpose-built places can have a much friendlier feel than some traditional resorts with big blocky buildings. And some places can be remarkably strung out, whereas others are surprisingly compact. The

85

landscape can have an important impact – whether the resort is at the bottom of a shady valley or on a sunny shelf with panoramic views. Some places are working towns as well as ski resorts. Some are full of bars, discos and shops. Others are peaceful backwaters. Traffic may choke the streets. Or the village may be traffic-free.

THE MOUNTAINS

The slopes Some mountains and lift networks are vast and complex, while others are much smaller and lacking variation.

Terrain-parks We summarise here the specially prepared fun-parks and other terrain features most resorts now arrange for freestylers.

Snow reliability This is a crucial factor for many people, and one that varies enormously. Ignore this at your peril.

For experts, intermediates, beginners Most (though not all) resorts have something to offer beginners, but relatively few will keep an expert happy for a week's holiday. As for intermediates, whether a resort will suit you really depends on your standard and inclinations.

For cross-country We don't pretend that this is a guide for avid cross-country skiers. But we do try to help.

Queues Monster queues are largely a thing of the past, but it still pays to avoid the resorts with the worst queues, especially in high season.

Mountain restaurants If you like a decent lunch, beware: some resorts offer miserable restaurants and food (eg many resorts in America). In some resorts, the mountain restaurants add an extra dimension.

Schools and guides This is an area where we rely heavily on readers' reports of their own or their friends' experiences.

Facilities for children Again, to be of real help we need first-hand reports from people whose children have actually used the facilities.

STAYING THERE

How to go The basic choice is between catered chalets, hotels and self-catering accommodation. These options are not all available in all resorts – in particular, some resorts have few hotels or few chalets. Note that we have a separate chapter on luxury chalets.

Eating out The range of restaurants varies widely. Even some big resorts, such as Les Arcs, may have little choice because most of the visitors stay in their apartments. American resorts offer lots of choice.

Après-ski Tastes and styles vary enormously. Most resorts have pleasant places in which to have an immediate post-skiing beer or hot chocolate. Some then go dead. Others have noisy bars and discos until the early hours.

Off the slopes This is largely aimed at assessing how suitable a resort is for someone who doesn't intend to use the slopes – eg, a non-skiing spouse.

Staying up the mountain/down the valley If there are interesting options for staying on the slopes above the resort village or in valley towns below it, we pick them out.

Resort ratings at a glance

ANDORRA / AUSTRIA

	ARINSAL	PAS DE LA CASA	SOLDEU	ALPBACH	BAD GASTEIN	ELLMAU	HINTERTUX	HOCHKÖNIG
Page	102	104	106	118	120	123	126	131
Fast lifts	**	***	***	**	**	**	***	**
Snow	****	****	****	**	***	**	*****	***
Extent	*	***	***	*	****	****	**	***
Experts	*	*	*	*	***	*	***	**
Intermediates	**	***	***	**	***	****	***	****
Beginners	***	****	****	****	**	****	**	****
Convenience	***	****	***	**	**	***	**	**
Queues	***	***	***	**	***	****	***	****
Restaurants*	**	**	**	***	****	**	**	***
Scenery	***	***	***	***	***	***	***	***
Resort charm	*	*	*	*****	***	***	***	***
Off-slope	*	*	*	***	****	***	*	***

	ISCHGL	KITZBÜHEL	LECH	MAYRHOFEN	NAUDERS	OBERGURGL	OBERTAUERN	SAALBACH-HINTERGLEMM
Page	138	144	150	157	166	168	173	175
Fast lifts	*****	**	***	***	**	****	*****	****
Snow	****	**	****	***	****	*****	****	***
Extent	****	***	****	***	**	**	**	***
Experts	***	***	****	*	***	**	***	**
Intermediates	****	****	****	***	****	***	****	****
Beginners	**	**	****	**	**	****	****	***
Convenience	***	**	***	*	**	****	****	****
Queues	****	**	****	*	****	*****	****	***
Restaurants*	****	****	***	***	***	**	****	****
Scenery	***	***	***	***	***	***	***	***
Resort charm	****	****	****	***	****	****	**	****
Off-slope	***	*****	***	****	***	**	**	**

	SCHLADMING	SÖLDEN	SÖLL	ST ANTON	ST JOHANN IN TIROL	WESTENDORF	WILDSCH'AU	ZELL AM SEE
Page	181	185	187	193	202	204	206	210
Fast lifts	***	*****	**	***	**	**	**	***
Snow	****	*****	**	****	**	**	**	**
Extent	***	***	****	****	*	*	*	**
Experts	**	***	*	*****	*	**	*	**
Intermediates	****	****	****	***	***	***	**	***
Beginners	***	**	***	*	****	***	***	***
Convenience	***	**	**	***	***	***	***	**
Queues	****	***	***	**	****	****	***	**
Restaurants*	****	***	**	***	****	***	**	***
Scenery	***	***	***	***	***	***	***	***
Resort charm	***	**	***	****	***	****	***	***
Off-slope	****	**	**	***	****	**	**	****

* Refers to mountain restaurants only

Resort ratings at a glance

	ALPE-D'HUEZ	LES ARCS	AVORIAZ	CHAMONIX	CHÂTEL	LA CLUSAZ	LES CONTAMINES	COURCHEVEL
Page	224	233	242	246	256	261	267	269
Fast lifts	**	**	***	***	*	**	**	****
Snow	****	****	***	****	**	**	****	****
Extent	****	***	*****	***	*****	***	***	*****
Experts	****	****	***	*****	***	***	***	****
Intermediates	****	****	****	**	****	****	****	*****
Beginners	*****	****	****	*	***	****	**	****
Convenience	****	****	*****	*	**	***	**	****
Queues	****	***	***	**	***	***	***	****
Restaurants*	****	***	****	**	***	****	****	****
Scenery	****	***	***	*****	****	***	****	***
Resort charm	*	*	**	****	***	****	****	**
Off-slope	****	*	*	*****	**	***	**	***

	LES DEUX-ALPES	FLAINE	LES GETS	LA GRAVE	MEGÈVE	LES MENUIRES	MÉRIBEL	MONTGENÈVRE
Page	280	286	292	294	296	302	304	314
Fast lifts	**	**	**	***	*	***	****	*
Snow	****	****	**	***	**	****	***	****
Extent	***	****	***	*	*****	*****	*****	****
Experts	****	****	***	*****	**	****	****	**
Intermediates	**	*****	****	*	****	*****	*****	****
Beginners	***	*****	****	*	***	***	****	*****
Convenience	***	*****	***	***	**	*****	***	****
Queues	**	***	***	****	****	****	****	****
Restaurants*	**	**	***	**	****	***	***	**
Scenery	****	****	***	****	*****	***	***	***
Resort charm	**	*	***	***	****	*	***	***
Off-slope	**	*	***	*	****	*	***	*

	MORZINE	LA PLAGNE	PUY-ST-VINCENT	RISOUL	LA ROSIÈRE	SAMOËNS	SERRE-CHEVALIER	STE-FOY
Page	318	327	338	340	343	345	347	354
Fast lifts	**	**	*	*	**	**	**	*
Snow	**	****	***	***	***	***	***	***
Extent	*****	****	**	***	***	****	****	*
Experts	***	***	***	**	**	****	***	****
Intermediates	****	*****	***	****	***	*****	****	***
Beginners	***	****	***	****	*****	**	****	**
Convenience	**	*****	*****	****	***	*	***	***
Queues	***	***	***	****	***	****	***	*****
Restaurants*	***	***	***	***	*	**	***	**
Scenery	***	****	***	***	***	****	***	***
Resort charm	***	*	**	**	***	****	***	***
Off-slope	***	*	*	*	*	***	**	*

	ST-MARTIN-DE-BELLEVILLE	LES SYBELLES	LA TANIA	TIGNES	VAL-D'ISÈRE	VALMOREL	VAL-THORENS	
Page	357	360	365	369	380	390	392	
Fast lifts	***	*	****	***	****	*	****	
Snow	***	***	***	*****	*****	***	*****	
Extent	*****	*****	*****	*****	*****	***	*****	
Experts	****	**	****	*****	*****	**	****	
Intermediates	*****	***	*****	*****	*****	****	*****	
Beginners	***	****	**	**	***	*****	****	
Convenience	***	***	****	****	***	*****	*****	
Queues	****	****	****	****	****	****	***	
Restaurants*	****	**	****	***	**	**	****	
Scenery	***	***	***	***	***	***	***	
Resort charm	****	*/****	***	**	***	****	**	
Off-slope	*	**	*	*	**	**	**	

	BORMIO	CERVINIA	CORTINA D'AMPEZZO	COURMAYEUR	LIVIGNO	MADONNA DI CAMPIGLIO	MONTEROSA SKI	SAUZE D'OULX
Page	409	411	416	421	426	430	432	436
Fast lifts	***	***	**	***	***	***	***	**
Snow	***	*****	***	****	****	***	****	**
Extent	**	***	***	**	**	***	***	****
Experts	*	*	**	***	**	**	****	**
Intermediates	***	****	***	****	***	****	****	****
Beginners	**	*****	*****	**	****	****	**	**
Convenience	***	***	*	*	**	***	***	**
Queues	***	***	****	***	****	****	****	***
Restaurants*	****	***	****	****	***	***	**	***
Scenery	***	****	*****	****	***	****	****	***
Resort charm	****	**	****	****	***	***	***	**
Off-slope	****	*	*****	***	**	***	*	*

	SELVA	SESTRIERE	LA THUILE					
Page	441	450	452					
Fast lifts	***	**	**					
Snow	****	***	****					
Extent	*****	****	***					
Experts	***	***	**					
Intermediates	*****	****	****					
Beginners	****	***	****					
Convenience	***	****	***					
Queues	***	***	****					
Restaurants*	****	**	*					
Scenery	*****	***	***					
Resort charm	***	*	***					
Off-slope	***	*	**					

Resort ratings at a glance

89

* Refers to mountain restaurants only

Resort ratings at a glance

90

	ANDERMATT	AROSA	CHAMPÉRY	CRANS-MONTANA	DAVOS	FLIMS	GRIN'WALD	MÜRREN
Page	468	470	472	474	476	483	485	489
Fast lifts	**	***	*	***	***	****	***	***
Snow	****	***	**	**	****	***	**	***
Extent	*	**	*****	***	*****	****	***	*
Experts	****	**	***	**	****	***	**	***
Intermediates	**	***	****	****	*****	*****	****	***
Beginners	*	****	**	***	**	****	***	**
Convenience	***	**	*	**	**	***	**	***
Queues	**	****	****	***	**	***	**	***
Restaurants*	*	***	***	***	***	***	***	**
Scenery	***	***	****	****	****	***	*****	*****
Resort charm	****	**	****	**	**	***	****	*****
Off-slope	**	****	***	****	*****	***	****	***

	SAAS-FEE	ST MORITZ	VERBIER	VILLARS	WENGEN	ZERMATT		
Page	493	499	505	515	518	523		
Fast lifts	***	****	**	***	***	*****		
Snow	*****	****	***	**	**	****		
Extent	**	*****	*****	***	***	****		
Experts	***	****	*****	**	**	*****		
Intermediates	****	****	***	***	****	****		
Beginners	*****	**	**	****	***	*		
Convenience	***	**	**	***	***	*		
Queues	***	**	***	***	***	***		
Restaurants*	***	****	***	***	****	*****		
Scenery	****	****	****	***	*****	*****		
Resort charm	*****	*	***	****	*****	*****		
Off-slope	****	*****	***	****	****	****		

| | CALIFORNIA | | | COLORADO | | | | |
	HEAVENLY	MAMMOTH		ASPEN	BEAVER CR'K	BRECK'RIDGE	COPPER MOUNTAIN	KEYSTONE
Page	542	547		555	561	563	568	570
Fast lifts	***	****		***	*****	****	**	****
Snow	****	****		*****	*****	*****	*****	*****
Extent	***	***		****	**	**	**	**
Experts	***	****		*****	****	****	****	***
Intermediates	****	****		*****	****	****	****	****
Beginners	****	****		*****	*****	****	****	****
Convenience	*	**		**	****	***	****	**
Queues	****	****		****	*****	****	****	****
Restaurants*	*	*		***	**	**	*	***
Scenery	****	***		***	***	***	***	***
Resort charm	*	**		****	**	***	**	**
Off-slope	**	*		****	***	***	*	**

	SNOWMASS	STEAMBOAT	TELLURIDE	VAIL	WINTER PARK			
Page	572	574	576	578	584			
Fast lifts	★★★	★★	★★★★★	★★★★	★★★			
Snow	★★★★★	★★★★	★★★★	★★★★★	★★★★★			
Extent	★★★★	★★★	★★	★★★★	★★★			
Experts	★★★★★	★★★	★★★★	★★★★	★★★★			
Intermediates	★★★★★	★★★★	★★★	★★★★★	★★★★			
Beginners	★★★★★	★★★★★	★★★★★	★★★	★★★★★			
Convenience	★★★★	★★★	★★★★	★★★	★★★			
Queues	★★★★	★★★★	★★★★★	★★	★★★★			
Restaurants*	★★★	★★★	★	★★	★★★			
Scenery	★★★★	★★★	★★★★	★★★	★★★			
Resort charm	★★	★★	★★★★	★★★	★★			
Off-slope	★★★	★★	★★	★★★	★			

	UTAH ALTA	THE CANYONS	DEER VALLEY	PARK CITY	SNOWBIRD	REST OF THE WEST BIG SKY	JACKSON HOLE	
Page	591	593	595	597	602	606	608	
Fast lifts	★★	★★★	★★★★	★★★★	★★★	★★★	★★★	
Snow	★★★★★	★★★★	★★★★	★★★★	★★★★★	★★★★	★★★★	
Extent	★★★	★★★	★★	★★★	★★★	★★★	★★★	
Experts	★★★★★	★★★★	★★★	★★★★	★★★★★	★★★★	★★★★★	
Intermediates	★★★	★★★★	★★★★	★★★★	★★★	★★★★	★★	
Beginners	★★★	★★	★★★★	★★★★	★★	★★★★	★★★	
Convenience	★★★★	★★★★	★★★★	★★	★★★★★	★★★★	★★★	
Queues	★★★	★★★★	★★★★	★★★★	★★	★★★★★	★★★	
Restaurants*	★★	★★★	★★★★	★★	★	★	★	
Scenery	★★★	★★★	★★★	★★★	★★★	★★★	★★★	
Resort charm	★★	★★	★★★	★★★	★	★★	★★★	
Off-slope	★	★★	★★	★★★	★	★★	★★★	

	NEW ENGLAND KILLINGTON	STOWE						
Page	617	621						
Fast lifts	★★	★★						
Snow	★★★	★★★						
Extent	★★	★						
Experts	★★★	★★★						
Intermediates	★★★	★★★★						
Beginners	★★★★	★★★★						
Convenience	★	★						
Queues	★★★★	★★★★						
Restaurants*	★	★★						
Scenery	★★★	★★★						
Resort charm	★	★★★★						
Off-slope	★	★						

Resort ratings at a glance

91

* Refers to mountain restaurants only

Resort ratings at a glance

92

	WESTERN CANADA BANFF	BIG WHITE	FERNIE	KICKING HORSE	LAKE LOUISE	PANORAMA	SUN PEAKS	WHISTLER
Page	628	634	636	641	643	648	650	652
Fast lifts	***	***	**	**	***	***	***	****
Snow	****	*****	*****	****	***	***	****	****
Extent	****	***	***	***	****	**	***	****
Experts	****	***	*****	****	****	****	***	*****
Intermediates	****	****	**	***	****	***	****	*****
Beginners	***	****	****	***	***	****	****	***
Convenience	*	****	****	*	*	****	****	****
Queues	****	*****	****	*****	****	*****	*****	***
Restaurants*	***	*	*	**	**	*	*	**
Scenery	****	***	***	***	*****	***	***	***
Resort charm	***	**	**	*	***	**	***	***
Off-slope	*****	**	**	*	****	*	**	**

	EASTERN CANADA TREMBLANT							
Page	664							
Fast lifts	****							
Snow	****							
Extent	*							
Experts	**							
Intermediates	***							
Beginners	****							
Convenience	****							
Queues	***							
Restaurants*	**							
Scenery	***							
Resort charm	****							
Off-slope	***							

	SPAIN BAQUEIRA	NORWAY HEMSEDAL	SWEDEN ÅRE	BULGARIA BANSKO	NEW ZEALAND QUEENST'WN			
Page	667	673	676	679	689			
Fast lifts	**	**	**	****	**			
Snow	***	****	***	***	**			
Extent	**	*	**	*	*			
Experts	***	**	**	**	***			
Intermediates	****	****	****	****	***			
Beginners	**	***	****	**	***			
Convenience	***	**	***	**	*			
Queues	***	****	****	****	***			
Restaurants*	**	*	***	***	*			
Scenery	***	**	***	***	****			
Resort charm	**	**	***	**	**			
Off-slope	*	*	***	*	*****			

* Refers to mountain restaurants only

Resort shortlists

To help you spot resorts that will suit you

To streamline the job of spotting the ideal resort for your own holiday, here are lists of the best ten or so resorts for 20 different categories. Some lists embrace European and North American resorts, but most we've confined to Europe, because America has too many qualifying resorts (eg for beginners) or because America does things differently, making comparisons invalid (eg for off-piste).

SOMETHING FOR EVERYONE
Resorts with everything from reassuring nursery slopes to real challenges for experts
Alpe-d'Huez, France p224
Les Arcs, France p233
Aspen, Colorado p555
Courchevel, France p269
Flaine, France p286
Mammoth, California p547
Vail, Colorado p578
Val-d'Isère, France p380
Whistler, Canada p652
Winter Park, Colorado p584

INTERNATIONAL OVERSIGHTS
Resorts that deserve as much attention as the ones we go back to every year, but don't seem to get it
Alta, Utah p591
Andermatt, Switzerland p468
Bad Gastein, Austria p120
Big Sky, Montana p606
Les Contamines, France p267
Copper Mountain, Colorado p568
Flims-Laax, Switzerland p483
Monterosa Ski, Italy p432
Risoul, France p340
Telluride, Colorado p576

RELIABLE SNOW IN THE ALPS
Alpine resorts with good snow records or lots of snowmaking, and high or north-facing slopes
Argentière/Chamonix, France p246
Cervinia, Italy p411
Courchevel, France p269
Hintertux, Austria p126
Lech/Zürs, Austria p150
Obergurgl, Austria p168
Saas-Fee, Switzerland p493
Val-d'Isère/Tignes, France pp380/369
Val-Thorens, France p392
Zermatt, Switzerland p523

OFF-PISTE WONDERS
Alpine resorts where, with the right guidance and equipment, you can have the time of your life
Alpe-d'Huez, France p224
Andermatt, Switzerland p468
Argentière/Chamonix, France p246
Davos/Klosters, Switzerland p476
La Grave, France p294
Lech/Zürs, Austria p150
Monterosa Ski, Italy p432
St Anton, Austria p193
Val-d'Isère/Tignes, France pp380/369
Verbier, Switzerland p505

SNOWPIX.COM / CHRIS GILL

Monterosa is one of two areas that appear in both of the lists immediately above →

POWDER PARADISES
Resorts with the snow, the terrain and (ideally) the lack of crowds that make for powder perfection
Alta/Snowbird, Utah pp591/602
Andermatt, Switzerland p468
Big Sky, Montana p606
Big White, Canada p634
Brighton/Solitude, Utah p604
Fernie, Canada p636
Grand Targhee, Wyoming p608
La Grave, France p294
Jackson Hole, Wyoming p608
Kicking Horse, Canada p641
Kirkwood, California, p552
Monterosa Ski, Italy p432
Red Resort, Canada p660
Snowbasin, Utah p604
Ste-Foy, France p354

BLACK RUNS
Resorts with steep, mogully, lift-served slopes within the safety of the piste network
Alta/Snowbird, Utah pp591/602
Andermatt, Switzerland p468
Argentière/Chamonix, France p246
Aspen, Colorado p555
Beaver Creek, Colorado p561
Courchevel, France p269
Jackson Hole, Wyoming p608
Whistler, Canada p652
Winter Park, Colorado p584
Zermatt, Switzerland p523

CHOPAHOLICS
Resorts where you can quit the conventional lift network and have a day riding helicopters or cats
Aspen, Colorado p555
Crested Butte, Colorado p589
Fernie, Canada p636
Grand Targhee, Wyoming p608
Lech/Zürs, Austria p150
Monterosa Ski, Italy p432
Panorama, Canada p648
Verbier, Switzerland p505
Whistler, Canada p652
Zermatt, Switzerland p523

WEATHERPROOF SLOPES
Alpine resorts with snow-sure slopes if the sun shines, and trees in case it doesn't
Les Arcs, France p233
Courchevel, France p269
Courmayeur, Italy p421
Flims, Switzerland p483
Schladming, Austria p181
Selva, Italy p441
Serre-Chevalier, France p347
Sestriere, Italy p450
La Thuile, Italy p452

HIGH-MILEAGE PISTE-BASHING
Extensive intermediate slopes with big lift networks
Alpe-d'Huez, France p224
Davos/Klosters, Switzerland p476
Flims/Laax, Switzerland p483
Milky Way: Sauze d'Oulx (Italy), Montgenèvre (France) pp436/314
Paradiski, France, p324
Portes du Soleil, France/Switz p336
Selva/Sella Ronda, Italy p441
Les Sybelles, France p360
Trois Vallées, France p378
Val-d'Isère/Tignes, France pp380/369
Whistler, Canada p652

MOTORWAY CRUISING
Long, gentle, super-smooth pistes to bolster the frail confidence of those not long off the nursery slope
Les Arcs, France p233
Breckenridge, Colorado p563
Cervinia, Italy p411
Cortina, Italy p416
Courchevel, France p269
Megève, France p296
La Plagne, France p327
Snowmass, Colorado p572
La Thuile, Italy p452
Vail, Colorado p578

RESORTS FOR BEGINNERS
European resorts with gentle, snow-sure nursery slopes and easy, longer runs to progress to
Alpe-d'Huez, France p224
Les Arcs, France p233
Bansko, Bulgaria p679
Cervinia, Italy p411
Courchevel, France p269
Flaine, France p286
Montgenèvre, France p314
La Plagne, France p327
Saas-Fee, Switzerland p493
Soldeu, Andorra p106

MODERN CONVENIENCE
Alpine resorts where there's plenty of slope-side accommodation to make life easy
Les Arcs, France p233
Avoriaz, France p242
Courchevel, France p269
Flaine, France p286
Les Menuires, France p302
Obertauern, Austria p173
La Plagne, France p327
Puy-St-Vincent, France, p338
La Tania, France, p365
Tignes, France, p369
Valmorel, France p390
Val-Thorens, France p392

BACK-DOOR RESORTS
Cute little Alpine villages linked to
big, bold ski areas, giving you the
best of two different worlds
Les Brévières (Tignes), France p369
Champagny (La Plagne), France p327
Leogang (Saalbach), Austria p175
Montchavin (La Plagne), France p327
Peisey (Les Arcs), France p233
Le Pré (Les Arcs), France p233
Samoëns (Flaine), France, p345
St-Martin (Three Valleys), France p357
Stuben (St Anton), Austria, covered in
Lech chapter p150
Vaujany (Alpe-d'Huez), France p224

SNOW-SURE BUT SIMPATICO
Alpine resorts with high-rise
slopes, but low-rise, traditional-
style buildings
Andermatt, Switzerland p468
Arabba, Italy p441
Argentière, France p246
Les Contamines, France p267
Ischgl, Austria p138
Lech/Zürs, Austria p150
Monterosa Ski, Italy p432
Obergurgl, Austria p168
Saas-Fee, Switzerland p493
Zermatt, Switzerland p523

SPECIALLY FOR FAMILIES
Alpine resorts where you can easily
find accommodation surrounded
by snow, not by traffic and fumes
Les Arcs, France p233
Avoriaz, France p242
Flaine, France p286
Lech, Austria p150
Montchavin (La Plagne), France p327
Mürren, Switzerland p489
Puy-St-Vincent, France p338
Risoul, France p340
Saas-Fee, Switzerland p493
Les Sybelles, France p360
Valmorel, France p390
Wengen, Switzerland p518

SPECIAL MOUNTAIN RESTAURANTS
Alpine resorts where the mountain
restaurants can really add an
extra dimension to your holiday
Alpe-d'Huez, France p224
La Clusaz, France p261
Courmayeur, Italy p421
Kitzbühel, Austria p144
Megève, France p296
St Johann in Tirol, Austria p202
St Moritz, Switzerland p499
Selva, Italy p441
Söll, Austria p187
Zermatt, Switzerland p523

DRAMATIC SCENERY
Resorts where the mountains are
not just high and snowy, but
spectacularly scenic too
Chamonix, France p246
Cortina, Italy p416
Courmayeur, Italy p421
Heavenly, California p542
Jungfrau resorts (Grindelwald,
Mürren, Wengen), Switzerland
pp485/489/518
Lake Louise, Canada p643
Megève, France, p296
Saas-Fee, Switzerland p493
St Moritz, Switzerland p499
Selva, Italy p441
Zermatt, Switzerland p523

VILLAGE CHARM
Resorts with traditional character
that enriches your holiday – from
mountain villages to mining towns
Alpbach, Austria p118
Champéry, Switzerland p472
Courmayeur, Italy p421
Crested Butte, Colorado p589
Lech, Austria p150
Mürren, Switzerland p489
Saas-Fee, Switzerland p493
Telluride, Colorado p576
Wengen, Switzerland p518
Zermatt, Switzerland p523

LIVELY NIGHTLIFE
European resorts where you'll have
no difficulty finding somewhere to
boogy, and someone to do it with
Chamonix, France p246
Ischgl, Austria p138
Kitzbühel, Austria p144
Saalbach, Austria p175
St Anton, Austria p193
Sauze d'Oulx, Italy p436
Sölden, Austria p185
Pas de la Casa, Andorra p104
Val-d'Isère, France p380
Verbier, Switzerland p505

OTHER AMUSEMENTS
Alpine resorts where those not
interested in skiing or boarding
can still find plenty to do
Bad Gastein, Austria p120
Chamonix, France p246
Cortina, Italy p416
Davos, Switzerland p476
Gstaad, Switzerland p535
Innsbruck, Austria p134
Kitzbühel, Austria p144
Megève, France p296
St Moritz, Switzerland p499
Zell am See, Austria p210

Resort shortlists

95

Our resort chapters

How to get the best out of them

FINDING A RESORT

The bulk of the book consists of chapters devoted to individual major resorts, plus minor resorts that share the same lift system. Sometimes we devote a chapter to an area not dominated by one resort (Les Sybelles, Monterosa). Chapters are grouped by country: first, the five major European countries; then the US and Canada (where resorts are grouped by states or regions); then minor European countries; then Australasia. Within each group, resorts are ordered alphabetically – except that each country/state/region section now ends with Short Turns: a handful of short chapters covering minor resorts.

There's a **chapter-by-chapter listing** on the facing page, and another at the front of the book.

Short cuts to the resorts that might suit you are provided by a table of comparative **star ratings** and a series of **shortlists** of resorts with particular merits. To find these, just turn back a few pages towards the front of the book.

At the back of the book is an **index** to the resort chapters, combined with a **directory** giving basic information on hundreds of other minor resorts. If the resort you are looking up is covered in a chapter devoted to a bigger resort, the page reference will take you to the start of that chapter, not to the exact page on which the minor resort is described.

There's further guidance on using our information in the chapter on 'Choosing your resort' – designed to be helpful particularly to people with little or no experience of resorts, who may not appreciate how big the differences between one resort and another can be (ie like chalk and cheese).

READING A CHAPTER

The **cost** of visiting each resort is rated on a scale of one to six – ①②③④⑤⑥ to ①②③④⑤⑥ – reflecting the typical cost of a one-week trip based on a half-board package from the UK, plus a lift pass and an allowance for lunch in mountain restaurants. We assume two people sharing a room – even in the US, where package prices are often based on four people sharing.

Star ratings summarise our view of the resort in 12 respects, including how well it suits different standards of skier/boarder. The more stars, the better. New this year is a rating based on the proportion of lifts that are fast.

We give phone numbers and internet addresses of the **tourist office** and phone numbers for recommended **hotels.** We give a cost rating for hotels: the higher the price, the more coins shown.

The UK tour operators offering **package holidays** in each resort are listed in the index at the back of the book, not in the main chapters.

Our **mountain maps** show the resorts' own classification of runs – so those for the US and Canada show green, blue and black runs, and no red ones (unlike Europe). On some maps we also follow the convention of using black diamonds to indicate expert terrain without defined runs. We do not distinguish single-diamond terrain from the steeper double-diamond.

We include on the map any lifts definitely planned for construction for the coming season.

We use the following symbols to identify **fast lifts**:

Ⓛ fast chair-lift

Ⓖ gondola

Ⓒ cable-car

Ⓕ funicular railway

THE WORLD'S BEST WINTER SPORTS RESORTS

To find a minor resort – or a major resort, if you don't know what country it's in – go to the index/directory at the back of the book

Our resort chapters

97

Andorra

More Brits now go to Andorra for winter holidays than to Switzerland, Canada and the USA combined – Andorra is almost level with Italy as the third most popular country to visit. Despite a continuing building boom, it is still often difficult to find a bed, even in low season. It's also difficult to get away from fellow Brits. And from traffic and construction sites – Andorra has lots of both.

Andorra used to be seen primarily as a cheap and cheerful holiday destination, aimed mainly at younger singles and couples looking for a good time in the duty-free bars and clubs as well as learning to ski or snowboard. And most of the resorts are still excellent for that market. Tour operator-organised pub crawls of 100+ guests are common. But there's more to it than that. The ski schools have always been excellent, with lots of native English-speaking instructors. In recent years, some more upmarket hotels have been built (though they often resemble Spanish summer package hotels and have self-service buffet meals). And lots of money has been pumped in to developing powerful lift systems and piste-grooming fleets that many well-known Alpine resorts would be proud of; this makes the slopes much more attractive to intermediates as well as beginners. Andorra no longer competes with eastern Europe for the budget market; it costs more, and what it delivers is in a different league – the Alpine league.

There are big differences in the characters of the resorts. Soldeu is the one that has tried hardest to move upmarket; chapters on Soldeu and the other two major resorts of Arinsal and Pas de la Casa follow.

This introduction includes some comments on the valley towns that are also marketed as ski resorts by some tour operators, and on the excellent out-of-the-way day skiing area of Arcalis.

Andorra has a relatively reliable snow record. Its situation close to both the Atlantic and the Mediterranean oceans, together with the high altitude of its resorts, means it usually gets substantial natural snowfalls. It has also invested heavily in snowmaking. This combination means you can book Andorra months in advance with some confidence. And an early reservation is necessary: late bookers can have difficulty finding an Andorra package.

Both package holiday prices and prices for drinks and extras such as instruction and equipment rental are generally lower than in the Alps. But some reporters have found duty-free luxury goods prices not the super-bargains they had expected.

Duty-free spirits prices and large, unmeasured helpings mean that nightlife can be very lively. If you want to spend your nights in the company of drunken young Brits, you will have no trouble finding places where you can. But you will also have no trouble avoiding such scenes, and finding more civilised places in which to relax.

The sight of cranes is still common, as hotels and apartments are built to keep up with demand. It is no longer true to say that the resorts resemble giant construction sites, but they all have construction sites within them (or on the edge of them as they expand in sprawling fashion along the roadside). And don't be surprised if a 'new' hotel you visit still has building work going on within it to finish it off.

ANDORRAN MINISTRY OF TOURISM
← Don't worry: this is not a ski resort – it's the capital city, Andorra La Vella

Adjacent resorts have been busy linking together, meaning bigger ski areas and a bit more variety. Arinsal and Pal were linked by a cable-car six seasons ago; since 2004/05 their lift pass has also covered Arcalis (an excellent but accommodation-free ski area 26km/16 miles away by road – see below). In 2003/04 the long-standing feud between the communities of Pas de La Casa and Soldeu was put aside to allow them to move in to the big league and market themselves together as the ski domain of Grandvalira, with one lift pass available to cover the whole area. The resorts' slopes had been physically linked by lift and piste for a few seasons before that, and they form an impressive area that is comparable with big-name resorts such as Kitzbühel and Les Deux-Alpes.

STAYING DOWN THE VALLEY

Several valley towns can be used as bases, either to use the slopes of one resort or to explore several resorts in the course of a week.

One obviously strong candidate here is **Encamp**, which has a powerful 18-seat gondola giving a quick way into the whole of the Grandvalira ski area. Encamp seemed to us the least attractive of the valley towns (not least because of its situation on the traffic-choked main road), but we can't claim to have examined it closely and a couple of reporters have recommend it. It is certainly cheap.

La Massana is a more appealing town, and since the 2004/05 season it has been linked to the Pal-Arinsal ski area by gondola. It is also 6km/4 miles closer to Arcalis. **Ordino** is slightly nearer Arcalis, and pleasantly rustic.

The capital of **Andorra la Vella** is not far down the valley from Encamp but is a more attractive base for someone wanting a more

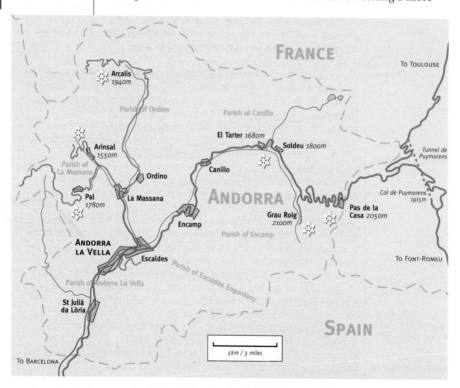

rounded holiday (though still choked by traffic and 'appalling' resultant fumes). The duty-free shopping could fill a page, but probably the most interesting feature is the Caldea spa 'probably the best off-slope activity in Andorra', according to a reporter. The interior is laid out in a 'Hanging Gardens of Babylon' style, and the facilities are very impressive – indoor and outdoor pools, with fountains and waterfalls, saunas, hot-tubs, Turkish baths, sunbeds, hydrotherapy, massage … even a grapefruit bath! There are plenty of high-quality, if relatively expensive, hotels. Andorra la Vella is not a big place, and most hotels are within easy walking distance of the centre. There is plenty of choice when it comes to dining out and plenty of bars and nightclubs that stay open until 4am. However, the clientele is generally a more sophisticated bunch, mainly Andorrans and Spaniards, and the 'drink-until-you-drop' attitude of the mountain resorts is rare.

SKIING AND BOARDING AWAY FROM THE MAIN RESORTS

Arcalis is the most remote area of slopes in Andorra, tucked away at the head of a long valley, and most British visitors to Andorra never hear about it. But it makes a very worthwhile day trip and from 2004/05 has been covered by a joint Vallnord lift pass with Arinsal and Pal. The variety of the terrain at Arcalis is greater than in most of the main resorts, the slopes are usually deserted except at weekends (when locals pour in) and the snow is usually the best you will find. It provides excellent intermediate and beginner terrain, but of all Andorra's resorts it has the most to offer experts, including lots of off-piste between the marked runs. There is no accommodation at the mountain, just a day lodge and a lot of car parking, but buildings are now springing up along the Vall d'Ordino leading up to it.

The Roc de les Bruixes restaurant at El Forn above Canillo has great views from the terrace and claims to be 'gastronomic', but we haven't had a chance to try it yet →

Arinsal

Cheap base for first-time skiers and boarders

NEWS

The long-awaited gondola from La Massana to Pal opened during the 2004/05 season, and a joint Vallnord lift pass was introduced, covering both the Arinsal-Pal and the Arcalis ski areas (26km/16 miles apart by road). These developments greatly increase the attractions of La Massana as a holiday base.

Hands-free, electronic lift passes were also introduced.

Snowmaking was extended in the Pal sector.

102

➕ Lively bars

➕ Ski school geared to British needs

➕ Cable-car link with Pal and shared lift pass with Arcalis useful for intermediates

➕ Pretty, tree-lined slopes in Pal

➖ Very confined and bleak local slopes

➖ Runs to village need good snow to be open, and don't lead to centre

➖ Long, linear and rather dour village, with no focus

➖ Obtrusive construction sites

Arinsal is the most British-dominated resort in Andorra, despite the fact that the village is the least attractive. This may be partly because the Spanish and French set their sights higher; but it is also because British tour operators offer packages here at tempting prices.

The resort attracts mainly first-time skiers and riders who come here for the cheap alcohol-fuelled nightlife as much as the experience on the slopes.

THE RESORT

Arinsal is a long, narrow village of grey, stone-clad buildings, near the head of a steep-sided valley north of Andorra la Vella. Development in recent years has been rapid.

The gondola from the village centre is the main way to and from the slopes and staying close to it is convenient; the alternative chair-lift, 1km/0.5 miles out of town, is largely irrelevant – though you can stay next to it and ski to the door in good conditions. Or you can drive to the top of the gondola. There is some accommodation at Pal, but it is a bus-ride from the lift base. There is also attractive accommodation in the lower town of La Massana (see previous spread); it is 6km/4 miles closer to Arcalis and now has a gondola link to Pal's slopes.

THE MOUNTAINS

The small local area above Arinsal's gondola is a narrow, east-facing bowl of open slopes. Pal's slopes, in contrast, are the most densely wooded of the Andorran resorts, calling to mind American resorts. They mainly face east; those down to the link with Arinsal face north.

Slopes Arinsal's slopes consist essentially of a single, long, narrow, rather bleak bowl above the upper gondola station at Comallempla, with runs leading straight back towards that point served by a network of chairs and drags. Almost at the top is the cable-car link to and from Pal. Pal's

slopes are widely spread around the mountain, with four main lift bases, all reachable by road. The main one, La Caubella, at the opposite extreme from the Arinsal link, is the arrival point of the new gondola from La Massana. The lift pass now covers Arcalis too – see previous page – but one 2005 reporter found it 'very difficult (but not impossible) to get transport over there'. **Terrain-parks** Arinsal's big freestyle area claims to be the most radical in southern Europe. It includes a huge half-pipe, big jump, terrain-park with spines, fun boxes, rails and quarter-pipes, boarder-cross and a chill-out area. **Snow reliability** With most runs above 1950m/6,400ft, north-easterly orientation and an impressive 370 snow-guns, snow is relatively assured. **Experts** These aren't great mountains for experts, but there are short, sharp black slopes at Arinsal – one now deliberately ungroomed – and quite long and challenging reds (and one black) as well as a new mogul area at Pal. There are also off-piste free-ride areas marked on the map in both Arinsal and Pal – the latter offering some great tree-skiing. **Intermediates** Arinsal offers a reasonable range of difficulty, but any confident intermediate is going to want to explore the much more interesting, varied and extensive Pal slopes. **Beginners** Around half the guests here are beginners. Arinsal and Pal both have gentle nursery slopes set apart from the main runs; they can get very crowded at peak times. There are long easy runs to progress to, as well.

KEY FACTS

Resort	1470m	
	4,820ft	
Slopes	1550-2560m	
	5,090-8,400ft	
Lifts	30	
Pistes	63km	
	39 miles	
Green	10%	
Blue	39%	
Red	39%	
Black	12%	
Snowmaking	19km	
	12 miles	

WEBSITES

For links to resort
sites, go to our own
new site at
www.wtss.co.uk

Phone numbers
From abroad use the
prefix +376.

TOURIST OFFICES

Arinsal
t 737000
palarinsal@palarinsal.
com
www.palarinsal.com
Pal
t 737000

Snowboarding It's a good place to
learn. But over half the lifts are drags,
and some of them are vicious. And
there are some tedious flat sections in
Pal too. We're told crash helmets are
compulsory in the terrain-park.
Cross-country There isn't any.
Queues Although its capacity was
boosted in 2002, Arinsal's gondola
builds queues to return to the village
at peak times. The cable-car link can
close if the wind is high.
Mountain restaurants Mainly self-
service, crowded, with snack food. The
restaurant at Comallempla is said to
run a barbie if the weather permits.
Schools and guides Arinsal's ski school
is geared to the British market – over
half the instructors are native English-
speakers. The reports we have are all
positive. A 2005 reporter said 'It's one
of the best ski schools I have used,
English fluently spoken, modern
teaching methods, proper initial
assessment before grouping.'
Facilities for children There is a ski
kindergarten for four- to eight-year-
olds at La Caubella (Pal) and nurseries
for younger children at Pal and Arinsal.

STAYING THERE

How to go There is a wide choice of
hotel and self-catering packages.
Hotels Rooms in the hotel Arinsal
(835640) are not large, but it is well
run, ideally placed and has a pleasant
bar. The Princesa Parc (736500) is a
big, glossy 4-star place close to the
gondola, with a swanky spa. The Xalet
Verdu (737140) is a smooth little 3-
star. The St Gotthard (836005) is big
but popular, except for its position a
long way down the hill from the
gondola. The Micolau (835052) is a
characterful stone house, close to the
centre, with simple rooms and a jolly,
beamed restaurant. If there is snow to
the valley, you can ski to the Crest
(835866) at the old chair-lift station.
Self-catering There is a reasonable
choice of places. Aparthotel Sant
Andreu is simple but comfortable, with
a relaxed bar-restaurant on site.
Eating out The Surf disco-pub does
grills. Cisco's is a Tex-Mex place in a
lovely wood and stone building. The
Rocky Mountain is popular for steaks.
El Rusc and Micolau do good food.
Borda Callisa does Indian.
Après-ski Arinsal has plenty of lively
bars and discos, such as Quo Vadis, El
Cau, Surf, Rocky Mountain and Cisco's,
(a major snowboarder hangout). El
Derbi is heaving on karaoke night. If,
like us, you prefer something quieter,
head for Borda Callisa – out of the way
and pleasantly relaxed – or the bar of
the hotel Arinsal.
Off the slopes There are lots of
activities. Or go shopping in Andorra la
Vella, half an hour away by infrequent
bus or inexpensive taxi.

Port Negre 2560m/8,400ft

Pic de Cubil 2360m/7,740ft

Pla de la Cot

La Massana

Setúria

La Caubella 1950m

Els Fontanals

Coll de la Botella 2065m

Comallempla 1950m

Cota 1550m

Pal 1780m/5,840ft

Arinsal 1470m/4,820ft

Pas de la Casa

Andorra's liveliest resort – we'd stay elsewhere

COSTS

① ② ③ ④ ⑤ ⑥

RATINGS

The slopes

Fast lifts	***
Snow	****
Extent	***
Expert	*
Intermediate	***
Beginner	****
Convenience	****
Queues	***
Mountain restaurants	**

The rest

Scenery	***
Resort charm	*
Off-slope	*

NEWS

The Coma Blanca 1 drag from Grau Roig back towards Pas de la Casa was replaced by a six-pack for 2004/05, helping to deal with weekend crowds. Hands-free electronic passes were also introduced.

For 2005/06 two beginner drag-lifts at Grau Roig are due to be replaced by a quad chair. There will also be more snowmaking. And it is planned that the signposting of the links between different sectors of the Grandvalira area will be improved.

REPORTS WANTED

Recently we have had few reports on this resort. If you go there, please do send us a report.

WEBSITES

For links to resort sites, go to our own new site at www.wtss.co.uk

---

+ The joint lift pass with Soldeu means the ski area now rivals many major resorts in the Alps for size

+ Andorra's liveliest nightlife

+ Attractive accommodation at Grau Roig

− Pas is an eyesore and the centre suffers from traffic (and fumes)

− Weekend crowds from France

− Very few woodland slopes – unpleasant in bad weather

The tour op brochures (and the few readers' reports we get) all say that Pas is Andorra's wildest party resort, and we don't doubt it. Having driven through it and skied down to it, we are quite happy to stay over the hill in Soldeu – or, for swift access to the heart of the Grandvalira ski area (as the combined Pas-Soldeu slopes are now called), at secluded Grau Roig.

THE RESORT

Sited right on the border between Andorra and France, Pas de la Casa owes its development as much to duty-free sales to the French as to skiing. It is a sizeable collection of concrete-box-style apartment blocks and hotels, a product of the late 1960s and early 1970s. As one reporter put it: 'The resort reminded us of Playa de las Americas in Tenerife – ugly, characterless with loads of restaurants with plastic-covered faded photos to show the discerning eater what a whopper-burger and chips actually looks like.' Most accommodation is conveniently placed near the lift base and slopes. The town centre boasts plenty of cheap shops and bars, as well as a sports centre. Reporters complain that that the heavy traffic generates fumes.

The resort attracts a lot of French and Spanish families, as well as Brits.

The road through from France goes on over the Port d'Envalira towards Soldeu and central Andorra but there is now a toll tunnel which avoids the pass and takes you to near Grau Roig (pronounced 'Rosh') in the next, attractively wooded valley. This is a mini-resort that acts as the access point for day visitors arriving by road, but it also makes a good base.

THE MOUNTAINS

The Grandvalira ski area, as it is now marketed, after Soldeu and Pas de la Casa finally agreed on a joint lift pass two seasons ago, offers an extensive 193km/120 miles of pistes – which compares with big-name Alpine resorts such as Kitzbühel and Les Deux Alpes.

With the exception of a couple of attractively wooded slopes in the central valley, the slopes above Pas are all open, and vulnerable to bad weather. Soldeu is more sheltered.

Slopes The home slopes, facing north-east, descend from a high, north–south ridge; lifts go up to it at four points. Runs on the far side of the ridge converge on Grau Roig, where there is some wooded terrain at the head of the valley. And a single lift goes on further west to the bowl of Llac del Cubill and the rest of the Grandvalira ski area. On the far side of this bowl is the arrival station of the 6km/4 mile gondola up from Encamp.

Terrain-parks There is a 'freestyle circuit' at Grau Roig and a terrain-park at Pas (both described as for beginners by the resort).

Snow reliability The combination of height and lots of snowmaking means good snow reliability and a season that often reaches late April. But on both our recent visits the snow has been better in Soldeu.

Experts There are few challenges on-piste – the black runs are rarely of serious steepness, and moguls are sparse. But there seem to be plenty of off-piste slopes inviting exploration – a reader recommends the bowls above Grau Roig, in particular.

Intermediates The local slopes cater for confident intermediates best, with plenty of top-to-bottom reds and blues on the main ridge, though they do rather lack variety. More timid intermediates will prefer Soldeu's slopes. The Grandvalira area as a whole can keep most intermediates amused for a week.

Beginners There are beginner slopes in

Grau Roig, the entry point for day visitors and a quiet place to stay to get away from the bars and discos of Pas →

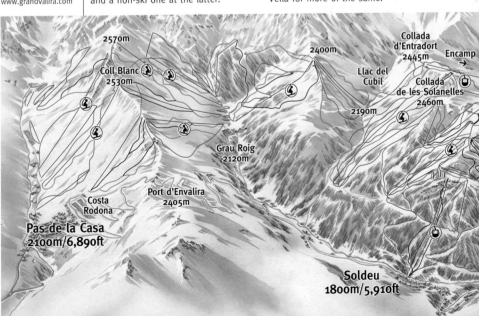

KEY FACTS

Resort	2100m
	6,890ft

GrandValira (Soldeu/El Tarter/Pas/Grau Roig)	
Slopes	1710-2570m
	5,610-8,430ft
Lifts	63
Pistes	193km
	120 miles
Green	16%
Blue	33%
Red	31%
Black	20%
Snowmaking	64km
	40 miles

Phone numbers
From abroad use the prefix +376.

Central reservations phone number
For all resort accommodation call 801060.

TOURIST OFFICE

t 871900
info@grandvalira.com
www.grandvalira.com

both Pas and Grau Roig. The Pas area is a short but inconvenient bus-ride out of town. Progression to longer runs is easier in Grau Roig, too.

Snowboarding Boarding is popular with the young crowd the resort attracts. Drags are usually avoidable.

Cross-country There are loops totalling 12km/7 miles below Grau Roig.

Queues Queues are rarely serious during the week. But at weekends and French school holidays some can develop, especially at Grau Roig.

Mountain restaurants There are routine places at the ridge above Pas and the top of the gondola from Encamp. The Rifugi dels Llacs dels Pessons at the head of the Grau Roig bowl is by far the best place – a cosy, beamed table-service restaurant with excellent food; best to book.

Schools and guides The ski school has a high reputation – good English.

Facilities for children There are ski kindergartens at Pas and Grau Roig, and a non-ski one at the latter.

STAYING THERE

How to go There are lots of apartments and hotels and a few chalets.

Hotels Himalaia-Pas has a pool and is 'comfortable and recommendable', says a reporter. The Grau Roig hotel is in a league of its own for comfort and seclusion (note that some tour ops list it under Soldeu). Beware of hotels catering to the 18-30 crowd – a reader in the Camelot reported vibrations from the basement disco until 5.30am.

Eating out It's not a resort for gourmets – though one reporter had 'good charcuterie and paella at the restaurant next to the Burger King' and another 'quail and foie gras' at Husky.

Après-ski Après-ski is very lively. The Marseilles, Milwaukee and Underground bars are popular. The Billboard is 'by far the best club'.

Off the slopes Off-slope activity is limited to shopping, visiting the leisure centre or taking a trip to Andorra la Vella for more of the same.

Pas de la Casa

105

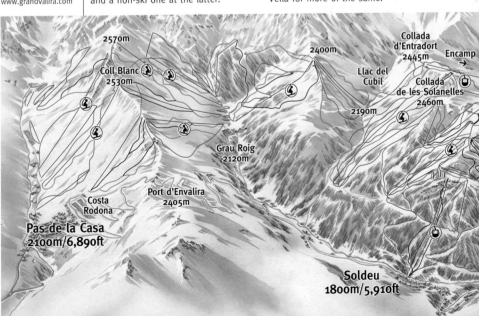

Collada d'Entradort
2445m
Encamp →

2570m

2400m

Llac del Cubil

Coll Blanc
2530m

Collada de les Solanelles
2460m

2190m

Grau Roig
2120m

Port d'Envalira
2405m

Costa Rodona

Pas de la Casa
2100m/6,890ft

Soldeu
1800m/5,910ft

Soldeu

Ideal for beginners and improvers, but check where you're staying

COSTS

① ② ③ ④ ⑤ ⑥

RATINGS

The slopes

Fast lifts	***
Snow	****
Extent	***
Expert	*
Intermediate	***
Beginner	****
Convenience	***
Queues	***
Mountain restaurants	**

The rest

Scenery	***
Resort charm	*
Off-slope	*

NEWS

For 2004/05 a 10-person gondola replaced the chair from El Tarter to Riba Escorxada, and the high-altitude link to Canillo was upgraded from a drag-lift to a chair.

For 2005/06 snowmaking is due to be increased with another 43 snow-guns in the Soldeu-El Tarter area. And it is planned that the signposting of the links between the different sectors of the Grandvalira area will be improved. A 5-star spa hotel, the Sport Hotel Hermitage, is due to open in December 2005.

➕ Joint lift pass with Pas de la Casa means the ski area now rivals many major resorts in the Alps for size

➕ Not as rowdy a resort as it once was

➕ Excellent beginner and early intermediate terrain

➕ Ski school has excellent British-run section for English-speaking visitors

➖ Slopes can get very crowded

➖ Very little to interest experts

➖ Village is on the main road through Andorra and suffers heavy traffic

➖ Some hotels are way out of town

➖ Not much to do off the slopes

If we were planning a holiday in Andorra, it would be in Soldeu (or the isolated hotel at Grau Roig, up the road – covered in the Pas de la Casa chapter). Despite the traffic, it is the least unattractive village, and its local slopes are the most interestingly varied (though crowded). It shares 193km/120 miles of pistes with neighbouring Pas de la Casa and the combined area is now known as Grandvalira, whose lift system includes four modern gondolas, eight six-packs and six high-speed quads. The alternative bases of El Tarter and Canillo, and accommodation being built along the busy main road that links them all, are often sold as Soldeu; they are much quieter, but also much cheaper.

THE RESORT

The village is an ever-growing ribbon of modern buildings – not pretty, but mainly with traditional stone cladding – on a steep hillside, lining the busy road that runs through Andorra from France to Spain. Most are hotels, apartments or bars, with the occasional shop; for serious shopping – or any other off-slope diversions – you have to head down to Canillo (see end of this chapter) or Andorra la Vella.

The steep hillside leads down to the river, and the slopes are on the opposite side. A gondola takes you from the heart of Soldeu to the heart of the slopes at Espiolets, and a wide bridge across the river forms the end of the piste home, with elevators to take you up to the gondola.

El Tarter, a few miles by road and 200m/66oft vertical down the valley, and Canillo, another 200m/66oft lower, offer alternative lifts into the slopes. Between all three resorts, hotels and apartments are being built along the main road and sold under the Soldeu banner – so check carefully where your proposed accommodation is. If you are staying a bus-ride from Soldeu, you can leave skis, boards and boots (for a fee) at the bottom or top (cheaper says a reporter) of the gondola.

THE MOUNTAINS

The Grandvalira ski area, as it is now marketed, after Soldeu and Pas de la Casa finally agreed on a joint lift pass two seasons ago, offers an extensive 193km/120 miles of pistes – which compares with big-name Alpine resorts such as Kitzbühel and Les Deux-Alpes. Soldeu's main local slopes are on open mountainsides above the woods, though there are runs in the woods back to all of the resort lift bases.

THE SLOPES
Pleasantly varied but crowded

The gondola rises over wooded, north-facing slopes to Espiolets, a broad shelf that is virtually a mini-resort – the ski school is based here, and there are extensive nursery slopes. A gentle run to the east takes you to an area of long, easy runs served by a six-pack. Beyond that is an extensive area of more varied slopes, served by a quad and another six-pack, that links with the Pas de la Casa area. Going west from Espiolets takes you to the open bowl of Riba Escorxada and the arrival point of the gondola up from El Tarter. From here, another six-pack serves sunny slopes on Tosa dels Espiolets and a fourth goes to the high-point of Tossal de la Llosada and the link with the slopes above Canillo. One problem is that, apart from the Canillo sector,

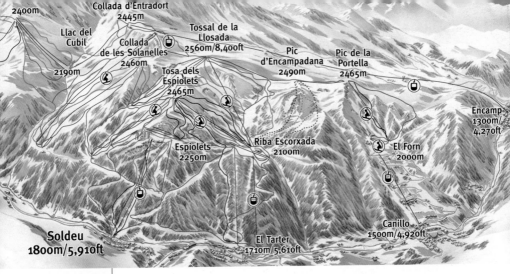

2400m
Collada d'Entradort 2445m
Llac del Cubil
2190m
Collada de les Solanelles 2460m
Tosa dels Espiolets 2465m
Tossal de la Llosada 2560m/8,400ft
Pic d'Encampadana 2490m
Pic de la Portella 2465m
Encamp 1300m/4,270ft
Espiolets 2250m
Riba Escorxada 2100m
El Forn 2000m
Canillo 1500m/4,920ft
Soldeu 1800m/5,910ft
El Tarter 1710m/5,610ft

KEY FACTS

| Resort | 1800m |
| | 5,910ft |

GrandValira (Soldeu/El Tarter/Pas/Grau Roig)	
Slopes	1710-2560m
	5,610-8,400ft
Lifts	63
Pistes	193km
	120 miles
Green	16%
Blue	33%
Red	31%
Black	20%
Snowmaking	64 km
	40 miles

many of the blue runs can get unpleasantly crowded.

TERRAIN-PARKS
A good one
The park, above Riba Escorxada, is large and impressive, with jumps, rails, a half-pipe, a boarder-cross run and a bumps area. Some lessons and free demonstrations are arranged for adults and children over six. For 2005/06 there are plans to expand its beginners' area and improve access from the Font Roiges drag-lift.

SNOW RELIABILITY
Much better than people expect
Despite its name (Soldeu means Sun God) the slopes enjoy reliable snow. Most slopes are north-facing, with a good natural snow record and snowmaking on over a third of the pistes. The excellent grooming helps maintain good snow too.

FOR EXPERTS
Hope for good off-piste
It's a limited area for experts, at least on-piste. The Avet black run down to Soldeu deserves its grading, but most of the others would be no more than reds (or even blues) in many resorts. The blacks on Tosa dels Espiolets, for example, are indistinguishable from the

neighbouring (and more direct) red and blue. But there is plenty of off-piste potential – notably in the bowl above Riba Escorxada, in the Espiolets and and Solanelles areas (we had a great time there in fresh powder on our last visit), and above El Forn. And the off-piste remains untouched for days because most visitors are beginners and early intermediates. When conditions permit at weekends, a snowcat takes people up to Pic d'Encampadana, from where four off-piste routes (dotted on our map) descend to Riba Escorxada.

FOR INTERMEDIATES
Explore Grandvalira
There is plenty to amuse all but the very keenest intermediates. The area east of Espiolets is splendid for building confidence, while those who already have it will be able to explore the whole mountain. Riba Escorxada is a fine section for mixed ability groups. The relatively new Canillo/El Forn sector has an easy, little-used blue run along the ridge with excellent views all the way to Pal and Arinsal and an easy black in the valley. Many of the blues and reds have short steeper sections, preceded by a 'slow' sign and netting in the middle of the piste to slow you down.

boarding

The excellent school and gentle beginner slopes make this a good place to learn. Intermediates may find the flattish areas of slopes irritating to scoot along but will welcome the many chair-lifts and few drags. Competent free-riders should enjoy the off-piste and weekend snowcat service when it's running (see Experts).

LIFT PASSES

GrandValira
Covers all lifts in Soldeu, El Tarter, Canillo, Grau Roig and Pas de la Casa

Beginners
Available for the Canillo sector only

Main pass
1 day €35
6 days €168

Children
Under 12: 6 days €129
Under 6: free pass

Notes
Pedestrian and local day and half-day passes available.

Alternative pass
The Ski Andorra pass covers all Andorran areas and allows skiing at any single one of them each day for five out of six consecutive days for €153 (under 12: €120).

ANDORRA

108

SCHOOLS

Soldeu
t 890591
El Tarter
t 890641
Canillo
t 890691

Classes
15hr: €95.50
Private lessons
€32 for 1hr for 1 or 2 people.

CHILDREN

Nurseries at Grau Roig and Soldeu
Ages 2 to 3; 2hr €15
Snow gardens run by ski schools
Ages 3 to 6; 2hr €18.50

Ski schools
15hr: €90.50

FOR BEGINNERS
One of the best
This is an excellent place to start. The Espiolets nursery area is huge, and served by moving carpet lifts (though one reader reckons the slope above El Tarter is even better). It is relatively snow-sure, and there are numerous easy pistes to move on to (though the crowds can be off-putting). And the ski school is top-notch.

FOR CROSS-COUNTRY
Er, what cross-country?
There is no cross country in Soldeu. There is some not far away at Grau Roig (see Pas de la Casa chapter), but Andorra's serious cross-country resort is La Rabassa, in the south-west corner of the country – 15km/9 miles of loops at an altitude of 2000m/6,560ft.

QUEUES
Crowds more of a problem
Most of Grandvalira's key lifts are high-speed chairs or gondolas, though there are a lot of slow lifts too. But the system seems to be able to cope. There are queues at the morning peak for the gondola out of Soldeu (though reporters are impressed by how quickly it moves because of staff ensuring all places are filled and loading skis and boards for you). The new gondola from El Tarter has eased problems there. Allow time for the queue-prone Cubil chair back from Grau Roig.

Another problem can be crowds on the blue slopes (including lots of ski school classes snaking along) – the reds and blacks are much quieter. The final bend on the Esquirol run to El Tarter was named 'carnage corner' by one reporter, who recommends a return to the resort by lift for the inexperienced. El Tarter is very busy with local skiers at the weekend.

MOUNTAIN RESTAURANTS
Not a highlight
The mountain restaurants are crowded and the food generally dull (a notable exception is Rifugi dels Llacs dels Pessons – see Pas de la Casa). There is a choice of places at Espiolets, including table-service at Gall de Bosc, which was recommended by a reporter. The Roc de les Bruixes at El Forn claims to be 'gastronomic' but we lack reports on it. Reporters favour descending to El Tarter, particularly to the snack bar in the Hotel del Clos.

SCHOOLS AND GUIDES
One of the best for Brits
The scale of the teaching operation here is very impressive. The ski school is effectively run as two units. One deals with English-speaking clients, is led by an Englishman and has mostly native-English-speaking instructors. 40% of the pupils are beginners, and the school has devised a special 'team-teaching' scheme to cope with this number of beginners. The school maintains its excellent reputation for teaching and friendliness. 'One of the reasons for returning to Soldeu', 'instructor was brilliant', 'everyone was very impressed, small classes of eight, English is first language, and good tuition' are typical comments from reporters.

FACILITIES FOR CHILDREN
With altitude
Children are looked after at the mid-mountain stations. There are nurseries at Espiolets, Riba Escorxada and El Forn for children from twelve months to three years old and Snow Gardens for three- to six-year-olds.

STAYING THERE

HOW TO GO
Be careful where you stay
A wide range of UK tour operators offer packages here, mainly in hotels but with some apartments and chalets. Location is important – many places are a bus-ride from town.
Hotels The best hotels are far removed from the standards of a decade ago.
(((4 **Sport Hotel Village** (870500) By far the best in town, with style and space in the public areas – comfortable chairs and sofas, high ceilings, beams and picture windows. Built over the gondola station by the family that sold the land to the lift company.
(((3 **Sport** (870600) Comfortable, good lounge areas, lively bar and a popular basement disco-bar. But dull buffet-style food.
(((3 **Piolets** (871787) Pleasant enough, with a pool. Central.
(((3 **Himalaia** (878515) Refurbished, central.
Self-catering Most reporters are hotel-based but apartments are available.

EATING OUT
Some gourmand delights
We enjoyed excellent, satisfying meals at three rustic restaurants. Borda del

GETTING THERE

Air Toulouse 196km/121 miles (3½hr).

Rail L'Hospitalet-Près-L'Andorre (25km/16 miles); buses and taxis to Soldeu

ACTIVITIES

Indoor Thermal spas, bowling (at Pas), leisure centre (pools, hot-tub, gym)

Outdoor Helicopter rides, Snowmobiling, dog-sledding, reindeer-sledding, snow-shoeing, paragliding, paintballing

SNOWPIX.COM / IAN STRATFORD

It's a good job there's no skiing on those south-facing slopes behind Soldeu. This is the home run, with the bridge across the river leading to the gondola station →

WEBSITES

For links to resort sites, go to our own new site at www.wtss.co.uk

Phone numbers From abroad use the prefix +376. **Central reservations phone number** Call 890501.

TOURIST OFFICE

t 890500 info@grandvalira.com www.grandvalira.com

Rector (Andorran-run, and with authentic Andorran cuisine), nearer to El Tarter than Soldeu, was our favourite. The other two were both British-run: Snails and Quails, 3km/2 miles up the road in Bordes d'Envalira, and Fat Albert's in downtown Soldeu. L'Esquirol (Indian) and Pussycat have had good reports.

APRES-SKI
Lively

Après-ski is lively 'but not loutish' – mainly bars and rep-organised events (such as pub crawls with maybe 100 participants). The bar at Fat Albert's has videos shot on the mountain and often a live band. The Pussycat is a good late-night place, with changing party themes. The Piccadilly, under the Sport hotel, is popular. The Aspen and the nearby Avalanche attract a younger crowd. We liked the Villager. Expect noise from late-night revellers.

OFF THE SLOPES
Head downhill

There is little to amuse non-skiers in Soldeu itself. Down in Canillo is the smart Palau de Gel, and in Andorra la Vella the impressive Caldea spa, and some very serious shopping opportunities. Some of the bigger hotels have excellent sports facilities.

El Tarter 1710m/5,610ft

El Tarter has grown over recent years and is rather sprawling, with no real centre. Reporters recommend the hotels del Clos ('good food but up a steep hill') and del Tarter and the local ski school – and we have a good review of the big new four-star Euro Esqui half-way to Soldeu ('very friendly staff, spacious rooms', with efficient minibus shuttle to El Tarter lifts). But they complain that the resort is 'dull at night'. The Mosquit pizzeria has been recommended .

Canillo 1500m/4,920ft

If you like the idea of deserted local slopes and don't mind riding a gondola down at the end of the day, consider Canillo, which looked an acceptably pleasant spot as we repeatedly drove through it. It has the impressive Palau de Gel – an Olympic ice rink plus swimming pool, gym and other amenities.

Soldeu

109

Austria's holiday recipe is quite distinctive. It doesn't suit everybody, but for many, nothing else will do; in particular, France won't do. Austria is the land of cute little villages clustered around onion-domed churches – there are no monstrous, purpose-built, apartment-block resorts of the kind that are so common in France. It's the land of friendly wooded mountains, reassuring to beginners and timid intermediates in a way that bleak snowfields and craggy peaks will never be. It's the land of friendly, welcoming people who don't find it demeaning to speak their guests' language (if it's English, at least). And it's the land of jolly, alcohol-fuelled après-ski action – in many resorts, starting in mid-afternoon with dancing in mountain restaurants and going on as long as you have the legs for it. For many visitors to Austrian resorts the partying is as important as the skiing or riding. Of course, there are exceptions to all these norms.

In general – and we should note here that Austria has some of the world's best glacier areas – Austria isn't the first place you'll want to consider if reliable snow is your top priority. Most resorts are relatively low, and conditions are more likely to be problematic here than in higher resorts. But Austrian resorts have made great strides in their attempts to catch up with their rivals – most have radically increased their snowmaking capacity in the last decade. In midwinter, especially, lack of snow generally coincides with low night-time temperatures, even at low altitudes, and snowmaking comes into its own. And recent seasons have been bumper natural snow years for much of Austria.

111

It's the après-ski that strikes most first-time visitors as being Austria's unique selling point. The few French resorts that have lively après-ski are dominated by British or Scandinavian holidaymakers (and resort workers); the French themselves are noticeable by their absence, and you could be in London or Stockholm rather than in France.

But Austrian après-ski remains very Austrian – or perhaps German. Huge quantities of beer and schnapps are drunk, German is the predominant language and German drinking songs are common. So is loud Europop music. People pack into mountain restaurants at the end of the day and dance in their ski boots on the dance floor, on the tables, on the bar – wherever there's room. There are open-air ice bars, umbrella bars and countless transparent 'igloo' bars in which to shelter from bad weather. In many resorts the bands don't stop playing until darkness falls, when the happy punters slide off in the general direction of the village to find another watering hole. After dinner the drinking and dancing starts again – for those who take time out for dinner, that is. Of course, not all Austrian resorts conform to this image. But lots of big-name ones with the best and most extensive slopes do. St Anton, Saalbach-Hinterglemm, Ischgl, Sölden and Zell am See, for example, fit this bill.

One thing that all Austrian resorts have in common is reliably comfortable accommodation – whether it's in 4-star hotels with pools, saunas and spas ('wellness centres'), or in great-value, family-run guest houses, of which Austria has thousands. Catered chalets and self-catering apartments are in general much less widely available (though there are one or two resorts, such as St Anton and

ALPENSZENE MONTAFON

← There are lots of cute little villages with onion-domed churches – this one is Bartholomäberg. The Hochjoch slopes above Schruns (in the Montafon) are in the background

Kitzbühel, where catered chalets are more easily come by).

One thing to beware of is Austria's strange aversion to credit cards. Reporter after reporter complains that many establishments do not accept cards – even quite upmarket hotels, as well as many ski lift companies. So check if they are accepted well in advance, and have access to plenty of cash.

Most Austrian resorts are real, friendly villages on valley floors, with skiing and boarding on the wooded slopes above them. They have expanded enormously since the war, but practically all the development has been in traditional chalet style, and the villages generally look good even without the snow that is the saving grace of many French and even some Swiss resorts. Unlike Courchevel and Verbier, many Tirolean resorts are as busy in August as in February.

Outside the big-name resorts, the skiing is often quite limited. There are many Austrian resorts that a keen skier could explore fully in half a day. Those who start their skiing careers in such resorts may not be worried by this; those who have tried the bigger areas of France and developed a taste for them may find the list of acceptable Austrian resorts quite a short one.

Unfortunately, several of the resorts on that shortlist bring you up against another problem – low altitude, and therefore the possibility of poor snow conditions. Kitzbühel is at 760m/2,490ft and Söll at 700m/2,300ft, for example. The top heights are relatively low, too – typically 1800m to 2000m (5,910ft to 6,560ft); as we note above, snowmaking is becoming more widespread, but it works only when the conditions are right. Many of these low resorts need only a shallow depth of snow to cover their smooth green pastures, but fluctuating temperatures bring the danger of slush and ice. The resorts of the Arlberg, at the western end of the Tirol – St Anton, Lech and Zürs – stand apart from these concerns, with excellent snow records and extensive skiing. And you can be fairly confident of good snow at Obergurgl, Obertauern and Ischgl, not to mention the year-round slopes on glaciers such as those at Hintertux, Neustift, Kaprun and Sölden. But for many other resorts our advice is to book late, when you know what the snow conditions are like.

There are some extensive areas of slopes that are little known in the UK and well worth considering. Bad Gastein, Schladming, Ischgl, Sölden and Lech spring to mind.

Nightlife is not limited to drinking and dancing. There are lots of floodlit toboggan runs, and UK tour operator reps organise Tirolean, bowling, fondue, karaoke and other evenings. And not all resorts are raucous. Lech and Zürs, for example, are full of rich, cool, 'beautiful' people enjoying the comfort of 4-star sophisticated hotels. And resorts such as Niederau in the Wildschönau and Westendorf and Alpbach in the Tirol are pretty, quiet, family resorts.

Austrian resorts are now easier to get to independently using cheap flights. The standard arrival airports are Munich and Salzburg, and for western resorts Zürich. But don't overlook less well-known airports such as Klagenfurt in Carinthia and Friedrichshafen, just over the German border and handy for resorts in western Austria.

GETTING AROUND THE AUSTRIAN ALPS

Austria presents few problems for the car-borne visitor, because practically all the resorts are valley villages which involve neither steep approach roads nor high altitude.

The dominant feature of Austria for the ski driver is the thoroughfare of the Inn valley, which runs through the Tirol from Landeck via Innsbruck to Kufstein. The motorway along it extends, with one or two breaks, westwards to the Arlberg pass and on to Switzerland. This artery is relatively reliable except in exceptionally bad conditions – the altitude is low, and the road is a vital transport link which is kept open in virtually any conditions.

The Arlberg – which divides Tirol from Vorarlberg, but which is also the watershed between Austria and Switzerland – is one of the

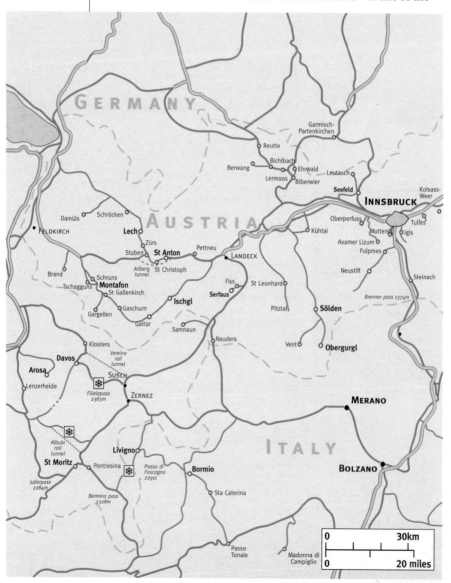

few areas where driving plans are likely to be seriously affected by snow. The east–west Arlberg pass itself has a long tunnel underneath it; this isn't cheap, and you may want to take the high road when it's clear, through Stuben, St Christoph and St Anton. The Flexen pass road to Zürs and Lech (which may be closed by avalanche risk even when the Arlberg pass is open) branches off just to the west of the Arlberg summit.

At the eastern end of the Tirol, the Gerlos pass road from Zell am Ziller over into Salzburg province can be closed. Resorts in Carinthia, such as Bad Kleinkirchheim, are usually reached by motorway, thanks to the Tauern and Katschberg tunnels. The alternative is to drive over the Radstädter Tauern pass through Obertauern, or use the car-carrying rail service from Böckstein to Mallnitz.

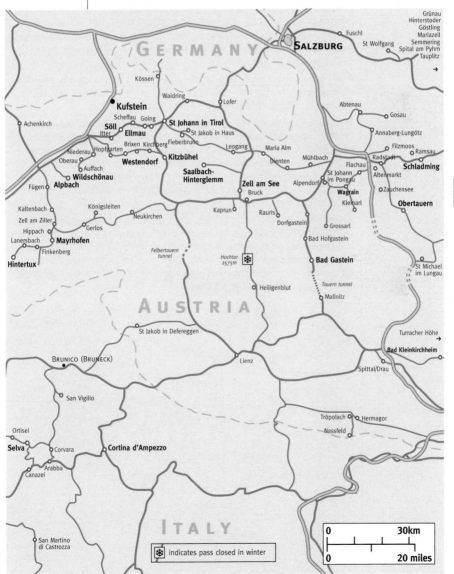

indicates pass closed in winter

0		30km

0		20 miles

There are more extensive lift passes in the Alps than Salzburgerland's Ski Amadé, but they are very few. What's more, with a car you really could aim to get around most of the resorts it covers – they are clustered close together, no high passes are involved in getting from one resort to another, and many areas are geared to people arriving by car, with out-of-town lifts and serious car parks. (They are also conveniently close to Salzburg airport – we got an early cheap flight there in 2004, and were on the slopes in Flachau before lunch time; when we left we skied till the end of the day, enjoyed some après-ski, had a leisurely drive to the airport and still had time to kill before our flight home.)

Some of the major components of the consortium are covered in their own chapters in the Austria section. In the Schladming chapter we also cover the smaller linked resorts of Haus in Ennstal and Pichl, as well as Schladming's elevated outpost of Rohrmoos. Also close to Schladming is Ramsau in Dachstein, which has slopes at village level but also a lift up to the lip of the Dachstein glacier. In the Bad Gastein chapter we cover not only the resorts in the Gastein valley, but also the next-door valley of Grossarl, which is linked over the hill to Dorfgastein.

This year we have a new chapter on the major area of Hochkönig's Winterreich. Though largely unknown on the British market, it has an extensive network of runs linking Muhlbach, Dienten and Maria Alm.

We have also given one of our half-page chapters (grouped at the end of each country section) to Wagrain, which is one of the main resorts in the biggest sub-region, the Salzburger Sportwelt. As well as the large three-valley system linking Wagrain to Flachau and Alpendorf/St Johann im Pongau, this area embraces a similarly extensive lift network linking Zauchensee, Flachauwinkl and Kleinarl, plus more modest lift systems at Filzmoos, Radstadt-Altenmarkt, Eben and Goldegg.

Considering the extent of the lift networks it covers (and the generally impressive efficiency of the lifts) the Ski Amadé pass is not expensive – last year, around 160 euros depending on the season. This is less than you'll pay for anything vaguely similar in France or Italy. Prices on the spot are not bad either – readers report prices in the mountain restaurants (which are very numerous) lower than in areas with a bigger international reputation.

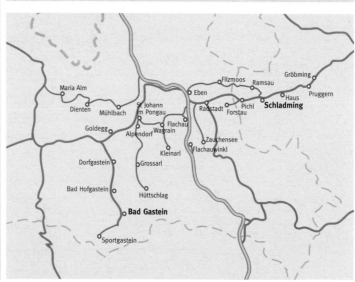

Alpbach

Traditional charm for those who like familiar slopes

COSTS

① ② ③ ④ ⑤ ⑥

RATINGS

The slopes
Fast lifts	**
Snow	**
Extent	*
Expert	*
Intermediate	**
Beginner	****
Convenience	**
Queues	***
Mountain restaurants	***

The rest
Scenery	***
Charm	*****
Off-slope	***

NEWS

For 2005/06 a new eight-person gondola is due to replace the two successive Pöglbahn double chairs from Inneralpbach to Wiedersbergerhorn. Also in Inneralpbach, a quad chair is planned to replace the Galtenberglift drag. A new lake is being built between Alpbach and Reith to provide water for the resort's snowmaking.

For 2004/05 a new red piste was built, which runs from the bottom of the Muldenlift drag to the bottom of the Kohlgrubenlift quad and a new beginners' lift was built on the Wiedersbergerhorn.

Snowmaking was further increased.

+ Charming traditional village with a relaxed atmosphere – great for young children

+ Handy, central nursery slopes

+ Several other worthwhile resorts within day-trip distance

+ Good, varied, intermediate terrain, not without challenges, but ...

– Slopes limited in extent and variety

– Main slopes are a shuttle-bus-ride away from the centre

– Few long easy runs for beginners to progress to

– Low altitude means lower slopes can suffer from poor snow – though a north-facing aspect and increased snowmaking help

Alpbach is an old British favourite – there is even a British ski club, the Alpbach Visitors. It is exceptionally pretty and friendly, and inspires great loyalty in the visitors who take to it – a regular reporter who has been going for over 20 years claims only junior status.

THE RESORT

Alpbach is near the head of a valley, looking south across it towards the Wiedersbergerhorn, where most of the slopes are to be found. It's an exceptionally pretty, captivating place; traditional chalets crowd around the pretty church (the graves are lit by candles at night), and the nursery slopes are only a few steps away.

Alpbach is small, but it's not necessarily convenient. The main village is the place to stay for atmosphere and après-ski, but involves using a free shuttle-bus to and from Achenwirt, a mile away, where the main gondola goes up to Hornboden. The backwater hamlet of Inneralpbach is much more convenient for the slopes, with its own lifts up to the heart of the slopes.

The Inn valley is a few miles north, and trips east to Kitzbühel or west to Innsbruck are possible. The Hintertux and Stubaier glaciers are within reach.

THE MOUNTAIN

Alpbach's slopes, on two flanks of the Wiedersbergerhorn, are small and simple. Piste grooming is excellent.
Slopes Chair-lifts and drags serve the open, north-facing slopes above the tree line, with black runs following the lift lines and reds (and a single blue) taking less direct routes. The runs are mostly of 200m to 400m (650ft to 1,300ft) vertical, but you can get 500m/1,650ft down the second stage

of the gondola, and 1000m/3,300ft when snow is good down to valley level. Behind Gmahkopf is a short blue west-facing slope and a new red run built for last season. The tiny area at Reith (about 3km/2 miles down the valley from Achenwirt) is on the lift pass and amazingly is accessed by an eight-seat gondola.
Terrain-parks There's a small terrain-park with half-pipe at the top of the main gondola.
Snow reliability Alpbach cannot claim great snow reliability, but at least most of the Wiedersbergerhorn faces north and two-thirds of the pistes are covered by snowmaking.
Experts Alpbach isn't ideal, but the reds and the three blacks are not without challenge, and runs of 1000m/3,300ft vertical are not to be sniffed at. There are a number of off-piste routes to the valley, short tours are offered, and the schools apparently take the top classes off-piste.
Intermediates There is fine intermediate terrain; the problem is that it's limited. This resort is for practising technique on familiar slopes, not high mileage.
Beginners Beginners love the sunny nursery slopes beside the village. But the main slopes are not ideal for confidence-building: most are classified red (there are only a couple of blues).
Snowboarding There's some good free-riding terrain, and the schools offer a range of options.
Cross-country 22km/14 miles of pretty cross-country trails rise up beyond

The pretty village is a
bus-ride from the
main mountain →
ALPBACH TOURIST OFFICE

KEY FACTS

Resort	1000m
	3,280ft
Slopes	670-2025m
	2,200-6,640ft
Lifts	20
Pistes	45km
	28 miles
Blue	15%
Red	70%
Black	15%
Snowmaking	31km
	19 miles

WEBSITES

For links to resort
sites, go to our own
new site at
www.wtss.co.uk

Phone numbers
From elsewhere in
Austria add the prefix
05336.
From abroad use the
prefix +43 5336.

TOURIST OFFICE

t 6000
info@alpbach.at
www.alpbach.at

Inneralpbach; the most challenging is
about 8km/5 miles long and climbs
300m/1,000ft.

Queues A 2005 reporter found 'queues
of around 40 minutes for the Achenwirt
gondola on several mornings'. The new
gondola planned for Inneralpbach for
2005/06 should ease this problem and
we have no recent reports of other
serious queues.

Mountain restaurants The small area
has squeezed in six mountain
restaurants – each worth a visit. A
2005 reporter recommends 'the spit-
roast chicken you order in advance at
the Böglalm above Inneralpbach'.

Schools and guides Alpbach and
Alpbach Aktiv are the two main ski
schools. We have had excellent reports
on both in the past.

Facilities for children Reporters find the
village very child-friendly, and
babysitters can be arranged by the
tourist office.

STAYING THERE

How to go Hotels and pensions
dominate in UK packages.

Hotels Of the smart 4-star places, the
Alpbacherhof (5237) – 'superb food
and excellent service' says a 2005
reporter – and ancient Böglerhof
(5227) get most votes. But simpler
Haus Thomas (5944) – 'very clean ...
you feel like part of the family' – Haus
Angelika (5339) and Haus Theresia
(5386) are recommended by visitors.
The Alphof (5371) is 'excellent' – and
its noisy disco has been replaced by
additional health facilities. Pension
Edelweiss (5268) is close to the
nursery slopes and is reported to offer

B&B and 'clean, spacious apartments
and excellent value'.

Self-catering There is quite a bit to
choose from now, easily bookable
through the tourist office web site.

Eating out The popular Post and
Alphof both provide 'excellent food'
according to a reporter, who also
favoured the 'superb' Jakober and its
non-smoking room. The
Wiedersbergerhorn in Inneralpbach has
been recommended, as has the
Rossmoos Inn for its lively Tirolean
evenings and 'superb' food.

Après-ski At peak times this is typically
Tirolean, with lots of noisy tea-time
beer-swilling in the bars of central
hotels such as the Jakober and the
Post. A 2005 reporter preferred the
Farmer's Pub to the Waschkuchl bar.

Off the slopes There are pretty walks
and trips to Innsbruck and Salzburg.
There are also an indoor swimming
pool and an outdoor ice rink.

Alpbach

Wiedersbergerhorn
2025m/6,640ft
Gmahkopf 1900m
Hornboden
1850m
1230m
Inneralpbach
1050m/3,440ft
Böglalm
1345m
1280m/4,200ft
Wölzenberg
Achenwirt
830m
Alpbach
1000m/3,280ft
Reith im
Alpbachtal
670m/ 2,200ft

Bad Gastein

Spa-town resort with extensive slopes and few British visitors

RATINGS

The slopes

Fast lifts	**
Snow	***
Extent	****
Expert	***
Intermediate	****
Beginner	**
Convenience	**
Queues	***
Mountain restaurants	****

The rest

Scenery	***
Resort charm	***
Off-slope	****

NEWS

Following on from Bad Hofgastein's spa revamp, Bad Gastein's Felsentherme was renovated for 2004/05 and has a new Adventure Area that includes two pools and seven different saunas/steam rooms. A new modern base facility in the Angertal is complete and includes an information centre, restaurant and children's facilities. A bottleneck on the Jungeralm run (B19) has been removed. For 2005/06 more snowmaking is planned at Sportgastein.

➕ Extensive, varied slopes above and below the tree line

➕ Excellent, testing long runs for confident intermediates, and some under-used off-piste

➕ More reliable snow than in most low-altitude Austrian resorts

➕ Lots of good, atmospheric, traditional mountain restaurants

➕ Ski Alliance Amadé lift pass covers wide range of nearby resorts

➕ Excellent thermal spas, but ...

➖ Main resorts are spa towns, without the usual Austrian resort ambience

➖ Bad Gastein itself has a weird, steep, confined setting, with narrow streets congested by local traffic

➖ Valley slopes are split into five areas, and bus services are inadequate – unless you take a car, budget for a lot of taxi-rides

➖ Timid intermediates will find most sectors too challenging – and beginners are better off elsewhere

The Gastein valley is beginning to attract more Brits, to judge by our readers' reports. Rightly so – the slopes form one of Austria's bigger and more varied areas, and snow is more reliable than average. Steeply tiered Bad Gastein itself is a difficult place to like; we much prefer rustic Dorfgastein or spacious Bad Hofgastein – described at the end of this chapter. The valley needs a top-notch public transport system, and it doesn't have one.

THE RESORT

Bad Gastein sits near the head of the Gastein valley. It is an old spa that has now spread widely, but still has a compact core. A bizarre combination of buildings is laid out in a cramped horseshoe, set in what is virtually a gorge. The central area is no pleasure at all to explore, and impossible for those with impediments (such as small children). Up the hill, above the centre of the town, is a modern suburb with more of a ski-resort feel and immediate access to the gondola up to the major sector, Stubnerkogel, which links via Angertal with Bad Hofgastein's Schlossalm sector. Across town, the double chair up Graukogel is a taxi-ride from the centre. A 25-minute bus-ride away, at the head of the valley, is Sportgastein, served by a gondola, with little other development.

A confusing range of ski-bus routes (covered by the lift pass) connects the villages and lift stations. There are trains, too. The ski-bus service is not super-efficient, and a car is a distinct asset here. It also allows exploitation of the Ski Alliance Amadé lift pass, which covers over 30 resorts in the region. Also worth visiting but not on the lift pass are snow-sure Obertauern and glacial Kaprun.

THE MOUNTAIN

Most of the runs are on the open slopes above the tree line, though there are some woodland runs.
Slopes Stubnerkogel has runs in all directions from the peak giving about 500m/1,640ft vertical on the open slopes above the tree line and rather more below it. There is night skiing once a week on the nursery slope. The much smaller Graukogel is unjustly neglected; its wooded runs are a great asset in bad weather, and quiet at other times. The high slopes of Sportgastein, in contrast, are more exposed both to wind and sun.

We cover the slopes above Bad Hofgastein and Dorfgastein below.
Terrain-parks See Dorfgastein.
Snow reliability The area is higher than many Austrian rivals, and there is snowmaking on crucial sections.
Experts The few black runs are not severe, but many reds are long and satisfying. Graukogel has some of the most testing slopes and is a great place to go in a blizzard. The other sectors have plenty of opportunities to go off-piste. Sportgastein is also worth the trip, not least for the shady 8km/ 5-mile Nord ski route.
Intermediates Good for the confident, who will find long, leg-sapping runs in

Bad Hofgastein's setting on the wide valley floor is a sharp contrast to Bad Gastein's in a narrow gorge →

BAD GASTEIN TOURIST OFFICE

all the sectors in the valley. The timid are better off sticking to Schlossalm (see Bad Hofgastein, below).

Beginners Nursery slopes are scattered and none is ideal. The main slope at Bad Gastein is simply too steep. And progression is tricky – the genuinely easy blue runs are often boring paths.

Snowboarding The valley hosts snowboard events, but doesn't seem to cater particularly well for holiday boarders. There's still a fairly high proportion of drag-lifts.

Cross-country There are 90km/56 miles of trails, but they are all low down.

Queues There are few problems outside the peak season.

Mountain restaurants Atmospheric, traditional huts abound – at least one reporter is pressing for a 5-star rating. The Jungerstube's 'excellent service and hospitality', Bergstadl, the cosy Stubneralm and the 'atmospheric' Hartlgut (from which you take a train or taxi back to town or to the lifts) have been recommended.

Schools and guides We lack recent reports.

Facilities for children There are facilities for all-day care and there's a 'Fun Center' for kids at the top of the Stubnerkogel gondola. There's also a snow adventure park at Angertal. Parents have found the facilities 'excellent', and the care of children, in small groups, 'attentive'.

KEY FACTS

Resort	1080m
	3,540ft

For the Gastein valley and Grossarl areas

Slopes	840-2685m
	2,760-8,810ft
Lifts	43
Pistes	201km
	125 miles
Blue	30%
Red	58%
Black	12%
Snowmaking	93km
	58 miles

For Bad Gastein and Bad Hofgastein only

Slopes	860-2685m
	2,820-8,810ft
Lifts	26
Pistes	121km
	75 miles

STAYING THERE

How to go British tour operators sell mainly hotel-based packages.

Hotels There are lots of smart 4- and 3-star hotels with spa facilities. The Wildbad (37610) was rated 'excellent' by a 2005 reporter. The Grüner Baum (25160) is a lovely retreat, but wildly inconvenient except for langlauf.

Eating out There is a fair range of restaurants. The central Wirtshaus Jägerhäusl does excellent food in a warm, traditional atmosphere (especially upstairs). The Vier Jahreszeiten, a short drive away in Böckstein, offers big portions, 'very good value and friendly service', according to a recent visitor.

Après-ski The town feels generally subdued, but there are numerous

Bad Gastein

Kreuzkogel
2685m/8,810ft

RAUKOGEL
2100m

Sportgastein
1600m

STUBNERKOGEL
2245m

Böckstein

Kötschachtal

Bad Gastein
1080m/3,540ft

Hohe Scharte
2300m/7,550ft

Angertal
1200m

SCHLOSSALM
2050m

Kleine Scharte

Grossarl

Dorfgastein ski area

Bad Hofgastein
860m/2,820ft

Kitzsteinalm
1300m

Dorfgastein ↓

popular bars and several discos to be found – plus a casino. Highlights from a recent report include the 'boisterous' Bergfex, the 'cosy, friendly, wood-panelled' Hexenhäusl, the 'vibrant, Wild-West-style' Silver Bullet, the 'friendlier' Eden and the Weinfassl for 'dancing and drinking games'. Places for a quiet late drink include the smart Bellini bar and the Ritz cocktail bar.
Off the slopes As well as extensive spa facilities there are plenty of other things to do, including coach trips.

Bad Hofgastein
860m/2,820ft

Bad Hofgastein is a sizeable, quiet spa village set spaciously in a broad section of the valley.

THE RESORT
Although sprawling, the village has a pleasant pedestrianised centre. The slopes are reached by a funicular to Kitzsteinalm starting a long walk or short shuttle-bus-ride away; or you can take a longer bus-ride to Angertal.

THE MOUNTAINS
Schlossalm is a broad, open bowl, with runs through patchy woods both to Bad Hofgastein and Angertal.
The slopes Schlossalm is the valley's gentlest area, with sunny open slopes graded blue and red. But the top lifts lead to some challenging terrain, and the Kleine Scharte cable-car serves a serious 750m/2,460ft vertical, with a splendid long red run from Hohe Scharte to Kitzsteinalm or the valley floor.
Terrain-parks See Dorfgastein.
Snow reliability Snowmaking is now fairly extensive, but snow-cover down to the bottom is unreliable, especially on the sunny Angertal slopes.
Experts There are no real challenges on the local pistes but there is ample opportunity to go off-piste.
Intermediates All intermediates will enjoy the Schlossalm slopes – and the more confident can go further afield.
Beginners You have to catch a bus to the limited nursery area at Angertal.
Snowboarding Pleasantly varied terrain, but no special facilities except at Grossarl (see Dorfgastein). Drag-lifts are dotted around every sector.
Cross-country Bad Hofgastein makes a fine base for cross-country when its lengthy valley-floor trails have snow.
Queues Crowds are not generally a problem, but the access funicular can

generate big queues at peak times (avoidable by bussing to Angertal).
Mountain restaurants Well up to the high local standards are Kleine Scharte, Hamburger Skihütte and Aeroplanstadl (its toilets 'in the form of a pristine mock cavern' are 'worth a visit'). Après-ski starts early at Aeroplanstadl.
Schools and guides No recent reports.
Facilities for children See Bad Gastein.

STAYING THERE
How to go Mostly hotels.
Hotels Reporters found the 4-star St Georg (61000) and the central Salzburgerhof (62300) excellent value. The 3-star Rauscher (64120) is handy for the shuttle-bus and provides 'clean, spacious rooms and good food'.
Self-catering Accommodation can be organised through the tourist office.
Eating out There is a good range of restaurants. Piccola Italia and Osteria Di Vino are 'well worth a visit'. The Wintergarten is an intimate restaurant, the Maier one of the better informal places. The Bertahof, on the way to Bad Gastein in Vorderscheeberg, has a high reputation. In the hamlet of Wieden is the Schmaranzgut – a splendidly rustic micro-brewery with cooking on an open fire.
Après-ski Quiet by Austrian standards. At close of play the central Piccolo ice bar is popular; there are several good places for cakes, among them Café Weitmoser, an historic little castle. Later on, the Glocknerkeller and the Gasteiner Discostadl are among the bars playing disco music.
Off the slopes The Alpen Therme Gastein spa is 'huge', with several pools, and a 'river' as well as saunas, steam baths and restaurants. Other amenities include ice skating.

Dorfgastein 830m/2,720ft

Dorfgastein is a rustic village further down the valley. It has its own extensive slopes, accessed by a two-stage gondola or chair-lifts starting 500m/1,640ft outside the village, linked with the slopes of Grossarl in the next valley. Runs are varied and long – from top to bottom, about 8km/5 miles to either village – with a good mix of open and wooded runs amid lovely scenery. The low nursery slopes can be cold and icy. Over in Grossarl is a boarders-only park with a half-pipe, two quarter-pipes and jumps. There are a few shops and après-ski places.

WEBSITES
For links to resort sites, go to our own new site at www.wtss.co.uk

Phone numbers
Bad Gastein
From elsewhere in Austria add the prefix 06434.
From abroad use the prefix +43 6434.

Bad Hofgastein
From elsewhere in Austria add the prefix 06432.
From abroad use the prefix +43 6432.

Dorfgastein
From elsewhere in Austria add the prefix 06433.
From abroad use the prefix +43 6433.

TOURIST OFFICE
For all resorts in the Gastein valley contact the Bad Hofgastein office.
t 3393
info@gastein.com
www.gastein.com

ALBIN NIEDERSTRASSER

Ellmau

A quiet base for exploration of the extensive Ski Welt area

COSTS

① ② ③ ④ ⑤ ⑥

RATINGS

The slopes

Fast lifts	**
Snow	**
Extent	****
Expert	*
Intermediate	****
Beginner	****
Convenience	***
Queues	****
Mountain restaurants	**

The rest

Scenery	***
Resort charm	***
Off-slope	***

KEY FACTS

Resort	800m
	2,620ft

For entire Ski Welt	
Slopes	620-1890m
	2,030-6,200ft
Lifts	93
Pistes	250km
	155 miles
Blue	43%
Red	48%
Black	9%
Snowmaking	180km
	112 miles

+ Part of Ski Welt, Austria's largest linked ski and snowboard area

+ Pretty, friendly slopes

+ Excellent nursery slopes (but snow reliability can be a problem)

+ Cheap by Austrian standards

+ Quiet, charming family resort – more appealing than neighbouring Söll

+ Massive recent investment in snowmaking has paid off, but ...

– Ski Welt is at low altitude, and has a poor natural snow record

– Main lift a bus-ride from village – though reachable via a drag-lift

– Upper-mountain runs are mostly short, and offer little for experts or adventurous intermediates

– Limited range of nightlife

– Ski Welt slopes can get crowded at weekends and in high season

If you like the sound of the large, undemanding Ski Welt circuit, Ellmau has a lot to recommend it as your base – quieter than Söll, but with more amenities than other neighbours such as Scheffau (covered in the Söll chapter). And Austria's largest snowmaking system makes the area less risky than it was.

THE RESORT

Ellmau sits at the north-eastern corner of the Ski Welt. Although sizeable and becoming more commercialised each year, it remains quiet, with traditional chalet-style buildings, welcoming bars and shops, and a pretty church.

Ellmau has a compact centre, but its accommodation is scattered – so the buses around the resort are important. Happily, recent reports suggest they are now better organised. There is accommodation out by the funicular to the main slopes but we prefer to stay near the heart of the village. Make sure you get a guest card entitling you to various discounts, including entry to the leisure centre.

THE MOUNTAIN

The Ski Welt is the largest mountain circuit in Austria. It links Going, Scheffau, Söll, Itter, Hopfgarten and Brixen. The piste map covering this huge area is, not surprisingly, difficult to comprehend. However, a 2005 reporter highly recommends the 'new plastic 3D map – a big improvement

Astberg 1265m · Hartkaiser · Eiberg 1675m · Zinsberg 1675m · Going 775m · Brandstadl 1650m · Hohe Salve 1830m/6,000ft · Hochbrixen 1240m · Ellmau 800m/2,620ft · Neualm · Kälbersalve 1545m · Brixen 800m · effau m · Rigi 1530m · 1200m · Westendorf 800m/2,620ft · Blaiken · Hochsöll · Salvenmoos · Söll 700m/2,300ft · Hopfgarten 620m · Itter 700m

on the huge paper version'. Most runs are easy, and short – which means that getting around the area can take time, despite increasing numbers of fast lifts. Westendorf is covered by the Ski Welt pass, though its local slopes are not linked. Kitzbühel, Waidring, Fieberbrunn and St Johann are in easy reach for day trips and are covered by the Kitzbüheler Alpenskipass.

Slopes Ellmau is close to the best slopes in the area, above Scheffau. The funicular railway on the edge of the village takes you up to Hartkaiser, from where a fine long red (a favourite with reporters) leads down to Blaiken (Scheffau's lift base station). A choice of gondolas take you up to Brandstadl.

Immediately beyond Brandstadl, the slopes become rather bitty; an array of short runs and lifts link Brandstadl to Zinsberg. From Zinsberg, excellent, long, south-facing pistes lead down to Brixen. Then it's a short bus-ride to Westendorf's pleasant separate area. Part-way down to Brixen you can head towards Söll, and if you go up Hohe Salve you get access to a long, west-facing run to Hopfgarten.

Ellmau and Going share a pleasant little area of slopes on Astberg, slightly apart from the rest of the area, and well suited to the unadventurous and families. One piste leads to the funicular for access to the rest of Ski Welt. The main Astberg chair is rather inconveniently positioned, midway between Ellmau and Going.

Terrain-parks This season Ellmau will have its own park with kickers and rails near the Kaiserexpress.

Snow reliability With a low average height, and important links that get a lot of sun, the snowmaking that the Ski Welt has installed is essential. And the Ellmau-Going sector now claims almost all its slopes are covered by snowmaking. This can, of course, only be used when it is cold enough and it cannot prevent slush and icy patches forming. The north-facing Eiberg area above Scheffau holds its snow well. A visitor in January this year found the snowmaking 'ace'. And grooming is reported to be 'excellent'. Several reporters also experienced great fresh powder all week in various 2005 visits.

Experts There are steep plunges off the Hohe Salve summit, and a little mogul field between Brandstadl and Neualm, but the area isn't really suitable unless you seek out off-piste opportunities. The ski route from Brandstadl down to

Scheffau is a highlight and was 'very challenging in half a metre of fresh snow and no one on it', says a 2005 reporter.

Intermediates With good snow, the Ski Welt is a paradise for those who love easy cruising. There are lots of blue runs and many of the reds deserve a blue grading ('pale blue', says a 2005 reporter). It is a big area and you get a feeling of travelling around. The main challenge is when the snow isn't perfect – ice and slush can make even gentle lower slopes seem tricky. For timid intermediates the easy slopes of Astberg are handy for Ellmau guests.

Beginners Ellmau has an array of good nursery slopes covered by snowmaking. The main ones are at the Going end, but there are some by the road to the funicular. The Astberg chair opens up a more snow-sure plateau at altitude. The Brandstadl-Hartkaiser area has a section of short easy runs, and a nice long piste running the length of the funicular, which even near-beginners can manage.

Snowboarding Ellmau is a good place to learn as its local slopes are easy.

Cross-country When there is snow, there are long, quite challenging trails (the Ski Welt area has a total of 170km/105 miles), but trails at altitude are lacking.

Queues Continued lift upgrades have greatly improved this once queue-prone area. With the exception of peak times, reporters comment on quiet and crowd-free slopes with 'few queues'.

Mountain restaurants The smaller places are fairly consistent in providing good-value food in pleasant surroundings. The Rübezahl above Ellmau is our favourite in the whole Ski Welt, but can be 'smoky and busy' according to a reporter last year. The Aualm, just below Brandstadl, is favoured especially for its cakes and glühwein, but a reporter last year felt 'disappointed' with the new layout and change of staff. The Jagerhütte (below Hartkaiser) is good for 'home-made strudel' and 'excellent for a drinks stop', says a 2005 reporter, before enjoying the 'quiet and pleasant' home-run. The Hausleitenstube is also worth a visit. The hut at Neualm, halfway down to Scheffau, has been recommended. The larger self-service restaurants are functional (the Jochstube at Eiberg is a pleasant exception) and suffer queues.

Schools and guides The three schools have good reputations – except that classes can be very large. Top is highly rated for children's lessons – and a 2005 reporter said, 'All our children had a great time in different classes with Top, who made sure they were in English-only speaking groups. It was a very busy week but only our youngest was in the maximum class size of 12.' As well as the main schools there are mountaineering schools that organise tours in the Wilder Kaiser and the Kitzbühel mountains.

Facilities for children Ellmau is an attractive resort for families, described by a regular visitor as 'so child-friendly'. Top ski school is recommended (see Schools). Kindergarten facilities seem to be satisfactory and include fun ideas such as a mini train to the lifts. Kinderland has its own fun-park and play areas. We have had no recent reports, however.

STAYING THERE

How to go Ellmau is essentially a hotel and pension resort, though there are apartments that can be booked locally.

Hotels The Bär (2395) is an elegant, relaxed Relais & Châteaux chalet, but twice the price of any other hotel. 'Very friendly and welcoming, wonderful food, reasonably priced house wine and a very good wellness centre,' wrote a 2005 reporter. 'Luxury without pretensions,' said another. The Hochfilzer (2501) is central, well equipped (with outdoor hot-tub) and popular with reporters (as is the simpler Pension Claudia, which it owns – use of hotel facilities allowed). Kaiserblick (2230), with good spa facilities and right by the piste, is recommended by a regular visitor who went with six families including 12 children.

Self-catering There is a wide variety. The Landhof apartments continue to impress – 'spacious, immaculately clean and well equipped' – and offer pool, sauna and steam room. Our regular reporter on these matters rates the supermarket on the way out of town towards Going as 'excellent'.

Eating out The jolly Gasthof Lobewein is a splendid central chalet, with cheerful service in countless rooms and excellent food. Hotel Hochfilzer has a reputation for good food. The Ellmauer Tenne has live music 'most nights'.

Après-ski Cafes Käiserstuberl and Bettina are good for coffee and cakes. There are several busy bars. Memory (which has internet facilities) is the early-evening riotous party pub. Pub 66 and Ötzi have regular events such as karaoke and 'erotic dancers'. Reporganised events include bowling, sleigh rides, Tirolean folklore and tubing. There's an Instructors' Ball and ski displays with 'a party atmosphere' each week, and the toboggan run from the Astberg lift is recommended.

Off the slopes The Kaiserbad leisure centre is good. There are many excursions available, including Salzburg and Vitipeno. Valley walks are spoiled by the busy main road. Heading up to Hartkaiser to relax on the terrace 'was a highlight for our non-skiers', writes a reporter.

Going 775m/2,540ft

Going is a tiny, attractively rustic village, ideal for families looking for a quiet time. It is well placed for the limited but quiet slopes of the Astberg and for the vast area of nursery slopes between here and Ellmau. Prices are low, but it's not an ideal base for covering the whole of the Ski Welt on the cheap unless you have a car for quick access to Scheffau and Söll. The Lanzenhof (2428) is a cosy central pension doing excellent traditional food in its woody dining rooms.

Hintertux/Tux valley

Powerful lifts, excellent snow, varied slopes and villages

COSTS

① ② ③ ④ ⑤ ⑥

RATINGS

The slopes

Fast lifts	★★★
Snow	★★★★★
Extent	★★
Expert	★★★
Intermediate	★★★
Beginner	★★
Convenience	★★
Queues	★★★
Mountain restaurants	★★

The rest

Scenery	★★★
Resort charm	★★★
Off-slope	★

NEWS

The self-service mid-mountain restaurant at Sommerbergalm is being rebuilt for 2005/06.

The slow Eggalm Nord double chair-lift, which links the end of the red run from Rastkogel to the Eggalm slopes, was replaced for 2004/05 by a fast six-seat chair with covers. It starts lower than the old lift, cutting out the short climb to reach it, and ends 100m/330ft higher, giving a choice of runs down.

A short drag now gives access to the top station of the Jumbo cable-car that forms the link with Mayrhofen – so skiers not up to the steep red run down no longer face a climb to the cable-car.

➕ Hintertux has one of the best glaciers in the world, open summer as well as winter, with some great runs for intermediates and experts on guaranteed good snow

➕ Massive investment in new lifts has linked Lanersbach to Mayrhofen and speeded up access to the glacier

➕ Some excellent off-piste opportunities

➕ A choice of quiet, unspoiled, traditional villages to stay in

➖ Lanersbach and Hintertux are a 15-minute bus-ride apart

➖ Not for those who want a huge choice of shops and throbbing nightlife on their doorstep

➖ Not ideal for beginners or timid intermediates, with few easy runs to valley level

➖ Glacier can be cold and bleak in midwinter, and there are lots of T-bars and slow chairs

The Tux valley has always had its attractions, chief among them the Hintertux glacier, which arguably has the most challenging and interesting runs of any lift-served Alpine glacier. For guaranteed good snow, Hintertux is simply one of the best places to go. But the valley acquired much broader appeal in 2001 when the quieter, friendlier, non-glacial slopes above Lanersbach and its nearby twin, Vorderlanersbach were linked by fast new lifts with those above Mayrhofen and Finkenberg, down in the Zillertal. Together, they form a fair-sized circuit. With the glacier only 20 minutes away by bus, these quiet, unspoiled, traditional villages are attractive bases – for many people, more attractive than either Hintertux or Mayrhofen (covered in its own chapter).

The Tux valley, an extension of Mayrhofen's Zillertal, has a variety of small villages, linked by regular free ski-buses. A free night-bus also runs until 2am. Vorderlanersbach is the first village you come to, and Lanersbach is just beyond it. Both are small, traditional places with rustic buildings, narrow roads and paths, their quiet centres bypassed by the main road.

Both have gondola links into the local slopes; the Vorderlanersbach sector links with the Penken-Horberg slopes above Mayrhofen – see separate chapter. Hintertux is 15 minutes by bus beyond Lanersbach, at the head of the valley, a few minutes from the glacier lifts. There is also accommodation in Juns and Madseit.

There are some good rustic restaurants and bars and a few places along the valley with discos or live music. But nightlife tends to be quieter than in many bigger Austrian resorts.

The Tux valley and Mayrhofen lifts now form what is called the Ski and Glacier World Zillertal 3000. Lift passes for four days or more also cover the countless resorts in the rest of the Ziller valley.

Hintertux 1500m/4,920ft

THE RESORT

Tiny Hintertux is bleakly set at the end of the Tux valley. It is little more than a small collection of hotels and guest houses; there is another, smaller group of hotels near the lifts, which lie a 15-minute walk away from the village, across a car park that fills with day-visitors' cars and coaches, especially when snow is poor in lower resorts.

THE MOUNTAINS

Hintertux's slopes are fairly extensive and, for a glacier, surprisingly challenging. The glacier is one of the best in the world, with varied terrain that attracts national ski teams for summer training.

Slopes A series of three speedy gondolas takes you up from the base to the top of the glacier (vertical rise 1750m/5,740ft) in under 20 minutes. The first stage is an eight-seater up to Sommerbergalm, while the second and third stages (linked by a short slope at Tuxer Ferner Haus) have 24-person cabins. On the two lower stages there is a parallel smaller gondola which is pressed into service to meet demand at peak times. From Sommerbergalm, a fast quad chair serves the slopes below Tuxer Joch; from the top of this sector, an excellent secluded off-piste run goes down to the base station. Between the top of the glacier and Tuxer Ferner Haus there are further chairs and drag-lifts to play on and links across to another 1000m/3,300ft-vertical chain of lifts below Grosser Kaserer on the west. Behind Gefrorene Wand is the area's one sunny piste, served by a triple chair. Descent to the valley involves a short ascent to Sommerbergalm on the way, now achieved by a six-seater chair-lift.

Terrain-parks Europe's highest World Cup half-pipe is on the glacier (a popular hang-out throughout the summer), and there is a terrain-park.

Snow reliability Snow does not come more reliable than this. Even off the glacier, the other slopes are high and face north, making for very reliable snow-cover. The runs from Tuxer Ferner Haus down to Sommerbergalm have snowmaking as well.

Experts There is more to amuse experts here than on any other glacier, with a couple of serious black runs at glacier level and steep slopes and ungroomed ski routes beneath. A lot of the off-piste is little used and one reporter said, 'We found untracked snow not far from the lifts two weeks after the last snowfall.'

Intermediates The area particularly suits good or aggressive intermediates. The long runs down from Gefrorene Wand and Kaserer are fun. And there is a pleasant, tree-lined ski route to the valley from Sommerbergalm and another from Tuxer Joch. Moderate intermediates will love the glacier.

Beginners There is a nursery slope at valley level, but the glacier isn't the ideal place to progress to.

Snowboarding There are some great off-piste opportunities, but boarders complain about the number of T-bars.

Cross-country See the Lanersbach information later in the chapter.

Queues There used to be huge queues at Hintertux when snow was poor elsewhere. Improved lifts have largely solved this problem. But the main runs can get crowded, and then it is best to head over to the quieter Kaserer lifts and runs.

Mountain restaurants The mountain restaurants tend to get very crowded and the big self-service places lack charm – 'rather soulless except for

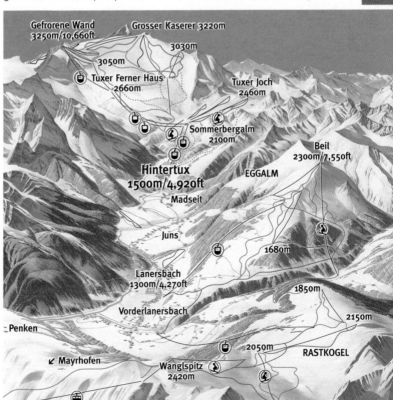

Lanersbach 1300m/4,270ft

Lanersbach and neighbouring Vorderlanersbach have long been attractive bases for anyone planning to explore the multiple resorts of the Zillertal and the higher Tuxertal. With the construction of direct links, via Rastkogel, with Mayrhofen's slopes their attractions are now greatly reinforced.

THE RESORT

Lanersbach is an attractive, spacious, traditional village largely unspoiled by the busy road up to Hintertux that passes the main lift. Happily, the quiet centre near the pretty church is bypassed by the road, yet is within walking distance of the gondola up to Eggalm. The village is small and delightfully uncommercialised, but it has all you need in a resort. And prices are relatively low. Vorderlanersbach is even smaller, with a gondola up to the Rastkogel area.

THE MOUNTAINS

Slopes The slopes of Eggalm, accessed by the gondola from Lanersbach, offer a small network of pleasantly varied, intermediate pistes, usually delightfully quiet. You can descend on red or blue runs back to the village or to Vorderlanersbach, where a gondola goes up to the higher, open Rastkogel slopes; here, two fast chair-lifts – one a covered eight-seater – serve some very enjoyable long red and blue runs and link with Mayrhofen's slopes. The linking run is classified red but is very tricky and many people opt to ride the 150-person cable-car down; a new short drag-lift cuts out the need to hike up to the top station. To get back from Rastkogel to Eggalm you have to take a red run which can suffer from poor snow and is shown on some local piste maps as a ski-route – a strange flaw in the system – or ride the gondola down to Vorderlanersbach (there are no pistes to the village) and catch the bus to Lanersbach.

Terrain-parks The Mayrhofen and Hintertux pipes and parks are easily accessed.

Snow reliability Snow conditions are usually good, at least in early season; by Austrian standards, these are high slopes and there is some snowmaking on Eggalm. But Rastkogel is basically south-facing, and the low links with Eggalm, in particular, are not reliable.

SCHOOLS

Hintertux/Madseit
t 87755
Happy Skiing
t 87240
Luggis
t 86808
Tux 3000
t 87747

Classes
(Hintertux prices)
5 days (2hr am and pm) €119
Private lessons
€48 for 1hr; each additional person €15

CHILDREN

Guest kindergarten
(in Tux Tourist Association building, Lanersbach)
t 872402
Ages 1 to 3

Ski school
All three ski schools run children's classes where lunch is provided. Hintertux school takes children from 10am to 3pm (5 days including lunch €169).

GETTING THERE

Air Salzburg 200km/124 miles (3½hr); Munich 176km/109 miles (3hr); Innsbruck 88km/55 miles (1½hr).

Rail Local line to Mayrhofen; regular buses from station.

Tuxerjochhaus,' as one visitor said. The 90-year-old Spannagelhaus is another exception, and there are great views from Gletscherhütte, at the top. There will be a new restaurant at Sommerbergalm for this season.

Schools and guides There are now four schools, which serve all the resorts in Tux, but we lack reports on them. The newest, Tux 3000, has special guiding, touring and race training programmes.

Facilities for children Most of the ski schools run classes for children aged 4 to 14 and lunch is provided.

STAYING THERE

How to go Most hotels are large and comfortable and have spa facilities, but there are also more modest pensions.

Hotels Close to the lifts are the 4-star Vierjahreszeiten (8525) and Neuhintertux (8580), in which a 2005 reporter enjoyed the 'large and modern spa' and 'unusually good and plentiful' fare. Another relished the 'comfort and hospitality' of the 4-star Alpenhof (8550). We have enjoyed staying in the 3-star Hintertuxerhof (85300); good food, sauna and steam room. Pensions Kössler (87490) and Willeiter (87492) are in the heart of the village.

Self-catering There are plenty of apartments.

Eating out Restaurants are mainly hotel-based. The Vierjahreszeiten is pleasant and informal.

Après-ski There can be a lively après-ski scene both at mid-mountain (Sommerbergalm) and at the base; the 'quite animated' Hohenhaus Tenne has several different bars, the Rindererhof has a popular tea dance, and there are a couple of local bars. The free night-bus gets you to and from the other villages until 2am, but Hintertux is not the place for keen clubbers.

Off the slopes The spa facilities are excellent, including a thermal indoor pool, but there are many more options in Mayrhofen.

100%
SNOW GUARANTEE

225 km of ski runs · 365 days of the year snowfun on the Hintertux Glacier

Rooms, Brochures, Information: Tourismusverband Tux, A-6293 Tux, Lanersbach 472, Tel. +43/5287/8506, Fax +43/5287/8508, e-mail: info@tux.at, **w w w . t u x . a t**

im Zillertal
tuX
1300 - 3250 m

↑ Probably the best glacier in the world, all things considered
TVB TUX / JP FANKHAUSER

ACTIVITIES

Indoor Bowling, tennis, squash, saunas, fitness rooms and pools in hotels open to public

Outdoor Ice rink, curling, winter hiking trails, paragliding, tobogganing, sleigh rides, snow-shoe tours

Phone numbers
From elsewhere in Austria add the prefix 05287.
From abroad use the prefix +43 5287.

TOURIST OFFICE

Tux
t 8506
info@tux.at
www.tux.at

Experts There are no pistes to challenge experts, but there is a fine off-piste route starting a short walk from Beil and finishing at the village.

Intermediates The slopes suit intermediates best – especially now that they are linked in to Mayrhofen's Penken slopes.

Beginners Both areas have nursery slopes (as do Madseit and Juns) but there are few ideal progression slopes – most of the easy runs are on the higher lifts of the Rastkogel sector.

Snowboarding The area isn't great for novices – there are drag-lifts dotted around, some in key places.

Cross-country There are 14km/9 miles of cross-country trails, alongside the Tux creek, between Madseit and Vorderlanersbach, and a 6km/4-mile skating track in Juns/Madseit.

Queues We have no reports of any problems. Indeed, Eggalm can be delightfully quiet.

Mountain restaurants There's no shortage but most, though fairly rustic, are self-service with simple food; the small Lattenalm on Eggalm is a table-service exception with a terrace that has splendid views of the Tux glacier.

Schools and guides There are four schools in the valley, but we lack recent reports on them.

Facilities for children The non-ski nursery takes children aged from one to three, and most of the schools take children from four years upwards

There's a new terrain-park, including a snow-tyre carousel and a bob-run, on the glacier.

STAYING THERE

How to go Lanersbach and Vorderlanersbach are essentially hotel-based resorts.

Hotels The Lanersbacherof (87256) is a good 4-star with pool, sauna, steam and hot-tub close to the lifts, but it is also on the main road. The cheaper 3-star Pinzger (87541) and Alpengruss (87293) are similarly situated. In Vorderlanersbach the 3-star Kirchlerhof (8560) is 'really friendly, with comfortable rooms and excellent food', says a regular visitor.

Self-catering Quite a lot of apartments are available.

Eating out Restaurants are mainly hotel-based, busy, and geared to serving dinner early.

Après-ski Nightlife is quiet by Austrian standards, which suits us. We enjoyed the jolly Hühnerstall in Lanersbach (an old wooden building with traditional Austrian music). There is a disco or two.

Off the slopes Off-slope facilities are fairly good considering the size of the resorts. Some hotels have pools, hot-tubs and fitness rooms open to non-residents. There is a tennis centre in Vorderlanersbach which also has squash and bowling. Innsbruck and Salzburg are possible excursions.

Hochkönig

A large ski area virtually unknown on the British market

COSTS

① ② ③ ④ ⑤ ⑥

RATINGS

The slopes

Fast lifts	**
Snow	***
Extent	***
Expert	**
Intermediate	****
Beginner	****
Convenience	**
Queues	****
Mountain restaurants	***

The rest

Scenery	***
Resort charm	***
Off-slope	***

KEY FACTS

Resorts	800-1070m
	2,620-3,510ft
Slopes	800-2000m
	2,620-6,560ft
Lifts	39
Pistes	150km
	93 miles
Blue	35%
Red	55%
Black	10%
Snowmaking	90km
	56 miles

➕ Traditional quiet villages

➕ Plenty of uncrowded beginner and easy intermediate terrain

➖ Little for experts except ski routes and off-piste

➖ Buses needed to explore full ski area

The picturesque Salzburgerland villages of Maria Alm, Hintermoos, Hinterthal, Dienten and Mühlbach combine to provide a sizeable ski area, best suited to beginners and intermediates. The lift system is not completely linked, so you'll have to drive or catch the ski buses to explore it all. The area is largely unknown on the British market and no big tour operators go there.

THE RESORT

Maria Alm is one of the two largest villages, and it houses the area's main tourist office. It's a pretty place with typically Austrian chalet-style architecture and a splendid old church boasting the highest spire in Salzburgerland. The peaks of the Selbhorn and Schonfeldspitze provide a dramatic backcloth. Hinterthal, the next real village up the valley, is smaller, with some big chalets owned by the rich and famous and a few smart 4-star hotels; it has some of the best mountain views in the region. Further up the road and over a pass is Dienten, a small, unspoiled, picturesque village with a handful of traditional hotels and guest houses. Mühlbach, at the eastern end of the ski area, is a similar size to Maria Alm and sprawls along the roadside for quite a distance. The spectacular Hochkönig massif, from which the region gets its name, overlooks the village but is not part of the ski area.

THE MOUNTAIN

The total ski area amounts to a respectable 150km/93 miles of piste, on a par with well-known names such as Kitzbühel.

Slopes The main slopes spread along several small mountains running east along the valley from Maria Alm to Mühlbach. Many of the runs are north-facing and have splendid views over to the high peaks opposite. Just to the west of Maria Alm is the tiny little area of Hinterreit, where the British and Austrian ski teams train. Maria Alm has its own small Natrun ski area of black and red runs, served by what was the world's first chondola (a mix of chairs and gondolas). An ungroomed ski route leads off the back to the main local Aberg-Langeck mountain, itself served by an eight-seat gondola and a number of chairs and drags; but most people catch the bus round to Aberg (you have to catch it back, too). You also need a bus from Aberg to the rest of the main ski area, starting at

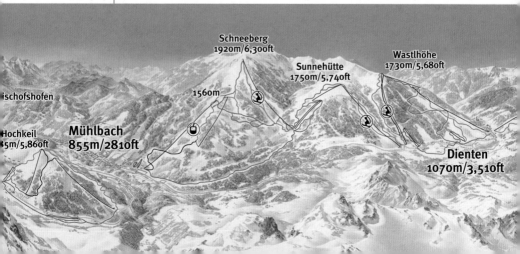

AUSTRIA!
Ski Chalets
www.ElevationHolidays.com
0845 6443578

NEWS

The resort plans to replace two drag-lifts on Aberg with a six-pack but was still waiting for government approval when we went to press.

Phone numbers
From elsewhere in Austria add the prefix 06584 (Maria Alm and Hinterthal), 06461 (Dienten), 06467 (Mühlbach). From abroad use the prefix +43 and omit the initial '0'.

TOURIST OFFICES

region@hochkoenig.at
www.hochkoenig.at
Maria Alm
t 7816
Dienten
t 263
Mühlbach
t 7235

AUSTRIA

132

Hinterthal – but you can ski back from Hinterthal to Aberg. From Hinterthal you can make your way over through Dienten right along the mountain to Mühlbach (where the gondola back up is a bus-ride from the centre of the sprawling village).

Terrain-parks There are five terrain-parks offering a variety of features.

Snow reliability Although low altitude, the region is in a snow pocket, so it tends to have better conditions than its height suggests. The runs towards Mühlbach are south-facing, so the snow can suffer here. Some 60% of the pistes are covered by snowmaking.

Experts There are several ungroomed but marked ski routes, the best of which is in a huge off-piste bowl behind the Aberg ridge. In the Hochmais area above Hinterthal there's another ski route down the side of a black run, with a variety of routes back to the lift. With a guide you can explore other excellent off-piste in these two areas, too.

Intermediates The whole area is ideal for easy intermediate cruising, and you really get a feeling of travelling around if you go from Hinterthal to Mühlbach and back in a day (or vice versa). For the more adventurous intermediate the sunny slopes from the top of the Aberg down to Hintermoos are a little steeper. The pistes down to Dienten from both directions are nicely varied from each other and usually quiet.

Beginners All the villages have good nursery slopes, and the runs at the foot of the Aberg and at Hinterthal are good progression runs.

Cross-country There are over 40km/ 25 miles of prepared tracks.

Queues Not usually a problem.

Mountain restaurants There are no fewer than 37, including some nice little huts. A local recommends the Tischlerhütte (Aberg), Griessbachhütte (on Aberg's ski route – great views), the Alm Bar (Hinterthal – good spare ribs) and Almhäust (just above Dienten – sun deck and umbrella bar).

Schools and guides All four main villages have schools, and many instructors speak good English.

Facilities for children The kindergartens at all the main base areas take children from the age of two. The ski schools take them from four.

STAYING THERE

How to go No big tour ops come here.

Hotels There are plenty of good hotels with spa and pool facilities. The Haus Salzburg (23497) in Hinterthal is a chalet-hotel run by an English couple.

Eating out The Ubergossene Alm just outside Dienten and the restaurant in the pretty hotel Thalerhof in Maria Alm have good menus. Most hotels have atmospheric stüberls. Haus Salzburg (see Hotels) serves international rather than traditional Austrian food.

Après-ski Maria Alm is by far the most animated village. The Dengl Alm gets packed and has zither music, dancing and jolly bar staff in lederhosen. Almer Tenne has live music and a disco. Bunny Bar and Chili's are good for a quieter time. The Alm Bar in Hinterthal can be lively and opens till late, as does the Haus Salzburg bar. Saustall is a decent 'pub' in Mühlbach.

Off the slopes Maria Alm is the main village for off-slope diversions. It has curling, tobogganing, bowling, sleigh rides, swimming and nice walks.

Aberg-Langeck
2000m/6,560ft

Wastlhöhe
730m/5,680ft

Gabühel
1635m/5,360ft

Hintermoos

Hinterreit

Saalfelde

Dienten
1070m/3,510ft

Natrun Höhe
1100m

Maria Alm
800m/2,620ft

Hinterthal

Innsbruck

A cultured city base for a range of little ski resorts – and a big glacier

COSTS

① ② ③ ④ ⑤ ⑥

KEY FACTS

Resort	575m
	1,890ft
Slopes	800-3210m
	2,620-10,530ft
Lifts	77
Pistes	266km
	165 miles
Blue	32%
Red	49%
Black	19%
Snowmaking	53km
	33 miles

NEWS

For 2005/06 a new fast quad is due to open on the Patscherkofel slopes above Igls. In Oberperfuss, the blue run from Stiglreith at 1400m/4,590ft at mid-mountain down to the valley is getting snowmaking.

It seems likely that the Mutters ski area will stay closed for the 2005/06 season.

Mountains rise up from the outskirts of this historic city ↓

Innsbruck is not a ski resort in the usual sense. It is an historic university city of 130,000 inhabitants, with a vibrant cultural life, and is a major tourist destination in summer. Its local slopes are mainly of local interest. But the city has twice hosted the Olympic Winter Games, and is surrounded by little resorts that share a lift pass and are accessible by efficient bus services. Among them is a glacier that is one of best in the world – the Stubaier Gletscher. Last year the portfolio was expanded by the addition of little Oberperfuss and the more distant Kühtai – at 2020m/6,63oft, one of Austria's highest resorts. Meanwhile, lower down, the slopes above Mutters are likely to remain closed, awaiting agreement on their redevelopment.

The Inn valley is a broad, flat-bottomed trench here, but Innsbruck manages to fill it from side to side. It is a sizeable city and, as you would expect from its Olympic background, it has an excellent range of winter sports facilities, as well as a captivating car-free medieval core. It has smart, modern, shopping areas, trendy bars and restaurants, museums (including, of course, one devoted to the Olympics), concert halls, theatres, a zoo and other attractions that you might seek out on a summer holiday, but normally wouldn't expect to find when going skiing.

Winter diversions off the slopes include 117km/72 miles of cross-country trails, some at valley level but others appreciably above it; curling and skating at the Olympic centre; several toboggan runs totalling 95km/59 miles, the longest (above Birgitz) an impressive 11km/7 miles and 1060m/3,480ft vertical; and rides on a four-man bob at Igls.

Not the least of the attractions of staying in such a place is that you don't pay ski resort prices for anything. There are hotels, inns and B&Bs of every standard and style, with 3-star and 4-star hotels forming the nucleus. Among the more distinctive hotels are the grand 5-star Europa Tyrol (59310), the ancient 4-star Goldener Adler (571111) and the 3-star Weisses Kreuz (59479) in the central pedestrian zone, and the 4-star art nouveau Best Western Neue Post (59476).

As well as traditional Austrian restaurants there are several Italians, plus a smattering of more exotic alternatives from Mexican to Japanese.

There is an impressive 1400m/ 4,600ft vertical of slopes on the south-facing slopes of **Seegrube-Nordkette**. The focus of the slopes at Seegrube is reached by cable-car rising 1050m/ 3,450ft from Hungerburg on the outskirts of the city (with buses and a funicular up to the cable-car departure station). Although there are red runs to the valley, the snow is not reliable. You go up here expecting to ski the red runs of 370m/1,210ft vertical below Seegrube, served by a chair-lift. A further stage of the cable-car rises 350m/1,150ft vertical to access the Karinne ski route, which is said to be fearsomely steep (up to 70% gradient). You can ski it with a guide and collect a T-shirt and certificate to prove it.

But for visitors, if not for residents, skiing usually means heading for the opposite side of the Inn trench.

The standard Innsbruck lift pass covers the lifts in all the resorts dealt with here, plus the slopes of Glungezer above Tulfes and Schlick 2000 above Fulpmes.

LIFT PASSES

Innsbruck Gletscher Skipass
Covers all resorts in this chapter.

Beginners
No special pass.

Main pass
6 days €155

Senior citizens
Over 60: 6 days €124

Children
Under 19: 6 days €124
Under 15: 6 days €93
Under 7: free

Other passes
Super-Skipass also covers days in the Arlberg (St Anton) and Kitzbühel.

Free ski-bus services run to and from all the lift-pass-covered areas, but only at the beginning and end of the day. A car makes life more convenient, especially if you are staying outside downtown Innsbruck.

There are terrain-parks at Seegrube, Axamer Lizum, the Stubaier Gletscher and Kühtai.

The runs on Glungezer are on north-facing slopes. A chair-lift from the bottom serves red and blue runs of 600m/1,970ft vertical. This leads to a drag up to the tree line serving a red run of 500m/1,640ft vertical. And this in turn leads to a drag and a chair-lift serving open red runs from the top at 2305m/7,560ft – almost 1400m/4,600ft above the village. On Schlick 2000, a two-stage gondola leads to a series of chair- and drag-lifts serving a few mainly short blue and red runs on the Sennjoch and two ski routes.

A major road runs southwards from Innsbruck over the Brenner pass to Italy – opening up the possibility of excursions to resorts in the Dolomites.

IGLS 900m/2,950ft
Igls seems almost a suburb of Innsbruck – the city trams run out to the village – but it is a small resort in its own right. Its famous downhill race course is an excellent piste.
The village of Igls is small and quiet, with not much in the way of diversions apart from the beautiful walks, an artificial ice rink, the Olympic bob run and the tea shops. You can stay in Igls, and a few UK operators sell packages there. Most hotels are small and in the centre of the village, a bit of a walk from the cable-car station. An exception is the family-run 5-star Sporthotel (377241), which occupies the prime site, centrally placed between the tram and the cable-car stations: 'Excellent facilities, good food and nice bar,' says a reporter.

The skiing on Patscherkofel is very limited and revolves around the excellent, varied, long red run that formed the men's downhill course in 1976, when Franz Klammer took ski racing (and the Olympic gold medal) by storm. There is a blue-run variation on this run, but few other pistes. A cable-car rises 1050m/3,450ft from the village (and you can take it down if the lower runs are poor or shut). At the top, a chair rises a further 275m/900ft to the summit offering wonderful views over Innsbruck and ski routes back down. Two fast quads (including a new one for 2005/06 which ends above the cable-car top station) and a couple of drags serve the other slopes. There is a short beginner lift at village level,

Innsbruck

135

↑ There's skiing all
year round on the
Stubaier glacier
TVB NEUSTIFT

AUSTRIA

TOURIST OFFICES

Innsbruck
t 59850
office@innsbruck.info
www.innsbruck.info

Tulfes
t 78324
info@tulfes.at
www.tulfes.at

Igls
t 377101
igls@innsbruck.tvb.
co.at
www.tiscover.com/igls

Fulpmes
t 62235
info@stubai.at
www.tiscover.com/
fulpmes

Neustift
t 2228
info@neustift.com
www.neustift.com

Axamer Lizum
t 68178
axams@innsbruck.info
www.tiscover.com/
axams

Oberperfuss
t 81489
oberperfuss@
innsbruck.info
www.tiscover.at/
oberperfuss

Kühtai
t 5222
info@kuehtai.co.at
www.kuehtai.co.at

and another a short bus-ride up the
hill. We have received mixed reports
on the grooming of the trails.

Après-ski is quiet. The resort suits
families but others might prefer to
stay in Innsbruck.

STUBAIER GLETSCHER

**The Stubaier Gletscher is one of the
best glacier ski and snowboard areas
in the world; it is open in summer as
well as in winter. The nearest place to
stay is picturesque Neustift, 20km/12
miles away and served by regular
buses.**

The glacier is accessed by two
alternative two-stage gondolas from
the huge car park at Mutterberg. A
third gondola, built a couple of
seasons ago, takes you right to the top
of the slopes.

On the glacier a variety of chair- and
drag-lifts (including three six-person
chairs) allow fabulous high altitude
cruising on blue and red runs, which
normally have excellent snow on
slopes between 3200m and 2300m
(10,500ft and 7,550ft). A lovely 10km/
6 mile ungroomed ski route through a
deserted bowl takes you down to the
valley – or, if you start at the top, a
descent of about 14km/9 miles and
1450m/4,760ft vertical is possible.
There is also good off-piste on the
glacier to be explored with a guide.

A recent reporter confirms that
improvements to the lifts have virtually
eliminated what used to be enormous
queues. On a busy weekend there
were only short delays mid-morning at
the gondola middle station and
occasionally at the Eisjoch six-pack.

There is a terrain-park and half-pipe,
a fun area for kids at Gamsgarten and
a 20m/66ft ice tower.

AXAMER LIZUM 1580m/5,180ft
**The mountain outpost of the Inn-side
village of Axams is a simple ski station
and nothing more, but it does have
some good slopes and reliable snow
conditions – and, as a reporter says,
'You feel as if you are in a wilderness.'**
Axamer Lizum could scarcely offer a
sharper contrast to Igls. It offers much
more varied slopes and a network of
lifts, with the base station at a much
higher altitude. The slopes here hosted
all the Olympic Alpine events in 1976
except the men's downhill, and this is
the standard local venue for weekends
– hence the huge car park, which is the
most prominent feature of the 'resort'.

The main slopes on Hoadl and
Pleisen are blues and reds, almost
entirely above the trees but otherwise
nicely varied, and there is scope to
'play in gullies and bumps, as well as
true off-piste', says a reporter. The
vertical of the main east-facing slopes
above the main lift station is 'only'
700m/2,300ft, but for good skiers at
least there is the possibility (given
good snow conditions) of a 1300m/
4,260ft descent at the end of the day
from Pleisen to the outskirts of Axams
– an easy 6.5km/4 mile black. On the
opposite side of the valley, a chair-lift
serves a fairly easy black slope.
Beyond it are the slopes of Mutters,
closed since 2001 and unlikely to re-
open for 2005/06. Snowmaking now
covers 70% of the slopes and there is
a new large restaurant with panoramic
views on Hoadl. There are two good
nursery lifts, and two ski schools.

You can stay up here – there is a 4-
star hotel, the Lizumerhof (68244) at
the lift base – 'nice rooms and decent
modern Austrian cuisine' – and there
are a couple of 3-stars, too. But there's
little in the way of après-ski apart from
a couple of bars – the Alm bar is the
most atmospheric – and you have to
eat in your hotel or go to Axams.

↑ Set at over 2000m/6,560ft, Kühtai is one of Austria's highest and most snow-sure resorts
TVB KUHTAI

WEBSITES

For links to resort sites, go to our own new site at www.wtss.co.uk

Phone numbers
Calling long-distance
Add the prefix given below for each resort. When calling from abroad use the country code 43 and omit the initial '0'.

Innsbruck and Igls
0512
Axamer Lizum
05234
Oberperfuss
05232
Kühtai
05239

INNSBRUCK TOURISMUS

The Seegrube-Nordkette slopes have impressive views over Innsbruck →

There is also accommodation not far away at lower altitude in Axams – including six 3-star hotels – and in other nearby villages such as Götzens (one 4-star hotel, two 3-star gasthofs) and Birgitz (two 3-star hotels).

OBERPERFUSS 815m/2,675ft
No, we hadn't heard of it, either – until the lifts on its local hill, Rangger Köpfl, were brought into the fold of the Innsbruck area lift pass.
The hill is a very limited one, with five lifts in a largely linear arrangement serving 17km/11 miles of easy-intermediate slopes – but an impressive vertical of 1200m/3,940ft. For 2005/06 the blue run from Stiglreith at 1400m/4,590ft at mid-mountain down to the valley is getting snowmaking. The village is small but self-sufficient, with one of most things you need (pharmacy, bakery) including a big 3-star hotel, the Krone (81465). It is prettily rustic, and targets the family market with the aid of a moving carpet lift on the nursery slopes.

KÜHTAI 2020m/6,630ft
A collection of comfortable hotels spread along a high road pass 25km/16 miles west of Innsbruck – higher than equally snow-sure Obergurgl or Obertauern, but cheaper than either.
Glaciers apart, Kühtai's altitude means it must be one of Austria's most snow-sure resorts. That is its main attraction, given the limited nature of the village.
Six drags and three fast quad chairs serve red cruisers of 400m/ 1,310ft to 500m/1,640ft vertical on either side of the road, plus some token blue and black runs (which may be easier than the reds because they get less traffic). There is a good nursery slope, but no easy blues to graduate to. There's also a terrain-park with kickers and rails. The resort attracts families during school holidays (notably carnival) and

crowds of day trippers on fine weekends – especially if lower resorts are short of snow – but is otherwise crowd-free. There are now three mountain restaurants. There are two ski schools.

The village is quiet in the evening, but for its size has 'a reasonable selection of bars and restaurants', says a report – practically all in hotels. The 4-star hotels include the Jagdschloss (5201) – a much-developed old hunting lodge. The 3-star hotel Elisabeth (5240) is recommended – 'Very friendly, excellent food.'

Reporters say that English is not spoken in one or two other hotels – and there is little resort information in English, either on paper or on the resort web site.

There are several free postbuses from Innsbruck morning and afternoon, but the journey takes over an hour.

Ischgl

One of Austria's best – and at last finding a place on the British market

COSTS

① ② ③ ④ ⑤ ⑥

RATINGS

The slopes
Fast lifts	*****
Snow	****
Extent	****
Expert	***
Intermediate	****
Beginner	**
Convenience	***
Queues	****
Mountain restaurants	****

The rest
Scenery	***
Resort charm	****
Off-slope	***

NEWS

For 2004/05 two six-packs with covers were installed: the Nachtweidebahn serves the beginner area at Idalp and the Viderjochbahn II provides another route to the Austrian border from Alp Trida Eck on the Swiss side.

In Galtür, a new eight-seat gondola to Alpkogel has replaced the longest T-bar in the resort.

➕ Charming old Tirolean village, expanded in sympathetic fashion

➕ High slopes with reliable snow

➕ Lots of good intermediate runs

➕ Superb modern lift system

➕ Wide range of accommodation from luxury hotels to simple B&Bs

➕ Very lively après-ski

➖ Not ideal for beginners or timid intermediates, for various reasons

➖ English less widely spoken than is usual in Austria

➖ Few seriously steep runs

➖ Very little wooded terrain to give shelter in bad weather

➖ Eurotrash-style après-ski – eg table dancing in plush 4-star hotels – and a lot of heavy drinking

For years we've been saying that Ischgl is unjustly neglected in Britain, mainly because of a shortage of package holidays to the resort. That's now changing, with three major operators going there – and a recent mini-flood of reports from readers. With one clear exception ('the place is full of maniacs') most enthusiastically endorse our view that this is one of Austria's best. The lift system is particularly impressive: 62% are fast lifts, putting the resort at the top of our new fast lift league table. Unless cost is an obstacle or you insist on the woodland runs that are the Tirolean norm, put it on your Austrian shortlist.

Samnaun, over the Swiss border, is tour-op-free (as well as duty-free), and likely to remain so. But it's a charming, relaxed village, and for a party booking independently and including novices it makes a better base than Ischgl.

THE RESORT

Ischgl is a quite compact village tucked away on the Swiss border in the long, narrow Paznaun valley, south of St Anton; the skiing is shared with Swiss Samnaun. It's set where a stream (the Fimbabach) joins the river Trisanna, and part of the village is built on high ground between the converging rivers. The wooded flanks of the valley rise steeply from the village, which gets almost no sun in early season.

The narrow main street plus a couple of side streets are traffic-free – the village is bypassed by the valley road

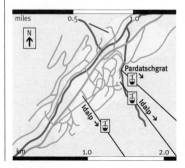

up to Galtür – and at the west end of the pedestrian zone is the main access lift, the 24-person Silvrettabahn, up to the main mid-mountain focus of Idalp. Two other gondolas – one to Idalp, the other to Pardatschgrat, higher up – start close together on the eastern fringe of the village. An underground moving walkway runs to these lifts from the heart of the village.

The buildings are practically all in traditional chalet style, and the place has a neat, prosperous air. There's a selection of lively bars and an excellent sports centre; shops are mainly confined to winter-sports. There is a lot of heavy drinking, but it rarely constitutes a nuisance.

The underground walkway makes choice of location less important than it was, but the best spot, overall, is on or near the main street. Beware of accommodation across the bypass road, a long way from the lifts.

There are frequent ski-buses down the valley to Kappl and up it to Galtür, described at the end of this chapter. A car makes trips to St Anton viable. It's a very long taxi-ride from Samnaun, should you get stuck there.

KEY FACTS

Resort	1400m
	4,590ft
Slopes	1400-2870m
	4,590-9,420ft
Lifts	42
Pistes	210km
	130 miles
Blue	18%
Red	61%
Black	21%
Snowmaking	168km
	104 miles

THE MOUNTAINS

Ischgl is a fair-sized, relatively high, snow-sure area. Practically all the slopes are above the tree line, and bleak in bad weather, the main exception being the steep lower slopes above the village and a couple of short runs low down in the Fimbatal.

We are pleased to note that several ski routes – unpatrolled runs, avalanche-controlled only 'in the immediate area of avalanche warning signs' – have been restored to piste status, so they are safe to ski alone.

Some reporters complain about the closure of lifts at about 4pm, even in late season. This is common in Austria.

THE SLOPES
Cross-border cruising

The sunny **Idalp** plateau, reached by two of the village gondolas, is the hub of the slopes. It can be very crowded, especially at ski school meeting time, lunchtime (lock up your skis!) and the end of the day. Pardatschgrat, reached by the third gondola, is about 300m/ 1,000ft higher. From here it's an easy run down to Idalp, where lifts radiate to a wide variety of mainly north-west- and west-facing runs. The main red runs from Idalp to Ischgl itself provoke regular complaints; neither is easy, conditions can be tricky, and beer-lubricated crowds don't help. The wide,

quiet run down the pretty Velilltal – now a piste, not a ski route – is much more pleasant. Quite a few people ride the gondolas down.

A short piste brings you from Idalp to the lifts serving the **Höllenkar** bowl, leading up to the area's south-western extremity and high point at Palinkopf. There are further lifts beyond here, on the west-facing flanks of the **Fimbatal**.

On the Swiss side the hub of activity is **Alp Trida**, surrounded by south- and east-facing runs with great views. From here a scenic red run goes down to Compatsch, where a short walk takes you to buses to Ravaisch – for the cable-car back – and Samnaun-Dorf. From Palinkopf there is a beautiful long run down an unspoiled valley to Samnaun-Dorf. It is not difficult, but it is excessively sunny in parts and prone to closure because of avalanche risk. There is a long flat stretch at the end.

TERRAIN-PARKS
One of Europe's best

Between Idjoch and Idalp is a championship half-pipe and an excellent terrain-park, 'Boarder's Paradise', with jumps, a quarter-pipe, rails, a boarder-cross course and a 'popular' timed race course. It is reported to be very quiet. There's a separate kids' snowboard area and another small park on the Swiss side.

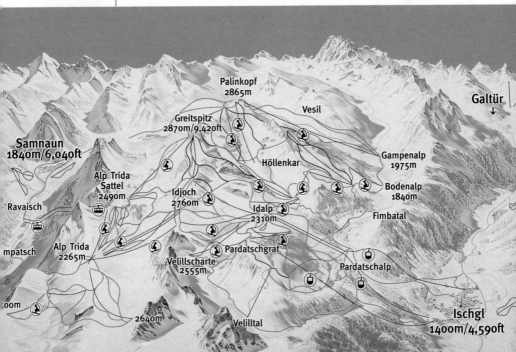

LIFT PASSES

VIP Skipass
Covers all lifts in Ischgl and Samnaun and local buses.

Beginners
No special pass.

Main pass
1 day €39
6 days €172.50

Senior citizens
Over 60: 6 days €146

Children
Under 16: 6 days €103.50
Under 7: free pass

Notes
Half-day pass available. Passes for two days and over available only to those staying in Ischgl, Samnaun or Mathon on presenting a guest card. Note that the lift pass office does not take credit cards.

Alternative passes
Regional (Silvretta) ski pass covers Ischgl, Samnaun, Galtür, Kappl and See.

boarding

Ischgl was one of the first resorts to wholeheartedly welcome boarders. It has one of the best terrain-parks in Europe and is constantly improving it. The use of speed boards and the carving courses are very popular. The lifts are generally boarder-friendly. The area is well-suited to beginners and intermediates; experts will love Ischgl after fresh snow, even if the gradients are less impressive than in St Anton. Silvretta Sports and Intersport Mathoy are recommended snowboard shops.

SNOW RELIABILITY
Very good
All the slopes, except the runs back to the resort, are above 2000m/6,56oft and many of those on the Ischgl side are north-west-facing. So snow conditions are generally reliable (which can lead to crowds when bus-loads of visitors arrive from lower resorts). There is snowmaking on various runs including several above Idalp, the two main descents to Ischgl and some key slopes on the Samnaun side. Piste grooming is reportedly 'very reliable'.

FOR EXPERTS
Not much on-piste challenge
Ischgl can't compare with nearby St Anton for exciting slopes, and some of the runs marked black on the piste map would be red elsewhere. But there is plenty of beautiful off-piste to be found with a guide (Alp Trida is popular) – and it doesn't get tracked out quickly. The best areas to head for are Greitspitz and Palinkopf – the wooded lower slopes of the Fimbatal are delightful in a storm. Ski route 39 is recommended to leave you 'suitably exhausted' after the testing 1000m/3,28oft descent. The best steep piste is 4, from Pardatschgrat towards Ischgl. The variant 4a, into Velilltal, is now a ski route. Black 14a, from Greitspitz, is steeper than most.

FOR INTERMEDIATES
Something for everyone
Most of the slopes are wide, forgiving and ideal for intermediates.

At the tough end of the spectrum our favourite runs are those from Palinkopf down to Gampenalp. There are also interesting and challenging black runs down the Höllspitz chair, and on Greitspitz. The reds from Pardatschgrat and Velillscharte down the beautiful Velilltal and the red from Greitspitz into Switzerland are great for quiet, high-speed cruising.

For easier motorway cruising, there is lots of choice, including those down to Alp Trida on the Swiss side.

FOR BEGINNERS
Not ideal
Beginners must go up the mountain to Idalp, where there are good, sunny, snow-sure nursery slopes served by drags and a new fast chair. The blue runs on the east side of the bowl offer pleasant progression for fast learners. Over at Alp Trida there are further easy expanses – you can return by lift.

FOR CROSS-COUNTRY
Plenty in the valley
There are 48km/30 miles of cross-country track in the Paznaun valley between Ischgl, Galtür and Wirl. This tends to be pretty sunless, especially in early season, and is away from the main slopes, which makes meeting downhillers for lunch inconvenient.

QUEUES
An amazing transformation
Ischgl tops our fast lift league table – 62% of its many lifts are fast ones. There are some flaws in the system, though, notably in the village – a reporter had a 30-minute wait at the Pardatschgratbahn, but the nearby Fimbabahn gets few queues. Up the mountain, the new Viderjochbahn II has relieved the afternoon queues for the Flimsattelbahn back from Alp Trida.

MOUNTAIN RESTAURANTS
Much improved
Mountain restaurants tend to be very crowded but quite good quality, with over half now offering table-service. The Paznauner Taja, above Bodenalp, is an attractive, rustic chalet with 'great spit-roasted chickens', but it gets very crowded. There is table-service upstairs and often a band playing on the terrace, or throbbing disco music. Down in Fimbatal is the Bodenalpe, a quieter, rustic table-service restaurant.

At Idalp there is a busy, big self-service cafeteria, and a good table-service alternative (splendid views from the terrace). The newly revamped Pardatschgrat (table- and self-service) tends to be quieter. The Schwarze

↑ Lots of glorious intermediate slopes above the tree line
ISCHGL TOURISMUS

SCHOOLS

Ischgl
t 5257/5404

Classes
5 days (2hr am and pm) €156
Private lessons
€114 for 2hr; each additional person €16

CHILDREN

Kindergarten
(run by ski school at Idalp)
t 5257/5404
For non-skiing children (no small infants); 10am to 4pm
Ski kindergarten
(run by ski school at Idalp)
t 5257/5404
Ages 3 to 5; €41 per day; lunch available

Ski school
Takes children from the age of 5 (5 full days €141)

Wand pizzeria at the top of Höllenkar is recommended by reporters, as is the Höllboden below it ('good desserts'). From Gampenalp you can be towed 5km/3 miles by snowmobile to the remote Heidelberger hütte – 'tough on the knees but exhilarating'. The way back involves 'a lot of poling, some climbs and a few gentle schusses'.

The restaurants on the Swiss side at Alp Trida are pleasant, quieter and generally recommended by reporters. The Alp Bella (table- or self-service) offers 'good views and local specialities'. Also highly rated are the Skihaus Alp Trida – 'best goulash soup ever' – and the Panorama Sattel (top of the Samnaun cable-car) – 'excellent food', 'splendid views'. Above the big Alp Trida self-service is the upmarket Marmotte, with table-service indoors and out (reservations needed).

SCHOOLS AND GUIDES
Good despite language problems
The school meets up at Idalp and starts very late (10.30 to 12.30 and 1.30 to 3.30) – perhaps to allow people to get over their hangovers. In the past we've had rave reports of both adult and children's classes, but recent reporters said class sizes were large at around 12 people and their instructor spoke limited English. But another found his private instructor 'helpful'. As well as normal lessons the school organises off-piste tours – this is a great touring area. You can try out the latest equipment at the newly built test centre at Idalp.

FACILITIES FOR CHILDREN
High-altitude options
The childcare facilities are all up at Idalp – there's an enclosed learning zone and adventure garden with cartoon characters, where children can safely enjoy their classes, but we have no first-hand reports of the service they provide.

STAYING THERE

HOW TO GO
Increasing choice of packages
Very few British tour operators have offered Ischgl in the past, but there is now a reasonable choice of mainstream and specialist operators.
Hotels There is a good selection from luxurious and expensive to basic B&Bs. Beware: some don't take credit cards.
(((((5 **Trofana Royal** (600) One of Austria's most luxurious hotels, with prices to match. A celebrity chef runs the kitchen. Sumptuous spa facilities.
(((((5 **Madlein** (5226) Convenient, 'hip', modern hotel. Pool, sauna, steam room. Nightclub and disco.
(((((5 **Elisabeth** (5411) Right by the Pardatschgrat gondola with lively après-ski. Pool, sauna and steam room.
(((((5 **Solaria** (5205) Near the Madlein and just as luxurious, but with a 'friendly family atmosphere'.
(((((5 **Brigitte** (5646) Highly recommended by a reporter. 'Central, but quiet', 'fantastic food'. Pool.
(((((4 **Piz Tasna** (5277) Up hill behind church: 'Quiet location, friendly, lovely views over village, excellent food.'

One of the 42 fast lifts that put Ischgl at the top of our fast lift league table →

GETTING THERE

Air Innsbruck 100km/62 miles (1½hr); Zürich 300km/186 miles (3hr); Munich 300km/186 miles (3hr).

Rail Landeck (30km/19 miles); frequent buses from station.

((((4) **Goldener Adler** (5217) Recommended by two recent reporters. Convenient, modern hotel, with 'outstanding food'. Sauna and whirlpool.

((((4) **Sonne** (5302) Highly rated by reporters. In the centre of the village. Lively stube. Sauna, hot-tub, solarium.

(((3) **Olympia** (5432) 'Well-appointed, family-run' with 'good-sized rooms'. Bar and restaurant.

(((3) **Jägerhof** (5206) 'Jewel of a hotel,' said a reporter. Friendly, good food, large rooms. Sauna and steam.

(((3) **Christine** (5346) Probably the best B&B in town. 'Huge rooms, nice views, good position near the lifts.'

((2) **Dorfschmeide** (5769) Small, central B&B recommended by a reporter. Other recommendations include the Albona (5500), the Sylvia (5690), the Ida (50005) and the Hotel (20150) – 'excellent food'.

Self-catering Some attractive apartments are available – the Golfais are conveniently placed by the Pardatschgrat gondola and are recommended.

EATING OUT
Plenty of choice

Most of our reporters eat in their hotels. For a lighter meal such as pizza try the Nona, the Schatzi or the Trofana Alm, which is as much a bar as a restaurant, and for fondue or ribs the Kitzloch, with its galleries over the dance floor. The Allegra and Salz & Pfeffer 'pasta and pizza' have been recommended (best to book). The Grillalm and Salnerhof are popular, 'traditional Austrian fare, huge portions'. A reporter pronounces The Nudel Himmel (above the Höllboden bar) his favourite – local dishes at reasonable prices. The Nevada is also recommended, 'friendly staff, but little English is spoken'.

APRES-SKI
Very lively

Ischgl is one of the liveliest resorts in the Alps, from early afternoon on. Lots of people are still in ski boots late in the evening. At close of play head for Trofana Alm near the Silvrettabahn or the Schatzi bar of the hotel Elisabeth by the Pardatschgratbahn – 'great fun', with indoor and outdoor bars and scantily clad dancing girls. The 'tremendously lively' Niki's Stadl across the road is a great place to sing along to live Austrian hits. The Kitzloch 'rocks', with dancing on the tables in ski-boots. The Sunn-Alm at the hotel Sonne gets crowded and has live music. The Kuhstahl under the Sporthotel Silvretta and Fire & Ice (expensive drinks) over the road are both lively all evening. The Hollboda bar is recommended for live music. Guxa, 'a cigars and cocktails type of place', and Allegra liven up after dinner, and the Golden Eagle is 'good for live bands'. The Coyote Ugly at the hotel Madlein – 'a lap dancing bar that just manages to avoid seediness' – has been recommended. There's a branch of the famous Pacha nightclubs, also in Ibiza and London (a bit 'tacky' says a visitor). The Living Room (hotel Grillalm) is allegedly 'more hands-on' than table dancing. And the club under the hotel Post has an ancient Roman theme. The Post also has a casino.

OFF THE SLOPES
No sun but a nice pool

The village gets little sun in the middle of winter, and the resort is best suited to those keen to hit the slopes. But there's no shortage of off-slope activities. There are 24km/15 miles of marked walks, a 7km/4 mile floodlit toboggan run and a splendid sports centre. And you can browse upmarket

ACTIVITIES

Indoor Silvretta Centre (bowling, billiards, swimming pool, sauna, solarium, massage), museums

Outdoor Skating, sleigh rides, hiking tours, 7km/4 miles floodlit toboggan run

WEBSITES

For links to resort sites, go to our own new site at www.wtss.co.uk

Phone numbers

Calling long-distance
Add the prefix given below for each resort. When calling from abroad use the country code 43 and omit the initial 0.

Ischgl
05444

Galtür
05443

Kappl
05445

Samnaun (Switzerland)
From elsewhere in Switzerland add the prefix 081.
From abroad use the prefix +41 81.

TOURIST OFFICES

Ischgl
t 5266
info@ischgl.com
www.ischgl.com

Galtür
t 8521
info@galtuer.com
www.galtuer.com

Kappl
t 6243
info@kappl.at
www.kappl.at

Samnaun (Switzerland)
t 868 5858
info@samnaun.ch
www.samnaun.ch

shops, which sell Versace and Bogner.

It's easy to get around the valley by bus, and there are restaurants that pedestrians can get to by gondolas. Ischgl has one of the most accessible lift systems to non-skiers and hikers. The 'excellent' Smuggler's Pass for pedestrians enables them to explore specially selected lifts for a day and lunch with skiing friends.

Samnaun 1840m/6,040ft

Samnaun is a small, quiet duty-free community in a corner of Switzerland more easily reached from Austria. A recent reporter saw no other Brits there all week.

There are four small components, roughly 1km/0.5 miles apart: Samnaun-Dorf, prettily set at the head of the valley is the main focus, with some swanky hotels and duty-free shops; Ravaisch, where the cable-car goes up; tiny Plan; and the hamlets of Laret and Compatsch, at the end of the main run down from the slopes (where there are several choices of lunchtime eateries). We've stayed happily on the edge of Dorf in the Waldpark B&B (8618310), and have eaten well at La Pasta. Reporters recommend the Hotel Post (8619200) ('good food but pricey') and the Stammerspitze Cafe. There's a smart AlpenQuell spa-pool-fitness centre.

The Schmuggler Alm is a popular après-ski spot.

Kappl 1260m/4,135ft

A couple of reporters recommend visiting Kappl, a 15-minute bus-ride down the valley from Ischgl. It is included on the area pass and has its own 40km/25 miles of piste. The slopes – served by an access gondola from the road and fast quads above it – offer plenty of variety, with several tough reds, including the 8km/5 mile Lattenabfahrt down a deserted valley from the top. Most of the slopes are open, but there are some woodland runs for bad-weather days. The village, with a couple of dozen hotels and guest-houses, is family-oriented – the Sunny Mountain development offering lots of attractions.

Galtür 1585m/5,200ft

Galtür hit the headlines when it was struck by a devastating avalanche in 1999, but the village centre has since been rebuilt and fortified and is now home to the Alpinarium, featuring an exhibition centre, climbing wall, internet and archive room, all built within the avalanche-protection structures.

Galtür is a charming, peaceful, traditional village clustered around a pretty little church, amid impressive mountain scenery. Sunnier, cheaper and much quieter than Ischgl, it is a good base for a quiet family holiday and mixed-ability groups – and the free buses to Ischgl are regular and quick. There are good 3- and 4-star hotels – the Almhof (8253), the Flüchthorn (8202) ('excellent, good food, family atmosphere'), the 'quiet and friendly' Alpenrose (8201) and Ballunspitze (8214) have been recommended. There are a couple of jolly bars – Tommy's Garage is recommended – 'good music and reasonably priced'.

Galtür's own slopes, above a lift base at Wirl, a short bus-ride from the village, are not very challenging and can be bleak in poor weather; but the black runs are ideal for intermediates and there are fine nursery slopes plus good 'graduation' pistes for improvers (now served by the Alpkogel gondola). Grooming is 'not great' though, according to a reporter. There is a small terrain-park at the top of the Soppalift drag but 'nobody seemed to use it'. The school has a high reputation and offers small classes. Children are well catered for – Kinderland has its own tow, carousel and magic carpet and the lifts have child-only lanes. Galtür has 60km/37 miles of cross-country loops, some quite testing.

Of the three mountain restaurants, the lively Wieberhimml oozes character and is recommended by a reporter. Or you could return to Wirl (Gasthof Alpkogel is suggested by a reporter) or the village.

Off-slope facilities are limited, but there's a natural ice rink and a sports centre with pool, tennis and squash. Night skiing and sledding are available every Wednesday evening on floodlit slopes and a popular local event is the Barrel Stave race – competitors strap wooden barrel pieces to their feet and race downhill.

The bus service to Ischgl finishes early in the evening (last bus leaves Ischgl at 7.30pm). But taxis are good value (20 euros one way), especially for groups, and are easily arranged.

Kitzbühel

Wonderful old town and extensive slopes, but unreliable snow

COSTS

① ② ③ ④ ⑤ ⑥

RATINGS

The slopes

Fast lifts	**
Snow	**
Extent	***
Expert	***
Intermediate	****
Beginner	**
Convenience	**
Queues	**
Mountain restaurants	****

The rest

Scenery	***
Resort charm	****
Off-slope	*****

NEWS

For 2005/06 the ski area of Westendorf is to be extended to meet the Kitzbühel area at Aschau, with an eight-seat gondola from there up to the Gampen sector of Westendorf.

Also a fast six-seat chair is to replace the Ehrenbachhöhe T-bar. And a new gondola is to be built to give access to Resterhöhe from Hollersbach near Mittersill, in the valley to the south.

The big news for last season was the new 30-person jumbo-gondola linking Pengelstein to Wurzhöhe above Jochberg, creating a much slicker link with the Resterhöhe sector above Pass Thurn. The first lift after the new gondola, heading to Pass Thurn, was also upgraded from a T-bar to a six-pack.

➕ Large, attractive, varied slopes offering a sensation of travel

➕ Beautiful medieval town centre

➕ Vibrant nightlife

➕ Plenty of off-slope amenities, both for the sporty and not-so-sporty

➕ A surprisingly large amount of cheap and cheerful accommodation

➕ Jolly mountain restaurants

➕ New gondola has improved access to the high Resterhöhe slopes, for the best snow in the area, but ...

➖ Snow in other, lower sectors is often poor, especially on runs to the valley (though there's now quite a bit of snowmaking)

➖ Surprisingly little challenging terrain – though plenty of off-piste

➖ Disappointing nursery area

➖ Some crowded pistes

Kitzbühel is one of the big names of the ski world, largely thanks to its Hahnenkamm downhill race course – the most spectacular on the World Cup circuit. And there is a lot to like about the resort – particularly the beautiful, traffic-free centre, complete with cobbled streets and lovely medieval buildings, including expensive, elegant hotels. The big drawback is the ski area's low altitude, which means the snow quality on the lower slopes is unreliable. In 2004 we encountered superb powder right down to the village, but that came after countless visits (over a 20-year period) blighted by ice and slush. Our advice is to book late, when you know the conditions are good.

Despite the glamorous reputation, this is no Gstaad: there is a huge amount of inexpensive accommodation which attracts low-budget visitors, many of whom are young and out to party in the resort's famous après-ski haunts.

THE RESORT

Set at a junction of broad, pretty valleys, Kitzbühel is a large, animated town, with separate areas of local slopes on each side. The beautiful walled medieval centre – with quaint church, cobbled streets and attractively painted buildings – is traffic-free and a compelling place to stay.

Many visitors love the sophisticated, towny ambience and swanky shops and cafes. But the resort spreads widely, and busy roads surround the old town, reducing the charm factor somewhat. Visitors used to peaceful little Austrian villages are likely to be disappointed by its urban nature. This year we also have a complaint about noisy trains passing through all night.

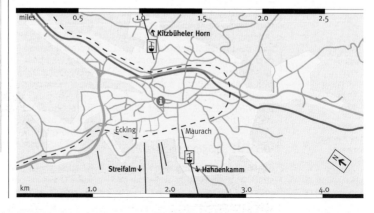

LIFT PASSES

Kitzbühel
Covers all lifts in Kitzbühel, Kirchberg, Jochberg, Pass Thurn, Bichlalm and Aschau, linking buses, and 50% reduction for swimming pool.

Beginners
Seven free lifts (three in Kitzbühel).

Main pass
1 day €35
6 days €165

Children
Under 19: 6 days €132
Under 16: 6 days €82.50
Under 7: free pass

Notes
Single ascent and hourly tickets, and graded prices for late-start day passes.

Alternative passes
Kitzbüheler Alpenskipass covers five large ski areas – Kitzbühel, Schneewinkel (St Johann), Wilder Kaiser, Alpbach and Wildschönau. Salzburg Super Ski Card covers 15 ski areas in the Salzburg province.

KITZBUHEL TOURIST OFFICE / ALBIN NIEDERSTRASSER

Kitzbühel's mix of wooded and open slopes is very attractive, given good snow like this ➔

boarding

Kitzbühel was slow off the mark with boarding, keeping to its image of World Cup downhill venue/skier party town. However, things have changed, and now there is a boarder-cross course (as well as a half-pipe and terrain-park) on the Kitzbüheler Horn, which the resort now styles as its 'Snowboard Area'. The Kasereck and Silberstuben runs on the Hahnenkamm are said to be a natural fun terrain-park. All major lifts are gondolas and chair-lifts – the area suits beginners and intermediates well.

The bus service around town was reported to be more overcrowded than ever in 2005 – the buses seemed to be running less often. A car is useful for visiting lots of other resorts covered by the Kitzbüheler Alpenskipass – though one of those, Westendorf, will now be linked by lift via Aschau.

The size of Kitz makes choice of location important. Many visitors prefer to be close to the Hahnenkamm gondola, south-west of the centre. Beginners should bear in mind that the Hahnenkamm nursery slopes are often lacking in snow, and then novices are taken up the Horn.

THE MOUNTAINS

Kitzbühel's extensive slopes – shared with Kirchberg and other, smaller villages – offer a very attractive mixture of entirely open runs higher up and patchy forest lower down. Most face north-east or north-west.

THE SLOPES
Big but bitty
The slopes are divided into five areas, but the two biggest are at last linked by the new 30-person gondola.

The **Hahnenkamm-Pengelstein** sector is by far the largest. After the Hahnenkamm gondola from the edge of the town, followed by a tedious walk along a flat piste, you descend into the bowl of Ehrenbachgraben, where several chair-lifts fan out. One goes up to Ehrenbachhöhe, the arrival point of lifts from Kirchberg. Another takes you to the gentle peak of Steinbergkogel, the high point of the sector. Beyond is the slightly lower peak of Pengelstein, whence several long west-facing runs go down to Aschau to meet the new extension of the Westendorf area (or ski-buses back towards Kirchberg) and Skirast where there is a gondola back up.

Pengelstein is also the start of the new cross-valley gondola to Wurzhöhe above Jochberg and so to the **Resterhöhe** sector above Pass Thurn. This impressive new link is much quicker than using the old routes down to the valley and a bus-ride back. Resterhöhe is well worth the excursion, for better snow and fewer crowds, though the new gondola may mean more people make the journey. Runs are short, but a couple of fast chairs have made the area more appealing.

The **Kitzbüheler Horn** is accessed by a gondola starting close to the railway station, some way from the centre. The second stage leads to the sunny Trattalm bowl, but the alternative cable-car takes you up to the summit

of the Horn, from where a fine, solitary piste leads down into the Raintal on the east side. There are blue, red and black runs back towards town.

The small and sunny **Bichlalm** area is now an entirely off-piste sector – no grooming, a few marked ski routes – accessed by an ancient single-person chair, with a snowcat to take you almost 300m/980ft higher.

There's floodlit skiing on Thursday and Friday on **Gaisberg**, a small area of slopes at Kirchberg, on the other side of the road from the main ski area.

Reporters still complain of confusion and poor piste signage around Pengelstein.

TERRAIN-PARKS
Take the Hornbahn

There is a half-pipe, with a music system, a terrain-park and a boarder-cross course on the Kitzbüheler Horn.

SNOW RELIABILITY
More snowmaking now

Even in an exceptionally good snow year such as 2004, some reporters complained of worn patches, ice and slush on the lower slopes. In a normal year, the lower slopes can be very tricky or bare at times (though the snow at the top is often OK). The problem is that Kitzbühel's slopes have one of the lowest average heights in the Alps. To make matters worse, the Horn is also sunny. The expansion of snowmaking in recent years has improved matters when it's cold enough to make snow – major runs right down to Kitzbühel, Kirchberg, Klausen and Jochberg are covered. But many slopes still remain unprotected. If snow is poor, head for Resterhöhe.

FOR EXPERTS
Plan to go off-piste

Steep slopes – pistes and off-piste terrain – are mostly concentrated around the bowl of Ehrenbachgraben. The most direct of these are challenging mogul fields. Nearby is the Streif red, the basis for the famous Hahnenkamm Downhill race – see the feature panel. When conditions allow, there is plenty of gentler off-piste potential elsewhere – some of it safely close to pistes, some requiring a guide. The off-piste-only Bichlalm area makes a refreshing change. The ancient single chair and small (maximum 14 people) snowcat make it feel like you are in a time-warp. We had a wonderful morning in fresh powder on here in January 2004, sharing the hill with only eight other people.

SCHOOLS

Rote Teufel (Red Devil)
t 62500

Hahnenkamm
t 63177

Kitzbüheler Horn
t 64454

Total
t 72011

Reith
t 65496

Aurach
t 65804

Classes
(Rote Teufel prices)
6 days (2hr am and pm) €135

Private lessons
€190 for 1 day; each additional person €20

FOR INTERMEDIATES
Lots of alternatives

The Hahnenkamm area is prime terrain. Good intermediates will want to do the World Cup downhill run, of course (see feature panel). And the long blues of around 1000m/3,300ft vertical to Klausen from Ehrenbachhöhe and to Skirast from Steinbergkogel or Pengelstein are also satisfying. The east-facing Raintal run on the Horn is excellent for good intermediates.

The runs above Jochberg are particularly good for mixed abilities and the short, high runs at Resterhöhe are ideal if you are more timid. There are also easy reds down to both Pass Thurn and Jochberg. Much of the Horn is good cruising.

FOR BEGINNERS
Not ideal

The Hahnenkamm nursery slopes are no more than adequate, and prone to poor snow conditions. The Horn has a high, sunny, nursery-like section, and quick learners will soon be cruising home from there on the long Hagstein piste. There are some easy runs to progress to if the snow is OK. But there are many more conveniently arranged places to start.

FOR CROSS-COUNTRY
Plentiful but low

There are nearly 40km/25 miles of trails scattered around, but all are at valley level and prone to lack of snow.

QUEUES
Still some problems

Since the old Hahnenkamm cable-car was replaced by a gondola, morning queues to get out of the town have been almost forgotten. However, once up the mountain there are bottlenecks at slow old chairs and drags, including the Steinbergkogel lift from Ehrenbachgraben. The Maierl chairs out of Kirchberg can also be tiresome. But we have had reports of queue-free weeks and maximum queues of ten minutes at half-term. Both the Horn and the Hahnenkamm can have crowded pistes – though reports suggest the new gondola link with Jochberg has spread the traffic across sectors.

MOUNTAIN RESTAURANTS
A highlight

There are many attractive restaurants – 'One of the reasons we keep going back,' says one of our Kitz regulars. On the Horn, Hornköpfl-Hütte's good food and sunny terraces still get praised

Kitzbühel

147

THE HAHNENKAMM DOWNHILL

Kitzbühel's Hahnenkamm Downhill race, held in mid-January each year, is the toughest as well as one of the most famous on the World Cup circuit. On the race weekend the town is packed and there is a real carnival atmosphere, with bands, people in traditional costumes and huge (and loud) cowbells everywhere.

The race itself starts with a steep icy section before you hit the famous Mausfalle and Steilhang, where even Franz Klammer used to get worried. The course (now thankfully served by snow-guns) starts near the top of the Hahnenkamm gondola and drops 860m/2,820ft to finish amid the noise and celebrations right on the edge of town. Ordinary mortals can now try most of the course after the race weekend, whenever the snow is good enough – it's an unpisted red ski route mostly. We found it steep and tricky in parts, even when going slowly – it must be terrifying at race speeds of 80mph or more. The course is normally closed from the start of the season until after the race.

↑ It may not look much from a distance, but Kitzbühel's car-free medieval centre is one of its key attractions

KITZBUHEL TOURIST OFFICE

GETTING THERE

Air Salzburg 80km/50 miles (1½hr); Munich 160km/99 miles (2hr); Innsbruck 95km/59 miles (1½hr).

Rail Mainline station in resort. Postbus every 15min from station.

CHILDREN

There is no non-ski nursery, but babysitters and nannies can be hired.

Ski school
Most schools cater for small children, offering lunchtime supervision as well as lessons – generally from the age of 3 or 4 (6 days approx €145).

WEBSITES

For links to resort sites, go to our own new site at www.wtss.co.uk

despite a slight climb to reach it. Alpenhaus 'does excellent self-service meals for great prices' but can get crowded; the Gipfelhaus is quieter with 'super views and a sheltered terrace'. Gasthof Hagstein is an attractive farmhouse. At Jochberg-Pass Thurn the Jägerwurzhütte and Trattenbachalm are recommended; Hanglalm has 'the best Kaiserschmarrn', and Panoramaalm great views. In the Hahnenkamm sector we loved the rustic Seidlalm, right by the lower part of the downhill course, and had a jolly meal at Berghaus Tyrol below Ehrenbachhöhe. Melkalm 'is worth the effort of finding'. The Hochbrunn has 'very friendly' staff and 'good strudel', the Steinbergkogel 'wonderful food'. The Kasereckhütte on the main run to Jochberg is 'brilliant'. The expensive table-service restaurant at the top of the gondola has good food, but service has been criticised.

SCHOOLS AND GUIDES
Mixed reviews

A 2005 report by adult beginners on the original school, Rudi Sailer's 200-strong Red Devils, was glowing: 'Enjoyable from start to finish. We progressed very quickly with our excellent instructor.' The other schools emphasise their small scale and personal nature. The Total school is the best established of these and includes video analysis. Lots of British instructors, reportedly.

FACILITIES FOR CHILDREN
Not an ideal choice

There is no non-ski nursery, but provided your children can take classes, you can deposit them at any of the schools. The Total school has supervision until 5pm.

STAYING THERE

HOW TO GO
Mainly hotels and pensions

Kitz is essentially a hotel resort.
Chalets A few tour operators run chalet-hotels here. One reporter has praised the 'ski to door' convenience of First Choice's chalet Karlberger.
Hotels There is an enormous choice, especially of 4-star and 3-star hotels.
(((((5) **Tennerhof** (63181) Luxurious former farmhouse, with renowned restaurant. Beautiful panelled rooms.
(((((5) **Schloss Lebenberg** (6901) Modernised 'castle' with smart pool; inconvenient location but free shuttle-bus. Free nursery for kids aged 3-plus.
(((((4) **Astron Sporthotel** (632110) 'Superb' says a 2005 visitor, with 'great' facilities.
(((((4) **Weisses Rössl** (625410) Smartly traditional exclusive 5-star aparthotel.
(((((4) **Goldener Greif** (64311) Historic inn, elegantly renovated; vaulted lobby-sitting area, panelled bar, casino.
(((((4) **Jägerwirt** (6981) Modern chalet with 'helpful staff and wonderful food'. Not ideally placed.
(((((4) **Schwarzer Adler** (6911) Traditional hotel, near centre, highly praised by a reporter: 'Great food and lovely leisure centre in basement.'
(((((4) **Schweizerhof** (62735) Comfortable chalet right by Hahnenkamm gondola.
(((((3) **Edelweiss** (75252) Recommended in 2005 for 'excellent food and accommodation'.
(((((3) **Strasshofer** (62285) A favourite with a regular reporter – 'central, family-run, friendly, good food, good with children, quiet rooms at back'.
(((((2) **Mühlbergerhof** (62835) Small, friendly pension in good position.
Self-catering Many of the best (and best-positioned) are attached to hotels.

EATING OUT
Something for everyone

There is a wide range of restaurants to suit all pockets, including pizzerias and fast-food outlets (even McDonald's). The Neuwirt in the Schwarzer Adler hotel is regarded as the best in town and wins awards in food guides. The Unterberger Stuben ('Excellent but expensive,' says a reporter) and Schwedenkapelle are also highly rated. Good, cheaper places include the traditional Huberbräu-Stüberl, Chizzo, Eggerwirt and, a little out of town with great views, Hagstein, which serves big

ACTIVITIES

Indoor Aquarena Centre (pools, slides, sauna, solarium, mud baths, aerated baths, underwater massage) – discounted entry with lift pass; indoor tennis hall, fitness centre, beauty centre, bridge, indoor riding school, bowling, museums, casino, cinema

Outdoor Ice rink (curling and skating), sleigh rides, toboggan run, ballooning, paragliding, hanggliding, helicopter flights, wildlife park, 40km/25 miles of cleared walking paths (free guided tours), copper mine tours

Phone numbers
Kitzbühel
From elsewhere in Austria add the prefix 05356.
From abroad use the prefix +43 5356.
Kirchberg
From elsewhere in Austria add the prefix 05357.
From abroad use the prefix +43 5357.

TOURIST OFFICES

Kitzbühel
t 777
info@kitzbuehel.com
www.kitzbuehel.com
Kirchberg
t 2309
info@kirchberg.at
www.kirchberg.at

pans of communal food for groups. Goldene Gams has a wide-ranging menu and both traditional and modern dining rooms. The Casino does a combined dinner/entry package. On Fridays and Saturdays you can dine at the top of the Hahnenkamm gondola.

APRES-SKI
A main attraction
Nightlife is a great selling point of Kitz. There's something for all tastes, from throbbing bars full of teenagers to quiet little places, nice cafes and smart spots for fur-coat flaunting.

Immediately after the slopes close, the town is jolly without being much livelier than many other Tirolean resorts. The Streifalm bar at the foot of the slopes is popular, with 'white pine and slate, open fire, widescreen TV and Europop music', as is the Sportcafe Hölzl. Cafes Praxmair, Kortschak, Langer and Rupprechter are among the most atmospheric tea-time places for cakes and pastries. Stamperl is a very lively bar. Later the American-style Highways bar and s'Lichtl (with thousands of lights hanging from the ceiling) get packed. Seppi's Pub is recommended for sport on TV, pizzas and the eccentric owner. Olympia and Take Five are the main discos. The Londoner Pub is a famous drinking place, well summarised by one visitor: 'Very crowded, very noisy and great fun, but the bar staff were mostly rude and arrogant.' The Casino is reportedly worth a visit – 'compact, casual, staff keen to explain how to lose/save money, expensive drinks'.

OFF THE SLOPES
Plenty to do
The lift pass gives a 50% reduction for the pools in the impressive Aquarena leisure centre. There's a museum and concerts are organised. The railway makes excursions easy (eg Salzburg).

Kirchberg 850m/2,790ft

THE RESORT
Kirchberg is a large, spread out, lively village. There are three ways into the slopes, all a bus-ride from the village.

THE MOUNTAIN
Slopes The Maierl chair-lifts and the gondola from Klausen take you to Ehrenbachhöhe, at the heart of the Kitzbühel slopes. The gondola from Skirast meets chairs to Pengelstein and the new gondola towards Pass Thurn. The separate small Gaisberg ski area is on the other side of the valley.
Snow reliability Kirchberg suffers from the same unreliable snow as Kitzbühel.
Experts Few challenging slopes.
Intermediates The main slopes back are easy cruises when snow is good.
Beginners There's a beginner lift and area at the foot of the Gaisberg slopes.
Snowboarding Kitzbühel has the edge, with the terrain-park on the Horn.
Cross-country There are plenty of trails – but they can suffer from lack of snow.
Queues There are some bottlenecks.
Mountain restaurants There are some good local huts.
Schools and guides We lack recent reports on the three schools.
Facilities for children There are non-ski and ski kindergartens.

STAYING THERE
How to go There's a wide choice of chalet-style hotels and pensions.
Hotels The 4-star Klausen (2128), close to the main gondola, and the Sporthotel Tyrol (2787), a bit out of the centre, have been recommended.
Self-catering There is some available.
Eating out Mostly in hotels, but there's a pizzeria and a steak house too.
Après-ski There's a toboggan run on Gaisberg. Nightlife is very lively.
Off the slopes Some hotels have swimming pools, saunas and so on.

Lech

Captivating blend of reliable snow and village charm

COSTS

① ② ③ ④ ⑤ ⑥

RATINGS

The slopes
Fast lifts	★★★
Snow	★★★★
Extent	★★★★
Expert	★★★★
Intermediate	★★★★
Beginner	★★★★
Convenience	★★★
Queues	★★★★
Mountain restaurants	★★★

The rest
Scenery	★★★
Resort charm	★★★★
Off-slope	★★★

NEWS

For 2005/06 the Hexenboden triple chairs at the north end of Zürs will be replaced by a six-pack. Like several other chair-lifts in the Lech-Zürs network, this will have heated seats. Another new heated six-pack will replace the slow triple-chair from Alpe Rauz, so that skiers heading for St Anton will no longer face queues there.

- Picturesque Alpine village
- Sunny and usually uncrowded slopes with excellent snow record and extensive snowmaking
- Fair-sized, largely intermediate piste network with some recently updated lifts, plus good, extensive off-piste
- Easy access by bus to the tougher slopes of St Anton and other Arlberg resorts
- Some very smart hotels
- Lively après-ski scene, but ...

- Very much hotel-dominated, with few non-hotel bars or restaurants
- Surprising shortage of seductive shopping, for a smart resort
- Local traffic intrudes on main street of Lech (and really spoils Zürs)
- Very few challenging pistes
- Nearly all slopes are above the tree line, and unpleasant in bad weather
- Blue runs back to the village are rather steep for nervous novices
- Generally expensive
- Inadequate ski-bus service
- Still a few slow, old lifts

Lech and its higher, linked neighbour Zürs are the most fashionable resorts in Austria, each able to point to a string of rich and/or vaguely royal visitors, and pulling in affluent Germans on an unmatched scale. But, like all such 'exclusive' resorts, they aren't actually exclusive in any real sense. A holiday here is unlikely to be cheap, but it doesn't have to cost any more than in countless other international resorts in the Alps. We don't feel out of place here, and neither would you. We often see Lech described as 'a very chic resort' – but it has none of the flash shops of St Moritz or Cortina, for example.

The real point about these resorts is that they offer a rare and attractive combination of impressive snowfall, traditional Alpine atmosphere and excellent hotels offering a truly personal service from their family owners.

THE RESORT

Lech is an old farming village set in a high valley that spent long periods of winter cut off from the outside world until the Flexen Pass road through Zürs was constructed at the end of the 19th century. (Even now, the road can be closed for days on end after an exceptional snowfall; a road tunnel is planned, but is not imminent.)

The village is attractive, with its upmarket hotels built in traditional chalet style, its gurgling river plus bridges, its adequately impressive scenery and the high incidence of snow on the streets. But its appeal is dimmed slightly by traffic on the main street that forms its spine: although the pavements have been widened and parking is controlled, it can still get very busy, especially at weekends.

Britain is the resort's third most important market, but Brits are outnumbered 10:1 by Germans and 3:1 by Austrians.

The heart of the village is a short stretch of the main street beside the river; most of the main hotels are clustered here. Right on this street is the base station of the Rüfikopf cable-car, departure point for exploration of the Zürs slopes. A short walk away, across the river, are the Schlegelkopf chair-lifts, leading up into Lech's main area of slopes. Chalets, apartments and pensions are dotted around the valley, and the village spreads along the main street for 2km/1.5 miles.

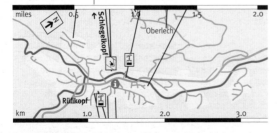

KEY FACTS

Resort	1450m
	4,760ft

For Arlberg region

Slopes	1305-2650m
	4,280-8,690ft
Lifts	83
Pistes	273km
	170 miles
Blue	36%
Red	42%
Black	22%
Snowmaking	72km
	45 miles

For Lech-Zürs only

Slopes	1450-2450m
	4,760-8,040ft
Lifts	33
Pistes	110km
	68 miles
Blue	40%
Red	40%
Black	20%

Some of the cheaper accommodation is quite a walk from the lifts.

Not far from the centre is the cable-car up to Oberlech: a small, traffic-free collection of 4-star hotels set on the mountainside, with an underground tunnel system linking the hotels and lift station – used routinely to move baggage, and by guests in bad weather. The cable-car works until 1am, allowing access to the mother resort's much livelier nightlife.

Zug is a hamlet 3km/2 miles from Lech, with a lift into the Lech-Oberlech area. The limited accommodation here is mostly bed and breakfast, with one pricey 4-star hotel.

Lech is linked by lifts and runs to higher Zürs, described at the end of this chapter. If you need to get the free ski-bus between the two at peak times of the day, be prepared for long waits and 'impossible' crowds, even in low season. Buses also run to St Anton, St Christoph and Stuben, all covered by the Arlberg lift pass. The Sonnenkopf area at Klösterle, reached by free ski-bus from Stuben, is also covered – 'Worth a trip,' say reporters, not least in bad weather for its combination of gondola rides and woodland runs.

THE MOUNTAINS

Practically all of the slopes are treeless, the main exception being the lower runs just above the village. Practically all the slopes are quite sunny – very few are north-facing.

The toughest runs are classed as unpatrolled 'ski routes' (as at St Anton – read that chapter for more on this), or 'high-alpine touring runs', which are not protected against avalanche and should be skied only with a guide. We don't have much of a problem with the latter category – in other resorts, these off-piste runs would simply not appear on the piste map at all. But the ski route concept is bad news, reducing the resort's responsibility for runs that are a key part of the area, and that should be patrolled pistes. The only ways down to Zug, for example, are ski routes; the only way to complete the Lech-Zürs-Lech circuit (the Madloch-Lech run) is a ski route; and of the eight identified runs from the Kriegerhorn, six are ski routes. To add to the confusion, these routes may be closed if avalanche conditions are dangerous; some of them are groomed after a heavy snowfall; and most

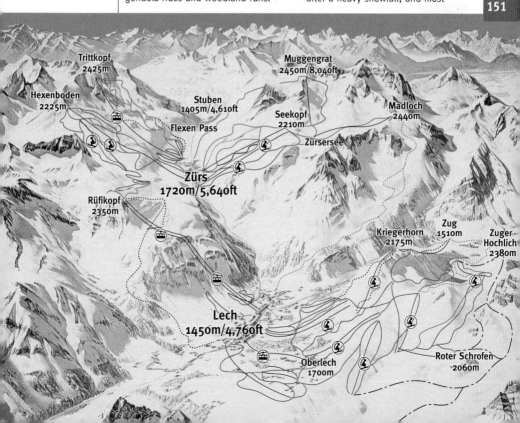

LIFT PASSES

Arlberg Ski pass
Covers all St Anton, St Christoph, Lech, Zürs and Stuben lifts, and linking bus between Rauz and Zürs.

Beginners
Points ticket

Main pass
1 day €39
6 days €184

Senior citizens
Over 65 (60 for women): 6 days €160
Over 75: €10

Children
Under 20: 6 days €160
Under 16: 6 days €111
Under 8: €10

Notes
Single ascent, half-day and afternoon 'taster' tickets available. Pass also covers Sonnenkopf (10 lifts) at Klösterle, 7km/4 miles west of Stuben (free bus link from Stuben).

people ski them (often into a piste-like state) without a guide or instructor.

The piste map, which attempts to cover the whole of the Arlberg region in one view, was redesigned for last season, but is still unclear or misleading in places – particularly above and around Oberlech.

THE SLOPES
One-way traffic
The main slopes centre on **Oberlech**, 250m/820ft above Lech (just below the tree line), and can be reached from the village by chair-lifts as well as the cable-car. The wide, open pistes above Oberlech are perfect for intermediates and there is also lots of off-piste. Zuger Hochjoch, the high point of this sector, gives stunning views.

The **Rüfikopf** cable-car takes Lech residents to the west-facing slopes of Zürs. This mountainside, with its high point at **Trittkopf**, is a mix of quite challenging intermediate slopes and flat/uphill bits. On the other side of Zürs the east-facing mountainside is of a more uniform gradient. Chairs go up to **Seekopf** with intermediate runs back down. There's a chair from below Zürsersee up to **Muggengrat** (the highest point of the Zürs area). This has a good blue run back under it and accesses a lovely long red (beware the steep top section) with lots of nearby off-piste options away from all the lifts back down towards Zürs – but it is a fair walk back to Zürs at the end. The long, scenic ski route back to Lech is accessed via the Madloch chair – which is slow and vulnerable to closure by wind. You can peel off part-way down and head for Zug and the slow chair-lift up to the Kriegerhorn above Oberlech, or continue to Lech – it comes out at the opposite end of town to the Oberlech cable-car, a walk from the centre. There are no lifts back towards Lech from Zürs, so the circuit is clockwise only. Those wanting to avoid the ski route can always get the bus from Zürs to Lech – but this can get over-subscribed.

TERRAIN-PARKS
In Lech only
There's a good terrain-park above Lech at the Schlegelkopf, with jumps, a boarder-cross and a half-pipe. It was recently extended and a separate children's park was added last season.

SNOW RELIABILITY
One of Austria's best
Lech and Zürs both get a lot of snow, but Austrian weather station records show a big difference between them despite their proximity. Lech gets an average of almost 8m/26ft of snow between December and March, almost twice as much as St Anton and three times as much as Kitzbühel; but Zürs gets 50% more than Lech. The altitude is high by Austrian resort standards and there is excellent snowmaking on Lech's sunny lower slopes.

This combination, together with excellent grooming, means that the Lech-Zürs area normally has good coverage from early December until late April. And the snow is frequently better here than on St Anton's predominantly south-facing slopes. Reporters suggest heading to Sonnenkopf for north-facing, tree-lined runs.

FOR EXPERTS
Off-piste is main attraction
There is only one black piste on the map, and there is no denying that for the competent skier who prefers to stick to patrolled runs the area is very limited. There are the two types of off-piste route referred to earlier, which most people are happy to undertake without guidance. But experts will get a lot more out of the area if they do have a guide, as there is plenty of excellent off-piste other than the marked ski routes, much of it accessed by long traverses. Especially in fresh snow, it can be wonderful.

Many of the best runs start from the top of the fast Steinmähder chair, which finishes just below Zuger Hochlicht. Some routes involve a short

boarding

Lech's upper-crust image has not stood in the way of its snowboarding development, and it continues to improve its facilities. Chairs and cable-cars, with hardly any drags, and perfectly manicured pistes make the area ideal for beginner and intermediate boarders, although the west-facing slopes at Zürs have many flat/uphill sections. Lessons are with the local ski school. More confident boarders should hire a guide and track some powder.

climb to access bowls of untracked powder. From the Kriegerhorn there are shorter off-piste runs down towards Lech and a very scenic long ski route down to Zug (followed by a slow chair and a rope tow to pull you along a flat area). Most runs, however, are south- or west-facing and can suffer from sun. At the end of the season, when the snow is deep and settled, the off-piste off the shoulder of the Wöstertäli from the top of the Rüfikopf cable-car down to Lech can be superb. There are also good runs from the top of the Trittkopf cable-car in the Zürs sector, including a tricky one down to Stuben.

Experts will also enjoy cruising some of the steeper red runs and will want to visit St Anton during the week, where there are more challenging pistes as well as more off-piste.

Heli-lifts are available to a couple of remote spots, at least on weekdays.

FOR INTERMEDIATES
Flattering variety for all
The pistes in the Oberlech area are nearly all immaculately groomed blue runs, the upper ones above the trees, the lower ones in wide swathes cut through them. It is ideal territory for leisurely cruisers not wanting surprises. And even early intermediates will be able to take on the circuit to Zürs and back, the only significant red involved being the beautiful long ski route back to Lech from the top of the Madloch chair in Zürs. It shouldn't be difficult but, because it's a ski route, it is groomed only occasionally, and several readers have found it unpleasantly mogulled. 'They should make it a proper pisted run,' complained one. We couldn't agree more.

It's worth noting that the final blue-run descents to Lech (as opposed to Oberlech) are uncomfortably steep for nervous novices.

More adventurous intermediates should take the fast Steinmähder chair to just below Zuger Hochlicht and from there take the scenic red run all the way to Zug (the latter part on a ski route rather than a piste). And if you feel ready to have a stab at some off-piste, Lech is a good place to try it.

Zürs has many more interesting red runs, on both sides of the village. We particularly like the west-facing reds from Trittkopf and the usually quiet east-facing Muggengrat Täli, which starts in a steep bowl – you can take the plunge, or skirt it on a catwalk.

FOR BEGINNERS
Easy slopes in all areas
The main nursery slopes are in Oberlech, but there is also a nice isolated area in Lech dedicated purely to beginners. There are good, easy runs to progress to, both above and below Oberlech.

FOR CROSS-COUNTRY
Picturesque valley trail
A 16km/10 mile trail starts from the centre of Lech and leads through the beautiful, but shady, Zug valley, following the Lech river to Zug and back. In Zürs there is a 4km/2.5 mile track to the Flexen Pass and back.

QUEUES
A few complaints
The resort proudly boasts that it limits numbers on the slopes to 14,000 for a more enjoyable experience. Most reporters also stress how much quieter Lech's slopes are than St Anton's. There have been significant lift improvements in the last few years, but there are still one or two bottlenecks – the Schlegelkopf fast quad out of Lech gets very busy first

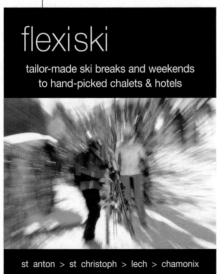

AUSTRIA

154

thing and the crucial Madloch double chair at the top of the Zürs area generates peak-time queues on the Lech-Zürs-Lech circuit. Some readers mention the Rüfikopf cable-car to Zürs as generating queues.

MOUNTAIN RESTAURANTS
On the up
The restaurants are scarcely a highlight, but they have definitely improved in recent years, persuading us to up the rating from ** to ***.

Rud-Alpe on the lower slopes above Lech is a rustic place, newly built using the timbers of an old hut. 'Excellent decor, food and service,' says one reporter; 'big roaring fire', enthuses another. The 'lively' Kriegeralpe, higher up, has been extended so it can open in winter as well as in summer. Rustic and charming, it is 'always full', writes a disappointed 2005 visitor. One reader commented that it has a 'limited menu, but is good for drinks'.

At Oberlech, there are several big sunny terraces set prettily around the piste. Quite often you'll find a live band playing outside one. The Ilga Stube is reported to have 'good food, rustic atmosphere, friendly staff and reasonable prices'. The Alter Goldener Berg is a lovely old building, 'We had an excellent lunch on the terrace, enhanced by a jazz band,' says a reporter. The Mohnenfluh, at the top of the nursery lift, does 'excellent' food.

The self-service Seekopf restaurant does 'quality food at decent prices' and has a good sun terrace – but you may have to queue to even get into the food serving area and it failed to impress one reporter this year. Also

popular is the cosy Palmenalpe above Zug ('stunning view', 'huge pizzas'), but it too gets crowded. The Schröfli Alm, just above the base of the Seekopf lift, is a pleasant chalet and the Cia (just above Lech) is also worth a try. The Petersboden Hotel's round tent is recommended for 'excellent soups and strudel'.

SCHOOLS AND GUIDES
Excellent in parts
The ski schools of Lech, Oberlech and Zürs all have good reputations and the instructors speak good English. Group lessons are divided into no fewer than 10 ability levels. One past visitor enjoyed 'the best lessons I have ever had'. In peak periods, you should book both instructors and guides well in advance, as many are booked regularly every year by an exclusive clientele.

FACILITIES FOR CHILDREN
Oberlech's fine, but expensive
Oberlech makes an excellent choice for families who can afford it, particularly as it's so convenient for the slopes. The Sonnenburg and the Goldener Berg have in-house kindergartens. Children of visitors staying in Oberlech have free access to the kindergarten there, Kinderland. Reporters tell us the Oberlech school is great for children, with small classes, good English spoken and lunch offered.

STAYING THERE

HOW TO GO
Surprising variety
There is quite a variety of accommodation from luxury hotels through to simple but spotless B&Bs.
Hotels There are three 5-star hotels, over 30 4-star and countless more modest places.
(((((5) **Arlberg** (2134-0) Patronised by royalty and celebrities. Elegantly rustic chalet, centrally placed. Pool.
(((((5) **Post** (2206-0) Lovely old Relais & Chateaux place on main street with pool, sauna. 'Absolutely first class,' says a recent visitor.
(((((4) **Krone** (2551) One of the oldest buildings, in a prime spot by the river. 'Food and service faultless,' says a 2005 report. 'Superb' wellness centre with pool and sauna.
(((((4) **Tannbergerhof** (2202-0) Splendidly atmospheric inn on main street, with outdoor bar and popular disco (tea time as well as later). Pool.

GETTING THERE

Air Zürich 200km/ 124 miles (2½hr); Innsbruck 120km/ 75 miles (1½hr). Friedrichshafen 130km/81 miles (1½hr).

Rail Langen (15km/ 9 miles); regular buses from station, buses connect with international trains.

ACTIVITIES

Indoor Tennis, hotel swimming pools and saunas, squash, museum, ice rink

Outdoor Cleared walking paths, ice-rink, toboggan run (from Oberlech), snow-shoeing, horse-drawn sleigh rides

Phone numbers

Lech and Zürs
From elsewhere in Austria add the prefix 05583.
From abroad use the prefix +43 5583.

Stuben
From elsewhere in Austria add the prefix 05582.
From abroad use the prefix +43 5582.

(((④ **Haldenhof** (2444-0) Friendly and well run, with antiques and fine paintings. 'Totally brilliant – probably the best food I have had anywhere in the world,' enthuses a 2005 reporter.

(((④ **Burg Vital** (Oberlech) (2291-930) 'Excellent – no criticism,' said a reporter of this plush luxury hotel.

(((④ **Burg** (Oberlech) (2291-0) Sister hotel of Burg Vital – same facilities and with famous outdoor umbrella bar.

(((④ **Sonnenburg** (Oberlech) (2147) Luxury on-piste chalet (popular for lunch). Good children's facilities. Pool.

(((④ **Monzabon** (2104) 'Characterful, with friendly staff,' says a reporter. Pool and an indoor ice rink.

(((③ **Pension Angerhof** (2418) Beautiful ancient pension, with wood panels and quaint little windows.

(((③ **Pension Fernsicht** (2432) Pension with spa facilities.

Other recommendations include **Gästehaus Lavendel** (2657) ('fantastic; huge breakfasts') and **Pension Sabine** (2718) in Oberlech – 'comfortable and charming with spa facilities'.

Self-catering There is lots available to independent bookers.

Chalets There are a couple run by British tour operators, including Total's chalet-hotel with pool and sauna.

EATING OUT
Mainly hotel-based

There are over 50 restaurants in Lech, nearly all of them in hotels. Reporter recommendations include the Krone, Ambrosius (above a shopping arcade), and the Post, which serves modern Austrian food. The Madlochblick has a typically Austrian restaurant, very cosy with good solid food, and Rudi's Stamperl is 'top-notch and reasonably priced'. Hûs Nr 8 is one of the best non-hotel restaurants and does good fondue, but you need to book (one recent reporter could not get in four days ahead in January). Schneggarei

does good pizza and Enzo does pasta. Bistro Casarole is a small casual place with a short menu of excellent grills. The Fux does 'excellent modern/Asian food, utterly un-Austrian'.

In Oberlech, hotel Montana has been highly recommended by a reporter and there is said to be good fondue at the Alter Goldener Berg.

In Zug the Rote Wand is excellent for fondues, kaiserschmarren (a delicious chopped pancake and fruit dessert) and a good night out, but is said to be 'frighteningly expensive'. Reporters also recommend the Alphorn, and the Gasthof Älpele 3km/ 2 miles from the road, up the valley on the cross-country route, reached by covered wagons attached to snowcats.

APRES-SKI
Good but expensive

At Oberlech, the umbrella bar of the Burg hotel is popular immediately after the slopes close, as is the champagne bar in hotel Montana.

Down in Lech the outdoor bars of hotels Krone (in a lovely setting by the river) and Tannbergerhof (where there's an afternoon disco) are popular. Later on, discos in the hotels Kristberg, Arlberg, Almhof-Schneider and Krone liven up too. The latter's Side Step specialises in 60s and 70s music. The Ilga is a good place for a drink, as is S'Pfefferkörndl. Schneggarei's music (rap to funky house) makes a change from Austrian drinking songs early and late. The smart, modern Fux bar and restaurant has live music, pop art in the toilets and a huge wine list. Archiv, in the Ambrosius shopping centre is good for cocktails and attracts a younger crowd.

From Lech, Zug makes a good night out: you can take a horse-drawn sleigh for a fondue at the Rote Wand, Klösterle or Auerhahn, followed by a visit to the Rote Wand disco.

Lech

155

LECH TOURIST OFFICE

Zürs has one of the
highest, bleakest,
snowiest settings of
any Austrian resort ↓

After 7.30pm the free resort bus
becomes a pay-for bus called James,
which runs until 4am.

OFF THE SLOPES
At ease
Many visitors to Lech don't indulge in
sports and the main street often
presents a parade of fur-clad strollers.
The range of shopping is surprisingly
limited, with Strolz's plush emporium
(including a champagne bar) right in
the centre the main attraction.

It's easy for pedestrians to get to
Oberlech or Zug to meet friends for
lunch. The village outdoor bars make
ideal posing positions. There are
various sporting activities and 29km/18
miles of walking paths – the one along
the river to Zug is especially beautiful,
and recommended by several readers.

There is a floodlit sledging run from
Oberlech to town: 'Loved by kids and
not to be missed,' says a reporter.

Zürs 1720m/5,640ft

Ten minutes' drive towards St Anton
from Lech, Zürs is almost on the Flexen
Pass, with good snow virtually
guaranteed. Austria's first recognisable
ski lift was built here in 1937.

The village is even more upmarket
than Lech, with no hotels of less than
3-star standing, and a dozen 4-star
and 5-star hotels. We stayed at the 5-
star Zürserhof (25130) and found it
excellent – great service, food and spa
facilities. But apart from the excellent
hotels, we find Zürs a difficult place to
like. It has nothing resembling a
centre, few shops and the traffic
doesn't so much intrude as ruin the
place. The Kaminstüble (Hotel

Mathie's) has been recommended for
lunch and Toni's Einkehr (Flexen Hotel)
is reported to be 'good value'. Nightlife
is quiet. Vernissage, at the Skiclub
Alpenrose (22710), is said to be the
best nightspot in town. There's a disco
in the Edelweiss hotel (26620) and a
piano bar in the Alpenhof (21910).
Serious dining means the Zürserhof
and the Lorünser (22540). All phone
numbers given are for 4- or 5-star hotels.

Many of the local Zürs instructors
are booked for the entire season by
regular clients, and more than 80% of
them are booked privately.

Stuben 1405m/4,610ft

Stuben is linked by lifts and pistes to
St Anton, but is on the Vorarlberg side
of the Arlberg pass (St Anton is in the
Tirol). There are infrequent but
timetabled buses between the village
and Lech and Zürs, and more frequent
ones from Rauz, reachable on skis.

Dating back to the 13th century,
Stuben is a small, unspoiled village,
where the only concessions to the new
era are a few unobtrusive hotels, a
school, two or three bars, a couple of
banks and a few little shops. The old
church and traditional buildings,
usually snow-covered, make Stuben a
really charming Alpine village.

The Albona mountain above Stuben
has north-facing slopes that hold
powder well and some wonderful,
deserted off-piste descents including
beautifully long runs down to Langen
and to St Anton (recommended by a
2005 reporter). These are, however,
'high-alpine touring runs' and should
be taken seriously. A regular reporter
recommends small Rasthaus Ferwall for
lunch (ask your guide to book) at the
end of a 'very easy off-piste run'. The
Berg-Klaus is said to serve 'excellent
rösti', and Willi's is recommended for
snacks. But a reporter who visited
Stuben on a Monday lunchtime was
surprised to find most places closed.
The slow village chair can be a cold
ride. A quicker and warmer way to get
to St Anton in the morning, if you have
a car, is to drive up the road to Rauz.
Stuben has sunny nursery slopes
separate from the main slopes, but
lack of progression runs make it
unsuitable for beginners.

Evenings are quiet, but several
places have a pleasant atmosphere.
The charming old Post (7610) is a very
comfortable 4-star with a fine restaurant.

Mayrhofen

Traditional British favourite with recently expanded area of slopes

RATINGS

The slopes

Fast lifts	★★★
Snow	★★★
Extent	★★★
Experts	★
Intermediates	★★★
Beginners	★★
Convenience	★
Queues	★
Mountain restaurants	★★★

The rest

Scenery	★★★
Resort charm	★★★
Off-slope	★★★★

NEWS

A short drag now gives access to the top station of the jumbo cable-car that forms the link with Rastkogel – so returning skiers not up to the steep red run down no longer face a climb to the cable-car. The return from the Horberg area is also made easier by the addition of a moving carpet across to the top of the Horberg gondola.

Last season's planned replacement of the Gerent T-bar in the Horberg sector by a fast six-pack didn't happen, but is due for 2005/06.

There are plans for a jumbo cable-car to Ahorn with a more centrally located base station, but this will probably not materialise until 2006/07.

+ The local terrain expanded by 40% four seasons ago and the area is now well served by high-speed lifts

+ Snow more reliable than usual in the Tirol, plus the snow guarantee of the Hintertux glacier nearby

+ Various nearby areas on the same lift pass, and reached by free bus

+ Lively après-ski – though it's easily avoided if you prefer peace

+ Excellent children's amenities

+ Wide range of off-slope facilities

− Often long queues for gondola to Penken – which is inconveniently sited for many visitors

− Slopes can be crowded

− Many short runs, though linked Lanersbach slopes are longer

− Few steep pistes – though they do include Austria's steepest

− No runs back to the village from Penken – the main area of slopes

− Smaller Ahorn area – the best bet for novices – is completely separate

Mayrhofen has long been a British favourite. Many visitors like it for its lively nightlife, but it's also an excellent family resort, with highly regarded ski schools and kindergartens and a fun pool with special children's area. The liveliest of the nightlife is confined to a few places, easily avoided by families. And there are quieter alternative bases, including Finkenberg (covered in this chapter) and Lanersbach (covered in the Hintertux chapter).

Mayrhofen's main Penken-Horberg slopes are entirely above the tree line, with no pistes down to valley level. The upside is better-than-average snow, for the Tirol; the downside, shorter-than-average runs (typically around 350m/1,150ft vertical). The link with Lanersbach opens up some welcome longer runs.

THE RESORT

Mayrhofen is a fairly large resort sitting in the flat-bottomed Zillertal. Most shops, bars and restaurants are on the one main, long, largely pedestrianised street, with hotels and pensions spread over a wider area. As the village has grown, architecture has been kept traditional.

Despite its reputation for lively après-ski, Mayrhofen is not dominated by lager louts. They exist, but tend to gather in a few easily avoided bars. The central hotels are mainly slightly upmarket, and overall the resort feels pleasantly civilised (though we have had a few complaints about traffic).

The main lift to Penken is set towards one end of the main street, while the cable-car to the much smaller and currently rather neglected Ahorn sector is out in the suburbs, about 1km/0.5 miles from the centre. The free bus service can be crowded and it finishes early (5pm), so location is important. The original centre, around the market, tourist office and bus/railway stations, is now on the

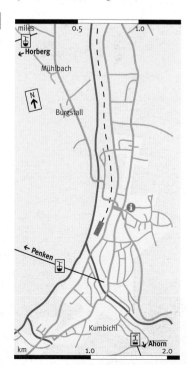

KEY FACTS

Resort	630m
	2,070ft

For Ski and Glacier World Zillertal 3000	
Slopes	630-3250m
	2,070-10,660ft
Lifts	62
Pistes	225km
	140 miles
Blue	26%
Red	60%
Black	14%
Snowmaking	93km
	58 miles

For Mayrhofen-Lanersbach only (ie excluding Hintertux glacier)	
Slopes	630-2500m
	2,070-8,200ft
Lifts	45
Pistes	147km
	91 miles

For Ziller valley	
Slopes	630-3250m
	2,070-10,660ft
Lifts	177
Pistes	620km
	385 miles

edge of things. The most convenient area is on the main street, close to the Penken gondola station.

Free buses linking the Zillertal resorts mean you can easily have an enjoyably varied week visiting different areas on the Ziller valley lift pass, including the extensive Arena slopes linking Zell to Königsleiten and Gerlos – and the excellent glacier up at Hintertux. But if you plan to spend a lot of time on the glacier, consider staying in Lanersbach (see Hintertux chapter).

The buses get packed at peak times, so it's worth planning your outings carefully ('Get the 8am bus and you'll be in Hintertux just as the lifts open,' recommends a reporter).

THE MOUNTAINS

Practically all Mayrhofen's slopes are above the tree line, and of moderate difficulty. When you buy a lift pass, make sure it covers the Hintertux glacier, unless you are absolutely confident that you won't want to try it.

THE SLOPES
Rather inconvenient
Lifts to the two main sectors are a longish walk or a bus-ride apart.

The larger area is **Penken-Horberg**,

accessed by the main jumbo gondola from one end of town. It is also accessible via gondolas at Hippach and Finkenberg, both a bus-ride away. You cannot get back to Mayrhofen on snow – you can catch the main gondola down or, if cover is good, you can descend to either Finkenberg or Hippach on unpisted ski routes. But the buses back from Finkenberg run only at hourly intervals.

A jumbo cable-car links the Penken area with the **Rastkogel** slopes above Vorderlanersbach, which is in turn linked to **Eggalm** above Lanersbach – see the Hintertux chapter. These links are a great asset, but getting to Eggalm depends on good snow on a low, sunny run. Getting back from Rastkogel on skis means braving a very tricky red run, but a new drag-lift up to the top station of the cable-car means you no longer face a climb to avoid that run.

The smaller, gentler **Ahorn** area had seemed to be going into decline: a reader who learned to ski there returned a couple of seasons ago to find the place deserted at 4pm. But we hear there are tentative plans to revive it by building a new access lift and extending the railway line to the bottom of it – and to create a new piste or two.

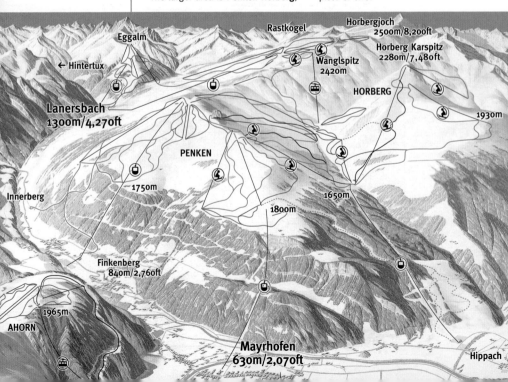

Ski and Glacier World Zillertal
1-, 2- or 3-day passes cover Penken, Eggalm, Rastkogel and Hintertux glacier areas; 4-day and over passes include all Ziller valley lifts, ski-bus and railway.

Beginners
No special pass.

Main pass
1 day €35
6 days €165

Children
Under 19: 6 days €132
Under 15: 6 days €82.50
Under 6: free pass

Notes
Part-day and pedestrian passes available.

boarding

Mayrhofen is not ideal for learning to snowboard – the nursery slopes are inconvenient and the lifts are mainly drags. For intermediates, the Penken slopes are good and the lifts are mainly gondolas and chairs. The terrain-park is popular and the British Snowboard Championships used to be held here. More advanced riders will enjoy the Hintertux glacier, further up the valley – see separate chapter.

TERRAIN-PARKS
Comprehensive
There is a good terrain-park, extended for 2003/04. It offers novice, intermediate and expert lines, rails, a half-pipe and a slalom course, beneath the Sun-Jet chair-lift on Penken.

SNOW RELIABILITY
Good by Austrian standards
Although the lifts go no higher than 2500m/8,200ft, the area is better than most Tirolean resorts for snow-cover because the slopes are mostly above 1500m/4,900ft. Snowmaking covers nearly all the main slopes in the Penken-Horberg area, though none on Rastkogel. And there is one of the best glaciers in the Alps at Hintertux. As mentioned above, poor snow on the run linking to Eggalm can be a problem.

FOR EXPERTS
Commit Harakiri
Austria's steepest piste, called Harakiri, was opened for 2003/04 under the Knorren chair, with a claimed gradient of 78% or 38°. Naturally, we rushed out to investigate on your behalf, and can confirm that it is certainly steep for a European piste. When we tried it, the run was mogul-free, but rock hard except near the edges – not

surprisingly, it was delightfully deserted. It does offer a worthwhile challenge for the brave but is quite short. The black run under the Schneekar chair on Horberg is a good, fast cruise when groomed, but there are few other steepish pistes. The long unpisted trail to Hippach is quite challenging but rarely has good snow because of its low altitude. There is, however, some decent off-piste to be found, such as from the top of the Horbergjoch at the top of Rastkogel – we had a great time there in fresh powder – and under the cable-car linking to Lanersbach. You can also try the other resorts covered by the valley lift pass.

FOR INTERMEDIATES
On the tough side
Most of Mayrhofen's slopes are on the steep side of the usual intermediate range – great for confident or competent intermediates. And the Lanersbach expansion made the area much more interesting for avid piste-bashers, with some good long runs on Rastkogel and delightfully quiet runs on Eggalm. But many of the runs in the main Penken area are quite short. And (except on Ahorn) there are few really gentle blue runs, making the area less than ideal for nervous intermediates or

SCHOOLS

**Die Roten Profis
(Manfred Gager)**
t 63800

Total (Max Rahm)
t 63939

**Mount Everest (Peter
Habeler)**
t 62829

**Mayrhofen 3000
(Michael Thanner)**
t 64015

Classes
(Roten Profis prices)
6 days (2½hr am or
pm) €102

Private lessons
1 day: €115 for 1
person

CHILDREN

Wuppy's Kinderland
t 63612
Ages 3mnth to 7yr;
9am to 5pm, Mon-Fri

Die Roten Profis
t 63800
Ages 3 upwards;
9.30-3.30

Total
t 63939
Ages 2 to 4, 9.30-
3.30

Ski school
All run classes for
children aged 4 or 5
to 14. Lunch can be
provided (6 days
including lunch
€180).

↑ The slopes of Rastkogel have made a
welcome addition to those of Penken-Horberg,
with longer, gentler runs – and the link has
been improved this year

SNOWPIX.COM / CHRIS GILL

near-beginners. The overcrowding on
many runs can add to the intimidation
factor.

If you're willing to travel, each of
the main mountains covered by the
Ziller valley pass is large and varied
enough for an interesting day out.

FOR BEGINNERS
Overrated: big drawbacks
Despite its reputation for teaching,
Mayrhofen is not ideal for beginners.
The Ahorn nursery slopes are excellent
– high, extensive and sunny – but it's a
rather tiresome journey to and from
them, and intermediate mates will
want to be on Penken. The Penken
nursery area is less satisfactory and
there are very few easy blues to
progress to.

FOR CROSS-COUNTRY
Go to Lanersbach
There is a fine 20km/12 mile trail along
the valley to Zell am Ziller, plus small
loops close to the village. But snow
down here is not reliable. Higher
Vorderlanersbach has a much more
snow-sure trail.

QUEUES
Still real problems
The Penken jumbo-gondola is very
oversubscribed at peak times. Reports
of queues of 45 or 60 minutes at the
morning peak are common. An
alternative is to take the bus to the
Horberg gondola at Hippach. There are
queues to get down at the end of the

day, too. The slopes can also get very
crowded, causing queues for some lifts
– a nuisance with so many short runs.

MOUNTAIN RESTAURANTS
Plenty of them
Most of Penken's many mountain
restaurants are attractive and serve
good-value food but can get crowded
in peak season. The Schneekar
restaurant at the top of the Horberg
section has been highly recommended
('table-service, traditional food, open
fire, wooden beams, leather sofa,
sometimes with a jazz pianist'). The
Almstüberl at the mid-station of the
Finkenberg gondola 'was usually quiet
when others were packed'. Vronis
Skialm remains a firm favourite with
reporters ('fabulous steaks'). Schiestl's
Sunnalm and Kressbrunnalm have also
been recommended.

SCHOOLS AND GUIDES
Excellent reputation
Mayrhofen's popularity is founded on
its schools, and a high proportion of
guests take lessons. We have received
many positive reports over the years,
but a few negative ones too –
including, strangely, reports of a
shortage of English-speaking
instructors. More reports would be
welcome.

FACILITIES FOR CHILDREN
Good but inconvenient
Mayrhofen majors on childcare and the
facilities are excellent. But there is a
lot to be said for resorts where
children don't have to be bussed
around and ferried up and down the
mountain.

AUSTRIA!
Ski Chalets

www.ElevationHolidays.com

0845 6443578

GETTING THERE

Air Salzburg 175km/109 miles (3hr); Munich 190km/118 miles (2½hr); Innsbruck 75km/47 miles (1hr).

Rail Local line through to resort; regular buses from station.

STAYING THERE

HOW TO GO
Plenty of mainstream packages
There is a wide choice of hotel holidays available from UK tour operators, but few catered chalets.
Hotels Most of the hotels packaged by UK tour operators are centrally located, a walk from the Penken gondola.
(((((5) **Elisabeth** (6767) The resort's only 5-star – 'Superb, with excellent food and service,' says a 2005 guest. Casino.
((((4) **Manni's** (633010) Well-placed, smartly done out; pool.
((((4) **Kramerwirt** (6700) Lovely hotel, oozing character, 'friendly and helpful staff, good rooms, interesting food'.
(((3) **Strass** (6705) Right by the Penken gondola. Lively bars, disco, fitness centre, pool; but very big and with a down-market feel ('Brits in football shirts') and rooms that lack style.
(((3) **Neuhaus** (6703) 'First-class facilities,' says a reporter; good food but rooms above the bar are not ideal.
(((3) **Rose** (62229) Well placed, near centre. Good food.
(((3) **Neue Post** (62131) Convenient family-run 4-star on the main street – 'good food and nice big rooms'.

(((3) **Waldheim** (62211) Smallish, cosy 3-star gasthof, near the gondola.

EATING OUT
Wide choice
Manni's is good for pizzas ('but expensive, especially for wine'). Wirthaus zum Griena is a 'wonderful old wooden building offering traditional farmhouse cuisine'. We had good lamb and pepper steak at Tiroler Stuben. A favourite with tour op reps is the Mount Everest in the Andrea hotel. The 'lively' Rundum is recommended for its 'good service'. A 2005 visitor enjoyed lunch at Mo's – 'cheerful and efficient service, plentiful portions'.

APRES-SKI
Lively but not rowdy
Après-ski is a great selling point. At close of play, the umbrella bar, at the top of the Penken gondola, the Ice Bar at the hotel Strass and Nicki's Schirmbar, in the Brücke hotel, get packed out. Some of the other bars in the Strass are rocking places later on, including the New Speak Easy, with live music. However, the Sport's Arena disco is said to be 'for the kids'.

Mayrhofen

161

Recent visitors have preferred the Apropos ('great music') and Brücke's Schlüssel Alm ('still the best all-round late-night venue'). Mo's American theme bar and Scotland Yard remain popular with Brits, but you might judge the latter to be 'dated, dirty and smoky'. Try Am Kamin or the small casino (both in the hotel Elisabeth) if you're after more Manhattan than Mayrhofen (though one reporter said the casino was 'usually deserted'). The Neue Post bar and the Passage are good for a quiet drink.

OFF THE SLOPES
Good for all
Innsbruck is easily reached by train. There are also good walks and sports amenities, including the swimming pool complex – with saunas, solariums and lots of other fun features. Pedestrians have no trouble getting up the mountain to meet friends for lunch.

Finkenberg 840m/2,760ft

Finkenberg is a much smaller, quieter village than Mayrhofen.

THE RESORT
Finkenberg is no more than a collection of traditional-style hotels, bars, cafes and private homes. There is a pretty central area around the church, but most of the buildings are spread along the busy, steep, winding main road up to Lanersbach. Beware slippery pavements. Some hotels are within walking distance of the gondola, and many of the more distant ones run their own minibuses; there is also an inefficient village minibus service.

THE MOUNTAIN
Finkenberg shares Mayrhofen's main Penken slopes.

Slopes A two-stage gondola gives direct access to the Penken slopes – and in good conditions you can ski back to the village on a ski route.
Snow reliability The local slopes are not as well-endowed with snowmaking as those on Mayrhofen's side.
Experts Not much challenge, except off-piste, the Harakiri piste and the run back from Lanersbach.
Intermediates The whole area opens up from the top of the gondola.
Beginners There's a village nursery slope, but it's a sunless spot, and good conditions are far from certain.
Snowboarding No special facilities.
Cross-country Cross-country skiers have to get a bus up to Lanersbach.
Queues The gondola to the Penken generates 20-minute queues at peak times – afternoon as well as morning.
Mountain restaurants See the recommendations given for Mayrhofen.
Schools and guides The Finkenberg School has a good reputation.
Facilities for children There's a non-ski nursery, and the ski nursery takes children from age four.

STAYING THERE
Hotels There are quite a few. The Sporthotel Stock (6775), owned by the family of former downhill champion Leonard Stock, enjoys pole position near the gondola station, and has great spa facilities. The Eberl is recommended by a 2005 reporter – 'attentive staff, excellent food' – but avoid the annexe rooms.
Eating out Mainly in hotels, notably the Eberl.
Après-ski The main après-ski spots are the Laterndl Pub at the foot of the gondola ('jumping as the lifts close') and Finkennest ('welcoming, cosy, weird decor').
Off the slopes Curling, ice-skating, swimming and good local walks.

Montafon

Extensive slopes, well off the beaten package path

For 2004/05 the new Aussergolmbahn quad chair-lift with covers replaced a T-bar; it extends up to Grüneck, where a ski tunnel links the slopes of Aussergolm with the main Golm slopes.

A new black run called Diabolo, previously a ski route, was opened last winter in the Golm sector.

The 40km/25 mile-long Montafon valley contains no less than eleven resorts and five main lift systems. Packages from the UK are few (accommodation to suit tour operators is not easy to find), but for the independent traveller the valley is well worth a look – especially the Silvretta Nova area (linking Gaschurn and St Gallenkirch) and high, tiny, isolated Gargellen.

The Montafon is neglected by the UK travel trade. Its location in Vorarlberg, west of the Arlberg pass, makes it a bit remote from the standard Austrian charter airport of Salzburg – and the valley is said to lack the large hotels that big operators apparently need.

The valley runs south-east from the medieval city of Bludenz – parallel with the nearby Swiss border. The first sizeable community you come to is Vandans, linked to its Golm ski area by gondola. Next are Schruns, at the foot of Hochjoch, and Tschagguns, across the valley at the foot of Grabs. Further on are St Gallenkirch and Gaschurn, at opposite ends of the biggest area, Silvretta Nova. Up a side valley to the south of St Gallenkirch is Gargellen, close to the Swiss border – a tiny village, but not unknown in Britain.

The valley road goes on up to Partenen. You can take a cable-car from Partenen to Trominier, and then a mini-bus (covered by the area lift pass) on up to Bielerhöhe and the Silvrettasee dam, at the foot of glaciers and Piz Buin (of sunscreen fame) – the highest peak in the Vorarlberg. Bielerhöhe is a great launch pad for ski-tours, and there are high, snow-sure cross-country trails totalling 22km/13 miles on and around the frozen lake. From here you can ski down to Galtür, near Ischgl. Some of the ski schools organise trips, with the return to Bielerhöhe by snow-cat; you end the day with a long run back down to Partenen.

There are more ordinary cross-country trails along the valley, and an 11km/7 mile woodland trail at Kristberg, above Silbertal – up a side valley to the east of Schruns Trails total over 100km/62 miles.

The shared valley lift pass covers the post-bus service ('comprehensive, and not too crowded') and the Bludenz-Schruns trains, as well as the 65 lifts – so exploration of the valley

does not require a car.

The top heights hereabouts are no match for the nearby Arlberg resorts; but there is plenty of skiing above the mid-mountain lift stations at around 1500m/4,920ft, and most of the slopes are not excessively sunny, so snow reliability (aided by snowmaking on quite a big scale) is reasonable. Practically all the pistes are accurately classified blue or red, but there are plentiful off-piste opportunities (including quite a few 'ski routes'). There are snowboard terrain-parks in most sectors, the newest being Nova Park at Silvretta Nova, which also features a half-pipe.

There are 12 ski schools in the valley, operating in each of the different ski areas. And eight ski kindergartens take kids from age three.

Tobogganing is popular, and there are several runs on the different mountains – the Silvretta Nova's 6km/4 mile floodlit run down to St Gallenkirch being the most impressive.

For those with a car, there is accommodation in various smaller villages in addition to those dealt with below. For example, a reader highly recommends the hotel Adler in St Anton im Montafon, at the entrance to the valley.

GARGELLEN 1425m/4,680ft

Gargellen is a real backwater – a tiny village tucked up a side valley, with a small but varied piste network on Schafberg that is blissfully quiet.
The eight-person gondola from the village up to the Schafberg slopes seems rather out of place in this tiny collection of hotels and guest houses, huddled in a steep-sided, narrow valley. The runs it takes you to are gentle, with not much to choose between the blues and reds; but there is lots of off-piste terrain. There are four unpatrolled ski-routes. A special feature is the day-tour around the

Most of the slopes
are above the trees –
this is Kreuzjoch,
above Schruns ➔

ARCHIV MONTAFON TOURISMUS

KEY FACTS

Resorts	655-1425m
	2,150-4,680ft
Slopes	680-2395m
	2,230-7,860ft
Lifts	64
Pistes	203km
	126 miles
Blue	54%
Red	32%
Black	14%
Snowmaking	97km
	60 miles

TOURIST OFFICE

Montafon
t 722530
info@montafon.at
www.montafon.at

The tourist office is in
Schruns, so from
elsewhere in Austria
add the prefix 05556,
from abroad use the
prefix +43 5556.

Phone numbers
Gargellen
From elsewhere in
Austria add the prefix
05557.
From abroad use the
prefix +43 5557.

Madrisa – a small-scale off-piste adventure taking you over to Klosters in Switzerland. It involves a 300m/1,000ft climb, but is otherwise easy.

The altitude of the village (the highest in the Montafon) and north-east facing slopes make for reasonable snow reliability. And there is snowmaking on one of the several pistes to the valley, which include a couple of excellent, scenic away-from-the-lifts runs at the extremities of the area. With care you can ski to the door of the hotel Madrisa (6331) among others. Behind the hotel is a rather steep nursery slope. There are four pleasant mountain restaurants, including two rustic huts at the tree line – the Obwaldhütte ('very traditional, good value') and the Kessl Hütte. The former holds a weekly après-ski party after the lifts close, followed by a torchlit descent. (Slide shows and bridge are more typical evening entertainments.) The Barga pizzeria at the foot of the Vergalden drag, can also be reached by walkers.

SCHRUNS 700m/2,300ft
Schruns is the most rounded resort in the valley – a towny little place, with the shops in its car-free centre catering for locals and for summer tourists.
A cable-car and gondola (which has just received a performance boost) go up from points outside the village into the Hochjoch slopes. Above the trees is a fair-sized area of easy blue runs, with the occasional red alternative, served by slow chairs and drags and the fast eight-seat Seebliga chair. There are restaurants at strategic points – the Wormser Hütte is a climbing refuge with 'stunning' views, while the Kapell restaurant has a good table-service section. Parents can leave their kids under supervision at the huge NTC Dreamland children's facility at the top of the cable-car, by the skier services building. The blue run from Kreuzjoch back to Schruns is exceptional: about 12km/7.5 miles long and over 1600m/5,250ft vertical. Snow-guns cover the lower half of this, plus the Seebliga area.

Easily accessible across the valley are the limited slopes of Grabs, above the rather formless village of Tschagguns, and the more extensive area of Golm, where a gondola goes from Vandans up to a handful of chairs and drags serving easy slopes above the trees, and offering a vertical descent of over 1400m/4,590ft. A six-pack now goes to the top of the area, linked via a ski tunnel to a new quad on the Aussergolm slopes on the back of the hill. This serves the new Diabolo black run, reputedly the steepest in the Montafon. Snow-guns cover two major upper slopes, and the run to the valley.

Piz Buin
3310m

Bielerhöhe

2010m

1720m

SILVRETTA
NOVA

1480m

enen

Gaschurn
oom/3,28oft

Gortipohl

2275m/7.46oft

2100m

1850m

St Gallenkirch
900m/2,950ft

2150m

Schafberg

Gargellen
1425m/4,68oft

Kreuzjoch
2395m/7,86oft

2300m

Hochegga
1600m

Grabs

Grüneck
2085m

1520m

GOLM

1000m

Tschagguns

Vandans
655m/251oft

Schruns
700m/2,300ft

1850m

Hochjoch

1335m

Silbertal 89om

Kristberg

Phone numbers
Schruns
From elsewhere in
Austria add the prefix
05556.
From abroad use the
prefix +43 5556.
Gaschurn
From elsewhere in
Austria add the prefix
05558.
From abroad use the
prefix +43 5558.

WEBSITES

For links to resort
sites, go to our own
new site at
www.wtss.co.uk

TOURIST OFFICES

Gargellen
t 6303
tourismus@gargellen.at
www.gargellen.at
Schruns
t 721660
info@schruns-
tschagguns.at
www.schruns-
tschagguns.at
Gaschurn
t 82010
info@gaschurn-
partenen.com
www.gaschurn-
partenen.com

As you are reminded frequently,
Ernest Hemingway ensconced himself
in Schruns in 1925/26, and his
favourite drinking table in the hotel
Taube (72384) can be admired. The
Löwen (7141) and the Alpenhof
Messmer (72664) are elegant, well-
equipped 4-stars with big pools, the
former a hub of the 'quite lively' après-
ski scene.

GASCHURN / ST GALLENKIRCH
1000m/3,28oft / 900m/2,950ft
**Silvretta Nova is the biggest lift and
piste network in the valley. As a result,
German cars fill to overflowing the
huge car parks at the valley lift
stations. Gaschurn is an attractive
place to stay.**
The two main resorts here are quite
different. Whereas St Gallenkirch is
strung along the main road and
spoiled by traffic, Gaschurn is a
pleasant village, bypassed by the
valley traffic, with the wood-shingled
Posthotel Rössle (8333) in the centre.
  The lift network covers two parallel
ridges running north-south, with most
of the runs on their east- and west-
facing flanks. The slopes are accessed
from three points along the valley. A
gondola from Gaschurn (prone to
serious peak-season queues) takes you
up to the east ridge, while another
gondola from St Gallenkirch goes up to
Valisera on the west ridge. A chair-lift

to Garfrescha gives access to the
central valley from Gortipohl – on the
road between the two resorts. Fast
though they are, the lifts out of the
central valley are queue prone. There
is snowmaking on one-third of the
area, with cover to two valley stations.
  This is generally the most
challenging area in the valley, with as
many red as blue runs, and some
nominal blacks. Most of the slopes are
above the tree line, typically offering a
modest 300m/98oft vertical. The
Rinderhütte six-pack serves more red
pistes from the top of the area. There
is lots of off-piste potential, including
steep (and quite dangerous) slopes
down into the central valley. The map
shows four 'ski routes'; outrageously,
their status is not explained.
  There are lots of mountain
restaurants, many impressive in
different ways. At the top of the east
ridge, the state-of-the-art Nova Stoba
has seats for over 1,500 people in
various rooms catering for different
markets, including splendid panelled
rooms with table service. The big
terrace bar gets seriously boisterous in
the afternoons. At the top of the other
ridge is the splendidly woody Valisera
Hüsli. A 2005 reporter recommends the
strudel and glühwein at Zur Brez'n and,
snow permitting, searching out the
unmapped Lamm Hütte on run 1a
down to Gaschurn: 'basic but lovely'.

Nauders/Reschenpass

Which country wil you ski today – Austria, Italy or Switzerland?

COSTS

① ② ③ ④ ⑤ ⑥

RATINGS

The slopes
Fast lifts	**
Snow	****
Extent	**
Expert	***
Intermediate	****
Beginner	**
Convenience	**
Queues	****
Mountain restaurants	***

The rest
Scenery	***
Charm	****
Off-slope	***

NEWS

For 2004/05 a new beginner area and a children's learning zone were created at mid-mountain in the Bergkastel sector above Nauders.

And there's a new linking red run from mid-station to the Ideal lift.

At Schöneben, a six-seat chair with covers replaced two drags above mid-station.

For 2005/06 a six-pack is planned to replace the Geissloch drag at Piengtal.

➕ High-altitude slopes, by Tirolean standards – so relatively snow-sure

➕ Attractively traditional village

➕ Grand views from the top lift

➕ Day trips to various places, including St Moritz in Switzerland, are a possibility, but ...

➖ That's just as well – the local slopes are rather limited in extent

➖ Main Nauders lifts are a bus-ride from the village, with Schöneben and Haider Alm further away still

Nauders is in the Tirol, but only just – it's 3km/2 miles from the Swiss border, and its lifts run up to the Italian one. And the Schiparadies Reschenpass area of which Nauders is the main element also includes two other small resorts just over the pass in Italy – Schöneben and Haider Alm. Swiss outings to Bad Scuol or even St Moritz are possible – or to Samnaun, which connects with Ischgl, back in Austria. All in all, it makes an interesting departure from the Tirolean norm.

THE RESORT

Nauders is a spacious, traditionally Alpine village not far short of the crest of the Reschenpass to Italy – but happily bypassed by the road. At 1400m/4,600ft, with lifts going up to 2850m/9,350ft, it is quite high by Tirolean standards. In other respects its own slopes are everyday Tirolean stuff, but the opportunity to visit other resorts covered by the Reschenpass lift pass effectively doubles the terrain. And if we were staying here for a week we would definitely be planning an outing to Switzerland. There aren't many resorts within day-trip range of St Moritz, and this is one of them.

The bit of Italy just over the pass is part of the Süd Tirol, with the usual duplication of place names in German and Italian. German dominates.

THE MOUNTAINS

Nauders' home slopes at Bergkastel start about 2km/1 mile outside the village, reached by a free shuttle-bus.
Slopes The main lift is a powerful gondola up to the mid-mountain meeting area (2200m/7,220ft), just above the tree-line. Beyond here there are three main options: take an eight-seat chair another 400m/1,310ft up the slopes of Bergkastelspitz; move across to a new six-pack on the next hill; or cross the side-valley of Piengtal to another six-pack chair on Tscheyeck, surmounted by a drag to the area

high-point at 2850m/9,350ft. There are a couple of red runs back to the valley – the Talabfahrt is a beautiful, wide swathe through trees.

Schöneben is not a village or a peak, but appears to be the name of a mountainside above the little village of Reschen and of the company operating lifts on it. From the valley station about 1km/0.5 miles outside Reschen a gondola goes up to a mid-mountain lift hub, just above the tree-line. There are wide, gentle slopes above and below this point, now served by a six-pack chair, a couple of more challenging runs served by two chairs beyond it, and an easy, undulating, highly enjoyable red run back to the valley.

The third area, Haider Alm, is named in the same fashion: Haider Alm is the tree-line focus of the lifts above the village of St Valentin. This is the most limited of the areas. But any mountain with 1200m/3,940ft vertical has to be worth a visit.
Terrain-parks There's a half-pipe and boarder-cross course at Nauders. More of the same at Haider Alm.
Snow reliability The slopes are quite good for snow. The pistes of Schöneben and Haider Alm are almost entirely covered by artificial back-up, as are a good proportion of those at Nauders, most of which get a lot of afternoon sun. The grooming at Nauders was immaculate when we visited.
Experts The Reschenpass area is not ideal for experts looking for a

KEY FACTS

Resort	1400m
	4,590ft
Slopes	1400-2850m
	4,590-9,350ft
Lifts	26
Pistes	111km
	69 miles
Blue	37%
Red	43%
Black	20%
Snowmaking	90km
	56 miles

WEBSITES

For links to resort
sites, go to our own
new site at
www.wtss.co.uk

Phone numbers
From elsewhere in
Austria add the prefix
05473.
From abroad use the
prefix +43 5473.

TOURIST OFFICE

t 87220
office@nauders.info
www.nauders.info

challenge, but there are satisfying runs. The one black classification at Nauders (Die Schwarze, on Tscheyeck) is just about justified. The blacks at Schöneben used to be red, and properly so. There is a lot of off-piste terrain accessible from the Tscheyeck chair (including ways down to Nauders itself), and there are red-classified ski routes from the Panorama drag above it and from the lower Geissloch lift.

Intermediates Basically, all the slopes here make excellent intermediate terrain. They don't add up to a huge amount, but with three areas to play in there is no lack of variety. The long descents to the valley at Nauders and Schöneben are very satisfying.

Beginners Nauders is not an ideal place for complete beginners because the village nursery slopes are some way out – and beginner lessons now take place at mid-mountain.

Snowboarding Facilities include the terrain-park on the Nauders slopes.

Cross-country There are four cross-country trails – amounting to 40km/25 miles of track in all – of differing levels of difficulty around Nauders itself. There are further accessible trails down in the (rather shady) Inn valley, over the Swiss border, and over in Italy.

Queues We should be surprised if lift queues were much of a problem.

Mountain restaurants At Nauders there are four, including two at the mid-mountain area; Goldseehütte is a pleasant self-service place . At Schöneben there are three restaurants at the mid-mountain, including a pleasant, woody self-service. A short plod from the far edge of the area is an extremely rustic Schihütte.

Schools and guides There are two ski schools at Nauders; among their offerings are off-piste courses.

Facilities for children There's a new learning area behind the children's restaurant at Bergkastel (classes from age three years), and a separate snow-garden. Nauderix Guest Kindergarten takes children from the age of two.

STAYING THERE

How to go Most of the hotels are comfortable 4-stars.

Hotels The Central (872210), Nauderer Hof (87704), Maultasch (86101) and Tirolerhof (86111) are well-equipped possibilities in the village. Nearer the lifts are the Neue Burg (87700), and the 3-star Erika (872170). The cheaper 3-star Gasthof Martha (87338) is right by the nursery slope.

Eating out Many of the options are hotel-based. The Almhof is an attractive, lively pizzeria, the Aladin is another pizza and pasta joint. The Stadlwirt is recommended for more traditional food. The Gasthof Goldener Löwe is a traditional old inn.

Après-ski The après-ski scene has typically Tirolean jollity in places such as the Almbar and Almhof (with live music). Maxi's Pub and Traktor Tenna in the Nauderer Hof hotel are said to be lively late on into the night.

Off the slopes There is quite a bit to do, including long toboggan runs from Bergkastel and Kleiner Mutzkopf (a separate hill), curling lanes, tennis, ice skating, squash, bowling, and public swimming pools in hotels. There are 50km/31 miles of marked walks shown on a special map.

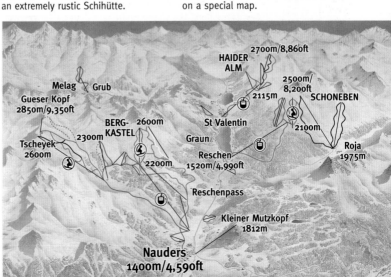

Nauders
1400m/4,590ft

Obergurgl

Chalet-style hotels on high, snow-sure slopes attract a loyal clientele

COSTS

① ② ③ ④ ⑤ ⑥

RATINGS

The slopes

Fast lifts	★★★★
Snow	★★★★★
Extent	★★
Expert	★★
Intermediate	★★★
Beginner	★★★★
Convenience	★★★★
Queues	★★★★★
Mountain restaurants	★★

The rest

Scenery	★★★
Resort charm	★★★★
Off-slope	★★

NEWS

The lift system has seen substantial investment in recent years. And for 2004/05 a fast six-seat chair with covers replaced the slow double chair out of Hochgurgl. Also for 2004/05 you could pay €10 extra when buying a week's lift pass to cover a day on the slopes of Sölden just down the road – free buses were included. The resort was not certain whether this would continue for 2005/06 when we went to press.

➕ Glaciers apart, one of the Alps' most reliable resorts for snow – especially good for a late-season holiday

➕ Excellent area for beginners, timid intermediates and families

➕ Mainly queue- and crowd-free

➕ Traditional-style village with very little traffic

➕ Jolly tea-time après-ski

➖ Limited area of slopes, with no tough pistes and no terrain-park or half-pipe

➖ Exposed setting, with few sheltered slopes for bad weather

➖ Few off-slope leisure amenities except in hotels

➖ Disappointing mountain restaurants

➖ Village is spread out and disjointed

➖ For a small Austrian resort, hotels are rather expensive

A loyal band of visitors go back every year to Obergurgl or higher Hochgurgl, booking a year in advance in recognition of the limited supply of beds. They love the high, snow-sure, easy intermediate slopes, the end-of-the-valley seclusion and the civilised atmosphere in the reassuringly expensive hotels.

We're unconvinced. If we're going to a bleak, high, snow-sure resort where there is not much to do but ski or board, we'd rather go somewhere with more skiing or boarding to do. But, of course, most such places aren't in Austria – important to some – and their hotels might be less reassuringly expensive.

THE RESORT

Obergurgl is based on a traditional old village, set in a remote spot, the dead end of a long road up past Sölden. It is the highest parish in Austria and is usually under a blanket of snow from November until May. The surrounding slopes are bleak, with an array of avalanche barriers giving them a forbidding appearance.

Obergurgl has no through traffic and few day visitors. The village centre is mainly traffic-free, and entirely so at night. Village atmosphere is relaxed during the day, jolly immediately after the slopes close, but rather subdued

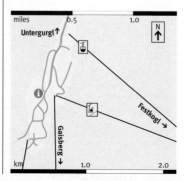

later at night; there are some nightspots, but most people stay in their hotels. The resort is popular with British families and well-heeled groups looking for a relaxing winter break.

Despite its small size, this is a village of parts. At the northern entrance to the resort is a cluster of hotels near the main Festkogl gondola, which takes you to all the local slopes. This area is good for getting to the slopes and for ease of access by car, but it's a long walk or a shuttle-bus ('excellent, prompt service,' says a 2005 visitor) from the village centre and the nursery slopes. The road then passes another group of hotels set on a little hill to the east, around the ice rink (beware steep, sometimes treacherous walks here). The village proper starts with an attractive little square with church, fountain, and the original village hotel (the Edelweiss und Gurgl). Just above are the Rosskar and Gaisberg chair-lifts to the local slopes. There is an underground car park in the centre of the village.

Hochgurgl, a gondola-ride away, is little more than a handful of hotels at the foot of its own slopes. It looks like it might be a convenience resort dedicated to skiing from the door, but

boarding

Obergurgl is a traditional ski destination, attracting an affluent and (dare we say it?) 'older' clientele. But the resort is actually pretty good for snowboarding and there are signs that the resort now wants to attract younger visitors. Beginners will be pleased to find that most of the slopes can be reached without having to ride drag-lifts. And there's some good off-piste potential for more advanced riders.

it isn't: from nearly all the hotels you have to negotiate roads and/or stairs to get to or from the snow. Hochgurgl is even quieter than Obergurgl at night.

In the valley below Hochgurgl (and linked by gondola) is Untergurgl, linked to Obergurgl by regular ski-buses. For a budget base, it is worth considering. For a day out, it's a short bus or car trip to Sölden (see separate chapter and News), and a long car trip to Kühtai (a worthwhile high area near Innsbruck). Much closer is the tiny touring launch-pad of Vent.

THE MOUNTAINS

The gondola between Obergurgl and Hochgurgl means that the two can be thought of as forming a single area. Even so, the slopes are surprisingly limited, and lacking interest or challenge for keen intermediates or experts. You don't get the sense of travel, as you do in bigger Alpine resorts. Most of the slopes are very exposed – there are few woodland runs to head to in poor conditions. Wind and white-outs can shut the lifts and, especially in early season, severe cold can curtail enthusiasm.

The lift pass is quite expensive for the relatively small area. In 2004/05 it

could be upgraded to cover a day in Sölden (see News), well worthwhile for a keen intermediate or expert. Piste grooming is very good. Some reporters have complained of poor signposting.

THE SLOPES
Limited cruising

Obergurgl is the smaller of the two linked areas. It is in two sections, well linked by piste in one direction, more loosely in the other. The gondola and the Rosskar fast quad chair from the village go to the higher Festkogl area. This is served by two drags and a chair up to 3035m/9,96oft (you can join the Rosskar lift at its mid-station too). From here you can head back to the gondola base or over to Gaisberg, with its high point at Hohe Mut, reached by a long, slow chair. On the lightly wooded lower part of this area, two fast chair-lifts have replaced three drag-lifts. A double chair up from Obergurgl's village square provides the other link on to the Gaisberg slopes. There are two 'ski routes', one of them the only run from Hohe Mut. The piste map used to explain that these are unpatrolled, but no longer does so. There is 8km/5 miles of night skiing.

The slopes of **Hochgurgl** consist of high, gentle bowls, either side of the

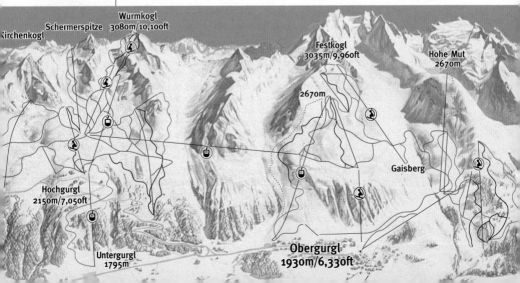

Wurmkogl
Schermerspitze 3080m/10,100ft
Kirchenkogl

Festkogl
3035m/9,96oft

Hohe Mut
2670m

2670m

2670m

Gaisberg

Hochgurgl
2150m/7,05oft

Untergurgl
1795m

Obergurgl
1930m/6,330ft

AUSTRIA

LIFT PASSES

Obergurgl ski pass
Covers lifts in Obergurgl and Hochgurgl, and local ski-bus.

Beginners
No special pass

Main pass
1 day €38
6 days €187

Senior citizens
Over 60: 6 days €150

Children
Under 16: 6 days €110
Under 8: free pass

Notes
Part-day passes available.

Schermerspitze. Wurmkogel is served by a two-stage gondola, which starts in Untergurgl, and chair-lifts. A covered six-seat chair – which was new for 2004/05 and which a reporter found 'comfortable and spacious' – allows you to access all the main areas easily from the village. From the top stations there are spectacular views of the Dolomites. A single run leads down through the woods from Hochgurgl to Untergurgl.

TERRAIN-PARKS
Still mothballed
We understand that there are still no plans to revive the terrain-park, half-pipe and quarter-pipe that were scrapped a few years ago.

SNOW RELIABILITY
Excellent
Obergurgl has high slopes and is arguably the most snow-sure of Europe's non-glacier resorts – even without its snowmaking, which is now impressively extensive. It has a longer season than most Austrian resorts.

FOR EXPERTS
Not generally recommendable
There are few challenges on-piste – most of the blacks could easily be red, and where they deserve the grading it's only for short stretches (for example, at the very top of Wurmkogl). But the Hohe Mut ski route can have big moguls, and there is a fair amount of enjoyable off-piste to be found with a guide – and the top school groups often go off-piste when conditions are right. This is a well-known area for ski touring, and we have reports of very challenging expeditions on the glaciers at the head of the valley.

FOR INTERMEDIATES
Good but limited
There is some perfect intermediate terrain here, made even better by the normally flattering snow conditions. The problem is, there's not much of it. Keen piste-bashers will quickly tire of travelling the same runs and be itching to catch the bus to Sölden, down the valley – last year you could upgrade a week's lift pass at the time of purchase to include a day on Sölden's slopes.

Hochgurgl has the bigger area of easy runs, and these make good cruising. For more challenging intermediate runs, head to the Vorderer Wurmkogllift, on the right as you look at the mountain. Less confident intermediates may find the woodland piste down from Hochgurgl to the bus stop at Untergurgl tricky.

The Obergurgl area has more red than blue runs but most offer no great challenge to a confident intermediate. There is some easy cruising around mid-mountain on the Festkogl. The blue run from the top of the Festkogl gondola down to the village, via the Gaisberg sector, is one of the longest cruises in the area. And there's another long enjoyable run down the length of the gondola, with a scenic off-piste variant in the adjoining valley.

In the Gaisberg area, there are very easy runs in front of the Nederhütte and back towards the village.

FOR BEGINNERS
Fine for first-timers or improvers
The inconveniently situated Mahdstuhl nursery slope above Obergurgl is adequate for complete beginners. And the gentle Gaisberg run – under the chair out of the village – is ideal to move on to as soon as a modicum of control has been achieved. The easy slopes served by the Bruggenboden chair are also suitable.

The Hochgurgl nursery slopes are an awkward walk from the hotels, but otherwise satisfactory. And there are good blue slopes to move on to.

The quality of the snow and piste preparation make learning here easier than in most lower Austrian resorts.

CROSS-COUNTRY
Limited but snow-sure
Three small loops, one each at Obergurgl, Untergurgl and Hochgurgl, give just 12km/7 miles of trail. All are relatively snow-sure and pleasantly situated. Lessons are available.

SCHOOLS

Obergurgl
t 6305

Hochgurgl
t 6265

Classes
(Obergurgl prices)
6 days (2hr am and
pm) €175

Private lessons
€115 for a half-day;
each additional
person €12

CHILDREN

**Kindergarten in
Obergurgl**
For non-skiing
children from age 3

**Alpina, Austria and
Hochfirst hotels**
Kindergartens in
these hotels

**Bobo's ski
kindergarten**
From age 3

Ski schools
Take children over the
age of 5 (6 full days
€175)

WEBSITES

QUEUES
Few problems
Major lift queues are rare. There can be
high-season queues for the village lifts
at the start of ski school, but these
tend to clear quickly, except in severe
weather when other lifts are closed.

MOUNTAIN RESTAURANTS
Little choice
Compared with most Austrian resorts,
mountain huts are neither numerous
nor very special. However, the jolly
Nederhütte at Gaisberg has a
'substantial menu', which more than
satisfied a visiting vegetarian, with
'tasty and huge portions'. David's
Skihütte is 'very friendly', cheerful and
good value. The small hut at Hohe Mut
serves 'good, tasty, local dishes' and
has excellent views.

At Hochgurgl, Wurmkogelhütte – a
big, but pleasantly woody and
spacious 'reasonably priced' self-
service – is the only place for a proper
meal, serving 'fine, standard Austrian'
fare. The tiny hut above it at
Wurmkoglgipfel is in an exceptional
position and does limited food. Many
people return to one village or the
other for lunch in the sun.

SCHOOLS AND GUIDES
Further good news
We continue to receive positive reports
of the Obergurgl school, with good
English spoken, a maximum of nine
per group and excellent lessons and
organisation. A 2005 reporter found
the instructors 'patient and supportive,
and chose routes that built confidence'
Demand for private instruction appears
to be increasing and it is advisable to
book ahead during peak periods.

FACILITIES FOR CHILDREN
Check out your hotel
Children's ski classes start at five years
and children from age three can join

Bobo's ski-kindergarten. There is also
a non-skiing kindergarten, the Pingu
Club, for kids aged three and up.
There's lunchtime supervision for ski
school and kindergarten children alike.
Many hotels offer childcare of one sort
or another, and the Alpina has been
particularly recommended.

STAYING THERE

HOW TO GO
Plenty of good hotels
Most tour operators feature hotels and
pensions. Demand exceeds supply, and
for once it is true that you should
book early to avoid disappointment.
Hotels Accommodation is of high
quality: most hotels are 4-stars, and
none is less than a 3-star. Couples
have been surprised to be asked to
share tables even at 4-star hotels.

A cheaper option is to stay down
the valley in Untergurgl, where the 4-
star Jadghof (6431) is recommended.
Some hotels don't accept credit cards.
((((4 **Edelweiss und Gurgl** (6223) The
focal hotel – biggest, oldest, one of
the most appealing; on the central
square, near the main lifts. Pool and
outdoor whirlpool.
((((4 **Alpina de Luxe** (600) Big, smart,
excellent children's facilities. Pool.
((((4 **Bergwelt** (6274) Recommended
as 'very smart'. Beauty and spa
facilities, including outdoor pool.
((((4 **Hochfirst** (63250) 'Superb
updated' spa facilities, comfortable,
four or five minutes from gondola. Ski
bus stop right outside. Casino.
((((4 **Crystal** (6454) Near the Festkogl
lift. If you don't mind the ocean-liner
appearance, it's one of the best.
((((4 **Gamper** (6545) 'Excellent,' says a
reporter – 'Good food, friendly staff.'
Far end of town, past the square.
((((4 **Gotthard-Zeit** (6292) 'Elegant',
spacious, comfortable, good food. Spa
facilities. Small pool. Sun terrace.

↑ The small hut at Hohe Mut has great views as well as tasty local dishes

OBERGURGL TOURIST OFFICE

GETTING THERE

Air Innsbruck 90km/56 miles (2hr); Salzburg 288km/179 miles (3hr); Munich 240km/149 miles (4hr).

Rail Train to Ötz; regular buses from station, transfer 1½hr.

ACTIVITIES

Indoor Pools, saunas, whirlpools, steam baths and massage in hotels; bowling, billiards, squash, library, table tennis

Outdoor Natural ice rink, snow-shoe outings, winter hiking paths

Phone numbers
From elsewhere in Austria add the prefix 05256.
From abroad use the prefix +43 5256.

TOURIST OFFICE

t 6466
info@obergurgl.com
www.obergurgl.com

Recommended too for skiing convenience but a 'steep walk back from the village' if you are on foot.
((((④ **Jenewein** (6203) 'Convenient with attractive spa facilities,' says a reporter.
(((③ **Wiesental** (6263) 'Excellent' said a 2005 visitor. Comfortable, well situated, good value. Sun terrace popular for lunch and après-ski.
(((③ **Granat-Schlössl** (6363) Amusing pseudo-castle, surprisingly affordable.
((② **Alpenblume** (6278) Good B&B hotel, well-placed for Festkogl lift.
((② **Gurgl** (6533) B&B near Festkogl lift; friendly, pizzeria, same owners as Edelweiss und Gurgl.
((② **Schönblick** (6251) B&B with downhill walk to main lifts, 'very clean, big rooms, hearty breakfast, friendly'.
Hochgurgl has equally good hotels.
(((((⑤ **Hochgurgl** (6265) The only 5-star in the area. Luxurious, with pool.
((((④ **Angerer Alm** (6241) 'Staff were really friendly and nothing was too much trouble,' said a reporter. Pool.
(((③ **Sporthotel Ideal** (6290) Well situated for access to the slopes. Pool.
(((③ **Laurin** (6227) Well equipped, traditional rooms, excellent food.
Self-catering The Lohmann is modern and well placed for the slopes, less so for the village centre below. The 3-star Pirchhütt (6390) has apartments close to the Festkogl gondola, and the Wiesental hotel has more central ones.

EATING OUT
Wide choice, limited range
Hotel à la carte dining rooms dominate. A reporter recommends the independent and rustic Krumpn's Stadl (where staff dress in traditional clothing). The Hexenkuchl in the Jenewein receives favourable reports, serving 'good quality Austrian food,

but not cheap'. The Romantika at the hotel Madeleine and the Belmonte are popular pizzerias. Hotels Alpina, Hochfirst ('food excellent, good wine selection') and Gotthard-Zeit have been recommended. The two restaurants in the Edelweiss und Gurgl are reportedly 'superb', and food at the Josl 'excellent'. Nederhütte (which has a fondue evening with live music, which 'rocks', says a reporter) and David's Skihütte up the mountain are both open in the evenings and popular snowmobile destinations. The 5-star hotel Hochgurgl is recommended for a 'delicious' treat. Remember, credit cards are not widely accepted.

APRES-SKI
Lively early, quiet later
Obergurgl is more animated in the evening than you might expect. The Nederhütte mountain restaurant has lively tea dancing – you ski home afterwards though (or ride down on a snowmobile, says a reporter). All the bars at the base of the Rosskar and Gaisberg lifts are popular at close of play – the Umbrella Bar outside the Edelweiss hotel is particularly busy in good weather. The Hexenkuchl at the Jenewein is also popular and a reporter last year enjoyed the 'excellent' and 'popular sun terrace' at the Wiesental.

Later on, the crowded Krumpn's Stadl barn is the liveliest place in town with live music on alternate nights. The Josl, Jenewein and Edelweiss und Gurgl hotels have atmospheric bars. The Bajazzo is a more sophisticated late-night haunt. When we visited, the Austria-keller disco attracted an extraordinary age range – 6 to 60. There's a casino at the Hochfirst.

Hochgurgl is very quiet at night except for Toni's Almhütte bar in the Olymp Sporthotel – one of three places with live music. There's also the African Bar disco.

OFF THE SLOPES
Very limited
There isn't much to do during the day, with few shops and limited public facilities. Innsbruck is over two hours away by post-bus. Sölden (20 minutes away) has a leisure centre and shopping facilities. Pedestrians can walk to restaurants in the Gaisberg area to meet friends for lunch and there are 15km/9 miles of hiking paths. The health suite at the Hochfirst is said to be open to non-residents.

Obertauern

Small, varied area, with great snow record and lively après-ski scene

COSTS

① ② ③ ④ ⑤ ⑥

RATINGS

The slopes

Fast lifts	*****
Snow	****
Extent	**
Expert	***
Intermediate	****
Beginner	****
Convenience	****
Queues	****
Mountain restaurants	****

The rest

Scenery	***
Resort charm	**
Off-slope	**

NEWS

Last season a new six-pack with covers replaced the Gamsleiten double from the valley.

For 2003/04 the Zehnerkar cable-car was replaced by an eight-seat gondola. The Kringsalm quad became a six-pack with covers and a fast quad replaced the Achenrain double chair. The lift company is now taking a break.

TVB OBERTAUERN

This is about all the forest there is – this is not a resort for bad-weather days ↓

- Excellent snow record
- Well-linked, user-friendly network of efficient modern lifts
- Slopes for all abilities
- Good mountain restaurants
- Lively but not intrusive après-ski
- Compact resort centre – family-friendly if you pick your spot

- Village lacks traditional charm
- Peaks are not high, so slopes are of limited vertical
- Lifts and snow can suffer from exposure to high winds

If you like the après-ski jollity of Austria but have a hankering for the good snow of high French resorts, Obertauern could be just what you're looking for. The terrain is a bit limited by French standards, and the village is no Alpbach. But if you've grown up on slush and ice in lower Austrian resorts, moving up in the world by 1000m/3,300ft or so will be something of a revelation.

THE RESORT

In the land of picture-postcard resorts grown out of rustic villages, Obertauern is different – a mainly modern development at the top of the Tauern pass road. Built in (high-rise) chalet style, it's not unattractive – but it lacks a central focus of shops and bars. Although the core is compact, there is accommodation spread widely along the road.

THE MOUNTAIN

The slopes and lifts form a ring around the village. The Tauern pass road divides them into two unequal parts; that apart, the slopes are well linked to make a user-friendly circuit that can be travelled either way in a couple of hours. Visitors used to big areas will soon start to feel they have seen it all. Runs are short and vertical is limited – most major lifts are in the 200m to

400m (660ft to 1,310ft) range. Reporters complain that while pistes are numbered on the mountain, they are not on the map.

Slopes Most pistes are on the sunny slopes to the north of the road and village: a wide, many-faceted basin of mostly gentle runs, some combining steepish pitches with long schusses. The slopes on the other side of the road – on Gamsleitenspitze, to the south-west – are generally quieter and have some of Obertauern's most difficult runs. There is floodlit skiing from the Edelweisbahn twice a week.

Terrain-parks There is a fun-park on the northern fringe of the area – the left-hand side of our piste map.

Snow reliability The resort has exceptional snow reliability because of its altitude. But lifts can be closed by wind (which may blow snow away too).

Experts There are genuinely steep black pistes from the top Gamsleiten chair, but it is prone to closure.

173

KEY FACTS

Resort	1740m
	5,710ft
Slopes	1630-2315m
	5,350-7,600ft
Lifts	26
Pistes	95km
	59 miles
Blue	50%
Red	35%
Black	15%
Snowmaking	85km
	53 miles

REPORTS WANTED

Recently we have had few reports on this resort. If you go there, please do send us a report.

WEBSITES

For links to resort sites, go to our own new site at www.wtss.co.uk

Phone numbers
From elsewhere in Austria add the prefix 06456.
From abroad use the prefix +43 6456.

TOURIST OFFICE

t 7252
info@obertauern.com
www.obertauern.com

Reporters recommend joining an off-piste guided group to explore the area. **Intermediates** Most of Obertauern's circuit is of intermediate difficulty. Stay low for easier pistes, or try the tougher runs higher up; you can't complete the whole circuit without venturing on to reds. In the Hochalm area, the Seekareck and Panorama chairs take you to challenging runs. The chair to Hundskogel leads to a red and a black. And over at the Plattenkar quad there are splendid black/red runs.
Beginners Obertauern has very good nursery slopes, but they are spread around and beginners must choose accommodation carefully to avoid long walks – there are no ski buses. The Schaidberg chair leads to a drag-lift serving a high-altitude beginners' slope and there is an easy run back home.
Snowboarding Drag-lifts are optional and Blue Tomato is a specialist school.
Cross-country There are 17km/11 miles of trails in the heart of the resort.
Queues When nearby resorts have poor snow, non-residents arrive by the bus-load. However, the modern lift system is impressively efficient. The Sonnenlift double chair from the bottom end of the resort is a bottleneck at ski school start time.
Mountain restaurants Mountain restaurants are plentiful and good, but crowded. A 2005 visitor recommends the Edelweisshütte, Treff 2000 and the Hochalm for 'lots of fun' in addition to food.
Schools and guides There are six schools. Frau Holle school has a

'caring attitude' and 'excellent English'. A recent visitor found Willi Grillitsch school 'very efficient'.
Facilities for children Most of the schools take children.

STAYING THERE

How to go Three major British tour operators offer packages here.
Hotels Practically all accommodation is in hotels (mostly 3-star and 4-star) and guest houses. The following have been recommended: Steiner (7306) – 'lavish spa facilities, magnificent food'; Frau Holle (7662) – 'comfortable rooms and great breakfast'; Kohlmayr (7272) – 'excellent, warm welcoming ambiance'; Enzian (72070) – 'very good facilities'; Schütz (72040) – pool and spa; Edelweiss (7245); Gamsleiten (72860) – 'definitely upmarket'; Alpina (7336).
Eating out The choices are mostly hotels and the busy après-ski bars at the foot of the lifts. The lively old Lürzer Alm does 'terrific food'.
Après-ski There's a lively and varied après-ski scene. The Latsch'n Alm, with terrace and dancing, is good at tea time. A 2005 visitor enjoyed the dancing later on at the new Monkey's Heaven and the People bar, both 'good fun'. The Lürzer Alm has farmyard-style decor and a disco. The Taverne has various bars, a pizzeria, and a disco. The Rosshimmel night-club and Römerbar are worth a look.
Off the slopes There's an excellent, large sports centre – no pool, though. Salzburg is an easy trip.

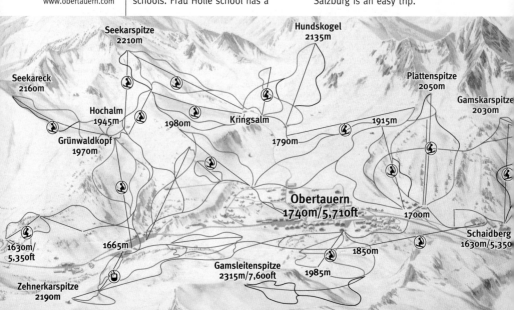

Saalbach-Hinterglemm

Attractive villages, lively nightlife and good intermediate circuit

RATINGS

The slopes

Fast lifts	★★★★
Snow	★★★
Extent	★★★
Expert	★★
Intermediate	★★★★
Beginner	★★★
Convenience	★★★★
Queues	★★★
Mountain restaurants	★★★★

The rest

Scenery	★★★
Resort charm	★★★★
Off-slope	★★

KEY FACTS

Resort	1000m
	3,280ft
Slopes	930-2095m
	3,050ft-6,870ft
Lifts	55
Pistes	200km
	124 miles
Blue	45%
Red	48%
Black	7%
Snowmaking	on all main slopes

➕ Large, well-linked, intermediate circuit with impressive lift system

➕ Saalbach is a big but pleasant, affluent village, lively at night

➕ Village main streets largely traffic-free

➕ Atmospheric mountain restaurants dotted around the slopes

➕ Sunny slopes

➕ Large snowmaking installation and good piste maintenance

➖ Large number of low, south-facing slopes that suffer from the sun

➖ Limited steep terrain

➖ Nursery slopes in Saalbach are not ideal – sunny, and crowded in parts

➖ Saalbach spreads along the valley – some lodgings are far from central

➖ Hinterglemm sprawls along a long street with no clearly defined centre

➖ Saalbach can get rowdy at night

Saalbach-Hinterglemm is one of Austria's major resorts, with a claimed 200km/ 124 miles of pistes. Compared with other big names nearby, it emerges well: it has more challenging intermediate terrain and better mountain restaurants than the Ski Welt (Söll, Ellmau etc), more impressive lifts and snowmaking than Kitzbühel, and has the edge on both in terms of village altitude and ski convenience.

If you cast the net wider, though, you become more aware of what a weakness it is to have most slopes facing south, especially when those slopes are mainly below the 1900m/6,230ft mark. There is a limit to what snowmaking can achieve, especially in February and March.

THE RESORT

Saalbach and Hinterglemm are separate villages, their centres 4km/ 2.5 miles apart, which have expanded along the floor of their dead-end valley. They haven't quite merged, but they have adopted a single shared marketing identity. This doesn't mean they offer a single kind of holiday.

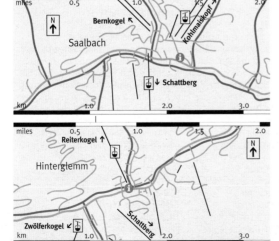

Saalbach is an attractive, typically Austrian village, with traditional-style (although mostly modern) buildings huddled together around a classic onion-domed church. But it is more convenient than most Austrian villages, with pistes coming right down to the traffic-free village centre; the result is close to an ideal blend of Austrian charm with French convenience.

Saalbach has a justified reputation as a party town – but those doing the partying seem to be a strangely mixed bunch. Big-spending BMW and Mercedes drivers, staying in the smart, expensive hotels that line the main street, share the bars with teenagers (including British school kids) spending more on alcohol than on their cheap and cheerful pensions out along the road to Hinterglemm. It can get very rowdy, with drunken revellers still in their ski boots long after dark.

Hinterglemm also has lifts and runs close to the centre, and offers quick access to some of the most interesting slopes. It is a more diffuse collection of hotels and holiday homes, where prices are lower and less cash is flashed. The main street, lined with bars and hotels, has been relieved of through traffic, which is not quite the

↑ This pic sums up the ski area: sunny south-facing slopes and shady north-facing ones

SAALBACH-HINTERGLEMM TOURIST OFFICE

NEWS

For 2005/06 two old T-bars to Kohlmais-kopf and Bründlkopf above Saalbach are due to be replaced by fast six-seat chairs with covers and heated seats. And a new eight-seat gondola is planned to replace the old double chair to Hochalm at the Lengau end of Hinterglemm's skiing.

This will bring the number of gondolas up to nine; in combination with 12 fast chairs, this amounts to an impressive system.

For the 2004/05 season the two successive Westgipfel double chairs from Hinterglemm up to Schattberg West were replaced by an eight-seat gondola.

More snowmaking was also added and a new reservoir built to provide sufficient water to keep the snow-guns working.

same as being traffic-free. It is lively without being rowdy, and for many people is the more attractive option.

In both villages, the amount of walking depends heavily on where you stay. There is an excellent valley bus service, but it isn't perfect: it finishes early, gets very busy at peak times and doesn't get you back to hotels in central Hinterglemm, or to hotels set away from the main road. Taxis are plentiful and not expensive.

Several resorts in Salzburg province are reachable by road – including Bad Hofgastein, Kaprun and Zell am See, the last a short bus-ride away.

THE MOUNTAINS

The slopes form a 'circus' almost entirely composed of intermediate, lightly wooded slopes.

THE SLOPES
User-friendly circuit
Travelling anticlockwise, you can make a complete circuit of the valley on skis, crossing from one side to the other at Vorderglemm and Lengau. You have to tackle a red run from Schattberg West, but otherwise can stick to blues. Going clockwise, you have to truncate the circuit because there is no lift on the south side at Vorderglemm – and there is more red-run skiing to do (and a black if you want to do the full circuit).

On the south-facing side, five sectors can be identified – from west to east, **Hochalm**, **Reiterkogel**, **Bernkogel**, **Kohlmaiskopf** and **Wildenkarkogel**. The last connects via Seidl-Alm to Leogang – a small, high, open area, leading to a long, north-

facing slope down to Leogang village. An eight-seat gondola brings you most of the way back.

The links across these south-facing slopes work well: when traversing the whole hillside you need to descend to the valley floor only once – at Saalbach, where the main street separates Bernkogel from the slopes of Kohlmaiskopf.

The north-facing slopes are different in character – two distinct mountains, with long runs from each to the valley. An eight-seat gondola rises from Saalbach to **Schattberg**, where the high, open, sunny slopes behind the peak are served by a fast quad.

From Schattberg, long runs go down to Saalbach, Vorderglemm and Hinterglemm. From the last, lifts go not only to Schattberg but also to the other north-facing hill, **Zwölferkogel**, served by a two-stage eight-seat gondola. A six-pack and drag-lift serve open slopes on the sunny side of the peak, and a gondola provides a link from Lengau and the south-facing Hochalm.

The Hinterglemm nursery slopes are well used, and floodlit every evening.

TERRAIN-PARKS
Excellent
There's a large half-pipe on Bernkogel above Saalbach, another below Seidl-Alm and terrain-parks on the north-facing slopes just above Hinterglemm (floodlit and 'loved' by a 2005 reporter's teenagers) and below Kl. Asitz on the way to Leogang. There are also dedicated 'carving' and 'mogul' zones on the pistes.

SNOW RELIABILITY
A tale of two sides
The south-facing slopes are in the majority, and can suffer when the sun comes out. Most are above 1400m/ 4,590ft, which helps. The north-facing slopes keep their snow better but can get icy. The long north-facing run down to Leogang often has the best snow in the area. Piste maintenance is good, and snowmaking – now serviced by a new reservoir – covers many top-to-bottom runs; but the low altitude is a problem that won't go away.

FOR EXPERTS
Little steep stuff
There are few challenging slopes. Off-piste guides are available, but snow conditions and forest tend to limit the

boarding

Saalbach is great for boarding. Slopes are extensive, lifts are mainly chairs and gondolas (though there are some connecting drags), and there are pistes to appeal to beginners, intermediates and experts alike – with few flats to negotiate. For experienced boarders, there's off-piste terrain between the lifts.

potential. The main attractions are the north-facing slopes. The long (4km/ 2.5 mile) Nordabfahrt run beneath the Schattberg gondola is a genuine black – a fine fast bash first thing in the morning if it has been groomed. The Zwölferkogel Nordabfahrt at Hinterglemm is less consistent, but its grading is justified by a few short, steeper pitches. The World Cup downhill run from Zwölferkogel is interesting, as is the 5km/3 mile Schattberg West-Hinterglemm red (and its scenic 'ski route' variant).

FOR INTERMEDIATES
Paradise for most

This area is ideal for both the mileage-hungry piste-basher and the more leisurely cruiser, although one nervous third-weeker found the slopes too challenging and gave up after two days, warns a 2005 visitor. For those looking for more of a challenge, the most direct routes down from Hochalm, Reiterkogel, Kohlmaiskopf and Hochwartalm are good fun. Only the delightful blue from Bernkogel into Saalbach – 'the ultimate cruiser', to quote a recent visitor – gets really crowded at times. The alternative long ski route is very pleasant, taking you through forest and meadows.

The north-facing area has some more challenging runs, with excellent relentless reds from both Schattberg West and Zwölferkogel, and a section of relatively high, open slopes around Zwölferkogel. None of the black runs is beyond an adventurous intermediate. The long, pretty cruise to Vorderglemm gets you right away from lifts.

Our favourite intermediate run is the long, off-the-main-circuit cruise on north-facing snow down to Leogang.

Saalbach-Hinterglemm

177

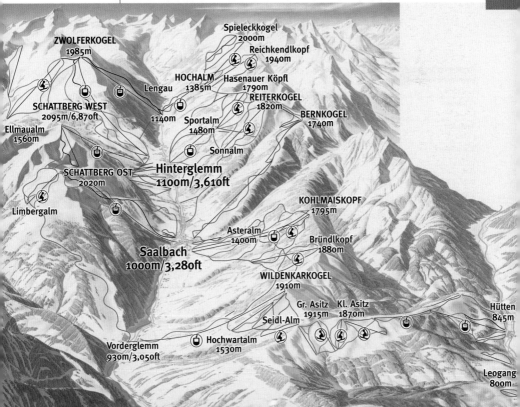

↑ You won't go hungry or thirsty in Saalbach-Hinterglemm – this is just one of 40 or so mountain huts to refuel at

SAALBACH-HINTERGLEMM TOURIST OFFICE

SCHOOLS

Saalbach
Fürstauer
t 8444
Aamadall
t 668256
Hinterholzer
t 7607
Zink
t 0664 162 3655
Snowboard
t 20047
easy ski
t 0699 111 80010
Hinterglemm
Hinterglemmer
t 63460
Activ
t 0676 517 1325

Classes
(Fürstauer prices)
6 days (4hr) €164
Private lessons
€90 for 2hr, for 1 or
2 people; extra
person €10

FOR BEGINNERS
Best for improvers

Saalbach's two nursery slopes are right next to the village centre. But they are south-facing and the upper one gets a lot of through-traffic. The lower one is very small but the lift is free.

Alternatives are trips to the short, easy runs at Bernkogel and Schattberg.

Hinterglemm's spacious nursery area is separate from the main slopes and 'very good', says a 2005 reporter. It is north-facing, so lacks sun in midwinter, but is more reliable for snow later on.

There are lots of easy blue runs to move on to, especially on the south-facing side of the valley.

FOR CROSS-COUNTRY
Go to Zell am See

Some 10km/6 miles of trails run beside the road along the valley floor from Saalbach to Vorderglemm, between Hinterglemm and the valley end at Lindlingalm, and there is a high trail on the Reiterkogel. In mid-winter the valley trails get very little sun, and are not very exciting. The area beyond nearby Zell am See offers more scope.

QUEUES
Only a problem in high season

Queues are a problem only in high season, when the lifts from Saalbach up the south-facing slopes can cause waits of up to 15 minutes at peak times, which include the end as well as the start of the day. A mid-February 2005 visitor found 30-minute queues for the Schönleiten gondola up from Vorderglemm 'all day except first thing in the morning'. High-season queues

can also arise for the chair to Hasenauer Köpfl. The new gondola that replaced the chairs towards Schattberg from Hinterglemm has ended queues there at the end of the day.

MOUNTAIN RESTAURANTS
Excellent quality and quantity

The area is liberally scattered with around 40 attractive huts that serve good food. Many have pleasant rustic interiors and a lively ambience.

On the south-facing slopes, the Panoramaalm on the Kohlmaiskopf slope, Thurneralm close to Bründlkopf and Walleggalm on Hochalm serve particularly good food. Across in the Hinterglemm direction, reporters recommend the 'enterprising' Rosswaldhütte, not least for its 'excellent rösti', and the Bärnalm near the top of the Bernkogel chair – 'good food, good value'.

The Wildenkarkogel Hütte has a big terrace and possibly the loudest mountain-top music we've heard, with resident DJ from mid-morning. The Alte Schmiede at the top of the Leogang gondola, with rustic decor including water wheels, is recommended for its 'good food' including 'the best pizza in the area', although you may have to wait for it.

The Simalalm at the base of the Limbergalm quad chair is 'great for the sun and the views'. On the north-facing slopes, the Bergstadl – halfway down the red run from Schattberg West – has stunning views and good food. Ellmaualm, at the bottom of the Zehner lift has been praised, the toilets being an 'outstanding' feature. The 12er-Treff

CHILDREN

Several hotels have nurseries

Ski schools
Some take children in miniclubs from about age 3 and can provide lunchtime care. From about age 4½, children can join ski school (€139 for 6 days – Fürstauer prices)

GETTING THERE

Air Salzburg 90km/ 56 miles (2hr); Munich 218km/135 miles (3½hr).

Rail Zell am See 19km/12 miles (40min); hourly buses.

---

umbrella bar at the top of the Zwölferkogel gondola is good for lounging in the sun.

SCHOOLS AND GUIDES
Plenty of choice
We're all in favour of competition, but visitors to Saalbach-Hinterglemm may feel that they are faced with rather too much of this particular good thing, with no fewer than nine schools to choose from. We have had conflicting reports of the Fürstauer school. One visitor said it was 'terrific' and the instructors 'took great care of our children', who made excellent progress – but an adult beginner had some complaints. We have also had conflicting reports of the Aamadall school. In 2005 a visitor had 'a very good instructor who took us from snowplough to parallel', but in 2004 a reporter did not like the 'wide ranging standard in the class'. A Hinterglemm boarder had 'worthwhile' lessons with Hinterglemmer.

FACILITIES FOR CHILDREN
Hinterglemm tries harder
Saalbach doesn't go out of its way to sell itself to families, although it does have a ski kindergarten. Hinterglemm has some good hotel-based nursery facilities – the one at the Theresia is reportedly excellent.

STAYING THERE

HOW TO GO
Cheerful doesn't mean cheap
Chalets We are aware of a few 'club hotels' but Saalbach isn't really a chalet resort.
Hotels There are a large number of hotels in both villages, mainly 3-star and above. Be aware that some central hotels are affected by disco noise and front rooms by all-night street noise.
Saalbach
((((4) **Alpenhotel** (6666) Luxurious, with open-fire lounge, disco, small pool.
((((4) **Berger's Sporthotel** (6577) Liveliest of the top hotels, with a daily tea dance, and disco. Small pool.
((((4) **Kendler** (62250) Position second to none, right next to the Bernkogel chair. Classy, expensive, good food.
((((4) **Saalbacher Hof** (71110) Retains a friendly feel despite its large size; 'excellent wellness centre'.
((((4) **Gartenhotel Eva** (71440) 'Small, good quality with sophisticated, simple, low calorie food,' said a 2004 reporter.

(((3) **Haider** (6228) Best-positioned of the 3-stars, right next to the main lifts.
(((3) **Kristiana** (6253) Near enough to lifts but away from night-time noise. 'Excellent food.' Sauna, steam bath.
(((3) **König** (6384) Cheaper 3-star and more basic rooms.
Hinterglemm
((((4) **Theresia** (71140) Hinterglemm's top hotel, and one of the best for families. Out towards Saalbach, but nursery slopes nearby. Pool.
((((4) **Egger** (63220) 'I'll stay here next time, on the slopes,' says a reader.
(((3) **Wolf** (63460) Small but well-equipped 4-star in excellent position. 'Superb food and gala dinners'. Pool.
(((3) **Sonnblick** (6408) Convenient 3-star in a 'quiet location' with 'friendly service' and 'the comfiest holiday beds I have slept in', says a guest. 'Buffet breakfast excellent and tasty choice at dinner,' says a 2005 visitor.
((2) **Haus Ameshofer** (8119) Beside piste at Reiterkogel lift. 'Great value ski-in, ski-out B&B,' says a reporter.
Self-catering There's a big choice of apartments for independent travellers.

EATING OUT
Wide choice of hotel restaurants
This is essentially a half-board resort, with few non-hotel restaurants. Peter's restaurant, at the top of Saalbach's main street, is atmospheric and serves excellent meat dishes cooked on hot stones. One reader enjoyed the excellent food, with 'an emphasis on the meatier, richer dishes', at the Hotel Neuhaus. The Wallner Pizzeria on the main street is good value. The Auwirt hotel on the outskirts of Saalbach has a good à la carte restaurant.

APRES-SKI
It rocks from early on
Après-ski is very lively from mid-afternoon until the early hours and can get positively wild. In Saalbach the

ACTIVITIES

Indoor Swimming pools, sauna, massage, solarium, tennis

Outdoor Ice-rink, curling, tobogganing, paragliding, sleigh rides, 40km/25 miles of cleared paths

WEBSITES

For links to resort sites, go to our own new site at www.wtss.co.uk

Phone numbers
Saalbach
From elsewhere in Austria add the prefix 06541.
From abroad use the prefix +43 6541.

Leogang
From elsewhere in Austria add the prefix 06583.
From abroad use the prefix +43 6583.

TOURIST OFFICES

Saalbach
t 680068
contact@saalbach.com
www.saalbach.com

Leogang
t 8234
info@saalfelden-leogang.at
www.leogang-saalfelden.at

rustic Hinterhagalm at the top of the main nursery slope is packed by 3.30. When it closes around 6pm, the crowds slide down to Bauer's Ski-alm and try to get into the already heaving old cow shed to continue drinking and dancing. The tiny Zum Turn (next door to the church and cemetery) is a medieval jail that also gets packed from 4pm until late.

Castello's 'at the bottom of the main street' is the place to be, according to a recent visitor. The Neuhaus Taverne has live music and attracts a mature clientele. Bobby's Pub is cheap, often full of British school kids, has bowling and serves Guinness. King's Disco livens up after midnight. Arena disco has go-go dancers and is very popular, as is Berger's Sporthotel Galerie. A reader recommends the Berger Hochalm: '3km up the toboggan track, marvellous atmosphere and reindeer steaks before a 1am descent.'

In Hinterglemm there are a number of ice bars, which are crowded immediately after the lifts close, including the Gute Stube of Hotel Dorfschmiede in the centre of town with loud music blasting out and people spilling into the street. A wider age group enjoys the live music later on at the smart, friendly Tanzhimmel – an open, glass-fronted bar with a dance floor. The Hexenhäusl gets packed and has an animated model of a witch revealing her undergarments. A similar fascination with moving models is demonstrated at the rustic Goasstall ('the best and loudest bar in the area,' according to a 2005 reporter) by the piste down from Sportalm, where a model goat is equally revealing (and where real goats graze behind glass near the men's toilet). Bla Bla is small, modern and smart, with reasonable prices. The Almbar has good music and some dancing.

Tour operator reps organise tobogganing, sleigh rides and bowling.

OFF THE SLOPES
Surprisingly little to do
Saalbach is not very entertaining if you're not into winter sports. There are few shops other than supermarkets and ski shops. Walks tend to be restricted to the paths alongside the cross-country trails or along the Saalbach toboggan run to Spielberghs. But there are excursions to Kitzbühel and Salzburg.

Leogang 800m/2,620ft

A much less expensive alternative to Saalbach-Hinterglemm.

THE RESORT
Leogang is quiet, attractive and rather scattered. It's best to stay at Hütten, near the lift.

THE MOUNTAIN
The village is linked to the eastern end of the Saalbach-Hinterglemm circuit.
Slopes A gondola from Hütten takes you into the ski area. The local slopes tend to be delightfully quiet.
Snow reliability The local slopes have some of the best snow in the region, being north- and east-facing, with snowmaking on the run home.
Experts Not much challenge locally.
Intermediates Great long red run cruise home from the top of the gondola. Plus the circuit to explore.
Beginners Good nursery slopes by the village, and short runs to progress to.
Snowboarding The whole area is great for boarding and there's a terrain-park.
Cross-country The best in the area. There are 20km/12 miles of trails, plus a panoramic high-altitude trail.
Queues No local problems.
Mountain restaurants A couple of good local huts. A 2005 visitor recommends the Forsthofalm – 'the nicest I have ever been in'.
Schools and guides Leogang Altenberger school has a high reputation – 'excellent service and lessons; highly recommended'.
Facilities for children There is a non-ski nursery, and children can start school at four years old.

STAYING THERE
Hotels The luxury Krallerhof (82460) has its own nursery lift, which can be used to get across to the main lift station. The 4-star Salzburgerhof (73100) is one of the best-placed hotels, within a two-minute walk of the gondola; sauna and steam.
Self-catering There are quiet apartments available.
Eating out Restaurants are hotel-based. The upscale Krallerhof has excellent food and the much cheaper Gasthof Hüttwirt has a high reputation.
Après-ski The rustic old chalet Kraller Alm is very much the focal tea-time and evening rendezvous.
Off the slopes Excursions to Salzburg are possible.

Schladming

Old valley town with extensive intermediate slopes

RATINGS

The slopes

Fast lifts	***
Snow	****
Extent	***
Expert	**
Intermediate	****
Beginner	***
Convenience	***
Queues	****
Mountain restaurants	****

The rest

Scenery	***
Resort charm	***
Off-slope	****

NEWS

The Gleiming gondola on Reiteralm is due to be replaced by a new eight-seat one for 2005/06.

For 2003/04 a six-pack with covers replaced two T-bars on Hauser Kaibling – part of a plan to encourage people eastwards towards Hauser Kaibling and so relieve the peak pressure on Planai and Hochwurzen.

➕ Extensive slopes in four sectors

➕ Excellent slopes for intermediates

➕ Very sheltered slopes, among trees

➕ Lots of good mountain restaurants

➕ Appealing town with friendly people and a life independent of tourism

➕ Ski Alliance Amadé lift pass covers a wide range of nearby resorts

➕ Extensive snowmaking, good grooming and shady slopes mean good piste conditions, but ...

➖ The mainly north-facing runs can be cold in early season

➖ Slopes lack variety

➖ Very little to entertain experts, on- or off-piste

➖ Nursery slopes (at Rohrmoos) are inconvenient unless you stay beside them – and beginners are expected to pay for a full lift pass

➖ Runs to valley level are not easy

Since its four previously separate mountains were linked by lifts and pistes, Schladming has been able to compete with major resorts that are better known internationally. A keen intermediate who wants to make the most of the links can get a real sense of travelling around on the snow. And as the list of plus-points suggests, we see many attractions in the place.

If you like your slopes to be reassuringly consistent, Schladming has a strong claim on your attention. If, on the other hand, you like the spice of variety and the thrill of a serious challenge, you might find it all rather tame.

The resort does not offer one of Austria's wildest après-ski scenes, but that doesn't seem to bother most of our reporters, who enjoy its established, valley-town ambience.

THE RESORT

The old town of Schladming has a long skiing tradition and has hosted World Cup races for many years.

The town has a pleasant, traffic-free main square, prettily lit at night, around which you'll find most of the shops, restaurants and bars (and some appealing hotels). The busy main road bypasses the town and is separated from it by a river. Much of the accommodation is close to the centre and can be noisy into the early hours because of nearby bars. The modern

sports centre and tennis halls are five minutes' walk from the centre.

Schladming sits at the foot of Planai, one of four mountains that are now linked to form a fair-sized network. A gondola starting a few minutes' walk from the centre goes most of the way up this home mountain. To the east is the small, attractively rustic village of Haus, where a cable-car and gondola go up to the highest of the four linked mountains, Hauser Kaibling. From the western suburbs of Schladming there are chair-lifts towards the next

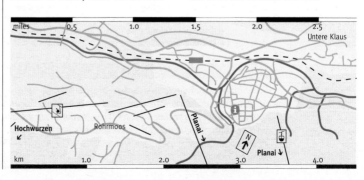

↑ Good views on a clear day – probably of Hochkönig (see our new chapter, a few pages back)

HAGSPIEL PHOTOGRAPHY / PLANAI-HOCHWURZEN-BAHNEN GMBH

AUSTRIA

LIFT PASSES

Ski Alliance Amadé Ski Pass
Covers over 270 lifts in more than 30 ski resorts in the Gastein valley and Grossarl; Salzburger Sportwelt; Hochkönig's Winterreich; also buses, trains and road tolls between the resorts.

Beginners
No special pass

Main pass
1 day €34
6 days €165

Children
Under 20: 6 days €153.50
Under 17: 6 days €82.50
Under 7: free pass

Notes
Part-day tickets are available.

Alternative pass
Salzburg Super Ski Card covers all lifts and pistes in Salzburgerland including Zell am See, Kaprun and Saalbach-Hinterglemm.

---

mountain to the west, Hochwurzen. The lifts pass through Rohrmoos, a quiet, scattered village set on an elevated slope that is effectively a giant nursery area. Rohrmoos makes an excellent base for beginners who aren't looking for lively nightlife.

There are timetabled buses between the villages and lift bases, but they are not as frequent as reporters wished.

Reporters have been impressed with the free photo e-mail service at the top of the Planai and Reiteralm gondolas. Another neat free souvenir is offered by the Skiline terminals at the Planai base. At the end of the day you can obtain a printout showing lifts used, height gained and distance covered.

THE MOUNTAINS

Most pistes are on the wooded north-facing slopes above the main valley, with some going into the side valleys higher up; there are a few open slopes above the trees. All four mountains have similar terrain, with mainly red runs of much the same pitch

Piste maps, and discrepancies between different versions (runs red on one, blue on the other; marked on one, not on the other) continue to provoke criticism.

Apart from the main slopes we describe here, there are several other

separate mountains nearby and shown on the main piste map – Fageralm, Galsterbergalm, Ramsau, the Dachstein glacier and Stoderzinken. The Ski Alliance Amadé lift pass also covers many other resorts. Trips to Bad Gastein are feasible by rail (with at least one change). Drivers can also visit Wagrain/Flachau, Kleinarl and Hochkönig. Tour operators organise day trips, too. Snow-sure Obertauern is not far away but is not on the lift pass.

THE SLOPES
Four linked sectors – and more
Each of the linked sectors is quite a serious mountain with a variety of lifts and runs to play on. **Planai** and **Hauser Kaibling** are linked at altitude via the high, wooded bowl between them. But the links with **Hochwurzen** (where you can try night skiing, boarding or tobogganing, though it is not included on the lift pass) and with the fourth linked mountain, **Reiteralm**, are at valley level. Getting around the whole area can take time – and involves some uninteresting linking runs. The link between Planai and Hochwurzen involves riding a lift through a tunnel, whichever way you are travelling.

Some people who want to spend time on Reiteralm prefer to get the bus, or a taxi, to one of the lift bases at Pichl or Gleiming.

There are handy ski lockers to rent at the Planai base station.

TERRAIN-PARKS
Three to try
There are two terrain-parks and half-pipes on the main linked area.

SNOW RELIABILITY
Excellent in cold weather
The northerly orientation of the slopes and good maintenance help keep the slopes in better shape than in some neighbouring resorts, and the serious snowmaking operation makes it a particularly good choice for early holidays; coverage is comprehensive, and the system is put to good use (to

---

boarding

Schladming is popular with boarders. Most lifts on the spread-out mountains are gondolas or chairs, with some short drags around. The area is ideal for beginners and intermediates, except when the lower slopes are icy, though there are few exciting challenges for expert boarders bar the off-piste tree runs. The Blue Tomato snowboard shop – reportedly 'well organised' – runs the specialist snowboard school.

KEY FACTS

Resort	745m
	2,440ft

For the Sportregion
Schladming-Ramsau/
Dachstein area

Slopes	745-2015m
	2,440-6,610ft
Lifts	81
Pistes	167km
	104 miles
Blue	29%
Red	61%
Black	10%
Snowmaking	100%

For Schladming only

Slopes	745-2015m
	2,440-6,610ft
Lifts	45
Pistes	115km
	71 miles

SCHOOLS

Tritscher
t 22647

Hopl
t 61268

Classes
(Tritscher prices)
5 half-days (2½hr am)
€110

Private lessons
Half day €90; each
additional person €15

the point that one January reporter found it 'a constant irritation'). The steep bottom part of the World Cup downhill run back to town can get extremely icy.

FOR EXPERTS
Strictly intermediate stuff
Schladming's status as a World Cup downhill venue doesn't make it macho. The steep black finish to the Men's Downhill course and the moderate mogul runs at the top of Planai and Hauser Kaibling are the only really challenging slopes. Hauser Kaibling's off-piste is good, but limited.

FOR INTERMEDIATES
Red runs rule
The area is ideal for intermediate cruising. The majority of runs are red but it's often difficult to distinguish them from many of the blues.

The open sections at the top of Planai and Hauser Kaibling have some more challenging slopes. And the two World Cup pistes, and the red that runs parallel to the Haus downhill course, are ideal for fast intermediates.

Hauser Kaibling has a lovely meandering blue running from top to bottom for the less confident intermediates, and Reiteralm has some gentle blues with good snow. Runs are well groomed, so intermediates will find the slopes generally flattering.

FOR BEGINNERS
Good slopes but poorly sited
The ski schools generally take beginners to the extensive but low-altitude Rohrmoos nursery area – fine

if you are based there, a discouraging bus-ride away if you are not. Another novice area near the top of Planai is more convenient for residents of central Schladming and has better snow, but the runs are less gentle.

FOR CROSS-COUNTRY
Extensive network of trails
Given sufficient snow-cover, there are 300km/186 miles of trails in the region, and the World Championships have been held at nearby Ramsau. There are local loops along the main valley floor and in the valleys between Planai and Hochwurzen.

QUEUES
Avoid peaks at Planai
The Planai gondola can have morning queues at peak-season and weekends, but generally reporters have found few problems. The upgraded gondola at Haus has relieved pressure there, and the slow Reiteralm gondola is due to be replaced for this season. Reporters recommend going to Fageralm on exceptionally busy days.

MOUNTAIN RESTAURANTS
Plenty of nice places
There are plenty of attractive rustic restaurants in all sectors ('too many,' says one reporter – 'we couldn't decide which to try'). A reporter returning to Austria after a decade skiing elsewhere said, 'It was an absolute delight to be reminded of what I had been missing!' 2005 reporters again enjoyed lunch in the 'spacious,' attractive Schladminger Hütte, at the top of the Planai gondola. The terrace of the

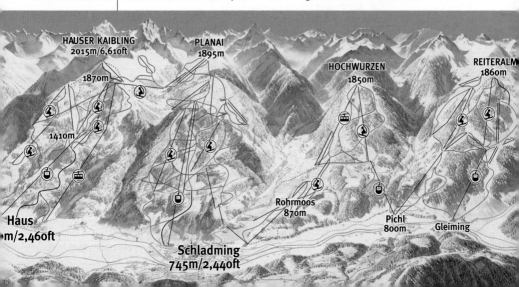

HAUSER KAIBLING
2015m/6,610ft

1870m

1410m

PLANAI
1895m

HOCHWURZEN
1850m

REITERALM
1886m

Rohrmoos
870m

Pichl
800m

Gleiming

Haus
m/2,46oft

Schladming
745m/2,44oft

ACTIVITIES

Indoor Swimming pool, fitness club, sauna

Outdoor Ice skating, curling, tobogganing, sleigh rides, 30km/19 miles of cleared paths

CHILDREN

Kinderclub Rohrmoos Takes children from 18mnth.

Ski schools Take children from age 4 (€190 for 5 days including lunch – Tritscher price).

GETTING THERE

Air Salzburg 90km/56 miles (1½hr).

Rail Main line station in resort.

WEBSITES

For links to resort sites, go to our own new site at www.wtss.co.uk

Phone numbers
Schladming
From elsewhere in Austria add the prefix 03687.
From abroad use the prefix +43 3687.
Haus
From elsewhere in Austria add the prefix 03686.
From abroad use the prefix +43 3686.

TOURIST OFFICES

Schladming
t 22777
info@schladming-rohrmoos.com
www.schladming-rohrmoos.com
www.skiamade.com
Haus
t 22340
info@haus.at
www.haus.at

Weitmoosalm is very pleasant in the sun, as is the one at the Schaf-Alm – a great spot for a vin chaud before the last run down. On Reiteralm 'you absolutely must visit' the Gasslhöh-Hütte to try the 'mega huge' spare ribs with jacket potato and garlic sauce. On Hauser Kaibling it's worth looking out for the sign to the tiny Kulmhoferhütte to experience real mountain hut atmosphere, complete with fur-lined walls. Higher up, the hut off the Almlift feels wonderfully isolated, with great views and soup. Mitterhausalm is good. The Knapplhof at Hauser Kaibling is full of ski-racing mementos.

SCHOOLS AND GUIDES
Generally okay reports
We have generally had good reports in the past, but a 2005 visitor found the Tritscher school 'badly organised'.

FACILITIES FOR CHILDREN
Rohrmoos is the place
The extensive gentle slopes of Rohrmoos are ideal for building up youngsters' confidence.

STAYING THERE

HOW TO GO
Packages mean hotels
Packaged accommodation is in hotels and pensions, but there are plenty of apartments for independent travellers.
Hotels Most of the accommodation is in modestly priced pensions but there are also a few more upmarket hotels.
《《《④ **Sporthotel Royer** (200) Big, smart and comfortable, a few minutes' walk from the main Planai lift. Pool, sauna.
《《③ **Alte Post** (22571) Characterful old inn with great position on the main square. Good food, but watch out for small rooms and sofa-beds.
《《③ **Zum Stadttor** (24525) Similarly priced, although less charming and well placed. 'Good food, good location,' says a reporter.
《《③ **Kirchenwirt** (22435) Just off the main square. 'Traditional atmosphere, wonderful food,' says a visitor. 'Great value for money,' adds a 2005 visitor.
《《③ **Neue Post** (22105) Large rooms, friendly, good food, central.
《《③ **Zum Kaiserweg** (22038) Family run. Very near the Planai West Tunnel lift. 'Good value, excellent food.'
《《③ **Rohrmooser Schlössl (61237)** Just downhill from the Planai West Tunnel lift. 'Really friendly', with 'excellent food and views'.

Self-catering Haus Girik (22663) is close to the gondola.

EATING OUT
Some good places
Recommendations include the Kirchenwirt hotel ('excellent home cooking'), Giovanni's (for pizza), Gasthof Brunner ('good value') and Talbachschenke ('good grills and atmosphere'). Hotels Neue Post and Alte Post are 'good but expensive'.

APRES-SKI
Explore the side streets
Some of the mountain restaurants are lively at the end of the afternoon, but down in the town there's a real lack of tea-time animation. Charly's Treff (with umbrella bar) opposite the Planai gondola is the main exception (and has great photos of local hero Arnold Schwarzenegger). The little Siglu also gets busy but quickly 'overcrowded and smoky'. A couple of central cafes are popular for coffee and cakes.

There is no lack of options later on – many of the central bars stay open until dawn. Popular spots include the brewpub, Schwalbenbräu. The Beisl is a smart bar but a 2005 visitor found it 'lifeless'. In contrast the Neiderl is 'small but friendly'. Szenario is 'quite cosy, with very eclectic music choices'. Hanglbar has occasional karaoke and 'generally a good atmosphere'. Maria's Mexican is 'relaxing' with chilled music and margueritas. The Porta is a 'smart place with the best music and ambience in Schladming'. The Sonderbar, a disco with three bars, is reportedly 'lacking in class'.

OFF THE SLOPES
Good for all but walkers
Non-skiers are fairly well catered for. Some mountain restaurants are easily reached on foot. The town shops and museum are worth a look. Train trips to Salzburg are easy (and worthwhile). Buses run to the old walled town of Radstadt. There's a pool and ice rink.

Haus 750m/2,460ft

Haus is a real village with a life of its own and its own ski schools and kindergartens. The user-friendly nursery slopes are between the village and the gondola. There's a railway station, so excursions are easy, but off-slope activities and nightlife are very limited. Hotel prices are generally lower here.

FRANK HEUER

Sölden

Dynamic, snow-sure, high-altitude area, with throbbing nightlife

NEWS

For 2004/05 the Seiterkar lift – the key lift back from the Tiefenbach glacier – was upgraded to a six-seat covered chair. And you could pay €10 extra when buying a week's lift pass to cover a day on the slopes of Obergurgl just up the road – free buses were included. The resort was not certain whether this would continue for 2005/06 when we went to press.

For 2005/06, the resort plans a considerable investment in new snowmaking.

KEY FACTS

Resort	1380m
	4,530ft
Slopes	1370-3250m
	4,490-10,660ft
Lifts	34
Pistes	149km
	93 miles
Blue	30%
Red	53%
Black	17%
Snowmaking	35 guns

➕ Excellent snow reliability, with access to two glaciers

➕ Fairly extensive network of slopes suited to adventurous intermediates

➕ Impressive lift system

➕ Very lively après-ski/nightlife

➖ Busy road through sprawling village

➖ Some central hotels are distant from the two main access lifts

➖ Inconvenient beginners' slopes

➖ Rowdy, drink-fuelled nightlife

➖ English not widely spoken

A couple of big UK tour operators have recently introduced Sölden to their brochures. But still very few Brits go there (and you might find the lack of English-speakers in the resort a drawback). Nevertheless, Sölden deserves a serious look from keen intermediates. It has recently invested massively in new lifts to link its glaciers to the lower slopes. There are some seriously long runs and some seriously rowdy après-ski (avoidable by staying off the main street).

THE RESORT

Despite its traditional Tirolean-style buildings and tree-filled valley, Sölden is no beauty: it is a large, traffic-filled place that sprawls along both sides of a river and busy main road. The resort attracts a young, lively crowd – mostly Dutch and German – bent on partying.

Gondolas from opposite ends of town go up to Sölden's home slopes – the peak of Gaislachkogl and the lift junction of Giggijoch, above the satellite resort of Hochsölden. A free, 'very efficient' shuttle-bus serves both lift stations. But reporters warn that you have to pay cash for lift passes – credit cards not accepted.

THE MOUNTAIN

The two similar-sized home sectors are linked by chair-lifts out of the Rettenbachtal that separates them. The Rettenbach and Tiefenbach glaciers are connected by a series of fast lifts from Rotkogl. Two 2005 reporters each commented that they skied all the runs in three days or less – so the day in Obergurgl (see News) is worthwhile.
Slopes Practically all the slopes you spend your days on are above the trees. But there are red runs through trees to the village – less confident intermediates should beware of the tricky one down from Hochsölden. Grooming is generally good.
Terrain-parks Two in winter above Giggijoch: one has a half-pipe, kickers and rails; the other a boarder-cross run with waves and jumps.

Snow reliability The slopes are high and mainly north-east- or south-east-facing; there is some snowmaking and more planned; and there are two extensive glaciers. So snow is usually good; but a late-season 2005 reporter found slush even on the Tiefenbach glacier due to warm weather.
Experts None of the black pistes dotted around Sölden's map is particularly serious, but there are quite a few non-trivial reds. And there are extensive off-piste possibilities with a guide. At the top of the valley is one of the Alps' premier touring areas.
Intermediates Most of Sölden's main slopes are red runs ideal for keen intermediates, and there are some serious verticals to be racked up; there is a drop of over 1800m/5,910ft from the top to the village. There are several easy blacks, and the long, quiet red down to Gaislachalm is ideal for high-speed cruising. Giggijoch offers gentler gradients, but gets extremely crowded.
Beginners The beginners' slopes are situated inconveniently – just above the village at Innerwald – and are prone to poor snow. Near-beginners can use the blues at Giggijoch.
Snowboarding Sölden is not ideal for beginners but there's great free-riding for experienced boarders. And all drag-lifts can be avoided.
Cross-country There are a couple of uninspiring loops by the river, plus small areas at Zwieselstein and Vent.
Queues 2005 reporters found big queues at the Einzeiger and Seekogl chairs on the way to and from the

WEBSITES

For links to resort sites, go to our own new site at www.wtss.co.uk

Phone numbers
From elsewhere in Austria add the prefix 05254.
From abroad use the prefix +43 5254.

TOURIST OFFICE

t 5100
info@soelden.com
www.soelden.com

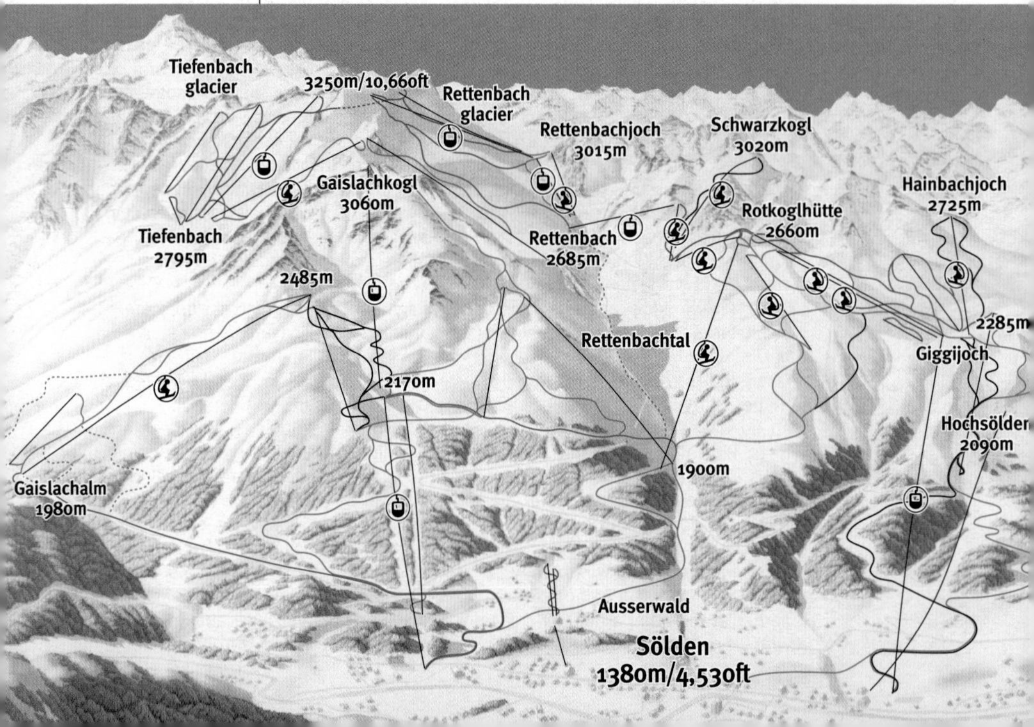

glacier – taking the ski route home allows you to avoid Seekogl.

Mountain restaurants The self-service places around Giggijoch can get very crowded. To escape the crowds try the cluster of places around Gaislachalm, Schwarzkogl on run 24 or head down piste 7 to the calm, rustic 'friendly' Pfandl at Ausserwald. Several reporters recommend the atmospheric old Gampealm, towards the end of piste 11. A couple of 2005 visitors enjoyed the rustic Eugens Obstlerhütte.

Schools and guides The three schools all restrict class sizes to seven or eight. A reporter this year had a 'good' private lesson with the main school.

Facilities for children The ski kindergarten takes children from the age of three. There are special family lift pass deals.

STAYING THERE

How to go There are few UK packages.

Hotels The 5-star Central (22600) is the best and one of the biggest in town. The 4-star Regina (2301) is recommended by a reporter. Several 2005 reporters enjoyed Gasthof Grauer Bar (2564). The Haus Grüner Karl B&B (2477) above town on run 7 is highly praised and has a 'suite of saunas and steam rooms'. Self-catering apartments at the Posthäusl (31380) are good.

Eating out Reporter recommendations include the Tavola in the hotel Rosengarten, Cafe Hubertus, Nudeltopf and Corso for pizza; and s'Pfandl at Ausserwald for Tirolean food.

Après-ski Sölden's après-ski is famous. It starts up the mountain, notably at Giggijoch, and progresses via bars in the main street – notably the greenhouse-style Dominic Bla-Bla – to countless places with live bands and throbbing discos (a 2005 reporter recommends the PartyHaus and Lawine), and table dancing and striptease at Rodelhütte. There are nightly toboggan evenings, with drinking and dancing before a 6km/ 4 mile floodlit run back to town from the Gaislachalm mountain restaurant.

Off the slopes There's a sports centre, swimming pool and an ice rink. Trips to Innsbruck are possible.

Tiefenbach glacier
3250m/10,66oft
Rettenbach glacier
Rettenbachjoch 3015m
Schwarzkogl 3020m
Gaislachkogl 3060m
Hainbachjoch 2725m
Tiefenbach 2795m
Rotkoglhütte 2660m
Rettenbach 2685m
2485m
2285m
Rettenbachtal
Giggijoch
2170m
Hochsölder 2090m
1900m
Gaislachalm 1980m
Ausserwald
Sölden
1380m/4,53oft

Söll

Lively but inconvenient base for the extensive Ski Welt slopes

COSTS

① ② ③ ④ ⑤ ⑥

RATINGS

The slopes
Fast lifts	**
Snow	**
Extent	****
Expert	*
Intermediate	****
Beginner	***
Convenience	**
Queues	***
Mountain restaurants	**

The rest
Scenery	***
Resort charm	***
Off-slope	**

NEWS

For 2004/05 a new fast six-seat chair with covers, the Hexen-6er, replaced a T-bar above Hochsöll. And at Hopfgarten, the double chair out of the village was replaced by an eight-seat gondola. A new 3D MountMap piste map of the Ski Welt was also on sale – the first ski region in Austria to have one.

For 2005/06, a six-seat chair-lift will replace a T-bar up to Eiberg. The extensive snowmaking will be increased yet again to cover 180km/112 miles of pistes in the Ski Welt (over 70 per cent of the total).

+ Part of Ski Welt, Austria's largest linked ski and snowboard area

+ Local slopes are the highest in the Ski Welt and north-facing, so they keep their snow relatively well

+ Plenty of cheap and cheerful pensions for those on a budget

+ Pretty village with lively après-ski

+ Massive recent investment in snowmaking has paid off, but ...

− Ski Welt is at low altitude, and has a poor natural snow record

− Long walk or infrequent buses from the village to the lifts

− Little to amuse experts or to challenge good intermediates

− Ski Welt slopes can get crowded at weekends and in high season – especially above Söll

− Mostly short runs in local sector

Söll has long been popular with British beginners and intermediates, attracting a mixture of singles looking for a fun week and families looking for a quiet time.

When the snow is good, as it has been for much of the last two seasons, Söll can be a great place for a holiday – cruising the attractive and undemanding pistes of Austria's largest linked area. Its main real drawback has always been the lack of altitude and the consequent danger of poor natural snow. But this problem has been tackled by a massive investment in snowmaking, and over 70% of the Ski Welt's 250km/155 miles of piste are now covered by snow cannons – the biggest snowmaking operation in Austria. This ensures the main pistes and links stay open, though it can't prevent slush and ice developing.

Many visitors are surprised by the small size of the village and the long distance between it and the slopes.

THE RESORT

Söll is a small, pretty, friendly village; you can explore it in a few minutes. New buildings are traditional in design and there's a huge church near the centre which, according to a reporter, is well worth a visit at dusk as the graveyard is lit with candles. The pretty scenery adds to Söll's charm, and it benefits from being off the main road. There aren't many shops.

The slopes are a bus- or taxi-ride or a 15-minute walk from the centre, the other side of a busy road with a pedestrian tunnel underneath. You can leave your equipment at the bottom of the gondola for a small charge.

There is some accommodation out near the lifts but most is in or around the village centre – a free (but 'too infrequent' say reporters) ski-bus-ride from the slopes. Being on the edge of the village nearest the lifts is best for those who are prepared to walk to the slopes. The other side of town has the advantage that you can board the bus there before it gets too crowded. Some guest houses are literally miles from the centre and lifts, and the ski-bus does not serve every nook and cranny of this sprawling community.

THE MOUNTAINS

The Ski Welt linked circuit includes Hopfgarten, Itter, Söll, Scheffau, Ellmau, Going and Brixen. It is the largest linked area in Austria, and will easily keep an early or average intermediate amused for a week. But that doesn't make it a Trois Vallées. It is basically a typically small, low, pastoral Austrian hill multiplied several times. One section is much like

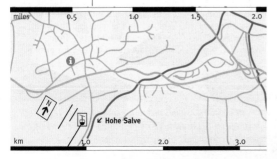

AUSTRIA

188

another, and most slopes best suit early to average intermediates. Runs are mostly short and scenery attractive rather than stunning – although the views from Hohe Salve are impressive.

Westendorf is separate (see separate chapter) but covered by the area pass. The Kitzbüheler Alpenskipass also covers many other resorts easily reached by car including Kitzbühel (which can be reached, from 2005/06, via Westendorf too) – an impressive total of 260 lifts and 680km/423 miles of pistes.

THE SLOPES
Short run network
A gondola takes all but complete beginners up to the mid-mountain shelf of Hochsöll, where there are a couple of short lifts and connections in several directions.

These include an eight-seat gondola to the high point of Hohe Salve. From here there are stunning views and runs down to Kälbersalve, Rigi and Hopfgarten. Rigi can also be reached by chairs and runs without going to Hohe Salve – to which it is itself linked by chairs. Rigi is also the start of runs down to Itter. From Kälbersalve you can head down south-facing runs to Brixen or up to Zinsberg and Eiberg and towards Ellmau.

A quicker way to Ellmau without taking as many south-facing slopes is by using a cable-car from Hochsöll.

We continue to receive criticism of the piste map, which is hopelessly over-ambitious in trying to show the

whole area in a single view. A reporter this year found the new 3D pop-up MountMap introduced for 2004/05 'excellent'. It cost 5 euros.

TERRAIN-PARKS
Not a major feature
None locally but there's a popular park at Westendorf and a new one planned for 2005/06 at Ellmau.

SNOW RELIABILITY
Artificial help saves the day
With a low average height, and important links that get a lot of sun, the snowmaking that the Ski Welt has installed in recent seasons is essential. At 180km/112 miles and covering over 70 per cent of the area's pistes, it is Austria's biggest snowmaking installation. We were there one January before any major snowfalls, and snowmaking was keeping the links open well. It did not, however, stop slush and ice forming. Several reporters also experienced great fresh powder all week in various 2005 visits.

FOR EXPERTS
Not a lot
The two black runs from Hohe Salve towards Hochsöll and Kälbersalve and the black run alongside the Brixen gondola are the only challenging pistes. There are further blacks in Scheffau and Ellmau, but the main challenges are off-piste – from Brandstadl down to Söll, for example.

boarding

Söll is a good place to try out boarding: slopes are gentle and there are plenty of gondolas and chairs. For competent boarders it's more limited – the slopes of the Ski Welt are tame. A reporter recommends the Scheffau school.

FOR INTERMEDIATES
Mainly easy runs

When blessed with good snow – not something to bank on – the Ski Welt is a paradise for early intermediates and those who love easy cruising. It is a big area and you really get a feeling of travelling around. There are lots of blue runs and many of the reds could be blue ('pale blue' says a 2005 reporter). The main challenge you may find is when the snow isn't perfect – ice and slush can make even gentle slopes seem tricky. In general the most difficult slopes are those from the mid-stations to the valleys – to Blaiken, Brixen and Söll, for example.

FOR BEGINNERS
Excellent when snow is good

The big area of nursery slopes between the main road and the gondola station is ideal when snow is abundant – gentle, spacious, uncrowded and free from good skiers whizzing past. But it can get icy or slushy. In poor snow the Hochsöll area is used. Near-beginners and fast learners can get home to the bottom station when the narrow blue from Hochsöll is not too icy.

FOR CROSS-COUNTRY
Neighbouring villages are better

Söll has 30km/19 miles of local trails but they are less interesting than those between Hopfgarten and Kelchsau or the ones around and beyond Ellmau. There is a total of 170km/105 miles in the Ski Welt area. Lack of snow-cover can be a problem.

QUEUES
Much improved

Lift upgrades have greatly improved this once queue-prone area. The gondola at Scheffau-Blaiken has cut the weekend queues there. When snow is poor, the links between Zinsberg and Eiberg get crowded. Hopefully, the new six-pack planned for 2005/06 will help matters.

MOUNTAIN RESTAURANTS
Good, but crowded

There are quite a few jolly little chalets scattered about, but we have had a few complaints of insufficient seating and long queues. The atmospheric Stöckalm (a converted cow shed), Kraftalm and Gründlalm are all near Hochsöll. The Hochsöll itself is reportedly 'excellent'. The highly rated Gasthof Hohe Salve (top of the gondola) offers a large, revolving terrace and 'stunning view', which is also accessible to non-skiers via a moving carpet. Above Brixen the Filzalm is a good place for a quick drink on the way back from the circuit. Check out our Ellmau chapter for more recommendations in that sector.

SCHOOLS AND GUIDES
More reports, please

The Söll-Hochsöll school has a fairly good reputation. But a 2005 reporter was 'not impressed' with his instructor 'who seemed to lose interest midweek'.

Söll

189

SCHOOLS

Söll-Hochsöll
t 5454

Classes
5 4-hr days: €123
Private lessons
€50 for 1hr; each
additional person €15

CHILDREN

Bobo's Mini-club
t 5454
9.45–4pm, Sat to
Thu; ages 3 to 5

Ski schools
Takes children from 5
to 14 for 4hr daily (5
days €123).

GETTING THERE

Air Salzburg 94km/58
miles (2hr); Innsbruck
73km/45 miles
(1½hr).

Rail Wörgl (13km/8
miles) or Kufstein
(15km/9 miles); bus
to resort.

ACTIVITIES

Indoor Swimming,
sauna, solarium,
massage, bowling,
squash

Outdoor Natural ice
rink (skating, curling),
sleigh rides, 3km/
2 miles of floodlit ski
and toboggan runs,
walks, paragliding

SKI WELT

Just one of over 70
mountain huts to
choose between in
the Ski Welt – but the
slope you ski down
afterwards seems
steeper than the local
norm ➔

FACILITIES FOR CHILDREN
Fast becoming a family resort
Söll has fairly wide-ranging facilities –
the Söll-Hochsöll ski kindergarten, a
Mini Club, which looks after children
aged three to five who don't want to
spend all day on the slopes, and a
special kids-only drag and slope on the
opposite side of the village to the
main lifts. Reports welcome.

STAYING THERE

HOW TO GO
Mostly cheap, cheerful gasthofs
The major mainstream tour operators
offer packages here
Hotels There is a wide choice of simple
gasthofs, pensions and B&Bs, and an
adequate amount of better-quality
hotel accommodation – mainly 3-star.
 Greil (5289) Attractive 4-star, but
out of the centre far from the lifts.
Postwirt (5081) Attractive, central,
traditional 4-star with built-in stube.
Bergland (5454) Small 3-star, well
placed between the village and lifts.
Panorama (5309) 3-star far from
lifts but with own bus stop; wonderful
views; pleasant rooms; good cakes.
Tulpe (5223) Next to the lifts.
Feldwebel (5224) Central 3-star.
Schirast (5544) Next to the lifts.
Gasthof Tenne (5282) B&B gasthof
between centre and main road.
Chalets There are few catered chalets

but a couple of big 'club hotels' run by
British tour operators.
Self-catering The central Aparthotel
Schindlhaus has nice accommodation,
though the best apartments in town
are attached to the Bergland hotel.

EATING OUT
A fair choice
Some of the best restaurants are in
hotels. The Greil and Postwirt are
good, but the Schindlhaus is said to
be the best. Giovanni does excellent
pizzas, while other places worth a visit
include the Dorfstub'n and the Venezia.

APRES-SKI
Still some very loud bars
Söll is not as raucous as it used to be,
but it's still very lively and a lot of
places have live music. The Salvenstadl
(Cow Shed) bar was recommended as
'the best with live music' by a recent
reporter. The Whisky Mühle is a large
disco that can get a little rowdy,
especially after other bars close.
Buffalo's is popular. There's a floodlit
piste and separate toboggan run – both
from top to bottom of the gondola.

OFF THE SLOPES
Not bad for a small village
You could spend a happy day in the
wonderfully equipped Panoramabad:
taking a sauna, swimming, lounging
about. The large baroque church would

be the pride of many tourist towns. There are numerous coach excursions, including trips to Salzburg, Innsbruck and even Vipiteno over in Italy.

Scheffau 745m/2,440ft

This is one of the most attractive of the Ski Welt villages.

THE RESORT
Scheffau is a rustic little place complete with pretty white church. It is spacious yet not sprawling and has a definite centre, a kilometre off the busy main road, which increases its charm at the cost of convenience – you can ski to the Ski Welt lifts at Blaiken (where there are several hotels) but need a bus to get back.

THE MOUNTAIN
Scheffau is well placed for the Ski Welt's best (and most central and snow-sure) section of pistes.

Slopes Two gondolas (including an eight-seater) give rapid access directly to Brandstadl.
Snow reliability Eiberg is the place to go when snow is poor.
Experts The pistes above Blaiken are some of the longest and steepest in the Ski Welt.
Intermediates This is as good a base as any in the area.
Beginners The nursery slope is in the village, making Scheffau a poor choice for mixed-ability parties; but a reporter rates the easy blues at Brandstadl as 'excellent for beginner snowboarders'.
Cross-country See Söll and Ellmau.
Queues The second gondola has cut weekend queues at Blaiken.
Mountain restaurants See Söll, Ellmau.
Schools and guides The school is well regarded, but groups can be large. A reporter's private snowboarding lesson was 'the best I've ever had'.
Facilities for children Both the ski kindergarten and non-ski nursery have good reputations. The children's ski area and school 'Kinder-Kaiserland' is also reported to be 'very good'. And excellent progress was made by a four-year-old at Ski Esprit's nursery.

STAYING THERE
How to go Major operators offer packages here.
Hotels The best hotels – both with pool, sauna and steam room – are the 4-star Kaiser (8000) and 3-star Alpin (85560) – 'excellent food, lots of

choice, spacious rooms'. Pool ('a bit cold') and sauna. The Wilden Kaiser (8118) – 'sauna and good fish dishes' – Blaiken (8126) and Waldhof (8122) are good value gasthofs near the gondolas. And the central Gasthof Weberbauer (8115) is said to be 'good value' and 'efficient'.
Eating out There aren't many village restaurants, and those staying in B&B places are advised to book tables. Donatello is a 'good pizza place' says a 2005 visitor
Après-ski 'Non-existent,' says one happy reporter – but another this year said the Red Bull had 'full-on hardcore music in a tent'. The usual reporganised events such as bowling and tobogganing are available.
Off the slopes Walking apart, there is little to do. Tour operators organise trips to Innsbruck and Salzburg.

Hopfgarten 620m/2,030ft

Hopfgarten is an unspoiled, friendly, traditional resort off the main road.

THE RESORT
The village is a good size: small enough to be intimate, large enough to have plenty of off-slope amenities. Most hotels are within five minutes' walk of the lift to Rigi.

THE MOUNTAIN
Hopfgarten is at the western extremity of the Ski Welt.
Slopes Hopfgarten offers queue-free access to Rigi and Hohe Salve – the high point of the main Ski Welt circuit.
Terrain-parks None locally but it's a short bus-ride to Westendorf, where there is a park, or Kelchsau, where there is a half-pipe.
Snow reliability The resort's great weakness is the poor snow quality on the south-west-facing home slope.
Experts Experts should venture off-piste for excitement.
Intermediates When snow is good, the runs down to Hopfgarten and the nearby villages of Brixen and Itter are some of the best in the Ski Welt.
Beginners There is a beginners' slope in the village, but it is sunny as well as low; lack of snow-cover means paying for a lift pass to higher slopes.
Snowboarding The Ski Welt is best suited to free-riding the extensive intermediate slopes.
Cross-country Hopfgarten is one of the best cross-country bases in the area.

Phone numbers
Calling long-distance
Add the prefix given below for each resort. When calling from abroad use the country code 43 and omit the initial 0.

Söll
05333
Scheffau
05358
Hopfgarten
05335
Itter
05335
Brixen
05334
Ski Welt TO
05358

There are fine trails to Kelchsau (11km/7 miles) and Niederau (15km/9 miles), and the Itter-Bocking loop (15km/9 miles) starts nearby. Westendorf's trails are close.

Queues Now that the promised eight-seat gondola is up and running, morning queues to leave the village should be a thing of the past.

Mountain restaurants See Söll.

Schools and guides Partly because Hopfgarten seems to attract large numbers of Australians, English is widely spoken in the two schools.

Facilities for children Hopfgarten is a family resort, with a nursery and ski kindergarten.

STAYING THERE

How to go Cheap and cheerful gasthofs, pensions and little private B&Bs are the norm here.

Hotels The comfortable hotels Hopfgarten (3920) and Sporthotel Fuchs (2420) are both well placed for the main lift.

Eating out Most of the restaurants are hotel-based, but there are exceptions, including a Chinese and a pizzeria.

Après-ski Après-ski is generally quiet, though a lively holiday can usually be ensured if you go with Aussie-dominated Contiki Travel.

Off the slopes Off-slope amenities include swimming, riding, bowling, skating, tobogganing and paragliding. The railway makes trips to Salzburg, Innsbruck and Kitzbühel possible.

Itter 700m/2,300ft

Itter is a tiny village halfway around the mountain between Söll and Hopfgarten, with nursery slopes close to hand and a gondola just outside the village into the Ski Welt, via Hochsöll.

There's a hotel and half a dozen gasthofs and B&Bs. The school has a rental shop, and when conditions are good this is a good beginners' resort.

Brixen 800m/2,620ft

It may not be pretty, but Brixen has a queue-free, high-capacity gondola up to the main Ski Welt slopes.

THE RESORT

Brixen im Thale is a very scattered roadside village at the south-east edge of the Ski Welt, close to Westendorf. The main hotels are near the railway station, a bus-ride from the lifts.

THE MOUNTAIN

Brixen is on the south side of the main Ski Welt circuit, and a short bus-ride from separate Westendorf.

Slopes The gondola takes you to Hochbrixen, where lifts diverge for Hohe Salve and Söll, or Astberg and Ellmau. There's a small area of north-facing runs, including nursery slopes, on the other side of the village. This year a regular visitor reported a nasty incident involving a liftie who was inside his hut and therefore failed to stop a chair-lift when her 10-year-old son slipped and fell under it and who then threw her son at the seat of the chair. We hope this was a one-off.

Terrain-parks None locally but there's a good park nearby at Westendorf.

Snow reliability A chain of snow-guns on the main south-facing piste helps to preserve the snow as long as possible and the area continues to benefit from major investment in snowmaking.

Experts The black run alongside the Brixen gondola is one of the few challenging pistes in the area.

Intermediates When snow is good, Brixen has some of the best slopes in the Ski Welt – including some challenging ones.

Beginners The nursery slopes are secluded and shady, but meeting up with friends for lunch is a hassle – the area is a bus-ride from the village.

Snowboarding See Söll.

Cross-country In addition to valley-floor trails, a 5km/3 mile loop up the mountain at Hochbrixen provides fine views and fairly reliable snow.

Queues Lift upgrades have improved the once queue-prone area.

Mountain restaurants The Filzalm above Brixen has been recommended.

Schools and guides The ski school runs the usual group classes, and mini-groups for five to seven people.

Facilities for children There is an all-day ski kindergarten.

STAYING THERE

How to go There are plenty of hotels and pensions.

Hotels Alpenhof (88320) and Sporthotel (8191) are both 4-stars with pools.

Eating out Mainly hotel-based, but the restaurant opposite the gondola has been recommended.

Après-ski Après-ski is quiet, but livelier Westendorf is a short taxi-ride.

Off the slopes Activities include tennis, hotel-based spa facilities and days out to Salzburg, Innsbruck and Kitzbühel.

TOURIST OFFICES

Söll
t 5216
info@soell.com
www.soell.at

Scheffau
t 7373
scheffau@skiwelt.at
www.scheffau.com

Hopfgarten
t 2322
info@hopfgarten.tirol.at
www.hopfgarten.at

Itter
t 2670
itter@skiwelt.at
www.itter.at

Brixen
t 8433
brixen@skiwelt.at
www.brixenimthale.at

Ski Welt
t 505
info@skiwelt.at
www.skiwelt.at

St Anton

Non-stop on- and off-slope action and pretty village base

COSTS

①②③④⑤⑥

RATINGS

The slopes
Fast lifts	***
Snow	****
Extent	****
Expert	*****
Intermediate	***
Beginner	*
Convenience	***
Queues	**
Mountain restaurants	***

The rest
Scenery	***
Resort charm	****
Off-slope	***

NEWS

For 2005/06 the overcrowded run down from the Steissbachtal to the village is to be improved to make it easier – though the overcrowding seems unlikely to be affected. A fast six-pack with covers and heated seats is to replace the Valfagehr triple chair from Alpe Rauz towards St Anton.

For 2004/05 the terrain-park on Rendl was improved to include areas for beginners. Next to it is the 'Fly In Rendl' development – a fun-sport, service and testing centre.

In St Christoph, a luxury health club and spa centre opened in the 5-star Hospiz hotel.

+ Extensive, varied slopes for experts and adventurous intermediates, with more to explore in Lech-Zürs, a bus-ride away

+ Heavy snowfalls, backed up by a fair amount of snowmaking

+ Very lively après-ski, from mid-afternoon onward

+ Despite expansion, the resort retains some traditional charm – and the animated village centre is mainly car-free

+ Improved lift system has made Nasserein a popular base and reduced queuing problems, but ...

– Still some serious lift queues, at resort level and at mid-mountain

– Slopes far from ideal for beginners or timid intermediates

– Most of the tough stuff is off-piste – and the distinction between piste and off-piste is unhelpfully blurred

– Pistes can get very crowded – some of them dangerously so

– Main slopes get a lot of sun, quickly affecting the snow conditions

– Resort spreads widely, with some long treks to key lifts and bars

– Can get rowdy, with noisy drunks in the central streets in the early hours

St Anton is undeniably a big-league resort. For competent skiers and riders with an appetite for non-stop action and the stamina to keep up with it, we'd rate it even higher: it is one of the great resorts, with an après-ski scene that can be as taxing as the splendid bowls below the Valluga. The combination draws ski bums from around the world, as well as lots of regular holiday visitors.

But it won't suit everyone, as our list of **–** points makes clear. Many people who might be thinking of trying an Austrian change from Val-d'Isère, or of taking a step up from Kitzbühel, are liable be put off by this list, and rightly so. The St Anton formula works brilliantly for some people, but very badly for others.

The 2001 Alpine World Ski Championships have left a legacy that is worthwhile, but not quite the transformation that is advertised. The improved lifts to Gampen have eased the queues and given the suburb of Nasserein a huge boost. The Arlberg-well.com leisure/conference centre is excellent, but looks as dreary as its name sounds silly. Shifting the divisive railway line across the river has certainly simplified access to the lifts, but in its place is a bit of a vacuum.

And nothing was done about St Anton's biggest problem – the spectacularly overcrowded piste down the Steissbachtal and on down to the village. For the last three years we've been saying 'the improvement that is most needed is a new piste or two back to the village from Galzig'. The improvements planned for this year sound like tinkering with the problem.

THE RESORT

St Anton is at the foot of the road up to the Arlberg pass, at the eastern end of a lift network that spreads across to St Christoph and across the pass to Stuben. The resort is a long, sprawling mixture of traditional and modern buildings crammed into a narrow valley. It used to be sandwiched between a busy road and the mainline railway – but the railway was moved in 2000, and where there were tracks there is now a little area of parkland.

Although it is crowded and commercialised, St Anton is full of character, its traffic-free main street lined by traditional-style buildings. It is an attractively bustling place, day and night. Several reporters have observed that it has better-than-usual everyday shopping with a 'wonderful Spar'.

The main hub of the resort is around the base stations of the two-stage cable-car up via Galzig to Valluga Grat and the fast quad chair up to Gampen. The attractive, lively main street and its hotels are only a short

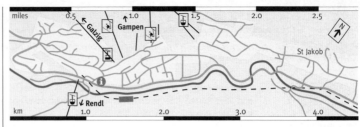

AUSTRIA

194

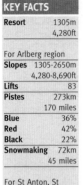
walk from these lifts, and for most purposes a location on or close to this main street is ideal.

The resort spreads down the valley, thinning out before broadening again to form the suburb of Nasserein. This backwater now has an eight-person gondola up to Gampen, and makes an appealing base for a quiet time. The nightlife action is a short bus-ride or 15-minute walk away ('quite a hike'). Staying between St Anton centre and Nasserein is also a more attractive idea since the Fang chair-lift, which gives access to the Nasserein gondola, was built.

On the other side of the main road a gondola goes up to the Rendl area. This is linked one-way by rope tows and a moving carpet from the end of St Anton's main street – but the return still involves a bus-ride or short walk.

St Anton spreads up the hill to the west of the centre, towards the Arlberg pass – first to Oberdorf, then Gastig, 10 minutes' walk from the centre. Further up the hill are the suburbs of Dengert and Moos – a long way out, but quite close to the slopes.

Regular buses go to Stuben, Zürs and Lech (all described in the Lech chapter) and the much less well-known but worthwhile Sonnenkopf area above Klösterle. These buses can get crowded early and late in the day and have provoked several complaints by reporters this year ('a complete nightmare', wrote one). Minibus-style taxis can be economic if widely shared.

Serfaus, Nauders, Ischgl and Sölden are also feasible outings by car.

THE MOUNTAINS

The main slopes are essentially open: only the run from Rendl to the valley offers much shelter from bad weather.

St Anton vies with Val-d'Isère for the title of 'resort with most underclassified slopes'. There are plenty of red pistes that would be black in many other resorts, and plenty of blues that would be red.

Many of the most popular steep runs marked on the piste map are classified as 'ski routes'. These have widely spaced markers, they may be groomed occasionally in part, but they

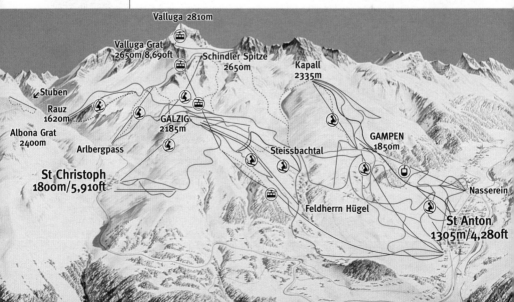

boarding

Though steeped in skiing tradition, St Anton is moving with the times and improving facilities for boarders. Although we don't really recommend it to beginners, for good boarders it is one of the best free-ride areas in the world, with lots of steep terrain and natural hits. There are still a few T-bars around but fast chair-lifts are now the main ways around the mountains. The Arlberg ski school has a special Snowboard Academy section. Rendl mountain is the place to experience park life.

are not patrolled and are protected from avalanches only 'in the immediate vicinity of the markers'.

Clearly you should not ski such runs alone, and the piste map recommends them only for people with 'alpine experience or with a ski instructor'. In theory this puts these routes out of bounds for many holidaymakers, but in practice many tackle them without the services of an instructor. One reader sums up the problem with admirable clarity: 'It is entirely unreasonable to expect everyone to take guides on these routes, and it seems irresponsible to ignore the fact that people will go on them. On some of the ski routes there were snow-guns. This doesn't fit with the idea that you're on your own.' A recent reporter comments: 'Ski routes offer endless possibilities for competent skiers and yet the authorities seem to leave them open or tape them off with no apparent consistent logic. There seems to be no indication of snow conditions off-piste, leaving the possibility of a crisis developing from a little adventure.' Another reader points out

that the routes vary from 'an easy red to a double-black-diamond nightmare'. On Rendl there is a lift serving no pistes but only a single ski route. The situation is, to quote another reader, 'absurd'.

Until 1999, the piste map also showed several 'high-alpine touring runs' not marked on the ground at all, and not protected against avalanche. Only one now appears on the map, though many runs of this kind are still shown over in Lech and Stuben. Read the Lech chapter for more on these.

The Arlberg piste map has long been a source of complaint. The basic problem is that the Arlberg lift companies appear determined to present all their terrain in a single view, despite the fact that it consists of four separate lift networks. For last season the map was redesigned, so that even distant isolated Sonnenkopf is now part of the main map. In terms of clarity, some parts are better – notably Galzig – but some are worse.

Fortunately the on-mountain maps and signs are clearer – although a 2005 visitor singles out those on Galzig as confusing. Reporters regularly complain of poor and limited piste grooming. The local cable TV, showing the state of some of the pistes and queues, can be very useful.

THE SLOPES
Large linked area
St Anton's slopes fall into three main sectors, two of them linked.

The major sector is that beneath the local high-spot, the **Valluga**, accessed by cable-car via **Galzig**. The tiny top stage of the cable-car to the Valluga itself is mainly for sightseeing – you can take skis or a board up only if you have a guide to lead you down the tricky off-piste run to Zürs. The slightly lower station of Valluga Grat gives access to St Anton's famous high, sunny bowls, and to the long, beautiful red/blue run to Rauz, at the western end of St Anton's own slopes. From

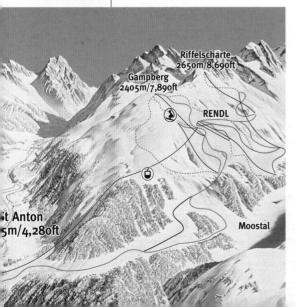

Riffelscharte
2650m/8,690ft

Gampberg
2405m/7,890ft

RENDL

St Anton
5m/4,28oft

Moostal

↑ The heart of St Anton's slopes – the Schindler Spitze, below the Valluga

JILL COOK

LIFT PASSES

Arlberg Ski Pass
Covers all St Anton, St Christoph, Lech, Zürs and Stuben lifts, and linking bus between Rauz and Zürs.

Beginners
Points ticket

Main pass
1 day €39
6 days €184

Senior citizens
Over 65 (60 for women): 6 days €160
Over 75: €10

Children
Under 20: 6 days €160
Under 16: 6 days €111
Under 8: €10

Notes
Single ascent, half-day and afternoon 'taster' tickets available. Pass also covers Sonnenkopf (10 lifts) at Klösterle, 7km/4 miles west of Stuben (free bus link from Stuben).

here you can go on to explore the rather neglected slopes of Stuben.

All of these high runs can also be accessed by riding the Schindlergrat triple chair. Other runs from Galzig go south-west to St Christoph and east into the Steissbachtal. Most of the runs in this whole sector funnel into this 'Happy Valley', producing incredible congestion, especially late in the day – see 'Queues'.

Beyond this valley, with lift and piste links in both directions, is the **Gampen-Kapall** sector, reachable by chair-lift from central St Anton or gondola from Nasserein. From Gampen at mid-mountain, pistes lead back to St Anton and Nasserein. Or you can ride a six-pack on up to Kapall to ski the treeless upper mountain.

A handful of lifts (including a fast six-pack to Gampberg) serve the west-facing runs at the top of **Rendl**, with a single north-facing piste returning to the gondola bottom station.

TERRAIN-PARKS
Head for Rendl
On Rendl, just below the top of the gondola, is St Anton's only terrain-park. Recently improved, it includes a half-pipe, quarter-pipe, jumps, rail slides and a washboard (several

humps in a row), some of which are now suitable for beginners. The new 'Fly in Rendl' centre offers park and pipe workshops.

SNOW RELIABILITY
Generally very good cover
If the weather is coming from the west or north-west (as it often is), the Arlberg gets it first, and as a result St Anton and its neighbours get heavy falls of snow. They often have much better conditions than other resorts of a similar height, and we've had great fresh powder here as late as mid-April. But many of the slopes face south or south-east, causing icy or heavy conditions at times. It's vital to time descents of the steeper runs off the Valluga to get decent conditions.

The lower runs are now well equipped with snowmaking, which generally ensures the home runs remain open. As a recent April visitor said, 'Pistes were kept open while surrounded by green fields.'

FOR EXPERTS
One of the world's great areas
St Anton vies with Chamonix, Val-d'Isère and a handful of other resorts for the affections of experts. There are countless opportunities for going off-

THE VALLUGA RUNS

The off-piste runs in the huge bowl beneath the summit of the Valluga, reached by either the Schindlergrat chair or the Valluga I cable-car, are justifiably world-famous. In good snow, this whole area is an off-piste delight for experts.

Except immediately after a fresh snowfall, you can see tracks going all over the mountain. There are two main ski routes marked on the piste map – both long, steep descents that quickly get mogulled. The Schindlerkar is the first you come to and it divides into two – the Schindlerkar gully being the steeper option. For the second, wider and somewhat easier Mattun run, you traverse further at the top. Both these feed down into the Steissbachtal gully where there are lifts back up to Galzig and Gampen. The Schweinströge – a high-alpine route no longer shown on the map – starts off in the same direction as the red run to Rauz, but you traverse the shoulder of the Schindler Spitze and descend a narrow gully.

The Arlberg region is an off-piste skier's dream – renowned for its consistently high snowfall record, incredible deep powder and enormous diversity of terrain. We invited Piste to Powder Mountain Guides to give us an introduction to the possibilities. Remember you should never explore far off-piste without a guide.

Runs from Rendl

After initial practice close to the pistes, the natural progression is to go beyond the furthest lift to access the wide rolling bowls of powder of Rossfall.

More serious routes from Rendl take you well away from all lifts. The North Face, accessed from the Gampberg six-seat chair, offers challenging terrain to the intermediate/confident off-piste skier. The Riffel chair-lifts access the imposing Hinter Rendl – a gigantic high-mountain bowl offering a huge descent down to St Anton, often in deep powder. A variant involves a climb to Rendl Scharte and a demanding descent with sections of 35° down the remote Malfontal to the village of Pettneu and a taxi back to St Anton.

Runs from Albona, above Stuben

Stuben's outstanding terrain, reached from the Albonagrat chair, is suited to the more experienced off-piste skier, as the descents are long. The open tree lines of the Langen forest, where the powder is regularly knee to waist deep, form some of the world's finest tree skiing. A 30-minute climb from Albonagrat, with skis on shoulder, opens up further outstanding terrain from Maroikopfe – either west, down undulating open slopes to Langen, or east, down steep 40° slopes to Ferwalltal, where this glorious run ends with a glass of wine at an old hunting lodge.

Runs from the Valluga

The legendary runs from the summit cable-car of the Valluga must be on the tick list of all keen and experienced off-piste skiers – the North Face, Bridge Couloir or East Couloir. Your pulse will race as you trace a steep ski line between cliff bands in the breathtaking scenery of the Pazieltal, leading down to Zürs. Here, at the top of the Madloch chair-lift and after a short hidden climb, you will be roped down into the steep Valhalla Couloir, accessing 1200m/3,940ft vertical of open slopes ending in the hamlet of Zug, close to Lech.

Piste to Powder
Mountain Guides
St. Anton – Austria

**Piste to Powder
Mountain Guides**

All day guiding 9am – 5pm. Choose from four skill levels. All safety equipment provided.

t 01661 824318
00 43 664 174 6282

info@pistetopowder. com
www.pistetopowder. com

St Anton

197

piste and guidance is very desirable. It has some of the most consistently challenging and extensive slopes in the world. The jewel in the crown is the off-piste terrain in the bowls beneath the Valluga – see feature panel. The ultimate challenge, perhaps, is to go with a guide off the back of the Valluga – see the Piste to Powder panel, above. Reporters who have tried this have loved it.

Lower down, there are challenging runs in many directions from both Galzig and Gampen-Kapall. These lower runs can be doubly tricky if the snow has been hit by the sun. Ski route 13 (Arlenmahder chair) is 'scary' writes a 2005 reporter – it follows a 'narrow, mogulled gully', rocky and exposed in parts.

The Rendl area across the road has plenty of open space beneath the top lifts and there is some delightful fun to be had on runs off the back of this ridge, away from the lift system – again, see panel above.

One of our reporters particularly liked the Sonnenkopf area down-valley from Stuben for its excellent off-piste route to Langen. See also the Stuben section at the end of the Lech chapter.

The few black pistes offer genuine challenges. These include the World Championship race courses – Kandahar from Kapall down to Gampen and the previously red Fang run from there down to the village.

On top of all this, bear in mind that many of the red runs on the piste map are long and challenging, too.

SCHOOLS

Arlberg
t 3411

St Anton
t 3563

Classes
(Arlberg prices)
6 days (2½hr am and
2hr pm) €199

Private lessons
€209 for full day;
each additional
person €18

GUIDES

Piste to Powder
t 0664 174 6282,
UK 01661 824318

Phone numbers
From elsewhere in
Austria add the prefix
05446.
From abroad use the
prefix +43 5446.

FOR INTERMEDIATES
Some real challenges
St Anton is well suited to good,
adventurous intermediates. They will
be able to try the Mattun run and the
easier version of the Schindlerkar run
from Valluga Grat (see feature panel).
The run from Schindler Spitze to Rauz
is very long (over 1000m/3,300ft
vertical), varied and ideal for good
(and fit) intermediates. Alternatively,
turn off from this part-way down and
take the Steissbachtal to the lifts back
to Galzig. The Kapall-Gampen section
is also interesting, with sporty bumps
among trees on the lower half. Good
intermediates may enjoy the men's
downhill run from the top to town.

Timid intermediates will find St
Anton less to their taste. There are few
easy cruising pistes. The most obvious
are the short blues on Galzig and the
Steissbachtal (aka 'Happy Valley').
These are reasonably gentle but get
uncomfortably crowded (see 'Queues').
The blue to St Christoph is generally
quieter and a 'wonderful confidence-
booster.' The narrowish blues between
Kapall and Gampen can have some
challenging bumps. For the best easy
cruising, take the bus to Lech.

In the Rendl area a variety of trails
suitable for good and moderate
intermediates criss-cross, including a
lovely long tree-lined run (over
1000m/3,300ft vertical from the top)
back to the valley gondola station.
This is the best run in the whole area
when visibility is poor, though it has
some quite awkward sections.

FOR BEGINNERS
Far from ideal
St Anton has better nursery slopes
now, near the Fang lift. But there are
no easy, uncrowded runs for beginners
to progress to. A mixed party of
experts, intermediates and novices
would be better off staying in Lech or

Zürs; those who want to explore St
Anton can get on the bus to Rauz.

FOR CROSS-COUNTRY
Limited interest
St Anton is not a great cross-country
resort, but trails total around 35km/
22 miles and snow conditions are
usually good. There are a couple of
uninspiring trails near town, another at
St Jakob 3km/2 miles away, and a
pretty trail through trees along the
Ferwalltal to the foot of the Albona
area. There is also a tiny loop at St
Christoph.

QUEUES
Improved, but still a problem
Queues are not the problem they once
were, since the replacement of several
lifts by fast chairs. But they can still be
tiresome in peak season and at
weekends. Recent reporters found long
queues for the cable-car to Galzig (one
2005 group barely made progress in
20 minutes, and gave up) and one hit
'massive' queues for the chair to
Gampen, which attracts crowds when
higher lifts are closed. At mid-
mountain, queues for the Schindlergrat
chair appear to have been eased by
the fast Arlenmähder chair allowing
access to the run to Rauz without
going to the top. The Zammermoos
chair out of the Steissbachtal can
generate short queues. There are US-
style 'singles lines' at some lifts; but,
despite taped exhortations in several
languages, the chairs are rarely filled.

Perhaps more of a worry than the
lift queues are the crowded pistes.
Clearly the worst has been the
Steissbachtal and the home run below
it, which can be uncomfortably
crowded even in January and a
nightmare on a peak weekend. So
acute has this problem been that
several reporters have recommended
heading down to Rauz or St Christoph

CHILDREN

Kindergarten
t 3451
From age 30mnth;
must be toilet trained

Ski schools
Both Austrian schools
take children aged
from 5 (6 days
including lunch €277
at Arlberg school)

and getting a bus back to town rather than tangling with the Steissbachtal. There is no sign of a proper solution to this long-standing problem, despite promised improvements to the piste for 2005/06.

MOUNTAIN RESTAURANTS
Plenty of choice
We often end up lunching in St Christoph at the atmospheric Hospiz Alm, famed for its slide down to the toilets as well as its food. It isn't cheap but most reporters love it – 'couldn't have chosen anywhere more cheering', 'excellent food and service'. Traxl's ice bar at the Maiensee Hotel, has also been recommended. Other recommendations include the self-service restaurant at Galzig for 'superb views and tasty food', Sennhütte on the Galzig home run ('excellent choices') and recently extended Rodelalm on Gampen: 'A real hut with good food at low prices and a lovely fire', 'great knuckles of pork'. Slightly lower still on Galzig, the Mooserwirt serves typical Austrian food at what seems a high price, but 'the portions are absolutely massive'; the Heustadl is 'getting very popular'; the Krazy Kanguruh does burgers, pizzas and snacks, as does Amalis in the village ('excellent salads' too); Taps Bar next door does 'good goulash soup'.
Over on Rendl, the self-service Rendl restaurant offers 'excellent food and value' and 'great views' with zero queuing even when busy. Bifang-Alm, near the end of the run to the valley, is 'friendly and atmospheric'.

SCHOOLS AND GUIDES
Mixed reports
The St Anton school and the Arlberg school are now under the same ownership but continue to operate separately. The Arlberg school generates conflicting reports: One reporter commented, 'Not enough attention was paid to putting equal standards together and groups were big.' Another complained of old-fashioned technique: 'They need to turn the clock forward.' But some reporters were very happy: 'Children and parents were delighted.' Another reader joined a top-level guided group and was impressed with the 'superb value' and 'non-stop high mileage covered'. We have skied with excellent guides from Piste to Powder, a specialist off-piste outfit run by British guide Graham Austick, and have had good reports from readers – 'A good balance of guiding to instruction and a professional attitude to safety,' writes a 2005 reporter. We also have reports of tour ops being stopped from supplying their own ski host to show guests around the pistes unless they hire an instructor too.

FACILITIES FOR CHILDREN
Getting better
The youth centre attached to the Arlberg school is excellent, and the special slopes both for toddlers (at the bottom) and bigger children (at Gampen) are well done. At Nasserein there is a moving carpet lift on the baby slope, and a reporter rates this an 'absolutely ideal' place to stay with young kids.

St Anton

199

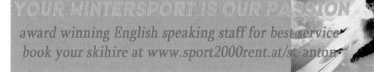

GETTING THERE

Air Innsbruck
100km/62 miles
(1½hr); Zürich
200km/124 miles
(3hr); Friedrichshafen
140km/87 miles
(1½hr).

Rail Mainline station
in resort.

AUSTRIA

200

WEBSITES

For links to resort
sites, go to our own
new site at
www.wtss.co.uk

JILL COOK

St Christoph makes a
rather isolated base,
but has one or two
splendid spots for
lunch ↓

STAYING THERE

HOW TO GO
Austria's main chalet resort
There's a wide range of places to stay,
from quality hotels to cheap and
cheerful pensions and apartments.
Chalets Plenty of catered chalets are
offered by UK operators. Nasserein
makes a convenient chalet base.

Hotels There is one 5-star hotel and
lots of 4- and 3-stars and B&Bs.
((((5) **Raffl's St Antoner Hof** (2910)
Best in town, but its position on the
bypass is less than ideal. Pool.
((((4) **Schwarzer Adler** (22440)
Centuries-old inn on main street.
Widely varying bedrooms.
((((4) **Alte Post** (2553) Atmospheric
place on main street with lively après-
ski bar. Endorsed by a reporter.
((((4) **Post** (2213) Comfortable if
uninspiring 4-star at the centre of
affairs, close to both lifts and nightlife.
((((4) **Sporthotel** (3111) Central position,
varied bedrooms, good food. Pool.
(((3) **Grischuna** (2304) Welcoming and
family-run in peaceful position up the
hill west of town; close to the slopes.

(((3) **Goldenes Kreuz** (22110)
A comfortable B&B hotel halfway to
Nasserein, ideal for cruising home.
(((3) **Nassereinhof** (3366) Close to the
Nasserein gondola. Family-run with
sauna and steam room. Recommended
for 'good home-cooked food'.
Other recommendations include: Haus
Pirker (2310), and the Rendlhof (3100)
a 'friendly' B&B in Nasserein.
Self-catering There are plenty of
apartments available but package
deals are few and far between. The
Bachmann apartments near the
Nasserein gondola received rave
reviews again this year ('really
excellent', 'spacious and comfortable').

EATING OUT
Mostly informal
Places such as the Trödlerstube and
Reselhof serve big portions of traditional
Austrian food. Fuhrmannstube is 'quiet,
relaxed and popular with the locals'.
The village museum's restaurant does
upmarket food and wine in elegant
panelled rooms. Quite different in style
is Ben.venuto ('good food', 'friendly
staff'), in the Arlberg-well.com building:
stark decor, eclectic menu and
excellent cooking. Scotty's and
Pomodoro have been endorsed by a
2005 reporter for pizza, and the Train
for fondue. The cosy Sonnbichl is
recommended for its 'superb home-
cooked food'. In Nasserein, the Tenne
is noted for game dishes, while Alt St
Anton is a cosy chalet doing a good
range of excellent traditional dishes.

APRES-SKI
Throbbing till late
St Anton's bars rock from mid-
afternoon until the early hours. Après-
ski starts in a collection of bars on the
slopes above the village. The Krazy
Kanguruh is probably the most famous,
but the Mooserwirt is now the 'in'
place, filling up with revellers as soon

ACTIVITIES

Indoor Swimming pool (also hotel pools open to the public, with sauna and massage), fitness centre, tennis, squash, bowling, museum, cinema in Vallugasaal

Outdoor Swimming pool, cleared walking paths, natural ice rink (skating, curling), sleigh rides, snow-shoeing, tobogganing, paragliding

TOURIST OFFICES

St Anton
t 22690
info@stantonam
arlberg.com
www.stantonamarlberg.
com

St Christoph
www.tiscover.com/
st.christoph

as the lunch trade finishes – reputedly dispensing more beer than any other bar in Austria. The Griabli opposite has 'great live rock music' and is almost as popular. All this is followed by a slide down the piste in the dark. The bars in town are in full swing by 4pm, too. Most are lively, with loud music; sophisticates looking for a quieter time are less well provided for. The Underground has live music (and does 'super ribs'), but gets packed. Equally popular are the Hazienda and, for late-night dancing, Stanton. The Picadilly is said to be 'a bit sad' and seems to have lost out to the other venues. Recent reporters have recommended Scotty's (in Mark Warner's chalet-hotel Rosanna, with extended happy hour), Bar Cuba (when Scotty's closes), Jacksy's, Pub 37, Bobo's, Alibi and Funky Chicken. In Nasserein, Tom Dooley's is 'relaxed and welcoming' and the Sonnegg is recommended.

OFF THE SLOPES
Some improvement
St Anton is a resort for keen skiers and riders. But the fitness, swimming and skating facilities of Arlberg-well.com are impressive and were enjoyed by

two 2005 reporters. The village is lively during the day, with a fair selection of shops. Getting by bus to the other Arlberg resorts is easy, as is visiting Innsbruck by train. Many of the best mountain huts are not readily accessible by lift for pedestrians. A reporter suggests using the winter walking trails to visit Pettneu.

STAYING DOWN THE VALLEY
Nice and quiet
Beyond Nasserein is St Jakob. It can be reached on snow, but is dependent on the free shuttle-bus in the morning. Pettneu is a quiet village further down the valley, with slopes that suit beginners most. It's best for drivers.

St Christoph 1800m/5,910ft

A small, exclusive collection of pricey hotels, restaurants and bars right by the Arlberg Pass, with drag-lifts for local slopes and a fast quad chair-lift to the heart of St Anton's slopes. It's quiet at night. The best hotel of all is the huge 5-star Arlberg-Hospiz (2611), with luxurious new health and spa facilities. Recommended by a reporter for expensive but fine gourmet dining.

St Anton

201

Individual holidays for individual people.

01276 61072
0871 666 1259
www.skistanton.net

SKI ST.ANTON

St Johann in Tirol

Relax on easy runs with plenty of pit stops and friendly locals

COSTS

① ② ③ ④ ⑤ ⑥

HOW IT RATES

The slopes

Fast lifts	**
Snow	**
Extent	*
Expert	*
Intermediate	***
Beginner	****
Convenience	***
Queues	****
Mountain restaurants	****

The rest

Scenery	***
Resort charm	***
Off-slope	****

NEWS

Night skiing off the Hochfeld chair was introduced on Monday, Wednesday and Friday evenings in 2005.

Spa facilities were added to the leisure centre.

+ Traditional traffic-free town centre

+ Lots of good mountain restaurants

+ Plenty of off-slope activities

+ Easy to visit neighbouring resorts, covered by the lift pass

+ Relatively good snow record

− Small area, with little to interest experts or keen piste-bashing intermediates

− Can be crowded on peak weekends, or when nearby resorts with less reliable snow are suffering

This friendly resort is an attractive place for beginners and leisurely part-timers who like to spend as much time having drinks and lunch as they do actually cruising the slopes. Keener and more proficient skiers and boarders will soon get bored unless they are prepared to visit surrounding resorts – nearby ones covered by the local pass, others by the Kitzbüheler Alpenskipass.

THE RESORT

St Johann is a sizeable valley town where life doesn't revolve entirely around skiing. Reporters emphasise the friendliness of the locals. The attractive traffic-free centre, where most of the hotels are found, is wedged between a railway track, main roads and rivers. The main access lift from the village is a gondola to the top; it's about a ten-minute walk from the centre, including a level crossing and walking beside a busy road. But there is the alternative of staying in hotels near the lift base. There is also accommodation in the hamlet of Eichenhof to the east, with drag-lifts into the slopes.

The local pass covers several other resorts to the north and east; Fieberbrunn and Waidring's Steinplatte are particularly worth a visit. The Kitzbüheler Alpenskipass covers the whole region, and Kitzbühel itself is only 10 minutes by car or train.

THE MOUNTAINS

St Johann's local slopes are on the north-facing side of the Kitzbüheler Horn – the 'back' side of Kitzbühel's 'second' and smaller mountain.

Slopes From the top of the gondola a choice of north-facing pistes lead back through the trees towards town – mainly reds on the upper mountain, blues lower down. A sunnier sector of west-facing pistes lead down to another gondola at Oberndorf.

Terrain-parks There is a half-pipe at the Eichenhof lift and a jumps area above the Hochfeld chairs.

Snow reliability St Johann gets more snow than neighbouring Kitzbühel and the Ski Welt, and this, together with its largely north-facing slopes, means that it often has better conditions. It also has substantial snowmaking.

Experts There is nothing here to challenge an expert. The long black run on the piste map is really a moderate red. Off-piste is limited.

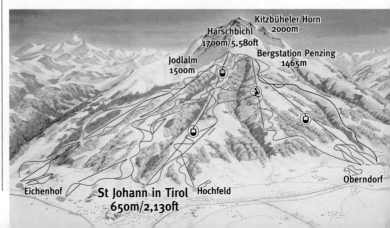

↑ Off-slope facilities
are excellent

TVB ST JOHANN IN TIROL

KEY FACTS

Resort	650m
	2,130ft
Slopes	670-1700m
	2,200-5,580ft
Lifts	17
Pistes	60km
	37 miles
Blue	41%
Red	47%
Black	12%
Snowmaking	28km
	17 miles

WEBSITES

For links to resort
sites, go to our own
new site at
www.wtss.co.uk

Phone numbers
From elsewhere in
Austria add the prefix
05352.
From abroad use the
prefix +43 5352.

TOURIST OFFICE

t 63335
info@stjohanntirol.at
www.stjohanntirol.at

Intermediates The slopes are varied. But keen piste-bashers will ski them all in a day and are likely to want to go on to explore nearby resorts. Decent intermediates have a fairly direct-running piste between Harschbichl and town, plus the black mentioned above. There are some easier red runs on the top part of the mountain, but the best (3a and 4b) are served by slow lifts. The Penzing red piste is served by a fast quad. The less adventurous can take gentle pistes from the mid-station of the village gondola.

Beginners Most beginners rate St Johann highly, but one dissenting voice this year says the nursery slopes at Eichenhof are a bit steep, while those who start from Hochfeld have to ride a tricky chair once off the nursery slope.

Snowboarding It's drag-lifts or nothing on the nursery slopes.

Cross-country Given good snow, St Johann is one of the best cross-country resorts in Austria. The wide variety of trails totals 75km/47 miles.

Queues Rare except at peak times – but slow lifts is a common complaint.

Mountain restaurants With 14 restaurants spread over its small area, St Johann must have the highest hut density in Europe. All those tried by one recent reporter had 'excellent food – especially the Hochfeld'. Harschbichlhütte is also recommended for 'excellent gulaschsuppe'. Our favourite is the Angerer Alm, just above the gondola mid-station, with good local food and an amazing wine cellar. Basgeigeralm is a rustic restaurant on the Oberndorf side.

Schools and guides The instructors of the St Johann school continue to impress reporters, but in the past we have heard of large classes and 'dreadful management and organisation'. No such problems with the new Wilder Kaiser school, though, rated 'very highly' again this year.

Facilities for children The village nursery, geared to the needs of workers rather than visitors, offers exceptionally long hours.

STAYING THERE

How to go British tour operators concentrate on hotels, but there are numerous apartments available.

Hotels All hotels are 3- or 4-star. There are dozens of B&B pensions. The 4-star Sporthotel Austria (62507) is near the lift, with pool, sauna and steam. The Post (62230) is a 13th-century inn on the main street – 'By far the nicest,' says a regular. 2005 visitors recommend the Park (62226), 'very well run, very friendly, food enjoyable and plentiful'. The Fischer (62332) is central, with 'friendly and helpful staff' and 'excellent' food.

Self-catering There are plenty of apartments to rent.

Eating out A 2005 reporter found 'plenty of places to eat', including good Italian food at the Rustica and Chinese at the Lange Mauer. Villa Masianco is said to be 'lovely' and 'very good value'. The Huber-Bräu brewery serves good food but closes early. For a special meal, locals recommend the Ambiente.

Après-ski Ice bars and tea dancing greet you as you come off the slopes – Max Pub at the bottom of the main piste has 'free-flowing alcohol and blaring euro-pop'. In town there are lots of bars that reporters have enjoyed, including Bunny's Pub with its 'good, alternative music' and 'youthful crowd'. Tour op reps organise outings and the resort itself puts on an event most evenings.

Off the slopes There's a public pool with sauna, steam-room, solarium and new spa facilities, indoor tennis, ice rink, curling, tobogganing and 40km/25 miles of cleared walks. Easy outings by rail to Salzburg or Innsbruck.

Westendorf

Charming Ski Welt resort with exciting expansion for 2005/06

RATINGS

The slopes

Fast lifts	**
Snow	**
Extent	*
Expert	**
Intermediate	***
Beginner	***
Convenience	***
Queues	****
Mountain restaurants	***

The rest

Scenery	***
Resort charm	****
Off-slope	**

NEWS

For 2005/06 the long-awaited link with the Kirchberg-Kitzbühel slopes is planned. There will be a new red piste down to Aschau from the Gampen area, with a new eight-seat gondola back. Shuttle buses will take you from Aschau (see piste map in Kitzbühel chapter) to the Pengelstein gondola at Skirast. All the Kirchberg-Kitzbühel and Ski Welt lifts are covered by the Kitzbüheler Alpenskipass (see 'Alternative passes' in the Söll chapter).

TVB WESTENDORF

There are great nursery slopes right by the village but most of the runs above are genuine reds →

- Charming traditional village
- Access to the extensive Ski Welt circuit via nearby Brixen and to Kitzbühel's slopes from this season
- Good local beginners' slopes
- Jolly if rather limited après-ski scene

- Local slopes are limited in extent, and mainly of genuine red gradient – so they suit neither keen intermediates nor novices
- Poor natural snow record, though now extensive snowmaking

Westendorf has long been on the Ski Welt lift pass, and its serious red slopes are worth visiting from Söll or Ellmau. As a base, it will become much more attractive for keen intermediates from this season, when it will be linked to the extensive area of slopes shared by Kitzbühel and Kirchberg.

THE RESORT

Westendorf is a small village with a charming main street and attractive onion-domed church (it was once declared 'Europe's most beautiful village' in a floral competition). The centre is close to the nursery slopes but a five-minute walk from the main gondola outside the village. A 2005 reader commented on how inexpensive the village is compared with resorts in France and Italy.

THE MOUNTAIN

The local slopes are small, but you can get into the Ski Welt circuit easily via a bus to Brixen and then a gondola – and into the Kitzbühel-Kirchberg slopes by taking the new piste to Aschau and then a bus.

Slopes A two-stage gondola takes you to Talkaser, from where one main north-west-facing red run goes back to the resort (with blue options on the lower half). Short west- and east-facing pistes at the top run below the peaks of Choralpe, Fleiding and Gampen. A couple of red runs from Fleiding go down past the lifts to hamlets served by buses; a reporter last year particularly enjoyed these. The piste grooming was excellent said a 2005 visitor. There's weekly floodlit skiing.

Terrain-parks There's a good terrain-park with jumps, boxes, rails and a half-pipe, with something for all levels.

Snow reliability Westendorf's snow reliability is a bit better than some other Ski Welt resorts and nearly all of its pistes now have snowmaking.

Experts The slopes are among the most testing in the Ski Welt area, and we guess it's possible to have a lot of fun off-piste with a guide.

KEY FACTS

For Westendorf only		
Resort	800m	
	2,620ft	
Slopes	800-1890m	
	2,620-6,200ft	
Lifts	12	
Pistes	45km	
	28 miles	
Blue	49%	
Red	40%	
Black	11%	
Snowmaking	40km	
	25 miles	

For Ski Welt		
Slopes	620-1890m	
	2,030-6,200ft	
Lifts	93	
Pistes	250km	
	155 miles	
Blue	43%	
Red	48%	
Black	9%	
Snowmaking	160km	
	99 miles	

ON YOUR OWN?

You can team up with other skiers/boarders by turning up at 10am or 1pm at one of seven designated points in the Ski Welt; there are stickers to identify participants, and even a website forum for making prior arrangements at www.skiwelt.at.

WEBSITES

For links to resort sites, go to our own new site at www.wtss.co.uk

Phone numbers
From elsewhere in Austria add the prefix 05334 (05358 for Ski Welt Tourist Office). From abroad use the prefix +43 5334 (+43 5358 for Ski Welt Tourist Office)

TOURIST OFFICES

Westendorf
t 6230
info@westendorf.com
www.westendorf.com
Ski Welt
t 505
info@skiwelt.at
www.skiwelt.at

Intermediates Nearly all the local terrain is genuinely red in gradient, though we see they have regraded some former reds to blues. The main Ski Welt area has lots of easier intermediate runs and Kitzbühel-Kirchberg a good mix of intermediate runs; but getting to either of those involves a bus.

Beginners Extensive village nursery slopes are Westendorf's pride and joy. There are a couple of genuine blues to progress to, but the reds are real reds (as are some of the regarded blues).

Snowboarding There are some tedious catwalks at altitude.

Cross-country There are 30km/19 miles of local cross-country trails along the valley but snow-cover is erratic.

Queues Given good conditions, queues are rare, and far less of a problem than in the main Ski Welt area. If poor weather closes the upper lifts, queues can become long.

Mountain restaurants Alpenrosenhütte is woody and warm, with good food; reporters enjoyed the quiet, pleasant Brechhornhaus; the Choralp (top of gondola) gets busy but is 'reasonably priced'; the Gassnerwirt is good but you have to bus back to town.

Schools and guides The three ski schools have quite good reputations, though classes can be large. One reporter tells of her teenager's 'excellent' private lesson with the Top school: 'He's been skiing since he was three, but this was a revelation.' Others praise the Westendorf school: 'teachers very good, good value, great prize-giving in town hall' and 'excellent instructor, good English'.

Facilities for children Westendorf sells itself as a family resort. The nursery and the ski kindergarten open all day.

STAYING THERE

How to go A couple of mainstream operators offer packages here.

Hotels There are central 4-star hotels – the Jakobwirt (6245) and the 'excellent' Schermer (6268) – and a dozen 3-star ones. The 3-star Post (6202) is good value, central and 'traditional and charming but the half-board dinner was bland with rushed service'. Among more modest guest houses, Haus Wetti (6348) is popular, and away from the church bells. Pension Ingeborg (6577) has been highly recommended and is next to the gondola station.

Self-catering The Schermerhof apartments are of good quality.

Eating out Most of the best restaurants are in hotels – the Schermer, Mesnerwirt and Jakobwirt are good. The Wastlhof and Klingler have also been recommended. Get a taxi to Berggasthof Stimlach for a good evening out.

Après-ski Nightlife is quite lively, but it's a small place with limited options. The One for the Road Bar and Liftstüberl, at the bottom of the gondola, are packed at the end of the day. The Moskito Bar has live music and theme nights but is said by one reporter to be 'a bit of a dive'. The Village Pub, next to the hotel Post, is very popular with 'good Irish craic' and sells draught Guinness. A 2005 reporter enjoyed the 'good atmosphere and live music' of In's Moment, run by a Scot.

Off the slopes There are excursions by rail or bus to Innsbruck and Salzburg. Walks and sleigh rides are very pretty. In February, the Jump and Freeze night is recommended viewing – 'all good fun' in a party atmosphere.

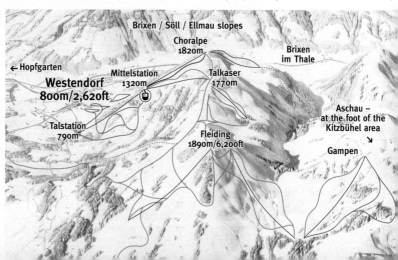

Wildschönau

Niederau and neighbours – family resorts with friendly slopes

COSTS

① ② ③ ④ ⑤ ⑥

RATINGS

The slopes
Fast lifts	**
Snow	**
Extent	*
Expert	*
Intermediate	**
Beginner	***
Convenience	***
Queues	***
Mountain restaurants	**

The rest
Scenery	***
Resort charm	***
Off-slope	**

NEWS

For 2005/06 a second six-pack will replace the two top drag-lifts on Schatzberg above Auffach.

+ Traditional, family-friendly villages

+ Good nursery slopes at Niederau and Oberau

+ Jolly après-ski scene

– Three separate ski areas, linked by ski-buses

– Each area has limited slopes

– Natural snow reliability not the best (but snowmaking covers 40% of runs)

Wildschönau is the dramatic-sounding name adopted by a group of small resorts in the Tirol – Niederau, Oberau and Auffach. The slopes may be limited, but the resorts suit families looking for a friendly, civilised atmosphere.

THE RESORT

Niederau has long been a favourite resort with British beginner and early intermediate skiers. It is the main resort in the Wildschönau and is quite spread out, with a cluster of restaurants and shops around the gondola station forming the nearest thing to a focal point. But few hotels are more than five minutes' walk from a main lift.

Auffach, 7km/4 miles away, is a smaller, quieter, attractive old village and has the area's highest and most extensive slopes.

On a low col between the two is **Oberau** – almost as big as Niederau and the valley's administrative and cultural centre.

The villages are unspoiled, with traditional chalet-style buildings. Roads are quiet, except on Saturdays, and the valley setting is lovely.

THE MOUNTAINS

Niederau's slopes are spread over a wooded mountainside that rises no higher than 1600m/5,250ft. The slopes at Auffach continue above the tree line to 1905m/6,250ft.

Slopes The main lift from Niederau is an eight-person gondola to Markbachjoch. A few minutes' walk away is the alternative chair-lift, and above it is a steep drag to the high point of Lanerköpfl. Beginner runs at the bottom of the mountain are served by several short drag-lifts. The whole area is very small, and we skied most of the area in less than two hours on our 2004 visit. There's a sizeable 'Race 'n' Boarder Arena' on the left of the mountain as you look at it. Races are run here, but you can also take race-training lessons.

A reliable free bus goes to Auffach. Its sunny, east-facing area, consisting almost entirely of red runs, goes up to Schatzberg, with a vertical of

Wildschönau's villages are all unspoiled, with traditional-style buildings →

wildschönau
exciting   relaxing

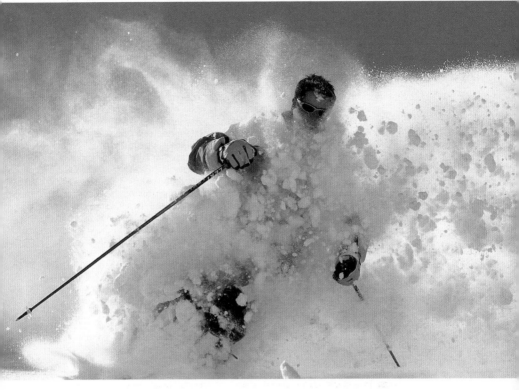

Wildschönau - Tyrol
Niederau - Oberau - Auffach - Thierbach

The 65km of piste give skiers everything they are looking for, steep slopes and gentle family runs. The Wildschönau offers its guests a lift capacity that sets it aside from other resorts. With two gondolas, three chair lifts and 20 drag lifts there is no time lost by queuing and there are no overcrowded lifts.

The gentle Wildschönau hills are particularly suitable for families but there are also plenty of opportunities for experienced skiers, e.g. the FIS runs for the giant slalom and Super G and some magnificent deep-snow slopes. There is also a measured section where skiers can test their top speed. Carvers and snowboarders are welcome on all pistes and the Schatzberg mountain offers an enormous fun park with a half pipe, high jump, fun-box, snake, quarter pipe and wave ride both for fun and competition.

WILDSCHÖNAUER BERGBAHNEN

Lift Company, A-6313 Wildschönau
Phone +43 5339 5353-0, Fax 5353-44
buero@schatzbergbahn.at www.schatzbergbahn.at

For more information contact:
Tourist Office
A-6311 Wildschönau
Phone +43 5339 8255-0, Fax 8255-50
E-Mail: info@wildschoenau.com
www.holidaytirol.com, www.wildschoenau.com

WILDSCHÖNAU
aufregend entspannend **Tirol**

1000m/3,280ft. The main lift up is a two-stage gondola and two six-packs (one new for 2005/06) serve the top runs. Again the area is very small.

The Kitzbüheler Alpen ski pass covers resorts in the Schneewinkel, Kitzbühel ski region, Ski Welt and Alpbachtal as well.

Terrain-parks There's a 90m/300ft half-pipe and a terrain-park with a quarter-pipe, jumps, snake, wave and fun-box served by a drag-lift on Schatzberg.

Snow reliability The low altitude means that natural snow reliability is relatively poor. But over 40% of the pistes have snowmaking, including the main runs down at both Niederau and Auffach from top to bottom. And Auffach has most of its runs above mid-mountain, making for more reliable snow there than at Niederau. Grooming is good.

Experts The several black pistes are short and not severe. We skied the main conventional black piste from the bottom of the drag-lift below Lanerköpfl to Niederau when it was well groomed and thought it great for fast carving, but of almost blue gradient for much of its length. A couple of Niederau's black pistes have now been converted to ungroomed and unpatrolled ski routes, which were bumpy and had patchy snow when we skied them. There are off-piste routes to be found, too – such as the Gern route, which is marked on the piste map, from the top of Schatzberg down a deserted valley to the road a little way from Auffach.

Intermediates Niederau's red runs generally merit their status but there's no blue run from top to bottom. The conventional black mentioned above is enjoyable, but the blue to reach it is just a path. Auffach has more intermediate terrain, with several short reds at the top, and the long main piste from the top to the village is attractive. But all this does not add up to very much – keen intermediate piste-bashers will be able to ski it all in a day. The slopes are best suited to confident but leisurely intermediates who are happy to take it easy and have a relaxing holiday.

Beginners There are excellent nursery slopes at the top and bottom of Niederau's main slopes, but the low ones don't get much sun in midwinter. Auffach has nursery slopes near the gondola mid-station. Oberau has its

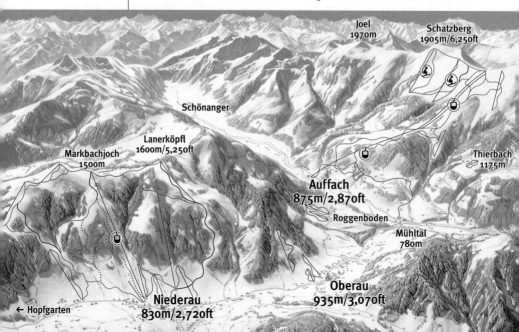

← Hopfgarten

Markbachjoch
1500m

Lanerköpfl
1600m/5,250ft

Schönanger

Joel
1970m

Schatzberg
1905m/6,250ft

Thierbach
1175m

Auffach
875m/2,870ft

Roggenboden

Mühltal
780m

Niederau
830m/2,720ft

Oberau
935m/3,070ft

↑ Niederau is a small place but quite spread out, right at the foot of its slopes

TVB WILDSCHONAU

WEBSITES

For links to resort sites, go to our own new site at www.wtss.co.uk

Phone numbers
From elsewhere in Austria add the prefix 05339.
From abroad use the prefix +43 5339.

TOURIST OFFICE

t 8255
info@wildschoenau.com
www.wildschoenau.com
www.holidaytirol.com

own nursery slopes, with a short black run above them. A problem is the lack of really easy longer runs to progress to.

Cross-country There are 50km/31 miles of trails along the valley, which are good when snow is abundant.

Queues One recent reporter said, 'Very little queueing.' Another complained of queues for the Niederau gondola. We saw long queues for the beginner drag-lifts at Niederau on our January visit.

Mountain restaurants These are scarce but good, causing lunchtime queues as ski schools take a break. Many people lunch in the villages.

Schools and guides The ski schools have good reputations both for English and for teaching beginners, and a recent reporter raved about his beginner lessons. But classes can be large.

Facilities for children The kindergarten and nursery take kids from age two.

STAYING THERE

How to go There are a number of attractive hotels and guest houses in the three main villages – many with pools. Several major operators run packages to Niederau and Oberau.

Hotels In Niederau the 4-star Sonnschein (8353) is reportedly the best hotel. The Austria (8188) is another central recommendation. A recent reporter gave the hotel Vicky, run by Thomson, a rave review – 'friendly staff, excellent food, brilliant crèche'. The oldest hotel in the valley – the 3-star Kellerwirt (8116), dating from 1200 – is in Oberau.

Eating out The restaurants at the hotels Alpenland and Wastl-Hof in Niederau have been recommended.

Après-ski Niederau has a nice balance of après-ski, neither too noisy for families nor too quiet for the young and lively. The Heustadl bar is popular at tea time. The Almbar and the Cave bar – 'where it all happens, live bands twice a week', says a reporter – are popular later on. The Drift-Inn bar at hotel Vicky is also recommended. Cafe Treff in Niederau is an internet cafe.

The other villages are quieter, once the tea-time jollity is over for the night.

Off the slopes There are excellent sleigh rides, horse-riding trips and organised walks as well as the Slow Train Wildschönau – on wheels not rails – which offers varied excursions. Several hotel pools are open to the public, and there's an outdoor ice rink. There's a long toboggan run at Auffach, from the mid-station of the gondola down to the bottom – a distance of 4km/2.5 miles. And on Wednesday and Thursday evenings tobogganing is organised next to the night skiing above Oberau. Shopping excursions to Innsbruck are possible.

Zell am See

Charming lakeside town, varied slopes and glacier option at Kaprun

RATINGS

The slopes

Fast lifts	***
Snow	**
Extent	**
Expert	**
Intermediate	***
Beginner	***
Convenience	**
Queues	**
Mountain restaurants	***

The rest

Scenery	***
Resort charm	***
Off-slope	****

NEWS

For 2005/06 a fast six-seat chair with covers is due to replace the Hochmaislift T-bar from the top of the cable-car at Sonnenalm. There will also be more snowmaking in the Sonnenalm area. In Kaprun a new 4-star hotel with pool and spa is planned for 2006/07.

At the local Maiskogel area at Kaprun for 2004/05 a quad chair replaced two T-bars from the village level.

➕ Pretty, tree-lined slopes with great views down to the lake

➕ Lively, but not rowdy, nightlife

➕ Charming old town centre with beautiful lakeside setting

➕ Lots to do off the slopes

➕ Huge range of cross-country trails

➕ Kaprun glacier nearby

➕ Varied terrain including a couple of steep black runs

➖ Sunny, low slopes often have poor conditions despite snowmaking, which makes the area more limited

➖ Trek to lifts from much of the accommodation, and sometimes crowded buses

➖ Less suitable for beginners than most small Austrian resorts

➖ The Kaprun glacier gets lengthy queues when it is most needed

Zell am See is not a rustic village like most of its Austrian rivals, but a lakeside summer resort town with a charming old centre. For a small area, Zell's slopes have a lot of variety and challenging terrain, but not enough to keep a keen intermediate or expert happy for long – only 75km/47 miles of pistes, if you ignore Kaprun's Kitzsteinhorn glacier. Zell is close to Kaprun, but if snow is in short supply, Zell visitors have no special claim: you have to queue for access along with visitors coming from Saalbach, Kitzbühel and other low resorts.

THE RESORT

Zell am See is a long-established, year-round resort town set between a large lake and a mountain. Its charming, traffic-free medieval centre is on a flat promontory, and the resort has grown up around this attractive core. A gondola at the edge of town (served by ski-buses) goes up one arm of the horseshoe-shaped mountain, and there are hotels here, too. 2km/1 mile away, in the Schmittental in the centre of the horseshoe, are two cable-cars; there is some accommodation as well.

A more radical alternative is to stay in Schüttdorf, 3km/2 miles away, where there is another gondola. But it is a characterless dormitory with little else going for it. Though closer to Kaprun, this is, perversely, a drawback unless you have a car. Trying to get on a glacier bus is tough, as they tend to be full when they leave Zell. Cross-country skiers and families wishing to use the Areitalm nursery stand to gain most from staying in Schüttdorf.

Kaprun's snow-sure glacier slopes are only a few minutes by crowded buses (best to get on at the bus station says a reporter); Saalbach is easily reached by bus and Bad Hofgastein by train. At a push, Wagrain, Schladming and Obertauern are car trips.

THE MOUNTAINS

Zell's mountain is horseshoe-shaped. The easiest runs are along the open ridges, with steeper pistes descending through woods to the Schmittental.

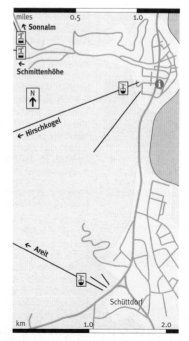

KEY FACTS

Resort	755m
	2,480ft

For Zell and Kaprun

Slopes	755-3030m
	2,480-9,940ft
Lifts	57
Pistes	130km
	81 miles
Blue	43%
Red	38%
Black	19%
Snowmaking	63km
	39 miles

For Zell only

Slopes	755-2000m
	2,480-6,560ft
Lifts	28
Pistes	75km
	47 miles
Snowmaking	50km
	31 miles

For Kaprun only

Slopes	785-3030m
	2,580-9,940ft
Lifts	29
Pistes	55km
	34 miles
Snowmaking	13km
	8 miles

Zell's mountain is horseshoe-shaped with easier slopes along the ridges and steeper ones descending through woods ↓

THE SLOPES
Varied but limited

The City Xpress gondola takes you to Mittelstation. From there it's either an easy or a steep run to the cable-car station in the Schmittental. Or you can take a fast chair up to Hirschkogel to meet the gondola up from Schüttdorf – you can ride this up further or ski down to take an alternative chair to Schmittenhöhe. This is also where the main Schmittental cable-car brings you. A gentle cruise and a single short drag-lift moves you to Sonnkogel. Here several routes lead down to Sonnenalm mid-station – where another cable-car from the Schmittental arrives. A black piste runs from here to the valley floor. At the end of the day you can take a gentle piste back to town or ride one of the lifts down.

TERRAIN-PARKS
Man-made and 'natural'

There's a half-pipe on Schmittenhöhe and a terrain-park on the Kaprun glacier.

SNOW RELIABILITY
Good snowmaking, but lots of sun

Zell am See's slopes get so much sun the snow can suffer as a result. Lots of slopes are now well covered by snow-guns, including the sunny home run to Schüttdorf and 70% of the lower slopes. But though reporters have seen 'lots of snowmaking in evidence', slush, ice and closed runs have still marred their holidays. The Kaprun glacier is snow-sure, but expect long queues there (and for buses there and back) when snow is short elsewhere.

FOR EXPERTS
Several blacks, but still limited

Zell has more steep slopes than most resorts this size, but can't entertain an expert for a week. When we were last

there it was fabulous speeding down the immaculately groomed black runs 13 and 14 – they were deserted first thing in the morning (and a January 2005 reporter also found them deserted). They aren't as steep as most French blacks though. Off-piste opportunities are limited.

FOR INTERMEDIATES
Bits and pieces for most grades

Good intermediates have a choice of fine, long runs, but this is not a place for mileage. All blacks are usually well groomed and within a brave intermediate's capability, and there's a lovely cruising run between Areit and Schüttdorf when conditions are good. Some Sonnkogel pistes are also suitable. The timid can cruise the ridge all day on quiet, attractive runs, or head past Mittelstation to Zell's cable-cars on an easy blue.

Kaprun's high, snow-sure glacier runs are also ideal for intermediates not looking for too great a challenge.

FOR BEGINNERS
Two low nursery areas

There are small nursery slopes at the cable-car area and at Schüttdorf, both covered by snow-guns. There are plenty of short, easy runs at Schmittenhöhe, Breiteck and Areit; some are used by complete beginners when snow conditions are poor lower down, but it means buying a lift pass.

FOR CROSS-COUNTRY
Excellent if snow allows

The valley floor has extensive areas – 40km/25miles – including a superb area on the Kaprun golf course. At altitude there are two short loops, one at the top of the Kaprun glacier, the other at the top of the Zell gondola.

Zell am See

211

LIFT PASSES

Europa–Sportregion Kaprun–Zell am See
Covers all lifts in Zell and Kaprun, and buses between them.

Beginners
Points card

Main pass
1 day €35
6 days €168

Children
Under 19: 6 days €134
Under 16: 6 days €84
Under 6: free pass

Notes
One-day pass price is for Schmittenhöhe (Zell) only. Kitzsteinhorn-only and Maiskogel-only day passes also available.

Alternative passes
Salzburg Super Ski Card covers huge area round Salzburg province from Abtenau to Zell and is available for three days or more.

boarding

Zell is well suited to boarders and most lifts are chairs, gondolas and cable-cars. You'll also find plenty of life in the evenings. The Kaprun glacier has powder in its wide, open bowl. But it also has a high proportion of drag-lifts – a day of this and the 'small walk' to enter the terrain-park exhausted some reporters who said 'a chair-lift would be most welcome'. Snowboard Academy is a specialist school.

QUEUES
A few bottlenecks
Zell am See doesn't have many problems except at peak times, when queues can form at the cable-cars (especially) and gondolas out of town. The chair at the top of the City Xpress gondola can have queues too and a 2005 visitor found trying to get on the gondola from Schüttdorf at the middle stations a lengthy business. One reporter recommends getting to Schmittenhöhe via the Sonnalm cable-car as a quieter route than others. When snow is poor there are few daytime queues at Zell – many people are away queueing at Kaprun. The queue for the bus back from Kaprun was said by a 2004 reporter to be 'chaotic – a heaving mass, all scrambling and fighting to get on'.

MOUNTAIN RESTAURANTS
Plenty of little refuges
There are plenty of cosy, atmospheric huts dotted around the Zell slopes, helpfully named on the piste map. Among the best are Glocknerhaus, Kettingalm, Areitalm, Breiteckalm and Blaickner's Sonnalm ('the best strudel'). Pinzgauer Hütte, in the woods at the back of Schmittenhöhe, is also recommended by reporters. The Berghotel at Schmittenhöhe is good, but expensive. Its bar with loud music is lively in the afternoons (see Après-ski). The Panorama-Pfiff gets crowded, but 'has wonderful views and quite good food'. The Ebenbergalm just above the village has 'excellent home cooked food,' says a reporter this year.

SCHOOLS AND GUIDES
A wide choice
There is a choice of schools in both Zell am See and Kaprun. We get few reports, but the daughter of a 2005 visitor had 'excellent' lessons with a 'delightful board instructor' at the main Zell school. There are also specialist cross-country centres at Schüttdorf and at Kaprun.

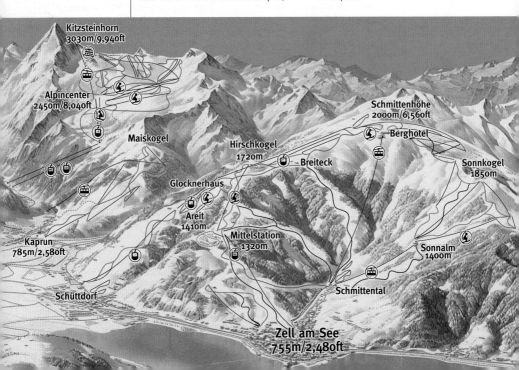

↑ The City Xpress gondola out of Zell am See, with the lake in the background

EUROPA SPORTREGION ZELL AM SEE-KAPRUN

SCHOOLS
Zell am See
t 56020
Sport Alpin
t 0664 453 1417
Snowboard Academy
t 0664 253 0381

Classes
(Zell prices)
5 days (2hr am and pm) €140
Private lessons
€50 for 1 hr; €10 for each additional person

CHILDREN
Kinderskiwelt Areit
t 56020
Ages from 2; with ski lessons for children over 3
Babysitter list
At the tourist office

Ski schools
Take children from age 4 (5 days including lunch €195)

GETTING THERE
Air Salzburg 80km/ 50 miles (2hr); Munich 230km/ 143 miles (3hr).

Rail Station in resort.

FACILITIES FOR CHILDREN
Schüttdorf's the place
We have no recent reports on the childcare provisions, but staying in Schüttdorf has the advantage of direct gondola access to the Areitalm snow-kindergarten. There's a children's adventure park on the mountain.

STAYING THERE

HOW TO GO
Choose charm or convenience
Lots of hotels, pensions and apartments.
Hotels A broad range of hotels (more 4- than 3-stars) and guest houses.

((((④ **Salzburgerhof** (7650) Best in town – the only 5-star. It is nearer the lake than the gondola, but has courtesy bus and pool.

((((④ **Tirolerhof** (7720) Excellent 4-star in old town. 'Greatly improved' pool, hot-tub and steam room. 'Very comfortable, very friendly and efficient staff,' 'good bar' say reporters.

((((④ **Eichenhof** (47201) On outskirts of town, but popular and with a minibus service, great food and lake views.

((((④ **Alpin** (7690) Modern 4-star chalet next to the Zell gondola.

((((④ **Zum Hirschen** (7740) Comfortable 4-star, easy walk to gondola. Sauna, steam, splash pool, popular bar.

((((④ **Schwebebahn** (724610) Attractive 4-star in secluded setting in the Schmittental, by the cable-cars.

((((④ **Romantikhotel Zell am See** (72520) 4-star close lake and centre. 'Very good, really wild decor, friendly,' says a visitor.

((((④ **Lebzelter** (7760) Is a family hotel in the pedestrian area – 'helpful reception and great Austrian food and service' says a reporter.

(② **Margarete** (72724) B&B in the Schmittental, by the cable-cars.

Self-catering Lots of options.

Apartment Hofer (80480) is mid-range and close to the Ebenberg lift (linking to the gondola). More comfortable are the 3-star Diana (72436) and Seilergasse (68787), both in the centre.

STAYING UP THE MOUNTAIN
Three options
As well as the Berghotel (72489) at the top of the Schmittenhöhe cable-car, the Breiteckalm (73419) and Sonnalm (73262) restaurants have rooms.

EATING OUT
Plenty of choice
Zell has more non-hotel places than is usual in a small Austrian resort. The Ampere is quiet and sophisticated; Giuseppe's is a popular Italian with excellent food; and Kupferkessel and Traubenstüberl both do wholesome regional dishes. There are Chinese restaurants in Zell and Schüttdorf. Car drivers can try the excellent Erlhof at Thumersbach.

APRES-SKI
Plenty for all tastes
Après-ski is lively and varied, with tea dances and high-calorie cafes, plus bars and discos aplenty. 'Even as a 55-year-old I had a great time pubbing,' says a reporter. When it's sunny, Schnapps Hans ice bar outside the Berghotel, up the mountain at Schmittenhöhe, really buzzes, with 'great music, a crazy DJ and dancing on tables and on the bar. All ages loved it.' The Diele disco bar rocks; Crazy Daisy on the main road has two crowded bars (one called Irish Daisy) and 'the group loved it' says one reporter; 'good Guinness' says another. Classic has a live band and 60s and 70s music. The Viva disco allows no under 18s; one reader proclaimed it 'excellent'. Or try the smart Hirschenkeller, the cave-like Lebzelter Keller and the Sportstüberl, with nostalgic ski photos adorning the walls. Lupo's has 'the cheapest beer in town and satellite TV, but is scruffy'.

OFF THE SLOPES
Lots of choices
There is plenty to do in this year-round resort. The train trip to Salzburg is a must, Kitzbühel is also well worth a visit and Innsbruck is within reach.

You can often walk across the frozen lake to Thumersbach, plus there are good sports facilities, a motor museum, sleigh rides and alpine flights.

ACTIVITIES

Indoor Swimming, sauna, solarium, massage, fitness centre, spa, tennis, squash, bowling, shooting gallery, museums, riding hall, cinema, library

Outdoor Ice rink, curling, walking, ice sailing, ice surfing, tobogganing, plane flights, sleigh rides, ballooning, paragliding, hang gliding

WEBSITES

For links to resort sites, go to our own new site at www.wtss.co.uk

Phone numbers
Zell am See
From elsewhere in Austria add the prefix 06542.
From abroad use the prefix +43 6542.
Kaprun
From elsewhere in Austria add the prefix 06547.
From abroad use the prefix +43 6547.

TOURIST OFFICE

Zell am See/Kaprun
t 7700
welcome@europa sportregion.info
www.europasport region.info

Kaprun 785m/2,580ft

THE RESORT
Kaprun is a spacious, charming and quite lively village. The main road to the glacier bypasses it, leaving the centre pleasantly quiet.

THE MOUNTAIN
There is a small area of slopes on the outskirts of the village at Maiskogel, served by a cable-car, a new quad, a couple of double chairs and a short drag-lift; it's best suited to early intermediates. There is also a separate nursery area. But most people will want to spend most of their time on the slopes of the nearby Kitzsteinhorn glacier or on Zell am See's slopes. Buses to and from both are often crowded. The lift pass covers only one ascent of the Kitzsteinhorn access gondola per day.
Slopes A 15-person, two-stage gondola has replaced the funicular, which suffered a tragic fire in autumn 2000. The first-stage runs parallel with an older eight-seat gondola, ending in the same mid-mountain area. The second stage, up to the Alpincenter and main slopes, runs parallel to a fast quad chair. The main slopes are in a big bowl above the Alpincenter, served by a cable-car, lots of T-bars and three chairs. The area above the top of the Alpincenter is open in summer and is particularly good for an early pre-Christmas or late post-Easter break.
Snow reliability Snow is nearly always good because of the glacier. And there's snowmaking too.
Queues Queues have always been a problem here. Recent reports tell of 15-minute waits for the access gondola (down as well as up) and up to 10 minutes for the upper lifts. See Zell am See for comments on the buses here.
Mountain restaurants There are three decent mountain restaurants – the

Gletschermühle and Krefelderhütte near the Alpincenter, and the Häusalm near the new gondola mid-station. All these get busy. Bella Vista at the top of the mountain has good views and is 'reasonably priced' says a 2005 reporter.
Experts There's little to challenge experts except for some good off-piste; the one slightly tough piste starts at the very top.
Intermediates Pistes are mainly gentle blues and reds and make for great easy cruising on usually good snow. From Alpincenter there is an entertaining red run down to the new gondola mid-station. This is our favourite run on the mountain, though it does get crowded. There's also a good unpisted ski route.
Beginners There are two nursery slopes in the village and some gentle blues on the glacier to progress to.
Snowboarding There's a terrain-park on the glacier and some excellent natural half-pipes.
Cross-country Trails on the Kaprun golf course are good, but at altitude there is just one short loop – at the top of the glacier.
Schools and guides There are several ski schools.
Facilities for children All of the schools offer children's classes and there's a kindergarten in the village.

STAYING THERE
How to go There are some catered chalets and chalet-hotels.
Hotels The Orgler (82050), 'spacious' Mitteregger (8207) and Tauernhof (8235) are among the best hotels.
Après-ski Nightlife is quiet, but the Baum bar is lively.
Eating out Good restaurants include the Dorfstadl, Hilberger's Beisl and Schlemmerstube.
Off the slopes Off-slope activities are good, and include a fine sports centre with outdoor rapids.

Bad Kleinkirchheim

BKK attracts surprisingly few British visitors – partly because it is tucked away in Carinthia, in the far south-east of Austria near the Italian and Slovenian borders. The slopes aren't easy but suit good intermediates well.

KEY FACTS

Resort		1090m
		3,580ft
Slopes		1100-2055m
		3,610-6,740ft
Lifts		26
Pistes		90km
		56 miles
Blue		17%
Red		72%
Black		11%
Snowmaking		75km
		47 miles

TOURIST OFFICE

t 04240 8212
info@badkleinkirch
heim.at
www.bkk.at

THE RESORT

BKK, as the locals call it, is home to Austrian super-hero Franz Klammer, 1976 Olympic downhill champion. This old spa town has mainly chalet-style buildings and is very spread out along the valley; the most convenient place to stay is near one of the main lifts. There are three 5-star and 17 4-star hotels, as well as cheaper options. Not surprisingly, there are superb spa facilities, but nightlife is rather quiet compared with many Austrian resorts.

THE MOUNTAINS

BKK's shady home slopes are reached by gondola or a fast quad from different parts of the village. They link in with St Oswald's sunnier slopes further along the valley, served by a further two gondolas. Despite Franz Klammer's endorsement, BKK has little to keep experts interested for a week. There are a few short black runs, including one that turns into the red Franz Klammer Downhill to the bottom of the gondola. Virtually all the slopes are ideal for intermediates. Over 70% are graded red and are wide, flattering and long – up to 1000m vertical. Most are sheltered in the trees. The lift pass covers all resorts in Carinthia.

There are nursery slopes and drag-lifts for beginners at both BKK and St Oswald – the St Oswald ones are much warmer and sunnier in midwinter. Once off the nursery slopes, there is an easy blue run at the top of St Oswald's Nockalm gondola and a long blue all the way from the top to the bottom.

Snowmaking is being extended for 2006, and is claimed to cover 95% of the runs. St Oswald, in particular, has many mountain restaurants.

Short turns

215

Fieberbrunn

Beginners could do worse than try Fieberbrunn, with its good nursery slopes, pretty tree-lined pistes and jolly Tirolean atmosphere. But adventurous intermediates will soon tire of its limited and unexciting slopes.

KEY FACTS

Resort		800m
		2,620ft
Slopes		835-2020m
		2,740-6,630ft
Lifts		11
Pistes		35km
		22 miles
Blue		35%
Red		60%
Black		5%
Snowmaking		15km
		9 miles

TOURIST OFFICE

t 05354 56304
fieberbrunn@
pillerseetal.at
www.pillerseetal.at

THE RESORT

Fieberbrunn sprawls along the valley road for 2km/1 mile, but has classic Tirolean charm: wooden chalets, pretty church, cosy bars and coffee shops. Most accommodation is in hotels and pensions. Much of the village is set back from the road and railway, so that peace is interrupted only by church bells. Light sleepers can stay in hotels out near the main lift station, served by regular but sometimes crowded buses from the village.

THE MOUNTAINS

The runs, on tree-lined north-facing slopes, are best for beginners and leisurely intermediates.

Two gondolas diverge from the lift base a little way outside the village, with lifts above them ultimately converging on the upper slopes of Lärchfilzkogel (1645m/5,400ft). One sector consists mainly of blue runs, the other mainly red – though they would be blue in many resorts. Across a valley behind this peak are separate lifts going up to the high point of 2020m/6,630ft on Hochhörndl, with further red slopes.

Beginners have broad nursery slopes conveniently close to the village centre. Graduation to long, gentle runs beneath one of the gondolas is easy.

Fieberbrunn has better snow-cover than is usual at this altitude, and it has snowmakers on the home slopes.

Weekday queues are rare outside the morning ski-school rush. Sunny weekends are busy.

There is a handful of good mountain restaurants at the main lift junctions, and a few more near the lift base – lively at the end of the afternoon.

Seefeld

Seefeld is a smart, all-round winter holiday resort in a pretty setting, with superb cross-country trails and off-slope activities, and a couple of small, separate areas of downhill slopes. Innsbruck is not far away.

KEY FACTS

Resort	1200m
	3,940ft
Slopes	1200-2100m
	3,940-6,890ft
Lifts	25
Pistes	45km
	28 miles
Blue	70%
Red	30%
Black	0%
Snowmaking	15km
	9 miles

AUSTRIA

216

TOURIST OFFICE

t 05212 2313
info@seefeld.at
www.seefeld.at

THE RESORT

A classic post-war Tirolean tourist development, Seefeld is well designed in traditional Tirolean style, with a large, pedestrian-only centre. Lots of people come here for the curling, skating and swimming rather than skiing. The upmarket nature of the resort is reflected in the hotels – there are four 5-stars and almost 30 4-stars. The village is on a main railway line.

THE MOUNTAINS

The slopes are in two main sectors – Gschwandtkopf and Rosshütte. Both are on the outskirts, served by a regular free shuttle-bus. The nursery slopes on Geigenbühel, close to the centre of the village are broad and gentle, with snowmaking.

Gschwandtkopf is a rounded hill of 300m/980ft vertical and intermediate runs on two main slopes. Rosshütte is more extensive, and has a terrain-park and half-pipe. The top of Rosshütte can be reached by a funicular – 'very efficient' says a reader – and then a cable-car. There is also a cable-car

across to the separate peak Härmelekopf, also reachable from the valley by two six-seat chairs. Both parts of the area have long runs of 800m vertical to the base station.

Rosshütte has some seriously steep off-piste challenges for experts and will offer intermediates an interesting day out from Innsbruck – but the terrain is too limited for a week's stay.

Seefeld's 285km/177 miles of excellent cross-country trails are some of the best in the Alps – one reason why nearby Innsbruck has been able to hold the Winter Olympics twice (and the Nordic World Ski Championships).

Serfaus

Serfaus offers the charm and nightlife of a typical Austrian village but with extensive slopes (shared with Fiss and Ladis), fairly reliable snow and the huge benefit of being largely traffic-free.

KEY FACTS

Resort		1430m
		4,690ft
Slopes	1200-2750m	
	3,940-9,020ft	
Lifts		53
Pistes		160km
		99 miles
Blue		20%
Red		70%
Black		10%
Snowmaking		75km
		47 miles

TOURIST OFFICE

t 05476 6239
info@serfaus.com
www.serfaus.com

THE RESORT

Serfaus is attractive and friendly, with chalet-style buildings set on a sunny shelf. It is largely traffic-free, with an underground railway running from a car park at one end to the lifts at the other, with two stops en route. Most accommodation is in comfortable, chalet-style hotels.

Most visitors are well-heeled Germans, many of them family groups. There are few British visitors. There are several après-ski bars, but evenings are not riotous. There is a 10km/6 mile toboggan run to the village.

THE MOUNTAINS

Three gondolas radiate from the village, including one to the mid-mountain focus of Komperdell (1980m/6,500ft). There's a broad area

of intermediate slopes above here, with some good long runs down to the village. There are a few black runs, lots of ski routes, and plenty of little-used off-piste. A chain of lifts and runs extends west over two more ridges, ending an extraordinary 11km/7 miles from the village. A new gondola has been built on the slopes of Pezid, opening up new black and blue runs.

One of the village gondolas leads to the slopes of Fiss (1435m/4,710ft), where there are extensive sunny slopes served by a long gondola to Schönjoch and shorter shady runs beyond.

Most of the slopes are above the tree line (ie above 1800m/5,910ft), and there is extensive snowmaking – so the area is reasonably snow-sure despite the sun. Queues are not a problem.

Both the village and mid-station nursery slopes are good, and there is ample opportunity for progression.

Short turns

217

Wagrain

Wagrain is a towny little resort at the centre of a lift system that is typical of many in Salzburger Land – spreading widely across several low, partly wooded ridges. Flachau and Alpendorf/St Johann are at its extremities.

KEY FACTS

Resort		850m
		2,790ft
Slopes	850-2190m	
	2,790-7,190ft	
Lifts		64
Pistes		200km
		124 miles
Blue		20%
Red		75%
Black		5%

TOURIST OFFICE

t 06413 8448
info@wagrain.info
www.wagrain.info
www.sportwelt-amade.com

THE RESORT

Wagrain is an unremarkable valley village where life does not revolve entirely around skiing. The lift stations are on the fringes of the village and served by ski-buses – one up at the elevated suburb of Kirchboden, along with the nursery slopes and the excellent Wasserwelt pool complex.

THE MOUNTAINS

It's an impressive lift system, with about a dozen eight fast chairs and several gondolas. From Wagrain, a gondola to Grafenberg leads to an area of short lifts and runs and so to Hirschkogel above Alpendorf, a satellite of St Johann im Pongau. To the east, from Kirchboden, another gondola goes to Griessenkareck, at the top of the slopes down to Flachau. It's

a big area – 15km/9 miles from end to end – with some good, long, although easy runs. The slopes are practically all graded red, with a few blues dotted around. The reds are generally not very testing, but they are genuine reds, and none of the home runs is really easy. The few stretches of black are for purely decorative purposes. Despite the altitude, most of the upper slopes are fairly open. Some get too much sun for comfort, and snow reliability is not a strong point. There are lots of attractive mountain restaurants.

The Salzburger Sportwelt lift pass area includes another similar lift system (tantalisingly close but connected only by buses) to the south, linking Zauchensee, Flachauwinkl and Kleinarl – much more easily accessed from Wagrain or Flachau than St Johann. There are also smaller areas at Filzmoos and Radstadt/ Altenmarkt.

France

Over one-third of British skiers and snowboarders choose France for their holidays each year, almost double the number who go to Austria, the next most popular country. It's not difficult to see what attracts us to France. The country has the biggest lift and piste networks in the world; for those who like to cover as many miles in a day as possible, these are unrivalled. Most of these big areas are also at high altitude, ensuring high-quality snow for a long season. And French mountains offer a mixture of some of the toughest, wildest slopes in the Alps and some of the longest, gentlest and most convenient beginner runs.

French resort villages can't be quite so uniformly recommended; but, equally, they don't all conform to the standard image of soulless, purpose-built service stations, thrown up without concern for appearance during the boom of the 1960s and 1970s. Many resorts are based on more traditional villages, or offer these as an option. Another advantage of smaller villages and less well-known resorts is that they tend to be cheaper. Some of the big-name resorts can now be very expensive – none more so than Courchevel 1850, where you can pay quite silly prices for hotel rooms, food and drink.

Towards the front of the book there is a special chapter on driving to the French Alps – still very popular, especially with people going self-catering, despite the growth of the budget airlines. The French Alps are easy to get to by car, and comfortable apartments are becoming more common as the French continue their retreat from the short-sighted ways of the 1960s.

ANY STYLE OF RESORT YOU LIKE

The main drawback to France, hinted at above, is the monstrous architecture of some of the purpose-built resorts. But not all French resorts are hideous. Certainly, France has its fair share of Alpine eyesores, chief among them central Les Menuires, central La Plagne, Flaine, Tignes, Isola 2000 and Les Arcs. But all these places have learned from past mistakes, and newer developments there are being built in a much more attractive, traditional chalet style. The later generation of purpose-built resorts, such as Valmorel, La Rosière and La Tania, have been built in much more sympathetic style than their predecessors. The big advantages of the high, purpose-built resorts are the splendid quality and extent of the slopes they serve, the reliability and quality of the snow, and the amazing slope-side convenience of most of the accommodation.

If you prefer, there are genuinely old mountain villages to stay in, linked directly to the big lift networks. These are not usually as convenient for the slopes, but they give you a feel of being in France rather than in a winter-holiday factory. Examples include Montchavin or Champagny for La Plagne, Vaujany for Alpe-d'Huez, St-Martin-de-Belleville, Les Allues or Brides-les-Bains for the Trois Vallées and Les Carroz, Morillon or Samoëns (now covered by its own chapter) for Flaine. There are also old villages with their own slopes that have developed as resorts while retaining some or all of their rustic ambience – such as Serre-Chevalier and La Clusaz.

SNOWPIX.COM / CHRIS GILL

← Méribel-Mottaret is a classic French purpose-built resort, with lots of ski-in, ski-out accommodation but a very limited range of après-ski and off-slope activity. Unlike many, it is built in traditional chalet style

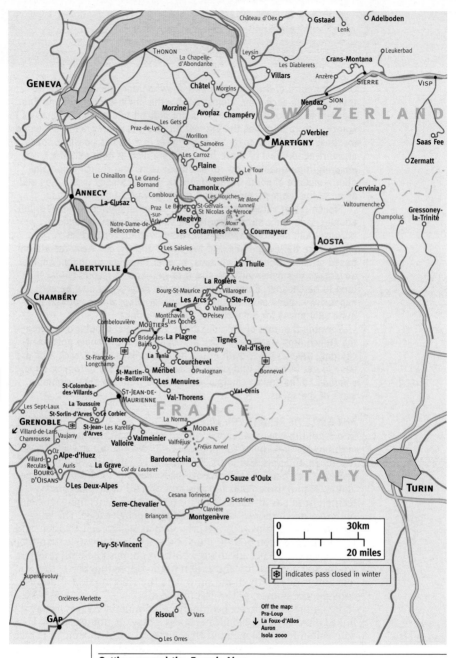

Getting around the French Alps

Pick the right gateway – Geneva, Chambéry or Grenoble – and you can hardly go wrong. The approach to Serre-Chevalier and Montgenèvre involves the 2060m/6,760ft Col du Lauteret; but the road is a major one and kept clear of snow or re-opened quickly after a fall. Crossing the French-Swiss border between Chamonix and Verbier involves two closure-prone passes – the Montets and the Forclaz. When necessary, one-way traffic runs beside the tracks through the rail tunnel beneath the passes.

Megève deserves a special mention – an exceptionally charming little town combining rustic style with sophistication; shame about the traffic.

And France has Alpine centres with a long mountaineering and skiing history. Chief among these is Chamonix, which sits in the shadow of Mont Blanc, Europe's highest peak, and is the centre of the most radical off-piste terrain in the Alps. Chamonix is a big, bustling town, where winter sports go on alongside tourism in general. At the opposite end of the vacation spectrum is tiny, simple La Grave, at the foot of mountains that are almost as impressive – the highest within France.

IMPROVING APARTMENTS

One of the most welcome developments on the French resort scene in recent years has been the availability of genuinely comfortable and stylish apartments, in contrast to the cramped and, frankly, primitive places that have dominated the market since the 1960s. Central to this shift has been a company called MGM, which has developed apartments (and some chalets) in several resorts; most of these have their own pool and spa, as well as rooms of normal size. We have also been very impressed by the Montagnettes apartments we've stayed in – they are spacious and well furnished. Other top-of-the-range operators include Soderev and Chalet de Neige.

Introduction

221

And now Intrawest – Canadian developer of Whistler and other pace-setting resorts in North America – has taken its first step into Alpine property development. The first phase of Arc 1950 – a brand new mini-village just below Arc 2000 – opened for 2003/04, offering an ambience and style rarely seen on a large scale in French resorts. See the Les Arcs chapter for more on this development.

Tour operator Erna Low offers an especially good range of comfortable apartments in its brochure and covers all the developers mentioned above.

PLAT DU JOUR

France has advantages over most rival destinations in the gastronomic stakes. While many of its mountain restaurants serve fast food, most also do at least a plat du jour that is in a different league from what you'll find in Austria or the US. It is generally possible to find somewhere to get a half-decent lunch and to have it served at your table, rather than queuing repeatedly for every element of your meal. In the evening, most resorts have restaurants serving good, traditional French food as well as regional specialities. And the wine is decent and affordable.

Many French resorts (though not all) have suffered from a lack of nightlife, but things have changed in recent years. In resorts dominated by apartments with few international visitors, there may still be very little going on after dinner, but places such as Méribel are now distinctly lively in the evening.

France is unusual among European countries in using four grades of piste (instead of the usual three) – a system of which we heartily approve. The very easiest runs are classified green; except in Val-d'Isère, they are reliably gentle. It's novices who care most about choosing just the right sort of terrain to build confidence, so this is a genuinely helpful system, which ought to be used internationally.

AVOID THE CROWDS

French school holidays mean crowded slopes, so they are worth avoiding if possible. The country is divided into three zones, with three fortnight holidays staggered over a four-week period – in 2006, 4 February to 6 March; from 11 to 27 February two zones overlap, so you can expect that period to be particularly busy.

Alpe-d'Huez

An impressive and sunny all-rounder with alternative bases to stay

224

COSTS

① ② ③ ④ ⑤ ⑥

RATINGS

The slopes

Fast lifts	**
Snow	****
Extent	****
Expert	****
Intermediate	****
Beginner	*****
Convenience	****
Queues	****
Mountain restaurants	****

The rest

Scenery	****
Resort charm	*
Off-slope	****

NEWS

For 2005/06 a six-pack is due to replace the three drag-lifts at Les Bergers. Also the Romains lift will be removed and a second tow added to the Rif Nel. This should improve access to the beginner slopes there, and is part of a long-term plan to upgrade lifts in the resort.

A moving carpet is planned for the beginner area at Oz-en-Oisans.

For 2004/05 the Marmottes III jumbo gondola opened to connect the existing Marmottes II lift with the Sarenne glacier.

There's a new sledding area at L'Eclose (floodlit twice a week) and a second terrain-park – next to the boarder-cross course.

+ Extensive, high, sunny slopes, split interestingly into various sectors

+ Huge snowmaking installation

+ Vast, gentle, sunny nursery slopes right next to the resort

+ Efficient, modern lift system

+ Some good, surprisingly rustic mountain restaurants

+ Short walks to and from the slopes

+ Livelier than most purpose-built resorts

+ Pleasant alternative bases in outlying villages and satellites

− In late season the many south-facing runs can be icy early and slushy later

− Some main intermediate runs get badly overcrowded in high season

− Many of the tough runs are very high, and inaccessible in bad weather

− Practically no woodland runs to retreat to in bad weather

− Run gradings can understate difficulty

− Sprawling resort with a hotchpotch of architectural styles, no central focus and very little charm

There are few places to rival Alpe-d'Huez for extent and variety of terrain – in good conditions it's one of our favourites. But, in late season at least, despite ever-expanding snowmaking, the 'island in the sun' suffers from the very thing it advertises: strong sun means that ice can spoil mornings on the main slopes, however alluring the prospect of slushy moguls in the afternoons.

The village has few fans, but if you don't like the sound of it you always have the alternative of staying in rustic Vaujany (with its mighty cable-car), Villard-Reculas, or in the modern ski-stations of Oz-en-Oisans or Auris. The whole area is increasingly being referred to as the Massif des Grandes Rousses.

THE RESORT

Alpe-d'Huez is a large village spread across an open mountainside high above the Romanche valley east of Grenoble, and it has grown in a seemingly unplanned way. Its buildings come in all shapes, sizes and designs (including a futuristic church which hosts weekly organ concerts). Many buildings look scruffy and in need of renovation, although some wood cladding and general smartening-up can now be seen. A couple of recent reporters remarked how friendly and welcoming the locals were, compared with other French resorts.

It is a large, amorphous resort; the nearest thing to a central focus is the main Avenue des Jeux in the middle, where you'll find the swimming pool, ice skating and some of the shops, bars and restaurants. The rest of the resort spreads out in a triangle, with lift stations at two of the apexes.

The bus service around the resort is free with the lift pass, and there's a bucket-lift (with a piste beneath it) running through the resort to the main lifts at the top. This is handy but slow, and some people don't like the need to jump on and off it as it moves. It doesn't operate in the evenings.

A short distance from the main body of the resort (and linked by chair-lift) are two satellite 'hamlets' – apartment blocks, mainly. Les Bergers, at the eastern entrance to the resort, is convenient for the slopes (with its own nursery area). It is fairly self-contained, with a couple of bar/restaurants and several shops near the slopes, but it's a trek from most of the other resort facilities. A chalet suburb is expanding this quarter uphill – convenient for skiing but even more remote from the village centre. L'Eclose, to the south of the main village, is less convenient and has even less to offer. There is also accommodation down the hill in the old village of Huez, linked by lift.

Outings by road are feasible to other resorts covered on a week's lift pass, including Serre-Chevalier and Les Deux-Alpes (the latter also reachable for the day by helicopter for a surprisingly modest fee). A bus now goes to Les Deux-Alpes, operating twice weekly (Wednesday and Thursday), but you need to book.

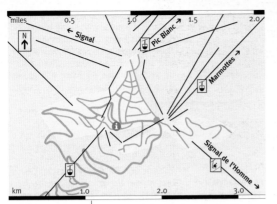

KEY FACTS

Resort	1860m
	6,100ft
Slopes	1120-3320m
	3,670-10,890ft
Lifts	87
Pistes	238km
	148 miles
Green	32%
Blue	29%
Red	27%
Black	12%
Snowmaking	
	700 guns

THE MOUNTAINS

Alpe-d'Huez is a big-league resort, ranking alongside giants like Val-d'Isère or La Plagne for the extent and variety of its slopes. Practically all the slopes are above the tree line, and there may be precious little to do when a storm socks in; the runs around Oz are your best bet (if you can get to them).

Reporters find the piste grading unreliable, making it a rather unnerving place for timid intermediates. For example, the Hirondelles run (now graded blue rather than green), is still singled out by reporters as being tricky, with a tendency to develop big bumps. You may find some reds rather tame, then find others 'steeply mogulled halfway down'.

THE SLOPES
Several well-linked areas

The slopes divide into four sectors, with good connections between them, though a recent reporter complained of having to pole or walk between lifts.

The biggest sector is directly above the village, on the slopes of **Pic Blanc**. The huge Grandes Rousses gondola, otherwise known as the DMC (a reference to its clever technology), goes up in two stages from the top of the village. Above it, a cable-car goes up to 3320m/10,890ft on Pic Blanc itself – the top of the Sarenne glacier. There is an alternative way to the glacier now that a third stage has been added to the Marmottes gondola, which also serves a lower area of challenging runs at Clocher de Macle. The longest piste in the Alps – the 16km/10 mile Sarenne – starts from Pic Blanc (see the feature panel).

The Sarenne gorge separates the main resort area from **Signal de l'Homme**. It is crossed by a down-and-up fast chair-lift from the Bergers part of the village. From the top you can take excellent north-facing slopes towards the gorge, or head south to Auris or west to tiny Chatelard.

On the other side of town from Signal de l'Homme is the small **Signal** sector, reached by drag-lifts next to the main gondola or by a couple of chairs lower down. Runs go down the other side of the hill to the old village of Villard-Reculas. One blue run back to

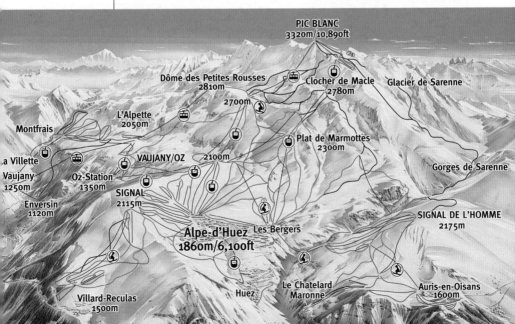

Alpe-d'Huez is floodlit twice a week.

The generally quieter **Vaujany-Oz** sector consists largely of north-west-facing slopes, accessible from Alpe-d'Huez via good red runs from either the mid-station or the top of the DMC gondola. At the heart of this sector is Alpette, the mid-station of the cable-car from Vaujany. From here a disastrously sunny red goes down to Oz, a much more reliable blue goes north to the Vaujany home slopes around Montfrais, and a shady black plunges down to Enversin, just below Vaujany, offering an on-piste descent of 2200m/7,220ft from Pic Blanc – not the biggest vertical in the Alps, but not far short. The links back to Alpe-d'Huez are by the top cable-car from Alpette, or a gondola from Oz.

TERRAIN-PARKS
A choice
There's a good boarder-cross course and new advanced park by the Babars drag, and a 1.5km/1 mile terrain-park with half-pipe, jumps and rollers near the main lift base – but it is reported to get busy: 'Schools frequently pass through without observing park etiquette, making it tricky to use.' There's another terrain-park near Auris.

SNOW RELIABILITY
Affected by the sun
Alpe-d'Huez is unique among major purpose-built resorts in the Alps in having mainly south- or south-west-facing slopes. The strong southern sun means that late-season conditions may alternate between slush and ice on most of the area, with some of the lower runs being closed altogether. There are shady slopes above Vaujany and at Signal de l'Homme. The small lift system on the Pic Blanc glacier has been enlarged, but is still too small to pin all your hopes on.

In more wintry circumstances the runs are relatively snow-sure, the natural stuff being backed up, in theory, by extensive snowmaking on the main runs above Alpe-d'Huez, Vaujany and Oz. But reports suggest that neither the grooming nor the snowmaking is as enthusiastic as we would wish.

FOR EXPERTS
Plenty of blacks and off-piste
This is an excellent resort for experts, with long and challenging black runs (and reds that ought to be black) as well as serious off-piste options (see panel on facing page).

The slope beneath the Pic Blanc cable-car, usually an impressive mogul-field, is reached by a 300m/1,000ft tunnel from the back side of the mountain. Despite improvements to the tunnel exit, the start of the actual slope is often awkward. The slope is of ordinary black steepness, but can be very hard in the mornings because it gets a lot of sun. The run splits part-way down – a couple of variants take you to the Lac Blanc chair back up to the cable-car.

The long Sarenne run on the back of the Pic Blanc is described in a special feature panel. We've never found the black Fare piste to Enversin open, but reporters rate it as one of the best – 'a demanding but highly enjoyable descent through the trees'. Some of the upper red pistes are tough enough to give experts a challenge. These include the Canyon and Balme runs accessed by the Lièvre Blanc chair-lift from the gondola mid-station – runs which are unprepared and south-facing, and steep enough to be classified black in many resorts.

boarding

The resort suits experienced boarders well – the extent and variety of the mountains mean that there's a lot of good free-riding to be had. And, if there's good snow, the off-piste is vast and varied and well worth checking out with a guide. Unfortunately for beginners, the main nursery slopes are almost all accessed by drag-lifts, but these can be avoided once a modicum of control has been achieved. Planète Surf is the main snowboard shop.

Above this, the Marmottes II gondola serves steep black runs from Clocher de Macle including the beautiful, long, lonely Combe Charbonniere.

FOR INTERMEDIATES
Fine selection of runs

Good intermediates have a fine selection of runs all over the area. In good snow conditions the variety of runs is difficult to beat. Every section has some challenging red runs to test the adventurous intermediate. The most challenging are the Canyon and Balme runs, mentioned previously. There are lovely long runs down to Oz and to Vaujany, with space for some serious carving. The Villard-Reculas and Signal de l'Homme sectors also have long challenging reds. The Chamois red from the top of the gondola down to the mid-station is quite narrow, and miserable when busy and icy and/or heavily mogulled. Fearless intermediates should enjoy the super-long Sarenne black run.

For less ambitious intermediates, there are usually blue alternatives, except on the upper part of the mountain. The main Couloir blue from the top of the big gondola is a lovely run, well served by snowmaking, but it does get scarily crowded at times.

There are some great cruising runs above Vaujany; but the red runs between Vaujany and Alpe-d'Huez can be too much for early intermediates. Unless you are prepared to travel via Oz on gondolas, you are effectively confined to one sector or the other.

Early intermediates will also enjoy the gentle slopes leading back to Alpe-d'Huez from the main mountain, and the Signal sector.

FOR BEGINNERS
Good facilities

The large network of green runs immediately above the village is as good a nursery area as you will find anywhere, and the drag-lifts at Les Bergers are due to be replaced by a new six-seat chair for 2005/06, making that part much easier for novices. Sadly, these slopes get very crowded and carry a lot of fast through-traffic. A large area embracing half a dozen runs has been declared a low-speed zone, but the restriction is not policed and so achieves very little. All in all, with a special lift pass covering 11 lifts, Alpe-d'Huez makes a good choice.

Alpe-d'Huez

OFF-PISTE FOR ALL STANDARDS

There are vast amounts of off-piste terrain in Alpe-d'Huez, from fairly tame to seriously adventurous. Here we pick out just a few of the many runs to be explored – always with guidance, of course.

One of the highlights of the resort is the Sarenne run – the longest black piste in the Alps (see separate feature panel). For an adventurous intermediate looking to try off-piste for the first time, the many off-piste variants that can be found on both sides of this valley are ideal. If you are feeling a bit more adventurous, ask your guide about the Combe du Loup, a beautiful south-facing bowl with views over the Meije. With a black-run gradient at the top, this itinerary again offers lots of variants, allowing guides to find excellent snow whatever the weather. You end up on long, gentle slopes leading back to the Sarenne gorge and the resort. La Chapelle Saint Giraud, which starts at Signal de l'Homme, is another excellent itinerary for off-piste novices. Its vertical drop of 630m/2,070ft includes a series of small confidence-boosting bowls, interspersed with gentle rolling terrain. You can descend straight into Auris or pass through the hamlet of Cluy further to the east, depending on the snow conditions.

For more experienced and adventurous off-piste skiers, the Grand Sablat is a classic which runs through a magnificently wild setting on the eastern face of the Massif des Grandes Rousses. This descent of 2000m/6,560ft vertical includes glacial terrain and some steep couloirs. You can either ski down to the village of Clavans, where you can take a pre-booked helicopter or taxi back, or traverse above Clavans back to the Sarenne Gorge. In the Signal sector, there are various classic routes down towards the village of Huez or to Villard-Reculas.

The north-facing Vaujany sector is particularly interesting for experienced off-piste enthusiasts. Route finding can be very tricky, and huge cliffs and rock bands mean this is not a place to get lost. From the top of Pic Blanc, a 40-minute hike takes you to Col de la Pyramide at 3250m/10,660ft, the starting point for the classic itinerary La Pyramide. With a vertical of over 2000m/6,560ft, the beauty of this run is the variety. Once at the bottom of the long and wide Pyramide snowfield, you can link into the Vaujany pistes. From the Dôme des Petites Rousses cable-car there are various routes, including the spectacular Canyon de la Fare, a long narrow passage between two huge walls of rock.

SCHOOLS

ESF
t 0476 809423

International
t 0476 804277

Classes (ESF prices)
6 days (3hr am and 2½hr pm) €170

Private lessons
€35 for 1hr, for 1 or 2 people.

GUIDES

Mountain guide office
t 0476 804255

FOR CROSS-COUNTRY
High-level and convenient

There are 50km/31 miles of trails, with three loops of varying degrees of difficulty, all at around 2000m/6,560ft and consequently relatively snow-sure.

QUEUES
Generally few problems

Even in French holiday periods, the modern lift system ensures there are few long hold-ups. The village bucket-lift is said to generate lengthy queues first thing. Queues can build up for the gondolas out of the village, but the DMC shifts its queue quickly and the bottom section can be avoided by taking alternative lifts to the quieter second stage.

The small Pic Blanc cable-car is no longer the bottleneck it was, thanks to the new Marmottes III gondola, which offers an alternative way to the glacier.

Although they may not cause queues, there are lots of old drag-lifts scattered around.

Over much of the area a greater problem than lift queues is that the main pistes can be unbearably crowded. We and many reporters rate the Chamois and Couloir runs from the top of the DMC among the most crowded we've seen. The red to Oz, beneath the Poutran gondola, is also singled out by reporters as being too busy for comfort – 'carnage all the way', said one.

MOUNTAIN RESTAURANTS
Some excellent rustic huts

Mountain restaurants are generally good – even self-service places are welcoming, and there are many more rustic places with table-service than is usual in high French resorts. One of our favourites is the cosy little Chalet du Lac Besson (endorsed by a 2005 visitor: 'fabulous place'), on the cross-country loops north of the DMC gondola mid-station; the route to it, now with piste status (the Boulevard des Lacs), is still not easy to follow.

The pretty Forêt de Maronne hotel at Chatelard, below Signal de l'Homme, is 'a delightfully quiet sun-trap', enthuses a reporter, and has a good choice of traditional French and International cuisine: 'The chicken satay kept us raving about the place all week.' The Bergerie at Villard-Reculas has good views and is 'highly recommended'.

The Combe Haute, at the foot of the

THE LONGEST PISTE IN THE ALPS – AND IT'S BLACK?

It's no surprise that most ski runs that are seriously steep are also seriously short. The really long runs in the Alps tend to be classified blue, or red at the most. The Parsenn runs above Klosters, for example – typically 12km to 15km (7 to 9 miles) long – are manageable in your first week on skis. Even Chamonix's famous Vallée Blanche off-piste run doesn't include steepness in its attractions.

So you could be forgiven for being sceptical about the 'black' Sarenne run from the Pic Blanc: even with an impressive vertical of 2000m/6,560ft, a run 16km/10 miles in length means an average gradient of only 11% – typical of a blue run. Macho-hype on the part of the lift company, presumably?

Not quite. The Sarenne is a run of two halves. The bottom half is virtually flat (boarders beware) but the top half is a genuine black if you take the direct route – a demanding and highly satisfying run (with stunning views) that any keen, competent skier will enjoy. The steep mogul-field near the top can be avoided by taking a newly created easier option (or by using the new Marmottes III gondola); and the whole run can now be tackled by an adventurous intermediate. The run gets a lot of sun, so pick your time with care – there's nothing worse than a sunny run with no sun.

CHILDREN

Les Crapouilloux
t 0476 113923
Ages 2 to 10; 9.30-
5.30

Les Intrépides
t 0476 112161
Ages 0 to 3; 8am-
6.30

Les Eterlous (ESF)
t 0476 806785
Ages 2½ to 5; 8.45-
5.30

Tonton Mayonnaise
(International school
Ages 2½ to 3½;
10am-12 noon

Jardin d'Enfants (ESF)
Ages 4 and over;
5½hr per day

Club des Marmottes
(International school)
Ages 4 to 12; 9.30-12
noon, 3pm-5pm

Club Med nursery
From age 4, with or
without lessons

Ski schools
Take children from 4
to 16 (ESF 6 days
€160)

GETTING THERE

Air Lyon 150km/
93 miles (3hr);
Geneva 220km/137
miles (4hr); Grenoble,
99km/62 miles
(1½hr).

Rail Grenoble (63km/
39 miles); daily buses
from station.

WENDY-JANE KING

There are quiet, rustic
hamlets on the
fringes of the area,
such as Chatelard ➔

Chalvet chair in the gorge towards the end of the Sarenne run, is welcoming but gets very busy. The Signal is quieter and has 'postcard views.' The terrace of the Perce-Neige, just below the Oz-Poutran gondola mid-station, attracts crowds. The Plage des Neiges at the top of the nursery slopes is one of the best places available to beginners. Chantebise 2100, at the DMC mid-station, offers slick and cheerful table service. The Cabane du Poutat, half-way down from Plat de Marmottes, is recommended for good food and service and the Marmottes itself is also recommended ('good value main courses').

The restaurants in the Oz and Vaujany sectors tend to be cheaper, but no less satisfactory. At Montfrais, the Airelles is a rustic hut, built into the rock, with a roaring log fire, atmospheric music and excellent, good-value food ('the best plat du jour I have ever eaten', says a 2005 reporter). The Auberge de l'Alpette also gets enthusiastic reviews emphasising it is 'really good value'. The P'Oz is also worth a visit.

SCHOOLS AND GUIDES
Contrasting reports

Recent reports on the ESF branches here are mixed: 'The kids progressed very well,' said one, but two others sound worrying alarms. 'Appalling,' said a reporter whose daughter was found 'sobbing after being shouted at' while another child 'was curled in a ball crying, totally ignored.' 'Don't even think about going to the ESF,' said another. Groups can be big: one reporter counted an astonishing 25 in one class. We continue to get favourable reports of Masterclass, an independent school run by British instructor Stuart Adamson – 'would go back to Alpe d'Huez just to ski with them,' says the latest. Class sizes are limited to eight. Advance booking for high season is necessary. The Bureau des Guides also has a good reputation.

FACILITIES FOR CHILDREN
Positive reports

Les Crapouilloux day-care centre is 'very well organised' and has been recommended, as has tour operator Crystal's childcare operation. The children's garden and nursery at Vaujany have been recommended.

STAYING THERE

HOW TO GO
Something of everything

Chalets UK tour operators run quite a few chalet-hotels, and some are offering smaller chalets in the new development above Les Bergers.

Hotels There are more hotels than is usual in a high French resort, and there's a clear downmarket bias, with more 1-stars than 2- or 3-stars, and only two 4-stars.

(((④ **Royal Ours Blanc** (0476 803550) Central. Luxurious, with good food. Superb fitness centre. Free (but often oversubscribed) minibus to the lifts.

(((③ **Au Chamois d'Or** (0476 803132) Good facilities, modern rooms, one of the best restaurants in town and well placed for main gondola.

(((③ **Cimes** (0476 803431) South-facing rooms, excellent food; close to cross-resort lift and pistes.

(((③ **Grandes Rousses** (0476 803311) A recent visitor says 'Great atmosphere, charming Madame, goodish food and a good guitarist.' Close to the lifts.

(② **Mariandre** (0476 806603) Comfortable hotel with good food, recommended by readers. Some small rooms. Next to the bucket-lift.

(② **Gentianes** (0476 803576) Close to the Sarenne gondola in Les Bergers; a range of rooms, the best comfortable.

Self-catering There is an enormous choice available. The Pierre et

Alpe-d'Huez

229

ACTIVITIES

Indoor Sports centre (tennis, gym, squash, aerobics, swimming, shooting range, climbing wall), cinemas, concerts, theatre, museum

Outdoor Ice rink, curling, cleared walking paths, swimming pool, snow-shoeing, microlight flights, sight-seeing flights, ice cave, off-road vehicle tours, hang-gliding, paragliding, ice driving school, all-terrain carts, quad-bikes

Vacances apartments near the Marmottes gondola in Les Bergers offer good facilities, but as usual in France they are too small if fully occupied. The Maison de l'Alpe close to the DMC has been recommended for its ideal location and good facilities.

EATING OUT
Good value
Alpe-d'Huez has dozens of restaurants, some of high quality; many offer good value by resort standards. Booking is often necessary. The Crémaillère is recommended by a frequent visitor. Au P'tit Creux got a similarly positive review for excellent food and ambience, though a reporter thought it was 'getting expensive'. The 'outstanding' Génépi is a friendly old place with good cuisine. The Pomme de Pin is repeatedly approved. Of the pizzerias, L'Origan 'served fabulous pizza and pasta'; Pinocchio 'gets very busy early', says a reporter, who also liked the 'enormous helpings' at Smithy's Tex-Mex. The Edelweiss is recommended for its 'excellent value set menus and grills'.

APRES-SKI
Getting better all the time
There's a wide range of bars, some of which get fairly lively later on. They are widely dispersed, making pub crawls hard work. Of the British-run bars, the Roadhouse in Crystal's hotel Vallée Blanche and the Underground in Neilson's hotel Chamois are established favourites – but a 2005 reporter thought the Underground 'smoke-filled and claustrophobic'. The Crowded House in Crystal's Hermitage hotel is a 'quiet' alternative with a pool table. The small but 'lively'

Sphere bar is popular after the lifts close. O'Sharkey's (with 'comfortable leather sofas') and the Pacific (sister bar to the one in Val d'Isère) are also popular. Smithy's can get pretty rowdy late on. The live bands at the Yeti make for 'some great nights'.

The Etalon and Free Ride cafes ('relaxed, cheery atmosphere with great sports videos') are also recommended. And the Dutch-run Melting Pot does good tapas and is great for a relaxed drink, as is the Zoo.

The Sporting is 'a great bar with class bands but the highest prices in town'; this and the Igloo disco liven up when the French hit town en masse.

OFF THE SLOPES
Good by purpose-built standards
There is a wide range of facilities, including an indoor pool, an open-air pool (boxer-style cozzies not allowed), Olympic-size ice rink and splendid sports centre – all of this covered by the lift pass. There's also an ice-driving school and a new sledding area at L'Eclose. Visits to the Ice Cave are highly recommended by reporters. Shops are numerous but limited in range. The helicopter excursion to Les Deux-Alpes is amusing. There are well-marked walkers' trails and there's a pedestrian lift pass. A special route map is also available. The better mountain restaurants are widely spread – some too remote for pedestrians.

Villard-Reculas

1500m/4,920ft
Villard-Reculas is a secluded village just over the hill (Signal) from Alpe-d'Huez, complete with an old church, set on a small shelf wedged between an expanse of open snowfields above and tree-filled hillsides below. Following the installation of a fast quad chair up to Signal a few years back, the village is becoming more popular as an access point and it is now beginning to find its feet as a 'resort'. Its visitor beds are mainly in self-catering apartments and chalets, booked either through the tourist office or La Source – an English-run agency that also runs a comfortable catered chalet in a carefully converted stone barn. There is one 2-star hotel, the Beaux Monts (0476 803032). There is a store 'almost like a trading post' and a couple of bars and restaurants.

The local slopes have something for

Phone numbers
From abroad use the prefix +33 and omit the initial '0' of the phone number.

TOURIST OFFICE

Alpe-d'Huez
t 0476 114444
info@alpedhuez.com
www.alpedhuez.com

everyone – including a nursery slope at village level – and there is a branch of the Ecole du Ski Français.

But a recent reporter warns 'the place is dull at night' and 'beginners will be stuck here because the runs that link to the rest of the wonderful skiing are very undergraded'. Two near-beginners in his party were 'very put off'.

Oz-en-Oisans

1350m/4,430ft

The purpose-built ski station above the attractive old village of Oz-en-Oisans apparently now takes its parent's name and is a 'thriving small resort', says a reporter who has an apartment there. It has a ski school, sports shops, nursery slopes, bars, restaurants, a supermarket and a skating rink. But another reporter complains that there is still no nightlife. There's a large underground car park, and attractive new chalets and apartment blocks have been built in a sympathetic style, with much use of wood and stone. There is a hotel, the Hors Piste (0476 798662). Two gondolas whisk you out of the resort – one goes to Alpette above Vaujany and the other goes in two stages to the mid-station of the DMC above Alpe-d'Huez. The main run home is liberally endowed with snow-guns, but it needs to be. One clear advantage of staying here is that the slopes above Oz are about the best in the area when heavy snow is falling – and those based elsewhere may not be able to reach them.

Phone numbers
From abroad use the
prefix +33 and omit
the initial '0' of the
phone number.

FRANCE

232

Auris 1600m/5,250ft

Auris is a series of wood-clad, chalet-style apartment blocks with a few shops, bars and restaurants pleasantly set close to the thickest woodland in the area. It's a fine, compact family resort, with a nursery and a ski kindergarten. There's also a ski school. Beneath it is the original old village, complete with attractive, traditional buildings, a church and all but one of the resort's hotels. Staying here with a car you can drive up to the lift base or make excursions to other resorts such as Serre-Chevalier.

Unsurprisingly, evenings are quiet, with a handful of bar-restaurants to choose from. The Beau Site (0476 800639), which looks like an apartment block, is the only hotel in the upper village. A couple of miles down the hill, the traditional Auberge de la Forêt (0476 800601) gives you a feel of 'real' rural France.

Access to the slopes of Alpe-d'Huez is no problem (but returning to Auris may prove difficult for novices – the top section of Signal de L'Homme is a bit steep). There are plenty of local slopes to explore, for which there is a special lift pass. Most runs are intermediate, though Auris is also the best of the local hamlets for beginners.

Vaujany 1250m/4,100ft

Vaujany is a quiet, small (though growing) village perched on the hillside opposite its own sector of the domain. Hydroelectric riches have financed huge continuing investment. There's a giant 160-person cable-car that whisks you into the heart of the Alpe-d'Huez lift system, a two-stage gondola that takes you to Vaujany's local slopes, a superb sports centre with a 'fantastic' pool and a newish village centre by the lifts (with smart ski shop, cafe, deli and underground car park) – quiet at lunchtime. The Igloo Gourmand cafe is well placed and recommended.

Vaujany has a handful of simple hotels – a reporter heartily recommends the Rissiou, run by British operator Ski Peak – and some smart self-catering developments up the mountainside; the 'huge' Perle d'Oisans apartments are highly rated by a 2005 visitor. Ski Peak also runs comfortable, tastefully decorated catered chalets in Vaujany and La Villette; a minibus service for guests is available. There are some lively bars (the Swallow holds some 'weird' theme nights) and a couple of discos. British, Dutch and Belgian visitors dominate.

A mile or two up the valley (at the mid-station of the gondola) is the even smaller and more rustic hamlet of La Villette (just one tiny bar-restaurant).

There are no village slopes, so even complete beginners have to ride the gondola to Montfrais, which has a mid-station at La Villette. There's a blue run back to La Villette, but it can be tricky enough to reduce early intermediates to tears. You normally have to ride from La Villette down to Vaujany. A 2005 reporter's daughter enjoyed the 'excellent' nursery (arranged through Ski Peak).

Les Arcs

Purpose-built convenience, with exciting recent developments

COSTS

① ② ③ ④ ⑤ ⑥

RATINGS

The slopes
Fast lifts	**
Snow	****
Extent	***
Expert	****
Intermediate	****
Beginner	****
Convenience	****
Queues	***
Mountain restaurants	***

The rest
Scenery	***
Resort charm	*
Off-slope	*

NEWS

For 2004/05, the whole of the Paradiski area moved to hands-free electronic passes. A new six-pack, the Grizzly, opened at Peisey-Vallandry (from the village to 2300m/7,550ft), along with a new blue piste from the top and additional snowmaking.

For 2005/06 more snowmaking is planned. The new Club Med at Peisey-Vallandry should open, as should two further buildings in Arc 1950, including the first to be managed by prestige hotel chain Radisson SAS.

+ A wide range of runs to suit intermediates and experts
+ Now has cable-car link to La Plagne
+ Excellent woodland runs
+ Mainly traffic-free villages with easy access to the slopes from most (but not all) of the apartments
+ Option of staying in quiet, more traditional, lower villages
+ Very easy rail access from UK
+ Splendid views of Mont Blanc massif

− Main village centres lack charm
− Few off-slope diversions
− Few confidence-building easy runs – yet lots of flats to annoy boarders
− Still a lot of slow old chairs
− Very quiet in the evenings, and limited choice of bars/restaurants
− Some apartments are quite a walk from the nearest lifts
− Accommodation in high villages is nearly all apartments

We've always liked Les Arcs' slopes: they offer impressive variety, including some of the longest descents in the Alps and plenty of steep stuff. The link with La Plagne means the combined Paradiski area can claim an impressive 425km/ 264 miles of runs – in the same league as the Three Valleys and Val-d'Isère/ Tignes. Keen mixed-ability groups should have Les Arcs on their shortlists.

The main villages are classic purpose-built resorts – functional but drab. But the new Arc 1950 village offers purpose-built convenience with a lot more style. And there are more traditional (still quiet) options at either extremity of the area.

THE RESORT

Les Arcs is made up of four modern resort units, linked by road, high above the railway terminus town of Bourg-St-Maurice. The four villages are all purpose-built and apartment-dominated, and offer doorstep access to the snow with no traffic hazards, but the original three lack Alpine charm, off-slope activities and much evening animation. There's a special feature panel on the fourth – the new, still-developing Arc 1950 – a couple of pages on.

Reporters repeatedly comment on the friendliness of the locals.

Arc 1600 was the original Arc. For rail travellers it is the obvious choice, with a funicular railway up from Bourg-St-Maurice. 1600 is set in the trees and has a friendly, small-scale atmosphere; and it enjoys good views along the valley and towards Mont Blanc. The central area is particularly good for families: uncrowded, compact, and set on even ground. But it is very quiet in the evening. Above the village, chair-lifts fan out over the lower slopes, leading to links to the other Arcs.

OT LES ARCS / PEDROTTI

Arc 1600 was the original Arc village and is the lowest →

KEY FACTS

Resort	1600-2000m
	5,250-6,560ft
Slopes	1200-3225m
	3,940-10,580ft
Lifts	56
Pistes	200km
	124 miles
Green	1%
Blue	51%
Red	30%
Black	18%
Snowmaking	12km
	7 miles

Paradiski area	
Slopes	1200-3250m
	3,940-10,660ft
Lifts	161
Pistes	425km
	264 miles
Green	5%
Blue	54%
Red	28%
Black	13%

Much the largest of the 'villages' is Arc 1800. It has three sections, though the boundaries are indistinct. Charvet and Villards are small shopping centres, mostly open-air but still managing to seem claustrophobic. Both are dominated by huge apartment blocks. More easy on the eye is Charmettoger, with smaller, wood-clad buildings nestling among trees. There are also apartments up the hillside in Le Chantel. The lifts depart from Villards – chair-lifts to mid-mountain, and a big gondola to Col de la Chal above Arc 2000.

Arc 2000 is just a few hotels, apartment blocks and the Club Med, huddled together in a bleak spot, with little to commend it but immediate access to the highest, toughest skiing. Although some more upmarket apartments have been built over the last few years, there is only a handful of restaurants and shops.

Just below Arc 2000 and now linked to it by open-top gondola, the new 'village' of Arc 1950 is part-complete – see feature panel later in this chapter.

There are lifts all around Arc 1950 and 2000, including the Varet gondola up towards the Aiguille Rouge.

At the southern end of the area, linked by pistes but reachable by road only by descending to the valley, is Peisey-Vallandry. The long-awaited cable-car link with La Plagne opened here for 2003/04. At the northern end of the ski area is the rustic hamlet of Le Pré. These outlying options are described at the end of the chapter.

THE MOUNTAINS

Les Arcs' terrain is notably varied; it has plenty of runs for experts and intermediates and a good mixture of high, snow-sure slopes and low-level woodland runs ideal for bad weather.

Day trips by car to Val-d'Isère-Tignes or the Three Valleys are possible – both covered for a day with a six-day Paradiski or Paradiski Découverte pass.

Several reporters this year have commented that the glossy, new Les Arcs piste map falls apart and they needed a few copies during the week.

THE SLOPES
Well planned and varied

The slopes are very well laid out, and moving around is quick and easy. Arc 1600 and Arc 1800 share a west-facing mountainside laced with runs leading down to one or other village. At the southern end is an area of woodland runs down to Peisey-Vallandry.

From various points on the ridge above 1600 and 1800 you can head down into the Arc 2000 bowl. On the opposite side of this bowl, lifts take you to the highest runs of the area, from the Aiguille Rouge and the Grand Col. As well as a variety of steep north-west-facing runs back to Arc 2000, the Aiguille Rouge is the start of a lovely long run (over 2000m/6,560ft vertical and 7km/4 miles long) right down to the hamlet of Le Pré near Villaroger. Arc 2000 has runs descending below village level, to the lift base, restaurant

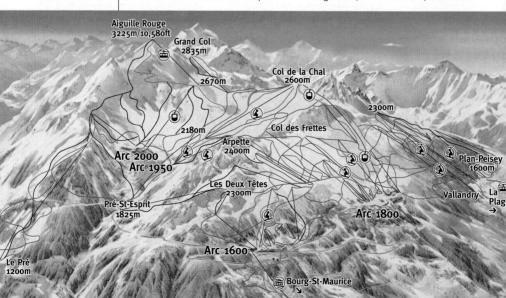

Aiguille Rouge
3225m/10,580ft

Grand Col
2835m

Col de la Chal
2600m

2670m

2300m

2180m

Arpette
2400m

Col des Frettes

Arc 2000
Arc 1950

Plan-Peisey
1600m

Les Deux Têtes
2300m

Pré-St-Esprit
1825m

Vallandry

La Plag

Arc 1800

Arc 1600

Le Pré
1200m

Bourg-St-Maurice

and car park at Pré-St-Esprit, about 200m/660ft lower. You can reach Le Pré from here, via a short drag-lift, and also via the Lanchettes chair at Arc 2000.

TERRAIN-PARKS
State of the art
The terrain-park – Apocalypse, just down from Arpette – is served by the Clair Blanc chair. Features change throughout the season, says the resort, and there are two areas. The Games zone has two boarder-cross runs as well as jumps and areas for novices. The more advanced Display zone has a big hip jump and rails. There is a half-pipe at Arc 2000 (floodlit at night), where you'll also find the Flying Kilometre – a speed skiing run on which you can try your luck travelling at 100kph/63mph or more.

SNOW RELIABILITY
Good – plenty of high runs
A high percentage of the runs are above 2000m/6,560ft and when necessary you can stay high by using lifts that start around that altitude. Most of the slopes face roughly west, which is not ideal. Those from the Col de la Chal and the long runs down to Le Pré are north-facing. The limited snowmaking is being gradually extended. Reporters are still finding that grooming can be 'economical'.

FOR EXPERTS
Challenges on- and off-piste
Les Arcs has a lot to offer experts – at least when the high lifts are open (the Aiguille Rouge cable-car, in particular, is often shut in bad weather).

There are a number of truly black pistes above Arc 2000, and a couple in other areas. After a narrow shelf near the top (which can be awkward), the Aiguille Rouge-Le Pré run is superb, with remarkably varying terrain

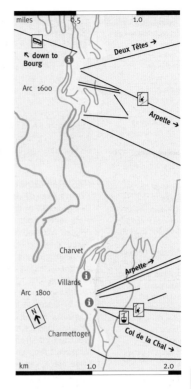

throughout its vertical drop of over 2000m/6,560ft. There is also a great deal of off-piste potential. There are steep pitches on the front face of the Aiguille Rouge, and secluded runs on the back side, towards Villaroger – the Combe de l'Anchette, for example. A short climb to the Grand Col from the chair-lift of the same name gives access to several routes, including a quite serious couloir and an easier option. The wooded slopes above 1600 are another attractive possibility and there are open slopes beside the pistes all over the place.

boarding

Les Arcs calls itself 'the home of the snowboard'. Local boy Regis Rolland played a big part in popularising the sport (not least with his 'Apocalypse Snow' movies), and the resort is constantly developing its boarding facilities – the terrain-park was moved and rebuilt recently and is excellently maintained. Boarders are attracted by the great mix of terrain served mainly by boarder-friendly lifts. However, getting around can involve some long traverses on near-flat cat-tracks and some of the blues at Arc 2000 are too flat for comfort. ('I wouldn't stay in Arc 2000 because it's too much of a pain to get to,' says one intermediate reporter.) Belvedère and Sources between 1600 and 1800 are also best avoided. Vallandry has great smooth runs for beginners and carvers. There are a couple of specialist board schools and shops.

FOR INTERMEDIATES
Plenty for all abilities

One strength of the area is that most main routes have easy and more difficult alternatives, making it good for mixed-ability groups. There are plenty of challenges, yet less confident intermediates are able to move around without getting too many nasty surprises. An exception is the solitary Comborcière black from Les Deux Têtes down to Pré-St-Esprit. This long mogul-field justifies its rating and can be great fun for strong intermediates. The Malgovert red, which starts from the same place, can be tricky – it is narrow and often mogulled.

The woodland runs at either end of the domain, above Peisey-Vallandry and Le Pré, and the bumpy Cachette red down to 1600, are also good for better intermediates. We especially like the Peisey-Vallandry area: its well groomed, tree-lined runs have a very friendly feel and are remarkably uncrowded much of the time, allowing great fast cruising. Good intermediates can enjoy the Aiguille Rouge-Le Pré run (with red and blue detours available to avoid the toughest bits of the black).

The lower half of the mountainside is good for mixed-ability groups, with a choice of routes through the trees. The red runs down from Arpette and Col des Frettes towards 1800 are quite steep but usually well groomed.

Cautious intermediates have plenty of blue cruising terrain. Many of the runs around 2000 are rather bland and prone to overcrowding. Edelweiss is a newish blue down to Arc 1950 from Col des Frettes. The blues above 1800 are attractive but also crowded. A favourite blue of ours is Renard, high above Vallandry, usually with excellent snow.

And, of course, you have the whole of La Plagne's slopes to explore if you get bored locally.

FOR BEGINNERS
1800 best for complete novices

There are nursery slopes conveniently situated just above all three villages. The ones at Arc 1600 are rather steep, while those at 2000 get crowded with intermediate through-traffic at times. The sunny, spacious slopes at 1800 are best. The 'Ski Tranquille' zones, served by free lifts, at the foot of each village are specially separated areas where novices can practise using the lifts before progressing onto the main runs. There is a lack of attractive, long, easy runs to move on to. But Mont Blanc, above 1600, is a beautiful, gentle blue, and you can take the gondola up to Col de la Chal and enjoy good snow on easy blues towards 2000.

FOR CROSS-COUNTRY
Very boring locally

Short trails, mostly on roads, is all you can expect unless you travel down to the Nancroix valley's 40km/25 miles of pleasant trails.

QUEUES
Slow chairs more of a problem

Reporters have few complaints about queues except in one or two places. In sunny weather, Arc 2000 attracts the crowds and readers comment on non-trivial queues for both the gondola and the chair to Col de la Chal. There are often lengthy waits for the Aiguille Rouge cable-car – 45 minutes, complained one high-season reporter; 'Beware, a large proportion of the queue is hidden inside the building,' warned another. A bigger issue than queues is the time taken riding slow old chair-lifts, some of them very long – Comborcière and Mont Blanc come in for particular criticism. At peak periods crowded pistes can be a problem, too. The cable-car link to La Plagne seems to cope with demand.

ARC 1950: WHERE NORTH AMERICA MEETS EUROPE

The first phase of the brand new resort of Arc 1950, a little way down the hill from Arc 2000 and linked to it by gondola until 9pm, opened two winters ago. For last winter three buildings were open; two more will open in time for the 2005/06 season, including one that will be managed by prestige hotel chain Radisson SAS. The resort was designed and built by Canadian company Intrawest, which specialises in developing stylish resort villages incorporating lots of upmarket accommodation. It has developed, for example, Whistler and Tremblant in Canada and the new Village at Squaw Valley in California. This is its first venture into Europe.

The buildings are attractively rustic, designed in curving shapes in wood and stone, around a traffic-free, cobbled square. The varied apartments are furnished to a much higher standard than is usual in French resorts. The living rooms we saw are spacious, but some incorporate tiny kitchens and the bedrooms conform more to the French norm than the spacious standards you get in North American condos. The outdoor hot-tubs and pools, saunas and steam rooms are added attractions – as are the 'animations' planned every evening, such as fireworks, live music and wine tastings.

Last winter there were three restaurants and bars, a disco, ski and snowboard shops, a ski school and a few shops including a convenience store, bread shop and gift shop. For 2005/06 a crêperie and either an Asian or a Tex-Mex restaurant as well as sweet shops and kids' clothing shops are planned.

Two more apartment-hotel buildings will open for 2006/07 and the final one for 2007/08 – and all these will be managed by Radisson SAS. Nearly all of the 750 apartments that will make up Arc 1950 have already been sold. All the apartments are sold to private purchasers before being built, and most of the owners (around 70% of them British) lease them back to a rental management company.

MOUNTAIN RESTAURANTS
Plenty of choice

There are some good places if you search them out. At the south end, a five-minute taxi-ride from Vallandry will bring you to the Ancolie, a delightful traditional auberge with superb food (there are only 20 covers, so call 0479 079320 to book). At the north end, the 500-year-old Belliou la Fumée at Pré-St-Esprit is charmingly rustic and given 'top marks' by a reporter. The Ferme, 'simple but excellent value', and Aiguille Rouge down at Le Pré are both friendly, with good food.

The restaurants scattered here and there on the main slopes are mainly unremarkable. An exception is the Chalets de l'Arc, above Arc 2000 towards Col de la Chal – built in traditional wood and stone and serving good French food. The little Blanche Murée, just down from the Transarc mid-station, has received mixed reports. The restaurant at Col de la Chal has fabulous views but is otherwise ordinary. The Aiguille Grive at the foot of the piste at 1800 is 'very French and worth booking' says a reader this year, while another recommends the Chalet de l'Arcelle at 1600 for 'beautiful decoration and great local food'. At 1950 'the plat du jour at the Belles Pintes is always good value', while the 'gastronomic' Chalet de Luigi is a 'convenient slope-side spot'. Above Vallandry, the Poudreuse has a 'fair choice of meals', although 'drinks at the bar are expensive – beware'. The Solliet above Le Pré has good views across the valley to La Rosière and Ste-Foy.

SCHOOL AND GUIDES
Several, including a Brit school

The ESF here is renowned for being the first in Europe to teach ski évolutif, where you start by learning parallel turns on short skis, gradually moving on to longer skis. We have had reports of several beginners whose progress astonished their experienced friends. But we have reports of a couple being left behind at chair-lifts, 'lousy service', and limited English being spoken by some instructors. Private boarding lessons with the ESF have been 'very highly recommended'. The International school (Arc Aventures) has impressed reporters over the years. Optimum's ski courses (based in a catered chalet in Le Pré) have been suspended and they

↑ The highest lift-served point of Les Arcs is the Aiguille Rouge, starting point for some great runs

OT LES ARCS / LEBEAU

GETTING THERE

Air Geneva 156km/ 97 miles (3½hr); Lyon 200km/125 miles (3½hr); Chambéry 127km/79 miles (2½hr).

Rail Bourg-St-Maurice; frequent buses and direct funicular to resort.

Phone numbers From abroad use the prefix +33 and omit the initial '0' of the phone number.

are recommending the British ski school New Generation based in Vallandry, which started up here two seasons ago – it has has operated in Courchevel and Méribel for several seasons (see those chapters). Reports welcome. The Spirit school in 1950 had 'good adult lessons' although 'children's lessons were large, and there was a steep walk up to their beginner area,' said a 2005 reporter.

FACILITIES FOR CHILDREN
Good reports
We have received good reports on the Pommes de Pin facilities in Arc 1800 – 'great care and attention', 'patient approach to teaching'. Comments on children's ski classes are favourable, too – 'nearly all instructors spoke English', 'classes were crowded but teaching/childcare was good'. There is a children's area at 1800, complete with moving carpet lifts, a sledging track and a climbing wall. There are also a couple of discovery pistes, at 1800 and 1600, for children to find out about flora and fauna of the Alps.

STAYING THERE

HOW TO GO
New chalets and apartments
Most resort beds are in apartments. There is a Club Med at Arc 2000 and another is due to open at Peisey-Vallandry for 2005/06.
Chalets There are now several catered chalets in the Peisey-Vallandry area (see the end of the chapter), and Le Pré has a couple, but there are hardly any in the high Les Arcs 'villages'.
Hotels The choice of hotels in Les Arcs is gradually widening.
(((4 **Mercure Coralia** (1800) (0479 076500) Locally judged to be worth four stars rather than its actual three.
((3 **Golf** (1800) (0479 414343) An expensive but good 3-star, with 'great

ambience around its Jazz Bar', a sauna, gym, kindergarten, covered parking. An outdoor pool is planned for 2005/06.
(((3 **Cachette** (1600) (0479 077050) Renovated in the mid-1990s. 'Very nice' but it can be 'dominated by kids', say reporters – not surprising as 1600's childcare facilities are here.
((2 **Aiguille Rouge** (2000) (0479 075707) Daily free ski guiding.
Self-catering The original apartments are mostly tight on space, so paying extra for under-occupancy is a sound investment. The MGM Alpages de Chantel apartments above 1800 and the new Arc 1950 apartments (both bookable through Erna Low) are attractive and comfortable by French standards, with pools, saunas and gyms. They are both very convenient for skiing, but the MGM ones not for much else – a couple of reporters have not enjoyed staying here. The Ruitor apartments, set among trees between Villards and Charmettoger, are reported to be 'excellent in all respects'. L'Aiguille Grive has been recommended for spacious apartments and excellent slope access. In Arc 2000 the Chalet des Neiges and Chalet Altitude have 'luxury' apartments, with pool etc.

EATING OUT
Good choice in Arc 1800
In Arc 1600 and 2000 there are very few restaurants, but deserving a mention is the Chez Eux (Arc 2000), which received the thumbs-up for the 'excellent' Savoie meals: 'All eight of us were complimentary – a rare event!' 1800 has a choice of about 15 restaurants; an ad-based (so not comprehensive) guide is given away locally. The Petit Zinc restaurant in the Golf hotel has haute cuisine and high prices; it has a Friday evening seafood buffet. Chalet Bouvier has been highly recommended by a reporter who knows his food. The Chalet de Milou

Les Arcs

FRANCE

240

CHILDREN

Arc 1600:
Garderie La Cachette
t 0479 077050
8.30 to 6pm; ages
4mnth to 11yr

Arc 1800: Les
Pommes de Pin
t 0479 042431
8.30 to 12 noon; 1.30
to 5pm; ages 3 to 6

Arc 2000:
t 0479 076425
8.30 to 12 noon; 1.30
to 5pm; ages 3 to 6

Club Med
(at Arc 2000) has full
childcare facilities –
this is one of their
'family villages'.

Ski school
The ESF branches in
all three stations take
children from 3:
6 days (3hr am or
pm) €125

ACTIVITIES

Indoor Squash (1800),
saunas, solaria, multi-
gym (1800), cinemas,
games rooms, concert
halls, bowling (1800)

Outdoor Natural
skating rinks (1800/
2000), tobogganing,
organised snow-shoe
outings, dog-sledding,
10km/6 miles cleared
paths, hang-gliding,
horse-riding, sleigh
rides, ice grotto,
'snowtubbing' (2000)

UK Representative
Erna Low Consultants
9 Reece Mews
London SW7 3HE
t 0870 750 6820
info@ernalow.co.uk
www.ernalow.co.uk

has gourmet cuisine, 'including
excellent fish'. The Gargantus is a
decent, informal place. Readers have
been satisfied by 'enormous portions'
at Equipage and 'good food and great
service' at the Triangle Noir. Casa Mia
is an excellent all-rounder with
exceptionally friendly service ('Good
food but expensive wine,' says one
recent visitor). The Mountain Café does
much more than the Tex-Mex it
advertises, and copes well with big
family parties. Chez les Filles is worth a
visit for 'exceptional views' and 'good
food'. A popular outing is to drive
halfway down the mountain to the
welcoming and woody Bois de Lune at
Montvenix, which has perhaps the best
food in the area (booking advised). At
1950, Hemingway's Café does an
'excellent value three-course dinner'.
There is also the gourmet Chalet de
Luigi, Chez Anne for Savoyard
specialities and the Casa for Italian.

APRES-SKI
Arc 1800 is the place to be
1800 is the liveliest centre. The J.O. bar
is open until the early hours and has a
friendly atmosphere with live music.
The friendly Red Hot Saloon has bar
games and 'surprisingly good' live
music. 'I danced until I couldn't stand
any more,' claimed one recent reporter,
who also enjoyed the cocktails,
atmosphere and live music at the
Jungle Café. The Fairway disco keeps
rocking until 4am most mornings and
the Apokalypse 'isn't terrible'.
Reporters also like the Jazz Bar in the
Hotel Golf – 'good ambience, great
Mexican Bloody Mary with tequila'. And
the Gabotte in Place Miravaldi is
favoured for its 'cosy upstairs bar'.
In 1600 the Bar des Montagnes
opposite (and belonging to) the hotel
Cachette has games machines, pool
and live bands, and can be quite lively
even in low season, and a reporter has

recommended the Beguin. Another
recommends the Aubreuvoir for 'good
live bands most nights'.
In 2000 the Red Rock is 'good for
youngsters but too crowded for grown-
ups'; a reporter's verdict is that the
Tavern (also at 2000) is 'best all
round'. The Whistler Dream, in the
Chalet des Neiges, could be worth a
try. There is bowling at 1800 and
skating at 1800 and 2000. The Chalet
de Luigi at 1950 has a nightclub,
Hemingway's a bar, and the Belles
Pintes is an Irish-style pub.
The cinemas at 2000, 1800 and
1600 have English-language films once
or twice a week.

OFF THE SLOPES
Very poor
Les Arcs is not the place for an off-the-
slopes holiday. There is very little to
do; the only public pool is at Bourg-St-
Maurice, though several of the newer
apartment blocks have pools. You can
visit the Beaufort dairy and go
shopping in Bourg-St-Maurice (cheaper
for buying ski equipment) and there
are a few walks – nice ones up the
Nancroix valley. There's also an ice
grotto at the top of the Transarc, which
pedestrians can reach.

Peisey-Vallandry
1600m/5,250ft
Plan-Peisey and Vallandry are recently
developed lift-base resorts above the
old village of Peisey, which has a
bucket-lift up to Plan-Peisey. They
market themselves as Peisey-Vallandry,
and the cluster of villages hereabouts
is known collectively as Peisey-
Nancroix. Clear as mud, eh?
Both Vallandry and Plan-Peisey are
still small and quiet, but more
development is planned, including a
Club Med (due to open in Plan-Peisey
for 2005/06) and some MGM

TOURIST OFFICES

Les Arcs
1600: 0479 077070
1800: 0479 076111
1950: 0479 071257
2000: 0479 071378
lesarcs@lesarcs.com
www.lesarcs.com

Bourg-St-Maurice
t 0479 070492

Peisey-Vallandry
t 0479 079428
info@peisey-
vallandry.com
www.peisey-vallandry.
com

apartments. Vallandry attracts a lot of Dutch guests.

The cable-car to La Plagne leaves from Plan-Peisey, which has one hotel, a few shops, bars and restaurants but no real focus other than the lift station. A high-speed six-seater chair takes you into the slopes. Ski Beat has nine chalets here (and one down in Peisey – see below). Family specialist Esprit Ski has seven chalets (and comprehensive childcare facilities). The hotel Vanoise (0479 079219) has been recommended by readers for its position, food and staff – 'very welcoming, very French,' with few British guests. Reporters recommend Cordée ('excellent, frequented by locals'), Armoise ('very, very good and good value') and Solan ('brasserie, cosy inside, large terrace'). The Flying Squirrel is British-run, has a popular happy hour, live music, 'gourmet-burgers', weekly quiz night and live sport on TV.

Vallandry is a few hundred metres away and linked by shuttle-bus. A fast quad takes you into the slopes. More development has gone on here recently, with lots of new chalets and a small pedestrian-only square at the foot of the slopes with a small

supermarket, a ski shop and several bars and restaurants. Reporters' recommendations include the Calèche for excellent duck, the Refuge and L'Ourson for pizzas. There is a crêperie by the Vanoise Express ('good for galettes'). Jimmy's bar is popular, especially with the Dutch, but 'noisy'. Mont Blanc Bar is a Brit hang-out and Marlu more French. Ski Olympic has a chalet-hotel towards the top of Vallandry with the Forêt, a Beatles-themed bar-restaurant, next to it. Erna Low has self-catered chalets just below the square, with great views.

The old village of Peisey dates back 1,000 years, and has a fine baroque church. The other, mostly old, buildings include a few shops and a couple of bars and restaurants – a reader enjoyed 'wonderful fondue' at the Ormelune. Ski Hiver has five chalets here, Ski Beat one.

Nancroix is a roadside hamlet notable only for the excellent Ancolie restaurant (a great place for dinner – see 'Mountain restaurants').

Le Pré 1200m/3,940ft

Le Pré is a charming, quiet, rustic little hamlet with three successive chair-lifts (the first two quite slow) up to above Arc 2000. It has a couple of small bar-restaurants and a couple of British-run chalets, including a rustic one that owners Martin and Deirdre Rowe renovated and run themselves under the Optimum brand. We can personally vouch for their good food, free-flowing wine, jolly bar and basic but adequate bedrooms. But Le Pré is not at all suitable for beginners.

Bourg-St-Maurice
850m/2,790ft

Bourg-St-Maurice is a real French town, with cheaper hotels and restaurants and easy access to other resorts for day trips. The funicular goes straight to Arc 1600 in seven minutes – but beware, the last one down is at 7.30pm. Hostellerie du Pt-St-Bernard (0479 070432) has been reported to be a reasonable 2-star hotel – 'looks rundown, but friendly with super food'. Another reporter enjoyed the cheap and cheerful Savoyard (0479 070403), despite the noise: 'Take earplugs to sell to other guests.' A restaurant recommended by a 2004 reporter is the Refuge – 'best food of our stay'.

Avoriaz 1800

Functional, relatively snow-sure base for the Portes du Soleil circuit

242

COSTS

① ② ③ ④ ⑤ ⑥

RATINGS

The slopes

Fast lifts	***
Snow	***
Extent	*****
Expert	***
Intermediate	****
Beginner	****
Convenience	*****
Queues	***
Mountain restaurants	****

The rest

Scenery	***
Resort charm	**
Off-slope	*

NEWS

For 2004/05 the Fornet chair, up towards the Swiss border, was upgraded to a six-pack.

There's a new children's learning area with boarder-cross course.

KEY FACTS

Resort	1800m
	5,900ft

Portes du Soleil	
Slopes	950-2300m
	3,120-7,550ft
Lifts	208
Pistes	650km
	404 miles
Green	14%
Blue	39%
Red	37%
Black	10%
Snowmaking	
	329 acres

Avoriaz only	
Slopes	1100-2275m
	3,610-7,460ft
Lifts	38
Pistes	150km
	93 miles

➕ Good position on the main Portes du Soleil circuit, giving access to very extensive, quite varied runs

➕ Generally has the best snow in the Portes du Soleil

➕ Accommodation right on the slopes

➕ Good children's facilities

➕ Snowy paths entirely free of cars are an attractive formula, but ...

➖ Non-traditional architecture, which some find ugly

➖ Much of Portes du Soleil is low for a major French area, with the risk of poor snow or bare slopes low down

➖ Can get very crowded at weekends

➖ Little to do off the slopes

➖ Few hotels or chalets – mostly no-frills, cramped apartments

If Avoriaz sounds like the kind of thing you like, you'll probably like it. Unlike many purpose-built resorts it is truly car-free, with cars kept completely separate from its reliably snow-covered paths and pistes. The snow is thanks to the altitude, which the resort is making a half-hearted attempt to emphasise by re-branding itself Avoriaz 1800. As for us – we're more at home lower down, in the cosy chalets of Châtel 1200 or Morzine 1000 (see separate chapters).

THE RESORT

Avoriaz 1800 is a purpose-built, traffic-free resort perched above a dramatic, sheer rock face. From the edge of town horse-drawn sleighs or snowcats transport people and luggage from car parks to the accommodation – or you can borrow a sledge for a small deposit and transport your own. The problem of horse mess has been cut since they now wear 'nappies' and staff on snowmobiles scoop up what escapes! Cars are left in paid-for outdoor or underground parking – choose the latter to avoid a chaotic departure if it snows. You can book space.

As our scale plan suggests, it's a compact place, with everything close to hand (turn forward to Chamonix, for a striking comparison). But the village is set on quite a slope; elevators inside the buildings (and chair-lifts outside, during the day) mean moving around is no problem except when paths are icy, but if you plan to go out much in the evening it's worth staying near the central focus. Wherever you stay, you should be able to ski from the door.

The village is all angular, dark, wood-clad, high-rise buildings, mostly apartments. But the snow-covered paths and pistes give the place quite a friendly Alpine feel, and one recent reporter was impressed by the effort made to make the best of the resort.

The evenings are not especially

lively, but reporters have enjoyed 'a good ambience, both day and night', and a 'brilliant parade in half-term week, with a fire-eating display'. Family-friendly events are laid on all season. A floodlit cliff behind the resort adds to its nocturnal charm.

You can also stay in the lower hamlets of Ardent and Les Prodains.

Avoriaz is on the main lift circuit of the Portes du Soleil – for an overview, look at our separate chapter, later. It has links to Châtel in one direction and Champéry (Switzerland) in the other – both covered in separate chapters. It is above the valley resort of Morzine, to which it is linked by gondola (but not by piste). The slopes of Morzine and Les Gets, on the far side of Morzine, are part of the Portes du Soleil but not on the core circuit; both are covered in their own chapters. Car trips are possible to Flaine and Chamonix.

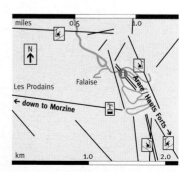

LIFT PASSES

Portes du Soleil
Covers all lifts in all resorts, and shuttle-buses.

Beginners
1 day €19.30 (Avoriaz area only)

Main pass
1 day €36
6 days €176

Senior citizens
Over 60: 6 days €141

Children
Under 16: 6 days €118
Under 5: free pass

Notes
Half-day pass available.

Alternative passes
Avoriaz-only pass available.
Snowboarder passes available for limited areas.

REPORTS WANTED

Recently we have had few reports on this resort. If you go there, please do send us a report.

THE MOUNTAINS

The slopes closest to Avoriaz are bleak and treeless, but snow-sure. The main linked Portes du Soleil circuit is easily done by intermediates of all abilities. Going clockwise avoids two snags in Morgins – the excessively sunny lower slopes of Bec de Corbeau, and the uphill walk to the next lift. The booklet-style piste map gives a reasonably clear picture of each resort along the way. The circuit breaks down at Châtel, where you need the frequent shuttle-bus.

THE SLOPES
Short runs and plenty of them
The village has lifts and pistes fanning out in all directions.

Facing the village are the slopes of **Arare-Hauts Forts** and, when snow conditions allow, there are long, steep runs down to Les Prodains.

The lifts off to the left go to the **Chavanette** sector on the Swiss border – a broad, undulating bowl. Beyond the border is the infamous Swiss Wall – a long, impressive mogul slope with a tricky start, but not the terror it is cracked up to be unless it's icy (it gets a lot of sun). It's no disgrace to ride the chair down – lots of people do. At the bottom of the Wall is the open terrain of Planachaux, above

Champéry, with links to the even bigger open area around Les Crosets and Champoussin.

Taking a lift up through the village of Avoriaz (or traversing from some of the highest accommodation) to the ridge behind the village is the way to the prettily wooded **Lindarets-Brocheaux** valley, from where lifts and runs in the excellent Linga sector lead to Châtel. A couple of reports suggest piste marking could be improved.

TERRAIN-PARKS
Still leading the way
In 1993 Avoriaz built the first French terrain-park, and now it boasts three. The Bleue du Lac up in the Arare area is aimed at experts, with advanced jumps such as tabletops, spines and hips, and a variety of rails. The Chapelle, in the resort centre, is better suited to novices. It has boarder-cross features as well as jumps. There's also a snow-skate park here, and a centrally positioned big air jump, where there's a competition at 7pm on Wednesdays. At the foot of the main slopes is the excellent Olympic-standard super-pipe, served by its own lift – 120m/390ft long with 4.5m/15ft walls. There is a special pass for those whose only interest is using the parks and the pipe.

SNOW RELIABILITY
High resort, low slopes
Although Avoriaz itself is high, its slopes don't go much higher – and some parts of the Portes du Soleil circuit are much lower. Considering their altitude, the north-facing slopes below Hauts Forts hold snow well. In general, the snow in Avoriaz is usually much better than over the border on the south-facing Swiss slopes.

Reporters generally say that grooming is good. More snow-guns have been installed, mostly in the Lindarets area, where we have had complaints of lack of snow in the past.

FOR EXPERTS
Several challenging runs
Tough terrain is scattered about. The challenging runs down from Hauts Forts to Prodains (including a World Cup downhill) are excellent. There is a tough red, and several long, truly black runs, one of which cuts through trees – useful in poor weather. Two chair-lifts serve the lower runs, which snow-guns help to keep open. The Swiss Wall at

↓ Champéry-Les Crosets   ↓ Champéry

Pointe de Mossettes
2275m

Chavanette   2215m   Hauts Forts

Châtel

Col du ssachaux
1920m

Avoriaz 1800

Les Lindarets
1495m

Ardent
1200m

Les Prodains
1145m

Morzine
1000m/3,280ft

SCHOOLS

ESF
t 0450 740565

International (L'Ecole de Glisse)
t 0450 740218

Emery (snowboard)
t 0450 741264

Avoriaz Alpine School
t 0450 747691

Classes
(ESF prices)
6 days (2½hr am and pm) €149

Private lessons
€32 for 1hr, for 1 or 2 people

CHILDREN

Les P'tits Loups
t 0450 740038
9am to 6pm; ages 3mnth to 5yr; 6 days €185

Annie Famose Children's Village and Le Village Snowboard
t 0450 740446
9am to 5.30 (skiing 9.30 to 12 noon and 1.30 to 4pm); ages 3 to 16; 6 days with meal €208

Club Med
This is a 'family village', with comprehensive childcare facilities

Ski schools
Take children from 4 to 12 (6 days €135)

WEBSITES

Chavanette will naturally be on your agenda, and Châtel is well worth a trip. The black runs off the Swiss side of Mossettes and Pointe de l'Au are worth trying and one reporter had a 'very good day' here exploring off-piste with a guide. Four 'snow-cross' runs – ungroomed but avalanche controlled and patrolled – have been introduced in the Hauts Forts (a 'safe favourite', writes a reporter), Lindarets, Chavanette and Mossettes areas. They are marked on the piste map, closed when dangerous and an excellent idea.

FOR INTERMEDIATES
Virtually the whole area
Although some sections lack variety, the Portes du Soleil is excellent for all grades of intermediates when snow is in good supply. Timid types not worried about pretty surroundings need not leave the Avoriaz sector; reporters recommend the 'wonderfully quiet' and 'scenic' blues to Prodains. Arare and Chavanette are gentle, spacious and above the tree-line bowls. The Lindarets area is also easy, with pretty runs through the trees, but several reporters complain about long flat sections where poling is required. Champoussin has a lot of easy runs, reached without too much difficulty via Les Crosets and Pointe de l'Au. Better intermediates have virtually the whole

area at their disposal. The runs down to Pré-la-Joux and L'Essert on the way to Châtel, and those either side of Morgins, are particularly attractive – as are the long runs down to Grand-Paradis near Champéry when snow conditions allow. Brave intermediates may want to take on the Wall, but Pointe de Mossettes offers an easier route to Switzerland.

FOR BEGINNERS
Convenient and good for snow
The nursery slopes seem small in relation to the size of the resort, but are adequate because so many visitors are intermediates. The slopes are sunny, yet good for snow, and link well to longer, easy runs. The main problem can be the crowded pistes. One recent reporter complains crowds and collisions on the Plateau area, made progress 'painfully slow' for novices taking classes there.

FOR CROSS-COUNTRY
Varied, with some blacks
There are 45km/28 miles of trails, a third classified as black, mainly between Avoriaz and Super-Morzine, with other fine trails down to Lindarets and around Montriond. The only drawback is that several trails are not loops, but 'out and back' routes.

QUEUES
Main problems now gone
Most of the bad queues have been eliminated by new high-speed lifts. But we still receive reports of long queues to get out of Les Lindarets towards Châtel on the slow Chaux Fleurie chair-lift to Bassachaux and for the cable-car at Prodains. Otherwise, 2005 visitors report few problems. At weekends crowds on the pistes (especially around the village) can be worse than queues for the lifts, with care having to be taken to avoid collisions.

boarding

Avoriaz has always encouraged snowboarding, opening France's first terrain-park in 1993 (the resort now has three parks, including a monster half-pipe – see 'Terrain-parks'). The snowboard pass (30 euros for two days) is excellent value if you're interested only in the parks. There's a specialist snowboard school (Emery) and a snowboard village for children aged 6 to 16. Chalet Snowboard, the first chalet company to target snowboarders, has a couple of chalets at Les Prodains. Only a few (mainly avoidable) drags are left, and the six-pack chairs make for a comfortable ride. Reporters warn of long flat stretches on the pistes. The snow-cross free-ride areas (see 'For experts') are a great innovation for riders who enjoy off-piste.

GETTING THERE

Air Geneva 80km/ 50 miles (2hr); Lyon 200km/124 miles (3½hr).

Rail Cluses (42km/ 26 miles) or Thonon (45km/28 miles); bus and cable-car to resort.

ACTIVITIES

Indoor Health centre 'Altiform' (sauna, gym, hot-tub), squash, ice rink, Turkish baths, cinema, bowling **Outdoor** Ice rink, snake slides, mountain biking on snow, dog-sledding, hot air ballooning, ice diving, walking paths, horse-drawn carriage tours, helicopter flights

Phone numbers
From abroad use the prefix +33 and omit the initial '0' of the phone number.

TOURIST OFFICE

t 0450 740211
info@avoriaz.com
www.avoriaz.com

MOUNTAIN RESTAURANTS
Good choice over the hill
The charming, rustic chalets in the hamlet of Les Lindarets form one of the great concentrations of mountain restaurants in the Alps. The jolly Crémaillière has wonderful chanterelle mushrooms and great atmosphere, but on a good day it's difficult to beat the Terrasse. Near the top of the gondola up from Morzine, the rustic Grenouille du Marais has good food, views and atmosphere. The 'friendly' table-service Abricotine does 'excellent galettes' and good-value main courses. The Refuge des Brocheaux at Les Brocheaux offers 'efficient service and a good menu'. Pas de Chavanette, at the top of the Swiss Wall, has been recommended. Don't forget to check out chapters on other Portes du Soleil resorts – particularly Châtel and Champéry.

SCHOOLS AND GUIDES
Try AAS
The ESF has a good reputation; classes can be large, but we have reports in 2005 of 'great instruction' and another of very successful private snowboard lessons. The Avoriaz Alpine School (formerly part of British Alpine Ski School) has British instructors and has been highly recommended, especially for 'quite excellent children's lessons'. They now operate in Ardent as well as Avoriaz. Emery is a specialist snowboard school.

FACILITIES FOR CHILDREN
'Annie Famose delivers'
The Village des Enfants, run by ex-downhill champ Annie Famose, is a key part of the family appeal of Avoriaz. Its facilities are excellent – a chalet full of activities and special slopes complete with Disney characters. There's a snowboard village too.

HOW TO GO
Self-catering dominates
Alternatives to apartments are few.
Chalets There are several available – comfortable and attractive but mainly designed for small family groups.
Hotels There is one good hotel and a Club Med 'village'.
⟨⟨3⟩ **Dromonts** (0450 740811) The original core of the resort, taken over and renovated by a celebrity French chef and now in the *Hip Hotels* guidebook. We stayed there recently and liked it, not least for the food.
Self-catering Past reporters have said that some apartments needed refurbishing, and others are typically 'basic and cramped'. But the Falaise apart-hotel, Douchka, Sepia and Datcha ('very basic') residences have all been recommended.

EATING OUT
Good; booking essential
There are more than 30 restaurants (though a reporter this year criticises 'limited variety'). The hotel Dromonts has a gastronomic restaurant with an excellent set-price six-course meal and a simpler Table du Marché restaurant. The Bistro and Cabane have been recommended for 'good food and value', as have the Fontaines Blanches and Douchka for Savoyard food, Intrêts for 'pizza and pasta', 'table-barbecues and Savoyard fare', and Au Briska, for a cosy night out. You can buy in advance meal vouchers for dinner in a range of five restaurants, when you book Pierre & Vacances apartments. 'Restricted menu but excellent value,' says a reporter.

APRES-SKI
Lively, but not much choice
A few bars have a good atmosphere, particularly in happy hour. The Yeti is busy at 4pm. The Tavaillon attracts Brits and has Sky TV, and the Fantastique is worth a visit. For late-night dancing the Choucas and The Place have bands. Going down to Morzine is possible.

OFF THE SLOPES
Not much at the resort
Those not interested in the slopes are better off in Morzine – though Avoriaz does have the Altiform Fitness Centre, with saunas and hot-tubs. Pedestrians are not allowed to ride the chair-lifts, which is a shame.

Chamonix

Views to die for and slopes that can kill: hire a guide to go off-piste

COSTS

① ② ③ ④ ⑤ ⑥

RATINGS

The slopes

Fast lifts	***
Snow	****
Extent	***
Expert	*****
Intermediate	**
Beginner	*
Convenience	*
Queues	**
Mountain restaurants	**

The rest

Scenery	*****
Resort charm	****
Off-slope	*****

NEWS

For 2004/05 a new eight-person gondola opened at Vallorcine, linking the village to the slopes of Le Tour. A blue run, Fôret Verte, goes down to the lift base.

The Nants black run from Brévent to the valley has been improved.

There are plans to upgrade the lift to L'Index at the top of Flégère, but the timing is not known.

- ➕ A lot of very tough terrain, especially off-piste
- ➕ Amazing cable-car, for the famous Vallée Blanche (or just the views)
- ➕ Stunning views of peaks and glaciers
- ➕ Lots of different resorts and areas covered on Mont Blanc lift pass
- ➕ Town steeped in Alpine traditions, with lots to do off the slopes
- ➕ Easy access by road, rail and air – excellent weekend destination

- ➖ Several separate mountains: mixed ability groups are likely to have to split up, and the bus service is far from perfect – we always take a car
- ➖ Pistes in each individual area are quite limited
- ➖ The few runs to the valley are often closed – and can be dangerous when open
- ➖ Crowds, queues, lots of road traffic
- ➖ Bad weather can shut the best runs

Chamonix could not be more different from the archetypal high-altitude, purpose-built French resort. Unless you are based next to one mountain and stick to it, you have to drive or take a bus each day. There are all sorts of terrain, but it offers more to interest the expert than anyone else, and to make the most of the area you need a mountain guide rather than a piste map. Chamonix is neither convenient nor conventional.

But it is special. The Chamonix valley cuts deeply through Europe's highest mountains and glaciers. The views are stunning and the runs are everything really tough runs should be – not only steep, but high and long. If you like your snow and scenery on the wild side, give Chamonix a try. But be warned: there are those who try it and never go home – including lots of Brits.

THE RESORT

Chamonix is a long-established tourist town that over the years has spread for miles along its valley in the shadow of Mont Blanc – the scale map below is one of the biggest in these pages.

On either side of the centre, just within walking distance, are lifts to two of the dozen slope areas in the valley – the famous cable-car to the Aiguille du Midi, and a gondola to Le Brévent. Also on the fringe of the centre is the nursery slope of Les Planards. All the other lift bases involve bus-rides – the nearest being the cable-car to La Flégère at the village of Les Praz.

Chamonix is a bustling town with scores of hotels and restaurants, visitors all year round and a lively Saturday market. The car-free centre of town is full of atmosphere, with cobbled streets and squares, beautiful old buildings, a fast-running river, pavement cafes crowded with shoppers and tourists sipping drinks and staring at the glaciers above. Not everything is rosy: unsightly modern buildings have been built on to the periphery (especially near the Aiguille du Midi cable-car station), some of the lovely old buildings have been allowed to fall into disrepair, and at times traffic clogs the streets around the car-free centre.

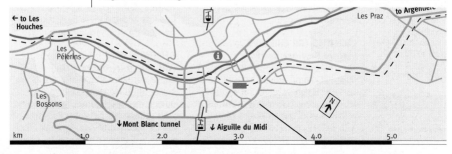

Once you get over the fact that the place is hopelessly disconnected, you come to appreciate the upside – that Chamonix has a good variety of slopes, and that each of the different areas is worth exploring. Practically all the slopes are above the tree line.

THE SLOPES
Very fragmented

The areas within the Chamonix valley – there are 11 in total – are either small, low, beginners' areas or are much higher up, above the wooded slopes that plunge to the valley floor, reached by cable-car or gondola.

The modern six-seat gondola for **Le Brévent** departs a short, steep walk from the centre of town, and the cable-car above takes you to the summit. The black run back to the valley was improved last year – not before time. At **La Flégère**, like Le Brévent, the runs are mainly between 1900m and 2450m (6,200ft and 8,040ft), and the stunning views of Mont Blanc are worth the price of the lift pass. The cable-car linking La Flégère and Le Brévent now makes this side of the valley more user-friendly – though reporters have found it's often closed by high winds.

A cable-car or chair-lift take you up to **Les Grands Montets** above Argentière. Much of the best terrain is still accessed by a further cable-car, of relatively low capacity. This costs extra – 5 euros a trip – though two free rides are included in a six-day pass. But it still attracts big queues (a 2005 reporter waited an hour at Easter).

Le Tour has an area of mainly easy pistes. It is also the starting point for good off-piste runs, some of which end up over the border in Switzerland. Sheltered pistes descend to Vallorcine from where you can return using the new gondola.

There is a valley piste map and an informative little Cham'Ski handbook, which includes all the local area piste maps, with brief descriptions of each run and assessments of suitability for different abilities. But for navigation purposes the individual piste maps available at each area are best.

Most of our reporters have been more impressed than they expected with the piste grooming, but not with the signposting of the runs ('virtually non-existent', said one reporter; 'horrendous' was the verdict in 2005).

↑ Prices may be high and service may not be special, but just look at that view
OT CHAMONIX-MONT BLANC

Chamonix's shops deal in everything from high-tech equipment to tacky souvenirs. But reporters often comment on the number and excellence of the former, and Chamonix remains essentially a town for mountain people rather than for poseurs.

Strung out for 20km/12 miles along the Chamonix valley are several separate lift systems, some with attached villages, from Les Houches at one end to Le Tour at the other. Regular buses link the lift stations and villages but can get very crowded and aren't always reliable – that to Les Houches is reportedly especially poor. There is an evening service, but it is said to finish too early. Like many reporters, we rate a car as essential. A car also means you can get easily to other resorts covered by the Mont Blanc pass, such as Megève and Les Contamines, and Courmayeur in Italy.

The obvious place to stay for the full Chamonix experience is in downtown Chamonix. If you plan to ski mainly Argentière, Le Tour or Les Houches, staying nearby obviously makes sense.

Chamonix

247

FRANCE

248

TERRAIN-PARKS
Competitive

Head for Argentière and the Grands Montets for the hairiest action – the terrain-park and half-pipe (not built last year) host regular competitions, and there's a boarder-cross course. There's also a natural half-pipe/gully at Le Tour.

SNOW RELIABILITY
Good high up; poor low down

The top runs on the north-facing Grands Montets slopes above Argentière are almost guaranteed to have good snow, and the season normally lasts well into May. The risk of finding the top lift shut because of bad weather is more of a worry (and is the excuse for not including unlimited use of the lift on the main pass). There's snowmaking on the busy Bochard piste and the run to the valley, which can now be kept open late in the season. Le Tour has a snowy location and a good late-season record. The largely south-facing slopes of Brévent and Flégère suffer in warm weather, and the steep runs to the resort are often closed. Don't be tempted to try these unless you know they are in good condition – they can be lethal. Some of the low beginners' areas have snowmaking.

FOR EXPERTS
One of the great resorts

Chamonix is justifiably renowned for its extensive steep terrain, and for impressively deep snow. To get the best out of the area without putting your life at risk you really need to have a local guide. There is also lots of excellent terrain for ski touring on skins. See the feature panel, facing.

The Grands Montets cable-car offers stunning views from the observation platform above the top station – if you've got the legs and lungs to climb the 121 steep metal steps. (But beware: it's 200 more steps down from the cable-car before you hit the snow.)

The ungroomed black pistes from here – Point de Vue and Pylones – are long and exhilarating. The Point de Vue sails right by some dramatic sections of glacier, with marvellous views of the crevasses.

The Bochard gondola serves a challenging red and a moderate black. Alternatively, head directly down the Combe de la Pendant bowl for 1000m/ 3,280ft vertical of wild, unpisted mountainside. The continuation down the valley side to Le Lavancher is equally challenging; it suffers frequently from lack of snow.

At Le Brévent there's more to test experts than the piste map suggests –

THE BEST OFF-PISTE SKIING IN THE WORLD?

Chamonix is renowned as an extreme sports Mecca, with arguably some of the best off-piste skiing in the world. And while thrill seekers and off-piste specialists are spoilt for choice, there is plenty for those looking for their first powder experience. Here, the guides of Chamonix Experience give us a tour.

Les Houches and Le Tour, at opposite ends of the Chamonix Valley, are ideal for a first taste off the beaten track. The forested slopes of Les Houches are easy to navigate on bad-weather days, with gentle blue runs bringing you back to the valley. Le Tour's open slopes are perfect for a foray into deep snow in between the pistes, with firmer ground just a few reassuring metres away.

Chamonix Experience offers a full range of mountain guiding and instruction. All guides are IFMGA qualified and have spent years climbing, skiing and snowboarding in the Mont Blanc region.

t 00 33 (0)450 540936
info@chamex.com
www.chamex.com

Snowboarders flock to La Flégère after a snowfall, its array of boulders and drop-offs turning it into a massive terrain-park. The open bowl of Combe Lachenal is easily accessed from the top of the Index lift, and the south-facing slopes of this ski area provide excellent spring skiing.

From the top of Les Grands Montets (3275m/10,740ft) skiing is mostly off-piste and on glacial terrain, so a good level of technique is required. The vast north-facing slope of La Face is fairly steep but with plenty of room for tracks. The steep, extensive area reached via the Point de Vue piste offers stupendous views, plus snow conditions that are often among the best in the valley. The Grands Montets also gives access to the steep Pas de Chèvre run. Skiing under the colossal granite spire of Le Dru, with views of Mont Blanc and the Vallée Blanche in the distance, is an unforgettable experience. The Couloir du Dru and the Rectiligne are also on this face, reserved for the adventurous – with some slopes of 40/45˚.

These are just some of the off-piste options in the Chamonix valley, but the possibilities are endless. Together with ski-touring itineraries like the Haute Route (Chamonix to Zermatt), and heli-skiing on the Italian side of Mont Blanc and in neighbouring Switzerland, the wealth of off-piste on offer could keep you skiing for a lifetime. We haven't mentioned here the Vallée Blanche, because it is covered in a separate feature panel in this chapter.

Chamonix

The Mountain Adventure Specialists

Heliskiing • Haute Route • Vallée Blanche
Avalanche Courses • Off Piste • Ice Climbing
Instructional Courses • Private Guiding

Photo © www.yakphoto.com

+33 4 50 54 09 36 • www.chamex.com • info@chamex.com

↑ The Vallée Blanche may be high-mountain territory, but there is, of course, a restaurant terrace waiting for you towards the end
SNOWPIX.COM / CHRIS GILL

LIFT PASSES

Cham'Ski pass
Covers all areas in the Chamonix Valley and the bus services between them, except Grands-Montets cable-car and Les Houches area.

Beginners
Cham'Start 6-day pass €85 and covers all valley floor lifts.

Main pass
1 day €43
6 days €181

Senior citizens
Over 60: 6 days €154

Children
Under 15: 6 days €154
Under 11: 6 days €127
Under 4: free pass

Notes
6-day pass includes four ascents on the Grands Montets cable-car and a day in Courmayeur.

Alternative passes
Skipass Mont Blanc covers lifts in the 13 resorts of the Mont Blanc area and Courmayeur in Italy.

there are a number of variations on the runs down from the summit. 'Superb when open,' said one visitor; 'Requires a lot of bottle,' writes another. Some are very steep and prone to ice. The runs in the sunny Col de la Charlanon are uncrowded and include one red piste and lots of excellent off-piste if the snow is good.

At La Flégère there are further excellent challenging slopes – in the Combe Lachenal, crossed by the linking cable-car, for example – and a pretty tough run back to the village when snow-cover permits. Le Tour boasts little tough terrain on-piste but there are good off-piste routes from the high points to the village and over the back towards Vallorcine or into Switzerland.

FOR INTERMEDIATES
It's worth trying it all
For less confident intermediates, the Col de Balme area above Le Tour is good for cruising and usually free from crowds. There are excellent shady runs on the north side of Tête de Balme, served by a quad. When conditions permit, you can head right down to Vallorcine and ride the new gondola.

More adventurous intermediates will also want to try the other three main areas, though they may find the Grands Montets tough going (and crowded). The bulk of the terrain at Le Brévent and La Flégère provides a sensible mix of blue and red runs; at Le Brévent the slopes have been redesigned to achieve this.

If the snow and weather are good, join a guided group and do the Vallée Blanche (see feature panel below).

A day trip to Courmayeur makes an interesting change of scene, especially when the weather is bad (it can be sunny there when Chamonix's high lifts are closed by blizzards or high winds).

THE VALLÉE BLANCHE

This is a trip you do for the stunning scenery. The views of the ice, the crevasses and seracs – and the spectacular rock spires beyond – are simply mind-blowing. The run, although exceptionally long, is not steep – mostly effortless gliding down gentle slopes with only the occasional steeper, choppy section to deal with. In the right conditions, it is well within the capability of a confident intermediate (rather flat for snowboarders, says a reporter). But if snow is sparse, the run can turn tricky – there can be patches of sheet ice, exposed stones and rocks, and narrow snow bridges over gaping crevasses. And if fresh snow is abundant, different challenges may arise. Go in a guided group – dangerous crevasses lurk to swallow those not in the know. The trip is popular – on a busy day 2,500 people do it; book in advance at the Maison de la Montagne or other ski school offices. To miss the worst of the crowds go very early on a weekday, or in the afternoon if you are a good skier and can get down quickly.

The amazing Aiguille du Midi cable-car takes you to 3840m/12,600ft. Across the bridge from the arrival station on the Piton Nord is the Piton Central; the view of Mont Blanc from the cafe – a stair-climb higher – should not be missed. It gives you the opportunity to adjust to the dizzying altitude. A tunnel delivers you to the infamous ridge-walk down to the start of the run. Be prepared for extreme cold up here. There is (usually) a fixed guide-rope for you to hang on to, and many parties rope up to their guides. You may still feel envious of those nonchalantly strolling down in crampons; you may wish you'd stayed in bed.

After that, the run seems a doddle. There are variants on the classic route, of varying difficulty and danger. Lack of snow often rules out the full 24km/15 mile run down to Chamonix; a stairway and slow gondola link the glacier to the station at Montenvers, for the half-hour mountain railway ride down to the town.

boarding

Chamonix is a place of pilgrimage for advanced boarders, but not the best place to learn. Most areas are equipped mainly with cable-cars, gondolas and chairs. However, there are quite a few difficult drags at Le Tour that cause boarders problems – though you can avoid these if you are ready to contend with cat tracks to take you to other lifts, according to a reporter. If you do the Vallée Blanche, be warned: the usual route is flat in places. If you're ready to tackle tougher off-piste, check out former British champ Neil McNab's excellent extreme backcountry camps (www.mcnab.co.uk) – 'fantastic' says a recent reporter.

FOR BEGINNERS
Best to learn elsewhere
If there is snow low down, the nursery lifts at La Vormaine, Les Chosalets, Les Planards and Le Savoy are fine for first-timers, who will not be bothered by speed-merchants there. But the separation of beginners' slopes from the rest inhibits the transition to real runs, and makes lunchtime meetings of mixed groups difficult. The slopes on the south side of the valley – Les Planards, in particular – can be dark and cold in mid-winter, as the editorial daughter can testify. Le Savoy is sunny, but devoid of restaurants. Better to learn elsewhere, and come to Chamonix when you can appreciate the tough terrain.

FOR CROSS-COUNTRY
A decent network of trails
Most of the 42km/26 miles of prepared trails lie along the valley between Chamonix and Argentière. There are green, blue, red and black loops. All these trails are fairly low; they're cold and shady in midwinter, and they fade fast in the spring sun.

QUEUES
Morning and afternoon problems
The main lifts from the valley at Chamonix and Argentière produce queues at peak times – and getting down when the home runs are closed can be as bad as getting up the mountain in the morning. At Flégère a booking system comes into operation

Chamonix

251

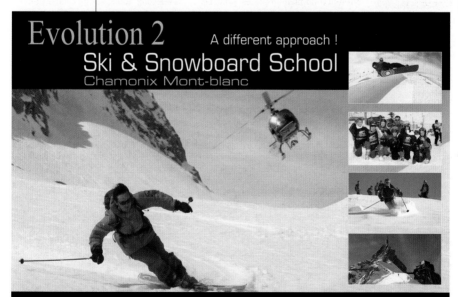

CHILDREN

Panda Club
t 0450 558612
Ages 3 to 12; 8.30-
5pm; includes ski
lessons

Babysitter list
Available from the
tourist office

Ski school
ESF takes children
aged 6 to 12 (6 half
days €210); Evolution
2 takes children from
age 3

SCHOOLS

ESF
t 0450 532257

Evolution 2
t 0450 559022

Classes
6 half days: €164

Private lessons
€36 for 1hr, for 1 or
2 people

GUIDES

**Compagnie des
Guides**
t 0450 530088

Chamonix Experience
t 0450 540936

at the end of the day.

In poor weather Les Houches gets crowded and the queues for the Bellevue cable-car can then be bad.

There are still long queues for the top cable-car on Les Grands Montets – often all day long. When they reach 30 minutes a booking system operates, so you can go skiing until it's your turn to ride – often an hour or more later. The replacement of the slow Herse chair by a six-pack has relieved the pressure there and on the Bochard gondola – a 2005 visitor confirms this. And the new gondola at Vallorcine seems to be queue-free 'even on Saturdays'. Crowded pistes are reported to be more of a problem in places – most notably at Lognan.

MOUNTAIN RESTAURANTS
Surprisingly dull

The Bergerie de Planpraz on Le Brévent is the most attractive option – built in wood and stone, with self- and table-service. Food and service are 'excellent'; but it gets very busy. The little Panoramic at the top enjoys amazing views over to Mont Blanc and the food is fine. Altitude 2000 provides table-service at rip-off prices and one reporter rates the attitude of the waiters as 'absolutely terrible'. There's a self-service place at La Flégère with a large terrace and excellent views.

On the Grands Montets the Plan Joran serves good food and does table- and self-service, but gets busy, according to a reporter. There's also an indoor picnic area. The restaurant at Lognan has been smartly renovated. The rustic Chalet-Refuge de Lognan, off the Variante Hôtel run to the valley, and overlooking the Argentière glacier, has marvellous food and is very popular.

At the top of the Le Tour gondola, the Chalet de Charamillon is an adequate self-service and there's a picnic area. The Refuge du Col de Balme

– a short hike from the lifts – is charming, but has 'appalling' service.

SCHOOLS AND GUIDES
The place to try something new

The schools here are particularly strong in specialist fields – off-piste, glacier and couloir skiing, ski-touring, snowboarding and cross-country. English-speaking instructors and mountain guides are plentiful, and specialist Chamonix tour operators can arrange them in advance for guests. At the Maison de la Montagne is the main ESF office and the HQ of the Compagnie des Guides, which has taken visitors to the mountains for 150 years. Both now offer ready-made week-long 'tours' taking clients to a different mountain or resort each day. We have a good report of the ESF Ski Fun Tour, where they ski a different Mont Blanc region resort each day, transport included: 'Fantastic – we cannot speak highly enough of the guides.' Competition is provided by a number of smaller, independent guiding and teaching outfits. Evolution 2 is recommended this year: 'never disappoints', writes a reporter. Chamonix Experience offers a full range of options, from classic itineraries and Italian heli-skiing to hidden off-piste routes and avalanche courses.

FACILITIES FOR CHILDREN
Better than they were

The Panda Club is used by quite a few British visitors and reports have been enthusiastic. The Argentière base can be inconvenient for meeting up with children for the afternoons. The Club Med nursery seems to go down well too. UK tour operator Esprit Ski has chalets here, with a nursery in the Sapinière chalet-hotel near the Savoy nursery slope.

Beware the tendency to keep children on the valley nursery slopes for the convenience of the school.

GETTING THERE

Air Geneva 86km/ 53 miles (1½hr). Lyon 226km/140 miles (3hr).

Rail Station in resort, on the St Gervais-Le Fayet/Vallorcine line.

Direct TGV link from Paris on Friday evenings and weekends.

STAYING THERE

HOW TO GO
Any way you like

There is all sorts of accommodation, and lots of it. The tourist office has a 'useful central booking system'. Call 0450 532333 or email reservation@ chamonix.com.

Chalets Many are run by small operators that cater for this specialist market. Quality tends to be high and value for money good by comparison with resorts that have wider appeal.

Hotels A wide choice, many modestly priced, and the vast majority with fewer than 30 rooms. Bookings for a day or two are no problem – the peak season is summer.

(((④ **Albert 1er** (0450 530509) Smart, 100-year-old chalet-style hotel with 'truly excellent' and 'reasonably priced' food (Michelin stars) but expensive rooms (especially in the farmhouse annexe). Indoor-outdoor pool.

(((④ **Auberge du Bois Prin** (0450 533351) A small modern chalet with a big reputation; great views; bit of a hike into town; closer to Le Brévent.

(((④ **Mont-Blanc** (0450 530564) Central, luxurious.

(((④ **Jeu de Paume** (Lavancher) (0450 540376) Alpine satellite of a chic Parisian hotel: a beautifully furnished modern chalet halfway to Argentière: 'Tasteful, friendly staff ... lovely.'

(((④ **Grand Hotel des Alpes** (0450 553780) Newly renovated, elegant central hotel with pool, sauna, hot-tub. Friendly, largely Italian staff.

(((③ **Alpina** (0450 534777) Much the biggest in town: modernist-functional place just north of centre.

(((③ **Gourmets & Italy** (0450 530138) Spot-on central mid-price B&B hotel.

(((③ **Labrador** (Les Praz) (0450 559009) Scandinavian-style chalet close to the Flégère lift. Good restaurant.

(((③ **Prieuré** (0450 532072) Mega-chalet on northern ring-road – handy for drivers, quite close to centre.

(((③ **Vallée Blanche** (0450 530450) Smart, low-priced 3-star B&B hotel, handy for centre and Aiguille du Midi.

(((② **Richemond** (0450 530885) Traditional, comfortable, with good public areas. 'Excellent, very good value, superb food,' says one reporter. 'Rather faded,' writes another.

(((② **Arve** (0450 530231) Central, by the river; small rooms. 'Good value and superb service from owners.'

Chamonix

ACTIVITIES

Indoor Sports complex (swimming pool, sauna, steam room, tennis, squash ice rink, fitness room, climbing wall), Alpine museum, library, casino, bridge, three cinemas, bowling

Outdoor Ice rink, panoramic flights, snow-shoeing, walking paths, ice-climbing

Ⓒ **Pointe Isabelle** (0450 531287) Not pretty, but central; friendly staff, good plain food and well-equipped rooms.
① **Faucigny** (0450 530117) Cottage-style; in centre.
Also recommended by a reporter is the 'friendly' Morgane (0450 535715). Pool.
Self-catering Many properties in UK package brochures are in convenient but cramped blocks in Chamonix Sud. The Balcons du Savoy are a cut above: great view, spacious rooms, use of a pool, a steam room and a solarium. The Splendid & Golf apartments in Les Praz are charming and close to the Flégère cable-car. Erna Low has some luxury places available.

EATING OUT
Plenty of quality places
The top hotels all have excellent restaurants and there are many other good places to eat. The Sarpé is a lovely 'mountain' restaurant and the Impossible is rustic but smart and features good regional dishes. We always enjoy the Atmosphere, by the river, despite its two-sitting system ('excellent', says a 2005 reporter). The National, next door, is also reported to be 'very good'. The Panier des Quatre Saisons is another favourite ('good food at reasonable prices') – much better than its shopping-gallery setting would suggest.

Reader recommendations include Maison Carrier in the Albert 1er hotel ('Bustling, rustic with great value traditional food'), the Crochon ('Good Savoyard fare, plus some varied and innovative dishes'), the Cabane next to the Labrador hotel in Les Praz ('excellent – set menu or à la carte'), the Calèche ('good food, atmosphere and service') and the Petit Moulin ('tiny, excellent, especially for veggies'). The Monchu is good for Savoyard specialities, as is the 'outstanding' Chaudron – a 2005 reporter's favourite ('excellent service'). The Bergerie is traditional and 'fantastic', according to another visitor. Separate reports this year endorse the popular Casa Valerio for 'fabulous pasta' and 'excellent pizza'. The Spiga d'Oro is another recommended Italian, over a 'lovely' deli.

There are a number of ethnic restaurants – Mexican, Spanish, Japanese, Chinese, Indian etc – which is not to say any of them are any good (the summer trade is not very discriminating). And lots of brasseries and cafes.

APRES-SKI
Lots of bars and music
Many of the bars around the pedestrianised centre of Chamonix get crowded for a couple of hours at sundown – none more so than the Choucas video bar. During the evening, The Pub ('friendly staff and good British/Irish beer'), Wild Wallabies, the Bar'd Up and the Bar du Moulin are busy. The Chambre Neuf at the Gustavia hotel remains so until late. The Micro Brasserie is 'very good', with live bands and DJs.

There are plenty of bars for a quieter drink, too. The Brit-run Dérapage has happy hours early and mid-evening; the Queen Vic is 'nice and dingy with a snug, pool table, good music and Beamish on tap'; L'Expedition is 'small and friendly'. There's a lively variety of nightclubs and discos. The Choucas (again), and Dick's Tea bar are popular. The Cantina sometimes has live music and is open late. Bar Terrasse has live music every night. Other bars include Privilege, TOF and BPM.

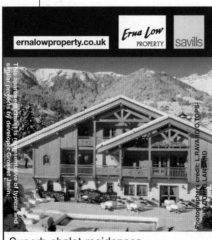

Phone numbers
From abroad use the
prefix +33 and omit
the initial '0' of the
phone number.

TOURIST OFFICES

Chamonix
t 0450 530024
info@chamonix.com
www.chamonix.com
Argentière
t 0450 540214
info@argentiere.
com
Les Houches
t 0450 555062
info@leshouches.com
www.leshouches.com

WEBSITES

For links to resort
sites, go to our own
new site at
www.wtss.co.uk

OFF THE SLOPES
An excellent choice
There's more off-slope activity here
than in many resorts, though one
reader complains that toddlers are not
well catered for. Excursion possibilities
include Annecy, Geneva, Martigny,
Courmayeur and Turin. The Alpine
Museum is 'very interesting' (also
includes entry to the Espace Tairraz
gallery), the library has a good
selection of English language books
and there's a good sports centre and
swimming pool.

Argentière 1240m/4,070ft

The old village is in a lovely setting
towards the head of the valley – the
Glacier d'Argentière pokes down
towards it and the Aiguille du Midi and
Mont Blanc still dominate the scene
down the valley. There's 'more
snowmaking on the lower runs',
according to one reporter. There's a
fair bit of modern development but it
still has a rustic appeal. A number of
the hotels are simple, inexpensive and
handy for the village centre – less so
for the slopes – but the Grands-
Montets (0450 540666) is a large
chalet-style building, right next to the
piste and the Panda Club for children.
The family-run Montana (0450 541499)
provides 'lovely rooms, excellent food'.
The Couronne (0450 540002) is basic
but 'good value'. Restaurants and bars
are informal and inexpensive. A 2005
reporter recommends Luigi's ('excellent
duck') – best to book. The Office is
always packed with Brits and
Scandinavians and has live bands and
'terrific cooked breakfasts'. The Savoy
bar is another traditional favourite –
'lively, friendly, well priced'. The
'friendly' Rencard plays reggae music
and serves food. The Rusticana is 'laid
back' and does 'excellent steaks'. The
Boomerang is large and packed till

2am and the Stone, near the top of the
village, is less busy, 'really friendly'
and is recommended by two reporters
this year.

Les Houches 1010m/3,310ft

Les Houches, 6km/4 miles from
Chamonix, is not on the valley pass,
but is covered by the regional Mont
Blanc pass. It's a pleasant village,
sitting in the shade of the looming
Mont Blanc massif. There is an old
core with a pretty church, but modern
developments in chalet style have
spread along the road at the foot of
the slopes, with the result that some
of them are quite a walk from the lifts.
  The wooded area above Les
Houches – popular when bad weather
closes other areas – is served by a
queue-prone cable-car and a gondola
(about to be upgraded). There are
open, gentle runs at the top of the
main lifts (including nursery slopes),
long, worthwhile blues and reds back
towards the village and some
particularly lovely woodland runs on
the back of the mountain towards St-
Gervais. It is the biggest single area of
pistes in the Chamonix valley.
  In good weather the slopes are
quiet, and the views superb from the
several attractive mountain restaurants,
which are noticeably cheaper than
others in the valley. Snow-cover on the
lower slopes is not reliable, but there
is a fair amount of snowmaking.
  The village is quiet at night, but
there are some pleasant bars and good
restaurants including Vieilles Luges and
the Terrain. Reporters enjoyed staying
in the 3-star Hotel du Bois (0450
545035), with its 'helpful staff and
excellent restaurant' and 'a good local
band in the bar on Saturday'. MGM has
some good apartments with their own
pool. Buses run to and from Chamonix
all evening.

Châtel

A distinctively French base for touring the Portes du Soleil

COSTS

① ② ③ ④ ⑤ ⑥

RATINGS

The slopes

Fast lifts	**
Snow	**
Extent	*****
Expert	***
Intermediate	****
Beginner	***
Convenience	**
Queues	***
Mountain restaurants	***

The rest

Scenery	****
Resort charm	***
Off-slope	**

NEWS

For 2004/05 a fast six-pack replaced the old two-seat chair at Pré-la-Joux. It starts below the car park and goes directly to Les Combes. For this season a new red run will be created to the base station.

A drag-lift was installed at Chermeu, cutting out poling on a flat section from Chalet-Neuf.

Also for 2004/05, a piste was created from the outskirts of the Vonnes quarter (on the road to Morgins) down to the Linga lift.

256

REPORTS WANTED

Recently we have had few reports on this resort. If you go there, please do send us a report.

The best reports earn a copy of the next edition, and can lead to free lift passes in future.

See page 10.

+ Very extensive, pretty, intermediate terrain – the Portes du Soleil

+ Wide range of cheap and cheerful, good-value accommodation

+ Pleasant, lively, French-dominated old village, still quite rustic in parts

+ Local slopes are among the best in the Portes du Soleil and relatively queue-free

+ Easily reached – one of the shortest drives from the Channel, and close to Geneva

− Village congestion can be a problem at weekends and in peak season, as can lift queues in parts of the Portes du Soleil circuit

− Both the resort and the slopes are low for a French resort, with the resulting risk of poor snow – though snowmaking is now extensive

− Most main lifts are a bus-ride from the village centre

− Best nursery slope is reached by bus or gondola

Châtel offers an attractive blend of qualities much like that of Morzine – another established valley village in the Portes du Soleil. Morzine is a bit more polished, Châtel (with a claimed 40 working farms) more rustic. But its key advantage is that it is part of the main Portes du Soleil (PdS) circuit. There is a gap in the circuit at Châtel, filled by buses; but this is more of an irritant to those passing through than for Châtel residents, for most of whom the excellent local bus services are part of the daily routine. At weekends it's worth trying the slopes of nearby Chapelle d'Abondance, which are pleasantly uncrowded.

THE RESORT

Châtel lies near the head of the wooded Dranse valley, at the north-eastern limit of the French-Swiss Portes du Soleil ski circuit.

It is a much expanded but still attractive old village. Modern unpretentious chalet-style hotels and apartments rub shoulders with old farms where cattle still live in winter.

Although there is a definite centre, the village sprawls along the road in from lake Geneva and the diverging roads out – up the hillside towards Morgins and along the valley towards the Linga and Pré-la-Joux lifts.

Lots of visitors take cars and the centre can get clogged with traffic – especially at weekends. Street parking is difficult but there is underground (paid-for) parking and day car parks at Linga and Pré-la-Joux (where the parking can still get very full in peak season despite the provision of new spaces). Other main French Portes du Soleil resorts are easy to reach by piste, but not by road.

The resort bus service is approved by reporters. A central location gives you the advantage of getting on the ski-bus to the outlying lifts before it gets very crowded, and simplifies

après-ski outings – the night bus finishes at 9.30pm. But there is accommodation near the Linga lift if first tracks are the priority.

A few kilometres down the valley is the rustic village of La Chapelle-d'Abondance (see end of chapter).

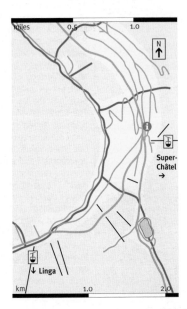

↑ The Torgon sector is unjustly neglected, probably because it is off the main Portes du Soleil circuit – it has some excellent testing slopes

SNOWPIX.COM / CHRIS GILL

KEY FACTS

Resort	1200m
	3,940ft

Portes du Soleil	
Slopes	950-2300m
	3,120-7,550ft
Lifts	208
Pistes	650km
	404 miles
Green	14%
Blue	39%
Red	37%
Black	10%
Snowmaking	
	329 hectares

Châtel only	
Slopes	1100-2205m
	3,610-7,230ft
Lifts	44
Pistes	83km
	52 miles
Green	30%
Blue	27%
Red	33%
Black	10%
Snowmaking	
	54 guns

THE MOUNTAINS

Châtel sits between two sectors of the main Portes du Soleil circuit, each offering a mix of open and wooded slopes, and linked by an 'excellent, practically continuous' free bus service. The circuit is easily done by intermediates of all abilities. How rewarding you will find it is another matter. There's no denying that it seems to involve a lot of time either on lifts or boring link runs. At least it gets you to other resorts, which you might want to revisit without doing a complete circuit again. The booklet-style piste map gives a fairly clear picture of each resort along the way.

THE SLOPES
The circuit breaks down here
Directly above the village is **Super-Châtel** – an area of easy, open and lightly wooded slopes, accessed by a gondola or two-stage chair. From here you can embark on a clockwise Portes du Soleil circuit by heading south to the Swiss resort of Morgins, travelling via Champoussin and Champéry to cross back into France above Avoriaz. Or you can head north for the slopes straddling a different bit of the Swiss border, above **Torgon**. You can also access these slopes by chair-lifts from

Petit Châtel, down the valley.

An anticlockwise circuit starts outside the village with a lift into the **Linga** sector – a gondola from Villapeyron or a choice of fast chairs from Pré-la-Joux. The fastest way to Avoriaz is via Pré-la-Joux. There is night-skiing on Linga every Thursday.

TERRAIN-PARKS
Head for Super Châtel
There's a terrain-park, with 15 features of varying difficulty, at Super Châtel, plus a 120m/390ft long half-pipe and an 800m/half-mile long boarder-cross course. Music blasts out to help motivate you for the tricks. There's a big air jump on the Stade de Slalom in the Linga sector, and La Chapelle d'Abondance also has a 360m/1,180ft long park with half-pipe. A special park-only pass is now available (18 euros a day).

SNOW RELIABILITY
The main drawback
The main drawback of the Portes du Soleil is that it is low, so snow quality can suffer when it's warm. Châtel is at only 1200m/3,940ft and some runs home can be tricky or shut. But a lot of snowmaking has been installed at Super-Châtel and on runs down to resort level. Linga and Pré-la-Joux are mainly north-facing and generally have the best local snow. The pistes to Morgins and Lindarets, in contrast, get full sun. Grooming could be better, according to a 2005 visitor.

FOR EXPERTS
Some challenges
The best steep runs – on- and off-piste – are in the Linga and Pré-la-Joux area. Beneath the Linga gondola and chair, there's a pleasant mix of open and wooded ground which follows the fall line fairly directly. And there's a mogul field between Cornebois and Plaine Dranse which has been described as 'steeper and narrower than the infamous Swiss Wall in Avoriaz'. An area under

boarding

Avoriaz is the hardcore destination in the Portes du Soleil. Châtel is not a bad place to learn or to go to as a budget option, and the terrain-park here might suit non-experts better (there's a park-only pass – 18 euros). But many lifts in the Super-Châtel sector are drags and reporters warn they can be a 'painful experience'. The Linga area also has good, varied slopes and off-piste possibilities, and the Stade de Slalom run there is floodlit every Thursday, is wired for sound and has a big air jump.

the Cornebois chair, known to the locals as Happy Valley, is also popular. There's also a great off-piste route from Tête du Linga down the valley of La Leiche – hire a guide. Two pistes from the Rochassons ridge are steep and kept well groomed. There are some genuine blacks and good off-piste opportunities on the way to Torgon from Super-Châtel, including a long run down to Barbossine which is quite narrow and tricky at the top.

FOR INTERMEDIATES
Some of the best runs in the area
When conditions are right the Portes du Soleil is an intermediate's paradise. Good intermediates need not go far from Châtel to find amusement; Linga and Plaine Dranse have some of the best red runs on the circuit. The moderately skilled can do the PdS circuit without problem, and will particularly enjoy runs around Les Lindarets and Morgins. Even timid types can do the circuit, provided they take one or two short-cuts and ride chairs down trickier bits. But some blues are said to be difficult: the 'narrow, steep and icy' route to Morgins provoked a complaint from one reporter this year, who witnessed skiers 'in tears' on its top section. The chair from Les Lindarets to Pointe de Mossettes leads to a red run into Switzerland, which is a lot easier than the 'Swiss Wall' from Chavanette and speeds up a journey round the circuit.

Expeditions to the Hauts-Forts runs above Avoriaz are worthwhile. Timid intermediates should note: the runs back to Plaine Dranse are real reds.

Don't overlook the Torgon sector, which has some excellent slopes including some challenging ones.

FOR BEGINNERS
Three possible options
There are good beginners' areas at Pré-la-Joux (a bus-ride away) and at Super-Châtel (a gondola-ride). And there are nursery slopes at village level if there is snow there. Reporters have praised the Super-Châtel slopes and lifts, which 'allow the beginner to progress' and 'safely practise' on gentle gradients away from the main runs. Getting up to them is a bit of an effort, though. The home run to the village at Super-Châtel is not recommended – it is narrow, busy and steep at the end which, coupled with often poor and icy conditions, makes it very tricky for beginners and timid intermediates. The Pré-la-Joux slopes are said to have 'less variety of slopes and quite a steep drag-lift'.

FOR CROSS-COUNTRY
Pretty, if low, trails
There are plenty of pretty trails along the river and through the woods on the lower slopes of Linga, but snow-cover can be a problem. The tourist office produces good maps with suggested routes and trail times.

QUEUES
Bottlenecks being eased
Queues to get to Avoriaz have been eased by the high-speed quad at Pré-la-Joux, and reaching Les Combes from there is much easier since a six-pack replaced the old two-seat chair. But

Morgins · Tête du Linga 2130m · Cornebois 2205m/7,230ft · Avoriaz · Chermeu · Linga · Tour de Don 2000m · Les Combes 1635m · Plaine Dranse 1650m · Super Châtel 1630m · Pré-la-Joux 1310m · Le Crêt · Villapeyron · Tête du Tronchet 1915m · Châtel 1200m/3,940ft · Col de Croix · Torgon · Barbossine · Petit Châtel

CHILDREN

Le Village des Marmottons
t 0450 733379
8.30 to 5.30; Mon-Fri; ages 3 to 8 or 10; 5 mornings €185 (with lunch)

Mouflets Garderie
t 0450 813819
ages 3mnth to 6yr; 8am to 7pm; half-day €18

Ski schools
ESF, International and Francis Sports take children from age 4 or 5 (ESF 6 half-days €117)

GETTING THERE

Air Geneva 75km/ 47 miles (1½hr).

Rail Thonon les Bains (40km/25 miles).

SCHOOLS

ESF
t 0450 732264
International
t 0450 733192
Stages Henri Gonon
t 0450 732304
Francis Sports
t 0450 813251
Snow Ride (Ecole de Glisse)
t 0608 337651
Bureau des Moniteurs Virages
t 0680 028763

Classes
(ESF prices)
6 half-days (2½hr am or pm) €108
Private lessons
€32 for 1hr, for 1 or 2 people

there are still a couple of bottlenecks, which tend to be worse at weekends (although we do have reports of little queuing even during half-term and New Year). The worst is at Les Lindarets, where there is often a lengthy wait for the Chaux Fleurie chair-lift to the Col du Bassachaux on the way back to Châtel – again provoking complaints from reporters this year. But the queue the other way up to Avoriaz has been eased since the introduction of the six-pack. You can face queues to get down from Super-Châtel if the slope back is shut by poor snow. Queues for the gondola out of the village form when school parties gather: 'It is common to share your lift with a buzz of hyperactivity,' writes a visitor. Reporters have also found lengthy queues at the Tour de Don and Chermeu drag-lifts at certain times of day, causing difficulties for skiers rushing back to Super-Châtel to pick up children from ski school.

MOUNTAIN RESTAURANTS
Some quite good local huts
Atmospheric chalets can be found, notably in a cluster at Plaine Dranse (the Bois Prin, Tan ô Marmottes, Vieux Chalet, Chaux des Rosées and Chez Denis have been recommended). A new restaurant, Fantaski, opened there last year. In the Linga area the Ferme des Pistes, 'a cosy alpine barn, complete with stable-door', is said to do 'simply the best tarte aux pommes'. The Perdrix Blanche at Pré-la-Joux scarcely counts as a mountain restaurant, but is an attractive (if expensive and crowded) spot for lunch. At Super Châtel the Portes du Soleil at the foot of the Coqs drags is much better than the big place at the top of the gondola. The Escale Blanche is worth a visit. Don't forget to check out chapters on other Portes du Soleil resorts – particularly Avoriaz.

SCHOOLS AND GUIDES
Plenty of choice
There are six ski and snowboard schools in Châtel. The International school has been recommended by a reporter, but another was 'very disappointed' with her private lesson. The ESF came in for praise, with comments such as 'very helpful and customer-focused instructors', and 'skiing progressed by leaps and bounds', reinforced recently by a regular reporter.

FACILITIES FOR CHILDREN
Increasingly sympathetic
The Marmottons nursery has good facilities, including toboggans, painting, music and videos, and children are reportedly happy there. Francis Sports ski school has its own nursery area with a drag lift and chalet at Linga: 'Very organised, convenient and reasonably priced.' The ESF had a rave report recently from a regular visitor: 'I continue to be very impressed.' His eight-year-old grandson has always received 'sympathetic instruction from English-speaking instructors' and made excellent progress.

STAYING THERE

HOW TO GO
A wide choice, including chalets
Although this is emphatically a French resort, packages from Britain are no problem to track down.
Chalets A fair number of UK operators have places here, including some Châtel specialists.
Hotels Practically all the hotels are 2-stars, mostly friendly chalets, wooden or at least partly wood-clad. None of the 3-stars is particularly well placed.
((©③ **Macchi** (0450 732412) Modern chalet, most central of the 3-stars.
((©③ **Fleur de Neige** (0450 732010) Welcoming chalet on edge of centre; Grive Gourmande restaurant is one of the best in town.
((©③ **Lion d'Or** (0450 813440) In centre, 'basic rooms, good atmosphere'.
((© **Belalp** (0450 732439) Simple chalet with small rooms, but 'very good food'. Carnotzet does good braserade.
((© **Choucas** (0450 732257) Recently refurbished. 'Friendly owner.'
((① **Kandahar** (0450 733060) One for peace-lovers: a Logis by the river, a walkable distance from the centre.
((① **Rhododendrons** (0450 732404) 'Great service, friendly, comfortable, clean.'
Self-catering Many of the better places are available through agencies specialising in Châtel or in self-drive holidays. The Gelinotte (out of town but near the Linga lifts and children's village) and the Erines (five minutes from the centre) look good. The Avenières is right by the Linga gondola. Châtel's supermarkets are reported to be small and over-crowded. There is a large supermarket out in the direction of Chapelle d'Abondance.

ACTIVITIES

Indoor Bowling, cinemas, library, painting and drawing lessons

Outdoor Ice rink, walks, salto trampolining, farm visits, cheese factory visits, ice-diving, snow-shoe excursions (60km/37 miles trails shared with Morgins – special route map available)

WEBSITES

Phone numbers From abroad use the prefix +33 and omit the initial '0' of the phone number.

TOURIST OFFICES

Châtel
t 0450 732244
touristoffice@chatel.com
www.chatel.com

La Chapelle-d'Abondance
t 0450 735141
ot.lachapelle@valdabondance.com
www.lachapelle74.com

EATING OUT
Fair selection

There is an adequate number and range of restaurants. Our favourite for a serious dinner is the Table d'Antoine, the restaurant of the hotel Chalet d'Alizée – excellent food, charming patronne. The Fleur de Neige hotel has a pricey gastronomic restaurant (La Grive Gourmand). The woody Vieux Four carries its rustic ornamentation a bit far for our taste, but it does ambitious dishes alongside Savoyard specialities and is approved by readers. The Pierrier and the Fiacre are more modest, everyday restaurants doing a range of grills as well as Savoyard specialities. The Moroccan chef at the Hotel Soldanelles cooks a 'veritable feast'. The Milles Pâtes does 'bargain' set menus. Out of town, the Ripaille, almost opposite the Linga gondola, is popular with the locals and highly rated by reporters, especially for its fish and the 'fantastic local Gamay wines'. The hotel Cornettes in La Chapelle-d'Abondance is worth a trip – see later section.

APRES-SKI
All down to bars

Châtel is getting livelier, especially at the weekends. The Tunnel bar is very popular with the British and has a DJ or live music every night (the caramel vodka is recommended). The Avalanche is a very popular English-style pub and has internet facilities. The Godille – close to the Super-Châtel gondola and crowded when everyone descends at close of play – has a more French feel. The 'small and cosy' Isba is the locals' choice, and shows extreme sports videos. The bar in the hotel Soldanelles has been recommended. The bowling alley, the Vieille Grange, also has a good bar.

OFF THE SLOPES
Better to stay in Morzine

Those with a car have some entertaining excursions available: Geneva, Thonon and Evian. Otherwise there is little to do but take some pleasant walks along the river, visit the cheese factory and the two cinemas, or join in the daily events organised by the tourist office.

The Portes du Soleil as a whole is less than ideal for those who like to meet their more active friends for lunch: skiers and boarders are likely to be above at some distant resort at

lunchtime and very few lifts are accessible to pedestrians.

La Chapelle-d'Abondance
1010m/3,310ft

This unspoiled, rustic farming community, complete with old church and friendly locals, is 5km/3 miles along a beautiful valley from Châtel. 'A car and a bit of French are virtually essential,' says a reporter. It's had its own quiet little north-facing area of easy wooded runs for some years, but has more recently been put on the Portes du Soleil map by an outlying gondola that links it to the slopes between Torgon in Switzerland and Super-Châtel.

Nightlife is virtually non-existent – just a few quiet bars, a cinema and torchlit descents.

The hotel Cornettes (0450 735024) is an amazing 2-star, run by the Trincaz family since 1894, with 2-star rooms but 4-star facilities, including an indoor pool, sauna, steam room and hot-tubs. It has an atmospheric bar and an excellent restaurant doing extremely good-value menus (but 'disappointing' desserts, comments one reporter). Look out for showcases with puppets and dolls and eccentric touches, such as ancient doors that unexpectedly open automatically.

La Clusaz – Le Gd-Bornand

Attractive, distinctively French all-rounders; all they lack is altitude

COSTS

① ② ③ ④ ⑤ ⑥

RATINGS

The slopes
Fast lifts	**
Snow	**
Extent	***
Expert	***
Intermediate	****
Beginner	****
Convenience	***
Queues	***
Mountain restaurants	****

The rest
Scenery	***
Resort charm	****
Off-slope	***

NEWS

A couple of seasons ago the Beauregard cable-car in La Clusaz was replaced by a gondola, more than tripling the capacity to 1,700 people an hour.

For 2005/06 snowmaking capacity is to be increased in La Clusaz, in Le Chinaillon and in the terrain-park at Le Grand-Bornand.

+ Mountain villages in a scenic setting, retaining traditional character

+ Extensive, interesting slopes – pistes best for beginners and intermediates

+ Very French atmosphere

+ Very short transfer from Geneva, and easy to reach by car from UK

+ Attractive mountain restaurants

+ Good cross-country trails

+ Slopes at La Clusaz and Le Grand-Bornand linked by shuttle-bus

− Snow conditions unreliable because of low altitude (by French standards)

− Not many challenging pistes for experts – though there are good off-piste runs

− Crowded at weekends

Few other major French resorts are based around what are still, essentially, genuine mountain villages that exude rustic charm and Gallic atmosphere. Combine that with more than 200km/125 miles of largely intermediate slopes, above and below the tree line, spread over five linked sectors in the two separate resorts of La Clusaz and Le Grand-Bornand, and there's a good basis for an enjoyable, relaxed week.

The area's one big problem is its height, or lack of it. Snowmaking is continually increased, but of course it makes no difference in mild weather; when we were last there it was raining. So pre-booking a holiday here remains a risky business.

THE RESORT

La Clusaz was once frequented almost entirely by the French. But it has developed into a major international resort – for both summer and winter seasons. And there is a substantial year-round presence of British residents in the area. As one of the most accessible resorts from Geneva and Annecy, it's good for short transfers, but it does get crowded, and there can be weekend traffic jams.

The village is built beside a fast-flowing stream at the junction of a number of narrow wooded valleys. It is now quite large and has had to grow in a rather rambling and sprawling way, with roads running in a confusing mixture of directions. But, unlike so many French resorts, La Clusaz has retained the charm of a genuine mountain village. It's the kind of place that is as attractive in summer as under a blanket of snow in winter.

In the centre is a large old church, and other original old stone and wood buildings; and, for the most part, the new buildings have been built in chalet style and blend in well. Les Etages is a much smaller centre of accommodation

south of (and quite a bit higher than) the main town, where two of the mountain sectors meet.

La Clusaz has a friendly feel to it. The villagers welcome visitors every Monday evening in the main square with vin chaud and a variety of local

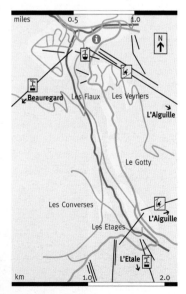

KEY FACTS

La Clusaz

Resort	1100m
	3,610ft
Slopes	1100-2500m
	3,610-8,200ft
Lifts	55
Pistes	132km
	82 miles
Green	30%
Blue	33%
Red	28%
Black	9%
Snowmaking	
	74 acres

Le Grand-Bornand

Resort	950m
	3,120ft
Slopes	1000-2100m
	3,280-6,890ft
Lifts	39
Pistes	90km
	56 miles
Green	31%
Blue	35%
Red	27%
Black	7%
Snowmaking	
	60 hectares

cheeses. There's a weekly market, tempting food shops and a wide choice of typically French bars.

For much of the season La Clusaz is a quiet and peaceful place for a holiday. But in peak season and at weekends the place gets packed out with French and Swiss families.

Le Grand-Bornand, also covered by the Aravis lift pass, is a much smaller and even more charming village, with a still greater sense that it remains a mountain community. This is partly because most of the development as a winter sports resort has gone on up the road at the satellite village of Le Chinaillon, which has been developed in chalet style. Le Grand-Bornand has quite extensive slopes and is worth exploring for a day or two, or considering as an alternative, quieter base.

Le Grand-Bornand and La Clusaz are linked by free buses doing the 10-minute journey every 30 minutes during the day – these become more erratic in peak-time traffic.

If you are taking a car, you might also consider basing yourself at **St-Jean-de-Sixt** – a small hamlet midway between La Clusaz and Le Grand-Bornand, with a small slope nearby, mainly used for sledging.

THE MOUNTAINS

Like the village, the slopes at **La Clusaz** are rather spread out – which makes them all the more interesting (and scenic). There are five main areas, each connecting with at least one other. At **Le Grand-Bornand** the slopes can be accessed from either the outskirts of the village or from Le Chinaillon, up the road.

THE SLOPES
Pretty and varied
Several points in **La Clusaz** have lifts giving access to the predominantly west- and north-west facing slopes of **L'Aiguille**. From here you can choose either a red or a black piste to reach the slightly higher and shadier slopes of the **La Balme** area and a gondola returns you to Côte 2000 on L'Aiguille. La Balme is a splendid, varied area with good lifts (a high-capacity gondola from the bottom leading to a quad chair); from the top there are wonderful views towards Mont Blanc.

Going the other way from L'Aiguille leads you to **L'Etale** via a choice of blue or red runs and then the Transval cable-car, which shuttles people between the two areas. From the

Aravis pass
Covers La Clusaz, Le Grand-Bornand, Saint-Jean-de-Sixt and Manigod, and shuttle service between resorts.

Beginners
6 days €91 (in La Clusaz only and issued in conjunction with group lesson card).

Main pass
1 day €27
6 days €152

Senior citizens
Over 60: 6 days €126
Over 75: free pass

Children
Under 15: 6 days €112
Under 5: free pass

Notes
One-day price is for La Clusaz only.

La Clusaz pass
Covers all lifts in La Clusaz.

Main pass
1 day €27
6 days €140.50

Senior citizens
Over 60: 6 days €115

Children
Under 15: 6 days €101

Le Grand-Bornand pass
Covers all lifts in Le Grand-Bornand.

Main pass
1 day €25
6 days €120.20

Senior citizens
Over 60: 6 days €111

Children
Under 15: 6 days €99.30
Under 9: 6 days: €70.00

bottom of L'Etale, you can head back along another path to the village and the gondola up to the fourth sector of **Beauregard** which, as the name implies, has splendid views and catches a lot of sunshine.

From the top of Beauregard you can link via an easy piste and a two-way chair-lift with the fifth area of **Manigod**. From here you can move on to L'Etale.

The main village at **Le Grand-Bornand** has two gondolas on the outskirts up to a gentle open area of easy runs (including nursery slopes) lying between 1400m and 1500m (4,600ft and 4,920ft). Chairs fan out above this point, one going up to the high point of **Le Lachat**, where there are serious red and black runs. Other lifts and runs go across the mountainside to the slopes above **Le Chinaillon**. Here there is a broad, open mountainside with a row of chairs and drags serving blue and red slopes, and links to the rest of the domain – a wide area of blue and red runs.

TERRAIN-PARKS
Twin parks – double the fun
Both resorts have terrain-parks, although boarders tend to prefer La Clusaz, which is more lively –

particularly at weekends. The park in La Clusaz is on the Aiguille, while Le Grand-Bornand's area is at Maroly. Both have quarter- and half-pipes, tables, rails and boarder-cross runs.

SNOW RELIABILITY
Variable because of low altitude
Most of the runs are west- or north-west facing and tend to keep their snow fairly well, even though most of the area is below 2000m/6,500ft. The best snow is usually on the north-west-facing slopes at La Balme, where a lift takes you up to 2500m/8,200ft. In late season, the home runs can be dependent on snowmaking – of which there is now virtually blanket coverage. However, the long paths linking La Balme and l'Etale to the village are devoid of snow-guns and can suffer as a result. The main lifts on Beauregard and Crêt du Merle can be used to descend. You can also ride the gondolas down to Le Grand-Bornand and the runs above Le Chinaillon have extensive snowmaking.

FOR EXPERTS
Plenty to do, especially off-piste
The La Clusaz piste map doesn't seem to have a lot to offer experts, but most

SCHOOLS

La Clusaz

ESF
t 0450 024083

Sno Academie
t 0450 326605

Aravis Challenge
t 0450 028129

Le Grand-Bornand

ESF
t 0450 027910

Starski (ESI)
t 0450 270469

Classes
(ESF prices)
6 days (2hr am and
2hr pm): €145

Private lessons
€32 for 1hr for 1 or 2
people

GUIDES

Bureau des guides
t 0450 633599

---

of the sectors present off-piste variants to the pistes, and there are more serious adventures to undertake – all the more attractive for being ignored by most visitors.

The best terrain is at La Balme, where there are several fairly challenging pistes above mid-mountain. The black Vraille run, which leads to the speed-skiing slope, is seriously steep. On the opposite side of the sector, the entirely off-piste Combe de Bellachat can be reached.

The Noire run down the face of Beauregard can be tricky in poor snow and is often closed. The Tétras on L'Etale and the Mur Edgar bumps run below Crêt du Loup on L'Aiguille deserve their black gradings. L'Aiguille has a good off-piste run down the neglected Combe de Borderan and the long Lapiaz black piste runs down the Combe de Fernuy from Côte 2000.

In Le Grand-Bornand there are worthwhile shady black runs on Le Lachat, and on the lower peak of La Floria, above Le Chinaillon.

FOR INTERMEDIATES
Good if snow is good
Most intermediates will love La Clusaz if the snow conditions are good. Early intermediates will delight in the gentle slopes at the top of Beauregard and over on La Croix-Fry at Manigod, where there's a network of gentle tree-lined runs. And they'll be able to travel all over the area on the gentle, green linking pistes, where poling or walking is more likely to be a problem than any fears about steepness.

L'Etale and L'Aiguille have more challenging but wide blue runs.

More adventurous intermediates will prefer the steeper red slopes and good snow of La Balme and the long red down Combe du Fernuy from L'Aiguille.

Le Grand-Bornand is full of good cruising blue and red intermediate runs stretching in both directions above Le Chinaillon – well worth a visit for a day or two if you are staying in La Clusaz.

FOR BEGINNERS
Splendid beginner slopes
There is a nursery slope at village level at La Clusaz, and a couple of others just above it, but the best nursery slopes are up the mountain at the top of the Beauregard cable-car and at Crêt du Merle. The Beauregard area has lovely gentle blue runs to progress to, including one long run around the mountain right back to the village. There are also some good beginner slopes at Le Grand-Bornand.

FOR CROSS-COUNTRY
Excellent
The region has much better cross-country facilities than many resorts, with around 70km/43 miles of loops of varying difficulty. In La Clusaz, one good area is near the Lac des Confins, reached by bus. There's also a lovely sunny area at the top of the Beauregard cable-car. At Le Grand-Bornand there are extensive trails in the Vallée du Bouchet and towards Le Chinaillon. These include a training circuit called the Nordic Park – complete with bumps, gradients and bends. And there are further trails at St-Jean-de-Sixt.

QUEUES
Not usually a problem
Lift queues aren't a problem, except on peak weekends or if the lower slopes are shut because of snow shortage. The chair-lifts up the front face of L'Aiguille are the main weekend black spots; they are avoidable.

MOUNTAIN RESTAURANTS
High standard
Mountain restaurants are one of the area's strong points. There are lots of them and most are rustic and charming, serving good, reasonably priced – often Savoyard – food. We have had excellent reports on the Télémark above the chair lift to L'Etale and the Chenons at the bottom of La Balme. There are several other good restaurants higher up in the Aiguille sector, of which the Bercail is said to

---

boarding

Snowboarding is popular in La Clusaz, and although there are still a lot of drag-lifts, most are avoidable. There are some good nursery slopes, served by chair-lifts, and great cruising runs to progress to. La Balme is a great natural playground for good free-riders. And both La Clusaz and Le Grand Bornand have decent terrain-parks to hang out in.

There are some good panoramic views (this one is taken at Le Grand Bornand) ➔

OT LE GRAND-BORNAND

CHILDREN

La Clusaz:
Club des Mouflets
t 0450 326520
Ages 8mnth to 4½yr; 8.30-12 noon, 2pm-6pm; 6 days €111.30
Club des Champions
t 0450 326950
Ages 3 to 5; 8.30-12 noon, 2pm-6pm
Piou-Piou Club
t 0450 024083
Up to 5yr; 9.30-12.30, 1.30-4.30; €10 for 1hr

Le Grand-Bornand:
Les P'tits Maringouins
t 0450 027905
Ages 3mnth up

Ski school
At La Clusaz ESF runs lessons for ages 5 to 11 (6 4hr days €135). At Le Gd-Bornand ESF runs lessons for ages 3 to 6 and for 6 to 12

GETTING THERE

Air Geneva 50km/ 31 miles (1½hr); Lyon 150km/93 miles (2½hr).

ACTIVITIES

Indoor Fitness centre, sauna, steam room; hotels with fitness rooms, saunas, etc; library, museum, bridge, cinema
Outdoor Ice rink, paragliding, snow-shoe excursions, ice carts, snowmobiling, tobogganing, dog-sledding, winter walks, quad-bikes, swimming pool (with indoor jacuzzi), farm visit, town tour, horse and buggy rides

WEBSITES

For links to resort sites, go to our own new site at www.wtss.co.uk

be the best. However a 2005 reporter was 'not impressed' and thought the place 'over-hyped and with slow service'. The 'very attractive' Chez Arthur at Crêt du Merle has a calm little table-service restaurant tucked away behind the crowded self-service. The Piste Bleue at Beauregard by the cross-country trail is sunny and peaceful, with good views, but a 2005 visitor thought it had high prices and 'was not worth the climb up'. The Relais de L'Aiguille at Crêt du Loup is also popular. In Le Grand Bornand, the Névé at Le Rosay and the Terres Rouges ('sunny terrace and good views') are recommended. The Vieille Ferme at Merdassier (see Eating out) is also open at lunchtime.

SCHOOLS AND GUIDES
Mixed reports
There are tales of large classes and poor instruction in the ESF, but we've heard from some satisfied customers too – especially those taking private lessons. According to reports, the smaller Sno Academie – with smaller class sizes – is much more reliable.

FACILITIES FOR CHILDREN
Good – in theory
We have had mixed reports about the kindergarten in La Clusaz and none about those in Le Grand-Bornand. But a recent visitor was impressed by the 'variety of activities to encourage the small ones to get used to the snow'. Generally the resorts are places where families can feel at home.

STAYING THERE

HOW TO GO
A fair choice of packages
La Clusaz is offered mostly by smaller operators, some of which go to Le Grand-Bornand too. The drive from the Channel and the transfer from Geneva airport are as short as they are.
Chalets There are some chalets, including some charmingly rustic ones.
Hotels Small, friendly 2- and 3-star family hotels are the mainstay of the area; luxury is not an option here.
((3 **Carlina** (0450 024348) A reporter says it's the best; central with pool and grounds.
((3 **Beauregard** (0450 326800) 'Spacious and comfortable'; on the fringe of the village. A reporter enthused about the pool area, the atmosphere and the 'excellent food'.
((3 **Alp'Hôtel** (0450 024006) Comfortable modern chalet close to the centre, with good restaurant. Pool.
((3 **Alpen Roc** (0450 025896) Big but stylish, central and comfortable, although one reporter said his room was 'very cramped'. Pool.
((3 **Saytels** (0450 022016) Only 3-star in Le Grand-Bornand. Close to church.
((3 **Cimes** (0450 270038) 3-star in Le Chinaillon.
(2 **Alpage de Tante Pauline** (0450 026328) Dinky chalet at foot of L'Etale slopes (bus stop outside).
Self-catering There's quite a good choice, including self-catering chalets as well as apartments. Some are out of town and best for those with a car.

La Clusaz

TOURIST OFFICES

La Clusaz
t 0450 326500
infos@laclusaz.com
www.laclusaz.com
Le Grand-Bornand
t 0450 027800
infos@legrandbornand.com
www.legrandbornand.com
St-Jean-de-Sixt
t 0450 022412
infos@saintjeandesixt.com
www.saintjeandesixt.com
Vallées des Aravis
t 0450 027874
infos@aravis.com
www.aravis.com

266

ARAVIS / NUTS-NOISILLIER

The rustic village charm is there; it's just a shame about the low altitude ↓

EATING OUT
Good choice
There's a wide choice of restaurants, some a short drive away, including the Vieux Chalet, which is one of our favourites – good food and service in a splendid, creaky old chalet. The St Joseph at the Alp'Hotel is regarded as the best restaurant in La Clusaz. Ecuelle is the place to go for Savoyard specialities. The Cordée and the Outa are simple places giving great value for money. At the other end of the price scale is the highly praised Symphonie restaurant in the hotel Beauregard.

We're told some of the best food in the area is at the Ferme de Lormay in La Vallée du Bouchet, about 5km/3 miles on from Le Grand-Bornand. But another reporter rates the Vieille Ferme at Merdassier his favourite place in the Alps – an old farm building with 'serious food, classy staff, perfect atmosphere'. The Foly, overlooking the Lac des Confins, is a firm favourite with both tourists and locals alike.

APRES-SKI
La Clusaz getting livelier
These resorts have always seemed to us typically quiet French family places, with the difference that La Clusaz is definitely the place to stay for a livelier time – especially at the weekend. The Caves du Paccaly, in the centre of La Clusaz, has woody 'olde worlde' decor and live music. The Pressoir is a focal bar, popular for sports videos. Pub le Salto is run by a British couple and has Sky TV and draught Guinness. The central Bali is a more typically French recommendation. The Ecluse disco has a glass dance floor; Club 18 rocks, often with live bands.

OFF THE SLOPES
Some diversions
The villages are pleasant. It's easy for pedestrians to get around the valley by bus and to several good mountain restaurants for lunch. There are good walks along the valleys, and a day trip to the beautiful lakeside town of Annecy is possible. And La Clusaz has an excellent aquatic centre with indoor and outdoor pools, jacuzzi, sauna and steam rooms.

STAYING UP THE MOUNTAIN
Cheap and panoramic
There are three places to stay at the top of Beauregard.

Les Contamines

A hidden gem: a charming, unspoiled French village with reliable snow

RATINGS

The slopes

Fast lifts	**
Snow	****
Extent	***
Expert	***
Intermediate	****
Beginner	**
Convenience	**
Queues	***
Mountain restaurants	****

The rest

Scenery	****
Resort charm	****
Off-slope	**

NEWS

For 2004/05 a fast quad, the Montjoie, replaced the drag-lift at Etape: it serves the lower Signal runs.

The super-pipe was moved to a new location lower down the mountain, on the Loyers piste. It is now floodlit twice a week.

Snowmaking was also increased.

+ Traditional, unspoiled French village
+ Fair-sized intermediate area
+ Good snow record for its height
+ Lift pass covers several nearby resorts, easily reachable by road

− Not ideal for beginners
− Quiet nightlife
− Lifts a bus-ride from main village
− Can be some lengthy queues if snow is in short supply elsewhere

Only a few miles from the fur coats of Megève and the ice-axes of Chamonix, Les Contamines is a charming contrast to both, with pretty wooden chalets, impressive old churches, a weekly market in the village square and prices more typical of rural France than of international resorts. Its position at the shoulder of Mont Blanc gives it an enviable snow record. What more could you want?

THE RESORT

The core of the village is compact, but the resort as a whole spreads widely, with chalets scattered over a 3km/2 mile stretch of the valley, and the main access lift is 1km/half a mile from the centre. There's expanding development by the lift at Le Lay but you can stay in the charming village centre, a shuttle-bus-ride away. Bizarrely, the local pass appears not to cover the buses. The Mont Blanc lift pass does cover them, as well as the lifts of Chamonix and Megève (among other resorts). A car is useful for such outings.

THE MOUNTAINS

Most of the slopes are above the tree line and there are some magnificent views, though the runs down from Signal are bordered by trees (as is the run from La Ruelle down to Belleville).

Slopes From Le Lay a two-stage gondola climbs up to the slopes at Signal. Another gondola leads to the Etape mid-station from a car park a little further up the valley, with a new fast quad above it. Above these, a sizeable network of open, largely north-east-facing pistes fans out, with lifts approaching 2500m/ 8,200ft in two places. You can drop over the ridge at Col du Joly to south-west-facing runs down to La Ruelle (very quiet, according to a 2005 reporter), with a single red run going on down to Belleville. From Belleville, a 16-person gondola runs back up to La Ruelle. A fast chair takes you the rest of the way back up to Col du Joly.

Terrain-parks There's a terrain-park with jumps, rails and boarder-cross on the Tierces slope, accessed by the fast Tierces chair-lift. A second area, on the Loyers piste, features a super-pipe − floodlit twice weekly.

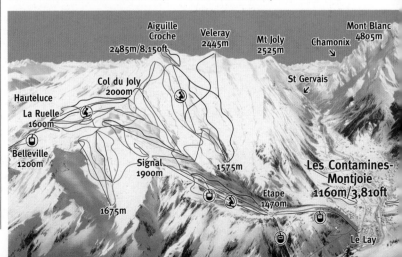

KEY FACTS

Resort	1160m
	3,810ft

For Les Contamines-Montjoie / Hauteluce

Slopes	1160-2485m
	3,810-8,150ft
Lifts	24
Pistes	120km
	75 miles
Green	19%
Blue	21%
Red	36%
Black	24%
Snowmaking	
	105 guns

WEBSITES

For links to resort sites, go to our own new site at
www.wtss.co.uk

Phone numbers
From abroad use the prefix +33 and omit the initial '0' of the phone number.

TOURIST OFFICE

t 0450 470158
info@lescontamines.com
www.lescontamines.com

AGENCE NUTS / OT LES CONTAMINES

Les Contamines is a traditional old village with pretty wooden chalets, a central square and impressive churches ↓

Snow reliability Many of the shady runs on the Contamines side are above 1700m/5,575ft, and the resort has a justifiable reputation for good snow late into the season, said to be the result of proximity to Mont Blanc. There's snowmaking on the home runs from Signal down to the valley.

Experts The steep western section has black runs, which are enjoyable but not terribly challenging. But there is substantial and varied off-piste terrain within the lift system and outside it – including a 'seriously steep and challenging' descent to Megève.

Intermediates Virtually all the runs are ideal for good intermediates, with a mix of blues and reds that one recent reporter described as 'very similar – more like purple'. Some of the best go from the gondola's top station to its mid-station and others are served by the Roselette and Bûche Croisée lifts. Given good snow, the south-facing runs down to La Ruelle are a delight. And the black runs are enjoyable for good intermediates. Timid intermediates might find sections of many blue runs too steep for comfort.

Beginners In good snow, the village nursery area is adequate for beginners. There are other areas at the mid-station and the top of the gondola. The piste map shows no long greens to progress to but reporters tell of a 'very gentle green run from Col du Joly back to Le Signal' that is not on the map. Beginners will want to take the gondola down to the village at the end of the day as the only run down is red.

Snowboarding There is excellent off-piste boarding on offer.

Cross-country There are trails of varying difficulty totalling 26km/16 miles. One loop is floodlit twice a week.

Queues There can be 15 to 20 minute peak-period queues for the gondolas, especially if people are bussed in from other resorts with less snow. The main bottleneck at Etape, where the lower gondolas meet, has been relieved by the fast quad parallel to the second stage. We've heard of minimal queues only, even at weekends.

Mountain restaurants There are quite a few lovely rustic mountain restaurants – not all of which are marked on the piste map. The Ferme de la Ruelle is a jolly barn, and the Grange just above it is rated in 2005 for its 'great-value plat du jour'. Roselette (a 2005 reporter's favourite: 'great food and service') and Bûche Croisée are two cosy chalets and the 'reasonably priced' Chez Gaston has great views.

Schools and guides We have mixed reports on the ESF – one expert was pleased with his 'fluent English-speaking' instructor but his brother was lost by the school and 'got a snooty remark' when he rejoined them. Excursions are offered, including trips to the Vallée Blanche. There's an alternative International school, and mountain guides are available.

Facilities for children The kindergarten, next to the central nursery slopes, takes children from age one. Children can join ski school from age three.

STAYING THERE

How to go There are some catered chalets and a dozen modest hotels.

Hotels The 3-star Chemenaz (0450 470244) at Le Lay is praised by reporters 'Comfortable, and best food in the village.'

Eating out There are restaurants and crêperies in town for eating out. Recommendations include the Husky, Auberge du Barattet and the Op Traken – and the Savoisien and the Auberge du Chalézan for Savoie specialities.

Après-ski Après-ski is quiet, but there are several bars. The Saxo near the gondola has been recommended, but the Ty Breiz has live music and is 'the only lively bar', according to reporters. Weekly events are organised, such as music and free vin chaud by the village fountain (on Saturdays) and torchlit descents.

Off the slopes There are good walks, a toboggan run, snowmobiling, dog-sledding, snow-shoeing, a climbing wall and a natural ice rink, but St-Gervais, Megève and Chamonix have more to offer.

Courchevel

Superb skiing and boarding – but sky-high prices in 1850

COSTS
① ② ③ ④ ⑤ ⑥

RATINGS

The slopes

Fast lifts	★★★★
Snow	★★★★
Extent	★★★★★
Expert	★★★★
Intermediate	★★★★★
Beginner	★★★★
Convenience	★★★★
Queues	★★★★
Mountain restaurants	★★★★

The rest

Scenery	★★★
Resort charm	★★
Off-slope	★★★

KEY FACTS

Resort	1260-1850m
	4,130-6,070ft

Three Valleys	
Slopes	1260-3230m
	4,130-10,600ft
Lifts	200
Pistes	600km
	373 miles
Green	21%
Blue	33%
Red	35%
Black	11%
Snowmaking	
	1500 guns

Courchevel/ La Tania only	
Slopes	1260-2740m
	4,130-8,990ft
Lifts	63
Pistes	150km
	93 miles
Green	25%
Blue	33%
Red	32%
Black	10%
Snowmaking	
	562 guns

OT COURCHEVEL /
JF MARIN EDITING

The Jardin Alpin above Courchevel 1850 is a very attractive wooded area full of smart chalets and hotels →

+ Extensive, varied local terrain to suit everyone from beginners to experts – plus the rest of the Three Valleys

+ Lots of slope-side accommodation

+ Impressive lift system, piste maintenance and snowmaking

+ Wooded setting is pretty, and useful in bad weather

+ Choice of four very different villages – only 1850 is notably expensive

+ Some great restaurants, and good après-ski by French standards

– Some pistes get unpleasantly crowded (but they can be avoided)

– Rather soulless villages with intrusive traffic in places

– 1850 has some of the priciest hotels, bars and mountain restaurants in the Alps and its getting pricier

– Losing a little of its French feel as more and more British visitors – and now Russians – discover its attractions

– Little to do away from the slopes, especially during the day

Courchevel 1850 – the highest of the four components of this big resort – has long been the favourite Alpine hangout of the Paris jet set and they have now been joined by wealthy Russians, who can fly directly to the mini-airport in the middle of the slopes. Its top hotels and restaurants have always been among the best and the most expensive in the Alps, and the influx of Russians has pushed up prices even further. We've also had reports of the service given to Brits in some restaurants being adversely affected. But don't be put off: a holiday here doesn't have to cost a fortune (especially in the lower villages), the atmosphere is not particularly exclusive, and the slopes are excellent.

Courchevel is the most extensive and varied sector of the whole Three Valleys, with everything from long gentle greens to steep couloirs. Many visitors never leave the Courchevel sector; but there is good access to the rest of the Three Valleys, too. Le Praz is an overgrown but still pleasant village, 1550 is quieter and good for families, 1650 has more of a village atmosphere than it seems from the road through, and the posh bits of 1850 are stylishly woody. But overall the resort is no beauty. Well, nothing's perfect. Courchevel's long list of important + points is enough to attract more and more Brits, but it remains much more French than Méribel, over the hill, as well as having better snow.

NEWS

THE RESORT

Courchevel is made up of four varied villages, generally known by numbers supposed to represent their altitudes. A road winds up the hill from Le Praz (1300) past 1550, through 1650 to 1850. From the skiing point of view, things work a bit differently: runs go down from 1850 to 1550 and 1300, but the slopes of 1650 form a distinct sector.

1850 is the largest village, and the focal point of the area, with most of the smart nightlife and shops. Two gondolas go over its lower slopes towards the links with Méribel and the rest of the Three Valleys. It's conspicuously upmarket, with some very smooth hotels on the slopes just above the village centre, and among the trees of the Jardin Alpin (a suburb served by its own gondola). There's a spreading area of smart private chalets.

You can pay through the nose to eat, drink and stay, but more affordable places are not impossible to find. One reporter has objected that preference is given in restaurants to Russian visitors, even to the extent of 'us being moved to a terrible table right by the kitchen. Abysmal service.' Early January and the second week in March are peak times for Russians with one local claiming there were over 18,000 there in January, making up 95% of resort visitors. And some signs in Russian are now appearing.

1650 by contrast is 'calm and uncrowded, a world away from 1850', as a reader puts it. The main road up to 1850 cuts through 1650 but there's also an attractive old village centre, lively bars and quietly situated chalets. Its local slopes (whose main access is an escalator-served gondola) are also relatively peaceful. 1650 isn't the most convenient base for exploration of the Three Valleys, but you can still reach Val-Thorens in 90 minutes or less.

1550 is a quiet dormitory, a gondola or chair ride below 1850. It has the advantage of having essentially the same position as 1850, with cheaper accommodation and restaurants. But it's a long trip to 1850 by road if you want to go there in the evening.

Le Praz (or 1300) is an old village set amid woodland and 'excellent for children'. It remains a pleasant spot despite expansion triggered by the 1992 Olympics – the Olympic ski jump is a conspicuous relic. Ancient gondolas go up over the forest to 1850

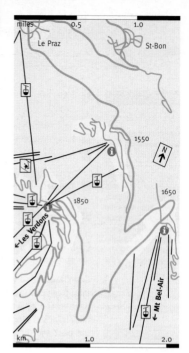

and towards Col de la Loze, for Méribel. Near-beginners face rides down as well as up: the pistes back to the village are red and black, and at this altitude snow conditions are often poor.

Efficient free buses run between and within the villages. Champagny is an easy road outing, for access to the extensive slopes of La Plagne.

THE MOUNTAINS

Although there are plenty of trees around the villages, most of the slopes are essentially open, with the notable exception of the runs down to 1550 and to Le Praz, and the valley between 1850 and 1650. These are great areas for experts when the weather closes in. Piste maintenance is good, and daily maps are available, showing which runs have been groomed overnight (normal in America but very rare in Europe). Snowmaking is abundant but the runs to Le Praz are still prone to closure in warm weather. Some slopes above 1850 get very busy, but you don't have to spend much time on them. Many reporters recommend buying only a Courchevel pass and then extensions for the Three Valleys as necessary. A visitor last year praised the piste marking, which 'above 1650 was the best we've seen'.

THE SLOPES
Huge variety to suit everyone

A network of lifts and pistes spreads out from **1850**, which is very much the focal point of the area. The main axis is the Verdons gondola, leading to a second gondola to **La Vizelle** and a nearly parallel cable-car up to **La Saulire**. Both the high points give access to a wide range of intermediate and advanced terrain (including a number of couloirs), Méribel and all points to Val-Thorens. You can also get over to 1650 from here.

To the right looking up from 1850 the **Chenus** gondola goes towards a second departure point for Méribel, the Col de la Loze. Easy and intermediate runs go back to 1850, with more difficult runs in the woods above **La Tania** (see separate chapter) and **Le Praz**. To the left of the Verdons gondola is the Jardin Alpin gondola, which leads to some great beginner terrain, and serves the higher hotels and runs until 8pm. It also gives access to 1650 via the valley of Prameruel.

1650 offers a good mix of beginner and intermediate slopes away from the crowds and is an ideal area for building confidence. There are still a few drag-lifts in this sector, but the trickiest have now been replaced by chairs (and for 2005/06 two more are due to be replaced by a six-pack).

TERRAIN-PARKS
Something for everyone

The Plantrey terrain-park – just below 1850 and accessed via the Epicea and Ecureuil lifts – is described by the tourist office as for 'experienced boarders' and includes a half-pipe. The

Courchevel

271

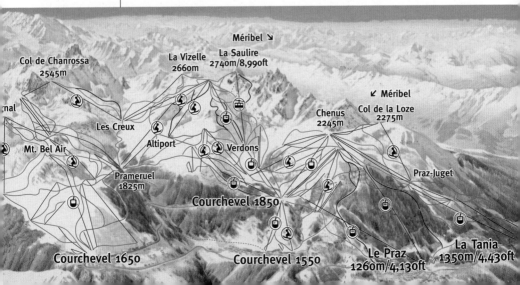

Col de Chanrossa 2545m · nal · Mt. Bel Air · Les Creux · Altiport · Prameruel 1825m · La Vizelle 2666m · La Saulire 2740m/8,99oft · Méribel ↘ · Verdons · Courchevel 1850 · Courchevel 1650 · Courchevel 1550 · Chenus 2245m · Col de la Loze 2275m · ↙ Méribel · Praz-Juget · Le Praz 1260m/4,13oft · La Tania 1350m/4,43oft

Verdons terrain-park, just above 1850, has rolling terrain suitable for all levels of ability to enjoy – as has the smaller Biollay area, which offers 'roller coasters' and 'big moguls to chew up, attack at your own speed, in your own style'. There's a boarder-cross at Pralong.

SNOW RELIABILITY
Very good
The combination of Courchevel's orientation (its slopes are north- or north-east-facing), its height, an abundance of snowmaking and generally excellent piste maintenance usually guarantees good snow down to at least the 1850 and 1650 villages. A reporter comments: 'On a week when snow was relatively scarce in the Alps, we were pleasantly surprised by the quality and quantity of the snow.' On countless visits we have found that the snow is usually much better than in neighbouring Méribel, where the slopes get the afternoon sun.

FOR EXPERTS
Some black gems
There is plenty to interest experts, even without the rest of the Three Valleys.

The most obvious expert runs are the couloirs you can see on the right near the top of the Saulire cable-car. The three main ways down were once designated black pistes (some of the steepest in Europe), but now only the Grand Couloir remains a piste – it's the widest and easiest of the three, but you have to pick your way along the narrow, bumpy, precipitous access ridge to reach it. There is a lot of steep terrain, on- and off-piste, on the shady

boarding

For an upmarket resort, Courchevel goes out of its way to attract boarders and last season there were no fewer than four terrain-parks to play in. It's easy to get around the Three Valleys using chairs and gondolas and there is some great free-riding available. RTM is a specialist snowboard school run by Brits that we've had good reports of. The big snowboard hangout in 1850 is 'Prends ta luge et tire toi', a combined shop/bar/internet cafe.

Courchevel's image is of up-market luxury and pampered piste skiing. But it is one of the world's best resorts for off-piste too. Manu Gaidet is a Courchevel mountain guide and a ski instructor with the Courchevel ESF. He is also one of the world's top free-riders and has won the Freeride World Championship for each of the last three years. We asked him to pick out a few of the best runs.

These suggested routes are limited to the Courchevel valley. In addition, there is great off-piste in the rest of the Three Valleys. And directly from the resort you can heli-ski in Italy and Switzerland (it is banned in France). But never venture off-piste without a qualified ski instructor or mountain guide and safety equipment.

For a first experience off-piste, the Tour du Rocher de l'Ombre is great. Access is easy from the left of the Combe de la Saulire piste and you are never far from the piste. It is very quiet, the slope is very broad and easy and you get a real sense of adventure as you plan your way between the rocks. And the view of the Croix des Verdons is impressive. Keep to the left for the best snow.

The Courchevel **ESF** is the largest ski school in Europe with over 700 instructors. They can help you find the best off-piste and explore it safely. For phone numbers see overleaf. The websites of the three different branches (1550, 1650, 1850) can be accessed through www.courchevel.com

Les Avals is one of my favourite routes. The easiest way to get to it is to take the Roc Merlet piste from the top of the Chanrossa chair-lift. Leave the piste on the right as soon as you can, then climb up and cross the ridge. Once you've arrived at a group of rocks (in the form of towers) descend the south side. This run is not technically difficult and is particularly beautiful in spring conditions. Another possibility from the Chanrossa chair is to traverse towards the Aiguille du Fruit. Almost anywhere along this very wide slope, you can choose your spot to start skiing down to rejoin the end of Chanrossa black piste at the bottom. A technically more difficult run, for experienced off-piste skiers only, is Plan Mugnier. This starts with a 20-minute walk from the top of the Chanrossa chair but you are normally rewarded by very good snow because the slope you ski down faces north. Le Curé is in the Saulire area: this narrow gully starts under a towering rock and offers a steady 35° slope and is only for expert skiers who don't mind climbing to the Doigt du Curé starting point.

Courchevel

273

slopes of La Vizelle, both towards Verdons and towards the link with 1650. Some of the reds on La Vizelle verge on black and the black M piste is surprisingly little used. If you love moguls, try the black Suisses and Chanrossa runs – and the off-piste moguls under the Chanrossa chair. For a change of scene and a test of stamina, a couple of long (700m/2,300ft vertical), genuinely steep blacks cut through the trees to Le Praz.

In good snow conditions you can ski all the way down (around 2000m/6,560ft vertical) from La Saulire to Bozel, way below Le Praz, over meadows and through trees on the final section and catch a bus back.

There is plenty of off-piste terrain to try with a guide – see the feature panel above.

FOR INTERMEDIATES
Paradise for all levels

The Three Valleys is the greatest intermediate playground in the world, but all grades of intermediates will love Courchevel's local slopes too.

Early intermediates will enjoy the gentle Pyramides and Grandes Bosses blues above 1650, and the Biollay and Pralong blues above 1850. Those of average ability can handle most red runs without difficulty. Our favourite is the long, sweeping Combe de la Saulire from top to bottom of the cable-car first thing in the morning, when it's well groomed and free of crowds; but it's a different story at the end of the day – cut up snow and very crowded. Creux, behind La Vizelle, is another splendid, long red that gets bumpy and unpleasantly crowded later on. Marmottes from the top of Vizelle is quieter and more challenging.

The Chenus sector has excellent blues and reds down towards 1850 and 1550 and through the trees towards La Tania – long, rolling cruises. Over at 1650, the Chapelets and Rochers reds right at the edge of the whole Three Valleys ski area are great fun for fast cruising, and usually quiet (though that might change when the new six-pack is in place).

FOR BEGINNERS
Great graduation runs

There are excellent nursery slopes above both 1650 and 1850. At the former, lessons are likely to begin on the short drags close to the village,

LIFT PASSES

Three Valleys
Covers all lifts in Courchevel, La Tania, Méribel, Val-Thorens, Les Menuires and St-Martin-de-Belleville.

Beginners
Eight free lifts in the Courchevel valley.

Main pass
1 day €41
6 days €204

Senior citizens
Over 60: 6 days €164
Over 72: free pass

Children
Under 13: 6 days €153.50
Under 5: free pass

Notes
Reductions for families. Half-day and pedestrian passes available. Six-day pass and over valid for one day in Espace Killy (Tignes-Val-d'Isère), Paradiski (La Plagne-Les Arcs), Pralognan and Les Saisies.

Alternative passes
Courchevel pass covers Courchevel and La Tania only.

but quick learners will soon be able to go up the gondola. The best nursery area at 1850 is at Pralong, above the village, near the airstrip. A reporter points out that getting to it from the village isn't easy, unless you go by road. A green path links this area with chairs to 1650, so adventurous novices can soon move further afield. The Bellecôte green run down into 1850 is an excellent, long, gentle slope – but it is used by skiers returning to the village and does get unpleasantly crowded. It is served by the Jardin Alpin gondola, and a drag that is one of eight free beginner lifts. 1550 and Le Praz have small nursery areas, but most people go up to 1850 for its more reliable snow.

FOR CROSS-COUNTRY
Long wooded trails
Courchevel has a total of 66km/41 miles of trails, the most in the Three Valleys. Le Praz is the most suitable village, with trails through the woods towards 1550, 1850 and Méribel. Given enough snow, there are also loops around the village.

QUEUES
There are always alternatives
Even at New Year and in mid-February, when 1850 in particular positively teems with people, queues are minimal, thanks to the excellence of the lift system. However, as one reporter points out, 'there can be a build-up at 1850 for the gondolas'. At such times 'it's best to avoid skiing back to 1850'. For example, try using the Plantrey chair, below 1850, or the Coqs chair, above it, to get over to the Col de la Loze, Le Praz and La Tania. The Biollay chair is very popular with the ski school (which gets priority) and can also be worth avoiding. Queues for the huge Saulire cable-car are rare. Many lifts have American-style singles lines, which seem

to be working better now than when they were first introduced.

MOUNTAIN RESTAURANTS
Good but can be very expensive
Mountain restaurants are plentiful and pleasant, but it is sensible to check the prices; for table-service restaurants reservations may be needed.

Cap Horn, near the airstrip, has now taken over from Chalet de Pierres as the biggest rip-off, according to a local who says it has a 'scarily' expensive wine list, specifically catering for the rich Russians. A reporter talks of food which was 'cold and dry' and says the place is 'like Cannes in the Alps'. Chalet de Pierres, on the Verdons piste is not far behind, pricewise, with one reporter calling it 'reassuringly expensive' and another forgoing 'a bottle of wine at 9,500 euros (over £6,000)'. But it is a comfortable, smooth place built in traditional style and reporters agree it does good food: 'great unfussy mountain food and very nice staff' is a typical comment. It has a wonderful array of desserts and is easily accessible for pedestrians. The Bergerie on the Bellecôte piste seems to attract a fashionable crowd.

The Verdons is well placed for piste-watching and La Soucoupe has good food and great views; there's an atmospheric self-service section with table-service upstairs where food is cooked on a log fire. The Panoramic at the top of Saulire also has self- and table-service restaurants and we had good confit de canard in the latter.

If we're paying the bill, our favourite Courchevel restaurant is the Bel Air, at the top of the gondola above 1650 – good simple food ('omelettes to die for'), friendly and efficient table-service, and a splendid tiered terrace; booking usually essential. The Casserole, at the bottom of the Signal chair, was found to be 'expensive, but efficient'.

SCHOOLS AND GUIDES
Size is everything

Courchevel's branches of the ESF add up to the largest ski school in Europe, with over 700 instructors. We lack recent reports.

Ski Academy is an independent group of French instructors – 'one brilliant, another OK', 'excellent and attentive', said two reporters. Magic in Motion was rated 'good, but not outstanding'. Supreme in 1850 (British owned and mainly staffed by British instructors) gets mixed reviews.

New Generation is another British-run school. We joined a group lesson with them last year and were very impressed by their US-style of teaching: they ask the students to set their goals for the lesson on the gondola ride up and then try to help them achieve them. We nearly all opted for skiing chopped-up, off-piste snow with style and all felt we had improved a lot by the end of the morning. We receive rave reviews about them from reporters, for adults and children alike: 'I joined a confident intermediate group (level 5) and learnt more in two days than I have for a long time,' said a 2005 visitor. 'We had

an absolutely brilliant week and our daughter, aged seven, had fun and progressed well,' said a 2004 reporter. 'Really excellent', 'young and highly motivated', 'learned more in the week than we had over many years previously' are other typical comments.

RTM is a specialist boarding school run and staffed by Brits, which a 2004 reporter said was 'great'.

The Bureau des Guides runs all-day off-piste excursions.

FACILITIES FOR CHILDREN
Lots of chalet-based options

In the past reporters have found the ski kindergarten at 1850 over-stretched, with 19 children in a class of five to seven-year-olds. But one reader last year said her three-year-old daughter was happy and 'skiing on reins quite well by the end of the week'. The ESF at 1850 offers VIC (Very Important Children) lessons for English-speaking children between 6 and 12 years with a maximum of six children per group. Several tour operators run their own nurseries using British nannies – an alternative that many families have found attractive.

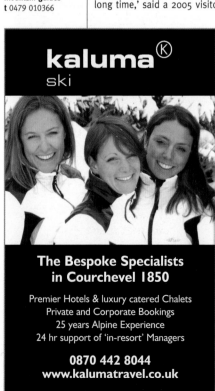

CHILDREN

Village des Enfants
(1850) **t** 0479 080847
Ages from 18mnth;
9am-5pm

Les Pitchounets (1650)
t 0479 083369
Ages from 18mnth;
9am-5pm

Babysitting list
Contact tourist office.

Ski schools
Most offer lessons
from the age of 3 or 4
(ESF 1850 prices
€234 for 6 days).

STAYING THERE

HOW TO GO
Value chalets and apartments
Huge numbers of British tour operators
go to Courchevel.
Chalets There are plenty of chalets and
some chalet-hotels available.

In 1850 several operators offer
notably comfortable chalets, and a few
genuinely luxurious ones. Kaluma has a
new Chalet Totara for 2005/06 – to be
run 'as an absolutely top-end product
in conjunction with Hotel Kilimanjaro'
and the splendid Chalet Vizelle.
Flexiski, Scott Dunn and Descent
International also have upscale and
convenient places. Lotus Supertravel
has a number of luxurious
'superchalets' – we loved our stay in
the splendid Chalet Founets.

Mark Warner's chalet-hotel Dahu in
1850 is convenient and reported to
serve 'excellent food'.

In 1650 Le Ski has 12 good-value
chalets; its flagship chalet Rikiki is all
en suite and set on the piste. We
stayed with them in 2004 and were
very impressed with the food, service
and ski guiding. A reporter this year
found 'the food excellent and the

chalet staff friendly, helpful and
unassuming'. Ski Olympic has two
chalets and a central chalet-hotel, Les
Avals, said to be 'just brilliant', and a
chalet-hotel in 1550. Small Scottish
operator Finlays has six chalets in
1550. Total has big chalets in both
1850 and 1650 and smaller ones in
1850. Family-specialist Esprit Ski has
several chalets down in Le Praz. As
does Simply Ski, which is also in 1850.
Crystal has places in all four villages.
Hotels There are nearly 50 hotels in
Courchevel, mostly at 1850 – including
more 4-stars than anywhere else in
France except Paris (14 at the last count).
((((⑤ **Les Airelles** (1850) (0479 003838)
'Super flash and over the top. The
most expensive hotel in the Alps.' On
the Jardin Alpin piste.
((((⑤ **St Joseph** (1850) (0479 081616)
Like a plush country house 'with 14 fab
rooms and two huge stunning
apartments, with awesome views'.
((((⑤ **Mélézin** (1850) (0479 080133)
Superbly stylish and luxurious – and in
an ideal position beside the bottom of
the Bellecôte home slope.
((((⑤ **Carlina** (1850) (0479 080030)
Luxury piste-side pad, next to Mélézin.
((((⑤ **Byblos Courchevel** (1850) (0479

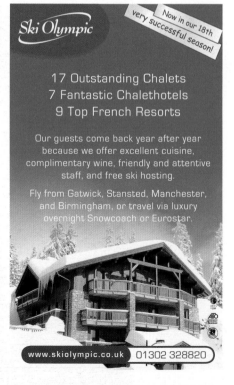

GETTING THERE

Air Geneva 149km/ 93 miles (3½hr); Lyon 187km/116 miles (3½hr); Chambéry 110km/68 miles (1½hr). Direct flights to Courchevel altiport from London on request only (contact tourist office for details).
Rail Moûtiers (24km/ 15 miles); transfer by bus or taxi.

ACTIVITIES

Indoor Artificial skating rink, climbing wall, gymnasium, bowling, exhibitions, concerts, cinemas, language and computer courses, cookery courses, library
In hotels: health and fitness centres (swimming pools, saunas, steam-room, hot-tub, water therapy, weight-training, massage), bridge (in the Chabichou)

Outdoor Hang-gliding, paragliding, flying lessons, snow-shoe excursions, ice-climbing, snowmobile rides, ice karting, horse-drawn sleigh rides, cleared paths, tobogganing, flight excursions

SNOWPIX.COM / CHRIS GILL

Vizelle, as seen from Chanrossa, with the Marmottes red run along the ridge and the Creux red in the shady valley. Nice and snowy, huh? ➔

009800) Next to first stop on Jardin Alpin gondola; spacious public rooms, good pool, sauna, steam complex.
Bellecôte (1850) (0479 081019) Our favourite among the more swanky places – it offers some Alpine atmosphere as well as sheer luxury.
Chabichou (1850) (0479 080055) Distinctive white building, right on the slopes; family-run, friendly and rustic with very good food plus the option of a restaurant with 2 Michelin stars.
Les Grandes Alpes (1850) (0479 000000) 4-star on piste by main lifts. Readers enthuse: 'Personal service. Luxurious rooms.' 'Brilliant food.'
Rond Point (1850) (0479 080433) Family atmosphere, central position.
Croisette (1850) (0479 080900) Next to main lifts above Le Jump bar. 'Simple and clean, staff very helpful.'
Courcheneige (1850) (0479 080259) On Bellecôte piste. 'A real find: lovely staff, good food.' Quiet.
New Solarium (1850) (0479 080201) Newly renovated, near first stop on Jardin Alpin gondola, 'sensible prices and very friendly service'.

Sivolière (1850) (0479 080833) Newly renovated, set among pines.
Golf (1650) (0479 009292) Rather impersonal 3-star, in a superb position on the piste next to the gondola.
Ancolies (1550) (0479 082766) 'A real find,' said a US visitor impressed by the friendly staff and excellent food.
Peupliers (1300) (0479 084147) Smartly renovated and expanded, good restaurant, cheap by local standards.
Self-catering There's a large selection, though high-season dates can sell out early. As usual in France, check room sizes and book a place advertised for more people than there are of you.

EATING OUT
Pick your price
There are a lot of good, very expensive French restaurants in Courchevel.

In 1850, among the best, and priciest, are the Chabichou (a 2004 visitor recommends the mini-dégustation menu of four courses), and the Bateau Ivre – both with two Michelin stars. Recommendations for Savoyard food include the cosy Saulire

Courchevel

and the Fromagerie. Other reporters praise the Chapelle ('fabulous and filling meal of lamb cooked on an open fire'). A reporter liked the pizzas but not the soup at the Via Ferrata and was concerned to watch the staff smoking in the kitchen. Also mentioned by readers are the Cloche ('good atmosphere'), the Tremplin ('delicious crêpes', but 'snooty and old-style French' in the evening) and the Cendrée ('a wonderful Italian', 'good value', but 'put Russians before us'). We've had mixed reports about the Locomotive with railway-theme decor and a varied menu: 'lots of character, good music, food and wine', said one 2005 reporter, 'very average food and service, overpriced', 'a lamentable meal', said others. The hotel Tovets is reported to have 'reasonable prices and delicious food'. A local recommends the Grand Café (underneath the hotel St Joseph) for good Asian cuisine. A 2005 visitor enjoyed the large helpings at the Tex Mex Kalico.

In 1550, the Oeil du Boeuf is good for grills. The Cortona does good-value pizza. In 1650 the Seizena has quickly built a good reputation; and the Eterlou, Montagne and the Petit Savoyard ('divine fillet steak and pâté de foie gras dish') do good French and Savoyard food and cheaper pizza and pasta. In Le Praz, Bistrot du Praz is expensive but excellent. The Ya-ca is small and 'very French'. We had an excellent meal at the Peupliers (good pepper steak).

APRES-SKI
1850 has most variety
If you want lots of nightlife, it's got to be 1850. There are some exclusive nightclubs, such as the Caves, with top Paris cabaret acts and sky-high prices. The popular Kalico has DJs and cocktails, and gets packed. The Bergerie has themed evenings – food, music, entertainment – but prices are high.

The Jump at the foot of the main slope is the place to be as the lifts close ('a very cool atmosphere but very

---

Selected chalet in Courchevel

WEBSITES

For links to resort
sites, go to our own
new site at
www.wtss.co.uk

Phone numbers
From abroad use the
prefix +33 and omit
the initial '0' of the
phone number.

TOURIST OFFICE

t 0479 080029
pro@courchevel.com
www.courchevel.com

expensive') and it does get impossibly packed. A reporter this year found the 'cool and trendy zinc look S'no Limit a good alternative to the Jump next door'. Another liked the new Milk Pub, set underground with live music 'sensible-ish prices and a young crowd'. One reader comments that there is 'no real large meeting place for après-ski'. The Saulire (aka Chez Jacques) and the cheap and cheerful Potinière (which has changed hands) are also popular. Piggys is described as 'fur coats, pampered dogs and sky-high prices' and as 'the world's only medieval themed French/Irish wine bar/pub/disco featuring a drawing room and library'; 'Four small beers cost me £45,' said a 2004 reporter. Mangeoire has 'an excellent Piano bar (with high Piggys-style prices) and is extremely lively from about 11pm'.

Cinemas in 1850 and 1650 show English-speaking films.

Last year a reader's 20-something kids found 'plenty to do' in 1650. The Bubble is the hub; with satellite TV, internet access, cheap bar prices, a happy hour, some strong local beers and frequent live music, it has a largely British clientele. Rocky's Bar (in chalet-

hotel Avals) is popular and 'good for watching sport' – and a reporter enjoyed the 'specialities, including flavoured vodkas'. Remonte Pente is a tiny French bar. The Space Bar has pool, games and live music or DJs and the local disco (now called La Godille) stayed open till 4am delighting a reporter's 20-year-old kids.

In 1550 the Chanrossa bar is British-dominated, with occasional live music, the Taverne also has English owners.

OFF THE SLOPES
1850 isn't bad
The Forum sports centre in 1850 includes a climbing wall in the shopping centre – good for spectating too. There are a fair number of shops in 1850, plus markets at most levels. There's an ice-driving circuit and an ice-climbing structure. Snow-shoeing among the trees is growing in popularity. A pedestrian lift pass for the gondolas and buses in Courchevel and Méribel makes it easy for non-slope users to meet up the mountain for lunch. And you can take joyrides from the altiport. A non-skier's guide to Courchevel, Méribel and La Tania is distributed by the tourist office.

Courchevel

Les Deux-Alpes

It's a long way up to the glacier and a narrow way down

COSTS

① ② ③ ④ ⑤ ⑥

RATINGS

The slopes
Fast lifts	**
Snow	****
Extent	***
Expert	****
Intermediate	**
Beginner	***
Convenience	***
Queues	**
Mountain restaurants	**

The rest
Scenery	****
Resort charm	**
Off-slope	**

NEWS

Two new runs were added last winter – the Grand Creux run on La Toura and a new red, Tête Moute, from the Bellecombes chair.

The La Toura chairlift at mid-mountain has been replaced by a fixed-grip quad with moving carpet to maximise its capacity.

➕ High, snow-sure slopes, including an extensive glacier area

➕ Varied high-mountain terrain, from motorways to steep off-piste slopes

➕ Excellent, sunny nursery slopes

➕ Stunning views of the Ecrins peaks

➕ Lively resort with varied nightlife

➕ Wide choice of affordable hotels

➖ Piste network modest by mega-resort standards – we're sceptical about the claimed 220km/137 miles – and badly congested in places

➖ The home runs are either steep and icy or dangerously overcrowded – so people queue for a lift down instead

➖ Virtually no woodland runs

➖ Spread-out, traffic-choked resort

➖ Few appealing mountain restaurants

We have a love–hate relationship with Les Deux-Alpes. We quite like the buzz of the village – arriving here is a bit like driving into Las Vegas from the Nevada desert – and we understand the appeal of its vibrant nightlife. We love the high-Alpine feel of its main mountain, and the good snow to be found on the north-facing pistes at mid-mountain. But we're very unimpressed by the extent of those pistes, and we hate the congestion that results when most of the town's 35,000 visitors are crammed on to them. Crowding apart, keen intermediates spoiled by high-mileage French mega-resorts (and not up to the excellent off-piste) will simply find the usable area of slopes rather small.

THE RESORT

Les Deux-Alpes is a narrow village sitting on a high, remote col. Access is from the Grenoble-Briançon road to the north. The village is a long, sprawling collection of hotels, apartments, bars and shops, most lining the busy main street and the parallel street that completes the one-way traffic system. The resort has a lively ambience.

The village has grown haphazardly over the years, and there is a wide range of building styles, from old chalets through 1960s blocks to more sympathetic recent developments. It looks better as you leave than as you arrive, because all the balconies face the southern end of the resort.

Lifts are spread fairly evenly along the village and there is no clear centre, but a couple of focal points are evident. Alpe de Venosc, at the south end of town, has many of the nightspots and hotels, the most character, the fewest cars, the best shops and the Diable gondola up to the tough terrain around Tête Moute. More generally useful is the Jandri Express, now with an improved second stage, from the middle of the resort, where there is a popular outdoor ice rink and some good restaurants and bars. The village straggles north from here, becoming less convenient the further you go.

The free shuttle-bus service saves on some very long walks from one end of town to the other.

The six-day pass covers a day in several nearby resorts including Alpe-d'Huez and Serre-Chevalier. Helicopter trips to Alpe-d'Huez are good value at £40 return – a 'must', says a reporter. More economical is the shuttle-bus service on Wednesdays and Thursdays.

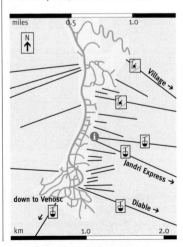

KEY FACTS

Resort	1650m
	5,410ft
Slopes	1300-3570m
	4,270-11,710ft
Lifts	59
Pistes	220km
	137 miles
Green	20%
Blue	40%
Red	21%
Black	19%
Snowmaking	
	105 guns

THE MOUNTAINS

For a big resort, Les Deux-Alpes has a disappointingly small piste area, despite recent improvements. Although extremely long and tall (it rises almost 2000m/6,560ft), the main sector is also very narrow, with just a few runs on the upper part of the mountain, served by a few long, efficient lifts. The piste-grading is rather inconsistent and some runs are graded differently on the map and on the mountain.

THE SLOPES
Long, narrow and fragmented
The western **Pied Moutet** side of Les Deux-Alpes is relatively little used. It is served by lifts from various parts of town but reaches only 2100m/6,890ft. As well as the short runs back to town, which get the morning sun, there's an attractive north-facing red run down through the trees to the small village of Bons. The only other tree-lined run in Les Deux-Alpes goes down to another low village, Mont-de-Lans.

On the eastern side of the resort, the broad, steep slope immediately above it offers a series of relatively short, challenging runs, down to the nursery slopes ranged at the bottom. With the exception of a long winding green run, which gets very crowded,

these runs are now all classified as black, and rightly so: they aren't groomed and are usually mogulled, and often icy when not softened by the afternoon sun. As a result, at the end of the day many visitors ride down the gondolas.

The ridge of **Les Crêtes** above the village has lifts and gentle runs along it, and behind it lies the deep, steep Combe de Thuit. Lifts span the combe to the main mid-mountain station at 2600m/8,530ft now known as **Toura**, at the foot of the slopes on La Toura. The middle section of the mountain, above and below this point, is made up primarily of blue cruising runs and is very narrow. At one point, there is essentially just a single run down the mountain – the Grand Nord, which is a real bottleneck late in the day. The only alternative is to take the roundabout (partly flat) blue Gours run to the bottom of the combe, where a chair-lift takes you up to Les Crêtes. This pleasant run passes the base of the Fée chair, serving an isolated (and neglected) black run, and a slightly easier parallel red run.

The top **Glacier du Mont de Lans** section, served by drag-lifts and the warmer underground funicular, has some fine, very easy runs, which afford great views and are ideal for beginners

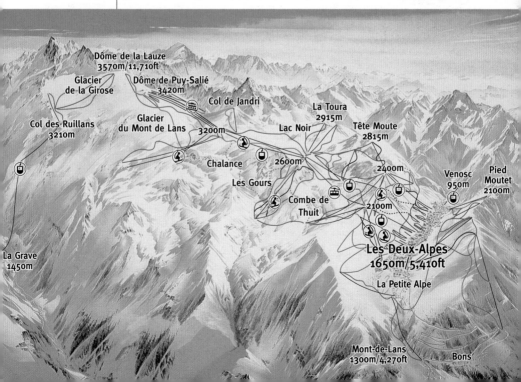

Dôme de la Lauze
3570m/11,710ft

Glacier
de la Girose

Dôme de Puy-Salié
3420m

Col de Jandri

La Toura
2915m

Col des Ruillans
3210m

Glacier
du Mont de Lans
3200m

Lac Noir

Tête Moute
2815m

Chalance

2600m

Les Gours

2400m

Venosc
950m

Pied
Moutet
2100m

Combe de
Thuit

2100m

**Les Deux-Alpes
1650m/5,410ft**

La Grave
1450m

La Petite Alpe

Mont-de-Lans
1300m/4,270ft

Bons

boarding

Les Deux-Alpes has been catering for snowboarders for years, and has built up an excellent reputation. There's a specialist Primitive school and lots of boarder-friendly facilities. Most of the lifts on the higher slopes are chairs. The terrain-park is relocated up to the glacier in the summer (access is by T-bar or funicular), which is where the Mondial du Snowboard competition is hosted each year. The ESF offers freestyle classes, using trampolines and a huge air-bag to practise on. But for beginner and timid intermediate boarders the narrow, flat crowded areas in mid-mountain and the routes down to the village are intimidating. There's some great off-piste in the local area for free-riders, and the link to La Grave offers some of the best off-piste terrain in the world for advanced riders – hire a guide.

LIFT PASSES

Super ski pass
Covers all lifts in Les Deux-Alpes and entry to swimming pool and ice rink.

Beginners
Four free drag-lifts

Main pass
1 day €34
6 days €161.50

Senior citizens
Over 60: 6 days €121.20
Over 72: free pass

Children
Under 13: 6 days €121.20
Under 5: free pass

Notes
Half-day and pedestrian passes available. Six-day pass includes access to La Grave and one day's skiing in Alpe-d'Huez, Serre-Chevalier, Puy-St-Vincent and the Milky Way.

Alternative passes
Ski Sympa covers 21 lifts.

WENDY-JANE KING

At mid-mountain there are two boarder-cross courses and a serious terrain-park ➔

and the less adventurous. You can go from the top here all the way down to Mont-de-Lans – a descent of 2270m/7,450ft vertical that is the world's biggest on-piste vertical, as far as we know. A walk (or snowcat tow) in the opposite direction takes you over to the slopes of La Grave – a splendid area for advanced skiers with a guide (now covered by the Deux-Alpes pass).

TERRAIN-PARKS
A real highlight
Terrain is taken seriously here. At mid-mountain on La Toura there are two boarder-cross courses and a big terrain-park including half-pipe, and higher up there are several innovative terrain features – ledges, gullies, canyons – all 'in tip-top condition'.

SNOW RELIABILITY
Excellent on higher slopes
The snow on the higher slopes is normally very good, even in a poor winter – one of the main reasons for the resort's popularity. Above 2200m/7,220ft most of the runs are north-facing, and the top glacier section guarantees good snow. More of a concern is bad weather shutting the lifts, or extremely low temperatures at the top. But the runs just above the village face west, so they get a lot of afternoon sun and can be icy at the beginning and end of the day. Snowmaking on some of the lower slopes helps keep them usable, when it's used – a January visitor skiing on rocky pistes saw it used 'not once'.

FOR EXPERTS
Off-piste is the main attraction
With good snow and weather conditions, the area offers wonderful off-piste sport – see the feature panel on the facing page. There are serious routes that end well outside the lift network, with verticals of over

2000m/6,56oft. One reporter recommends the renowned descent to St-Christophe (hire a guide, who will arrange transport back).

A weekly Free Respect event promotes off-piste safety, with free advice and free-ride competitions.

The Super Diable chair-lift, from the top of the Diable gondola, serves the steepest black run around. The brave can also try off-piste variations here.

If the conditions are right, an outing to the slopes of La Grave is a must.

FOR INTERMEDIATES
Limited cruising
Les Deux-Alpes can disappoint keen intermediates. A lot of the runs are either rather tough – some of the blues could be reds – or boringly bland.

The runs higher up generally have good snow, and there is some great fast cruising, especially on the mainly

The off-piste routes in Les Deux-Alpes are numerous and varied in difficulty, the easiest permitting skiers even of an intermediate level to enjoy their first 'free-ride experience'. We've asked Jeremy Edwards of the European Ski and Snowboard School to share some of his favourites.

For something slightly technical, both sides off the Bellecombe red piste – 2800m-2300m (9,190ft-7,550ft) – offer a wide range of varying terrain; it's important to take care here – there are several small cliff faces. For those keen to tackle couloirs – steep, narrow slopes between rocks – this descent offers small ones that are ideal for your first attempts; they can be avoided, though.

The **European Ski and Snowboard School** does classes and guiding in small groups. Its instructors are of several nationalities, but all speak excellent English.
t 00 33 476 797455
europeanskischool@
worldonline.fr
www.europeanskischool.
co.uk

Traversing across the top of the black Grand Couloir piste leads to the North Rachas area, with off-piste faces that offer cold snow conditions all winter. The first large valley leads to three couloirs – one fairly broad and easy, the other two much narrower and steeper, and certainly not for the timid. Traversing further leads to a much wider descent that avoids the three couloirs.

For tree skiing it's best to head for the Vallée Blanche area, reached via the lifts on Pied Moutet. The north-east face, towards the chair-lift at Bons, offers great routes over generally deserted wooded terrain with excellent cold snow conditions.

Strong skiers will enjoy the famous Chalance run, which starts just below the glacier and descends 1000m/3,280ft vertical to the Gours run; there are several variations, mixing wide open slopes and rocky pitches. These faces are at times subject to quite a high avalanche risk because of wind slab.

Traversing above the north face of the Chalance leads to the couloir Pylone Electrique – a steep, narrow 200m/660ft-long couloir with the reward below it of an excellent wide powder field of moderate gradient. A rest on the Thuit chair-lift is a must after this adrenalin-charged descent.

These routes and many more play a large part in the off-piste free-ride courses offered by the European Ski and Snowboard School.

Les Deux-Alpes

283

SCHOOLS

ESF
t 0476 792121
International St-Christophe
t 0476 790421
European
t 0476 797455
Primitive
t 0607 907135
Ski Privilege
t 0476 792344
Easiski
t 0476 795884
Burton Connexion
t 0615 079442

Classes
(ESF prices)
6 half days (2¼hr am or pm) €125
Private lessons
€31 for 1hr

GUIDES

Guides office
t 0476 113629

CHILDREN

Crèche du Clos des Fonds
t 0476 790262
Ages 6mnth to 2yr;
8.30-5.30
Bonhomme de Neige
t 0476 790677
Ages 2 to 6; 9am-5.30 (also activity centre for ages 6 to 17)
Jardins des Neiges
t 0476 792121
Ages 3 to 6; 9.15-12 noon, 2.30-5pm; 6 mornings €105.50

Ski schools
Classes for ages 6 to 12 (6 mornings €105.50 with ESF)

---

north-facing pistes served by the chair-lifts off to the sides. You can often pick gentle or steeper terrain in these bowls as you wish, but avid piste-bashers will explore all there is to offer in a couple of days. Many visitors take the opportunity of excursions to Alpe-d'Huez and Serre-Chevalier.

Less confident intermediates will love the quality of the snow and the gentleness of most of the runs on the upper mountain. Their problem might lie in finding the pistes too crowded.

FOR BEGINNERS
Good slopes
The nursery slopes beside the village are spacious and gentle. The run along the ridge above them is excellent, too. The glacier also has a fine array of very easy slopes. But there is a lot of lift-riding to do between these various possibilities.

FOR CROSS-COUNTRY
Needs very low-altitude snow
There are three small, widely dispersed areas. La Petite Alpe, near the entrance to the village, has a couple of snow-sure but very short trails. Given good snow, Venosc, reached by a gondola down, has the only worthwhile picturesque ones. Total trail distance is 25km/16 miles. You can ski the Mont de Lans glacier with a qualified guide.

QUEUES
Can be a problem
Les Deux-Alpes has some impressive lifts, but the village is large, and queues at the mid-morning peak can be 'diabolically' long for the Jandri Express and Diable gondolas. The eight-seat chair from the mid-station to the glacier has reduced the bottleneck for the second stage. Problems can also occur when people are bussed in because snow is in short supply elsewhere. The top lifts are prone to closure if it's windy, putting pressure on the lower lifts. We have repeated reports of queues for the gondolas back to the village when people decline to tackle the tricky blacks or the crowded green run back down.

MOUNTAIN RESTAURANTS
Still limited
There are mountain restaurants at all the major lift junctions, but they are generally pretty poor. The Diable au Coeur, opened at the top of the Diable gondola last season but the Chalet de

---

la Toura, in the middle of the domain at about 2600m/8,530ft, is still said to be 'probably the best restaurant on the mountain', with a big terrace, a welcoming woody interior and 'very friendly staff'. The Panoramic has been recommended again this year – 'but it gets very crowded and there's no queuing system'.

SCHOOLS AND GUIDES
We are all Europeans now
We get relatively few reports on the many schools operating here. We have a positive recent report on the tuition and organisation of the European school, a dynamic outfit composed of instructors of various nationalities, all (we are assured) speaking good English. Class sizes are small – as few as four pupils if you go for their advanced classes.

FACILITIES FOR CHILDREN
Fine for babies
Babies from six months to two years old can safely be entrusted to the village nursery. The kindergarten takes kids from two to six years, and there are chalet-based alternatives run by UK tour operators. There are also four free T-bars for children at the village level.

STAYING THERE

HOW TO GO
Wide range of packages
Les Deux-Alpes has something for most tastes, including that rarity in high-altitude French resorts, reasonably priced hotels.
Chalets There are a number of catered chalet packages available from UK tour operators, but some use apartments.
Hotels There are over 30 hotels, of which the majority are 2-star or below. There's a Club Med 'village' here, too.
⟨⟨⟨3⟩ **Bérangère** (0476 792411) Smartest in town (but dreary exterior) with an excellent restaurant and pool; on-piste, at less convenient north end of resort.
⟨2⟩ **Mariande** (0476 805060) Highly recommended, especially for its 'excellent' five-course dinners. At Venosc end of resort.
⟨2⟩ **Chalet Mounier** (0476 805690) Smartly modernised. Good reputation for its food, and well placed for the Diable bubble and nightlife. Swimming pool and fitness room.
⟨2⟩ **Souleil'or** (0476 792469) Looks like a lift station, but pleasant and comfortable, and well placed for the

The resort spreads a couple of miles from one end to the other →

SNOWPIX.COM / CHRIS GILL

WEBSITES

For links to resort sites, go to our own new site at www.wtss.co.uk

GETTING THERE

Air Lyon 160km/ 99 miles (3½hr); Grenoble 120km/ 75 miles (2½hr); Chambéry 126km/ 78 miles (3hr); Geneva 230km/ 143 miles (4½hr).

Rail Grenoble (70km/43 miles); four daily buses from station.

ACTIVITIES

Indoor Swimming pool, hot-tub, sauna, sports centres (Club Forme, Tanking Center), cinemas, games rooms, bowling, museum, library

Outdoor Ice rink, ice gliders (dodgems), ice driving, donkey rides, snowmobiles, helicopter flights, paragliding, quad bikes, snow-shoeing, Kanata (Inuit) village visit

Phone numbers From abroad use the prefix +33 and omit the initial '0' of the phone number.

TOURIST OFFICE

t 0476 792200 les2alp@les2alpes.com www.les2alpes.com

Jandri Express gondola. The rooms and food are reportedly 'fantastic'.

② **Les Lutins** (0476 792152) Central. Reportedly the 'best value accommodation' and 'best location in the resort'.

② **Brunerie** (0476 792223) 'Basic and cheerful', large 2-star with plenty of parking and quite well positioned.

Self-catering Many of the apartments are stuck out at the north end of the resort – well worth avoiding. However the new Prince des Ecrins (0492 840000) 'luxury apartments' are apparently at the south end of town.

EATING OUT
Plenty of choice
The hotel Bérangère has an excellent restaurant and the Chalet Mounier has a high reputation. The Petite Marmite has good food and atmosphere at reasonable prices. Bel'Auberge does classic French and is 'quite superb' – booking is advised. The Patate, the Cloche (formerly the Dahu) and Crêpes à Gogo are also recommended. Visitors on a budget can get a relatively cheap meal at Bleuets bar, the Vetrata or the Spaghetteria. One regular visitor says that Smokey Joe's Tex Mex is the best value for money in the resort.

APRES-SKI
Unsophisticated fun
Les Deux-Alpes is one of the liveliest of the French resorts, with plenty of bars, several of which stay open until the early hours. The Windsor bar is another noisy British enclave. Corrigans and Smokey Joe's are recommended. The Baron has changed hands and is now said to be the haunt of inebriated

teenagers. Bar Brésilien is apparently quieter than in previous years. The Avalanche is reportedly 'still the best club' and the Opera is recommended by locals but a 2005 visitor found it to be too far out of the resort. There are quieter places, too – the 'cosy, friendly' Bleuets is recommended.

The resort has contrived a couple of ways of dining at altitude – you can snowmobile to the glacier and back, eating on the way, or at full moon you can ski or board back to town after dinner (accompanied by ski patrollers).

OFF THE SLOPES
Not recommended
Les Deux-Alpes is not a particularly good choice for people not hitting the slopes. The pretty valley village of Venosc is worth a visit by gondola, and you can take a scenic helicopter flight to Alpe-d'Huez. There is a good pool and lots of scenic walks. Several mountain restaurants are accessible to pedestrians. Snowcat tours across the glacier provide wonderful views.

STAYING DOWN THE VALLEY
Worth considering
Close to the foot of the final ascent to Les Deux-Alpes are two near-ideal little hotels for anyone thinking of travelling around to Alpe-d'Huez, La Grave and Serre-Chevalier, both Logis de France – the cheerful Cassini (0476 800410) at Le Freney, and the even more appealing Panoramique (0476 800625), at Mizoën – approved by a reporter this year for 'hearty food, informative Dutch hosts' and (not least) the 'wondrous' panorama.

Les Deux-Alpes

Flaine

Extensive slopes, with traditional villages but bleak main resort

COSTS

①②③④⑤⑥

RATINGS

The slopes
Fast lifts	**
Snow	****
Extent	****
Expert	****
Intermediate	*****
Beginner	*****
Convenience	*****
Queues	***
Mountain restaurants	**

The rest
Scenery	****
Resort charm	*
Off-slope	*

NEWS

For 2004/05 the Kedeuze gondola out of Les Carroz was upgraded to eight-seat cabins.

Flaine is spending over a million euros on upgrading its snowmaking system. Last season it was overhauled and the system was extended on the lower slopes.

There are plans to expand Flaine by up to 4,500 beds over the next decade. Canadian developer Intrawest recently announced that the first phase of its projected 2,500 beds will go on sale in 2006.

➕ Big, varied area, with plenty of terrain to suit everyone

➕ Reliable snow in the main bowl

➕ Compact, convenient, mainly car-free village, right on the slopes

➕ Excellent facilities for children

➕ You can stay in traditional villages on the lower fringes of the area

➕ Scenic setting, and glorious views

➕ Very close to Geneva but ...

➖ Weekends can be busy as a result

➖ Austere 1960s Bauhaus buildings of Flaine itself are not easy to like

➖ In bad weather main Flaine bowl offers little to do, and links to outer sectors of the area may be closed

➖ No proper hotels in Flaine itself – only club hotels and apartments

➖ Nightlife not a highlight

➖ Little to do off the slopes (in Flaine)

Flaine is best known as a convenient resort catering particularly well for families, but it has a much broader appeal than that. The Grand Massif may not be quite in the same league as the Three Valleys and the new Paradiski area, but in extent its slopes are almost a match for Val-d'Isère/Tignes.

Flaine's family orientation is underlined by the domination of self-catering accommodation. Its few hotels have now all been taken over by tour operators such as Club Med and Crystal. But you open up more accommodation options by considering the outlying villages – Les Carroz, Samoëns and Morillon (the last two now covered in our new Samoëns chapter). Not only are they more attractive, rounded places to stay in, but also they offer some sheltered forest slopes for bad-weather days.

THE RESORT

The concrete Bauhaus-style blocks that form the core of Flaine were conceived in the sixties as 'an example of the application of the principle of shadow and light'. They look particularly shocking from the approach road – a mass of blocks nestling at the bottom of the impressive snowy bowl. From the slopes they are less obtrusive, blending into the rocky grey hillside. For us, the outdoor sculptures by Picasso, Vasarely and Dubuffet do little to improve Flaine's austere ambience.

The relatively new development of Hameau-de-Flaine is built in a much more attractive chalet style – but is inconveniently situated 1km/0.5 miles from the slopes and main village.

In Flaine proper, everything is close by: supermarket, sports rental shops, ski schools, main lifts out etc. The resort itself is also easy to get to – only 70km/43 miles from Geneva, and about 90 minutes from the airport.

There are two parts to the main resort. The 'club' hotels and some apartments, are set in the lower part, Forum. The focus of this area is a snow-covered square with buildings on three sides, the open fourth side blending with the slopes. Flaine Forêt, up the hillside and linked by lift, has its own bars and shops, and most of the apartment accommodation.

There are children all over the place; they are catered for with play areas, and the resort is supposed to be traffic-free. In fact, roads penetrate the village and you don't have to go far to encounter traffic; but the central Forum itself, leading to the pistes, is pretty safe. A car gives you the option of visiting the Portes du Soleil, Chamonix, Megève or Courmayeur (via the Mont Blanc tunnel). The bus service to/from Hameau is 'excellent'.

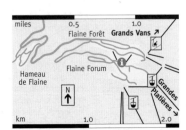

KEY FACTS

Resort	1600m
	5,250ft

Grand Massif ski area (Flaine, Les Carroz, Morillon, Samoëns, Sixt)	
Slopes	700-2480m
	2,300-8,140ft
Lifts	78
Pistes	265km
	165 miles
Green	11%
Blue	40%
Red	38%
Black	11%
Snowmaking	25%

For Flaine only	
Slopes	1600-2480m
	5,250-8,140ft
Lifts	28
Pistes	120km
	75 miles
Green	13%
Blue	37%
Red	42%
Black	8%

THE MOUNTAINS

The Grand Massif is an impressive area, with plenty of scope for any level of skier or boarder, provided you can get to all of it – the greater part of the domain lies outside the main Flaine bowl and the links can be closed by excessive wind or snow.

THE SLOPES
A big white playground

The day begins for most people at the **Grandes Platières** jumbo gondola, which speeds you in a single stage up the north face of the Flaine bowl to the high-point of the Grand Massif, and a magnificent view of Mont Blanc.

Most of the runs are reds (though there are some blues curling away to the right as you look down the mountain, and one direct black). There are essentially four or five main ways down the barren, treeless, rolling terrain back to Flaine, or to chairs in the middle of the wilderness going back to the summit.

On the far right, the Cascades blue run leads away from the lift system behind the Tête Pelouse down to the outskirts of Sixt, dropping over 1700m/5,58oft vertical in its exceptional 14km/9 mile length. The gentle/flat top half

is hard work, so we're not greatly concerned that the run isn't reliably open – it's not a run we are itching to do again. There is no lift back, but there are buses to the lifts at Samoëns or Morillon. The timetable is on the piste map; buses are often crowded. The end of the Cascades is also the foot of the slopes of Sixt – very quiet, with a non-trivial 700m/2,300ft vertical. End your exploration at Salvagny in the middle of the slopes and get a less crowded bus.

On the other side of the Tête Pelouse, a broad catwalk leads to the experts-only **Gers** bowl. At the bottom, a flat trail links with the lower (and more interesting) half of the Cascades run or there's a drag back to the ridge.

Back at Platières, an alternative is to head left down the long red Méphisto (many of the runs in this area have diabolic names – Lucifer, Belzébuth etc) to the **Aujon** area. This opens up another sector of the bowl, again mostly red runs but with some blues further down. The lower slopes here are used as slalom courses. This sector is also reachable by gondola or drag-lifts from below the resort.

The eight-seat Grands Vans chair, reached from Forum by means of a slow bucket-lift (aka télébenne), gives

Flaine

Les Grandes Platières
248om/8,14oft

Tête Pelouse

Tête des Lindars

Tête de Véret
2315m

Aujon
2035m

Gers
1715m

Les Grands Vans
2205m

Flaine
1600m/5,25oft

Tête des Saix
2120m

Vernant

Les Molliets

Sixt

1900m

1500m

Les Carroz
1140m/3,74oft

Samoëns Village
72om/2,36oft

Samoëns
1600m

Vercland

Morillon
1100m

Morillon
700m ↓

LIFT PASSES

Grand Massif
Covers all the lifts in Flaine, Les Carroz, Morillon, Samoëns and Sixt.

Beginners
Day pass €15

Main pass
1 day €33.50
6 days €168

Senior citizens
Over 60: 6 days €143
Over 75: free pass

Children
Under 16: 6 days €135
Under 12: 6 days €123
Under 5: free pass

Alternative passes
Flaine area only – half and day passes available. 4, 5 and 6 out of 7 day passes available.

access to the extensive slopes of Samoëns, Morillon and Les Carroz. You come first to the wide Vernant bowl equipped with three fast chair-lifts, one starting from a car park on the road up to Flaine. Beyond here the lie of the land is complicated, and the piste map does not represent it clearly. In good snow there is a choice of blues and reds winding down to **Les Carroz** or **Morillon**, the latter with a halfway point at 1100m/3,610ft. While there is a choice of blue, red and black runs on the top section above **Samoëns 1600**, the runs below here to Vercland are challenging blacks and reds (without snowmaking, so often closed).

We have had past reports of lifts breaking down too often and being too easily closed because of high winds, cutting off links with the lower villages. Piste signing and grooming have, however, been praised.

The piste map is rubbish – hopelessly ambitious in trying to cover such a big and complex area in a single view. In the middle of the area are several distinct bowls that are simply not detectable on the map.

TERRAIN-PARKS
Cater for kids to experts
There's a big terrain-park (called the JamPark Pro – standing for Jib and Air Maniacs) in the Aujon area of Flaine. Watch out for the 'downright dangerous' Aujon drag-lift, though, which is reportedly as much of a challenge as the park. There's also an

intermediates' park under the Charionde 2 chair on the Samoëns side, with green, red and black options and a variety of rails. And there's a kids' park, JamPark Kids, with a boarder-cross run under the Esserts quad on the Morillon side.

SNOW RELIABILITY
Usually keeps its whiteness
The main part of Flaine's slopes lie on the wide north- and north-west-facing flank of the Grandes Platières. Its direction, along with a decent height, means that it keeps the snow it receives. There is snowmaking on the greater part of the Aujon sector and on the nursery slopes. The runs towards Samoëns 1600 and Morillon 1100 are north-facing too, and some lower parts have snowmaking, but below here can be tricky or closed. The Les Carroz runs are west-facing and can suffer from strong afternoon sun, but a couple of runs have snowmaking.

FOR EXPERTS
Great fun with guidance
Flaine's family-friendly reputation tends to obscure the fact that it has some seriously challenging terrain. But much of it is off-piste and, although some of it looks like it can safely be explored without guidance, this impression is mistaken. The Flaine bowl is riddled with rock crevasses and potholes, and should be treated with the same caution that you would use on a glacier. We are told that these hazards cause deaths most years.

All the black pistes on the map deserve their grading. The Diamant Noir, down the line of the main gondola, is a challenging 850m/2,790ft descent, tricky because of moguls, narrowness and other people, rather than great steepness; the first pitch is the steepest, with spectators applauding from the chair-lift.

To the left of the Diamant Noir as you look down are several short but steep off-piste routes through the crags of the Grandes Platières.

boarding

Flaine suits boarders quite well – there's lots of varied terrain and plenty of off-piste with interesting nooks and crannies, including woods outside the main bowl. The key lifts are all now chairs or gondolas – with few unavoidable drag-lifts (beware of the absurdly vicious Aujon drag-lift though, which serves the terrain-park). There are two other terrain-park options, including one for kids. Black Side is the local specialist shop, in the central Forum.

SCHOOLS

ESF
t 0450 908100

International
t 0450 908441

Flaine Super Ski
Advanced skiers only
t 0681 061906

Independent instructors
t 0607 195609

Stages François Simond
t 0450 908097

Classes (ESF prices)
6 days (3hr per day)
€115

Private lessons
€30 for 1hr, for 1 or 2 people

The Lindars Nord chair serves a shorter slope that often has the best snow in the area, and some seriously steep gradients if you look for them.

The Gers drag-lift, outside the main bowl beyond Tête Pelouse, serves great expert-only terrain. The piste going down the right of the drag is a proper black, but by departing from it you can find slopes of up to 45°. To the left of the drag is the impressive main Gers bowl – a great north-facing horseshoe of about 550m/1,800ft vertical, powder or moguls top to bottom, all off-piste. You can choose your gradient, from steep to very steep. As you look down the bowl, you see more adventurous ways into the bowl from the Grands Vans and Tête de Véret lifts.

There are further serious pistes on the top lifts above Samoëns 1600.

Touring is a possibility behind the Grandes Platières, and there are some scenic off-piste routes from which you can be retrieved by helicopter – such as the Combe des Foges, next to Gers.

FOR INTERMEDIATES
Something for everyone

Flaine is ideal for confident intermediates, with a great variety of pistes (and usually the bonus of good snow conditions, at least above Flaine itself). As a reporter puts it, 'There may not be many challenging runs, but there are very few dull ones.' The diabolically named reds that dominate the Flaine bowl are not really as hellish as their names imply – they tend to gain their status from short steep sections rather than overall difficulty, and they're great for improving technique. The relatively direct Faust is great carving territory, at least in January when it isn't cluttered by other people. There are gentler cruises from the top of the mountain – Cristal, taking you to the Perdrix chair, or Serpentine, all the way home. The blues at Aujon are excellent for confidence-building, but the drag serving them is just the opposite.

The connections with the slopes outside the main bowl are classified blue but several blue-run reporters have found them tricky because of narrowness, crowds or poor snow. Once the connection has been made, however, all intermediates will enjoy the long tree-lined runs down to Les Carroz, as long as the snow is good. The Morillon slopes are also excellent

intermediate terrain – the long green Marvel run to Morillon 1100 is an easy cruise with excellent signs along the way explaining (in English as well as French) the local wildlife.

FOR BEGINNERS
Fairly good

There are excellent nursery slopes right by the village, served by free lifts which make a pass unnecessary until you are ready to go higher up the mountain. The area is roped off, but it is still used as a short cut back to the village by other skiers. There are no long green runs to progress to in the Flaine bowl – if you have a really nervous intermediate to deal with, it's worth driving or bussing down the access road to the Lac chair at Vernant – but there are one or two gentle local blues.

CROSS-COUNTRY
Very fragmented

The Grand Massif claims 64km/40 miles of cross-country tracks but only about 17km/10 miles of that is around Flaine itself. The majority is on the valley floor and dependent on low snow. There are extensive tracks between Morillon and Les Carroz, with some tough uphill sections. Samoëns 1600 has its own tracks and makes the best base for cross-country enthusiasts.

QUEUES
A few problems

Recent investment in new lifts has eliminated some trouble spots, and several reporters have had queue-free weeks, even in high season. But there can be problems when the resorts are full and at weekends (the area is very close to Geneva). Towards the end of the day expect delays at the Vernant chair to get back to the Flaine bowl (an alternative is to descend to one of the lift-bases along the access road, and catch a bus) and at Les Molliets – 'horrendous' at times. The main Grandes Platières gondola is prone to queues at the start of the day, but they move quickly. The other main lift out of Flaine, the old Aup de Veran gondola, also gets busy.

Queues elsewhere can build up at weekends and when the lifts out of the Flaine bowl are shut due to high winds or when the weather is warm and the lower resorts have poor snow. (When this happens, the queues to go down can be worse than those to go up.)

↑ You can make out the two levels of central Flaine in this shot – and the chalet roofs of Hameau, to the left
SNOWPIX.COM / CHRIS GILL

CHILDREN

Les P'tits Loups
t 0450 908782
Ages 6mnth to 3yr

Rabbit Club and Fantaski
t 0450 908100
Ages 3 to 12; 9am-5pm; 6 days with lunch €215

La Souris Verte
t 0450 908441
Ages 3 to 12

MMV Hotels Flaine and Aujon
t 0492 126212
Ages 18mnth to 14yr

Club Med Flaine
t 0450 908166
For babies aged from 4mnth

Ski school
For ages 5 to 12: €95 for 6 days, 3hr per day (ESF prices)

MOUNTAIN RESTAURANTS
Back to base, or quit the bowl
In the Flaine bowl, there are few restaurants above the resort's upper outskirts. The rustic Blanchot, at the bottom of the Serpentine run, has 'friendly staff' and 'excellent food', but it can get crowded. At Forum level, across the piste from the gondola, is the welcoming Michet ('definitely worth a visit'), with very good Savoyard food and table service, and the Eloge – 'fast table service, tasty food, reasonable value'. Up the slope a bit, the Cascade is self-service but with a good terrace and 'very pleasant' proprietors. Epicéa has a rustic atmosphere, a terrace and gets rave reviews. Up at Forêt level, the Bissac has a good atmosphere, traditional decor and excellent food.

Outside the Flaine bowl, we love the remote Chalet du Lac de Gers (book in advance and ring for a snowcat to tow you up from part way down the Cascades run) – simple food but splendid isolation and views of the frozen lake. We also had an excellent plat du jour at the cosy and rustic Igloo above Morillon, but service gets overstretched. The rustic Chalet les Molliets near the bottom of the Molliets chair offers 'exemplary food and service'. But this year's find is the Cuprese on the Timalets red piste down to Les Carroz – 'unanimous praise' in one party for 'excellent food and jovial service'.

SCHOOLS AND GUIDES
Getting better
We've had few reports recently on the ESF but a 9-year old visitor in 2004 was happy to return for a second year. Recent reporters have praised the International school, although a 2004 pupil said some found it a little too demanding: 'They refused to take hot chocolate breaks, which led to people dropping out early.' The small specialist Super Ski school apparently has 'small class sizes, good instruction'.

FACILITIES FOR CHILDREN
Parents' paradise?
Flaine prides itself on being a family resort, and the number of English-speaking children around is a bonus. There are some free children's lift passes available in low season weeks.

Club Med has good childcare facilities open to residents only, as does Crystal's hotel Le Totem, said to be 'well organised and popular'.

STAYING THERE

HOW TO GO
Plenty of apartments
Accommodation is overwhelmingly in self-catering apartments.
Chalets There are few catered chalet options, but they include a couple of Scandinavian-style huts in Hameau. Crystal's Totem club-hotel continues to impress reporters, even if some find the rooms a little small.
Hotels All the hotels are now run by tour operators. B&B is available at the Cascade restaurant.
Self-catering The best apartments are out at Hameau. In Flaine Forêt, the Forêt and Grand Massif apartment buildings are attractively woody inside and there are hotel facilities.

EATING OUT
Enough choice for a week
The Perdrix Noire in Forêt, a past recommendation, was judged pricey by a 2004 visitor. Its bar is popular. Chez Daniel offers a good range of Savoyard specialities, and is good with kids. The 'lively' Brasserie les Cîmes is recommended for 'very good local food, good prices, very friendly service'. There are several pizzerias. A couple of places close to the village and described under 'Mountain restaurants' are open in the evening – the Michet and the Bissac. The Ancolie

GETTING THERE

Air Geneva 90km/
56 miles (1½hr).

Rail Cluses (30km/
19 miles); regular bus
service.

ACTIVITIES

Indoor Swimming
pool, sauna, solarium,
gymnasium, massage,
bowling, cinema,
billiards, climbing
wall, cultural centre
with art gallery and
library

Outdoor Ice rink,
snowshoe excursions,
dog-sledding,
paragliding, helicopter
rides, snow scooters,
quad bikes, ice-
driving

WEBSITES

For links to resort
sites, go to our own
new site at
www.wtss.co.uk

Phone numbers
From abroad use the
prefix +33 and omit
the initial '0' of the
phone number.

TOURIST OFFICES

Flaine
t 0450 908001
welcome@flaine.com
www.flaine.com

Les Carroz
t 0450 900004
info@lescarroz.com
www.lescarroz.com

in Hameau is said to be worth the trip
for its 'great food' and 'beautiful
wooden chalet interior'. If you don't
mind a drive or taxi ride, Chalet les
Molliets gets rave reviews.

APRES-SKI
Signs of life

You can eat and drink into the early
hours here if you move around a bit –
but you don't have much choice of
venues. The White Grouse pub has a
big screen TV, rock music and punters
trying to get pints in before the end of
happy hour. The Flying Dutchman is
'very lively 5-7pm, very friendly, tends
to wind down around 11'. The bar at
the bowling alley has a 'family
atmosphere earlier on, turns into a pub
after 11' and is 'the only place still
serving food until 3am'. The Texa is
Flaine's only nightclub but the drinks
are 'very expensive' and the 'music not
up to much'. The 'very French' Diamant
Noir pool hall is open late and
sometimes has 'good live music'.

OFF THE SLOPES
Curse of the purpose-built

Flaine is not recommended for people
who don't want to hit the slopes. But
there is a great ice-driving circuit where
you can take a spin (literally) in your
car or theirs. Snowmobile tours and
dog-sledding excursions are popular,
and there's a cinema, gymnasium and
swimming pool. Save your souvenir
shopping in the few upper gallery
shops in Forum for the one evening a
week when there is a free hands-on
display of large wooden games,
enjoyed by visitors of all ages.

Les Carroz 1140m/3,740ft

This is a sprawling, sunny, traditional,
family resort where life revolves
around the village square with its
pavement cafes, restaurants and
interesting little shops. It has a lived-in
feel of a real French village, with more
animation than Flaine, at least in the
afternoon – 'a delight' says a recent
visitor. But a thorough report this year
confirms that the après-ski scene
doesn't amount to much: the Marlow
pub is popular at close of play but
soon becomes quiet; the next-door
Pinot Noir is cheaper and more
animated; Carpe Diem is devoid of
customers until the other places close.

We have a rave 2005 review of the
Brit-run hotel Belles Pistes (0450
900017) – 'ideal: staff A1, food good,
close to lifts'. Readers also recommend
the hotel Arbaron (0450 900267) for
food, views, and airport transfer
service, and the Bois de la Char (0450
900618): 'Perfectly situated beside the
piste; the food was good, the staff
friendly and it was excellent value for
money'. Apartments include the
'superior' new MGM units with indoor
pool, sauna and spa facilities.

The recently upgraded gondola
starts a steep 300m/1,000ft walk up
from the centre – the nursery drag is a
help or you can catch the free ski-bus.
It serves some excellent slopes in the
woods above the village as well as
launching you off into the Grand
Massif, so this is a great place to be
on a bad-weather day.

The ski school's torchlit descent is
'not to be missed' – ending with vin
chaud and live jazz in the square.

Les Gets

Friendly village amid extensive friendly (but low-altitude) slopes

292

➕ Good-sized, varied local piste area shared with slightly lower Morzine – plus excellent, neglected Mont Chéry

➕ Attractive chalet-style village, with through-traffic kept on fringes

➕ Relatively short drive from the UK

➕ Few queues locally

➕ Part of the vast Portes du Soleil ski pass region, but ...

➖ To get to Avoriaz and the main Portes du Soleil circuit is a real slog, unless you drive to Ardent

➖ Modest altitude means there is always a risk of poor snow, though increased snowmaking has helped

➖ Few challenging pistes

➖ Too many slow, old chairs

➖ Weekend crowds

The area that Les Gets shares with Morzine offers the most extensive slopes in the Portes du Soleil, and in some respects Les Gets is the better base for them. But if the main Portes du Soleil circuit is a priority, stay closer to it.

THE RESORT

Les Gets is an attractive, sunny, much-expanded village of traditional chalet-style buildings, on the low pass leading from the A40 autoroute at Cluses to Morzine. The main road bypasses the village centre, which is partly car-free and has plenty of attractive food and other shops and restaurants lining the main street. There's also a popular outdoor ice rink, which adds to the charm.

Although the village has a scattered appearance, most facilities are close to the main lift station – and the free 'petit train' road-train shuttle is a cute way of travelling around. It is fairly quiet in the evenings but gets busier and livelier at weekends.

THE MOUNTAINS

Les Gets is not an ideal base for the Portes du Soleil, but its local slopes are extensive. The local pass saves a fair bit on a Portes du Soleil pass, and makes a lot of sense for many visitors.
Slopes The main local slopes – accessed by a gondola and fast chair-lift from the nursery slopes beside the village – are shared with Morzine, and are mainly described in that chapter. On the opposite side of Les Gets is Mont Chéry, accessed by a gondola and parallel chair. The slopes include some of the most challenging in the area, and are usually very quiet. Both sectors offer wooded and open slopes.
Snow reliability The nursery slopes benefit from a slightly higher elevation

than Morzine, but otherwise our general reservations about the lack of altitude apply. A lot more snow-guns have improved runs to the resort. The front slopes of Mont Chéry face south-east – bad news at this altitude; but grooming is good, and the other two flanks are shadier. On our January 2005 visit, when snow was sparse, we found the Les Gets pistes much better than in the higher Three Valleys resorts (largely because the grassy slopes need less snow cover) and better than in neighbouring Morzine.
Terrain-parks There's a park on the upper slopes of Mont Chéry with kickers, hip jumps, a gap jump and a couple of quarter-pipes. There is also boarder-cross here.
Experts Black runs on the flank and back of Mont Chéry chair are quite steep and often bumped. In good snow there is plenty to do off-piste, including some excellent wooded areas.
Intermediates High-mileage piste-bashers might prefer direct access to the main Portes du Soleil circuit, but the local slopes have a lot to offer – including excellent reds on Mont Chéry.
Beginners The village nursery slopes are convenient, and there are better, more snow-sure ones up at Chavannes. Although the only longer greens are up the mountain, there are plenty of easy blues lower down.
Snowboarding The local Les Gets and Morzine slopes are good for beginners and intermediates.
Cross-country There are 18km/11 miles of good, varied loops on Mont Chéry and Les Chavannes.

KEY FACTS

Resort	1170m
	3,840ft

Portes du Soleil	
Slopes	950-2300m
	3,120-7,550ft
Lifts	208
Pistes	650km
	404 miles
Green	14%
Blue	39%
Red	37%
Black	10%
Snowmaking	
	329 acres

Morzine-Les Gets only	
Slopes	1000-2010m
	3,280-6,590ft
Lifts	48
Pistes	110km
	68 miles

WEBSITES

For links to resort sites, go to our own new site at www.wtss.co.uk

Phone numbers
From abroad use the prefix +33 and omit the initial '0' of the phone number.

TOURIST OFFICE

t 0450 758080
lesgets@lesgets.com
www.lesgets.com

Queues See the Morzine chapter for general observations. Mont Chéry is crowd-free. But there are still a lot of slow, old chairs which reporters complain about.

Mountain restaurants See Morzine.

Schools and guides Mixed reports of the ESF – a 2005 reporter enjoyed her private lessons but her four-year-old daughter 'was bored after a couple of days as the class was too big'. Another 2005 visitor had private lessons with Ecole International and thought the instructor 'brought me on'. The 'good but pricey' British Alpine Ski & Snowboard School has a branch here.

Facilities for children There are comprehensive resort facilities, and several family-oriented tour operators. The British-run Snowkidz nursery takes babies as well as infant skiers, and our latest report describes it as 'superb – absolutely faultless'.

STAYING THERE

How to go Several tour operators have catered chalets, including Ski Activity and Total Ski (of which we've heard good reports).

Hotels We stayed at the Ferme de Montagne (0450 753679) in 2005 and loved it. It is a beautifully renovated farmhouse with eight luxury bedrooms, gourmet food, ski guiding, sauna, outdoor hot-tub and a brilliant massage therapist (try the hot stones); on the edge of town at La Turche. The 3-star Crychar (0450 758050), 100m/330ft from central Les Gets at the foot of the slopes, is one of the best 3-star hotels. The 2-star Alpen Sports (0450 758055) is a friendly, family-run hotel – 'excellent food and good value for money', says a reporter, but 'sound-proofing and room size not good', says another. We've had good reports of the Nagano (0450 797146) and the Marmotte (0450 758033) –

'great maître d'; large, warm pool' – both 3-star.

Self-catering The tourist office has a list of apartments. A recent reporter was happy with the Lion D'Or.

Eating out The Ferme de Montagne (see Hotels) has wonderful food, beautifully presented in a splendid renovated wooden dining room. The Tyrol and the Schuss are good for pizza; the rustic Vieux Chêne for Savoyard specialities. The Flambeau, Tanière and Tourbillon have been recommended. Book ahead, especially at weekends.

Après-ski Après-ski is quiet, especially on weekdays. The Irish Pub, the Canadian Bar above it, the Boomerang, the Copeaux and the Bush (Scottish owned) are recommended by reporters. The Igloo is a popular disco.

Off the slopes There's a well-equipped fitness centre with a pool, and an artificial ice rink. The Mechanical Music Museum is strongly recommended by a reporter (barrel organs and music boxes, for example, with guided tours in English). There's a cinema; husky rides and snow-shoeing are possible. There is a good selection of shops and visits to Geneva, Lausanne and Montreux are feasible.

OT LES GETS / GILLES LANSARD / FOC

Les Gets is an attractive, friendly village with a rustic feel. Lifts go up from and slopes come down to both its centre and its outskirts ↓

La Grave

A superb mountain for good skiers and free-riders

COSTS

①②③④⑤⑥

RATINGS

The slopes

Fast lifts	***
Snow	***
Extent	*
Expert	*****
Intermediate	*
Beginner	*
Convenience	***
Queues	****
Mountain restaurants	**

The rest

Scenery	****
Resort charm	***
Off-slope	*

NEWS

La Grave does not change much, and that is half the charm of the place.

294

- ➕ Legendary off-piste mountain
- ➕ Usually crowd-free
- ➕ Usually good snow conditions
- ➕ Link to Les Deux-Alpes
- ➕ Easy access by car to other nearby resorts

- ➖ Rather dour village
- ➖ Poor weather means lift closures – on average, two days per week
- ➖ Suitable for experts only, despite some easy slopes at altitude
- ➖ Nothing to do off the slopes

La Grave enjoys legendary status among experts. It's a quiet old village with around 500 visitor beds and just one serious lift – a small stop-start gondola serving a high, wild and almost entirely off-piste mountainside. The result: an exciting, usually crowd-free area. Strictly, you ought to have a guide, but in good weather many people go it alone.

THE RESORT

La Grave is a small, unspoiled mountaineering village set on a steep hillside facing the impressive glaciers of majestic La Meije. It's rather drab, and the busy road through to Briançon doesn't help. But it has a rustic feel, some welcoming hotels, friendly inhabitants and prices that are low by resort standards. The single serious lift starts just below the centre. Storms close the slopes on average two days a week – so a car is useful for access to nearby resorts.

THE MOUNTAIN

A slow two-stage 'pulse' gondola (with an extra station at a pylon halfway up the lower stage) ascends into the slopes and finishes at 3200m/10,500ft. Above that, a short walk and a drag-lift give access to a second drag serving twin blue runs on a glacier slope of about 350m/1,150ft vertical – from here you can ski to Les Deux-Alpes. But the reason that people come here is to explore the legendary slopes back towards La Grave. These slopes offer no defined, patrolled, avalanche-protected pistes – but there are two marked itinéraires (with several variations now indicated on the 'piste' map) of 1400m/4,590ft vertical down to the pylon lift station at 1800m/5,910ft, or all the way down to the valley – a vertical of 2150m/7,050ft.

Slopes The Chancel route is mostly of red-run gradient; the Vallons de la Meije is more challenging but not too steep. People do take these routes without a guide or avalanche protection equipment, but we couldn't possibly recommend it.

There are many more demanding runs away from the itinéraires, including couloirs that range from the straightforward to the seriously hazardous, and long descents from the glacier to the valley road below the village, with return by taxi, bus, or strategically parked car. The dangers are considerable (people die here every year), and good guidance is essential. You can also descend southwards to St-Christophe, returning by bus and the lifts of Les Deux-Alpes.

very limited slopes with a handful of intermediate and beginner runs.

Beginners Novices tricked into coming here can go up the valley to the beginner slopes at Le Chazelet, which has two cannons for snowmaking.

Snowboarding There are no special facilities for boarders, but advanced free-riders will be in their element on the open off-piste powder.

Cross-country There is a total of 20km/12 miles of loops in the area.

Queues Normally, there are short queues only at weekends. If snow conditions back to the valley are poor, queues can build up for the gondola down from the mid and lower stations.

Mountain restaurants Surprisingly, there are three decent mountain restaurants; the best is the refuge on the Chancel itinéraire. A 2005 reporter enjoyed the food at the Haut-Dessus, at the top, 'particularly the pizzas'.

Schools and guides There are a dozen or so guides in the village, offering a wide range of services through their bureau. See also Hotels below.

Facilities for children Babysitting can be arranged through the tourist office.

STAYING THERE

How to go There are several simple hotels.

Hotels The Edelweiss (0476 799093) is a friendly 2-star with 'comfortable rooms and a phenomenal wine list' as well as a cosy bar and restaurant. The long-established Skiers Lodge operation – all-inclusive week-long packages, including guiding – has moved into the old hotel des Alpes in the centre of the village (reservations 0450 533119). A 2005 visitor had an 'excellent' week, advising that 'you need to get really fit beforehand'.

Self-catering Bookable through the tourist office.

Eating out Most people eat in their hotels, though there are alternatives.

Après-ski The standard tea-time après-ski gathering place is the central Glaciers bar, known to habitués as chez Marcel. The Vieux Guide gets crowded later. The Vallons and Bois des Fées are two other possibilities.

Off the slopes Anyone not using the slopes will find La Grave much too small and quiet.

La Grave

295

KEY FACTS

Resort	1450m
	4,760ft
Slopes	1450-3550m
	4,760-11,650ft
Lifts	4
Pistes	5km
	3 miles
Green/Blue	100%

The figures above relate only to pistes; practically all the skiing – at least 90% – is off-piste

| **Snowmaking** | none |

Phone numbers
From abroad use the prefix +33 and omit the initial '0' of the phone number.

TOURIST OFFICE

t 0476 799005
ot@lagrave-lameije.com
www.lagrave-lameije.com

Terrain-parks There aren't any.

Snow reliability The chances of powder snow on the high, north-facing slopes are good, but if conditions are tricky there are no pistes to fall back on apart from the three short blue runs at the top of the gondola.

Experts La Grave's uncrowded off-piste slopes have earned it cult status among hard-core skiers. Only experts should contemplate a stay here – and then only if prepared to deal with bad weather by sitting tight or struggling over the Col du Lautaret to the woods of Serre-Chevalier.

Intermediates The itinéraires get tracked into a piste-like state, and adventurous intermediates could tackle the Chancel. But the three blue runs at the top of the gondola won't keep anyone occupied for long. The valley stations of Villar d'Arène and Lautaret, around 3km/2 miles and 8km/5 miles to the east respectively, and Chazelet, 3km/2 miles to the north-west, offer

Megève

One of the traditional old winter holiday towns

296

COSTS

① ② ③ ④ ⑤ ⑥

RATINGS

The slopes
Fast lifts	*
Snow	**
Extent	*****
Expert	**
Intermediate	****
Beginner	***
Convenience	**
Queues	****
Mountain restaurants	****

The rest
Scenery	*****
Resort charm	****
Off-slope	****

NEWS

For 2004/05 the slopes of Le Jaillet were linked to the slopes of La Torraz above Le Plan, near La Giettaz. A fast six-pack has replaced the old double chair up to Le Christomet, and the Pres chair on the way back is now a quad equipped with a moving carpet – so not slow, but not really fast.

A shuttle-bus now runs between Praz-sur-Arly and Megève.

We are told that there are medium-term plans to link Praz-sur-Arly to Megève.

➕ Extensive slopes, with miles of easy pistes, ideal for intermediates

➕ Scenic setting, with splendid views

➕ Charming old village centre, with very swanky shopping

➕ Some lovely luxury hotels

➕ Both gourmet and simple mountain lunches in attractive surroundings

➕ Excellent cross-country trails

➕ Different lift pass options cover other worthwhile resorts nearby

➕ Great for weekends – co-operative hotels, short drive from Geneva

➕ Great when it snows – woodland runs with no one on them

➕ Plenty to do off the slopes

➖ With most of the slopes below 2000m/6,560ft there's a risk of poor snow, especially on runs to the village – although the grassy terrain does not need a thick covering, and snowmaking has improved a lot

➖ Lots of slow, old lifts remain – a real irritant to mileage-hungry skiers

➖ Three separate mountains, two linked by lift but not by piste, and the third not linked at all

➖ Not many challenging pistes – though there is good off-piste

➖ Very muted après-ski scene

➖ Traffic jams and fumes at weekends and peak season

Megève is the essence of rustic chic. It has a medieval heart but it was, in a way, the original purpose-built French ski resort – developed in the 1920s as an alternative to St Moritz. And, although Courchevel took over as France's swank resort ages ago, Megève's smart hotels and chalets still attract 'beautiful people' with fur coats and fat wallets. Happily, you don't need either to enjoy it. And it is enjoyable – the list of plus points above is as long as they come.

The risk of poor snow still makes us wary of low resorts like this. But it is true that a few inches of snow is enough to give skiable cover on the grassy slopes, and when a storm socks in this is a great place to be, as we have confirmed more than once in recent years.

The resort's managers can't do much about the altitude. What they could do, though, is drag the lift system into this century. Only one in seven of the area's lifts is fast, putting Megève close to the bottom of our fast lifts league table. For such an affluent resort, the lack of investment is disgraceful.

THE RESORT

Megève is in a lovely sunny setting and has a beautifully preserved, traditional, partly medieval centre, which is pedestrianised and comes complete with open-air ice rink, horse-drawn sleighs, cobbled streets and a fine church. Lots of smart clothing, jewellery, antique, gift and food shops add to the chic atmosphere.

The main Albertville-Chamonix road bypasses the centre, and there are expensive underground car parks. But the resort's clientele arrives mainly by car and the resulting traffic jams and fumes are a major problem. It's worst at weekends, but can be serious every afternoon in high season.

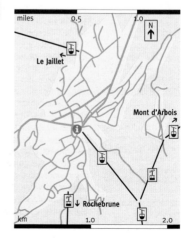

KEY FACTS

For Megève only		
Resort	1100m	
	3,610ft	
Slopes	850-2355m	
	2,790-7,730ft	
Lifts	88	
Pistes	320km	
	198 miles	
Green	17%	
Blue	30%	
Red	40%	
Black	13%	
Snowmaking		
	185 guns	

The clientele are mainly well-heeled French couples and families, who come here as much for an all-round winter holiday as for the slopes themselves. What they don't come for is après-ski action. The tea-time atmosphere is muted, and later on the nightlife is smart rather than lively.

A gondola within walking distance of central Megève gives direct access to one of the three mountains, Rochebrune. This sector can also be reached directly by a cable-car from the southern edge of town. The main lifts for the bigger Mont d'Arbois sector start from an elevated suburb of the resort – though there is also a cable-car link from Rochebrune. The third sector, Le Jaillet, starts some way out on the north-west fringes of the town.

Staying close to one of the main lifts makes a lot of sense. Some accommodation is a long walk from the lifts, and the half-hearted free bus services are a source of complaints. There are several alternative bases on the fringes of the area, but beware slow access lifts from otherwise attractive spots such as St-Nicolas and Combloux. St-Gervais and Le Bettex above it have gondola access. St-Gervais is described at the end of this chapter. No doubt La Giettaz offers low prices, but it is out on a limb.

The standard weekly lift pass covers Les Contamines, and the Mont Blanc pass also covers Chamonix and Courmayeur, reached through the Mont Blanc road tunnel. A car is handy for visiting these resorts.

THE MOUNTAINS

The three different mountains provide predominantly easy intermediate cruising, much of it prettily set in the woods and with some spectacular views. The wooded slopes make it a great resort to head for in poor weather. Some reporters complain that the piste grading is inconsistent. Signposting is poor, not helped by an imprecise piste map.

Megève

297

THE SLOPES
Pretty but low

The biggest, highest and most varied sector is **Mont d'Arbois**, accessible not only from the town but also by a gondola from La Princesse, way out to the north-east of town. It offers some wooded slopes but is mainly open, especially higher up.

The slopes above the resort are sunny, but there are north-east-facing slopes to Le Bettex and on down to St-Gervais. A two-stage gondola returns you to the top. You can work your way over to Mont Joux and up to the small Mont Joly area – Megève's highest slopes. And from there you can descend to the backwater village of St-Nicolas-de-Véroce (there's a splendid red run along the ridge with spectacular views of Mont Blanc); tediously slow chair-lifts bring you back to Mont Joux.

From the Mont d'Arbois lift base, the Rocharbois cable-car goes across the valley to **Rochebrune**. Alpette is the starting point for Megève's historic

LIFT PASSES

Evasion Mont Blanc
Covers lifts at Les
Contamines as well as
Megève.

Beginners
No special pass.

Main pass
1 day €32
6 days €154

Senior citizens
Over 60: 6 days €139
Over 80: free pass

Children
Under 15: 6 days
€123
Under 5: free pass

Alternative passes
Day and half-day
passes for Megève
only; weekly Mont
Blanc passes (all
resorts in the Mont
Blanc area plus
Courmayeur in Italy);
Jaco pass (Le Jaillet,
Christomet, la Giettaz
and Combloux);
pedestrian pass for
Megève.

downhill course, now revived as an off-piste route, and narrow enough to be quite tricky. A network of gentle, wooded, north-east-facing slopes, served by drags and chair-lifts, lead across to the high-point of Côte 2000.

The third area is **Le Jaillet**, accessed by gondola from just outside the north-west edge of town. This neglected area got a bit of a boost last season. A link was created via the sector high-point of Le Christomet to the slopes of **Le Torraz**, outside La Giettaz, a tiny resort half-way to La Clusaz. As part of the development, a very welcome fast chair-lift was installed on Le Christomet. The slopes of La Torraz are worth visiting, but the link is a bit of a mess – miles of skating and poling plus an awkward bit of narrow steep stuff. In the other direction, a series of long, gentle tree-lined runs go down to Combloux.

TERRAIN-PARKS
Music to motivate
There is a 320m/1,050ft slope on Mont Joux with a half-pipe, quarter-pipe, pyramid and a section of challenging moguls. A sound system at the bottom helps to motivate the faint-hearted. And there's a small park, Snowtap – on the upper slopes at Combloux.

SNOW RELIABILITY
The area's main weakness
The problem is that the slopes are low,

with very few runs above 2000m/6,560ft, and partly sunny – the Megève side of Mont d'Arbois gets the afternoon sun. So in a poor snow year, or in a warm spell, snow on the lower slopes can suffer badly.

Fortunately, the grassy slopes don't need much depth of snow, and the resort has expanded its snowmaking network to 252 snow-guns at the last count. Some runs are now entirely covered, including the long red Olympique run at Rochebrune. There is also a high standard of piste grooming.

FOR EXPERTS
Off-piste is the main attraction
One of Megève's great advantages for expert skiers is that there is not much competition for the powder – you can often make first tracks on challenging slopes many days after a fresh dump.

The Mont Joly and Mont Joux sections offer the steepest slopes. The top chair here serves a genuinely black run, and the slightly lower Epaule chair has some steep runs back down and also accesses some good off-piste, as well as pistes, down to St-Nicolas.

The steep area beneath the second stage of the Princesse gondola can be a play area of powder runs among the trees. Cote 2000 has a small section of steep runs, including good off-piste.

The terrain under the Christomet chair could be a good spot to practise off-piste technique, given decent snow.

boarding

Boarding doesn't really fit with Megève's traditional, rather staid, upmarket image. But free-riders will find lots of untracked off-piste powder for days after new snowfalls. It's a good place to try boarding for the first time, with plenty of fairly wide, quiet, gentle runs and a lot of chair-lifts and gondolas; though there are a fair number of drag-lifts, they are generally avoidable. There are no specialist snowboard schools, but all the ski schools offer boarding lessons. There's a terrain-park on Mont Joux and a smaller one above Combloux.

FOR INTERMEDIATES
Superb if the snow is good
Good intermediates will enjoy the whole area – there is so much choice it's difficult to single out any particular sectors. Keen skiers are likely to want to focus on the fast lifts, and happily several of these serve excellent terrain – the Princesse and Bettex gondolas on Mont d'Arbois, the Fontaine chair on Rochebrune and the new Christomet chair in the Le Jaillet sector. But don't confine yourself to those – there are lots of other interesting areas, including the shady north-east-facing slopes on the back of Mont d'Arbois and Mont Joux and the front of Rochebrune, and the genuinely red/black slopes of La Giettaz.

It's a great area for the less confident. A number of comfortable runs lead down to Le Bettex and La Princesse from Mont d'Arbois, while nearby Mont Joux accesses long, problem-free runs to St-Nicolas. Alpette and Cote 2000 are also suitable.

Even the timid can get a great deal of mileage in. All main access lifts have easy routes down to them (there is now a blue down the Princesse gondola). There are some particularly good, long, gentle cruises between Mont Joux and Megève via Mont d'Arbois. But in all sectors you'll find long, easy blue runs.

FOR BEGINNERS
Good choice of nursery areas
There are beginner slopes at valley level, and more snow-sure ones at altitude on each of the main mountains. There are also plenty of very easy longer green runs to progress to – one reporter favoured those at Combloux.

FOR CROSS-COUNTRY
An excellent area
There are 75km/47 miles of varied trails spread throughout the area. Some are at altitude (1300m–1550m/ 4,270ft–5,090ft), making lunchtime meetings with Alpine skiers simple.

QUEUES
Few weekday problems
Megève is relatively queue-free during the week, except at peak holiday time. But school holidays and sunny Sunday crowds can mean some delays. The Lanchettes drag between Cote 2000 and the rest of the Rochebrune slopes gets busy ('ridiculously long waits', writes a 2005 visitor) – as does the cable-car linking the two mountains. Crowded pistes at Mont Joux and Mont d'Arbois can also be a problem. But slow lifts and breakdowns (eg of the gondola from St Gervais) provoke more complaints than queues or crowds.

MOUNTAIN RESTAURANTS
Something for all budgets
Megève has some chic, expensive, gourmet mountain huts but plenty of cheaper options too. Booking ahead is advisable for table-service places.

The Mont d'Arbois area is very well endowed with restaurants. There are two suave places popular with poseurs with small dogs and fur coats – the Club House and the Idéal 1850. The Mont d'Arbois self-service is a 'useful meeting point' with a varied menu. Chez Tartine, 'beautifully located' half-way down the Princesse gondola, may be getting too popular for the kitchen to cope. The Ravière, tucked away in the woods near La Croix chair, is a tiny rustic hut that does a set meal and where booking is essential. The Igloo, 'quiet but expensive', with wonderful views of Mont Blanc, has both self- and table-service sections. At the base of the Mont Joux lift, Chez Marie du Rosay is recommended.

Prices are lower on the back side of the hill. The hut at the bottom of the Mont Rosset chair offers 'great food' and 'friendly staff', say recent reporters. Alpage at Les Communailles is good, too – although a regular reckons 'the place has lost something' under its newish management. Above St-Nicolas are several little chalets offering great charm and good food

↑ Le Plan, the base of the slopes of La Giettaz, is no more than a few apartment blocks and a snack bar or two – the slopes, though, are worth exploring

CHILDREN
Meg'Accueil
t 0450 587784
Ages 18mnth to 12yr;
from €40 a day
Club des Piou-Piou
t 0450 589765
Ages 3 and 4
La Princesse
t 0450 930086
Ages from 2½

Ski schools
The schools run classes for ages from 3 or 4 (ESF prices: 5 mornings €94 for ages 3 and 4, €114 for ages 5 to 12).

WEBSITES
For links to resort sites, go to our own new site at www.wtss.co.uk

GETTING THERE
Air Geneva 70km/ 43 miles (1hr); Lyon 180km/112 miles (2½hr).

Rail Sallanches (12km/7 miles); regular buses from station.

and views at modest prices.

Our favourite on Rochebrune is Alpette, atop the ridge – excellent all-round views outside, a good atmosphere inside, friendly people, good food. At the foot of the Cote 2000 slopes is the popular Auberge de la Cote 2000, a former farm ('We went in for a drink and staggered out three hours and five courses later,' writes a reporter); Radaz, up the slope a little, enjoys better views but can get busy. A reporter enjoyed his Christmas Day lunch at the Super Megève. And Chalet Forestier is a 'cosy' retreat.

On Le Jaillet the Auberge du Christomet is highly rated for its 'plats du jour' and 'touches of real originality' about the food. It is also accessible to walkers, and gets booked out. We hear the Face au Mont Blanc at the top of the gondola does a great fixed-price buffet.

SCHOOLS AND GUIDES
Several good options
The International school has traditionally been more popular with readers than the ESF, but we have several reports of successful private lessons with the ESF. White Sensations is a small school with eight BASI-trained instructors, recommended recently for its 'fun' children's classes – 'my six-year old progressed quickly'. Both main schools offer expeditions to the Vallée Blanche and heli-skiing (in Italy), as well as normal teaching. Individual guides are available. We had a great morning powder skiing in the trees with Alex Périnet (06 8542 8339).

FACILITIES FOR CHILDREN
Language problems
The kindergartens offer a wide range of activities. But lack of English-speaking staff could be a drawback. The slopes are family-friendly and the schools rated by reporters (see above). There's a snow garden at Le Bettex.

STAYING THERE

HOW TO GO
Few packages
Relatively few British tour operators go to Megève, but there is an impressive range of accommodation.

Chalets A few UK tour operators offer catered chalets. For a cheap and very cheerful base, you won't do better than Stanford's Sylvana – a creaky, unpretentious old hotel, reachable on skis, run along chalet lines.

Hotels Megève offers a range of exceptionally stylish and welcoming hotels. There are simpler places, too.
((((4 **Mont Blanc** (0450 212002) Megève's traditional leading hotel – elegant, fashionable, central.
((((4 **Chalet du Mont d'Arbois** (0450 212503) Prettily decorated Relais & Châteaux hotel in a secluded position near the Mont d'Arbois gondola.
((((4 **Fer à Cheval** (0450 213039) Rustic-chic at its best, with a warmly welcoming wood-and-stone interior and excellent food. Close to the centre. 'A memorable stay,' writes a reporter.
(((3 **The Prairie** (0450 214855) Central, 'reasonably priced' B&B. Close to the Chamois lift.
(((3 **Coin du Feu** (0450 210494) 'Very well managed' chalet midway between Rochebrune and Chamois lifts.
(((3 **Grange d'Arly** (0450 587788) Wrong side of the road, but still quite close to the centre; a beautifully furnished chalet.
(((3 **Ferme Hôtel Duvillard** (0450 211462) Smartly restored farmhouse, perfectly positioned for the slopes, at the foot of the Mont d'Arbois gondola.
((2 **Mourets** (0450 210476) Poor location but a favourite of readers: 'basic but spacious, good food and views'; 'very friendly'; 'excellent hosts'.
((2 **Sévigné** (0450 212309) Ten minutes from the centre, but 'really delightful – very quaint, excellent food'.
Self-catering There are some very comfortable and well-positioned apartments – not cheap. Prices are lower in Combloux.

EATING OUT
Very French
Lots of upmarket restaurants – many recommended in the gastro guides. The multi-starred Ferme de Mon Père and the restaurants in all the best hotels are excellent but very pricey. The fashionable Cintra, also expensive, is 'great for fresh seafood'. Michel

Gaudin is one of the best in town – 'excellent', with good-value set menus.

The Brasserie Centrale 'serves almost anything you ask for,' says an impressed reporter. The Flocons de Sel is recommended for its 'excellent service'. The Prieuré is 'highly recommended – lots of atmosphere, excellent food, good value', as is the Bistrot ('great salads and pizzas'). The Delicium is also popular. Some reporters wish for more variety. The Phnom-Penh is one of the few less conventional possibilities.

APRES-SKI
Strolling and jazz
Megève is a pleasant place to stroll around after the lifts close, but exciting it isn't. If there are atmospheric bars for a post-piste beer, they have eluded us. And those looking for loud disco-bars later on will also be disappointed. Our favourite place was the Club de Jazz (aka the 5 Rues) – a very popular, if rather expensive, jazz club-cum-cocktail bar, that gets some big-name musicians and opens from tea-time to late. But a change of management has not impressed a 2005 reporter: 'it's cold, impersonal, and the pure jazz seems to have given way to more rock and roll'. The Cocoon is popular with Brits. The casino is more slot machines than blackjack tables.

OFF THE SLOPES
Lots to do
There is a 'fantastic' sports centre with pool, an outdoor ice rink, plenty of outdoor activities, three cinemas and a weekly market. Trips to Annecy and Chamonix are possible. Walks are excellent, with 50km/30 miles of marked paths classified for difficulty on a special map. Meeting friends on the slopes for lunch is easy.

STAYING UP THE MOUNTAIN
Several possibilities
As well as mid-mountain Le Bettex, a small collection of hotels, private chalets and modern apartments, there are hotels further up on Mont d'Arbois.

St-Gervais 850m/2,790ft

St-Gervais is a handsome 19th-century spa town set in a narrow river gorge, on the far side of Mont d'Arbois, with access to the slopes via a 20-person gondola from just outside the town. It's an urban but pleasant place, with interesting food shops and cosy bars, thermal baths and an Olympic skating rink. Prices are noticeably lower than in Megève. Buses are reported to be regular and convenient. Two hotels convenient for the gondola are the Liberty Mont Blanc (0450 934521), a pleasantly traditional 2-star, and the 'quite charming' 3-star Carlina (0450 934110), the best in town, with a small pool and sauna. A 2005 reporter recommends the Val d'Este (0450 936591) and its restaurant ('outstanding').

On the opposite side of St-Gervais is a rack-and-pinion railway, which in 1904 was intended to go to the top of Mont Blanc but actually takes you to the slopes of Les Houches.

Les Menuires

The bargain base for the Trois Vallées – but pick your spot with care

COSTS

① ② ③ ④ ⑤ ⑥

RATINGS

The slopes

Fast lifts	✱✱✱
Snow	✱✱✱✱
Extent	✱✱✱✱✱
Expert	✱✱✱✱
Intermediate	✱✱✱✱✱
Beginner	✱✱✱
Convenience	✱✱✱✱✱
Queues	✱✱✱✱
Mountain restaurants	✱✱✱

The rest

Scenery	✱✱✱
Resort charm	✱
Off-slope	✱

NEWS

For 2005/06 a new eight-seat gondola is planned to replace the Combes chair and the ancient Mont de la Chambre gondola out of Les Menuires, which should improve access to St-Martin and Méribel. The following year a new chair is planned from the top of the gondola up to Roc des 3 Marches. A new leisure centre is due to open for 2005/06, with pools, saunas, steam room, hot-tubs and gym. A new hands-free electronic lift pass system will be introduced.

- ➕ The cheapest base for the 3V
- ➕ Great local slopes on La Masse, and quick links with Val-Thorens
- ➕ Extensive snowmaking
- ➕ Lots of slope-side accommodation
- ➕ New, outlying parts of the resort are much more attractive than the core
- ➕ Good specialist food shops, although they are found in ...

- ➖ Gloomy indoor shopping malls
- ➖ Resort core is dominated by big, dreary apartment blocks
- ➖ Main intermediate and beginner slopes get a lot of sun
- ➖ No woodland slopes
- ➖ Some of the lower slopes get dangerously crowded as well as over-exposed to the sun

Les Menuires is developing in the right way, adding traditional-style satellites where you can ignore the brutal architecture at the core of the resort. And the Belleville valley has a lot of terrain, including the excellent, challenging slopes on La Masse, rarely used by visitors from the other valleys.

THE RESORT

The original buildings that surround the main lift base, La Croisette, are among the worst examples of the thoughtless building of the 1960s/70s. The main centre has a particularly dire indoor shopping gallery. But the resort is trying hard to lose its reputation as one of the ugliest in the Alps. In outposts such as Reberty and Hameau des Marmottes, the latest additions are in stone-and-wood chalet style – and there are some luxury developments. These outposts have their own shops and bars – Les Bruyères is now a more-or-less self-contained resort.

THE MOUNTAINS

Les Menuires is set at about the tree line, with almost entirely open slopes.
Slopes The major part of the network spreads across the broad, west-facing mountainside between Les Menuires and St-Martin, with links to the Méribel valley at four points (mostly red runs, but there is one blue) as well as a link up the valley to Val-Thorens. The new gondola and a fast chair go up from La Croisette. Lifts to La Masse, a more challenging mountain, start below the village – a gondola and a chair-lift.
Terrain-parks There's a new terrain-park with slides, pyramids, tables and snowcross in the Combes-Becca sector.
Snow reliability La Masse's height and orientation ensure good snow for a long season. The west-facing slopes have lots of snowmaking but the snow

lower down is often icy or slushy.
Experts The upper slopes of La Masse are virtually all of stiff red/soft black steepness. Dame Blanche is a particularly fine black, on the front of the hill – we'd love to catch it when groomed, or after fresh snow. There is also a huge amount of off-piste, though it gets tracked out quickly after a fresh snowfall. Vallon du Lou is a broad, sweeping route towards Val-Thorens that used to be marked as an itinerary on the piste map. Other off-piste routes go in the opposite direction to various villages.
Intermediates With good snow, you may be content with the local slopes, which are virtually all blue and red. In poor snow you can head up to Val-Thorens, and there's blue-run as well as red-run access. Don't miss La Masse – the blacks are not super-steep – but beware the steep Masse drag-lift.
Beginners There are wide and gentle slopes and a special lift pass for beginners, but the snow quality on the nursery slopes is a worry. The blue slopes you progress to can get extremely crowded.
Snowboarding The number of drags is low and dwindling further year by year; but there are some flattish sections of piste in places. There are huge amounts of terrain to suit free-riders.
Cross-country There are 28km/17 miles of prepared trails along the valley floor between St-Martin and Val-Thorens.
Queues The fast lifts up from La Croisette seem to have largely solved the problem of queues there, but have

The newer parts of Les Menuires (on the right) are much more attractive than the original development (on the left) ↗

SNOWPIX.COM / CHRIS GILL

KEY FACTS

Resort	1850m
	6,070ft

For the Three Valleys

Slopes	1260-3230m
	4,130-10,600ft
Lifts	200
Pistes	600km
	373 miles
Green	21%
Blue	33%
Red	35%
Black	11%
Snowmaking	
	1500 guns

For Les Menuires / St-Martin only

Slopes	1450-2850m
	4,760-9,350ft
Lifts	39
Pistes	160km
	99 miles
Green	10%
Blue	40%
Red	38%
Black	12%
Snow-guns	365

WEBSITES

For links to resort sites, go to our own new site at www.wtss.co.uk

Phone numbers
From abroad use the prefix +33 and omit the initial '0' of the phone number.

TOURIST OFFICE

t 0479 007300
lesmenuires@lesmenuires.com
www.lesmenuires.com

perhaps contributed to the worsening problem of acute overcrowding on the slopes down to the resort centre.

Mountain restaurants There are few remarkable places in this sector of the 3V. Just above Les Menuires is the very pleasant but quite pricey Etoile. At higher altitude there is 'excellent food and below average prices' at the Alpage, on the 4 Vents piste. Many people head down to the villages for lunch; you retain some sense of being on the mountain at the 'good value' Ferme, beside the piste at Reberty and a regular reporter recommends the 'good, reasonably priced' food at the Ours Blanc hotel.

Schools and guides The ESF has the monopoly here; we lack recent reports.

Facilities for children This is very much a family resort, but a 2003 visitor reports that no English was spoken at the 'generally grubby' resort nursery and that her children were not allowed to stay together. Family Ski Company has its own nursery in Reberty – and sends a minder with kids going to ski-school, to make up for ESF 'brutality'.

STAYING THERE

How to go Some big UK tour operators offer holidays here, and some chalet operators have a presence in Reberty. There is a Club Med above Reberty, praised by a recent reporter.

Chalets Reberty Village has been virtually taken over by UK chalet operators. Family Ski Company has three attractive properties; Cabaniols has a splendid living room.

Hotels None of the hotels is above 3-star grading. Ours Blanc (0479 006166) is the best – a chalet-style 3-star on the slopes above Reberty 1850. Les Bruyères (0479 007510) is set on the lower fringe of Les Bruyères.

Self-catering The newer apartments are more attractive. The Montagnettes and Alpages (with a pool), both in Reberty, are among the best. Les Cotes d'Or is 'very spacious for a French resort'. Choose apartments with care though – a 2004 reporter tells of 'cheap bunk beds, insufficient crockery and linen, a two-foot square bath and nowhere to store or wax a snowboard'.

Eating out Though some restaurants lack atmosphere, most serve good food. Alternatives to Savoyard include Italian and Tex-Mex. The Trattoria, with its 'good menu' and 'rustic French' ambience, has been recommended. The set menus at Le Refuge are 'reasonably priced' with 'particularly good' tartiflette. The La Marmite de Géant has 'excellent food and pleasant atmosphere' and 'is good value'. Chalet-boy night off is no problem in Reberty: La Ferme is one of the best places in the resort.

Après-ski There is no shortage of bars in La Croisette, but many are within the dreadful shopping gallery and a 2004 reporter says, 'Too many had a British feel and advertised big-screen football.' The Taverne bar in Les Bruyères is 'lively and welcoming'. There are discos.

Off the slopes This is a resort for keen skiers and boarders.

Les Menuires

303

Méribel

Big chalet-style resort in the centre of the wonderful Three Valleys

COSTS

① ② ③ ④ ⑤ ⑥

RATINGS

The slopes
Fast lifts	****
Snow	***
Extent	*****
Expert	****
Intermediate	*****
Beginner	****
Convenience	***
Queues	****
Mountain restaurants	***

The rest
Scenery	***
Resort charm	***
Off-slope	***

NEWS

A six-pack replaced the slow Plan de l'Homme quad from Méribel to halfway up Tougnète last season and has taken pressure off the Tougnète gondola in the morning peak. A new terrain-park, the Family Park, was built on the Burgin sector. It is designed for children aged 5 to 12. The Plattières terrain-park was extended. Some pistes in the Mottaret sector linking to and from Mont Vallon were remodelled, and snowmaking was increased, with another 62 machines on Burgin-Saulire and at Plattières.

For 2005/06, the metal staircase between Le Pub and the tourist office will be replaced by a lift to make access to the piste easier, and a new hands-free electronic lift pass system will be introduced throughout the Three Valleys.

➕ In the centre of the biggest linked lift network in the world – ideal for intermediates, great for experts, too

➕ Impressive lift system, piste maintenance and snowmaking

➕ Pleasant chalet-style architecture

➖ Not the best snow in the Three Valleys, and pistes can get crowded

➖ Sprawling main village, with lots of accommodation far from the slopes

➖ Expensive and full of Brits

➖ Méribel-Mottaret and Méribel Village satellites are rather lifeless

For keen piste-bashers who like big resorts but dislike tacky purpose-built ones, Méribel is difficult to beat. The Three Valleys can keep anyone amused for a fortnight – and Méribel-Mottaret, in particular, has quick access to every part. And, unlike other purpose-built resorts, Méribel has always insisted on chalet-style architecture. What more could you ask? Well, our ➖ points are mostly non-trivial. And other Three Valleys resorts have the edge in some respects. For better snow opt for Courchevel or Val-Thorens. For less crowded runs, Courchevel 1650. For a smaller village St-Martin or La Tania. For lower prices, Les Menuires. But these resorts have their drawbacks too. Regular visitors love Méribel.

THE RESORT

Méribel occupies the central valley of the Three Valleys system and consists of two main resort villages.

The original resort is built on a single steepish west-facing hillside with the home piste running down beside it to the main lift stations at the valley bottom. All the buildings are wood-clad, low-rise and chalet style, making it one of the most tastefully designed of French purpose-built resorts. A road winds up from the village centre to the Rond Point des Pistes, and goes on through woods to the outpost of the Altiport (an airstrip with snow-covered runway for little planes with skis).

The resort was founded by a Brit, Peter Lindsay, in 1938, and has retained a strong British presence ever since – 'More like Kensington than France,' commented a reporter. It has grown enormously over recent years, and although some accommodation is right on the piste, much of the newer building is more than a walk away – check your location carefully if you don't like having to rely on buses (or tour operator minibuses). One clear exception is Belvédère, an upmarket enclave built on the opposite side of the home piste (there's a tunnel for road access). There are collections of shops and restaurants at a couple of points on the road through the resort – Altitude 1600 and Plateau de Morel.

The hotels and apartments of Altiport enjoy splendid isolation in the woods, and are convenient for the slopes.

The satellite village of Méribel-

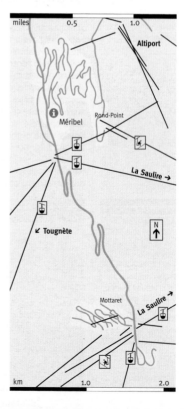

The original part of Mottaret was built in attractive chalet style in the early 1970s. As you can see, it's on a steep hillside ↗

OT MERIBEL

Mottaret was developed in the early 1970s and is very centrally placed in the Three Valleys ski area, offering swift access in one direction to Courchevel and in another to Mont du Vallon, Val-Thorens and Les Menuires.

The original development was beside the piste on the east-facing slope, but the resort has spread up the opposite hillside and further up the valley. Both sides are served by lifts for pedestrians – but the gondola up to the original village stops at 7.30pm and it's a long, tiring walk up.

Mottaret looks modern, despite wood cladding on its apartment blocks. Even so, it's more attractive than many other resorts built for slope-side convenience. It has far fewer shops and bars and much less après-ski than Méribel. Some visitors have found it 'lacking in atmosphere', but we are getting an increasing number of positive reports on it.

The hamlet of Méribel-Village, on the road from Méribel to La Tania and Courchevel, has a chair-lift up to Altiport with a blue run back and has developed into a mini-resort. There are some luxury chalets and apartments here but little else apart from a fitness centre, bar, pizzeria and a couple of restaurants; but if nightlife is not a priority it's a pleasant place to stay.

There are some alternative bases lower down the mountain (and price scale) – see the end of this chapter.

Local buses are free (though some readers complain they are not frequent enough and are overcrowded at peak times), and many UK tour operators run their own minibus services to and from the lifts. A car is mainly of use for outings to other resorts.

Lift passes for six days or more give you a day in each of Val-d'Isère-Tignes and Paradiski.

THE MOUNTAINS

Most of the slopes are above the tree line, but there are some sheltered runs for bad-weather days. The lift system is well planned to cut out walks and climbs. Piste grading is not always reliable – there are some testing blues – and in an area where some slopes get the afternoon sun, snow conditions have a huge impact on difficulty. In warm weather, the west-facing slopes down from La Saulire can be frozen rock-hard first thing in the morning. Daily maps are available showing which runs were groomed overnight.

KEY FACTS

Resort	1400-1700m	
	4,590-5,580ft	

Three Valleys		
Slopes	1260-3230m	
	4,130-10,600ft	
Lifts	200	
Pistes	600km	
	373 miles	
Green		16%
Blue		38%
Red		36%
Black		10%
Snowmaking		
	1500 guns	

Méribel only		
Slopes	1400-2950m	
	4,590-9,680ft	
Lifts	53	
Pistes	150km	
	93 miles	
Green		11%
Blue		46%
Red		31%
Black		12%
Snowmaking		
	650 guns	

THE SLOPES
Highly efficient lift system
The Méribel valley runs north-south. On the eastern side, gondolas leave both Méribel and Mottaret for **La Saulire**. From here you can head back down towards either village or down the other side towards Courchevel.

From Méribel a gondola rises to **Tougnète**, on the western side of the valley, from where you can get down to Les Menuires or St-Martin-de-Belleville. You can also head for Mottaret from here. From there, a fast chair then a drag take you to another entry point for the Les Menuires runs.

The **Plattières** gondola rises up the valley from Mottaret to the south, ending at yet another entry point to the Les Menuires area. To the east of this is the big stand-up gondola to the top of **Mont du Vallon** (there are wonderful views from the top). A fast quad from near this area goes south up to **Mont de la Chambre**, giving direct access to Val-Thorens.

TERRAIN-PARKS
There's a choice
The Plattières terrain-park – accessed from the second stage of the Plattières gondola – has two half-pipes (one for experts, one for novices), two quarter-pipes, three tables, a spine and a 650m/2,130ft boarder-cross and was extended in 2004/05. The Moon Park, near the Arpasson drag above the Tougnète gondola mid-station, has two half-pipes and a boarder-cross with various toys to play on. The new Family Park on Burgin caters specially for kids aged 5 to 12.

SNOW RELIABILITY
Not the best in the Three Valleys
Méribel's slopes aren't the highest in the Three Valleys, and they mainly face east or west; the latter get the full force of the afternoon sun. So snow conditions are often better elsewhere. And grooming seems to be rather better in neighbouring Courchevel.

The lower runs have substantial snowmaking and lack of snow is rarely a problem, but ice or slush at the end of the day can be. The north-west-facing slopes above Altiport generally have decent snow. See 'For intermediates' for criticisms of the so-called blue runs back into Mottaret.

At the southern end of the valley, towards Les Menuires and Val-Thorens, a lot of runs are north-facing and keep their snow well, as do the runs on Mont du Vallon.

FOR EXPERTS
Exciting choices
The size of the Three Valleys means experts are well catered for. In the Méribel valley, head for Mont du Vallon – voted 'the best skiing in the whole of the Three Valleys' by one reporter's group. The long, steep Combe du Vallon run here is classified red; it's a wonderful, long, fast cruise

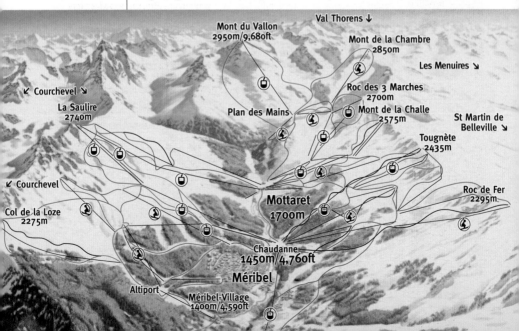

LIFT PASSES

Three Valleys
Covers all lifts in Courchevel, La Tania, Méribel, Val-Thorens, Les Menuires and St-Martin-de-Belleville.

Main pass
1 day €41
6 days €204

Senior citizen
Over 60: 6 days €164
Over 72: free pass

Children
Under 13: 6 days €153.50
Under 5: free pass

Notes
Reductions for families. Half-day and pedestrian passes available. Six-day pass and over valid for one day in Espace Killy (Tignes-Val-d'Isère), Paradiski (La Plagne-Les Arcs), Pralognan and Les Saisies.

Alternative passes
Méribel pass covers Méribel and Méribel-Mottaret only.

when groomed, but presents plenty of challenge when mogulled. And there's a beautiful off-piste run in the next valley to the main pistes, leading back to the bottom of the gondola.

A good mogul run is down the side of the double Roc de Tougne drag-lift which leads up to Mont de la Challe. And there is a steep black run all the way down the Tougnète gondola back to Méribel. Apart from a shallow section near the mid-station, it's unrelenting most of the way.

At the north end of the valley the Face run was built for the women's downhill in the 1992 Olympics. Served by a fast quad, it's a splendid cruise when freshly groomed, and you can terrify yourself just by imagining what it must be like to go straight down.

Nothing on the Saulire side is as steep or as demanding as on the other side of the valley. The Mauduit red run is quite challenging, though – it used to be black.

Throughout the area there are good off-piste opportunities – see feature panel later in this chapter.

FOR INTERMEDIATES
Paradise found
Méribel and the rest of the Three Valleys is a paradise for intermediates; there are few other resorts where a keen piste-basher can cover so many miles so easily. Virtually every slope in the region has a good intermediate run down it, and to describe them would take a book in itself. For less adventurous intermediates, the run

from the second station of the Plattières gondola above Mottaret back to the first station is ideal, and used a lot by the ski school. It is a gentle, north-facing, cruising run and is generally in good condition. Below that can get tricky and bumpy later in the day; 'Carnage when the beginner classes went up,' said a 2004 reporter. 'People spreadeagled everywhere, with the bloodwagons overwhelmed,' said another. We think the run into Mottaret on the other side of the valley gets dangerously icy and crowded too. The lift company needs to solve both these problems, which spoil an otherwise ideal intermediate area.

Even early intermediates should find the runs over into the other valleys well within their capabilities, opening up further vast amounts of intermediate runs. Go to Courchevel or Val-Thorens for the better snow.

Virtually all the pistes on both sides of the Méribel valley will suit more advanced intermediates. Most of the reds are on the difficult side.

FOR BEGINNERS
Strengths and weaknesses
Méribel has an excellent slope for beginners, but it's out of the resort at Altiport, which is a bit of a nuisance. There is a small nursery slope at Rond-Point, at the top of the village, mainly used by the children's ski school.

The Altiport area is accessible from the village by the Morel chair-lift, or by free bus. Once you have found your feet, a free drag-lift takes you half-way

Méribel

307

boarding

Méribel is increasingly boarder-oriented. The terrain locally and further afield has lots to offer and you rarely have to take a drag-lift – but there are quite a lot of flat sections on some of the main ways to/from Val-Thorens. The resort hosts a number of big-air and boarder-cross competitions. Specialist shops include Board Brains (in Méribel), and Quiksilver Gotcha Surf (in Mottaret).

SCHOOLS

ESF Méribel
t 0479 086031

ESF Méribel-Mottaret
t 0479 004949

Magic in Motion
t 0479 085336

New Generation
t 0479 010318
www.skinewgen.com

Snow Systems
t 0479 004022

Classes
(ESF prices)
6 half-days (2½hr per
day): €154.80

Private lessons
From €80 for 2hr for
1 to 4 people

GUIDES

Mountain guide office
t 0479 003038

up a long, gentle, wide, tree-lined
green run – ideal except that it can get
crowded and have good skiers
speeding through. Next, a longer drag
takes you to the top of this run, then a
chair a bit higher, then another chair
higher still, on to an excellent blue
usually blessed with good snow.

FOR CROSS-COUNTRY
Scenic routes
There are about 33km/21 miles in total.
The main area is in the pine forest
near Altiport, a pleasant introduction
to those who want to try cross-country
for the first time. There's also a loop
around Lake Tuéda, in the nature
reserve at Mottaret, and for the more
experienced an itinéraire from Altiport
to Courchevel.

QUEUES
3V traffic a persistent problem
Huge lift investment over the years has
paid off in making the area virtually
queue-free most of the time, despite
the huge numbers of people. Generally,
if you do find a queue, there is an
alternative quieter route you can take.
The real problems result from the tidal
flows of people between the three
valleys, in the morning (when the tide
coincides with the start of ski school)
and in the late afternoon. One 2004
reporter, who also said the 'lifts kept
stopping while I was on them', thought
the queues 'horrendous'. The queue
for the Tougnète gondola at Méribel
towards Les Menuires has been eased
by the installation of the new fast chair
in 2004/05 – 'an excellent
improvement' says a local; but the
Plattières gondola at Mottaret towards
Les Menuires, the Côte Brune chair to
Mont de la Chambre; the Plan des
Mains chair (used by everyone
returning from Val-Thorens) can still
generate big queues.

MOUNTAIN RESTAURANTS
Less than wonderful
There are lots of places on the piste
map, but few that are worth singling
out – and not enough to meet the
demand, so many get very crowded (so
you might want to take lunch early or
late). The Chardonnet, at the mid-
station of the Mottaret-Saulire gondola,
has table-service and excellent food,
but is expensive. The large terrace at
the Rhododendrons, at the top of the
Altiport drag, is also expensive but
remains a popular spot. The Rond
Point, just below the mid-point of the
Rhodos gondola, offers tasty paninis
as well as delicious rösti. The cosy
Crêtes, below the top of the Tougnète
gondola, continues to provide 'good
food and service'. Lower down, at the
bottom of the Roc de Tougne drags,
the Tougniat has 'very good self-
service food'. The pricey Altiport hotel
scarcely counts as a mountain
restaurant, but has a great outdoor
buffet in good weather and the 'best
tarts in town'. Two self-service places
notable for their views are the Pierres
Plates, at the top of Saulire, and the
Sittelle ('good choice of cooked and
cold buffet lunches') above the first
section of the Plattières gondola. The
Blanchot, next to the road to the
altiport, is recommended as 'a good
place to meet non-skiers'.

SCHOOLS AND GUIDES
No shortage of instructors
The main schools all have English-
speaking instructors.

The ESF is by far the biggest, with
over 300 instructors. It has a special
international section with instructors
speaking good English. Recent reports
have been mixed; a 2005 reporter said,
'A couple in our chalet had two private
lessons with an ESF instructor who was
late both times and smelt strongly of
alcohol (at 11.30am!),' but a 2004

Méribel has a lot of very good off-piste to discover, as well as the pistes that the Three Valleys is famous for. We asked Pierre François Papet, head of Méribel's Snow Systems ski school, to pick out some of the best off-piste runs.

Snow Systems is a ski school that operates from both Méribel and Mottaret. As well as group and private on- and off-piste lessons, they run children's lessons, snowboard lessons and Instructor training.

t 0479 004022
www.snow-systems.com

For your first time off piste, an easy and accessible area is from the Dent de Burgin chair-lift. Take the Renard slope for 50m/165ft and turn right off-piste. This is a very broad area of gentle slopes close to the piste, perfect for off-piste beginners to practise their skills on before reaching the Blanchot piste in the Altiport area.

For intermediate skiers with some off-piste experience the run from near Roc de Fer to Le Raffort, a small village below Méribel, is an adventure. From the top of the Olympic chair-lift turn right and follow the ridge, then drop off into a gentle bowl, ski through that and finish among the trees. The views over the Les Allues valley are exceptional. Take the Olympe gondola back to Méribel.

Accomplished off-piste skiers can take the Plattières gondola to the top. Follow the Mouflon run for 100m/330ft, then on the right go up and follow the ridge to a cairn, which identifies the top. The descent, known as The Cairn, starts in a fairly steep couloir and becomes wider with a consistent pitch until the Sittelle run. An area we call the Spot is a great playground in powder snow. You reach it from Mont de La Challe, at the top of the Roc de Tougne drag-lift, then follow the Lagopéde run for 50m/165ft and turn right off the piste. This is for good skiers only – the descent is rather technical and steep. You end up on the Sittelle run. The Col du Fruit is a great classic of the Méribel valley, far away from the lifts and resort. Access is by the Creux Noirs chair-lift in Courchevel; you then walk along the ridge for 15 minutes before starting the descent through the national park to Lac de Tueda and the cross-country tracks ... 800m/2,625ft of flat ground from the Mottaret lifts.

Mont Vallon offers a big choice of routes and exposures – quite steep at the top but with easier slopes from the middle. The northern couloir, for excellent skiers who want to push their limits, starts at the top of the Campagnol run, before plunging down to the right.

You should, of course, never venture off-piste without safety equipment and a qualified guide or instructor.

Méribel

visitor found their instructor 'very thorough'. The ESF offers useful alternatives to standard classes, such as off-piste groups, heli-skiing on the Italian border and Three Valleys tours.

Magic in Motion, the second largest school, also offers heli-skiing, couloir and extreme sessions as well as normal lessons. But recent reports have been poor, including a 2005 reporter who says, 'Every day we had to push both kids to go to their classes. The instructors had very little enthusiasm.'

New Generation, a British school which expanded from Courchevel to Méribel four seasons ago, is now well-established and receives excellent reports. One reader said, 'I cannot recommend them highly enough, they were patient and kept groups small.' A 2005 reporter 'progressed quickly in a group of only three; the instructor explained and demonstrated techniques clearly'.

FACILITIES FOR CHILDREN
Tour operators rule
We guess readers needing childcare use the facilities of chalet operators who run their own nurseries – we rarely get reports on resort facilities.

STAYING THERE

HOW TO GO
Huge choice but few bargains
Package holidays are easy to find, both with big UK tour operators and smaller Méribel specialists.
Chalets Méribel has more chalets dedicated to the British market than any other resort, and over 50 operators offering them. What really distinguishes Méribel is the range of recently built luxury chalets. Some are perfectly positioned for the slopes, but many have minibuses on hand to compensate for their inconvenient locations. Méribel specialists include Meriski, Purple Ski and Bonne Neige and all have smart-looking chalets. At the top of the luxury end of the market, VIP has several sumptuous looking places, mostly with saunas and hot-tubs; sister company Snowline has some not far behind; Kaluma runs the splendid Lodge; and Descent International has four of the best chalets. Lotus Supertravel has a couple of places. Of the few chalet-hotels, Mark Warner's Tarentaise (with a sauna and hot-tub) has a great position, right on the piste at Mottaret. Other companies to check out are those advertising here and others listed in our Resort directory/index at the back of the book.
Hotels Méribel has some excellent hotels, but they're not cheap.
(((4 **Grand Coeur** (0479 086003) Our favourite almost-affordable hotel in Méribel. Just above the village centre. Welcoming, mature building with plush lounge. Magnificent food. Huge hot-tub, sauna, etc.
(((4 **Altiport** (0479 005232) Modern and luxurious hotel, isolated at the foot of the Altiport lifts. Convenient for Courchevel, not for Val-Thorens.
(((4 **Mont-Vallon** (0479 004400) The best hotel at Mottaret; good food, and excellently situated for the Three Valleys' pistes. Pool, sauna, squash, fitness room, etc.
(((3 **Arolles** (0479 004040) Right on the slopes at Mottaret. 'Friendly, unpretentious, good food, highly recommended,' says a 2004 visitor. Pool and sauna.
(((3 **Adray Télébar** (0479 086026) Welcoming piste-side chalet with pretty, rustic rooms, good food and popular sun terrace.
(((3 **Parc Alpin** (0479 082963) Newly renovated luxury B&B at 1600 with

Phone numbers
From abroad use the prefix +33 and omit the initial '0' of the phone number.

pool, sauna and wi-fi internet.
② **Roc** (0479 086416) A good-value B&B hotel, in the centre, with a bar-restaurant and crêperie below.

Self-catering There is a huge number of apartments and chalets to let in both Méribel and Mottaret. Make sure that the place you book is conveniently situated and has enough space. A reader recommends the Merilys apartments in Méribel: 'A fine place with very helpful staff.'

EATING OUT
Fair choice
There is a reasonable selection of restaurants, from ambitious French cuisine to relatively cheap pizza and pasta. For the best food in town, in plush surroundings, there are top hotels – Grand Coeur ('so pleased, we ate

there several times'), Allodis and Kouisena ('beef fondue excellent') in the Eterlou. Other reader recommendations include: Chez Kiki – 'the best steaks'; the Taverne – 'relaxed atmosphere' but 'can be expensive'; the Tremplin – 'good for families, friendly service, reasonably priced'; the Enfants Terribles – 'wonderful roast beef carvery'; the Refuge – 'lovely crêpes'; the Grange 'excellent food and service'; Oasis – 'good meals at a reasonable price'; and the Cactus Café – 'always busy and friendly, mainly British staff', 'cheap meals, quieter in the evenings'.

Alternatives include the Galette, the Fromagerie, the Cava and Cro-Magnon up the hill in Morel – all popular for raclette and fondue. The Marie Blanche specialises in seafood and the Blanchot, just below Altiport, offers the

---

CHILDREN

Les Saturnins
t 0479 086690
Ages 18mnth to 3yr;
6 days €198

Les P'tits Loups
t 0479 086031 (Mér)
t 0479 004949 (Mot)
Ages 3 to 5; 9am-
5pm; 6 days €198

Childminder list
Available from the
tourist office.

Ski school
The ESF runs classes
for ages 5 to 13: 6
half-days (2½hr) from
€94.80

choice of two dining areas, one dedicated to dishes of the region. Scott's does good American-style food.

At Les Allues, the Tsaretta will provide a free taxi service to transport you to enjoy the imaginative creations of the Australian chef. The Chaumière offers 'good value inclusive menus in pleasant, rustic surroundings'. The Chemina is another recommendation as is the Martagon at Le Raffort between Méribel and Les Allues.

APRES-SKI
Méribel rocks – loudly

Méribel's après-ski revolves around British-run places. Dick's Tea Bar is well established but is remote from the slopes. At close of play it's the piste-side Rond Point that's packed – happy hour starts around 4pm – and has live music and 'tasty toffee vodka'. The sun terrace of Jack's (under new ownership) near the main lift stations, remains very popular.

The ring of bars around the main square do good business at tea time. The Taverne (run by the same company that owns Dick's Tea Bar) gets packed. Just across the square is the Pub, with videos, pool and sometimes a band.

There are a couple of alternatives to the loud pubs complained about in the past. The Poste 'serves the best vin chaud' and is a 'more French option than the bars closer to the slopes'. The Barometer has a good atmosphere and lots of leather seating.

There is late dancing at Scott's (next to the Pub) and, of course, there's Dick's Tea Bar. One reader was put off by the queues at the Pub, another liked its 'busy atmosphere'.

In Mottaret the bars at the foot of the pistes get packed at tea time – Rastro ('as good as ever' and 'good value', comment regular visitors) and Down Town are the most popular, though reporters say that Zig-Zag has lower prices. Later on the Rastro disco gets going.

Both villages have a cinema.

OFF THE SLOPES
Flight of fancy

Méribel is not really a resort for people who want to languish in the village, but it is not unattractive. There's a good public swimming pool and an Olympic ice rink. You can also take joyrides in the little planes that operate from the altiport.

GETTING THERE

Air Geneva 135km/ 84 miles (3½hr); Lyon 185km/115 miles (3½hr); Chambéry 95km/59 miles (1½hr)

Rail Moûtiers (18km/11 miles); regular buses to Méribel.

ACTIVITIES

Indoor Parc Olympique (ice rink, swimming pool, climbing wall, karting on ice), fitness centres in hotels, bowling, library, two cinemas, museum, heritage tours

Outdoor Flying lessons and excursions, snow-mobiles, snow-shoe excursions, cleared paths, paragliding, dog-sledding, hot air ballooning, paintball

TOURIST OFFICE

t 0479 086001 info@meribel.net www.meribel.net

OT MERIBEL

Méribel seen from the Tougnète side: it's a spread-out village (and there's a lot more of it you can't see, hidden by the slope) ➔

The pedestrian's lift pass covers all the gondolas, cable-cars and buses in the Méribel and Courchevel valleys, and makes it very easy for pedestrians to meet friends for lunch. There are pleasant, marked walks in the Altiport area and a signposted trail through some of the hamlets down to Les Allues (return from there or Le Raffort in the Olympic gondola).

A non-skier's guide to Courchevel, Méribel and La Tania is distributed free by the tourist office.

STAYING DOWN THE VALLEY
Quieter, cheaper choices

For the 1992 Olympics the competitors were accommodated in **Brides-les-Bains** (600m/1,970ft), an old spa town way down in the valley, and a gondola was built linking it to Méribel. It is much cheaper than the higher resorts and has some simple hotels, adequate shops and 'plenty of good-value restaurants and friendly bars used by locals', says a reporter. 'It's a nice place to be based if you want to be away from the crowds,' says another. Ski Weekends runs a chalet-hotel here. There is a casino, but evenings are distinctly quiet. The long gondola ride

to and from Méribel (about 25 minutes) is tedious, can be cold, stops early ('ridiculously early at 5pm' said a 2005 reporter) and the top station is still a bit of a trek from the main lifts up the mountain; but in good conditions you can ski off-piste to one or other of the mid-stations at the end of the day (or even down to Brides itself if conditions are exceptional). Given a car, Brides makes a good base for visiting other resorts.

Some UK tour operators have places in the old village of **Les Allues**, down the road from the resort and close to a mid-station on the gondola up from Brides-les-Bains. The pick of the chalets is probably Bonne Neige's Les Allodis, a carefully converted barn ('Absolutely brilliant, the best chalet holiday ever, excellent food,' said a 2004 reporter) plus one other chalet, St Joseph – there's a hot-tub and a sauna in each. Ski Blanc have six good-looking chalets too, including one with a hot-tub. Next door to one of them is an independent British-run playgroup. There are a couple of bars – and a good-value, well-renovated hotel, the Croix Jean-Claude (0479 086105); rooms are small, though.

Montgenèvre

The snowiest part of the Franco-Italian Milky Way circuit

SNOWPIX.COM / CHRIS GILL

COSTS

① ② ③ ④ ⑤ ⑥

RATINGS

The slopes

Fast lifts	*
Snow	****
Extent	****
Expert	**
Intermediate	****
Beginner	*****
Convenience	****
Queues	****
Mountain restaurants	**

The rest

Scenery	***
Resort charm	***
Off-slope	*

NEWS

A tunnel is being built to take the through-traffic out of Montgenèvre. It is due for completion in December 2006.

For 2003/04 the Tremplin drag was replaced by a chair. The new Tremplin red slope was added, too. Snowmaking was extended.

REPORTS WANTED

Recently we have had few reports on this resort. If you go there, please do send us a report.

The best reports earn a copy of the next edition, and can lead to free lift passes in future.

See page 10.

+ Good snow record, and local slopes largely north-facing – often the best snow in the Milky Way area

+ Plenty of intermediate cruising and good, convenient nursery slopes

+ Few queues on weekdays, unless people are being bussed in from other resorts with poor snow

+ A lot of accommodation close to the slopes, and some right on them

+ Great potential for car drivers to explore other nearby resorts

– Poor base for exploring the Italian Milky Way resorts unless you have use of a car

– Lots of slow lifts and mainly short runs in local area

– Busy road lined by tatty bars reduces village charm and family appeal – a problem due to be solved for the 2006/07 season

– Little to challenge experts on-piste

Montgenèvre is set at one end of the big Milky Way network, reaching over into Italy. On snow, it's a time-consuming trek from here to Sestriere and Sauze d'Oulx at the far end (you may have to ride some slow lifts down as well as up). But you can get to these worthwhile resorts much more quickly by car, which also facilitates day trips in the opposite direction to other excellent French resorts such as Serre-Chevalier. The local slopes shared with Claviere (in Italy, but very close) will probably have the best snow in the region.

The village is quite pleasant once you get away from the main road. Sadly, you can't avoid the road altogether if you want to make use of the bigger area of slopes on the south side of the pass. Most visitors don't seem to find that it spoils their enjoyment. But in our view the road tunnel due for completion at the end of 2006 will transform the place.

THE RESORT

Montgenèvre is a narrow roadside village set on a high pass only a mile from the Italian border – this is an area where the euro has really simplified things. At first glance the resort appears a rather inhospitable place – a collection of tatty-looking bars and restaurants lining the side of the sometimes windswept and often busy main road over the col. But the cheap and cheerful cafes and bars add an animated atmosphere sometimes missing from French resorts. And tucked away off the main road is a quite pleasant old village, complete with quaint church and friendly natives. The place gets a lot of snow, which adds to the charm factor.

The slopes are convenient, despite the road; most of the accommodation is less than five minutes from a lift. Some of the newer accommodation is uphill, away from the slopes – but there is a free shuttle-bus. The main lifts are gondolas from opposite ends

of the village. On the village side of the road are the south-facing slopes of Le Chalvet. The more extensive north-facing slopes of Les Anges and Le Querelay are across the main road, with nursery slopes at the bottom. Both sectors have piste links with Claviere, gateway to the other Italian resorts of the Milky Way – Sansicario, Sestriere and Sauze d'Oulx.

The best way to get to other resorts is by car. Serre-Chevalier and Puy-St-Vincent, with lift pass sharing arrangements, are easily reached, and well worth an outing each. Different lift pass options cater for most needs.

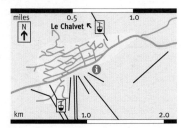

KEY FACTS

Resort	1850m
	6,070ft

For Montgenèvre-Monts de la Lune (Claviere)

Slopes	1850-2630m
	6,070-8,630ft
Lifts	40
Pistes	100km
	62 miles
Green	11%
Blue	27%
Red	42%
Black	20%
Snowmaking	
	40 hectares

For the whole Milky Way area

Slopes	1390-2825m
	4,560-9,270ft
Lifts	93
Pistes	400km
	249 miles
Blue	25%
Red	55%
Black	20%
Snowmaking	
	1000 guns

THE MOUNTAINS

Montgenèvre's local slopes are best suited to leisurely intermediates, with lots of easy cruising on blues and greens, both above and in the woods.

Run gradings on the local area and Milky Way piste maps have differed in the past, which can be confusing – however, none of the blacks is much more than a tough red.

THE SLOPES
Nicely varied

The major north-facing Les Anges sector offers easy intermediate slopes above the mid-mountain gondola station, with more of a mix of runs lower down. It has a high-altitude link via Collet Vert (reached by a quad chair) to the slopes above Claviere, in Italy (covered on the Monts de la Lune lift pass). The main complaint about the Claviere area is the number of long, steep and awkward drag-lifts (we have reports of kids 'dropping like flies'). But this whole area around the border is attractively broken up by rocky outcrops and woods and the scenery is quite spectacular.

The runs of the sunny Chalvet sector are mainly on open slopes above its mid-mountain gondola station. When conditions permit, a 'charming' long blue run from this sector goes down to Claviere, for access to Italy. But on some maps this run is marked as an itinéraire, which would normally mean that it is not patrolled. Check the situation before you start if skiing alone.

TERRAIN-PARKS
High and remote

There's a terrain-park – with quarter-pipe, jump and rope tow – and a boarder-cross near the Gondrans chair-lift at the top of the Les Anges sector.

SNOW RELIABILITY
Excellent locally

Montgenèvre has a generally excellent snow record, receiving dumps from westerly storms funnelling up the valley. The high north-facing slopes naturally keep their snow better than the south-facing area, but both have snowmaking on the main home pistes.

FOR EXPERTS
Limited, except for off-piste

There are very few challenging pistes locally. Many of the runs are overclassified. There is, however, ample off-piste terrain. The remote north-east-facing bowl beyond the Col de l'Alpet on the Chalvet side is superb in good snow and has black and red pistes, too. The open section between La Montanina and Sagnalonga on the Italian side is another good powder area. Those with a car should visit Sestriere for the most challenging runs. Heli-skiing can be arranged on the Italian side.

FOR INTERMEDIATES
Plenty of cruising terrain

The overclassified blacks are just right for adventurous intermediates, though none holds the interest for very long. The pleasantly narrow tree-lined runs to Claviere from Pian del Sole, the

Montgenèvre

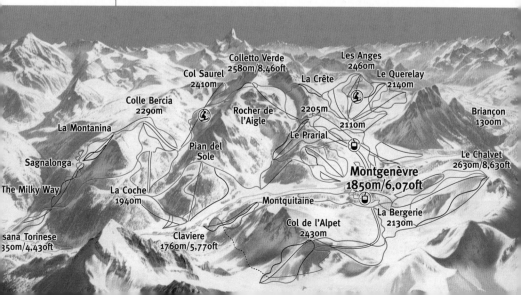

LIFT PASSES

Montgenèvre-Monts de la Lune
Covers Montgenèvre and Claviere lifts.

Beginners
6 days €78 if taking ESF lessons

Main pass
1 day €26.50
6 days €126

Senior citizens
Over 60: 6-day pass €100.50
Over 75: free pass

Children
Under 12: 6-day pass €100.50
Under 6: free pass

Notes
6-day and over Galaxie pass allows free day at Alpe-d'Huez, Deux-Alpes, Puy-St-Vincent and Serre-Chevalier.

Alternative passes
Montgenèvre only and Voie Lactée (Milky Way) area passes available.

SCHOOLS

ESF
t 0492 219046
esf.montgenevre@wanadoo.fr
www.esf-montgenevre.com

A-Peak
t 0492 218330
info@a-peak.com
www.a-peak.com

Classes (ESF prices)
6 half days (2½hr)
€91

Private lessons
€32 for 1hr

boarding

There's plenty to attract boarders to Montgenèvre. There are good local beginner slopes and long runs on varied terrain for intermediates. The only real drawback is that many of the lifts in the area are drags, and you will have to use them to get around – getting over to Sestriere and back involves lots (and some flat sections to skate along as well). There are some excellent off-piste areas for more advanced boarders. Snow Box is the local specialist shop.

steepest of the routes down in the Chalvet sector and the runs off the back of Col de l'Alpet are all fine in small doses.

Average intermediates will enjoy the red runs, though most are short. On the major sector, both the runs from Collet Vert – one into Italy and one back into France – can be great fun.

Getting to Cesana via the lovely sweeping run starting at the top of the Serra Granet double-drag, and heading home from Pian del Sole, is easier than the gradings suggest, and can be tackled by less adventurous intermediates, who also have a wealth of cruising terrain high up at the top of the Les Anges sector. The runs down to the village are flattering cruises.

Further afield, the run down to Claviere from the top of the Gimont drags, on the Italian side, is a beautifully gentle cruise.

FOR BEGINNERS
Good for novices and improvers
There is a fine selection of convenient nursery slopes with reliable snow at the foot of the north-facing area. Progression to longer runs could not be easier, with a very easy blue starting at Les Anges, leading on to a green and finishing at the roadside 600m/1,970ft below.

FOR CROSS-COUNTRY
Having a car widens horizons
Montgenèvre is the best of the Milky Way resorts for cross-country enthusiasts, but it's useful to have a car. The two local trails, totalling 17km/11miles, offer quite a bit of variety, but a further 75km/47 miles of track starts in Les Alberts, 8km/5 miles away in the Clarée valley.

QUEUES
No problems most of the time
The slopes are wonderfully uncrowded during weekdays, provided surrounding resorts have snow. Some lifts become crowded at weekends and when nearby Bardonecchia is lacking snow.

And queues for the two gondolas out of the village can occur first thing. Links with Italy have improved but some walking can be involved and many of the lifts are still old and slow. Reporters praise the lift attendants.

MOUNTAIN RESTAURANTS
Head for Italy
The few mountain restaurants in the Montgenèvre sector are of the large self-service canteen variety, but a 2005 visitor was pleasantly surprised by the 'healthy and impressive fare' served up by some. In the Claviere sector there is a choice of atmospheric little mountain huts, such as the 'cosy' and 'friendly' Montanna Restaurant at the top of the chair lift from Sagnalonga. Alternatively there are plenty of places to eat back in the village.

SCHOOLS AND GUIDES
Encouraging reports
Latest reports on the ESF seem to suggest that language is the key issue. A couple whose instructor spoke 'excellent' English applauded his tuition, patience and encouragement. Another group also had 'delightful' instructors but found 'it was sometimes difficult to grasp what they meant' and none of them lasted the week.

FACILITIES FOR CHILDREN
Pity about the traffic
The intrusive main road apart, Montgenèvre would seem a fine family resort. Reports on the school's children's classes have been complimentary of both class size and spoken English.

STAYING THERE

HOW TO GO
Limited choice
UK tour operators concentrate on cheap and cheerful catered chalets, though some apartments are also available and a few operators also package hotels.

CHILDREN

Village kindergarten
t 0492 215250
Ages 3mnth to 6yr
ESF kindergarten
t 0492 219046
www.esf-montgenevre.com
Ages 3 to 5

Ski school
For ages 5 to 12
(6 half days €88)

GETTING THERE

Air Turin 98km/ 61 miles (2hr); Grenoble 145km/ 90 miles (3hr); Lyon 253km/157 miles (4½hr).
Rail Briançon (12km/ 7 miles) or Oulx (15km/9 miles); buses available from both five times a day.

ACTIVITIES

Indoor Cinema

Outdoor Natural ice rink, snow-shoeing, snowmobiling, walking, heritage tours, horse-riding

WEBSITES

For links to resort sites, go to our own new site at www.wtss.co.uk

Phone numbers
From abroad use the prefix +33 and omit the initial '0' of the phone number.

TOURIST OFFICE

t 0492 215252
info@montgenevre.com
www.montgenevre.com

Hotels There is a handful of simple places offering good value.
② **Valérie** (0492 219002) Central rustic old 3-star. 'Quiet and nicely French.'
② **Napoléon** (0492 219204) 3-star on the roadside.
① **Alpet** (0492 219006) Basic 2-star near the centre.
① **Chalet des Sports** (0492 219017) Among the cheapest rooms in the Alps.
Self-catering Résidences La Ferme d'Augustin are simple, ski-to-the-door apartments on the fringes of the main north-facing slopes, five minutes' walk (across the piste) from town.

EATING OUT
Cheap and cheerful
There are a dozen places to choose from. The Cesar reportedly has 'the best pizzas I have every tasted' and the Estable is highly praised for 'fantastic' food and service. The Jamy has an authentic French feel. The 3-star Napoléon is the only hotel with a restaurant open to non-residents – a pizzeria. A trip to Claviere is worthwhile – reporters have testified to the excellence of the restaurants.

APRES-SKI
Mainly bars, but fun
The range is limited. The Graal is a friendly, unsophisticated place; the Ca del Sol bar is a cosy place with open fire. Pub Chaberton is recommended. The Blue Night disco is popular. The Refuge, the Crepouse and the Jamy are the focal cafe-bars at tea-time.

OFF THE SLOPES
Very limited
There is a weekly market and you can walk the cross-country routes, but the main diversion is a bus-trip to the beautiful old town of Briançon.

STAYING UP THE MOUNTAIN
Easily arranged, recommended
The Sport Hotel at Sagnalonga, halfway down the piste to Cesana (on the Italian side of the border) and reached by chair-lift or snowmobile, is recommended by two reporters – 'good-value self-service meals', but 'it's in need of redecoration'. Even at half-term you get the immaculately groomed local slopes to yourself until skiers based elsewhere arrive, mid-morning. It's quiet in the evenings, but livens up considerably when Italian weekenders arrive to party. It's in the First Choice package programme.

Claviere 1760m/5,770ft

Claviere is a small, traditional village, barely a mile to the east of Montgenèvre and just over the border in Italy. It's no great beauty, and the main road to Montgenèvre and Briançon that divides it in two has an obvious impact, but visitors seem to like its quiet, relaxed ambience, and are ready to go again.

The slopes of Montgenèvre are as easily reached as those on the Italian side of the border. Stupidly, there is no shared pass sold here; you have to buy day extensions for the French slopes, or buy a shared pass up the road in Montgenèvre.

Claviere's nursery slope is small and steep but usually uncrowded and snow-reliable. We have had mixed reports of its ski school – from 'lovely instructors, brilliant with the kids' to 'only average' and 'big classes'.

Morzine

A lively, year-round resort linked by lift to the Portes du Soleil

COSTS

①②③④⑤⑥

RATINGS

The slopes
Fast lifts	**
Snow	**
Extent	*****
Expert	***
Intermediate	****
Beginner	***
Convenience	**
Queues	***
Mountain restaurants	***

The rest
Scenery	***
Resort charm	***
Off-slope	***

NEWS

Morzine and Les Gets have benefited from a lot of new fast lifts recently. But a lot of slow, old ones remain.

For 2005/06 the Nabor double chair used by beginners at Le Pléney is due to be replaced by a quad. A new mountain restaurant at the bottom of the Pointe de Nyon is also planned.

A new activity area called Indiana Winter Games was created for 2004/05. Open from 3pm to 10pm, it has skiing, tubing, big air, is floodlit and has music.

+ Part of the vast Portes du Soleil

+ Larger local piste area than other Portes du Soleil resorts

+ Good nightlife by French standards

+ Quite attractive old town – a sharp contrast to purpose-built Avoriaz

+ One of the easiest drives from the Channel (a car is very useful here)

+ Few queues locally

− Takes a while to get to Avoriaz and the main Portes du Soleil circuit

− Bus-ride or long walk to lifts from much of the accommodation

− Low altitude means there is an enduring risk of poor snow, despite increased snowmaking

− Choice of low-altitude or inconvenient nursery slopes

− Not a great resort for experts

− Weekend crowds

Morzine is a long-established year-round resort, popular for its easy road access, traditional atmosphere and gentle wooded slopes, where children do not get lost and bad weather rarely causes problems. For keen piste-bashers wanting to travel the Portes du Soleil circuit, the main drawback is having to take a bus and cable-car or several lifts to get to Avoriaz and the main circuit.

Such problems can be avoided by taking a car or using a tour operator who will drive you around. The little-used Ardent gondola, a short drive from Morzine, is a particularly neat option, giving the alternative of a shorter circuit that misses out Avoriaz, where the worst crowds tend to be found.

THE RESORT

Morzine is a traditional mountain town sprawling along both sides of a river gorge. In winter, under a blanket of snow, its chalet-style buildings look charming, and in spring the village quickly takes on a spruce appearance.

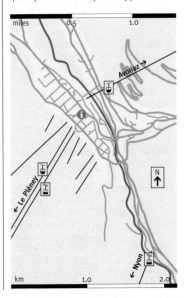

Morzine is a family resort, and village ambience tends to be fairly subdued – but there is plenty of après-ski action to be found.

The centre is close to the river, around the tourist office. Restaurants and bars line the street up to the Le Pléney lifts, where a busy one-way street runs along the foot of the slopes. Accommodation is widely scattered, and a good multi-route bus service (including two electric buses, introduced a couple of seasons ago) links all parts of the town to outlying lifts, including those for Avoriaz.

As the extensive network of bus routes and a growing number of hotel mini-buses imply, Morzine is a town where getting from A to B can be tricky. The best plan is to stay near the gondola and cable-car to Le Pléney and accept that any trips to the Portes du Soleil circuit are going to involve a bus-ride or a drive.

Our view that the resort suits car drivers is widely shared. But the roads are busy and the one-way system takes some getting used to; parking problems should be alleviated by a new central underground car park for 2005/06 to join others built quite recently near Le Pléney.

KEY FACTS

Resort	1000m
	3,280ft

Portes du Soleil	
Slopes	950-2300m
	3,120-7,550ft
Lifts	208
Pistes	650km
	404 miles
Green	14%
Blue	39%
Red	37%
Black	10%
Snowmaking	
	329 hectares

Morzine-Les Gets only	
Slopes	1000-2010m
	3,280-6,590ft
Lifts	48
Pistes	110km
	68 miles
Green	12%
Blue	35%
Red	44%
Black	9%

BERTRAND BODIN / FOC

There are some scenic
cross-country trails
near Morzine ↗

THE MOUNTAINS

The local slopes suit intermediates
well, with excellent areas for beginners
and near-beginners too. Reporters
have praised the system of Discovery
Routes around the Portes du Soleil –
choose an animal that suits your ability
and follow the signs displaying it
around the circuit.

THE SLOPES
No need to go far afield

Morzine is not an ideal base for the
Portes du Soleil main circuit (described
in the Avoriaz, Châtel and Champéry
chapters). But it has an extensive local
area shared with Les Gets (covered in
a separate chapter).

A cable-car and parallel gondola rise
from the edge of central Morzine to **Le
Pléney**, where numerous routes return
to the valley, including a run down to
Les Fys – a quiet junction of chairs
which access **Nyon** and, in the opposite
direction, the ridge separating Morzine
from the Les Gets slopes. The Nyon
sector has two peaks – Pointe de Nyon
and Chamossière – accessible from
Nyon and Le Grand Pré respectively.
Nyon can also be accessed by cable-
car, situated a bus-ride from Morzine.
Beyond Chamossière are two more
ridges – Le Ranfolly and La Rosta. In
the valley between these two, no fewer
than five chair-lifts have their base
stations clustered together.

Beyond Les Gets, **Mont Chéry** is
notably quiet, and well worth a visit.

Across town from the Le Pléney
sector – a handy 'petit train' shuttle
service runs between the two – is a
gondola leading (via a long chain of
lifts and runs) to Avoriaz and the main
Portes du Soleil circuit. This is a
painless way to get back to Morzine at
the end of the day, but a slow way to
get to the circuit. Better alternatives
are a bus-ride or short drive to either
Les Prodains (from where you can get

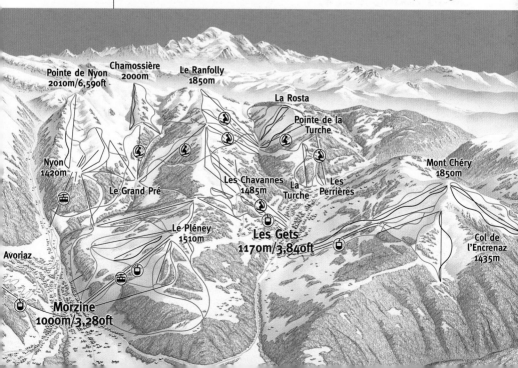

LIFT PASSES

Portes du Soleil
Covers all lifts in all resorts, and shuttle-buses.

Beginners
No special pass

Main pass
1 day €36
6 days €176

Senior citizens
Over 60: 6 days €141

Children
Under 16: 6 days €118
Under 5: free pass

Notes
Half-day passes available.

Alternative passes
Morzine-Les Gets pass (free for over-75s) and Morzine-Avoriaz pass available, also special snowboard. pass for Mont Chéry area €15.50 a day.

a cable-car to Avoriaz or a chair-lift into the **Hauts Forts** slopes above it), or to Ardent, where a gondola accesses Les Lindarets for lifts towards Châtel, Avoriaz or Champéry. The tree-lined slopes at Les Lindarets are good in poor visibility and the area at the top of the gondola is a good one for mixed ability groups to meet up. Car trips to Flaine and Chamonix are feasible. Reporters agree with us that piste maps, piste signposting and grooming are all good.

TERRAIN-PARKS
Mont Chéry, or head for Avoriaz
There's another boarder-cross, aimed at children, in the Zone Enfant at the top of Les Chavannes. Avoriaz has much more to offer (see Avoriaz chapter).

SNOW RELIABILITY
Poor
Morzine has a very low average height, and it can rain here when it is snowing higher up. It had no snow at Christmas and New Year 2002/03, for example. A reporter who visited in January 2004 speaks of 'three days of heavy rain up to 1800m'. But on our 2005 visit, when

snow was sparse throughout the Alps, we found the skiing good because little coverage is needed on the rock-free grassy pastures that you ski on. There is some snowmaking, most noticeably on runs linking Nyon and Le Pléney, and on the home runs.

FOR EXPERTS
A few possibilities
The runs down from Pointe de Nyon and Chamossière are quite challenging, as are the black runs down the back of Mont Chéry. Don't overlook the excellent Hauts Forts black runs at Avoriaz. There is plenty of off-piste scope throughout the area; the open slopes of Chamossière offer some of the best local possibilities, and Mont Chéry at Les Gets is also worth exploring. For further off-piste ideas, see the feature box on the facing page.

FOR INTERMEDIATES
Something for everyone
Good intermediates will enjoy the challenging red and black down from Chamossière. Mont Chéry has some fine steepish runs which are usually very quiet as everyone heads from Les Gets towards Morzine.

boarding

Avoriaz is the hard-core boarding HQ of the Portes du Soleil. But there's a boarding presence in Morzine, too – Chalet Snowboard (0870 800 4020 UK), who were the first chalet company to target snowboarders rather than skiers, has Morzine chalets, and former British champ Becci Malthouse teaches with the British Alpine Ski & Snowboard School. With interesting, tree-lined runs and few drags, the local Morzine slopes are good for beginners and intermediates. And there's a terrain-park over in Mont Chéry that might seem less intimidating than the big one in Avoriaz. There's a special snowboarder's pass if you just want to ride that area and there's a snow-park map. The specialist shop Misty Fly runs big air comps every Monday – and broadcasts them on the internet.

Those of average ability have a great choice, though most runs are rather short. Le Pléney has a compact network of pistes that are ideal for groups with mixed abilities: mainly moderate intermediate runs, but with some easier alternatives for the more timid, and a single challenging route for the aggressive.

Less experienced intermediates have lots of options on Le Pléney, including a great away-from-it-all, snow-gun-covered blue cruise from the top to the valley lift station. Heading from Le Ranfolly to Le Grand Pré on the blue is a nice cruise. And the slopes down to Les Gets from Le Pléney are easy when conditions allow (they face south).

The fast chairs on Le Ranfolly and La Rosta now make these sectors more attractive, serving easy blacks and cruising reds.

And, of course, there is the whole of the Portes du Soleil circuit to explore by going up the opposite side of the valley to Avoriaz or via Ardent to Les Lindarets.

FOR BEGINNERS
Good for novices and improvers
The wide village nursery slopes are convenient, and benefit from snow-guns, though crowds are reported to be a problem. Some of the best

---

OFF-PISTE RUNS IN THE PORTES DU SOLEIL AREA

The Portes du Soleil offers a lot of great lift-served off-piste terrain. We asked the ESF Morzine to give us a run-down on some of the highlights on the French side. Like all serious off-piste runs, these should not be done without guidance.

The **ESF** Morzine has 155 instructors offering group and private lessons at every level. For off-piste guiding, instructors can be hired for groups of up to six people, by the day and half day.

t 0450 791313
f 0450 791770
info@esf-morzine.com
www.esf-morzine.com

Morzine – Nyon/Chamossière area
From the Chamossière chair-lift (2000m/6,560ft), heading north brings you to two runs – one on the same north-west slope as the pistes, the other via a col down the north-east slope to the the Nyon cable-car (1020m/3,350ft) in the Vallée de La Manche – a wild area, with a great view of Mont Blanc at first.

Avoriaz area – two suggestions
From the the Fornet chair-lift (2220m/7,280ft) on the Swiss border, you head west to descend a beautiful, unspoiled bowl leading down to the village of L'Erigné (1185m/3,890ft). In powder snow you descend the west-facing slopes of the bowl; when there is spring snow, you traverse right to descend the south-facing slopes. Medium-pitch slopes, for skiers and snowboarders.

From the top of the Machon chair-lift (2275m/7,460ft) you traverse west, beneath the peaks of Les Hauts Forts, across Les Crozats de la Chaux – a steep, north-facing slope. You then turn north to descend through the forest to the cable-car station at Les Prodains (1150m/3,770ft). Testing terrain, for very good skiers – the traverse is dangerous following a snowfall.

Châtel area
From the top of the Linga chair-lift (2040m/6,690ft), you head north-west to cross the ridge on your right at a recognisable col and then head down the La Lèche slope to the drag-lift of the same name (1550m/5,090ft). It's a north-facing slope with powder snow. This run starts in a white wilderness, taking you through trees back to civilisation. Steep slopes – for good skiers only.

FRANCE

322

SCHOOLS

ESF
t 0450 791313
International
t 0450 790516
BASS
t 0871 7801500 (UK)

Classes
(ESF prices)
6 half days (2½hr am or pm) €113
Private lessons
€33.50 for 1hr for 1 to 3 people

GUIDES

Mountain Office
t 0450 747223

CHILDREN

L'Outa nursery
t 0450 792600
Ages 3mnth to 6yr; 6 days €166; meals €5.50
Club des Piou-Piou
t 0450 791313
Ages 3 to 12; with ESF instruction and lunch

Ski school
ESF takes children from age 5: 6 half-days €105

progression runs are over at Nyon and the slopes between Avoriaz and Morzine are also recommended. Adventurous novices also have the option of easy pistes around Le Pléney. Near-beginners can get over to Les Gets via Le Pléney, and return via Le Ranfolly.

FOR CROSS-COUNTRY
Good variety
There are 95km/60 miles of varied cross-country trails, not all at valley level. The best section is in the pretty Vallée de la Manche beside the Nyon mountain up to the Lac de Mines d'Or, where there is a good restaurant. The Pléney-Chavannes loop is pleasant and relatively snow-reliable.

QUEUES
Few problems when snow is good
Queues are not usually a problem in the local area. But we have had complaints of overcrowding, particularly in the Ranfolly-Rosta area and of waits for the old Rosta chair. The Nyon cable-car and Belvédère chair-lift (Le Pléney) are weekend bottlenecks. Long waits at the Morzine to Pléney gondola can be avoided by using the adjacent chairs, suggests a reporter. Queues to and from Avoriaz are much improved in recent times, but are still bad when snow is in short supply.

MOUNTAIN RESTAURANTS
Within reach of some good huts
We have had several very enjoyable Savoyard lunches at the rustic Chez Nannon near the top of the Troncs chair between Nyon and Chamossière. The nice little place at the foot of the d'Atray chair is also good. The tiny Lhottys hut has had mixed reviews ('amazing fresh seafood', 'mediocre spaghetti Bolognese', 'inadequate toilets'). The Vaffieu at the top of the

Folliets chair has had several recommendations ('We liked the food, service, location and atmosphere,' says a 2005 reporter) as has the Nabor (Pléney). The self-service on Mont Chéry is 'one of the better examples of the breed'. The Tanière in Les Gets at the bottom of the Chavanette chair is recommended for its 'varied food and lower prices'. A 2005 reporter found many small huts overcrowded even midweek in January.

SCHOOLS AND GUIDES
Good reports this year
The British Alpine Ski & Snowboard School (BASS), staffed by BASI-qualified instructors, is pricey but gets good reports: 'Absolutely first class; personalised, friendly service,' says a 2005 reporter, and his wife felt '£100 for a 2-hour private lesson with Becci Malthouse a bargain!' The beginners in a 2005 reporter's group had private lessons with 'great instructors' from the ESF (which is half the price). Another 2005 visitor and his grown-up daughter had a private lesson with 'an excellent instructor' at International: 'It was money very well spent.'

FACILITIES FOR CHILDREN
Various possibilities
The facilities of the Outa nursery are quite impressive, but we've received reports of poor English and low staff ratios. There is a big children's area, the Zone Enfant, in the Les Chavannes area. An ESF childcare centre, Club des Piou-Piou looks after children between the ages of 3 and 12 after skiing. The Dérêches Farm offers days learning about animals, snow-shoeing and tobogganing. The tour operator Esprit Ski has good facilities. Ski Famille and Ski Hillwood are other family specialists, based in Les Gets.

↑ In good snow, Morzine has some great off-piste slopes over the meadows. Sadly, the snow is not always this good

PIERRE JACQUES / FOC

GETTING THERE

Air Geneva 75km/ 47 miles (1½hr); Lyon 195km/121 miles (3½hr).

Rail Cluses or Thonon (30km/19 miles); regular bus connections to resort.

ACTIVITIES

Indoor Ice rink, fitness centre, sauna, hot-tub, climbing wall, library, cinemas

Outdoor Sleigh rides, snow-shoe classes, fitness trail, helicopter flights, ballooning, snowmobiles, bungee jumping, ice-diving, tobogganing, paragliding, cheese factory visits

WEBSITES

For links to resort sites, go to our own new site at www.wtss.co.uk

Phone numbers
From abroad use the prefix +33 and omit the initial '0' of the phone number.

TOURIST OFFICE

t 0450 747272
touristoffice@
morzine-avoriaz.com
www.morzine-avoriaz.com

STAYING THERE

HOW TO GO
Good-value hotels and chalets
The tour operator market concentrates on hotels and chalets.

Chalets There's a wide choice, but position varies enormously. Snowline has five central, luxurious places (three with hot-tub and sauna). A regular reporter always stays at the independently run Farmhouse: 'Excellent service, good ski guide.'
Hotels The handful of 3-star hotels includes some quite smart ones; and there are dozens of 2-stars and 1-stars.
(((4) **Airelles** (0450 747121) Central 3-star close to Pléney lifts and Prodains and Nyon bus routes. Good pool.
(((4) **Champs Fleuris** (0450 791444) Comfy 3-star next to Pléney lifts. Pool.
(((4) **Dahu** (0450 759292) 3-star linked to centre by footbridge over river; good restaurant; pool. Private shuttle to lifts.
(((3) **Tremplin** (0450 791231) Next to lifts; 'friendly, good food, small rooms'.
(((3) **Viking** (0450 791169) On the slopes at top of gondola. Evening entertainment. 'Fantastic food; good pool; great for families.'
(((3) **Bergerie** (0450 791369) Rustic chalet, in centre. Friendly staff. Pool.
((2) **Côtes** (0450 790996) Simple 2-star on the edge of town. Pool.
((2) **Equipe** (0450 791143) One of the best 2-stars; next to the Pléney lift.
Self-catering The Télémark apartments, close to the Super-Morzine gondola, and the Udrezants, by the Prodains cable-car, have been recommended.

EATING OUT
A reasonable choice
The best restaurant in town is probably in hotel Samoyede, which offers traditional and modern cuisine – we enjoyed lobster ravioli, truffle risotto and scallops. The hotel Airelles has a fine restaurant and the hotel Dahu also has good food. The Chamade looks the part (elegant table settings) but reports are mixed. The Grange does 'excellent food, but at a price'. Locals rate the Chalet Philibert highly. The Etale is a good, popular, unpretentious all-rounder. Café Chaud is popular for fondue and the Pique Feu does Savoyard food at 'reasonable prices'. The Tyrolien has 'tartiflette to die for' says a 2005 visitor. And the Clin d'Oeil has been recommended.

APRES-SKI
One of the livelier French resorts
On Tuesday evenings there's a 'ski retrospective' on the Le Pléney slopes, and on Thursdays there's a torchlight descent, followed by floodlit skiing. There are two cinemas.

Nightlife is good by French resort standards. The Dixie has sport on TV, MTV, a cellar bar and some live music. Between the slopes and the centre, and all in the same building are: the Cavern, which is popular with resort staff; the Coyote Bar for arcade games and DJ; the 'relaxed' Boudha Café, with Asian decor, for a quieter drink. At the nearby Crépuscule dancing on the tables in ski boots to deafening music seems compulsory. L'Opéra (which advertised 'nuits torrides' of striptease and lap dancing last time we heard) and Laury's are late-night haunts.

OFF THE SLOPES
Quite good; excursions possible
There is an excellent ice rink, with ice hockey matches and skating galas. Some hotels have pools open to non-residents. 'Morzine is a shopper's paradise,' says a 2005 visitor. Buses run to Thonon for more shopping, and car owners can drive to Geneva, Annecy or Montreux. There are lots of pretty walks, and other activities include horse-drawn sleigh rides, paragliding, and a cheese factory visit.

Paradiski

The new mega-area formed by linking Les Arcs and La Plagne

December 2003 saw the opening of the world's largest cable-car – a double-decker holding 200 people – which swoops low across a wooded valley to link the French resorts of Les Arcs and La Plagne. The result is that the two resorts can claim a joint ski area, called Paradiski, that is one of the biggest in the world. With 425km/264 miles of pistes and 161 lifts, it beats most of the established mega-areas; only the Three Valleys and the Portes du Soleil are significantly bigger. Add in a lot of off-piste terrain and you could argue the new area is bigger than either.

The new cable-car, called the Vanoise Express, spans the 2km/1 mile-wide valley between Plan-Peisey (in the Les Arcs area) and a point 300m/980ft above Montchavin (in La Plagne).

The linking of these two major resorts is good news for the great British piste-basher who likes to cover as much ground as possible. In truth, both La Plagne and Les Arcs on their own have enough pistes to keep anyone happy for a week. But readers report that a visit or two to the other resort during the week adds interest and variety. We've included some of their comments in our chapters on each resort.

For those who like a bit of a challenge, getting from your home base to both far-flung outposts of the Paradiski area – Villaroger in Les Arcs and Champagny-en-Vanoise in La Plagne – would make quite a full day.

The new link is good for expert skiers and boarders based in Les Arcs wanting to tackle the north face of La Plagne's Bellecôte. In the past, you had to get to Montchavin and the La Plagne lift system by taxi. For those doing the run from La Plagne it has benefits, too: you are now able to descend all the way to Nancroix, have lunch at the excellent restaurant Ancolie and catch the free bus or a taxi for the short ride back up to the Vanoise Express.

If you want to make the most of the new link it makes sense to stay near one of the cable-car stations. But once you start to study the piste maps you realise that it's easily accessible from many other bases.

On the Les Arcs side, **Plan-Peisey** and nearby **Vallandry** are in pole position. They are basically small, low-rise, modern developments, but built in a much more sympathetic style than the original Les Arcs resorts. They have

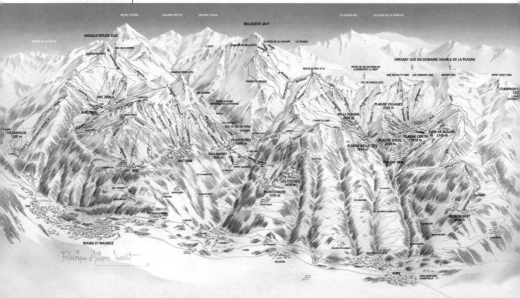

Frédérique et Pierre Novat

LIFT PASSES

Paradiski

Covers lifts in whole Paradiski area.
6-day pass €225 (over 60 €191; under 14 €169). Also covers a day in the Three Valleys, Val-d'Isère-Tignes, Les Saisies and Pralognan-en-Vanoise.

Paradiski Découverte

Covers lifts in Les Arcs area or La Plagne area plus one day Paradiski extension.
6-day pass €205 (over 60 €174; under 14 €154). Pass also covers a day in the Three Valleys, Val-d'Isère-Tignes, Les Saisies, Pralognan.

One day extension to normal Les Arcs or La Plagne 6-day pass
€25 Mon-Fri
€18 Sat-Sun

a few bars, restaurants and shops at the moment and are quiet places to stay, but are expanding rapidly and a few UK operators have chalets there. There is also accommodation in the old village of **Peisey**, 300m/980ft below and linked by bucket-lift to Plan-Peisey. Peisey is still unspoiled by tourism, with two bars and two restaurants.

It's easy to get to the cable-car station at Plan-Peisey from the main resort parts of Les Arcs. One lift and a blue run is all it takes to get there from **Arc 1800**, which is the most attractive of the main resort units. From quieter **Arc 1600**, along the mountainside from 1800, it takes two lifts. **Arc 2000** and the stylish new **Arc 1950** development seem further away, over the ridge that separates them from 1600 and 1800; but all you have to do is ski down a little way, ride one fast chair to the ridge and enjoy the long blue run down the other side. Beyond and below the bowl of Arc 2000, **Le Pré** and **Villaroger** are not ideal starting points.

On the La Plagne side, the obvious place to stay is **Montchavin**, which is below the Vanoise Express station.

Montchavin is a well-restored traditional old village with modern additions built in traditional style. **Les Coches**, across the mountain from the station, is most easily reached with the help of a lift. It is entirely modern, but built in a traditional style. Between them Montchavin and Les Coches have several restaurants and bars and a nightclub. From either village one lift brings you to the cable-car.

The other parts of La Plagne are some way from the cable-car, over in the main bowl of the area. But one long lift is all it takes to get from monolithic **Plagne-Bellecôte** up to L'Arpette, from which point it's a single long blue descent. The most attractive of the resort villages, **Belle-Plagne**, is only a short run above Plagne-Bellecôte. From the villages further across the bowl – **Plagne-Villages**, **Plagne-Soleil**, dreary **Plagne-Centre**, futuristic **Aime-la-Plagne** – you have to ride a lift to get to Plagne-Bellecôte. From **Plagne 1800**, below the bowl, add another lift. From the villages beyond the bowl – rustic, sunny **Champagny-en-Vanoise** and expanding **Montalbert** – it's going to be pretty hard work.

UK Representative
Erna Low Consultants
9 Reece Mews
London SW7 3HE
t 0870 750 6820
info@ernalow.co.uk
www.ernalow.co.uk

RIDING THE VANOISE EXPRESS

The cable-car ride from one resort to the other takes less than four minutes. There are no pylons between the lift-stations. The cabins give spectacular views through the transparent walls. The two cars operate independently, on separate cables, so you don't have to wait for one to fill before the other can set off; and if one is out of action the other can still operate.

The system is designed to be able to operate in bad weather and high winds, so the risk of getting stranded miles from home is low. Each car shifts 1,000 people an hour in each direction – which means the system can shift 2,000 an hour – effectively the same capacity as a small gondola.

At the outset, there was some concern that the system could be overloaded at the end of the day taking people back to the resort they started from. But these worries have proved to be unfounded, and few of those who reported to us this year encountered crowds.

The lift company offers a six-day pass covering the whole Paradiski region, which is perhaps most likely to appeal to people based in the villages at either end of the lift, who might choose to go in one direction on one day, and the other direction the next.

But it also offers a pass (Paradiski Découverte) which includes just one day's use of the Vanoise Express and the lifts in the other resort.

These two passes both give you a free day in the Three Valleys, Val-d'Isère-Tignes, Les Saisies and Pralognan-en-Vanoise if you want it – but why would you?

Alternatively, you can also buy one-day extensions to a Les Arcs or La Plagne six-day lift pass. These cost less at weekends (18 instead of 25 euros) because demand is less then.

OT LES ARCS

The Montchavin end of the Vanoise Express with the big double-decker cable-car about to dock ↘

La Plagne

A huge variety of villages spread across a vast playground

RATINGS

The slopes

Fast lifts	**
Snow	****
Extent	****
Expert	***
Intermediate	*****
Beginner	****
Convenience	*****
Queues	***
Mountain restaurants	***

The rest

Scenery	****
Resort charm	*
Off-slope	*

NEWS

For 2004/05 access from Montchavin to L'Arpette was improved by two new six-pack chairs – replacing the Bijolin chair and the two Salla drags. Also, the whole of the Paradiski area moved to hands-free electronic passes.

For 2005/06 the Arpette chair (the route from Plagne-Bellecôte towards Montchavin and the Vanoise Express) will be upgraded to an eight-seater, hopefully alleviating queues here. Snowmaking will also be further extended – for this season in Champagny and Montchavin.

➕ Extensive intermediate slopes, plus plentiful, excellent off-piste terrain

➕ Now linked with Les Arcs

➕ Good nursery slopes

➕ High and fairly snow-sure – and with some wonderful views

➕ Purpose-built resort units are convenient for the slopes

➕ Attractive, traditional-style villages lower down share the slopes

➕ Wooded runs of lower resorts are useful in poor weather

➖ Pistes in the main bowl don't have much to offer experts

➖ Pistes get very crowded in places

➖ Lower villages can suffer from poor snow – Champagny especially

➖ Unattractive architecture in some of the higher resort units

➖ Not many green runs for nervous beginners to go on to – though some blues are very easy

➖ Nightlife very limited

With 225km/140 miles of its own slopes and 85% of these being blue or red, the La Plagne area is an intermediate's paradise. And with much-needed lift improvements over the last few years, plus the link with Les Arcs, the resort is going up in our estimation. It has a reputation for plug-ugly, soulless, purpose-built villages and some of them justify that view. But there are 10 different villages to choose from – and as well as delightful old mountain villages at the foot of the slopes, there are some quite attractive purpose-built centres, too.

Experts prepared to hire a guide can have a splendid time off-piste, with some long descents which are often deserted and untracked compared with the classic off-piste runs of more macho resorts like Val-d'Isère.

THE RESORT

La Plagne consists of no fewer than 10 separate 'villages'; six are purpose-built at altitude in the main bowl, on or above the tree line and linked by road, lifts and pistes; the other four are scattered around outside the bowl. Each is self-contained, with its own shops, bars, restaurants, schools and lift pass offices.

Even the core resorts vary a lot in character. The first to be built, in the 1960s, was Plagne-Centre – still the focal point for shops and après-ski.

Typical of its time, it has ugly blocks and dreary indoor 'malls' that house a reasonable selection of shops, bars and restaurants. Recent developments just above Plagne-Centre are more pleasing to the eye.

Lifts radiate from Centre to all sides of the bowl, the major one being the big twin-cable gondola to Grande Rochette. A cable-car goes to the even more obtrusive 'village' of Aime-la-Plagne – a group of monolithic blocks. Below these two, and a bit of a backwater ('a dormitory', says one reader), is Plagne 1800, where the

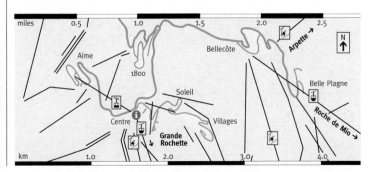

KEY FACTS

Resort	1800-2100m
	5,900-6,890ft

For La Plagne only

Slopes	1250-3250m
	4,100-10,660ft
Lifts	105
Pistes	225km
	140 miles
Green	8%
Blue	57%
Red	28%
Black	7%
Snowmaking	
	98 hectares

For Paradiski area

Slopes	1200-3250m
	3,940-10,660ft
Lifts	161
Pistes	425km
	264 miles
Green	5%
Blue	54%
Red	28%
Black	13%

buildings are small-scale and chalet-style – indeed many are offered as catered chalets on the UK market. Access to the main bowl from here is by lifts to Aime-la-Plagne and reporters comment on a drag-lift, the Lovatière, which links with no other lifts.

A little way above Plagne-Centre is the newest development, Plagne-Soleil, with attractive modern chalets. This area is officially attached to Plagne-Villages, which is a rather strung-out but attractive collection of small-scale apartments and chalets in traditional style, handy for the slopes but for nothing else.

The two other core resort units are a bus-ride away, on the other side of a low hill. The large apartment buildings of Plagne-Bellecôte form a wall at the foot of the slopes leading down to it. Some way above it is Belle-Plagne – as its name suggests, easy on the eye, with a neo-Savoyard look, and entirely underground parking. Reporters have complained of exhaustion when moving between the different levels in Belle-Plagne (the bars and other facilities are mainly in the lower part, but are serviced by public lifts).

Lifts from Plagne-Bellecôte provide links to two of the lower resorts in the valleys outside the bowl – the old village of Montchavin (above which is

the cable-car to Les Arcs) and its more recently developed neighbour Les Coches, at the northern extremity of the area. Beyond Grande Rochette, at the southern extremity, is rustic Champagny. Beyond Aime-la-Plagne, at the western extremity, is little Montalbert. For a description of these villages, see the end of this chapter.

A free bus system between the core villages within the bowl runs until after midnight. But you may have to change in Plagne-Centre. Lifts from Belle-Plagne to Plagne-Bellecôte, Aime-la-Plagne to Plagne-Centre, and Plagne-Centre to Plagne-Villages all run until 1am.

Trips by car to Val-d'Isère-Tignes or the Three Valleys are possible – and each is covered for a day with a 6-day Paradiski or Paradiski Découverte pass.

THE MOUNTAINS

The majority of the slopes in the main bowl are above the tree line, though there are trees scattered around most of the resort centres. The slopes outside the bowl are open at the top but descend into woodland. The gondola up to the exposed glacier slopes on Bellecôte, to the west of the main bowl, is prone to closure by high winds or poor weather, and the top Glacier chair is normally shut in winter.

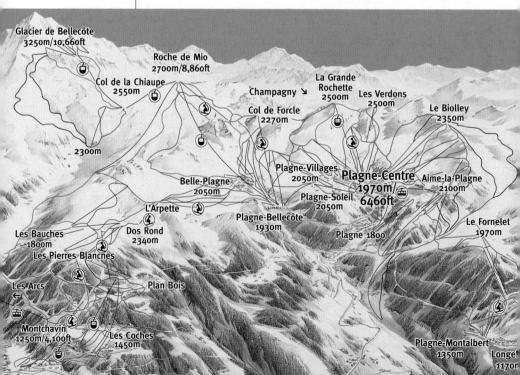

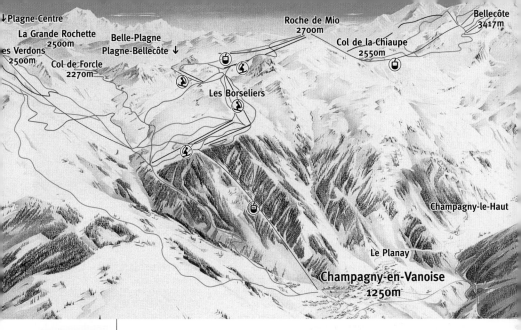

Plagne-Centre
La Grande Rochette 2500m
es Verdons 2500m
Belle-Plagne
Plagne-Bellecôte
Col de Forcle 2270m
Les Borseliers
Roche de Mio 2700m
Col de la Chiaupe 2550m
Bellecôte 3417m
Champagny-le-Haut
Le Planay
Champagny-en-Vanoise 1250m

THE SLOPES
Multi-centred; can be confusing

La Plagne boasts 225km/140 miles of pistes over a wide area that can be broken down into seven distinct but interlinked sectors. From Plagne-Centre you can take a lift up to **Le Biolley**, from where you can head back to Centre, to Aime-la-Plagne or down gentle runs to **Montalbert**, from where you ride several successive lifts back up. But the main lift out of Plagne-Centre leads up to **La Grande Rochette**. From here there are good sweeping runs back down and an easier one over to Plagne-Bellecôte, or you can drop over the back into the mainly south-facing **Champagny** sector. From the Champagny sector there are great views over to Courchevel.

From Plagne-Bellecôte and Belle-Plagne, you can head up to **Roche de Mio**, and have the choice of a gondola, or two successive fast chairs (the first of which also links with the Champagny sector). From Roche de Mio, runs spread out in all directions – towards La Plagne, Champagny or **Montchavin/Les Coches** and the link with Les Arcs. Montchavin/Les Coches can also be reached by taking a chair from Plagne-Bellecôte to L'Arpette. This journey should be speedier when the chair is replaced by an eight-seater this year, and the return has already been improved by the Salla six-pack.

From Roche de Mio you can also take a gondola down then up to the

Bellecôte glacier. The top chair is normally shut in winter – but if open, it offers excellent snow and stunning views. You can descend 2000m/6,560ft vertical from the glacier to Montchavin, with a not-difficult off-piste stretch in the middle.

Several reporters have complained that some runs are more difficult than their grading suggests, others are easier. Some also complain that the signing can be confusing. And there are a lot of slow old lifts still around.

TERRAIN-PARKS
Lots of choices

There are terrain-parks at Belle-Plagne, Montchavin-Les Coches and Champagny. The biggest is at Belle-Plagne, with big air, loads of kickers and rails – plus deckchairs to chill in and shovels to build your own kickers if you want. The other two have a selection of jumps. Plagne-Bellecôte has a 100m/328ft half-pipe and a ski-and boarder-cross run.

SNOW RELIABILITY
Generally good except low down

Most of La Plagne's runs are snow-sure, being at altitudes between 2000m and 2700m (6,560ft and 8,860ft) on the largely north-facing open slopes above the purpose-built centres. And although poor conditions early last season attracted a few comments about inconsistent piste grooming, in general comments about

LIFT PASSES

La Plagne
Covers all lifts in all
La Plagne areas.

Beginners
Some free lifts and a
reduced day-pass
price.

Main pass
1 day €38
6 days €181

Senior citizens
Over 60: 6 days €154
Over 72: free pass

Children
Under 14: 6 days
€136
Under 5: free pass

Notes Also available:
individual village-area
and half-day passes,
and Paradiski
extension.

Paradiski Découverte
Covers lifts in all La
Plagne areas and
one-day Paradiski
extension.

Main pass
6 days €205

Senior citizens
Over 60: 6 days €174
Over 72: free

Children
Under 14: 6 days
€154
Under 6: free

Notes Also covers a
day in each of the
Three Valleys, Val-
d'Isère-Tignes, Les
Saisies, Pralognan.

Paradiski
Covers all lifts in Les
Arcs area and La
Plagne area.

Main pass
1 day €45
6 days €225

Senior citizens
Over 60: 6 days €191
Over 72: free

Children
Under 14: 6 days
€169
Under 6: free pass

Notes 6-day pass
covers a day in each
of the Three Valleys,
Val-d'Isère-Tignes, Les
Saisies, Pralognan.

grooming have improved. The resort is in the middle of a four-year plan to increase snowmaking on the links to all the villages. The north-facing runs to Montchavin/Les Coches and Montalbert, plus a few runs around Plagne-Centre and most of those into Plagne-Bellecôte, have guns at the moment. But even here cover can be patchy if the weather is warm. The two sunny runs to Champagny are often closed.

FOR EXPERTS
A few good blacks and off-piste
There are two great black runs from Bellecôte to the chair-lift up to the gondola mid-station at Col de la Chiaupe – both beautiful long runs with a vertical of some 1000m/3,280ft that take you away from the lift system. But these are often closed because of too much or too little snow.

The Charmettes black at the end of the long Emile Allais red down from above Aime-la-Plagne is little used, north-facing and very enjoyable in good snow. A couple of drag-lifts take you back up. The Coqs and Morbleu runs also in the Aime-la-Plagne sector are seriously steep.

But experts will get the best out of La Plagne if they hire a guide and explore the vast off-piste potential – which takes longer to get tracked out than in more 'macho' resorts.

FOR INTERMEDIATES
Great variety
Virtually the whole of La Plagne's area is a paradise for intermediates, with blue and red runs wherever you look.

For early intermediates there are plenty of gentle blue motorway pistes in the main La Plagne bowl, and a long, interesting run from Roche de Mio back to Belle Plagne, Les Inversens (involving a tunnel). The blue runs either side of L'Arpette, on the Montchavin side of the main bowl, are glorious cruises. In poor weather the best place to be is in the trees on the gentle runs leading down to Montalbert. The easiest way over to Champagny is from the Roche de Mio-Col de Forcle area rather than from Grande Rochette.

Better intermediates have lots of delightful long red runs to try. There are challenging red mogul pitches down from the glacier. Roche de Mio to Les Bauches is a drop of 900m/2,950ft – the first half, Le Clapet, is a fabulous varied run with lots of off-piste diversions possible; the second half, Les Crozats, was changed from

boarding

La Plagne offers terrain for all levels of rider – there's a good mix of long, easy runs and high, open slopes with some fantastic off-piste options that should be done with a guide. The broad, gentle pistes are ideal for beginners and carvers (crowds permitting). There are also lots of areas to play in between the pistes, as well as three terrain-parks, a boarder-cross and a half-pipe. Whether on- or off-piste, be prepared for some flat areas, including the tunnel in the middle of the Inversens run and the linking blue down to Montchavin from Les Bauches. And while most lifts are gondolas or chairs, there are still some difficult drag-lifts. More difficult drag-lifts are conveniently marked on the map – it's not a good idea to go all the way down Emile Allais, for example, unless you're very experienced at riding them. Some reporters faced a long walk back to 1800!

SCHOOLS

ESF
Schools in all centres.
t 0479 900668 (Belle Plagne)
Oxygène (Plagne-Centre)
t 0479 090399
EL Pro (Belle-Plagne)
t 0479 091162
Reflex (Plagne 1800)
t 0479 091607
Magic in Motion (Plagne Centre)
t 0617 803311
Evolution 2 (Montchavin)
t 0479 078185

Classes (ESF prices)
6 half-days €172
Private lessons
€68 for 2hr for 1-2 people

black to red for 2003/04 – but a reporter comments that it is 'narrow and mogulled' and tricky for timid intermediates. A blue run carries on to Montchavin, but much of this is flattish, and hard work.

The Champagny sector has a couple of tough reds – Kamikaze and Hara-Kiri – leading from Grande Rochette. And the long blue cruise Bozelet has one surprisingly steep section. The long, sweeping Mont de la Guerre red, with 1250m/4,100ft vertical from Les Verdons to Champagny, is also a great run in good snow (a rare event).

FOR BEGINNERS
Excellent facilities for the novice

La Plagne is a good place to learn, with generally good snow and above-average facilities for beginners, especially children. Each of the main centres has nursery slopes on its doorstep. There's a free drag-lift in each resort as well. There are no long green runs to progress to, but no shortage of easy blues. The Plan Bois area above Les Coches has good gentle slopes. But the blue runs back into Plagne 1800 and Montchavin are difficult for novices.

CROSS-COUNTRY
Open and wooded trails

There are 85km/53 miles of prepared cross-country trails scattered around. The most beautiful of these are the 30km/19 miles of winding track set out in the sunny valley around Champagny-le-Haut. The north-facing areas have more wooded trails that link the various centres. It's best to have a car if you want to make the most of it all.

QUEUES
Main problems being sorted

La Plagne used to have some big bottlenecks. Recent lift improvements have eased some of the worst problems, and hopefully the upgrading of the Arpette chair towards Montchavin from Plagne-Bellecôte will reduce the queues for that. But reporters still complain of queues for the Roche de Mio gondola, despite its renovation, and there are still several lifts that can generate queues that you can't avoid, once you've descended to them – at Les Bauches for example, and in the Champagny sector. The gondola to the glacier is queue-prone when snow is poor lower down. Crowds on the pistes are now as much of a problem as lift queues, particularly above Plagne-Bellecôte and Belle-Plagne in the afternoon, and at Roche de Mio – 'very crowded, quite dangerous' comments a recent reporter, while another advises retreating to the quieter slopes of Montalbert, Les Coches or Montchavin.

MOUNTAIN RESTAURANTS
An enormous choice

Mountain restaurants are numerous, varied and crowded only in peak periods, as many people prefer to descend to one of the resorts – particularly Champagny or Montchavin/ Les Coches – at the end of the

La Plagne

331

CHILDREN

Nursery (Belle-Plagne)
t 0479 090668
Ages 18mnth to 3yr

Les P'tits Bonnets
(Plagne-Centre)
t 0479 900083
Ages from 10wk

Marie Christine
(Centre)
t 0479 091181
Ages 2 to 6

ESF nurseries and snow nurseries (ages from 2 or 3):
Aime: 0479 900475
Village and Soleil:
0479 090440
Belle: 0479 090668
Centre: 0479 090040
Bellecôte: 0479 091033
1800: 0479 090964

Ski schools
Children's classes are available up to 12 or 16 depending on the village: ESF Belle-Plagne 6 full days €184 (€245 during French February school holidays).

morning. Recommendations by readers include the Bergerie above Plagne-Villages, Crystal des Neiges, Carroley, Plan Bois, Arpette, Dou du Praz and the 'friendly' Plein Soleil on the Montchavin/Les Coches slopes. Two great rustic restaurants in which to hole up in poor weather for a long lunch of Savoyard dishes are the Chez Pat du Sauget, above Montchavin, and Au Bon Vieux Temps, just below Aime-la-Plagne. Reservations may be required at either. Chalet des Colosses above Plagne-Bellecôte and Chalets des Inversens at Roche de Mio ('fabulous views, good food') have been highly recommended. We love Rossa, at the top of the Champagny gondola – friendly staff, both table- and self-service, beautiful views over to Courchevel from the terrace and good, basic cooking. And reporters recommend the Roc des Blanchets at the top of the Borseliers chair-lift – 'fondue strongly recommended; great views'. The little Breton cafe at the bottom of the Quillis lift has been recommended as has the 'very French' Chalet du Friolin at Les Bauches. The Forperet, an old farm above Montalbert, is popular ('superb views, good value') and does good tartiflette.

SCHOOLS AND GUIDES
Better alternatives to ESF
Each centre has its own ESF school, offering classes for all abilities. But high-season classes can be much too large (up to 20) and good spoken English cannot be relied upon. In the past a reporter complained of a 'mainly French class of 14', with an instructor disinclined to speak English. Another received good tuition in her group but her previously keen young daughter 'was left in floods of tears, with her confidence completely destroyed'. But reports about private lessons are generally positive, and the school in

Les Coches has come in for praise. However, the consensus seems to be that the alternatives are preferable. The Oxygène school in Plagne-Centre has impressed reporters: 'Worked very hard with us, and was very patient.' 'Superb with our children, very friendly, made everything into a game.' We have had glowing reports on the El Pro school in Belle-Plagne ('good English, asked us what we wanted to do, strong focus on technique and safety'). We have also had good reports on Evolution 2 (based in Montchavin): 'One of the most positive and best value experiences I've had in a while.' Reflex is the newest school (based in 1800), and a reporter said of a private lesson, 'The best for several years; humorous, pitched at the right level to test and enjoy.' Antenne Handicap offers private lessons for skiers with any kind of disability.

FACILITIES FOR CHILDREN
Good choice
Children are well catered for with facilities in each of the villages. The nursery at Belle-Plagne is 'excellent, with good English spoken'. Be wary, however, of ESF classes (see 'Schools and Guides'). A Club Med at Aime-la-Plagne is one of their 'family' villages. Several UK chalet operators run childcare services.

STAYING THERE

HOW TO GO
Plenty of packages
For a resort that is very apartment-dominated, there is a surprising number of attractive chalets available through British tour operators. There are few hotels, but there are some attractive, simple 2-stars in the lower villages. There are two Club Meds. Accommodation in the lower resorts is described at the end of the chapter.

GETTING THERE

Air Geneva 149km/
93 miles (3½hr); Lyon
196km/122 miles
(3½hr); Chambéry
92km/57 miles
(2½hr).

Rail Aime (18km/
11 miles) and Bourg-
St-Maurice (35km/
22 miles) (Eurostar
service available);
frequent buses from
stations.

UK Representative
Erna Low Consultants
9 Reece Mews
London SW7 3HE
t 0870 750 6820
f 020 7589 9531
info@ernalow.co.uk
www.ernalow.co.uk

Phone numbers
From abroad use the
prefix +33 and omit
the initial '0' of the
phone number.

Chalets There's a large number
available – the majority are fairly
simple, small, and located in 1800. But
new chalets in the lower villages are
proving very popular now that La
Plagne is linked with Les Arcs.
Hotels There are very few, all of 2-star
or 3-star grading. For 2005/06 two new
3-stars are planned, one in Plagne-
Centre (the Araucaria) and another in
Belle-Plagne (the Carlina).
② **Balcons** (0479 557655) 3-star at
Belle-Plagne. Pool.
② **Eldorador** (0479 091209) Adequate
hotel in Belle-Plagne – 'Single rooms
tiny, food good but service chaotic.'
② **Terra Nova** (0479 557900) Big,
120-room 3-star in Plagne-Centre.
Self-catering This is the ultimate
apartment resort, but some are fairly
grotty. The best we have seen are the
Montagnettes in Belle-Plagne (spacious
and with good views) and the MGM
Les Hauts Bois apartments in Aime-la-
Plagne, 'highly recommended' by a
reader – 'friendly, not a bad size'. A
new 4-star residence, the Pelvoux, is
set to open in Plagne-Centre this year.

EATING OUT
A surprising amount of choice
Throughout the resort there is a good
range of casual restaurants including
pizzerias and traditional Savoyard
places serving raclette and fondue.

Reader recommendations in Plagne-
Centre include the Métairie ('the most
enjoyable we've encountered in the
Alps'), the Vega ('pricey but friendly
with excellent food') and the Refuge
('great meal in charming, rustic
atmosphere', 'very reasonable').

In Plagne-Villages, the Chevrette is
good for pizzas and steaks, the Grizzli
for Savoyard food. In Plagne 1800, the
Loup Garrou, the Petit Chaperon Rouge
and the Mama Mia pizzeria have been
praised as has the Loup Blanc – 'great
food, good service'. At Aime-la-Plagne,
Au Bon Vieux Temps (see Mountain
restaurants) is open in the evening and
the Soupe au Schuss, buried deep in
the main block, has 'exceptional' food.

In Plagne-Bellecôte, the Ferme and
Chalet des Colosses have been
recommended. In Belle-Plagne, so have
Pappagone pizzeria, the Chalet Maître

La Plagne

333

Selected chalets in La Plagne

FRANCE

334

ACTIVITIES

Indoor Sauna and solarium in most centres, squash (1800), fitness centres (Belle-Plagne, 1800, Centre, Bellecôte), library (Centre), climbing wall, cinemas, bowling

Outdoor Heated swimming pool (Bellecôte), bob-sleigh (La Roche), marked walks, paragliding, snowmobiles, ice-climbing, ice rink, hang-gliding, snow quad-bikes, paintball, snow-shoeing, dog-sledding

Kanter ('good value'), the Cloche ('good duck breast in bilberry sauce') and the Face Nord ('very friendly, lovely rabbit').

APRES-SKI
Bars, bars, bars

Though fairly quiet during low season, La Plagne has a wide range of après-ski, catering particularly for the younger crowd.

In Belle-Plagne, Mat's (an English 'pub') and the Cheyenne are the main bars. The Maître Kanter has been recommended. The King Café (with a massive TV and occasional live music) is the liveliest bar in Plagne-Centre. Plagne-Centre also has night skiing thanks to the floodlights on the Stade de Slalom. Plagne 1800 is fairly quiet at night – though the Mine (complete

with old train and mining artifacts) is an exception: 'Get there early for a seat. Quiz night and rock bands made for a very sociable week,' says a reporter. Another reader recommends upstairs at the Loup Garrou. The Lincoln Pub in Plagne-Soleil has also been recommended. Plagne-Bellecôte is very limited at night, with only one real bar – Showtime, which is popular for karaoke. But one reporter's group enjoyed the bowling, and another enjoyed the tubing. Aime-la-Plagne is also quiet.

Neal's and the Luna (Plagne-Centre), the Jet 73 (Plagne-Bellecôte) and the Saloon (Belle-Plagne) are the main discos. There are cinemas at Aime, Bellecôte and Plagne-Centre.

TRY THE OLYMPIC BOB-SLEIGH RUN – YOU CAN NOW DO IT SOLO

If the thrills of a day on the slopes aren't enough, you can round it off by having a go on the bob-sleigh run that was built specially for the 1992 Winter Olympics. Note that it is open on certain afternoons and early evenings only. The floodlit 1.5km/1 mile run drops 125m/410ft and has 19 bends. You can go in a proper four-man 'taxi-bob' (100 euros in 2004/05), a padded driverless bob-raft (33 euros), or, the latest craze, a mono-bob, 95 euros.

We tried the mono-bob and hurtled down solo at 100kph/62mph (in excess of the advertised speed!) lying almost horizontally – a great thrill, though we have to admit that we did close our eyes on a couple of the sharper bends (the pressure in the turns can be as high as 3g). Whether it is worth £70 to scare yourself silly is your shout! With the taxi-bob, you are one of three passengers wedged in a real four-man bob behind the driver. You reach a maximum advertised speed of 110kph/68mph. Most people find the bob raft's 80kph/50mph quite thrilling enough. Be sure your physical state is up to the ride. It's a good idea to book ahead – and there are minimum age limits. Additional insurance is available (holiday policies may not be valid).

Plagne-Centre: the
original part of La
Plagne. Its ugly 1960s
blocks and gloomy
indoor malls were
trendy 40 years
ago ↗

OT LA PLAGNE / D SCHMITT

OFF THE SLOPES
OK for the active

As well as the sports and fitness facilities, winter walks along marked trails are pleasant: 'There are enough walks to keep you busy for six days,' says one reporter. It's also easy to get up the mountain on the gondolas, which both have restaurants at the top. The Olympic bob-sleigh run is a popular evening activity (see feature box). Excursions are limited.

STAYING IN THE LOWER RESORTS
A good plan

Montchavin (1250m/4,100ft) is based on an old farming hamlet and has an attractive traffic-free centre. The cable-car link with Les Arcs starts from 300m/980ft above the village, and is reached by a fast chair. There are adequate shops, a kindergarten and a ski school. Reaching the La Plagne slopes involves a series of lifts; but the local slopes have quite a bit to offer – pretty, sheltered runs, well endowed with snowmaking, with nursery slopes at village level and up at Plan Bois. Those who venture further can return from Roche de Mio or the Bellecôte glacier (off-piste) in one lovely long swoop. The more usual way home involves some of the trickiest blue runs we have encountered. Après-ski is quiet, but the village doesn't lack atmosphere and has a couple of nice little bars, a nightclub, cinema and night skiing. The Bellecôte hotel (0479 078330) is convenient for the slopes.

Les Coches (1450m/4,760ft) is 2km/1 mile away and shares the same slopes. It is a sympathetically designed modern mini-resort that reporters have liked for its 'small, quiet and friendly' feel and its traffic-free centre. It has its own school and kindergarten. The Last One pub is good for après-ski, with a big screen TV and live bands. Poze (for pizza) and Taverne du Monchu are recommended for eating out. There's a shuttle to the cinema in Montchavin.

Montalbert (1350m/4,430ft) is a traditional but much expanded village with quicker access into the main area – though it's a long way from here across to the Bellecôte glacier or the Les Arcs link. The local slopes are easy and wooded – a useful insurance against bad visibility. The Aigle Rouge (0479 555105) is a simple hotel.

Champagny-en-Vanoise (1250m/4,100ft) is a charming village in a pretty, wooded setting, with its modern expansion done sensitively. It is at the opposite end of the slopes from the link to Les Arcs but well placed for an outing by taxi or car to Courchevel (or the beautiful Vanoise national park, with its 500km/310 miles of marked walking paths). Given good snow, there are lovely runs home (though a reporter doesn't recommend them for near-beginners). There are several hotels, of which the two best are both Logis de France. The Glières (0479 550552) is a rustic old hotel with varied rooms, a friendly welcome and good food. The Ancolie (0479 550500) is smarter, with modern facilities (recommended by a 2004 reporter). The village is quiet in the evenings but the restaurant Poya is highly rated again this year for a 'terrific atmosphere and traditional dishes at a good price'. Good views too. An artificial ice-climbing site in Champagny-le-Haut opened in a couple of seasons ago (25 euros for a two hour introduction, including equipment).

Portes du Soleil

Low altitude cross-border cruising

The Portes du Soleil vies with the Trois Vallées for the title of World's Largest Ski Area, but its slopes are very different from those of Méribel, Courchevel, Val-Thorens and neighbours. The Portes du Soleil's slopes are spread out over a large area, and not all are linked – but most are part of an extensive circuit straddling the French-Swiss border. You can travel the circuit in either direction, with a short bus-ride needed at Châtel. There are smaller areas to explore slightly off the main circuit. The runs are great for keen intermediates who like to travel long distances and through different resorts. There are few of the tightly packed networks of runs that encourage you to stay put in one area – though there are exceptions in one or two places. The area also has some nice rustic mountain restaurants, serving good food in pleasant, sunny settings.

The lifts throughout the area have been improved in recent years, with several new high-speed chair-lifts eliminating some bad bottlenecks – though there are still plenty of drags and slow chairs. But the slopes are low by French standards, with top heights in the range 2000m to 2300m (6,560ft to 7,550ft), and good snow is far from assured (though snowmaking has been expanded in recent years). When the snow is good you can have a great time racing all over the circuit. But the slopes can get very crowded, especially at weekends and in the Avoriaz area.

Purpose-built **Avoriaz** has the most snow-sure slopes and is especially good for families, with a big snow-

On the Swiss side of the main circuit are broad, open snowfields – in the bottom of the bowl here is Les Crozets →

Those Swiss snowfields get tough at the top, though – in the distance is the infamous Swiss Wall, more notable for its length and big moguls than extreme steepness ↓

garden right in the heart of the car-free village. And it is good for snowboarders and freestylers, with three terrain-parks and now snow-cross areas.

The other French resort on the main circuit is **Châtel**. Given good snow, it has some of the best runs in the area – though they are mostly quite short. It is an old and quite characterful village, but traffic is a nuisance at times. It has some good beginner areas – at resort level and up the mountain.

Morzine is close to Avoriaz. It is linked by lift but there's no piste all the way back to town. It's a summer as well as a winter resort – a pleasant, bustling little town with good shops and restaurants, busy traffic and long walks to the lifts from much of the accommodation – countered by increasing use of hotel minibuses. The local slopes are extensive, and linked to those of the slightly higher, quieter, traditional village of Les Gets. But they are low, and good snow is certainly not assured. You can use Morzine as a base to ski the main Portes du Soleil circuit, but it's not ideal. Linked **Les Gets** is another attractive family resort, at slightly higher altitude; it is even further off the main circuit, and if skiing that circuit is a priority you are better off elsewhere – unless you have a car to drive to Ardent's gondola.

On the Swiss side, **Champéry** is a classic, charming Swiss village – but again just off the main circuit. You have to take a cable-car down from the main slopes as well as up to them – or, if there is enough snow, take a piste that ends out of town and then ride a bus.

Champoussin and **Les Crosets** are purpose-built mini-resorts set on the very extensive open slopes between Champéry and Morgins, with fairly direct links over to Avoriaz. **Morgins**, in contrast to Champéry, has excellent local slopes – but they are low and the linking runs from Châtel are very sunny and prone to poor conditions or even closure. Its more serious local runs on the Swiss side are enjoyable and prettily wooded, but they are also limited in extent.

On a spur off the main circuit are the slopes above **Torgon** in Switzerland (with splendid views over Lake Geneva). This area can be reached from above Châtel and is usually quiet even when the rest of the circuit is packed. Almost linked, too, is **La Chapelle d'Abondance** in France – down the valley from Châtel.

SHOWPIX / CHRIS GILL

Puy-St-Vincent

Underrated small modern resort with some serious slopes

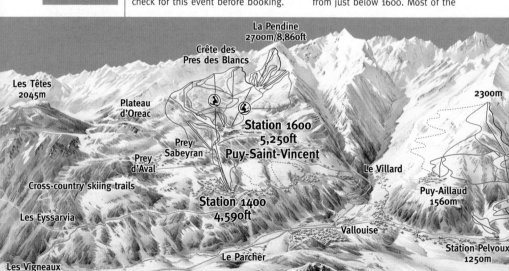

338

COSTS

① ② ③ ④ ⑤ ⑥

RATINGS

The slopes
Fast lifts	*
Snow	***
Extent	**
Expert	***
Intermediate	***
Beginner	***
Convenience	*****
Queues	***
Mountain restaurants	***

The rest
Scenery	***
Resort charm	**
Off-slope	*

REPORTS WANTED

Recently we have had few reports on this resort. If you go there, please do send us a report.

The best reports earn a copy of the next edition, and can lead to free lift passes in future. See page 10.

+ Mostly convenient, purpose-built resort that isn't too hideous
+ Good variety of slopes with challenges for all abilities
+ Low prices by resort standards
+ Friendly locals
+ Some great cross-country routes

– Slopes very limited in extent
– Upper village has only apartment-based accommodation
– Huge queues in French holidays
– Lots of slow old lifts
– Limited après-ski/restaurants
– Not a lot to do off the slopes

Puy-St-Vincent's ski area may be limited, but we found ourselves liking it more than we expected before we went. It offers a decent vertical and a lot of variety, including a bit of steep stuff. Provided you pick your spot with care, it makes an attractive choice for a family not hungry for piste miles.

THE RESORT

Puy-St-Vincent proper is an old mountain village. The modern resort of PSV is a two-part affair – the minor part, Station 1400, is just along the mountainside from PSV proper at 1400m/4,590ft; the major part, Station 1600, is a few hairpins (or a chair-lift ride) further up (yes, at 1600m/5,250ft), and there are buildings in various styles scattered around the hillside. Compact it may be, but 1600 is not perfectly laid out; depending on where you stay, beware walks to the lifts. We and our reporters have found PSV friendly ('even the lift operators').

Some 2005 holidays were spoilt by the drunken antics of 800 French dental students. Get your operator to check for this event before booking.

THE MOUNTAINS

Within its small area, PSV packs in a lot of variety, with runs from green to black that justify their gradings.
Slopes There are gentle slopes between the two villages, but most of the runs are above 1600. A fast quad goes up to the tree line at around 2000m/6,560ft. Entertaining red runs go back down, and a green takes a less direct route. The main higher lift is a long chair to 2700m/8,860ft, serving excellent open slopes of red and genuine black steepness. The shorter Rocher Noir drag serves another steep slope, but also accesses splendid cruising runs that curl around the eastern edge of the area. These runs are also reached by a fast quad chair from just below 1600. Most of the

KEY FACTS

Resort	1400-1600m
	4,590-5,250ft
Slopes	1250-2700m
	4,100-8,860ft
Lifts	15
Pistes	60km
	37 miles
Green	16%
Blue	37%
Red	41%
Black	6%
Snowmaking	10km
	6 miles

WEBSITES

For links to resort
sites, go to our own
new site at
www.wtss.co.uk

Phone numbers
From abroad use the
prefix +33 and omit
the initial '0' of the
phone number.

TOURIST OFFICE

t 0492 233580
courrier@puysaint
vincent.net
www.puysaintvincent.
com

OT PUY-ST-VINCENT

In winter, at least, the
white main blocks fit
in surprisingly well ➔

other lifts are drags. The six-day Galaxie pass covers a series of major resorts beyond Briançon. More to the point for most visitors, it also covers a day's skiing above the valley hamlet of Pelvoux, 10 minutes' drive away. This area has blue, red and black runs, often used for race training, and a vertical of over 1000m/3,280ft served by a chair and a drag.

Terrain-parks There is a floodlit terrain-park with half-pipe at 1600.

Snow reliability The slopes face north-east and are reasonably reliable for snow. Snowmaking has increased and now covers one run down to 1400 and several above 1600.

Experts The black runs are short but genuinely black, and are 'totally ungroomed, with serious moguls'. There are off-piste routes to be tackled with guidance. There are itinéraires outside the piste network, including one to the valley.

Intermediates Size apart, it's a good area for those who like a challenge – but there aren't many very easy runs.

Beginners Beginners should be happy on either of the nursery slopes, and on the long green from 2000m/6,560ft.

Snowboarding Boarders are not allowed on the Rocher Noir drag-lift.

Cross-country There are 30km/19 miles of cross-country trails, including some splendid routes between 1400m and 1700m (4,590ft and 5,575ft), ranging from green to black difficulty.

Queues One reporter suggests avoiding all French school holidays, as 'the lifts can't cope', leading to 'awful' queues. At other times, no problems.

Mountain restaurants There is a modern but pleasantly woody restaurant at mid-mountain, but in good weather the sunny terraces down at 1600 are the natural choice.

Schools and guides You have a choice of French and International ski schools, and a British tour operator, Snowbizz, has its own school, which a recent reader found 'excellent'; it provides free guiding in the afternoons, as well as 'good instruction' in 'great English' and in small groups.

Facilities for children There are nurseries taking children from 18 months in both villages, and both schools run ski kindergartens.

STAYING THERE

How to go A number of UK operators now offer accommodation here.

Hotels There are three cheap hotels in 1400, but none in 1600.

Self-catering 1600 consists entirely of apartments, and there are more in 1400. The cheaper apartments may be rather cramped.

Eating out The bar-restaurants serve 'a rather monotonous range of dishes'.

Après-ski Après-ski amounts to a few bar-restaurants in each village.

Off the slopes There are 30km/19 miles of walking trails. Paragliding, dog-sled rides, floodlit toboganing and outdoor skating are available. The cinema shows English-speaking films.

Risoul

Villagey modern resort in an attractive setting – and a big shared area

COSTS

①②③④⑤⑥

RATINGS

The slopes
Fast lifts	*
Snow	***
Extent	***
Expert	**
Intermediate	****
Beginner	****
Convenience	****
Queues	****
Mountain restaurants	***

The rest
Scenery	***
Resort charm	**
Off-slope	*

NEWS

The six-seat Peyrol chair replaced twin drag-lifts last season, greatly improving the journey up from Ste-Marie to La Mayt.

For 2005/06 the Peyrefolle drag-lift in the Risoul sector is due to be replaced by a chair.

There is also a plan to replace the Sibières drag-lift at Vars-les-Claux with a fast chair.

+ One of the more attractive and convenient purpose-built resorts

+ Scenic slopes linked with Vars add up to a fair-sized area

+ High resort, reasonably snow-sure

+ Good resort for beginners, early intermediates and families

+ Plenty of good-value places to eat

− Not many modern lifts – lots of long drag-lifts

− Not too much to challenge expert skiers and boarders

− Long airport transfers

− Little to do off the slopes

Slowly but surely the international market is waking up to the merits of the southern French Alps. Were they nearer Geneva, Risoul and its linked neighbour Vars would be as well known as Les Arcs and Flaine – the village of Risoul is more attractive than either.

THE RESORT

Risoul, purpose-built in the late 1970s, is a quiet, apartment-based resort, popular with families. Set among the trees, with excellent views over the Ecrins national park, it is made up of wood-clad buildings – mostly bulky, but with some concessions to traditional style. It has a busy little main street that, surprisingly, is very far from traffic-free. But the village meets the mountain in classic style with sunny restaurant terraces facing the slopes. Reporters have commented on the friendliness of the natives. The village does not offer many resort amenities. Airport transfers (usually from Turin) can take four hours.

THE MOUNTAINS

Together with neighbouring Vars, the area amounts to one of the biggest domains in the southern French Alps – marketed as the Forêt Blanche.
Slopes The slopes, mainly north-facing, spread over several minor peaks and bowls, and connect with the sunnier slopes of neighbouring Vars via the Pointe de Razis and the lower Col des Saluces. The upper slopes are open, but those back to Risoul are prettily wooded, and good for bad-weather days. Improvements in the lift system mean that the link can now be made in both directions without using drag-lifts. But the system as a whole still has too many long and steep drag-lifts. Piste grooming is reportedly poor, and the gradings are unreliable.

Terrain-parks There are two good terrain-parks – with half-pipes, boarder-cross, hand-rail and big air – one near the base, the other high-up.
Snow reliability Risoul's slopes are all above 1850m/6,070ft and mostly north-facing, so despite its southerly position snow reliability is reasonably good. Snowmaking is fairly extensive and is being extended. Visitors recommend going over to the east-facing Vars slopes for the morning sun, and returning to Risoul in the afternoon.
Experts The pistes in general do not offer much to interest experts. However, Risoul's main top stations access a couple of steepish descents. And there are some good off-piste opportunities if you take a guide.
Intermediates The whole area is best suited to intermediates, with some good reds and blues in both sectors. Almost all Risoul's runs return to the village, making it difficult to get lost.
Beginners Risoul's local area boasts some good, convenient, nursery slopes with a free lift, and a lot of easy longer pistes to move on to.
Snowboarding There is a lot of good free-riding to be done throughout the area, although beginners might not like the large proportion of drag-lifts. There are weekly competitions.
Cross-country There are 45km/28 miles of cross-country trails in the whole domain. A trail through the Peyrol forest links the two resorts together.
Queues Outside French school holidays, the slopes are impressively quiet. There may be a wait to get back from Vars at the end of the day.

KEY FACTS

Resort	1850m
	6,070ft

For the entire Forêt Blanche ski area

Slopes	1660-2750m
	5,450-9,020ft
Lifts	57
Pistes	180km
	112 miles
Green	16%
Blue	38%
Red	36%
Black	10%
Snowmaking	29km
	18 miles

Mountain restaurants Most people return to the village terraces, but the mountain restaurants have increased in quantity and quality. Snack Attack, near the Forêt Blanche apartments pleased a recent visitor. The newish Tetras is a stylish chalet and the Refuge de Valbel is recommended.
Schools and guides We have had mainly positive reports on the ESF and Internationale schools. However some older beginners in 2005 gave up on their class after three days – 'if you were a little slow you got ignored'.
Facilities for children Risoul is very much a family resort. It provides an all-day nursery for children over six months. Both ski schools operate ski kindergartens, slightly above the village, reached by a child-friendly lift. One parent reckons many other drags have a dangerous 'whiplash' effect.

STAYING THERE

How to go Most visitors stay in self-catering apartments, but there are a few hotels and more chalets are becoming available from UK operators. A 2005 reporter was very impressed with Crystal's club hotel Le Morgan, although it could be very noisy.
Hotels The Chardon Bleu (0492 460727) is handy for the slopes. You can also stay overnight at the Tetras mountain refuge (0492 460983) at 2000m/6,560ft.
Self-catering The Constellation Forêt Blanche apartments, although small, are said to be 'in an excellent position, well-equipped and pristine'; the Bételgeuse and Pégase are new.
Eating out There's plenty of choice for

eating out, from pizza to good French food, and it's mostly good value – the Ecureuil ('very friendly, excellent food, good prices') is highly recommended this year, as is the 'excellent' Chalet.
Après-ski Après-ski in the centre is reportedly now 'very lively' and goes on through the night, with half a dozen 'extremely friendly' bars and three clubs to move between. The best bars are apparently, the Place, 'noisy and fun', and the 'trendy' Caribbean-themed Babao. For a quieter drink, try the Chalet or the Eterlou.
Off the slopes There is little to do; excursions to Briançon are possible.

Vars 1850m/6,070ft

THE RESORT
Vars includes several small, old villages on or near the road running southwards towards the 2110m/6,920ft Col de Vars. But for winter visitors it mainly consists of purpose-built Vars-les-Claux, higher up the road. The resort has convenience and reasonable prices in common with Risoul, but is bigger and has far more in the way of amenities. There are a lot of block-like apartments, but Vars-les-Claux is not a complete eyesore, thanks mainly to surrounding woods. There are two centres: the original, geographical one – where the main gondola starts – has most of the accommodation and shopping; Point Show is a collection of bars and shops, 10 minutes' walk away at another main lift station.

Vars-Ste-Marie makes a more attractive base now that fast chairs take you to the top of La Mayt.

Risoul has the classic 'front de neige' of a French purpose-built resort →

SNOWPIX.COM / CHRIS GILL

THE MOUNTAINS

There are slopes on both sides of the village, linked by pistes and by chair-lift at the lower end of Les Claux. Lifts also run up from both sides of Ste-Marie, lower down the mountain.

Slopes The wooded, west-facing Peynier area is the smaller sector, and reaches only 2275m/7,460ft – though there are good long descents down to Les Claux and Ste-Marie. The main slopes are in an east-facing bowl beneath the Pic de Chabrières, with direct links to the Risoul slopes at the top and at the Col des Saluces. There's a speed-skiing course at the top (to have a go, ask the ski school). Beneath it are easy runs, open at the top but descending into trees.

Terrain-parks There's a terrain-park above Les Claux.

Snow reliability The main slopes get the morning sun, and are centred at around 2000m/6,560ft, so snow reliability is not as good as in Risoul, but snowmaking is widespread.

Experts There is little of challenge for experts, though the Crête de Chabrières top section accesses some off-piste, an unpisted route and a tricky couloir at Col de Crevoux. The Olympic red run from the top of La Mayt down to Ste-Marie is a respectable 920m/3,020ft vertical.

Intermediates Most of the area is fine for intermediates, with a good mixture of comfortable reds and easy blues, particularly in the main bowl.

Beginners There is a nursery area close to central Vars, with lots of 'graduation' runs throughout the area. Quick learners will be able to get over to Risoul by the end of the week.

Snowboarding There is good free-riding to be done throughout the area, although beginners might find the number of drag-lifts a problem.

Cross-country There are 25km/16 miles of trails in Vars itself. Some start at the edge of town, but those above Ste-Marie are more extensive.

Queues Queues are rare outside the French holidays, and even then Vars is not overrun as some family resorts are.

Mountain restaurants There are several in both sectors, but a lot of people head back to the villages for lunch. The Cassette, at the bottom of the Mayt chair, 'delighted' a 2005 visitor.

Schools and guides Lack of English speaking has been a problem.

Facilities for children The ski school runs a nursery for children from two years old. There is also a ski kindergarten.

STAYING THERE

How to go There are a few small hotels, but Les Claux is dominated by apartment accommodation.

Hotels The Caribou (0492 465043) is the smartest of the hotels and has a pool. The Ecureuil (0492 465072) is an attractive, modern chalet (no restaurant). There are more hotels in the lower villages, including Ste-Marie.

Eating out The range of restaurants is impressive, with good-value pizzerias, crêperies and fondue places. A 2005 reporter says the Taverne du Torrent is 'excellent with reasonable prices' and found the food at Chez Plumot to be 'truly haute cuisine'.

Après-ski Après-ski is animated at tea-time, less so after dinner – except at weekends when the discos warm up.

Off the slopes The amenities are rather disappointing, given the size of Vars: 35km/22 miles of walking paths, a cinema and an ice rink – and that's it.

La Rosière

Pop over to Italy from the sunniest slopes in the Tarentaise

COSTS

① ② ③ ④ ⑤ ⑥

RATINGS

The slopes
Fast lifts	**
Snow	***
Extent	***
Expert	**
Intermediate	***
Beginner	*****
Convenience	***
Queues	***
Mountain restaurants	*

The rest
Scenery	***
Resort charm	***
Off-slope	*

NEWS

For 2004/05 two six-packs were installed, replacing the drag-lift at Les Eucherts and the main chair out of the village. Both chairs will now be open to pedestrians, with paths prepared at the top.

For 2005/06 new MGM apartments are planned to open at Les Eucherts.

KEY FACTS

Resort	1850m
	6,070ft

Espace San Bernardo	
Slopes	1175-2610m
	3,850-8,560ft
Lifts	37
Pistes	150km
	93 miles
Green	9%
Blue	36%
Red	40%
Black	15%
Snowmaking	
	275 guns

For La Rosière only	
Slopes	1175-2385m
	3,850-7,820ft
Lifts	20
Pistes	47km
	29 miles

➕ Attractive purpose-built resort with glorious views towards Les Arcs

➕ Fair-sized area of slopes shared with La Thuile in Italy

➕ Sunny home slopes

➕ Heli-skiing over the border in Italy

➕ Good nursery slope

➕ Gets big dumps of snow when storms sock in from the west, but...

➖ Winds can close lift links with Italy

➖ Snow affected by sun in late season

➖ Lots of slow old lifts

➖ Few on-piste challenges for experts

➖ One run is much like another – though La Thuile is more varied

➖ Limited après-ski

➖ Few off-slope diversions

Like Montgenèvre, a long way to the south, La Rosière enjoys a position on the watershed with Italy that brings the twin attractions of big dumps of snow and access to cheap vino rosso. The former is crucial: given the sunny orientation of the slopes – very unusual in a modern French resort – average snowfalls wouldn't do the trick. The Chianti is less significant, because there are few attractive restaurants in which to consume it (see La Thuile chapter).

THE RESORT

La Rosière has been built in attractive, traditional chalet style beside the road that zigzags its way up from Bourg-St-Maurice to the Petit-St-Bernard pass to Italy (closed in winter). It's a quiet place with a few shops and friendly locals; don't expect lively nightlife. The most convenient accommodation is in the main village near the lifts, or just below, in Le Gollet or Vieux Village. Growth continues, notably by the second main lift at Les Eucherts – including some new upmarket apartments from MGM.

THE MOUNTAINS

La Rosière and La Thuile in Italy share a big area of slopes, now called Espace San Bernardo. La Rosière's sunny home slopes are south-facing with great views over the valley to Les Arcs and La Plagne. The link with Italy's slopes is prone to closure because of high winds or heavy snow.

Slopes Two fast chairs out of the village take you into the heart of the slopes, from where a series of drags and chairs, spread across the mountain, takes you up to Col de la Traversette. From there, you can get over the ridge and to the lifts, which link with Italy at Belvedere.

Terrain-parks There is a terrain-park served by the Poletta drag lift, just above the village centre.

Snow reliability Surprisingly good, despite its south-facing direction (you may find it has much more snow than the Italian side).

Experts Other than excellent heli-skiing from just over the Italian border (see La Thuile) and guided off-piste, there is little excitement for experts. The steepest terrain is on the lowest slopes, down the Marcassin run to Le

343

FRANCE

344

Vaz and down the Ecudets and Eterlou runs close to the village.

Intermediates La Rosière would be nothing special on its own, but there's a fair amount to explore if you take into account La Thuile. The main part of La Rosière's area is a broad open mountainside offering straightforward red and blue pistes. More interesting is the Fontaine Froide red, dropping 750m vertical through woods to the Ecudets chair, far below the village.

The red over the ridge from Col de la Traversette has good snow and views, but is narrow along its top section. Weaker intermediates can avoid it by taking a chair down.

Beginners There are good nursery slopes and short lifts near the village and near Les Eucherts.

Snowboarding The long drag-lift to Italy means the resort is best-suited to beginners content to stay on the La Rosière side.

Cross-country There are 8km/5 miles of trails near the altiport.

Queues Queues are not usually a problem. Morning queues to get out of

the village should be a thing of the past now that the lift is a six-pack.

Mountain restaurants There is little choice unless, like most people, you descend to the village for lunch. A reporter recommends the self-service Plan du Repos for its 'friendly staff, huge pasta portions and lovely salads'. The San Bernardo on the border is recommended. In the village, reporters recommend the Relais du Petit St Bernard – 'good value, wide menu choice' – and the P'tit Relais – 'lots of choice'.

Schools and guides There are three schools. Evolution 2 is praised again in 2005 for its 'small groups and friendly instructors', who are especially good with children. Reports of the ESF have been less favourable: 'large groups' and 'insufficient supervision of small children'.

Facilities for children Club des Galopins has a snow garden, and British tour operators Esprit and Thomson run nurseries.

STAYING THERE

How to go A number of British tour operators now offer packages here.

Hotels There are a few 2-star hotels in the village, and more in the valley.

Chalets There are now several companies operating chalets here.

Self-catering You can book through the resort's central booking service. Les Balcons at Les Eucherts offers smart accommodation for larger groups in spacious apartments, some with wood-burning stoves and all with hot-tubs.

Eating out The Chalet, Yéti, L'Oustal, Le Plein Soleil and the 'charming' Ancolie have all been recommended.

Après-ski Après-ski is limited to a couple of bars in the village.

Off the slopes There are scenic flights and walks, an indoor climbing wall and a cinema. The ski schools offer paragliding and organise various non-skiing expeditions on foot. Children might enjoy a visit to see the St Bernard dogs. Mountain restaurants are essentially inaccessible on foot.

Staying up the mountain The Hotel San Bernardo, on the border and reachable only on skis, provided a memorable two-night stay for an adventurous recent reporter – 'Simple, comfortable and peaceful', with a 'spectacular collection of grappas'.

La Thuile

Col du Petit Saint Bernard 2190m

Belvedere 2610m/8,560ft

Le Roc Noir 2400m

Col de la Traversette 2385m

Le Gollet

1175m

Les Eucherts

La Rosière 1850m/6,070ft

Le Vaz 1500m

Samoëns

The prettiest base for the extensive and varied Grand Massif

COSTS

① ② ③ ④ ⑤ ⑥

RATINGS

The slopes

Fast lifts	**
Snow	***
Extent	****
Expert	****
Intermediate	*****
Beginner	**
Convenience	*
Queues	****
Mountain restaurants	**

The rest

Scenery	****
Resort charm	****
Off-slope	***

NEWS

For 2003/04 a gondola from village level was at last built, speeding access to Samoëns 1600.

SNOWPIX.COM / CHRIS GILL

Cheese is a speciality at the Wednesday morning market ↓

- ✚ Lovely historic village, with traffic-free centre and weekly market
- ✚ Lift into big, varied area shared with Flaine and Les Carroz, with slopes to suit everyone
- ✚ Glorious views from top heights
- ✚ Very close to Geneva, but ...

- ▬ Weekends can be busy as a result
- ▬ Access lift is way outside the village
- ▬ Slow lifts above mid-mountain
- ▬ Not ideal for beginners
- ▬ Traffic around the central car-free area needs better control
- ▬ Nightlife not a highlight

The impressive Grand Massif area is chiefly associated in Britain with high, purpose-built, apartment-dominated Flaine; but the network can also be accessed from much more attractive traditional villages – Les Carroz, Morillon and Samoëns. And the cutest of these, if not the most convenient, is Samoëns.

THE RESORT

Samoëns is the only resort in France to be listed as a 'Monument Historique' – once a thriving centre for stone-masons, with their work much in evidence. There is a small traffic-free centre of narrow streets lined by appealing food shops, and nearby a pretty square (sadly not traffic-free) with a stone fountain, an ancient linden tree, a fine church and other medieval buildings. Also nearby is a nominally car-free area of modern resort development. Despite recent growth, the village as a whole retains the feel of 'real' rural France. There is a good weekly market.

The long-awaited eight-seat gondola from village level was opened in 2003, supposedly transforming Samoëns into a proper ski resort. Well, not quite. The base station is a drive or a bus-ride from most accommodation – and yet there is no run back to it. For non-beginners with a car, the slow old gondola at Vercland is still worth considering: only a couple of minutes' drive up the hill, it is now queue-free, and you can ski back to the base.

THE MOUNTAINS

Most of the skiing directly above Samoëns is on open slopes beneath Tête des Saix, from which point there are links to the next-door Morillon sector (see end of this chapter) and the slightly more distant sectors of Les Carroz and Flaine (both covered in the Flaine chapter).

Slopes The two gondolas from the valley arrive at separate points on the 'hilly plateau' of Samoëns 1600. This mini-resort is also reachable by road. Tête des Saix, point of departure for the other Grand Massif resorts, is reached by parallel chair-lifts in two stages. These slow lifts are a real drawback to Samoëns as a base: a couple of six-packs are urgently needed here. From the Tête you can descend to Morillon or Les Carroz; one more (fast) chair is needed for access to the Flaine bowl.

Terrain-parks There is a terrain-park beside one of the chairs above 1600, and another above Morillon 1100.

Snow reliability The slopes above Samoëns face due north, so above 1600 snow is fairly reliable. There is snowmaking around 1600.

Experts The upper pistes on Tête des Saix are among the most testing in the Grand Massif, and there is lots of good off-piste in the valleys and bowls between Samoëns and Flaine.

Intermediates If you can put up with the slow lifts mentioned above, Samoëns makes a perfectly satisfactory base for all but the most timid intermediates, who might be better off in Morillon. From Tête des Saix you

PISTE MAP

Samoëns is covered
on the Flaine map

KEY FACTS

| Resort | 720-1600m |
| | 2,360-5,250ft |

Grand Massif ski area
(Samoëns and all
linked resorts)

Slopes	700-2480m
	2,300-8,140ft
Lifts	78
Pistes	265km
	165 miles
Green	11%
Blue	40%
Red	38%
Black	11%
Snowmaking	25%

Massif ski area
(excluding Flaine)

Slopes	700-2120m
	2,300-6,700ft
Lifts	54
Pistes	145km
	90 miles

Phone numbers
From abroad use the
prefix +33 and omit
the initial '0' of the
phone number.

TOURIST OFFICES

Samoëns
t 0450 344028
infos@samoens.com
www.samoens.com

Morillon
t 0450 901576
info@ot-morillon.fr
www.ot-morillon.fr

have a wide choice of good long runs
in various directions. In good snow the
valley runs to Vercland are highly
enjoyable – the black is very little
steeper than the red, and used less.

Beginners Beginners must buy a pass
(there is a special one at about 15
euros a day) and go up to 1600. There
are snow-sure, gentle slopes for
absolute beginners up there – excellent
when not crowded at peak times – but
no long green runs to progress to.
Morillon or Flaine are better bets.

Snowboarding Beware drag-lifts on the
nursery slopes.

Cross-country There are trails on the
flat valley floor around Samoëns, and
more challenging ones up the valley
beyond Sixt and up at Col de Joux
Plane (1700m/5,580ft).

Queues We have no reports of
particular problems in this sector.

Mountain restaurants There are places
to eat at Samoëns 1600, but the most
captivating places are above Morillon
and Les Carroz – see Flaine chapter.

Schools and guides There is a sizeable
branch of the ESF, on which we lack
reports.

Facilities for children There is a newly
built kindergarten, and ski lessons are
available.

STAYING THERE

How to go A few specialist operators
now include Samoëns in their
programmes.

Hotels We and readers have enjoyed
the Neige et Roc (0450 344072), a
walk from the centre – 'friendly staff,
excellent food, big spa area'. Avoid the
annexe, though. The central hotel les
Glaciers and the Letenires B&B are
recommended.

Chalets We don't know of any.

Self-catering Apartments are available

locally and through UK operators and
agencies.

Eating out The Table de Fifine is a
short drive from the centre, but a fine
spot – beautiful wooden interior,
satisfying food. A reporter recommends
the La Louisiane for its wood-oven
pizzas and alcoholic ice creams.
Visitors in 2005 enjoyed the 'excellent'
Relais Gourmand; earlier reports also
recommend the Pierrot des Neiges.

Après-ski There are several bars,
including an Irish pub, Covey's, rated
by an Irish reporter as 'authentic' –
even 'great craic' one night.

Off the slopes Samoëns offers quite a
range of activities. We enjoyed a highly
informative guided tour of the church
one evening. Snowmobiling up at
Samoëns 1600 is wilder and more
exciting than is usual in the Alps.
There is an outdoor, covered ice rink.

Morillon 700m/2,300ft

Morillon is a couple of miles down the
valley from Samoëns, at the foot of its
own branch of the Grand Massif lift
network. Not quite in the Samoëns
league but still a pretty, rustic village,
Morillon makes a good base, with an
efficient gondola from the upper
fringes of the village to the mid-
mountain mini-resort of Morillon 1100
(Les Esserts) – also reachable by road.
Up here there is a large and 'delightful'
ski kindergarten plus good slopes for
adult beginners – including a fabulous
long green run (Marvel) through the
forest, away from the lifts. There are
new apartments right on the piste up
here – but it's 'dead as a dodo in the
evenings', says a reporter. Back in the
village, the 'very friendly' hotel
Morillon, a short walk from the
gondola, is 'thoroughly recommended',
not least for its 'superb food'.

SNOWPIX.COM / CHRIS GILL

Serre-Chevalier

One of a kind, with a growing band of enthusiastic visitors

COSTS

①②③④⑤⑥

RATINGS

The slopes
Fast lifts	**
Snow	***
Extent	****
Expert	***
Intermediate	****
Beginner	****
Convenience	***
Queues	***
Mountain restaurants	***

The rest
Scenery	***
Resort charm	***
Off-slope	**

NEWS

Two new six-seat chairs are to be installed for 2005/06, replacing the Clos Gauthier chair above Fréjus and the Foret and Rouge drags above L'Aravet. Plans for a third six-pack, replacing the Grande Serre double chair above Grand Alpe, seem less certain.

The red Cucumelle run is to be remodelled. A new blue piste down to Chantemerle, parallel to the existing red and black, is planned.

MGM is apparently starting work on a new apartment block in Chantemerle this summer.

➕ Big, varied mountain, with something for everyone	➖ Serious crowds in central sectors in French holidays
➕ Interesting mixture of wooded runs and open bowls with lots of off-piste	➖ Despite current improvements, still too many slow, old lifts on upper mountain – some vicious drags
➕ One of the few big French areas based on old villages with character	➖ Busy road runs through the resort villages, with traffic jams at times
➕ Good-value and atmospheric old hotels, restaurants and chalets	➖ A lot of indiscriminate new building
➕ Lift pass covers days elsewhere	➖ Limited nightlife, especially in Le Monêtier and smaller hamlets
➕ Generally quiet slopes, but ...	➖ Few off-slope diversions

Serre-Chevalier is a big-league resort, but isn't well known internationally. It doesn't lend itself to marketing hype – the slopes are not super-high, the lifts are not super-efficient, the hotels are far from super-smooth. But we like it a lot: it's one of the few French resorts where you can find the ambience you might look for on a summer holiday – a sort of Provence in the snow, with lots of small, family-run hotels and restaurants housed in old stone buildings.

The slopes are likeable, too. They are split into different segments, so you get a real sensation of travel. What really sets the area apart from the French norm are the woodland runs, making Serre-Chevalier one of the best places to be when snow is falling or wind is blowing – though there are plenty of open runs, too.

The lift system, on the other hand, is far from likeable. For years we've been calling for an injection of six-packs to disperse high-season queues at mid-mountain. Happily, two or maybe three are going in as we speak, but more are needed.

347

THE RESORT

The resort is made up of a string of 13 villages set on a valley floor running roughly north-west to south-east, below the north-east-facing slopes of the mountain range that gives the resort its name. From the north-west – coming over the Col du Lautaret from Grenoble – the three main villages are Le Monêtier (or Serre-Che 1500), Villeneuve (1400) and Chantemerle (1350), spread over a distance of 8km/5 miles. Finally, at the extreme south-eastern end of the mountain, is Briançon (1200) – not a village but a town (the highest in France). Nine

smaller villages can be identified, and some give their names to the communes: Villeneuve is in the commune of La Salle les Alpes, for example. Confusing.

Serre-Chevalier is not a smart resort, in any sense. Although each of its parts is based on a simple old village, there is a lot of modern development, which ranges from brash to brutal, and even the older parts are roughly rustic rather than chocolate-box pretty. (A ban on corrugated iron roofs would help.) Because the resort is so spread out, the impact of cars and buses is difficult to escape, even if you're able to manage without them yourself. But

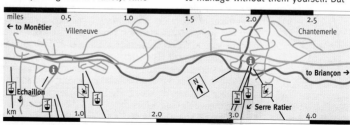

miles | 0.5 | 1.0 | 1.5 | 2.0 | 2.5
← to Monêtier | Villeneuve | | | | Chantemerle
| | | | | to Briançon →
Echaillon | | | | Serre Ratier |
km | 1.0 | 2.0 | 3.0 | 4.0

Villeneuve, its quiet main street lined by cosy bars, hotels and restaurants.

Not far down the valley, **Chantemerle** gives access to opposite ends of the mid-mountain plateau of Serre Ratier via a gondola and a cable-car, both with second stages above. Chantemerle has some tasteless modern buildings in the centre and along the main road. The old sector is a couple of minutes' walk from the lifts, with a lovely church and most of the small hotels, restaurants, bars and nightlife. However, a lot of accommodation is across the main road – 'Quite a long walk from the lifts,' says a weary visitor.

At the top of the valley, **Le Monêtier** has one main access lift – a fast quad chair to mid-mountain, reached from the village by bus or a steepish 10-minute walk, tricky when ice is around (though you can leave your boots at the lift base). Le Monêtier is the smallest, quietest and most unspoiled of the main villages (or 'deadly dull', to put it another way), with a bit of a Provençal feel to its narrow streets and little squares, and new building which is mostly in sympathetic style. Sadly, the through-road to Grenoble, which skirts the other villages, bisects Le Monêtier; pedestrians stroll about bravely, hoping the cars will avoid them.

Briançon has a gondola from right in the town to mid-mountain and on almost to the top. The area around the lift station has a wide selection of modern shops, bars, hotels and restaurants, but no character. In contrast, the 17th-century fortified upper quarter is a delight, with narrow cobbled streets and traditional restaurants, auberges and patisseries. Great views from the top, too.

Ski-buses, covered on the free guest card, circulate around each village and link all the villages and lift bases along the valley. But they finish quite early, and at least one reporter found the service inadequate; taxis aren't cheap.

A six-day area pass (or rather your receipt) covers a day in each of Les Deux-Alpes, Alpe-d'Huez, Puy-St-Vincent and the Milky Way. All of these outings are possible by public transport, but are more attractive to those with a car. If driving through France, you are likely to approach over the high Col du Lautaret, which required chains on our recent visit and is very occasionally closed because of avalanche danger.

Turin airport is closer than Lyon, with easier road access.

when blanketed by snow the older villages and hamlets do have an unpretentious charm, and we find the place as a whole easy to like. Reporters talk of 'wonderfully friendly people' who 'made us very welcome' – hardly the norm in France.

There are few luxury hotels or notably swanky restaurants; on the other hand, there are more hotels in the modestly priced Logis de France 'club' here than in any other ski resort. This is a family resort, which fills up (even more than most others) with French children in the February high season. You have been warned.

The heart of the resort is **Villeneuve**, which has two gondolas and a fast quad chair going up to widely separated points at mid-mountain. The central area of new development near the lifts is brutal and charmless. But not far away is the peaceful hamlet of Le Bez, which has a third gondola, and across the valley is the old stone village of

KEY FACTS

Resort	1350-1500m
	4,430-4,920ft
Slopes	1350-2735m
	4,430-8,970ft
Lifts	74
Pistes	250km
	155 miles
Green	17%
Blue	29%
Red	41%
Black	13%
Snowmaking	40km
	25 miles

LIFT PASSES

Grand Serre-Che
Covers all lifts in Briançon, Chantemerle, Villeneuve and Le Monêtier.

Beginners pass
No special pass

Main pass
1 day €33
6 days €160

Senior citizens
Over 65: 6 days €113
Over 75: free pass

Children
Under 12: 6 days €113
Under 6: free pass

Notes
Passes of six days or more give one day in each of Les Deux-Alpes, Alpe-d'Huez, Puy-St-Vincent and Voie Lactée (Milky Way). Reductions for families.

Alternative passes
Passes covering individual areas of Serre-Chevalier.

THE MOUNTAINS

Trees cover almost two-thirds of the mountain, providing some of France's best bad-weather terrain (we had a great day here despite the upper lifts all being closed by high winds). The Serre-Chevalier massif is not particularly dramatic, but from the peaks there are fine views of the Ecrins massif, the highest within France (ie not shared with Italy).

The trail map is supposed to have been improved, but it remains infuriatingly unclear and imprecise in places. Readers have found navigation is made even more challenging by 'atrocious' signposting and the tendency of runs to 'change colour halfway down'. We ourselves have found that the signposting at altitude is not up to the job when a storm socks in; take great care.

Piste classification is unreliable – many reds, in particular, could be classified blue, but there are occasional stiff blues, too.

THE SLOPES
Interestingly varied and pretty

Serre-Chevalier's 250km/155 miles of pistes are spread across four main sectors. The sector above **Villeneuve** is the most extensive, reaching back a good way into the mountains and spreading over four or five identifiable bowls. The main mid-station is Fréjus. This sector is reliably linked to the slightly smaller **Chantemerle** sector well below the tree line. The link from Chantemerle to **Briançon** is over a high, exposed col via a six-pack. The link between Villeneuve and **Le Monêtier** is liable to closure by high winds or avalanche

danger. Travelling from here towards Villeneuve involves a red run, so timid intermediates have to use the bus.

TERRAIN-PARKS
Fully featured

There are big airs in Briançon and near the Echaillon piste, a boarder-cross in Villeneuve and Chantemerle and a half-pipe in Villeneuve (though it's not always open), all with sound systems.

SNOW RELIABILITY
Good – especially upper slopes

Most slopes face north or north-east and so hold snow well, especially high up (there are lots of lifts starting above 2000m/6,560ft). The weather pattern is different from that of the northern Alps and even that of Les Deux-Alpes or Alpe-d'Huez, only a few miles to the west. Serre-Che can get good snow when there is a shortage elsewhere, and vice versa. There is snowmaking on long runs down to each village. Piste grooming is generally excellent.

FOR EXPERTS
Deep, not notably steep

There is plenty to amuse experts – except those wanting extreme steeps.

The broad black runs down to Villeneuve and Chantemerle are only just black in steepness, but they are fine runs with their gradient sustained over an impressive vertical of around 800m/2,620ft. One or the other may be closed for days on end for racing or training. The rather neglected Tabuc run, sweeping around the mountain away from the lifts to Le Monêtier, has a couple of genuinely steep pitches but is mainly a cruise; it makes a fine end to the day. For moguls, look higher up the mountain to the steeper slopes

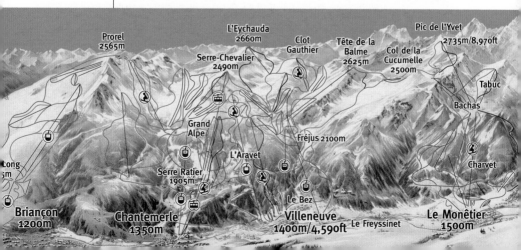

served by the two top lifts above Le Monêtier and the three above Villeneuve. The runs beside these lifts – on and off-piste – form a great playground in good snow. The more roundabout Isolée black is a reader's favourite – 'scenic and challenging' after a rather scary ridge start.

There are huge amounts of off-piste terrain throughout the area; on a recent visit we had a great morning in the trees above Villeneuve and Chantemerle. There are plenty of more serious off-piste expeditions including: Tête de Grand Pré to Villeneuve (a climb from Cucumelle); off the back of L'Eychauda to Puy-St-André (isolated, beautiful, taxi-ride home); L'Yret to Le Monêtier via Vallon de la Montagnolle; Tabuc (steep at the start, very beautiful). The experts' Mecca of La Grave is nearby. And the Compagnie des Guides runs heli-skiing excursions to Italy, not far away, where the practice is legal.

FOR INTERMEDIATES
Ski wherever you like
Serre-Chevalier's slopes ideally suit intermediates, who can buzz around without worrying about nasty surprises on the way. On the trail map red runs far outnumber blues – but most reds are at the easy end of the scale and the grooming is usually good, so even nervous intermediates shouldn't have problems with them.

There's plenty for more adventurous intermediates, though. Many runs are wide enough for a fast pace. Cucumelle on the edge of the Villeneuve sector is a favourite – a beautiful long red, away from the lifts, with a challenging initial section. The red runs off the little-used Aiguillette chair in the Chantemerle sector (which we dubbed the 'Lost Chair' on our last visit because it was so quiet while other areas were packed) are worth seeking out – quiet, enjoyable fast cruises. Aya and Clos Galliard at Le Monêtier and the wonderful long run from the top to the bottom of the gondola at Briançon (with great views of the town) are other favourites.

If the reds are starting to seem a bit tame, there is plenty more to progress to. Unless ice towards the bottom is a problem, the (often well-groomed) blacks on the lower mountain should be first on the agenda, and the bumpier ones higher up can be tackled if snow is good.

FOR BEGINNERS
All three areas OK
All three main villages have nursery areas (at Chantemerle the area is small, and you generally go up to Serre Ratier or Grand Alpe – both rated

boarding

Serre-Che is a snowboarding hot spot, popular with advanced boarders because of the off-piste, but it is not without problems for others. For beginners, local slopes are limited and drag-lifts must soon be faced; progression from the nursery slope up at Fréjus, for example, is tricky. The diverse pistes, with open and tree-lined runs, also suit intermediates, though there are some annoying flat sections – notably on the way to Le Monêtier – and descents to the valley can involve a choice between winding paths and unpleasantly steep runs. In some areas there are a lot of difficult-to-avoid and violent drag-lifts – one reporter's group stayed mostly in the Chantemerle sector, simply because they could cover a lot of ground using three major chair-lifts.

as good by a beginner reporter) and there are some easy high runs to progress to. Villeneuve has excellent green runs above Fréjus. Both sectors have green paths down from mid mountain. But they are narrow, and not enjoyable when the runs become rutted and others are speeding along. Le Monêtier's easy runs are at resort level, next to excellent nursery slopes, and beginners have recommended it for 'better snow and fewer people'. But progression to long runs here isn't so easy, and the link to Villeneuve involves the red Cucumelle run.

FOR CROSS-COUNTRY
Excellent if the snow is good
There are 35km/22 miles of tracks along the valley floor, mainly following the gurgling river between Le Monêtier and Villeneuve and going on up towards the Col du Lautaret.

QUEUES
Investment at last
A range of big lifts means there are few problems getting out of the valley. But the many old, slow lifts at altitude still cause queues, as well as slowing down the whole process of exploration. The new lifts going in this summer will help, but remaining bottlenecks include the slow and unreliable Balme chair on the way to Le Monêtier and the Fréjus chair above the Pontillas gondola. The Grande Serre chair to the peak of Serre-Chevalier may or may not be upgraded in time for this season.

More than most resorts, Serre-Chevalier seems to fill up with French families in the February holidays, producing serious mid-mountain queues, especially in the central sectors.

The lower slopes above Chantemerle, in particular, can get hideously crowded, particularly when snow conditions are poor and progress therefore slow – head for the Aiguillette chair in these circumstances (see 'For Intermediates').

MOUNTAIN RESTAURANTS
Choose carefully
Mountain restaurants are quite well distributed, but if lunch is an important part of your day, you need to plan it carefully.

The Villeneuve sector holds the aces. L'Echaillon, just below the the top of the Casse du Boeuf quad is a lofty chalet with open fire and a table-service section doing excellent food. Just above here, the Bivouac de la Casse. is another attractive chalet with both self-service and 'first-class' table-service (inside and out), recommended again by a 2005 reporter. Pi Maï in the hamlet of Fréjus, a fine retreat on a bad day, set a little way below the Fréjus lift station, is back in business once again and 'highly acclaimed'.

In the Chantemerle sector, the busy Soleil continues to please reporters – 'good food, sun trap' and 'excellent food for good prices' are comments this year. The Relais de Ratier is said to be 'cheaper than elsewhere' and has in the past been praised for 'excellent fresh-cooked food'.

In the Briançon sector, the 'attractive' Pra Long chalet at the gondola mid-station has great views, food in both table- and self-service sections is 'excellent', and self-service prices are 'very reasonable'. The little chalet just down from the top of Prorel has great views and is reasonably priced. Above Le Monêtier the choice is between the self-service Bachas at mid-mountain, 'ideal for those who want to get back on the slopes as soon as possible', and the cosy and 'friendly' Peyra Juana much lower down, which we and readers alike have enjoyed, although a 2005 visitor found it 'somewhat expensive'. Both get packed on bad-weather days.

SCHOOLS AND GUIDES
Nearly all good
We have received a number of reports on the Ecole de Ski Buissonnière over the years – most of them full of praise. But last year a couple of early-intermediate boarders report being put together with a couple of experts, with predictably distressing results.

EurekaSki, British-run by BASI instructors, gets consistently good reports. It was 'the main reason for returning to the resort' for some 2005 visitors, and they are going back in 2006. One reporter who took two private lessons 'learned more than I have previously in a week'. Classes with a maximum size of six range from beginner to free-ride masterclass. Skiers at all levels report good results. EurekaSki also offer special one-day Avalanche Awareness courses, including training on how to use transceivers and how to choose the safest routes off-piste, as well as some fun off-piste skiing.

CHILDREN

Les Schtroumpfs
t 0492 247095
Ages 6mnth upwards;
9am-5pm

Les Poussins
t 0492 244003
Ages 8mnth upwards;
9am-5pm

Les Eterlous
t 0492 244575
Ages 18mnth to 6yr
(6mnth to 6yr out of
school holidays);
9am-5pm

Le Toupidek
For children age 6 to
14 years.

Ski school
Snow gardens for
ages 3 to 5; from age
7 children can join ski
school classes (ESF 6
half-days €89).

We lack recent reports of group classes with the ESF, but a 2005 reporter was 'very concerned' on observing 'large groups' and 'terrified children'. Some 2005 visitors had private lessons and found that the 'instructors were very friendly and gave good advice'.

The Internationale school 'gave the impression of being rather more professional than the ESF'.

On our 2004 visit we had a great morning skiing off-piste with Bertrand Collet of Axesse ski school and guiding service (which specialises in off-piste and advanced techniques).

FACILITIES FOR CHILDREN
Facilities at each village
We have had no very recent reports, but the Ecole de Ski Buissonnière (see above) has been praised in the past, as has Les Schtroumpfs in Villeneuve.

There are quite extensive cross-country trails following the river along the valley floor, organised into eight loops – with plenty of provision for skating-style skiers as well as plodders ⬎

STAYING THERE

HOW TO GO
A good choice of packages
There's a wide choice of packages from UK tour operators, offering all kinds of accommodation.

Chalets Several operators offer chalets in the different parts of the resort. A 2005 visitor found ' imaginative' food and a 'friendly team' of staff at Inghams' club hotel Lièvre Blanc. Chez Bear is a wonderful conversion of an 18th-century farmhouse into a luxury chalet for 10 – remotely set above Briançon, but the owners will ferry you around in their minibus.

Hotels One of the features of this string of little villages is the range of attractive family-run hotels – many of them part of the Logis de France.
In Monêtier:
⑶ **Auberge de Choucas** (0492 244273) Smart, wood-clad rooms, and 'excellent, seven-course dinners in stone-vaulted restaurant – but mediocre breakfast and erratic service'.
⑵ **Europe** (0492 244003) Simple well-run Logis in heart of old village, with pleasant bar and 'very good' food.
⑵ **Alliey** (0492 244002) 'Excellent

Serre-Chevalier

GETTING THERE

Air Turin 108km/ 67 miles (1½hr); Grenoble 92km/ 57 miles (2hr); Lyon 208km/129 miles (3hr).

Rail Briançon (6km/ 4 miles); regular buses from station.

ACTIVITIES

Indoor Swimming pool, sauna, fitness centres, tennis, thermal baths, theatre, cinemas, bowling, libraries, bridge

Outdoor Ice rinks, swimming pool, paragliding, cleared paths, snow-shoeing, snowmobiling, ice-driving, ice-climbing, ski-joring

WEBSITES

For links to resort sites, go to our own new site at www.wtss.co.uk

Phone numbers From abroad use the prefix +33 and omit the initial '0' of the phone number.

TOURIST OFFICE

t 0492 249898 contact@ot-serrechevalier.fr www.serre-chevalier.com

rooms with an indoor/outdoor spa.' Our favourite places to eat (see Eating out).
In Villeneuve:
② **Christiania** (0492 247633) Civilised, family-run hotel on main road, crammed with ornaments.
② **Vieille Ferme** (0492 247644) Stylish conversion on the edge of the village.
② **Cimotel** (0492 247822) Modern and charmless, with good-sized rooms and 'excellent' food.
① **Chatelas** (0492 247474) Prettily decorated simple chalet by river.
In Chantemerle:
② **Plein Sud** (0492 241701) Modern; pool and sauna.
② **Boule de Neige** (0492 240016) Comfortable, friendly, in the old centre.
① **Ricelle** (0492 240019) Charming, but across the valley from the slopes in Villard-Laté. Good food.
Self-catering There are plenty of modern apartment blocks in Villeneuve, Briançon and Chantemerle. Few have charm.

EATING OUT
Unpretentious and traditional
In Le Monêtier, there are several good hotel-based options. Our favourite is the panelled restaurant of the Alliey, which offers excellent food at astoundingly moderate prices and an impressive wine list. The Auberge du Choucas considers itself the best in Le Monêtier and is certainly the most expensive. The Europe has reliable French cooking at reasonable prices. The Boîte à Fromages is said to do a 'magnificent' fondue. Barbin is a bit out of town, in a rustic setting.

In Villeneuve the Swedish-run Vieille Ferme is a 'great, stylish eating place'. The Marotte, a tiny stone building with classic French cuisine in the old part of Villeneuve, 'offers a wide choice of very good food at very reasonable prices'. The Refuge specialises in fondue and raclette. And there are good crêperies – try the Petit Duc, or the Manouille. Over in Le Bez, the Bidule is said to have 'first-class food and service, at good value'. Two new restaurants which opened last season have been highly recommended: L'Ours Blanc and Passé Simple.

In Chantemerle, the Couch'où is good value for fondue and raclette, and has a pizzeria upstairs. The candlelit Crystal is the smartest, most expensive place in Chantemerle; the rustic Ricelle offers 'amazing value'.

APRES-SKI
Quiet streets and few bars
Nightlife seems to revolve around bars, scattered through the various villages and several reporters complain of it being too quiet (though that doesn't bother us personally).

In Le Monêtier the British-run Alpen has a happy hour, free nibbles and welcoming staff; the Que Tal warms up later on.

In Villeneuve, Loco Loco in the old village was reportedly 'the place to go, with funky music and a French atmosphere'; but a 2005 visitor took a dim view, reporting 'tedious music and high prices'. The Frog has 'good local beer'. In Chantemerle the Kitzbühel shows sporting events on TV, 'does good pizzas' and is 'not too full of fellow Brits' (though that may change now that the Underground and Yeti, which used to be run by Thomson, are no more). After everything else has closed, a karaoke bar with 'an erratic door policy' may still let you in.

In Briançon, the Auberge Mont Prorel, right by the gondola base, had live music and was full of Brits and Danes rounding off their day when we paid a tea-time visit.

OFF THE SLOPES
Try the hot baths
Serre-Chevalier doesn't hold many attractions for non-slope-users, and it's certainly not for avid shoppers, but the old town of Briançon is well worth a visit. There is a leisure complex with pools, sauna, hot-tub and steam room. Briançon also has an ice hockey team – their games make 'a good night out', says one reporter. Visitors have enjoyed walking in the valley on 'well-prepared trails', and the indoor-outdoor thermal bath in Le Monêtier makes a great place to watch the sun go down – you need to book. (There are ambitious plans to develop the bath into a swanky spa for 2007.) There is a public swimming pool and health spa near the hotel Sporting in Villeneuve. Each of the main villages has a cinema. Chantemerle and Villeneuve have outdoor skating rinks.

STAYING UP THE MOUNTAIN
Worth considering
You can stay at Pi Maï (0492 248363) in Fréjus, above Villeneuve (see Mountain restaurants). We understand that the Chalet-Hôtel de Serre-Ratier, above Chantemerle, has re-opened.

Ste-Foy-Tarentaise

Off-piste haven now becoming better known – get there soon!

COSTS

① ② ③ ④ ⑤ ⑥

RATINGS

The slopes
Fast lifts	*
Snow	***
Extent	*
Expert	****
Intermediate	***
Beginner	**
Convenience	***
Queues	*****
Mountain restaurants	**

The rest
Scenery	***
Resort charm	***
Off-slope	*

NEWS

The promised new six-pack to the east of the resort's bowl is now scheduled for 2006/07. There will be a new children's area for 2005/06, and the nursery drag at the base of the slopes is set to be upgraded to a moving carpet. Plus there should be another ski shop, another bar, a new car park and yet more new chalets and apartments, including one block with a pool. Another phase of building is now planned in the satellite village of La Bataillettaz.

Rumours continue that Val-d'Isère may buy the lift company.

For 2004/05, a new blue piste was created at the top of the second lift, and two new restaurants and a deli opened at the station. The deli will be offering a catering service for 2004/05, delivering meals to your accommodation.

+	No crowds
+	Lots of off-piste and untracked powder
+	Cheap lift pass and good-value lodging
+	Other resorts you can visit nearby
–	Fledgling resort with limited après-ski and few off-slope diversions
–	Very limited piste network
–	To make the most of other resorts it's best to have a car

This small area has been developed only since 1990; but there has been a recent building boom. The millions who flock to the nearby mega-resorts of Val-d'Isère, Tignes and Les Arcs still rarely give it a thought. But those in the know – and that includes an increasing number of Brits – are well rewarded. It's an uncrowded gem with some wonderful off-piste slopes for experts and intermediates. Lots of instructors from the big resorts come here on their days off and some bring their off-piste groups here to escape the crowds back home.

THE RESORT

Until a few seasons ago there was not much accommodation at the ski station. Now more and more is being built, all in the traditional Savoyard style of wood and stone.

Ste-Foy Station (sometimes called Bonconseil) is set 4km/2.5 miles off the main road between Val-d'Isère and Bourg-St-Maurice: turn off at La Thuile, just after the village of Ste-Foy. A complex at the foot of the lifts houses the tourist and ticket office, a couple of cafe/bars, a pizzeria, a small supermarket and a couple of well-equipped ski/snowboard shops. Zigzags has been there for years and gets both positive and negative reports. The newly established competition is part of the Skiset chain and a second shop is planned for this season.

An alternative focus is emerging on the other side of the lift, with the new children's area, the new ski school, the new Balcons de Ste-Foy apartments (with pool, spa, sauna, steam room and fitness centre), a new piano bar and the gourmet Bergerie restaurant.

If you don't have a car, it's most convenient to stay at the ski station, as the free buses to and from Ste-Foy village and other local hamlets aren't very frequent. To make the most of nearby resorts, however, and some excellent but not local restaurants, it's a good idea to have a car. Parking can be rather challenging, but a new car park with 60 free places is set to open in the centre of the resort.

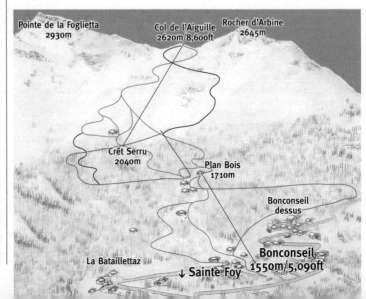

KEY FACTS

Resort	1550m	
	5,090ft	
Slopes	1550-2620m	
	5,090-8,600ft	
Lifts	5	
Pistes	25km	
	16 miles	
Green	7%	
Blue	20%	
Red	53%	
Black	20%	
Snowmaking Minimal		

THE MOUNTAIN

Off-piste guides from Val regularly impress clients by bringing them to Ste-Foy's deserted slopes, accessed by three quad chairs, rising one above the other to the Col de l'Aiguille. But Ste-Foy is also popular with families who like its quiet slopes and easy navigation. Impressive as the off-piste can be, you may want to spread your wings from the tiny resort during a week's stay, particularly if the snow is unkind. Luckily Val d'Isère, Tignes, Les Arcs (via Villaroger) and La Rosière are all within easy reach (with a car). You are entitled to a day at each of them for around 21 euros a time on presentation of a Ste-Foy six-day pass – which at 100 euros last season was around half the price of neighbouring Val d'Isère. A day pass was a bargain 18.5 euros – compared to 39 in Val.

Slopes The top lift accesses almost 600m/1,970ft of vertical above the tree line and superb, long off-piste routes on the back of the mountain. The two lower chairs serve a few pleasant runs through trees and back to the base station. Most reporters have been amazed by the amount of terrain the few lifts access: 'Most of my ski career I've been in Verbier, Zermatt and Vail. Skiing in Ste-Foy is better,' said one. But don't come here for miles of groomed pistes or modern lifts.

Terrain-parks There has not been one for the last couple of seasons.

Snow reliability The slopes face north or west. Snow reliability is good on the former but can suffer on the latter, especially as there is snowmaking only on the run down to the resort.

Experts Experts can pass happy times on and off the sides of Ste-Foy's black and red runs, exploring lots of easily accessible off-piste and trees in the huge bowl (the long Crystal Dark black run usually seems pretty much off-piste). If there's been fresh snow, Ste-Foy can't be beaten for snaring first tracks. The lack of crowds means you can still make fresh tracks days after a storm. There's more serious off-piste on offer too, for which you need a guide. There are wonderful runs from the top of the lifts down through deserted old villages, either to the road between Ste-Foy and Val-d'Isère or back to the base, and a splendid route which starts with a hike up to the Pointe de la Foglietta, and takes

you through trees and over a stream down to the tiny village of Le Crot. The ESF runs group off-piste trips, with transport back to the station. There's also a Bureau des Guides which can arrange heli-skiing (0614 629024).

Intermediates Intermediates can enjoy 1000m/3,280ft vertical of uncrowded reds – ideal for confidence building and sharpening technique. The higher slopes are the more difficult – the red Aiguille is a superb test for confident intermediates, who would also be up to the off-piste routes, especially the Monal route back to base. Anyone who doesn't fancy experimenting with off-piste will tire of the limited runs in a day or two and be champing at the bit to get to Val d'Isère or Les Arcs.

Beginners Not the best place, but there is a small nursery slope (with a new moving carpet lift planned for this season) at the base, and another area with a rope tow at the top of the first lift. After that you can progress to a green run off the first chair and a couple of gentle blues off the second – and the slopes will be pleasantly quiet.

Snowboarding Great free-riding terrain, with lots of trees and easily accessed powder between the pistes to play in.

Cross-country No prepared trails, but ask the tourist office about marked itinerary routes such as Planay Dessus.

Queues Except in peak season and on fresh powder days, despite all the new building, reporters have still failed to find queues at Ste-Foy. Even at peak times you won't wait long.

Mountain restaurants There are two rustic restaurants at the top of the first chair. A reporter recommends Chez Léon as 'a winner'; you need to book. The Brevettes does good omelettes. The Maison à Colonnes, at the base of the first lift, gets consistently good write-ups. There's also an open-air snack-bar, the Chalet La Foglietta, at the top of the second lift.

Schools and guides We've had good reports of ski school, especially for children (from age four). There's a good chance classes will not be large, and reporters say that your instructor is likely to speak good English.

Facilities for children Children under seven ski free. There is a nursery, Les P'tits Trappeurs, which takes children from age three to eleven. The UK tour operator Première Neige also runs a nursery (its own guests take priority). The new children's area should be out of the way of general skiing traffic.

STAYING THERE

How to go Various small tour operators can organise chalets and hotels here. Ste-Foy is about 20 minutes from the Eurostar terminal at Bourg-St-Maurice.

Hotels We have had several glowing reports of Auberge sur la Montagne (0479 069583), just above the turn-off at La Thuile, which has excellent food and atmosphere and is run by an English couple. It has a sauna and hot-tub. Yellow Stone Chalet (0479 069606) is a Gîte de France at the ski station run by an American, and has been highly recommended, though some visitors find it rather expensive. For a more French experience try the Ferme du Baptieu (0479 069752). Hotel Monal (0479 069007), in Ste-Foy village, is a basic 2-star, with a games room, bar and two restaurants.

Chalets and self-catering Gîte de Sainte Foy station and Première Neige both have several chalets and apartments here, with catered and self-catered options. Chalet Number One, in the village of La Masure, is run by former British snowboard champion Lloyd Rogers. And one of our assistant editors has one of the MGM chalets to rent, 100m/330ft from the lift (see www.ste-foy-chalet.co.uk).The tourist runs a central reservation system.

Eating out In the village of Le Miroir, Chez Mérie is excellent (for lunch as well as dinner). So is the Auberge sur la Montagne. In Ste-Foy village, the Grange at the Monal does 'good food'. Chez Léon, up the mountain, opens by arrangement in the evenings. At the station the Maison à Colonnes is good, and the Bec de l'Ane pizzeria does takeaway as well as eat-in. Two new restaurants opened at the base last season: Chez Alison and the Bergerie ('Beautiful, with lovely food, though it wasn't busy when we were there and it lacked atmosphere,' said one reporter).

Après-ski Pretty quiet apart from the restaurants – Chez Alison is also a bar. The Pitchouli at the ski station is the place to go for a drink later on, though its liveliness is unpredictable. It has table football and sometimes live music. The bar of the Monal can get busy, too, and may have live music.

Off the slopes There's not a lot to do off the slopes, but paragliding, dog-sledding and snow-shoeing are available – four new snow-shoe trails opened last season.

St-Martin-de-Belleville

Explore the Three Valleys from a traditional old village

COSTS

① ② ③ ④ ⑤ ⑥

RATINGS

The slopes

Fast lifts	★★★
Snow	★★★
Extent	★★★★★
Expert	★★★★
Intermediate	★★★★★
Beginner	★★★
Convenience	★★★
Queues	★★★★
Mountain restaurants	★★★★

The rest

Scenery	★★★
Resort charm	★★★★
Off-slope	★

NEWS

For 2004/05 the long-promised improvements to the Chef Lieu drag-lift, now called the Village, from the church up to the main slope have finally been made. And the Granges six-pack to Roc des 3 Marches replaced two drag-lifts. It allows the run from Méribel and St-Martin to Les Menuires to be a proper ski rather than a traverse (though the traverse is still the quickest route). The blue Grand Lac run from the top will be equipped with snowmaking for 2005/06.

+ Attractively developed traditional village with pretty church

+ Easy access to the whole of the extensive Three Valleys network

+ Long, easy intermediate runs on rolling local slopes

+ Extensive snowmaking keeps local runs open in poor conditions, but ...

− Snow at resort level suffers from altitude, and sun in the afternoon

− No green runs for beginners to progress to

− The climb up from the lower part of the village can be taxing

− Limited après-ski

− Few off-slope diversions

St-Martin is a lived-in, unspoiled village with an old church (prettily lit at night), small square and buildings of wood and stone, a few miles down the valley from Les Menuires. As a quiet, inexpensive, attractive base for exploration of the Three Valleys as a whole, it's unbeatable.

THE RESORT

In 1950 St-Martin didn't even have running water or electricity. Later, while new resorts were developed nearby, St-Martin was a bit of a backwater. But in the 1980s chair-lifts were built, linking it to the slopes of Méribel and Les Menuires. The old village has been developed, of course, but the new buildings fit in well, and it remains small – you can walk around it in a few minutes. The main feature of the centre remains the lovely old 16th-century church – prettily floodlit at night. There are some good local shops and few 'touristy' ones. A regular visitor was pleased to report how 'unobtrusive' the newish gondola station is.

THE MOUNTAINS

The whole of the Three Valleys can easily be explored from here.

Slopes A gondola, which opened three seasons ago, followed by a fast quad take you to a ridge from which you can access Méribel on one side and Les Menuires on the other.

Terrain-parks There isn't a terrain-park in the St-Martin sector, but you can get to the Les Menuires one or those above Méribel relatively easily.

Snow reliability The local slopes face west and get the full force of the afternoon sun, and the village is relatively low. But there is now snowmaking from top to bottom of the main run to the village, and reporters agree that it is impressively effective at keeping the run open. Many people

ride the gondola down if snow is poor. A 2005 visitor found piste marking an issue: 'In poor visibility it is quite easy to go off-piste unintentionally.'

Experts Locally there are large areas of gentle and often deserted off-piste. A reader recommends the descent from Roc de Fer to the village of Béranger. And the new Granges chair provides an alternative, more interesting route to La Masse for steep north-facing slopes.

Intermediates The local slopes are pleasant blues and reds, mainly of interest to intermediates – including one of our favourite runs in the Three Valleys: the long, rolling, wide Jerusalem red. The Verdet blue from

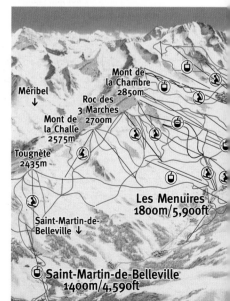

Méribel ↓

Mont de la Chambre 2850m

Roc des 3 Marches 2700m

Mont de la Challe 2575m

Tougnète 2435m

Les Menuires 1800m/5,900ft

Saint-Martin-de-Belleville ↓

Saint-Martin-de-Belleville 1400m/4,590ft

KEY FACTS

Resort	1400m
	4,590ft

For the Three Valleys

Slopes	1260-3230m
	4,130-10,600ft
Lifts	200
Pistes	600km
	373 miles
Green	21%
Blue	33%
Red	35%
Black	11%
Snowmaking	
	1500 guns

For Les Menuires / St-Martin only

Slopes	1450-2850m
	4,760-9,350ft
Lifts	39
Pistes	160km
	99 miles
Green	10%
Blue	40%
Red	38%
Black	12%
Snowmaking	
	355 guns

the top of the Méribel lifts is a wonderful easy cruise with great views and is usually very quiet. The whole of the Three Valleys is, of course, an intermediate's paradise.

Beginners St-Martin is far from ideal – there's a nursery slope but no easy green runs to progress to.

Snowboarding There is some great local off-piste free-riding available.

Cross-country There are 28km/17 miles of trails in the Belleville valley.

Queues Queues are not usually much of a problem – 'We didn't queue all week,' comments one visitor.

Mountain restaurants There are three atmospheric old places on the run down to the village. Chardon Bleu and Corbeleys near the mid-mountain lift junction are good for lunch, and the Loy, lower down, is busy as the lifts close. The new Grand Lac at the bottom of the Granges chair is 'friendly with good food'. Brewski's terrace is good for 'good value, filling pies' and burgers. For a real treat, La Bouitte in St-Marcel is one of the best restaurants in the Three Valleys (see Eating out) – you ski to it off-piste, and the owners will ferry you to a lift afterwards (though a regular visitor with corporate groups 'prefers to book a helicopter to take us back to Courchevel after such a blow-out meal').

Schools and guides The husband of a 2005 reporter had a private ESF lesson on off-piste skiing and said the instructor was 'good at analysing his faults but not so good at teaching him how to improve'. Friends of another visitor found the 'instructors spoke English and were helpful' and enjoyed their lessons.

Facilities for children The Piou Piou club and ESF take children from two-and-a-half years old from 9am to 5pm.

STAYING THERE

How to go For a small village there's a good variety of accommodation.

Hotels The Alp Hôtel (0479 089282), at the foot of the slope by the main lift and close to the nursery, is deservedly popular, but a visitor this year was disappointed with the food. The Saint Martin (0479 008800) is right on the slope, and the Edelweiss (0479 089667) is in the village itself. All are 3-stars. We stayed a night in 2005 at La Bouitte (0479 089677) in St-Marcel (see Eating out) which has four delightful and remarkably spacious rooms beautifully designed using wood that looks centuries old and furnished with antiques. Not cheap – but excellent for a quiet, civilised or romantic break. Breakfast is a gourmet delight as well as dinner – served in your room or in a rustic breakfast room/ residents lounge. Kaluma is the only UK tour operator you can book it through.

Chalets Les Chalets de St Martin has operated here ever since the first lift was built – 'I'd recommend them,' says a 2005 visitor. The Alpine Club has a chalet in the heart of St Martin's old village, nicely renovated, combining original features with a contemporary twist, from a 17th century building. There's a large vaulted living-dining room, some smallish bedrooms and good food. It is personally run by the proprietors, a British couple who go out of their way to provide personal

Les Chalets de St. Martin

We have been in St. Martin since the first lift was built in 1984 and for the last two decades have been offering outstanding hospitality and service to our guests.

Catered Chalet Roussette (Sleeps 10) This beautiful timber and stone chalet is set in mature grounds with some of the best views in the valley. All bedrooms have balconies and en-suite bathrooms. Public areas are spacious and comfortable with satellite TV, video library, piano and a games compendium. Furnished throughout with antique pine and a host of early skiing memorabilia, the chalet also has a spa and sauna room. The food and wines are outstanding; for 20 years the proprietors owned a restaurant that was highly recommended by the Michelin Guide and the Good Food Guide. The all-inclusive tariff includes a mountain guide service and a Land Rover Defender to take guests to and from the piste.

Self Catered Accommodation All our chalets and apartments are a cut above the rest and include many things that you normally pay extra for, such as bed linen, towels, tourist tax, etc. We are also the UK agents for two other ski accommodation companies in St. Martin, one French and one German, who have apartments and chalets sleeping from 6 to 28 people.

Chalet Marie Pierre Two apartments, each sleeps 8/10 with 4 bedrooms, 2 bathrooms. Combined can sleep up to 20.

Chalet Myosotis Sleeps 8/9, 4 bedrooms, 3 bathrooms **Apartment Etoile** Sleeps 7/9, 3 bedrooms, 3 bathrooms

Chez Simon Sleeps 6, 3 bedrooms, 2 bathrooms **Apartment Patrick** Sleeps 5, 2 bedrooms, 1 bathroom

Chez Sue Sleeps 2/4, 1 bedroom/mezzanine, 1 bathroom

John or Hazel 00 33 (0) 479089177   les.chalets@virgin.net   www.leschalets.co.uk

service including running you to and from the lifts and allowing flexible breakfast times.

Self-catering Les Chalets de St Martin has a variety of self-catered chalets and apartments to rent, and plenty of others are available. A reporter this year liked the 'peaceful location' of Les Balcons de St Martin.

Eating out For such a small village there is a good variety of restaurants on hand. Several readers enjoyed the Montagnard's 'fabulous', Savoyard food, but 'it's moving up the price scale'. The Voûte is good value and 'high quality' and is recommended for its salads and pizzas. The Lachenal is said to do 'good mid-priced food' and the Grenier, in the hotel St Martin, 'is great for an expensive lunch'.

The Etoile des Neige is a smart, traditionally French restaurant, but a 2005 reporter thought that it was a bit over-priced for what you get when compared to the more expensive La Bouitte, just up the road in St-Marcel and now boasting a Michelin star. We dined at the family-run Bouitte in 2005 and the food was truly superb – warm foie gras, pigeon casserole and desserts to die for – served in a lovely old wooden dining room with attentive service and excellent wine. The 'amuse bouche' is like a starter on its own – seven different dishes and advice from the waiter on the order to eat them in. They ask you to order dessert when you order the entrée – don't overestimate your capacity (there's a delicious tasting selection of several which we ordered and struggled to

finish). A 2005 reporter comments 'the food is unique in the area' and advises you to 'stick to the fixed price menus'. A bit further up the valley, at Les Granges, is the rustic Chez Bidou – popular with locals and 'highly recommended for a Savoyard evening'.

Après-ski Après-ski centres around two bars. The Pourquoi Pas? is cosy, with a roaring log fire and comfortable easy chairs and sofas. Brewski's is a more animated bar with more basic wooden chairs, live bands, karaoke evenings and the like.

Off the slopes If you don't use the slopes, there are better places to base yourself. There are pleasant walks and a sports hall, and classical concerts take place in the church.

Les Sybelles

Big linked areas, now starting to get the new lifts they need

COSTS

① ② ③ ④ ⑤ ⑥

RATINGS

The slopes

Fast lifts	*
Snow	***
Extent	*****
Expert	**
Intermediate	***
Beginner	****
Convenience	***
Queues	****
Mountain restaurants	**

The rest

Scenery	***
Resort charm	
– Le Corbier	*
– La Toussuire	**
– St-Jean	****
– St-Sorlin	****
Off-slope	**

NEWS

For 2004/05 four much-needed fast chair-lifts were installed to improve links between resorts – all six-packs. Two go from St-Sorlin up to Les Perrons, two from La Toussuire via Grande Verdette to Tête de Bellard.

On the lower slopes a new drag-lift was added at Le Corbier.

Two new red runs opened above La Toussuire; there are now floodlit slalom runs here and above Le Corbier.

A new mountain restaurant opened above St-Sorlin.

Snowmaking was increased, the slopes linking Le Corbier and St-Jean-d'Arves being the main focus.

➕ Extensive area of largely easy intermediate slopes and gentle, uncrowded off-piste

➕ Inexpensive by French standards

➕ Unusual mixture of stark, purpose-built resorts and old villages

➖ Few pistes steep enough to interest adventurous intermediates

➖ Après-ski limited and quiet

➖ Mainly simple accommodation

➖ Few off-slope diversions

Les Sybelles? No, we hadn't heard of it, either, until word began to get around that a group of little-known ski resorts in the Maurienne massif in the French Alps were linking to form an impressively large network for the 2003/04 season. In terms of the extent of pistes, Les Sybelles' 310km/193 miles of pistes puts it straight into the big league, alongside such giants as Val-d'Isère-Tignes.

We knew the major resorts of old, so we knew the slopes were going to be a bit tame. What came as a bit of a shock, though, was the lift system – just one fast chair among scores of slow chairs and drags. We had forgotten just how slow progress around a mountain can be on slow lifts. Happily, a big step in the right direction was taken last year, at least for visitors to La Toussuire and St-Sorlin, with the installation of four more fast chairs. But Les Sybelles still languishes at the bottom of our fast lift league table; more six-packs, please.

The resorts are sharply contrasting in character. Of the major ones, La Toussuire and Le Corbier are most politely described as functional and modern, selling on price and convenience, particularly for families, while St-Sorlin-d'Arves and St-Jean-d'Arves are largely unspoiled, traditional mountain villages which have recently expanded tastefully and attracted some major UK tour operators.

The creation of the new linked area involved construction for the 2003/04 season of nine new lifts and five new pistes linking the existing resorts to the hill at the hub of the new area, L'Ouillon. The new links are high – mostly between 2000m and 2600m (6,560ft and 8,530ft) – so they are relatively snow-sure, safe and are easily negotiated by intermediates. The drawback is that getting from one resort to another can be slow going.

LE CORBIER 1550m/5,090ft
Le Corbier is centrally placed, with direct links to St-Jean-d'Arves in one direction and La Toussuire in the other, as well as a new link to St-Sorlin-d'Arves via L'Ouillon.

THE RESORT
Designed in the 1960s, Le Corbier is a no-compromise functional resort. Most of its accommodation is in eight inner-city-style tower blocks – one as high as 19 storeys – with subterranean shops beneath. To our eye, it looks like a mistake. But it does accommodate its 9,000 visitors efficiently in the

minimum space, and in functional terms it is hard to criticise – it is compact, family-friendly and traffic-free with all ski-in/ski-out accommodation. The apartment blocks line the foot of the slopes, and in the other direction the resort's balcony setting gives good views of the valley. It sells itself firmly as a family resort and runs a French Family Championship with teams made up of mother, father and one child. And the resort assures us that all new building will be in traditional style.

THE MOUNTAIN
Le Corbier's local ski area has 90km/56 miles of gentle pistes. Although the altitudes are modest (top height 2265m/7,430ft, resort 1550m/5,090ft), there are hardly any trees.

Slopes Two successive slow chairs rise over 700m/2,300ft vertical to Pte du Corbier from where you use some of the new pistes and lifts along the ridge to Pte de L'Ouillon and the links to St-Sorlin-d'Arves or La Toussuire. Runs spread across a wide, north-east-facing mountainside return to the resort, and there are links at the extremities to La

The Combe Balme had reasonable snow cover when we visited, but in January 2005 it was reportedly 'very icy, and in need of closure' →

SNOWPIX.COM / CHRIS GILL

Toussuire and St-Jean-d'Arves.

Terrain-park There's a park on the lower slopes just above the resort.

Snow reliability The mix of reasonable altitude and lack of crowds cutting up the pistes means the snow tends to stay in fairly good condition. The slopes get the morning sun, but there is snowmaking on all the main pistes back to the resort. The sunny link to St-Jean-d'Arves was bare and rocky on our January 2004 visit but should be improved by new snowmaking facilities installed last season. The low connection from La Toussuire is another problem spot, but there is also a higher link.

Experts The area lacks challenges – the one short black piste scarcely deserves a red grading. There are off-piste options in the valley between Le Corbier and La Toussuire.

Intermediates Le Corbier's gentle slopes are ideal cruising terrain, though the runs aren't very long and they rather lack variety.

Beginners There is an extensive nursery area with a moving carpet right in front of the resort, with gentle progression runs directly above.

Snowboarding The wide, open terrain is ideal for riders, as long as they don't want anything too challenging.

Cross-country There are narrow loops across the mountainside either side of the resort, one of which leads to La Toussuire and back. It's all a bit bleak.

Queues The area is renowned for its uncrowded slopes, and the system is free of bottlenecks.

Mountain restaurants A 2004 reporter says Le Charmun, at the foot of the Vadrouille area, 'was the restaurant of the week for us, with delicious crozets with wild mushrooms and lardons' and Chalet 2000 near the top was 'notable for its playful golden labrador as well as its welcome and food'.

Schools Our one past reporter judged the ESF 'disdainful, uncaring, very disorganised; bad tuition'.

Facilities for children The Nursery takes children from six months. A reporter praised the ski kindergarten (for age three up): 'Nice, well-equipped ski-park; good instructors'. Its location up on the pistes means a bit of a hike.

STAYING THERE

How to go There are several UK operators selling packages here.

Chalets Equity Ski runs its own chalet hotel, described by one reporter as 'clean, comfortable and very good value' and approved by others, too.

Self-catering There's nothing larger than cramped two-bedroomed units on offer from central reservations.

Eating out Le Grillon, 3km/2 miles away in the Villarembert, makes a pleasant, rustic change from Le Corbier's tower blocks – and serves traditional French food.

Après ski Very quiet. The Equity Ski chalet-hotel bar is popular. Roches Blanches restaurant in the centre includes a cosy bar area with an open fire. For dancing, the Président gets busy only at peak holiday periods.

Off the slopes There's a nice natural ice rink and a new fitness centre. The outdoor pool is open, and you can go snowmobiling, among other things.

LA TOUSSUIRE 1700m/5,580ft

La Toussuire, along with Le Corbier, is one of the central resorts of the new network – the two have been linked at low altitude since 1986.

THE RESORT

La Toussuire has grown up over many years but is predominantly modern, with a car-free and snow-covered main street lined by dreary-looking buildings dating from the 1960s and 1970s and plagued by piped muzak and a DJ coming via speakers attached to the lamp posts. The resort has now spread widely from here, with recently built wooden chalets as well as older hotels

and small apartment blocks scattered across the mountainside.

THE MOUNTAIN

The local slopes amount to 45km/ 28 miles of pistes.

Slopes The resort sits in the pit of a wide bowl. Drags and chair-lifts (including two new fast six-packs planned for 2004/05) rise just over 500m/1,640ft vertical to the high point of Tête de Ballard in the centre of the bowl and the link to L'Ouillon and onwards to St-Sorlin. At one end of the bowl is the low-level link to Le Corbier and at the other the start of a long red run to Les Bottières of 900m/2,950ft vertical.

Terrain-park There's a boarder-cross course in the centre of the bowl.

Snow reliability With every run above 1800m/5,910ft snow-cover is fairly assured, but some of the slopes are rather exposed to the sun – particularly the low-level connection to Le Corbier.

Experts There are few challenges here, and not much space left between the pistes. The main interest is the ungroomed black Vallée Perdue run, which descends the valley separating La Toussuire from Le Corbier, away from the lifts. But it gets a lot of sun, and snow conditions can suffer. The new lifts towards L'Ouillon opened up new off-piste routes down this valley.

Intermediates This is ideal terrain for cruisers who don't mind mainly short runs. The longer runs that go down to Les Bottières are some of the most appealing in the whole area.

Beginners There are nice, gentle nursery slopes immediately above the centre of the village, and good, easy progression slopes.

Snowboarding There are quite a few drag-lifts in the area.

Cross-country A narrow loop goes to Le Corbier, but it is in bleak surroundings close to the road. There

are also loops on the lower slopes of Le Grand Truc.

Queues We have not heard of any problems.

Mountain restaurants A reporter recommends the Foehn at Le Marolay for its 'friendly service', the good views and an interesting interior of old photos, carvings, etc. A recent reporter endorses its 'stunning views' and says Les Cigales, near the foot of the bowl, had 'good basic food and was friendly'.

Schools A lack of English-speaking tuition can be a problem, though we understand that English classes are often laid on for Dutch visitors. The classes are no larger than 10.

Facilities for children The nursery accepts children from three to six. Language may be a problem.

STAYING THERE

How to go A few UK tour operators serve the resort.

Hotels There are several small 3-star and 2-star places. The 3-star Ruade (0479 830179) and Soldanelles (0479 567529) both have pools and saunas.

Self-catering The Ecrins chalets are large 3-star apartments. Most others are cheap and not so cheerful.

Eating out The options are mostly inexpensive pizzerias and bar-restaurants.

Après-ski Fairly dire. There are a few bars, including the Tonneau. The Alpen Rock nightclub can get busy at peak French holiday time.

Off the slopes There's a reasonable amount to do, including snow-shoeing, snowmobiling, dog-sledding, skating (the rink on the roof of a building in the main street pumps out loud music) and hang-gliding.

ST-SORLIN D'ARVES 1500m/4,920ft
St-Sorlin is the major beneficiary of last season's investment in new fast chairs, gaining a slick link right to the top of the most interesting slopes in the area, on Les Perrons. If it suits you in other respects, this is now an excellent base for the area – especially for keen, experienced intermediates.

THE RESORT

St-Sorlin-d'Arves is a real, medium-sized village with a year-round life outside skiing. It's a picturesque collection of well-preserved traditional farmhouses, with a baroque church and long-established shops – fromagerie, boulangerie, crafts, etc – alongside more modern resort development. Its setting on a narrow shelf gives fine views of the Aiguilles d'Arves but doesn't allow much room for expansion, so the village has grown in a ribbon-like fashion along its main street. A 2004 reporter warns that the road up from the valley is in poor repair and narrow in places, with precipitous drops and no petrol station. He also warns that, in March at least, the bus link between St-Sorlin and St-Jean stops before the lifts. A visitor in January 2005 found the bus service unreliable and was irritated that it stopped altogether at 7pm, given that the village does not lend itself to strolling on foot to find a place to eat.

THE MOUNTAIN

St-Sorlin's local slopes form the biggest single sector of the new network, with 120km/75 miles of piste. Although very much an intermediate mountain, it does offer much more variety, including some steeper options, than the rest of the area.

Slopes There are two distinct sections. The lower, gentler left side on La Balme, reached by a choice of slow chairs from the village, is crammed with lots of short, easy runs. The higher, right side on Les Perrons, now reached by two successive fast six-packs that opened in 2004/05, has long, sweeping, generally steeper pistes. The new Vallons run off the

back of Les Perrons (which forms the first part of the link to L'Ouillon and from there to La Toussuire, Le Corbier or St-Colomban) and the runs from Petit Perron have added a lot of interest to the local skiing, even for those who have no intention of setting off towards a different resort.

Snow reliability Not bad. Les Perrons slopes are the highest in the area and the main runs back to the village are covered by snowmakers.

Experts There isn't much on-piste challenge, but Les Perrons had the best off-piste in the whole pre-existing area and the slopes beneath the new Petit Perron chair look interesting.

Intermediates The long top-to-bottom reds on both sides of Les Perrons are the best pistes in the whole area. There is only one on the back and a couple on the front, but they have the whole mountain to themselves, giving a great away-from-it-all feel. La Balme has shorter, more leisurely runs.

Beginners The nursery slope is right by the village, and there are plenty of slopes to progress to on La Balme.

Snowboarding La Balme has a lot of drag-lifts.

Cross-country There's a narrow 16km/10 mile loop along a side valley past the foot of La Balme's Alpine area, with good views of the Aiguilles d'Arves.

Queues We have received no reports of any problems and the only queue

Les Sybelles

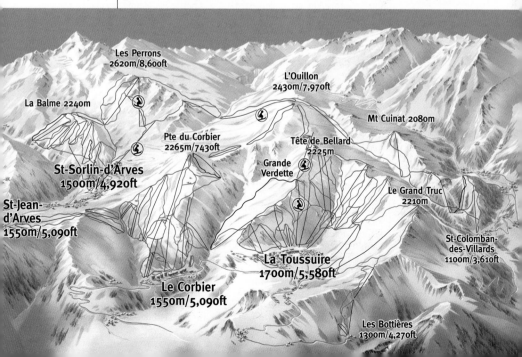

Les Perrons 2620m/8,600ft

L'Ouillon 2430m/7,970ft

La Balme 2240m

Mt Cuinat 2080m

Pte du Corbier 2265m/7430ft

Tête de Bellard 2225m

Grande Verdette

St-Sorlin-d'Arves 1500m/4,920ft

Le Grand Truc 2210m

St-Jean-d'Arves 1550m/5,090ft

St-Colomban-des-Villards 1100m/3,610ft

La Toussuire 1700m/5,580ft

Le Corbier 1550m/5,090ft

Les Bottières 1300m/4,270ft

↑ Le Toussuire spreads quite widely across its shelf
SNOWPIX.COM / CHRIS GILL

Phone numbers
From abroad use the prefix +33 and omit the initial '0' of the phone number.

TOURIST OFFICES

info@les-sybelles.com
www.les-sybelles.com
La Toussuire
t 0479 830606
info@la-toussuire.com
www.la-toussuire.com
Le Corbier
t 0479 830404
info@le-corbier.com
www.le-corbier.com
St-Sorlin-d'Arves
t 0479 597177
info@saintsorlin
darves.com
www.saintsorlindarves.
com
St-Jean-d'Arves
t 0479 597330
info@saintjeandarves.
com
www.saintjeandarves.
com
**St-Colomban-des-
Villards**
t 0479 562453
info@saint-colomban.
com
www.saint-colomban.
com
Les Bottières
t 0479 832709
info@bottieres-
jarrier.com
www.maurienne-
tourisme.com

we saw was for the popular but slow chair up to Les Perrons. Pressure on this should be eased by the new fast chairs installed in 2004/05.

Mountain restaurants We enjoyed lunch and stunning views of the Aiguilles d'Arves on the sunny terrace of the rustic Bergerie at the top of the Plan Moulin chair at La Balme.

Schools A recent visitor reports 'exceptionally friendly and helpful instructors but big classes of up to 20'. A 2005 visitor was annoyed that the ESF shortened his child's pre-booked lessons with no matching cut in the price.

Facilities for children The Petits Diables nursery accepts children from three months. The ski kindergarten accepts kids from three-and-a-half years. Language is a likely problem.

STAYING THERE

How to go Some major UK tour operators now offer holidays here – see the index at the back of book.

Hotels There are three small 2-star places – all attractive chalets. The Beausoleil (0479 597140) and Balme (0479 597021) look the best bets.

Self-catering There are scores of small properties (and the Grignotte bakery sells 'the best bread ever encountered in the Alps', says one reporter).

Eating out The choice is limited to cheap and cheerful pizzerias and raclette/fondue places. The Table de Marie, Gargoulette ('friendly, decent food, but frenetic and disorganised service') and pizza and pasta above the Avalanche bar have been recommended. The Kalico, in the Fermes de Saint Sorlin residence, is said to have 'very good food' and 'a good atmosphere'.

Après-ski St-Sorlin-d'Arves is even quieter than the other resorts. A 2004 reporter says 'the Avalanche bar was lively with a student-age clientele and the Godille was more frequented by locals but essentially dead. We did not think the guide's warning that there isn't much nightlife or many bars would matter to us oldies, but it did.' You have been warned – again.

Off the slopes There is not much to do. Dog-sledding and snow-shoeing are options, but it's fairly tame territory.

ST-JEAN-D'ARVES 1550m/5,090ft
Although small, St-Jean-d'Arves is quite a scattered community. The original old village, with the usual ancient church, is set across the valley from the main slopes, at the foot of a north-facing ridge with two drag-lifts.

Across the valley is the mid-mountain hamlet of La Chal. Here, where a tasteful development of new chalet-style buildings is still expanding, you will find the lift link to and piste back from Le Corbier. It is not directly affected by the new lifts: as in the past, it remains linked to Le Corbier by lifts and runs, and to St-Sorlin-d'Arves by shuttle-bus along the valley.

Off-slope diversions are few – dog-sledding, cheese farm visits, snow-shoeing. Après-ski is basic, with a few bars, an Irish pub and night-tobogganing with music. The attractive Chalets Les Marmottes and La Fontaine du Roi apartments are by far the best self-catering option in the whole area.

ST-COLOMBAN-DES-VILLARDS
1100m/3,610ft
St-Colomban-des-Villards is a tiny old village in the next valley to La Toussuire, only a few miles up from the Maurienne valley.

In recent years it has developed a chain of drags and chair-lifts on north- and east-facing slopes to the south of the village, with a high point at Mt Cuinat, and is now linked to L'Ouillon, at the hub of Les Sybelles. A battery of snowmakers keeps the home slope down to the village open for most of the season.

LES BOTTIERES 1300m/4,270ft
Down the mountain from La Toussuire, this tiny hamlet offers little infrastructure and extremely indirect access to the main network – it takes three lifts to get over to La Toussuire, before setting off for L'Ouillon.

La Tania

Small, family-friendly base for exploring the Three Valleys

NEWS

For 2004/05 work finally began on building the much-needed new green piste from Courchevel 1850 back through the trees into the village, and this is due for completion for the 2005/06 season. When it opens, it should transform the attraction of La Tania for beginners and timid intermediates.

Also for 2004/05 the new hotel Telemark with Le Bistro restaurant opened beside the slopes.

- Part of the Three Valleys – the world's biggest linked ski area
- Quick access to the slopes of Courchevel and Méribel
- Long, rolling, intermediate runs through woods back to the village
- New green run back to village should make it attractive for beginners and timid intermediates
- Greatly improved snowmaking
- Attractive, small, traffic-free village

- Small development without much choice of après-ski – and no doctor or pharmacy
- Main nursery slope is part of the blue run to the village, and gets a lot of through-traffic
- Runs home are too steep for those progressing from the nursery slopes (though this will change when the promised new green run opens)
- Some accommodation is a long walk from the centre and the main lifts

La Tania does not try to compete with its more upmarket neighbours, Courchevel and Méribel. It has carved out its own niche as a good-value, small, quiet, family-friendly base from which to hit the snow-sure slopes of Courchevel and to explore the whole of the Three Valleys. It is prettily set in the trees, and the wood-clad buildings make it one of the more attractive French purpose-built resorts (development started in the early 1990s, by which time lessons had been learned from the resorts that were developed in the 1960s and 70s, with their tiny apartments and uncompromisingly functional architecture). As a budget base for the Three Valleys, it has a lot to be said for it.

THE RESORT

La Tania is set just off the minor road linking Le Praz (Courchevel 1300) to Méribel. It has grown into a quiet, attractive, car-free collection of mainly ski-in, ski-out chalets and apartments set among the trees, most with good views. There are few shops other than food and sports shops and you can walk around it in a couple of minutes. But for such a small place there is a fair selection of bars and restaurants.

A gondola leads up into the slopes, and there are two wonderful sweeping intermediate runs down. The nursery slope is on your doorstep, and visitors say that La Tania is 'very child friendly'. The steepness of the runs back to the village has, until now, been its key weakness though this should be rectified for 2005/06 as work on a new beginner piste from the links with Courchevel and Méribel down to the village is planned.

Free buses go to Courchevel, which reporters find punctual in the daytime, but one warns that the service is erratic in the evenings. For those with a car Méribel is probably a bigger draw – and a lot nearer than Courchevel 1850.

THE MOUNTAINS

As well as good, though limited, local slopes, the whole of the Three Valleys can be explored easily from here, with just two lifts needed to get to either the Courchevel or the Méribel slopes.

Slopes The gondola out of the village goes to Praz-Juget. From here a drag-lift takes you to Chenus and the slopes above Courchevel 1850 and a fast quad goes to the link with Méribel via Col de la Loze. An alternative way to the slopes above 1850 is to take two successive drag-lifts from the village to Loze. From all these points, varied, interesting intermediate runs take you back into the La Tania sector.

Terrain-parks There is no local terrain-park or half-pipe, but you can get to Courchevel's four parks easily.

Snow reliability Good snow-cover down to Praz-Juget is usual all season. Snowmaking now covers the whole of the blue run back to the village; some reporters found this satisfactory, but others found the run became icy in the afternoon and preferred to ride the gondola down at times.

Experts There are no particular challenges directly above La Tania, but the Jean Blanc and Jockeys blacks from

KEY FACTS

Resort	1350m 4,430ft
For the Three Valleys	
Slopes	1260-3230m 4,130-10,600ft
Lifts	197
Pistes	600km 373 miles
Green	21%
Blue	33%
Red	35%
Black	11%
Snowmaking	1500 guns
For Courchevel/ La Tania only	
Slopes	1260-2740m 4,130-8,990ft
Lifts	63
Pistes	150km 93 miles
Green	25%
Blue	33%
Red	32%
Black	10%
Snowmaking	562 guns

Loze to Le Praz are genuine challenges and there is good off-piste terrain beneath the Col de la Loze ridge and close by in the Courchevel sector.
Intermediates There are two lovely, long, undulating intermediate runs back through the trees to La Tania – though there's little difference in gradient between the blue and the red and timid intermediates may find them too steep for their liking. On the higher slopes you have a choice of three or four pistes. Both Lanches and Dou des Lanches (now reclassified from red to black) are excellent and challenging. The quick access to the rest of the Three Valleys' 600km/373 miles of well-groomed pistes makes the area an adventurous intermediate's paradise.
Beginners There is a good beginner area and lift right in the village and beginner children, in particular, are well catered for. But there's a lot of through traffic on the main slope and, until now, there have been no easy, long, local slopes to progress to; the intermediate runs back to the village are quite challenging. But the new green, due to be ready for 2005/06, should make La Tania a lot more suitable for beginners.
Snowboarding It's easy to get around on gondolas and chairs, avoiding drags.
Cross-country There are trails at altitude with links through the woods to Méribel and Courchevel, which has an extensive 66km/41 miles of trails. To our non-specialist eye, this looks a good base.
Queues A queue can build up for the village gondola but it is quick-moving, and one of the attractions of La Tania in general is the lack of crowds. Elsewhere in the Three Valleys there are a few remaining bottlenecks.
Mountain restaurants The Bouc Blanc, near the top of the gondola out of La Tania, has friendly table-service in a wood-clad dining room, good food and a big terrace. Roc Tania, higher up at Col de la Loze, is tiny, but very pretty inside – good for a scenic coffee stop; one reader found the food good at lunch time, another was disappointed with food and service. A visitor this year found them all a bit pricey so 'tended to come back to the village for lunch towards the end of the holiday for a cheaper meal'. Check out the Courchevel and Méribel places, too.
Schools and guides Several 2005 reporters rave about the ESF: 'excellent but the instructor allowed one or two dominant people to overshadow the rest' and 'unequivocally the lessons for myself and children were excellent'. One of the satisfied ESF clients went

there because of 'appalling service' from Magic in Motion, which 'repeatedly asked me to phone back' when he tried to book: 'I got the feeling they were coasting on a good reputation.' We have no recent reports of the other schools, Supreme (a Brit-run school which has operated out of Courchevel 1850 for years and started up in La Tania last season) and Snow Ball.

Facilities for children We have had excellent reports of tour operator Le Ski's nursery here and they are opening a second, larger one for 2005/06. The local Maison des Enfants kindergarten takes non-skiing children from the age of three; the Jardin des Neiges takes skiing children from the age of four. A list of babysitters is available from the tourist office.

STAYING THERE

How to go Over 30 British tour operators go here.

Hotels The Montana (0479 088008) is a slope-side 3-star next to the gondola with a sauna and fitness club. The Mountain Centre (01273 897525 in the UK or www.themountaincentre.com) has 'cheap backpacker-style accommodation and food'.

Chalets Several tour operators have selections of splendid newish ski-in, ski-out chalets with fine views, which reporters generally enjoy though we have had complaints of 'poor sound-proofing' in some. The choice gets wider every year; Le Ski, for example, will have an additional two newly built slope-side chalets (for 19 and 22) for 2005/06, bringing its total to five. We

La Tania

Col de Chanrossa 2545m

Méribel ↘

La Vizelle 2660m

La Saulire 2740m/8,990ft

↙ Méribel

Chenus 2245m

Col de la Loze 2275m

Les Creux

Altiport

Verdons

Mt. Bel Air

Prameruel 1825m

Praz-Juget

Courchevel 1850

Courchevel 1650

Courchevel 1550

Le Praz 1260m/4,130ft

La Tania 1350m/4,430ft

FRANCE

Phone numbers
From abroad use the prefix +33 and omit the initial '0' of the phone number.

have had especially good reports of them and of Snowline.

Self-catering There are lots of apartments – and most are more spacious and better equipped than usual in France. The Saboia and the Christiania have been recommended. There is a deli and a bakery, as well as a small supermarket.

Eating out The Ferme de la Tania gets generally good reviews for its Savoyard fare – 'good service, good food'. The Farçon was considered 'outrageously expensive and not all that good' by several reporters. Le Ski Lodge has 'damn good chilli burgers' and 'will do a deal for groups including all-you-can-eat-and-drink salad, chips and wine'. The Chanterelles is 'highly recommended' for crêpes and pizzas ('first-class meals at knockdown prices') and the Taïga does 'very good pizzas and is friendly and quite cheap'. A 2004 reporter recommends the Marmottons for its tartiflette and a 2005 one the Telemark as having 'a very good new restaurant'.

Après-ski Le Ski Lodge has long been the focal après-ski place and has live bands. But it also now has some rivals. The Telemark, new last season, has 'civilised live music nightly' and the Taïga 'is quite smart, with cocktails and live music', according to 2005 reporters. The hotel Montana bar is also worth trying for a quiet drink and the French-run L'Arbatt, in the centre of the village, is popular as the slopes close.

Off the slopes Unless you have a car, La Tania is not the best place for someone not intending to hit the slopes. However, snowmobile trips, snow-shoeing, paragliding and husky dog-sledding are possibilities, and the hotel Montana has a fitness club with a swimming pool. A non-skier's guide to Courchevel, Méribel and La Tania is distributed free by the tourist office.

Selected chalets in La Tania

Tignes

Good snow, great varied terrain and a resort that's ... er ... improving

- Good snow guaranteed for a long season – about the best Alpine bet
- One of the best areas in the world for lift-served off-piste runs
- Huge amount of terrain for all abilities, with swift access to the slopes of Val-d'Isère
- Lots of accommodation close to the slopes (though there is also quite a bit that involves some walking)
- Efforts to make the resort villages more welcoming are paying off

- Resort architecture not to everyone's taste (including ours)
- Bleak, treeless setting – and many slopes liable to closure during and after storms
- Still a few long, slow chair-lifts – though they are part way through an upgrading programme
- Near beginners looking for long green runs have to buy an area pass and go to the Val-d'Isère slopes
- Limited, but improving, après-ski

The appeal of Tignes is simple: good snow, spread over a wide area of varied terrain, shared with Val-d'Isère. Together the two resorts form the enormous Espace Killy – a Mecca for experts, and ideal for adventurous intermediates. The height of Tignes is crucial: a forecast of 'rain up to 2000m' means 'fresh snow down to village level in Tignes'.

We prefer to stay in Val, which is a more human place. But in many ways Tignes makes the better base: appreciably higher, more convenient, surrounded by intermediate terrain, with quick access to the Grande Motte glacier. And the case for Tignes gets stronger as results flow from the resort's campaign to reinvent itself in a more cuddly form. Cars have been largely pushed underground, new buildings are being designed in traditional styles and some old ones are getting a facelift. It all helps to combat the impression that you've landed on the Moon.

They have been improving their lifts as well, and in the last few seasons have, at last, got around to installing some fast chairs on the western side of the Tignes bowl, allowing more time to be spent on skis or board and less on slow lifts. But there are still a few key links that need upgrading.

369

THE RESORT

Tignes was created before the French discovered the benefits of making purpose-built resorts look acceptable. But things are improving. Traffic is now discouraged (and in places routed underground), and the villages are gradually acquiring a more traditional look and feel.

The original and main village – Tignes-le-Lac – is still the hub of the resort. Some of the smaller buildings in the central part, Le Rosset, are being successfully revamped in chalet style. But the place as a whole is dreary, and the blocks overlooking the lake from the quarter called Le Bec-

The Arbina hotel in Le Lac is popular for après-ski and has one of the best restaurants in town. It's a good place to stay too – and no, we don't have shares in it ➔

NEWS

For 2004/05 two lifts
on the wide expanse
of slopes west of
Tignes were
upgraded. The Merle
Blanc and Grattalu
up towards Col du
Palet were replaced
by six-packs. Also, a
SPOT (Skiing the
Powder of Tignes)
area was created on
the Col de Ves with a
black run and various
free-ride zones
(which are marked on
the map but are not
avalanche
controlled). There's
an avalanche
transceiver training
area, with
information about
the SPOT area and
the latest avalanche
hazard bulletin.
There's also a
boarder-cross course
(served by a drag-
lift).

For 2005/06 the
Tichot chair out of
Val Claret on the
western side is due
to be replaced by a
high-speed six-pack.

A new sports centre
is due to be ready
for the 2006/07
season.

Rouge will remain monstrous until the
day they are demolished. It's at the
point where these two sub-resorts
meet – now a snowy pedestrian area,
with valley traffic passing through a
tunnel beneath – that the lifts are
concentrated: two slow, old chair-lifts
up the western slopes and a powerful
gondola towards Tovière and Val-
d'Isère. Some attractive new buildings
are being added both in the centre and
on the fringes, in a suburb built on the
lower slopes known as Les Almes. A
nursery slope separates Le Rosset from
the fourth component part, Le
Lavachet, below which there are now
good fast lifts up both sides of the
valley. Like Le Rosset, Le Lavachet is
an apartment development, but one
that is much easier on the eye.

Val-Claret (2km/1 mile up the valley,
beyond the lake) was also mainly
developed after Le Rosset, and is a bit
more stylish – though we don't side
with those readers who claim to
actually like the look of it. The main
part of the village, Centre, is an
uncompromisingly modern-style
development on a shelf above the
valley floor. Below this, from 2005/06 a
high-speed chair up the western slopes
will join the existing ones towards Val
d'Isère and the Grande Motte and the
Grande Motte underground funicular.

Beside the road along the valley to
the lifts is a ribbon of more recent
development in traditional style,
known as Grande Motte. The two
levels of Val-Claret are linked by a
couple of (unreliable) indoor elevators
and stairs and by hazardous paths.

Below the main resort villages are
two smaller places. Tignes-les-Boisses,
quietly set in the trees beside the road
up consists of a barracks and a couple
of simple hotels. Tignes-les-Brévières is
a renovated old village at the lowest
point of the slopes – a favourite lunch
spot, and a friendly place to stay.

Location isn't crucial, as a regular
and very efficient free bus service
connects all the villages until midnight
– though in the daytime the route runs
along the bottom of Val-Claret, leaving
residents of Val-Claret Centre with
some uphill hiking.

A six-day pass covers a day in some
other resorts, including Paradiski (Les
Arcs and La Plagne) and the Three
Valleys, most easily reached with the
aid of a car. Keep your pass and you'll
get a loyalty discount off next year's.

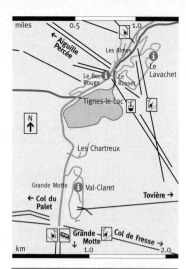

THE MOUNTAINS

The area's great weakness is that it
can become unusable in bad weather.
There are no woodland runs except
immediately above Tignes-les-Boisses
and Tignes-les-Brévières. Heavy snow
produces widespread avalanche risk
and wind closes the higher chairs.

Piste classification here is more
reliable than in Val-d'Isère.

THE SLOPES
High, snow-sure and varied

Tignes' biggest asset is the **Grande
Motte** – and the runs from, as well as
on, the glacier. The underground
funicular from Val-Claret whizzes you
up to over 3000m/9,840ft in seven
minutes. There are blue, red and black
runs to play on up here, as well as
beautiful long runs back to the resort.

The main lifts towards Val-d'Isère
are efficient: a high-capacity gondola
from Le Lac to **Tovière**, and a fast chair
with covers from Val-Claret to **Col de
Fresse**. You can head back to Tignes
from either: the return from Tovière
to Tignes-le-Lac is via a steep black
run but there are easier blue runs to
Val-Claret.

Going up the opposite side of the
valley takes you to a quieter area of
predominantly east-facing slopes split
into two main sectors, linked in both
directions – **Col du Palet** and **l'Aiguille
Percée**. This whole mountainside is at
last being given the fast lifts it has
needed for years – by 2005/06 there
will be four of them.

The Col des Ves chair-lift, at the
south end of the Col du Palet sector,

now serves the new SPOT area – see 'News'. You can descend from l'Aiguille Percée to Tignes-les-Brévières, on blue, red or black runs. There's an efficient gondola back.

TERRAIN-PARKS
New but not improved
Tignes has moved its snow-park to Val-Claret, much to the annoyance of many boarders. There are two half-pipes, a 120m/395ft expert one and a 70m/230ft beginner one, plus jumps, ribs and rails. There's also a boarder-cross course as part of the SPOT area below Col du Palet. Both the park and the boarder-cross were heavily criticised in 2005 by a regular reporter for being badly designed with inadequate access lifts. For the summer season, Tignes builds a big terrain-park on the Grande Motte glacier.

SNOW RELIABILITY
Difficult to beat
Tignes has all-year-round runs (barring brief closures in spring or autumn) on its Grande Motte glacier. And the resort

height of 2100m/6,89oft generally means good snow-cover right back to base for most of the long winter season – November to May. The west-facing runs down from Col de Fresse and Tovière to Val-Claret suffer from the afternoon sun, although they now have serious snowmaking. Some of the lower east-facing and south-east-facing slopes on the other side of the valley can suffer late in the season, too.

FOR EXPERTS
An excellent choice
Tignes has converted many of its black runs into 'Naturides', which means they are never groomed (a neat way of saving money!) but they are marked, patrolled and avalanche protected. Many of them are not especially steep (eg the Ves run was only recently promoted from red status). Perhaps the most serious challenge is the long black run from Tovière to Tignes-le-Lac, with steep, usually heavily mogulled sections (the top part, Pâquerettes, is now a 'Naturide' but the bottom part, Trolles, is a normal black). Parts of this run get a lot of afternoon sun. Our

Tignes

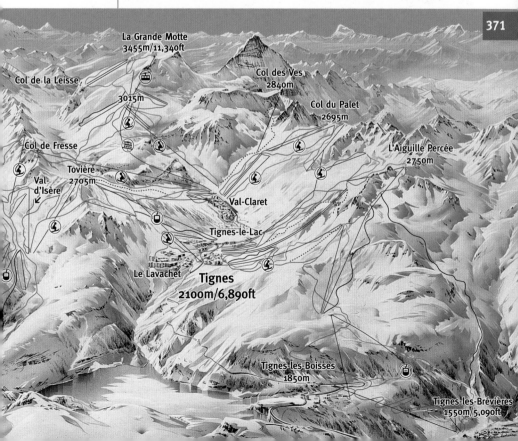

La Grande Motte
3455m/11,340ft

Col de la Leisse

Col des Ves
2840m

3015m

Col du Palet
2695m

Col de Fresse

L'Aiguille Percée
2750m

Tovière
2705m

Val-
d'Isère

Val-Claret

Tignes-le-Lac

Le Lavachet

Tignes
2100m/6,89oft

Tignes-les-Boisses
1850m

Tignes-les-Brévières
1550m/5,09oft

favourite black run (still a 'normal' black) is the Sache, from l'Aiguille Percée down a secluded valley to Tignes-les-Brévières, which can become very heavily mogulled at the bottom.

But it is the off-piste possibilities that make Tignes such a draw for experts. Go with one of the off-piste groups that the schools organise, and in good snow you'll have a great time. The feature box opposite explains some of the options.

One of the big adventures not mentioned there is to head for Champagny (linked to the La Plagne area) or Peisey-Nancroix (linked to the Les Arcs area) – very beautiful runs, and not too difficult.

The whole western side of the bowl has lots of off-piste possibilities. The terrain served by the Col des Ves chair has been redesignated Le SPOT (Skiing the Powder of Tignes) area and has various ungroomed off-piste zones: Hardride for experts, Softride for the less experienced and Backcountry freestyle with jumps. It is explained at length on the back of the piste map. At Chalet Freeride you can learn to use an avalanche transceiver, practise searching for avalanche victims, read

the avalanche bulletins and study maps and photos of the terrain.

Schools and guides offer the bizarre French form of heli-skiing: mountaintop drops are forbidden, but from Tovière you can ski down towards the Lac du Chevril to be retrieved by chopper.

FOR INTERMEDIATES
One of the best
For the keen intermediate piste-basher the Espace Killy is one of the top three or four areas in France, or the world.

Tignes' local slopes are ideal intermediate terrain. The red and blue runs on the Grande Motte glacier nearly always have superb snow. The glacier run from the top of the cable-car has been regraded from blue to red but is wide and mostly easy on usually fabulous snow. The Leisse run down to the chair-lift is now classified black and can get very mogulled but has good snow. The long red run all the way back to town is a delightful long cruise – though often crowded. The roundabout blue alternative (Génépy) is much gentler and quieter.

From Tovière, the blue 'H' run to Val-Claret is an enjoyable cruise and generally well groomed. But again, it

Tignes is renowned for offering some of the best lift-served off-piste skiing in the world. There is a tremendous choice, with runs to suit all levels, from intermediate skiers to fearless free-riders and off-piste experts. We invited the ESF to give us a guided tour. Although some of these runs are heavily skied, we don't recommend anyone to undertake them without proper guidance.

*For a first experience of off-piste, perhaps for a family, **Lognan** is ideal. These slopes – down the mountainside between the pistes to Le Lac and the pistes to Val-Claret – are broad and not very difficult.*

*One of our favourite routes is the **Tour de Pramecou**. After few minutes' walking at the bottom of the Grande Motte glacier, we pass around a big rock called Pramecou. There is then a multitude of possibilities, differing in difficulty – so a route can be found for skiers of different abilities.*

*There is an **ESF** in each part of Tignes:*

Val Claret
t 0479 063128

Le Lac
t 0479 063028

Le Lavachet
t 0479 400884

Les Brévières
t 0479 065113

www.esf-tignes.com

***Petite Balme** is a run for good skiers only – access is easy, but leads to quite challenging north-facing slopes in real high-mountain terrain, far from the pistes.*

*To ski **Oreilles de Mickey** (Mickey's Ears) you start from Tovière and walk north along the ridge to the peak of Lavachet, where you get a great view of Tignes. The descent involves three long couloirs, narrow and pretty steep, which bring you back to Le Lavachet.*

*The best place to find fresh snow is the **Chardonnet** couloirs – they face north, and never get the sun. The snow is always very good here. The route involves a 20-minute walk from the top of the Merle Blanc chair-lift.*

*The **Vallons de la Sache** is one of the most famous off-piste routes – a descent of 1200m/3,940ft vertical down a breathtaking valley in the heart of the National Park, overlooked by the magnificent Sache glacier. Starting from l'Aiguille Percée at 2750m/9,020ft you enter a different world, high up in the mountains, far away from the ski lifts. You arrive several hours later down in Les Brévières at 1550m/5,090ft, below the Tignes dam.*

This valley offers a multitude of routes to suit intermediate skiers or highly experienced free-riders – gentle slopes, steep slopes, couloirs, rock-faces and tree skiing. The north-facing slopes offer powder skiing while the south-facing slopes are perfect for spring snow skiing. Highly experienced skiers and snowboarders can climb up and pass through the Trou de la Souris (Mouse Hole) to ski the steep slopes of the 3 Murs (3 Walls). And the really fearless can ski through the sheer-sided Gorges de la Sache.

Tignes

373

can get very crowded. There is lots to do on the other side of the valley, including explore the Ves run (which we loved when it was a red piste). As part of the creation of Le SPOT (see 'For experts') this has now been reclassified a Naturide. The runs down from l'Aiguille Percée to Tignes-les-Boisses and Tignes-les-Brévières are also scenic and fun. There are red and blue options as well as the beautiful Sache black run – adventurous intermediates shouldn't miss it – 'very exciting', says a visitor this year. The runs down from l'Aiguille Percée to Le Lac are gentle, wide blues.

FOR BEGINNERS
Good nursery slopes, but ...
The nursery slopes of Tignes-le-Lac and Le Lavachet (which meet at the top) are excellent – convenient, snow-sure, gentle, free of through-traffic and served by a slow chair and a drag. The

ones at Val-Claret are less appealing: an unpleasantly steep slope within the village served by a drag, and a less convenient slope served by the fast Bollin chair. All of these lifts are free.

Although there are some fairly easy blues on the west side of Tignes, for long green runs you have to go over to the Val-d'Isère sector. You need an Espace Killy pass to use them, and to get back to Tignes you have a choice between the blue run from Col de Fresse (which has a tricky start) or riding the gondola down from Tovière. And in poor weather, the high Tignes valley is an intimidatingly bleak place – enough to make any wavering beginner retreat to a bar with a book.

FOR CROSS-COUNTRY
Interesting variety
The Espace Killy has 40km/25 miles of cross-country trails. There are tracks on the frozen Lac de Tignes, along the

LIFT PASSES

L'Espace Killy
Covers all Tignes and Val-d'Isère.

Beginners
5 free lifts.

Main pass
1 day €39
6 days €187

Senior citizens
Over 60: 6 days €159
Over 75: free pass

Children
Under 13: 6 days €140.50
Under 5: free pass

Notes
Half-day and pedestrian passes available. Discount on presentation of lift pass from any of previous three seasons. Six-day passes and over are valid for one day in the Three Valleys, Valmorel and Paradiski, half-price pass in Ste-Foy and reduced price in La Rosière.

Alternative passes
Tignes-only pass available.

valley between Val-Claret and Tignes-le-Lac, at Les Boisses and Les Brévières and up on the Grande Motte.

QUEUES
Very few
The queues here depend on snow conditions. If snow low down is poor, the Grande Motte funicular generates queues; the fast chairs in parallel with it are often quicker, despite the longer ride time. These lifts jointly shift a lot of people, with the result that the run down to Val-Claret can be unpleasantly crowded. The worst queues now are for the cable-car on the glacier – half-hour waits are common.

Of course, if higher lifts are closed by heavy snow or high winds, the lifts on the lower slopes have big queues.

The famous afternoon queues for the slow Tommeuses chairs bringing Tignes residents back from the Val slopes to Tovière are now a fond memory, thanks to the fast eight-seat replacement. It has also cut queues at the Borsat quad to Col de Fresse, the easiest way back to Val-Claret. Post-lunch queues at Les Brévières are not unknown.

MOUNTAIN RESTAURANTS
Adequate
The restaurants at the top of the Chaudannes chair – the Alpage for self-service and Lo Soli for table-service – represented a huge improvement on the western side of the bowl when they were built a few seasons back. Their adjacent terraces share a superb view of the Grande Motte, and Lo Soli provides 'superb service' with 'sensible portions and reasonable prices'.

The opposite side of the bowl has two places offering both table- and self-service. The atmospheric chalet at the top of Tovière is 'fairly basic' but does 'very good portions'. Table-service meals at the modern but pleasantly woody Chalet du Bollin – just a few metres above Val-Claret – are 'first class', and 'worth the little extra cost', though a 2005 visitor found the 'service just OK, but food very good'. At the top of the Tichot chair from Val Claret, the Palet 'serves good food at good prices'.

The big Panoramic self-service restaurant at the top of the Grande Motte funicular has great views from its huge terrace, but it is traversed every few minutes by the next funicular-full of people. There's an excellent table-service 'cuisine gourmande' restaurant here too with 'exceptionally good service and hospitality', says a recent reporter.

There are lots of easily accessible (and often cheaper) places for lunch in the resorts. One ski-to-the-door

boarding

This is a big area, with a big boarder reputation, and it's a cheaper place to stay than Val-d'Isère. There are a few flat areas (avoid Génépy and Myrtilles warns a 2005 boarding reporter) but the lift system relies more on chairs and gondolas than drags (though a long drag serves the boarder-cross area – 'Nuts!' says a 2005 reporter). There are long, wide pistes to blast down, with acres of powder between them to play in such as Grattalu, Carline and Piste H). There are three specialist snowboard schools (Kebra, Snocool and Surf Feeling). Reporters have been impressed with the Evolution 2 boarding instructors: 'First class, with a really innovative approach.' Hiring a guide and exploring the off-piste is recommended for good free-riders.

SCHOOLS

ESF
t 0479 063028

Evolution 2
t 0479 064378

Snocool
t 0479 400858

Kebra
t 0479 064337

333
t 0479 062088

Surf Feeling
t 0479 065363

Classes (ESF prices)
6 half days: €119
Private lessons
€34 for 1hr

GUIDES

Bureau des Guides
t 0479 064276

Tetra
t 0479 419707

CHILDREN

Les Marmottons
t 0479 065167
Ages 3 to 8. €110 for
5 half days

Ski schools
Evolution 2 takes
children from age 3
and ESF takes
children from age 4 (6
half-days €123).

OT TIGNES / C TATIN

High, snow-sure,
open slopes, way
above the tree line –
that's what you go to
Tignes for →

favourite of ours in Le Lac is the
ground-floor restaurant of the hotel
Montana, on the left as you descend
from l'Aiguille Percée. In Val-Claret the
Fish Tank is described as 'very good
value', the Carline self-service
restaurant as having 'cheerful staff and
hearty portions', and the Taverne des
Neiges as having 'good food and
service'. In Le Lac, the 'excellent'
Arbina is popular (see 'Eating out'). In
Les Brévières, a short walk round the
corner into the village brings you to
places much cheaper than the two by
the piste. Sachette, for example, is
crowded with artefacts from mountain
life and offers 'lots of good cheese
dishes' including 'superb tartiflette'.
The Etoile des Neiges 'serves great,
typical Savoyard food'.

SCHOOLS AND GUIDES
Plenty of choice
There are over half-a-dozen schools,
including three specialist snowboard
schools, plus various independent
instructors. Reporters advise that pre-
booking is 'essential' at busy times

like Easter. A 2005 visitor heard 'good
reports of ESF; individuals were moved
groups as they improved; usually
maximum of eight in a class.' And a
reporter on Evolution 2 said: 'Our
beginner boarders got on well in the
group lessons despite a class size of
ten and the instructor's poor English.
We had a selection of private ski and
boarding lessons, which were excellent.'

FACILITIES FOR CHILDREN
Mixed reports
We have had good reports on the
Marmottons kindergartens – 'brilliant'
says a father of a four-year-old this
year – and the Spritelets ski classes
arranged by Esprit Ski and Evolution 2:
'She loved her class and could
snowplough by the end of the week.'
But we have had a few poor reports on
Evolution 2 in the past – eg a young
girl at the back of one class got
detached from the group and left on
the mountain, to be rescued by
passers-by, and another young girl in a
different class was 'delivered to her
father with white, frost-bitten cheeks'.

Tignes

375

GETTING THERE

Air Geneva
165km/103 miles
(3½hr); Lyon 240km/
149 miles (3½hr);
Chambéry 130km/
81 miles (2½hr)

Rail Bourg-St-Maurice
(30km/19 miles);
regular buses or taxi
from station

ACTIVITIES

Indoor 'Vitatignes'
(sauna, Turkish baths,
hot-tub, etc), Bains
du Montana (pool,
sauna, etc), Fitness
Centre (spa
treatments, weight
training, fitness),
Aquatonic Centre (spa
and beauty
treatments, fitness
etc), cinemas,
multisports hall, yoga,
bowling, squash,
networked games
tournaments,
computer and video
editing lessons

Outdoor Natural
skating-rink, hang-
gliding, paragliding,
helicopter rides,
snow-mobiles, husky
dog-sledding, ice-
diving, bungee
trampolining, mini
quad bikes, snow
rafting, ice-climbing,
snow-shoeing, aircraft
and microlight flights,
ski-joring

STAYING THERE

HOW TO GO
Unremarkable range of options
All three main styles of accommodation
are available through tour operators.
And more luxury options are appearing.
Chalets The choice of catered chalets is
increasing. Total Ski and Neilson both
have several smart chalets, including
some with pool, hot-tub and sauna.
Child specialist Esprit Ski has a chalet
hotel and several chalets here. Ski
Olympic's Chalet Rosset has been
recommended by reporters: 'Superb,
with a lovely lounge with views.'
Crystal's hotel-style Curling, plumb in
the centre of Val-Claret, has neat
public areas and spacious bedrooms.
Snowstar's Chalet Chardon has a vast
living room and was once owned by
the late Robert Maxwell.
Hotels The few hotels are small and
concentrated in Le Lac. There are Club
Meds at Val-Claret and Les Brévières.
(((3) **Campanules** (0479 063436)
Smartly rustic chalet in upper Le Lac,
with good restaurant. One reporter was
impressed enough to suggest that it
deserved a 4-star rating.
(((3) **Village Montana** (0479 400144)
Stylishly woody 3-star on the east-
facing slopes above Le Lac, with 4-star
suites section. Outdoor pool and sauna,
steam and hot-tub. Reporters praise it
but warn there are 'lots of children'.
(((3) **Lévanna** (0479 063294) Smart 3-
star in central position in Le Lac –
comfortable, with a 'generous hot-tub'.
(((3) **Diva** (0479 067000) Biggest in
town (121 rooms). On lower level of
Val-Claret, a short walk from lifts. 'Very
comfy rooms, excellent meals.' Sauna.
((2) **Arbina** (0479 063478) Well-run
place close to the lifts in Le Lac, with
lunchtime terrace, crowded après-ski
bar and one of the best restaurants.
((2) **Marais** (0479 064006) Prettily
furnished, simple hotel in Les Boisses.

(1) **Génépy** (0479 065711) Simple
Dutch-run chalet in Les Brévières.
Self-catering There are lots of
apartments available. MGM's wood-
clad L'Ecrin des Neiges apartments in
lower Val-Claret are probably the best,
with a pool. The Chalet Club in Val-
Claret is a collection of simple studios,
but has a free indoor pool, sauna and
in-house restaurant and bar. The
supermarket at Le Lac is reported to
be 'comprehensive but very expensive'.

EATING OUT
Good places scattered about
The options in Le Lavachet are rather
limited, though a 2005 reporter
enjoyed Le Grenier with its 'excellent
cold meats and tartiflette'. Finding
anywhere with some atmosphere is
difficult in Le Lac, though the food in
some of the better hotels is good. The
Campanules is 'a gastronomic delight',
said a reporter last year. The Arbina
continues to provide 'outstanding
food, very good value and first-class
service'. Two 2005 visitors recommend
the 'delicious food' at the 'quirky' Clin
d'Oeil. Two others recommend Bagus
Cafe's 'eclectic cuisine'.

In Val-Claret the Caveau is
recommended for a special treat. You
may have to wait at Petit Savoyard but
the food and service are said to be
worth it. The buffet at the Indochine
has been strongly recommended by
several reporters. Pizza 2000 has
'reasonable prices and helpful staff'
but a 2005 reporter says La Pignatta
'slightly trumps it'. The Auberge des 3
Oursons was recommended for
'massive portions, friendly service'.

The Cordée in Les Boisses is said to
offer unpretentious surroundings, great
traditional French food, modest prices.

APRES-SKI
Hidden away
Recent reporters agree that there is
plenty going on if you know where to
find it. Val-Claret has some early-
evening atmosphere and happy hours
are popular. Reporters differ on the
merits of the Crowded House and Fish
Tank (both popular with Brits), with
the latter getting marginally more
votes. Grizzly's is 'cosy and atmospheric,
but you pay for the ambience'.

Le Lac is a natural focus for
immediate après-ski drinks. Again this
year's favourite is the 'lively' Loop,
with pool table, and its 'two for one
happy hour 4 to 6pm, which is popular

Val-Claret, seen from the run down from the Grande Motte. There will be a new fast chair for 2005/06 heading up the western slopes on the left ➔

SNOWPIX.COM / CHRIS GILL

with the younger set'. The bar of the hotel Arbina is our kind of spot – adequately cosy, friendly service. It's a great place to sit outside and people-watch. The Alpaka Cocktail Bar is recommended as 'a real gem later on' with 'a staggering array of cocktails'. Embuscade is said to be 'the only proper French bar in town'. The Red Lion in Les Almes has satellite TV, pool and 'a good range of beers'. What was the most animated bar in Le Lavachet – Harri's – is now called Censored and still has a 'good atmosphere'. TC's bar is 'very friendly, with good music'.

Le Lac, Café de la Poste and Jack's are popular late haunts.

OFF THE SLOPES
Forget it

Despite the range of alternative activities, Tignes is a resort for those who want to use the slopes, where anyone who doesn't is liable to feel like a fish out of water. Some activities do get booked up quickly as well – a reporter said it was impossible to find a free dog-sledding slot in April. A sports centre is under construction but won't be finished until summer 2006. Meanwhile, the big pools at the Village Montana and Suites du Montana are open to the public (though they may require advance booking).

Tignes

377

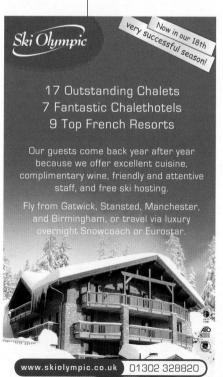

Les Trois Vallées

The biggest lift-linked ski area in the world – and it undersells itself

Despite competing claims, notably from the Portes du Soleil, in practical terms the Three Valleys cannot be beaten for sheer quantity of lift-served terrain. There is nowhere like it for a keen skier or boarder who wants to cover as much mileage as possible while rarely taking the same run repeatedly. It has a lot to offer everyone, from beginner to expert. And its resorts offer a wide range of alternatives – not only the quite widely known attractions of the big-name mega-resorts but also the increasingly appreciated low-key appeal of the smaller villages.

What's more, the area deliberately undersells itself. It should actually be known as the Four Valleys because several years ago it expanded into a fourth valley – the Maurienne. And the figures the individual resorts give us for their local ski areas add up to 630km/391 miles – but the Three Valleys claims only 600km/ 373 miles. So we'll forgive the fact that the lifts add up to a mere 185 when 200 are claimed. After spending millions on marketing itself as Three Valleys with 600km of pistes and 200 lifts why should it change? Whatever, it's huge!

The runs of the Three Valleys and their resorts are dealt with in six chapters. The four major resorts are Courchevel, Méribel, Les Menuires and Val-Thorens, but we also give chapters to St-Martin- de-Belleville, a small village down the valley from Les Menuires, and La Tania, a relatively recent development between Courchevel and Méribel.
None of the resorts is cheap. **Les**

Menuires has some budget accommodation but its original buildings are hard on the eye (new developments are now being built in a much more acceptable style). The slopes around the village get too much sun for comfort, but across the valley are some of the best (and quietest) challenging pistes in the Three Valleys on its north-facing La Masse. Down the valley from Les Menuires is **St-Martin-de-Belleville**, a charming traditional village which has been expanded in a sympathetic style. It has good-value accommodation and lift links into the slopes of Les Menuires and Méribel.

Up rather than down the Belleville valley from Les Menuires, at 2300m/ 7,550ft, **Val-Thorens** is the highest resort in the Alps, and at 3230m/ 10,600ft the top of its slopes is the high point of the Three Valleys. The snow in this area is almost always good, and it includes two glaciers where good snow is guaranteed. But the setting is bleak and the lifts are vulnerable to closure in bad weather. The purpose-built resort is very

convenient. Visually it is not comparable to Les Menuires, thanks to the smaller-scale design and more thorough use of wood cladding, but it still isn't to everyone's taste.

Méribel is a two-part resort. The higher component, **Méribel-Mottaret**, is the best placed of all the resorts for getting to any part of the Three Valleys system in the shortest possible time. It's now quite a spread-out place, with some of the accommodation a long way up the hillsides – great for access to the slopes, less so for access to nightlife. **Méribel** itself is 200m/660ft lower and has long been a British favourite, especially for chalet holidays. It is the most attractive of the main Three Valleys resorts, built in chalet style beside a long winding road up the hillside. Parts of the resort are very convenient for the slopes and the village centre; parts are very far from either. The growing hamlet of **Méribel-Village** has its own chair-lift into the system but is very isolated and quiet.

Courchevel has four parts. 1850 is the most fashionable resort in France, and can be the most expensive resort in the Alps (though it doesn't have to cost a fortune to stay there). The less expensive parts – Le Praz (aka 1300), 1550 and 1650 – don't have the same choice of nightlife and restaurants. Many people rate the slopes around Courchevel the best in the Three Valleys, with runs to suit all standards. The snow tends to be better than in neighbouring Méribel.

La Tania was built for the 1992 Olympics, just off the small road linking Le Praz to Méribel. It has now grown into an attractive, car-free collection of chalets and chalet-style apartments set among the trees, and is popular with families. It has a good nursery slope and lovely long intermediate runs, with a green run back due to open for winter 2005/06.

Les Trois Vallées

379

Val-d'Isère

On- and off-piste playground, with smart new lifts and reliable snow

COSTS

① ② ③ ④ ⑤ ⑥

RATINGS

The slopes

Fast lifts	****
Snow	*****
Extent	*****
Expert	*****
Intermediate	*****
Beginner	***
Convenience	***
Queues	****
Mountain restaurants	**

The rest

Scenery	***
Resort charm	***
Off-slope	**

NEWS

For 2005/06 a new six-pack is due to open. This will go from the roadside at Le Laisinant up to above the top of the cable-car from Le Fornet, and will mean you no longer have to catch a bus if you ski one of the lovely runs down to Le Laisinant. It will also be an alternative way of getting up the mountain in the morning.

Snowmaking should be installed on the Pissaillas glacier to make the summer skiing season last longer.

For 2004/05 Piste M down from Solaise to the village – one of the tough blue runs that we have complained about as being undergraded – was at last regraded to red. And the alternative Piste A down was switched from red to black.

Also for 2004/05 a new nightclub called Le Graal opened.

➕ Huge area linked with Tignes, with lots of runs for all abilities

➕ Big recent investment in new lifts

➕ One of the great resorts for lift-served off-piste runs

➕ High altitude of most slopes means snow is more or less guaranteed

➕ Wide choice of schools, especially for off-piste lessons and guiding

➕ For a high resort, the town is attractive, very lively at night, and offers a good range of restaurants

➕ Wide range of package holidays and accommodation

➕ Piste grooming and staff attitudes have improved noticeably

➖ Some green and blue runs are tricky – and often hazardous for early or timid intermediates

➖ You're quite likely to need the bus at the start and end of the day

➖ Most lifts and slopes are liable to close when the weather is bad

➖ Nursery slopes not ideal

➖ Still some lifts in need of upgrading

➖ Main off-piste slopes get tracked out very quickly

➖ Seems at times more British than French – especially in low season

➖ Few good mountain restaurants

➖ Increasingly pricey

Val-d'Isère is one of the world's best resorts for experts – attracted by the extent of lift-served off-piste – and for confident, mileage-hungry intermediates. But you don't have to be particularly adventurous to enjoy the resort.

The many drawbacks listed above are mainly not serious complaints, whereas most of the plus-points weigh heavily in the balance, The lift company has made a concerted effort in recent years to deal with key criticisms. Heavy investment in new lifts has eliminated bad bottlenecks, the piste grooming has been improved and they have even started to regrade some of their pistes, which should help timid intermediates to have more confidence in the piste map. But more regrading is needed, and the green run down to La Daille remains one of the most seriously undergraded we have come across. The village ambience has been improved recently too; and the resort has a huge selection of both chalet and hotel holidays on offer by UK tour operators – with some very luxurious options indeed. Overall, this is one of our favourite resorts in the world.

THE RESORT

Val-d'Isère spreads along a remote valley, which is a dead end in winter. The road in from Bourg-St-Maurice brings you dramatically through a rocky defile to the satellite mini-resort of La Daille – a convenient but hideous slope-side apartment complex and the base of lifts into the major Bellevarde sector of the slopes. The outskirts of Val proper are dreary, but as you approach the centre recent improvements become more evident: new wood- and stone-cladding, culminating in the tasteful pedestrian-only Val Village complex. The few remnants of the original old village are tucked away behind this. Many first-

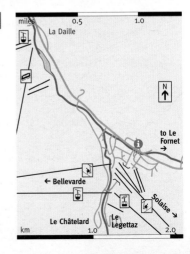

The centre of Val has pleasant chalet-style buildings →

OT VAL-D'ISERE / NUTS

KEY FACTS

Resort	1850m
	6,070ft
Entire Espace Killy area	
Slopes	1550-3455m
	5,090-11,340ft
Lifts	90
Pistes	300km
	186 miles
Green	15%
Blue	46%
Red	27%
Black	12%
Snowmaking	26km
	16 miles

time visitors find the resort much more pleasant than they expect a high resort to be, and returning visitors generally find things improving.

Turn right at the centre and you drive under the nursery slopes and Val's big lifts up to Bellevarde and Solaise to a lot of new development beyond. Continue up the main valley instead, and you come to Le Laisinant, a peaceful little outpost with a new lift out of the valley for 2005/06, and then to Le Fornet and the fourth major lift station.

There is a lot of traffic around, but the resort is working to get cars under control and make the centre more pedestrian-friendly.

The location of your accommodation isn't crucial. The main lift stations are linked by efficient free shuttle-buses; even in peak periods you never have to wait more than a few minutes. But in the evening frequency plummets and dedicated après-skiers will want to be within walking distance of the centre. The developments up the side valley beyond the main lift station – Le Châtelard and La Legettaz – are mainly attractive, and some offer ski-in/ski-out convenience. But you pay the price in the evening when the buses stop running – the farthest-flung places are a long slog from the village. La Daille and Le Fornet have their (quite different) attractions for those less concerned about nightlife.

A car is of no great value around the resort, but simplifies outings to other resorts. A six-day lift pass gives a day in the Paradiski area (Les Arcs and La Plagne combined) and in the Three Valleys and 50% off a pass in Ste-Foy, the locals' favourite outing.

THE MOUNTAINS

Although there are wooded slopes above the village on all sectors, in practice most of the runs here are on open slopes above the tree line.

Piste grooming is clearly better than it used to be, but we continue to get complaints about the poor signing (particularly at piste junctions) and the piste grading – 'a joke' reiterated a 2005 visitor. Many blue and some green runs are simply too steep, narrow and even bumpy; we are pleased to see that some pistes have been regraded (see 'News'), but more need to be.

If you plan a return visit, keep your lift pass – those with a week's pass

bought in the last three years are entitled to a 'loyal customer' reduction.

The local radio carries weather reports in English as well as in French. Precision Ski was a highly regarded British-run ski shop, but the management changed last season and we have no current reports.

THE SLOPES
Vast and varied

Val-d'Isère's slopes divide into three main sectors. **Bellevarde** is the mountain that is home to Val-d'Isère's famous downhill course – the OK piste, which opens each season's World Cup Alpine circus in December (in 2005, on the weekend of 10/11 December for men and 17/18 December for women). You can reach Bellevarde quickly by funicular from La Daille, but the powerful new gondola from near the centre of town is now the preferred route for those based near it. From the top you can descend to the valley, play on a variety of drags and chairs at altitude or take a choice of lifts to the Tignes slopes, including the fast Tommeuses eight-seat chair-lift.

Solaise is the other mountain accessible directly from Val-d'Isère. The Solaise Express fast quad chair-lift takes you a few metres higher than the parallel cable-car. Once up, a short drag takes you over a plateau and down to a variety of chairs that serve this very sunny area of predominantly gentle pistes. From near the top of this

LIFT PASSES

L'Espace Killy
Covers Tignes and
Val-d'Isère.

Beginners
All seven lifts on the
nursery slopes are
free.

Main pass
1 day €39
6 days €187

Senior citizens
Over 60: 6 days €159
Over 75: free pass

Children
Under 13: 6 days
€140.50
Under 5: free pass

Notes
Half-day and
pedestrian passes
available. Discount on
presentation of lift
pass from any of
previous three
seasons. Six-day
passes and over are
valid for one day in
the Three Valleys,
Valmorel and
Paradiski (La Plagne-
Les Arcs), half-price
pass in Ste-Foy and
reduced price in La
Rosière.

Alternative passes
There is no separate
pass for Val-d'Isère's
lifts only.

area you can catch the fast Leissières
six-pack (which climbs over a steep
ridge and then drops suddenly down
the other side) over to the third main
area, above and below the **Col de
l'Iseran**. The area can also be reached
by the new chair-lift for 2005/06 from
Le Laisinant or by cable-car from Le
Fornet. The runs at Col de l'Iseran are
predominantly easy, with spectacular
views and access to the region's most
beautiful off-piste terrain.

TERRAIN-PARKS
Beginners and experts welcome
We continue to get rave reports on the
very good terrain-park above the La
Daille gondola. It is served by the
Mont Blanc chair, two drag-lifts and a
rope-tow. As well as a half-pipe, two
quarter-pipes and boarder-cross
courses there are assorted bumps,
jumps, hips and railslides catering to
park-beginners and park-experts alike.
'Enough to keep you entertained for
many hours,' said one reporter. 'My
sons spent much of the week hanging
out there,' another. But a reporter who
was staying in Tignes said, 'It
appeared to be open on only one day
during our stay.' Four snow-guns are
used to ensure good snow-cover.

SNOW RELIABILITY
Difficult to beat
In years when lower resorts have
suffered, Val-d'Isère has rarely been
short of snow. Its height means you
can almost always get back to the
village, especially because of the
snowmaking on the main routes home.
But even more important is that in
each sector there are lots of lifts and
runs above mid-mountain, between
about 2300m and 2900m (7,550ft and
9,510ft). Many of the slopes face
roughly north. And there is access to
glaciers at Pissaillas or over in Tignes,
although both take a while to get to.

FOR EXPERTS
One of the world's best
Val-d'Isère is one of the top resorts in
the world for experts. The main
attraction is the huge range of
beautiful off-piste possibilities – see
the feature panel over the page.

There may be better resorts for
really steep pistes – there are certainly
lots in North America – but there is
plenty on-piste to amuse the expert,
despite the small number of blacks on
the piste map. Many reds and blues
are steep enough to get mogulled.

On Bellevarde the famous Face run
is the main attraction – often mogulled
from top to bottom, but not worryingly
steep. Epaule is the sector's other
black run – where the moguls are hit
by long exposure to sun and can be
slushy or rock-hard (it is prone to
closure for these reasons too). There
are several challenging ways down
from Solaise to the village: all steep,
though none fearsomely so (Piste X
has now been regraded from a normal
black run to a 'Naturide' – see Tignes
chapter for what this means).

Wayne Watson of off-piste school
Alpine Expérience puts a daily diary of
off-piste snow conditions and runs on
the web at www.alpineexperience.com.

FOR INTERMEDIATES
Quantity and quality
Val-d'Isère has even more to offer
intermediates than experts. There's
enough here to keep you interested for
several visits – though pistes can be
crowded in high-season, and the less
experienced should be aware that
many runs are under-graded.

In the Solaise sector is a network of
gentle blue runs, ideal for building
confidence. And there are a couple of
beautiful runs from here through the
woods to Le Laisinant – ideal in bad
weather, though prone to closure in
times of avalanche danger.

Val-d'Isère is good for boarders, though Tignes is a more popular boarder destination. Most of the main lifts are cable-cars, chair-lifts and gondolas, with very few drag-lifts. But there are a few flat areas where you'll need to scoot or walk. Experts will revel in the off-piste. There are several specialist snowboard shops and schools, including Misty Fly. The village nursery area is ideal for trying out boarding and Le Fornet is good to progress to. The terrain-park is great.

Val-d'Isère

3300m/10,830ft
Glacier de Pissaillas
Col Pers
2950m
Col de l'Iseran
2765m   2900m
Col de la Leisse
Col de Fresse
2770m
Tour Charvet
Tignes ↘
Le Manchet
1940m
Tovière
2705m
2325m
Bellevarde
2705m
Solaise
2560m
Le Châtelard
Le Fornet
1930m
Le Laisinant
Val d'Isère
1850m/6,070ft
La Daille
1785m

Most of the runs in the Col de l'Iseran sector are even easier – ideal for early and hesitant intermediates. Those marked blue at the top of the glacier could really be classified green.

Bellevarde has a huge variety of runs ideally suited to intermediates of all levels. From Bellevarde itself there is a choice of green, blue and red runs of varying pitch. And the wide runs from Tovière normally give you the choice of groomed piste or moguls.

A snag for early intermediates is that runs back to the valley can be challenging. The easiest way is to head down to La Daille, where there is a green run – but it should be classified blue (in some resorts it would be red). It gets very crowded and mogulled by the end of the day. None of the runs from Bellevarde and Solaise back to Val itself is really easy. The blue Santons run from Bellevarde takes you through a long, narrow gun barrel, which often has people standing around plucking up courage, making things even trickier. On Solaise there isn't much to choose between the black and red ways down. At the top, there's no option other than the red run in full view of the lifts. Many early intermediates sensibly choose to ride the lifts down – take the chair for a spectacular view.

FOR BEGINNERS
OK if you know where to go
The nursery slope right by the centre of town is 95% perfect; it's just a pity that the very top is unpleasantly steep. The lifts serving it are free.

Once off the nursery slopes, you have to know where to find easy runs; many of the greens should be blue, or even red. One local instructor admits: 'We have to have green runs on the map, even if we don't have so many green slopes – otherwise beginners wouldn't come to Val-d'Isère.'

A good place for your first real runs off the nursery slopes is the Madeleine green run on Solaise – served by a fast six-pack. The Col de l'Iseran runs are also gentle and wide, and not overcrowded. There is good progression terrain on Bellevarde, too. From all sectors, it's best to take a lift down back to the valley.

FOR CROSS-COUNTRY
Limited
There are a couple of loops in each of three areas – towards La Daille, on Solaise and out past Le Laisinant. More picturesque is the one going from Le Châtelard (on the road past the main cable-car station) to the Manchet chair. But keen cross-country enthusiasts should go elsewhere.

QUEUES
Few problems
Queues to get out of the resort have been kept in check by new lifts – most recently the big new gondola to Bellevarde and for 2005/06 by the new six-pack from Le Laisinant. At Solaise the slow Lac chair up to the Tête Solaise can generate queues. Getting back from Col de l'Iseran to Solaise at the end of the day is no longer a problem thanks to the new Leissières Express six-pack. Crowded pistes in high season is a more common complaint than queues these days.

THE BEST LIFT-SERVED OFF-PISTE IN THE WORLD?

Few resorts can rival the extent of lift-served off-piste skiing in Val-d'Isère.

Some runs are ideal for adventurous intermediates looking to try off-piste for the first time. The Tour du Charvet goes through glorious scenery from the top of the Grand Pré chair-lift on the back of Bellevarde. For most of the way it is very gentle, with only a few steeper pitches. It ends up at the bottom of the Manchet chair up to the Solaise area. The Pays Désert is a very easy run from the top of the lift system on the Pissaillas glacier. The views are superb. You end up at the Pays Désert T-bar.

For more experienced off-piste skiers, Col Pers is one of our favourite runs. Again, it starts a traverse away from the Pissaillas glacier. You go over a pass into a big, wide, fairly gentle bowl with glorious views and endless ways down. If the snow is good, you can drop down into the Gorges de Malpasset, and ski over the frozen Isère river back to the Le Fornet cable-car.

There are endless other off-piste options such as Cugnai and Danaides on Solaise, Banane and the Couloir des Pisteurs on Bellevarde – and of course many more in Tignes.

But don't dream of doing any off-piste runs without a fully qualified guide or instructor. Route finding is difficult, avalanche danger can be high and hidden hazards such as cliffs and crevasses lurk.

MOUNTAIN RESTAURANTS
Getting better – slowly

The mountain restaurants mainly consist of big self-service places with vast terraces at the top of major lifts. But there are exceptions, and they are gradually growing in number.

The Fruitière at the top of La Daille gondola, a table-service place kitted out with stuff rescued from a dairy in the valley, is still popular. Reports on the Folie Douce next door range from 'a fine lunch with live music' to 'overpriced' and 'cold chips and lukewarm soup'. Later, après-ski starts here. The 'friendly' but busy Trifollet, about halfway down the OK run, 'serves one of the best tartiflettes in the Alps' and good plats du jour. If you are in a hurry, Marmottes, in the middle of the Bellevarde bowl, is an efficient self-service with a big sunny terrace. A visitor this year found its coffee and hot chocolate machines much cheaper than buying them conventionally. The small and friendly Bar de L'Ouillette, at the base of the Madeleine chair-lift, does good food at reasonable prices and the Datcha, at

the bottom of the Cugnai lift, 'excellent salads, if expensive'. A reporter last year found the Tanière better value, set between the two chairs going up Face de Bellevarde. It is popular with the locals and is 'a welcome change from the usual cafeteria crush', and a visitor this year noted it had the 'best toilets on the mountain – and the only ones where you didn't have to pay'. Several reporters last year were excited by the discovery of 'a smashing little place with a nice landlady' and 'very nice cooking' – the 'pleasantly woody' Edelweiss, above Le Fornet.

On the lower slopes at La Daille and reachable on snow and by pedestrians, Tufs is one of the best places around, with good pizzas and a good-value buffet on the first floor.

Of course there are lots of places actually in the resort villages. When at Col de l'Iseran, one idea for lunch on a wintry day is to descend to the rustic Arolay at Le Fornet. The terrace of the Brussel's hotel in Val d'Isère, right by the nursery slopes, was recommended by a 2005 reporter for its 'good food and excellent service'.

Val-d'Isère

OT VAL-D'ISERE / NUTS

The outlying hamlets of Le Fornet and Le Laisinant have some very nice recently built accommodation, their own lifts straight into the Le Fornet slopes and their own runs back; very pleasant for a quiet time ↘

SCHOOLS AND GUIDES
A very wide choice

There is a huge choice of schools, guides and private instructors. But as they all get busy, at peak periods it's best to book in advance. Practically all the schools run off-piste groups at various levels of competence, as well as on-piste lessons. Outside the ESF, practically all the instructors and guides speak good English, and many are native English-speakers.

The big news in the schools business a few years ago was the launch of The Development Centre, based in the Precision Ski shop in the heart of the village. This group of British instructors offers intensive clinics for all levels of skier and has been highly praised. Last season New Generation, another British-run school, also opened up – after successfully starting up in Courchevel and then expanding to Méribel and Les Arcs. See Méribel and Courchevel chapters for reports from satisfied customers.

Mountain Masters is a group of highly qualified British and French instructors and guides.

The Oxygène school gets mixed reviews. A 2005 reporter said that one adult had 'three instructors in six days' and that the 'children's tuition was good for the advanced classes but not for beginners'. They added, 'The adult beginners class was very poor indeed and 50% of the class dropped out on the first day.'

Over recent years we've heard from lots of satisfied pupils of Snow Fun and Evolution 2. A visitor this year found Evolution 2 'very good and really improved my skiing' when he turned to them after 'being abandoned' by his ESF instructor 'in limited visibility'. A reporter last year was mightily impressed by Bernard Chesneau of Ski Mastery: 'He transformed the balance of the upper intermediates – and gave confidence to a nervous intermediate.' Misty Fly is a specialist snowboard school.

There are two outfits specialising in guided off-piste groups – an excellent way to get off-piste safely without the cost of hiring a guide as an individual. We have had excellent mornings out with Alpine Expérience (Canadian, French, Italian, British guides) who also do 'excellent off-piste lessons' in the afternoons, and with Top Ski (mostly French guides) founder, Pat Zimmer.

CHILDREN

Le Village des Enfants
t 0479 400981
Ages 3 to 8; 9am-5.00 (Sun-Thu); 9am-2pm (Fri)

Le Petit Poucet
t 0479 061397
Ages from 3; 9am-5.30

Babysitter list
Contact tourist office.

Ski schools
Most offer classes. For example ESF runs classes for ages 5 to 17 (€188 to €240 for five days depending on age and ability). Snow Fun's Club Nounours takes children aged 3 to 6.

GETTING THERE

Air Geneva 180km/112 miles (4hr); Lyon 220km/137 miles (4hr); Chambéry 130km/81 miles (3hr)

Rail Bourg-St-Maurice (30km/19 miles); regular buses from station.

The weekly Henry's Avalanche Talks in Dick's Tea Bar are 'both entertaining and informative'. Heli-trips can be arranged from over the border in Italy – heli-drops are banned in France.

FACILITIES FOR CHILDREN
Good tour op possibilities
Many people prefer to use the facilities of UK tour operators such as Mark Warner or Ski Beat. But there's a 'children's village' for 3- to 8-year-olds, with supervised indoor and outdoor activities on the village nursery slopes. A past reporter was 'very pleased' with the childcare there: 'The staff speak English, and are very organised, in particular about the children's safety.'

STAYING THERE

HOW TO GO
Lots of choice
More British tour operators go to Val-d'Isère than to any other resort. The choice of chalets and chalet-hotels is vast. There is a Club Med 'village'.
Chalets This is Planet Chalet. There is everything from budget chalets to the most luxurious you could demand. Some of the most impressive are in the side-valley running south from the village. Companies with properties at the top end of the market include VIP, Scott Dunn and Descent International.

YSE is a Val d'Isère specialist, with 27 chalets. Le Ski has seven splendid all-en-suite chalets grouped together just behind the main street (and is putting in a big outdoor hot-tub for 2005/06), plus another two including a brand new one on the main street. Ski Beat has five en-suite chalets. Finlays has half-a-dozen properties, with especially luxurious looking ones in Le Fornet and Le Laisinant. There are several chalet hotels. Mark Warner has four, including the family-friendly Cygnaski, the nightlife hot spot Moris and the Val d'Isère in the centre, which has its own outdoor swimming pool.
Hotels There are about 40 to choose from, mostly 2- and 3-star, but for such a big international resort surprisingly few are notably attractive.
((((4) **Barmes de L'Ours** (0479 413710) 4-star 'luxury' hotel, the best in town. Central, with excellent indoor pool, numerous spa treatments, outdoor hot-tub planned for 2005/06. The fabulous rooms are in a different style on each floor. Three restaurants. Hugh Grant stayed here in 2005.
((((4)**Christiania** (0479 060825) Big chalet. Chic but friendly. Pool, sauna.
((((4) **Blizzard** (0479 060207) Comfortable. Convenient. Indoor-outdoor pool and sauna. Good food.
(((3) **Savoyarde** (0479 060155) Rustic decor. Newly refurbished leisure centre.

Val-d'Isère

387

FRANCE

388

ACTIVITIES

Indoor Swimming pool, sports hall (badminton, gym etc), climbing wall, weights room, library, fitness and health clubs, bridge, art gallery, yoga

Outdoor Ice rink, quad-bikes, all-terrain karts, farm visits, snowmobiles, paragliding, scenic flights, walking

Good food (but 'extremely disappointing' for vegetarians, said a 2005 reporter, who complained they made 'virtually no effort'). Rooms a bit small.

(((③ **Brussels** (0479 060539) Excellent location, right on nursery slope with big terrace. Sauna, steam room, hot-tub.

(((③ **Grand Paradis** (0479 061173) Next to Brussels. Recent refurbishment includes a new, imported Austrian wine cellar! Good food.

(((③ **Kandahar** (0479 060239) Smart, newish building above Taverne d'Alsace on main street.

(((③ **Mercure** (0479 061293) Highly recommended by one of our most reliable reporters: 'It doesn't look much from the outside, but the food and the wine list are excellent.'

(((③ **Sorbiers** (0479 062377) Modern but cosy B&B hotel, not far out. 'Clean, comfortable, good-sized rooms.'

(((③ **Samovar** (0479 061351) In La Daille. Traditional, with good food. 'Very friendly and helpful staff.'

Self-catering There are thousands of properties to choose from. UK operators offer lots of them, but they tend to get booked up early. The MGM Chalets du Laisinant apartments, out of town on the road to Le Fornet, look good. Local agency Val-d'Isère Agence (0479 067350) has a large selection of places and a good brochure. The local supermarkets are well stocked.

EATING OUT
Plenty of good, affordable places
The 70-odd restaurants offer a wide variety of cuisines and there's a helpful free *Guide des Tables* booklet.

Sadly, our favourite restaurant in town, the Chalet du Crêt, closed down at the end of last season. But the Grande Ourse, by the nursery slope, is one place to head for, for a top-of-the-range meal. Another is Les Clochetons, out in the Manchet valley (they run a free minibus to pick up and drop off clients) – we ate there in 2005 and enjoyed the foie gras and duck.

There are plenty of pleasant mid-priced places. But the popular Perdrix Blanche got very mixed reviews in 2005. Head for the Taverne d'Alsace – 'atmospheric and vibrant, good food but pricey'. Tufs, on the snow at La Daille, is open in the evenings (see 'Mountain restaurants'). The 'impressive' Austrian-influenced menu of the Schuss restaurant in the Grand Paradis hotel comes highly recommended. Those on tight budgets should try Chez Nano (next to Dick's Tea Bar) and the Lodge. Family-run Chez Paolo is praised for its 'excellent pizzas and pastas', the Corniche for being 'traditional French, very enjoyable'; Casa Scara for 'good food, though the service was slow', and Grand Cocor for 'excellent food and choice'.

APRES-SKI
Very lively

Nightlife is surprisingly energetic, given that most people have spent a hard day on the slopes. There are lots of bars, many with happy hours followed by music and dancing later on.

The Folie Douce, at the top of the La Daille gondola, has become an Austrian-style tea-time rave, with music and dancing; you can ride the gondola down. At La Daille the bar at the Samovar hotel is 'a good spot for a beer after skiing'. In downtown Val, Bananas (cosy wooden chalet with nice terrace), Café Face ('warm and friendly') and the Moris pub fill up as the slopes close; the 'friendly' Boubou, Bar Jacques and the Perdrix Blanche are popular with locals. Victor's bar is popular before it turns into a restaurant later on – black-and-white decor, stainless steel toilets. The Pacific Bar has sport on big screen TVs. Bar des Sports has some mountain atmosphere. The basement Taverne d'Alsace is quiet and relaxing.

Later on, the famous Dick's Tea Bar is the main disco and gets packed, but it receives mixed reports, with one reporter complaining about extortionate prices after 11pm. The nearby Petit Danois is a good alternative and somewhat less frenetic than Dick's. A new club called Le Graal opened last season, but we have no reports on it. Live music at Café Fats was enjoyed by a 2004 reporter who described it as 'a haphazard place but nevertheless a good atmosphere'.

On a quieter note, the Pub draws a 'more conversational crowd' and the Lodge is 'quite cosy', or there are hotel bars, piano bars and cocktail lounges.

OFF THE SLOPES
Not much

Val is primarily a resort for those keen to get on to the slopes – though one non-skiing reporter was 'very satisfied' with the facilities. The sports facilities, renovated swimming pool included, are not particularly impressive. The range of shops is better than in most high French resorts. Lunchtime meetings present problems: the easily accessible mountain restaurants are few, and your friends may prefer lunching miles away in places like Les Brévières. One reporter suggests that it's worth watching out for 'spectacular' firework displays and torchlit descents.

Val-d'Isère

389

JEANNE CATTINI

Valmorel

Pretty, purpose-built resort with fair-sized area of slopes

COSTS

① ② ③ ④ ⑤ ⑥

RATINGS

The slopes
Fast lifts	*
Snow	***
Extent	***
Expert	**
Intermediate	****
Beginner	*****
Convenience	*****
Queues	****
Mountain restaurants	**

The rest
Scenery	***
Resort charm	****
Off-slope	**

NEWS

For 2004/05, some pistes were improved and snowmaking was increased on the terrain-park.

+ The most sympathetically designed French purpose-built resort
+ Largely slope-side accommodation
+ Beginners and children particularly well catered for

− Few challenging pistes
− Fairly low, so snow can suffer
− Little variety in accommodation
− Still too many slow lifts and drags

Built from scratch in the mid-1970s, Valmorel was intended to look and feel like a mountain village: a traffic-free main street with low-rise hamlets grouped around it. The end result is an attractive, friendly sort of place. The slopes are extensive by most standards and with good snow conditions there's enough here to keep everyone except real experts happy; but the lift system is starting to look old-fashioned with only one fast chair and one gondola on the local slopes. Unashamedly aimed at the middle ground (intermediates, families and mixed-ability groups), Valmorel otherwise has considerable appeal.

THE RESORT

Valmorel is the main resort in 'Le Grand Domaine' – a ski area that links the Tarentaise with the Maurienne, by way of the Col de la Madeleine. Bourg-Morel is the heart of the resort – a traffic-free street where you'll find most of the shops and restaurants. It's pleasant and usually lively, with a distinctly family feel – but a reporter says the main street can get very crowded. Scattered here and there on the hillside are the six 'hameaux' with most of the accommodation. Hameau-du-Mottet is convenient – it is at the top of the Télébourg (the cross-village lift) with good access to the main lifts and from the return runs. All the mega-ski areas of the Tarentaise are within driving distance.

THE MOUNTAINS

Variety is provided by sectors of distinctive character, and the extent is enough to provide interesting day-trips. There are still a lot drag-lifts (you can't get back from Longchamp without taking one) and slow chairs.
Slopes The pistes are spread over a number of minor valleys and ridges either side of the Col de la Madeleine. The most heavily used route out of the village is the fast Altispace quad chair. From the top, a network of lifts and pistes takes you to the Col de la Madeleine and beyond that to Lauzière or the slopes of St-François and Longchamp. The Mottet and Gollet area have their own runs back towards the village, or you can work your way to the Beaudin and Madeleine sectors.

Terrain-parks There's a terrain-park, with a boarder-cross course, rails, quarter- and super-pipes, at the top of the Crève Coeur chair; a special park-only pass is available. There's also a boarder-cross by the Lune Bleue chair-lift at St-François.

Snow reliability With many runs below 2000m/6,560ft, good snow is not guaranteed. Mottet is north-facing and usually has the best snow. There's snowmaking on the nursery slopes and the main runs back to base.

Experts There are a few challenging pistes, but the off-piste is attractive because the resort does not attract experts, so powder can lie untracked for days after a snowfall. Gollet is usually a good place for moguls. There are steep black runs below the top section of the Mottet chair.

Intermediates The whole area except the steepest black runs is ideal, though part of the main run back to the village can be quite daunting at the end of the day. We have had conflicting reports about piste grooming with a reporter last year finding it 'erratic, which can make some red runs tricky'.

Beginners There are dedicated learning areas ('Still the best we've seen, 10/10,' according to one reporter) right by the village for both adults and children.

Snowboarding There are decent intermediate runs – but new boarders will find some of the drag-lifts tricky.

Cross-country Trails adding up to 23km/14 miles can be reached by bus.

Queues There can be 10- to 15-minute waits for the Altispace chair out of town at the morning peak, but those staying in the Mottet or Forêt areas can avoid this by taking the Lanchettes chair. The Frêne drags can't cope when everyone is returning from St-François.

Mountain restaurants There are half a dozen or so. Banquise 2000, with a great location at Col de la Madeleine, and Prariond have been recommended.

Schools and guides A 2005 reporter wrote, 'The charming teacher was excellent and spoke good English. She took us off-piste, on blacks and carving – great variety.' Teaching for first-timers is a speciality of the resort.

Facilities for children Piou-Piou club is a comprehensive childcare facility run by the ski school, and children taking ski lessons can have lunch there, too. Advance booking is essential.

STAYING THERE

How to go Self-catering packages are the norm but there are some catered chalets, mainly aimed at families. One regular prefers staying in Combelouvière below Valmorel – 'sunnier and quieter'.

Hotels A reporter last year described the Soleil La Fontaine (0825 826205) as 'Excellent; great food, friendly staff, sunny location right on the slopes.'

Self-catering The Athamante et Valeriane apartments have been praised.

Eating out The Grange and Ski Roc win approval again from a 2005 reporter.

Après-ski Immediate après-ski centres on the lively outdoor cafes; after-dark activities centre on the main street.

Off the slopes It's very pretty but not a great place to hang around if you're not using the slopes. There's a fitness centre, cinema and ice climbing is possible with a guide.

Valmorel

391

Val-Thorens

Europe's highest resort, with guaranteed good snow

COSTS

① ② ③ ④ ⑤ ⑥

RATINGS

The slopes

Fast lifts	****
Snow	*****
Extent	*****
Expert	****
Intermediate	*****
Beginner	****
Convenience	*****
Queues	***
Mountain restaurants	****

The rest

Scenery	***
Resort charm	**
Off-slope	**

NEWS

For 2005/06 a new hands-free electronic lift pass system will be introduced throughout the Three Valleys.

An ice-driving school opened for the 2004/05 season and runs courses from beginner to competition level. A toboggan run for young children also opened in the Place de Péclet. More snowmaking was installed and it will be increased again for 2005/06.

392

- Extensive local slopes to suit all abilities, and good access to the rest of the vast Three Valleys
- The highest resort in the Alps and one of the most snow-sure, with north-facing slopes guaranteeing good snow for a long season
- Convenient, gentle nursery slopes
- Not as much of an eyesore as most high, purpose-built resorts
- Compact village with direct slope access from most accommodation

- Can be bleak in bad weather – not a tree in sight
- Parts of the village are much less attractive to walk through in the evening than to ski past in the day
- Not much to do off the slopes
- Some very crowded pistes and dangerous intersections
- Still some queues – especially for the Cîme de Caron cable-car

For the enthusiast looking for the best snow in the Alps, it's difficult to beat Val-Thorens. That wonderful snow lies on some pretty wonderful slopes, and the village – always one of the better-designed high-altitude stations – gets more attractive as it continues to develop, and has some smart accommodation now.

But we still prefer a cosier base elsewhere in the Three Valleys. That way, if a storm socks in, we can play in the woods; if the sun is scorching, we have the option of setting off for Val-Thorens. The formula simply doesn't work the other way round. For a pre-Christmas or an April trip, though, it's the best base.

THE RESORT

Val-Thorens is built high above the tree line on a sunny, west-facing mountainside at the head of the Belleville valley, surrounded by peaks, slopes and lifts. The village streets are supposedly traffic-free. Practically all visitors' cars are banished to car parks, except on Saturday. But workers' cars still generate a fair amount of traffic, and weekends can be mayhem with people arriving and leaving. A 2005 reporter recommends booking parking in advance: 'It's cheaper and you are less likely to get a far distant parking spot.'

Many parts of the resort are designed with their 'fronts' facing the slopes, and their relatively dreary backs facing the streets. There are quite extensive shopping arcades, a

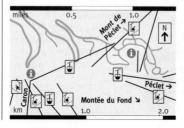

fair choice of bars and restaurants, and a good sports centre.

It is a classic purpose-built resort, with lots of convenient slope-side accommodation. It's quite a complex little village; but since it's very compact – our scale plan is one of the smallest in these pages – it doesn't matter much where you stay and there is a free bus service which visitors praise. At its heart is the snowy Place de Caron, where pedestrians mix with skiers and boarders. Many of the shops and restaurants are clustered here, along with the best hotels, and the sports centre is nearby. The village is basically divided in two by a little slope (with a drag-lift) that leads down from here to the broad main nursery slope running the length of the village. The upper half of the village is centred on the Place de Péclet. A road runs across the hillside from here to the chalet-style Balcons development. The lower half of the village is more diffuse, with the Rue du Soleil winding down from the dreary bus station to the big Temples du Soleil apartments.

Seen from the slopes, the resort is not as ugly as many of its rivals. The buildings are mainly medium-rise and wood-clad; some are distinctly stylish.

Gentle slopes lead
past nearly all the
accommodation; and
you get good views
into some apartments
from the chair-lifts ↗

OT VAL-THORENS /
BRUNO BOISSIERE

KEY FACTS

Resort	2300m
	7,550ft

Three Valleys	
Slopes	1260-3230m
	4,130-10,600ft
Lifts	200
Pistes	600km
	373 miles
Green	16%
Blue	38%
Red	36%
Black	10%
Snowmaking	
	1500 guns

Val-Thorens only	
Slopes	1800-3230m
	5,900-10,600ft
Lifts	30
Pistes	170km
	106 miles
Green	12%
Blue	38%
Red	42%
Black	8%
Snowmaking	
	200 guns

THE MOUNTAINS

Take account of the height, the extent
of its local slopes and the easy access
to the rest of the Three Valleys, and
the attraction of Val-Thorens becomes
clear. The main disadvantage is the
lack of trees. Heavy snowfalls or high
wind can shut practically all the lifts
and slopes, and even if they don't
close, poor visibility can be a problem.

THE SLOPES
High and snow-sure
The resort has a wide piste going right
down the front of it, leading down to a
number of different lifts. The big **Péclet**
gondola, with 30-person cabins, rises
700m/2,300ft to the Péclet glacier, with
a choice of red runs down. One links
across to a wide area of intermediate
runs served by lifts to cols either side
of the **Pointe de Thorens**. You can take
red or blue runs into the 'fourth
valley', the Maurienne, from one of
these – the **Col de Rosaël**, now served
by the Grand Fond 30-person gondola.
In the Maurienne valley two
successive chairs go up to 3230m/
10,600ft on the virgin flanks of **Pointe
du Bouchet** – the highest lift-served
point in the Three Valleys and with
stunning views. The former black run
off the back of here is now off-piste

because of crevasse and avalanche
danger and the snow gets very
windblown and icy – nice!
The 150-person cable-car to **Cîme de
Caron** is one of the great lifts of the
Alps, rising 900m/2,950ft in no time at
all. It can be reached by skiing across
from mid-mountain, or by coming up
on the gondola, which starts below the
village. From the top there is the
choice of red and black pistes down
the front, or a black into the
Maurienne.
The relatively low **Boismint** sector is
overlooked by many visitors, but is
actually a very respectable hill, with a
total vertical of 860m/2,820ft.
Chair-lifts heading north from the
resort serve sunny slopes above the
village and also lead to the Méribel
valley. Les Menuires can also be
reached via these lifts; the alternative
Boulevard Cumin along the valley floor
is nearly flat, and can be hard work,
especially for kids – as the editorial
offspring can confirm.

TERRAIN-PARKS
Adequate
The terrain-park just above the resort,
served by a fast chair, has a half-pipe,
jumps and a sound system. There is
also a boarder-cross course in the
Maurienne valley.

boarding

*The best resort-level snow in Europe appeals to boarders as well as skiers – and
pulls in considerable numbers. There are pistes to suit all abilities, and the good
snow is great for beginners and carvers. There's plenty of off-piste choice for
free-riders, though if you want trees you'll have to travel. The lifts are now mainly
chairs and gondolas, although one or two drags remain.*

LIFT PASSES

Three Valleys
Covers all lifts in Courchevel, La Tania, Méribel, Val-Thorens, Les Menuires and St-Martin-de-Belleville.

Beginners
5 free lifts in Val-Thorens.

Main pass
1 day €41
6 days €204

Senior citizens
Over 60: 6 days €164
Over 72: free pass

Children
Under 13: 6 days €153.50
Under 5: free pass

Notes
Reductions for families. Half-day and pedestrian passes available. Six-day pass and over valid for one day in Espace Killy (Tignes-Val-d'Isère), Paradiski (La Plagne-Les Arcs), Pralognan and Les Saisies.

Alternative passes
Pass for Val-Thorens-Orelle only.

SNOW RELIABILITY
Difficult to beat

Few resorts can rival Val-Thorens for reliably good snow-cover, thanks to its altitude and generally north-facing slopes. Snowmaking covers a lot of the key pistes, including the crowded south- and west-facing runs on the way back from the Méribel valley, and is increased each year with more planned for 2005/06.

FOR EXPERTS
Lots to do off-piste

Val-Thorens' local pistes are primarily intermediate terrain. The fast Cascades chair serves a short but steep black run that quickly gets mogulled. The pistes down from the Cîme de Caron cable-car are challenging, but not seriously steep and there's a sunny black run off the back into the fourth valley. The black Chamois and red Falaise and Variente runs from Col de Rosaël can get heavily mogulled and challenging (and a 2005 reporter found them 'full of out of control skiers and boarders who are not prepared for the conditions they find'). The sunny Marielle run, one of the routes from the Méribel valley, is one of the easiest blacks we've come across, but it can get crowded and be icy in the morning.

There is a huge amount of off-piste to explore with a guide – see the feature panel opposite.

FOR INTERMEDIATES
Unbeatable quality and quantity

The scope for intermediates throughout the Three Valleys is enormous. It will take a keen intermediate only 90 minutes or so to get to Courchevel 1650 at the far end, if not distracted by the endless runs on the way.

The local slopes in Val-Thorens are some of the best intermediate terrain in the region. Most of the pistes are easy reds and blues, made even more enjoyable by the excellent snow.

The snow on the red Col run is always some of the best around. The blue Moraine below it is gentle and popular with the schools. The runs on the top half of the mountain are steeper than those back into the resort. The Grand Fond gondola serves a good variety of red runs. The recently improved Pluviomètre from the Trois Vallées chair is a glorious varied run, away from the lifts. Adventurous intermediates shouldn't miss the Cîme de Caron runs. The black run is not intimidating – it's very wide, usually has good snow, and is a wonderful fast cruise when freshly groomed.

FOR BEGINNERS
Good late-season choice

The slopes at the foot of the resort are very gentle and provide convenient, snow-sure nursery slopes, now with moving walkway lifts. There are no long green runs to progress to, but the blues immediately above the village

FABULOUS OFF-PISTE IN VAL-THORENS

Val-Thorens offers a huge choice of off-piste. And because of the high altitude, the snow stays powdery longer here than in lower parts of the Three Valleys.

For an adventurous intermediate looking to try off-piste for the first time, or with a little off-piste experience already, the Pierre Lory Pass run is ideal. It is a very large and gentle slope and you access the pass by doing an easy traverse (20 minutes maximum) on the Chavière glacier from the top of the Col chair-lift. When you arrive at Pierre Lory Pass there are breathtaking views of the Aiguilles d'Arves in the Maurienne valley, and you will be just above the Du Bouchet glacier, which you then ski down, rejoining the lift system at Plan Bouchet.

For those with more off-piste under their belt already, the Lac du Lou is a famous off-piste run of 1400m/4,590ft vertical. It is easily accessible from the top of the Cîme de Caron cable-car, from where you have a view of 1,000 summits. The many ways into this long, wide valley allow plenty of variety and opportunities for making first tracks; because many of the slopes face north or north-west it is not unusual to find good powder most of the ski season, even in late April. The views are stunning and you'll notice the quietness and vastness of the whole valley.

La Combe sans Nom on the Maurienne side in the fourth valley, also accessible from the Cîme de Caron cable-car, usually offers superb skiing and snowboard conditions. There's a choice of south-, west- and, on the far side, some east-facing slopes, which makes for excellent spring skiing conditions.

For the more adventurous there are many options, including hiking up from the top of the Col chair-lift and skiing a long run over the Gébroulaz glacier down to Méribel.

But don't even think about doing any off-piste runs without a fully qualified guide or instructor. Route finding can be difficult, there can be avalanche danger, and hidden hazards such as cliffs and crevasses lurk.

are easy. The resort's height and bleakness make it cold in midwinter, and intimidating in bad weather.

FOR CROSS-COUNTRY
Try elsewhere
Val-Thorens is a poor base for cross-country, with only 4km/2.5 miles of local trails.

QUEUES
Persistent at the Cîme de Caron
Recent reports suggest that the longest queues are for the largest and most rewarding lifts, notably the Cîme de Caron cable-car, but also the gondolas. The queues move fairly quickly, but reporters warn that visits to the Cîme de Caron really need to be timed to miss the crowds (the view at the top is worth the wait, emphasise a couple of 2005 reporters).

The Plein Sud six-pack chair-lift does a good job of getting the crowds out of the village towards Méribel and Courchevel, and delivers you to just above the Bouquetin gondolas. But a 2004 reporter says that in the morning there are still massive queues as

people head out to the rest of the Three Valleys. Check the Méribel chapter for bottlenecks there.

When snow is in short supply elsewhere, the pressure on the Val-Thorens lifts can increase markedly.

MOUNTAIN RESTAURANTS
Lots of choice
For a high, modern resort, the choice of restaurants is good. The Bar de la Marine, on the Dalles piste, does excellent food (we had good pot au feu), but it's pricey and service can be stretched. The Moutière, near the top

SCHOOLS

ESF
t 0479 000286

Ski-Cool
t 0479 000492

Prosneige
t 0479 010700

International
t 0479 000196

Classes (ESF prices)
6 half-days (3hr am)
from €99

Private lessons
from €32 for 1hr

GUIDES

t 0689 292336

CHILDREN

Le Montana
t 0479 000286
Ages from 3mnth

Le Roc
t 0479 000286
Ages from 18 mnth.
Skiing tuition for 3
and over (Bambi club)

Ski school
All the schools offer
classes for children
aged 4 or 5 and over
(ESF: 6 mornings from
€90).

of the chair of the same name, is one of the more reasonably priced huts. The Chalet Plan Bouchet refuge in the Maurienne valley is very popular and welcoming, but bar service can be slow. You can stay the night there, too. The Chalet Plein Sud, below the chair of the same name, has excellent views but a 'rather limited menu'. The big Chalet de Thorens has been praised for its food and reasonable prices, but is in need of refurbishment, according to one reporter. The Chalet des 2 Lacs has 'the best food and is the best value – the potato pie is a must', says a 2005 reporter. Another found the Deux Ours half way down the Blanchot run 'a dream; excellent quality food, large portions and reasonably priced'.

SCHOOLS AND GUIDES
A mixed bag
The ESF, has a Trois Vallées group for those who want to cover a lot of ground while receiving lessons – available by the day or the week, and can include off-piste. The children of a 2005 visitor had snowboard lessons with the ESF but found the language mainly French despite 'being guaranteed that lessons would be in English'. Prosneige was 'good with children' and provided 'great instruction and low group numbers', said two 2005 reporters; but another's son had a bad experience as he was the only British kid with the rest French. Ski-Cool class sizes are guaranteed not to exceed 10. They also have off-piste courses. There are several specialist guiding outfits.

FACILITIES FOR CHILDREN
Coolly efficient
Our most recent reporter on the ESF nursery found the facilities convenient and the service efficient. In spite of the fact that the staff were 'not particularly warm or friendly', by the end of the

week all the children were 'comfortable' on skis. The Prosneige takes children from the age of five.

STAYING THERE

HOW TO GO
Surprisingly high level of comfort
Accommodation is of a higher standard than in many purpose-built resorts.
Chalets These are catered apartments, and many are quite comfortable.
Hotels There are plenty of hotels, and there's a Club Med, too.
〔〔〔〔5 **Fitz Roy** (0479 000478) The sole 4-star is a swanky but charming Relais & Châteaux place with lovely rooms. Pool. Well placed.
〔〔〔〔4 **Val Thorens** (0479 000433) Next door to Fitz Roy. 'Good service, good food and an excellent on the slopes location.' 'Comfortable and friendly.'
〔〔〔3 **Sherpa** (0479 000070) Highly recommended for atmosphere and food. Less-than-ideal position at the top of the resort.
〔〔〔3 **Val Chaviere** (0479 000033) Friendly, convenient, 'good food and plenty of it'.
〔〔〔3 **Bel Horizon** (0479 000477) Friendly, family-run 3-star, popular with reporters – 'cuisine wonderful'.
Self-catering The options include apartments of a higher standard than usual in France. The luxurious Oxalys (with pool, sauna, steam room and open fire in all living rooms), Montagnettes and Chalets du Soleil are all said to be outstanding. 2005 reporters enjoyed Temples de Soleil, Orsiere and Village Montana.

EATING OUT
Surprisingly wide range
Val-Thorens has something for most tastes and pockets. Top of the range is the gourmet restaurant in the Oxalys apartment building. Last year a reporter said it was 'out of this world.

The chalet-style Balcons development, like the rest of Val-Thorens, is set among snowy, treeless slopes ➔

BASILE / JC PIRONON

GETTING THERE

Air Geneva 160km/ 99 miles (3½hr), Lyon 193km/120 miles (3½hr), Chambéry 112km/70 miles (2½hr).

Rail Moûtiers (37km/23 miles); regular buses from station.

ACTIVITIES

Indoor Sports centre (spa, sauna, fitness room, hot-tub, tennis, squash, swimming pool, volleyball, table tennis, squash, badminton, football), games rooms, music recitals

Outdoor Paragliding, sightseeing microlight flights, snowmobiles, snow-shoeing, ice-driving, walks, tobogganing

Phone numbers
From abroad use the prefix +33 and omit the initial '0' of the phone number.

TOURIST OFFICE

t 0479 000808
valtho@valthorens.com
www.valthorens.com

In over half a century of French gastronomy I have never had a meal to compare with the inventiveness of this smart but friendly establishment. It is expensive but worth every penny.' A 2005 visitor agrees: 'A genuinely innovative menu with cuisine of a high order.' We can't wait to try it ourselves.

The Fitz Roy and Val Thorens hotels do classic French food and were the best in town before Oxalys appeared. For something more regional, the best bets are the 'excellent' Vieux Chalet and the Chaumière. Other readers' recommendations include the Cabane ('very high quality cooking with real innovation and reasonably priced'), the Ferme de Rosalie ('good but limited menu'), the Montana ('good food and service'), El Gringo's ('great for Tex-Mex food' and 'very popular so get there early'), Auberge des Balcons ('wonderful raclette'), Le Toit au Monde ('particularly good' and 'excellent value for money') and the Joyeuse Fondue. The Galoubet has been recommended for local specialities, including pierrades. The Blanchot is an unusually stylish wine bar with a simple but varied carte and of course an excellent range of wines. Several pizzerias are recommended, including the Grange ('good food and friendly staff') in the Temples du Soleil.

APRES-SKI
Livelier than you'd imagine
Val-Thorens is more lively at night than most high-altitude ski-stations. The

Red Fox up at Balcons is crowded at close of play, with karaoke. At the opposite extreme the Sherlock in the Temples du Soleil is 'always lively'. The Frog and Roastbeef at the top of the village is a cheerful British ghetto with a live band at tea time and half-price beer while it plays; real ale is sold, but several reporters were disappointed with the food. It claims to be the highest pub in Europe. The Friends and the Viking pub are all lively bars on the same block. The Underground nightclub in Place de Péclet has an extended happy hour but 'descends into Europop' when its disco gets going. The Malaysia cellar bar is recommended for good live bands, and gets very crowded after 11pm. Quieter bars include the 'atmospheric without being overcrowded' O'Connells and the cosy Rhum Box (aka Mitch's).

OFF THE SLOPES
Forget it
There's a good sports centre, which was renovated for 2003/04, a small cinema and twice-weekly street markets. You can get to some mountain restaurants by lift, and the 360° panorama from the top of the Cîme de Caron cable-car is not to be missed. But it is not a good bet for a holiday off the slopes.

The French Pyrenees

Decent skiing and boarding at half the price of the Alps

NEWS

For 2004/05, Barèges built a new fast quad to replace a drag, and snowmaking was increased. For 2005/06 a new eight-seat gondola is planned to replace the cable-car from Cauterets to the slopes. And a fast six-pack is due to replace two old chairs.

At Font-Romeu, a six-pack was added last season. This season a new piste is due to be built.

Phone numbers
From abroad use the prefix +33 and omit the initial '0' of the phone number.

TOURIST OFFICES

www.pyrenees-online.fr

Barèges
t 0562 921600
www.tourmalet.fr
www.bareges.com

La Mongie
t 0562 919084
www.tourmalet.fr
www.bagneresdebigorre
-lamongie.com

Cauterets
t 0562 925050
www.cauterets.com

Font-Romeu
t 0468 306830
www.font-romeu.fr

St-Lary-Soulan
t 0562 395081
www.saintlary.com

It took us a long time to get round to visiting the resorts of the French Pyrenees – mainly because we had the idea that they were second-rate compared with the Alps. Well, it is certainly true that they can't compete in terms of size of ski area with the mega-resorts of the Three Valleys and Paradiski. But don't dismiss them: they have considerable attractions, including price – hotels cost half as much as in the Alps, and meals and drinks are cheap.

The Pyrenees are serious mountains, with dramatic, picturesque scenery. They are also attractively French. Unlike the big plastic mega-resorts, many Pyrenean bases have a rustic, rural Gallic charm.

The biggest ski area – shared by **Barèges** and **La Mongie** – is called **Domaine Tourmalet**. Between them they have 100km/62 miles of runs (69 pistes) and 43 lifts. Most lifts are drags and slow chairs but they have three high-speed chairs. There is 20km/12 miles of cross-country.

The runs are best suited to intermediates, with good tree-lined runs above Barèges and open bowl skiing above La Mongie. The best bet for an expert is to try off-piste with a guide – one beautiful run away from all the lifts starts with a scramble through a hole in the rocks. There is a terrain-park. Rustic mountain huts are scattered around the slopes.

Barèges is a spa village set in a narrow, steep-sided valley, which gets little sun in midwinter; the lift base is at Tournaboup, 4km/2.5 miles up the valley and served by ski-bus. It's the second oldest ski resort in France and the pioneer of skiing in the Pyrenees. Accommodation is mainly in 2-star hotels such as the Igloo, Central and Europe, which reporters recommend for good food and a friendly welcome. One reporter stayed in nearby Luz in the Chimes hotel, describing the food as 'divine'. The rather drab buildings and one main street of Barèges grow on you, though there's little to do in the evenings other than visit the thermal spa and a restaurant. La Mongie, on the other hand, is a modern, purpose-built resort reminiscent of the Alps.

Cauterets is another spa town but a complete contrast to Barèges. It is much bigger and set in a wide, sunny valley. It is a popular summer destination, and even in March we were able to sit at a pavement cafe with a drink after dinner. A new gondola for 2005/06 will take you up to the slopes 850m/2,790ft above the town – you have to ride it down as well as up. There are only 35km/22 miles of slopes (mainly intermediate), and a terrain-park, set in a bowl that can be cold and windy.

But Cauterets' jewel is its cross-country, a long drive or bus-ride from town at Pont d'Espagne and served by a gondola. It is the start of the Pyrenees National Park and the old smugglers' route over the mountains between France and Spain. The 36km/22 miles of snow-sure cross-country tracks run up this beautiful deserted valley, beside a rushing stream and a stunning waterfall.

Font-Romeu has 54km/33 miles of pistes and 26 lifts, serving mainly easy and intermediate pistes (13 of its 38 pistes are green) and is popular with families. The slopes get a lot of sun but it has the biggest snowmaking set-up in the Pyrenees. Weekend crowds arrive from nearby Perpignan and over the border from Spain and both lifts and pistes can get crowded. It has 100km/62 miles of cross-country skiing. The village is a bus-ride from the slopes and hotels are mainly 2- and 3-star.

The other major Pyrenean resort is **St-Lary-Soulan**, a traditional village with houses built of stone, with a cable-car at the edge going up to the slopes, of which there are 100km/62 miles, mainly suiting intermediates. It has a terrain-park and half-pipe. There's a satellite called **St-Lary-Espiaube**, which is purpose-built and right at the heart of the slopes.

A recent reporter also visited other small resorts such as Formiguères, Eyne and Les Angles, and suggests staying down in a small valley town and visiting different resorts daily.

Isola 2000

An EasyJet flight and a short drive from Nice makes Isola easy and cheap to reach for a short break. It has slope-side accommodation and some snow-sure slopes. But the core of the resort village is dire: block-like and tatty.

KEY FACTS

Resort	2000m
	6,560ft
Slopes	1840-2610m
	6,035-8,560ft
Lifts	23
Pistes	120km
	75 miles
Green	15%
Blue	39%
Red	35%
Black	11%
Snowmaking	15km
	9 miles

TOURIST OFFICE

t 0493 231515
info@isola2000.com
www.isola2000.com

THE RESORT

Isola is a small, high, purpose-built resort close to the Côte d'Azur and easy to combine with a couple of days by the sea.

Built by a British property company at the end of the 1960s, the slope-side centre is a complex of block-like apartments, with shops, bars and restaurants in dark and tatty underground tunnels. Various owners have since worked hard to polish the image of the resort with new hamlets of more luxurious, wood-clad buildings. The Diva hotel (0493 231771) looks the best place to stay.

THE RESORT

The ski area spreads around the resort in a horseshoe shape, with the main access lift being a gondola to Pélevos at 2320m/7,610ft. But there are still a lot of drag-lifts and slow chairs.

Due to the great base height of Isola – the lowest of the slopes is at 1840m/ 6,035ft – most of the runs are above the tree line. Isola gets different weather from other major French resorts, so it can have masses of snow when the rest of the French Alps have none, and vice versa. Regular visitors say that they never find all the lifts open, but there is always snow – and plenty of sun.

Many of the runs suit confident intermediates best. They and experts will find the toughest runs in the St-Sauveur sector. There is more choice of blue runs in the Pélevos sector and excellent beginner slopes near the resort base. There are some surprisingly attractive restaurants on the slopes, including some just above the base, such as the Bergerie.

Short turns

399

Val-Cenis

Val-Cenis is a marketing concept rather than a place. It comprises two quiet villages in the high and remote part of the Maurienne valley – Lanslebourg and Lanslevillard. A good place for half-term holidays, say readers.

KEY FACTS

Resort	1400m
	4,590ft
Slopes	1400-2800m
	4,590-9,190ft
Lifts	18
Pistes	80km
	50 miles
Green	21%
Blue	23%
Red	42%
Black	14%
Snowmaking	84 guns

TOURIST OFFICE

t 0479 052366
info@valcenis.com
www.valcenis.com

THE RESORT

Lanslebourg is a long, linear place, spreading along the RN6 (a dead end in winter, when the road over the Col du Mont-Cenis becomes a piste). It's pleasant enough, but no beauty. Up the valley, Lanslevillard is more captivating – off the road, randomly arranged and rustic, with a neat 'front de neige'. There are modest hotels and a dozen restaurants in each village, and plenty of modern apartments. Lanslevillard has a leisure centre with rink and pool. Evenings are quiet.

THE MOUNTAIN

There are lifts from base stations in and between the two villages – the main one a gondola starting near Lanslevillard. Above mid-mountain is a good range of open runs, served by chairs and drags. Below mid-mountain

all the runs are prettily wooded – there is usually an easy blue or green alternative to the various red runs back down as well. Most of the runs are north-facing, and there is snowmaking on the runs back to the base stations, so snow reliability is quite good. There is ample off-piste and a few bump runs to challenge experts. For intermediates there are top-to-bottom cruises of up to 1400m/4,600ft vertical. Lanslevillard has excellent nursery slopes; higher options include a splendid green following the road from the Col.

There are extensive cross-country trails at Bessans, further up the valley.

Queues are rare, and bearable even at half-term – 'mainly at the gondola in the afternoon' – and tend to move quite quickly.

We have encouraging reports of the ESF ski school – 'friendly, really seems to care'.

BERNARD GRANGE / OT VALLOIRE

Valloire

The old mountain village of Valloire is the best known, internationally, of a bunch of resorts sitting high above the Maurienne valley that lie to the south of Val-Thorens and the Trois Vallées.

THE RESORT

Valloire still feels like a real mountain village, with a year-round population of 1,000, a 17th-century baroque church and market square in the centre, crêperies, fromageries and reasonably priced restaurants. Various events such as street markets and ice carving competitions add to its lively ambience and, because the Col du Galibier pass beyond it closes in winter, the place is mercifully free of through-traffic – its one-way system is there only because of its narrow streets. It is 17km/ 11 miles up a winding road from the valley town of St-Michel-de-Maurienne.

The hotel Aux Oursons (0479 590137) near the centre is comfortable and friendly, and has a small pool, hot-tub and sauna – and teddy bears everywhere (*ourson* means bear). The hotel de la Poste (0479 590347) is recommended. The Galibier (0479 590045) – 1km/0.5 miles from the centre but close to the Verneys chair-lift – and the central Valmonts apartments are both relatively new, with pool, sauna and steam room.

The Gastilleur restaurant in the Sétaz hotel on the main street is the gourmet choice, while Bistrot Chez Fred's reasonably priced brasserie food attracts such numbers that the place has been forced to expand into a heated tent on the terrace. The Grange is a rustic bar/crêperie, and the Asile des Fondues serves what you'd expect from the name in a beautiful old building with stone walls. Valloire is not the place to go if you want lively nightlife, though the Touring Bar attracts the teens and 20s with table football, a pool table and loud music.

THE MOUNTAINS

Two gondolas from different parts of town access Valloire's two linked mountains. The Setaz sector's shady slopes, the lower part tree-lined and the upper section open, generally have the best snow and the toughest slopes. The broad, open, west-facing slopes of Crey du Quart offer a choice

of routes to link to the Valmeinier valley (see next page). A gentle blue heads down from Grand Plateau to Valmeinier 1800, while a delightfully scenic and even gentler blue (with green alternative) leads to the Armera chair lift, which goes down and then up to Valmeinier 1500.

Lift queues are rarely a problem. Watch out for some tricky drag-lifts, which can lift you in the air at the start – not good for boarders.

Experts will find the area limited. The long Grandes Droze black run down to Valmeinier 1500 can present a challenge when the bumps build up, and the area from Crey du Quart down into the Valmeinier valley has some decent off-piste if the snow is good.

The vast majority of the slopes are ideal for intermediates of all standards. For easy cruising, head for the Crey du Quart sector which has gentle blues and almost-as-gentle reds everywhere. The Neuvache blue along the valley from Valmeinier 1800 is flat enough to be a green. The rather out-of-the way red Praz Violette piste from the top of the Combe drag-lift (which, be warned, has some very steep pitches and a huge bend of over 90° in it) can be a wonderful cruise away from the crowds. For more of a challenge, head over to Cretaz and try the highest runs, including the Cascade black, which often has excellent snow. The Marmottes, down the gondola, is an excellent genuine red.

Valloire suits beginners well, with nursery slopes both at village level and up the mountain at the top of both gondolas, followed by very easy green runs to progress to.

Few of the mountain restaurants are memorable. We and readers have had decent meals in the crowded self-service Chateau Ripaille in the Crey du Quart sector.

A 2005 reporter had 'superb' private lessons from an ESF instructor.

The six-day lift pass allows a cut-price day in the Trois Vallées (the Val-Thorens sector can be accessed easily by gondola from Orelle, around 30 minutes away by bus).

Valmeinier

Valmeinier's two villages share slopes which are linked to those of Valloire (see opposite). Purpose-built Valmeinier 1800 attracts most of the visitors, though the lower Valmeinier 1500 was the traditional base.

KEY FACTS

Resort	1500-1800m
	4,920-5,900ft
Valloire/Valmeinier	
Slopes	1430-2595m
	4,690-8,510ft
Lifts	33
Pistes	150km
	93 miles
Green	26%
Blue	28%
Red	38%
Black	8%
Snowmaking	
	375 guns

TOURIST OFFICE

t 0479 595369
info@valmeinier.com
www.valmeinier.com

OT VALLOIRE / BERNARD GRANGE

Valloire has a lovely setting, ringed by mountains ↓

THE RESORT

The original old village of Valmeinier 1500 has expanded somewhat, with low-rise buildings that blend in well, and is closer to the link with Valloire. But the vast majority of visitors stay up the valley in the purpose-built satellite of Valmeinier 1800, which was started in 1986. Its low-rise chalet-style buildings line the bottom and side of the main slope and fit in well with their surroundings. It is a small, quiet, sunny place that mainly attracts French families on a budget looking for a hassle-free time and undemanding slopes. A reporter who stayed at the hotel Aigle (0479 592431) praised its childcare facilities but found 'over 60 children staying there' too many. The Pierre & Vacances apartments are above average for the chain, right on the piste, with outdoor pool and sauna.

THE MOUNTAINS

The local slopes get a lot of sun, though the nursery slopes and a fair number of the main pistes have snowmaking. They are served almost entirely by chair-lifts (a welcome contrast with some of the vicious drag-lifts you'll encounter in the Valloire sector). An easy green route runs from top to bottom of the mountain, and it is difficult to tell the difference in gradient between many of the blues and reds. The area suits beginners and undemanding intermediates best. The link to Valloire starts with a chair-lift reached by an almost flat track from Valmeinier 1800 or a down-and-then-up chair from Valmeinier 1500. See opposite for details of the Valloire slopes. There's a shortage of good mountain restaurants. Don't count on English-speaking instructors.

Short turns

Italy's recent development as an international winter sports destination owed a lot to prices that were appreciably lower than those in other Alpine countries. It is still the cheapest of the four major Alpine countries, but it is not quite the bargain it was, so it now has to compete in terms of the quality of the holidays offered. And it is trying hard to do so – many resorts now have powerful, modern lifts and huge snowmaking systems. It has some enduring attractions, such as its good food and wine, jolly atmosphere and splendid scenery – especially in the Dolomites.

Italian resorts vary as widely in their characteristics as they do in location – and they are spread along the full length of the Italian border, from Sauze d'Oulx to the Dolomites. There are high, snow-sure ski stations and charming valley villages, and mountains that range from one-run wonders to some of the most extensive lift networks in the world.

A lot of Italian runs, particularly in the north-west, seem flatteringly easy. This is partly because grooming is immaculate, and partly because piste classification seems to overstate difficulty. Nowhere is this clearer than in the linked area of La Rosière in France and La Thuile – in Italy, despite the French-sounding name.

THE AMAZING DOLOMITI SUPERSKI LIFT PASS

The Dolomiti Superski lift pass is one of the wonders of the world, covering 45 resorts and 460 lifts. We describe the most important resorts in our chapters on Cortina d'Ampezzo, Selva and Trentino, but there are countless others worth a visit and we can only touch on a few here.

The Superski region, which straddles the provinces of Veneto, Trentino and Alto Adige/Südtirol (predominantly German-speaking, hence the alternative names), is broken down into 12 areas, each embracing a number of resorts.

One of the most interesting areas is in the north-east corner of the region, the Val Pusteria/Pustertal, which leads off eastwards towards the Slovenian border from the Brenner motorway. The main town is Brunico/Bruneck; we have fond memories of one of our first weeks on skis, spent near here on Plan de Corones/Kronplatz – an extraordinary dome-shaped mountain with easy, open slopes around its bare summit, and more testing stuff lower down. Brunico now has lift access to the mountain by gondola from an outlying suburb, and what looks like an exciting black run through the woods to the base.

Just to the east is the area known as the Alta Val Pusteria/Hochpustertal. There are three small towns dotted along the valley. Westernmost is Villabassa/Niederdorf, chiefly of interest to cross-country skiers. At the watershed of the gently sloping valley, where it starts to descend towards Slovenia, is Dobbiaco/Toblach, with some short slopes on its fringes and very scenic cross-country trails. And further east is San Candido/Innichen, with a long chair-lift serving intermediate slopes.

Up an elevated side valley from here (again with scenic cross-country trails) is the main resort of this area, the village of Sesto/Sexten. This has nursery slopes all around it, and two major lifts. From close to the village a cable-car gives access to a variety of open intermediate slopes on Gallo Cedrone/Hahnspiel, with a long red of 1100m/3,610ft vertical to the base of a gondola up from the Val Pusteria.

← The scenery in many Italian resorts is impressive. This is the 'wrong' side of the Matterhorn, but it is still pretty striking by normal standards. Resort villages range from the cute to the fairly brutal and tatty. Cervinia is nearer the latter than the former

South Tyrol ...

sun-soaked

South Tyrol Information • Pfarrplatz 11 • 39100 Bozen|Bolzano • Italy
phone: +39 0471 999 999
info@suedtirol.info

Italian Alps

www.suedtirol.info

SÜDTIROL

The magic of diversity

Venturing from the Italian motorways to the French moguls is like moving from the shelter of the harbour to the open sea.

Many Italians based in the northern cities ski mainly at weekends, and it's very noticeable that many resorts become busy only at weekends. It's a great advantage for those of us who are there for the whole week. This pattern is especially noticeable at the chic resorts, such as Cortina, Courmayeur and Madonna, and resorts which have not yet found international fame such as the Monterosa region; it's much less pronounced in parts of the Dolomites favoured by German visitors who, like Brits, tend to go for a week.

In general, Italians don't take their skiing or boarding too seriously. A late start, long lunch and early finish are the norm – leaving the slopes delightfully quiet for the rest of us. Almost everywhere mountain restaurants are welcoming places, encouraging leisurely lunching. Pasta – even in the most modest establishment – is delicious. And eating and drinking on the mountain is still cheaper than in other Alpine resorts. But one drawback that many reporters remark upon is the primitive hole-in-the-ground toilets that are the norm in mountain restaurants (and sometimes in resorts too).

One thing that Italian resorts do have to contend with is erratic snowfall. While the snow in the northern Alps tends to come from the west, Italy's tends to come from storms arriving from the south. So it can have great conditions when other countries are suffering; or vice versa. Italian resorts have extensive snowmaking, and our observation is that they tend to use it more effectively than other

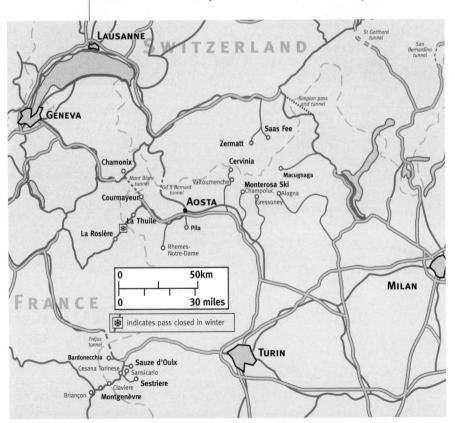

Alpine countries. We have skied in Courmayeur and in the Dolomites when little natural snow had fallen, and in each case there was excellent cruising on man-made snow.

Italy seems to be in the grip of a legislation fever at present, with worthwhile results. As we note in the editorial introduction to this edition, Italian bars and restaurants are now smoke-free – and unlike French ones, they really are. And it is now compulsory for children (under 14, we understand) to wear helmets on the slopes.

DRIVING IN THE ITALIAN ALPS

There are four main geographical groupings of Italian resorts, widely separated. Getting to some of these resorts is a very long haul, and moving from one area to another can involve very long drives (though the extensive motorway network is a great help).

The handful of resorts to the west of Turin – Bardonecchia, Sauze d'Oulx, Sestriere and neighbours in the Milky Way region – are easily reached from France via the Fréjus tunnel from Modane, or via the good road over the pass that the resort of Montgenèvre sits on.

Further north, and somewhat nearer to Turin than Milan, are the resorts of the Aosta valley – Courmayeur, Cervinia, La Thuile and the Monterosa area are the best known. These (especially Courmayeur) are the easiest of all Italian resorts to reach from Britain (via the Mont Blanc tunnel from Chamonix in France). The Aosta valley can also be reached from Switzerland via the Grand St Bernard tunnel. The approach is high and may require chains. The road down the

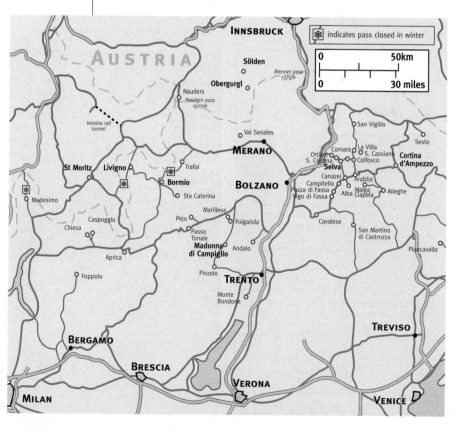

Aosta valley is a major thoroughfare, but the roads up to some of the other resorts are quite long, winding and (in the case of Cervinia) high.

To the east is a string of scattered resorts, most close to the Swiss border, many in isolated and remote valleys involving long drives up from the nearest Italian cities, or high-altitude drives from Switzerland. The links between Switzerland and Italy are more clearly shown on our larger-scale Switzerland map at the beginning of that section than on the map of the Italian Alps included here. The major routes are the St Gotthard tunnel between Göschenen (near Andermatt) and Airolo – the main route between Basel and Milan – and the San Bernardino tunnel reached via Chur.

Finally, further east still are the resorts of the Dolomites. Getting there from Austria is easy, over the Brenner motorway pass from Innsbruck. But getting there from Britain is a very long drive indeed – allow at least a day and a half. We wouldn't lightly drive there and back for a week's skiing, though we routinely do as part of a longer tour including some Austrian resorts. It's also worth bearing in mind that once you arrive in the Dolomites, getting around the intricate network of valleys linked by narrow, winding roads can be a slow business – it's often quicker to get from village to village on skis. Impatient Italian driving can make it a bit stressful, too.

SNOWPIX.COM / CHRIS GILL
Italian lifts are now pretty slick. But you'll occasionally come upon a real relic that does not inspire confidence. This 'bucket' lift above Alagna is due for replacement we hear – or well overdue, depending on your point of view ↘

ITALY

408

Bormio

A tall, narrow mountain above a very unusual, historic resort town

COSTS

① ② ③ ④ ⑤ ⑥

RATINGS

The slopes
Fast lifts	***
Snow	***
Extent	**
Expert	*
Intermediate	***
Beginner	**
Convenience	***
Queues	***
Mountain restaurants	****

The rest
Scenery	***
Resort charm	****
Off-slope	****

NEWS

For 2004/05 two fast quads with covers replaced four old lifts serving Cima Bianca from the mid-station at Ciuk. A new mountain restaurant, Heaven 3000, was opened at the top.

Over at Santa Caterina, an eight-seat gondola and a new mountain restaurant opened.

+ Good mix of high, open pistes and woodland runs adding up to some good long descents

+ Worthwhile neighbouring resorts

+ Attractive medieval town centre – quite unlike any other winter resort

+ Good mountain restaurants

– Slopes all of medium steepness

– Rather confined main mountain, with second area some way distant

– Long airport transfers

– Crowds on Sundays

– Central hotels inconvenient

If you like ancient Italian towns and don't insist on a traditional Alpine resort atmosphere, you'll find the centre of Bormio very appealing – though you're unlikely to be staying right in the centre. Given the limited slopes of Bormio's own mountain, plan on taking the free bus out to the Valdidentro area and perhaps make longer outings, to Santa Caterina at least.

THE RESORT

Bormio, a spa since Roman times, has a splendid 17th-century town centre, with narrow cobbled streets and grand stone facades – very colourful during the evening promenade. It is in a remote spot, close to the Swiss border – though road improvements have cut the airport transfer to three hours.

The town centre is a 15-minute walk from the gondola station across the river to the south. There are reliable free shuttle-buses, but many people walk. Closer to the lifts is a suburban sprawl of hotels for skiers. Several major hotels are on Via Milano, leading out of town, which is neither convenient nor atmospheric.

THE MOUNTAINS

There's a nice mix of high, snow-sure pistes and lower wooded slopes. The main slopes are tall (vertical drop 1800m/5,900ft) and narrow. Most pistes face north-west.

Both the piste map and the piste marking need substantial improvement. The policy of opening certain lift links only at weekends and busy times (much same thing) also provokes complaints.

The Valdidentro area, a short bus-ride out of Bormio, shouldn't be overlooked. The open and woodland runs are very pleasant and usually empty (and have great views). Day trips to Santa Caterina (20 minutes by bus) and Livigno (90 minutes) are covered by the Alta Valtellina lift pass. A six-day pass entitles you to a discount rate on a one-day pass in St Moritz (three hours away).

Slopes The main access lift is an eight-seat gondola to the mid-mountain mini-resort of Bormio 2000, with a cable-car going on up to the top at over 3000m/9,840ft. An alternative gondola goes to Ciuk, and above this two fast chairs now serve the top.

Terrain-parks There aren't any.

Snow reliability Runs above Bormio 2000 are usually snow-sure, and there is snowmaking on the lower slopes, though this doesn't necessarily help in late March. The Valdidentro area is more reliable, and the high, shaded, north-facing slopes of Santa Caterina usually have good snow.

na Bianca
m/9,88oft

2550m

2200m

Valdidentro

Val di Sotto

Oga
1475m

Isolaccia

Bormio 2000

Le Motte
1430m

Ciuk
1620m

Bormio
1225m/4,020ft

terrace and a play area for children. And a new restaurant, Heaven 3000, opened at the top of Cima Bianca last year. Several reporters recommend the very welcoming Baita de Mario, at Ciuk, as a great place for a long lunch.

Schools and guides The only recent report we have is of the Nazionale school, which offered 'satisfactory lessons in English'.

Facilities for children The ski school takes children from the age of three, from 10am to 4pm. The Bormio 2000 branch of the school has a roped-off snow garden at mid-mountain with a moving carpet lift.

KEY FACTS

Resort	1225m
	4,020ft

Bormio and Valdidentro		
Slopes	1225-3010m	
	4,020-9,880ft	
Lifts		26
Pistes		44km
		27 miles
Blue		28%
Red		65%
Black		7%
Snowmaking		30km
		19 miles

Bormio only		
Slopes	1225-3010m	
	4,020-9,880ft	
Lifts		16
Pistes		25km
		16 miles

WEBSITES

Phone numbers
From abroad use the prefix +39 (and do **not** omit the initial '0' of the phone number).

TOURIST OFFICE

t 0342 903300
aptbormio@provincia.
so.it
www.valtellinaonline.
com

Experts There are a couple of short black runs in the main area, but the greatest interest lies in off-piste routes from Cima Bianca to both east and west of the piste area.

Intermediates The men's downhill course starts with a steep plunge, but otherwise is just a tough red, ideal for strong intermediates. Stella Alpina, down to 2000, is also fairly steep. Many runs are less tough – ideal for most intermediates. The longest is a superb top-to-bottom cruise. The outlying mountains are also suitable for early intermediates.

Beginners The nursery slopes at Bormio 2000 offer good snow, but there are no very easy longer pistes to move on to. Novices are better off at nearby Santa Caterina.

Snowboarding The slopes are too steep for novices, and there's little to attract experienced boarders either.

Cross-country There are some trails either side of Bormio, towards Piatta and beneath Le Motte and Valdidentro, but cross-country skiers are better off at snow-sure Santa Caterina.

Queues The gondola that replaced the cable-car from the main car park to Bormio 2000 a couple of years ago should have dealt with the problems low-down, and the fast chairs which now go up to Cima Bianca should relieve the pressure on the top cable-car – but we've no recent reports on this. There should now be few problems outside carnival week.

Mountain restaurants The mountain restaurants are generally good. Even the efficient self-service at Cafe Bormio 2000 has a good choice of dishes. At the Rocca, above Ciuk, there is a welcoming chalet and a smart, modern place with table- or self-service. Cedrone, at Bormio 2000, has a good

STAYING THERE

How to go There are plenty of apartments, but hotels dominate the package market.

Hotels Most of Bormio's 40-plus hotels are 2- and 3-star places. The 4-star Palace (0342 903131) is the most luxurious in town. The Posta (0342 904753) is in the centre of the old town – rooms range from adequate to very good. The Baita dei Pini (0342 904346) is the best placed of the top hotels – on the river, between the lifts and centre. The Ambassador (0342 904625) is close to the gondola to Ciuk.

Self-catering The modern Cristallo apartments have been recommended.

Eating out There's a wide selection of restaurants. The atmospheric Taula at Valfurva does excellent modern food with great service. The Kuerc and the Vecchia Combo are also popular. The Rododendri (at Valfurva) is recommended and there are excellent pizzerias, including the Jap.

Après-ski The après-ski starts on the mountain at the Rocca, and there are popular bars around the bottom lift stations. The Clem Pub, Cafe Mozart and the Aurora are popular. Shangri-La is a friendly bar. The King's Club is said to be the best disco.

Off the slopes Diversions include thermal baths (including reopened Roman baths), riding and walks in the Stelvio National Park. There is also an excellent sports centre, ice rink and 'superb' swimming pool. St Moritz and Livigno are popular excursions.

Staying up the mountain The modern Girasole 2000 (0342 904652), at Bormio 2000, is simple but well run by an Anglo-Italian couple; lots of events for evening entertainment.

Cervinia

Mile after mile of high-altitude, easy, snow-sure cruising

NEWS

For 2004/05 a moving carpet replaced the Cretaz IV baby drag-lift that served the nursery slope.

Snowmaking was increased above Laghi Cime Bianche.

Cervinia and Zermatt have agreed to promote their linked slopes under the name Matterhorn Ski Paradise. More importantly, they have produced a single, fairly clear piste map for the whole linked area.

- Extensive mountain with miles of long, consistently gentle runs – ideal for early intermediates and anyone wary of steep slopes or bumps
- High, sunny and snow-sure slopes amid impressive scenery
- Excellent village nursery slope
- Link with Zermatt in Switzerland provides even more spectacular views and good lunches

- Very little to interest good or aggressive intermediates and above
- Little to do in bad weather – almost entirely treeless, and lifts prone to closure by wind
- Too many slow old lifts
- Steep climb to main lifts, followed by lots of steps in station
- Rather dreary-looking village
- Few off-slope amenities

If there is a better resort than Cervinia for those who like gentle cruising in spring sunshine on mile after mile of easy, snow-sure, well-groomed slopes, we have yet to find it. And then there's the easiest of Zermatt's slopes just over the Swiss border, and linked by lift and piste.

But what about the rest of us? Well, to be frank, the rest of us are better off elsewhere. In particular, those who might be harbouring thoughts about bumps or powder over in Zermatt should probably think about staying there, not here. The link between the two resorts is unreliable, and the best of Zermatt's slopes take a long time to reach.

THE RESORT

Cervinia is at the head of a long valley leading off the Aosta valley on the Italian side of the Matterhorn. The old climbing village developed into a winter resort in a rather haphazard way, and it has no consistent style of architecture. It's an uncomfortable hotchpotch, neither pleasing to the eye nor as offensive as the worst of the French purpose-built resorts. The centre is pleasant, compact and traffic-free. But ugly surrounding apartment blocks and hotels make the whole place feel less friendly and welcoming.

A lot of people stay near the village centre, at the foot of the nursery slopes, which is obviously best for après-ski purposes but not necessarily for ski purposes. You can take a series of slow drags and chairs from here into the slopes, or peel off after the first and ski down to the main gondola and cable-car to Plan Maison. Otherwise these main lifts are an awkward uphill walk away, above the village.

There are modern developments above the main village, which can in practice be more convenient. Some hotels run their own shuttle-bus and the public bus from the Cieloalto complex, for example, is reported to be 'efficient and well-used'.

At weekends and public holidays, the resort can fill up with day trippers and weekenders from Milan and Turin. There are surprisingly few off-slope amenities, such as marked walks and spa facilities.

The slopes link to Valtournenche further down the valley (covered by the lift pass) and Zermatt in Switzerland (covered by a daily supplement, or a more expensive weekly pass).

Day trips by car are possible to Courmayeur, La Thuile and the Monterosa Ski resorts of Champoluc and Gressoney (all covered by the Aosta valley lift pass).

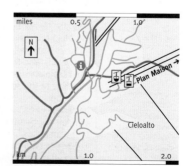

KEY FACTS

Resort	2050m
	6,730ft

Cervinia/ Valtournenche	
Slopes	1525-3480m
	5,000-11,420ft
Lifts	28
Pistes	200km
	124 miles
Blue	30%
Red	59%
Black	11%
Snowmaking	21km
	13 miles

Cervinia/ Valtournenche/ Zermatt combined	
Slopes	1525-3820m
	5,000-12,530ft
Lifts	58
Pistes	383km
	238 miles
Blue	21%
Red	58%
Black	21%
Snowmaking	69km
	43 miles

LIFT PASSES

Breuil-Cervinia
Covers all lifts on the Italian side of the border including Valtournenche.

Beginners
Day pass for limited number of lifts €11.50.

Main pass
1 day €32
6 days €170

Senior citizens
Over 65: 6 days €128

Children
Under 12: 6 days €128
Under 8: 6 days €43

Notes
Half-day pass and individual section passes available. Also daily extension for Zermatt lifts.

Alternative passes
International pass covers all lifts on the Italian side plus Zermatt.

THE MOUNTAINS

Cervinia's main slopes are high, open, sunny and mostly west-facing. If the weather is bad, the top lifts often close because of high winds – and even the lower slopes may suffer poor visibility because of the lack of trees.

THE SLOPES
Very easy
Cervinia has the biggest, highest, most snow-sure area of easy, well groomed pistes we've come across, though we're very sceptical of the claimed total of 200km/124 miles. The area has Italy's highest pistes and some of its longest (a claimed 13km/8 miles from Plateau Rosa to Valtournenche, interrupted only by a short drag-lift part-way – but see 'Snow reliability'). Nearly all the runs are accessible to average intermediates. The high proportion of red runs on the piste map is misleading: most of them would be classified blue elsewhere. There is now a handy quick-folding piste map that covers both Cervinia's and Zermatt's slopes fairly clearly, ending past confusion over different names for the same point on the border. The slopes just above the village are floodlit some evenings.

The main lifts take you to the mid-mountain base of **Plan Maison**. From there a further gondola goes to Laghi Cime Bianche and then a giant cable-car goes up to **Plateau Rosa** and one link with Zermatt. The alternative link goes via three successive fast quads (all with covers) from Plan Maison up to a slightly lower point on the border. Between the fast quads and Laghi Cime Bianche, and going all the way back to the village, is a deep gorge that separates Cervinia's slopes into two main sections.

Plateau Rosa is the start of the splendid wide Ventina run. Part-way down you can branch off left down towards **Valtournenche**. The slopes here are served by a number of slow old lifts above the initial modern gondola from Valtournenche to Salette.

There is also the very small, little-used **Cieloalto** area, served by a slow old chair to the south of the cable-car at the bottom of the Ventina run. This has some of Cervinia's steeper pistes and (on the bottom half) the only trees in the area.

Several reporters complain of poor information and signing.

TERRAIN-PARKS
Winter and summer
The terrain-park at Plan Maison has jumps, rails, boxes, a boarder-cross course and a half-pipe, and the resort claims it is designed for everyone from beginners to experts. But boarding reporters thought it was 'intimidating' and lacked accessibility to intermediates. Another who is a skier had a go but saw a sign saying 'no skiers'. There's an even bigger park over the Swiss border on Zermatt's Klein Matterhorn glacier slopes, open all year round.

SNOW RELIABILITY
Superb
The mountain is one of the highest in Europe and, despite getting a lot of afternoon sun, can usually be relied on to have good snow conditions.

The village nursery slopes, the bottom half of the Ventina run, above Laghi Cime Bianche and the runs under the top chair-lifts down to Plan Maison have snowmaking. But the run below the top of the gondola to lower-lying Valtournenche doesn't – and so is prone to bare patches and closure. We've found it closed in March, despite excellent snow elsewhere.

FOR EXPERTS
Forget it
This is not a resort for experts. There is little readily accessible off-piste and high winds can blow the snow off what there is (though 'good-value' heli-drops with guides can be arranged). There are a few black runs scattered here and there, but most of them would be classified red elsewhere. Many reporters head over to Zermatt for more challenging slopes but don't necessarily find them – see 'The Zermatt connection' box overleaf.

FOR INTERMEDIATES
Miles of long, flattering runs
Virtually the whole area can be covered comfortably by average intermediates. But as a recent reporter so aptly put it, 'Strong, aggressive intermediates will get bored quickly.' If you like wide, easy, motorway pistes, you'll love Cervinia: it has more long, flattering runs than any other resort. The easiest slopes are on the left as you look at the mountain. From top to bottom there are gentle blue runs and almost equally gentle reds in the beautiful scenery at the foot of the

boarding

Cervinia has great slopes for learning to snowboard – gentle, wide and usually with good snow. And the main lifts around the area are chairs, gondolas and cable-cars, but there are a lot of drag-lifts and some long flat bits as well. There's not much to interest better boarders – just as there's not much to interest better skiers.

south face of the Matterhorn. A reporter warns that the start of the run from Plan Maison has been reclassified from red to blue but is 'very tricky in parts and I saw children in trouble'.

The area on the right as you look at the mountain is best for adventurous intermediates. The Ventina red is a particularly good fast cruise. You can use the cable-car to do the top part repeatedly, or go all the way down to Cervinia (8km/5 miles and over 1400m/4,600ft vertical). The long run down to Valtournenche is mostly easy, though the snow conditions on the lower part can be challenging.

FOR BEGINNERS
Pretty much ideal
Complete beginners will start on the good village nursery slope (which now has an excellent, long moving carpet), and should graduate quickly to the fine flat area around Plan Maison and its gentle blue runs. Fast learners will be going all the way from the top to the bottom of the mountain by the end of the week.

FOR CROSS-COUNTRY
Hardly any
There are a couple of short trails, but this is not a cross-country resort.

QUEUES
Not as bad as they were
Our 2005 reporters did not find queues a problem, at least on weekdays. But the two main access lifts from Cervinia to Plan Maison can get crowded at the peak morning rush, especially on Sundays and public holidays (waits of an hour or more are reported), and the alternative series of drags and chairs need upgrading ('continually stopping and uncomfortable', writes one). There are still some antiquated lifts around in other sectors, too: the series of slow lifts back up from Valtournenche is a particular source of complaint – one 2005 visitor was 'stuck' there when the drag-lifts closed without warning ('absolute chaos'). There can also be queues for many lower lifts when upper lifts are shut due to wind, concentrating Cervinia residents in a relatively small area.

Cervinia

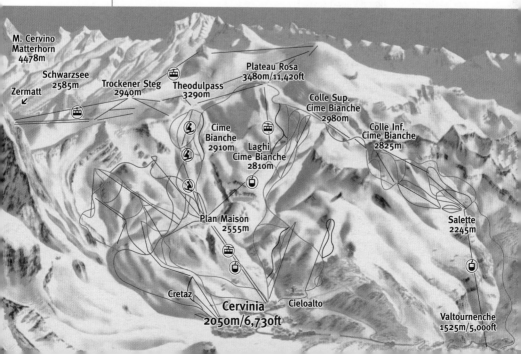

M. Cervino
Matterhorn
4478m

Schwarzsee
2585m

Zermatt

Trockener Steg
2940m

Theodulpass
3290m

Plateau Rosa
3480m/11,420ft

Colle Sup.
Cime Bianche
2980m

Colle Inf.
Cime Bianche
2825m

Cime
Bianche
2910m

Laghi
Cime Bianche
2810m

Plan Maison
2555m

Salette
2245m

Cretaz

Cervinia
2050m/6,730ft

Cieloalto

Valtournenche
1525m/5,000ft

THE ZERMATT CONNECTION

If the weather is good, you'll want to go over to Zermatt. And quite right – the restaurants are simply the best, and it's only from the Swiss side that you get the classic view of the Matterhorn. But don't expect to have time to savour either the lunch or the view.

You come first of all to glacier motorways even gentler than those on the Cervinia side. There are more challenging pistes once you get below Trockener Steg and below Schwarzsee. But to ski Zermatt's classic terrain on the Rothorn/Stockhorn you have to descend to the village, and then get a bus or taxi to other lifts.

Once there, you have the worry of queues on the way back to the border. There can be long queues for the Klein Matterhorn cable-car (a reporter writes of an hour's wait) and for the alternative T-bars.

We did a tour from Cervinia last March. Without rushing or dawdling too much, it went like this:

0840 Cervinia
0930 Swiss border
1030 Zermatt
1200 Rothorn
1300 Hohtälli
1400 Furi
1415 Trockener Steg
1445 Schwarzsee for late rösti lunch
1500 left Schwarzsee
1530 Trockener Steg
1615 Italian border

So in addition to making the tour we got an hour's skiing off the circuit, around Trockener Steg, and 15 minutes for a late lunch. A worthwhile day, but not one you are likely to want to repeat.

MOUNTAIN RESTAURANTS
OK if you know where to go

The mountain restaurants are not as appealing as you might expect in an Italian resort. Toilet facilities have been a traditional cause of complaints from reporters, but several have been improved according to this year's visitors. Some reporters head over to Zermatt for lunch.

Our favourite restaurant, and readers', is the Chalet Etoile, beneath the Rocce Nere chair-lift above Plan Maison: 'Top quality cuisine in an authentic Italian style – absolutely super,' says one reader. The more basic table-service section of Rifugio Teodulo at Theodulpass is also recommended – excellent pasta. Booking is recommended at both.

Other reporter recommendations include the British-run Igloo, near the top of the Bardoney chair just off the Ventina piste, which serves huge burgers and has 'a UK-style toilet'. Baita Cretaz, near the bottom of the Cretaz pistes, is good value ('the best bombardinos'). The Bontadini at the top of the Fornet chair was praised again recently ('good value and superb view').

The restaurants are cheaper and less crowded on the Valtournenche side. On the upper slopes there, the Motta does excellent food including goulaschsuppe that is 'out of this world' (and speciality hot white wine), and Lo Baracon dou Tene does a 'magnificent polenta con funghi'.

SCHOOLS AND GUIDES
Generally positive reports

Cervinia has three main schools, Cervino, Breuil and Nuova Cielo Alto. Recent reviews are fairly positive. The Breuil school is recommended for 'just the right mix of technical tuition and tour of the runs', as well as good-value private lessons. English speakers can be in short supply, though. A 2005 reporter's children made 'excellent progress' with the Cervino ski school: 'We couldn't fault the instructor'.

FACILITIES FOR CHILDREN
Could be better

The Cervino ski school runs a ski kindergarten. And there's a babysitting and kindergarten area at Plan Maison. Another kindergarten, Bianca Neve, opened last season. The slopes, with their long gentle runs, should suit families.

HOW TO GO
Plenty of hotel packages

Most of the big operators come here, offering a wide selection of hotels, though other types of accommodation are rather thin on the ground.

Hotels There are almost 50 hotels, mostly 2- or 3-stars, but there are a few 4-stars. Unless they run their own mini-bus to the slopes, choose your location with care.

(((((4) **Hermitage** (0166 948998) Small, luxurious Relais et Château just out of the village on the road up to Cieloalto. Great views, pool, free bus to lifts. 'First class, good ambiance and service,' says a recent reporter.

((((3) **Excelsior Planet** (0166 949426) Regularly recommended by reporters: 'Fantastic food and comfortable facilities,' said one visitor this year. Pool, spa facilities and minibus to lift. In centre near Cretaz lifts.

((((3) **Sporthotel Sertorelli** (0166 949797) Excellent food, sauna and hot-tub. Ten minutes from lifts.

((((3) **Europa** (0166 948660) Friendly and family run; near Cretaz lifts. Pool.

((((2) **Astoria** (0166 949062) Right by main lift station. Family run and simple. 'Comfortable but that's all,' says a reporter.

((((2) **Marmore** (0166 949057) Friendly, family run, with 'quite good food'; on main street – an easy walk to the lifts.

((((1) **Al Piolet** (0166 949161) A flood of approval this year for this 'friendly' budget place, recently refurbished 'to a high standard'. 'Excellent – ski-in location', 'good meals'.

Self-catering There are many apartments, but few are available via UK tour ops. The Escargot ones in Cieloalto are 'very spacious'.

EATING OUT
Plenty to choose from

Cervinia's 50 or so restaurants allow plenty of choice. The Chamois and Matterhorn are excellent, but quite expensive. Casse Croute also serves good pizzas. The Copa Pan has a lively atmosphere and is recommended by several reporters. The Bricole and the Nicchia have also been praised, and the Maison de Saussure does 'very good local specialities – quite cosy'. The Vieux Grenier at the hotel Grivola does 'an excellent pizza and is lively' and you'll find 'good pizza and pasta' at Capanna Alpina. The Ski d'Oro is

CHILDREN

Bianca Neve
t 0166 940201
Ages 2 to 8; 9am-
5pm daily
Ski school
Classes for children
over 5

GETTING THERE

Air Turin 118km/
73 miles (2½hr);
Geneva 220km/
137 miles (2½hr).

Rail Châtillon
(27km/17 miles);
regular buses from
station.

ACTIVITIES

Indoor Hotels with
swimming pools and
saunas, fitness centre,
squash, bowling,
climbing wall

Outdoor Natural ice
rink, paragliding,
hang-gliding, hiking,
mountaineering,
snowmobiles, snow-
shoeing, quad biking,
ice climbing, ice cave
visits

WEBSITES

For links to resort
sites, go to our own
new site at
www.wtss.co.uk

Phone numbers
From abroad use the
prefix +39 (and do
not omit the initial '0'
of the phone
number).

TOURIST OFFICE

t 0166 949136
breuil-cervinia@
montecervino.it
www.montecervino.it
www.cervinia.it

'good value' and the Jour et Nuit is
praised for its 'excellent hospitality'
and wine tasting experience. An
evening out at the Baita Cretaz
mountain hut makes a change.

APRES-SKI
Disappoints many Brits

Plenty of Brits come here looking for
action but find there isn't much to do
except tour the bars in and around the
main street. 'The best thing to do is
take a good book,' said a recent
reporter. The bar of the hotel Grivola,
next to the Vieux Grenier restaurant, is
attractively woody. The Copa Pan (see
'Eating out') has live music and is
good value. The Dragon Bar is popular
with Brits and Scandinavians and has
satellite TV and videos ('It's great if
you're homesick,' says a reporter).
Other recommendations include Lino's,
by the ice rink ('excellent pizzas and
cheap beer'), the Yeti, Torette and
Hostellerie des Guides (with mementos
of the owner's Himalayan trips). The
discos liven up at weekends. Events
are organised by tour-op reps, such as
snowmobiling on the old bob-sled run,
quiz nights, bowling, fondue nights.

OFF THE SLOPES
Little attraction

There is little to do for those who
don't plan to hit the slopes. The
pleasant town of Aosta is a four-hour
round trip. Village amenities include
hotel pools, a fitness centre and a
natural ice rink. The walks are

disappointing. The mountain
restaurants that are reachable by
gondola or cable-car are not special.

STAYING UP THE MOUNTAIN
To beat the queues

Up at Plan Maison, the major lift
junction 500m/1,640ft vertical above
the resort, Lo Stambecco (0166
949053) is a 50-room 3-star hotel
ideally placed for early nights and early
starts. Less radically, the Cime Bianche
(0166 949046) is a rustic 3-star chalet
on the upper fringes of the resort (in
the area known as La Vieille).

STAYING DOWN THE VALLEY
Great home run

Valtournenche, 9km/5.5 miles down
the road, is cheaper than Cervinia. The
village spreads along the steep,
winding road up to Cervinia, which is
often very busy.

A gondola speeds you out of town.
But the slow lifts above it mean it
takes quite a time to reach the top.
The exceptionally long run back down
is a nice way to end the day – when it
is all open (the bottom section is often
closed due to lack of snow). There's a
fair selection of simple hotels, of which
the 3-star Bijou (0166 92109) is the
best. There's a leisure centre and pool.

On the road between the two
resorts, Les Neiges d'Antan (0166
948775 was strongly recommended to
us by during a chair-lift ride in 2005. It
operates a non-stop shuttle bus to the
lifts. Short cross-country trail nearby.

Cortina d'Ampezzo

The scenery will take your breath away even if the slopes don't

COSTS

① ② ③ ④ ⑤ ⑥

RATINGS

The slopes
Fast lifts	**
Snow	***
Extent	***
Expert	**
Intermediate	***
Beginner	*****
Convenience	*
Queues	****
Mountain restaurants	****

The rest
Scenery	*****
Resort charm	****
Off-slope	*****

NEWS

For 2005/06 on the Cristallo area the old double is due to be replaced with a fast quad, the Paedon.

In 2004/05 the old Pian di Ra Bigontina chair-lift towards Faloria, above Rio Gere, was replaced by a fast quad. And a new hands-free electronic lift pass system was introduced for all Cortina's lifts.

Also for 2004/05, 10km/6 miles of new cross-country tracks opened at Passo Tre Croci, bringing the total in the area to 85km/53 miles.

And the new Adrenalin Park amid the trees behind the bob-sleigh track offers over 40 platforms for zipwire rides etc on cables and ropes.

You can now arrive in style – helicopter transfers will be available to whisk you from Venice (Marco Polo) to the resort in 35 minutes.

416

+ Magnificent Dolomite scenery – perhaps the most dramatic anywhere

+ Marvellous nursery slopes and good long cruising runs

+ Access to the vast area covered by the Dolomiti Superski pass

+ Attractive, although rather towny, resort, with lots of upmarket shops

+ Good off-slope facilities

+ Remarkably uncrowded slopes

– Several separate areas spread around all sides of the resort and linked by buses

– Erratic snow record

– Expensive by Italian standards

– Gets very crowded in town and in restaurants during Italian holidays

– Very little to entertain experts

– Mobile phones and fur coats may drive you nuts

Cortina is one on its own. Sure, it has a quantity of well-maintained, enjoyable intermediate slopes, and in one or two sectors it has efficient lifts. But you shouldn't even think about a holiday here if matters like these are top of your agenda – if skiing or riding from dawn to dusk is your priority.

If, on the other hand, you like lazy days centred around long lunches on sunny terraces, gazing at scenery that is just jaw-droppingly wonderful, this is the place. Dramatic pink-tinged cliffs and peaks rising vertically from the top of the slopes ring the town, giving picture-postcard views wherever you look. Every time we go back, the memory has faded and our jaws drop again.

Cortina has a regular upmarket clientele from Rome and Milan, many of whom have second homes here and enjoy the strolling, shopping, people-watching and lunching as much as the slopes. A good proportion of visitors don't go near the slopes except to drive up to a 'mountain restaurant' for lunch.

As an occasional change from serious ski resorts, we love it.

THE RESORT

In winter, more people come to Cortina for the clear mountain air, the stunning views, the shopping, the cafes and to pose and be seen than for the winter sports – 70% of all Italian visitors don't bother taking to the slopes. Cortina attracts the rich and famous from the big Italian cities. Fur coats and glitzy jewellery are the norm.

The resort itself is a widely spread town rather than a village, with exclusive chalets scattered around the outskirts. The centre is the traffic-free, Corso Italia, full of chic designer clothes, jewellery and antique shops, art galleries and furriers – finding a ski shop can seem tricky. The cobbles and picturesque church bell tower add to the atmosphere. By 5pm, hardly anyone is still in ski gear; the streets are packed with people parading up and down in their evening finery and shouting and gesticulating into their mobile phones.

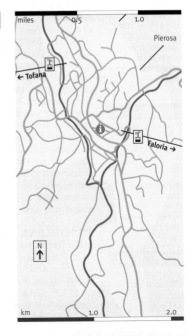

↑ The top chair serving the south-facing black run at Forcella Staunies is spectacularly set but rarely open

CORTINA TURISMO / PAOLA DANDREA

THE MOUNTAINS

Cortina first leapt to fame as host of the 1956 Winter Olympics. At the time, it was very modern; now its facilities feel dated. There is a good mixture of slopes above and below the tree line.

THE SLOPES
Inconveniently fragmented

All Cortina's smallish separate areas are a fair trek from the town centre. The largest is **Socrepes**, accessed by chair- and drag-lifts a bus-ride away. You can reach it by piste from **Tofana**, Cortina's highest area, accessed by cable-car from near the Olympic ice rink.

On the opposite side of the valley is the tiny **Mietres** area. Another two-stage cable-car from the east side of town leads to the **Faloria** area, from where you can head down to chairs that lead up into the limited but dramatic runs beneath **Cristallo**.

Other areas are reachable by road – in particular the road west over Passo Falzarego towards San Cassiano and the Sella Ronda area. (Taxis are an affordable means of access if shared.)

First is the small but spectacular Cinque Torri area. Its excellent, north-facing slopes are accessed by a high-speed quad, followed by an ancient one-person chair and a rope tow – also leading to a long red run on the sunny side of the hill to Passo Giau.

Then comes the tiny Col Gallina area – north-facing, again – from where you can take a pleasant green to Cinque Torri. The cable-car from nearby Passo Falzarego up to Lagazuoi accesses a beautiful red run down a 'hidden valley' to Armentarola on the fringe of the Alta Badia area. (For more on this run and another excellent red run back down to the cable-car base station see the Selva chapter.)

Reporters consistently praise the excellent grooming and quiet slopes but complain about other things: the piste map not showing some runs, the way runs are named on the mountain but numbered on the map, poor piste marking, some runs being marked blue on the piste map but red on the mountain, some blacks that should be reds and vice versa, World Cup races disrupting January skiing, having to take some cable-cars down as well as up if snow is poor or you want to avoid poling.

It's certainly a fairly long list of grumbles. But most reporters judge

Unlike the rest of the Dolomites, Cortina is pure Italy. It has none of the Germanic traditions of the Sud Tirol and you'll hear Italian rather than German being spoken by most locals and visitors.

Surrounding the centre is a horrendous one-way system, often traffic-clogged and a nasty contrast to the stunning scenery everywhere else you look. The lifts to the two main areas of slopes are a fair way from the centre, and at opposite sides of town. Other lifts are bus-rides away. There's a wide range of hotels, both in the centre and scattered on the outskirts. Staying centrally is best.

The local bus service is good, and free to ski-pass holders. A car can be useful, especially for getting to the outlying areas and to make the most of other areas on the Dolomiti Superski pass, but a 2005 visitor found parking 'inadequate'. San Cassiano is not far to the west, with links from there to Corvara and the other Sella Ronda resorts (see Selva chapter).

KEY FACTS

Resort	1225m
	4,020ft
Slopes	1225-2930m
	4,020-9,610ft
Lifts	51
Pistes	140km
	87 miles
Blue	33%
Red	62%
Black	5%
Snowmaking	90%

LIFT PASSES

Dolomiti Superski
Covers 450 lifts and
1220km/758 miles of
piste in the
Dolomites, including
all Cortina areas.

Beginners
No special pass

Main pass
1 day €38
6 days €190

Senior citizens
Over 60: 6 days €161

Children
Under 16: 6 days
€133

Alternative pass
Cortina d'Ampezzo
covers all lifts in
Cortina, San Vito di
Cadore, Auronzo and
Misurina, and ski-
buses.

ITALY

418

boarding

Despite its upmarket chic, Cortina is a good resort for learning to board. The Socrepes nursery slopes are wide, gentle and served by a fast chair-lift. And progress on to other easy slopes is simple because you can get around in all areas using just chairs and cable-cars – though there are drags, they can be avoided. A specialist snowboard shop, Boarderline, organises instruction as well as equipment hire. There's little off-piste to interest experienced boarders, but the best is to be found off the back of Cinque Torri, and the tiny Col Gallina area. There are some nice trees and natural undulations under the one-person chair at Cinque Torri.

that Cortina's other charms more than make up for them.

One way to tour the area is to use special ski itineraries, maps for which are available at the tourist and ski pass offices. 'Skitour Olympia' takes you on the 1956 Olympic downhill, GS and slalom courses and the Bobsled run. 'Skitour Romantic Views' covers the Lagazuoi-Cinque Torri area.

TERRAIN-PARKS
Not a bad one
There is a terrain-park at Faloria that has some decent kickers and rails, and a half-pipe. We're told it's open to snowboarders only.

SNOW RELIABILITY
Lots of artificial help
The snowfall record is erratic – it can be good here when it's poor on the north side of the Alps (and vice versa). But 90 per cent of the pistes are now covered by snowmaking, so cover should be good if it is cold enough to make snow. When we visited a few years ago, the link from Tofana to Socrepes was closed because of lack of snow on a key south-facing slope – which made the areas even more

fragmented. Last season, however, though natural snow was scarce temperatures were low, and the pistes had ample artificial cover.

FOR EXPERTS
Limited
The run down from the second stage of the Tofana cable-car at Ra Valles is deservedly graded black; it goes through a gap in the rocks, and a steep, narrow, south-facing section gives wonderful views of Cortina way down in the valley below. It can be tricky in poor snow conditions.

Cortina's other steep run goes from the top of the Cristallo area at Forcella Staunies. A chair-lift takes you to a south-facing couloir that is often shut due to avalanche danger or poor snow.

Other than these two runs there are few challenges. There are some great long red runs though, and if it snows, you'll also have very little competition for first tracks. Heli-skiing is available.

FOR INTERMEDIATES
Fragmented and not extensive
To enjoy Cortina you must like cruising in beautiful scenery, and not mind doing runs repeatedly.

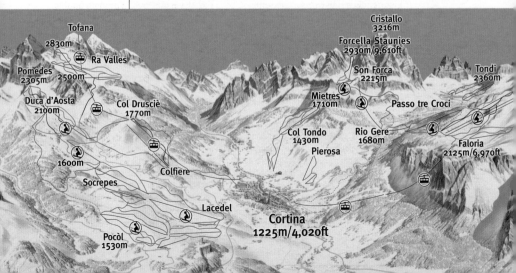

The runs at the top of Tofana are short but normally have the best snow. The highest are at over 2800m/9,190ft and mainly face north. But be warned: the only way back down is by the tricky black run described above or by cable-car. The reds from the linked Pomedes area offer good cruising.

Faloria has a string of fairly short north-facing runs – we loved the Vitelli red run, round the back away from the lifts. And the Cristallo area has a long blue run served by a fast quad.

It is well worth making the trip to Cinque Torri for wonderful, deserted fast cruising on usually excellent north-facing snow. And do not miss the wonderful 'hidden valley' red run from Lagazuoi (at the top of the Passo Falzarego cable-car) – covered in more detail in the Selva chapter. Shared taxis take you back to Passo Falzarego (if you've time, try the slopes of Alta Badia, accessed from Armentarola).

FOR BEGINNERS
Wonderful nursery slopes
The Socrepes area has some of the biggest nursery slopes and best progression runs we have seen. Some of the blue forest paths can be icy and intimidating. But you'll find ideal gentle terrain on the main pistes.

FOR CROSS-COUNTRY
One of the best
Cortina has around 85km/57 miles of trails suitable for all standards, mainly in the Fiames area, where there is a cross-country centre and school. Trails include a 30km itinerary following an old railway from Fiames to Cortina, and there is a special beginner area equipped with snowmaking. Passo Tre Croci offers more challenging trails, and 10km/6 miles of new ones will open there in 2004/05.

QUEUES
No problem
Most Cortina holidaymakers rise late, lunch lengthily and leave the slopes early – if they get on to them at all. That means few lift queues and generally uncrowded pistes – a different world from the crowded Sella Ronda circuit. 'Lack of queues was one of the highlights of our holiday,' said one reporter. Another visitor was delighted to find the slopes got emptier in the afternoons, as the Italians left the slopes, but that lifts stayed open as late as 5pm.

MOUNTAIN RESTAURANTS
Good, but get in early
Lunch is a major event for many Cortina visitors. At weekends you often need to book or turn up very early to be sure of a table. Many restaurants can be reached by road or lift, and fur coats arrive as early as 10am to sunbathe, admire the views and idle the time away on their mobile phones.

Although prices are high in the swishest establishments, we've found plenty of reasonably priced places, serving generally excellent food (now in a no-smoking environment due to new laws). A 2005 visitor says they are all 'brilliant – never found a bad one'. In the Socrepes area, the Rifugio Col Taron is highly recommended and the Pié de Tofana, Rifugio Pomedes and El Faral are also good. At Tofana, the Col Drusciè re-opened in 2003 and a new place for 2004/05, El Soréi, opened by the Olympic chair above Lacedèl.

At Cristallo the Rio Gere at the base of the quad chair and Rifugio Son Forca, with fabulous views at the top of it (and owned by Alberto Tomba's former trainer), are both worth a visit.

The restaurants at Cinque Torri, the Scoiattoli ('magnificent home-made pastas') and the Rifugio Averau, offer fantastic views as well as good food – 'splendid pasta'. The Rifugio Fedare, over the back of Cinque Torri, is also recommended – 'great pasta with hare sauce'. Rifugio Lagazuoi, a short hike up from the top of the Passo Falzarego cable-car, also has great views.

SCHOOLS AND GUIDES
Mixed reports
Of the four ski schools, we've had mixed reports of the Cortina school over the years – though we lack recent reports. The Gruppo Guide Alpine offers off-piste and touring.

FACILITIES FOR CHILDREN
Better than average
By Italian standards childcare facilities are outstanding, with all-day care arrangements for children of practically any age. However, given the small number of British visitors, you can't count on good spoken English. And the fragmented area can make travelling around with children difficult. A 2005 reporter commented how well the lift staff and instructors look after children. Note that it is compulsory for skiing or snowboarding children under 14 to wear helmets.

GETTING THERE

Air Venice 160km/ 100 miles (2hr). Treviso 132km/ 82 miles (1³/₄hr). Saturday and Sunday transfers available for hotel guests; advance booking required. 35-minute heli-transfers from Venice also available.

Rail Calalzo (35km/ 22 miles) or Dobbiaco (32km/20 miles); frequent buses from station.

ACTIVITIES

Indoor Swimming pool, saunas, health spa, fitness centre, ice stadium, museums, art gallery, cinema, indoor tennis court, library

Outdoor Rides on Olympic bob run, snowrafting down Olympic ski jump, crazy sledging, snow-shoe tours, sleigh rides, horse-riding school, 6km/4 miles of walking paths, tobogganing

WEBSITES

For links to resort sites, go to our own new site at www.wtss.co.uk

Phone numbers
From abroad use the prefix +39 (and do **not** omit the initial '0' of the phone number).

TOURIST OFFICE

t 0436 866252
cortina@dolomiti.org
www.cortina.dolomiti.org

STAYING THERE

HOW TO GO
Now with more packages
Hotels dominate the market but there are some catered chalets.

Hotels There's a big choice, from 5-star luxury to 1-star and 2-star pensions.
(((((5) **Miramonti** (0436 4201) Spectacularly grand hotel, 2km/1 mile south of town. Pool.
(((((5) **Cristallo** (0436 881111) Newish, with a spa-health clinic. A hike from the lifts and town centre, but there's a shuttle bus.
(((((4) **Poste** (0436 4271) Reliable 4-star, at the heart of the town.
(((((4) **Ancora** (0436 3261) Elegant public rooms. On the traffic-free Corso Italia.
(((((4) **Victoria Parc**(0436 3246) Rustic, family-run 4-star with small rooms but good food – at the Faloria end of the town centre.
(((((4) **Corona** (0436 3251) Family run 4-star, very friendly with good food and lots of original art. Near Tofana lift.
(((((4) **Park Faloria** (0436 2959) Near ski jump, splendid pool, good food.
(((((3) **Olimpia** (0436 3256) Comfortable B&B hotel in centre, near Faloria lift.
(((((3) **Menardi** (0436 2400) Welcoming roadside inn, a long walk from centre and lifts.
(((((3) **Villa Resy** (0436 3303) Small and welcoming, just outside centre, with British owner.
(((((3) **Des Alpes** (0436 862021) On the edge of town. 'Excellent food and service and friendly staff.'
((2) **Montana** (0436 862126) 'Excellent B&B. Amazing value and central location,' says a reporter.
Self-catering There are some chalets and apartments – usually out of town – available for independent travellers.

EATING OUT
Huge choice
There's an enormous selection, both in town and a little way out, doing mainly Italian food. The very smart and expensive El Toulà is in a beautiful old barn, just on the edge of town. Many of the best restaurants are further out – such as the Michelin-starred Tivoli, Meloncino, Leone e Anna, Rio Gere and Baita Fraina. Reasonably priced central restaurants include the Cinque Torri and the Passetto for pizza and pasta. The Tavernetta is a new restaurant in the centre. You can also arrange a night-time jaunt for a meal at a rifugio, travelling by snowmobile and sledge.

APRES-SKI
Lively in high season
Cortina is a lively social whirl in high season, with lots of well-heeled Italians staying up very late.

The Lovat is one of several high-calorie tea-time spots. There are many good wine bars: Enoteca has 700 wines and good cheese and meats; Osteria has good wines and local ham; and Villa Sandi, Dok-Dall' Ava and Brio di Vino have been recommended. The liveliest bar is the Clipper, with a bob-sleigh by the door. Discos liven up after 11pm.

OFF THE SLOPES
A classic resort
Cortina attracts lots of people who don't use the slopes. The setting is stunning, the town attractive, the shopping extensive and many mountain restaurants are accessible by road (a car is handy). And there's plenty more to do, such as swimming, ice skating and dog-sledding.

There is an observatory at Col Drusciè that has star-gazing tours (call 0436 3146 to book). You can have a run (with driver!) down the Olympic bob-sleigh run and try Adrenalin Park (see News). There's horse jumping and polo on the snow occasionally. Excursions to Venice are easy. You can visit World War 1 tunnels at Lagazuoi or the memorial at Pocol.

Courmayeur

Seductive village, stunning scenery, limited slopes

COSTS

① ② ③ ④ ⑤ ⑥

RATINGS

The slopes
Fast lifts	***
Snow	****
Extent	**
Expert	***
Intermediate	****
Beginners	**
Convenience	*
Queues	***
Mountain restaurants	****

The rest
Scenery	****
Resort charm	****
Off-slope	***

NEWS

For 2004/05 a new blue piste was created between the tops of the Aretu and Plan de la Gabba chair-lifts, linking the latter with the runs at Col Checrouit.

For 2005/06 there are plans to open a rail park on the Lavechon run – a second facility for boarders or freestylers to complement the recently-opened boarder-cross course.

The Swiss International Ski Championships, in association with Momentum Ski, are run here annually. This season's dates are 16 to 19 March 2006.

➕ Charming old village, with car-free centre and stylish shops and bars

➕ Stunning views of Mont Blanc massif

➕ Day trips to Chamonix (including doing the Vallée Blanche run) possible

➕ Heli-skiing available

➕ Comprehensive snowmaking

➕ Some good mountain restaurants

➖ Relatively small area, with mainly short runs; high-mileage piste-bashers should stay away

➖ Lack of nursery slopes and easy runs for beginners to progress to

➖ No tough pistes

➖ Slopes very crowded on Sundays

➖ Tiresome walk and cable-car journey between village and slopes

Courmayeur is a great place for a weekend away from Milan or Turin (or a day-trip to escape bad weather in Chamonix), and we always look forward to a quick visit here. (That the village bars are among the most civilised in the skiing world is a factor, we admit.) Whether it makes sense for a week's holiday is another matter. Its pistes are best suited to competent intermediates, who are likely to have an appetite for mileage that Courmayeur will arouse but not satisfy. Off-piste, there is more to do. And with a car you can explore several other worthwhile resorts further down the Valle d'Aosta.

THE RESORT

Courmayeur is a traditional old Italian mountaineering village that, despite the nearby Mont Blanc tunnel road and modern hotels, has retained much of its old-world feel.

The village has a charming traffic-free centre of attractive shops, cobbled streets and well-preserved buildings. An Alpine museum and a statue of a long-dead mountain rescue hero add to the historical feel.

The centre has a great atmosphere, focused around the Via Roma. As the lifts close, people pile into the many bars, some of which are very civilised. Others wander in and out of the many small shops, which include a salami specialist and a good bookshop. At weekends people-watching is part of the evening scene, when the fur coats of the Milanese and Torinese take over.

The village is quite large, and its huge cable-car to Plan Checrouit is on the southern edge. There is no bus alternative to walking or driving to the lift, so having accommodation close to it is handy. Some hotels are a long walk away. Parking at the cable-car is very limited, but drivers can go to Entrèves, up the valley, where there is a large car park at the cable-car.

Up at Plan Checrouit there is another short walk to the other lifts

before you can get going. You can leave skis, boards and boots in lockers up the mountain – highly recommended by reporters.

Buses, infrequent but timetabled, go to La Palud, just beyond Entrèves, for the Punta Helbronner-Vallée Blanche cable-car. Taxis are easily arranged for evenings out.

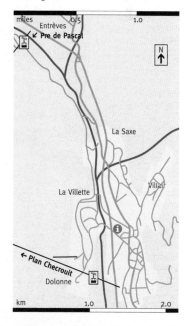

KEY FACTS

Resort	1225m
	4,020ft
Slopes	1210-2755m
	3,970-9,040ft
Lifts	16
Pistes	100km
	62 miles
Blue	26%
Red	57%
Black	17%
Snowmaking	20km
	12 miles

ITALY

422

LIFT PASSES

Courmayeur Mont Blanc
Covers all lifts in Val Veny and Checrouit, and the lifts on Mont Blanc up to Punta Helbronner.

Beginners
Two free nursery lifts.

Main pass
1 day €36
6 days €186

Senior citizens
Over 65: 6 days €136.50

Children
Under 12: 6 days €139.50
Under 8: €46.50
Under 6 free

Notes
Single ascent on some lifts and half-day pass available. Passes for four days plus allow for at least one day in the Aosta valley, Flaine and Chamonix.

THE MOUNTAINS

The pistes suit intermediates, but are surprisingly limited for such a well-known, large resort. They are varied in character, if not gradient. Piste marking could be improved.

La Thuile and Pila are an easy drive or bus ride to the south, and Cervinia is reachable.

THE SLOPES
Small but interestingly varied

There are two distinct sections, both almost entirely intermediate. The east-facing **Checrouit** area, accessed by the Checrouit gondola, catches morning sun, and has open, above-the-tree-line pistes. The 25-person, infrequently running Youla cable-car goes to the top of Courmayeur's pistes. There is a further tiny cable-car to Cresta d'Arp. This serves only long off-piste runs but it is no longer compulsory to have a guide with you to go up it.

Most people follow the sun over to the north-west-facing slopes towards **Val Veny** in the afternoon. These are interesting, varied and tree lined, with great views of Mont Blanc and its glaciers. Connections between the

Checrouit and Val Veny areas are complex, with many alternative routes. The Val Veny slopes are also accessible by cable-car from Entrèves, a few miles outside Courmayeur.

A little way beyond Entrèves is La Palud, where a cable-car goes up in three stages to Punta Helbronner, at the shoulder of **Mont Blanc**. There are no pistes from the top, but you can do the famous Vallée Blanche run to Chamonix from here without the horrific ridge walk that forms the start on the Chamonix side. There are buses back from Chamonix through the Mont Blanc tunnel. Or you can tackle the tougher off-piste runs on the Italian side of Mont Blanc. None of these glacier runs should be done without a guide.

TERRAIN-PARKS
At last, there's a boarder-cross

Like a lot of Italian resorts, Courmayeur has no terrain-park or half-pipe. However, the resort created a 500m/1,640ft boarder-cross run recently near the top of the Plan de la Gabba high-speed chair and a rail park is planned for the Lavechon run this year.

Cresta d'Arp
2755m/9,040ft

Cresta Youla
2625m

Lago Checrouit
2255m

COLLE CHECROUIT

Courba Dzeleuna

VAL VEN

Plan Checrouit
1700m

Dolonne
1210m

Pre de Pascal
1910m

Zerotta
1525m

Courmayeur
1225m/4,020ft

Entrèves

La Palud
1370m

a deserted valley to Dolonne or Pré St Didier; or south through the Youla gorge to La Thuile.

On Mont Blanc, the Vallée Blanche is not a challenge (though there are more difficult variations), but the Toula glacier route on the Italian side from Punta Helbronner to Pavillon most certainly is, often to the point of being dangerous. There are also heli-drops available, including a wonderful 20km/12 mile run from the Ruitor glacier down into France – you ride the lifts back up from La Rosière and descend to La Thuile (a taxi-ride from Courmayeur). And you can do a day trip to Chamonix through the Mont Blanc tunnel.

FOR INTERMEDIATES
Ideal gradient but limited extent
The whole area is suitable for most intermediates, but it is small. The avid piste-basher will ski it in a day. It also lacks long, easy runs to suit the more timid.

The open Colle Checrouit section is pretty much go-anywhere territory, but it is basically a red slope. Timid skiers should head up the Pre Neyron chair for access to the area's few blues. The Val Veny side of the mountain is basically steeper, with manageable blacks going close to the fall line and good reds and the occasional blue taking less direct routes. These runs link in with the pretty, wooded slopes heading down to Zerotta. The fast Zerotta chair dominates Val Veny, serving runs of varying difficulty over a decent vertical of 560m/1,800ft – including a long blue. But boarders should beware flat sections down here, according to a 2005 reporter.

The Vallée Blanche, although off-piste, is easy enough for adventurous, fit intermediates to try. So is the local heli-skiing (from £90 a drop including a guide); you are picked up on the piste so there's no wasted time.

SNOW RELIABILITY
Good for most of the season
Courmayeur's slopes are not high – mostly between 1700m and 2250m (5,600ft and 7,400ft). Those above Val Veny face north or north-west, so keep their snow well, but the Plan Checrouit side is rather too sunny for comfort in late season. There is snowmaking on most main runs, so good coverage in early- and mid-season is virtually assured – we were there in the January 2002 snow drought and enjoyed decent skiing entirely on man-made snow.

FOR EXPERTS
Off-piste is the only challenge
Courmayeur has few challenging pistes. The black runs on the Val Veny side are not severe, and few moguls form elsewhere. But if you're lucky enough to find fresh powder – as we have been several times – you can have fantastic fun among the trees.

Classic off-piste runs go from Cresta d'Arp, at the top of the lift network, in three directions – a clockwise loop via Arp Vieille to Val Veny, with close-up views of the Miage glacier; east down

boarding

Courmayeur's pistes suit intermediates, and most areas are easily accessible by novices as the main lifts are cable-cars, chairs and gondolas – but it's all a bit steep for absolute beginners. The biggest draws for the more experienced are the off-piste routes to be done with a guide. And there's a boarder-cross run – the first special facility for boarders. A rail park is due this season.

MOUNTAIN RESTAURANTS
Lots – some of them good

The area is lavishly endowed with 27 establishments ranging from rustic little huts to larger self-service places. Most huts do table-service of delicious pizza, pasta and other dishes and it is best to reserve tables in advance. But there are also snack bars selling more basic fare and relying on views and sun to fill their terraces.

Several restaurants are excellent. Maison Vieille, at the top of the chair of the same name and run by the charming mountain man Giacomo, is our favourite – a welcoming rustic place with superb home-made pastas. Chiecco, next to the drag-lift with the same name at Plan Checrouit, has good food and friendly service. The pick of the Plan Checrouit places is the Christiania (book a table downstairs) – also recommended this year for 'the best custard-filled bombolina ever'.

In Val Veny is another clutch of places worth trying. The jolly Grolla has good food and a sunny terrace with excellent views; the Fodze (just below Grolla) is a nice snack bar with some hot food; the Zerotta, at the foot of the eponymous chair, has a sunny terrace and good food; the nearby Petit Mont Blanc has also been recommended.

One of the better snack bars is Courba Dzeleuna, just below the top of Dzeleuna chair, with incredible views and delicious home-made myrtle grappa (beware the alcohol-soaked berries left in the bottom of your glass). A 2005 visitor enjoyed an 'excellent lunch of charcuterie and cheese' there.

SCHOOLS AND GUIDES
Good reports

'We had the best instructor for ages – possibly ever,' said a reporter about the Monte Bianco ski school. There is a thriving guides' association ready to help you explore the area's off-piste; it has produced a helpful booklet showing the main possibilities.

FACILITIES FOR CHILDREN
Good care by Italian standards

Childcare facilities are well ahead of the Italian norm, but Courmayeur is far from an ideal resort for a young family.

SCHOOLS

Monte Bianco
t 0165 842477
Courmayeur
t 0165 848254

Classes
(Monte Bianco prices)
5 days (3hr per day)
€146
Private lessons
€33 to €42 for 1hr
for 1 person; each
additional person €10

CHILDREN

Kinderheim at Plan Checrouit
t 0165 842477
From age 6mnth; 9.30 to 4pm
Kinderheim at the Sports Centre
From age 6mnth
'Fun park' at Dolonne
9am-4.30

Ski schools
Takes children from age 4 who can be looked after for the whole day (lesson am, play pm) (5 days incl. lunch €180)

FOR BEGINNERS
Consistently too steep

Courmayeur is not well suited to beginners. There are several nursery slopes, none ideal. The area at Plan Checrouit gets crowded, and there are few easy runs for the near-beginner to progress to. The small area served by the short Tzaly drag, just above the Entrèves cable-car top station, is the most suitable beginner terrain, and it tends to have good snow.

FOR CROSS-COUNTRY
Beautiful trails

There are 35km/22 miles of trails scattered around Courmayeur. The best are the four covering 20km/12 miles at Val Ferret, served by bus. Dolonne has a couple of short trails.

QUEUES
Sunday crowds pour in

The Checrouit and Val Veny cable-cars suffer queues on Sundays and peak periods – a 2005 reporter experienced an 'absolutely awful' wait at 8am. There can be queues to go down as well as up. The infrequent Youla cable-car may require patience – mainly worth it for those heading off-piste. Overcrowded slopes on Sundays, particularly down to Zerotta, can also be a problem.

STAYING THERE

HOW TO GO
Plenty of hotels
Courmayeur's long-standing popularity
ensures a wide range of packages
(including some excellent weekend
deals), mainly in hotels. Tour op
Interski has cheap hotels out of town,
and buses people in. One or two UK
operators have catered chalets.
Hotels There are nearly 50 hotels,
spanning the star ratings.
((((4) **Grand Hotel Courmaison** (0165
831400) Luxury hotel 2km/1 mile from
town, with 'excellent food'. Pool.
((((4) **Gallia Gran Baita** (0165 844040)
Luxury place with antique furnishings,
panoramic views and 'superb food'.
Pool. Shuttle-bus to cable-car.
((((4) **Pavillon** (0165 846120)
Comfortable 4-star near cable-car, with
a pool. Friendly staff.
(((3) **Auberge de la Maison** (0165
869811) Small atmospheric 3-star in
Entrèves under same ownership as
Maison de Filippo (see Eating Out).
(((3) **Bouton d'Or** (0165 846729) Small,
friendly B&B near main square.
(((3) **Berthod** (0165 842835) Friendly,
family-run hotel near centre.
(((3) **Grange** (0165 869733) Rustic,
stone-and-wood farmhouse in Entrèves.
(((3) **Triolet** (0165 846822) 'Excellent
location near lift. Comfy, well- furnished.'
((2) **Edelweiss** (0165 841590) Friendly,
cosy, good-value; close to the centre.
((2) **Lo Scoiattolo** (0165 846721) Good
rooms, good food, shame it's at the
opposite end of town to the cable-car.
Self-catering There is quite a lot
available to independent bookers.

EATING OUT
Jolly Italian evenings
There is a great choice, both in
downtown Courmayeur and within taxi
range; there's a handy promotional
booklet describing many of them (in
English as well as Italian). The touristy
but very jolly Maison de Filippo in
Entrèves is rightly famous for its fixed-
price, 36-dish feast. Also in Entrèves,
the Brenva has a separate Steakhouse
serving huge steaks. We've been
impressed by the traditional Italian
cuisine of both Pierre Alexis and
Cadran Solaire. The Terrazza ('excellent
pasta and very friendly, jolly service')
is a rising star. The Tunnel pizzeria
does a good job. The Mont-Fréty
('good value', 'its antipasti is a must'),
the Padella ('great pizza, raclette and

fondue') and the Vieux Pommier ('the
place to go for fondue and raclette')
have been recommended by reporters.

APRES-SKI
Stylish bar-hopping
Courmayeur has a lively evening scene
– at weekends, at least – centred on
stylish bars with comfy sofas or
armchairs to collapse in, often serving
free canapés in the early evening. Our
favourites are the Roma, the back
room of the Caffè della Posta and the
Bar delle Guide. The Cadran Solaire is
where the big money from Milan and
Turin hangs out. The Prive is excellent
for cocktails. The American Bar has
good music and a fine selection of
wines. Poppys is recommended for
drinks and pizza. Maquis is the better
of the two night clubs in Entrèves.

OFF THE SLOPES
Lots on for non-slope users
If you're not interested in hitting the
snow you'll find the village pleasant –
parading up and down is a favourite
pastime for the many non-slope users
the resort attracts (especially at
weekends). You can go by cable-car up
to Punta Helbronner, by bus to Aosta,
or up the main cable-car to Plan
Checrouit to meet friends for lunch.
The huge sports centre is good (indoor
tennis, climbing wall, skating, squash,
gym, sauna, steam, but no pool).

STAYING UP THE MOUNTAIN
Why would you want to?
Visiting Courmayeur and not staying in
the charming village seems perverse –
if you're that keen to get on the slopes
in the morning, this is probably the
wrong resort. But at Plan Checrouit,
the 1-star Christiania (0165 843572 –
see 'Mountain restaurants') has simple
rooms and the 3-star Baita (0165
843570) is smarter; you need to book
way in advance.

Livigno

Lowish prices and highish altitude – a tempting combination

COSTS

① ② ③ ④ ⑤ ⑥

RATINGS

The slopes
Fast lifts	***
Snow	****
Extent	**
Experts	**
Intermediates	***
Beginners	****
Convenience	**
Queues	****
Mountain restaurants	***

The rest
Scenery	***
Resort charm	***
Off-slope	**

NEWS

The most recent development was the opening of a fast six-pack at Federia in 2004, which replaced the double drag-lifts. Over half of the chair-lifts are now high-speed.

REPORTS WANTED

Recently we have had few reports on this resort. If you go there, please do send us a report.

The best reports earn a copy of the next edition, and can lead to free lift passes in future.

See page 10.

KEY FACTS

Resort	1815m
	5,950ft
Slopes	1815-2800m
	5,950-9,190ft
Lifts	32
Pistes	110km
	68 miles
Blue	25%
Red	58%
Black	17%
Snowmaking	70km
	43 miles

➕ High altitude plus snowmaking means reliable snow

➕ Large choice of beginners' slopes

➕ Impressive modern lift system

➕ Cheap by the standards of high resorts, with the bonus of duty-free shopping (eg for new equipment)

➕ Cosmopolitan, friendly and quite smart village with some Alpine atmosphere

➕ Long, snow-sure cross-country trails

➖ No challenging pistes

➖ Long airport transfer – around 5hr

➖ Slopes split into two quite widely separated areas

➖ Village is very long and straggling

➖ Few off-slope amenities

➖ Bleak setting – wind can easily close upper lifts

➖ Not many really comfortable hotels bookable through UK tour operators

➖ Nightlife can disappoint

Livigno offers the unusual combination of a fair-sized mountain, high altitude and fairly low prices. Despite its vaunted duty-free status, hotels, bars and restaurants are not much cheaper than in other Italian resorts, but shopping is – there are countless camera and clothes shops. As a relatively snow-sure alternative to the Pyrenees or to the smallest, cheapest resorts in Austria, Livigno seems attractive. But don't overlook the long list of drawbacks.

THE RESORT

Livigno is an amalgam of three villages in a wide, remote valley near the Swiss border – basically a string of hotels, bars, specialist shops and supermarkets lining a single long street. The buildings are small in scale and mainly traditional in style, giving the village a pleasant atmosphere. The original hamlet of San Antonio is the

nearest thing Livigno has to a centre, and the best all-round location. Here, the main street and those at right angles, linking it to the busy bypass road, are nominally traffic-free. The road that skirts the 'traffic-free' area is constantly busy, and becomes intrusive in the hamlets of Santa Maria, 1km/0.5 miles to the north, and San Rocco, a bit further away to the south (and uphill).

Lifts along the length of the village access the western slopes of the valley. The main lift to the eastern slopes is directly across the flat valley floor from the centre.

The bus services, on three colour-coded routes, are free and fairly frequent, but can get overcrowded at peak times and stop early in the evening. A 2005 reporter found them confusing: 'there is no way to tell which way around they will go'. Taxis (including minibus taxis for groups) are an affordable alternative.

The lift pass covers Bormio and Santa Caterina, an easy drive or free bus-ride if the high pass is open, and a six-day pass entitles you to a discount rate on a one-day pass in St Moritz, reached via a road tunnel – a 'fantastic' day out, says a reader.

The airport transfer from Bergamo is long – five hours with a snack stop.

Alta Valtellina
Covers all lifts in
Livigno, Bormio,
Valdidentro and
Valfurva

Main pass
1 day €32
6 days €159

Senior citizens
Over 60: 6 days
€110.50

Children
Under 13: 6 days
€110.50
Under 8: free pass

Notes
6-day pass entitles
you to a discount on
a 1-day pass for St
Moritz.

Alternative passes
Half-day passes for
Livigno only are
available. Natura
skipass classic covers
lift pass, tuition, ski
hire and a full day's
pass for St Moritz.

boarding

Livigno attracts a fair number of boarders. There are some good, long, high runs for free-riders and carvers, as well as ample off-piste opportunities for intermediate riders. Most of the resort can be accessed by cable-cars and chairs; however, the excellent beginner slopes are mainly served by drags.

THE MOUNTAINS

The mainly open slopes, on either side of the valley, are more extensive than in many other budget destinations.

THE SLOPES
Improved links
There are three sectors, all of them suitable for moderate and leisurely intermediates, and two of them are reasonably well linked.

A two-seat chair from the nursery slopes at the north end of the village take you up to **Costaccia**, where a long fast quad chair-lift goes along the ridge towards the **Carosello** sector. The blue linking run back from Carosello to the top of Costaccia is flat in places and may involve energetic poling if the snow conditions and the wind are against you. Carosello is more usually accessed by the optimistically named Carosello 3000 gondola at San Rocco, which goes up, in two stages, to 2750m/9,020ft. Most runs return towards the village, but there are a couple on the back of the mountain, on the west-facing slopes of Val Federia – now served by a six-pack.

The ridge of **Mottolino** is reached by an efficient gondola from Teola, a tiresome walk or a short bus-ride across the valley from San Antonio. From the top, you can descend to fast quads on either side of the ridge or, if you must, take a slow antique chair up the ridge to Monte della Neve. There is the alternative of a fast quad starting a little way up the Bormio road, and linking with a six-pack above.

Signposting is patchy and the piste map isn't always entirely accurate.

TERRAIN-PARKS
There, but empty
There's a half-pipe, a beginner's half-pipe and a good, if under-used, terrain-park/boarder-cross in the Mottolino area. The park hosts regular snowboarding events.

SNOW RELIABILITY
Very good, despite no glacier
Livigno's slopes are high (you can spend most of your time around 2500m/8,200ft), and with snow-guns on the lower slopes of Mottolino and Costaccia, the season is long.

Livigno

427

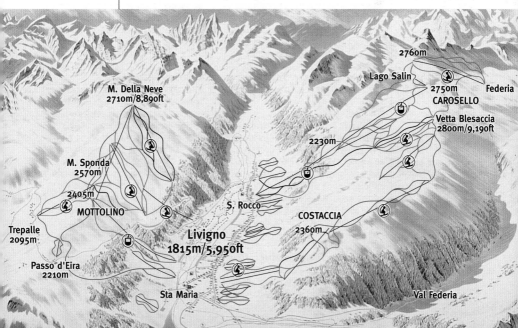

M. Della Neve
2710m/8,890ft

Lago Salin

2760m

2750m   Federia
CAROSELLO

Vetta Blesaccia
2800m/9,190ft

M. Sponda
2570m

2230m

2405m
MOTTOLINO

S. Rocco

COSTACCIA

Trepalle
2095m

Livigno
1815m/5,950ft

2360m

Passo d'Eira
2210m

Sta Maria

Val Federia

↑ There are trees, but most of the pistes are above or below them

SCHOOLS

Livigno Inverno/Estate
t 0342 996276
Azzurra Livigno
t 0342 997683
Livigno Italy
t 0342 996767
Livigno Galli Fedele
t 0342 970300
Top Club Mottolino
t 0342 970822

Classes
(Livigno Inverno/
Estate prices)
6 days (2hr per day)
€83
Private lessons
€30 for 1hr; each
additional person €6

CHILDREN

Alì Babà
t 0342 978050
Ages 3 and over
**Miniclub Top Club
Mottolino**
t 0342 970822
**Spazio Gioco
Peribimbi**
t 0342 970711
Ages 18mnth to 3yr;
8.30-1pm

FOR EXPERTS
Not recommended
The piste map shows a few black runs but these are not particularly steep. Even the all-black terrain served by the six-pack on Monte della Neve is really no more than stiff red in gradient. There is off-piste to be done, but guidance would be needed.

FOR INTERMEDIATES
Flattering slopes
Good intermediates will be able to tackle all the blacks without worry. The woodland black run down from Carosello past Tea da Borch is narrow in places and can get mogulled and icy at the end of the day. The red runs at Federia are now reportedly well groomed. Moderate intermediates have virtually the whole area at their disposal. The long run beneath the Mottolino gondola is one of the best – and there is also a long, under-used blue going less directly to the valley. Leisurely types have several long cruises available. The run beneath the fast chair at the top of Costaccia is a splendid slope for building confidence.

FOR BEGINNERS
Excellent but scattered slopes
A vast array of nursery slopes along the sunny lower flanks of Costaccia, and other slopes around the valley, make Livigno excellent for novices – although some of the slopes at the northern end are steep enough to cause difficulties. There are lots of longer runs to progress to.

CROSS-COUNTRY
Good snow, bleak setting
Long snow-sure trails (40km/25 miles in total) follow the valley floor, making Livigno a good choice, provided you don't mind the bleak scenery. There is a specialist cross-country school, and the resort organises major cross-country races.

QUEUES
Few problems these days
Despite reports of queues for the Costaccia chair at midday and short delays for the Carosello gondola in peak season, lift queues are not generally a problem. A total of nine fast chairs is impressive for an area of this size. A bigger problem is that strong winds often close the upper lifts, causing overcrowding lower down.

MOUNTAIN RESTAURANTS
More than adequate
On Mottolino, the refuge at the top of the gondola is impressive, with smart self- and table-service sections, a solarium and a nursery, but 'immense' lunch-time queues. The rustic restaurants at Passo d'Eira and Trepalle are a good option for a quiet stop – the Trela is recommended for pizza. And there are some more charming places lower down. The welcoming Tea del Vidal is at the base of the same sector. Costaccia's Tea del Plan is pleasantly rustic and sunny, with good food and a great atmosphere. The self-service place at the top of Carosello is acceptable and Tea da Borch, in the trees lower down, serves great food in a Tirolean-style atmosphere, though the run down can be tricky. Lunch in the valley is popular – recommendations include the hotel Sporting (near the Carosello gondola) the Vecchia Lanterna and the hotel Mòta, at the base of Costaccia.

SCHOOLS AND GUIDES
Watch out for short classes
There are several schools. English is widely spoken, and recent reports are complimentary. A common complaint is that most of the classes are short (two-hours). Another is that beginners spend too long on the nursery slopes before progressing up the mountain. It also seems to be the case that the schools on the Costaccia-Carosello side avoid the Mottolino sector altogether.

FACILITIES FOR CHILDREN
Not bad for Italy
The schools run children's classes. The Livigno Inverno/Estate school's Alì-Babà nursery offers all-day care and the staff speak English.

GETTING THERE

Air Bergamo 200km/124 miles (5hr).

Rail Tirano (48km/ 30 miles), Zernez (Switzerland, 28km/ 17 miles); regular buses from station, weekends only.

ACTIVITIES

Indoor Saunas and fitness rooms (in hotels), swimming pool (hotel Spöl), badminton, basketball, billiards, climbing wall, bowls, bowling, cinema

Outdoor Cleared paths, ice rink, snow-shoeing, horse-riding, ice climbing, snowmobiling, ice driving, paragliding

WEBSITES

For links to resort sites, go to our own new site at www.wtss.co.uk

Phone numbers From abroad use the prefix +39 (and do **not** omit the initial '0' of the phone number).

TOURIST OFFICE

t 0342 996379
info@aptlivigno.it
www.aptlivigno.it

STAYING THERE

HOW TO GO
Lots of hotels, some apartments
Livigno has an enormous range of hotels and a number of apartments. There are some attractively priced catered chalets from UK operators.
Hotels Most of the hotels are small 2- and 3-star places, with a couple of 4-stars out of the centre.

(((3 **Intermonti** (0342 972100) Modern 4-star with all mod cons (including a pool); some way from the centre, on the Mottolino side of the valley.

(2 **Bivio** (0342 996137) The only hotel in central Livigno with a pool.

(2 **Steinbock** (0342 970520) Nice little place, far from major lifts but a short walk from some nursery slopes.

(2 **Loredana** (0342 996330) Modern chalet on the Mottolino side. 'Pleasant food, good rooms.'

(2 **Larice** (0342 996184) Stylish little 3-star B&B well placed for Costaccia lifts and slopes.

(2 **Montanina** (0342 996060) Good central 3-star.

(2 **Alpi** (0342 996408) In San Rocco, not far from Carosello gondola. 'Absolutely the best; exquisite food.'

(2 **Camana Veglia** (0342 996904) Charming old wooden chalet. Popular restaurant, well placed in Santa Maria.

(2 **Silvestri** (0342 996255) 2-star in the San Rocco area. 'Great staff, comfortable rooms, filling meals.'

Self-catering All the big tour operators that come here have apartment options. Most are cheap and cheerful.

EATING OUT
Improving, still value for money
Livigno has lots of traditional, unpretentious restaurants, many hotel-based. Hotel Concordia has some of the best cooking in town. The Baita and Astoria are recommended for 'good food and service'. Mario's wide-ranging menu includes seafood, fondue and steaks. Bait dal Ghet and the Bivio restaurant are popular with the locals, and the Rusticana does wholesome, cheap food. Pesce d'Oro is good for seafood and Italian cuisine. The Bellavista, Ambassador, Mirage, Grolla and the Garden are also recommended.

APRES-SKI
Lively, but disappoints some
It's not that there isn't action in Livigno, but simply that the scene is quieter than some people expect in a duty-free resort. Pas de la Casa it is not – to the relief of most reporters. Also, the best places are scattered about, so the village lacks evening buzz. At tea time many people return to their hotels for a quiet drink. But Tea del Vidal, at the bottom of Mottolino, gets lively, as does the Stalet bar at the base of the Carosello gondola. The Caffè della Posta umbrella bar, near the centre, is also popular. We hear Europe's highest brewery is in production at the Echo. Nightlife gets going only after 10pm. Galli's pub, in San Antonio, is 'a full-on party pub', popular with Brits. The Kuhstall under the Bivio hotel is an excellent cellar bar with live music, as is the Helvetia, over the road. The San Rocco end is quietest, but Daphne's ('good fun') and Marco's are popular. The stylish Art Cafe is also recommended. Kokodi and the Cielo are the main discos.

OFF THE SLOPES
Look lively, or go shopping
Livigno offers a small range of outdoor alternatives to skiing and boarding – horse-riding among them. Walks are uninspiring and there is no sports centre or public swimming pool. However, the duty-free shopping more than makes up for this. Trips to Bormio and St Moritz are popular.

Madonna di Campiglio

Extensive, easy slopes amid stunning scenery

- ➕ Pleasant town in a pretty valley with splendid views at altitude
- ➕ Fairly extensive network of slopes, best for beginners and intermediates
- ➖ Spread-out village and infrequent shuttle-bus service
- ➖ Quiet après-ski

Like Cortina, Madonna is a pleasant Dolomite town with an affluent, almost exclusively Italian, clientele – though the scenery isn't in quite the same league. Folgarida and Marilleva, to which Madonna's slopes are linked, are quite different – and are covered in our chapter on Trentino.

THE RESORT

Madonna is a long-established, traditional-style but now largely modern town, set in a prettily wooded valley beneath the impressive Brenta Dolomites, with slopes in three linked sectors. The centre is fairly compact: the cable-car to Cinque Laghi (to the west) and the gondola to Pradalago (to the north) bracket most of the central hotels, and are about a five-minute walk apart. Five minutes outside the centre is a gondola to Monte Spinale, leading to the Grostè sector, to the

east; there is another gondola to Grostè starting a short bus-ride outside the town, to the north. Beyond this lift station are the main nursery slopes at Campo Carlo Magno. The town spreads a long way south from the centre, past a frozen lake.

Madonna attracts an affluent Italian clientele; it has lots of smart shops. The village is busy all day, and promenading is an early evening ritual.

The free ski-bus runs to a timetable, but is not frequent. Some hotels run minibuses. There's underground parking by the Spinale lift.

RATINGS

The slopes

Fast lifts	★★★
Snow	★★★
Extent	★★★
Expert	★★
Intermediate	★★★★
Beginner	★★★★
Convenience	★★★
Queues	★★★★
Mountain restaurants	★★★

The rest

Scenery	★★★★
Resort charm	★★★
Off-slope	★★★

NEWS

For 2004/05 a six-pack replaced the two parallel chairs serving the top slopes at Passo Grostè.

Terrain-park improvements included a new 85m/280ft half-pipe on the slopes of Panciana, above Marilleva.

A shuttle-bus now operates on Sundays, between the resort and Milan or Verona airports – providing a convenient transfer for independent travellers.

WEBSITES

For links to resort sites, go to our own new site at www.wtss.co.uk

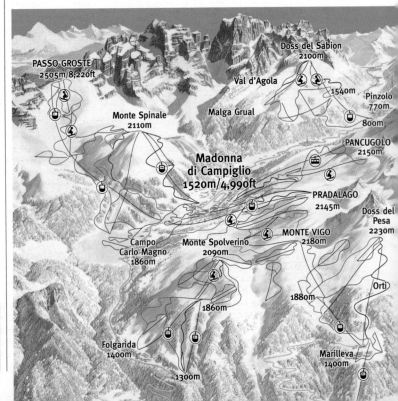

PASSO GROSTE
2505m/8,220ft

Monte Spinale
2110m

Malga Grual

Val d'Agola

Doss del Sabion
2100m

1540m

Pinzolo
770m

800m

PANCUGOLO
2150m

Madonna
di Campiglio
1520m/4,990ft

PRADALAGO
2145m

Doss del
Pesa
2230m

Campo
Carlo Magno
1860m

Monte Spolverino
2090m

MONTE VIGO
2180m

Orti

1880m

1860m

Folgarida
1400m

Marilleva
1400m

1300m

KEY FACTS

Resort	1520m
	4,990ft
Madonna, Folgarida, and Marilleva combined area	
Slopes	1520-2505m
	4,990-8,220ft
Lifts	45
Pistes	120km
	75 miles
Blue	35%
Red	50%
Black	15%
Snowmaking	77km

REPORTS WANTED

Recently we have had few reports on this resort. If you go there, please do send us a report.

The best reports earn a copy of the next edition, and can lead to free lift passes in future.

See page 10.

Phone numbers
From abroad use the prefix +39 (and do **not** omit the initial '0' of the phone number).

TOURIST OFFICE

t 0465 447501
info@campiglio.to
www.campiglio.to

THE MOUNTAINS

The Pradalago sector is linked by lift and piste to Monte Vigo, and so to the slopes of Folgarida and Marilleva.
Slopes The terrain is mainly intermediate, both above and below the tree line. Recent reporters were very impressed with the grooming. Some recommend skiing the Marilleva and Folgarida slopes in the afternoon to avoid crowds of ski school classes.
Terrain-parks The Ursus park, at Grostè, includes boarder-cross, half- and quarter-pipes and big air jumps. There's a new 85m/280ft half-pipe above Marilleva.
Snow reliability Although many of the runs are sunny, they are at a fair altitude, and there has been hefty investment in snowmaking. As a result, snow reliability is reasonable. Grooming is excellent.
Experts Experts should plan on heading off-piste. The trees under the Genziana chair are 'a good spot for untracked snow'. But the 3-Tre race course and the Spinale Direttissima are steep. Pista Nera, above Folgarida, can be a challenging mogul field. And a reporter enjoyed the Orti/ Marilleva black at Marilleva.
Intermediates Cinque Laghi, Madonna's racing mountain, is ideal: early or timid intermediates will love the area and have no difficulty exploring most of the network, though the connection to Folgarida is a bit trickier. Grostè and Pradalago have long, easy runs, though the former can get crowded.
Beginners The nursery slopes at Campo Carlo Magno are excellent, but do involve a bus-ride. Progression to longer runs is easy.
Snowboarding The resort is popular with boarders and some major events have been held here.
Cross-country There are 30km/19 miles of pretty trails through the woods.

Queues Two recent reporters did not find queuing a worry, but there are one or two bottlenecks. The Cinque Laghi 'Express' cable-car is tiny; it produces half-hour queues which can be avoided by using the two nearby chairs. The new six-pack at Grostè should help to relieve any queues there.
Mountain restaurants 'Small and crowded', was one 2005 reporter's comment. But the Malga Montagnoli in the lower part of Grostè is a 'charming old refuge' (self-service). Other recommendations include the Cinque Laghi ('stunning views'), the Boch and Cascina Zeledria (table-service).
Schools and guides One group 'got on well' with the Nazionale school recently – an improvement on the past.
Facilities for children Very limited.

STAYING THERE

How to go There is a wide choice of hotels and some self-catering.
Hotels The 4-star Spinale (0465 441116) is convenient. The Savoia Palace (0465 441004) is also 4-star but without a pool; 'comfortable and friendly', but the location can be noisy. The central Arnica (0465 442227) does only breakfast but does it very well and got a rave review last year – 'super', with 'very friendly owners'. The central 3-star Milano (0465 441210) is also recommended. At Campo Carlo Magno the Zeledria (0465 441010) is 'a good 4-star with friendly staff'. Recently refurbished.
Eating out There are around 20 restaurants. 'All the ones we tried were good,' says a reporter, and Belvedere, the Antico Focolare, the Roi and Stube Diana have all been recommended. Another reporter enjoyed the 'artistic dishes' at the pricey Alfiero, and Locanda degli Artisti is 'worth the expense for a special night out'. Some of the mountain huts are also open.
Après-ski Après-ski is quiet. At tea-time, the Maturi is said to have the 'best cakes and chocolates in town'. Franz-Joseph Stube, Bar Suisse and Cantina del Suisse are recommended. The Alpes is perhaps the smartest club. There's also a well-known disco – the Zangola – which reportedly gets going very late.
Off the slopes Window-shopping, skating on the lake and walking are popular. There's also paragliding. A reporter recommends taking the bus out to Campo Carlo Magno for lunch.

Monterosa Ski

Europe's best kept secret – an undiscovered gem

COSTS

①②③④⑤⑥

RATINGS

The slopes
Fast lifts	***
Snow	****
Extent	***
Expert	****
Intermediate	****
Beginner	**
Convenience	***
Queues	****
Mountain restaurants	**

The rest
Scenery	****
Resort charm	***
Off-slope	*

NEWS

For 2005/06 a new 8-seat gondola is planned above Champoluc to replace the two slow chairs up to Colle Sarezza. This should reduce queues and speed access to the upper slopes.

For 2004/05 Alagna was linked to Gressoney properly: a cable-car opened between Pianalunga and Passo dei Salati, with a red piste back down.

There are plans to build another lift from Passo dei Salati to Cresta Rosa at 3500m/11,480ft, replacing the tiny, ancient cable-car to Punta Indren; and for a new gondola to replace the Stafel/ St. Anna chair at Gressoney.

432

➕ Fabulous intermediate and advanced off-piste, including heli-skiing

➕ Slopes usually very quiet weekdays

➕ Panoramic views

➕ Good snow reliability and grooming

➕ Quiet, unspoiled villages

➕ Three-valley lift/piste network gives a sensation of travel, but ...

➖ Virtually no choice of route when touring the three valleys on-piste

➖ Few challenging pistes – mainly easy cruising

➖ High winds can close links

➖ Few off-slope diversions

➖ Limited après-ski

Monterosa Ski's three resorts – Champoluc, Gressoney and Alagna – are popular with Italians weekenders, who drive up from Milan and Turin, but are hardly heard of on the international market. As a result, they retain a friendly, small-scale, Italian ambience that we and a growing band of readers like a lot.

The three-valley network of lifts and pistes is anything but small-scale: Alagna and Champoluc, at opposite ends, are no less than 17km/11 miles apart – slightly further apart than Courchevel and Val-Thorens. A glance at the piste map reveals that the Italian network between the two extremes is skeletal compared to the full-bodied French one. But outside the piste network is a lot of great off-piste terrain, some lift-served, which has long attracted experts.

It was only last season that Alagna became accessible by piste from the top of the Gressoney lifts. Expert skiers may be inclined to regret the fact that a splendid off-piste run was sacrificed; but that's progress. They have plenty more bowls to play in – and the new Olen red piste is a cracker.

THE RESORT

There is one main village in each of the area's three long valleys. Champoluc in the western valley and Gressoney in the central one are both about an hour's drive up from the Aosta valley, to the south. Alagna is even more remote, and approached from the Italian lakes, to the east.

Champoluc is a pleasant but not notably pretty place, strung out along the valley road without much ski resort ambience – the centre, where there are a couple of good hotels, is more or less devoid of bars and inviting shops. The village gondola starts from a kind of micro-resort several minutes' walk up the road. You can store boots and skis/board there overnight. The valley road continues past several new hotels towards Frachey, where there is a chair-lift into the slopes.

Gressoney La Trinité is a quiet, neat little village, with cobbled streets, wooden buildings and an old church. It is about 800m/0.5 miles from the chair-lift into the local slopes, where there are a few convenient hotels. Links with

the other valleys revolve around Stafal at the head of the valley, reached by bus (5 euros for a pass). There is accommodation here, too. Gressoney St Jean, a bigger village, is 5km/3 miles down the valley and has its own separate slopes.

Alagna is a peaceful, rustic village with a solid church and some lovely old wooden farmhouses built in the distinctive Walser style. It bears no resemblance to a conventional ski resort. We visited on a sunny morning last March, and found the place deserted. The recently built gondola starts from an amazingly central station; it must be losing a fortune.

Trips to Cervinia, La Thuile and Courmayeur (covered by the Aosta Valley pass) are possible by car.

THE MOUNTAINS

The slopes of Monterosa Ski are relatively extensive, and very scenic. The pistes are almost all intermediate (and well groomed), and the lifts are mainly chairs and gondolas, with few drag-lifts. The terrain is undulating and

runs are long, but many lifts serve only one or two pistes.

The piste map is appalling – the worst in the northern hemisphere, and possibly the world. But the signposting on the pistes is clear. Reporters visiting at various times have found the top lifts making the connection between valleys closed by wind, severely limiting the available terrain.

Slopes If all goes according to plan, Champoluc residents will now be whisked 1150m/3,770ft up the mountain by two successive gondolas. From the top a steep, narrow, bumpy run (which a lot of timid intermediates find very difficult) is the link with the long cruising runs below Colle Bettaforca. Taking the bus to the Frachey chair avoids the tricky top run and has traditionally been the quicker

way to Colle Bettaforca, but the new gondola may change that.

At Stafal a cable-car followed by a fast chair bring you back towards Champoluc and two successive gondolas opposite take you to Passo dei Salati. From there runs lead back down to Stafal and to Gressoney La Trinité and Orsia, both served by chair-lifts. Or you can head towards Alagna on the new pistes there.

From Alagna a modern gondola goes to Pianalunga at mid-mountain. From here, a cable-car (able to pause at a mid-station where a new blue run theoretically ends) now takes you to Passo dei Salati. The alternative from Pianalunga is a double chair leading to the tiny, ancient cable-car to Punta Indren (due for replacement soon; see News). This serves a long ungroomed

KEY FACTS

Resort	1640m
	5,380ft
Slopes	1200-3260m
	3,940-10,700ft
Lifts	36
Pistes	180km
	112 miles
Blue	22%
Red	67%
Black	11%
Snowmaking	70km
	43 miles

black run ending in the middle of nowhere; an antique 'bucket' lift goes back up to the bottom of the cable-car. There are also lots of off-piste routes from Punta Indren, including routes to the Gressoney valley.

Gressoney St Jean and Antagnod, near Champoluc, have their own small areas of slopes. The St Jean slopes have only one lift but two recent reporters enjoyed half-days there. Antagnod is used by local instructors on bad-weather days and has some good off-piste terrain.

Terrain-parks No park, but big air jumps are sometimes constructed near the top of the Champoluc gondola.

Snow reliability Generally good, thanks to altitude, extensive snowmaking and good grooming.

Experts The attraction is the off-piste, with great runs from the high points of the lift system in all three valleys and some excellent heli-drops. Among the adventures we're enjoyed here was a heli-drop on Monte Rosa, skiing down to Zermatt and returning off-piste from the top of the Cervinia lifts.

Intermediates For those who like to travel on easy, undemanding pistes, the area is great, with long cruising runs from the ridges down into the valleys ('wonderful, care-free carving'). The new red Olen piste down towards Alagna is a great blast. There isn't much on-piste challenge for more demanding intermediates, but those willing to take a guide and explore some of the gentler off-piste will have a great time.

Beginners The high nursery slopes at mid-mountain above Champoluc, served by two moving carpets, are better than the lower ones at Gressoney. But neither area has ideal gentle runs to progress to.

Snowboarding There is great off-piste free-riding.

Cross-country There are long trails around St Jean, and shorter ones up the valley; Brusson, in the Champoluc valley, has the best trails in the area.

Queues Few problems, say reporters. Usually they occur only at weekends. The worst bottleneck is the tiny top cable-car on the Alagna side, where waits of over an hour are possible and where queues can form even in mid-week. The double chair to Belvedere, on the way back from Frachey/Bettaforca to Champoluc, can have long queues at the end of the day. The

new gondola planned above Champoluc should relieve any queues to reach Col Sarezza. Pistes can get crowded at weekends, too, but the off-piste is still delightfully quiet.

Mountain restaurants The mountain restaurants are generally simple, but there are plenty of them. The following have been enjoyed by reporters: the 'lively' Belvedere (one of the few mountain restaurants in the region to have a sit-down loo); the Ostafa ('excellent pasta') and the Tana del Loup above Champoluc; the Mandria and the 'small but charming' Chamois at Punta Jolanda; the Bedemie above Orsia; the Del Ponte above Gabiet; the Baita just below Pianalunga; and the Sitten above Stafel ('excellent specials and stunning view'). Stadl Soussun above Frachey is a bit out of the ordinary – 'charming, with an excellent limited menu; booking essential'. A diversion to the right at the top of the run to Alagna brings you to the Rifugio Guglielmina – see the picture on the previous page. There's a welcoming new restaurant, Morgenrot, at Bedemie above Orsia, with table service.

Schools and guides We have had mixed reports on the Italian ski schools but universally good reports about the Monterosa mountain guides ('Really excellent day,' said a recent reporter) and the ski school run by tour operator Ski 2 ('good, friendly instructors').

Facilities for children There is a special kids' ski school and snow-park at Antagnod near Champoluc and a mini-club at Gressoney St Jean.

STAYING THERE

How to go More tour operators are discovering the area. We've had good reports of Monterosa specialists Ski 2 ('great from pick-up to drop-off').

Hotels For a small place, Champoluc has a striking range of attractive hotels. A 2005 reporter liked the central Relais des Glaciers (0125 308721) – a welcoming 4-star with spa and shuttle to the gondola. The central, creaky old Castor (0125 307117) is 'an absolute gem' with 'good food and magnificent puddings'; it is managed by a British guy who married into the family that has owned it for generations. The Breithorn (0125 08734), just up the road, is the luxury option, with beautifully furnished public areas, beamed bedrooms and good spa facilities. 'It's a gem,' says

one well-travelled reporter – 'superb service'. Food in the elegant dining room or more casual brasserie is excellent. Out beyond the lift base are several interesting places. The California (0125 307977) is chiefly notable for the pop music themes applied to the rooms, and the big saloon bar. The new Rocher (0125 308711) is recommended by reporters as friendly and welcoming, with good food, spa and sauna facilities.

At Gressoney La Trinité several reporters recommend the recently extended Jolanda Sport (0125 366140), with gym, saunas, new pool; it's right by the lift. But one 2005 visitor was disappointed by the food – limited choice, especially for vegetarians. Another says of the nearby Residence (0125 366148), 'Friendliest hotel I've ever stayed at in the Alps.' The Dufour (0125 366139) and the 'extremely pleasant' Lysjoch (0125 366150) have also been mentioned. In Alagna, try the Monterosa (0163 923209) or Cristallo (0163 91285).

Eating out Both Gressoney and Champoluc have a few stand-alone restaurants; most are in hotels. The Walserchild in Gressoney got a good review from a recent reporter.

Après-ski Après-ski is quiet. In Champoluc, the bar of the hotel Castor is cosy and popular with resort workers; the Golosone is a small atmospheric, authentic Italian wine bar; the Galion opposite the gondola is busy as the lifts close; the Saloon del Branco in the hotel California has karaoke some nights. At weekends, the disco beneath the California gets going. Gressoney is even quieter; 'Schnee Blume bar is the best, but it has nothing to beat,' says a reporter, 'and the tour-op organised wine tasting at Hirschstube was excellent.'

Off the slopes There is little to amuse those who don't head for the slopes.

SNOWPIX.COM / CHRIS GILL

↙ Eagle's Gully, one of the standard off-piste routes from Punta Indren to Gabiet – a run of almost 1000m/3,280ft vertical. It must be fabulous in powder.

WEBSITES

For links to resort sites, go to our own new site at www.wtss.co.uk

Phone numbers
From abroad use the prefix +39 (and do **not** omit the initial '0' of the phone number).

TOURIST OFFICE

t 0125 303111
kikesly@monterosa-ski.com
www.monterosa-ski.com

Sauze d'Oulx

'Suzy does it' still, but with more dignity than in the past

COSTS

① ② ③ ④ ⑤ ⑥

RATINGS

The slopes

Fast lifts	**
Snow	**
Extent	****
Expert	**
Intermediate	****
Beginner	**
Convenience	**
Queues	***
Mountain restaurants	***

The rest

Scenery	***
Resort charm	**
Off-slope	*

NEWS

Turin is hosting the 2006 Winter Olympic Games between 10 and 26 February: freestyle events will be at Sauze d'Oulx, the women's downhill, super-g and combined events at Sansicario.

For 2005/06 a fast quad is expected to replace the extremely antiquated chair between the village and Clotes – a much needed improvement.

For 2004/05 a two-stage gondola opened between the valley (near Cesana) and Sansicario.

Also last season, two drag-lifts replaced the old one at Monte Fraiteve; they link the slopes of Sansicario with those of Sauze and Sestriere.

Snowmaking was increased throughout the region.

+ Extensive and uncrowded slopes, great intermediate cruising

+ Linked into Milky Way network

+ Mix of open and tree-lined runs is good for all weather conditions

+ Entertaining nightlife

+ Some scope for off-piste adventures

+ One of the cheapest major resorts there is – and more attractive than its reputation suggests

− Still lots of ancient lifts, making progress around the slopes slow

− Erratic snow record – and far from comprehensive snowmaking

− Crowds at weekends

− Getting to the French end of the Milky Way takes forever

− Very few challenging pistes – and hardly a mogul to be seen

− Mornings-only classes, and the best nursery slopes are at mid-mountain

− Steep walks around the village, and an inadequate shuttle-bus service

In the 1980s Sauze became known as prime lager-lout territory. But it always was a resort of two halves – young Brits on a budget alongside mature second-home owners from Turin – and these days the two halves seem to be much more in balance, at weekends at least. It still has lively bars and shops festooned in English signs, but sober Brits like you and us need not stay away. When we visit, we always find ourselves liking it more than we expect to – as do many reporters.

We are slightly haunted, though, by the memory of the bare slopes of our first visit, in the mid-1980s – and cover has been thin in some recent seasons too. Good use is made of the snowmaking system, but it needs expanding.

THE RESORT

Sauze d'Oulx sits on a sloping mountain shelf facing north-west across the Valle di Susa to the impressive mountains forming the border with France. Most of the resort is modern and undistinguished, made up of block-like hotels relieved by the occasional chalet, spreading down the steep hillside from the slopes. Despite the decline in lager sales, the centre is still lively at night; the late bars are usually quite full, and the handful of discos do brisk business – at the weekend, at least. Noise can be a problem in the early hours.

Sauze also has an attractive old core, with narrow, twisting streets and houses roofed with huge stone slabs. There is a central car-free zone, but traffic roams freely through most of the village, which can be congested morning and evening. The roads have few pavements and can become icy and treacherous at night.

Out of the bustle of the centre, there are quiet, wooded residential areas full of secluded apartment blocks, and a number of good restaurants are also tucked away from the front line.

Most of the hotels are reasonably central, but the lifts are less so: the Clotes chair is at the top of the village, up a short but steep hill, and the Sportinia chair is an irritatingly long walk beyond that. Ski-buses (not covered by the lift pass) are infrequent and can't cope with high-season crowds. The service around lunch-time is particularly poor. Getting to other resorts involves public buses with multiple changes in some cases. A car simplifies excursions, eg to Montgenèvre and other French resorts.

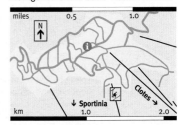

The upper slopes have a pleasant scattering of trees, and grand views towards France →

KEY FACTS

Resort	1510m
	4,950ft

For Milky Way

Slopes	1390-2825m
	4,560-9,270ft
Lifts	91
Pistes	400km
	249 miles
Blue	25%
Red	55%
Black	20%
Snowmaking	100km
	62 miles

For Sauze d'Oulx-Sestriere-Sansicario only

Slopes	1390-2825m
	4,560-9,270ft
Lifts	51
Pistes	300km
	186 miles
Snowmaking	90km
	56 miles

LIFT PASSES

La Via Lattea
Covers all lifts in Sauze d'Oulx, Sestriere, Sansicario, Cesana and Claviere.

Beginners
No special pass

Main pass
1 day €31
6 days €163

Children
Under 12: 6-day pass €81.50
Under 10: free pass

Notes
4-hour pass available; also one-day extension for Montgenèvre.

THE MOUNTAINS

Sauze's mountains provide excellent intermediate terrain. The piste grading fluctuates from year to year – we're never sure we've caught up with the latest changes from blue to red and red to blue. But most reporters agree that many runs graded red or even black should really be graded blue; challenges are few and far between.

THE SLOPES
Big and varied enough for most
Sauze's local slopes are spread across a broad wooded bowl above the resort, ranging from west- to north-facing. The main lifts are chairs, from the top of the village up to **Clotes** and from the western fringes to **Sportinia** – a sunny mid-mountain clearing in the woods, with a ring of restaurants and hotels (see 'Staying up the mountain') and a small nursery area.

The high point of the system is **Monte Fraiteve**. From here you can travel west on splendid broad, long runs to **Sansicario** – and on to a two-stage gondola near **Cesana Torinese** that links with **Claviere** and then **Montgenèvre**, in France, the far end of the Milky Way (both are reached more quickly by car).

You normally get to **Sestriere** from the lower point of Col Basset, on the shoulder of M Fraiteve – but snow cover is unreliable and in our experience you normally have to use the gondola to descend the bottom half of the mountain. In bad weather, on the other hand, the gondola may be closed by strong winds (twice in one 2005 reporter's week). The alternative of descending the slope from M Fraiteve itself has been reinstated, at least in theory; but snow again is not reliable, and our attempts to check out this slope were frustrated by closure of the piste.

As in so many Italian resorts, piste marking, direction signing and piste map design are not taken seriously and receive regular complaints from our reporters ('a joke', writes one).

TERRAIN-PARKS
Jump and grind
The Double Black terrain-park opened a couple of seasons ago in the Rio Nero bowl, just below Col Basset. There's no half-pipe, but a selection of jumps, spines and rails provide a choice for freestylers. Its location on the mountain means that it is probably easier to reach from Sestriere, via the gondola, than it is from Sauze. There is another park in Sestriere.

SNOW RELIABILITY
Can be poor, affecting the links
The area is notorious for erratic snowfalls, occasionally suffering acute droughts. Another problem is that many of the slopes get a lot of afternoon sun. At these modest altitudes, late-season conditions are far from reliable. Reporters have found icy, bare slopes at vital link points earlier in the season, too – particularly from M Fraiteve. There's snowmaking on the central section of slopes, above and below Clotes. Reporters are impressed by the efforts to keep runs open, despite poor conditions ('they worked miracles').

FOR EXPERTS
Head off-piste
Very few of the pistes are challenging. The best slopes are at virtually opposite ends of Sauze's local area – a short, high, north-facing run from the

boarding

Sauze has good snowboarding slopes – it's got local tree-lined slopes (with space in the trees, too), high, undulating, open terrain, and links to other resorts in the Milky Way. But although it has a fair number of chair-lifts, there are also lots of drags – a serious drawback for novice riders. There's a terrain-park just off the Col Basset chair, at Rio Nero (see 'Terrain-parks').

shoulder of M Fraiteve, and the sunny slopes below M Moncrons.

The main interest is in going off-piste. There are plenty of minor opportunities within the piste network, but the highlights are long, top-to-bottom descents of up to 1300m/ 4,270ft vertical from M Fraiteve, ending (snow permitting) at villages dotted along the valleys. The best known of these runs (which used to be marked on the piste map but is no longer – presumably to encourage the use of guides) is the Rio Nero, down to the road near Oulx. When snow low down is poor, some of these runs can be cut short at Jouvenceaux or Sansicario.

FOR INTERMEDIATES
Splendid cruising terrain
The whole area is ideal for confident intermediates who want to clock up the kilometres. For the less confident, the piste map doesn't help because it picks out only the very easiest runs in blue – there are many others that are

manageable. The Belvedere and Moncrons sectors at the east of the area are served only by drags but offer some wonderful, uncrowded high cruising, some of it above the tree line.

The long runs down to Jouvenceaux are splendid, confidence-boosting intermediate terrain.

The slopes above Sansicario are also excellent – served by two fast quad chair-lifts, installed for the benefit of Olympic racers – but the link via the steep shoulder of M Fraiteve is problematic for those lacking confidence. You have to tackle a seriously steep double drag-lift on the way out, and a short but genuine black run – the steepest pitch in the whole area – on the way back. This is a serious shortcoming in the circuit, which ought to have been dealt with years ago by installation of a chair-lift.

At the higher levels, where the slopes are above the tree line, the terrain often allows a choice of route. Lower down are pretty runs through

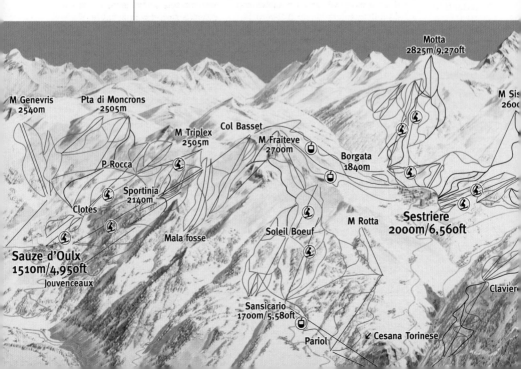

the woods, where the main complication can be route-finding. The mountainside is broken up by gullies, and pistes that appear to be quite close together but may in fact have no easy connections between them.

FOR BEGINNERS
There are better choices
Sauze is not ideal for beginners: its village-level slopes are a bit on the steep side and the main nursery area is up the mountain, at Sportinia. Equally importantly, the mornings-only classes don't suit everyone. Once off the nursery slopes, the main problem is a psychological one – that most of the mountain is classified red, though the gradient is generally blue.

FOR CROSS-COUNTRY
Severely limited, even with snow
There is very little cross-country skiing, and it isn't reliable for snow.

QUEUES
Slow lifts the biggest problem
There can be irritating waits at Sportinia, especially when school classes set off, or just after lunch; otherwise the system has fewer, though still some noticeable, bottlenecks. Despite the introduction of fast quads over recent years, most of the lifts are ancient and terribly slow. But the antiquated chair-lift from the village to Clotes is due to be replaced by a fast quad for 2005/06 – so you will no longer have to carry your skis on your lap. Breakdowns of elderly lifts may be a nuisance. And a February visitor reports that several lifts were opened only at weekends, when the Italian crowds arrive.

MOUNTAIN RESTAURANTS
Some pleasant possibilities
Restaurants are numerous and generally pleasant, though few are particularly special. If you like a civilised table-service lunch head for the hotel Capricorno, at Clotes. It is not cheap, and midweek in low season it can be amazingly quiet. Reporters recommend the Ciao Pais, further up the hill, 'a superb rustic restaurant, ideal when the weather closes in', writes one, but 'a bit pricey', according to another. The Clot Bourget has also pleased visitors. There are several places at Sportinia; Capanna Kind does 'an awesome all-day breakfast' and the Rocce Nere is highly rated this year

('good food, excellent service'). The Marmotta on M Triplex is one reader's tip for 'drinks and service with a smile'. The Soleil Boeuf above Sansicario is 'good value, with a nice sun terrace'.

SCHOOLS AND GUIDES
Lessons variable
A recent reporter found his daughter enthusiastic about her lesson (in a group of eight, in low season), and another writes of 'patient instructors with good English spoken', though past reports have been mixed.

FACILITIES FOR CHILDREN
Tour operator alternatives
The village kindergarten, La Cinciarella, can be booked for evenings so long as there are at least three children using the facility. You might also want to look at the nursery facilities offered by major UK tour operators in the chalets and chalet-hotels that they run here – Crystal and Neilson, for example.

STAYING THERE

HOW TO GO
Packaged hotels dominate
All the major mainstream operators offer hotel packages here, but there are also a few chalets.
Hotels Simple 2-star and 3-star hotels form the core of the holiday accommodation, with a couple of 4-stars and some more basic places.
((((4) **Torre** (0122 858301) Cylindrical 4-star landmark 200m/650ft below the centre. Excellent rooms, 'good food', 'plenty of choice'; mini-buses to lifts.
(2) **Hermitage** (0122 850385) Neat chalet-style hotel beside the home piste from Clotes.
(2) **Gran Baita** (0122 850183) Comfortable place in quiet, central backstreet, with excellent food and good rooms, some with sunset views.
(2) **Biancaneve** (0122 850160) Pleasant, with smallish rooms. Near the centre.
(2) **Des Amis** (0122 858488) Down in Jouvenceaux, but near bus stop; simple hotel run by Anglo-Italian couple.
(2) **Stella Alpina** (0122 858731) Between Clotes and Sportinia lifts. Friendly Anglo-Italian family doing 'excellent food'.
(2) **Vila Cary** (0122 850191) Recommended by a 2005 reporter as 'cosy and welcoming' with good food.
Self-catering Apartments and chalets available, some through UK operators.

EATING OUT
Caters for all tastes and pockets

Typical Italian banquets of five or six courses can be had in the upmarket Godfather and Cantun restaurants. The Falco does a particularly good three-course 'skiers' menu'. In the old town, the Borgo and the Griglia are popular pizzerias. The Lampione is the place to go for 'pub grub' – good-value Chinese, Mexican and Indian food. Sugo's spaghetteria provides delicious, filling and economic fare. The Pecore Nere also gets good reviews.

APRES-SKI
Suzy does it with more dignity

Once favoured almost solely by large groups of youngsters, some of whom were very rowdy, Sauze's bars now impress reporters young and old.

The Assietta terrace is popular for catching the last rays of the sun at the end of the day. The New Scotch bar in the hotel Stella Alpina serves English beer and is also popular ('high standard of service'), as is the Lampione, in the old town.

After dinner, more places warm up. One of the best is the smart, atmospheric cocktail bar Moncrons,

which holds regular quiz nights. Reporters also like the Village Café (first beer free with freely available vouchers); you can eat here too ('excellent pizzas'). The Cotton Club provides good service, directors' chairs, video screen and draught cider; and Max's shows football. Miravallino is a 'very Italian' cafe bar. Paddy McGinty's offers 'a good variety of meals including Mexican and steaks'. The 'very cosy' Derby is nice for a quiet drink and a 'civilised chill-out'. The Grotta offers free sandwiches with your drinks. Of the discos, the Bandito is a walk away, and popular with Italians. Schuss runs theme nights and drink promotions – entrance is normally free.

Tour operators' resort reps organise the usual range of activities.

OFF THE SLOPES
Go elsewhere

Sauze is not a particularly rewarding place in which to while away the days if you don't want to hit the slopes. Shopping is limited, there are no gondolas or cable-cars for pedestrians and there are few off-slope activities. Turin or Briançon are worth a visit.

STAYING UP THE MOUNTAIN
'You pays your money ... '

In most resorts, staying up the mountain is an amusing thing to do and is often economical – but usually you pay the price of accepting simple accommodation. Here, the reverse applies. The 4-star Capricorno (0122 850273), up at Clotes, is one of the most comfortable hotels in Sauze, certainly the most attractive and by a wide margin the most expensive. It's a charming little chalet beside the piste, with only eight bedrooms.

Not quite in the same league are the places up at Sportinia – though reporters who stayed here enjoyed the isolation and ski convenience.

Sansicario 1700m/5,580ft

If any resort is ideally placed for exploration of the whole Milky Way, it is Sansicario. It is a modern, purpose-built, self-contained but rather soulless little resort, mainly consisting of apartments around the small shopping precinct. The 45-room Rio Envers (0122 811333) is a comfortable, expensive hotel. Visitors recommend the Enoteca in the evening for fondue and grappa.

Selva/Sella Ronda

Endless intermediate slopes amid spectacular Dolomite scenery

COSTS

① ② ③ ④ ⑤ ⑥

RATINGS

The slopes
Fast lifts	✱✱✱
Snow	✱✱✱✱
Extent	✱✱✱✱✱
Expert	✱✱✱
Intermediate	✱✱✱✱✱
Beginner	✱✱✱✱
Convenience	✱✱✱
Queues	✱✱✱
Mountain restaurants	✱✱✱✱

The rest
Scenery	✱✱✱✱✱
Resort charm	✱✱✱
Off-slope	✱✱✱

KEY FACTS

Resort	1565m
	5,130ft

The linked lift network of Val Gardena, Alta Badia, Arabba, and the Canazei and Campitello slopes of Val di Fassa

Slopes	1235-2520m
	4,050-8,270ft
Lifts	186
Pistes	395km
	245 miles
Blue	38%
Red	53%
Black	9%
Snowmaking	276km
	172 miles

Val Gardena-Alpe di Siusi only
Slopes	1005-2520m
	3,300-8,270ft
Lifts	82
Pistes	175km
	109 miles
Blue	30%
Red	60%
Black	10%
Snowmaking	90km
	56 miles

➕ Vast network of connected slopes – suits intermediates particularly well
➕ Stunning, unique Dolomite scenery
➕ Superb snowmaking and grooming
➕ Jolly mountain huts with good food
➕ Lift system now pretty efficient
➕ Mix of open and wooded slopes
➕ Excellent value

➖ Very few tough runs
➖ Crowds on Sella Ronda circuit
➖ Most runs are rather short
➖ Selva is not the ideal base in the area for novices
➖ Bus services are far from ideal
➖ Erratic snow record; slopes vulnerable to warm weather

This is an area unlike any other. The Sella Ronda is an amazing circular network of lifts and pistes taking you around the spectacular Gruppo Sella – a mighty limestone massif with villages scattered around it, the biggest of them being Selva (aka Wolkenstein) in Val Gardena (aka Gröden). As well as this impressive main circuit, there are major lift systems leading off it at four main points. In overall scale, the network rivals the famed Trois Vallées in France.

The Dolomite scenery is fabulous. But the geology that provides the visual drama also dictates the nature of the slopes. Sheer limestone cliffs rise out of gentle pasture-land; you spend your time on the latter, gazing at the former. There is scarcely a black run to be seen, and runs of more than 500m/1,640ft vertical are rare, whereas runs of under 300m/980ft vertical are not.

Don't overlook the several alternatives to Selva as a base. Experts and confident intermediates should consider Arabba, where classic Dolomite terrain gives way to longer, steeper slopes. For less confident intermediates the obvious choice is Corvara, where the gentlest part of the Sella Ronda meets the Alta Badia.

THE RESORT

Selva is a long roadside village at the head of the Val Gardena, almost merging with the next village of Santa Cristina. It suffers from traffic but has traditional-style architecture and an attractive church. The valley is famed for wood carvings, which are on display (and sale) wherever you look.

The village enjoys a lovely setting under the impressive pink-tinged walls of Sassolungo and the Gruppo Sella – a fortress-like massif about 6km/4 miles across that lies at the hub of

the Sella Ronda circuit (see the feature box later in the chapter). Despite the World Cup fame of Val Gardena and animated atmosphere, Selva is neither upmarket nor brash. It's a good-value, civilised family resort – and the biggest and liveliest of the places to stay right on the Sella Ronda circuit.

For many years the area was part of Austria, and reporters admire the Tirolean charm of the resort. German is the main language, not Italian, and most visitors are German, too. Most places have two names: Selva is also known as Wolkenstein and the

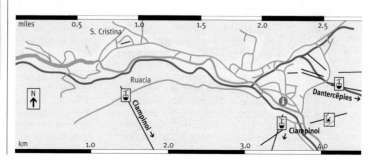

Gardena valley as Gröden. We do our bit to help with Italian unity by using the Italian place names. The local dialect, Ladin, also survives.

Ortisei is the administrative centre of Val Gardena but it is not so convenient for the Sella Ronda slopes. For a brief description of this and the other villages on or near the circuit, see the end of this chapter.

From Selva, gondolas rise in two directions. The Dantercëpies gondola, starting outside the main village at the top of the nursery slopes (but easily accessed via a central chair-lift and short run down), goes east towards Colfosco and Corvara, forming the start of the clockwise Sella Ronda route. The Ciampinoi gondola goes south from near the centre of the village to start the anti-clockwise route. The most convenient position is near one of these gondolas. There are regular buses until early evening – three euros for a weekly card – but they generate complaints from reporters about infrequency, inadequate capacity (especially at the end of the day), poorly sited stops and lack of services to Corvara and Plan de Gralba. Last season a nightbus was introduced between Selva and Ortisei. Many reporters use taxis, although they are expensive unless you share. Some hotels run their own free transport.

The Dolomiti Superski pass covers not only the Sella Ronda resorts but dozens of others. It's an easy road trip to Cortina – worth it for the fabulous scenery alone. But many other drives in this area are very tortuous and slow – it's often quicker on skis.

THE MOUNTAIN

The slopes cover a vast area, all amid stunning scenery and practically all ideally suited to intermediates. 'The fact that you never had to ski the same piste twice throughout the week is enough to draw me back for several years to come,' said one recent reporter. There are different piste maps for different areas; you need to collect each one as you pass through if you want to explore that area. Some reporters complain that they are inadequate and confusing. Piste marking and signing also come in for criticism, though the Sella Ronda route itself is well signposted. Most of the lifts stay open until around 5pm in high season.

THE SLOPES
High mileage piste excursions

The **Ciampinoi** gondola accesses several pistes, including the famous World Cup Downhill run, leading back down to Selva, **Santa Cristina** and **Plan de Gralba** – and leads to the anti-clockwise Sella Ronda circuit via **Passo Sella** and **Canazei**.

The Dantercëpies gondola serves the Ladies' Downhill course and accesses the clockwise Sella Ronda circuit. From the top you head down to **Colfosco**, then lifts link with **Corvara**.

At the far corner of the circuit, opposite Selva, is **Arabba**.

At Passo Pordoi, between Canazei and Arabba, is the one breach in the defences of the Gruppo Sella: a cable-car goes up to Sass Pordoi at 2950m/9,680ft, giving access to off-piste routes – and spectacular views.

There are several linked areas that are not directly on the Sella Ronda circuit that are worth exploring. The biggest is the **Alta Badia** area to the east of Corvara – a lovely area of gentle slopes from which you can go down to **La Villa** or to **San Cassiano** and Armentarola on the road to Cortina. You can go by taxi from here to Passo Falzarego to ride the Lagazuoi cable-car and do the lovely (and easy) 'hidden valley' run back to Armentarola.

Not far from Selva is the **Col Raiser/Seceda** area, accessed by a gondola on the outskirts of Santa Cristina. This is now accessible by descending from Ciampinoi to ride the underground funicular across the valley. Runs descend to Santa Cristina or to **Ortisei**. And from Ortisei a cable-car goes up the other side of the valley to **Alpe di Siusi** – a gentle elevated area of quiet, easy runs, cross-country tracks and walks. This area can also be accessed via the big gondola from the village of **Siusi**, to the west.

The **Marmolada** glacier beyond Arabba is open most of the winter and is included on the main lift pass. It's a trip to do more for its spectacular views than for skiing, though the red run from top to bottom is a notable 1490m/4,900ft vertical. The first two stages of the inadequate antique cable-car were replaced for 2004/05, which reporters found made a dramatic difference to queues. Hopefully the final top stage will be replaced for 2005/06. Alternatively, 'spectacular' early morning helicopter rides are available to the top.

TERRAIN-PARKS
A few widely spread options

Near Selva, there are boarder-cross
runs at Passo Sella by the Grohmann-
Cavazes chair and at Piz Sella by the
Comici chair, and there's a natural half-
pipe near the Sotsaslong lift at Piz
Sella. At Alpe di Siusi, there's a half-
pipe by the Laurin chair and a kids'
terrain-park by the Euro chair. Alta
Badia has a terrain-park near the
Brancia restaurant and the Dolomites
Fun Park at Piz la Villa. There's a half-
pipe, boarder-cross and new kids' park
at Belvedere above Canazei. Timed
slalom runs are located in several
areas – free to try.

SNOW RELIABILITY
Excellent when it's cold

The slopes are not high – there are few
above 2200m/7,220ft and most are
between 1500m and 2000m (5,000ft
and 6,500ft). And natural snowfalls are
erratic. But the area has one of the
largest snowmaking systems in Europe,
and we have enjoyed excellent pistes

here in times of severe natural snow
shortage. Most areas have snow-guns
on the main runs to the resorts. World-
class piste grooming adds to the
effect. Typical reporter comments on
the snowmaking are 'a revelation –
quite superb', 'wonderful' and
'stunning'. A 2005 reporter arrived 'in a
heatwave but still skied fantastic pistes
owing to the unbelievable coverage
and the quality of the snowmaking.'

Problems arise only in poor snow
years if it is too warm to make snow.

FOR EXPERTS
A few good runs

In general, experts may find the region
too tame, especially if they're looking for
lots of steep challenges or moguls.

Arabba has the best steep slopes
(and snow). North-facing blacks and
reds from Porta Vescovo back to
Arabba are served by an efficient high-
capacity gondola and are great fun.
The black run down to La Villa is worth
a visit, too – 'long, consistently steep,
but crowded', writes a reporter.

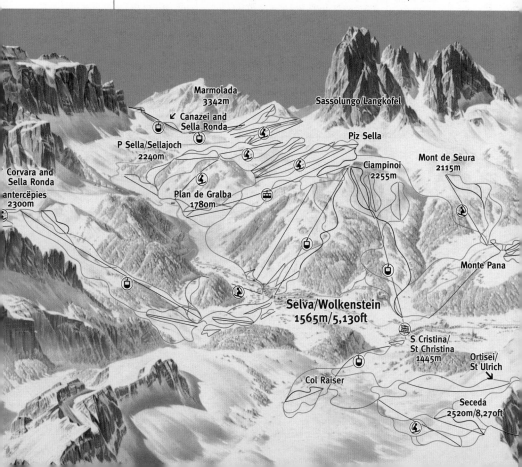

Marmolada
3342m

← Canazei and
Sella Ronda

Sassolungo/Langkofel

P Sella/Sellajoch
2240m

Piz Sella

Corvara and
Sella Ronda
antercëpies
2300m

Ciampinoi
2255m

Mont de Seura
2115m

Plan de Gralba
1780m

Monte Pana

Selva/Wolkenstein
1565m/5,130ft

S Cristina/
St Christina
1445m

Ortisei/
St Ulrich
→

Col Raiser

Seceda
2520m/8,270ft

Another enjoyed the short black at Colfosco. The Val Gardena World Cup piste, the Saslong, is one of several steepish runs between Ciampinoi and both Selva and Santa Cristina. Unlike many World Cup pistes it is kept in racing condition for Italian team practices, but it is open to the public much of the time. It's especially good in January, when it's not too crowded. The unpisted trail down to Santa Cristina, accessed from the Florian chair on Alpe di Siusi, is not difficult, but is pleasantly lonely.

Off-piste is limited because of the sheer-drop nature of the mountain tops in the Dolomites, but for the daring – and with a guide – there is excitement to be found. The itinerary from Sass Pordoi back to the cable-car station is not too difficult; the much longer route to Colfosco ends in a spectacular narrow descent through the Val de Mesdi.

FOR INTERMEDIATES
A *huge network of ideal runs*
The Sella Ronda region is famed for easy slopes. For early or timid intermediates, the runs from Dantercëpies to Colfosco and Corvara, and over the valley from there in the Alta Badia, are superb for cruising and confidence-boosting. Alta Badia is easy to reach from Selva, but returning from Dantercëpies may be a little daunting. Riding the gondola down is an option.

THE SELLA RONDA

The Sella Ronda is one of the world's classic intermediate circuits. The journey around the Sella massif is easily managed in a day by even an early intermediate. The slopes you descend are almost all easy, and take you through Selva, Colfosco, Corvara, Arabba and Canazei. You can do the circuit in either direction by following very clear coloured signs. The clockwise route is slightly quicker and offers more interesting slopes; but at Porta Vescovo above Arabba timid intermediates should be sure to find the red run and not struggle down the black. Reporters have found the anti-clockwise route tends to be less crowded though. There are two free maps available; map-literate people will want the proper topographical one with contour lines, from the tourist office (not lift stations).

The runs total around 23km/14 miles and the lifts around 14km/9 miles. The lifts take a total of about two hours (plus any queuing). We've done it in just three and a half hours plus some diversions and hut stops; five or six hours is a realistic time during busy periods, when there are crowds both on the pistes and on the lifts. If possible, choose low season or a Saturday, and set out early.

Not everyone likes it. 'It's a bit of a slog,' said one reporter. Others have found the circuit 'boring', and 'too busy and crowded'. 'Queuing was appalling – spent more time queuing than skiing,' says a 2005 reporter. Boarders beware: there are quite a few flat bits.

If you set out early, you can make more of the day by taking some diversions from the circuit. Among the most entertaining segments are the long runs down from Ciampinoi to Santa Cristina and Selva, from Dantercëpies to Selva, from the top of the Boe gondola back down to Corvara and from the top of the Arabba gondola. Take in all those in a day doing the circuit and you'll have had a good day.

Intermediates could take time out to explore the off-the-circuit Alta Badia area from Corvara. Groups of different abilities can do the circuit and arrange to meet along the way at some of the many welcoming rifugios.

The region is not especially boarder-friendly because of some frustratingly flat sections where you have to scoot or walk (reporters recommend the anti-clockwise Sella Ronda route as best) and the lack of off-piste opportunities. Some snowboarders in a reporter's group last season exchanged their boards for skis after two days. But the main lifts out of Selva are all gondolas or chairs.

Nearer to Selva, the runs in the Plan de Gralba area are gentle – but the red run to get there from Ciampinoi is a real obstacle – steep and crowded. Recent reporters found it worth the struggle though. The Alpe di Siusi above Ortisei is ideal for confidence-building – very gentle, quiet, amid superb scenery. A 2004 reporter loved the 'long red' down to Saltria from Punta d'Oro and those at Spitzbuhl were 'enjoyable and never busy'. The runs at Mont de Seura, between this area and Ciampinoi, are also recommended for avoiding the crowds. On the rather neglected Seceda sector there is a splendid easy blue back to Santa Cristina (the lower half is marked red on maps but is of blue gradient).

Average intermediates have a very large network of suitable pistes, though there are few long runs. One notable one is the beautiful red swoop Cucasattel on Seceda to Ortisei. The Plan de Gralba area, the runs from the Florian chair on Alpe di Siusi and the main pistes to San Cassiano and La Villa in the Alta Badia area are other recommended cruises. Don't neglect the Edelweiss valley, off the Sella Ronda circuit at Colfosco – gentle, normally very quiet pistes ideal for fast cruising. The red underneath the Boè cable-car in Corvara is usually uncrowded and retains good snow. The area above Canazei, below the Belvedere is also worth exploring: the red to Lupo Bianco is a beautiful run through the trees.

The runs back to Selva direct from Ciampinoi are a bit more challenging, as are the descents from Dantercëpies to Selva. Those at Arabba can be tricky and a reporter warns of the red run from Passo Padon – narrow, steep and unnerving in places – which is the only way back from Marmolada.

The very easy 'hidden valley' red run from Lagazuoi (at the top of the Passo Falzarego cable-car on the road to Cortina and an easy taxi-ride from Armentarola or San Cassiano) back to Armentarola is a must. It is one of the most beautiful runs we've come across, and usually delights reporters. It offers isolation amid sheer pink-tinged Dolomite peaks and frozen waterfalls. Make time to stop at the atmospheric Scotoni rifugio ('an absolute must' writes a reporter) near the end; then it's a long pole, skate or walk to the welcome sight of a horse-drawn sled (with ropes attached) which tows the weary (for a few euros) to Armentarola and the Alta Badia lifts.

FOR BEGINNERS
Great slopes, but ...
The village nursery slopes are excellent – spacious, convenient, and kept in good condition. In the area as a whole, near-beginners have lots of splendid gentle long runs to progress to, but Selva isn't the ideal base for access to them – Corvara or Colfosco are much better placed. You could take a bus or taxi to Ortisei and the cable-car up to Alpe di Siusi, where runs are marked red but of only blue gradient. A 2005 reporter recommends getting a taxi to the blues at Plan de Gralba.

FOR CROSS-COUNTRY
Beautiful trails
There are 98km/61 miles of trails, all enjoying wonderful scenery. The 12km/7 mile trail up the Vallunga-Langental valley is particularly attractive, with neck-craning views all around. Almost half the trails have the advantage of being at altitude, running between Monte Pana and Seiseralm, and across Alpe di Siusi.

Selva/Sella Ronda

445

APT VAL DI FASSA

The stunning scenery is a major attraction of this whole area ↓

QUEUES
Still a few problems
New lifts have vastly improved the area, and there are now fewer bottlenecks. Most recently, the fast quad out of Arabba has greatly improved matters there, and 2005 reporters tell us the new gondola out of San Cassiano, and the upgrading of the first two stages of the Marmolada cable-car, have solved the serious queue problems there. However, problems 2005 reporters mention are the Dantercëpies gondola ('an absolute scrum till after 10'), the Sodlisia chair in Colfosco, the Ciampinoi gondola, the Piz Seteur chair at Plan de Gralba, the two-way Borest chair between Corvara and Colfosco and the T-bar in Passo Campolongo. You may find the length of queues on the Sella Ronda circuit less of a problem than their character ('Lots of pushing and shoving,' says one reporter) and the crowds on the pistes. Many reporters find queues don't pose a problem away from the main Sella Ronda circuit.

MOUNTAIN RESTAURANTS
One of the area's highlights
There are lots of huts all over the area, and virtually all of them are lively, with helpful staff, good food, lots of character and modest prices. Reporters love them, even more so now that they are non-smoking due to a new Italian law.

In Val Gardena the Panorama is a small, cosy, rustic suntrap at the foot of the Dantercëpies drag. On the way down to Plan de Gralba from Ciampinoi, the Vallongia Rolandhütte is tucked away on a corner of the piste. In the Plan de Gralba area the top station of the cable-car does excellent pizza; the Comici is atmospheric, with a big terrace. Piz Seteur has 'superb lasagne' and is also recommended late in the day (see Après-ski).

In the Colfosco area the little Forcelles, Edelweiss and Pradat huts are all pleasant but can get very busy. A 2005 reporter recommends the rustic Jimmy's at the top of the Frara gondola – especially for egg and bacon fry up.

At Alta Badia the Piz Sorega above San Cassiano gets very crowded – a reporter suggests going down to the Pic Prè, which is 'badly marked on the map and consequently quiet'. La Brancia does 'wonderful polenta and delicious blackberry grappa'. The Saraghes is 'friendly and popular' and 'serves generous portions'. Cherz

above Passo di Campolongo has great views of Marmolada. The Pralongia is 'welcoming and cosy' with 'a wonderful array of pastries and strudels'.

Around Arabba, Bec de Roces and Col de Burz are both suntraps (with 'amazing Bombardinos' at the latter). The rifugio at the top of the Porta Vescovo lifts has been recommended for 'excellent food' and 'stunning panoramic views', as have the 'lively' Rifugio Plan Boè, the Fodom ('first class, good value pizza') at the bottom of the Lezuo Belvedere chair below Passo Pordoi and Capanna Bill, near the Marmolada lifts, on the way back to Arabba ('good food, table-service').

In the Seceda sector there are countless options. The cosy Sangon 'has bags of atmosphere', though another reporter pronounces Baita Gamsblut her favourite: 'Super rustic hut with a good menu and a warm, friendly atmosphere.' The Seceda does 'wonderful food, served by waitresses in miniskirts or leather shorts', which brightened one reporter's day.

On Alpe di Siusi the rustic Sanon refuge gets a good review, particularly since 'the barman came out to serenade us with his accordion'. The table-service restaurant at the bottom of the Monte Piz lift is also highly rated – 'good value', 'huge portions', say recent visitors. And the Williams hut at the top of the Florian chair has 'superb views'.

Above Canazei there are at least six huts scattered around the Belvedere bowl. Baita Belvedere is 'a good place for lunch, with excellent service' and a 'superb view'. Rifugio Salei offers table- or self-service and is recommended. Lower down, Lupo Bianco is a notable rendezvous point and suntrap (though a 2005 reporter had 'the longest wait I've ever had for lunch' here). As well as restaurants, there are lots of little snow bars for a quick grappa.

SCHOOLS AND GUIDES
Positive reports
A skier in a 2005 reporter's group was 'happy enough' with lessons with the 2000 school. Another 2005 reporter had a private lesson with Ski & Boarders Factory in Selva and said it was good and that there were lots of English speakers – but advises booking ahead as it gets busy. Another reporter rated the ski school at Pecol, above Canazei 'excellent'.

SCHOOLS

Factory Selva Gardena
t 0471 795156

2000
t 0471 773125

Peter Runggaldier
t 0471 773282

Classes
(Selva prices)
6 days (5 half days
and one full day)
€155
Private lessons
€34 for 1hr

CHILDREN

Kindergarten
(run by ski school)
For ages 2 up; skiing
available for ages
3 upwards

Ski school
For age 4 to 12:
6 days €269, lunch
included (Selva
school price)

GETTING THERE

Air Verona 190km/
118 miles (3hr);
Bolzano 40km/
25 miles (45min);
Treviso 130km/81
miles (2½hr)

Rail Chiusa (27km/
17 miles), Bressanone
(35km/22 miles),
Bolzano (40km/
25 miles); frequent
buses from station

FACILITIES FOR CHILDREN
Good by Italian standards
There are comprehensive childcare
arrangements, but German and Italian
are the main languages here and
English is not routinely spoken. That
said, in the past we have had reports
of very enjoyable lessons and of
children longing to return.

STAYING THERE

HOW TO GO
A reasonable choice
These resorts now feature in quite a
few tour op brochures.
Chalets There is a fair choice of
catered chalets, including some good
ones with en suite bathrooms. Family
specialist Esprit has chalets here.
Hotels There are a dozen 4-stars in
Selva, over 30 3-stars and numerous
lesser hotels. Few of the best are well
positioned.
Gran Baita (0471 795210) Large,
luxurious sporthotel, with lots of mod
cons including indoor pool. A few
minutes' walk from centre and lifts.
Granvara (0471 795240) 'Just out
of town but free hotel bus, great food
and views and a spa. Recommended.'
Aaritz (0471 795011) Best-placed
4-star, opposite the Ciampinoi
gondola, and with an open fire.
Tyrol (0471 774100) 'Friendly and
fantastic value, handy for nursery
slopes but bit of a way to Sella Ronda.'
Rodella (0471 794553) Just outside
Selva but friendly pensione, with free
taxi, spa and delicious meals.'
Linder (0471 795242) 'Friendly,
family-run with good food.'
Pralong (0471 795370) An uphill
walk from the centre, but 'one of the
best hotels we've visited', says a
reporter – endorsed again in 2004.
Solaia (0471 795104) 3-star chalet,
superbly positioned for lifts and slopes.

Self-catering There are plenty of
apartments to choose from. We have
had excellent reports of the Villa
Gardena (0471 794602) and Isabell
(0471 794562) apartments.

EATING OUT
Plenty of good-value choices
Selva offers both Austrian and Italian
food at prices to suit all pockets. The
higher-quality restaurants are mainly
hotel-based – recent reporters highly
recommend the Armin Grill in the hotel
of the same name, and the Sal Fëur in
the Broi B&B. The Bellavista is good for
pasta and Costabella 'highly
recommended' for Tirolean specialities
and 'large measures of spirits'. Rino's
has 'excellent pizza'.

APRES-SKI
Above average for a family resort
Nightlife is lively and informal, though
the village is so scattered there is little
on-street atmosphere. La Stua is an
après-ski bar on the Sella Ronda route,
with live music on some nights. For an
early drink we are told that the Piz
Seteur bar, above Plan de Gralba, is
worth a little detour from the route –
'fun, loud and a bit raunchy' (you may
find scantily clad girls dancing on the
bar). For a civilised early drink try the
good-value ski-school bar at the base
of the Dantercëpies piste. Or the
Costabella – cosy, serving good
glühwein. Café Mozart on the main
street is 'a great place for cakes'.

For thigh-slapping in Selva later on,
the Laurinkeller has good atmosphere
though it's 'quite expensive', while the
popular Luislkeller is 'very German',
'lively' and 'packed', with loud music
and barmaids in Tirolean garb.

The place to go later is Dali, where a
mixed British and Italian crowd dances
till the small hours – but 'it doesn't get
going until about midnight'.

Selva is a spread-out village but built in attractive chalet style architecture ➔

APT VAL GARDENA

ACTIVITIES

In Val Gardena:

Indoor Swimming pool, sauna, bowling, squash, ice rink, ice hockey, museum, concerts, cinema, billiards, tennis, climbing wall, fitness centre

Outdoor Sleigh rides, snow-shoeing, toboggan runs, paragliding, extensive cleared paths, climbing

OFF THE SLOPES
Good variety

There's a sports centre, snow-shoeing, lovely walks, tobogganing and sleigh rides on Alpe di Siusi. There is a bus to Ortisei, which is well worth a visit for its large hot-spring swimming pool, shops, restaurants and lovely old buildings.

Pedestrians can reach numerous good restaurants by gondola or cable-car. Car drivers have Bolzano and Innsbruck within reach and tour operators do trips to Cortina.

Ortisei 1235m/4,050ft

Ortisei is an attractive, prosperous market town with a life of its own, and its local slopes aren't on the main Sella Ronda circuit. It's full of lovely buildings, pretty churches and pleasant shops. The lift to the Seceda slopes is easily reached from the centre by a 300m/980ft-long series of underground moving walkways and escalators; the Alpe di Siusi lifts are a similar distance out – but the cable-car is now accessed via a long pedestrian footbridge, an improvement over the previous steep, icy uphill walk. The nursery area, school and kindergarten are at the foot of these slopes, but there's a fair range of family accommodation on the piste side of the road. The fine public indoor pool and ice rink are also here.

There are hotels and self-catering to suit all tastes and pockets and many good restaurants, mainly specialising in local dishes. A reporter recommends the Hotel Alpenheim (0471 796515): 'luxurious rooms', 'excellent food' but not central. Another says the Adler (0471 775000), which has a very impressive spa, is 'an excellent hotel'. Après-ski is quite jolly, and many bars keep going till late.

Corvara 1570m/5,150ft

Corvara is the most animated village east of Selva, with plenty of hotels, restaurants, bars and sports facilities.

It's well positioned, with village lifts heading off to reasonably equidistant Selva, Arabba and San Cassiano, and has gentle slopes for beginners. The main shops and some hotels cluster around a small piazza, but the rest of the place sprawls along the valley floor – a recent reporter warns that some accommodation can be far from the lifts. The Posta Zirm in Corvara does a ski-boot tea dance but support may depend on tour ops organising group transport back to other villages. The hotel Tablè is recommended by reporters for its piano bar and good cakes. Other suggestions from a 2005 reporter are the smart bar in the Perla hotel (which also houses the Michelin-starred Stüa de Michil restaurant) and the 'self-consciously trendy' cocktail bar at the Marmolada. Accommodation wise, the hotel Posta Zirm has a large spa facility, and is recommended by a 2005 reporter: 'Very good food, ski-in, ski-out, comfortable rooms.' Also recommended is the pensione Villa Tony: 'Very reasonably priced half-board, conveniently located on the main street.' There's a covered ice rink, indoor tennis courts and an outdoor artificial climbing wall.

WEBSITES

For links to resort sites, go to our own new site at www.wtss.co.uk

Phone numbers

From abroad use the prefix +39 (and do **not** omit the initial '0' of the phone number).

TOURIST OFFICES

VAL GARDENA
t 0471 792277
info@valgardena.it
www.valgardena.it

Selva
t 0471 795122
selva@valgardena.it

Ortisei
t 0471 796328
ortisei@valgardena.it

ALTA BADIA
www.altabadia.org

Corvara
t 0471 836176
corvara@altabadia.org

Colfosco
t 0471 836145
colfosco@altabadia.org

San Cassiano
t 0471 849422
s.cassiano@altabadia.org

La Villa
t 0471 847037
lavilla@altabadia.org

ARABBA
t 0436 780019
info@arabba.it
www.arabba.it

VAL DI FASSA
www.fassa.com

Canazei
t 0462 601113
infocanazei@fassa.com

Campitello
t 0462 750500
infocampitello@fassa.com

Colfosco 1645m/5,400ft

Colfosco is a smaller, quieter version of Corvara, 2km/1 mile away. It has a fairly compact centre with a sprawl of large hotels along the road towards Selva. It's connected to Corvara by a horizontal chair-lift. In the opposite direction, a gondola goes to Passo Gardena, from where you can then press on to Selva.

Arabba 1600m/5,250ft

Arabba is a small, traditional-style village. But it is growing fast (and we are getting many more reports on it). It is well placed for exploring the Sella Ronda circuit while avoiding the worst of the crowds starting from Selva and Corvara, and set at the foot of high, north-facing slopes, which have the best natural snow and steepest pistes in the Dolomites. It is not a good choice for beginners or timid intermediates – there is a small nursery slope, but access to longer easy runs is tricky.

There are several chalets here, including a good selection from Neilson. Of the dozen or so hotels, reporters recommend the 3-star Portavescovo (0436 79139): 'Excellent: wonderful food, nicely furnished rooms and a well-equipped fitness centre' (with the only pool in the village). The 3-star B&B hotel Royal (0436 79293) is 'a real gem' and offers 'incredible value for money' – large rooms, sauna, hot-tub and Turkish bath. The 3-star Al Forte (0436 79329) is 'well appointed with good food, and built around the old fort, with fascinating public rooms'. The 3-star Malita (0436 79103) is 'comfortable with good food, at reasonable prices'. Self-catering accommodation is available.

The après-ski is limited but cheap. The atmospheric Rifugio Plan Boè up the mountain is good for a last drink on the pistes before heading back to the village – 'loud 70s, 80s and Europop music', The 'friendly' Bar Peter and cosy hotel bars are the focal points in the village. The lively Stube bar attracts tour op reps, instructors and young teenagers, say recent reporters. The Treina is recommended as the liveliest bar by a couple of 2005 reporters and the Albergio Pordoi has 'the biggest selection of drinks in town'. Restaurant choice is limited, too. The central hotels all have busy restaurants. 7 Sass does 'wonderful enormous pizzas and little else'. Miky's

Grill in the Hotel Mesdì (which opened in December 2004) has 'steaks cooked to perfection' and, asserts our reporter, is 'the best restaurant in Arabba'. You can go up to Rifugio Plan Boè by snowmobile for a 'special' 3-course dinner and dancing – 'the best meal we had'.

San Cassiano 1530m/5,020ft

San Cassiano is a pretty little village, set in an attractive, tree-filled valley. It's a quiet, slightly upmarket resort, full of well-heeled Italian families and comfortable hotels. The local slopes, the sizeable and attractive Alta Badia, form a spur off the main Sella Ronda circuit. Adventurers who want to do the circuit repeatedly will find getting to it a tiresome business. At least the new gondola gets you off to a quick start. Trips to the Hidden Valley are also easily arranged.

The best hotel is the 4-star Relais & Chateau Rosa Alpina (0471 849500).

Mountainsun has a jumbo chalet here – 'brilliantly located' on the piste, according to one guest. Après-ski starts up the mountain with loud music at Las Vegas. Nightlife is very limited: the Rosa Alpina has dancing and there's a bowling alley. There are also two Michelin-starred restaurants – Siriola in the Ciasa Salares, and St Hubertus in the Rosa Alpina. Walking in the pretty scenery is the main off-slope activity; swimming is the other.

La Villa 1435m/4,710ft

La Villa is similar to neighbouring San Cassiano in most respects – small, quiet, pretty, unspoiled – but it is slightly closer to Corvara, making it rather better placed for the main Sella Ronda circuit. The home pistes are challenging – genuine red and black. Village amenities include a pool and skating on a frozen lake.

Canazei 1465m/4,810ft

Canazei is a sizeable village at the south-west corner of the Sella Ronda circuit. It is covered in the chapter on Trentino.

Campitello 1445m/4,740ft

Campitello is a pleasant, unremarkable village, smaller and quieter than next-door Canazei and still unspoiled. It is covered in the chapter on Trentino.

Sestriere

Altitude is the main attraction; for some, the only attraction

NEWS

Turin is hosting the 2006 Winter Olympic Games in February.

For 2005/06 a new eight-seat gondola is being built up Monte Fraiteve for access to Sansicario.

For 2004/05 the Clos dell' Acqua drag-lift at Sises was replaced.

Snowmaking was also increased.

KEY FACTS

Resort	2000m
	6,560ft

For Milky Way	
Slopes	1390-2825m
	4,560-9,270ft
Lifts	91
Pistes	400km
	249 miles
Blue	25%
Red	55%
Black	20%
Snowmaking	100km
	62 miles

For Sestriere-Sauze d'Oulx-Sansicario	
Slopes	1390-2825m
	4,560-9,270ft
Lifts	51
Pistes	300km
	186 miles
Snowmaking	90km
	56 miles

+ Snow reliability is usually good, with extensive snowmaking back-up

+ Local slopes suitable for most levels, with some tougher runs than most neighbouring resorts

+ Part of the extensive Milky Way area, with its links being improved by gondola access to Sansicario

– The purpose-built village is an eyesore, and much of it is rather scruffy, though being improved for the 2006 Winter Olympics

– Weekend and peak-period queues

– For a purpose-built resort, not conveniently arranged

– Little après-ski during the week

Sestriere was built for snow – high, with north-west-facing slopes – and it has very extensive snowmaking, too. So even if you are let down by the notoriously erratic snowfalls in this corner of Italy, you should be fairly safe here – certainly safer than in Sauze d'Oulx, over the hill. Whether this is a sensible basis for choosing to stay here is another question. When we go to Italy, we generally aim to go somewhere a bit more captivating.

THE RESORT

Sestriere was the Alps' first purpose-built resort, developed by Giovanni Agnelli in the 1930s. It sits on a broad, sunny and windy col, and neither the site nor the village, with its large apartment blocks, looks very hospitable – though the buildings have benefited from recent investment. New building work, including a large residential building close to the Cit Roc chair, has taken shape in preparation for the 2006 Olympics. There are some interesting buildings, but much of the village still seems rather scruffy. This is not the most convenient of purpose-built resorts, either – some of the walks are non-trivial. The satellite of Borgata, 200m/66oft lower, is less convenient for nightlife and shops.

THE MOUNTAINS

The local slopes have two main sectors: Sises, directly in front of the village, and more varied Motta, above Borgata – to the north-east and 225m/740ft higher. Sestriere is at one extreme of the big Franco-Italian Milky Way area. Access to Sansicario and the rest of the Milky Way should be transformed this season by the new gondola to Monte Fraiteve – one concrete benefit of the Olympics. In theory the return to Sestriere is via the red run down from Monte Fraiteve to the northern side of the village or via a long red from the top of the gondola

at Col Basset, but we've yet to see these runs open – usually you have to ride the gondola down – our reporters in 2005 agree.

Slopes There are mainly drag- and chair-lifts on the local north-west-facing slopes. Signposting and the piste map are poor. There's night skiing twice a week.

Terrain-parks There's a terrain-park next to the Cit Roc chair on Sises and another at Sauze d'Oulx.

Snow reliability With most of the local slopes facing north-west and ranging from 1840m to 2825m (6,040ft to 9,270ft), and an extensive snowmaking network covering most of the Sises sector and over half of Motta, snow-cover is usually reliable for most of the season. The notoriously erratic snowfalls in the Milky Way often leave the rest of the area seriously short of snow. The sunny runs down from Col Basset and Monte Fraiteve do not benefit from artificial back-up.

Experts There is a fair amount to amuse experts – steep pistes served by the drags at the top of both sectors (though don't go hoping for moguls, which are erased religiously), and off-piste slopes in several directions from here and Monte Fraiteve.

Intermediates Both sectors also offer plenty for confident intermediates, who can explore practically all of the Milky Way areas, conditions permitting. The runs in the Motta sector offer more of a challenge.

Beginners The terrain is good for

PISTE MAP

Sestriere is covered on the Sauze d'Oulx map a few pages back.

Phone numbers
From abroad use the prefix +39 (and do **not** omit the initial '0' of the phone number).

TOURIST OFFICE

t 0122 755444
sestriere@montagne
doc.it
www.sestriere.it
www.montagnedoc.it
www.vialattea.it

↑ There are resorts that look worse than Sestriere; but they are few, and most are much more conveniently arranged

SNOWPIX.COM / CHRIS GILL

beginners, with several nursery areas and the gentlest of easy blue runs down to Borgata. But there is a lack of easy intermediate runs to progress to.
Snowboarding Sestriere has a reasonable number of chairs, but there are also lots of drag-lifts.
Cross-country There are two loops covering a total of 10km/6 miles.
Queues The lifts are mainly modern, though there are still some inadequate old ones. But queues for the main lifts occur at the weekends and holidays. A 2005 reporter experienced a half-hour wait for the Cit Roc chair, which could be avoided by taking the Garnel chair instead. The lifts from Borgata to Sestriere should now be less of a bottleneck at the end of the day. Queues occur when poor weather closes the gondola link to Sauze. Reporters here, as in Sauze, complain that some lifts may be kept closed during the week, either to conserve money or snow – when crowded pistes can also become a problem.
Mountain restaurants The Raggio di Sole in the Anfiteatro sector is a 'cosy log cabin'. Reporters also recommend the Tana della Volpe at the top of the Banchetta chair, the Alpette ('good portions, spectacular view') and the busy Gargotte at Garnel ('excellent hot chocolates'). The Teit pizzeria at Borgata has 'good choices at reasonable prices', and the Capret is also worth a try. But on the whole the local restaurants are only fair. There are better ones further afield.
Schools and guides Lack of spoken English can be a problem. 'Well organised,' says a 2005 visitor.
Facilities for children There are no special facilities for children.

STAYING THERE

How to go Most accommodation is in apartments.
Hotels There are a dozen hotels, mostly 3-star or 4-star. The Savoy Edelweiss (0122 77040) and the Du Col (0122 76990) are central, and just out of the village is the luxurious Principi di Piemonte (0122 7941). Grangesises offers an alternative base – it's 3km/1 mile from Sestriere and linked by bus.
Eating out There are plenty of options. Try Lu Periol for home-made ravioli and atmosphere. Tre Rubinetti is highly recommended for 'outstanding cooking' and enormous wine list. The Spelonca is 'cosy with an interesting menu.' Last Tango and the Baita are well regarded.
Après-ski Après-ski is quiet during the week but the Prestige and Palace are two of the many little bars that liven up at weekends. The Pinky is one of the best of the bars that double as eateries, with low sofas in the classic Italian casual-chic style, an antipasto buffet and 'great choices of pizzas'.
Off the slopes There are some smart shops and there's a fitness centre, an ice rink, a sports centre and pool.

La Thuile

Little-known resort with extensive, easy slopes and link with France

COSTS

①②③④⑤⑥

RATINGS

The slopes

Fast lifts	**
Snow	****
Extent	***
Expert	**
Intermediate	****
Beginner	****
Convenience	***
Queues	****
Mountain restaurants	*

The rest

Scenery	***
Resort charm	***
Off-slope	**

NEWS

The Belvedere chairlift, which was out of action when we visited in 2004, is being replaced, presumably by a fast chair.

A new red piste is being created down the Piccolo San Bernardo fast chair.

- Fair-sized area with good lift system linked to La Rosière in France
- Free of crowds and queues
- Excellent beginner and easy intermediate slopes
- Heli-skiing available, opening up some notably long descents
- Some slope-side accommodation

- Most of the seriously tough pistes are low down, and most of the low, woodland runs are tough
- Mountain restaurants are generally disappointing
- Winds can close lift links with France
- Not the place for lively après-ski

La Thuile deserves to be better known internationally. The slopes best suit beginners and intermediates not seeking challenges, but are not devoid of interest for experts, particularly if the snow conditions are good. Those who try it seem to appreciate the quiet village as much as the quiet slopes.

THE RESORT

La Thuile is a resort of parts. At the foot of the lifts is the modern Planibel complex, with places to stay, a leisure centre, bars, shops and restaurants – like a French purpose-built resort, but with a distinctly Italian atmosphere. But many people find this rather soulless and prefer to stay in the old village across the river (served by a regular free bus service). Much of the old village has been restored and new buildings (and an underground car park) tastefully added. There are reasonable restaurants and bars.

The slopes link with La Rosière, over the border in France. Courmayeur is easily reached by car, and Cervinia is about an hour away.

THE MOUNTAINS

La Thuile has quite extensive slopes, with the great attraction that they are normally very uncrowded. Many runs are marked red, but deserve no more than a blue rating. The link with La Rosière adds adventure; but the runs of La Rosière tend to be more challenging than those of La Thuile – steeper, and exposed to sun – and the start of the route back is a fairly tricky red. One reporter describes La Thuile as 'like Heaven' compared to La Rosière for lifts and slope maintenance – endorsed by others in 2005. Strong winds can close the higher lifts, including the link to France.

Slopes The lifts out of the village take you to Les Suches, with shady black runs going back down directly to the village through the trees, and reds taking a more roundabout route. From here chairs and drags take you to Chaz Dura for access to a variety of gentle bowls facing east. You can go off westwards from here to the Petit St Bernard road. The high-point of Belvedere is the launch pad for excursions to La Rosière in France.

Terrain-parks There aren't any.

Snow reliability Most of La Thuile's slopes are north- or east-facing and above 2000m/6,56oft, so the snow generally keeps well. There's also a decent amount of snowmaking and 'grooming is immaculate'.

Experts The only steep pistes are those down through the trees from Les Suches: the steepest – the Diretta and Tre – are serious stuff. The area above

Chaz Dura
258om

Col de Fourclaz

Belvedere
2610m/8,56oft

Col de la
Traversette
2385m

↙ La Rosière

Cerellaz

Les
Suches
2200m

La Thuile
1440m/4,72oft

KEY FACTS

Resort	1440m
	4,720ft

For Espace San Bernardo (La Rosière and La Thuile)

Slopes	1175-2610m
	3,850-8,560ft
Lifts	35
Pistes	150km
	93 miles
Green	9%
Blue	36%
Red	40%
Black	15%
Snowmaking	
	Over 300 guns

WEBSITES

For links to resort sites, go to our own new site at www.wtss.co.uk

Phone numbers
From abroad use the prefix +39 (and do **not** omit the initial '0' of the phone number).

TOURIST OFFICE

t 0165 883049
info@lathuile.it
www.lathuile.it

Respectable nursery slope at the lift base – there's another at mid-mountain ↓

the Petit St Bernard road has some genuinely black terrain and plenty of off-piste – the fast quad means you can do quick circuits in this area. The new black, Maisonettes, by the Arnouvaz chair, is reported to be quiet.

Heli-lifts are available. One of the best, to the Ruitor glacier, has a 20km/12 mile run into France ending near Ste-Foy, a short taxi-ride from La Rosière and the lifts back to La Thuile.

Intermediates La Thuile has some good intermediate runs. The bowls above Les Suches have many gentle blue and red runs, ideal for cruising. There are also long reds through the trees back to the resort. The red runs on the other side of the top ridge, down towards the Petit St Bernard road, offer a greater challenge – as do the slopes of La Rosière. But beware the 'long and boring' roundabout San Bernardo red back to the village: 'It took us over two hours to pole back,' complains a reporter.

Beginners There are nursery slopes at village level and up at Les Suches. There's a good gentle green run above there, and easy blues. Promenade is 'a very easy blue and good for beginners', but is served by drag-lifts. You ride the gondola back down.

Snowboarding These are great slopes for learning. You need ride only chair-lifts and the gondola, and most of the slopes are easy. For the more experienced there are great tree runs, and the link with France offers off-piste possibilities. There is good free-riding, and some good carving runs.

Cross-country La Thuile has four loops of varying difficulty on the valley floor, adding up to 20km/12 miles of track.

Queues The lift system is excellent in general: a fast chair or gondola takes you up the mountain, and there are fast chairs to the top. There may be some weekend queues at the gondola first thing, but not at the chair.

Mountain restaurants There are few notable places – disappointing, for Italy. But 'functional and filling', was one 2005 reporter's verdict. La Clotze at the foot of the Chalets chair-lift does 'tasty, reasonably priced food' and has a 'good atmosphere'. The Offshore below the Belvedere quad does a 'hearty soup' and is recommended by two visitors this year ('excellent atmosphere'). The newish Mélèze, near the top of the gondola, serves 'generous portions'.

Schools and guides A 2005 reporter's parents received 'patient and effective tuition' and made excellent progress. They were 'delighted by the growth of confidence their instructors fostered'. Another reader had small classes early in the season ('really good').

Facilities for children There's an 'excellent' nursery, a Miniclub, and children over the age of five can join adult ski classes.

STAYING THERE

How to go The number of tour operators going there is increasing.

Hotels The choice is between the characterless 4-star Planibel, a few 3-stars and some simpler places. The 'quiet, friendly, family-run' hotel du Glacier, a short walk to the slopes above the lifts, is again recommended by reporters. Chalet Eden (3-star, near the main gondola) is also praised ('excellent value').

Self-catering The Planibel apartments are spacious, right by the lifts and great value. Some 'have been refurbished and are quite smart', but others are 'tired and urgently need refurbishing'.

Eating out Reader recommendations include the Bricole ('excellent house pasta'), the Créton ('the gorgonzola and walnut fagottini was outstanding'), the Lune for good value steaks and salads, and the Rascard ('tremendous jumbo prawns'). Early on, head for Chocolat and indulge in all things sweet – a cafe 'not to be missed'.

Après-ski Nightlife is 'not vibrant' and 'even quieter' than one reporter expected. The Cage aux Folles is popular from 4pm till late. The Bricole is the liveliest bar. The Fantasia disco at the Planibel warms up well after midnight.

Off the slopes The Planibel complex has a good pool, but there are few attractive walks or shops. Pedestrians can ride up the gondola for lunch.

The province of Trentino is a fabulously scenic region that is rather neglected by the British. It has a great many small ski areas that you won't have heard of, as well as a few large ones that are better known. The following guide is not comprehensive; but it certainly includes all the places that are likely to be of international interest, and more. Several areas spread across the borders of Trentino into Alto Adige, Lombardia or Veneto.

EAST OF TRENTO

Canazei and Campitello in the Val di Fassa are in Trentino and the slopes above them are part of the famous Sella Ronda circuit (see separate chapter for a description of the skiing).

CANAZEI 1465m/4,810ft

Canazei is a sizeable, bustling, pretty, roadside village of narrow streets, rustic old buildings, traditional-style hotels and nice little shops, set in the Sella Ronda's most heavily wooded section of mountains. There's plenty going on generally – and it has been recommended by many reporters.
The grand 3-star hotel Dolomiti (0462 601106) in the middle of town is one of the original resort hotels; the chalet-style Diana (0462 601477) is charming, and five minutes from the centre.

There are numerous restaurants. The Stala, Melester and Te Cevana are all worth a try. And après-ski is really animated. La Stua di Ladins serves good local wines. The Husky and Roxy bars are worth a visit.

Off-slope entertainment consists of beautiful walks and shopping. There's also a pool, sauna, Turkish baths and skating in neighbouring Alba.

A 12-person gondola is the only mountain access point, but it shifts the queues (which can be long) quickly.

A single piste runs back to the village but it is often closed. The local Belvedere slopes are easy, with mountain restaurants scattered here and there. The village nursery slope is good but inconvenient, and so unlikely to be used after day one.

Lack of spoken English in the school and kindergarten can be a problem.

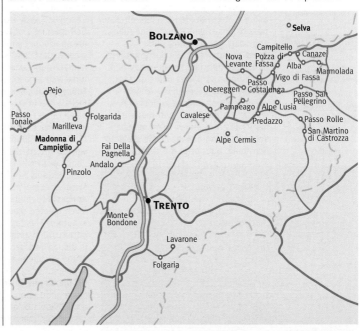

454

↑ The scenery in
Trentino is simply
stunning
APT VAL DI FASSA

CAMPITELLO 1445m/4,740ft
Campitello is a pleasant, unremarkable
village, smaller and quieter than next-
door Canazei, and still unspoiled. It's
quiet during the day, having no slopes
back to the village.
A reporter recommends the 4-star hotel
Soroghes (0462 750060): 'Superb food
and accommodation, helpful staff,
excellent facilities.' Another enjoyed a
stay at the hotel Sella Ronda (0462
750525). Campitello has quite lively
après-ski – we've had trouble getting
near the bar of the throbbing Da Giulio
in the early evening, and a reporter
says it's even busier later on. There's
an ice rink. A cable-car takes you up to
the slopes. To get home you can take
the cable-car down or take the piste to
Canazei and catch a bus.

The well-known glacier of **Marmolada**,
on the border with Veneto, is
reachable on skis from Arabba on the
Sella Ronda circuit. Close to Canazei,
Alba has its own slopes, linked to
Pozza di Fassa further down the Val di
Fassa; over the road from Pozza
another small area of slopes is linked
to **Vigo di Fassa.** Not far from the
valley town of Moena is the lift system
of **Alpe Lusia**, but off to the east are
more extensive slopes at **Passo San
Pellegrino**, linked with **Falcade** – again,
over the border in Veneto. Off to the
east is another fair-sized lift network at
Passo Costalunga, linked with **Nova
Levante** (Welschnofen) in Alto Adige.
Continuing downstream, you are
now in the Val di Fiemme. Near
Predazzo there is a lift up to the
slopes shared with **Pampeago** and with
Obereggen, across the border in Alto
Adige. Finally, the town of **Cavalese**
has lifts up to the **Alpe Cermis** slopes.
To the south of the Val di Fassa/Val
di Fiemme axis, a steep road over the
high **Passo Rolle** – where there is a
small network of drags and chairs

serving easy slopes on either side of
the road – leads down to the resort of
San Martino di Castrozza (1470m/
4,820ft). San Martino has a fabulous
setting beneath a wall of Dolomite
cliffs and peaks – the Pale di San
Martino – soaring to over 3000m/
9,840ft. The village is not notably cute
– there are quite a few large, block-
like buildings – but it is pleasant
enough. The slopes, modest in extent
and entirely intermediate in difficulty,
are split into three sectors, only two of
them linked (at altitude). Restaurant
terraces in two of these sectors give
magnificent views of the Pale.

AROUND TRENTO

Trento's local hill – only a few minutes'
drive from the town – is **Monte
Bondone**. And for a local hill it is
excellent: half a dozen roadside chair-
lifts serve partly wooded slopes here
on Palon (2090m/6,860ft), with a
longest run of 4km/2.5 miles dropping
800m/2,620ft and served by a fast
quad chair. About 90% of the small
area is covered by snowmaking. There's
a terrain-park. And great views to the
Brenta Dolomites around Madonna.
To the south-east of Trento, and
closer to the town of Rovereto, are the
small resorts of **Folgaria** (1165m/3,820ft
– not to be confused with Folgarida
near Madonna) and **Lavarone**. Lavarone
has a handful of lifts, but Folgaria has
more like 20, serving 60km/37 miles of
runs with 100% snowmaking cover.
To the north-west are the slopes on
Paganella (2125m/6,970ft) shared by
Fai della Paganella (1000m/3,280ft)
and **Andalo** (1050m/3,440ft). Andalo is
a sizeable resort that a couple of UK
tour ops feature. Runs radiate from the
peak, and end up in one of the two
resorts. The direct red run to Fai, 1100m/
3,610ft vertical and almost directly
north-facing, has great Dolomite views.

Trentino

455

In Trentino.
A holiday on and
off the slopes.

Breezing up and down the sunny slopes of Trentino will become a habit you will never want to break: the breathtaking pistes, panoramic views, the enchantment of the Dolomites, the warm, friendly welcome and the great tradition of food and wine all combined in this beautiful region of Italy. **www.trentino.to**

TRENTINO

ITALIA

Trentino's largest and best-known ski area is here in the Brenta Dolomites, shared by the big resort of **Madonna di Campiglio** (which has its own separate chapter) and the much smaller resorts of **Marilleva** and **Folgarida**.

Marilleva is a modern resort, the main part (largely consisting of a few functional low-rise buildings) built on a mid-mountain shelf at 1400m/4,590ft and reached by road or gondola from the lower part of the resort at 900m/2,950ft, on the valley floor. From 1400, lifts diverge to Doss della Pesa (2230m/7,320ft) and Monte Vigo, where the slopes link with those of Folgarida and Madonna. Folgarida is also a purpose-built two-part resort, but both parts are at about the same altitude beside the road up to Madonna – clustered around gondola stations at 1300m/4,270ft and at 1400m/4,590ft – and the resort is more traditional in style.

A 20-minute drive south of Madonna – and possibly to be linked one day by lifts and pistes – is **Pinzolo** (780m/2,560ft), not a conventional ski resort but the main town of the Val Rendena, with half-a-dozen lifts on Doss del Sabion (2100m/6,890ft). There are great views of the Brenta massif from the top, and some quite steep terrain.

Further up the Val di Sole is **Pejo** (1400m/4,590ft), a spa village with a narrow but tall slope area close to the border with Lombardia. Actually straddling the border is high, snow-sure Passo Tonale, described below.

PASSO TONALE 1885m/6,180ft
Passo Tonale offers that all too rare combination of a fair-sized, uncrowded, snow-sure ski area and slope-side hotels at a bargain price. The resort lacks many traditional ski-village amenities, but who cares? Reporters are unanimous that it's a great place for beginners.
Passo Tonale sits on a wide, treeless pass. The village is a compact, functional affair, purpose built for skiing, with its hotels, shops, bars and restaurants spread along both sides of the busy through-road. There are 26 hotels, almost all of which are in the 2- to 3-star category. Practically everyone stays on half-board terms, so there are few restaurants other than in hotels. There are plenty of bars but they seem very quiet. Snowmobiles are for hire

and there's a good swimming pool and skating rink down in Ponte di Legno.

Tonale's slopes are spread over two unconnected sections, far enough apart at their bases to be linked by efficient buses. The broad, south-facing area is much the larger, starts right in the village and is entirely novice and intermediate terrain served by a well-laid-out mix of chairs and drags, mostly between 2000m and 2400m (6,560ft and 7,870ft). The north-facing area is steeper, narrower and taller. First, there is an 8-seater gondola (new for 2004/05) of 700m/2,300ft vertical; above that a double chair-lift; and at the top, four drag-lifts on the Presena glacier going just over the 3000m mark (just short of 10,000ft). Both areas are completely open terrain, but down in the village of Ponte di Legno in Lombardia is a tree-lined area that's good for poor visibility days and due to be expanded for 2005/06 by five new lifts and 20km of new pistes.

Given a glacier, no low altitude slopes and a lot of snowmaking, Tonale is difficult to beat for snow.

It's an excellent resort for novices. The sunny lifts on gentle slopes right by the village are ideal for beginners, and there are good longer progression runs higher up. Reports on the ski schools are good, too.

For intermediates, Tonale is rather limited. The south-facing slopes offer gentle terrain ideal for cruising; the 4.5 km/3 mile Alpino piste down a deserted valley to the village is a highlight. The glacier runs are short and easy, while the rest of the north-facing side is more challenging but not extremely so. You could use the regional pass and visit the Marilleva/Madonna area down the valley.

Experts will need to look off-piste. The black piste down the gondola is not seriously steep except at the top, but the more direct ski route next to it is more of a challenge. In the right conditions there are epic off-piste runs to be done from the glacier, including the impressive 16km/10 mile Pisgana run towards Ponte di Legno (a vertical of 1650m/5,410ft). Guidance needed.

The lift system is impressive – well able to cope with the demand, and with half-a-dozen fast chairs in key positions it provides fast uplift. Unlike many Italian resorts, Tonale does not seem to get invaded at weekends.

The half-dozen mountain restaurants generally meet with readers' approval.

Bardonecchia

A fairly extensive area, worth considering as a base for touring other nearby French and Italian resorts. The local slopes, and the town itself, tend to be fairly quiet during the week, but lots of weekenders pour in from Turin.

BARDONECCHIA TOURIST OFFICE

KEY FACTS

Resort	1310m
	4,300ft
Slopes	1290m-2750m
	4,230-9,020ft
Lifts	20
Pistes	110km
	68 miles
Blue	41%
Red	49%
Black	10%
Snowmaking	26km
	16 miles

TOURIST OFFICE

t 0122 99032
bardonecchia@
montagnedoc.it
www.comune.
bardonecchia.to.it

BARDONECCHIA TOURIST OFFICE

The town is no beauty, but the setting helps ↓

THE RESORT

Bardonecchia is a sizeable old railway town, with little Alpine charm but with a pleasant old quarter. It is hosting the snowboard events of the 2006 Olympics. A regular visitor enthuses about the hotel des Geneys (0122 99001) – 'friendly, excellent food'. Après-ski is quiet, but not absent – there are some good-value bars and a couple of discos, at weekends at least. There is an 'excellent' ski-bus service.

THE MOUNTAINS

Two separate areas of slopes, either side of town, are each a free bus-ride away. The larger sector is a wide mountainside of north-facing runs, mostly in trees, above three valley lift stations – Campo Smith, Les Arnauds and Melezet. Most runs here are below 2200m/7,220ft. The other sector – Jafferau – is a tall, thin mountain of long, partly open, west-facing runs going appreciably higher. There are no maintained pistes to the bottom here. Despite an Olympics-inspired injection of four fast chairs on the larger sector, most lifts (all at Jafferau) are still slow. There are few queues during the week, though. The snow record isn't particularly good, but there is now extensive snowmaking on the larger sector, with mid-stations meaning you can stay above 1800m/5,910ft. There is little challenge for experts, but virtually the whole area is good for intermediates. Campo Smith and Melezet have nursery areas for beginners. For boarders there is a terrain-park and half-pipe but there are a lot of awkward drag-lifts to cope with. Mountain restaurants are generally pleasant and uncrowded.

Short turns

459

Macugnaga

Macugnaga consists of a pair of quiet, pretty villages dramatically set at the head of a remote valley, across the mountains from Zermatt and Saas-Fee. It's a place for a cheap holiday away from it all, with some skiing thrown in.

KEY FACTS

Resort	1325m
	4,350ft
Slopes	1325-2800m
	4,350-9,190ft
Lifts	12
Pistes	38km
	24 miles
Blue	30%
Red	65%
Black	5%
Snowmaking	some

TOURIST OFFICE

t 0324 65119
info@macugnaga.it
www.macugnaga.it

THE RESORT

The villages of Staffa and slightly higher Pecetto have a lot of traditional charm and enjoy a splendid setting close to the the the towering east wall of Monte Rosa. Reporters remark on the friendly people and the good food. There is a 'lovely' wine shop, too. The bus service between the villages is reliable. There are a dozen small hotels; most manage 3-star status. The Girasole (0324 65052) is approved by a reporter this year – 'friendly, homely'.

THE MOUNTAINS

The slopes are in two separate sectors above the two villages.

Pecetto's lifts run up to Belvedere (1930m/6,330ft), at the foot of the Belvedere glacier. A chair-lift rises gently and very slowly from the village to Burky, in the middle of the small, woody area of gentle runs.

Staffa has a couple of drags on an excellent nursery slope beside the village and a two-stage cable-car going over sunny slopes almost to the Swiss border. Drag-lifts up here serve short blue and slightly longer red and black runs, and there are good, varied red runs down the 1100m/3,610ft vertical of the top cable-car – the longest curling away to notch up 7.5km/5 miles. In the right conditions, off-piste possibilities from the cable-car are considerable, including a run north ending below Saas-Fee. Whether it's worth the long bus- or taxi-ride back ...

Reporters have approved of the piste grooming, the lack of queues, the 'very patient' and 'enthusiastic' ski instructors and the 'lovely, inexpensive' lunches in the several mountain restaurants.

Madesimo

Madesimo's mountain is great for Italian weekenders, who arrive in numbers. If you're planning a week, it's far from ideal. But we have a sneaking affection for the place – and we'd really like to do the run to Fraciscio.

KEY FACTS

Resort	1545m
	5,070ft
Slopes	1545-2880m
	1545-9,450ft
Lifts	16
Pistes	60km
	37 miles
Blue	30%
Red	55%
Black	15%
Snowmaking	some

TOURIST OFFICE

t 0343 53015
aptmadesimo@
provincia.so.it
www.madesimo.com

THE RESORT

Madesimo sits in a remote, pretty side valley, a three-hour drive north from Bergamo that ends in a very dramatic hairpin-bend ascent. The village has some old farm buildings, but is mainly a piecemeal modern development. The delightful central church, narrow streets and little shops appear to be overlooked by an airport control tower (actually the hotel Torre, about to be truncated). A fair choice of hotels is available. Eating out is a highlight. Après-ski is fairly quiet.

THE MOUNTAINS

The venerable two-stage cable-car is due to be replaced by an eight-seat gondola for 2005/06, accessing the west-facing front and east-facing back of the mountain. This should solve existing queue problems. From mid-mountain are very pleasant runs to the village, passing through pretty woodland, or you can cut across to the open slopes above Motta, now equipped with fast quads to deal with the weekend influx on the funicular from the valley town of Campodolcino. There is snowmaking on lower front runs, which get the afternoon sun. The top of the gondola serves the famous Canalone, a long, sweeping, easy black, but classed as off-piste. In theory there is also an off-piste route of 1600m/5,250ft vertical to Fraciscio, next to Campodolcino. The gondola also accesses the best intermediate runs, on the back of the mountain in the high Val di Lei. The nursery slopes are fine, but there are few really easy pistes to graduate to. The mountain restaurants are not particularly appealing.

Pila

Pila is little known outside Italy and offers a worthwhile surprise to those who visit. A fair-sized area of well-groomed, snow-sure slopes rises around a purpose-built resort, linked by gondola to the old Roman town of Aosta.

PILA TOURIST OFFICE

KEY FACTS

Resort	1800m
	5,910ft
Slopes	1550-2710m
	5,090-8,890ft
Lifts	12
Pistes	70km
	43 miles
Blue	12%
Red	73%
Black	15%
Snowmaking	15km
	9 miles

TOURIST OFFICE

t 0165 521055
info@pilaturismo.it
www.pilaturismo.it

SNOWPIX.COM / CHRIS GILL

Pila looks every inch the modern French ski resort. The snow was not at its best in March 2005 ↓

THE RESORT

Pila is a car-free, purpose-built, ski-in ski-out resort, with a mix of chalet-style buildings and large apartment blocks. Après-ski is quiet. Below the resort at 570m/1,870ft, 20 minutes away by gondola, 30 minutes by road, is Aosta, founded by the Romans. Aosta is a big, generally dreary town, but it has a pleasant traffic-free old centre, with cobbled streets and squares lined by shops and cafes (largely for locals). Aosta attracts large numbers of British school groups.

THE MOUNTAINS

Chair-lifts (some fast, but most slow) and a cable-car fan out from the village. There is an interesting mix of slopes. The tree line is notably high (about 2300m/7,550ft) and most runs are below it, making this an excellent bad-weather resort. Lifts go on up over open slopes to the top heights, where there are stunning views stretching from Mont Blanc in the west to the Matterhorn in the east. There are runs for all standards, but mostly they are reds, ranging from easy to stiff. The blacks don't amount to much, but there is extensive off-piste. There are two short beginner lifts, but progression seems to involve use of the very busy central run of the area. Most of the slopes are north- or north-east facing and above 2000m/6,560ft, so snow reliability is good (as is the grooming). There is extensive snowmaking. There are few queues, except at weekends and to descend to Aosta – 'huge from 3.30pm onwards'.

There are several good rustic mountain restaurants. La Châtelaine is a cosy retreat with a friendly owner.

Short turns

461

Switzerland

Switzerland is home to some of our favourite resorts. We award ✶✶✶✶ for resort charm and for spectacular scenery to only three resorts in this book – the essentially traffic-free Swiss villages of Wengen, Mürren and Zermatt. Many other Swiss resorts are not far behind. Many resorts have impressive slopes, too – including some of the biggest, highest and toughest runs in the Alps as well as a lot of good intermediate terrain. For fast, queue-free lift networks, Swiss resorts rarely match French standards, but the real bottlenecks are steadily disappearing. And there are compensations – the world's best mountain restaurants, for one.

People always seem to associate Switzerland with high prices. In the recent past, we haven't found most Swiss resorts appreciably more expensive than most French ones – though some Swiss resorts, such as Zermatt, Verbier and St Moritz, do tend to be pricey. What is clear is that what you get for your money in Switzerland is generally first class.

While France is the home of the purpose-built resort, Switzerland is the home of the mountain village that has transformed itself from traditional farming community (or health retreat) into year-round holiday resort. Many of Switzerland's most famous mountain resorts are as popular in the summer as in the winter, or more so. This creates places with a more lived-in feel to them and a much more stable local community. Many villages are still dominated by a

463

handful of families lucky or shrewd enough to get involved in the early development of the area.

This has its downside as well as advantages. The ruling families are able to stifle competition and prevent newcomers from taking a slice of their action. Alternative ski schools, competing with the traditional school and pushing up standards, are much less common than in other Alpine countries, for example.

Switzerland means high living as well as high prices, and the swanky grand hotels of St Moritz, Gstaad, Zermatt and Davos are beyond the dreams of most ordinary holidaymakers. Even in more modest places, the quality of the service is generally high. The trains run like clockwork to the advertised timetable (and often they run to the top of the mountain, doubling as ski-lifts – see our introductory photo). The food is almost universally of good quality and much less stodgy than in neighbouring Austria. In Switzerland you get what you pay for: the cheapest wine, for example, is not cheap, but it is reliable.

GETTING AROUND THE SWISS ALPS

Access to practically all Swiss resorts is fairly straightforward when approaching from the north – just pick your motorway. But many of the high passes that are perfectly sensible ways to get around the country in summer are closed in winter, which can be inconvenient if you are moving around from one area to another.

There are very useful car-carrying trains in various places. One key link is between the Valais (Crans-Montana, Zermatt etc) and Andermatt via the Furka tunnel, and another is from Andermatt to the Grisons (Flims, Davos etc) via the Oberalp pass – closed to road traffic in winter but open to trains except after very heavy snowfalls. Another rail tunnel that's very handy is the Lötschberg, linking Kandersteg in the Bernese Oberland with Brig in the Valais.

St Moritz is more awkward to get to than other resorts. The main road route is over the Julier pass. This is normally kept open, but at 2285m/7,500ft it is naturally prone to heavy snowfalls that can shut it for a time. Fallbacks are car-carrying rail tunnels under the Albula

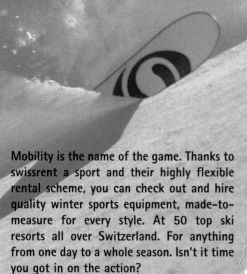

pass and the Vereina tunnel from near Klosters.

These car-carrying rail services are generally painless. Often you can just turn up and drive on. But capacities are obviously limited, and at peak times there may be long queues – particularly for the Furka tunnel from Andermatt, which Zürich residents use to get to the big Valais resorts. There is a car-carrying rail tunnel linking Switzerland with Italy – the Simplon. But most routes to Italy are

kept open by means of road tunnels. See the Italy introduction for more information.

To use Swiss motorways (and it's difficult to avoid doing so if you're driving serious distances within the country) you have to buy a permit to stick on your windscreen (costing SF40 in 2005, and lasting from December 2004 to the end of January 2006). They are sold at the border, and are, for all practical purposes, compulsory.

indicates pass closed in winter

Andermatt

An old-fashioned resort with some great off-piste (and snow)

COSTS

① ② ③ ④ ⑤ ⑥

RATINGS

The slopes
Fast lifts	**
Snow	****
Extent	*
Expert	****
Intermediate	**
Beginner	*
Convenience	***
Queues	**
Mountain restaurants	*

The rest
Scenery	***
Resort charm	****
Off-slope	**

NEWS

There are plans for a new chair-lift on Gemsstock, but not until 2006/07.

The increase in snowmaking capacity will mean coverage of 11km/7 miles of runs by next season.

We flew SWISS to this resort. 11 flights a day between London and Zürich. www.swiss.com

WEBSITES

For links to resort sites, go to our own new site at www.wtss.co.uk

KEY FACTS

Resort	1445m
	4,740ft
Slopes	1445-2965m
	4,740-9,730ft
Lifts	12
Pistes	74km
	46 miles
Blue	12%
Red	48%
Black	40%
Snowmaking	7km
	4 miles

+ Attractive, traditional village

+ Excellent snow record

+ Some excellent steep pistes, and great off-piste terrain – plus ski-touring opportunities

+ Easy access from Zürich

− Three separate areas of slopes are all fairly limited if you stay on-piste

− Unsuitable for beginners

− Limited off-slope diversions

− Little English spoken

− Cable-car queues at weekends

Little old Andermatt was rather left behind in the mega-resort boom of the 1960s and 70s. But its attractions have not faded for those who like their mountains tall, steep and covered in deep powder. At first sight, it makes a tempting spot for a weekend break – but you'll be joined by the residents of Zürich, who arrive by the coachload and trainload. For a midweek break, it's superb.

THE RESORT

Andermatt is quite busy in summer and gets weekend winter business, but at other times seems deserted apart from soldiers from the local barracks. The town is quietly attractive, with wooden houses lining the dog-leg main street that runs between railway and cable-car stations, and some imposing churches. There are good road and rail links from Zürich, but in winter east-west links with the Grisons and the Valais rely on car-carrying trains. The town is big enough for reporters to appreciate the good minibus service to Gemsstock and Winterhorn.

THE MOUNTAINS

Andermatt's skiing is split over three unlinked mountains, all limited in extent. The slopes are almost entirely above the trees. The Gotthard-Oberalp lift pass also covers Sedrun and Disentis, reached by train over the Oberalp pass – a good outing.
Slopes A two-stage cable-car from the edge of the village serves magnificent, varied slopes on the open, steep, north-facing and usually empty slopes of Gemsstock. Across town is the gentler, sunny Nätschen/ Gütsch area. And a bus- or train-ride along the valley is north-facing Winterhorn (above Hospental). There is also an isolated nursery slope further along at Realp. Piste marking is slack, which on such a steep hill is bad news in a white-out.
Terrain-parks There are facilities (park and pipe) on Gemsstock.

Snow reliability The area has a justified reputation for reliable snow. Piste grooming is generally good.
Experts It is most definitely a resort for experts. The north-facing bowl beneath the top Gemsstock cable-car is a glorious, long, steep slope (about 900m/2,950ft vertical), usually with excellent snow, down which there are countless off-piste routes and one marked run that branches into two. Outside the bowl, the Sonnenpiste is a fine open red run curling around the back of the mountain to the Gurschen mid-station, also flanked by off-piste opportunities. From Gurschen to the village there is a black run, not steep but often tricky because of poor snow or moguls. Routes off the back of Gemsstock lead to the village, or to Hospental. Nätschen and Winterhorn both have black pistes and off-piste opportunities, including worthwhile itinerary routes.
Intermediates Intermediates needn't be put off Gemsstock: the Sonnenpiste can be tackled (especially as there are immaculately groomed sections of the piste 'created especially for carvers'), and there is a pleasant red run and some short blues at mid-mountain. Winterhorn's modest lift system offers pistes to suit all abilities down the 1000m/3,280ft vertical, while Nätschen's south and west-facing mountain is perfect for confidence-building – and for first experiments off-piste.
Beginners The lower half of Nätschen has a good, long, easy run. But this is not a good resort for beginners.
Snowboarding The cable-car accesses some great free-ride terrain.

↑ The shady Gemsstock, looming above the village

ANDERMATT GOTTHARD SPORTBAHNEN AG

Phone numbers
From elsewhere in Switzerland add the prefix 041.
From abroad use the prefix +41 41.

TOURIST OFFICE

t 887 1454
info@andermatt.ch
www.andermatt.ch

Cross-country There are 40km/24 miles of loops along the valley.

Queues The Gemsstock cable-car can generate morning queues in the village and at mid-mountain when conditions are attractive, especially at weekends. Things take a while to get going after heavy snow.

Mountain restaurants They are present, but are still no more than adequate. The Gemsstockbar, at Gurschen, opened last winter, but seems to be only a bar.

Schools and guides Bergschule Uri/ Mountain Reality, a guiding outfit run by local big wheel Alex Clapasson, is very pricey, and a reporter last year did not regret hiring a guide from the Swiss ski school instead.

Facilities for children There are slopes they can handle at Nätschen and the Swiss school does classes.

STAYING THERE

How to go Andermatt's accommodation is in cosy 2- and 3-star hotels.

Hotels Gasthaus Sternen (887 1130) is an attractive central chalet with a cosy restaurant and bar. The lovely old 3-star Sonne (887 1226), between the centre and the lift, is welcoming and comfortable, with 'excellent service'. The neighbouring 2-star Bergidyll (887 1455) is a British favourite. Alpenhotel Schlüssel (888 7088) is 'good value', with spacious rooms.

Eating out A recent reporter praises the Sternen (see above) for 'generous portions, nicely cooked and very cosy surroundings'. The hotel Kronen's 'quite formal' Tre Passi restaurant has also been mentioned in dispatches.

Après-ski There are several cosy bars, which come alive on Saturdays – the Spycher and the Piccadilly in particular. The Curva at the hotel Monopol is 'very pleasant'. At weekends the Gotthard disco is said to be 'lively'.

Off the slopes There's a toboggan run at Nätschen. The churches and the museum of local history are worth a visit. The fitness centre at the hotel Drei König is open to the public. There are maintained footpaths.

Andermatt

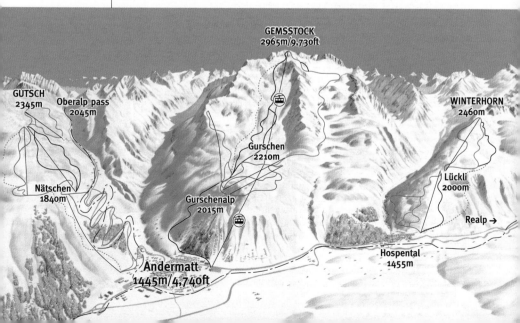

Arosa

Classic all-round winter resort – walkers are as welcome as skiers

470

COSTS

①②③④⑤⑥

RATINGS

The slopes
Fast lifts	***
Snow	***
Extent	**
Expert	**
Intermediate	***
Beginner	****
Convenience	**
Queues	****
Mountain restaurants	***

The rest
Scenery	***
Resort charm	**
Off-slope	****

NEWS

The FIS Snowboard World Championships are to be held in Arosa in 2007.

There are plans for two new pistes on Brüggerhorn for 2005/06.

A new half-pipe opened late last season, near the Mittelstation.

There are still plans to link Arosa to Lenzerheide-Valbella, but not imminently.

KEY FACTS

Resort	1800m
	5,910ft
Slopes	1800-2655m
	5,910-8,710ft
Lifts	13
Pistes	60km
	37 miles
Blue	27%
Red	60%
Black	13%
Snowmaking	10km
	6 miles

We flew SWISS to this resort. 11 flights a day between London and Zürich. www.swiss.com

➕ Classic winter sports resort ambience, with lots going on other than skiing and boarding

➕ Some of the best cross-country loops in the Alps

➕ Few queues

➕ Relatively good snow reliability

➕ Prettily wooded setting, but ...

➖ Some very block-like buildings in main village

➖ Spread-out village lacks a heart, and means some accommodation is inconveniently situated

➖ Slopes too limited for mileage-hungry intermediates

➖ Few challenging pistes for experts – though there is good off-piste

The classic image of a winter sports resort is perhaps an isolated, snow-covered Swiss village, surrounded by big, beautiful mountains, with skating on a frozen lake, horse-drawn sleighs jingling along snowy streets and people in fur coats strolling on mountain paths. Arosa is exactly that. It's just a pity that many of its comfortable hotels date from a time when pitched roofs were out of fashion.

THE RESORT

High and remote, Arosa is in a sheltered basin at the head of a beautiful wooded valley, in contrast to the open slopes above it. It's a long, winding drive or splendid rail journey from Chur (both take just under an hour). The main resort development is around Obersee – a pretty spot, spoilt by the surrounding block-like buildings. Lifts go up from here into the Weisshorn sector of the slopes. The rest of Arosa is scattered, much of it spreading up the steep road separating Obersee from the older, prettier Inner-Arosa, where lifts from opposite extremities go up into both sectors of the slopes. Arosa is quiet; its relaxed ambience attracts an unpretentiously well-heeled clientele of families and older people. Very few of them are British.

Some accommodation is a long walk from the lifts, but there is an excellent free shuttle-bus.

THE MOUNTAINS

Arosa's slopes are situated in a wide, open bowl, facing north-east to south-east, with all the runs returning eventually to the village at the bottom. All the slopes are above the tree line, except just above Obersee.

Slopes The slopes are spread widely over two main sectors. The major lift junction in the Weisshorn sector is Tschuggen (strangely un-named on the resort piste map), 500m/1,640ft away from the Mittelstation of the Weisshorn cable-car, and reachable from both Obersee and Inner-Arosa. From Mittelstation, you can take a chair to the lower peak of Brüggerhorn. The main access to the Hörnli sector is a slow gondola from below Inner-Arosa. Well-used walking paths wind across the mountainsides, and great care is needed where they cross the pistes.

Terrain-parks There is a park and a half-pipe.

Snow reliability The slopes are quite high, but the Weisshorn sector gets a lot of sun; the shadier Hörnli slopes hold their snow well. Grooming is good, and snowmaking on the home runs is often put into use.

Experts Arosa isn't an obvious target for experts, but there is plenty of gentle off-piste terrain and several ungroomed 'free-ride' routes – and Brüggerhorn is subtitled 'Free Ride Mountain'. The status of these routes is sadly unclear.

Intermediates This is a good area for intermediates who aren't looking for high mileage or huge challenges. The runs from Hörnli are enjoyable cruises, the black including a short steeper pitch. The Weisshorn runs are generally steeper, with some rewarding reds. The long blue to Obersee from Brüggerhorn via Prätschli is a great way to end the day, with fab views of sunlit peaks from the shady piste.

Beginners The Tschuggen nursery slopes are excellent and usually have

the main schools. Class sizes can be large. There's a lot of demand for private lessons.

Facilities for children Arosa's appeal as a family resort has led to Disney endorsement, with 13 hotels and the Swiss Ski school forming the Alpine Club Mickey Mouse.

STAYING THERE

How to go Arosa is a hotel resort, with a high proportion of 3- and 4-stars.
Hotels The sensitively modernised 4-star Waldhotel National (378 5555) with 'really special food' and direct access to the slopes is 'quite delightful'. The 4-star Sporthotel Valsana (378 6363) is recommended.
Eating out Most restaurants are hotel-based, some with a very high reputation. The Kachelofa-Stübli at the Waldhotel National is excellent.
Après-ski Après-ski is quite lively. The Carmenna hotel by the ice rink has a popular piano bar. The Sitting Bull is busy and cheerful. Recommended bars include the Grischuna for grown-ups and Mexicalito for kids (both with restaurants attached). The BLU club (formerly the Casino) has a dance floor, games and snooker tables, and is said to be 'good fun'.
Off the slopes There's an indoor pool and plenty of outdoor alternatives. You can get a pedestrian's lift pass, and many mountain restaurants are reachable via 60km/37 miles of cleared, marked paths shown on a special map. Sleigh rides in the mountains are popular, and there are indoor and outdoor ice rinks.

good snow, but they get a lot of through traffic. Inner-Arosa has a quieter area for children.
Snowboarding Bananas is the specialist school and Mountain Surf Club offers two-day free-ride training camps.
Cross-country Arosa's modest 26km/16 miles of loops include some of the best and most varied in the Alps.
Queues Arosa does not suffer from serious queues – even in half-term. There can be waits for the Weisshorn cable-car, though recent reporters have had no problems.
Mountain restaurants There's a reasonable choice, several equipped with seriously indulgent sunbeds whereon you can lunch while sunbathing. Carmennahütte has scores. Tschuggenhütte expanded into a new log cabin last winter. Alpenblick does 'very good food' and Hörnli is a 'welcoming hut in a dramatic position'.
Schools and guides Swiss and ABC are

Arosa

471

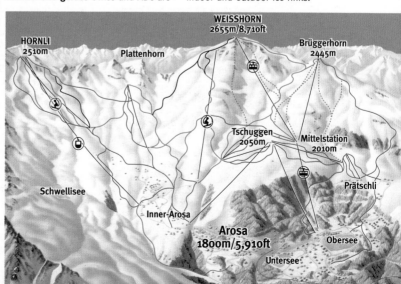

WEISSHORN 2655m/8,710ft
HORNLI 2510m
Plattenhorn
Brüggerhorn 2445m
Tschuggen 2050m
Mittelstation 2010m
Prätschli
Schwellisee
Inner-Arosa
Arosa 1800m/5,910ft
Obersee
Untersee

Champéry

Picture-postcard village, with access to the Portes du Soleil circuit

COSTS

① ② ③ ④ ⑤ ⑥

RATINGS

The slopes

Fast lifts	*
Snow	**
Extent	*****
Expert	***
Intermediate	****
Beginner	**
Convenience	*
Queues	****
Mountain restaurants	***

The rest

Scenery	****
Resort charm	****
Off-slope	***

NEWS

For 2004/05 two fast six-packs with covers replaced old lifts – from Grand Paradis to Planachaux and from there on up to Croix de Culet.

The already good sports facilities will be further improved for 2005/06 with the opening of the Palladium – the new Swiss national ice-sports centre.

472

CHAMPERY TOURIST OFFICE

A classic Swiss mountain village, in a lovely setting ↓

- ➕ Charmingly rustic mountain village
- ➕ Cable-car or fast new six-packs take you into the Portes du Soleil circuit
- ➕ Quiet, relaxed – yet plenty to do off the slopes

- ➖ Local slopes suffer from the sun
- ➖ No runs back to the village – and sometimes none back to the valley
- ➖ Not good for beginners
- ➖ Not many tough slopes nearby

With good transport links and sports facilities, Champéry is great for intermediate skiers looking for a quiet time in a lovely place, especially if they have a car. Access to the Portes du Soleil circuit is not bad: Avoriaz is fairly easy to get to – and there may be fresh powder there when Champéry is suffering.

THE RESORT

Set beneath the dramatic Dents du Midi, Champéry is a village of old wooden chalets. Friendly and relaxed, it would be ideal for families if it wasn't separated from its slopes by a steep, fragmented mountainside.

Down a steepish hill, away from the main street, are the cable-car, sports centre and railway station.

THE MOUNTAINS

Once you get up to them, the local slopes are open, friendly and relaxing.

Slopes Champéry's sunny slopes are part of the big Portes du Soleil circuit, which links Avoriaz, Châtel (in France) Les Crosets and Morgins (see Avoriaz and Châtel chapters). The village cable-car or fast six-seat chair-lift from Grand Paradis, a short free bus-ride from Champéry, go up to Croix de Culet, above the bowl of Planachaux. If snow is good there are a couple of pistes back to Grand Paradis, with an efficient bus service back to the village, but no pistes back to Champéry.

Terrain-parks There is a good terrain-park at Les Crosets (which a reporter

rates as the best in the area), half of which is natural. The 17 features include a quarter-pipe, gaps and kickers. There's also a half-pipe that's floodlit twice a week.

Snow reliability The snow on the north-facing French side of the link with Avoriaz is usually better than on the sunnier Swiss side to the south. The local Champéry area would benefit from more snowmaking.

Experts Few local challenges and badly placed for most of the tough Portes du Soleil runs. The Swiss Wall, on the Champéry side of Chavanette, is intimidatingly long and bumpy, but not terrifyingly steep. There's scope for off-piste at Chavanette and on the broad slopes of Les Crosets and Champoussin.

Intermediates Confident intermediates have the whole Portes du Soleil at their disposal. Locally, the runs home to Grand Paradis are good when the snow conditions allow. Les Crosets is a junction of several fine runs. There are slightly tougher pistes from Mossettes and Pointe de l'Au, Champoussin's leisurely cruising, and delightful tree-lined meanders to Morgins. A highlight is the quiet, beautiful, long blue from Col des Portes du Soleil to Morgins via the 'cute' restaurant at Tovassière.

Beginners The Planachaux runs, where lessons are held, are steepish and limited in extent.

Snowboarding Not ideal for beginners, and access to the Portes du Soleil circuit involves drag-lifts, many of which are quite steep. Good terrain-parks for experts though, and some good between-the-pistes powder areas.

Cross-country It's advertised as 10km/ 6 miles with 4km/2 miles floodlit every night, but it's very unreliable snow.

Queues Few local problems – and the new chair-lifts should provide speedier

KEY FACTS

Resort	1050m
	3,440ft

Portes du Soleil	
Slopes	950-2300m
	3,120-7,550ft
Lifts	208
Pistes	650km
	404 miles
Green	14%
Blue	39%
Red	37%
Black	10%
Snowmaking	
	329 hectares

Swiss side only	
Slopes	1050-2275m
	3,440-7,460ft
Lifts	35
Pistes	100km
	62 miles

Phone numbers
From elsewhere in
Switzerland add the
prefix 024.
From abroad use the
prefix +41 24.

TOURIST OFFICES

Champéry
t 479 2020
info@champery.ch
www.champery.ch
Les Crosets
t 479 1400
lot.illiez@chablais.info
www.valdilliez.ch
Champoussin
t 477 2727
champoussintourisme
@bluewin.ch
www.valdilliez.ch
Morgins
t 477 2361
touristoffice@morgins.ch
www.morgins.ch

access – but Les Crosets is still a bottleneck at peak times. If snow is poor, end-of-the-day queues for the cable-car down are inescapable.

Mountain restaurants The local favourite is Chez Coquoz at Croix de Culet – lovingly prepared food, and a knockout wine list. Chez Gaby above Champoussin does 'marvellous rösti'. The tiny Lapisa on the way to Grand Paradis is delightfully rustic (they make cheese and smoke their own meats on site). Chez Hermann and the Marmottes ('excellent fresh soup buffet') are recommended.

Schools and guides The few reports that we've had on the Swiss school are free of criticism ('professional but friendly'). The Freeride Company provides healthy competition.

Facilities for children The tourist office has a list of childminders. The Swiss ski school takes three- to six-year-olds.

STAYING THERE

How to go Limited packages available. Easy access for independent travellers.
Chalets Tour op Piste Artiste has some.
Hotels Prices are low compared with smarter Swiss resorts. The Beau Séjour (479 5858) is friendly, family-run, with 'large rooms'. The National (479 1130) has 'friendly staff, lovely breakfast'. The Auberge du Grand Paradis (479 1167) is 'charmingly rustic but noisy'.
Self-catering Some apartments are available to independent travellers.
Eating out A fair choice. Two excellent non-traditional places: Mitchell's bar has a good restaurant and the Café du Centre – 'modern Asian menu in a wonderfully restored building'. The Vieux Chalet (hotel Beau-Séjour) is recommended, as is the bistro in the hotel National ('friendly service'). Two

of the best for local specialities are just outside the village: Cantines des Rives and Auberge du Grand Paradis. Twice a week, the slopes are floodlit and the restaurant at the top of the cable-car opens.

Après-ski Mitchell's is popular at tea time – big sofas and a fireplace. Below the 'rather seedy' Pub, the Crevasse disco is one of the liveliest places. The Café du Centre has its own micro brewery. Try the Bar des Guides in the hotel Suisse, or the Farinet's spacious cellar nightclub.

Off the slopes Walks are pleasant and the railway allows excursions to Montreux, Lausanne and Sion. There's a big sports centre (see 'News').

Les Crosets 1660m/5,450ft

A good base for a quiet time and slopes on the doorstep. The Télécabine hotel (479 0300) is homely, with good food in a rustic dining room.

Champoussin 1580m/5,180ft

A good family choice – no through traffic, near the slopes, no noisy late-night revellers and the comfortable Royal Alpage Club hotel (pool, gym, disco, two restaurants – 476 8300).

Morgins 1350m/4,430ft

A fairly scattered, but attractive, quiet resort. The hotel Reine des Alpes (477 1143) is well thought of, and there are catered chalets. There are now two ski schools – a reporter found the ESS 'very satisfactory'. The village kindergarten and nursery are recommended this year, but can be a fair walk from some accommodation. There's also a gentle nursery slope.

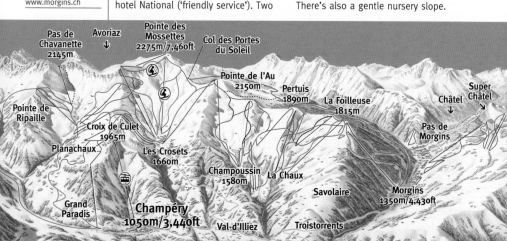

Crans-Montana

Sun-soaked slopes, stunning long-distance views and big town base

COSTS

① ② ③ ④ ⑤ ⑥

RATINGS

The slopes

Fast lifts	★★★
Snow	★★
Extent	★★★
Expert	★★
Intermediate	★★★★
Beginner	★★★
Convenience	★★
Queues	★★★
Mountain restaurants	★★★

The rest

Scenery	★★★★
Resort charm	★★
Off-slope	★★★★

NEWS

For 2004/05 the Toula chair-lift was upgraded to a fast six-seater.

REPORTS WANTED

Recently we have had few reports on this resort. If you go there, please do send us a report.

KEY FACTS

Resort	1500m
	4,920ft
Slopes	1500-3000m
	4,920-9,840ft
Lifts	33
Pistes	140km
	87 miles
Blue	38%
Red	50%
Black	12%
Snowmaking	17km
	11 miles

WEBSITES

For links to resort sites, go to our own new site at www.wtss.co.uk

---

- ☑ Large, varied piste area
- ☑ Splendid setting and views
- ☑ Fair number of woodland slopes – good in bad weather
- ☑ Modern, well-designed lift system, with few queues
- ☑ Excellent, gentle nursery slopes
- ☑ Excellent cross-country trails
- ☑ Very sunny slopes, but ...

- ☒ Snow badly affected by sun – ice in morning and slush in afternoon
- ☒ Large town (rather than village) composed partly of big chalet-style blocks but mainly of dreary cubic blocks – and therefore entirely without Alpine atmosphere
- ☒ Bus- or car-rides to lifts from much of the accommodation
- ☒ Few challenges except off-piste

When conditions are right – clear skies above fresh, deep snow – Crans-Montana takes some beating: the mountains you bounce down are charmingly scenic, the mountains you gaze at are mind-blowing, and you can forgive Crans-Montana its inconvenient, linear layout and the plain, towny style of its twin resort centres. Sadly, conditions are more often wrong. Except in the depths of winter, the strong midday sun bakes the pistes.

THE RESORT

Set on a broad shelf facing south across the Rhône valley, Crans-Montana is really two towns, their centres a mile apart and their fringes merging. Strung along a busy road, the resort's many hotels, villas, apartments and smart shops are mainly dull blocks with little traditional Alpine character, though the resort's many trees make some areas positively attractive.

The resort is reached by good roads, and by a fast funicular railway from Sierre. It depends heavily on summer conference business, so hotels tend to be formal, and visitors dignified. Crans is the more upmarket; Montana has somewhat cheaper restaurants and bars. The main gondola stations are above the main road – there is a free shuttle-bus during the day but it can get very crowded.

There are other gondola bases and places to stay at Les Barzettes and at Aminona. Anzère is nearby, and you can get to Zermatt, Saas-Fee and Verbier by road or rail.

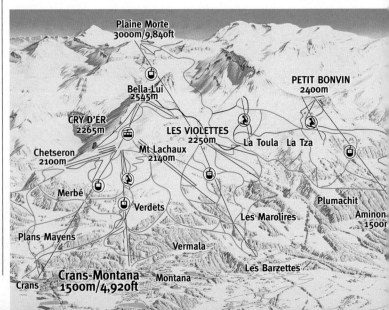

Phone numbers
From elsewhere in Switzerland add the prefix 027.
From abroad use the prefix +41 27.

THE MOUNTAINS

Crans-Montana has slopes with few challenges and no nasty surprises, and there is a pleasant mix of open and wooded slopes. The views over the Valais trench to the peaks bordering Italy are breathtaking.

The slopes The slopes are spread over a broad mountainside, with lifts from four valley bases. Gondolas from Crans and Montana meet at Cry d'Er – an open bowl descending into patchy forest. There is free night skiing here one night a week. The next sector, focused on Les Violettes, is accessed from Les Barzettes. A jumbo gondola goes up to the Plaine Morte glacier. The fourth sector is served by a gondola up from Aminona. Some of the runs down to the valley are narrow woodland paths, and signing is ridiculously slack.

Terrain-parks Aminona has a terrain-park, and there's a half-pipe in the more central Cry d'Er area.

Snow reliability The runs on the Plaine Morte glacier are limited and practically all the other slopes get a lot of direct sun. There is snowmaking on the main runs, but we have never found good snow on the runs down to the valley.

For experts There are few steep pistes and the only decent moguls are on the short slopes at La Toula. There's plenty of off-piste, particularly beneath Chetseron and La Tza.

For intermediates Pistes are mostly wide, and many of the red runs don't justify the grading. They tend to be uniform in difficulty from top to bottom, with few surprises. Avid piste-bashers enjoy the length of many runs, plus the fast lifts and good links that allow a lot of mileage. The 11km/7 mile run from Plaine Morte to Les Barzettes starts with top-of-the-world views and powder, and finishes among pretty woods. The Piste Nationale downhill course is a good test of technique.

For beginners There are three excellent nursery areas, with slopes of varying difficulty. Near-beginners can try the little run up at Plaine Morte.

Snowboarding Despite the resort's staid image, boarding is very popular. There are a number of specialist shops and the Stoked snowboard school. The main lifts are chairs and gondolas, and the drag-lifts are usually avoidable.

For cross-country There are 40km/25 miles of cross-country trails altogether, including snow-sure ones on the glacier.

Queues Investment in gondolas has helped, though bottlenecks can occur at the Nationale drag-lifts.

Mountain restaurants There are 20 mountain restaurants; the Merbé is one of the most attractive. Bella-Lui's terrace offers good views, as does the Chetseron eatery and Petit Bonvin, at the top of the Aminona sector. The Cabane des Violettes has 'good food at fairly reasonable prices'.

Schools and guides The Swiss schools have attracted mainly favourable comments over the years.

Facilities for children These seem adequate, but we lack recent reports.

STAYING THERE

How to go There is a wide choice of hotels and apartments.

Hotels This conference resort has over 50 mainly large, comfortable, expensive hotels. Pas de l'Ours (485 9333) is our favourite – chic, attractive, wood and stone. Aïda Castel (485 4111) is also beautifully furnished in chic rustic style. Beau-Site (481 3312) is a friendly, family-run hotel.

Self-catering There are many apartments available.

Eating out There is a good variety of places, from French to Lebanese. The best is the Bistrot in the Pas de l'Ours hotel. The Chalet, the Plaza and the Padrino are also recommended.

Après-ski Amadeus 2006 and Chez Nanette are tents on Cry d'Er, serving close-of-play vin chaud. The George & Dragon in Crans is one of the liveliest bars. Reporters recommend Bar 1900 and the Grange.

Off the slopes There are swimming pools (in hotels), two ice rinks and a cinema. Sierre and Sion are close.

Davos

A big, grey town surrounded by a glorious Alpine playground

COSTS

① ② ③ ④ ⑤ ⑥

RATINGS

The slopes

Fast lifts	★★★
Snow	★★★★
Extent	★★★★★
Expert	★★★★
Intermediate	★★★★★
Beginner	★★
Convenience	★★
Queues	★★
Mountain restaurants	★★★

The rest

Scenery	★★★★
Resort charm	★★
Off-slope	★★★★★

NEWS

The long awaited Klosters bypass road is due to open in December 2005.

The Madrisa gondola at Klosters Dorf is to be upgraded for 2005/06. This will apparently result in a 20% reduction in travelling time up to the slopes.

➕ Very extensive slopes

➕ Some superb, long, and mostly easy pistes away from the lifts

➕ Lots of accessible off-piste terrain, with several marked itineraries

➕ Good cross-country trails

➕ Plenty to do off the slopes – from sports to shopping

➕ Some cute mountain restaurants

➕ Klosters is an attractively villagey alternative base

➖ Dreary block-style buildings of Davos spoil the views

➖ Davos is a huge, city-like place, plagued by traffic, lacking Alpine atmosphere and après-ski animation

➖ The slopes are spread over five separate areas

➖ Preponderance of T-bars is a problem for some visitors

➖ The only pistes back to Davos from the main Parsenn area are black runs finishing on the outskirts

Davos was one of the original mega-resorts, with slopes on a scale that few resorts can better, even today. But it's a difficult resort to like. You can easily put up with slopes spread over separate mountains, some queue-prone lifts and lots of T-bars if that's the price of staying in a captivating Alpine village. But Davos is far from that.

Whether you forgive the flaws probably depends on how highly you value three key plus-points: the distinctive, super-long runs of the Parsenn area; being able to ski different runs each day; and the considerable off-piste potential. We value all three, and we always look forward to visiting, especially since the upgraded funicular to the Parsenn slopes removed what was the Alps' worst lift queue.

But you don't have to stay in Davos to enjoy its slopes: villagey Klosters offers a much more attractive alternative, with the bonus of arguably better mountain access. Despite royal connections, it is not particularly exclusive. Its cable-car still produces queues. Its main drawbacks, as a recent reporter emphasises, are an excess of traffic (especially at weekends) and a lack of life in the streets. The splendid new bypass will remedy the first this season; maybe it will go some way to remedy the second, too, by encouraging pedestrians.

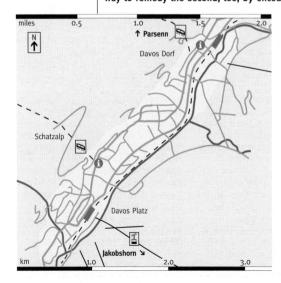

THE RESORT

Davos is set in a high, broad, flat-bottomed valley, with its lifts and slopes either side. Arguably it was the very first place in the Alps to develop its slopes. The railway up the Parsenn was one of the first built for skiers (in 1931), and the first drag-lift was built on the Bolgen nursery slopes in 1934. But Davos was already a health resort; many of its luxury hotels were built as sanatoriums.

Sadly, that's just what they look like. There are still several specialist clinics and it is for these, along with its conferences and sporting facilities, that Davos has become well known. The place has the grey, neat, rectilinear feel of a Swiss city rather than that of a mountain village.

KEY FACTS

Resort	1550m
	5,090ft
Slopes	810-2845m
	2,660-9,330ft
Lifts	50
Pistes	310km
	193 miles
Blue	27%
Red	43%
Black	29%
Snowmaking	19km
	12 miles

It has two main centres, Dorf and Platz, about 2km/1 mile apart. Although transport is good, with buses around the town as well as the railway linking Dorf and Platz to Klosters and other villages, location is important. Easiest access to the slopes is from Dorf to the main Parsenn area, via the funicular railway; Platz is better placed for the Jakobshorn area, the big sports facilities, the smarter shopping and evening action.

Davos shares its slopes with the famously royal resort of Klosters, down the valley – an attractive village with good links into the Parsenn area and its own separate sector, the sunny Madrisa. Klosters is described in more detail at the end of this chapter.

Trips are possible by car or rail to St Moritz (the Vereina rail tunnel offers access to the Engadine area without having to negotiate the snowy Flüelapass) and Arosa, and by car to Flims-Laax and Lenzerheide.

THE MOUNTAINS

The slopes here have something for everyone, though experts and nervous intermediates need to choose their territory with care.

THE SLOPES
Vast and varied
You could hit a different mountain around Davos nearly every day for a week, but the out-of-town areas tend to be much quieter than the ones directly accessible from the resort. Lots of reporters remark on the immaculate grooming of the slopes.

The Parsennbahn funicular from Davos Dorf ends at mid-mountain, where a choice of fast six-pack or old funicular take you on up to the major lift junction of Weissfluhjoch, at one end of the **Parsenn**. The only run back to the valley is a black to the outskirts of Dorf. At the other end of the wide, open Parsenn bowl is Gotschnagrat,

reached by cable-car from the centre of Klosters. There are excellent, exceptionally long intermediate runs down to Klosters, and to other villages (see feature panel). From Davos Platz, a funicular goes up to Schatzalp, where there is a hotel, but the lifts above here are now closed.

Across the valley, **Jakobshorn** is reached by cable-car or chair-lift from Davos Platz; this is popular with snowboarders but good for skiers too. **Rinerhorn** and **Pischa** are reached by bus or (in the case of Rinerhorn) train.

Beyond the main part of Klosters, a gondola goes up from Klosters Dorf to the sunny, scenic **Madrisa** area.

There are too many T-bars for the comfort of some reporters – Rinerhorn, Pischa and Madrisa have little else.

boarding

Intermediate and advanced boarders will get the most out of Davos's vast terrain and off-piste potential. The established boarder mountain is the Jakobshorn, with its pipe and park facilities and funky Jatzhütte. But there are some lengthy flattish bits elsewhere, including on the long runs down the Schifer gondola on the main Parsenn area. Top Secret is a specialist snowboard shop and school. There are several cheap hotels specially for boarders, including the 180-bed Bolgenhof near the Jakobshorn, the Snowboardhotel Bolgenschanze and the Snowboarder's Palace.

TERRAIN-PARKS
Lots of choice

The Jakobshorn has traditionally been
the main boarder hang-out and has
two half-pipes, one near the bottom in
the Bolgen area and another at the top
at Jatz – which is 100m/330ft long.
There is also a terrain-park, a boarder-
cross course and the funky Jatzhütte
nearby. The Rinerhorn and Pischa each
have a park and the Parsenn has a
boarder-cross area.

SNOW RELIABILITY
Good, but not the best

Davos is high by Swiss standards. Its
mountains go respectably high, too –
though not to glacial heights. Not
many of the slopes face directly south,
but not many face directly north either.
Snow reliability is generally good
higher up but can be poor lower down
– you may have to take the lifts down
after using the Parsenn slopes. Snow-
guns cover a couple of the upper runs
on the Parsenn and several on the
Jakobshorn, and the home runs from
the Parsenn to Davos Dorf and
Klosters. And piste grooming is
excellent, helping to preserve snow.

FOR EXPERTS
Plenty to do, on- and off-piste

A glance at the piste map may give the
misleading impression that this is an
intermediate's resort – there aren't
many black runs. But there are some
excellent runs among them – the
Meierhofer Tälli run to Wolfgang is a
favourite. There are also half a dozen
off-piste itineraries (marked but not
prepared or patrolled). These are a key

feature, adding up to a lot of expert
terrain that can be tackled without
expensive guidance. Some are on the
open upper slopes, some in the woods
lower down, some from the peaks right
to the valley. Two of the steepest
routes go from Gotschnagrat down
beside the infamous Gotschnawang
slope – Drostobel and Chalbersäss.

There is also excellent 'proper' off-
piste terrain, for which guidance is
needed, and some short tours. Arosa
can be reached with a bit of help from
a train or taxi and from there you can
travel on snow to Lenzerheide, but
you'll need a train back. From Madrisa
you can make tours to Gargellen in
Austria. A reader also recommends the
descent to St Antönien, north of
Küblis, not least for 'spectacular
views', returning by bus and train.

FOR INTERMEDIATES
A splendid variety of runs

For intermediates of any temperament,
this is a great area. There are good
cruising runs on all five mountains, so
you would never get bored in a week.
This variety of different slopes, taken
together with the wonderful long runs
to the Klosters valley, makes it a
compelling area with a unique
character.

The epic runs to Klosters and other
places (described in the feature panel
on the facing page) pose few
difficulties for a confident intermediate
or even an ambitious near-beginner
(one of your editors did the run to
Klosters on his third day on skis, and
we have heard from reporters who did
the run to Küblis on their second

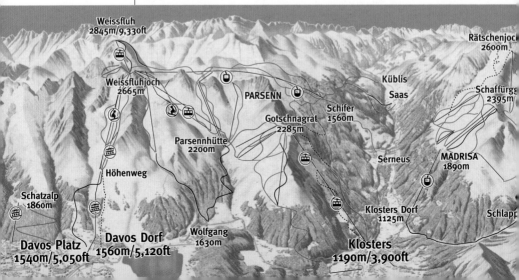

THE PARSENN'S SUPER-RUNS

The runs from Weissfluhjoch that head north, on the back of the mountain, make this area special for many visitors. The pistes that go down to Schifer and then to Küblis, Saas and Serneus, and the one that curls around the mountain to Klosters, are classified red but are not normally difficult – though the latter parts can be challenging if they are not groomed. What marks them out is their sheer length (10-12km/6-7 miles) and the sensation of travel they offer – plus the welcoming huts in the woods towards the end. You can descend the 1100m/ 3,610ft vertical to Schifer as often as you like and take the gondola back. Once past there, you're committed to finishing the descent. If you're based in Klosters, or one of the lower villages, it's a fabulous way to end the day. If based in Davos, the return journey is by train (included in the lift pass).

holiday). And there are one or two other notable away-from-the-lifts runs to the valley. In particular, you can travel from the top of Madrisa back to Klosters Dorf via the beautiful Schlappin valley (it's an easy black – classified red until the mid-1990s).

Pischa is a relatively gentle area, whereas the Jakobshorn has some genuine challenges. Rinerhorn comes somewhere between the two.

FOR BEGINNERS
Platz is the more convenient

The Bolgen nursery slope is adequately spacious and gentle, and a bearable walk from the centre of Platz. But Dorf-based beginners face more of a trek out to Bünda – unless staying out at the hotel of the same name.

There is no shortage of easy runs to progress to, spread around all the sectors. The Parsenn sector probably has the edge, with long, early intermediate runs in the main Parsenn bowl, as well as in the valleys down from Weissfluhjoch.

FOR CROSS-COUNTRY
Long, scenic valley trails

Davos has a total of 75km/47 miles of trails running in both directions along the main valley and reaching well up into Sertigtal, Dischmatal and Flüelatal. There is a cross-country ski centre and special ski school on the outskirts.

QUEUES
Worst one now gone

Some of the longest queues in the Alps were ended three seasons ago, with the upgrade of the first stage of the Parsenn funicular railway, tripling the lift's capacity. The existing lifts from the mid-station — a six-pack and second stage of the original railway — seem to be coping with the increased loading, too, although there was some queuing over the New Year period. Queues can build up elsewhere for some cable-cars (including the one out of Klosters) at peak periods, although a 2005 visitor found more problems up the mountain at the Totalp chair and the Parsennhüttenbahn.

Davos

479

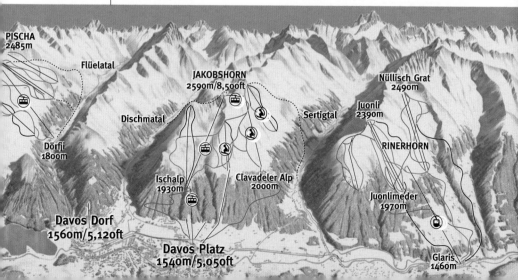

SCHOOLS

Swiss Davos
t 416 2454

New Trend
t 413 2040

**Top Secret
(snowboard)**
t 413 4043

Classes
(Swiss prices)
5 4hr days SF240

Private lessons
Half day SF190

CHILDREN

Pischa nursery
t 417 6767
Ages from 3

Bobo Club
t 416 5969
Ages 4 to 7; 10am-
noon, 2pm-4pm; SF60
per day

Kinderland Madrisa
t 410 2330
Ages 2 to 6

Kinderhotel Muchetta
(at Wiesen)
t 404 1424
Ages from 6mnth

Babysitter list
At tourist office

Ski school
Takes ages 5 to 14 (5
days SF218)

MOUNTAIN RESTAURANTS
Stay low down

The main high-altitude restaurants are dreary self-service affairs. The main exception is the highest of all: Bruhin's at Weissfluhgipfel – a great place for a hang-the-cost blow-out on a snowy day, with table-service of excellent rustic as well as gourmet dishes, and some knockout desserts. The table-service Gastro Alpin at Weissfluhjoch is also is said to be 'particularly good'.

There are other compelling places lower down in the Parsenn sector. A reader recommends 'big portions of chicken and noodles' at the Höhenweg bar at the Parsennbahn mid-station. The rustic 'schwendis' in the woods on the way down to the Klosters valley from the Parsenn still attract crowds. The Chesetta remains 'a particular favourite' with its 'super sun terrace' and 'very cosy interior'. Nearby, the Alte Conterser Schwendi is 'very friendly with good food'. These are fun places to end up as darkness falls – some sell wax torches to illuminate your final descent.

On Jakobshorn the Jatzhütte near the boarders' terrain-park is wild – with changing scenery such as mock palm trees, parrots and pirates. The Chalet Güggel on Jakobshorn is 'small and cosy – nice atmosphere but slow service'. Both restaurants on the Madrisa slopes have been pronounced 'disappointing'. On Pischa, the Mäderbeiz at Flüelameder is a friendly and spacious woody hut, cheering on a cold day. On the Rinerhorn, the Hubelhütte is the best bet.

SCHOOLS AND GUIDES
Decent choice

A reporter says that 'nearly all instructors spoke English and were skilled and friendly — both my kids had a terrific time'. There is an alternative ski school called New Trend (maximum of six in a class) and Top Secret is the competing snowboard school.

FACILITIES FOR CHILDREN
Not ideal

Davos is a rather spread-out place in which to handle a family – and indeed the school's nursery is in a rather isolated spot, at Dorf's Bünda nursery slope. A reporter tells us the nursery is 'well organised, but even good instructors forget at times that your child doesn't speak German'.

STAYING THERE

HOW TO GO
Hotels dominate the packages

Although most beds are in apartments, hotels dominate the UK market.

Hotels A dozen 4-star places and about 30 3-stars form the core of the Davos hotel trade, though there are a couple of 5-stars and quite a few cheaper places, including B&Bs. You can book any hotel by calling 415 2121.

(((((5) **Flüela** (410 1717) The more atmospheric of the 5-star hotels, in central Dorf. Pool.

((((4) **Waldhuus** (417 9333) Convenient for langlaufers. Quiet, modern, tasteful. Pool.

((((4) **Sunstar Park** (413 1414) At far end of Davos Platz. Pool, sauna, games room. Recommended for 'excellent' food. Due to have new spa facilities for the coming winter.

(((3) **Davoserhof** (414 9020) Our favourite. Small, old, beautifully furnished, with excellent food; well placed in Platz.

(((3) **Parsenn** (416 3232) Right opposite the Parsenn railway in Dorf. An attractive chalet marred by the big McDonald's on the ground floor.

(((3) **Berghotel Schatzalp** (415 5151) On the tree line 300m/1,000ft above Platz; reached by funicular (free to guests).

((2) **Alte Post** (414 9020) Traditional and cosy; in central Platz. Popular with boarders.

((2) **Hubli's Landhaus** (417 1010) 5km/3 miles out at Laret, towards Klosters. Quiet country inn with sophisticated, expensive food, which a 2005 reporter describes as 'really special', and an 'attentive, friendly and helpful' owner.

(1) **Snowboarder's Palace** (414 9020) Close to Schatzalp funicular, offers good-value dormitory accommodation.

EATING OUT
Wide choice, mostly in hotels

In a town this size, you need to know where to go – if you just walk around hoping to spot a suitable place to eat, you may starve. For a start, get the tourist office's Gastroführer booklet. The more ambitious restaurants are mostly in hotels. There is a choice of two good Chinese restaurants – the lavish Zauberberg in the Europe and the Zum Goldener Drachen in the Bahnhof Terminus. Good-value places include the jolly Al Ponte (pizza and steak both approved of), La Carretta (good for home-made pasta), the small

GETTING THERE

Air Zürich 160km/
99 miles (2hr by car,
3hr by rail or bus).

Rail Stations in Davos
Dorf and Platz. 20
minutes from Davos
to Klosters.

ACTIVITIES

Indoor Ice rink,
fitness centre, tennis,
squash, swimming
pool, sauna, solarium,
wellness centres,
cinema, casino,
galleries, museums,
libraries, massage,
badminton, pool, golf-
driving range

Outdoor Over 80km/
50 miles of cleared
paths (mostly at
valley level), snow-
shoe trekking,
tobogganing, ice rink,
curling, horse-riding,
sleigh rides,
paragliding

and cosy Gentiana (with an upstairs stübli), and the Hotel Dischma's Röstizerria. For local specialities try Heidi's und Haui's Bündnerstübli. An evening excursion for dinner out of town is popular. A reporter this year enjoyed a fondue evening at Höhenweg, half-way up the Parsenn – 'excellent food, very friendly and good service' – but warns that your ski pass isn't valid in the evening. Schatzalp (reached by a funicular), the Schneider and Landhaus in Frauenkirch have also been recommended.

APRES-SKI
Lots on offer, but quiet clientele
There are plenty of bars, discos and nightclubs, and a large casino in the hotel Europe. But we're not sure how some of them make a living – Davos guests tend to want the quiet life. At tea time, mega-calories are consumed at the Weber, and the Schneider might be worth a look. The Scala has a popular outside terrace. The liveliest place in town is the rustic little Chämi bar (popular with locals); it has 'the best atmosphere later in the evening', according to a reporter. The smart Ex-Bar attracts a mixed age group.

Nightclubs tend to be sophisticated, expensive and lacking atmosphere during the week. The most popular are the Cabanna and the Cava Grischa (both in the hotel Europe), the Rotliechtli, Paulaner's and Bar Senn.

Bolgenschanze and Bolgen-Plaza are popular boarder hang-outs.

OFF THE SLOPES
Great apart from the buildings
Provided you're not fussy about building style, Davos can be unreservedly recommended for those not planning to hit the slopes. The towny resort has shops and other diversions, and transport along the valley and up on to the slopes is good – though the best of the mountain restaurants are well out of range for pedestrians. The sports facilities are excellent; the natural ice rink is said to be Europe's biggest, and is supplemented by artificial rinks, both indoor and outdoor. Spectator events include speed skating as well as 'hugely popular' ice hockey. And there are lots of walks up on the slopes as well as around the lake and along the valleys.

Klosters 1190m/3,900ft

In a word association game, 'Klosters' might trigger 'Prince of Wales'. The enlarged cable-car to Gotschna – and the Parsenn – is named after him.

Don't be put off. We don't know why HRH likes to ski in Klosters particularly, but it is certainly not because the place is the exclusive territory of royalty. Most of the really smart socialising goes on behind closed doors, in private chalets.

THE RESORT
Klosters is a comfortable, quiet village with a much more appealing Alpine flavour than Davos. Klosters Platz is the main focus – a collection of upmarket, traditional-style hotels around the railway station, at the foot of the steep, wooded slopes of Gotschna. Traffic on the road through, leading to Davos, is a long-standing problem, due to be solved by a bypass opening in December 2005.

The village spreads along the valley road for quite a way before fading into the countryside; there's then a second concentration of building in the even quieter village of Klosters Dorf, base of the gondola to Madrisa.

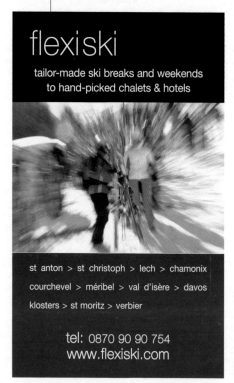

← The railway station in the foreground is central to life in Klosters Platz; the main cable-car station is right next to it, and the main après-ski bars are close by

skifreshtracks.co.uk

holiday
adventures
for all standards

+44 (0)20
8410 2022
atol 2911 abtot 5064

THE MOUNTAIN

Slopes A cable-car takes you to the Gotschnagrat end of the Parsenn area and a gondola from Klosters Dorf takes you up to the scenic Madrisa area.

Terrain-parks The Madrisa area has a park, and there are more options on the other mountains.

Snow reliability It's usually reliable higher up but can be poor lower down – you may have to take the lifts down after using the Parsenn slopes.

Experts The off-piste possibilities are the main appeal for experts.

Intermediates There are excellent cruising runs in all five ski areas shared with Davos.

Beginners There are some nursery lifts at valley level, but the wide sunny slopes of Madrisa are more appealing.

Snowboarding Local slopes are good, but more boarders stay in Davos.

Cross-country There are 35km/22 miles of trails and a Nordic ski school offers lessons. Further trails are easily accessible at Davos.

Queues Queues for the Gotschna cable-car have been reduced by a doubling of its capacity, but can still be a problem at weekends and peak holiday times.

Mountain restaurants There are a number of atmospheric huts in the woods above the village.

Schools and guides There is a choice of three ski and snowboard schools. One reader recommends the Saas, with 'excellent English-speaking instructors'.

Facilities for children The ski schools offer classes for children from the age of four and the Madrisa Kids' Club takes children aged two to six.

STAYING THERE

How to go There is a wide choice of packages offered by UK tour operators.

Hotels There are some particularly attractive hotels – all bookable on the

central reservations phone number, 410 2020. The central Chesa Grischuna (422 2222) is still a firm favourite, combining traditional atmosphere with modern comfort – and a lively après-ski bar. The Albeina (423 2100) is cheaper than the other 4-stars, runs a mini-bus to the lifts, has a good spa and is 'friendly, with good food' says a fourth-time visitor. We get good reports of the 3-star Cresta (423 2600) and a 2005 visitor enjoyed 'extremely good value' half board at the 2-star Bündnerhof (422 1450). The very cosy old Wynegg (422 1340) is popular with British visitors.

Eating out Good restaurants abound, but a reporter comments that there is a shortage of the cheap and cheerful variety. Top of the range is the Walserhof. Al Berto's serves the best pizza in town and the rösti at the Alpina is recommended. The Chesa Selfranga is 20 minutes' walk from the centre of town, but is noted for fondue.

Après-ski In the village, the Chesa Grischuna is a focus from tea-time onwards, with its live music, bowling and restaurant. A reporter enjoyed the music 'at a volume which allowed you to converse'. The hotel Vereina is recommended for its piano bar.

Gaudi's at the foot of the slopes is a popular stop after skiing 'if you're happy to drink in a tent', as is the lively bar at the four-star Alpina and the warmly panelled Wynegg. The 'popular' new Gotschna bar, near the base station, is 'friendly' and colourful inside. The Rossli bar is a 'nicely busy' place to watch sport on TV.

The Casa Antica is a small disco that livens up on Saturday night. The Kir Royal, under the hotel Silvretta Park, is bigger and more brash.

Off the slopes Klosters is an attractive base for walking and cross-country skiing, and tobogganing is popular – there is an exceptional 8.5km/5 mile run from Madrisa to Saas. There is a sport and leisure centre with an ice rink, and some hotels have pools with public access. There are spas in the hotel Bad Serneus just down the valley and further afield at Scuol Tarasp. You can take the train to the interesting old town of Chur.

Phone numbers
From elsewhere in Switzerland add the prefix 081.
From abroad use the prefix +41 81.

TOURIST OFFICES

Davos
t 415 2121
info@davos.ch
www.davos.ch

Klosters
t 410 2020
info@klosters.ch
www.klosters.ch

Flims

Splendid slopes that deserve to be better known outside Switzerland

- ➕ Extensive, varied slopes ideal for intermediates, shared with Laax
- ➕ Impressive lift system
- ➕ Virtually queue-free on weekdays

- ➖ Sunny orientation can cause icy or slushy pistes and bare lower runs
- ➖ Village very spread out, which can mean long walks or bus-rides
- ➖ Weekend crowds in high season

Flims is virtually unknown outside the Swiss and German markets and deserves much more international recognition. It has an impressive 220km/137 miles of mainly intermediate pistes and some good off-piste. The resort is popular with weekenders but can be very quiet during the week.

THE RESORT

Flims is set on a sunny mountain terrace and has two parts: Dorf is the main village and lift base, spread along a busy road; Waldhaus is a leafy suburb with the smart hotels (which run efficient courtesy buses). The slopes spread across to a lift station outside the smaller village of Laax. There's also a high-speed quad at even smaller Falera, 5km/3 miles away.

THE MOUNTAINS

Flims has extensive, varied slopes and some high, exposed peaks, including a small glacier. In poor visibility there are plenty of tree-lined runs. Trips are possible by car to Lenzerheide, Davos-Klosters and Arosa.

After fooling around with various innovations, the resort has reverted to a normal piste map. It shows 'downhill/free-ride routes' in yellow without explaining what they are – in particular, whether they are avalanche-protected, and patrolled: scandalous. Don't be tempted to tackle the green runs – they are footpaths.

Slopes There are powerful gondolas going into the heart of the slopes from both Flims Dorf and Laax (where there's a cable-car too, of exceptional length). Above mid-mountain, there is a complex web of lifts and runs. Some chairs (eg to Naraus) are designed as much for walkers as skiers – skis are taken off.

Terrain-parks The terrain-park at Crap Sogn Gion is claimed to be Europe's best. As well as the two half-pipes, with walls up to 6.7m/22ft, there are drops, jumps, quarter-pipes, rails for

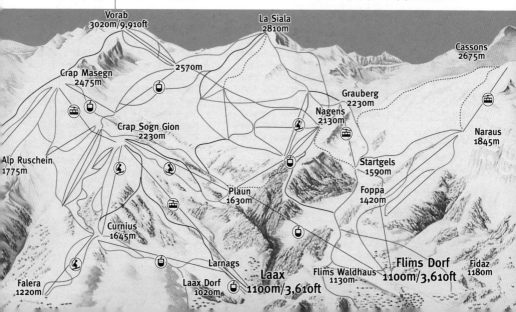

KEY FACTS

Resort	1100m
	3,610ft
Altitude	1100-3020m
	3,610-9,910ft
Lifts	29
Pistes	220km
	137 miles
Blue	35%
Red	40%
Black	25%
Snowmaking	13km
	8 miles

Phone numbers
From elsewhere in Switzerland add the prefix 081.
From abroad use the prefix +41 81.

TOURIST OFFICES

Flims
t 920 9200

Laax
t 921 8181

Falera
t 921 3030

For all three resorts:
tourismus@alpen arena.ch
www.alpenarena.ch

all levels and a boarder-cross. A Pipe & Park day pass is available. There's a park and a half-pipe on the glacier.

Snow reliability Upper runs are snow-sure, but those back to Flims can suffer from sun. There is snowmaking on the main runs from Crap Sogn Gion, from Segnes-Hütte to Flims and on part of the run to Alp Ruschein.

Experts The few black pistes are not seriously steep except in patches, but the 'free-ride routes' add an extra dimension and there is abundant off-piste terrain too. In such a sunny area, timing your runs can be crucial to avoid rock-hard moguls.

Intermediates This is a superb area for all intermediates. There are easy snow-sure blue runs on the Vorab glacier and good blue cruising lower down – the bowl below La Siala is huge and gentle. For the more adventurous and confident, there are plenty of reds and some blacks worth trying – especially the superb, long Sattel run from the Vorab glacier, and the men's World Cup Downhill piste from Crap Sogn Gion to Larnags, which is often beautifully groomed. Flims is also a good area to learn off-piste.

Beginners There's a nursery area in Dorf, and alternatives at Crap Sogn Gion and Nagens if snow is poor. The Foppa and Curnius areas have good easy runs to move on to.

Snowboarding This is a snowboard hot spot. Crap Sogn Gion is a popular meeting point, with loud music from the bars that overlook half-pipes.

Cross-country There are 60km/37 miles of trails scattered around.

Queues At weekends coach loads of day visitors arrive at the Laax lift base, although this did not affect a 2005 visitor. Lifts closing because of wind has been a common complaint.

Mountain restaurants All 15 are briefly described on the piste map. There are some stylish modern table-service places at altitude – Das Elephant and Capalari. We prefer the huts lower down, such as the smartly rustic Tegia Larnags and cosy Runcahöhe (which attracts as many walkers as skiers).

Schools and guides The school has a good reputation. It offers several innovative programmes such as special free-riding and park-and-pipe courses.

Facilities for children Children aged three and over can be looked after at one of the Dreamland centres. And there is a Snow Kids Village in the ski school. Nannies are available.

STAYING THERE

How to go Only a handful of UK tour operators feature Flims.

Hotels In Waldhaus the Adula (928 2828) and Cresta (911 3535) have been recommended. The award-winning Park Hotel (928 4848) has an ultra-modern wellness centre. In Dorf the Bellevue (911 3131) is 'highly recommended'.

Self-catering The tourist office has a long list of available apartments.

Eating out Most Flims restaurants are in hotels. Reporters recommend the Alpina (Waldhaus) and the Pomodoro.

Après-ski Flims is pretty quiet. If you want action, head for Laax lift base and the Crap Bar, the Riders Palace bar and its club. The 'friendly' Iglu and the Stenna bar are packed at close of play. Casa Veglia has live bands.

Off the slopes There's an enormous sports centre, with ice rink, and 60km/37 miles of marked walks. Historic Chur is a bus-ride away.

Laax 1100m/3,610ft

The modern development at the base of the Crap Sogn Gion cable-car, Murschetg, now seems to be called Laax. Here, the high-tech Riders Palace (927 9700) is a trendy place to stay – with dorm as well as normal rooms. The village of Laax, now called Laax Dorf, is a quiet place a short drive/bus-ride away with a rustic centre and pleasant suburbs spreading around a lake Here, the little Posta Veglia (921 4466) is the place to stay or eat – excellent food in a lovely old stube, and in a plainer restaurant behind.

Falera 1220m/4,000ft

This tiny village is quiet and traffic-free and has good views over three valleys. Most accommodation is in apartments. Two successive fast quad chairs take you to the heart of the slopes.

Grindelwald

Traditional town in spectacular scenery at the foot of the Eiger

485

COSTS

① ② ③ ④ ⑤ ⑥

RATINGS

The slopes

Fast lifts	***
Snow	**
Extent	***
Expert	**
Intermediate	****
Beginner	***
Convenience	**
Queues	**
Mountain restaurants	***

The rest

Scenery	*****
Resort charm	****
Off-slope	****

NEWS

For 2004/05 the railway from Grindelwald to the Kleine Scheidegg got new panoramic rolling stock and a 'more sophisticated' timetable. But it is still slow.

For 2003/04 the Läger double chair-lift on Männlichen was replaced by a fast quad with covers, doubling capacity.

➕ Dramatically set in magnificent scenery, directly beneath the towering north face of the Eiger

➕ Lots of long, gentle runs, ideal for intermediates, with links to Wengen

➕ Pleasant old village with long mountaineering history

➕ Fair amount to do off the slopes, including splendid walks

➖ Village gets very little midwinter sun

➖ Few challenging pistes for experts

➖ Inconvenient for visiting Mürren

➖ Snow-cover unreliable

➖ Major area accessed by a painfully slow, queue-prone (especially at weekends) gondola or by slow trains

For stunning views from the town and the slopes, there are few places to rival Grindelwald. The village is nowhere near as special as Wengen or Mürren, just over the hill, but staying here does give you direct access to Grindelwald's own First area. But you can spend ages queueing for, waiting for or sitting in the gondola or trains up into the Kleine Scheidegg area shared with Wengen. (The gondola ride – the longest in Europe according to Grindelwald's literature – takes half an hour. The train to Kleine Scheidegg from Grindelwald takes about the same.) Grindelwald regulars accept all this as part of the scene.

THE RESORT

Grindelwald is set either side of a road along a narrow valley. Buildings are mainly traditional chalet-style. Towering mountains rise steeply from the valley floor, and the resort and main slopes get very little sun in January.

Grindelwald can feel very jolly at times, such as during the ice-carving festival in January, when huge ice-sculptures are on display along the main street. The village is livelier at night than the other Jungfrau resorts of Wengen and Mürren. There's live music in several bars and hotels, but it isn't a place for bopping until dawn.

The main lifts into the slopes shared with Wengen are at Grund, right at the bottom of the sloping village. Near the opposite end of the village, a gondola goes to the separate First area. Trains run from the centre to Grund or direct to Kleine Scheidegg, and buses link the lift stations – but these get congested at times and reporters say they are too infrequent.

The most convenient place to stay for the slopes is at Grund. But this is out of the centre and rather charmless. There's a wide range of hotels in the heart of the village, handy enough for everything else, including the First area, at the foot of which are nursery slopes, ski school and kindergarten.

Trips to other resorts are not very easy, but you can drive to Adelboden. Getting to the tougher, higher slopes of Mürren is a lengthy business unless you go to Lauterbrunnen by car.

THE MOUNTAINS

The major area of slopes is shared with Wengen and offers a mix of wooded slopes and open slopes higher up. The smaller First area is mainly open, though there are wooded runs to the village. The Aletsch glacier, which can be seen from the Jungfraujoch station (see feature panel later in this chapter), has been declared a UNESCO World Nature Heritage Site.

THE SLOPES
Broad and mainly gentle

From Grund, near the western end of town, you can get to **Männlichen** by an

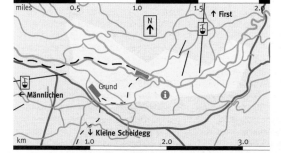

SWITZERLAND

KEY FACTS

Resort	1035m
	3,400ft

Jungfrau region

Slopes	945-2970m
	3,100-9,740ft
Lifts	44
Pistes	213km
	133 miles
Blue	25%
Red	61%
Black	14%
Snowmaking	60km
	37 miles

First-Männlichen-Kleine-Scheidegg only

Slopes	945-2485m
	3,100-8,150ft
Lifts	30
Pistes	150km
	93 miles

LIFT PASSES

Jungfrau Top Ski Region
Covers Grindelwald, Wengen and Mürren lifts, trains between them and Grindelwald ski-bus.

Beginners
No special pass

Main pass
1 day SF56
6 days SF288

Senior citizens
Over 62: 6 days SF259

Children
Under 20: 6 days SF230
Under 16: 6 days SF144
Under 6: free pass

Notes
Day pass price is for Grindelwald and Wengen area only.

Alternative passes
Passes available for Grindelwald and Wengen only and for Mürren only. Non-skiers pass available.

appallingly slow two-stage gondola or to **Kleine Scheidegg** by an equally slow cog railway. The slopes of the separate south-facing First area are reached by a long, slow three-stage gondola starting a bus-ride east of the centre. From all over the slopes there are superb views, not only of the Eiger but also of the Wetterhorn and other peaks. Piste marking is poor, especially at First complains a reporter, who twice failed to find the new Schwarzer Traum (Black Dream) run down from Oberjoch, and another who says it is difficult to determine which run you are on – and therefore easy to end up at the wrong point in the valley.

TERRAIN-PARKS
First things first
There is a terrain-park at Oberjoch and a super-pipe at Schrekfeld, both on First.

SNOW RELIABILITY
Poor
Grindelwald's low altitude (the slopes go down to below 1000m/3,280ft and few are above 2000m/6,560ft) and the lack of much snowmaking mean this is not a resort to book far in advance or for a late-season holiday. First is sunny, and so even less snow-sure than the main area. We have also had reports of 'patchy' piste grooming.

FOR EXPERTS
They are trying
The area is quite limited for experts, but there is some fine off-piste if the snow is good. Heli-trips with mountain guides are organised. The black run on First beneath the gondola back to town is quite tough, especially when the snow has suffered from the sun.

FOR INTERMEDIATES
Ideal intermediate terrain
In good snow, First makes a splendid intermediate playground, though the general lack of trees makes the area less friendly than the larger Kleine Scheidegg-Männlichen area. The runs to the valley are great fun. Nearly all the runs from Kleine Scheidegg are long blues or gentle reds. On the Männlichen there's a choice of gentle runs down to the mid-station of the gondola up from Grund. In good snow, you can get right down to the bottom on easy red runs – 'barely deserving the grade', says a reporter (and one of these runs used to be marked black).

For tougher pistes, head for the top of the Lauberhorn lift and the runs to Kleine Scheidegg, or to Wixi (following the start of the downhill course). You could also try the north-facing run from Eigergletscher to Salzegg, which often has the best snow late in the season.

FOR BEGINNERS
Depends where you go
The Bodmi nursery slope at the bottom of First is scenic but can suffer from the sun and its low altitude – a 2004 reporter said Grindelwald instructors used it despite it being icy, full of craters and spoiled by fast skiers and tobogganers racing through. Kleine Scheidegg has a better, higher beginner area and splendid long runs to progress to, served by the railway.

FOR CROSS-COUNTRY
Good but shady
There are 25km/16 miles of prepared tracks. Almost all of this is on the valley floor, so it's shady in mid-winter and may have poor snow later on.

SCHOOLS

Grindelwald Sports
t 854 1280

**Buri Sport
(snowboard)**
t 853 3353

**Snowsports Kleine
Scheidegg**
t 855 1545

Classes
(Sports prices)
5 full days SF270

Private lessons
SF320 for 1 day

CHILDREN

Kinderhort Sunshine
t 853 0440
Ages from 1mnth;
9.30-4pm (SF62 per
day)

Kidsclub Bodmi
t 854 1280
Ages from 3; 9.15-
3.30; SF50 per day

Ski school
Takes children from
age 4 (5 days SF270)

REPORTS WANTED

Recently we have
had few reports on
this resort. If you
go there, please do
send us a report.

boarding

Intermediates will enjoy the area most – the beginners' slopes can be bare, while experts will hanker for Mürren's steep, off-piste slopes. First is the main boarders' mountain, not only because of the terrain-park and big pipe but also the open free-ride terrain accessed via the top lifts. There are still quite a few drag-lifts.

QUEUES
Can be dreadful at peak times
The queues for the gondola and train at Grund can be very bad in high season, especially at weekends. And Saturday queues are exacerbated because children up to 15 can ski free if a parent buys a one-day pass on Saturday. A recent reporter told of half-hour waits for the gondola. But the upgrading of the Läger chair cut queues on the top half of the Männlichen. And a Christmas 2005 visitor tells us, 'I never queued once for a lift or train.' You may find long waits for the gondola down from First when the lower runs are closed.

MOUNTAIN RESTAURANTS
Wide choice
See the Wengen chapter for options around Kleine Scheidegg and down towards Wengen. Brandegg, on the railway, is recommended for 'wonderful' apple fritters and its sunny terrace. Berghaus Bort does very good rösti, but the 'best rösti anywhere' is at the Jägerstubli, off the Rennstrecke piste. There are splendid views from Mannlichen, and the Spycher there has a cosy indoor bar plus deckchairs and an ice-bar, which also serves sandwiches. At First, Café Genepi at the bottom of the Oberjoch chair serves 'tasty pasta', and has a splendid terrace.

SCHOOLS AND GUIDES
Mixed views
One report declares the main school, Grindelwald Sports, 'very good'; spoken English is normally excellent. But a 2005 reporter had a 'wasted' first day, because abilities were not assessed before the class. However, 'the teachers (three in three days!) were excellent'. And a 2004 reporter criticised the school for taking her children to the First beginner area when the Kleine Scheidegg 'is better and more convenient for families who want to ski together'.

FACILITIES FOR CHILDREN
Good reputation
See above, but a past reporter who put four children through the Grindelwald mill praised caring and effective instructors. The First mountain restaurant runs a day nursery, which is a neat idea, and the Sunshine nursery is at the top of Männlichen.

Grindelwald

487

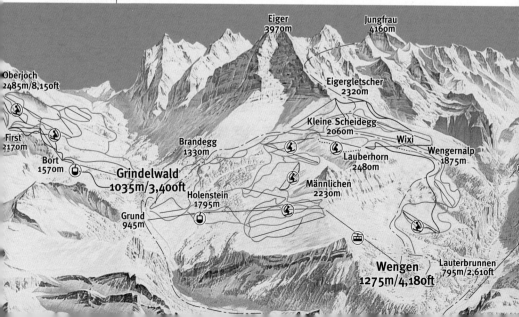

GETTING THERE

Air Zürich 195km/
121 miles (3hr); Bern
70km/43 miles
(1½hr).

Rail Station in resort.

ACTIVITIES

Indoor Sports centre
(swimming pool,
sauna, steam, fitness
room, games room),
indoor ice rink,
bowling, curling,
concerts, cinema

Outdoor 80km/
50 miles of cleared
paths, train rides to
Jungfraujoch, ice rink,
tobogganing, snow-
shoe excursions,
climbing, snow
tubing, paragliding,
glacier tours, sleigh
rides, husky rides

Phone numbers
From elsewhere in
Switzerland add the
prefix 033.
From abroad use the
prefix +41 33.

TOURIST OFFICE

t 854 1212
touristcenter@
grindelwald.ch
www.grindelwald.com

STAYING THERE

HOW TO GO
Limited range of packages
The hotels UK tour operators offer are
mainly at the upper end of the market.
Hotels There's a 5-star, a dozen 4-stars
and plenty of more modest places.
((((5) **Grand Regina** (854 8600) Big
and imposing 5-star; right next to the
station. Nightly music in the bar. Pool.
((((4) **Belvedere** (854 5757) Family-run,
close to the station. 'Wonderful' pool.
(((4) **Schweizerhof** (853 2202) 4-star
chalet at west end of the centre, close
to the station. Pool.
((((4) **Spinne** (854 8888) Central 4-star
which a reporter 'cannot praise enough:
friendly, superb food, good rooms'.
(((3) **Hirschen** (854 8484) Family-run 3-
star by nursery slopes. Good food.
(((3) **Derby** (854 5461) Popular, modern
3-star next to station, with 'first-class'
service, good food and great views.
(((3) **Eigerblick** (854 1020) A bit away
from the station but 'great service,
including free taxi'. Huge bedrooms.
(1) **Hotel Wetterhorn** (853 1218) Cosy,
simple chalet way beyond the village,
with great views of the glacier.
Self-catering Reporters recommend the
apartments of the hotels Hirschen (854
8484) and Eiger (854 3131).

EATING OUT
Hotel based
There's a wide choice of good hotel
restaurants. Among the more traditional
places are: the Bistro-Bar Memory in the
Eiger; Schmitte in the Schweizerhof;
Challi-Stübli in the Kreuz; and the Alte
Post. The Fiescherblick's Swiss Bistro is
'brilliant but expensive'. The Kirchbühl
and Oberland are good for vegetarians,
the Bahnhof in the Derby for fondue
and raclette. Hotel Spinne has many
options: Italian, Mexican, Chinese and
the candlelit Rôtisserie for a special
romantic meal. Onkle Tom's Hutte is

recommended for pizza. The Latino
does Italian home cooking.

APRES-SKI
Getting livelier
Tipirama at Kleine Scheidegg is a fun
place immediately after skiing,
sometimes with DJs and live bands.
Pumuckl's offers a similar experience
on First. In town, the terrace of the
C&M Café is good for coffee and cake,
and the Down Town teepee has live
music and DJs. There are at least three
discos and a handful of bars that aim
to keep going late. The Espresso bar in
the Spinne hotel seems to be the
liveliest. There's also a cinema, and ice
hockey and curling matches to watch.
There's an excellent sports centre with
pool. Tobogganing and tubing are
organised on First, and some evenings
a 'Sledge Express' train takes people
up to Brandegg/Alpiglen for fondues.

OFF THE SLOPES
Plenty to do, easy to get around
There are many cleared paths with
magnificent views, especially around
First – and there's a special (though
expensive) pedestrian bus/lift pass. A
trip to Jungfraujoch is spectacular (see
below), and excursions by train are
easy to Interlaken and possible to
Bern. Tobogganing has undergone a
renaissance, with runs up to 15km/9
miles on First (the world's longest –
bear in mind it's a two-and-a-half-hour
uphill walk from the top of the
gondola) and 57km/35 miles of runs in
total. Helicopter flights from
Männlichen are recommended.

STAYING UP THE MOUNTAIN
Several possibilities
See the Wengen chapter for details of
rooms at Kleine Scheidegg. The
Berghaus Bort (853 3651), at the
gondola station in the middle of the
First area, is an attractive alternative.

THE JOURNEY TO THE TOP OF EUROPE

*From Kleine Scheidegg you can take a train through the Eiger to the highest
railway station in Europe – Jungfraujoch at 3454m/11,332ft. The journey is a bit
tedious – you're in a tunnel except when you stop to look out of two galleries
carved into the sheer north face of the Eiger. From the first there are magnificent
views over to Männlichen and the village; from the second you overlook the
glacier. At the top is a big restaurant complex. There's an 'ice palace' carved out
of the glacier, an outdoor 'plateau' to wander around and a viewing tower with
fabulous views of the Aletsch glacier (a UNESCO World Heritage Site).*

*The cost is SF50.50 with a Jungfrau lift pass for three days or more. At the top
the air is thin, and some people have breathing or balance problems.*

Mürren

Stupendous views, an epic run, and a chocolate-box village

RATINGS

The slopes

Fast lifts	***
Snow	***
Extent	*
Expert	***
Intermediate	***
Beginner	**
Convenience	***
Queues	***
Mountain restaurants	**

The rest

Scenery	*****
Charm	*****
Off-slope	***

NEWS

There isn't much that changes in Mürren. That's one of the things that makes it so special. However, more snowmaking was installed down to Mürren for 2004/05, and is expected on runs via Winteregg towards Lauterbrunnen for the coming season.

➕ Tiny, charming, traditional 'traffic-free' village, with snowy paths and chocolate-box chalets

➕ Stupendous scenery, best enjoyed on the challenging run from the panoramic Schilthorn

➕ Good sports centre

➕ Good snow high up, even when the rest of the region is suffering

➖ Extent of local pistes very limited, no matter what your level of expertise

➖ Lower slopes can be in poor condition

➖ Quiet, limited nightlife

Mürren is one of our favourite resorts. There may be other mountain villages that are equally pretty, but none of them enjoys views like those from Mürren across the deep valley to the rock faces and glaciers of the Eiger, Mönch and Jungfrau: simply breathtaking. Then there's the Schilthorn run – 1300m/4,270ft vertical with an unrivalled combination of varied terrain and glorious views.

Our visits are normally one-day affairs; holidaymakers, we concede, are likely to want to explore the extensive intermediate slopes of Wengen and Grindelwald, across the valley. And you have to accept that getting there takes time.

It was in Mürren that the British more or less invented modern skiing. Sir Arnold Lunn organised the first ever slalom race here in 1922. Some 12 years earlier his father, Sir Henry, had persuaded the locals to open the railway in winter so that he could bring the first winter package tour here. Sir Arnold's son Peter, who first skied here in November 1916, still skis here with his children and grandchildren. He still takes part in the annual Inferno race and you may bump into him around the village bars.

THE RESORT

Mürren is set on a shelf high above the Lauterbrunnen valley floor, across from Wengen, and can be reached only by cable-car from Stechelberg (via Gimmelwald) or by funicular and then railway from Lauterbrunnen. Once you get there you can't fail to be struck by Mürren's tranquillity and beauty. The tiny village is made up of paths and narrow lanes weaving between tiny wooden chalets and a handful of bigger hotel buildings. The roofs and paths are normally snow-covered.

Two further stages of the cable-car take you up to the high slopes of Birg and the Schilthorn. Last season, however, these were out of action until mid-March, severely restricting the available terrain. Hopefully they will be fully operational for 2005/06. Nearby lifts go to the main lower slopes, and a funicular halfway along the village accesses the other lower slopes.

Mürren's traffic-free status is being somewhat eroded and there are now a few delivery trucks. But the place still isn't plagued by electric carts and taxis in the way that most other traditional 'traffic-free' resorts now are.

It's not the place to go for lively nightlife, shopping or showing off your latest gear to admiring hordes. It is the place to go if you want tranquillity and stunning views. The village is so small that location is not a concern. Nothing is more than a few minutes' walk.

THE MOUNTAIN

Mürren's slopes aren't extensive (53km/33 miles in total). But it has something for everyone, including one of our favourite runs, and a vertical of some 1300m/4,270ft. And those happy to take the time to cross the valley to Wengen-Grindelwald will find plenty of options. These resorts are covered by the Jungfrau lift pass.

THE SLOPES
Small but interesting

There are three connected areas around the village, reaching no higher than 2145m/7,040ft. The biggest is

KEY FACTS

Resort	1650m
	5,410ft

Jungfrau region

Altitude	945-2970m
	3,100-9,740ft
Lifts	44
Pistes	213km
	133 miles
Blue	25%
Red	61%
Black	14%
Snowmaking	60km
	37 miles

Mürren-Schilthorn only

Slopes	1650-2970m
	5,410-9,740ft
Lifts	12
Pistes	53km
	33 miles

LIFT PASSES

Jungfrau Top Ski Region
Covers Wengen, Mürren and Grindelwald, trains between them and Grindelwald ski-bus.

Beginners
No special pass

Main pass
1 day SF56
6 days SF288

Senior citizens
Over 62: 6 days SF259

Children
Under 20: 6 days SF230
Under 16: 6 days SF144
Under 6: free pass

Notes
Day pass price is for Mürren-Schilthorn area only.

Alternative passes
Passes available for Grindelwald and Wengen only and for Mürren. Non-skiers pass available.

SCHOOLS

Swiss
t 855 1247

Classes
6 2hr days SF180

Private lessons
SF120 for 2hr for 1-4 persons

boarding

Like many Swiss resorts, Mürren has a traditional image, but it is trying to move with the times and offer a more snowboard-friendly attitude – and the major lifts are cable-cars and chair-lifts. The terrain above Mürren is suitable mainly for good free-riders – it's steep, with a lot of off-piste. Intermediates will find the area tough and limited; nearby Wengen is ideal, and much better for beginners.

Schiltgrat, served by a fast quad chair behind the cable-car station. You can also get there from the top of the funicular that goes from the middle of the village to the nursery slope at **Allmendhubel** – from where a run and a fast chair take you to the slightly higher **Maulerhubel**. Runs go down from here to the Winteregg stop on the railway. These lower slopes take you up to around 2000m/6,560ft.

Much more interesting are the higher slopes reached by cable-car. The first stage takes you to Birg and the **Engetal** area, where an old T-bar serves short, steep, shady slopes. Two chair-lifts below the Engetal serve some snow-sure intermediate slopes. To get back to the Birg cable-car station and avoid the tricky black run down to the village, you face an annoying walk up from these chairs to the old T-bar.

The final stage of the cable-car takes you up to the summit of the **Schilthorn** and the Piz Gloria revolving restaurant, made famous by the James Bond film *On Her Majesty's Secret Service*. In good snow you can go all the way from here to Lauterbrunnen – almost 16km/10 miles. The Inferno race (see separate box) takes place over this course, conditions permitting. Below Winteregg station, it's all boring paths down to Lauterbrunnen.

TERRAIN-PARKS
Affirmative
There is a terrain-park on the lower slopes of Schiltgrat.

SNOW RELIABILITY
Good on the upper slopes
The Jungfrau region does not have a good snow record – but Mürren always has the best snow in the area. When Wengen-Grindelwald (and Mürren's lower slopes) have problems, the Schilthorn and Engetal often have packed powder snow because of their height and orientation – north-east to east. The runs from below Engetal to Allmendhubel and parts of the lower slopes have snowmaking – and a 2004 reporter complains of it being left on at midday forming 'lumps of wet icing sugar' while another tells of bare patches on the lower slopes being left that way. A 2005 reporter tells of 'random piste grooming despite half of Mürren being closed because of the cable-car problems'.

FOR EXPERTS
One wonderful piste
The run from the top of the Schilthorn starts with a steep but not terrifying slope, in the past generally mogulled but now often groomed. It flattens into a schuss to Engetal, below Birg. Then there's a wonderful, wide run with stunning views over the valley to the Eiger, Mönch and Jungfrau. Since the chair-lifts were built here you can play on these upper runs for as long as you like. Below the lifts you hit the Kanonenrohr (gun barrel). This is a very narrow shelf with solid rock on one side and a steep drop on the other – protected by nets. After an open slope and scrappy zig-zag path,

THE INFERNO RACE

Every January 1,800 amateurs compete in Mürren's spectacular Inferno race. Conditions permitting, and they usually don't, the race goes from the top of the Schilthorn right down to Lauterbrunnen – a vertical drop of 2175m/7,140ft and a distance of almost 16km/10 miles, incorporating a short climb at Maulerhubel. The racers start individually at 12 second intervals; the fastest finish the course in around 15 minutes, but anything under half an hour is very respectable.

The race was started by Sir Arnold Lunn in 1928, when he and his friends climbed up to spend the night in a mountain hut and then raced down in the morning. For many years the race was organised by the British-run Kandahar Club, and there is still a strong British presence among the competitors.

CHILDREN

Snowgarden
Ages 1mnth to 5yr

Ski school
Takes ages 5 and
over (6 2hr days
SF180).

you arrive at the 'hog's back' and can descend towards the village on either side of Allmendhubel.

From Schiltgrat a short, serious mogul run – the Kandahar – descends towards the village, but experts are more likely to be interested in the off-piste runs into the Blumental – both from here (the north-facing Blumenlucke run) and from Birg (the sunnier Tschingelchrachen) – or the adventurous runs from the Schilthorn.

FOR INTERMEDIATES
Limited, but Wengen nearby
Keen piste-bashers will want to make a few trips to the long cruising runs of Wengen-Grindelwald. The best easy cruising run in Mürren is the north-facing blue down to Winteregg. The reds on the other low slopes can get mogulled, and snow conditions can be poor. The area below the Engetal normally has good snow, and you can choose your gradient.

FOR BEGINNERS
Not ideal, but adequate
The nursery slopes at Allmendhubel, at the top of the funicular, are on the steep side. And there are not many easy runs to graduate to – though the blue down the Winteregg chair is easy,

and a couple of blues are served by the long Gimmeln drag and the less tiring Schiltgrat chair.

FOR CROSS-COUNTRY
Forget it
There is one small loop above the village in the Blumental, and more extensive loops down at Lauterbrunnen or Stechelberg. But snow is unreliable at valley height.

QUEUES
Generally not a problem
Mürren doesn't get as crowded as Wengen and Grindelwald, except on sunny Sundays. There can be queues for the cable-cars – usually when snow shortages bring in people from lower resorts. The top stage has only one cabin.

MOUNTAIN RESTAURANTS
Nothing outstanding
Piz Gloria revolves once an hour, displaying a fabulous 360° panorama of peaks and lakes. We don't like the ambience here, but a 2004 reporter tells of 'a very nice goulash soup' and says, 'It is incredible value for money just for the view (and cheaper than Méribel).' By the Engetal chair-lifts, the Schilthornhütte is small and rustic and

The pretty, car-free village sits on a shelf high above the Lauterbrunnen valley →

SNOWPIX.COM / CHRIS GILL

GETTING THERE

Air Zürich 195km/ 121 miles (3½hr); Bern 70km/43 miles (1½hr).

Rail Lauterbrunnen; transfer by mountain railway and tram.

ACTIVITIES

Indoor Alpine Sports Centre: swimming pool, sauna, solarium, steam bath, massage, fitness room, gymnasium, squash, library, museum

Outdoor Ice rink, curling, ice-climbing, tobogganing, 12km/ 7 miles cleared paths, snow-shoeing

WEBSITES

For links to resort sites, go to our own new site at www.wtss.co.uk

Phone numbers
From elsewhere in Switzerland add the prefix 033.
From abroad use the prefix +41 33.

TOURIST OFFICE

t 856 8686
info@muerren.ch
www.wengen-muerren.ch

'does excellent special coffees'. Lower down, the Suppenalp in the Blumental is rustic and quietly set but gets no sun in January. A 2005 reporter talks of 'friendly service' and 'fantastic goulash soup and macaroni with apple sauce'. As you might expect, Sonnenberg is sunnier and a reporter enjoyed 'marvellous rösti'. Gimmeln is a self-service place with a large terrace, famous for its apple cake. Winteregg does something similar, as well as 'superb rösti' and 'the best burger east of the Rockies'. Both have little playgrounds to amuse kids.

SCHOOLS AND GUIDES
Long tradition
We lack recent reports, but the school has a long tradition of teaching Brits.

FACILITIES FOR CHILDREN
Adequate
There is a baby slope with a rope tow. And there is a children's club at the sports centre. The ski school takes children from five years.

STAYING THERE

HOW TO GO
Mainly hotels, packaged or not
A handful of operators offer packages to Mürren.
Hotels There are fewer than a dozen hotels, ranging widely in style.
((((④ **Anfi Palace** (856 9999) Victorian pile near station.
((((④ **Eiger** (856 5454) Plain-looking 'chalet' blocks next to railway station, widely recommended; good blend of efficiency and charm; good food; pool.
(((③ **Alpenruh** (856 8800) Attractively renovated chalet next to the cable-car.
(((③ **Edelweiss** (856 5600) Block-like but friendly; good food and facilities.
(((③ **Jungfrau** (855 4545) Perfectly placed for families, in front of the baby slope and close to the funicular.
((② **Alpenblick** (855 1327) Simple, small, modern chalet near station.
Self-catering There are plenty of chalets and apartments in the village for independent travellers to rent.

EATING OUT
Mainly in hotels
The main alternative to hotels is the rustic Stägerstübli – a bar as well as restaurant. The locals eat in the little diner at the back. The food at the Eiger hotel is good, and the Bellevue and Alpenruh get good reports.

APRES-SKI
Not devoid of life
The Eiger Bar (in the Eiger guest house, not the hotel) is the Brits' meeting place. The new Iglu bar near the bottom of the Allmendubel train makes a good stop at the end of the day. The tiny Stägerstübli is cosy, and the place to meet locals. The Anfi Palace's Balloon bar is an attempt at a trendy cocktail bar; it also has a weekend disco, the Inferno. The Bliemli Chäller disco in the Blumental hotel caters for kids, the nightly Tachi disco in the Eiger for a more mixed crowd.

OFF THE SLOPES
Tranquillity but not much else
There isn't a lot to amuse people who don't hit the slopes except the scenery and a very good sports centre with an outdoor ice rink. Excursions to Bern and Interlaken are easy and friends can return to the village for lunch easily. The only problem with meeting at the top of the cable-car is the expense.

STAYING DOWN THE VALLEY
A cheaper option
Lauterbrunnen is a good budget base, with a resort atmosphere and access to both Wengen and Mürren until late. We've happily stayed at the Schützen (855 3026) and Oberland (855 1241); the Silberhorn (856 2210) has been recommended. It's fairly quiet in the evenings.

Saas-Fee

Beautiful car-free village with slopes on top of the world

COSTS

① ② ③ ④ ⑤ ⑥

RATINGS

The slopes
Fast lifts	★★★
Snow	★★★★★
Extent	★★
Expert	★★★
Intermediate	★★★★
Beginner	★★★★★
Convenience	★★★
Queues	★★★
Mountain restaurants	★★★

The rest
Scenery	★★★★
Charm	★★★★★
Off-slope	★★★★

NEWS

For 2005/06 a big new restaurant is due to open at Morenia, at mid-mountain.

Also for this winter we are told that the Längfluh chair will be replaced by a quad.

For 2006/07 the slopes around Britanniahütte are to be developed, with a six-pack and a T-bar.

With surprisingly little fuss, the resort has acquired four electric buses – a much cheaper alternative to the electric taxis.

＋ Spectacular setting amid high peaks and glaciers

＋ Traditional, 'traffic-free' village

＋ Most of the runs are at exceptionally high altitude, and snow-sure

＋ Good off-slope facilities – even a mountain specially for walking and tobogganing

－ Disappointingly small area of slopes, with mainly easy runs

－ Glacier limits off-piste exploration

－ Much of the area is in shadow in midwinter – cold and dark

－ Bad weather can shut the slopes

－ Long village can mean long walks

－ Some visitors suffer altitude problems at top of mountain

Saas-Fee is one of our favourite places – a sort of miniature Zermatt without the conspicuous consumption. And good snow is guaranteed, even late in the season: the altitude you spend most of your time at – between 2500m and 3500m (8,200ft and 11,480ft) – is unrivalled in the Alps.

But we tend to drop in here for a couple of days at a time, so the limited extent of the slopes never becomes a problem; for a week's holiday, it would. Top to bottom there is an impressive 1800m/5,900ft vertical – but there aren't many alternative ways down. Keen, mileage-hungry intermediates should look elsewhere, as should experts (except those prepared to go touring). For the rest, it's a question of priorities and expectations. Over to you.

THE RESORT

Like nearby Zermatt, Saas-Fee is a high-altitude mountain village centred on narrow streets lined by attractive old chalets and free of cars (there are car parks at the resort entrance) but not free of electric milk floats posing as taxis. On most other counts, Saas-Fee and its more exalted neighbour are a long way apart in style.

There are some very smart hotels (plus many more modest ones) and plenty of good eating and drinking places. But there's little of the glamour and greed that, for some, spoil Zermatt – and even the electric taxis here are driven at a more considerate pace. Saas-Fee still feels like a village, with its cow sheds more obviously still containing cows. The village may be chilly in January, but when the spring sun is beating down, Saas-Fee is a quite beautiful place in which to just stroll around and relax.

Depending on where you're staying and which way you want to go up the mountain, you may do more marching through the village than strolling, though. It's a long walk from one end to the other. Three major lifts start from the southern end of the village, at the foot of the slopes, and lots of the hotels and apartments (particularly cheaper ones) are 1km/0.5 miles or more away. The biggest lift, though – the Alpin Express gondola – starts from a more central location. Your hotel may run a courtesy taxi, and there are now affordable little public buses. You can store kit near the lifts, which helps.

The village centre has the school and guides' office, the church and a few more shops than elsewhere, but it doesn't add up to much. On a sunny day, though, the restaurant terraces fronting the nursery slopes at the south end of the village are a magnet,

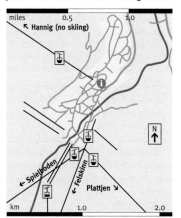

miles   0.5   1.0
↖ Hannig (no skiing)

N ↑

← Spielboden

← Felskinn

Plattjen ↘

km   1.0   2.0

KEY FACTS

Resort	1800m
	5,910ft
Slopes	1800-3500m
	5,910-11,480ft
Lifts	22
Pistes	100km
	62 miles
Blue	25%
Red	50%
Black	25%
Snowmaking	8km
	5 miles

LIFT PASSES

Saas-Fee area
Covers all lifts in Saas-Fee only.

Beginners
Cheap pass for nursery lifts in village.

Main pass
1 day SF60
6 days SF299

Children
Under 16: 6 days SF179
Under 6: free pass

Notes
Single and return tickets on most main lifts. Afternoon pass available. Free passes for second and all further children when two adults purchase for 6 days or more.

Alternative passes
Separate passes for each of the other Saastal ski areas (Saas-Grund, Saas-Almagell, Saas-Balen). Pass for all four villages also available; includes ski-bus between them.

with breathtaking views up to the ring of 4000m/13,120ft peaks – you can see why the village is called 'The Pearl of the Alps'.

The slopes of Saas-Almagell and Saas-Grund are not far away, and you can buy a lift pass that covers all these resorts and frequent buses between the villages. There is a footpath down to Saas-Almagell, which one reporter enjoyed skiing down. Day trips by car/train to Zermatt are also possible.

THE MOUNTAIN

The area is a strange mixture of powerful modern lifts (a two-stage 30-person gondola followed by an underground funicular which take you up 1700m/5,580ft vertical) and a lot of old-fashioned T-bars (there's only one chair-lift). Blame the glaciers, which move too quickly for chair-lifts. Readers complain about the 'walks and climbs' involved in getting from one lift to another. Take it easy when climbing out of the top lift station: the altitude of 3500m/ 11,480ft means some people feel faint because of the thin air.

The upper slopes are largely gentle, while the lower mountain, below the glacier, is steeper and rockier, needing good snow-cover. There is very little shelter in bad weather: during and after heavy snowfalls you may find yourself limited to the nursery area.

Saas-Fee is one of the leading resorts for mountaineering and ski touring from valley to valley. Several nearby peaks can be climbed, and the extended Haute Route from Chamonix via Zermatt ends here.

THE SLOPES
A glacier runs through it
There are two routes up to the main **Felskinn** area. The 30-person Alpin Express jumbo gondola, starting across the river from the main village, takes you to Felskinn via a mid-station at Morenia (where you have to change

cabins). The alternative is a short drag across the nursery slope at the south end of the village, and then the Felskinn cable-car. From Felskinn, the Metro Alpin underground funicular hurtles up to **Allalin**. From below here, the top two drag-lifts access the high point of 3500m/11,480ft.

Also from the south end of the village, a gondola leaves for Spielboden. This is met by a cable-car which takes you up to **Längfluh**. Between Felskinn and Längfluh is an off-limits glacier area. A very long drag-lift from Längfluh takes you to a point where you can get down to the Felskinn area. These two sectors are served mainly by drag-lifts, and you can get down to the village from both.

Another gondola from the south end of the village goes up to Saas-Fee's smallest area, **Plattjen**.

TERRAIN-PARKS
Well developed
Saas-Fee was early into the fun-park business, and has well-established facilities in the Felskinn sector including an 'excellent' big half-pipe, a fun-park and a 'half-hearted' boarder-cross course. The nearby Morenia bar is the place for a break.

SNOW RELIABILITY
Good at the highest altitudes
Most of Saas-Fee's slopes face north and many are above 2500m/8,200ft, making this one of the most reliable resorts for snow in the Alps. The glacier is open most of the year. There has been substantial recent investment in snow-guns but reporters say they aren't used enough. Piste grooming remains 'excellent'.

FOR EXPERTS
Not a lot to keep your interest
There is not much steep stuff, except on the bottom half of the mountain where the snow tends not to be as good. There is a short black run from

boarding

Saas-Fee encourages boarding in a big way. In summer, in particular, its glacier slopes are dominated by boarders. While the gentle glacier slopes are ideal for learning, only the main access lifts are boarder-friendly (gondolas, cable-cars and a funicular); nearly all the rest are drags. There are a couple of specialist schools. Expert free-riders may be frustrated by the limits imposed on off-piste riding by the glacier. The slopes above Längfluh and Morenia offer great carving space. Getting to the base of the Alpin Express from the slopes involves a hike.The Popcorn board shop and bar is popular.

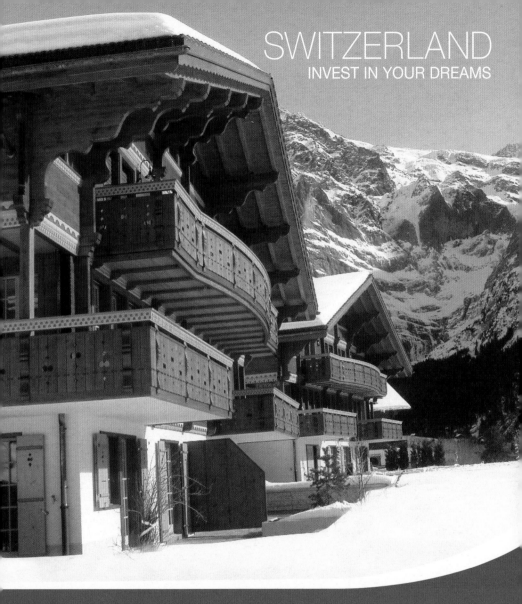

SWITZERLAND
INVEST IN YOUR DREAMS

CHALETS AND APARTMENTS FOR SALE

Villars Saas Fee Zermatt-Täsch Verbier
Grindelwald Grimentz Leukerbad Wengen

www.investorsinproperty.com

SKI PROPERTY SPECIALISTS SINCE 1986   +44 (0) 20 8905 5511

Felskinn that certainly deserves its grading. The slopes around the top of Längfluh often provide good powder, and there are usually moguls above Spielboden. The blacks and trees on Plattjen are worth exploring. The glacier puts limits on the local off-piste even with a guide – crevasse danger is extreme. But there are extensive touring possibilities.

FOR INTERMEDIATES
Great for gentle cruising
Saas-Fee is ideal for early intermediates and those not looking for much of a challenge. For long cruises, head for Allalin. The top of the mountain, down as far as Längfluh in one direction and as far as Morenia in the other, is ideal, with usually excellent snow. Gradients range from gentle blues to slightly steeper reds which can build up smallish bumps. For more of a challenge, head across to Längfluh.

The 1800m/5,900ft vertical descents from the top to the village are great tests of stamina – or, if you choose, an enjoyable long cruise with plenty of view stops. The lower runs have steepish, tricky sections and can have poor snow, especially if it isn't cold enough to make artificial snow – timid intermediates might prefer to take a lift down from mid-mountain.

Plattjen has a variety of runs, all of them fine for ambitious intermediates, and often under-used.

FOR BEGINNERS
A great place to start
We say 'great' – a reporter who took a beginner this year says 'perfect'. There's a good, large, out-of-the-way nursery area at the edge of the village, as snow-sure as any you will find. Those ready to progress can head for the gentle blues on Felskinn just above Morenia – it's best to return by the Alpin Express. There are also gentle blues at the top of the mountain, from where you can head down to Längfluh. Again, use the lifts to return to base.

A useful beginners' pass covers all the short lifts at the village edge, for those not ready to go higher.

FOR CROSS-COUNTRY
Good local trail and lots nearby
There is one short (6km/4mile) pleasant trail at the edge of the village. It snakes up through the woods, providing about 150m/490ft of climb and nice views. There are more options in the Saas valley.

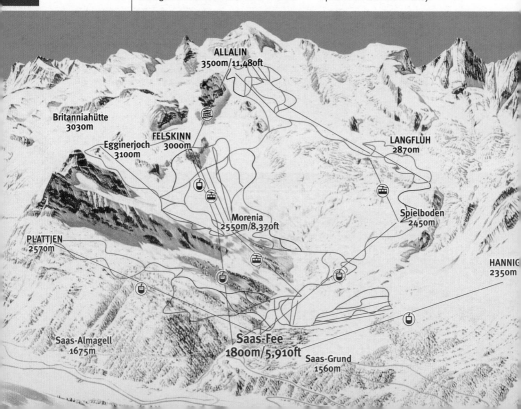

Allalin 3500m/11,480ft

Britanniahütte 3030m

Egginerjoch 3100m

Felskinn 3000m

Langfluh 2870m

Morenia 2550m/8,370ft

Spielboden 2450m

Plattjen 2570m

Hannig 2350m

Saas-Almagell 1675m

Saas-Fee 1800m/5,910ft

Saas-Grund 1560m

QUEUES
Persistent problems
Reporters still complain of an 'uncomfortable scrum' to get on the Alpin Express gondola first thing in the morning, and note that the whole journey to the top may take over an hour – but it is quite a long way. A 2005 reporter confirms that the Felskinn cable-car still regularly produces big queues, and another waited for 30 minutes during the afternoon up at Längfluh. The drag-lifts at the top of the mountain are persistent offenders.

MOUNTAIN RESTAURANTS
Fair choice, but it's no Zermatt
The restaurants at the main lift stations are functional; at least the one at Allalin revolves – see separate box. The best places are slightly off the beaten track: the Berghaus Plattjen (just down from Plattjen) and the cosy Gletschergrotte, halfway down from Spielboden (watch for the arrow from the piste). A reporter says it does 'good food but is popular, so you have to wait'. If you're up for a trek – about 15 minutes each way – the Britanniahütte is special: a real climbing refuge, with atmosphere and views. The restaurant at the top of Plattjen has 'friendly service and the best rösti in the resort'. At Spielboden there are 'great views' of tricky slopes and a 'good selection of rösti'. At Längfluh the large terrace has spectacular views of huge crevasses and inside is 'very cosy' and atmospheric, but the food is 'basic'. Several reporters again recommend the Morenia (about to be replaced by a new giant eatery) for 'cheap and very good' pizza. If you have made the trip to Saas-Grund a 2005 visitor says that

the restaurant on top of Hohsaas is good – 'feels more like an Alpine climbing hut than a ski eatery'.

SCHOOLS AND GUIDES
No choice; mixed reactions
For skiing, it's the Swiss school or nothing. Reports of adult classes this year suggest that 'the standard of English and actual instruction was OK but apart from that people weren't too impressed'. Members of one over-stretched group 'dropped out for various reasons', whilst those in another got ahead so quickly that their instructor seemed to run out of things to teach them and 'refused to go any further'. Private lessons were found to be 'good'. We hear positive things about the Eskimos snowboard school, with private lessons being 'rewarding'.

FACILITIES FOR CHILDREN
Good reports
The school takes children from four years old, and reports are generally positive. This year some children 'really enjoyed' their lessons, while another was less keen but 'stuck it out'. Classes as big as 15 have been spotted. For younger ones, several hotels have an in-house kindergarten.

EUROPE'S HIGHEST LUNCH?

There is something beautifully Swiss about the idea of a revolving restaurant – and all three pivoting pubs in the Alps are in Switzerland. 'Customers not getting a share of the views? Can't have that. Only one thing for it: spin the whole restaurant about once an hour.' Actually, they spin only the bit of floor with the tables on it; the stairs stay put (along with the windows – watch your gloves). Only the table-service section revolves; there is stationary self-service downstairs.

This is the world's highest revolving restaurant – a good 500m/1,640ft higher than the famous original on Mürren's Schilthorn. We don't rate the views from Allalin all that highly, but it's an amusing novelty that most visitors enjoy, and lunch is OK too – confirmed by a reporter who rates the place highly for food, service and value. To reserve a table next to the windows phone 957 1771.

And the third spinning speisesaal? At Leysin.

GETTING THERE

Air Sion 70km/
43 miles (1hr);
Geneva 234km/
145 miles (3½hr);
Zürich 246km/
153 miles (4hr);
Milan 250km/
155 miles (3hr).

Rail Brig (38km/
24 miles); regular
buses from station.

ACTIVITIES

Indoor Bielen leisure
centre (swimming,
hot-tub, steam bath,
whirlpool, solarium,
sauna, aerobics,
massage, tennis,
badminton, gym,
bodyforming,
aquafitness), cinema,
museums

Outdoor 30km/
19 miles of cleared
paths, ice rink
(skating, curling,
snowbowling),
tobogganing, snow
tubing, climbing, ice-
climbing, snow-
shoeing, dog-sledding

Phone numbers
From elsewhere in
Switzerland add the
prefix 027.
From abroad use the
prefix +41 27.

TOURIST OFFICE

t 958 1858
to@saas-fee.ch
www.saas-fee.ch

SWITZERLAND

498

STAYING THERE

HOW TO GO
Check the location
Quite a few UK tour operators sell
holidays to Saas-Fee. But there are
surprisingly few chalet holidays.
Hotels There are over 50.

((((⑤ **Fletschhorn** (957 2131) Elegant
chalet in woods, with original art and
individual rooms, a trek from the
village and lifts, but fabulous food.

((((⑤ **Ferienart** (958 1900) Formerly the
Walliserhof. Lovely relaxed place,
despite 5-star status. Central, with
excellent facilities including swish spa.
A 2005 reporter found some rooms not
up to scratch and judges the food
'good but not exceptional'.

(((④ **Schweizerhof** (958 7575) Stylish,
in quiet position above the centre.
'Fantastic food, friendly staff, excellent
kindergarten, wonderful service.' Pool
and new health facilities.

(((③ **Beau-Site** (958 1560) 'First-rate' if
quiet 4-star in central, but not
convenient, position. Good food. Pool
and relaxation suite.

(((③ **Christiania** (957 3166) 'Thoroughly
recommended' 3-star 'delivering much
more than our expectations', says a
2005 visitor.

(((③ **Alphubel** (958 6363) At the wrong
end of town, praised by reporters for
its own 'brilliant nursery'.

(((③ **Waldesruh** (958 6464) Strongly
recommended by a reporter: 'Best
situation for the Alpin Express.'

(((③ **Astoria** (957 1133) 'Very handy for
the Alpin Express, excellent, friendly',
says a reporter. Whirlpool and sauna.

(((③ **Hohnegg** (957 2268) Small rustic
alternative to the Fletschhorn, in a
similarly remote spot.

(((③ **Jägerhof** (957 1310) Adjacent to
nursery slopes. 'The service was simply
phenomenal', says a 2005 visitor.

((② **Belmont** (958 1640) The most
appealing of the hotels looking directly
on to the nursery slopes.

Self-catering Most apartments featured
by UK operators are at the north end
of the village, but they are generally
spacious and well equipped.

EATING OUT
Good variety – but book a table
Gastronomes will want to head for the
highly acclaimed Fletschhorn –
expensive but excellent. Our favourite
is the less formal Bodmen, along a
path into the woods. It has great food
(from rösti to fillet steak) and rustic

ambience. The hotel Ferienart's several
restaurants include a Thai one that we
have enjoyed. Boccalino is cheap and
does pizzas – book or get there early.
The rustic Alp-Hitta does 'reasonable'
food. The hotel Dom's restaurant does
endless varieties of rösti. The Ferme is
'excellent'. Arvu Stuba, Zur Mühle,
Gorge, Feeloch and the Sport-Hotel's
Tischgrille have all been recommended.

APRES-SKI
Excellent and varied
Late afternoon, Nesti's Ski-Bar, Zur
Mühle and the little snow-bars near the
lifts are all pretty lively, especially if
the sun's shining. The Black Bull, with
outdoor seating only, is reportedly still
the 'in place'. Later on, Nesti's and the
Alpenpub keep going till 1am. Popcorn
is 'relaxed' and as popular as ever. The
night club, Poison (formerly Go-Inn),
advertises 'legendary parties' fuelled
by shots and shakers. The Metro Bar is
'like being in a 19th-century mine shaft
full of outgoing people trying to share
the few stools'. Why-Not is the place
for a Guinness. The Happy bar's cheap
drinks sessions are popular. The 'large
and popular' Metropol, with American
diner, Crazy Night disco and other
bars, 'doesn't liven up till late'.

OFF THE SLOPES
A mountain for pedestrians
The whole of the Hannig mountain is
dedicated to walking, paragliding and
tobogganing, which a 2005 reporter
rates as 'terrific – all visitors should try
it'. Hannig offers 'great views' of the
glacial slopes. In the village, the
splendid Bielen leisure centre boasts a
25m/80ft pool, indoor tennis courts
and a lounging area with sunlamps.
There's also the interesting Saas
museum and the Bakery Museum,
where children can make bread. Don't
miss the largest ice cave in the world,
carved out of the glacier at Allalin.

St Moritz

Luxury living – on and off the flatteringly easy slopes

COSTS

RATINGS

The slopes

Fast lifts	★★★★
Snow	★★★★
Extent	★★★★★
Expert	★★★★
Intermediate	★★★★
Beginner	★★
Convenience	★★
Queues	★★
Mountain restaurants	★★★★

The rest

Scenery	★★★★
Resort charm	★
Off-slope	★★★★★

NEWS

For last season a one-way link was created from the Diavolezza sector to Lagalb. A new red piste splits from the black piste on the lower slopes, leading to a short lift bringing you to the Lagalb base station. Moving between the sectors in the opposite direction still depends on a shuttle-bus. But the new link should be quite popular, because Diavolezza gets the morning sun while Lagalb gets more afternoon sun.

➕ Wonderful panoramic scenery

➕ Off-slope activities second to none

➕ Extensive, mainly intermediate slopes

➕ Fairly snow-sure

➕ Good après-ski, for all tastes

➕ Good mountain restaurants, some with magnificent views

➕ Painless rail access via Zürich

➖ Some hideous block buildings

➖ A sizeable town, with little traditional Alpine character

➖ Several unlinked mountains, with a bus, train or car needed to most

➖ Runs on two main mountains all fairly easy and lacking variety

➖ Expensive

St Moritz is Switzerland's most famous 'exclusive' winter resort: glitzy, expensive, fashionable and, above all, the place to be seen – a place for an all-round winter holiday, with an unrivalled array of wacky diversions such as polo, golf and cricket on snow, and gourmet and music festivals. It has long been popular with upper-crust Brits, who stay in the top hotels. The slopes on the two main mountains are almost uniformly easy intermediate – experts must venture off-piste for their fun. But for cross-country, it is superb.

The town of St Moritz doesn't have the chocolate-box image of a Swiss mountain resort, all wooden huts and cows with bells round their necks. Many buildings resemble council flats (extremely neat and clean ones – it is Switzerland, after all).

But you may find, as some readers have, that St Moritz's spectacular setting blinds you to the town's aesthetic faults. This is one of those areas where our progress on the mountain is regularly interrupted by the need to stand and gaze. And the cross-country skiing, walking and other activities on the frozen lake give it a real 'winter wonderland' feel.

THE RESORT

St Moritz has two distinct parts. Dorf is the fashionable main part, on a steep hillside above the lake. It has two main streets – lined with boutiques selling Rolex watches, Cartier jewellery and Hermes scarves – a few side lanes and a small main square. A funicular takes you from Dorf to the slopes of Corviglia, also reached by gondola from down the road at Celerina, and by cable-car from Dorf's other half, the spa resort of St Moritz Bad, spread around one end of the lake.

Everything in Bad is less prestigious. Many of the modern buildings are uncompromisingly rectangular and spoil otherwise superb views. In winter the lake is used for eccentric activities including horse and greyhound racing, show jumping, polo, 'ice golf' and even cricket. It also makes a superb setting for walking and cross-country skiing.

Other downhill slopes, at Corvatsch, are reached via lifts at Surlej and Sils

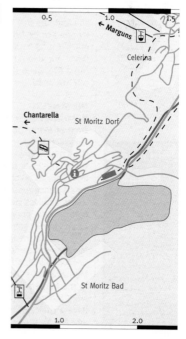

KEY FACTS

Resort	1770m
	5,810ft
Slopes	1730-3305m
	5,680-10,840ft
Lifts	56
Pistes	350km
	217 miles
Blue	16%
Red	71%
Black	13%
Snowmaking	70km
	43 miles

For Corviglia only	
Slopes	1730-3055m
	5,680-10,020ft
Lifts	23
Pistes	158km
	98 miles

LIFT PASSES

Upper Engadine
Covers all lifts in
Corviglia (St Moritz,
Celerina, Samedan),
Corvatsch (Silvaplana,
Sils, Surlej),
Diavolezza-Lagalb
(Pontresina), and
Zuoz.

Beginners
No special pass

Main pass
1 day SF69
6 days SF332

Children
Under 20: 6 days
SF299
Under 16: 6 days
SF166
Under 6: free pass

Alternative passes
Half-day and day
passes available for
individual areas
within Upper
Engadine.

Maria. Cross-country skiing is the main activity around the outlying villages of Samedan and Pontresina.

The town's clientele is typified by the results of a Cresta Run race we saw on one of our visits. In the top 29 were three Lords, one Count, one Archduke and a Baronet. But the race was won by a local Swiss guy.

For high society and a better choice of bars and restaurants, stay in Dorf. Bad has the advantage that you can get back to it from Corvatsch and Corviglia. Celerina is the obvious alternative, and an attractive one, but there are other options – a reader heartily recommends 'chocolate-box-pretty' Sils Maria, with immediate access to the Corvatsch slopes.

THE MOUNTAINS

Like the resort, most of the slopes are made for posing. There are lots of long, wide, well-groomed runs with varied terrain – practically all on open slopes above the trees. The piste map is poor, with 'several pistes not marked' according to one reporter. The several distinct areas add up to a substantial 350km/217 miles of pistes. The main slopes, shown on our maps, are nearby Corviglia-Marguns and Corvatsch-Furtschellas, a bus-ride away (you can get back to Bad on snow). But some of the more distant slopes are well worth an outing. It helps to have a car, although the free bus service is reported to be fairly efficient. Trips to other resorts such as Klosters and Davos (around 90 minutes by train or car) and Livigno (around an hour by car) are possible.

THE SLOPES
Big but broken up
From St Moritz Dorf a two-stage railway goes up to **Corviglia**, a fair-sized area with slopes facing east and south. The peak of Piz Nair, reached from here by a cable-car, splits the area – sunny runs towards the main valley, and less sunny ones to the north. From Corviglia you can head down (snow permitting) to Dorf and Bad, and via the lower lift junction of Marguns to Celerina.

From Surlej, a few miles from St Moritz, a two-stage cable-car takes you to the north-facing slopes of **Corvatsch**. From the mid-station at Murtèl you have a choice of reds to Margun-Vegl and Alp Margun. From the latter you

can work your way to **Furtschellas**, also reached by cable-car from Sils Maria.

Diavolezza (2980m/9,78oft) and Lagalb (2960m/9,710ft), the main additional areas, are on opposite sides of the road to the Bernina pass to Italy, less than half an hour away by bus. The two are now linked in one direction (see 'News'). **Diavolezza** has excellent north-facing pistes of 900m/2,950ft vertical, down under its big 125-person cable-car, and a very popular and spectacular off-piste route across a glacier and down a valley beneath Piz Bernina to Morteratsch. **Lagalb** is a smaller area with quite challenging slopes, and an 80-person cable-car serving the west-facing front slope of 850m/2,790ft vertical.

TERRAIN-PARKS
Not a clear picture
The resort's information is inconsistent, and it doesn't have a great record of delivering what it promises in this area, but we believe on Corviglia there is a half-pipe above the Signal area and a terrain park towards Marguns.

SNOW RELIABILITY
Improved by good snowmaking
This corner of the Alps has a rather dry climate, but the altitude means that any precipitation is likely to be snowy. The top runs at Corvatsch are glacial. There is snowmaking in every sector and piste grooming is excellent.

FOR EXPERTS
Dispersed challenges
If you're looking for challenges, you're liable to find St Moritz disappointing on-piste. Red runs (many of which should really be classified blue) far outnumber black, and mogul-fields are scarce. The few serious black runs are scattered about in different sectors and few are seriously steep; those at Lagalb and Diavolezza are the most challenging. The Minor run down the Lagalb cable-car has 850m/2,790ft vertical of non-stop moguls. But there is good off-piste terrain, and it doesn't get tracked out as it does in more macho resorts. There is an excellent north-facing slope immediately above Marguns, for example. Experts often head for the tough off-piste runs on Piz Nair or the Corvatsch summit. More serious expeditions can be undertaken – such as down the Roseg valley from Corvatsch. To get the most out of the area, you will need to hire a guide.

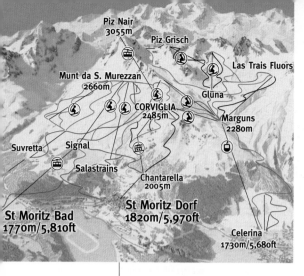

Piz Nair 3055m
Piz Grisch
Las Trais Fluors
Munt da S. Murezzan 266om
Glüna
CORVIGLIA 2485m
Marguns 2280m
Suvretta
Signal
Salastrains
Chantarella 2005m
St Moritz Bad 1770m/5,81oft
St Moritz Dorf 1820m/5,97oft
Celerina 1730m/5,68oft

the run to the cable-car up to Corviglia.

Diavolezza is mostly intermediate stuff, too. There is an easy open slope at the top, served by a fast quad, and a splendid long intermediate run back down under the lift. The popular off-piste run to Morteratsch requires a bit of energy and nerve. After a gentle climb, you cross the glacier on a narrow ledge, with crevasses waiting to gobble you up on the right. When we last did it, there were ice picks and shovels at intervals along the path, put there by the enterprising proprietors of the beautifully laid out, welcoming ice bar which greets you at the end of the 30-minute slog. After that, it's downhill through the glacier, with splendid views. Lagalb has more challenging pistes.

FOR INTERMEDIATES
Good but flattering

St Moritz is great for intermediates. Most pistes on Corviglia and Corvatsch are very well groomed, easyish reds that could well have been classified blue – ideal cruising terrain. One reporter takes the view that Corvatsch is the more varied and interesting area, and we don't dispute that; it is certainly higher and wider, and well worth the excursion from St Moritz. If you're lucky with the snow, you can end the day there with the splendid Hahnensee run, from the northern limit of the Corvatsch lift system at Giand'Alva down to St Moritz Bad – a black-classified run that is of red difficulty for most of its 6km/4 mile length and 900m/2,95oft vertical drop. It's a five-minute walk from the end of

FOR BEGINNERS
Not much to offer

St Moritz is not ideal for beginners. It sits in a deep, steep-sided valley, with very little space for nursery slopes at the lower levels. Beginners start up at Salastrains or Corviglia, or slightly out of town, at Suvretta. Celerina has good, broad nursery slopes at village level. Progression from the nursery slopes to intermediate runs is rather awkward – these always include a difficult section.

FOR CROSS-COUNTRY
Excellent

The Engadine is one of the premier regions in the Alps for cross-country, with 180km/112 miles of trails, including floodlit loops, amid splendid scenery and with fairly reliable snow. A reporter recommends the lessons at

St Moritz

501

PIZ CORVATSCH 3450m
3305m/10,84oft
Culöz das las Furtschellas 2800m
Fuorcla Surlej 2760m
Murtèl 2700m
Val Fex
Giand'Alva 2645m
Margun-Vegl 2405m
Hahnensee 2155m
Alp Margun 2270m
Furtschellas 2310m
Surlej 1870m
St. Moritz Bad 1770m/5,81oft
Sils Maria 1795m

↑ The valley offers fabulous panoramic views

ST MORITZ TOURIST OFFICE

SCHOOLS

Swiss
t 830 0101
Suvretta
t 836 3600

Classes
(Swiss prices)
6 2hr days SF230
Private lessons
SF90 for 1hr

CHILDREN

Schweizerhof hotel
t 837 0707
Ages from 3; 9.30-
5.30; Mon-Sat; SF34
per day

Ski school
Ages from 5; pick-up
service and all-day
care available

WEBSITES

For links to resort
sites, go to our own
new site at
www.wtss.co.uk

the Langlauf Centre near the Hotel Kempinski. The Engadine Ski Marathon is held here every March – over 12,000 racers take part. Pontresina makes a great base for cross-country.

QUEUES
Not much of a problem
St Moritz has invested heavily in new lifts in recent years. Once you get up the mountain, Corviglia has fast chairs everywhere. But the area as a whole has a lot of cable-cars – both for getting up the mountain from the resort and for access to peaks from mid-mountain. Queues can result, though reporters have had good experiences lately – the enlarged cable-car from Surlej to Murtèl is a big improvement at Corvatsch, although a reporter recommends avoiding Surlej and going to Sils Maria instead. The upgraded cable-car to Piz Nair above Corvatsch seems to have cut the queues there, but not eliminated them. Happy reporters comment that many St Moritz visitors are late risers and don't ski after lunch, leaving the slopes quiet at the start and end of the day. 'Peak period is 11 to 12.30, when congestion can be a problem above Marguns on Corviglia and on the run down from Murtèl on Corvatsch,' says a reporter.

MOUNTAIN RESTAURANTS
Some special places
Mountain restaurants are plentiful, and include some of the most glamorous in Europe. Prices can be high, and

reservations are advisable. But there are plenty of cheaper places too.

On Corviglia, the top lift station (known locally as the highest post office in Switzerland because of its bright yellow paint) houses several restaurants run under the umbrella title of Mathis Food Affairs, including the famous Marmite. Much better for charm is the Paradiso, with panoramic views from the terrace; or the inviting terrace of the Chamanna, or the Lej de la Pêsch, in the valley behind Piz Nair.

On the Corvatsch side, we've heard good reports about the self-service place at the top of the area and of the sunny bar, with live music, at the bottom of Rabguisa. Fuorcla Surlej is delightfully secluded, as is Hahnensee, on the lift-free run of the same name down to Bad – a splendid place to pause in the sun on the way home at the end of the day. On stormy days, most captivating is the rustic Alpetta, near Alp Margun – 'nice food, lovely atmosphere and a great bar' (table-service inside).

The hotel-restaurant up at Muottas Muragl, between Celerina and Pontresina, is well worth a visit. It has truly spectacular views overlooking the valley – a fabulous sunset, if you are lucky – as well as good food.

Morteratsch restaurant (at the end of the off-piste run from Diavolezza) is splendid – sunny, by the cross-country area and tiny railway station, and with excellent, good-value food.

SCHOOLS AND GUIDES
Internal competition
As well as the St Moritz and Suvretta schools, there is The Wave snowboarding school and The St Moritz Experience, for heli-trips. Some hotels have their own instructors for private lessons.

FACILITIES FOR CHILDREN
Choose a hotel with a nursery
Children wanting lessons have a choice of schools, but others must be deposited at a hotel nursery. Club Med has its usual good facilities.

boarding

Despite the high prices and its glitzy image, the terrain in St Moritz is boarder-friendly and there's a special boarders' booklet with lots of good information and profiles of local riders. The Corvatsch area has links that rely on drags – otherwise, most lifts are chairs, gondolas, cable-cars and trains. There are several specialist snowboard shops, including Playground in Paradise.

ACTIVITIES

Indoor Swimming pool, sauna, solarium, golf range, tennis, squash, museums, cinema (with English films), beauty/health centre, casino, library

Outdoor Ice skating, sleigh rides, ski-jumping, curling, cricket on snow, tobogganing, hang-gliding, paragliding, golf on frozen lake, bobsleigh rides, Cresta run, 180km/ 112 miles cleared paths, greyhound racing, horse-riding, polo tournaments

STAYING THERE

HOW TO GO
Several packaged options

Packages are available, but many people make their own arrangements. There is a Club Med – its all-inclusive deal cuts the impact of high prices. The tourist office can provide a list of apartments.
Hotels Over half the hotels are 4-stars and 5-stars – the highest concentration of high-quality hotels in Switzerland. We don't like any of the famous 5-stars or their jacket-and-tie policies. If made to choose we'd prefer the glossy, secluded Carlton or even more secluded Suvretta House to the staid Kulm or Gothic Badrutt's Palace.
(((((4) **Crystal** (836 2626) Big 4-star in Dorf, as close to the Corviglia lift as any. Recently renovated and now part of the 'Small Luxury Hotels' group.
(((((4) **Schweizerhof** (837 0707) 'Relaxed' 4-star in central Dorf, five minutes from the Corviglia lift, with 'excellent food and very helpful staff'.
(((((4) **Albana** (836 6161) 4-star in Dorf, with walls adorned with big game trophies bagged by proprietor's family.
(((((3) **Monopol** (837 0404) Good value (for St Moritz) 4-star in centre of Dorf.

Excellent breakfasts, hot-tub, sauna.
(((((3) **Steinbock** (833 6035) 'Friendly, understated, comfortable,' says a reporter. In Dorf.
(((((3) **Nolda** (833 0575) One of the few chalet-style buildings, close to the cable-car in St Moritz Bad.
(((((2) **Bellaval** (833 3245) A two-star between the station and the lake.

EATING OUT
Mostly chic and expensive

It's easy to spend £50 a head eating out in St Moritz – without wine – but you can eat more cheaply. We liked the excellent Italian food at the down-to-earth Cascade in Dorf and the (pricier) three restaurants in the Chesa Veglia, though one reporter considers it a rip-off – 'the staff lost interest when we ordered only two pizzas and turned down the wine, which started at £35 a bottle'. Another reporter had a 'week of gourmet eating'. The two top restaurants, Jöhri's Talvo at Champfèr and Bumanns Chesa Pirani in La Punt, both approach the top restaurants in London or Paris for quality and price – we spent SF200 a head in each. We also liked the rustic Landhotel Meierei, in a bay of the lake opposite Bad. If you want something less pricey and like fondue, reporters recommend the restaurant in the hotel Schweizerhof.

Try an evening up at Muottas Muragl for the spectacular views, splendid sunset and unpretentious dinner. The food at the Chesa Rosatsch hotel at Celerina attracts non-resident diners and is recommended this year.

APRES-SKI
Caters for all ages

There's a big variety of après-skiing age groups here. The fur coat count is high – people come to St Moritz to be seen.

At tea time, head for Hanselmann's 'fabulous tea and strudels' but 'the place is a bit dull'. Or try Café Hauser.

Bobby's Pub (with internet access) attracts a young crowd, as does the loud music of the Stübli, one of three bars in the Schweizerhof: the others are the Muli, with a country and western theme and live music, and the chic Piano Bar. The Cresta, at the Steffani, is popular with the British, while the Cava below it is louder, livelier and younger. The Diamond (formerly the Prince) has a bar and a disco. Readers rate the piano bar at the Albana Hotel 'cosy and welcoming'. It is also amusing to put on a jacket and

St Moritz

503

↑ The railway climbs 600m/1,970ft to Corviglia at the heart of the slopes directly above St Moritz Dorf

ST MORITZ TOURIST OFFICE

GETTING THERE

Air Zürich 200km/ 124 miles (3hr); Upper Engadine airport 5km/3 miles.

Rail Mainline station in resort.

Phone numbers
From elsewhere in Switzerland add the prefix 081.
From abroad use the prefix +41 81.

TOURIST OFFICES

St Moritz
t 837 3333
information@stmoritz.ch
www.stmoritz.ch

Celerina
t 830 0011
info@celerina.ch
www.celerina.ch

Pontresina
t 838 8300
info@pontresina.com
www.pontresina.com

tie and explore bars in Badrutt's Palace and the Kulm.

The two most popular discos are Vivai (expensive) at the Steffani, and King's at Badrutt's Palace (even more expensive; jackets and ties required). And if they don't part you with enough of your cash, try the casino.

OFF THE SLOPES
Excellent variety of pastimes
Even if you lack the bravado for the Cresta Run, there is lots to do. In midwinter the snow-covered lake provides a playground for bizarre events (see earlier in chapter) but in March the lake starts to thaw. There's an annual 'gourmet festival', with chefs from all over the world.

Some hotels run special activities, such as a curling week. Other options are hang-gliding, indoor tennis and trips to Italy (Milan is four hours by car). There's a public pool in Bad.

St Moritz gets a lot of sun – 322 sunny days a year, they claim – so lounging on sunny terraces is popular. One reporter was bowled over by a train trip on the Bernina Express, with 'amazing bends, gradients and scenery. The high-spot of our visit.'

STAYING UP THE MOUNTAIN
Excellent possibilities
Next door to each other at Salastrains are two chalet-style hotels, the 3-star Salastrains (833 3867), with 60 comfy beds, and the slightly simpler and much smaller Chesa Chantarella (833 3355). Great views, and no queues.

Celerina 1730m/5,680ft

At the bottom end of the Cresta Run, Celerina is unpretentious and villagey, if quiet, with good access to Corviglia. It is sizeable, with a lot of second homes, many owned by Italians (the upper part is known as Piccolo Milano). There are some appealing small hotels (reporters recommend Chesa Rosatsch 837 0101) and a couple of bigger 4-stars.

Pontresina 1805m/5,920ft

Pontresina is small and sedate, and an excellent base for the extensive cross-country skiing on its doorstep.

It's a sheltered, sunny village with one main street, spoiled by the predominant sanatorium-style architecture. Location of accommodation is unimportant – all downhill skiing involves travel by car or bus.

Pontresina's own hill, Languard, has a single long piste. Five minutes away towards Celerina is the Muottas Muragl area, where a funicular railway serves a tiny mountain-top area with marvellous views and a single long run to the bottom station.

It can be somewhat cheaper to stay here than St Moritz and there is a Club Med (offering its usual all-inclusive deal). Dining is mostly based in hotels and nightlife is quiet. A reporter found restaurant prices here compared favourably with the UK and recommends the Bernina Hotel and the Thai restaurant at the Collina Hotel.

THE CRESTA RUN

No trip to St Moritz is really complete without a visit to the Cresta Run. It's the last bastion of Britishness (until recently, payment had to be made in sterling) and male chauvinism (women have been banned since 1929 – unless you can secure an invitation from a club member for the last day of their season).

Any adult male can pay around £200 for five rides on the famous run (helmet and lunch at the Kulm hotel included). Watch out for Shuttlecock corner – that's where most people come off and the ambulances ply for trade. You lie on a toboggan (aptly called a 'skeleton') and hurtle head-first down a sheet ice gully from St Moritz to Celerina. David Gower and Sandy Gall are among the Cresta's many addicts.

Verbier

Great for nightlife-loving powder hounds with cash

RATINGS

The slopes

Fast lifts	**
Snow	***
Extent	*****
Expert	*****
Intermediate	***
Beginner	**
Convenience	**
Queues	***
Mountain restaurants	***

The rest

Scenery	****
Resort charm	***
Off-slope	***

KEY FACTS

Resort	1500m
	4,920ft

4 Valleys area	
Slopes	1500-3330m
	4,920-10,930ft
Lifts	95
Pistes	410km
	255 miles
Blue	33%
Red	41%
Black	26%
Snowmaking	50km
	31 miles

Verbier, Bruson and Tzoumaz/Savoleyres sectors only (covered by Verbier pass)

Slopes	1500-3025m
	4,920-9,920ft
Lifts	38
Pistes	150km
	93 miles
Blue	33%
Red	33%
Black	34%
Snowmaking	20km
	12 miles

➕ Extensive, challenging slopes with a lot of off-piste potential and some good, very long bump runs

➕ Upper slopes offer a real high-mountain feel plus great views

➕ Pleasant, animated village in a sunny, panoramic setting

➕ Lively, varied nightlife

➕ Good advanced-level lessons

➕ Much improved lift system, piste grooming and on-mountain signposting, but ...

➖ Pistes still do not have names or numbers – it would help if they did

➖ Still many slow lifts and and some queues on 4 Valleys links

➖ Some overcrowded pistes and areas

➖ The 4 Valleys network is much less wonderful than it looks on paper

➖ Sunny lower slopes will always be a problem, even with snowmaking

➖ Some long walks/rides to lifts

➖ Lots of off-piste is tracked out quickly

We have been criticising Verbier ever since the first edition of this book back in 1994. At last we feel we're getting somewhere. Its lift system has been improved considerably and its queues have shrunk except for a couple of key, but optional, lifts. Its grooming, ski schools and snowmaking have got better. And now it has completely renewed its formerly atrocious on-mountain signposting and linked it to its piste map. Well done Téléverbier – but there's still a lot of further improvement we'd like to see (see the panel on page 508).

For experts prepared to hire a guide to explore off-piste, Verbier is one of the cult resorts worldwide. And for vibrant nightlife it is difficult to beat. With its claimed 410km/255 miles of pistes, Verbier also seems at first sight to rank alongside the French mega-resorts that draw keen piste skiers, such as the Three Valleys and Paradiski. But it doesn't; Three Valleys and Paradiski devotees will be sorely disappointed by the 4 Valleys network, which is an inconveniently sprawling affair, with lots of traversing to get to the far end and back. And Verbier's local pistes are confined and crowded.

THE RESORT

Verbier is an amorphous sprawl of chalet-style buildings, without too much concrete in evidence, in an impressive setting on a wide, sunny balcony facing spectacular peaks. It's a fashionable, informal, very lively place that teems with cosmopolitan visitors. Most are younger than visitors to other big Swiss resorts.

Most of the shops and hotels (but not chalets) are set around the Place Centrale and along the sloping streets stretching down the hill in one direction and up it in the other to the main lift station at Médran 500m/ 1,640ft away. Much of the nightlife is here, too, though bars are rather scattered. These central areas get unpleasantly packed with cars at busy times, especially weekends.

More chalets and apartments are built each year with many newer properties inconveniently situated along the road to the lift base for the secondary Savoleyres area, about 1.5km/1 mile from Médran.

The Médran lift station is a walkable distance from the Place Centrale, so staying there has attractions. There is accommodation close to the Médran lift station, which is sufficiently distant

NEWS

For 2005/06 a major new lift – a 'chondola', which consists of gondolas and fast chairs on the same lift – is planned between Les Ruinettes and La Chaux via the ridge at Côte de Brunet. It will replace the Combes 2, Chaux 1 and Fontanys chairs, and you will be able to ride it both ways and get off at the Brunet ridge or at the terminus.

A programme to increase snowmaking to cover 60% of the pistes is being started; La Chaux and Lac des Vaux are the first areas due to get more snow-guns.

The slope from Col des Gentianes to La Chaux is being remodelled so the run straight down can be groomed.

A new fast quad from Siviez to Cambatzeline en route to Greppon Blanc is planned to replace the Novelli double.

At long last, for 2004/05 the lift company made the signposting on the slopes clearer and linked them up with the piste map. Four new marked trails for snow-shoeing were set up, and a new map showing the winter-hiking, snow-shoeing and cross-country trails was published.

A new hotel, the Central, was built in the Place Centrale.

Slow skiing zones were introduced on two pistes – one on Savoleyres and one at La Chaux.

from nightlife to avoid late-night noise. If nightlife is not a priority, staying somewhere near the upper (north-east) fringes of the village may mean that you can almost ski to your door – and there is a piste linking the upper nursery slopes to the one in the middle of the village.

But in practice most people just get used to using the free buses, which run efficiently on several routes until 7pm. Some areas have quite an infrequent service. We are told that from 7pm to 8.30 there is a special taxi service that will drop you at any of the usual bus stops within the resort for five francs per person.

Verbier is at one end of a long, strung-out series of interconnected slopes, optimistically branded the 4 Valleys and linking Verbier to Nendaz, Veysonnaz, Thyon and other resorts. These other resorts have their own pros and cons. All are appreciably cheaper places to stay than Verbier, and some are more sensible bases for those who plan to stick to pistes rather than venture off-piste – the Veysonnaz-Thyon sector, in particular, is much more intermediate-friendly than Verbier. As bases for exploration of the whole 4 Valleys, only Siviez is much of an advance on Verbier. They are much less lively in the evening. You can also stay down in the valley village of Le Châble, which has a gondola up to Verbier and on into the slopes. Across the valley, Bruson is more attractive as a place to visit for a day than to stay in. These alternatives are all described at the end of the chapter.

Chamonix and Champéry (Portes du Soleil) are within reach by car. But a car can be a bit of a nuisance in Verbier itself. Parking is tightly controlled; your chalet or hotel may not have enough space for all guests' cars, which means a hike from the free parking at the sports centre or paying for garage space.

THE MOUNTAINS

Essentially this is high-mountain terrain. There are wooded slopes directly above the village, but the runs here are either bumpy itinéraires or winding paths. There is more sheltered skiing in other sectors – particularly above Veysonnaz.

THE SLOPES
Very spread out
Savoleyres is the smaller area, reached by a gondola from the north-west end of the village. This area is underrated and generally under-used. It has open, sunny slopes on the front side, and long, pleasantly wooded, shadier runs on the back. You can take a catwalk across from Savoleyres to the foot of Verbier's main slopes. These are served by lifts from Médran, at the opposite end of the village.

Two gondolas rise to **Les Ruinettes** and then on to **Les Attelas**. From Les Attelas a small cable-car goes up to Mont Gelé, for steep off-piste runs only. Heading down instead, you can go back westwards to Les Ruinettes, south to La Chaux or north to Lac des Vaux. From Lac des Vaux chairs go back to Les Attelas and up to Chassoure, the top of a wide, steep and shady off-piste mogul field leading down to **Tortin**, with a gondola back.

For 2005/06 the link between Les Ruinettes and La Chaux will be greatly improved by the new chondola (see News). The local La Chaux slopes are served by an additional slow chair-lift and is the departure point of a jumbo cable-car up to Col des Gentianes and the glacier area. A second, much smaller cable-car then goes up to **Mont-Fort**, the high point of the 4 Valleys. From the glacier is another off-piste route down to Tortin, a north-facing run of almost 1300m/4,270ft vertical. A cable-car returns to Col des Gentianes.

Below Tortin is the gateway to the rest of the 4 Valleys, **Siviez**, where one

chair goes off into the long, thin
Nendaz sector and a new fast quad for
2005/06 heads for the **Thyon-
Veysonnaz** sector, via a couple of lifts
and a lot of catwalks.

Allow plenty of time to get to and
from these remote corners – the taxi-
rides home are expensive.

The slopes of **Bruson** are described
briefly at the end of this chapter.

TERRAIN-PARKS
A couple of options

There are two terrain-parks – one at La
Chaux and another at Savoleyres.

SNOW RELIABILITY
Improved snowmaking

The slopes of the Mont-Fort glacier
always have good snow. The runs to

Tortin are normally snow-sure too. But
nearly all of this is steep, and much of
it is formally off-piste. Most of
Verbier's main local slopes face south
or west and are below 2500m/8,200ft –
so they can be in poor condition at
times. There is snowmaking on the
main run down all the way from Attelas
to Médran; and Lac des Vaux and La
Chaux will get extra snowmaking for
2005/06, as part of a plan to have 60
per cent of the pistes covered. The
north-facing slopes of Savoleyres
generally hold their snow well.

FOR EXPERTS
The main attraction

Verbier has some superb tough slopes,
many of them off-piste and needing a
guide – see the separate feature panel
on this. There are few conventional
black pistes; most of the runs that
might have this designation are now
defined as itinéraires – which means
they are 'marked, not maintained and
not controlled'. But they do seem to
be closed if unsafe or if snow cover is
insufficient. We'd like to see them
given official black piste status, so you
know where you stand better. The
blacks that do exist are mostly
indistinguishable from nearby reds. The
front face of Mont-Fort is an exception:
a long mogul field, with a choice of
gradient from seriously steep to
intimidatingly steep. The World Cup
run at Veysonnaz is a steepish, often

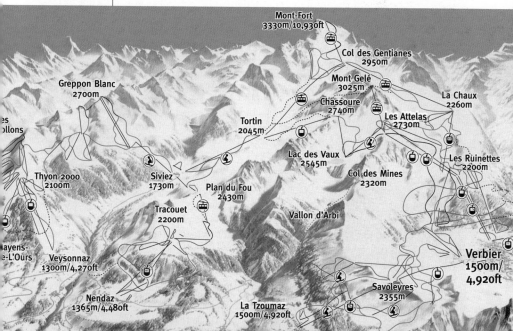

LIFT PASSES

4 Valleys/Mont-Fort
Covers all lifts and
ski-buses in Verbier,
Mont-Fort, Bruson, La
Tzoumaz, Nendaz,
Veysonnaz and
Thyon.

Beginners
No special pass.

Main pass
1-day SF61
6 days SF314

Senior citizens
Over 65: 6 days
SF228

Children
Under 20: 6 days
SF267
Under 16: 6 days
SF220
Under 6: free pass

Notes
Afternoon pass
available. Reductions
for families.

Alternative passes
Verbier pass, La
Tzoumaz/Savoleyres
pass and Bruson only
pass available.

icy red, ideal for really speeding down.
The two itinéraires to Tortin are both
excellent in their different ways. The
one from Chassoure is just one wide,
steep slope, normally a huge mogul
field. The north-facing itinéraire from
Gentianes is longer, less steep, but
feels much more of an adventure (keep
left for quieter and shallower slopes
and better snow, right for steeper
moguls where the crowds go). There is
an entertaining itinéraire from Greppon
Blanc, at the top of the Veysonnaz-
Thyon sector, into the next valley.

FOR INTERMEDIATES
Hit Savoleyres – or Veysonnaz
Many mileage-hungry intermediates
find Verbier disappointing. The
intermediate slopes in the main area
are concentrated between Les Attelas
and the village, above and below Les

Ruinettes, plus the little bowl at Lac
des Vaux and the sunny slopes at La
Chaux. This is all excellent and varied
intermediate territory, but there isn't
much of it – to put it in perspective,
this whole area is no bigger than the
tiny slopes of Alpbach – and it is used
by the bulk of the visitors staying in
one of Switzerland's largest resorts. So
it is often very crowded, especially the
otherwise wonderful sweeping red from
Les Attelas to Les Ruinettes served by
the big gondola. Even early
intermediates should taste the perfect
snow on the glacier. The red run
served by the T-bars is really of gentle
blue steepness. And the red path from
Col des Gentianes to La Chaux is not
too difficult, but its high-mountain feel
can be unnerving and it's no disgrace
to ride the cable-car down instead.

There is excellent easy blue-run
skiing at La Chaux (including a 'slow
skiing' piste, though this is not heavily
policed). Thankfully, getting back from
La Chaux to Les Ruinettes will be a lot
easier from 2005/06 as you'll be able
to ride the new 'chondola' instead of
taking a tricky red run.

Intermediates should exploit the
under-used Savoleyres area. This has
good intermediate pistes, usually
better snow and far fewer people
(especially on Sundays). It is also a
good hill for mixed abilities, with
variations of many runs. From here,

NEW SIGNPOSTING AT LAST – BUT WHY NOT NAME OR NUMBER THE PISTES?

*For years we've been campaigning for Verbier to improve its shambolic piste map
and on-mountain signposting. At last it has. New signs for 2004/05 at the top of
all major lifts and at key piste junctions show the colour-grading of the slopes
going in each direction, together with the name and number of the lift that each
goes to. These names and numbers tie up with those on the piste map (a huge
advance!). They also have white signs showing the direction to take to get to a
particular destination (eg Verbier, La Tzoumaz, Boarder Cross) and the grading
of the slopes towards them. This is all a great improvement and helped us find
our way around on our 2005 visit. But we have three further suggestions for
Téléverbier (the lift company). Please mark each individual piste on the mountain
and on the map with a name or number (as nearly all other resorts do), otherwise
it is too easy to be confused as to where you are part way down a
run. Mark with an arrow on the piste map the direction of some key
pistes (eg from Savoleyres to the top of Verbier's nursery slopes) to
eliminate confusion about access possibilities. And please show the
La Chaux and Savoleyres areas more clearly. Instead of the existing
4 Vallées map, which tries to show the entire area on one sheet,
perhaps what is needed is a good multi-part map similar to the
ones provided in other big areas such as the Three Valleys and the
Portes du Soleil (Téléverbier did attempt to produce one a few years
ago, but the result was poor). So our end of term report is: Huge
improvement made but still a lot further to go to score a Grade A.*

Verbier has some of the best, most extensive and varied off-piste in the world, and major free-ride competitions are held there every year. Here, with the help of Luca Voisin from Adrenaline, we pick out just a few of the runs on offer.

For adventurous intermediates who want to try off-piste for the first time, Adrenaline ski school runs off-piste courses, including avalanche transceiver training, the use of wide skis specially designed to make off-piste easier and other essential safety equipment such as shovel and probe. Then you can try relatively easy runs such as Col des Mines and Vallon d'Arby (both start from Lac des Vaux and are itinéraires) – the former is a long, open slope back to Verbier and the latter a very beautiful run in a steep-sided valley down to La Tzoumaz. For better skiers who can ski in every type of snow and who do not mind steep slopes there is the Rock Garden, which starts with a 20-minute walk from Lac des Vaux, or Col de la Mouche, which starts from Chassoure with a traverse over the normal Tortin itinéraire to a wide, quieter alternative.

Adrenaline ski and snowboard school organises off-piste and heli-skiing groups and provides safety equipment. It also offers ski-touring, freestyle lessons in the park and pipe, ice-climbing, snow-shoeing and group and private lessons for every standard of skier and snowboarder.

t 00 41 27 771 74 59
www.adrenaline-verbier.ch

Experts have endless off-piste to choose from. From the top of the Mont Fort cable-car you can drop off the back and negotiate a very, very steep initial pitch followed by crevasses before dropping into a beautiful deserted valley and ending up at Siviez. If you'd like to follow in the tracks of the best free-riders in the world, you can try the legendary Bec des Rosses, where the Xtreme free-ride contest takes place each year. Or head for the very steep couloirs between Mont Gelé and Les Attelas.

Heli-skiing is permitted in Switzerland and allows you to reach virgin slopes on which you can make first tracks – magic if there's fresh powder. Some of the most famous runs are Petit-Combin, Trient and Rosablanche.

Off-piste skiing is great fun, but don't even think about going off-piste without a fully qualified guide or instructor and the right safety equipment: route finding is difficult, avalanche danger can be high and hidden hazards such as cliffs and crevasses lurk. Adrenaline ski school can provide all you need.

Verbier

509

there is an easy way to Médran but there may be no easy way down to that link from the top of Savoleyres.

The Thyon-Veysonnaz and Nendaz sectors are worth exploring (those not willing to take on the itinéraires have to ride down to Tortin; and down from Plan du Fou to get to Nendaz).

FOR BEGINNERS
OK but not ideal
There are sunny nursery slopes close to the middle of the village and at Les Esserts, at the top of it. These are fine provided they have snow (they have a lot of snowmaking, which helps). For progression, there are easy blues at La Chaux (and you'll be able to ride the new chondola back to Les Ruinettes) and the back side of Savoleyres (from where you can ride the gondola down).

FOR CROSS-COUNTRY
Surprisingly little on offer
Verbier is limited for cross-country. There's a 4km/2.5 mile circuit in Verbier, 6km/3.5 miles at Les Ruinettes-La Chaux and 30km/19 miles down at Le Châble/Val de Bagnes.

QUEUES
Not the problem they were
Verbier's queue problems have been greatly eased by recent investment. The jumbo gondola to Les Attelas – its capacity increased recently – has cut queues at Les Ruinettes, but it has increased the overcrowding on the pistes back down (and at the top where we have had to search hard to find space to put our skis on amidst a horde of others). The mega-queues at Tortin for Chassoure are a thing of the past, thanks to the upgraded gondola. The fast chair at Lac des Vaux has greatly eased the bottleneck there. Queues at La Chaux should disappear when the new chondola is in place. But the cable-car from Tortin to Col des Gentianes can produce queues, and the Mont-Fort cable-car above it can still generate very long ones. Some queues at the main village lift station at Médran can arise if Sunday visitors fill one of the gondolas down at Le Châble, but the crowds shift quickly.

We have reports of queues for outdated double chairs and for inadequate drag-lifts in the outlying 4 Valleys resorts – notably the Greppon Blanc drags on the way to Veysonnaz.

CHILDREN

Schtroumpfs
t 771 6585
Ages 3mnth to 4yr;
8.30 to 5.30; SF60
per day

Kids Club
t 775 3363
From age 3; 8.30-
5pm; 6 days SF435
including lunch

Ski school
Takes children aged 4
to 12 (5 half days
SF155)

SCHOOLS

**Swiss (Maison du
Sport)**
t 775 3363

Fantastique
t 771 4141

Adrenaline
t 771 7459

Altitude
t 771 6006

European Snowsport
t 771 6222

Powder Extreme
t 020 8675 5407 (UK)

**Warren Smith Ski
Academy**
t 01525 374757 (UK)

Classes
(Swiss prices)
5 2½hr days SF200

Private lessons
SF140 for 2hr for 1 or
2 people

GUIDES

Bureau des guides
t 775 3363

Olivier Roduit
t 771 5317

MOUNTAIN RESTAURANTS
Disappointing in main area

There are not enough huts, which means queues and overcrowding in high season. Savoleyres is the best area. The Poste hotel by the Tzoumaz chair takes some beating for value and lack of crowds. Also worth trying are Chez Simon ('simple and cheap'), Au Mayen (beneath the Combe 1 chair – 'good service, sunny terrace') and the rustic Marmotte ('wicked, excellent rösti'). The Namasté is recommended by a 2005 reporter – 'the best restaurant on the mountain, reservations almost always essential'. Le Sonalon, on the fringe of the village, is 'excellent, with great views', but reached off-piste.

In the main area, the rustic Chez Dany at Clambin, on the off-piste run on the southern fringe of the area, is about the best, and gets packed – booking needed. Carrefour, with a large terrace, is popular and well-situated at the top of the village. The restaurants at Les Ruinettes – table-service upstairs – have big terraces with splendid views. The Olympique at Les Attelas is a good table-service restaurant. Everyone loves the Cabane Mont Fort – a proper mountain refuge off the run to La Chaux from Col des Gentianes; cosy on a bad day, and great views on a good one, but very busy – get there early or book a table.

SCHOOLS AND GUIDES
Good reports

Verbier is an excellent place for advanced skiers, in particular, to get lessons. Several reporters have praised off-piste lessons with the Swiss ski school. Of the others, Adrenaline gets rave reviews, particularly for its private lessons; a 2004 reporter said it was 'the one bright spot about the resort – highly recommended'. Another had a private lesson with European Snowsport and found the English instructor 'was brilliant at spotting faults and an excellent communicator'. A 2005 reporter also recommends European Snowsport for 'their snowboard instructors for private lessons'. British instructor Warren Smith runs his Ski Academy here (www.warrensmith-skiacademy.com). Powder Extreme was a new school for 2004/05 that specialises in off-piste. We skied with both Warren Smith and Powder Extreme in 2005 and thought them both good.

FACILITIES FOR CHILDREN
Wide range of options

The Swiss school's facilities in the resort are good, and the resort attracts quite a lot of families. The playground up at La Chaux has also received favourable reports. Space on the bus back is limited, and priority is given to school groups. The possibility of leaving very young babies at the Schtroumpfs nursery is valuable.

There are considerable reductions on the lift pass price for families on production of your passports.

STAYING THERE

HOW TO GO
Plenty of options

Given the size of the place there are surprisingly few apartments and pensions available, though those on a budget have inexpensive B&B options in Le Châble. Hotels are expensive in relation to their grading. Given a sleeping bag you can bed down at the sports centre for about £10 a night – and that includes the use of the pool. **Chalets** Verbier is the chalet-party capital of the Switzerland. Companies large and small have properties here, including Verbier specialists such as Ski Verbier who have 14 chalets including some with an indoor pool and several with steam, sauna and

← Well ... you have to take a breather to admire the views on the runs down to Tortin

SNOWPIX.COM / CHRIS GILL

Air Geneva 170km/106 miles (2hr)

Rail Le Châble (7km/ 4 miles); regular buses to resort or gondola

---

outdoor hot-tub. Flexiski has the deeply comfortable chalet Bouvreuil. Right at the top of the market, Descent has two superb chalets.

Hotels There is one 5-star hotel, five 4-star, 13 3-star and a few simpler places.

(((((5) **Chalet d'Adrien** (771 6200) Relais & Chateaux. A beautifully furnished low-rise 25-room chalet, with top-notch cooking to match. Right next to the Savoleyres lift.

(((4) **Rosalp** (771 6323) Relais & Chateaux. Comfortable rooms but the great attraction is the food in Roland Pierroz's Michelin-starred restaurant, which is as good as you'll find in any Swiss resort. Sauna, steam room, hot-tub. Good position midway between centre and Médran.

(((4) **Montpelier** (771 6131) Very comfortable 4-star, but out of town (a courtesy bus is provided). Pool.

(((4) **Vanessa** (775 2800) Central 4-star with spacious apartments as well as rooms; 'Great food,' says a reporter.

(((3) **Rotonde** (771 6525) Much cheaper, well positioned 3-star between centre and Médran; some budget rooms.

(((3) **Verbier Lodge** (771 6666) Novel log-built 3-star with stylish modern fittings, offering packages with tuition

or heli-skiing. On southern fringe, beyond Médran – reachable on skis.

(((3) **Poste** (771 6681) Well placed 3-star midway between centre and Médran; pool. Some rooms small.

((2) **Farinet** (771 6626) Central 3-star hotel, British-owned, with a focal après-ski bar on its elevated terrace.

Self-catering Few UK tour operators offer apartments, but they can be booked locally.

EATING OUT
Plenty of choice
There is a very wide range of restaurants; a pocket guide is given away locally which would be much more useful if all its advertisers gave some clues about price.

Hotel Rosalp is clearly the best (and most expensive) in town, and among the best in Switzerland, with an awesome wine cellar to match its excellent Michelin-starred food – splash out on the seven-course Menu Gastronomique if you can afford it. We have had two delicious meals there. The Pinte bistro in the hotel basement is a less expensive option – worth trying. The 5-star Chalet d'Adrien also has two tempting options, with a

Verbier

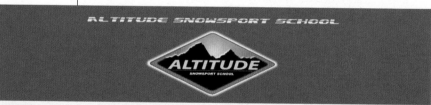

Phone numbers
From elsewhere in
Switzerland add the
prefix 027.
From abroad use the
prefix +41 27.

starred chef at work in the
gastronomique Astrance. The Grange is
another place serious about its food.

King's is one of our favourites –
innovative food in a stylish, clublike
setting. We've also had excellent meals
in the stylish Millénium.

For Swiss specialities, try the Relais
des Neiges, the Robinson, the Caveau,
Au Vieux Verbier by the Médran lifts or
Esserts by the nursery slopes. Au
Mignon does an 'excellent fondue',
said a 2004 reporter. The ever-popular
Fer à Cheval does reasonably priced
pizza and other simple dishes.
Arguably the best-value Italian food in
town is at Al Capone out near the
Savoleyres gondola. Harold's Snack
internet cafe is a 'reasonable burger
joint', says a 2005 visitor.

You can be ferried by snowmobile
up to Chez Dany or the Marmotte for a
meal, followed by a torchlit descent.

APRES-SKI
Throbbing but expensive
It starts with a 4pm visit to the
Offshore Café at Médran, for people-
watching, milk shakes and cakes. The
nearby Big Ben pub is 'great and lively
on a sunny afternoon'. Au Mignon at

the bottom of the golf course has
become popular since it was given a
large sun deck.

Then if you're young, loud and
British it's on to the Pub Mont-Fort –
there's a widescreen TV for live
sporting events. The Nelson is popular
with locals. The Farinet is particularly
good in spring, its live band playing to
the audience on a huge, sunny terrace
– there's a conservatory-type cover
over it when it's cold. Fer à Cheval is a
fun place full of regulars.

After dinner the Pub Mont-Fort is
again popular (the shots bar in the
cellar is worth a visit). Crok No Name
has good live bands or a DJ and is
entertaining for its cosmopolitan
crowd. Murphy's Irish bar in the Garbo
hotel is popular, with a good resident
DJ. The much-loved King's is a quiet
candlelit cellar bar with 60s' decor –
'hip crowd, good music'. New Club is a
sophisticated piano bar, with
comfortable seating and a more
discerning clientele. The Farm Club is
seriously expensive – on Friday and
Saturday packed with rich Swiss paying
SF220 for bottles of spirits. You'll find
us having a quiet nightcap in the
basement Bar'Jo, across the road.

ACTIVITIES

Indoor Sports centre (swimming pools, ice rink, curling, squash, sauna, solarium, steam bath, hot-tub), cinema, ice hockey, indoor golf

Outdoor 25km/ 16 miles of cleared walking paths, paragliding, hang-gliding, ice-climbing, snow-shoeing, horse-riding, tobogganing, mountaineering

TOURIST OFFICES

Verbier
t 775 3888
info@verbier.ch
www.verbier.ch
Nendaz
t 289 5589
info@nendaz.ch
www.nendaz.ch
Siviez
www.siviez-nendaz.ch
Veysonnaz
t 207 1053
tourism@veysonnaz. ch
www.veysonnaz.ch
Thyon 2000 / Les Collons
t 281 2727
info@thyon-region.ch
www.thyon-region.ch
Le Châble and **Bruson**
t 776 1682
bagnestourisme@ verbier.ch

The Casbah, in the basement of the Farinet hotel, has a North African theme. Taratata is a friendly club that seems to be growing in popularity. Scotch is the cheapest disco in town and popular with teenagers. Big Ben is 'lively, crowded and friendly'.

OFF THE SLOPES
No great attraction
Verbier has an excellent sports centre, some nice walks and a big alpine museum, but otherwise not much to offer if you don't want to hit the slopes. Montreux is an enjoyable train excursion from Le Châble, and Martigny is worth a visit for the Roman remains and art gallery. The spa complex at Lavey-les-Bains has been highly recommended by a reporter. Various mountain restaurants are accessible to pedestrians. Both toboggan runs – on the shady side of Savoleyres and from Les Ruinettes – are an impressive 10km/6 miles long. The nursery slope at Les Esserts is floodlit for tubing etc on Saturday and Sunday evenings.

Nendaz 1365m/4,480ft

Nendaz is a big resort with over 17,000 beds, but is little-known in Britain. Although it appears to be centrally set in the 4 Valleys, getting to and from the other sectors is a slow business unless you drive/take a bus to Siviez. In other respects it has attractions, relatively low prices among them. Airport transfers are quick.

THE RESORT
Nendaz itself is a large place on a shelf above and with great views of the Rhône valley. Most of the resort is modern but built in traditional chalet-style and the original old village of Haute-Nendaz is still there, with its narrow streets, old houses and barns, and baroque chapel dating from 1499.

THE MOUNTAIN
Nendaz has its own area of slopes and a rather tenuous link with rest of the 4 Valleys via Siviez.
Slopes There's a 12-person gondola straight to the top of the local north-facing slopes at Tracouet. Here there are good, snow-sure nursery slopes plus blue and red intermediate runs back to town through the trees.

Intermediate and better skiers and boarders can head off down the back of Tracouet to a cable-car which takes you to Plan du Fou at 2430m/7,970ft. From there you can go down to Siviez and the links to Verbier one way and Thyon and Veysonnaz in the other.
Terrain-parks There is a terrain-park.
Snow reliability Nendaz sits on a north-facing shelf so its local slopes don't get the sun that affects Verbier.
Experts Access to the tough stuff is a bit slower from here than from Verbier.
Intermediates The local slopes are quite varied, but not very extensive.
Beginners There are good nursery slopes at Tracouet where two new lifts were built for 2004/05.
Snowboarding There is a half-pipe.
Cross-country There are 15km/9 miles of cross-country tracks.
Queues There may be queues at Siviez at the end of the day.
Mountain restaurants The most compelling are in the Verbier area.
Schools and guides Families seem pleased with the school.
Facilities for children The school has a nursery area at Tracouet.

STAYING THERE
How to go Interhome has properties.
Hotels There are a few traditional hotels. Reporters recommend the Sourire (288 2616): 'Simple, but good food.'
Self-catering There is no shortage of apartments bookable locally.
Eating out Readers recommend the hotel Sourire and the Mont Rouge.

Verbier

Après-ski There are plenty of bars and four discos; a 17-year-old reporter recommends the Cactus Saloon as one of the livelier spots.

Off the slopes Nendaz has 70km/43 miles of winter walks, an open-air rink, a fitness centre and squash courts.

Siviez 1730m/5,680ft

Siviez is a small huddle of buildings in an isolated spot, where the slopes of Verbier, Nendaz and Veysonnaz/Thyon meet. Among them is the 2-star hotel de Siviez (288 1623). Not surprisingly, this is an ideal base from which to explore the whole 4 Valleys lift network and the new fast quad to Cambatzeline planned for 2005/06 should make this easier. But, being set a little way down the valley from Tortin, at the foot of the steep itinerary runs from Chassoure and Mont-Fort, it is also an excellent base for exploration of the tough skiing of Verbier – you can end the day with a descent of 1600m/5,250ft vertical from Mont-Fort; no noise in the evenings; perfect.

Veysonnaz 1300m/4,270ft

Veysonnaz is a small, quiet resort, sunny in the afternoon, at the foot of an excellent long red slope from the ridge above Thyon. It is an attractive old village complete with church. It has adequate bars, cafes and restaurants, a disco and a 'good' sports centre with swimming pool. Accommodation is mainly in apartments. Of the two hotels, the 'very comfortable' Chalet Royal (208 5644) is preferable to the 'tired-looking' Magrappé, which is the focus of noisy après-ski. Taking a car means you can drive to Siviez for quick access to the Verbier or Nendaz slopes – a slow business by lift and piste.

Thyon 2000 2100m/6,890ft

Thyon 2000 (why not Thyon 2100, we wonder?) is a functional, purpose-built collection of plain, medium-rise apartment blocks just above the tree line at the centre of the Thyon-Veysonnaz sector of the 4 Valleys. It has the basics – bakery, supermarket, newsagent, a couple of bar-restaurants. There's a terrain-park and a kindergarten as well as a ski school, and indoor pool.

Les Collons 1800m/5,910ft

At the foot of a broad, east-facing slope down from Thyon 2000 – a couple of strings of chalets along roads following the hillside, mostly apartments but also a couple of modest hotels including the 3-star Cambuse (281 1883). There's a much wider range of bars, restaurants and other diversions than up in Thyon.

Le Châble 820m/2,690ft

Le Châble is a busy roadside village in the valley, at the bottom of the hairpin road up to Verbier. It is linked to Verbier by a queue-free gondola that goes on (without changing cabins) to Les Ruinettes and Les Attelas, which means access to the slopes can be just as quick as from Verbier. Le Châble is on the rail network, and is also convenient for drivers who want to visit other resorts in the Valais or further afield. And it is handy for Bruson, just a short bus-ride up the mountainside facing Verbier. There are several modest hotels, of which the 2-star Giétroz (776 1184) is the pick.

Bruson 1000m/3,280ft

Bruson is a small village on a shelf just above Le Châble, and reached by a short free bus-ride. Its lifts are covered by the Verbier pass. From the village a slow chair goes up over gentle east-facing slopes dotted with chalets to Bruson les Forêts (1600m/5,250ft).

The open slopes above Bruson les Forêts are served by a quad chair up to the ridge, on the far side of which is a short drag-lift serving a tight little bowl. This may not sound much, but in addition to the intermediate pistes served by these lifts there are large amounts of underused off-piste terrain, notably through woods on the front side accessed by the drag on the back side. Off-piste descents down the back towards Orsières are possible, with the return by train. For years there have been great plans to develop Bruson – building a lift from Le Châble to mid-mountain, extending the lift network across the north-east-facing slopes of Six Blanc and on to the shoulder of Mt Rogneux at 2800m/9,190ft, and building a lift up from Orsières. A new Intrawest village is rumoured to be at the planning stages here. For now, it remains a great place to escape Verbier crowds.

Villars

Traditional old resort with a much-needed but far-flung glacier

COSTS

① ② ③ ④ ⑤ ⑥

RATINGS

The slopes

Fast lifts	***
Snow	**
Extent	***
Expert	**
Intermediate	***
Beginner	****
Convenience	***
Queues	***
Mountain restaurants	***

The rest

Scenery	***
Resort charm	****
Off-slope	****

NEWS

A new lift with increased capacity is planned to replace the Villars-Roc d'Orsay gondola, but timing is uncertain.

+ Pleasant, relaxing year-round resort
+ Fairly extensive intermediate slopes linked to Les Diablerets
+ Good nursery slopes
+ Quite close to Geneva airport
+ Good range of off-slope diversions

− Unreliable snow-cover
− Overcrowded mountain restaurants
− Short runs on the upper slopes
− Getting up the mountain may mean a slow, often crowded train journey or a bus-ride out to the gondola

With its mountain railway and gentle low-altitude slopes, Villars is the kind of place that has been overshadowed by modern mega-resorts. But for a relaxing and varied family holiday the attractions are clear – and the link with Les Diablerets and its high glacier, now known as Glacier 3000, adds to the appeal.

THE RESORT

Villars sits on a sunny shelf, looking across the Rhône valley to the Portes du Soleil. A busy high street lined with a variety of shops gives it the air of a pleasant small town; all around are chalet-style buildings, with just a few block-like hotels. You can travel to the centre of Villars on a picturesque cog train which goes on up to the slopes. It leaves from Bex in the valley, which is served by direct trains from Geneva airport (as is Aigle, a bus-ride from

Villars). A gondola at one end of town is the main lift; stay nearby if you can, since shuttle-buses get crowded at peak times. You can also stay in Gryon.

The Glacier-Alpes Vaudoises pass covers Villars, the linked slopes of Les Diablerets and Glacier 3000, plus Leysin and Les Mosses, both of which are easy jaunts by rail or road. Other resorts (eg Champéry and Verbier) are within driving distance. Les Diablerets, Leysin and Les Mosses have extended entries in our resort directory, at the back of the book.

Runs are mostly short – Grand Chamossaire rises only 300m/980ft vertical above the train terminus at Bretaye ↗

SNOWPIX.COM / CHRIS GILL

SWITZERLAND

516

KEY FACTS

| Resort | 1300m |
| | 4,270ft |

Villars, Gryon and Les Diablerets, but excluding Glacier 3000

Slopes	1115-2120m
	3,660-6,960ft
Lifts	36
Pistes	100km
	62 miles
Blue	40%
Red	50%
Black	10%
Snowmaking	10km
	6 miles

WEBSITES

For links to resort sites, go to our own new site at www.wtss.co.uk

Phone numbers
From elsewhere in Switzerland add the prefix 024.
From abroad use the prefix +41 24.

TOURIST OFFICE

t 495 3232
information@villars.ch
www.villars.ch

THE MOUNTAINS

There's a good mix of open and wooded slopes throughout the area.
Slopes The train goes up to the col of Bretaye, which has intermediate slopes on either side, with a maximum vertical of 300m/980ft back to the col and much longer runs back to the village. To the east, open slopes (often spoilt by sun) go to La Rasse and the link to the Les Chaux sector. The gondola from town takes you to Roc d'Orsay, from where you can head for Bretaye or back to Villars. From Bretaye you can head for the slow two-way chair-lift which is the connection to Les Diablerets. The piste map and marking are both poor. 'If you don't know the resort, skiing in bad visibility would be stressful,' says a reader this year.
Terrain-parks There are parks at Les Chaux and Chaux Ronde and a half-pipe at Les Diablerets.
Snow reliability Low altitude and sunny slopes mean snow reliability isn't good. There is some snowmaking but the SF12m investment planned is badly needed. If local snow is poor, head for Glacier 3000 – a long trek.
Experts The main interest for experts is off-piste. Heli-skiing is available.
Intermediates The local slopes and Les Diablerets offer a good variety and add up to a fair amount of terrain. The lengthy trip to Glacier 3000 for the splendid red run down the Combe d'Audon is worth it for the adventurous.
Beginners Beginners will enjoy the village nursery slopes and riding the train to Bretaye. There are gentle runs here, too, but it's also very crowded.
Snowboarding There are quite a few drag-lifts, including some on the link with Les Diablerets.
Cross-country The trails up the valley past La Rasse are long and pretty, and there are more in the depression beyond Bretaye (44km/27 miles in all).

Queues Queues appear for the lifts at Bretaye mainly at weekends and peak periods, and the buses and train can get overcrowded.
Mountain restaurants They are often oversubscribed, especially at Bretaye and the Meilleret sector of Les Diablerets. The Golf is expensive but good, as is the Col-de-Soud ('best rösti ever'); Lac des Chavonnes (open at peak periods) is worth the walk.
Schools and guides The Villars ski school – aka Ecole Moderne (using the ski évolutif method) – and the Swiss ski school get good reports. A past reporter gave the Swiss School '10 out of 10'. Riderschool is a specialist snowboard outfit.
Facilities for children Both ski schools run children's classes. There is also a non-ski nursery for children up to six and a Club Med with good facilities.

STAYING THERE

How to go Several tour operators offer packages here. We have received glowing reports on the Club Med. If you fancy sleeping in a hi-tech tent out in the wilds, go to www.whitepod.com.
Hotels The Golf (496 3838) is popular ('great, family tries hard'). The Eurotel Victoria (495 3131) lacks style but is near the gondola. The Bristol (496 3636) is not, but offers 'comfort, good food and service'. All are 4-star.
Eating out Many restaurants are based in hotels. Apart from these, the Sporting is recommended for pizza and the Vieux-Villars for local specialities.
Après-ski Charlie's, the Central, the Sporting and the Mini-Pub are popular bars. The Bowling bar can be a laugh; El Gringo and Fox are the discos.
Off the slopes Paragliding and hang-gliding are available, plus tennis, skating, curling, swimming, 'excellent' walks, and trips on the train – to Lausanne for instance.

SWITZERLAND
INVEST IN YOUR DREAMS

Wengen

Charming village, stunning views and extensive intermediate terrain

COSTS

① ② ③ ④ ⑤ ⑥

RATINGS

The slopes

Fast lifts	*******
Snow	******
Extent	*******
Expert	******
Intermediate	********
Beginner	*******
Convenience	*******
Queues	*******
Mountain restaurants	********

The rest

Scenery	*********
Charm	*********
Off-slope	********

NEWS

For 2005/06 snowmaking is to be improved on the slopes from Kleine Scheidegg via Wengernalp to Wengen.

For 2004/05 the old double chair from Innerwengen to Allmend was replaced by a high-speed quad with covers.

- ✚ Some of the most spectacular scenery in the Alps
- ✚ Traditional, nearly traffic-free Alpine village, reached only by cog railway
- ✚ Lots of long, gentle runs, ideal for intermediates, leading down to Grindelwald
- ✚ Rebuilt cable-car an attractive alternative to slow trains up to the slopes above Grindelwald
- ✚ Nursery slopes in heart of village
- ✚ Calm, unhurried atmosphere

- ▬ Limited terrain for experts and adventurous intermediates
- ▬ Despite some snowmaking, snow conditions are unreliable – especially on the sunny home run and village nursery slope
- ▬ Trains to slopes from here and from Grindelwald are slow
- ▬ Getting to Grindelwald's First area can take hours
- ▬ Subdued in the evening, with little variety of nightlife

Given the charm of the village, the friendliness of the locals and the drama of the scenery, it's easy to see why many people – including large numbers of middle-aged British people who have been going for decades – love Wengen. But non-devotees should think carefully about the lack of challenge, the unreliable snow and the number of slow lifts before signing up.

The Männlichen cable-car station, destroyed in the devastating avalanches of 1999, was rebuilt in the heart of the village, where it is less vulnerable to avalanche band much more convenient. Of course, it is now more popular, and gets queues at peak times but it does offer a useful alternative to living with the train timetable.

THE RESORT

Wengen is set on a shelf high above the Lauterbrunnen valley, opposite Mürren, and reached only by a cog railway, which carries on up the mountain as the main lift. Wengen was a farming community long before skiing arrived; it is still tiny, but it is dominated by sizeable hotels, mostly of Victorian origin. So it is not exactly pretty, but it is charming and relaxed, and almost traffic-free. The only traffic is electric hotel taxi-trucks, which gather at the station to pick up guests, and a few ordinary engine-driven taxis. (Why, we wonder?)

The short main street is the hub of the village. Lined with chalet-style shops and hotels, it also has the ice rink and village nursery slopes right next to it. The nursery slopes double as the venue for floodlit ski-jumping and parallel slalom races.

The views across the valley are stunning. They get even better higher up, when the famous trio of peaks comes fully into view – the Mönch (Monk) protecting the Jungfrau (Maiden) from the Eiger (Ogre).

The main way up the mountain is the regular, usually punctual trains from the southern end of the street to Kleine Scheidegg (about a half-hour journey), where the slopes of Wengen meet those of Grindelwald. The cable-car is a much quicker way to the Grindelwald slopes, and now starts conveniently close to the main street.

Wengen is small, so location isn't as crucial as in many other resorts. The main street is ideally placed for the station. There are hotels on the home piste, convenient for the slopes. Those who don't fancy a steepish morning climb should avoid places down the hill below the station.

You can get to Mürren by taking the train down to Lauterbrunnen, followed by a funicular and connecting train to Winteregg (where you can get a chair-lift up and ski down to the village) or to Mürren itself and then walk though the village to the other lifts. Alternatively you can take an (infrequent) bus to Stechelberg followed by a cable-car up. The Jungfrau lift pass covers all of this. Outings further afield aren't really worth the effort.

miles 0.5

Männlichen

down to Lauterbrunnen

N ↑

Kleine Scheidegg

km 0.5

Jungfrau Top Ski Region
Covers Wengen, Mürren and Grindelwald, trains between them and Grindelwald ski-bus.

Beginners
No special pass

Main pass
1 day SF56
6 days SF288

Senior citizens
Over 62: 6 days SF259

Children
Under 20: 6 days SF230
Under 16: 6 days SF144
Under 6: free pass.

Notes
Day pass price is for First-Kleine Scheidegg-Männlichen area only.

Alternative passes
Passes available for Grindelwald and Wengen only and for Mürren only. Non-skiers pass available.

THE MOUNTAINS

Although it is famous for the fearsome Lauberhorn Downhill course – the longest and one of the toughest on the World Cup circuit – Wengen's slopes are best suited to early intermediates. Most of the Downhill course is now open to the public. But the steepest section (the Hundschopf jump) can be avoided by an alternative red route, for those who don't fancy it. The majority of Wengen's runs are gentle blues and reds, ideal for cruising.

THE SLOPES
Picturesque playground
Most of the slopes are on the Grindelwald side of the mountain. From the railway station at Kleine Scheidegg you can head straight down to Grindelwald or work your way across the mountain with the help of a couple of lifts to the top of the Männlichen. This area is served by drag- and chair-lifts, and can be reached directly from Wengen by the cable-car. There are a few runs back down towards Wengen from the top of the Lauberhorn, but below Kleine Scheidegg there's really only one.

TERRAIN-PARKS
None last season
There was no terrain-park marked on the Wengen piste map last season and the parks at Mürren and First take quite a time to get to.

SNOW RELIABILITY
How well do they use the guns?
Most slopes are below 2000m/6,560ft, and at Grindelwald they go down to less than 1000m/3,280ft. Very few slopes face north and the long blue run back to the village suffers from sun and lack of altitude. In the past reporters have been critical that the resort's snowmaking wasn't made enough use of in times of dire need. We also have a 2005 report of 'patchy' piste grooming. More reports please!

FOR EXPERTS
Few challenges
Wengen is quite limited for experts. The only genuine black runs in the area are parts of the Lauberhorn World Cup Downhill (which, for most of its length, is merely of intermediate red run gradient) and a couple of pistes from Eigergletscher towards Wixi including Oh God (which used to be off-piste).

There are some decent off-piste runs such as White Hare from under the north face of the Eiger and more adventurous runs from the Jungfraujoch late in the season (see the Grindelwald chapter for more about going to the Jungfraujoch).

For more serious challenges it's well worth going to nearby Mürren, around an hour away. Heli-trips with mountain guides are organised if there are enough takers.

Wengen

519

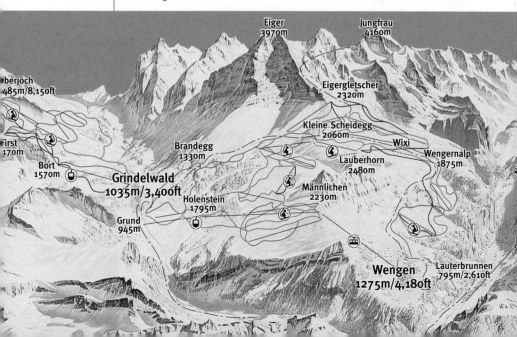

Eiger 3970m
Jungfrau 4160m
berjoch 485m/8,150ft
Eigergletscher 2320m
First 170m
Kleine Scheidegg 2060m
Bort 1570m
Brandegg 1330m
Wixi
Wengernalp 1875m
Grindelwald 1035m/3,400ft
Lauberhorn 2480m
Männlichen 2230m
Holenstein 1795m
Grund 945m
Wengen 1275m/4,180ft
Lauterbrunnen 795m/2,610ft

The Männlichen cable-
car leaves from the
centre of the village
near the nursery
slopes →

WENGEN-MUERREN-
LAUTERBRUNNENTAL AG /
SWISS-IMAGE.CH

SWITCHERLAND

520

KEY FACTS

Resort	1275m
	4,180ft

Jungfrau region	
Slopes	945-2970m
	3,100-9,740ft
Lifts	44
Pistes	203km
	126 miles
Blue	25%
Red	61%
Black	14%
Snowmaking	60km
	37 miles

First-Männlichen-
Kleine-Scheidegg
only

Slopes	945-2485m
	3,100-8,150ft
Lifts	30
Pistes	150km
	93 miles

REPORTS WANTED

Recently we have
had few reports on
this resort. If you
go there, please do
send us a report.

The best reports
earn a copy of the
next edition, and
can lead to free lift
passes in future.

See page 10.

FOR INTERMEDIATES
Wonderful if the snow is good
Wengen and Grindelwald share superb
intermediate slopes. Nearly all are long
blue or gentle red runs – see
Grindelwald chapter. The run back to
Wengen is a relaxing end to the day,
as long as it's not too crowded.

For tougher pistes, head for the top
of the Lauberhorn lift and then the
runs to Kleine Scheidegg, or to Wixi
(following the start of the Downhill
course). You could also try the north-
facing run from Eigergletscher to
Salzegg, which often has the best
snow late in the season.

FOR BEGINNERS
Not ideal
There's a nursery slope in the centre of
the village – it's convenient and gentle,
but the snow is unreliable. There's a
beginners' area at Wengernalp and
another on the Grindelwald side of
Kleine Scheidegg, but to get back to
Wengen you either have to take the
train or tackle the run down, which can
be tricky. There are plenty of good,
long, gentle slopes to progress to on
the Grindelwald side.

FOR CROSS-COUNTRY
There is none
There's no cross-country in Wengen
itself. There are 17.5km/11 miles of

tracks down in the Lauterbrunnen
valley, where the snow is unreliable.

QUEUES
Improving, but a long way to go
The Männlichen cable-car has helped
cut the queues for the trains but both
can still be crowded at peak periods. It
is best to avoid travelling up at the
same time as the ski school. Weekend
invasions can increase the crowds on
the Grindelwald side, especially on a
Saturday, because children up to 15
can ski free if a parent buys a one-day
pass on Saturday. Queues up the
mountain have been alleviated a lot in
the last few years by the installation of
fast chairs. A 2005 reporter says that
last year's new Innerwengen quad is 'a
big improvement'.

MOUNTAIN RESTAURANTS
Plenty of variety
A popular but pricey place for lunch is
the Jungfrau hotel at Wengernalp,
where the rösti is excellent and the
views of the Jungfrau are superb. The
highest restaurant is at Eigergletscher.
If you get there early on a sunny day,
you can grab a table on the narrow
outside balcony and enjoy magnificent
views of the glacier, and 'lovely menu
of the day – lamb, beans and potato'
says a 2005 reporter. The station
buffet at Kleine Scheidegg gets

boarding

*Wengen is not a bad place for gentle boarding – the nursery area is not ideal, but
beginners have plenty of slopes to progress to, with lots of long blue and red runs
served by the train and chair-lifts. Getting from Kleine Scheidegg to Männlichen
means an unavoidable drag-lift though. And the slope back to Wengen is narrow
and almost flat in places, so you may have to scoot. For the steepest slopes and
best free-riding, experts will want to head for Mürren.*

SCHOOLS

Swiss
t 855 2022
Privat
t 855 5005

Classes
(Swiss prices)
6 3hr days SF242
Private lessons
SF139 for 2hr

CHILDREN

Playhouse
t 855 1414
From 18mnth; 9pm-5pm; Sun-Fri
Sunshine
t 853 0440
Ages 1mnth upwards

Ski school
The Swiss school takes ages 4 up
(6 3hr days SF242)

GETTING THERE

Air Zürich 195km/ 121 miles (3½hr); Bern 70km/43 miles (1½hr).

Rail Station in resort.

---

repeated rave reviews, so it's not surprising that it also gets packed – the take-away rösti and sausage are a popular option. The Grindelwaldblick is a worthwhile trudge uphill from Kleine Scheidegg, with great food and views of the Eiger.

The Allmend, near the top of the Innerwengen chair and the train stop, is reportedly 'delightful', with 'friendly service' and wonderful views of the valley from the terrace. We've had conflicting reviews for Mary's Cafe situated at the end of the World Cup runs. One 2004 reporter says it is 'cosy and serves excellent food'; another found it had 'lost its character now it is owned by the Regina hotel'; a 2005 visitor found it 'very comfy, with open fires', but was disappointed by the food. For restaurants on the slopes towards Grindelwald, see that chapter.

SCHOOLS AND GUIDES
Healthy competition
A reporter says, 'The Swiss school is definitely trying harder than a few years ago.' The lessons and the standard of English are usually good. The independent Privat school has been recommended for private lessons. Guides are available for heli-trips and powder excursions.

FACILITIES FOR CHILDREN
Apparently satisfactory
Our reports on children's facilities are from observers rather than participants, but are all favourable. It is an attractive and reassuring village for families, with the baby slope in the very heart of the village.

The train gives easy access to higher slopes.

STAYING THERE

HOW TO GO
Wide range of hotels
Most accommodation is in hotels. There is only a handful of catered chalets (and no especially luxurious ones). Self-catering apartments are few, too.
Hotels There are about two dozen hotels, mostly 4-star and 3-star, with a handful of simpler places.
((((4) **Beausite Park** (856 5161) Reputedly the best in town. Good pool, steam and massage. But poorly situated at top of nursery slopes – a schlep up from the main street.
((((4) **Wengener Hof** (856 6969) No

---

prizes for style or convenience, but recommended for peace, helpful staff and spacious, spotless rooms with good views.
((((4) **Sunstar** (856 5200) Modern hotel on main street right opposite cable-car. Comfortable rooms which are gradually being refurbished; lounge has a log fire. Live music most evenings. Pool with views. 'Excellent meals, friendly.'
((((4) **Silberhorn** (856 5131) Comfortable, modern 4-star in central position opposite station, with a choice of restaurants, frequently praised by reporters.
((((4) **Caprice** (856 0606) Small, smartly furnished chalet-style hotel just above the railway. Sauna and steam room. 'Comfortable and friendly'; 'fabulous views, children's menu'. Kindergarten.
((((3) **Belvédère** (856 6868) Some way out, but we have good reports of buffet-style meals ('good for families'), spacious rooms and grand art nouveau public rooms.
((((3) **Alpenrose** (855 3216) Long-standing British favourite; eight minutes' climb to the station. Small, simple rooms, but good views; 'first-class' food; friendly staff.
((((3) **Eiger** (856 0505) Very conveniently sited, right next to the station. Focal après-ski bar. Comfy modern rooms.
(((2) **Falken** (856 5121) Further up the hill. Another British favourite, known affectionately as 'Fawlty Towers'.
Self-catering The hotel Bernerhof's decent Résidence apartments are well positioned just off the main street, and hotel facilities are available to guests.

EATING OUT
Lots of choice
Most restaurants are in hotels. They offer good food and service. The Eiger has a traditional restaurant and a stube with Swiss and French cuisine. The Bernerhof has good-value traditional dishes. The little hotel Hirschen has good steaks. There's no shortage of fondues in the village. Several bars do casual food, including good-value pizza at Sina. Cafe Gruebi has been recommended for 'the most wonderful cakes'. The Jungfrau at Wengernalp has an excellent restaurant – but you have to get back on skis or on a toboggan.

APRES-SKI
It depends on what you want
People's reactions to the après-ski scene in Wengen vary widely,

SWITZERLAND

522

ACTIVITIES

Indoor Swimming pool (in Beausite Park and Sunstar hotels), sauna, solarium, whirlpool, massage (in hotels), cinema (with English films), billiards

Outdoor Ice rink, curling, 50km/ 31 miles of cleared paths, tobogganing, snow-shoeing, paragliding, glacier flights, sledging excursions, hang-gliding, ice-climbing, helicopter flights

WEBSITES

For links to resort sites, go to our own new site at
www.wtss.co.uk

Phone numbers
From elsewhere in Switzerland add the prefix 033.
From abroad use the prefix +41 33.

TOURIST OFFICE

t 855 1414
info@wengen.ch
www.wengen-muerren.ch

according to their expectations and appetites. If you're used to raving in Kitzbühel or Les Deux-Alpes, you'll rate Wengen dead, especially for young people. If you've heard it's dead, you may be pleasantly surprised to find that there is a handful of bars that do good business both early and late in the evening. But it is only a handful of small places. The bar at the Bumps section of the home run is a popular final run stop-off. And the stube at the Eiger hotel and the tiny, 'always welcoming' Eiger Bar are popular at the end of the day. The traditional Tanne and the funky Chili's, almost opposite each other on the main street, are generally lively. Sina's, a little way out by Club Med, usually has live music. The Caprice bar is also recommended. There are discos and live music in some hotels. The cinema often shows English-language films.

OFF THE SLOPES
Good for a relaxing time
Wengen is a superb resort for those who want a completely relaxing holiday, with its unbeatable scenery and pedestrian-friendly trains and cable-car (there's a special, though expensive, pass for pedestrians). There are some lovely walks, ice skating and a curling club. Several hotels have health spas. Excursions to Interlaken and Bern are possible by train, as is

the trip up to the Jungfraujoch (see the Grindelwald chapter). Helicopter flights from Männlichen are recommended.

STAYING UP THE MOUNTAIN
Great views
You can stay at two points up the mountain reached by the railway: the expensive Jungfrau hotel (855 1622) at Wengernalp – with fabulous views – and at Kleine Scheidegg, where there are rooms in the big Scheidegg Hotels (855 1212) and dormitory space above the Grindelwaldblick restaurant (855 1374) and the station buffet. The big restaurant at Männlichen has rooms.

STAYING DOWN THE VALLEY
The budget option
Staying in a 3-star hotel like the Schützen (855 2032) or Oberland (855 1241) down in Lauterbrunnen will cost about half as much as similar accommodation in Wengen. And the Silberhorn (856 2210) is recommended by a 2005 reporter as 'good and outstanding value, and two minutes from the train station'. The trains from Wengen run until 11.30pm and are included in your lift pass. Staying in Lauterbrunnen also improves your chances of getting a seat on the morning train to Kleine Scheidegg rather than joining the scramble at Wengen – though of course it also means a much longer journey time. Lauterbrunnen is also much better placed for visits to Mürren. Another 2005 reporter last year enjoyed his stay, but 'wouldn't recommend it for those wanting après-ski'. There is a fairly lively bar in the Horner hotel.

You can save even more by staying in Interlaken. Choose a hotel near Interlaken Ost station, from which you can catch a train to Lauterbrunnen (22 minutes) or Grindelwald (36 minutes). Driving can take longer at weekends, when the roads get very busy.

THE BRITISH IN WENGEN

There's a very strong British presence at Wengen. Many Brits have been returning for years to the same rooms in the same hotels in the same week, and treat the resort as a sort of second home. There is an English church with weekly services, and a British-run club, the DHO (Downhill Only) – so named when the first Brits persuaded the locals to keep the summer railway running up the mountain in winter so that they would no longer have to climb up in order to ski down again. That greatly amused the locals, who until then had regarded skiing in winter as a necessity rather than a pastime to be done for fun. The DHO is still going strong and organises regular events throughout the season.

Zermatt

Magical in many respects – both on and off the slopes

COSTS

① ② ③ ④ ⑤ ⑥

RATINGS

The slopes

Fast lifts	*****
Snow	****
Extent	****
Expert	*****
Intermediate	****
Beginner	*
Convenience	*
Queues	***
Mountain restaurants	*****

The rest

Scenery	*****
Charm	*****
Off-slope	****

NEWS

For 2005/06 the old Sunnegga-Blauherd gondola is to be replaced by a 'chondola' – a fast lift offering a choice of travelling in eight-seat cabins or on six-seat chairs.

For 2004/05 snowmaking was increased across all sectors – mainly on lower linking runs.

Cervinia and Zermatt have agreed to promote their linked slopes under the name Matterhorn Ski Paradise. More importantly, they have produced a single, fairly clear piste map for the area.

For the next few years there are plans for new lifts improving access to the Gornergrat sector, both from Sunnegga and from Furi, at the foot of the Glacier sector.

+ Wonderful, high and extensive slopes in three/four varied areas

+ Spectacular high-mountain scenery, dominated by the Matterhorn

+ Charming, if rather sprawling, old mountain village, largely traffic-free

+ Reliable snow at altitude

+ World's best mountain restaurants

+ Extensive helicopter operation

+ Nightlife to suit most tastes

+ Smart shops

+ Linked to Cervinia in Italy

− Main lifts may be a long walk, or a crowded bus- or taxi-ride from home

− Beginners should go elsewhere

− Europe's most expensive lift pass

− Some restaurants and hotels very expensive – so choose carefully

− One-way link between Gornergrat and Glacier sectors (for the moment)

− Slow train up to Gornergrat annoys some people, but can be avoided

− Some lift queues at peak periods

− Annoying electric taxis detract from the car-free village ambience

You must try Zermatt before you die. Few places can match its combination of excellent advanced and intermediate slopes, reliable snow, magnificent scenery, Alpine charm and mountain restaurants with superb food and stunning views.

Zermatt has its drawbacks – see the long list above. But for us, and for virtually all our reporters (after taking a few days to get used to its inconvenience, in some cases), these pale into insignificance compared to its attractions, which come close to matching perfectly our notion of the ideal winter resort. It's one of our favourites – and one of the editors regularly takes his annual holiday here.

THE RESORT

Zermatt started life as a traditional mountain village, developed as a mountaineering centre in the 19th century, then became a winter resort. Summer is as important as winter here.

The central part of the village is car-free. But the village doesn't have the relaxed, rustic feel of other car-free resorts, such as Wengen and Saas-Fee. Zermatt is big business, and it shows. The clientele is more overtly part of the jet set, and the electric taxis ferrying people around are more intrusive and aggressive. Most restaurants and hotels are owned by a handful of families. Many of the workers are brought in from outside the area – but that is probably one of the reasons many reporters have remarked on the increased friendliness and improved service in recent years.

The village sprawls along either side of a river, mountains rising steeply on each side. It is a mixture of chocolate-box chalets and modern buildings, most in traditional style. You arrive by rail or taxi from Täsch, where cars have to be left for a fee. They can be left for free at more distant Visp, from where you can also get a train. The main street runs away from the station, lined with luxury hotels, shops and restaurants. Many of the narrow side-streets and paths are hilly and treacherous if icy.

For a resort with such good and extensive slopes, the clientele is remarkably 'mature'. Most visitors seem to be over 40, maybe 50, and there's little of the youthful vitality you get in rival resorts with comparable slopes, such as Val-d'Isère or St Anton.

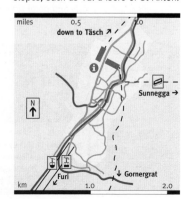

KEY FACTS

Resort	1620m
	5,310ft

Zermatt only	
Slopes	1620-3820m
	5,310-12,530ft
Lifts	28
Pistes	183km
	114 miles
Blue	25%
Red	59%
Black	16%
Snowmaking	48km
	30 miles

Zermatt-Cervinia-Valtournenche combined	
Slopes	1525-3820m
	5,000-12,530ft
Lifts	58
Pistes	383km
	238 miles
Blue	21%
Red	58%
Black	21%
Snowmaking	69km
	43 miles

The cog railway to Gornergrat starts from near the main station. The Sunnegga underground funicular towards Rothorn is a few minutes' walk away but the gondola to the Glacier and Schwarzsee areas (and the link to Cervinia) is at the opposite end of the long village. Walking from the station to the Glacier lifts can take 15 to 20 minutes and can be unpleasant because of treacherous icy paths. There are solar-powered shuttle-buses, covered by the lift pass, but they get very crowded; 'totally inadequate', 'confusing' and 'infrequent', say reporters. You can take an electric taxi instead (and keep costs down by sharing).

Choosing where to stay is very important. The best spot to stay is near the Gornergrat and Sunnegga railways, near the station end of the main street. Some accommodation is up the steep hill across the river in Winkelmatten – you can ski back to it from all areas and it has its own reliable bus service.

Getting up to the village from Täsch is no problem. The trains run on time and have automatically descending ramps that allow you to wheel luggage trolleys on and off. You are met at the other end by electric and horse-drawn taxis and hotel shuttles.

THE MOUNTAINS

Practically all of the slopes are open, above the trees – the runs served by the Sunnegga funicular are the main exception.

A single piste map now covers both Cervinia's and Zermatt's slopes fairly clearly, ending past confusion over different names for the same point on the border. The handy quick-folding version given out in Cervinia wasn't in evidence in Zermatt when we visited last season. The bigger Zermatt version is not only cumbersome, but also fails to name lifts and runs; bizarre. The piste-marking is 'vague and inadequate', says a 2005 visitor.

Some runs in all sectors and all the runs on Stockhorn are now 'ski runs' rather than normal pistes. On the resort piste map this classification is defined as 'protected' (from avalanches, we presume) 'and marked, but not prepared and not checked at the end of the day'. If it's correct that these runs are not checked, you should of course never descend them alone.

On our recent visits we have been impressed by service improvements: the lift staff are polite and helpful, there are useful announcements in several languages (including English) on the train and some cable-cars and there are free tissues at most lift stations (just as in America).

THE SLOPES
Beautiful and varied

Zermatt now divides its slopes into five branded areas, but we reckon it's clearer to divide them into four. The **Rothorn** sector (incorporating the lift company's Sunnegga sector) is reached by an underground funicular starting by the river, not far from the centre. A new 'chondola' (chair/gondola hybrid) will now go on up to Blauherd, where a cable-car goes up to Rothorn.

From the top of this area you can make your way – via south-facing slopes served by snowmaking – to Gant in the valley between Sunnegga and the second main area, **Gornergrat**. A 125-person cable-car links Gant to Hohtälli, on the ridge above Gornergrat. A gondola makes the link back from Gant to Sunnegga. Gornergrat can be reached directly from Zermatt by cog railway trains which leave every 24 minutes and take 30 or 40 minutes to get to the top – arrive at the station early to get a seat

Stockhorn: 1200m/ 3,940ft vertical, north-facing, steep. Gant is at bottom right, Hohtälli near the top, left of centre. Behind are the higher peaks of Lisskamm and Breithorn →

LIFT PASSES

Zermatt
Covers all lifts on the Swiss side of the border.

Beginners
No special pass.

Main pass
1 day SF67
6 days SF332

Senior citizens
Over 65: 6 days SF282

Children
Under 20: 6 days SF282
Under 16: 6 days SF166
Under 9: free pass

Notes
Half-day passes and single-ascent tickets on some lifts also available.

Alternative passes
International pass covers all lifts on the Swiss side plus Cervinia; Peak Pass available for pedestrians.

on the right-hand side and enjoy the fabulous views. It can be a long journey if you have to stand.

From Gornergrat there's a piste, followed by a short walk, to Furi where a cable-car goes up to Trockener Steg and the spectacular Klein Matterhorn cable-car to the top of the third and highest sector – now known as the **Glacier** area. There are plans for a link back to Gornergrat from Furi, but for now you have to descend to the village to catch a lift up. The Glacier area gives access to Cervinia – make sure you have an appropriate pass.

From Furgg, towards the bottom of the Glacier area, a stop-start gondola goes up to the top of the small but worthwhile **Schwarzsee** area.

There are pistes back to the village from all four areas – though some of them can be closed or tricky due to poor snow conditions. They can be hazardous at the end of the day due to crowds and speeding skiers – particularly the black from Furgg.

TERRAIN-PARKS
Two fun winter options
There's a world-class terrain-park (Gravity Park) between the six-pack and T-bar above Trockener Steg in the Glacier area. It includes kickers, rails, wall ride, box, rainbow, boarder-cross course, and 'a wondrous pipe' says a reporter. There's an excellent park just a bit higher up the glacier in the summer.

Zermatt

525

SNOW RELIABILITY
Good high up, poor lower down

Zermatt has rocky terrain and a relatively dry climate. But it also has some of the highest slopes in Europe, and quite a lot of snowmaking.

Three of the four sectors go up to over 3000m/9,840ft, and the Glacier area has summer skiing. There are loads of runs above 2500m/8,200ft, many of which are north-facing, so guaranteeing decent snow except in freak years.

Snowmaking machines serve some of the pistes on all four areas, from about 3000m to under 2000m (about 10,000ft down to under 6,500ft). The runs back to the village can still be patchy, as can the lower part of the south-facing run from Rothorn to Gant. Coverage was increased last year. Piste grooming is excellent.

FOR EXPERTS
Good – with superb heli-trips

If you've never been, Zermatt has to be on your shortlist. If you have been, we're pretty sure you'll want to return.

If you love long mogul pitches, the 'ski runs' (see opposite) at Triftji, below Stockhorn, are the stuff of dreams. From the top of the Stockhorn cable-car there's a run down to the T-bar that serves a wide, long face that can be one vast mogul field – steep, but not extremely so. Being north-

boarding

Boarders in soft boots have one big advantage over skiers in Zermatt – they have much more comfortable walks to and from the lift stations! Even so, there aren't many snowboarders around. The slopes are best for experienced free-riders, because tough piste and off-piste action is what Zermatt is really about; plus there's the world-class terrain-park. There is, however, an excellent little beginner area at Blauherd, complete with moving carpet lift, which we've seen many beginner snowboarders having lessons on. The main lifts are boarder-friendly: train, funicular, gondolas and cable-cars, and there aren't too many flat bits. But there are still a few T-bars. Stoked is a specialist snowboard school.

OFF-PISTE RUNS FROM THE ACCESSIBLE TO THE EPIC

Zermatt offers a wide variety of off-piste runs for all levels of skier, from off-piste beginner to expert. And if the runs reached from the lift system aren't enough, heli-skiing is available (and popular). We asked Ralph Schmidhalter, head of the Ski and Snowboard School Zermatt, to give us a run-down.

The 'ski runs' marked on the mountain and on the piste map open up a lot of ungroomed terrain. There are 'ski runs' in all sectors of the ski area. But there are also vast areas of off-piste mountainside waiting to be explored. These slopes present serious hazards, and should be tackled only with the help of a mountain guide or instructor.

The fast Patrullarve chair-lift in the Rothorn sector serves some excellent terrain, between Tuftern and the National pistes, for off-piste beginners to start developing their technique.

The slopes of Stockhorn offer some of the best runs, and generally open in late January, depending on the snow conditions. Descending from Stockhorn towards Gant, one special run goes down 'the lost valley'. In the other direction from Stockhorn there is an excellent descent to the Gornergletscher, starting with a short uphill hike and ending at Furi, at the bottom of the Glacier lift network.

In the Schwarzsee sector there are many good off-piste slopes. These include the area known as 'innru waldieni', right underneath the Matterhorn, reached from the top of the Hörnli T-bar.

There is nothing to beat the kick you can get from heli-skiing. Air Zermatt's helicopters can take you to the 3845m/12,620ft Alphubel. Or you can go higher still, to the 4250m/13,940ft Monte Rosa, for the longest descent here in Zermatt – a run of 2300m/7,550ft vertical. The run descends through wonderful glacier scenery to Furi; it is not steep, and does not require great expertise, but we suggest this for expert skiers only because of the physical demands of such a long run.

The **Ski & Snowboard School Zermatt** is the resort's original ski school, now with 200 instructors, the majority of them English-speakers. It provides group or private lessons for all standards.

t 966 2466
www.skischulezermatt.ch

facing and lying between 3400m and 2700m (11,150ft and 8,860ft), the snow keeps in good condition long after a new snowfall. But be warned: this whole area does not open until February. There's another great 'ski run' down from Hohtälli to Gant.

There are two wonderful 'ski runs' from Rothorn, with spectacular views of both the village and the Matterhorn. But they need good snow-cover to be really enjoyable.

At Schwarzsee there are several steep north-facing gullies through the woods. The gondola from Furi has improved access to these runs.

There are marvellous off-piste possibilities from the top lifts in each sector, but they aren't immediately obvious to those without local knowledge. They are also dangerous because of rocky and glacial terrain. See the feature panel above. You can join daily ski touring groups, but there aren't straightforward off-piste groups as there are in resorts such as Val-d'Isère and Méribel; you have to hire a guide privately for a full day, so to make it economic you need to form your own group. The Ski Club of Great Britain usually hires a guide for off-piste skiing once a week – a recent reporter had 'an awesome day of powder' with them.

Zermatt is the Alps' biggest heli-trip centre; the helipad resembles a bus station at times, with choppers taking off every few minutes. There are only two or three main drop-off points, so you are likely to encounter other groups on the mountain.

FOR INTERMEDIATES
Mile after mile of beautiful runs
Zermatt is ideal for adventurous intermediates. Many of the blue and red runs tend to be at the difficult end of their grading. There are very beautiful reds down lift-free valleys from both Gornergrat (Kelle) and Hohtälli (White Hare) to Gant – we love these first thing in the morning, before anyone else is on them. A variant to Riffelalp (Balmbrunnen) ends up on a narrow wooded path with a sheer cliff and magnificent views to the right.

On Rothorn, the 5km/3 mile Kumme run, from Rothorn itself to the bottom of the Patrullarve chair, also gets away from the lift system and has an interesting mix of straight-running and mogul pitches. The reds served by the

↑ We've managed to keep the Matterhorn out of this shot of the Chämi-Hitta, on the run down to Furi from Gornergrat. But the terrace has a fab view of the peak, of course – and the fact that the restaurant is not mentioned in the panel on the right doesn't mean you should pass it by

THE WORLD'S BEST MOUNTAIN RESTAURANTS

Even reporters who don't normally stop long for lunch usually succumb to temptation here. The choice of restaurants is enormous, the food usually excellent (but it helps not to be vegetarian), the small hut-based places very atmospheric (some with spectacular views), the table-service friendly (if over-worked). It is impossible to list here all those worth a visit – so don't limit yourself to those we mention. It is best to book; check prices are within your budget when you do!

Down at Findeln below Sunnegga are several attractive, busy, expensive, rustic restaurants, including the Findlerhof (aka Franz & Heidy's) where we have enjoyed excellent lamb, Chez Vrony ('Fab lunch with wine for about SF40,' says a reporter), Paradies ('good views, great rösti') and Enzian ('less busy than others'). The simple hut at Tuftern has great views from the terrace, sells good Heida wine from the highest vineyard in Europe and does a basic menu of home-made soup, cheese and cold sausage and 'wonderful apple spice cake'.

The restaurants at Fluhalp (which often has live music on the terrace) and Grünsee have beautiful, isolated situations, and the large terraces at Sunnegga and Rothorn have great views. All these are part of the Matterhorn Group and do decent food.

The Kulmhotel, at 3100m/10,170ft at Gornergrat, has both self-service and table-service restaurants, with amazing views of lift-free mountains and glaciers. Readers also rate the Riffelberg at Gornergrat ('fabulous soups') and Moos (home run from Riffelberg) for coffee and cakes.

At Furi, the Restaurant Furri (excellent rösti and scrumptious tarts) and Simi's on the road below both have large sun terraces and good food. The Aroleid is also recommended. The hotel at Schwarzsee is right at the foot of the Matterhorn, with staggering views and endless variations of rösti. Down the hill from here Stafelalp is simple, but it is charmingly situated and does 'huge portions'. Up above Trockener Steg, Gandegghütte has stunning views of the glacier. On the way back to the village below Furi, Zum See is a charming old hut serving the best mountain food in Zermatt (which means it is world-class: we've had delicious beef, lamb and raspberry tart here). Blatten is 'excellent' too.

Wherever you go, don't miss the local alcoholic coffee – in its many varieties.

Hörnli drag at Schwarzsee are excellent. In the Glacier sector the reds served by the fast quad chair from Furgg are long, testing and gloriously set at the foot of the Matterhorn. The Furggsattel chair from Trockener Steg serves more pistes with stunning views, notably the 1100m/3,610ft-vertical Matterhorn piste – a red that is of no more than blue gradient for much of its considerable length.

For less adventurous intermediates, the best runs to head for are the blues from Blauherd on Rothorn and above Riffelberg on Gornergrat, and the runs between Klein Matterhorn and Trockener Steg. Of these, the Riffelberg area often has the best combination of good snow and easy cruising, and is understandably popular with the school. Blauherd gets afternoon sun, but the snowmaking means that the problem is more often a foot or more of heavy snow near the bottom than bare patches.

In the Glacier sector most of the runs, though marked red on the piste map, are very flat and represent the easiest slopes Zermatt has to offer, as well as the best snow. The problem here is the possibility of bad weather

because of the height – high winds, extreme cold and poor visibility can make life very unpleasant (and if you are skiing into a head-wind downhill progress can be very slow).

Even an early intermediate can make the trip to Cervinia, crossing at Theodulpass rather than taking the more challenging Ventina run from Testa Grigia/Plateau Rosa.

Beware the run from Furgg to Furi at the end of the day, when it can be chopped up, mogulled in places and very crowded (the only reason it is graded black that we can see, because it isn't very steep). A much more relaxed way is the beautifully scenic Weiss Perle run from Schwarzsee (the Stafelalp variant is even more scenic but has a short uphill section). Or you can ride the gondola from Schwarzsee.

FOR BEGINNERS
Learn elsewhere

Zermatt is to be avoided by beginners. The best snow-sure nursery slope area is at Blauherd – but even this can get very busy. And there are no long easy runs to progress to except above Trockener Steg, which can be bitterly cold and windy.

Zermatt

↑ The glacier slopes are easy reds. The foreground buildings are Theodulpass, the distant ones on the skyline Testa Grigia/ Plateau Rosa

SNOWPIX.COM / CHRIS GILL

SCHOOLS

Swiss
t 966 2466

Stoked
t 967 7020

Classes (Swiss prices)
5 days (10am to 3.30 with lunch break)
SF295

Private lessons
SF160 for 2hr for 1 or 2 people

CHILDREN

Kinderparadies
t 967 7252
Ages from 3mnth

Hotel Nicoletta
t 966 0777
Ages 2 to 8

Kinderclub Pumuckel (Hotel Ginabelle)
t 966 5000
Ages from 30mnth

Kinderhort (Stoked)
t 967 7020
Ages from 3; 9am-3.30

Private babysitters
Tourist office has list.

Ski school
Both schools take children from age 4; 5 full days incl. lunch SF385 (Swiss prices).

FOR EVERYONE
Spectacular cable-car and ice cave
The Klein Matterhorn cable-car is an experience not to miss if the weather is good. There are stupendous views from the left side down to the glacier and its crevasses, as the car swings steeply into its hole blasted out of the mountain at the top. When you arrive, you walk through a long tunnel, to emerge on top of the world for the highest piste in Europe – walk slowly, the air is thin here and some people have altitude problems. The ice grotto cut into the glacier here is well worth a visit, with 'incredible ice carvings'.

FOR CROSS-COUNTRY
Fairly limited
There's a 4km/2.5 mile loop at Furi, 3km/2 miles of trails near the bottom of the gondola to Furi and another 12 to 15km/7 to 9 miles down at Täsch (don't count on good snow). There are also 'ski walking trails', best tackled as part of an organised group.

QUEUES
Main problems being solved
Zermatt has improved its lift system hugely in recent years, eliminating major bottlenecks. But a few problems remain. The Sunnegga funicular shifts large numbers rapidly which has caused queues for the gondola above it – but this is due to be upgraded for 2005/06. Both the lifts out of Gant are prone to queues at times. The high-speed quad from Furgg can get busy now that the Schwarzsee gondola is dumping people nearby. The Klein Matterhorn cable-car has queues much of the time. You may find there's only standing room on the Gornergrat train, which can be tiring and uncomfortable:

'Better to wait for the next one,' says a reporter. One thing we love about Zermatt is getting the 8am train with the lifties and restaurant staff. It arrives at the top just as they are dropping the rope to open the pistes, and you have the slopes to yourself for an hour or two.

The village buses, not surprisingly, cannot handle demand at the end of the day ('The chaos resulted in a fight over a taxi – not what you would expect in a location like this,' says a reporter).

SCHOOLS AND GUIDES
Competition paying off
The main Swiss school has a history of critical reports from readers. This year we have one encouraging report, from someone observing rather than receiving instruction, who noted 'individual advice' to each pupil in 'good English'.

There's a separate Stoked snowboard school, of which we generally have good reports. This has combined with The SkiSchool, which started in 2000/01 and is made up of talented young instructors, some of whom are British and all of whom speak good English. One reader says they had 'a complete beginner confident on reds after three lessons', but another in 2005 was disappointed by the initial 'lack of instruction' in the group classes. Group sizes are said to be small.

FACILITIES FOR CHILDREN
Good hotel nurseries
The Nicoletta and Ginabelle hotels have nurseries. The Kinderparadies, 200m/660ft from the station, takes children from three months. Stoked/ The SkiSchool runs Snowflakes, for children aged at least four years old, at Trockener Steg and a kindergarten for kids from three years at Schwarzsee. There's a snow-garden at Riffelberg.

GETTING THERE

Air Geneva
244km/152 miles
(4hr by rail); Zürich
248km/154 miles
(5hr by rail); Sion
80km/50 miles
(1½hr).

Rail Station in resort.

STAYING THERE

HOW TO GO

A wide choice, packaged or not
Chalets Several operators have places here, many of the most comfortable contained in large apartment blocks. Reporters have praised Total Ski's operation here. And Simply Ski has some good-looking small places.
Hotels There are over 100 hotels, mostly comfortable and traditional-style 3-stars and 4-stars, but taking in the whole range.

((((5)) **Mont Cervin** (966 8888) Biggest in town. Elegantly traditional. Good pool and new wellness centre.

((((5)) **Zermatterhof** (966 6600) Traditional 'grand hotel' style with piano bar and pool.

((((5)) **Riffelalp Resort** (966 0555) Up the mountain, recent smart extension, pool and spa, own evening trains.

(((4)) **Alex** (966 7070) Close to station. Reporters love it. 'Wonderful,' says one. Pool. Dancing.

(((4)) **Ambassador** (966 2611) Peaceful position near Gornergrat station. Large pool; sauna. But reports on the food are mixed.

(((4)) **Monte Rosa** (966 0333) Well-modernised original Zermatt hotel, near southern end of village – full of climbing pictures and mementos.

(((4)) **Ginabelle** (966 5000) Smart pair of chalets not far from Sunnegga lift; has own ski nursery as well as day care.

(((4)) **Nicoletta** (966 0777) Modern chalet quite close to centre, with nursery.

(((4)) **Sonne** (966 2066) Traditionally decorated, in quiet setting away from main street; 'Roman Bath' complex.

(((4)) **Beau-Site Parkhotel** (966 6868) Highly recommended by a recent reporter. 'Faultless service with nouvelle meals of four to five courses.'

(((3)) **Julen** (966 7600) Charming, modern-rustic chalet over the river, with Matterhorn views from some rooms.

(((3)) **Butterfly** (966 4166) 'Small, friendly, as well furnished as the Alex, but much better food,' says a reporter.

(((3)) **Atlanta** (966 3535) No frills, but 'friendly service'; close to centre, with Matterhorn views from some rooms.

((2)) **Alpina** (967 1050) Modest but very friendly, and close to centre.

((2)) **Bahnhof** (967 2406) Right by Gornergrat station. Cheapest place to stay in town (SF95 a night for twin room with shower, SF30 a night for a dormitory bed; with communal kitchen).

ACTIVITIES

Indoor Sauna, tennis, squash, hotel swimming pools (some open to public), salt water pool, fitness centre, indoor golf, climbing wall, casino, billiards, bowling, gallery, library, concerts, Alpine museum, cinema

Outdoor Ice rinks, curling, sleigh rides, 30km/19 miles cleared paths, snow-shoeing, helicopter flights, paragliding, climbing, ice-climbing

WEBSITES

For links to resort sites, go to our own new site at www.wtss.co.uk

---

Other recommendations include the Mirabeau (966 2660), highly praised this year – 'sophisticated and friendly', huge breakfasts, new wellness centre; also the Derby (966 3999) ('good value'), the Biner (966 5666) ('organic food') and the Mischabel (967 1131) ('cheap for Zermatt').

Self-catering There is a lot of apartment accommodation, but not much finds its way to the UK package market. We have enjoyed staying in the hotel Ambassador apartments, with free use of all its facilities such as a pool and a sauna. The Vanessa complex was recommended by a reporter. The tourist office web site has apartments.

EATING OUT
Huge choice at all price levels
There are over 100 restaurants to choose from, ranging from top-quality haute cuisine, through traditional Swiss food, Chinese, Japanese and Thai to egg and chips. There is even a McDonald's – heaven knows why.

Mood's (see Après-ski) does 'outstanding' fish. The Mazot is highly rated and highly priced. At the other end of the scale, Du Pont has good-value pasta and rösti; Grampi's ('sensibly priced'), Broken and Postli do good pizzas. The Schwyzer Stübli has local specialities and live Swiss music and dancing.

Rua Thai in the basement of the hotel Abana Real has been recommended for 'excellent Thai in attractive surroundings'. Fuji in the same building is a good Japanese.

Chez Heini serves excellent lamb and the owner sings after dinner. Giuseppe's doesn't look much, but has the best Italian food in town – book before your trip, it gets so busy. Avena and the Pipe ('refreshingly different') are recommended for curry. The Zur Alten Muhle does 'excellent steaks and venison' and the Schäferstube (Hotel Julen) is the place for a gourmet meal according to a reporter, who enjoyed 'heavenly lamb' there this year.

Da Mario, Casa Rustica, the Swiss Chalet, the Derby, the Avenstube ('good trout'), the Old Spaghetti Factory (in the hotel Post complex), the Stockhorn Grill ('excellent local lamb'), Tony's Grotta ('expensive but excellent Italian'), the Walliserkanne ('fine pizza'), and the Walliserhof ('good value set menu') have all been recommended by readers.

APRES-SKI
Lively and varied
There's a good mix of sophisticated and informal fun, though it helps if you have deep pockets. On the way back from the Glacier or Schwarzsee sectors there are lots of restaurants below Furi for a last drink and sunbathe. Hennu Stall blasts out loud music in a very un-Zermatt-like fashion but attracts huge crowds ('a beer and toffee vodka chaser sets you up to tackle the slush below,' says a recent reporter). We preferred the delicious red wine and fruit tarts at Zum See. On the way back from Rothorn, Othmar's Hütte has great views and organises dinners (followed by tobogganing down), and the Olympia Stübli often has live music. Near the church at Winkelmatten, the Sonnenblick is 'a great place to watch the sun set'.

Promenading the main street checking out expensive shoes and watches is a popular early-evening activity. The Papperla Pub is one of the few popular early places (it's crowded after dinner, too, and has a nightclub downstairs). Elsie's bar is wood-panelled, atmospheric and gets packed with an older crowd both early and late. The North Wall is frequented by seasonal workers.

Later on, the hotel Post complex has something for everyone, from a quiet, comfortable bar (Papa Caesar's) to a lively disco (Broken) and live music (Pink) and a selection of restaurants.

Grampi's is 'relaxed' and has a good restaurant. Z'Alt Hischi (in an old house, serves huge measures of spirits) and the Little Bar (crowded if there are ten people in) are good for a quiet drink. The Hexen Bar is cosy too. The hotel Alex draws a mature clientele for eating, drinking and dancing. The Hotel Pollux has 'lively music in its bar', says a reporter.

The Vernissage is our favourite bar

Phone numbers
From elsewhere in
Switzerland add the
prefix 027.
From abroad use the
prefix +41 27.

TOURIST OFFICE

t 966 8100
zermatt@wallis.ch
www.zermatt.ch

in town for a quiet evening drink. It is an unusual and stylish modern place, with the projection room for the cinema built into the upstairs bar and displays of art elsewhere. Mood's was designed by the same guy and is run by the team that used to run the Post complex (recommended by a 2005 visitor). There's a good cocktail bar downstairs, wood-panelled restaurant above and a comfortable bar done out in nautical fashion at the top.

OFF THE SLOPES
Considerable attractions
Zermatt is an attractive place to spend time. As well as pricey jewellery and clothes shops, there are interesting places selling food, wine, books and art. It is easy (but expensive) for pedestrians to get around on the lifts (purchase the Peaks Pass) and meet others for lunch, and there are some nice walks (highly recommended by a 2005 reporter) – a special map is available. The Ice Grotto at Klein Matterhorn and the Alpine museum in town are worth seeing (both regularly recommended by reporters). You can take a helicopter trip around the Matterhorn. There is a cinema, and a

reader tells us the free village guided tour is 'well worth doing'. For an icy experience, visit (or stay at) the Igloo up on Gornergrat.

STAYING UP THE MOUNTAIN
Comfortable seclusion
There are several hotels at altitude, of which the pick is the Riffelalp Resort at the first stop on the Gornergrat railway (see 'Hotels', above) – but the evening train service is a bit limited. At the top of the railway, at 3100m/10,170ft, is the Kulmhotel Gornergrat (966 6400) – an austere building with basic rooms.

STAYING DOWN THE VALLEY
Attractive for drivers
In Täsch, where visitors must leave their cars, there are five 3-star hotels, costing less than half the price of the equivalent in Zermatt. The Täscherhof (966 6262) ('Very comfortable, good food and spa facilities,' says a recent reporter) is next to the station; the City (967 3606) is close by. Täsch is very quiet at night, a 13-minute ride from Zermatt, with trains every 20 minutes for most of the day; the last train down is 11.10. Taxis can operate up to the edge of Zermatt.

Zermatt

SKI & FUN

FUJI OF ZERMATT

RESTAURANTS

WELLNESS

★ ★ ★
Hotel Albana Real
Zermatt - Matterhorn

RUA THAI

► www.hotelalbanareal.com ▲ info@hotelalbanareal.com ▲ Tel +41 27 966 61 61 ▲ Fax +41 27 966 61 62

ADELBODEN TOURIST OFFICE

Adelboden

For intermediates who find relaxing, pretty surroundings more important than convenience for the slopes, chocolate-box-pretty Adelboden has a lot of appeal. The slopes are extensive, and the lifts are impressive.

KEY FACTS

Resort	1355m
	4,450ft
Slopes	1070-2355m
	3,510-7,730ft
Lifts	56
Pistes	170km
	106 miles
Blue	41%
Red	52%
Black	7%
Snowmaking	40km
	25 miles

TOURIST OFFICE

t 033 673 8080
info@adelboden.ch
www.adelboden.ch

THE RESORT

Adelboden is a classic Swiss mountain village: old chalets line the quiet main street (cars are discouraged), with a backdrop of 3000m/9,840ft peaks. The village is compact, with efficient buses to the outlying areas. There are some 30 pensions and hotels (mainly 3- and 4-star). The après-ski is low-key, based on bars and tea rooms. Eating out possibilities are varied, and include a couple of mountain restaurants. There is a fair bit to do off the slopes, including skating and curling.

THE MOUNTAINS

Adelboden's slopes are split into five sectors – two of them a bus-ride away. The others are linked, by piste if not by lift, and stretch across the mountain to Lenk in the next valley.

Most pistes are below 2000m/ 6,560ft and snowmaking is limited – so snow reliability is not ideal. At Geils there are some genuine black pistes, and good off-piste possibilities down to both Adelboden and Lenk that are under-used. All five sectors deserve exploration by intermediates. At Geils there is a lot of ground to be covered – including trips across to Lenk's own gentle Betelberg area. There are good nursery slopes in the village and at nearby sectors. At Geils there are long, glorious, easy runs to progress to.

There are extensive cross-country trails along the valley and up at snow-sure Engstligenalp.

The main gondola isn't entirely free of queues. And the old Hahnenmoos gondola is a bottleneck, overdue for replacement. There are pleasant mountain restaurants with terraces in the Geils sector.

ENGELBERG TOURIST OFFICE

Engelberg

Engelberg is an easy 2.5 hour train ride from Zürich airport (even less by car), which makes it great for short breaks. It has one of the biggest verticals in the Alps, awesome off-piste and some good intermediate slopes.

KEY FACTS

Resort	1050m
	3,440ft
Slopes	1050-3020m
	3,440-9,910ft
Lifts	24
Pistes	82km
	51 miles
Blue	30%
Red	67%
Black	3%
Snowmaking	some

MOMENTUM SKI

Weekend & a la carte ski holiday specialists in Engelberg

020 7371 9111
www.momentumski.com

TOURIST OFFICE

t 041 639 7777
welcome@engelberg.ch
www.engelberg.ch

THE RESORT

Engelberg was popular with Brits in the early 20th century but its grand Victorian hotels have a faded look and have been joined by chalet-style buildings and concrete blocks. It is more of a town than a village. The 12th-century monastery and its cheese-making shop are worth a visit. It's a bus-ride or long walk to the lifts from most hotels. The Europe (041 639 7575) is central, the Terrace (041 639 6666) is served by a funicular and run on club-hotel lines. The Yucatan is the main après-ski bar.

THE MOUNTAINS

The main slopes rise almost 2000m/ 6,560ft above the town by three successive lifts: a gondola and two cable-cars, the top one rising above glacial crevasses and rotating 360° on

the way. Weekend queues can be long.

Pistes are limited and fragmented by the glaciers and rugged terrain, and they suit strong intermediates best: most runs are steep reds and there are few easy cruises. Beware of the seriously steep and usually mogulled black between Titlis and Stand. There's a good isolated beginner area near the mid-station of the gondola.

There is superb off-piste for experts who hire a guide. The classic Laub run is 1000m/3,280ft vertical down an immensely wide face with a consistent pitch and magnificent views of town. But we enjoyed even more the 2000m/ 6,560ft vertical Galtiberg run, which starts over glaciers and ends among mountain streams and trees: we saw only three other people on it. There's plenty more off-piste, too. The Ritz (at the bottom of the Laub) and Jochpass mountain restaurants are rustic.

Gstaad

Despite its exclusive reputation, Gstaad is an attractive, traditional village where anyone could have a relaxing holiday. But the slopes are very fragmented, and not snow-sure – most are below 2100m/6,890ft.

KEY FACTS

Resort	1050m
	3,440ft
Slopes	950-3000m
	3,120-9,840ft
Lifts	62
Pistes	250km
	155 miles
Blue	48%
Red	36%
Black	16%
Snowmaking	some

TOURIST OFFICE

t 033 748 8181
gst@gstaad.ch
www.gstaad.ch

THE RESORT

Gstaad is a year-round resort in a spacious, sunny setting amid friendly, wooded mountains, its traffic-free main street lined by chalet-style hotels, smart shops and cafes. Most of the accommodation is in private chalets and apartments, the rest in 3-star hotels and above – including the landmark 5-star Palace. Restaurants are mainly hotel-based, and expensive. In season après-ski is lively. Off-slope activities are good – the tennis centre and pool complex are impressive.

THE MOUNTAINS

There are four main areas of slopes, covered by a single, confusing map. Most slopes are below the tree line.

Three sectors are accessed via lifts scattered around the fringes of Gstaad and served by a shuttle-bus. The largest sector is accessed from lifts reached by train at Saanenmöser and Schönried, which also has a separate sunny area of slopes across the valley.

Low altitude means that snow-cover can be unreliable except on the Glacier des Diablerets – also covered by the area pass, but 15km/9 miles away.

Few runs challenge experts. Black runs rarely exceed red or even blue difficulty. There is off-piste potential – some steep. Given good snow, this is a superb area for intermediates, with long, easy descents in the major area to the villages scattered around its edges. The nursery slopes at the bottom of Wispile are adequate, and there are plenty of runs to progress to. Time lost on buses or trains is more of a problem than queues. Mountain restaurants are plentiful, and most are attractive.

Short turns

Lenzerheide

Lenzerheide is the senior partner with Valbella in an extensive area of intermediate slopes in a pretty setting around a lake, all at a decent altitude – worth considering, although the villages are not chocolate-box pretty.

KEY FACTS

Resort	1470m
	4,820ft
Slopes	1230-2865m
	4,040-9400ft
Lifts	28
Pistes	155km
	96 miles
Blue	35%
Red	45%
Black	20%

TOURIST OFFICE

t 081 385 1120
info@lenzerheide.ch
www.lenzerheide.ch

THE RESORTS

Lenzerheide is a sprawling village – a pleasant enough place once you get away from the minor through-road that is at its centre. The road runs past a prettily wooded lake to Valbella, a more amorphous collection of holiday accommodation on the sunny slopes north of the lake, and over a low pass to the smaller village of Parpan. There are plenty of comfortable hotels, and a wonderful luxury rustic retreat in the Guarda Val. An influx of weekend visitors enlivens the après-ski scene.

THE MOUNTAINS

The slopes are on the two sides of the valley, facing due east and west. Links across the valley are by bus, but within each sector there are links across the mountainside – so a circuit is possible.

All around the circuit there are separate lifts serving the wooded lower slopes and the open upper slopes – with lots of appealing restaurants dotted around at the mid-mountain stations where they meet, and at some of the tops. The east-facing, morning-sun slopes are mainly fairly gentle, with top heights around the 2300m/7,550ft mark. Piste classification overstates difficulty. The west-facing slopes have more character, both in skiing and visual terms, including a run on the back of the dramatic peak of the Rothorn (2865m/9,400ft), reached by cable-car.

The lift system is a mix of new and old – there are a couple of six-packs but there are also quite a few old chairs and drags. But queues are rare except at weekends. Snow reliability is reasonable, at least on the upper east-facing slopes.

In general, people who try American skiing and snowboarding for the first time are captivated by the experience and by the contrasts with European resorts. Nearly everyone is struck by the high standards of service and courtesy, the relatively deserted pistes, the immaculate piste grooming and the quality of accommodation. Depending on the resort, you may also be struck by the cute Wild West ambience and the superb quality of the snow.

But don't fall into the trap of lumping all US resorts together – they differ enormously. That's one reason why we have organised our American chapters in regional sections – California, Colorado, Utah, Rest of the West, and New England. US skiing does have some distinct disadvantages, too. Read on.

Most American resorts receive serious amounts of snow – average snowfall is typically in the region of 6m to 12m (20ft to 40ft) in a season. And most have serious snowmaking facilities too. What's more, they use them well – they lay down a base of snow early in the season, rather than patching up shortages later.

There are wide differences in quantity and quality of snowfall, both between individual resorts and between regions – we discuss some of these in our regional introductions.

Piste grooming is taken very seriously – most American resorts set standards that the best Alpine resorts are only now attempting to match. Every morning you can expect to step out on to perfect 'corduroy' pistes. But this doesn't mean that there aren't moguls – far from it. It's just that you get moguls where the resort says you can expect moguls, not everywhere. Some resorts even go so far as to groom half the width of some runs, leaving the other half mogulled.

The slopes of most American resorts are blissfully free of crowds – a key advantage that becomes more important every year as the pistes of Europe become ever more congested. If you want to ride those new shaped skis through turns at the speeds they were designed for, take them to the States. And, because the slopes are mostly below the tree line, they offer good visibility in bad weather.

Most American resorts offer free guided tours of the area. Lift queues are short, partly because they are highly disciplined: spare seats on chair-lifts are religiously filled, with the aid of cheerful, conscientious attendants. Piste maps and tissues are freely available at the bottom of most lifts. Mountain 'hosts' are on hand to advise you about the best possible routes to take. School standards are uniformly high, with the added advantage that English is the native language. And facilities for children are impressive, too.

Many Europeans have the idea that American resorts don't have off-piste terrain, but this seriously misrepresents the position. It's true that resorts practically always have a boundary, and that venturing beyond it into the 'backcountry' may be discouraged or forbidden. But within the boundary there is often very challenging terrain that is very much like off-piste terrain in an Alpine resort, but with the important advantage that it is patrolled and avalanche-controlled – so you don't need to hire a guide. We rate this as one of the great attractions of American resorts.

← One of the key attractions of the States for experts is that there are steep, snowy, ungroomed slopes like this that are avalanche-protected. You do sometimes have to hike up to get to the best snow or slopes – as here, at Aspen's Highland Bowl

537

There are drawbacks to the US, of course. One is that many resorts
have slopes that are very modest in extent compared with major
Alpine areas. But many US resorts (in Colorado and California, in
particular) are very close to each other – so if you are prepared to travel
a bit, you won't get bored. Roads are good, and car hire is cheap
(though you should budget for buying snow-chains – we've yet to find
a US rental company that will provide them). A more serious problem
is that the day is ridiculously short. The lifts often shut at 3pm or 3.30.
That may explain another drawback for those who like a good lunch –
the dearth of decent mountain restaurants. The norm is monster self-
service refuelling stations – designed to minimise time off the slopes.
Small restaurants with table-service and decent food are rare.

It's also true that in many resorts the mountains are slightly
monotonous. You don't get the spectacular mountain scenery and
the distinctive high-mountain runs of the Alps. Most trails have
clearly been cut through the forest; whereas in the Alps the artificial
nature of the runs is rarely obvious when they are blanketed by
snow, in the Rockies it is inescapable.

The classification of pistes (or trails, to use the local term) is
different from that in Europe. Red runs don't exist. The colours used
are combined with shapes. Green circles correspond fairly closely to
greens in Europe (that is, in France, where they are mainly found).
American blue squares largely correspond to blues in Europe, but also
include tougher intermediate runs that would be red in the Alps;
these are sometimes labelled as double-blue squares, although in
some resorts a hybrid blue-black grading is used instead. Black
diamond runs correspond to steeper European reds and easier
European blacks. But then there are multiple diamonds. Double-
diamond runs are seriously steep – often steeper than the steepest

SNOWPIX.COM / CHRIS GILL

If you are getting
tired of weaving
through crowds of
other skiers on Alpine
pistes, give the USA a
try. This is the main
run down to
Arrowhead, at Beaver
Creek in Colorado ➔

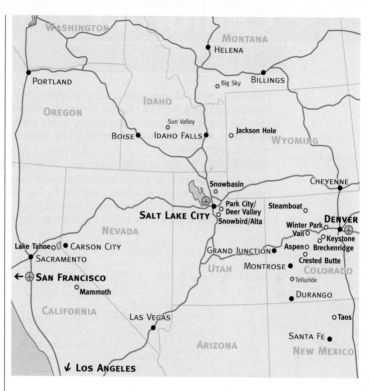

pistes in the Alps – and include high, open bowls. A few resorts have wildly steep triple-diamonds.

US resort towns vary widely in style and convenience. There are old restored mining towns such as Telluride, Crested Butte and Aspen, genuine cowboy towns such as Jackson Hole, purpose-built monstrosities such as Snowbird, and even skyscraping gambling dens such as Heavenly. There is an increasing number of cute, car-free base villages such as Keystone's River Run, Copper Mountain's revamped base and the fledgling village at Squaw Valley. Two important things that they all have in common are good-value, spacious accommodation and good, reasonably priced restaurants. One point for young people to watch is that the legal age for buying or consuming alcohol is 21; and the law is rigorously enforced – anyone under 40 is well advised to carry evidence of age.

In the end, your reaction to skiing and snowboarding in America may depend mainly on your reaction to America. If repeated cheerful exhortations to have a nice day wind you up – or if you like to ride chair-lifts in silence – perhaps you'd better stick to the Alps.

What about the cost? It's never going to be cheap, but the basic cost of getting there is lower than you might think: you can get room-plus-hire-car February packages to California for under £600; with the £ at over $1.70, eating out is not expensive; and it's not difficult to find rooms with kitchenettes where you can economise by doing some of your own catering. But lift passes, tuition and childcare are very expensive by European standards – they can be double what you would pay in the Alps. You can often save, especially on lift passes, by buying in advance through tour operators – look out for these deals.

California

California? It means surfing, beaches, wine, Hollywood, Disneyland and San Francisco cable-cars. But it also has the highest mountains in continental USA and some of America's biggest winter resorts, usually reliable for snow from November to May. What's more, winter holidays in California are less expensive than you might expect.

For most visitors, Californian skiing means the Lake Tahoe area. Spectacularly set high in the Sierra Nevada 322km/200 miles east of San Francisco, Lake Tahoe is ringed by skiable mountains containing 14 downhill and 7 cross-country centres – the highest concentration of winter sports resorts in the USA. Then, a long way south and more often reached from LA, there is Mammoth.

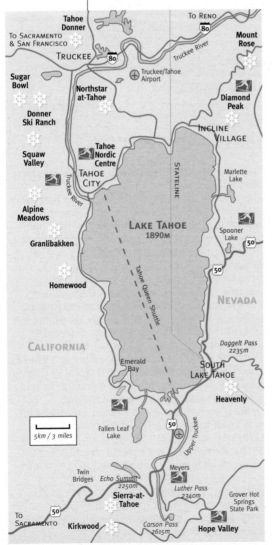

One or two of the Lake Tahoe resorts may have the extent and variety of slopes to keep you amused for a week, but the real appeal of a holiday in this area is that you can easily visit several resorts, spending a day or two at each. You could visit them all from a single base using a car, and most using buses and boats.

Two resorts stand out from the herd, at least in terms of size. **Heavenly** (covered in detail in its own chapter) is the biggest in the area, and has at the foot of its slopes much the biggest development – the bizarre gambling-based town of South Lake Tahoe. It makes an obvious base for visiting a range of resorts, both south and north of the lake.

Squaw Valley, the biggest north-shore resort, comes a close second to Heavenly in terms of area, but is only now developing a wide choice of accommodation. Squaw gets a half-page Short Turns entry at the end of the California section, along with the three next-most-interesting resorts – **Alpine Meadows**, **Kirkwood** and **Northstar**. All are appreciably smaller than Heavenly and Squaw, but all offer a worthwhile 2,000 to 2,500 acres of terrain.

Most of the resorts around Tahoe are not fully formed 'destination' resorts of the kind that you find in Colorado or the Alps. A few have no nearby accommodation at all; but there are lots of B&Bs and motels scattered around the lake, and a couple of quite pleasant small towns.

The obvious alternative to staying in South Lake Tahoe is the small tourist town of Tahoe City, on the lake's north-west shore – especially handy for

Squaw Valley and Alpine Meadows. It has a range of touristy shops and some good restaurants and bars. One regular Tahoe reporter suggests Incline Village at the north-east corner of the lake (handy for Diamond Peak and Mount Rose) for its 'country charm and ambience, and friendly people'.

Sierra-at-Tahoe is only a half-hour drive from South Lake Tahoe – though the road passes over the 2250m/7,380ft Echo Summit, which may require chains. It's a densely wooded area with a vertical of 675m/2,210ft, 2,000 acres, and 11 lifts including three fast quads. Sierra claims an impressive average of 420 inches of snow a year. The Backside area is gentle, but slopes are generally quite challenging. There is nothing at the base but a day lodge and a car park.

Sugarbowl (460m/1,510ft vertical, 1,500 acres, nine lifts include five fast quads) was the first Sierra Nevada area to be developed. It is a few miles away from the lake, and claims the most snow in the region with an annual average of 500 inches. It is said by an experienced local reporter to be a place 'for serious skiers', and it certainly has a row of double diamond chutes – but also plenty of single black and blue slopes. There is lodging at the base in the Inn at Sugarbowl.

Visitors recommend two areas north-east of the lake particularly for their quiet slopes. **Diamond Peak** (560m/1,840ft vertical, 650 acres, six chairs, one fast) offers 'breathtaking views and a fab restaurant'. Its terrain park was revamped last season. The relatively high and steep **Mount Rose** (550m/1,800ft vertical, 1,200 acres, seven lifts including two six-packs) is recommended for its 'great snow always and carving runs'. Last season saw big changes here: installation of the second six-pack, and relocation of the quad it replaced to open up The Chutes – a shady bowl mainly of serious double-diamond steepness.

At least one reporter reckons **Homewood** (500m/1,640ft vertical, 1,250 acres, eight lifts) has the best views of all from its position right on the western shore of the lake, as well as the quietest slopes of all, suitable for all abilities.

The other Californian resort we cover in detail, **Mammoth**, has the real drawback that it is rather isolated – it's a long drive from Tahoe, or from Los Angeles airport. But it is an impressive mountain that is worth considering – it's much higher than the Tahoe resorts, for one thing – and it's well placed if you fancy a couple of days at Disneyland as part of the trip.

Holidays in California are relatively cheap because winter is low season for much of the accommodation and also for scheduled flights from Britain into Los Angeles and San Francisco. There is huge capacity available for the massive summer tourist trade to the Lake Tahoe area, in particular, and hotel owners and airlines are happy to offer cut-price deals to keep a contribution coming in towards their overheads.

California's mountains get a lot of snow. In several recent seasons, Californian resorts have recorded the deepest snow-cover in North America. Connoisseurs of Rockies powder are inclined to brand the snow that falls in California as wet 'Sierra Cement'. Our fat file of reports from visitors has some complaints about that – especially late in the season – but most people have found the snow just fine, particularly in comparison with what you would expect in the Alps. So have we: on our last visit we enjoyed two of the best days of our season skiing powder in the trees of Heavenly and Mammoth.

Most of the resorts mainly attract weekend visitors from the cities of California's coastal area. Peak weekends apart, the slopes are uncrowded, and queues are rare.

In the past our main reservation has been the character of the resorts themselves; they don't have the traditional mountain-town ambience that we look for in the States. That's partly because this is California, where walking is regarded as an eccentric way to get around. In compensation, Heavenly, at least, offers uniquely big-time entertainment in its casinos.

But things are changing, with several new pedestrian 'villages' being developed. At Heavenly a gondola now goes from a new car-free 'village' in the centre of South Lake Tahoe right into the heart of the slopes. The new village at Squaw Valley continues to develop, making this an increasingly attractive base. Kirkwood and Northstar have developed small, attractive slope-side villages. And a new pedestrian village opened a couple of years back in Mammoth, too, linked to the slopes by gondola.

Heavenly

Knockout views over Lake Tahoe, and a unique nightlife scene

RATINGS

The slopes

Fast lifts	***
Snow	****
Extent	***
Expert	***
Intermediate	****
Beginner	****
Convenience	*
Queues	****
Mountain restaurants	*

The rest

Scenery	****
Resort charm	*
Off-slope	**

NEWS

For 2005/06 the North Bowl and Olympic chairs on the Nevada side will be replaced by a fast quad. This new North Bowl Express may open up more on- and off-piste possibilities

Also for next winter, the Skyline Trail is to be regraded to facilitate the journey from the top of the gondola to the Nevada side.

For 2004/05 the slow Powderbowl and Waterfall chairs on the California side were replaced by a six-pack. At the top Heavenly's fourth terrain-park was added – the Rail Yard. Snowmaking was increased on the black Face run and in the Adventure Peak beginners' area.

The East Peak Lodge was renovated, including weather protection for the terrace.

+ Spectacular setting, with amazing views of Lake Tahoe and Nevada

+ Fair-sized mountain which offers a sensation of travelling around – common in the Alps, not in the US

+ Large areas of widely spaced trees, largely on intermediate slopes – fabulous in fresh powder

+ Some serious challenges for experts

+ Numerous other worthwhile resorts within an hour's drive

+ A unique nightlife scene

+ Good snow record plus impressive snowmaking facilities

− South Lake Tahoe, where you stay, is a bizarre and messy place spreading along a busy highway

− Tediously flat links between some sectors of the slopes

− No trail back to South Lake Tahoe

− Gondola can be stopped by high winds

− Very little traditional après-ski activity – though the new 'village' at the gondola base helps

− If natural snow is in short supply, most of the challenging terrain is likely to be closed

A resort called Heavenly invites an obvious question: just how close to heaven does it take you? Physically, close enough: with a top height of 3070m/10,070ft and vertical of 1075m/3,530ft, it's the highest and biggest of the resorts clustered around scenic Lake Tahoe. Metaphorically, it's not quite so close. In particular, anyone who (like us) is drawn to Heavenly partly by its exceptionally scenic setting is likely to be dismayed by the appearance and atmosphere of South Lake Tahoe.

The official line is that the place has been transformed into something like a European ski resort by the gondola from downtown up to the mountain, and by the opening of a pedestrian 'village' around its base. We don't buy that. Unless you stay there, the 'village' is just somewhere to spend time and money at the end of the day – the general feel of South Lake Tahoe isn't much affected.

THE RESORT

Heavenly is on California's border with Nevada, at the south end of Lake Tahoe. Other resorts around the lake are easily visited from a base here.

Heavenly's base-town – South Lake Tahoe – is primarily a summer resort. In this respect it is unusual, but not unique. What really sets it apart is that its economy is driven by gambling. The Stateline area at its centre is dominated by a handful of monstrous hotel-casinos located just inches on the Nevada side of the line. These brash but comfortable hotels offer good-value accommodation (subsidised by the gambling), swanky restaurants and big-name entertainers, as well as roulette wheels, craps and card games – and endless slot machines into which gambling-starved Californians feed bucketloads of quarters.

The casinos are a conspicuous part of the amazing lake views from the lower slopes (though not from above mid-mountain). They look like a classic American downtown area, which you'd expect to be full of shops and bars. But they are actually just a cluster of high-rise blocks bisected by the seriously busy US Highway 50. The rest of the town spreads for miles along this pedestrian-hostile road – dozens of low-rise hotels and motels (some quite smart, but many rather shabby), stores, wedding chapels and so on. The general effect is less dire than it might be, thanks to the camouflage of the tall trees that blanket the area.

The new 'village' built on the California side of the stateline is an improvement, providing an après-ski focus and pedestrianised area that the resort has lacked, and this is now the obvious place to stay – right next to the base of the gondola into the heart of the slopes.

KEY FACTS

Resort	1995m
	6,540ft
Slopes	1995m-3070m
	6,540-10,070ft
Lifts	30
Pistes	4,800 acres
Green	20%
Blue	45%
Black	35%
Snowmaking	70 %

Some of the casino-hotels are within five minutes' walk of the 'village' and gondola, making these an attractive choice even for those not keen on the gambling and entertainment, but others are enough of a hike away to justify using the shuttle buses. And much of the cheaper accommodation is literally miles away. If that's where you're staying, you may prefer to access the mountain from the original lift base, the refurbished California Lodge, up a heavily wooded slope 2km/1 mile out of South Lake Tahoe. That way, you'll be able to ski down at the end of the day instead of riding a lift down to the town base.

Like the town, the slopes spread across the border into Nevada – and there are two other lift bases, which can easily be reached by road, around the mountain in Nevada. There are 'adequate' free shuttle-bus services to the three out-of-town bases (and more buses will be in service this year). A car is still handy to explore the other resorts around Lake Tahoe and to get to many of the best restaurants.

An amusing way to visit Squaw Valley is to go by boat on the skier/boarder shuttle. The service runs from Tuesday to Friday from 7am.

THE MOUNTAIN

Practically all of Heavenly's slopes are cut through forest, but in many areas the forest is not dense and there is excellent tree skiing. As always in America, this 'off-piste' terrain is avalanche controlled. But it's 'patrolled' only by hollering; since collision with a tree may render you unconscious, don't ski the trees alone.

THE SLOPES
Interestingly complex

Heavenly's mountain is complicated, and getting from A to B requires more careful navigation than is usual on American mountains. Quite a few of the links between different sectors involve flat tracks, which attract complaints from reporters.

There is a fairly clear division between the California side of the mountain (directly above South Lake Tahoe) and the Nevada side (above Stagecoach Lodge and Boulder Lodge). The gondola is efficient but it can be closed by high winds. Some reporters are disappointed to find that there is a bit of a plod from the top to the base of the fast Tamarack six-seat chair, above it. Near the Nevada border you

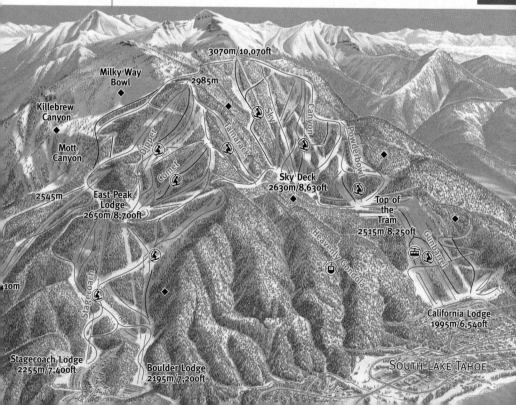

Milky Way Bowl

3070m/10,070ft

2985m

Killebrew Canyon

Mott Canyon

Dipper

Comet

Tamarack

Sky

Canyon

Powderbowl

Sky Deck
2630m/8,630ft

East Peak Lodge
2650m/8,700ft

2545m

Top of the Tram
2515m/8,250ft

Gunbarrel

Heavenly Gondola

California Lodge
1995m/6,540ft

Stagecoach

Stagecoach Lodge
2255m/7,400ft

Boulder Lodge
2195m/7,200ft

SOUTH LAKE TAHOE

LIFT PASSES

Heavenly
Covers all lifts on Heavenly mountain.

Beginners
Combined lesson/ limited lift pass/ equipment deals available.

Main pass
1 day $65
6 days $390 ($312)

Senior citizens
Over 65: 6 days $270 ($180)

Children
Under 19: 6 days $324
Under 13: 6 days $192 ($144)
Under 5: free pass

Notes
Prices quoted are what you pay at a ticket window in the resort. The reduced prices in brackets are available to international visitors who pre-book through a UK tour operator. It is not necessary to buy a complete holiday package to obtain these prices.

can see beautiful views over Lake Tahoe in one direction and the arid Nevada 'desert' in the other.

On the California side there are four fast chairs on the upper mountain, each serving its own runs, with links between the sectors. The steep lower slopes served by the Tramway (cable-car) and Gunbarrel fast chair.

On the Nevada side there are three main bowls. The central one, above East Peak Lodge, is an excellent intermediate area, served by two fast quad chairs, with a downhill extension of the bowl served by the Galaxy chair. On one side of this central bowl is the steeper, open terrain of Milky Way Bowl, leading to the seriously steep Mott and Killebrew canyons, served by the Mott Canyon chair. On the other side is the North Bowl, with fast chairs up from Nevada's two base lodges – one, new for this season, providing a link back to the California side.

TERRAIN-PARKS
Big improvements
Recent expansion has resulted in four good terrain-parks on the Groove, High Roller and Cascade runs, and the latest addition, the Rail Yard, above the Powderbowl Express. The resort boasted the country's first tri-level box and has a 120m/390ft super-pipe.

SNOW RELIABILITY
No worries
Heavenly was one of the first resorts to invest heavily in snowmaking. The system now covers around 70% of the trails and ensures that most sections are open most of the time. In recent years California has consistently recorded some of the deepest snow-cover of any North American resorts, and Heavenly is now able to claim a five-year average of an impressive 360 inches – a figure likely to rise when 2005's record snowfall is worked in.

FOR EXPERTS
Some specific challenges
The black runs under the California base lifts – including The Face and Gunbarrel (often used for mogul competitions) – are seriously steep and challenging. Ellie's, at the top of the mountain, may offer continuous moguls too. There's even steeper stuff on the Nevada side. Milky Way Bowl provides a gentle single-diamond introduction to the emphatically double-diamond terrain beyond it. The extremely steep Mott and Killebrew canyons have roped gateways and the less expert are steered to lower gates. The Mott Canyon chair is slow, but you may welcome the rest it affords.

All over the mountain there is excellent off-piste among widely spaced trees – tremendous fun when conditions are right. Some wooded slopes are identified on the trail map, but you are not confined to those. The trail map gives a good indication of the density of trees, and the grading of nearby trails gives a good idea of steepness.

FOR INTERMEDIATES
Lots to do
Heavenly is excellent for intermediates, who are made to feel welcome and secure by excellent piste grooming and signposting. The California side offers a progression from the relaxed cruising of the long Ridge Run, starting right at the top of the mountain, to more challenging blues dropping off the ridge towards the Sky Deck restaurant. Confident intermediates will want to spend more time on the Nevada side, where there is more variety of terrain, some longer runs down to the lift bases and more carving space. There are some great top-to-bottom cruises down to Stagecoach Lodge, and the excellent runs down to Boulder Lodge will be more attractive now that the return lift is a fast quad.

SCHOOLS

Heavenly
775 586 4400

Classes
3-day (3 x 2¾hr)
learn-to ski package
(includes equipment
and pass) $310

Private lessons
$185 for 2hr

CHILDREN

Day Care Center
t 775 586 7000
Ages 6wk to 6yr;
8.30-4pm; $96
including lunch; book
ahead

Ski school
For ages 4 to 13
(snowboarding 7 to
13); full 5hr day
(including lesson,
equipment, pass and
lunch) $135

FOR BEGINNERS
An excellent place to learn
Beginners are rather spoilt for choice.
We have had no first-hand experience
or reports of the new beginner area at
the top of the gondola, but it sounds
good. Lower down on California side
there are gentle green runs served by
the various lifts at the top of the cable-
car. There are good nursery slopes at
the California base lodge, and at
Boulder Lodge in Nevada, too.

FOR CROSS-COUNTRY
A separate world
You can try cross-country at Adventure
Peak at the top of the gondola. But
the serious stuff is in other areas
dotted around the lake – notably at
the Spooner Lake Cross Country Area
on the eastern shore: an extensive
meadow area of over 100km/60 miles
and 21 prepared trails. Organised
moonlit tours are a popular.

QUEUES
Some at weekends
Lift lines are generally not a problem,
except during some weekends and
public holidays. Thanks to the
gondola, the key lifts from the base
lodges are now under less pressure on
busy days. But the gondola does get
weekend queues, and then it's worth
taking the shuttle to the much quieter
Stagecoach Lodge. A 2005 visitor
found queues to ride the gondola
down, and advises getting there before
the ski school groups.

MOUNTAIN RESTAURANTS
Even refuelling is problematic
We have long considered the on-
mountain catering grossly inadequate,
especially in bad weather. The only
recommendable restaurant is the table-
service Lake View Lodge at the top of
the tram from California Lodge
(reservations necessary). East Peak
Lodge was renovated last season, the
menu widened and the terrace covered
but a 2005 reporter says, 'it can still
be pretty chilly'. The other options
consist of outdoor decks serving BBQs
and pizzas (hugely unenjoyable in a
blizzard, as we can testify) and grossly
overcrowded cafeterias.

SCHOOLS AND GUIDES
Innovative programmes
A 2004 reporter joined the school for
two days and was delighted to find
only two in her class. However, a 2005
skier, looking for advanced tuition,
found the attitude of the organisers
'terrible, really patronising' and didn't
feel he got what he'd paid for.
Programmes on offer include guided
adventures, such as four hours on
unmarked runs, and skiing corduroy
before the lifts officially open.

FACILITIES FOR CHILDREN
Comprehensive
We lack recent feedback but a past
reporter praised the day care and ski
school facilities: 'Excellent – very
convenient and very professionally run.
I would thoroughly recommend it.'

boarding

Lake Tahoe is quickly becoming known as the snowboarding hub of North
America and, as you would expect, boarders are very well catered for at Heavenly.
The off-piste in trees and double-black-diamond bowls make a great playground
for good free-riders. Beginners and intermediates will enjoy great cruising runs and
the easy-to-ride chair-lifts. There are a couple of specialist shops in South Lake
Tahoe. Learn some 'hot new moves' in Pipe and Park classes offered by the school.

GETTING THERE

Air San Francisco
274km/170 miles
(3¹/₂hr); Reno
89km/55 miles
(1¹/₄hr); South Lake
Tahoe, 15min.

ACTIVITIES

Indoor Casinos, spas,
art galleries, multiplex
cinema, museums

Outdoor Lake cruises,
snowmobiling, snow-
shoeing, snowtubing,
sleigh rides, dog-
sledding, hot springs,
fishing, hot-air
ballooning, ice
skating, factory outlet
shops

CALIFORNIA

546

WEBSITES

For links to resort
sites, go to our own
new site at
www.wtss.co.uk

Phone numbers
Different area codes
are used on the two
sides of the stateline.
For this chapter,
therefore, the area
code is included with
each number.

From distant parts of
the US, add the prefix
1. From abroad, add
the prefix +1.

TOURIST OFFICE

t 775 586 7000
info@vailresorts.com
www.skiheavenly.com

STAYING THERE

HOW TO GO
Hotel or motel?
Accommodation in the South Lake
Tahoe area is abundant and ranges
from the glossy casinos to small
motels. Rooms are easy to find midweek, but weekends can be busy.
Chalets UK tour operators run some
good catered chalets, including some
lakeside ones.
Hotels Of the main casino hotels,
Harrah's (775 558 6611) and Harveys
(775 558 2411) are the closest to the
gondola. Rooms booked on the spot
are expensive; packages are cheaper.
((((**Embassy Suites** (530 544 5400)
Luxury suites in a modern, traditional-
style building close to the gondola.
((((**Marriott's Timber Lodge** (530 542
6600) Part of the new 'village'.
(((**Forest Suites** (530 541 6655) Right
by the gondola, pools, hot-tubs,
'enormous rooms, very luxurious'.
(((**Holiday Inn Express** (530 544 5900)
'Eight minutes walk to gondola, modern,
comfortable, plenty of facilities.'
((**Holiday Lodge** (530 544 4101)
Opposite the gondola. 'Clean,
comfortable, breakfast included, indoor
and outdoor pools, hot-tub.'
((**Station House Inn** (530 542 1101)
Recommended again in 2005: 'Very
good, shuttle bus stops outside.'
((**Tahoe Chalet Inn** (530 544 3311)
Clean, friendly, near casinos. Back
rooms (away from highway) preferable.
((**Timber Cove Lodge** (530 541 6722)
Bland but well run, with lake views
from some rooms.
Self-catering Plenty of choice. Some
are available from tour operators.
We've had a rave report about The
Ridge Tahoe condos near Stagecoach
Lodge: 'Luxury accommodation. The
bathroom was big enough for
waltzing.' There's an indoor-outdoor
pool and hot-tub – and a private
gondola to whisk you to the slopes.

EATING OUT
Good value
The casino hotels' all-you-can-eat
buffets offer fantastic value. They have
some more ambitious 'gourmet'
restaurants too – some high enough to
give superb views (try Harrah's 18th
floor). A 2005 visitor enjoyed the Grills
in Harvey's and Caesar's. At the new
'village' Fire and Ice (with an outdoor
seating area with fires and heaters)
was 'heartily recommended' by one

visitor, although a 2005 reporter found
it 'very popular and busy, but not for
me'. The sprawling resort area offers a
great choice, from cosy little pizza
houses to large, traditional American
diners, Mexican tequila-and-tacos
joints, and English and Irish pubs.
Visitors' suggestions include
Applebee's ('the best value meals'),
Hunan Garden ('best Chinese buffet
ever') and Fresh Ketch at Tahoe Keys
Marina for 'wonderful fresh fish and
harbour views'. For breakfast, join the
locals at the Driftwood Cafe.

APRES-SKI
Extraordinary
The casinos on the Nevada side of the
stateline aren't simply opportunities to
throw money away: top-name pop and
jazz stars, comedians, circus acts and
Broadway revues are also to be found
in them – designed to give gamblers
another reason to stay. A 2005
reporter found a 'good atmosphere' in
Harvey's Casino bar and at Applebee's.
The Embassy Resort has a 'formal'
piano bar. You can dance and dine
your way across the lake aboard an
authentic paddle steamer.

OFF THE SLOPES
Luck be a lady
If gambling is your weakness, you're in
luck. Or then again, perhaps not. If you
want to get away from the bright
lights, try a boat trip on Lake Tahoe,
snowmobiling a short drive from South
Lake Tahoe, or a hot-air balloon ride.
Pedestrians can use the cable-car or
the gondola to share the lake views
and at Adventure Peak, at the top of
the gondola, you can try tubing, snowbiking, tobogganing and snow-shoeing.

Mammoth Mountain

A big, sprawling mountain above a car-oriented, sprawling resort

547

COSTS

① ② ③ ④ ⑤ ⑥

RATINGS

The slopes
Fast lifts	****
Snow	****
Extent	***
Expert	****
Intermediate	****
Beginner	****
Convenience	**
Queues	****
Mountain restaurants	*

The rest
Scenery	***
Resort charm	**
Off-slope	*

NEWS

For 2004/05 a fast quad, the Schoolyard Express, replaced the old triple Chair 17, serving the easy runs and family fun-park above Canyon Lodge.

A new condo-hotel, the Grand Sierra Lodge, opened at The Village.

+ One of North America's bigger ski hills, with something for everyone

+ Good mix of open Alpine-style bowls and classic American wooded slopes

+ Combination of location and altitude means a good snowfall record

+ Uncrowded slopes except on peak-season weekends

+ Mightily impressive terrain parks

+ Good views, including more Alpine drama than usual in the US

− Mammoth Lakes, though not unpleasant, is a rather straggling place with no focus, where life generally revolves around your car

− Most accommodation is miles from the slopes – though development is taking place at the lift bases

− Weekend crowds in high season

− Trail map and signing still poor

− Wind can close high lifts, and upper runs can be icy and wind blown

Mammoth may not be giant in Alpine terms – from end to end, it measures less than one-third of the size of Val-d'Isère-Tignes, in area more like one-sixth – but it is among the bigger resorts in the US, and big enough to amuse many people for a week. It can be a superb mountain for anyone who is happy in deep snow, but is equally suited to families and mixed-ability groups looking for groomed runs. The main thing it has lacked is a real village at the base.

You have to applaud the efforts of Intrawest, owner of Whistler and now of various key plots of land here, to put this right by building a new pedestrian 'village' (which we are encouraged to call The Village) on the edge of sprawling Mammoth Lakes, connected by a gondola to one of the main lift bases. If your lodgings are at The Village, no doubt its restaurants and boutiques will attract your custom. But we'd be surprised if it ever has much impact on the resort as a whole. You can't ski down to The Village, so most visitors based elsewhere (ie the majority) will ignore it. Mammoth will remain what it has always been: a resort that expects you to arrive by car, and get around by car.

THE RESORT

The mountain is set above Mammoth Lakes, a small year-round resort town that spreads over a wide area of woodland. The place is entirely geared to driving, with no discernible centre – hotels, restaurants and little shopping centres are scattered along the four-lane highway called Main Street and Old Mammoth Road, which crosses it. The buildings are generally timber-clad in traditional style – even McDonald's has been tastefully designed – and are set among trees, so although it may be short on village ambience, the place has a pleasant enough appearance – particularly when under snow.

The town meets the mountain at two lift bases, both a mile or two from most of the hotels and condos. The major base is Canyon Lodge, with a big day lodge and four chair-lifts; there are hotels, condos and individual

MAMMOTH MOUNTAIN SKI AREA

The Village is a typically thorough Intrawest job. The development is connected to Canyon Lodge by gondola, so staying here makes sense; for the rest of us, it's a pity it's not at the foot of the slopes →

KEY FACTS

Resort	2425m
	7,950ft

Mammoth only

Slopes	2425-3370m
	7,950-11,050ft
Lifts	27
Pistes	3,500 acres
Green	25%
Blue	40%
Black	35%
Snowmaking	
	477 acres

June Mountain only

Slopes	2290-3075m
	7,510-10,090ft
Lifts	7
Pistes	500 acres
Green	35%
Blue	45%
Black	20%
Snowmaking	none

homes in the area below the lodge. Not far from here, Intrawest has built phase 1 of its pedestrian development, The Village, which is linked to Canyon Lodge by a gondola. The minor base, with a single six-pack, is Eagle Lodge (previously Little Eagle – also known as Juniper Springs, which strictly is the name of the condos built at the base).

A road runs along the north fringe of the mountain past an anonymous chair-lift base to two major base areas: The Mill Cafe, with two fast chairs, and Main Lodge, a mini-resort with three fast access lifts and a big day lodge. You can stay here, in the newly refurbished Mammoth Mountain Inn; but who wants to be based four miles from practically all of the resort's 50 restaurants? Not us.

Shuttle-buses run on several colour-coded routes serving the lift bases (though they are reported to be erratic in the mornings). Night buses run via The Village until midnight. A car is useful.

The Mammoth lift pass also covers June, a small mountain half an hour's drive north, chiefly attractive for its astonishingly people-free slopes. See feature box, later in this chapter.

The drive up from Los Angeles takes six hours (more in poor conditions); but it is not without interest. You pass through the Santa Monica mountains close to Beverly Hills, then the San Gabriel mountains and Mojave Desert (with the world's biggest jet-plane parking lot) before reaching the Sierra Nevada range.

There are plans to extend Mammoth Lakes' small airport to take jet flights, but progress seems slow.

THE MOUNTAIN

The 27 lifts access an impressive area, suitable for all abilities. The highest runs are open, the lower ones more sheltered by trees.

Finding your way around is not easy at first. Most of the chair-lifts now have names (the traditional practice was to give them numbers), but the trail map still shows trails by means of isolated symbols, not continuous lines, so it's difficult to see where a run starts and finishes. The signposting of runs on the mountain leaves a lot to be desired, too. On the lower part of the mountain this doesn't matter a lot: head downhill, and you'll come to a lift. But higher up there are real dangers, especially in poor visibility. The map uses a six-point trail difficulty scale, with green/blue and blue/black categories – pointless when you often end up on the wrong trail anyway.

THE SLOPES
Interesting variety
From **Main Lodge** the two-stage Panorama gondola goes via McCoy Station right to the top. The views are great, with Nevada to the north-east and the jagged Minarets to the west. From the top, there are essentially three ways down. The first, with countless variations, is down the front of the mountain, which ranges from steep to very steep – or vertical if the wind has created a cornice, as it often does. The second is off the back, down to **Outpost 14**, whence chairs 14 or 13 bring you back to lower points on the ridge. The third is to follow the ridge, which eventually brings you down to

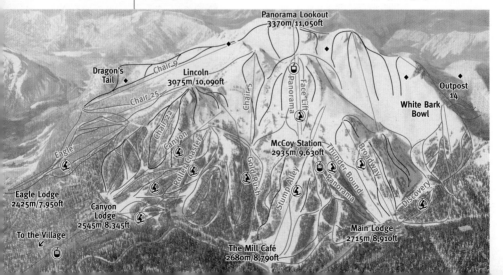

LIFT PASSES

Mammoth Mountain
Covers all lifts at
Mammoth and June
Mountains.

Beginners
Pass covering Chair 7
and Discovery only.

Main pass
1 day $63
6 days $310

Senior citizens
Over 65: 6 days $155
Over 80: free pass

Children
Under 19: 6 days
$232
Under 13: 6 days
$155
Under 7: free pass

Notes
Afternoon pass
available.

Alternative passes
Pass covering June
Mountain only.

boarding

Mammoth's slopes are ideal for all abilities, with some excellent free-riding in the high bowls and perfect beginner and intermediate runs below. There's only one tiny drag-lift, and none of the flat linking runs that make some American resorts hard work to get around. Competent boarders will revel in the resort's extensive terrain parks (see below).

the Main Lodge area. This route brings you past an easy area served by a double chair, and a very easy area served by the Discovery fast quad.

McCoy Station can also be reached using the Stump Alley fast chair from **The Mill Cafe**, on the road up from town. The fast Gold Rush quad from here takes you into the more heavily wooded eastern half of the area. This has long, gentle runs served by lifts up from **Canyon Lodge** and **Eagle Lodge** and seriously steep stuff as well as some intermediate terrain on the subsidiary peak known as Lincoln (un-named on the resort trail map), served by lifts 25 and 22.

TERRAIN-PARKS
Among the best
Mammoth initially set out to attract boarders and freestylers to its sister mountain June, where there are three good terrain-parks and a half-pipe. But Mammoth itself now has three impressive 'Unbound' terrain-parks and half-pipes for different abilities – more than 60 acres in all. Novices get a taster at the Family Fun park and the Discovery Zone, and there's an ever-expanding selection of urban-style rails, jumps and 'impressively large kickers' at Unbound South and Main. Highlights are the astonishing Super-Duper pipe, 183m/600ft long and boasting 7m/22ft walls, and 'The Wall' – a 5m/16ft tall steel structure for advanced jibbers.

SNOW RELIABILITY
A long season
Mammoth has an impressive snow record – an annual average of 385 inches, which puts it ahead of major Colorado resorts and about on a par with Jackson Hole. Mammoth is appreciably higher than other Californian resorts, and it has an ever-expanding array of snow-guns, so it enjoys a long season – staying open as late as 4 July in many years. The mountain faces roughly north; the relatively low and slightly sunny slopes down to Eagle Lodge are affected by warm weather before others. Strong winds are not uncommon on the upper mountain; some lifts are kept going in surprisingly breezy conditions. One reporter was blown over and another complains of 'extreme conditions'. The snow quality can be affected by these strong winds, too. This is not always a bad thing – the 'wind-compacted powder' can be 'just like spring snow'.

FOR EXPERTS
Some very challenging terrain
The steep bowls that run the width of the mountain top provide wonderful opportunities for experts. There are one or two single-diamond slopes, but runs such as Hangman's Hollow and Wipe-Out Chutes are emphatically double-diamond affairs requiring a lot of bottle. Route-finding can be tricky – marking is virtually non-existent.

There is lots of challenging terrain

JUNE MOUNTAIN: THE WORLD'S QUIETEST SLOPES?

June Mountain, a scenic half-hour drive from Mammoth, is a small resort in the same ownership and covered by the Mammoth lift pass. It makes a pleasant day out, especially if Mammoth is busy. When Mammoth isn't busy, June is quite incredibly quiet; when we visited on a March weekday morning we rode chair after chair, skied run after run, without seeing another person.

A double chair goes up from the car park at 2290m/7,510ft over black slopes that are often short of snow to the main lodge, June Meadows Chalet. From here, a quad chair serves a gentle blue-run hill, and a double chair goes right over very gentle green runs to the foot of a quad serving short but genuinely black slopes on June Mountain itself (3100m/10,175ft). There are a couple of double-diamond runs, but they don't really deserve the grading. June is very sensibly going for the freestyle market, with three terrain-parks, two jib-parks and a super-pipe.

SCHOOLS

Mammoth Mountain
934 0745

Classes
1 3hr morning $60
Private lessons
$140 for 1hr for 1 to
5 people

CHILDREN

Small World
t 934 0646
Ages newborn to 12;
8am-4.30

Ski school
Takes ages 4 to 6 at
Woollywood ($45 for
2hr; $109 all day
(10am-3pm) and ages
7 to 12 at **Canyon
Kids** ($109 for a day
(10am-3pm).

REPORTS WANTED

Recently we have
had few reports on
this resort. If you
go there, please do
send us a report.

The best reports
earn a copy of the
next edition, and
can lead to free lift
passes in future.

See page 10.

lower down, too; Chair 5, Chair 22 and Broadway are often open in bad weather when the top is firmly shut, and their more sheltered slopes may in any case have the best snow. (The top of Chair 22 is higher than the very top of Heavenly, remember.) There are plenty of good slopes over the back towards Outpost 14, too.

Many of the steeper trails are short by Alpine standards (typically under 400m/1,300ft vertical), but despite this we've enjoyed some great powder days here (with guidance).

FOR INTERMEDIATES
Lots of great cruising
Although there are exceptions, most of the lower mountain, below the tree-line, is intermediate cruising territory. What's more, Mammoth's piste maintenance is generally good, and many slopes that might become mogulled are kept easily skiable. 'Very flattering', says one visitor.

As you might hope, the six-point trail difficulty scale – which we haven't tried to replicate on our own small trail map – is a good guide to what you'll find on the mountain.

Some of the mountain's longest runs, blue-blacks served by chairs 9 and 25, are ideal for good intermediates. There are also some excellent, fairly steep, woodland trails down to The Mill Cafe.

Most of the long runs above Eagle Lodge, and some of the shorter ones above Canyon Lodge, are easy cruises. There is a variety of terrain, including lots of gentle stuff, at the western extremity of the slopes, both on the front side and on the back side.

June mountain is great for a leisurely day out – see feature box.

FOR BEGINNERS
Excellent
Chair 7 and the new fast Chair 17 replacement, named the Schoolyard Express, at Canyon Lodge and Discovery Chair at Main Lodge serve quiet, gentle green runs – so as soon as you're off the nursery slopes you can get an encouraging taste of real skiing. Excellent instruction, top-notch grooming and snow quality usually make progress speedy.

FOR CROSS-COUNTRY
Very popular
Two specialist centres, Tamarack and Sierra Meadows (ungroomed), provide lessons and tours. There are 45km/28miles of trails at Tamarack, and lots of scenic ungroomed tracks, including some through the pretty Lakes Basin area: 70km/43 miles of trails in all.

QUEUES
Normally quiet slopes
During the week the lifts and slopes are usually very quiet, with no queues; 'empty', 'deserted', say reporters. But even the efficient lift system can struggle when 15,000 visitors arrive from LA on fine peak-season weekends. That's the time to try the wonderfully uncrowded June Mountain, half an hour away.

MOUNTAIN RESTAURANTS
Not a lot of choice
The only real mountain restaurants are at mid-mountain McCoy Station. This offers 'a good choice' of roasts, Italian, Asian and other dishes – but does get 'very busy'. The Parallax table-service restaurant next door does satisfying food with a calm atmosphere and a splendid view. The other on-mountain possibility in good weather is the primitive outdoor BBQ at Outpost 14, on the back of the hill.

Most people eat at the lift bases. Talons at Eagle Lodge has its fans. The Mill Cafe is 'pleasant' but the 'choice of food was limited', according to a 2004 visitor. The Mountainside Grill at the revamped Mammoth Mountain Inn is also recommended. And Canyon Lodge offers Mexican, Italian, Asian and more.

SCHOOLS AND GUIDES
Excellent reports
Past and recent reporters alike are favourably impressed by the school, which apparently contains growing numbers of Scottish instructors. There is the general American problem that you usually get a different instructor every day. There are some special 'camps' for experts, and for women.

FACILITIES FOR CHILDREN
Family favourite
Mammoth is keen to attract families. The Woollywood school, based in the Panorama gondola station, works closely with the nearby Small World childcare centre. We've had glowing reports; one reporter noted the 'family feel of the resort'. Another rated the facilities as 'second to none'.

↑ Main Lodge, with genuine double-diamond slopes rising above it

MAMMOTH MOUNTAIN SKI AREA

GETTING THERE

Air Los Angeles 494km/307 miles (5hr); Reno 270km/168 miles (3hr).

ACTIVITIES

Indoor Museum, art galleries, cinema, concerts

Outdoor Ice rink, snowmobiling, snowshoeing, dog-sledding

WEBSITES

For links to resort sites, go to our own new site at www.wtss.co.uk

Phone numbers
From distant parts of the US, add the prefix 1 760.
From abroad, add the prefix +1 760.

TOURIST OFFICE

t 934 0745
info@mammoth-mtn.com
www.mammoth
mountain.com

STAYING THERE

HOW TO GO
Good value packages

A good choice of hotels (none very luxurious or expensive) and condos. The condos tend to be out of town, near the lifts or on the road to them. ((((④ **Mammoth Mountain Inn** (934 2581) Way out of town at Main Lodge. Recently refurbished. 'Spacious and comfortable, perfect for access to the slopes but rather isolated'. (((③ **Quality Inn** (934 5114) Good main street hotel with a big hot-tub. (((③ **Alpenhof Lodge** (934 6330) Comfortable and friendly, in central location. Shuttle-bus stop and plenty of restaurants nearby. (((③ **Austria Hof Lodge** (934 2764) Ski-out location near Canyon Lodge, recommended by a reporter despite modest-sized rooms. (((③ **Sierra Nevada Rodeway Inn** (934 2515) Central, good value, 'great spa'. (((③ **Holiday Inn** (924 1234) Central location, large, comfortable rooms and 'great restaurant'. Pool.
Self-catering The Juniper Springs Lodge is near lifts and town. Close to the Canyon Lodge base-station, the 1849 Condominiums are spacious and well equipped. The Mammoth Ski and Racquet Club, a 10-minute walk from the same lifts, is very comfortable. There is an 'excellent' supermarket in the Minaret Mall, with good discounts.

EATING OUT
Outstanding choice

Reporters continue to be impressed by the wide choice available – over 50 restaurants, scattered over a wide area, catering for most tastes and pockets. Start with a copy of the local menu guide, and book what you fancy. One reporting couple had a great time dining in a different restaurant every day for a fortnight. Meshing their findings with other reports, we offer the following guidance: Slocums Grill – very good meal in wood-panelled room; Angel's – popular, good-value diner; Ocean Harvest – great atmosphere and wonderful fish; Nevados – best in town, excellent modern cooking; Chart House – excellent seafood, varied meat dishes; Alpenrose – intimate chalet-style place, good food; Matsu – small, simple, with delicious Asian food; Berger's – 'excellent monster-sized burgers'; Old Mammoth Grill – traditional family diner, 'good bar'.

Also recommended are Shogun for Japanese and Gomez's for 'good' Mexican food 'and over 30 different tequilas'. A 2005 visitor says that the meal he had at the Lakefront up at Twin Lakes was 'the best I've ever had in any ski resort'. We've had excellent dinners at Skadi and Whiskey Creek, too. Several new eateries have opened in The Village.

APRES-SKI
Lively at weekends

The liveliest immediate après-ski spot is the Yodler, at the Main Lodge base – a chalet transported from Switzerland (so they say). Later on, things revolve around a handful of bars, which come to life at weekends. The Clocktower Cellar is reported to be 'best in town – lively, friendly, good music, great choice of beers'. Whiskey Creek is the liveliest (and stays open latest); it has live bands at weekends. Slocums is popular with locals and 'ideal for an after-dinner drink'. Grumpy's is a sports bar (big-screen TVs). A 2005 visitor enjoyed the new venues in The Village . He says you shouldn't miss Hawaiian-style Lakanuki's with its 'bikini tree' or Dublin's Irish Pub (with Fever disco).

OFF THE SLOPES
Mainly sightseeing

There are various things to be done outdoors, including skating. Or you can go sightseeing by car (preferably 4WD). The town of Bishop, 40 minutes' drive south, makes an amusing day out. Factory outlet shopping is recommended for bargains. Mono Lake is reported to be 'well worth a visit'.

SNOWPIX.COM / CHRIS GILL

Alpine Meadows

Squaw Valley's next-door neighbour has similar, lightly wooded terrain, with runs of all classifications and an impressive snow record, but a modest total vertical of 550m/1,800ft. There's nothing but a day lodge at the base.

KEY FACTS

Resort	2085m
	6,840ft
Slopes	2085-2635m
	6,840-8,640ft
Lifts	14
Pistes	2,400 acres
Green	25%
Blue	40%
Black	35%
Snowmaking	runs
served by 12 of 14	
lifts	

TOURIST OFFICE

t 530 583 4232
info@skialpine.com
www.skialpine.com

THE RESORT?

There is no resort in the European sense of the word. The base day-lodge has 'uninspiring' self-service and table-service restaurants. Lots of lodgings close-by in lakeside Tahoe City.

THE MOUNTAIN

The base is surrounded by excellent beginner slopes with a variety of slow lifts. The major mountain access lifts are a fast quad going half-way up the broad bowl under Ward Peak, and a six-pack to the top of it; this accesses a wide range of black runs (single and double diamond) at the top of the bowl, some of them involving long traverses, but there are blue runs, too, down to the generally blue terrain lower down the bowl. There is also a double chair on the upper slopes.

Separated from Ward Peak by a low saddle is Scott Peak; a double chair goes up over the steep black slopes on the front, and on the back pleasant blue runs are served by a triple. The open lower slopes on the back of Ward Peak are getting a new fast quad for 2005/06; steeper areas are accessed by the Alpine Bowl chair on the front of the hill. The resort boundary is open – expeditions require guidance.

There's a terrain-park, a half-pipe and a super-pipe just above the base. With a good average snowfall of 460 inches, Alpine Meadows is known for its long season and excellent spring snow – but when it closes depends on ticket sales.

There is a little Mid-Mountain Chalet on the hill – self-service, but pleasantly woody and welcoming.

A regular visitor warns of '10-minute lift lines on weekends'.

KIRKWOOD MOUNTAIN RESORT

Kirkwood

Kirkwood is renowned for its powder, and has a lot to offer experts and confident intermediates; reports from day-visitors are highly enthusiastic. The small base village includes a growing range of condos.

KEY FACTS

Resort	2375m
	7,800ft
Slopes	2375-2985m
	7,800-9,800ft
Lifts	12
Pistes	2,300 acres
Green	15%
Blue	50%
Black	35%
Snowmaking	4 runs

TOURIST OFFICE

t 209 258 6000
info@kirkwood.com
www.kirkwood.com

THE RESORT

Kirkwood is reached from South Lake Tahoe over two high passes; heavy snowfall often closes the road. There is a cheap shuttle-bus, arriving at 9.30.

A small 'village' with ski-in, ski-out apartment accommodation is taking shape at the base. There are several bars and restaurants, a recreation centre with outdoor pool, spa and sun deck, and an ice rink on the edge of the village plaza. Après-ski is limited.

THE MOUNTAIN

The resort sits at the centre of a semicircle of slopes, lightly wooded at the top, more densely at the bottom. The lift system consists almost entirely of slow chair-lifts. One goes up to the top of the main bowl above the base, as does the resort's one fast quad.

These two long lifts also give access to bowls to left and right of the main one. All three bowls have black slopes at the top, and easier runs lower down, served by their own shorter chairs. Beyond the left-hand bowl is a lightly wooded mountainside of blue/black gradient served by two more chairs, with various fairly adventurous ways back to the front mountain. The separate Timber Creek beginner area, with its own base lodge, gets its first fast quad chair for 2005/06.

Kirkwood is an excellent resort for experts and adventurous intermediates, and fine for beginners, but rather limited for less confident intermediates who are not happy to tackle black runs. Deep snow is part of the attraction: Kirkwood claims an annual average snowfall of over 500 inches, and readers report 'top class snow – far better than Heavenly'.

Northstar-at-Tahoe

Northstar is a classic US-style mountain, with runs cut through dense forest – and lacking variety, to some extent. The lift system is slicker than at other minor Tahoe resorts, with a high fast-lift quotient.

KEY FACTS

Resort	1930m
	6,330ft
Slopes	1930-2625m
	6,330-8,610ft
Lifts	17
Pistes	2,420 acres
Green	25%
Blue	50%
Black	25%
Snowmaking	50 %

TOURIST OFFICE

t 530 562 1010
verticalplus@northstar
attahoe.com
www.skinorthstar.com

THE RESORT

Northstar is in the middle of constructing what amounts to a new village at the base. Phase one, with around 100 condos and quite a few new shops, is planned for completion for 2005/06. There will eventually be an ice rink with pedestrian plaza. The gondola station is at one end of the village, a short walk from the highly organised drop-off zone and the premium parking lot – free parking is a bit further away, served by buses.

THE MOUNTAIN

The whole area is very sheltered and good for bad-weather days. It enjoys long views in various directions.

A short gondola and a chair – being upgraded to a fast quad for 2005/06 – go up to a mid-mountain lodge at Big Springs, only 160m/525ft above the village. From this point two fast chairs and one slow one radiate to serve a broad bowl with some short steep pitches at the top, with easier blue runs lower down and around the ridges – these giving excellent runs to the village of almost 700m/2,300ft vertical. On the back-side of the mountain is a second, steeper bowl with a central fast quad chair rising 575m/1,880ft; on either side of it are three or four runs that are at the easy end of the black spectrum .

A fast quad serves the most recently opened area – another four black runs with a modest vertical of 390m/1,280ft on Lookout Mountain. The two runs close to the chair are seriously steep.

You can eat on the hill – there are several options at Big Springs, and an over-busy but otherwise good Mexican place at The Summit.

Squaw Valley

The major resort at the north end of Lake Tahoe, with 4,000 acres of open and lightly wooded bowls on six linked peaks. The small base village has undergone major development by Intrawest, with considerable success.

KEY FACTS

Resort	1890m
	6,200ft
Slopes	1890-2665m
	6,200-8,700ft
Lifts	34
Pistes	4,000 acres
Green	25%
Blue	45%
Black	30%
Snowmaking	
	400 acres

TOURIST OFFICE

t 530 583 6985
squaw@squaw.com
www.squaw.com

THE RESORT

Until recently, Squaw has had very little accommodation at the base. The main options were Squaw Valley Lodge and the self-contained, luxurious conference-oriented Resort at Squaw Creek, linked into one end of the lift network by its own chair-lift. But a new resort village has been built by Intrawest, of Whistler fame, and with phase 2 complete reporters tell us it now has a real village atmosphere.

THE MOUNTAINS

There are two powerful lifts from the base – a twin-cable jumbo Funitel gondola (as in Verbier and Val-Thorens) and a big cable-car. Both rise 610m/2,000ft to the twin mid-mountain stations of Gold Coast and High Camp – an incredible mid-mountain complex (open in the evening), with bars and restaurants, outdoor pool, ice skating, tennis, bungee jumping and tubing. Above these two points is a superb area of long, gentle, snow-sure beginner slopes. Intermediates have a choice of some lovely cruises in the Emigrant and Snow King sectors, and a three-mile top-to-bottom run. The possibilities for experts are huge, with lots of steep slopes, chutes and big mogul fields. There are several distinct sectors, each offering different challenges. Some sectors – notably the steep slopes down the Silverado chair – we wouldn't go into without a guide.

The peaks and high bowls of the area are treeless, but much of the terrain is lightly wooded – a very attractive compromise between the usual US wooded terrain and the open Alpine style of terrain. The average snowfall is an impressive 450 inches.

Colorado

Colorado was the first US state to market its resorts internationally and is still the most popular American destination for UK visitors. And justifiably so: it has the most alluring combination of attractive resorts, slopes to suit all abilities and excellent, reliable snow – dry enough to justify its 'champagne powder' label. It also has daily direct scheduled British Airways flights from Heathrow to Denver and for the 2005/06 season there will be a two charter flights a week from Gatwick to Denver too, run for Crystal and Thomson.

Colorado has amazingly dry snow. Even when the snow melts and refreezes, the moisture seems to be magically whisked away, leaving it in soft powdery condition. Even in times of snow shortage, the artificial snow is of a quality you'll rarely find in Europe.

Colorado resorts vary enormously, both in the extent and variety of slopes and in the character of the villages. If you want cute restored buildings from the mining boom days of the late 1800s, try the dinky old towns of Telluride or Crested Butte or the much bigger Aspen. Others major on convenience – such as Aspen's modern satellite, Snowmass, which is covered in its own chapter. Some

resorts deliberately pitch themselves up-market, with lots of glitzy, pricey hotels – such as Vail and Beaver Creek – while others are much more down to earth and affordable – such as Winter Park and Copper Mountain (which has a great 'free ski pass' offer – see Copper Mountain chapter).

Like most north American rivals, Colorado resorts generally have excellent, steep, ungroomed terrain that has enormous appeal to the adventurous.

Some resorts, such as Steamboat, Crested Butte and Telluride, are rather isolated, but there is a cluster of resorts west of Denver which can be combined in a holiday tour by car. You could visit these while staying in cheaper accommodation in a valley town such as Frisco. As well as the resorts we cover in detail, you could think about quick visits to some others – notably high, steep Arapahoe Basin, up the valley from Keystone; and snow-sure Loveland, which you can see from the main I70 highway. If visiting Crested Butte, you could take in Monarch, which has snowcat as well as lift-served slopes

Further south, Durango (which used to be called Purgatory) is a covered in a half-page entry at the end of the Colorado section. If approaching from the north, be warned: the road over Red Mountain pass is quite the scariest we have driven – do it only in daylight and good weather. We hear good things about Silverton, with steep, ungroomed runs that you tackle in guided groups, and Wolf Creek, which claims the most snow in Colorado – an average of 465 inches a year.

Aspen

Don't be put off by the ritzy image – this is America's best resort

COSTS

① ② ③ ④ ⑤ ⑥

RATINGS

The slopes
Fast lifts	★★★
Snow	★★★★★
Extent	★★★★
Expert	★★★★★
Intermediate	★★★★★
Beginner	★★★★★
Convenience	★★
Queues	★★★★
Mountain restaurants	★★★

The rest
Scenery	★★★
Resort charm	★★★★
Off-slope	★★★★

Our extent rating relates to the whole Aspen-Snowmass area. Aspen alone would rate ★★

NEWS

For 2005/06 a new triple chair called Deep Temerity will open at Aspen Highlands. It will serve new advanced and expert terrain below Highland Bowl and Steeplechase.

Work has begun to replace the gondola cabins on Aspen Mountain for the 2006/07 season.

Your choice of swanky hotels near the lift base widens further for 2005/06 with the opening of the Hyatt Grand Aspen.

For 2004/05 a fast quad replaced the old West Buttermilk chair. A mid-station allows easier access to the beginner terrain on the mountain.

➕ Notably uncrowded slopes, even by American standards

➕ Attractive, characterful old mining town, with lots of smart shops

➕ Lively, varied nightlife

➕ Great range of restaurants

➕ Excellent Snowmass just up the road

➖ Slopes split over three separate mountains (four if you count Snowmass, as you should), though there's efficient, free transport

➖ Some accommodation in Aspen town is a bus-ride from the lifts

➖ Expensive

Aspen is our favourite American resort. We love the town and we love the extensive and varied skiing. We admit that this affection for the skiing depends heavily on the presence of Snowmass a little way down the valley, which is covered in a separate chapter, and Aspen Highlands – so to get to most of the slopes you have to ride a bus. That doesn't put us off, and doesn't seem to worry readers who report on the place – so it shouldn't deter you, either.

You can forget the filmstar image. Yes, many rich and famous guests jet in to the local airport, and for connoisseurs of cosmetic surgery the bars of Aspen's top hotels can be fascinating places. But most celebs keep a low profile; and, like all other 'glamorous' ski resorts, Aspen is actually filled by ordinary holidaymakers.

THE RESORT

In 1892 Aspen was a booming silver-mining town, source of one-sixth of the USA's silver, with 12,000 inhabitants, six newspapers, an opera house and a red-light district. But Aspen's fortunes took a nose-dive when the silver price plummeted in 1893, and by the 1930s the population had shrunk to 700 or so, and handsome Victorian buildings – such as the Hotel Jerome – had fallen into disrepair.

Development of the skiing started on a small scale in the late 1930s. The first lift was opened shortly after the Second World War, and Aspen hasn't looked back since. Now, the historic centre – with a typical American grid of streets – has been beautifully renovated to form the core of the most fashionable ski town in the Rockies. There's a huge variety of bars, restaurants, shops and art galleries – some amazingly upmarket. Spreading out from this centre, you'll find a mixture of developments, ranging from the homes of the super-rich to the mobile homes for the workers. Though the town is busy with traffic, it moves slowly and pedestrians effectively have priority in much of the central area.

Aspen is very unusual in being a cute town with a major lift close to the centre: the Silver Queen gondola straight to the top of Aspen Mountain is only yards from some of the top hotels, and the streets running away from the lift base are lined by the restaurants and shops that make Aspen what it is. Stay close to this lift if you can. Downtown Aspen is quite compact by American resort standards, but it spreads far enough to make the free ski-bus a necessity for many visitors staying less centrally.

Aspen Highlands, a couple of miles out of town, now has limited accommodation. Twelve miles away is Snowmass, which now gets its own chapter. Buses for these mountains and Buttermilk leave from near the gondola station.

LIFT PASSES

Four Mountain Pass
Covers Aspen Mountain, Aspen Highlands, Buttermilk and Snowmass, and shuttle-bus between the areas.

Beginners
Included in price of beginners' lessons.

Main pass
1 day $74
6 days $420

Senior citizens
Over 65: 6 days $378
Over 70: Unlimited period $199

Children
Under 18: 6 days $378
Under 13: 6 days $252
Under 7: free pass

Notes
Substantial savings on lift passes for 4 days or more if you purchase them more than 7 days in advance or through certain tour operators.

COLORADO

556

THE MOUNTAINS

Aspen has lots for every ability; you just have to pick the right mountain. All of them have regular, free guided tours, given by excellent amateur ambassadors. The ratio of acres to visitor beds is high, and the slopes are usually blissfully uncrowded. Lift passes are discounted heavily for purchase in advance or through tour operators – check out your options well in advance of travelling.

THE SLOPES
Widely dispersed
Each of the three local mountains is worth a visit – though novices should note that Aspen Mountain has no green runs. Most of the slopes are in the trees. Much the most extensive mountain is at Snowmass – see separate chapter.

Once you are up the gondola, a series of chairs serves the ridges of **Aspen Mountain**. In general, there are long cruising blue runs along the valley floors and short, steep blacks down from the ridges.

Buttermilk is the least challenging mountain, served by a fast quad from the fairly primitive main base lodge. The runs fan out from the top in three directions – back to the base, or down to the slow Tiehack chair, or down to the fast quad at West Buttermilk.

Aspen Highlands consists essentially of a single ridge served by three fast quad chairs, with easy and intermediate slopes along the ridge itself and steep black runs on the flanks – very steep ones at the top. And beyond the lift network is Highland Bowl, where gates give access to a splendid open bowl of entirely double-black gradient. There are free snowcat rides from the top of the lifts to the first access gate of Highland Bowl, but if these are not operating, it's a 20-minute hike. All the other gates require further hiking. This season the new Deep Temerity triple chair will access new advanced and expert terrain below Highland Bowl and Steeplechase. The views from the upper part of Highlands are the best

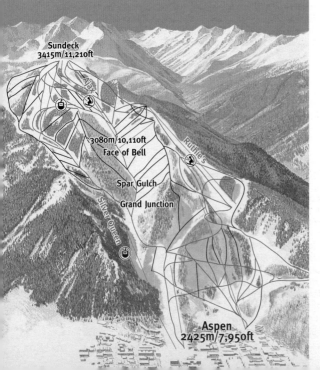

Sundeck
3415m/11,210ft

3080m/10,110ft
Face of Bell

Spar Gulch

Grand Junction

Aspen
2425m/7,950ft

<table>
<tr><th colspan="3">KEY FACTS</th></tr>
<tr><td>Resort</td><td></td><td>2425m</td></tr>
<tr><td></td><td></td><td>7,950ft</td></tr>
<tr><td colspan="3">Aspen Mountain</td></tr>
<tr><td>Slopes</td><td colspan="2">2425-3415m</td></tr>
<tr><td></td><td colspan="2">7,950-11,210ft</td></tr>
<tr><td>Lifts</td><td></td><td>8</td></tr>
<tr><td>Pistes</td><td></td><td>673 acres</td></tr>
<tr><td>Green</td><td></td><td>0%</td></tr>
<tr><td>Blue</td><td></td><td>48%</td></tr>
<tr><td>Black</td><td></td><td>52%</td></tr>
<tr><td>Snow-guns</td><td></td><td>210 acres</td></tr>
<tr><td colspan="3">Aspen Highlands</td></tr>
<tr><td>Slopes</td><td colspan="2">2450-3560m</td></tr>
<tr><td></td><td colspan="2">8,040-11,680ft</td></tr>
<tr><td>Lifts</td><td></td><td>4</td></tr>
<tr><td>Pistes</td><td></td><td>790 acres</td></tr>
<tr><td>Green</td><td></td><td>18%</td></tr>
<tr><td>Blue</td><td></td><td>30%</td></tr>
<tr><td>Black</td><td></td><td>52%</td></tr>
<tr><td>Snow-guns</td><td></td><td>110 acres</td></tr>
<tr><td colspan="3">Buttermilk</td></tr>
<tr><td>Slopes</td><td colspan="2">2400-3015m</td></tr>
<tr><td></td><td colspan="2">7,870-9,900ft</td></tr>
<tr><td>Lifts</td><td></td><td>9</td></tr>
<tr><td>Pistes</td><td></td><td>430 acres</td></tr>
<tr><td>Green</td><td></td><td>35%</td></tr>
<tr><td>Blue</td><td></td><td>39%</td></tr>
<tr><td>Black</td><td></td><td>26%</td></tr>
<tr><td>Snow-guns</td><td></td><td>108 acres</td></tr>
<tr><td colspan="3">Total with Snowmass</td></tr>
<tr><td>Slopes</td><td colspan="2">2400-3815m</td></tr>
<tr><td></td><td colspan="2">7,870-12,510ft</td></tr>
<tr><td>Lifts</td><td></td><td>42</td></tr>
<tr><td>Pistes</td><td></td><td>4,900 acres</td></tr>
<tr><td>Green</td><td></td><td>10%</td></tr>
<tr><td>Blue</td><td></td><td>45%</td></tr>
<tr><td>Black</td><td></td><td>45%</td></tr>
<tr><td>Snow-guns</td><td></td><td>608 acres</td></tr>
</table>

that Aspen has to offer – the famous Maroon Bells that appear on countless postcards. There is a base lodge with underground parking and a Ritz-Carlton aparthotel.

TERRAIN-PARKS
Some of the world's best
Buttermilk has a 3km/2 mile-long terrain-park (claimed to be the world's longest) with a beginner and intermediate area, more than 25 rails and 40 jumps and hits, a boarder-cross course, a 100m/330ft long super-pipe and 'motivating' sound system. The park is currently home to the ESPN Winter X games and now incorporates a permanent X Games-style course. The Crazy T'Rain and Jacob's Ladder parks are also on Buttermilk.

SNOW RELIABILITY
Rarely a problem
Aspen's mountains get an annual average of 300 inches of snow – not in the front rank, but not far behind. In addition, all areas have substantial snowmaking. Immaculate grooming adds to the quality of the pistes.

FOR EXPERTS
Buttermilk is the only soft stuff
There's plenty to choose from – all the mountains except Buttermilk offer lots of challenges.

Aspen Mountain has a formidable array of double-black-diamond runs. From the top of the gondola, Walsh's, Hyrup's and Kristi are on a lightly wooded slope and link up with

Gentleman's Ridge and Jackpot to form the longest black run on the mountain. A series of steep glades drops down from Gentleman's Ridge. The central Bell ridge has less extreme single-diamonds on both its flanks. On the opposite side of Spar Gulch is another row of double-blacks, collectively called the Dumps, because waste was dumped here in the silver-mining days.

At Highlands there are challenging runs from top to bottom of the mountain. Consider joining a guided group as an introduction to the best of them. Highland Bowl, beyond the top lift, is superb in the right conditions: a big open bowl with pitches from a serious 38° to a terrifying 48° – facts you can check in the very informative Highlands Extreme Skiing Guide leaflet. Within the lift system, the Steeplechase area consists of a number of parallel natural avalanche chutes, and their elevation means the snow stays light and dry. The Olympic Bowl area on the opposite flank of the mountain has great views of the Maroon Bells and some serious moguls. Thunderbowl chair from the base serves a nice varied area that's often underused.

FOR INTERMEDIATES
Grooming to die for
Most intermediate runs on Highlands are concentrated above the mid-mountain Merry-Go-Round restaurant,

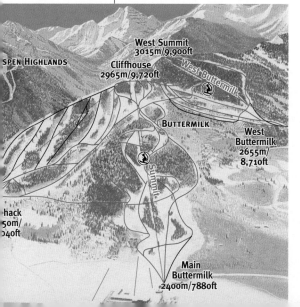

SCHOOLS

Aspen
t 923 1227

Classes
Full day (5hr) $125,
incl.tax

Private lessons
$340 for a half day
(3hr) for up to 5
people.

boarding

There is great snowboarding for every ability. The ban on snowboarding on Aspen Mountain was lifted back in April 2001. All the mountains offer excellent boarding, with few flat sections and almost all lifts being chairs or gondolas. There are world-class terrain-parks, and regularly hosting the Winter X Games has boosted Aspen's image as boarder-friendly.

many served by the Cloud Nine fast quad chair. But there are good slopes higher up and lower down – don't miss the vast, neglected expanses of Golden Horn, on the eastern limit of the area.

Aspen Mountain has its fair share of intermediate slopes, but they tend to be tougher than on the other mountains. Copper Bowl and Spar Gulch, running between the ridges, are great cruises early in the morning but can get crowded later. Upper Aspen Mountain, at the top of the gondola, has a dense network of well-groomed blues. The unusual Ruthie's chair – a fast double, apparently installed to rekindle the romance that quads have destroyed – serves more cruising runs and the popular Snow Bowl, a wide, open area with moguls on the left but groomed on the right and centre.

The Main Buttermilk runs offer good, easy slopes to practise on. And good intermediates should be able to handle the relatively easy black runs – when groomed, these are a real blast on carving skis. It's also a great place for early experiments off-piste.

FOR BEGINNERS
Can be a great place to learn
Buttermilk is a great mountain for beginners. West Buttermilk has beautifully groomed, gentle, often deserted runs, which got a new quad last season. The easiest slopes of all, though, are at the base of the Main Buttermilk sector – on Panda Hill.

Despite its macho image, Highlands boasts the highest concentration of green runs in Aspen.

FOR CROSS-COUNTRY
Backcountry bonanza
There are 60km/37 miles of groomed trails between Aspen and Snowmass in the Roaring Fork valley – the most extensive maintained cross-country system in the US. And the Ashcroft Ski Touring Centre maintains around 35km/21 miles of trails around Ashcroft, a mining ghost-town. The Pine Creek Cookhouse (970 925 1044) – excellent food and accessible by ski, snow-shoe or horse-drawn sleigh only – reopened last season following a devastating fire. Aspen is at one end of the famous Tenth Mountain Division Trail, heading 370km/230 miles north-east almost to Vail, with 12 huts for overnight stops.

QUEUES
Few problems
There are rarely major queues on any of the mountains. At Aspen Mountain, the gondola can have delays at peak times, but you have alternative lifts to the top. Aspen Highlands is almost always queue-free, even at peak times. The two lifts out of Main Buttermilk sometimes get congested.

MOUNTAIN RESTAURANTS
Good by American standards
On Aspen Mountain the Sundeck has

GET THE BEST OF THE SNOW, ON- AND OFF-PISTE

Aspen offers special experiences for small numbers of skiers or riders.

Fresh Tracks *The first eight skiers to sign up each day get to ride the gondola up Aspen Mountain at 8am the next morning, and to get first tracks on perfect corduroy or fresh powder. Free!*

Off-piste Tours *On Wednesdays backcountry guides lead expert skiers and riders around the famous expert terrain of Highlands – the same deal is available in Snowmass. 10am–3pm, $109 (2004/05).*

Powder Tours *Spend the day finding untracked snow in 1,500 acres of backcountry beyond Aspen Mountain, with a 10-passenger heated snowcat as your personal lift. You're likely to squeeze in about 10 runs in all. You break for lunch at an old mountain cabin. Full day, $295 (2004/05).*

Some of the smaller
bumps on Aspen
Mountain, with some
of Aspen Highlands'
steepest runs in the
background ➔

SNOWPIX.COM / CHRIS GILL

GETTING THERE

Air Aspen 5km/3
miles; Eagle 113km/
70 miles (1½hr);
Denver 355km/
220 miles (4hr).

Rail Glenwood
Springs (63km/40
miles).

CHILDREN

Buttermilk:
Powder Pandas
t 920 0935
Ages 3 to 6 (5 to 7
for snowboarding);
shuttle-bus from
Aspen.

Snowmass:
Big Burn Bears
t 923 0570
From age 3½

Snow Cubs
t 923 0563
Ages 8wk to 3½yr

Nighthawks
t 923 0570
Ages 3 to 10; 4pm to
11pm.

Grizzlies
t 923 0580
Ages 5 and 6
(snowboarding for 5
to 7).

All-day non-skiing
nurseries
Several

Ski school
Takes ages 7 to 17,
US$350 for 5 days
(5¼hr per day, lunch
included).

'one of the best self-service restaurants
you'll find', with great views. And a
couple of seasons ago a table-service
area – Benedict's – was opened,
offering 'wonderful food'.

At Highlands the Cloud Nine Alpine
bistro is the nearest thing you will find
in the States to a cosy Alpine hut, with
great views and excellent food –
thanks to an Austrian chef.

On Buttermilk the mountaintop
Cliffhouse is known for its 'Mongolian
Barbecue' stir-fry bar and great views.

SCHOOLS AND GUIDES
Simply the best?
There's a wide variety of specialised
instruction – mountain exploration
groups, off-piste tours, adrenaline
sessions, women's groups, and so on.
Reporters rave about the small group
lessons ('they say average of three
people, but we did five days and my
wife had one-to-one the whole time';
'the best class ever'; 'wonderful
instruction'). The Wizard Ski Deck is an
indoor ski and snowboard simulator
used in combination with some classes
or available for a private lesson.

FACILITIES FOR CHILDREN
Choice of nurseries
We have no recent reports, but past
reports on the childcare arrangements
have always been first class. Young
children are bused to and from
Buttermilk's very impressive Fort Frog.
The Kids' Trail Map is a great idea. But
Snowmass has clear advantages for
families with young children.

STAYING THERE

HOW TO GO
Accommodation for all pockets
There's a mixture of hotels, inns,
B&Bs, lodges and condos.
Chalets Several UK tour operators have
chalets here – some very luxurious.
Hotels There are places for all budgets.
Most smaller hotels provide an après-
ski cheese and wine buffet, which can
be quite a spread. A new hotel by the
gondola, the Hyatt Grand Aspen, is
scheduled to open in time for the
2005/06 season.

((((5) **St Regis Aspen** (920 3300)
Opulent city-type hotel, near gondola.
A fancy new spa facility opened last
season.

((((5) **Little Nell** (920 4600) Stylish,
modern hotel right by the gondola with
popular bar. Fireplaces in every room,
outdoor pool, hot-tub, sauna.

((((5) **Jerome** (920 1000) Step back a
century: Victorian authenticity
combined with modern-day luxury.
Several blocks from the gondola.

((((4) **Lenado** (925 6246) Smart modern
B&B place with open-fire lounge,
individually designed rooms.

(((3) **Hotel Aspen** (925 3441) Best
'moderate' place in town, 10 minutes
from lifts; comfortable, pool, hot-tubs.

(((3) **Boomerang Lodge** (925 3416)
Lloyd-Wright inspired architecture,
seven blocks from the centre,
comfortable, pool, hot-tub.

(((3)**The Mountain Chalet** (925 7797)
Cosy lodge five minutes from gondola;
breakfast included. Pool, sauna and
fitness room.

ACTIVITIES

Indoor The Aspen
Club and Spa (racquet
ball, swimming,
weights, aerobics,
sauna, steam room,
hot-tubs, ice skating);
new Aspen Recreation
Centre (swimming
complex and ice rink),
cinemas, theatre,
naturalists' evenings,
paintballing

Outdoor Ice skating,
snowcat tours, snow-
shoe tours, sleigh
rides, dog sledding,
tubing, snowmobiles

Phone numbers
From distant parts of
the US, add the prefix
1 970.
From abroad, add the
prefix +1 970.

WEBSITES

For links to resort
sites, go to our own
new site at
www.wtss.co.uk

TOURIST OFFICE

t 925 1220
intlres@skiaspen.com
www.aspensnowmass.
com

Self-catering The standards here are
high, even in US terms. Many of the
smarter developments have their own
free shuttle-buses. The Gant is luxurious
and close to the gondola. Chateau
Roaring Fork and Eau Claire, four
blocks from the gondola, are spacious
and well furnished. A reader says the
two small supermarkets are
'exceptionally well stocked'.

EATING OUT
Dining dilemma
As you'd expect, there are excellent
upmarket places, but also plenty of
cheaper options – and an easy way to
economise in many smarter places is
to choose from the bar menu.

Piñons serves innovative American
food. Syzygy is a suave upstairs place
with live jazz from 10pm. Pacifica
Seafood Brasserie is top-notch. The
basement Steak Pit is a long-
established and reliable favourite. The
Elevation features 'original Andy
Warhol artworks on the wall' and
'superb modern food'. L'Hostaria, The
Mother Lode, Campo de Fiori and
Manrico are good Italians. Cache Cache
does good-value Provençal. Ute City
Bar & Grill is good for local game.

Cheaper recommendations include:
Bentley's (main courses $8 upwards),
Boogie's (a 50s-style diner, great for
families), Main Street Bakery & Café,
Mezzaluna, Red Onion, Hickory House
('very good ribs'), the Skier's Chalet
Steak House and Woody Creek Tavern
– apparently a favourite of famous
Aspen resident the late Hunter S
Thompson.

APRES-SKI
Lots of options
As the lifts shut, a few bars at the
bases get busy. At Highlands the
terrace of Iguana's is busy. In Aspen
the Ajax Tavern is popular. The
Greenhouse bar at the Little Nell is a
great place for gazing at face-lifts.

Many of the restaurants are also
bars – Jimmy's (spectacular stock of
tequila), Mezzaluna, Red Onion, and
Ute City, for example. The J-bar of the
Jerome hotel still has a traditional feel.
Shooters Saloon is a splendid country-
and-western dive with pool and line-
dancing. For pool in more suave
circumstances, there's Aspen Billiards
adjoining the fashionable Cigar Bar,
with its comfortable sofas (and
smoking permitted!). The Popcorn
Wagon is the place for munchies after

↑ Aspen Mountain rises from the heart of
the beautifully restored 19th century silver
mining town
PETER MCBRIDE / ASPEN SKIING COMPANY

the bars close. We're told a great place
to be seen sipping a botox Martini is
the swanky 39 Degrees (located in the
Sky Hotel). You can get a week's
membership of the famous members-
only Caribou club.

OFF THE SLOPES
Silver service
Aspen has lots to offer, especially if
you've got a high credit card limit.
There are literally dozens of art
galleries, some of them world class, as
well as the predictable clothes and
jewellery shops. Just wandering around
town is pleasant. It's a shame that all
the best mountain restaurants are
awkward for pedestrians to get to.
Many hotels have excellent spa
facilities. The Aspen Recreation Center
at the base of Highlands has a huge
swimming complex and an indoor ice
rink.

Beaver Creek

The Rolls Royce of resorts: very expensive but smooth and spacious

561

COSTS

① ② ③ ④ ⑤ ⑥

RATINGS

The slopes

Fast lifts	★★★★★
Snow	★★★★★
Extent	★★
Expert	★★★★
Intermediate	★★★★
Beginner	★★★★★
Convenience	★★★★
Queues	★★★★★
Mountain restaurants	★★

The rest

Scenery	★★★
Resort charm	★★
Off-slope	★★★

NEWS

For 2005/06 the Larkspur triple will be replaced by the resort's 10th high-speed quad.

For 2004/05 a new base area, Beaver Creek Landing, was created close to the valley town of Avon. Two fast quads now link this new entry point with the main slopes at the top of Strawberry Park via Bachelor Gulch.

WEBSITES

For links to resort sites, go to our own new site at www.wtss.co.uk

➕ Blissfully quiet slopes, in sharp contrast to nearby Vail

➕ Mountain has it all, from superb novice runs to daunting mogul-fields

➕ Fast chair-lifts all over the place

➕ Compact, traffic-free village centre

➖ Rather urban feel to the village core – far from the Wild West atmosphere Europeans might look for

➖ Very expensive

➖ Disappointing mountain restaurants – the best ones are members-only

In contrast to its better-known neighbour, Vail, Beaver Creek is a haven of peace – both on and off the slopes. It gets rather overshadowed by big sister, but we wouldn't dream of making a trip to Vail without spending a day or two in Beaver. If money were no object and we wanted a quiet time, we'd tempted to do it the other way round – but lodging is very pricey in this exclusive resort.

THE RESORT

Beaver Creek, 10 miles to the west of Vail, was developed in the 1980s. It is unashamedly exclusive, with a choice of top-quality hotels and condos right by the slopes. It centres on a smart but rather severe pedestrian area with escalators to the slopes, exclusive shops, exquisite bronze statues and an open-air ice rink.

The lift system spreads across the mountains through Bachelor Gulch, with its Ritz-Carlton hotel, to Arrowhead, a slope-side hamlet with luxury condos which are less pricey than Beaver Creek. Most of the nightlife, bars and restaurants are in Beaver Creek and the choice is much more limited than in Vail, a 25-minute bus-ride away.

Staying in the valley town of Avon became much more attractive last season with the opening nearby of a new lift base, Beaver Creek Landing, with two fast new chairs linking to the heart of the Beaver Creek slopes. This also forms the natural access point for day visitors.

THE MOUNTAINS

Beaver Creek, Bachelor Gulch, Arrowhead and Beaver Creek Landing offer a small-scale version of the linked lift networks of the Alps. Free mountain tours are held four days a week. Sadly, the free tours that used to be offered by former British downhiller Martin Bell have ended, as he has left the area.

Slopes The slopes immediately above Beaver Creek divide into two sectors, each accessed by a fast quad chair. The major sector is centred on Spruce Saddle, with lifts above it reaching 3485m/11,430ft. The other is Strawberry Park, which forms the link with Bachelor Gulch and the other lift bases. Between these two sectors is Grouse Mountain.

Resorts within a two-hour drive include Vail, Breckenridge and Keystone (owned by Vail Resorts and covered by multi-day lift passes), Arapahoe Basin, Aspen, Steamboat and Copper Mountain.

Terrain-parks There are three: Park 101 is a small beginners' park, Moonshine includes a 120m/400ft long super-pipe and the Zoom Room is for progressing intermediates and beginners. Park-ology is a park and pipe programme designed to offer tuition mainly to kids.

Snow reliability An impressive annual snow record (average 310 inches) plus extensive snowmaking means you can relax. Grouse Mountain can suffer from thin cover (some call it Gravel Mountain). Grooming is excellent.

Experts There is quite a bit of intimidatingly steep double-diamond terrain. In the Birds of Prey and Grouse Mountain areas most runs are long, steep and mogulled from top to bottom (but watch the grooming map – when one of these is groomed it makes a great fast cruise, especially the World Cup Downhill run). The Larkspur Bowl area has three short, steep mogul runs.

KEY FACTS

Resort	2470m
	8,100ft
Slopes	2255-3485m
	7,400-11,440ft
Lifts	16
Pistes	1,625 acres
Green	34%
Blue	39%
Black	27%
Snowmaking	
	624 acres

REPORTS WANTED

Recently we have had few reports on this resort. If you go there, please do send us a report.

LIFT PASSES

See Vail chapter.

Central reservations phone number
1 800 427 8308
(toll free from within the US).

Phone numbers
From distant parts of the US, add the prefix 1 970.
From abroad, add the prefix +1 970.

TOURIST OFFICE

t 845 9090
bcinfo@vailresorts.com
beavercreek.snow.com

Intermediates There are marvellous long, quiet, cruising blues almost everywhere you look, including top-to-bottom runs with a vertical of 1000m/3,280ft from the top of the Cinch chair. The Larkspur and Strawberry Park chairs serve further cruising runs – and lead to yet more ideal terrain, served by the Bachelor Gulch and Arrowhead fast chairs.

Beginners There are excellent nursery slopes at resort level and at altitude (there's a family zone at the top of the Cinch chair) – 'snow stayed light and powdery here all week' says a 2005 visitor. And there are plenty of easy longer runs to progress to, including runs from top to bottom of the mountains.

Snowboarding Good riders will love the excellent gladed runs and perfect carving slopes. The resort is great for beginners, too, with special teaching methods and equipment that claim to help you learn quicker.

Cross-country There's a splendid, mountain-top network of tracks at McCoy Park (over 32km/20 miles), reached via the Strawberry Park lift.

Queues The slopes are delightfully deserted and virtually queue-free, even at peak times – it is amazing that more skiers don't come here from Vail.

Mountain restaurants There's not much choice. The 'pleasant' and 'good-value' Spruce Saddle at mid-mountain is the main place – a food court in a spectacular log and glass building. Red Tail Camp does decent barbecues. The Broken Arrow at Arrowhead base is recommended.

Schools and guides We've had good reports. This year one 'timid intermediate changed into a daredevil' because the 'care and attention' she received in her 'expensive to a fault' group lesson.

Facilities for children Small World Play School looks after non-skiing kids from two months to six years from 8.30 to 4.30. We've had good reports on the children's school and there are splendid adventure trails and play areas.

STAYING THERE

How to go There's a reasonable choice of packages.

Hotels There are lots of upmarket places, including the Ritz-Carlton, Inn at Beaver Creek and Park Hyatt.

Self-catering There's a wide choice of condos available.

Eating out SaddleRidge is luxurious and packed with photos and Wild West artefacts. A good evening out is to take a sleigh ride to one of the beautiful log cabins that are open for dinner – Beano's, Allie's or Zach's. Toscanini, the Golden Eagle Inn, Dusty Boot, Beaver Creek Chophouse and Blue Moose have all been recommended.

Après-ski Try the Coyote Cafe, Whiskey Elk and McCoys (live bands).

Off the slopes There are smart boutiques and galleries, an impressive ice rink, hot-air balloon rides and some great shows and concerts.

Staying up the mountain Trappers Cabin is a luxurious private enclave up the mountain, which a group can rent (for a small fortune) by the night.

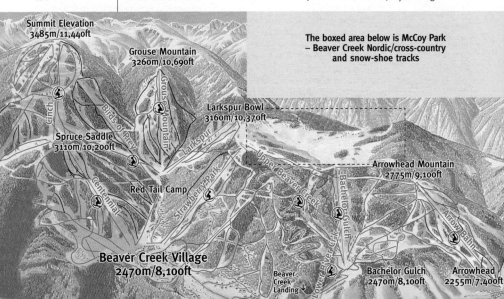

The boxed area below is McCoy Park – Beaver Creek Nordic/cross-country and snow-shoe tracks

Summit Elevation 3485m/11,440ft

Grouse Mountain 3260m/10,690ft

Larkspur Bowl 3160m/10,370ft

Spruce Saddle 3110m/10,200ft

Red Tail Camp

Arrowhead Mountain 2775m/9,100ft

Beaver Creek Village 2470m/8,100ft

Beaver Creek Landing

Bachelor Gulch 2470m/8,100ft

Arrowhead 2255m/7,400ft

Breckenridge

Four linked mountains, reached from a village with Wild West roots

COSTS

① ② ③ ④ ⑤ ⑥

RATINGS

The slopes
Fast lifts	****
Snow	*****
Extent	**
Expert	****
Intermediate	****
Beginner	****
Convenience	***
Queues	****
Mountain restaurants	**

The rest
Scenery	***
Resort charm	***
Off-slope	***

NEWS

Work started in August 2005 on a new high-speed quad called Imperial Express, which will run from the top of Chair 6 to just below the top of Peak 8. This will be North America's highest chair-lift, reaching 3915m/12,840ft, and will open up 400 acres of steep terrain previously accessible only by a 45-minute hike. We are also promised some groomed intermediate terrain here and when we went to press the resort was 'optimistic the new lift will be ready to ride this winter'.

Further in the future, new villages at the bases of Peaks 7 and 8 are planned. A new Skyway Skiway connecting Peak 8 with the town is due to be completed for 2006/07.

- ➕ Local mountains have something for all abilities
- ➕ Shared lift pass with nearby Keystone and Arapahoe Basin and not-so-nearby Vail and Beaver Creek
- ➕ Efficient lifts mean few queues
- ➕ Lively bars, restaurants and nightlife by US standards
- ➕ Some slope-side accommodation
- ➕ Restored Victorian mining town, with mainly sympathetic new buildings
- ➕ One of the nearest major resorts to Denver, so relatively short transfer

- ➖ Limited intermediate terrain, and few long runs
- ➖ Best advanced slopes can be windy
- ➖ At 2925m/9,600ft the village is one of the highest you will encounter. At this extreme altitude there is a real risk of sickness for visitors coming straight from lower altitudes
- ➖ The 19th century style gets a bit overblown in places, and there are some out-of-place modern buildings
- ➖ Main Street is just that – always busy with traffic

Breckenridge is very popular with first-time visitors to Colorado, and it's not a bad introduction to the place. We're not registered fans, though – no doubt partly because our first visit was spoiled by altitude sickness, and partly because some of our subsequent attempts to explore the steep stuff at the top have been thwarted by high winds – a regular feature, apparently.

For intermediates not interested in tackling the steep stuff, the slopes lack character as well as extent. If you base yourself here for a week or more, you should do so with the expectation that you'll want to explore other resorts (covered by the lift pass) by car or bus.

THE RESORT

Breckenridge was founded in 1859 and became a booming gold-mining town. The old clapboard buildings have been well renovated and form the bottom part of Main Street. New shopping malls and buildings have been added in similar style – though they are obvious modern additions.

The town centre is lively in the evening, with over 100 restaurants and bars. Christmas lights and decorations remain throughout the season, giving the town an air of non-stop winter festivity. This is enhanced by a number of real winter festivals such as Ullr Fest – a carnival honouring the Norse God of Winter – and Ice Sculpture championships, which leave sculptures for weeks afterwards.

Hotels and condominiums are spread over a wide, wooded area and are linked by regular, free shuttle-buses (less frequent in the evening). If you stay in a condo and don't have a car, shopping at the local supermarket can be hard work – it is not in the centre of town. Although there is a lot of slope-side accommodation – more than any other Colorado resort, it is claimed – there is also a fair amount that's inconveniently distant from Main Street and the lift base-stations.

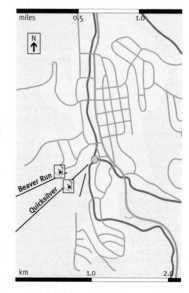

Just one of the four
terrain-parks, which
between them have
something for
everyone from park
novices to world-class
experts →

VAIL RESORTS, INC /
NATE ABBOTT

KEY FACTS

Resort	2925m
	9,600ft
Slopes	2925-3915m
	9,600-12,840ft
Lifts	28
Pistes	2,208 acres
Green	15%
Blue	33%
Black	52%
Snowmaking	
	540 acres

THE MOUNTAINS

The slopes are mainly cut through the forest, with some open runs at the top. Breckenridge is in the same ownership as Vail, Beaver Creek and Keystone. A multi-day lift ticket covers all four resorts plus Arapahoe Basin. Copper Mountain is not covered by the same ticket. All six of these resorts are linked by regular buses (free except for the trips to Vail or Beaver Creek).

THE SLOPES
Small but fragmented
There are four sectors, linked by lift and piste, named Peaks 7, 8, 9 and 10 – going from right to left as you look at the mountain. The grooming is excellent and the signposting very clear. There are free mountain tours at 9.30am daily.

Two high-speed chair-lifts go from the top end of town up to **Peak 9**, one accessing mainly green runs on the lower half of the hill, the other mainly blues higher up. From there you can get to **Peak 10**, which has a large number of blue and black runs served by one high-speed quad.

The **Peak 8** area – tough stuff at the top, easier lower down – can be reached by a fast quad from Peak 9. The new Imperial Express quad chair (see 'News') will improve access to lots of the toughest terrain. The base lifts of Peak 8 at the Bergenhof can also be reached by the town shuttle-bus or the Snowflake lift from the edge of town. Beyond here the lower slopes of **Peak 7** are served by a single six-pack. A T-bar on Peak 8 gets you to the resort's open ski-anywhere bowls, on 8 and 7. The resort claims a top height of 3960m/13,000ft, but that involves a hike of 260m/850ft vertical.

TERRAIN-PARKS
Something for everyone
There are now four terrain-parks and half-pipes – one of the best in the US is on Peak 8, Freeway, with a series of great jumps, obstacles and an enormous championship half-pipe, which one reporter described as 'massive, steep, well kept and awesome'. Less intimidating is the Gold King park on Peak 9, with jumps and railslides designed for intermediates. The Country Boy half-pipe is also on Peak 9.

The most recent addition is the small park, Trygves, on Peak 8, with

gentle jumps and an introductory pipe. Eldorado is a mini-terrain-park with a half-pipe on Peak 9.

SNOW RELIABILITY
Excellent
With its high altitude, Breckenridge boasts an excellent natural snow record – annual average 300 inches. That is supplemented by substantial snowmaking (used mainly early in the season to form a good base). There are a lot of east- and north-east-facing slopes, which hold snow well.

FOR EXPERTS
Quite a few short but tough runs
A remarkable 52% of Breckenridge's runs are classified black – either 'most difficult' (single-black-diamond) or 'expert' (double-black-diamond) terrain. That's a higher proportion than the famous 'macho' resorts, such as Jackson Hole, Taos and Snowbird. But it's a high proportion of what is a fairly small area.

The new Imperial Express quad (see 'News') will cut out the hiking needed to access much of the steepest terrain, including Imperial Bowl and Lake Chutes on Peak 8 and the Peak 7 Bowl. It will also cut down dependence on the T-bar to reach other good ungroomed terrain on Peak 8 in Horseshoe and Contest bowls, where the snow is normally good, and in

LIFT PASSES

The Colorado Ticket
Covers all Vail, Beaver
Creek, Breckenridge
and Keystone resorts,
plus Arapahoe Basin.

Beginners
Three beginner lifts

Main pass
1 day $77
6 days $462 ($378)

Senior citizens
Over 65: 6 days $402
($321)

Children
Under 13: 6 days
$282 ($224)
Under 5: free pass

Notes
Prices are regular
season rates that you
pay in the resort. The
reduced prices in
brackets are available
to international
visitors who pre-book
the ticket through a
UK tour operator. It is
not necessary to buy
a complete holiday
package to obtain
these prices.

Alternative pass
Breckenridge/
Keystone Ticket
available to
international visitors
pre-booking through
UK tour operators;
allows half their
skiing days in Vail
and Beaver Creek (6
days $354).

North Bowl and Art's Bowl on Peak 7.
On our last visit, we particularly liked
the lightly wooded back bowls of Peak
8, beneath Chair 6 – picturesque and
not too steep. Steep black mogul fields
lead further to the junction with Peak 9.

Peak 9's North Slope under Chair E
has very steep blacks (so steep that
we have never seen them retaining
good snow). The double diamond Peak
9 chutes are reached by hiking up from
the peak.

On Peak 10, at the edge of the area,
is a network of interlinking steep
mogul runs. To skier's left of the chair
is a lovely, lightly wooded off-piste
area called The Burn.

FOR INTERMEDIATES
Nice cruising, limited extent
Breckenridge has some good blue
cruising runs for all intermediates. But
dedicated piste-bashers are likely to
find the runs short and limited in
extent. Peak 9 has the easiest slopes.
It is nearly all gentle, wide, blue runs
at the top and almost flat, wide, green

runs at the bottom. And the ski patrol
is supposed to enforce slow-speed
skiing in narrow and crowded areas,
though a 2005 reader did not see
much evidence of this.

Peak 10 has a couple of more
challenging runs classified blue-black,
such as Crystal and Centennial,
which make for good fast cruising.
Peaks 7 and 8 both have a choice of
blues on trails cut close together in
the trees. Adventurous intermediates
will also like to try some of the high
bowl runs.

FOR BEGINNERS
Excellent
The bottom of Peak 9 has a big,
virtually flat area and some good,
gentle nursery slopes. There's then a
good choice of green runs to move on
to. Beginners can try Peak 8 too, with
another selection of green runs and a
choice of trails back to town. Reporters
praise the good-value beginner
package which includes lessons,
equipment rental and lift pass.

boarding

*Breckenridge is pretty much ideal for all standards of boarder and hosts several
major US snowboarding events. Beginners have ideal nursery slopes and greens to
progress to. Intermediates have great cruising runs, all served by chairs. The
powder bowls at the top of Peaks 7 and 8 make great riding – and access by the
new Imperial Express quad will end the need to ride the awkward T-bar. Boarders
of all levels will enjoy the choice of four excellent terrain-parks and half-pipes (see
'Terrain-parks'). Nearby Arapahoe Basin is another area for hardcore boarding in
steep bowls and chutes. Breckenridge pays homage to the early pioneers of the sport
with a history of snowboarding display in the Vista Haus restaurant on Peak 8.*

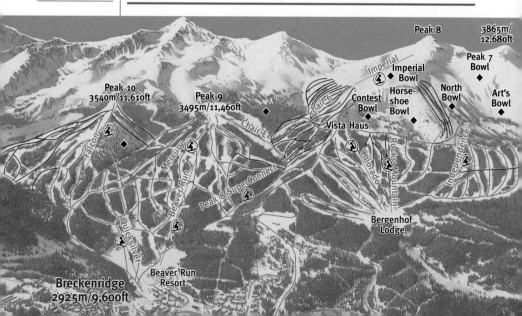

CHILDREN

Children's Center, Peak 8
t 453 3258

Children's Center, Peak 9
t 496 7449
Complex array of options for all-day care from 8.30 to 4.30 for children from age 2mnth – prior reservation essential.

Ski school
For ages 3 to 12, 9.45 to 3.45 daily ($100 for full day, incl. lunch).

SCHOOLS

Breckenridge
t 453 3272

Classes
Half day (2¼hr) $70
Private lessons
$335 for 3hr

FOR CROSS-COUNTRY
Specialist centre in woods
There are 50km/31 miles of groomed trails in total. Breckenridge's Nordic Center is prettily set in the woods between the town and Peak 8 (served by the shuttle-bus). It has 30km/19 miles of trails and 20km/12 miles miles of snow-shoeing trails. Some 20km/12 miles more cross-country trails are located at the golf course.

QUEUES
Not normally a problem
Breckenridge's eight high-speed chair-lifts make light work of peak-time crowds. Neither we nor our reporters have come across serious queues, apart from exceptional times, such as President's Day weekend and on powder days – when the T-bar at Peak 8 can get crowded.

MOUNTAIN RESTAURANTS
Varied but nothing special
Breckenridge is making an effort to improve on the standard US cafeterias: both Tenmile Station, where Peak 9 meets 10, and the Vista Haus – 'smartened up but food uninspiring' – at the top of Peak 8 are food-court operations. Border Burritos ('huge portions') is now located at Vista Haus.

SCHOOLS AND GUIDES
Excellent reports
Our reporters are unanimous in their praise for the school: classes of five to eight (sometimes smaller), doing what the class, not the instructor, wants. 'Superb, fantastic value for money. One nice aspect is that you can buy three days of lessons and take them whenever you want,' says a 2005 reporter. Special clinics include bumps, telemark and powder.

FACILITIES FOR CHILDREN
Excellent facilities
Every report on the children's school and nursery is full of plaudits. Typical comments: 'excellent, combining serious coaching with lots of fun', 'our boys loved it', 'so much more positive than ski schools in Europe'.

STAYING THERE

HOW TO GO
Lots of choice
A lot of tour operators feature Breckenridge.
Chalets Several tour operators have very comfortable chalets. A reporter described Whispering Pines (sold through Ski All America) as, 'an absolutely top notch place to stay'.
Hotels There's a good choice of style and price range.
(((4 **Great Divide Lodge** (453 4500) Owned by Vail Resorts. Prime location, vast rooms. Pool, tubs.
(((4 **Main Street Station** (800-869-9172) Closest thing Breckenridge has to a luxury hotel. On Main Street, close to slopes. Hot-tub, outdoor pool, sauna.
(((4 **Lodge at Breckenridge** (453 9300) Stylish luxury spa resort set out of town among 32 acres, with great views. Private shuttle-bus. Pool, tubs.
(((4 **Little Mountain Lodge** (453 1969) Luxury B&B near ice rink.
(((4 **Village** (547 5725) Central 3-star. 'Good value with spacious rooms.'
(((3 **Beaver Run** (453 6000) Huge, resort complex with 520 spacious rooms. Great location, by one of the main lifts up Peak 9. Pool, hot-tubs.
(((3 **Barn on the River** (800 795 2975) B&B on Main St. Said to do one of the best breakfasts in town.
Self-catering There is a huge choice of condominiums, many set conveniently off the aptly named Four O'Clock run. There are lots of houses to rent, too .

GETTING THERE

Air Denver 167km/
104 miles (2½hr).

ACTIVITIES

Indoor Spas, theatre,
museum, ice skating,
recreation centre
(pool, tubs, gym,
tennis, climbing wall)
on the outskirts of
town – accessible by
bus

Outdoor Horse-drawn
sleigh rides, dog-
sledding, fishing,
snowmobiles, snow-
shoeing, ice skating,
hot-air balloon rides

Phone numbers
From distant parts of
the US, add the prefix
1 970.
From abroad, add the
prefix +1 970.

TOURIST OFFICE

t 453 5000
breckguest@vail
resorts.com
www.breckenridge.
snow.com

WEBSITES

For links to resort
sites, go to our own
new site at
www.wtss.co.uk

VAIL RESORTS, INC

The Main Street is
mainly cute 19th
century mining town
architecture, but a lot
of the slope-side and
other buildings are
most definitely not ➜

EATING OUT
Over 100 restaurants
There's a very wide range of eating
places, from typical American food to
fine dining. The Breckenridge Dining
Guide lists a full menu of most places.

The Brewery is famous for its
enormous portions of appetisers such
as buffalo wings – as well as its
splendid brewed-on-the-spot beers –
and is still 'the liveliest spot in town'.

The sophisticated food at both Café
Alpine and Pierre's Riverwalk Café have
been recommended. Mi Casa (Mexican)
has had good reviews as has the
Kenosha steakhouse – 'specials at
great prices'. The owners of previously
recommended Sushi Breck have
opened a new sushi place, Wasabi.
Mountain Flying Fish also does sushi.
The Hearthstone is said to do 'lovely
food in good surroundings', the Blue
River Bistro to offer 'a wide selection
of food at affordable prices', and
Bubba Gump Shrimp Company to have
'good food and exceptional service'.
Michael's Italian is recommended for
'extensive menu, large portions and
reasonable prices'. Rasta Pasta offers
pasta dishes with a Jamaican twist.

APRES-SKI
The best in the area
The Breckenridge Brewery, Tiffany's,
Liquid Lounge, Fatty's and Sherpa &
Yetti's are popular. The Gold Pan
saloon dates from gold rush days, and
is reputedly the oldest bar west of the
Mississippi. Cecilia's serves good
cocktails; Gracy O'Malley's is an Irish
bar and Downstairs at Eric's is a disco
sports-bar. Mount Java is a relaxed
cafe-bookshop with internet access.

OFF THE SLOPES
Pleasant enough
Breckenridge is a pleasant place to
wander around, with plenty of souvenir
and gift shops. Silverthorne (about 30

minutes away) has excellent bargain
factory outlet stores – 'well worth a
visit' writes a reporter. It is easy to get
around and visit other resorts.

STAYING DOWN THE VALLEY
Good for exploring the area
Staying in Frisco makes sense for
those touring around or on a tight
budget. It's a small town with decent
bars and restaurants. There are cheap
motels, a couple of small hotels and
some B&Bs; Hotel Frisco (668 5009) is
'comfortable, spacious and friendly',
says a 2005 reporter, who recommends
the 'excellent' Backcountry Brewery
for drinking and eating, the 'basic'
Moose Jaw bar, 'good Italian' at
Tuscato and American food at Farrellys
and Silverlode.

Copper Mountain

Great terrain for all ability levels, above a born-again resort

COSTS

① ② ③ ④ ⑤ ⑥

RATINGS

The slopes

Fast lifts	**
Snow	*****
Extent	**
Expert	****
Intermediate	****
Beginner	****
Convenience	****
Queues	****
Mountain restaurants	*

The rest

Scenery	***
Resort charm	**
Off-slope	*

NEWS

For 2005/06 (as in 2004/05) if you book a week's holiday in the resort through most UK tour operators, you will get a free lift pass, which includes the queue-busting Beeline Advantage (see 'Queues') and a day at Winter Park.

For 2004/05 a free night-time jib park was built at the base of the American Eagle lift, open from 5pm to 9pm on designated Saturdays. The three terrain-parks were upgraded with new rails, boxes and jibs.

568

KEY FACTS

Resort	2955m
	9,700ft
Slopes	2955-3750m
	9,700-12,300ft
Lifts	22
Pistes	2,450 acres
Green	21%
Blue	25%
Black	54%
Snowmaking	
	380 acres

➕ Convenient purpose-built resort, transformed by owners Intrawest (of Whistler fame)

➕ Fair-sized mountain, with good runs for all abilities

➕ Free lift pass offer (see News)

➕ Few queues on weekdays, but ...

➖ Can be long lift queues at weekends (avoided by Beeline Advantage pass)

➖ Village still very limited

➖ Black-diamond bowls at the top offer only limited vertical

➖ Risk of altitude sickness

➖ One mediocre mountain restaurant

Copper's slopes are some of Colorado's best, and now there's a much-improved village at the base. But expect weekend crowds, and watch out for that altitude sickness; Copper's village is even higher than Breckenridge.

THE RESORT

Rather like the French resorts of the 1960s, Copper Mountain was originally high on convenience, low on charm. But new owner, Intrawest, has done a typically thorough job with the new Village at Copper, a small group of wood-and-stone-clad condo buildings with shops, restaurants and car-free walkways and squares, forming the heart of the resort. There is also the separate East Village – with some accommodation and base lodge. A regular free shuttle-bus runs between these bases and the family skiing and beginners' area at Union Creek.

Keystone, Breckenridge and Arapahoe Basin are all nearby, and Vail and Winter Park a bit further.

THE MOUNTAIN

The area is medium-sized by American standards, and has great runs for all ability levels, with an attractive mix of wooded, gladed and open slopes. Guided tours are available twice daily.
Slopes The area divides into slopes below Copper Peak and below Union Peak, with fast quads towards each from the main base area. Between the two is Union Bowl, and on the back of the hill are the high Spaulding and

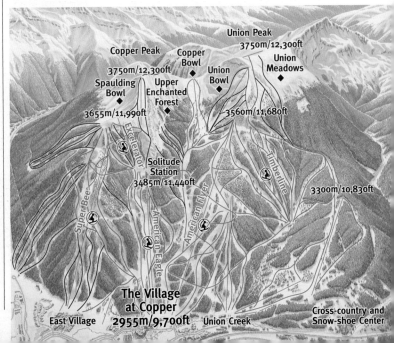

Union Peak
3750m/12,300ft

Copper Peak
3750m/12,300ft

Copper Bowl

Union Meadows

Union Bowl

Spaulding Bowl
◆

Upper Enchanted Forest
◆

3655m/11,990ft

3560m/11,680ft

Excelerator

Solitude Station
3485m/11,440ft

Timberline

3300m/10,830ft

Super Bee

American River

American Eagle

The Village at Copper
2955m/9,700ft

East Village

Union Creek

Cross-country and Snow-shoe Center

Central reservations
Call 968 2882.
Toll-free number
(from within the US)
1 888 219 2441.

Phone numbers
From distant parts of
the US, add the prefix
1 970.
From abroad, add the
prefix +1 970.

SNOWPIX.COM / CHRIS GILL

The Village at Copper
forms the heart of the
resort →

Copper Bowls – open slopes, in contrast to the wooded lower runs.

Terrain-parks There are three. The main Catalyst park is beside the American Flyer chair and has areas for beginners, intermediates and experts, plus a super-pipe and 62m/100ft rail. There's also the special kid's park, and a park for experts, with big jumps. A free night-time jib park opened last season (see News).

Snow reliability Height and extensive snowmaking give Copper an early opening date and excellent reliability. Snowfall averages 28oin a year.

Experts There is a lot of good expert terrain. Spaulding and Copper bowls offer gradients ranging from moderate to seriously steep, but with limited vertical. The wooded bump runs lower down are much longer.

Intermediates There are runs to suit everyone, from top-to-bottom greens on the right of the map through similarly long blues to easy black runs in various sectors.

Beginners The nursery slopes are excellent, and there are plenty of very easy green runs to graduate to.

Snowboarding There are great slopes for all abilities, plus three terrain-parks.

Cross-country There are 25km/15 miles of trails through the White River forest.

Queues On weekdays you may find no queues, but weekend visitors pour in from Denver and cause 20-minute queues. You can buy a (pricey) Beeline Advantage pass to jump the queues (you get it free if you book a holiday through most UK tour operators – see News). But a visitor this year found people 'got upset when we went in front of them'.

Mountain restaurants Grim. The only place worth considering is a food court at Solitude Station.

Schools and guides The school offers a wide variety of courses and has a fine reputation, especially for children.

Facilities for children The Belly Button childcare facility takes children from two months old and ski school takes children from age three. On the mountain, there are dedicated fun trails and a special kids' map.

STAYING THERE

How to go A number of tour operators offer packages to Copper.

Hotels and condos There are no hotels but some condos are splendidly luxurious, with outdoor hot-tubs, etc.

Eating out Alexander's on the Creek does excellent sophisticated food. Blue Moose pizza, Endo's and JJ's Rocky Mountain Tavern are popular. The Imperial Palace, Creekside Pizza and Salsa Mountain Cantina were recommended by a 2005 visitor. Sleigh rides take people out to Western-style dinners in tents.

Après-ski Après-ski is lively as the lifts close. Later on, Endo's Adrenaline Cafe and JJ's Rocky Mountain Tavern (with live music) are popular. Pravda is a Russian-style club and Larkin's Cross a traditional Irish pub. McGillycuddy's is an Irish bar with live music.

Off the slopes There's a good sports club, with a huge pool and indoor tennis, and ice skating on the lake.

Copper Mountain

Keystone

For those who want a peaceful, quiet, pampered time

COSTS

① ② ③ ④ ⑤ ⑥

RATINGS

The slopes

Fast lifts	****
Snow	*****
Extent	**
Expert	***
Intermediate	****
Beginner	****
Convenience	**
Queues	****
Mountain restaurants	***

The rest

Scenery	***
Resort charm	**
Off-slope	**

NEWS

During the past two years Keystone has concentrated on terrain-park improvements and upgrading snowmaking and grooming equipment. It has also expanded its ungroomed gladed terrain.

570

KEYSTONE RESORT

River Run is the cutest base village, but it is very limited in size and facilities ↓

+ Good mountain with something for everyone

+ Huge night-skiing operation

+ Other nearby resorts on lift pass

+ Luxurious condominiums

– Very scattered resort, with a lot of bussing or driving for most visitors, and no village atmosphere except in small River Run development

– Risk of altitude sickness for visitors coming straight from sea level

Keystone's slopes are impressive from many points of view, but there isn't a proper village at the foot of them. Luxurious condos are scattered over a wide area, and the nearest thing to a 'village' is the limited River Run development. We prefer to stay elsewhere and visit Keystone's slopes for a day.

THE RESORT

Keystone is a sprawling resort of condominiums spread around a partly wooded valley floor. It has no clear centre and is divided into seven 'neighborhoods'. Some are little more than groups of condos, while others have shops, restaurants and bars (though no supermarkets or liquor stores – they are on the main highway).

River Run, at the base of the main gondola, is the nearest thing to a conventional ski resort village, with condo buildings, a short main street, a square and a few restaurants, bars and shops. A second lift base area half a mile to the west, Mountain House, is much less of a village. Another mile west is Lakeside Village, which is not a village at all but a hotel and condo complex, weirdly lacking animation, beside a lake – a huge natural ice rink.

Buses link all the component parts. At weekends, overflow parking lots come into operation and the bus services become overstretched.

THE MOUNTAINS

By US standards Keystone offers extensive intermediate slopes and some challenging steeper stuff, further expanded last season with the opening of Erickson and Bergman Bowls. The resort is owned by Vail Resorts, and the lift pass covers Vail, Beaver Creek, Breckenridge and Arapahoe Basin (a few minutes away by road). Copper Mountain is also nearby.

Slopes Three wooded mountains form Keystone's local slopes. Lifts depart from Mountain House and River Run to the one above the resort, Dercum Mountain. The front face of the mountain has Keystone's biggest network of lifts and runs by far, mainly of easy and intermediate gradient. From the top you can drop over the back down to Keystone Gulch, where there are lifts back on to the next hill, North Peak. Or you can ride the Outpost gondola directly to the shoulder of North Peak. Beyond North Peak is the third peak, The Outback. Keystone has the biggest floodlit skiing operation in the US, covering Dercum Mountain top to bottom up to 8pm on certain nights of the week.

Terrain-parks The terrain-park is huge; it was trebled in size a couple of seasons ago and has features for all levels including a half-pipe and super-pipe. The park has its own chair-lift, and is floodlit several nights a week.

Snow reliability Snow shortage is rarely a problem, and there's one of the world's biggest snowmaking systems.

Experts Keystone has a lot of steeper, ungroomed terrain. The Windows is a 60-acre area of experts-only glade runs on Dercum Mountain's back side. From

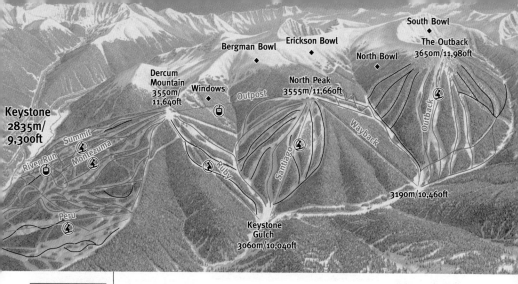

KEY FACTS

Resort	2835m
	9,300ft
Slopes	2835-3650m
	9,300-11,980ft
Lifts	19
Pistes	2,870 acres
Green	19%
Blue	32%
Black	49%
Snowmaking	
	650 acres

REPORTS WANTED

Recently we have had few reports on this resort. If you go there, please do send us a report.

WEBSITES

For links to resort sites, go to our own new site at www.wtss.co.uk

Central reservations phone number
1 877 753 9786
(toll free from within the US).
Phone numbers
From distant parts of the US, add the prefix 1 970.
From abroad, add the prefix +1 970.

TOURIST OFFICE

t 496 2316
keystoneinfo@
vailresorts.com
www.keystone.snow.
com

The Outback there are black runs with all sorts of challenges, route-finding being one of them. You can hike to open and gladed runs in the North and South Bowls, Erickson Bowl and Bergman Bowl, but you pay extra for snowcat access and guidance ($71 for four hours with guides from the top of Dercum; $5 for a one-off ride but no guide on the Outback).

Intermediates Keystone is ideal. The front face of Dercum Mountain itself is a network of beautifully groomed blue and green runs through the trees. The Outback and North Peak also have easy cruising and some steeper blues. Some of the blacks are groomed, and are tremendous fun early in the day.

Beginners There are good nursery slopes at the top and bottom of Dercum Mountain, although a reporter found the area at the top rather 'disorganised' and a 'little daunting' for novices arriving from the gondola. There are excellent long green runs to progress to.

Snowboarding Keystone is ideal for beginners and intermediates, with mainly chair-lifts and gondolas, good beginner areas and cruising runs. Expert riders will love The Outback.

Cross-country There are 16km/10 miles of groomed trails and 57km/35 miles of unprepared trails.

Queues Except at the morning peak, there are few queues and the trails are usually beautifully quiet, except for Mozart, the only blue run down from Dercum Mountain to North Peak.

Mountain restaurants The table-service Alpenglow Stube (North Peak) is a delightfully cosseting place, and one of our favourites in the US: the fixed-price lunch is a bargain at about $20. The alternatives, at the top of Dercum and at the lift base between the two hills, are not appealing.

Schools and guides As well as the normal lessons, there are bumps, race and various other advanced classes. A 2004 reporter enjoyed 'excellent' instruction in very small groups.

Facilities for children Excellent, with programmes tailored to specific age groups, dedicated children's teaching areas and organised kids' nights out.

STAYING THERE

How to go Regular shuttles operate from Denver airport. Most accommodation is in condominiums.

Hotels There isn't a great choice but they're all of a high standard.

Self-catering All the condominiums are large and luxurious – and we've stayed in some fabulous ones.

Eating out Disappointing: the restaurants are scattered around, and there isn't the range of mid-market restaurants that makes eating out such a pleasure in many American resorts. You can eat up the mountain at the Summit House or Alpenglow Stube.

Après-ski The Summit House has live music and caters for night skiing customers too. But this is not the resort for late-night revellers.

Off the slopes There are plenty of activities, including skating on the frozen lake, tubing and indoor tennis. Silverthorne has a leisure centre, swimming pool and skate park, as well as the factory outlet shopping.

Snowmass

Aspen's modern satellite – with impressively varied and extensive slopes

+ Big, varied mountain with a vertical of 1340m/4,400ft – biggest in the US

+ Aspen's three mountains also accessible by frequent free bus

+ Uncrowded slopes

+ Lots of slope-side lodgings

− Snowmass 'village' offers very limited shopping and nightlife, though the new Base Village being built should improve things

− Diversions of Aspen town are a bus-ride away

The slopes of Snowmass are a key part of the attraction of nearby Aspen as a destination. Whether Snowmass makes sense as a base depends on what's more important to you: great bars and restaurants, or great nursery slopes and green runs on your doorstep. For many families, the choice is clear.

THE RESORT

Snowmass is a modern, purpose-built resort with most of the accommodation in low-rise buildings set alongside the gentle home slope. At the heart of these buildings is Snowmass Village Mall, with a small cluster of shops and restaurants. There are also lots of private homes set along roads that wind up into the lower slopes.

The Mall contains the essentials of resort life, but not much more. But work has started on a new base village as part of a development plan that should make Snowmass an even more compelling base for families.

Aspen is some 12 miles away, its Highlands and Buttermilk mountains slightly less. Efficient free bus services link the resorts and mountains. The service to Aspen town runs to 1am.

THE MOUNTAIN

Snowmass has over 60% of the total acreage covered by the Aspen ski pass – it is almost five miles across, and has the biggest vertical in the US. Many of the Snowmass runs are wide, sweeping cruisers. But it also has some of the toughest terrain in the Aspen portfolio. Most of the slopes are in the forest, but the higher ones are open or only lightly wooded.

Slopes Chair-lifts fan out from the purpose-built village at the base towards four linked sectors – Elk Camp, High Alpine, Big Burn and Sam's Knob. There is also access from Two Creeks, which is much nearer to Aspen town and has free slope-side parking.

Terrain-parks The Snowmass Pipeline terrain-park is 2.5km/1.5 miles long and incorporates a super-pipe and a rail yard. There are also separate parks and pipes for beginners and kids.

Snow reliability With 300 inches a year plus snowmaking, it's good.

Experts Our favourite area is around the Hanging Valley Wall and Glades – beautiful scenery and steep, tree-covered slopes. The other seriously steep area is the Cirque. The Cirque drag-lift takes you well above the tree line to Aspen's highest point. From here, the Headwall is not terrifyingly steep, but there are also narrow, often rocky, chutes – Gowdy's is one of the steepest. All these runs funnel into a pretty, lightly wooded valley. Consider joining a guided group as an introduction to the best of Snowmass.

Intermediates Snowmass is the best mountain in the Aspen area for intermediates. The Big Burn is a cruising paradise – a huge, lightly wooded area with a satisfying variety of terrain, including the Powerline Glades for the adventurous. The easiest intermediate slopes are from the Elk Camp lift all the way down to Two Creeks. Long Shot is a glorious, ungroomed, 5km/3 mile run, lost in the forest, and well worth the short hike up to get to the start. In the centre of the area, the two chair-lifts below High Alpine serve yet more intermediate slopes – a little trickier and more varied. The Sam's Knob sector offers slightly more challenge, including some regularly groomed single-black runs. And Green Cabin, from the High Alpine lift, is a magical top-to-bottom cruise.

Beginners In the heart of the resort is a broad, gentle beginners' run. An even easier slope is the wide Assay Hill, at the bottom of Elk Camp. From

It's great for families and has wide, gentle nursery slopes →

NEWS

Work has started on a new Base Village, to be connected to the existing village by an open-top gondola. For 2005/06 the main chair from the village will be replaced by a six-pack that will go higher.

Phone numbers
From distant parts of the US, add the prefix 1 970.
From abroad, add the prefix +1 970.

TOURIST OFFICE

t 925 1220
intlres@skiaspen.com
www.aspensnowmass.com

Sam's Knob there are long, gentle cruises leading back to the resort.
Snowboarding A great mountain, whatever your boarding style.
Cross-country Excellent trails between here and Aspen – see Aspen chapter.
Queues Snowmass has so many alternative lifts and runs that you can normally avoid problems. Some long, slow chairs can be cold in mid-winter. The home slope gets very crowded.
Mountain restaurants There are refuelling stops at several key points, but also some places worth seeking out. Gwyn's High Alpine is an elegant table-service restaurant serving above-average food. The best views are from Sam's Knob, with self-service and table-service restaurants. Cafe Suzanne on Elk Camp has a French flavour and does 'exceptionally good crêpes'.
Schools and guides A 2004 reporter had three rewarding days, but warns that the advertised off-piste groups turned out to be just standard school classes, which will go off-piste only if the whole group is up to it.
Facilities for children We lack recent reports, but the facilities for kids here look good to us. The village has special family skiing zones.

STAYING THERE

How to go Most accommodation is self-catering.
Hotels The focal hotel is the Silvertree (923 3520) – an ocean liner parked next to the home slope and the Mall – with 'disappointing rooms', excellent top-floor Brothers' Grille restaurant and pools. Stonebridge Inn (923 2420) is a good-value alternative; nice restaurant, pool, hot-tub.
Self-catering The Tamarack Townhouses, Terrace House and Top of the Village have been highly recommended by reporters.
Eating out The choice is adequate. As well as the excellent Brothers' Grille and a nearby steakhouse there are Italian, Tex-Mex, Provençal and 'pan-Asian' restaurants. Butch's Lobster Bar 'is by far the best restaurant in town – garlic prawns to die for', says a regular reporter. The Blue Door (see below) does Cajun food. Sno Beach Café is good for breakfast.
Après-ski The Cirque next to the home slope has live bands most days but closes at 6pm. The restaurants (above) have bars – the Margarita keeps 30 tequilas. The Mountain Dragon is popular. The Blue Door is a new nightclub, sometimes with live music.
Off the slopes Diversions include tubing on Assay Hill 1pm to 8pm, snow-shoe trails, nature tours, piste-basher rides, paintball, dog-sled rides.

Snowmass

573

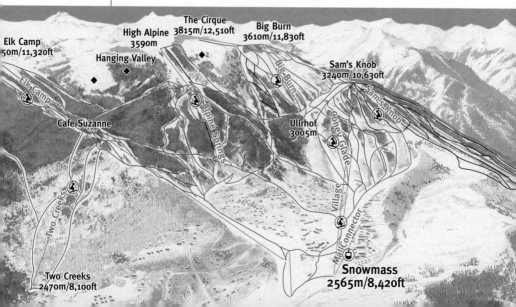

Steamboat

Where they invented the term Champagne Powder™

- Excellent easy runs
- Famed for its gladed powder terrain
- Good snow record
- Table-service mountain restaurants
- Plenty of slope-side lodging
- Town has some Western character

- Town is a drive from the slopes
- Modern base 'village' is sprawling, with some eyesore buildings
- Not enough runs to amuse keen intermediates for a week
- Not a huge amount of double-black terrain – some of it is a hike away

Sadly, there is very little of the Wild West about Steamboat's base village – and the 'cattle town' of Steamboat Springs doesn't merit more than the occasional excursion. The mountain may not match some of its competitors for extent, but it's one of the best for powder fun among the trees.

THE RESORT

The resort village is a 10-minute bus-ride from the old town of Steamboat Springs. Near the gondola there are a few shop- and restaurant-lined multi-level squares, some of which are receiving a much-needed facelift over the next few years. Some lodgings are up the sides of the piste, but the resort also sprawls across the valley. The old town can be a bit of a disappointment. It may be a working cattle town, but the Wild West isn't much in evidence. The wide main street is lined with bars, hotels and shops in a mixture of styles, from old wooden buildings to concrete plazas.

THE MOUNTAINS

Steamboat's slopes are prettily set among trees, with extensive views over rolling hills and the wide Yampa valley. The place is relatively isolated, but you could combine it with resorts west of Denver, from Winter Park to Vail.
Slopes The gondola from the village rises to the low peak of Thunderhead. Beyond it are lifts to Storm Peak and Sunshine Peak. On the back of the hill is the Morningside Park area, with a lift up to the highest point at Mt Werner, also accessing some of the highest runs on the front side. Below these is an area served by the Pony Express chair.
Terrain-parks The SoBe terrain-park includes rails, jumps, a mini-pipe and the Mavericks super-pipe, claimed to be the longest in North America. Beehive is a special park for kids.
Snow reliability Steamboat is low for

Colorado but it has an excellent snow record with a 10-year annual average of 335 inches. The term Champagne Powder™ was invented here. There is snowmaking from top to bottom, too.
Experts The main attraction is the challenging terrain in the glades. A great area is on Sunshine Peak below the Sundown chair. Morningside Park and Pioneer Ridge also have excellent gladed runs. Three steep chutes are easily accessed via the lift back from Morningside, and a short hike gets you to the tree runs of Christmas Tree Bowl. For bumps, try the runs off Four Points.
Intermediates Much of the mountain is ideal, with long cruising blue runs. Morningside Park is a great area for easy black as well as blue slopes. The Sunshine area is very gentle. Keen intermediates will find the area is limited in extent, but if you catch the area with fresh powder, it offers a great introduction to tree skiing.
Beginners There's a big nursery area at the base of the mountain, with a variety of gentle greens to progress to.
Snowboarding There's a special learning area, gentle slopes to progress to and you can get around using chair-lifts and the gondola. For experienced riders, riding the glades in fresh powder is unbeatable.
Cross-country A free shuttle service takes you to 30km/19 miles of groomed tracks at the Touring Center.
Queues Queues form for the gondola first thing, but they move quickly; the slow Sunshine lift can be crowded. Noticeboards indicate waiting times.
Mountain restaurants There are food courts and table-service restaurants at

The resort village is functional and modern →

Central reservations phone number
1 800 922 2722
(toll free in the US).

Phone numbers
Calling long-distance, add the prefix 1 970. From abroad, add the prefix +1 970.

TOURIST OFFICE

t 879 6111
info@steamboat.com
www.steamboat.com

WEBSITES

For links to resort sites, go to our own new site at
www.wtss.co.uk

both Thunderhead and Rendezvous Saddle – much better than the American fast-food norm.
Schools and guides Reports are very positive. 'Very good indeed ... even by the standards of the USA,' enthused a couple who had separate lessons.
Facilities for children Arrangements are exceptional, including evening entertainment. Kids under 12 ski free with a parent or a grandparent buying a pass for at least five days.

STAYING THERE

How to go A fair number of UK tour operators feature Steamboat.
Chalets There are some catered chalets run by UK tour operators.
Hotels There are smart hotels at the base, including the 'excellent' Steamboat Grand (871 5050) and the Ptarmigan Inn (879 1730) – more characterful ones in town. The Rabbit Ears Motel (879 1150) has been recommended.
Self-catering There are countless condos, many with good pool/hot-tub facilities, all on a free bus route. Ski Inn Condos at the base of the gondola and Antlers ('the best luxury ski-in, ski-out accommodation'), Eagleridge, Canyon Creek, Timber Run and The Lodge have all been recommended.

Eating out There are over 70 bars and restaurants. Pick up a dining guide booklet to check out the menus. You can dine in three restaurants up the mountain. At the base area the Tugboat Grill and Bar and Cafe Diva have been recommended (as has the Wired internet cafe for breakfast). In downtown Steamboat Springs try Antares for Asian fusion cuisine, Old West Steakhouse, or the Cottonwood Grill for its 'fabulously tasty Pacific Rim cuisine'. For a budget meal, head for Double Z (pronounced Zee).
Après-ski The base lodge area is livelier than the old town in the evening. At close of play the Slopeside Grill is popular. The Bear River Bar has a comedy club, and the Tugboat has live music and dancing.
Off the slopes Getting to Thunderhead restaurant complex is easy for pedestrians. Visiting town is, too.

Steamboat

575

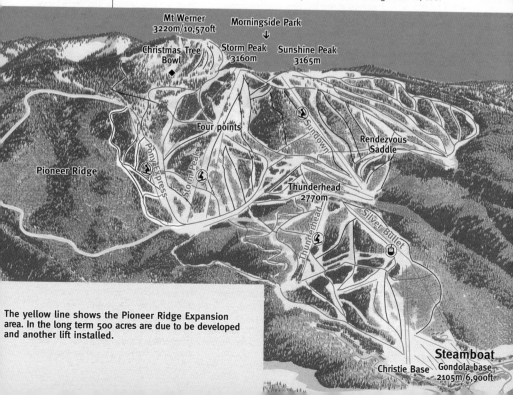

The yellow line shows the Pioneer Ridge Expansion area. In the long term 500 acres are due to be developed and another lift installed.

Mt Werner
3220m/10,570ft

Morningside Park

Christmas Tree Bowl

Storm Peak
3160m

Sunshine Peak
3165m

Four points

Pioneer Ridge

Rendezvous Saddle

Thunderhead
2770m

Silver Bullet

Power Express

Storm Peak

Sundown

Thunderhead

Steamboat

Christie Base

Gondola base
2105m/6,900ft

Telluride

One of the best Colorado has to offer, in every respect except size

COSTS

① ② ③ ④ ⑤ ⑥

RATINGS

The slopes

Fast lifts	*****
Snow	****
Extent	**
Expert	****
Intermediate	***
Beginner	*****
Convenience	****
Queues	*****
Mountain restaurants	*

The rest

Scenery	****
Resort charm	****
Off-slope	**

NEWS

For 2004/05 a new super-pipe was built above Mountain Village and guided backcountry tours in Prospect Bowl, bookable through the Ski and Snowboard School, were introduced.

KEY FACTS

Resort	2665m
	8,750ft
Slopes	2660-3735m
	8,730-12,260ft
Lifts	16
Pistes	1,700 acres
Green	24%
Blue	38%
Black	38%
Snowmaking	
	204 acres

REPORTS WANTED

Recently we have had few reports on this resort. If you go there, please do send us a report.

The best reports earn a copy of the next edition, and can lead to free lift passes in future.

See page 10.

+ Charming restored Victorian mining town with a Wild West atmosphere
+ Slopes for all, including experts
+ Dramatic, craggy mountain scenery – unusual for Colorado

− Isolated location
− Despite expansion, still a small area
− Mountain Village a little quiet
− Limited mountain restaurants

We love the old town of Telluride and always enjoy its scenic, varied slopes; but their limited extent makes the place difficult to recommend for a holiday except in combination with another resort – which means travelling some distance.

THE RESORT

Telluride is an isolated resort in south-west Colorado. The town first boomed when gold was found – and Butch Cassidy robbed his first bank here. The town's old red-brick and timber buildings have been well restored, and it has more Wild West charm than any other resort. Shops and restaurants have gone decidedly up-market since its 'hippy' days of a few years ago and a lot of celebrities have plush holiday-homes in the area now. But Telluride is still friendly and small-scale. On the slopes, the Mountain Village is a development of lavish modern condos and hotels. A gondola links the town and village and runs until midnight.

THE MOUNTAINS

There is something for everyone here.
Slopes Two chair-lifts and a gondola serve steep wooded slopes above the town, and access the bowl beyond which leads down to Mountain Village. This bowl is almost all wooded, with steep open slopes at the very top.
Terrain-parks The huge, 10-acre Sprite Air Garden terrain-park above the Mountain Village has a super pipe and all the features you could dream of. The separate Pocket Park off the Ute Park lift is suitable for beginners.
Snow reliability With an average of 309 inches of snow a year and some snowmaking, reliability is good, but there have been some slow starts to recent seasons.
Experts The double-black bump runs are well-known tests, and there are steep gladed runs from all along the ridge between Giuseppe's and Gold Hill – no longer a hike, thanks to the Gold Hill lift. Gold Hill has some truly

challenging terrain, from wide open steeps to narrow chutes and gnarly wooded trails. You can now try hike-to backcountry terrain with the ski school. Helitrax claims to be Colorado's only heli-skiing operation.
Intermediates There are ideal blue cruising runs with awesome views from the top down to Mountain Village (including the aptly-named See Forever). Some of the blacks above the town get groomed – worth catching if you can. Prospect Bowl has some great intermediate terrain, with dozens of rolling pitches that meander and weave their way through thickets of trees – a very relaxing and pretty area. Even so, keen piste-bashers could get bored after a couple of days.
Beginners There are ideal runs in the Meadows below Mountain Village, and splendid long greens and blues served by the Sunshine fast chair.
Snowboarding The lift system means it is easy to get about, and the huge terrain-park offers plenty of scope.
Cross-country The beauty of the area makes it splendid for cross-country – both in the valley and at altitude with 30km/19 miles in total. There are 10km/6 miles of trails at the wonderfully elevated Topaten Center.
Queues These are rarely a problem.
Mountain restaurants Gorrono Ranch is the main on-mountain restaurant, with a big terrace, live music and a BBQ. There are a couple of snack shacks higher up, with great views. Allred's, a civilised table-service place at St Sophia gondola station, is meant to be members only – but there's no harm in asking if they can squeeze you in.
Schools and guides The resort is proud of its Telluride Teaching System. Bump clinics are a speciality and they now offer some backcountry guiding.

↑ The Prospect Bowl slopes seen from the Gold Hill area

SNOWPIX.COM / CHRIS GILL

Wyndham Peaks Resort in the Mountain Village is enormous but has a spectacular lounge area and impressive spa facilities.

Self-catering There are plenty of condos. The Inn At Lost Creek in Mountain Village is the most lavish of the self-catering options.

Eating out The Cosmopolitan in the Hotel Columbia is renowned as the best in town. Other sophisticated options include the Marmotte and Harmon's (in the old station). Allred's at the top of the gondola is open for gourmet dining in the evenings.

Après-ski There's a lively bar-based après-ski scene. The West End Tavern has a popular happy hour from 4pm to 6pm. The New Sheridan has a lovely old bar dating from 1895. The Last Dollar has been recommended by locals. The Fly Me to the Moon Saloon has live music and stays open late. There's a swanky candlelit lounge called the Noir Bar attached to the Blue Point Grill. There are often concerts at the historic Sheridan Opera House. The Nugget Theatre shows latest cinema releases. Thrill Hill at the Mountain Village has floodlit tubing, sledding and snowbiking.

Off the slopes There's quite a lot to do around town if you are not skiing or boarding, such as dog sledding, horse riding, snow-shoeing, ice skating, snowmobiling and glider rides. The Golden Door Spa in the Wyndham Peaks Resort was voted one of the top 10 spas in the world by *Condé Nast Traveller* readers.

Facilities for children The Adventure Club provides indoor and outdoor play before and after children's lessons. The Mountain Village Activity Center has a nursery for toddlers.

STAYING THERE

Telluride is tricky to get to from the UK, involving two or three flights or a long 540km/335 mile drive from Denver.

How to go Packages fly into nearby Montrose or the tiny Telluride airport (prone to closure by the weather).

Hotels Hotel Columbia is luxurious, as is the plush yet friendly Camel's Garden Hotel and Spa. The New Sheridan is actually old – a Main Street USA classic, and comfortable too. The

WEBSITES

For links to resort sites, go to our own new site at www.wtss.co.uk

Central reservations
Call 728 7507.
Toll-free number
(from within the US)
1 888 827 8050.

Phone numbers
From distant parts of the US, add the prefix 1 970.
From abroad, add the prefix +1 970.

TOURIST OFFICE

t 728 6900
info@tellurideskiresort.com
www.tellurideskiresort.com

Telluride

577

Palmyra Peak

Gold Hill

3735m/12,26oft

3600m/11,81oft

3650m

Giuseppe's

Gold Hill 10

Prospect Bowl 12

3280m

3315m

Station St Sophia
3210m

Palmyra 5

Sunshine 10

Telluride
2665m/
8,750ft

Coonskin Base
2660m/8,730ft

Mountain Village
2910m/9,540ft

Big Billie's
2790m/9,16oft

Vail

Luxury living, high prices and the US's biggest single ski area

COSTS

① ② ③ ④ ⑤ ⑥

RATINGS

The slopes

Fast lifts	****
Snow	*****
Extent	****
Expert	****
Intermediate	*****
Beginner	***
Convenience	***
Queues	**
Mountain restaurants	**

The rest

Scenery	***
Resort charm	***
Off-slope	***

NEWS

For 2004/05 a yurt was built at Two Elk, providing additional seating for the children's ski school and for picnic lunches. Snowmaking was improved on eastern areas of Golden Peak.

The Lionshead area is being completely redeveloped (in typical US fashion they have dubbed this 'Vail's New Dawn'). Plans include a luxury hotel and a car-free plaza with shops, restaurants and outdoor ice rink. They hope it will be finished for the 2007/08 season.

➕ Biggest area in the US – great for confident intermediates, especially

➕ The Back Bowls are big areas of treeless terrain – unusual in the US

➕ Fabulous area of ungroomed, wooded slopes at Blue Sky Basin

➕ Largely traffic-free resort centres, very pleasant in parts – but ...

➖ Resort as a whole is a vast sprawl, and Lionshead is a dreary mess, though it's being redeveloped

➖ Slopes can be crowded by American standards, with some lift queues

➖ Blue Sky Basin and the Back Bowls may not be open in early season; warm weather can close the Bowls

➖ Inadequate mountain restaurants

➖ Expensive

Blue Sky Basin, an area of shady, wooded, largely ungroomed slopes, has transformed Vail's attraction for good skiers and riders. Not only does it bring a much-needed bit of spice to the resort, but it gets you away from the crowds that are Vail's most serious drawback.

Vail's slopes are undeniably compelling, especially when you take account of nearby sister-resort Beaver Creek (see separate chapter). What continues to push Vail down our American shortlist are its style and its atmosphere – a curious mixture of pseudo-Tirol and sprawling, anonymous suburbs. The resort works well, largely thanks to the efficient buses. But if you hope to be captivated, Vail can't compete with the distinctive Rockies resorts based on old mining or cowboy towns. If we're going that far West, we like it to be a bit Wild.

THE RESORT

Standing in the centre of Vail Village, surrounded by chalets and bierkellers, you could be forgiven for thinking you were in the Tirol – which is what Vail's founder, Pete Seibert, intended back in the 1950s. But Vail Village is now just part of an enormous resort, mostly built in anonymous modern style, stretching for miles beside the I-70 freeway running west from Denver.

The vast village benefits from a free and efficient bus service – 'superb', says a 2005 reporter – which makes choice of location less than crucial. But there's no denying that the most convenient – and expensive – places to stay are in mock-Tirolean Vail Village, near the Vista Bahn fast chair, or in functional Lionshead, near the gondola – a much less attractive area that really needs the revamp that is now starting. There is a lot of accommodation further out – the cheapest tends to be across the I-70.

Beaver Creek, 10 miles away, is covered by the lift pass and is easily reached by bus. A short drive gets you to Breckenridge and Keystone (both owned by Vail Resorts and covered by the lift pass), and Copper Mountain. Each of these resorts is covered in its own chapter in this guide.

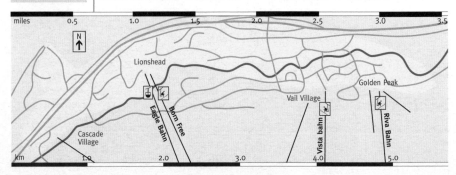

KEY FACTS

Resort	2500m
	8,200ft
Slopes	2475-3525m
	8,120-11,570ft
Lifts	34
Pistes	5,289 acres
Green	18%
Blue	29%
Black	53%
Snowmaking	
	390 acres

bowls – Mid-Vail in the centre, with Game Creek to the south-west and Northeast Bowl to the, er, north-east. Lifts reach the ridge at three points, all giving access to the **Back Bowls** (mostly ungroomed and treeless) and through them to the **Blue Sky Basin** area (mostly ungroomed and wooded).

The slopes have yellow-jacketed patrollers who stop people speeding recklessly. There's a New Technology Center where you can test the latest equipment.

TERRAIN-PARKS
Head for Golden Peak

There is an excellent terrain-park with lots of rails and jumps and a super-pipe (130m/425ft long with 5.5m/18ft walls) at Golden Peak, accessed by the Riva Bahn Express. There's also a deck where you can chill out. A log rail park is located in the trees near the Golden Peak park. Two smaller parks were added a couple of seasons ago – Mule Skinner (also served by the Riva Bahn) has four jumps, boxes and two rails while Bwana Park, under the Eagle Bahn gondola, has a few more. The schools will also use the parks for their new 'speciality' classes.

SNOW RELIABILITY
Excellent, except in the Bowls

As well as an exceptional natural snow record, Vail has extensive snowmaking facilities, normally needed only in early season. Both the Back Bowls and Blue Sky Basin usually open later in the season than the front mountain. Blue Sky is largely north-facing (and wooded) and keeps its snow well, but the Bowls are sunny, and in warm weather snow can deteriorate to the point where they are closed or a traverse is kept open to allow access to Blue Sky Basin – boring for boarders especially.

THE MOUNTAINS

Vail has the biggest area of slopes in the US, with immaculately groomed trails and ungroomed terrain in open bowls and among the trees. There are runs to suit every taste, and you get a real sense of travelling around the mountain – something missing in many smaller American resorts. The main criticism is that some of the runs (especially blacks) are overclassified. Trail marking has been praised – 'good directions', 'large map boards'.

THE SLOPES
Something for everyone

The slopes above **Vail** can be accessed via three main lifts. From right next to Vail Village, the Vista Bahn fast chair goes up to the major mid-mountain focal point, Mid-Vail; from Lionshead, the Eagle Bahn gondola goes up to the Eagle's Nest complex; and from the Golden Peak base area just to the east of Vail Village, the Riva Bahn fast chair goes up towards the Two Elk area.

The front face of the mountain is largely north-facing, with well-groomed trails cut through the trees. At altitude the mountainside divides into three

Vail

BLUE SKY BASIN

When Blue Sky Basin opened six seasons ago it transformed the attraction of Vail for good skiers. There are now 645 acres of terrain, served by three fast quads. There are some easy blue runs that are frequently groomed, but most of the area is left ungroomed and the runs among the trees – some widely spaced, some very tight – are delightful for strong skiers and boarders. Few of the runs are very steep, but because you are basically finding your own way much of the time, there is a great feeling of adventure. The snow is usually much better than in the Back Bowls because of the shelter given by the trees and the generally north-facing aspect. A reporter recommends the free daily tours, which start at 10am at the Blue Sky Basin sign at the top of the Mountaintop and Northwoods Express lifts.

Two Elk Lodge
3420m/11,220ft

Patrol Headquarters
3430m/11,250ft

Wildwood
3345m/10,98oft

Northeast Bowl

Northwoods

Mountaintop

Wildwood

Game Creek Bowl

Game Creek

Mid-Vail
3095m/10,150ft

Avanti

Eagle's Nest
3155m/10,350ft

Riva Bahn

Vista Bahn

Pride

Born-Free

Eagle Bahn

Golden Peak

Vail Village
2500m/8,200ft

Lionshead
2475m/8,120ft

Cascade
Village

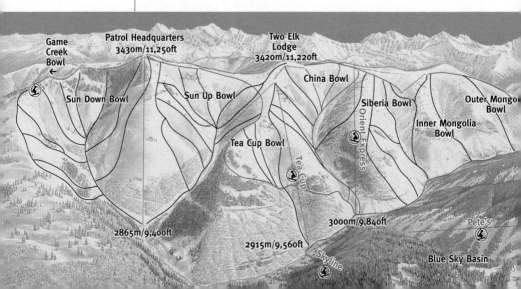

Game Creek Bowl ←

Patrol Headquarters
3430m/11,250ft

Two Elk Lodge
3420m/11,220ft

China Bowl

Sun Down Bowl

Sun Up Bowl

Siberia Bowl

Outer Mongo
Bowl

Orient Express

Inner Mongolia
Bowl

Tea Cup Bowl

Tea Cup

3000m/9,840ft

Pete's

2865m/9,400ft

2915m/9,56oft

Skyline

Blue Sky Basin

LIFT PASSES

The Colorado Ticket
Covers all Vail, Beaver Creek, Breckenridge and Keystone resorts, plus Arapahoe Basin.

Beginners
3-day learn-to-ski course includes reduced-cost lift pass.

Main pass
1 day $77
6 days $462 ($378)

Senior citizens
Over 65: 6 days $402 ($321)

Children
Under 13: 6 days $282 ($224)
Under 5: free pass

Notes
Prices are regular season rates that you pay in the resort. The reduced prices in brackets are available to international visitors who pre-book the ticket through a UK tour operator. It is not necessary to buy a complete holiday package to obtain these prices.

boarding

Vail has been wooing boarders with excellent facilities for years. With beautifully groomed, gentle slopes and lots of high-speed chairs, this is a great area for beginners, and there's plenty for experts too, including some wonderful gladed runs. There are specialist board shops and good instruction. Vail's Burton Learn to Ride Program uses special equipment designed to help you learn. It claims to minimise falls and accelerate the learning curve. There's a Burton test centre at the New Technology Centre at the top of the Mountaintop Express chair.

FOR EXPERTS
Transformed by Blue Sky Basin

Vail's Back Bowls are vast areas, served by three chair-lifts and a couple of short drag-lifts. You can go virtually anywhere you like in the half-dozen identifiable bowls, trying the gradient and terrain of your choice. There are interesting, lightly wooded areas, as well as the open slopes that dominate the area. Some 87% of the runs in the Back Bowls are classified black but are not particularly steep, and they have disappointed some of our expert reporters. They are best in fresh powder and the snow can deteriorate rapidly in warm, sunny weather.

Blue Sky Basin has some great adventure runs in the trees – see feature panel earlier in this chapter.

On the front face there are some genuinely steep double-black-diamond runs which usually have great snow; they are often moguled but sometimes groomed to make wonderful fast cruising. The Highline lift on the extreme east of the area serves three – a 2004 reporter had 'great fun' here on 'deserted' trails. Prima Cornice, served by the Northwoods Express, is one of the steepest runs on the front side.

If the snow is good, try the back-country Minturn Mile – you leave the ski area through a gate in the Game Creek area for an off-piste run starting with a powder bowl and finishing on a path by a river – ending up at the atmospheric Saloon (see Après-ski).

FOR INTERMEDIATES
Ideal territory

The majority of Vail's front face is great intermediate territory, with easy cruising runs. Above Lionshead, especially, there are excellent long, relatively quiet blues – Born Free and Simba both go from top to bottom. Game Creek Bowl, nearby, is excellent, too. Avanti, underneath the chair of the same name, is a nice cruiser.

As well as tackling some of the easier front-face blacks, intermediates will find plenty of interest in the Back Bowls (given good visibility). Some of the runs are groomed and several are classified blue, including Silk Road, which loops around the eastern edge, with wonderful views. Some of the unpisted slopes make the ideal introduction to powder. Confident

Vail

581

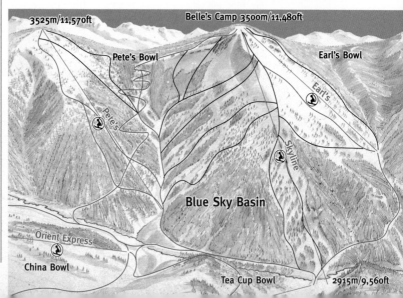

3525m/11,570ft · Belle's Camp 3500m/11,480ft · Pete's Bowl · Earl's Bowl · Earl's · Pete's · Skyline · Blue Sky Basin · Orient Express · China Bowl · Tea Cup Bowl · 2915m/9,560ft

The original part of
Vail was built to
resemble an Austrian
or Bavarian village.
Most newer parts
have more modern
buildings with less
character ↗

VAIL RESORTS INC

CHILDREN

Small World Play School
t 479 3285
Ages 2mnth to 6yr;
8am to 4.30;
reservations essential

Ski school
Ages 3 to 12 at
Golden Peak and
Lionshead (full day
including lift pass and
lunch US$122)

SCHOOLS

Vail
t 476 3239

Classes
Full day (9.45-3.30)
$100
Private lessons
$150 for 1hr for 1 to
6 people

intermediates will also enjoy Blue Sky
Basin's clearly marked blue runs.

FOR BEGINNERS
Good but can be crowded
There are excellent nursery slopes at
resort level and at altitude and easy
longer runs to progress to. But they
can be rather crowded.

FOR CROSS-COUNTRY
Some of the best
Vail's cross-country areas are at the
foot of Golden Peak and at the Nordic
Center on the golf course. Cross-
country and telemark lessons are
available at Golden Peak.

QUEUES
Can be bad
Vail has some of the longest lift
queues we've hit in the US, especially
at weekends because of the influx from
Denver. At Mid-Vail, 15-minute waits
are common and we have reports of
45-minute queues both here and for
the slow chairs in the Back Bowls. The
Northwoods Express lift can also have
queues of 15-minutes or more.

MOUNTAIN RESTAURANTS
Surprisingly poor (though pricey)
As other major American resorts are
gradually improving their mountain
restaurants, Vail's are slipping further
behind: demand is increasing to the
point where the major self-service
restaurants can be unpleasantly
crowded from 11am to 2pm. They are
also expensive (especially the huge
Two Elk, where a reporter said 'a hot
dog, fries and coke cost £10'). There's
table-service (with limited menu) at
Eagle's Nest – the Blue Moon (book
ahead). A 2005 reporter recommends
the Wildwood Smokehouse at the top
of Wildwood Express lift –
'atmospheric, slightly different food
and very good value'. 'Good
barbecues,' says another. Don't rely on
Belle's Camp on Blue Sky Basin: 'Very
few toilets and only sells sandwiches
and cold drinks,' says a 2005 reporter.

SCHOOLS AND GUIDES
Among the best in the world
The Vail-Beaver Creek school generates
many glowing reports. Class sizes are
usually small. A 2005 reporter says,
'Wonderful. The grading into classes is
done carefully. Our son was begging to
go back after his first three booked
days. The instructor really made it fun.

We did a two-day workshop called
Vail's 3 Sides which was a mixture of
touring and lessons; there were only
four in our group and it was the best
ski lesson I've ever had.' Another
found both the skiing and the
snowboarding classes 'excellent', with
class sizes of five and four
respectively. Unusually, we also had a
critical 2005 report: 'A useless teacher.
It was a let down,' from a visitor who
also had a satisfactory lesson with
another instructor. You can sign up for
lessons on the mountain.

FACILITIES FOR CHILDREN
Excellent
The comprehensive arrangements for
young children look excellent, and
we've had good reports on the
children's school. There are splendid
children's areas with adventure trails
and themed play areas. There's even a
special kids' cafe area at Mid Vail. The
Night Owl programme gives parents an
evening off and includes supervised
activities and dinner at Adventure
Ridge at the top of the gondola.

STAYING THERE

HOW TO GO
Package or independent
There's a big choice of packages to
Vail. It's easy to organise your own
visit, with regular airport shuttles.
Chalets Several UK tour operators offer
catered chalets. Many are out of the
centre at East Vail or West Vail or
across the busy I-70 freeway.
Hotels Vail has a fair choice of hotels,
though nearly all are expensive. Check
online for the best deals.
(((((5) **Vail Cascade** One of the best in
town. A resort within a resort – lots of
facilities and a chair-lift right outside.

GETTING THERE

Air Eagle 56km/
35 miles (1hr);
Denver 193km/
120 miles (2½hr).

ACTIVITIES

Indoor Athletic clubs
and spas, massage,
ski museum

Outdoor Ice skating,
sleigh rides, fishing,
snowmobiles, snow-
shoe excursions, dog-
sledding, tubing hill

**Central reservations
phone number**
Call 1 800 404 3535
(toll-free from within
the US).

Phone numbers
From distant parts of
the US, add the prefix
1 970.
From abroad, add the
prefix +1 970.

WEBSITES

For links to resort
sites, go to our own
new site at
www.wtss.co.uk

TOURIST OFFICE

t 476 5601
vailinfo@vailresorts.
com
vail.snow.com

Sonnenalp Bavaria Haus Very
smart and central. Large spa and
splendid piano bar-lounge.
Lodge at Vail Owned by Vail
Resorts, right by the Vista Bahn in Vail
Village. Some standard rooms small.
Huge buffet breakfast. Outdoor pool.
'A real treat,' writes a reporter.
Marriot Mountain Resort Also
owned by Vail Resorts, near the Eagle
Bahn gondola. Impressive spa facilities.
Manor Vail Resort At Golden
Peak. Suites with sitting area, fireplace,
kitchen and terrace. Spa and pool.
Breakfast included. 'I definitely
recommend it,' says a 2005 visitor.
Evergreen Lodge Cheaper (for
Vail!) option. Between village and
Lionshead. Outdoor pool. Sports bar.
Self-catering The Racquet Club at East
Vail has lots of amenities. Mountain
Haus has high-quality condos in the
centre of town.

EATING OUT
Endless choice
Whatever kind of food you want, Vail
has it – but most of it is pricey.
   Fine-dining options include the
Wildflower, in the Lodge, the Tour
(modern French) – recommended
highly by a 2004 reporter – and
Ludwig's, in the Sonnenalp Bavaria
Haus. Other recommendations for good
food and service in an Alpine ambience
are the Alpenrose and Pepi's in the
hotel Gramshammer.
   For better value, we've found Blu's
'contemporary American' food
satisfactory; a reader recommends the
Ore House and Billy's Island Grill
('superb steaks at moderate prices').
Bart & Yeti's or Bogart's Bar and Bistro
are good for local ales and no-frills,
filling American food.
   Other recommendations from
readers include May Palace (Chinese)
in West Vail, Sapphire (seafood),
Montauk (seafood), the Bistro at the

Racquet Club, Los Amigos, Russell's, La
Bottega, Vendetta's and Pazzo's ('good
pizzas, relatively cheap'). For a bit of a
treat try Game Creek Lodge, reached by
snowcat from the top of the gondola.

APRES-SKI
Fairly lively
Lions Den at Lionshead is popular at
the end of the day, with live music.
Nearby Garfinkel's has a DJ, sun deck
and happy hour. The Red Lion in the
village centre has live music, big-
screen TVs and huge portions of food.
The George tries to be an English-style
pub. The Ore House serves 'mean
margaritas and hot wings'. The Tap
Room in the Vista Bahn building is a
relaxed woody bar – 'good range of
wines by the glass'.
   King's Club is the place to go for
high-calorie cakes, and becomes a
piano bar later; and Los Amigos and
Bogart's Bar and Bistro are other lively
places at four o'clock.
   You can have a good night out at
Adventure Ridge at the top of the
gondola. As well as bars and
restaurants, there's lots to do on the
snow – though a reporter reckons the
tubing hill is no match for Keystone's.
   Later on, Fubar is a popular disco.
8150 is also good, with a suspended
floor that moves with the dancing; the
Bully Ranch at the Sonnenalp has great
'mudslide' drinks; The Bridge is a
snowboard hangout; Vendetta's does
good pizza and beer. The Sanctuary
club is above the Tap Room bar.
   Out of town in Minturn, the Saloon
is worth a trip – genuine old-West style
with photos of famous skier patrons.

OFF THE SLOPES
A lot to do
Getting around on the free bus is easy,
and there are lots of activities to try.
The factory outlets at Silverthorne are
a must if you can't resist a bargain.

Vail

Winter Park

Good value, great terrain, huge snowfalls, unpretentious town

COSTS

① ② ③ ④ ⑤ ⑥

RATINGS

The slopes

Fast lifts	★★★
Snow	★★★★★
Extent	★★★
Expert	★★★★
Intermediate	★★★★
Beginner	★★★★★
Convenience	★★★
Queues	★★★★
Mountain restaurants	★★★

The rest

Scenery	★★★
Resort charm	★★
Off-slope	★

NEWS

For 2005/06 the Summit quad up Mary Jane is due to be upgraded to a six-pack. New gladed terrain is also due to open in this area.

For 2004/05 the learning zone in Sorensen Park, at the base area, was expanded to cover five acres, and new lifts were installed.

Intrawest has unveiled its plans for expanding the base village, with the first phase of construction expected to begin in 2006, at a cost of $70 million, and be ready for the 2008/09 season.

➕ The best snowfall record of all Colorado's major resorts

➕ Superb beginner terrain and lots of groomed cruises

➕ Lots for experts, including countless mogul slopes and great tree skiing – at least when conditions are right

➕ Quiet on weekdays, and impressive lift system copes with weekends

➕ Leading resort for teaching people with disabilities to ski and ride

➕ Largely free of inflated prices and ski-resort glitz, but ...

➖ Also lacking the range of shops and restaurants you might expect

➖ Town is a bus-ride from the slopes, and strung-out along the main road

➖ 'Village' at the lift base is still very limited, and dead in the evening

➖ Access to high advanced/expert terrain depends on conditions

➖ Trails tend to be either easy cruises or stiff mogul fields

➖ One or two slow lifts in key spots

➖ The nearest big resort to Denver, so can get crowded at weekends

When we first visited Winter Park – developed for the recreation of the citizens of nearby Denver, and still owned by the city – we were surprised by what we found: a mountain of world class. Now there seems to be the prospect of a world-class resort at the base, too: dynamic Intrawest (developers of famously wonderful Whistler) has signed a long-term agreement to operate and develop the whole resort. The future looks bright.

For the present, if value for money and snow are more important to you than glamour or variety of shops and restaurants, the place should be high up on your Colorado shortlist. Some of our reporters rate it their favourite Colorado resort, partly because it makes such a refreshing change from the norm. Both the mountain and the town have a distinct character, which even Intrawest will be hard pushed to iron out. But for now, the 'village' at the base is very limited.

THE RESORT

Winter Park started life around the turn of the century as a railway town, when Rio Grande railway workers climbed the slopes to ski down. One of the resort's mountains, Mary Jane, is named after a legendary 'lady of pleasure' who is said to have received the land as payment for her favours.

The railway still plays an important part in Winter Park's existence, with a station right at the foot of the slopes where trains deposit Denverites every Saturday and Sunday morning; there's apparently quite an après-ski party on the homebound leg.

Most accommodation is a shuttle-bus-ride away in spacious condos scattered around either side of US highway 40, the road through the town of Winter Park, or a few miles down the road around the town of Fraser. Drive into Winter Park at night, and it seems to resemble an established ski resort town, with brightly lit shops,

motels, bars and restaurants along the road – but in the daytime it's clear that the place doesn't amount to much.

In the last few years, stylish accommodation has been developed at or near the foot of the slopes, including a car-free mini-resort known as The Village at Winter Park Resort.

Confusingly, an area between the mountain and the town is known as Old Town.

Shuttle-buses (reportedly rather primitive, with unhelpful drivers) run between the town and the lift base, and the hotels and condos also provide shuttles. A car simplifies getting around what is a very spread-out resort area as well as day trips to Denver or other resorts such as Copper Mountain, Breckenridge and Keystone.

The approach road is more like the Alps than Colorado, going over the Continental Divide at Berthoud Pass (3450m/11,320ft). Sadly, the mini-resort that operated here in the past – most recently using snowcats – has closed.

THE MOUNTAINS

Winter Park has a mountain that's big by US standards, and an excellent mix of terrain that suits all abilities – when it's all open.

THE SLOPES
Interestingly divided

There are five distinct, but well-linked, sectors. From the main base, a fast quad takes you to the peak of the original **Winter Park** mountain. From there, you can descend in all directions. Runs lead back towards the main base and over to the **Vasquez Ridge** area on the far right, served by the Pioneer fast quad.

You can also descend to the base of **Mary Jane** mountain, where four chairs up the front face serve tough runs; other chairs serve easier terrain on the flanks. From the top you can head up to **Parsenn Bowl**, via the slow Timberline chair, for intermediate terrain above and in the trees. This chair is exposed at the top, and can be closed for long periods in bad weather. From here, conditions permitting, you can hike for up to half

an hour to access the advanced and extreme slopes of **Vasquez Cirque**. A long ski-out takes you to the bottom of Vasquez Ridge and the Pioneer lift.

TERRAIN-PARKS
Bigger and better...

The Rail Yard park, with over 12 rails, 15 jumps and a 130m/420ft long super-pipe, runs down much of the front of Winter Park mountain for over 1110m/3,650ft. Halfway down it crosses a bridge so that those on the Cranmer Cutoff green run can cross the park safely. For the lower half, you can choose to continue on traditional park features such as table-tops and spines or go on the slope-style park designed for skier- and boarder-cross events. There's also a beginner's park at Jack Kendrick's and a mini-park in the Discovery area.

SNOW RELIABILITY
Among Colorado's best

'Copious amounts of beautiful, dry powder,' enthuses a reporter. 'So much snow, we were delayed a day getting to the resort,' says another. Winter

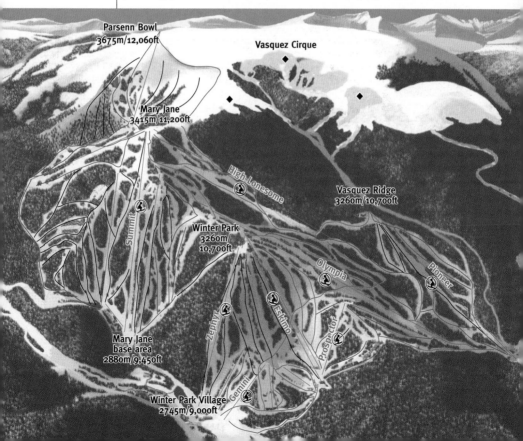

Parsenn Bowl
3675m/12,060ft

Vasquez Cirque

Mary Jane
3415m/11,200ft

High Lonesome

Vasquez Ridge
3260m/10,700ft

Summit

Winter Park
3260m/
10,700ft

Olympia

Pioneer

Zephyr

Eskimo

Prospector

Gemini

Mary Jane
base area
288om/9,450ft

Winter Park Village
2745m/9,000ft

LIFT PASSES

Winter Park Resort
Covers all lifts in
Winter Park.

Beginners
No special pass.

Main pass
1 day $65
6 days $348

Senior citizens
Over 65: 6 days $342
Over 70: free pass
(Mon-Thu)

Children
Under 14: 6 days
$192
Under 6: free pass

Notes
Special rates for
disabled skiers.

SCHOOLS

Winter Park
t 1 800 729 7788

**National Sports
Center for the
Disabled**
t 726 1518
Special programme
for disabled skiers
and snowboarders.

**Classes (Winter Park
prices)**
Half day (2½hr) $62

Private lessons
$229 for 2hr for 1 to
3 people

boarding

There is some great advanced and extreme boarding terrain and a high probability of fresh powder to ride. The Rail Yard park (see Terrain-parks) makes Winter Park even more attractive to advanced riders. The resort is also an ideal beginner and intermediate boarder area, with excellent terrain for learning. A good school provides classes for all levels, including learning to jump and ride rails, and special lessons for children aged 7-17.

Park's position, close to the watershed of the Continental Divide, gives it an average yearly snowfall of over 350 inches – the highest of any major Colorado resort. Snowmaking covers a lot of Winter Park mountain's runs.

FOR EXPERTS
Some hair-raising challenges
Mary Jane has some of the steepest mogul fields, chutes and hair-raising challenges in the US. On the front side are a row of long black mogul fields that are quite steep enough for most of us. There are some challenges on Winter Park Mountain, too.

Some of the best terrain is open only when there is good snow and/or good weather – so it's particularly unreliable early in the season. The fearsome chutes of Mary Jane's back side – all very steep, narrow and bordered by rocks – are accessed by a control gate.

Parsenn Bowl, served by the high, exposed Timberline chair, has superb blue/black gladed runs and tougher tree skiing on the back side. Vasquez Cirque, the least reliably open area, has excellent ungroomed expert terrain with extensive views. You don't get much vertical before you hit the forest, though.

FOR INTERMEDIATES
Choose your challenge
From pretty much wherever you are on Winter Park mountain and Vasquez Ridge you can choose a run to suit your ability. Most are well groomed every night, giving you perfect early morning cruising on the famous Colorado 'corduroy' pistes.

For bumps, try Mary Jane's front side. Parsenn Bowl has grand views and some gentle cruising pistes as well as more challenging ungroomed terrain. It's also an ideal place to try ungroomed powder for the first time. When it's actually snowing, though, you are better off lower down, sticking to the edges of tree-lined runs to find the best powder and visibility.

FOR BEGINNERS
About the best we've seen
Discovery Park is a 25-acre dedicated area for beginners, reached by a high-speed quad and served by two more chairs. As well as a nursery area and longer green runs, it has an adventure trail through trees and a special terrain park. Once out of the Park, there are easy runs back to base. And the Sorensen learning zone at the base area was expanded and improved for last season.

NATIONAL SPORTS CENTER FOR THE DISABLED

If you are able-bodied, the most striking and humbling thing you'll notice as you ride your first chair-lift is the number of people with disabilities hurtling down the mountain faster than many of us could ever hope to. There are blind skiers, skiers with one leg, people with paralysis – whatever their problem, they've cracked it.

That's because Winter Park is home to the US National Sports Center for the Disabled (NSCD) – the world's leading centre for teaching skiing and snowboarding to people with disabilities. As well as full-time instructors, there are 1,000 trained volunteers who help in the programme. More than 40 disabilities are specially catered for. If you are disabled and want to learn to ski or snowboard, there's no better place to go. It's important to book ahead so that a suitably trained instructor is available. The NSCD can help with travel and accommodation arrangements:

NSCD, PO Box 36, Winter Park, CO 80482, USA. Tel: 726 1540.

↑ There are two good beginner areas: one is at the base area and the other – the 25-acre Discovery Park shown here – is up the mountain
SNOWPIX.COM / CHRIS GILL

CHILDREN

Children's Center
t 1 800 420 8093
Ages 2mnth to 6yr; $89 per day

Ski school
Takes ages 3 to 17 ($112 per day including lift ticket and lunch)

GETTING THERE

Air Denver 145km/ 90 miles (1½hr).

Rail Denver, Sat and Sun only. Journey time 2¼hr.

ACTIVITIES

Indoor Fitness clubs, hot-tubs, climbing wall, comedy club

Outdoor Dog-sledding, ice rink, snow-shoeing, sleigh rides, tubing, snowmobiling, snowcat tours, hot air ballooning, hot springs

FOR CROSS-COUNTRY
Lots of it

There are several different areas, all with generally excellent snow, totalling over 200km/125 miles of groomed trails, as well as backcountry tours.

QUEUES
Rarely a problem

During the week the mountain is generally quiet. 'We had whole runs to ourselves for a couple of miles,' says one delighted reporter. However, there may be a crowd waiting for the opening of the Zephyr Express from the main base and there can be queues on the slow chair up Parsenn Bowl. At weekends the Denver crowds arrive – even then the network of more than 20 lifts (including eight fast chairs) makes light work of the people.

MOUNTAIN RESTAURANTS
Some good facilities

The highlight is the Lodge at Sunspot, at the top of Winter Park mountain. This wood and glass building has a welcoming bar with a roaring log fire, a table-service restaurant and very good self-service food – but it gets very busy. Lunch Rock Cafe at the top of Mary Jane does quick snacks and has a deli counter, and there is a self-service at Snoasis, by the beginner area. Mama Mia's Pizzeria is on the lower level of Snoasis – you can order food in advance from a special kiosk on top of Winter Park mountain so that the food is waiting for you on arrival.

Otherwise, it's down to the bases. The Club Car at the base of Mary Jane offers table-service and 'a good atmosphere and more varied menu' than the American norm. The Box Car Deli at the West Portal Station does sandwiches, pastries and coffees. Moffat Market food court (also at West Portal) offers a wider selection in a railway-themed setting.

SCHOOLS AND GUIDES
A good reputation

'The ski school was a delight and class sizes averaged three!' says a reporter. Another was put in the wrong class 'and was given an extra day's lesson, ski hire and lift pass' to compensate. Yet another found the teaching 'lacklustre – it depends on who you get'. As well as standard classes there are ideas such as Family Private, for different abilities together, themed lessons such as Bump Jamboree, Park and Pipe and women-only clinics.

FACILITIES FOR CHILDREN
Some of the best

The Children's Center at Winter Park base area houses day-care facilities and is the meeting point for children's classes, which have their own areas, including moving carpets. 'They couldn't do enough for children,' says a reporter.

↑ Downtown Winter Park straddles the main highway and is a shuttle-bus-ride away from the slopes
BYRON HETZLER PHOTOGRAPHY / WINTER PARK RESORT

WEBSITES

For links to resort sites, go to our own new site at www.wtss.co.uk

Central reservations
Call 726 5587.
Toll-free number
(from within the US)
1 800 729 5813.

Phone numbers
From distant parts of the US, add the prefix 1 970.
From abroad, add the prefix +1 970.

TOURIST OFFICE

t 726 5514
wpinfo@skiwinterpark.com
www.skiwinterpark.com

STAYING THERE

HOW TO GO
Fair choice
Several UK operators offer Winter Park.
Chalets Several operators offer them.
Hotels There are a couple of outstanding hotel/condo complexes.
(((4) **Iron Horse Resort** Slope-side, comfortable, liked by reporters.
(((4) **Vintage** Near resort entrance; good facilities but some poor past reports of it (and it will be used as employee housing from 2006/07).
(((3) **Winter Park Mountain Lodge** Inconveniently positioned across the valley from the lifts; incorporates a micro-brewery; gets mixed reports.
Self-catering There are a lot of comfortable condos, including the slope-side Zephyr Mountain Lodge. 'Large comfortable rooms and couldn't be more convenient,' says a reporter, but it has no bar or restaurant.

EATING OUT
A fair choice
The range of options is gradually improving, but still isn't a match for that in more established 'destination' resorts. Get hold of the giveaway Grand County menu guide – but don't expect to find the contents wildly appetising unless you're starving for a 16oz steak. Reporters are keen on the long-established Deno's – seafood, steaks etc (also popular après-ski bar). Smokin' Moe's offers sports TV and grills plus 'a great salad bar'. Nearby in the Cooper Creek Square area is New Hong Kong (for 'tasty' Chinese) and

the Divide Grill (for pasta, seafood and grills). Readers also recommend the Shed ('excellent steak and seafood, reasonably priced'), for Tex-Mex Carlos and Maria's, for pizza/pasta the 'dark but rustic' Hernandos, with open fires. Gasthaus Eichler does 'very good' German-influenced food, at slightly higher prices. Try the Crooked Creek Saloon at Fraser for atmosphere and typical American food. The Lodge at Sunspot, up the mountain, is open some nights, with a 'fantastic' five-course fine-dining option on Saturday. They put gondola cabins on the chair-lift to get you up there in comfort.

APRES-SKI
If you know where to go ...
At close of play, there's action at Doc's Roadhouse and the 'quite jolly' Derailer Bar at the main lift base, as well as the Club Car (being renovated for 2005/06) at the base of Mary Jane. Later on, the Shed ('excellent food') and Randi's Irish Saloon can be lively. The Crooked Creek is popular with locals and the Winter Park Pub attracts the younger crowd. Buckets is a funky sports-bar and 'the liveliest in town', says a 2005 reporter.

OFF THE SLOPES
Mainly the great outdoors
Most diversions involve getting about on snow in different ways. If you like shopping, you'll rapidly exhaust the local possibilities and will want to visit Silverthorne's factory outlet stores (around 90 minutes away) – but you'll need a car to do so.

Crested Butte

Crested Butte has one of the cutest old Wild West towns in Colorado. It enjoys cult status among experts who enjoy steep, gnarly terrain, but there isn't enough suitable terrain for keen, mileage-hungry intermediates.

KEY FACTS

Resort	2860m
	9,380ft
Slopes	2775-3620m
	9,100-11,880ft
Lifts	15
Pistes	1,073 acres
Green	23%
Blue	57%
Black	20%
Snowmaking	
	300 acres

TOURIST OFFICE

t 970 349 2286
info@cbmr.com
www.skicb.com

THE RESORT

This small town in a remote corner of Colorado takes its name from the local mountain – an isolated peak (a butte, pronounced 'beaut') with a distinctive shape. It was a mining town in the late 1800s and is now one of the cutest resorts in the Rockies – a few narrow streets with beautifully restored wooden buildings and sidewalks and a good selection of bars and restaurants. You can stay there or at the mountain, a couple of miles away, with its modern characterless resort 'village' (due to receive a revamp from its new owners).

THE MOUNTAINS

It's a small area, but it packs in an astonishing mixture of perfect beginner slopes, easy cruising runs and expert terrain. Two fast quad chairs leave the base. Snowfall is modest by Colorado standards – an average of 240 inches compared with over 300 for many other resorts. But for those who like steep, ungroomed terrain, if the snow is good, Crested Butte is idyllic – the 448 acres of the Extreme Limits at the top of the mountain offer seriously steep, prettily wooded terrain; but it is not unusual for it to be closed until late January to allow the snowpack to build up. Though there are also some 'ordinary' black runs, these are few.

Good intermediates will find the area limited, with few challenging groomed trails. For early intermediates, there are lots of wide, fairly gentle, well-groomed and normally uncrowded cruising runs. There are excellent nursery slopes near the village and lots of good long runs to progress to. The ski school has an excellent reputation and there are a couple of mountain restaurants.

Short turns

Durango Mountain Resort

Durango Mountain Resort (not to be confused with Durango, a nearby city) is not a resort you would cross the Atlantic to visit – but if you're passing, you could do worse than give it a day or two.

KEY FACTS

Resort	2680m
	8,790ft
Slopes	2680-3300m
	8,790-10,820ft
Lifts	11
Pistes	1,200 acres
Blue	23%
Red	51%
Black	26%
Snowmaking	
	250 acres

TOURIST OFFICE

t 970 247 9000
info@durango
mountainresort.com
www.durango
mountainresort.com

THE RESORT

The heart of the resort is Purgatory Village, a modern, purpose-built affair with hotel and condo accommodation – as convenient and soulless as the many similar developments in France. Evening options in the 'village' are extremely limited. Fortunately, Hamilton's Chop House down on the roadside at The Inn at DMR is a surprisingly competent restaurant. There is tubing and snowmobiling. The city of Durango has a historic district and is worth a look. Other diversions a drive away include hot springs, Sky Ute Casino and a steam railroad.

THE MOUNTAIN

Practically all the runs are cut through dense forest. It's a small area even by US standards, and won't amuse most non-beginners for more than a day or two. Directly above the resort is a steepish slope served by a six-pack, with a slow double chair off to the right serving gentle green runs. Both link to the shady mountainside that forms the main part of the area, served by a row of three chairs with a vertical of not much over 350m/1,150ft. The first, a fast quad, serves a handful of pleasant blue runs. The others serve steeper terrain that provides some genuine blacks – including a nice little gladed area – and some very short double-diamond pitches. Snowcat skiing is said to operate from the top.

The snowfall record isn't Colorado's best, but an average of 260 inches is not bad. There are two terrain-parks with all the usual features, including a half-pipe. Amazingly, the mountain restaurants include a highly regarded table-service place, Café de los Piños.

Utah

Salt Lake City and the resorts just to the east of it got a bit of a boost to their international profile a while back, hosting the 2002 Winter Olympics. Now it's back to business as usual – playing second fiddle to Colorado on the international market, despite a marketing slogan that ought to bring in the customers in bigger numbers than it does: The Greatest Snow on Earth.

590

Utah's extravagant climatic claim (which features on many local car number plates) has some basis. Some Utah resorts do get huge dumps – up to twice the amount, over the season, that falls on some big-name Colorado resorts. And by Alpine standards the snow here is wonderful. If you like the steep and deep, you should at some point make the pilgrimage to Utah.

The biggest dumps are reserved for **Snowbird** and **Alta** – an average of 500 inches a year that has made these small resorts the powder capitals of the world. Recently their snow record has been matched by that of **Brighton**, in the next valley, and almost matched by that of **Solitude**, next door. And in these less well known places the snow gets tracked out less quickly, because the resorts attract far fewer experts.

Park City is the main 'destination' resort of the area, and an excellent holiday base because it has upmarket **Deer Valley** next door and **The Canyons** only a short drive away. As the crow flies these resorts are only a few miles from Alta/Snowbird (and indeed you can ski between them off-piste – see Park City chapter) but they get 'only' 300 to 350 inches of snow.

It was unknown **Snowbasin** (400 inches of snow), well to the north, that hosted the Olympic downhill events.

Separate chapters follow on these resorts. The other resort that gets a bit of international attention – not least because it's owned by Robert Redford – is **Sundance** (1860m/6,100ft, 450 acres, 655m/2,150ft vertical, four lifts and a small tow). It gets 'only' 320 inches of snow a year. It's a small, narrow mountain but the vertical is respectable, the setting beneath Mt Timpanogos is spectacular and there is terrain to suit all abilities. The lower mountain is easy-intermediate, served by a quad chair, the upper part, with two triple chairs, has blue and black trails and a double-diamond area. Bearclaw's Cabin, at the top of it, is a proper log cabin with spectacular views. The 'village' is designed for summer visitors: the comfortable rooms are in welcoming cabins dotted around the hillside above the base; paths are long and icy, so you end up driving down to ski in the morning and to eat in the evening, which rather conflicts with Redford's eco-philosophy. There's a pleasant bar and two restaurants to choose from.

Utah is the Mormon state, which means that sale and consumption of alcohol is tightly controlled. We've never found this to be a problem in practice; depending on the kind of establishment you're aiming to drink in, you may need to acquire temporary membership of a club, and this may sometimes involve a payment.

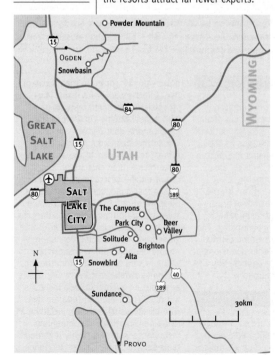

Alta

Cult powder resort, now sharing one of America's biggest areas

COSTS

① ② ③ ④ ⑤ ⑥

RATINGS

The slopes

Fast lifts	**
Snow	*****
Extent	***
Expert	*****
Intermediate	***
Beginner	***
Convenience	****
Queues	***
Mountain restaurants	**

The rest

Scenery	***
Resort charm	**
Off-slope	*

KEY FACTS

Resort	2600m
	8,530ft
For Alta and	
Snowbird combined	
area see Snowbird	
For Alta only	
Slopes	2600-3215m
	8,530-10,550ft
Lifts	12
Pistes	2,200 acres
Green	25%
Blue	40%
Black	35%
Snowmaking	
	50 acres

REPORTS WANTED

Recently we have had few reports on this resort. If you go there, please do send us a report.

+ Phenomenal snow and steep terrain mean cult status among experts (but there's great beginner terrain, too)

+ Link to Snowbird, making one of the largest ski areas in the US

+ Ski-almost-to-the-door convenience

− 'Resort' is no more than a scattering of lodges – not much après-ski atmosphere, and few off-slope diversions

− Limited groomed runs for intermediates, though the link with Snowbird doubles the terrain

Alta has long been famous for remarkable amounts of powder snow arriving with great regularity. It used to be famous also for its stubborn refusal to develop or modernise, but things have changed on that front: the Sunnyside fast triple chair, installed specially for beginners, was followed in 2001 by the resort's first fast quad, to give access to Snowbird. Now another fast quad has been installed, going from bottom to top of the mountain, and they have built their first terrain-park. How long, we wonder, before Alta really joins the modern world, and admits snowboarders to its hallowed slopes?

THE RESORT

Alta, which celebrated its 65th year of operation recently, sits at the craggy head of Little Cottonwood Canyon, 2km/1 mile beyond Snowbird and less than an hour's drive from downtown Salt Lake City. Both the resort and the approach road are prone to avalanches and closure: visitors can be confined indoors for safety. Where once there was a bustling and bawdy mining town, now there is just a strung-out handful of lodges and parking areas. Life revolves around the two separate lift base areas – Albion and Wildcat – linked by a bi-directional rope tow along the flat valley floor. There are about a dozen places to stay.

SNOWPIX.COM / CHRIS GILL

The slopes are lightly wooded; the Supreme area gets afternoon sun ↓

THE MOUNTAINS

Alta's slopes are lightly wooded, with some treeless slopes. Check out the Snowbird chapter for the linked slopes. **Slopes** The dominant feature of Alta's terrain is the steep end of a ridge that separates the area's two basins. To the left, above Albion Base, the slopes stretch away over easy green terrain towards the blue and black runs from Point Supreme and from the top of the Sugarloaf quad (also the access lift for Snowbird). To the right, above Wildcat Base, is a more concentrated bowl with blue runs down the middle and blacks either side, now served by the fast two-stage Collins chair. The two sectors are linked at altitude, and by the flat rope tow along the valley floor. **Terrain-parks** There's a park with jumps, boxes and rails above Albion Base, near the Sunnyside lift. **Snow reliability** The quantity and quality of the snow and the northerly orientation put Alta in the top rank. **Experts** Even without the Snowbird link Alta had cult status among local experts, who flocked to the high ridges after a fresh snowfall. There are dozens of steep slopes and chutes. **Intermediates** Adventurous intermediates who are happy to try ungroomed slopes and learn to love powder should like Alta, too. There are good blue bowls in both Alta and Snowbird and not-so-tough blacks to progress too. But if it is miles of

NEWS

For 2005/06 the Watson Shelter lodge above Wildcat is to be replaced by a new building at the mid-station of the Collins chair, which will incorporate a large cafeteria, a sun deck and a table-service restaurant.

For 2004/05 the Collins fast quad replaced two old chairs above Wildcat.

Also last season, a terrain-park opened above Albion base, by the Sunnyside lift.

Phone numbers
From distant parts of the US, add the prefix 1 801.
From abroad, add the prefix +1 801.

TOURIST OFFICE

t 359 1078
info@alta.com
www.alta.com

UTAH

592

perfectly groomed piste you are after, there are plenty of better resorts.

Beginners Timid intermediates and beginners will be very happy on the gentle lower slopes of the Albion side. But it's hard to recommend such a narrowly focused resort to beginners.

Snowboarding Boarding is banned (but guided snowcat boarding is available in nearby Grizzly Gulch).

Cross-country There's a 5km/3 mile groomed track and the Alta Nordic Centre offers lessons and equipment.

Queues The slopes are normally uncrowded, but the new Collins lift is said to be increasing numbers on the Wildcat side, with 'everybody skiing top to bottom, making it impossible to load at the mid-station'.

Mountain restaurants There's a basic mountain restaurant in each sector of the slopes, offering mainly fast food. Alf's on the Albion side 'serves very good sandwiches'. The Wildcat side is getting a new cafeteria and restaurant for 2005/06, replacing the old Watson Shelter cafeteria and Collins Grill. Several lodges at the base do lunch.

Schools and guides The ski school naturally specialises in powder lessons – though there are regular classes, too.

Facilities for children Day care for children over three months is available at the Children's Center at Albion Base.

STAYING THERE

How to go None of the hotels is luxurious in US terms. Most get booked up well in advance by repeat visitors. Unusually for America, most lodges (as they're called) operate half-board deals, with dinner included.

Hotels The venerable Alta Lodge (742 3500) has comfortable rooms and an atmospheric bar, and has developed a cult following in the US by serving a limited dinner menu at shared tables, in two sittings, instead of enlarging its dining room. Ingenious. Rustler Lodge (742 2200) is more luxurious, with a big outdoor pool, but impersonal. The comfortable, modern and conveniently located Goldminer's Daughter (742 2300) and the basic Peruvian Lodge (742 3000) are cheaper. The Snowpine Lodge (742 2000) is 'convenient, comfortable and friendly' but rather 'old-fashioned'.

Eating out It is possible, but eating in is the routine.

Après-ski This rarely goes beyond a few drinks in one of the hotel bars and possibly a video in your lodge. The Goldminer's Daughter has the main après-ski bar, with pool table etc.

Off the slopes There are few options other than a sightseeing trip to Salt Lake City, or the spa at Snowbird.

The Canyons

Potentially the biggest mountain in the US, and already impressive

COSTS

① ② ③ ④ ⑤ ⑥

RATINGS

The slopes

Fast lifts	✶✶✶
Snow	✶✶✶✶
Extent	✶✶✶
Experts	✶✶✶✶
Intermediate	✶✶✶✶
Beginner	✶✶
Convenience	✶✶✶✶
Queues	✶✶✶✶
Mountain restaurants	✶✶✶

The rest

Scenery	✶✶✶
Resort charm	✶✶
Off-slope	✶✶

NEWS

For 2005/06 an additional 200 acres of intermediate and advanced terrain will be opened to the north-east of the Dreamscape area, served by a quad chair.

A second terrain-park will be constructed, specifically aimed at beginners.

➕ Extensive area of slopes for all abilities – and continuing to grow

➕ Modern lift system with few queues

➕ Convenient purpose-built resort village taking shape at the base

➕ Very easy access to Park City and Deer Valley next door

➕ Excellent snow in general, but ...

➖ Snow on the many south-facing slopes affected by sun

➖ Many runs are short

➖ Few green runs suitable for those progressing from nursery slopes

➖ Resort village offers limited après-ski and dining possibilities, and few off-slope diversions

The American Skiing Company (ASC) intends to make The Canyons' slopes the most extensive in the US, and with another lift going in this season to serve an additional 200 acres the resort is now claimed to be the fourth biggest – amazing, considering its low international profile. Anyone having a holiday in Park City should plan to spend some time here. Whether staying in the purpose-built resort village at the lift base makes sense is another question.

THE RESORT

The Canyons has been transformed by the ASC over the last decade. As well as doubling the area of the slopes, the company has built a car-free village at the base which now offers a basic selection of shops, restaurants and bars as well as accommodation. The main access gondola starts from one end of the compact village. Although the accommodation at the base is convenient, the village isn't a very appealing place to spend time, and we would much rather stay in Park City – regular shuttle-buses run to the resort, and there is also a car park below the village from which you get a cabriolet lift up to the lift base.

THE MOUNTAINS

The Canyons gets its name from the valleys between the eight mountains that make up the ski area.

Slopes Red Pine Lodge, at the heart of the slopes, is reached by an eight-seat gondola from the village. From here you can move in either direction across a series of ridges and valleys. Runs come off both sides of each ridge and generally face north or south. Most runs finish on the valley floors, with some long, relatively flat run-outs. The core of the lift system either side of Red Pine Lodge consists of fast quads, but the left-hand third of the trail map has no fast lifts. Free daily mountain tours start at 10.30am.

593

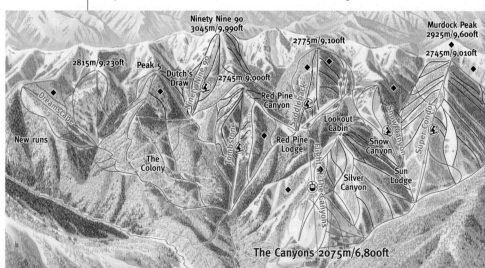

Ninety Nine 90
3045m/9,990ft

Murdock Peak
2925m/9,600ft

2775m/9,100ft

2745m/9,010ft

2815m/9,230ft   Peak 5

Dutch's Draw

2745m/9,000ft

Dreamscape

Red Pine Canyon

Lookout Cabin

Snow Canyon

Super Condor

New runs

Red Pine Lodge

Snow Canyon

Sun Lodge

The Colony

Silver Canyon

Flight of the Canyons

The Canyons 2075m/6,800ft

The southern end of the area (on the left of the trail map) has no crowds, slow chair-lifts, roads winding up to access the grand homes of The Colony, and views back to Ninety Nine 90 →
SNOWPIX.COM / CHRIS GILL

KEY FACTS

Resort	2075m
	6,800ft
Slopes	2075-3045m
	6,800-9,990ft
Lifts	17
Pistes	3,700 acres
Green	14%
Blue	44%
Black	42%
Snowmaking	
	160 acres

Central reservations
Call 1 866 604 4171 (toll-free from within the US).
Phone numbers
From distant parts of the US, add the prefix 1 435.
From abroad, add the prefix +1 435.

TOURIST OFFICE

t 649 5400
info@thecanyons.com
www.thecanyons.com

Terrain-parks There are five natural half-pipes across the mountain. The SoBe terrain-park, which includes a super-pipe, jumps and rails, is near the Sunpeak Express. A second park, better suited to beginners, is planned for 2005/06.

Snow reliability Snow is not the best in Utah. The Canyons gets as much on average as Park City (350 inches) and more than Deer Valley. But the south-facing slopes suffer in late-season sun.

Experts There is steep terrain all over the mountain. We particularly liked the north-facing runs off Ninety Nine 90, with steep double-black-diamond runs plunging down through the trees to a pretty but almost flat run-out trail. There is also lots of double-diamond terrain on Murdock Peak. The runs off the Peak 5 chair are more sheltered.

Intermediates There are groomed blue runs for intermediates on all the main sectors except Ninety Nine 90. Some are quite short, but you can switch from valley to valley for added interest. From the Super Condor and Tombstone fast chairs there are excellent double blue square runs. The Dreamscape area can be blissfully quiet, and a great area for experiments off-piste.

Beginners There are good areas with magic carpets up at Red Pine Lodge. But the run you progress to is rather short and very busy.

Snowboarding It's a great area, with lots of natural hits. Canis Lupis is a mile-long, tight gully with high banked walls and numerous obstacles – like riding a bob-sleigh course.

Cross-country There are prepared trails on the Park City golf course and the Homestead Resort course.

Queues The gondola can be busy at peak times. No problems in 2005,

according to a reporter.

Mountain restaurants Satisfactory, by US standards. Red Pine Lodge is a large, attractive log-and-glass building with a busy cafeteria and a table-service restaurant. Reporters found the Dreamscape Grill 'much quieter and more relaxing, with good soup'. The Lookout Cabin has wonderful views, and we've had excellent table-service food there.

Schools and guides The ski school uses the American Skiing Company's Perfect Turn formula, which focuses on an individual's strengths and builds on them (rather than correcting faults). The 'Perfect Kids' clinics are available for children from 4 to 12 years.

Facilities for children There's day care for children from 6 weeks to 4 years, located in the Grand Summit Hotel.

STAYING THERE

How to go Accommodation at the resort village is still fairly limited.

Hotels The luxurious Grand Summit is right at the base of the gondola, and has a pool on the roof.

Self-catering The Sundial Lodge condos are in the resort village, with a rooftop hot-tub and plunge pool.

Eating out The Cabin restaurant, in the Grand Summit, serves eclectic US cuisine; Smokie's in the village is more casual. The Westgate Grill does steak and seafood. There is a Viking yurt for 'gourmet' dining after a sleigh ride.

Après-ski The Cabin Lounge in the Grand Summit has live entertainment, and Smokie's is good for après-ski.

Off the slopes There's a factory outlet mall nearby and a fair bit going on in Salt Lake City and Park City (see that chapter for more details).

Deer Valley

The ultimate upmarket ski resort

DEER VALLEY RESORT

COSTS

① ② ③ ④ ⑤ ⑥

RATINGS

The slopes

Fast lifts	****
Snow	****
Extent	**
Expert	***
Intermediate	****
Beginner	****
Convenience	****
Queues	****
Mountain restaurants	****

The rest

Scenery	***
Resort charm	***
Off-slope	**

NEWS

For 2005/06 a fast quad is to replace the Sultan triple chair on Bald Mountain, adding 75 acres of new terrain.

Last season, two new chairs were installed on Flagstaff Mountain – one triple and one fast quad. Two new runs were cut. A terrain-park was built in Empire Canyon.

SNOWPIX.COM / CHRIS GILL

Deer Valley has lots of accommodation (mainly private) at mid-mountain ↓

+ Immaculate piste grooming, good snow record and lots of snow-guns
+ Good tree skiing
+ Many fast lifts and no queues
+ Good mid-mountain restaurants (and accommodation)
+ Very easy access to Park City and The Canyons

– Relatively expensive
– Small area of slopes
– Mostly short runs of less than 400m vertical
– Deer Valley itself is quiet at night – though Park City is right next door

Deer Valley prides itself on pampering its guests, with valets to unload your skis, gourmet dining, immaculately groomed slopes, limited numbers on the mountain – and no snowboarding. But it also has has some excellent slopes, with interesting terrain for all abilities, including plenty of ungroomed stuff.

The slopes of Deer Valley and Park City are separated by nothing more than a fence which, given Deer Valley's ethos, seems likely to be permanent. Any skier visiting the area should try both; for most people, Park City is the obvious base – but there are some seductive hotels here at mid-mountain Silver Lake.

THE RESORT

Just a mile from the end of Park City's Main Street, Deer Valley is unashamedly upmarket – famed for the care and attention lavished on both slopes and guests. It's very obviously aimed at people who are used to being pampered and can pay for it.

There is no village as such. The lodgings – luxurious private chalets and swanky hotels – are scattered around the fringes of the slopes, with more concentrated clusters on the valley floor near the main lift base and at Silver Lake Lodge (mid-mountain but accessible by road). For ski-town animation, head for Park City, or base yourself there. There are free buses.

THE MOUNTAINS

The slopes are varied and interesting. Deer Valley's reputation for immaculate grooming is justified, but there is also a lot of exciting tree skiing (great when snow is falling) – and some steep mogul runs, too.

Slopes Two fast quads take you up to Bald Eagle Mountain, just beyond which is the mid-mountain focus of Silver Lake Lodge. You can ski from here to the isolated Little Baldy Peak, served by a gondola and a quad chair-lift, with mainly easy runs to serve property developments there, and also some short black runs. But the main skiing is on three linked peaks beyond Silver Lake Lodge, all served by fast quads – Bald Mountain, Flagstaff Mountain and Empire Canyon. The top of Empire is just a few metres from the runs of the Park City ski area.

Terrain-parks The new Tricks n' Turns park on Empire Mountain offers rails, jumps and boxes, as well as a skier-cross course.

Snow reliability As you'd expect in Utah, snow reliability is excellent, and there's plenty of snowmaking too.

Experts Despite the image of pampered luxury there is excellent expert terrain on all three main mountains, including fabulous glade skiing, bumps, chutes and open bowl slopes. And the snow doesn't get skied

out quickly. The Ski Utah Interconnect Tour to Alta now starts here (see Park City chapter).

Intermediates There are lots of immaculately groomed blue runs all over the mountains.

Beginners There are nursery slopes at Silver Lake Lodge as well as the base, and gentle green runs (some, like Bandana, with great views from the top) to progress to on all mountains.

Snowboarding Boarding is banned.

Cross-country There are prepared trails on the Park City golf course and the Homestead Resort course, just out of town. There is also lots of scope for backcountry trips.

Queues Waiting in lift lines is not something that Deer Valley wants its guests to experience, so it limits the number of lift tickets sold. But a recent visitor found the area 'crowded compared with nearby resorts'.

Mountain restaurants There are attractive wood-and-glass self-service places at both Silver Lake and the base lodge, with free valet ski storage (you can store them free overnight too). The food is fine (but expensive). The grill restaurant at the Empire Canyon Lodge has been recommended. For a bit of a treat, try the restaurants at Stein Eriksen Lodge (including an all-you-can-eat buffet which was 'very highly recommended' by a recent reporter) or the Goldener Hirsch.

Schools and guides The ski school is doubtless excellent. Classes have a maximum of four pupils. Telemark lessons are now available. The Mahre Training Center (run by Olympian brothers Steve and Phil) is based here.

Facilities for children Deer Valley's newly-expanded Children's Center gives parents complimentary pagers. The free 'early drop' system means you can leave your kids at 8.30am.

STAYING THERE

How to go A car is useful for visiting the other nearby Utah resorts, though Deer Valley, Park City and The Canyons are all linked by regular shuttle-buses.

Hotels Stein Eriksen Lodge and the Goldener Hirsch at Silver Lake are two of the plushest hotels in any ski resort.

Self-catering There are many luxury apartments and houses to rent.

Après-ski The Lounge of the Snow Park Lodge at the base area is the main après-ski venue, with live music. Then there's Main Street in Park City.

Eating out Of the gourmet restaurants, the Mariposa is the best. The Seafood Buffet is also recommended. 'Fireside Dining' evenings at the Empire Canyon Lodge are held two days a week.

Off the slopes Park City has lots of shops, galleries etc. Salt Lake City has concerts, sights and shopping. Balloon rides and snowmobiling are popular.

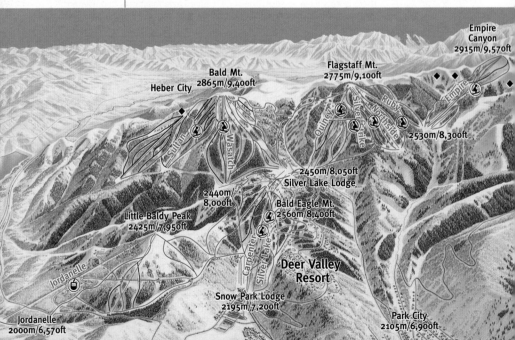

Park City

An entertaining base for excursions into Utah's famous powder

COSTS

① ② ③ ④ ⑤ ⑥

RATINGS

The slopes

Fast lifts	****
Snow	****
Extent	***
Expert	****
Intermediate	****
Beginner	****
Convenience	**
Queues	****
Mountain restaurants	**

The rest

Scenery	***
Resort charm	***
Off-slope	***

NEWS

For 2005/06 a new area lift pass, the Three Resorts International Pass, will be available to visitors wishing to ski Park City, The Canyons and Deer Valley.

For 2004/05 a fast quad replaced the First Time triple chair, improving access to the lower beginner runs. And safety bars were fitted to several other chairs-lifts.

+ Entertaining, historic Main Street, convenient for slopes

+ Lots of bars and restaurants make nonsense of Utah's Mormon image

+ Well maintained slopes, with lots of snowmaking

+ Good lift system, with four six-packs

+ Easy to visit other resorts – Deer Valley and The Canyons (covered by area pass) are effectively suburbs

– Away from Main street, town is an enormous (still expanding) sprawl – inconvenient as well as charmless

– The blue and black runs tend to be rather short

– Most lodgings involve driving or bussing to Main Street and slopes

– Snowfall record comes nowhere near that of Alta, Snowbird et al

– Lack of spectacular scenery

Park City has clear attractions, particularly if you ignore its sprawling suburbs and stay near the centre to make the most of the lively bars and restaurants in Main Street. And it's an excellent base for touring other resorts – notably next-door Deer Valley and The Canyons, both covered by the Three Resort Pass.

Deer Valley is separated from Park City's slopes by a fence between two pistes, and by separate ownership with different objectives. They could be linked by removing the fence – but it stays in place. To European eyes, all very strange. The Canyons is only a little further away, and reached by free buses.

Then there are the famously powdery resorts of Snowbird and Alta, less than an hour away by car or bus. Even the Olympic downhill slopes of Snowbasin are within easy reach if you have a car.

THE RESORT

Park City is about 45 minutes by road from Salt Lake City. It was born with the discovery of silver in 1872. By the turn of the century the town boasted a population of 10,000, a red-light area, a Chinese quarter and 27 saloons.

Careful restoration has left the town with a splendid historic centre-piece in Main Street, now lined by a colourful selection of art galleries, boutiques, bars and restaurants – some a bit tacky, but many quite smart. New buildings have been tastefully designed to blend in smoothly. But away from the centre the resort is an amorphous sprawl, still expanding.

The Town chair-lift goes up to the slopes from Main Street, but the main lift base is on the fringes at Resort Center; there are lodgings out there.

Deer Valley, The Canyons and Park City are linked by free shuttle-buses, which also go around town and run until late. A car is useful for visiting other ski areas on the good roads.

If you're not hiring a car, pick a location that's handy for Main Street and the Town chair or the free bus.

Main Street is based on the original 19th century silver mining town; the old buildings have been well restored →

KEY FACTS

Resort	2105m
	6,900ft
Slopes	2105-3050m
	6,900-10,000ft
Lifts	15
Pistes	3,300 acres
Green	18%
Blue	44%
Black	38%
Snowmaking	
	475 acres

THE MOUNTAIN

Mostly the area consists of blue and black trails cut through the trees on the flanks of rounded mountain ridges, with easier runs running along the ridges and the gullies between. The more interesting terrain is in the lightly wooded bowls and ridges at the top of the resort's slopes.

THE SLOPES
Bowls above the woods

A fast six-seat chair-lift whisks you up from Resort Center, and another beyond that up to Summit House, the main mountain restaurant.

Most of the easy and intermediate runs lie between the Summit House and the base area, and spread along the sides of a series of interconnecting ridges. Virtually all the steep terrain is

above Summit House in a series of ungroomed bowls, and accessed by the McConkey's six-pack and the old Jupiter double chair.

There are free, twice-daily Mountain History Tours of the slopes, looking at the area's silver mining heritage (including old mine workings). A long floodlit run and a floodlit terrain-park and half-pipe are open until 7.30pm.

TERRAIN-PARKS
Is four enough?

There are four terrain-parks, created with the help of the Park City All Stars (big-name skiers and snowboarders who regularly ride them), and two half-pipes (including the 105m/350ft long Eagle Superpipe used in the 2002 Olympics). All are now wired for sound.

SNOW RELIABILITY
Not quite the Greatest on Earth

Utah is famous for the quality and quantity of its snow. Park City's record doesn't match those of Snowbird and Alta, but an annual average of 350 inches is still impressive, and ahead of most Colorado figures. And snowmaking covers about 15% of the terrain.

FOR EXPERTS
Lots of variety

There is a lot of excellent advanced and expert terrain at the top of the lift system. It is all marked as double-diamond on the trail map, but there are many runs that deserve only a single-diamond rating – so don't be put off. We particularly like the prettily wooded McConkey's Bowl, served by a six-pack and offering a range of open pitches and gladed terrain. The old Jupiter lift accesses the highest bowls, which include some serious terrain – with narrow couloirs, cliffs and cornices – as well as easier wide-open slopes. The Jupiter bowl runs are under the chair, but there is a lot more terrain accessible by traversing and hiking – turn left for West Face, Pioneer Ridge and Puma Bowl, right for Scott's Bowl and the vast expanse of Pinecone Ridge, stretching literally for miles down the side of Thaynes Canyon.

Lower down, the side of Summit House ridge, serviced by the Thaynes and Motherlode chairs, has some little-used black runs, plus a few satisfying trails in the trees. There's a zone of steep runs towards town from further round the ridge. And don't miss Blueslip Bowl near Summit House – so

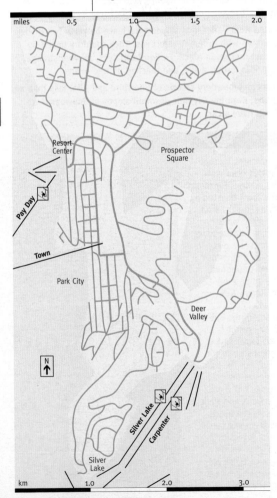

LIFT PASSES

Park City
Covers all lifts in Park City Mountain Resort, with free ski-bus.

Beginners
No special pass.

Main pass
1 day $71
6 days $366

Senior citizens
Over 65: 1 day $40
Over 70: free

Children
Under 13: 6 days $204
Under 7: free

Notes
Six-day prices are advance purchase prices. Additional discounts if purchased in advance with lodging.

Alternative passes
Three Resorts International Pass covering Park City, The Canyons and Deer Valley (from $300 for a 6-days-in-10 booklet).

boarding

It's difficult to believe that boarding was banned here until the late 1990s. Park City now works hard to attract boarders. 'Great boarding area,' says a recent reporter; and no wonder – the resort has wonderful free-ride terrain and high powder bowls. Beginners have their own excellent area, good easy cruising and a lift system which is entirely chair-lifts. And there are no fewer than four terrain-parks and the Olympic half-pipe.

called because in the past when it was out of bounds, ski company employees caught skiing it were fired, and were given their notice on a blue slip.

Good skiers (no snowboarders, due to some long flat run-outs and hikes) should not miss the Utah Interconnect – see feature panel. For bigger budgets, Park City Powder Guides offers heli-skiing on 20,000 acres of private backcountry land.

FOR INTERMEDIATES
OK for a day
There are blue runs served by all the main lifts, apart from Jupiter (the blue Jupiter Access is worth a go though, even if you don't ride the chair, for the sight of people coming down the chutes). The areas around the King Con high-speed quad and Silverlode high-speed six-pack have a dense network of great (but fairly short) cruising runs. There are also more difficult trails close by, for those looking for a challenge.

But there are few long, fast cruising runs – most trails are around 1 to 2km/0.5 to 1 mile, and many have long, flat run-outs. The Pioneer and McConkey's chair-lifts are off the main drag and serve some very pleasant, often quiet runs. The runs under the Town lift have great views of the town.

Intermediates will certainly want to visit The Canyons and Deer Valley for a day or two (see separate chapters).

FOR BEGINNERS
A good chance for fast progress
Novices start on short lifts (the First Time chair is now a fast quad) and a beginners' area near the base lodge. Classes graduate up the hill quite quickly, and there's a good, gentle and wide 'easiest way down' – the three-and-a-half-mile Home Run – clearly marked all the way from Summit House. It's easy enough for most to manage after only a few lessons. The Town chair can be ridden down.

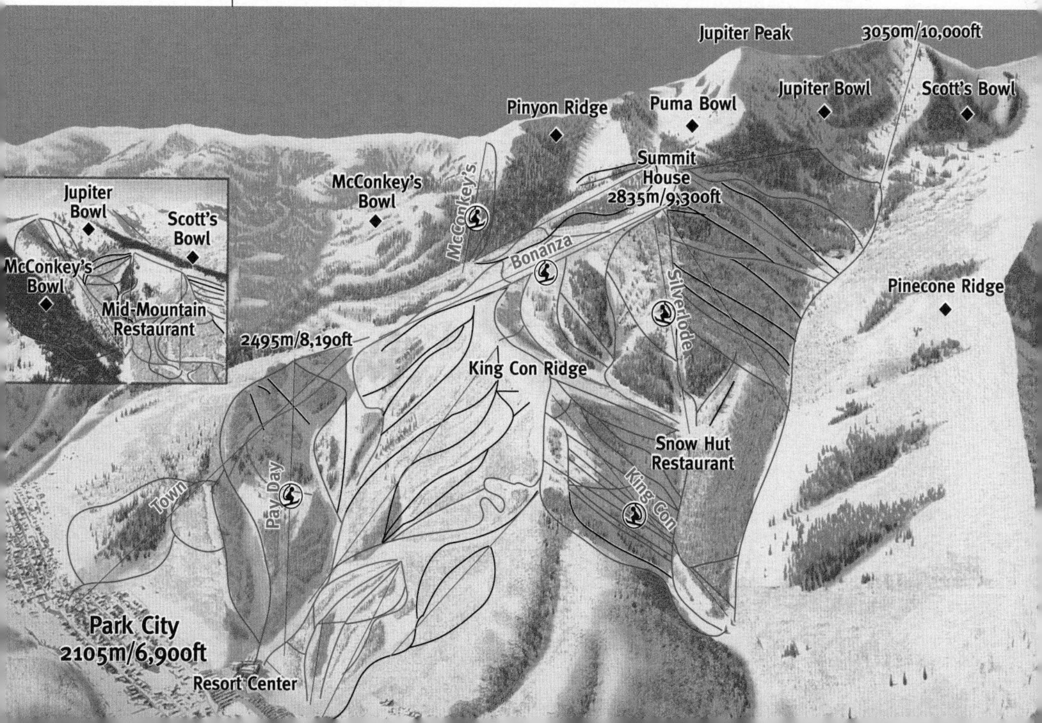

Park City

599

SCHOOLS

Park City
t 1-800-227-2754
pcinfo@pcski.com

Classes
3 3hr days $215
Private lessons
$120 for 1hr

CHILDREN

Little Groomers
(run by ski school)
t 1 800 227 2754
9am-3pm or 9.45-
3.45; ages 3½ to 5; 5
days $650, includes
ski tuition, lunch and
indoor activities
The Clubhouse
t 940 1607
Licensed day care
centre
Guardian Angel
t 783 2662
Babysitting service

Ski school
The school offers
classes for ages 6 to
13, 9.30-3.30, $122
per day including
lunch

GETTING THERE

Air Salt Lake City
58km/36 miles (½hr).

FOR CROSS-COUNTRY
Some trails; lots of backcountry
There are prepared trails on both the
Park City golf course, next to the
downhill area, and the Homestead
Resort course, just out of town. There
is lots of scope for backcountry trips.

QUEUES
Peak period problems only
Lift queues aren't normally a problem
with so many six-packs. But it can get
pretty crowded (on some trails as well
as the lifts) at weekends, particularly
on the Payday lift from Resort Center.
With a pass for four days or more, the
Fast Track system means you can jump
the queues on four main lifts.

MOUNTAIN RESTAURANTS
Standard self-service stuff
The Mid-Mountain Lodge is a 19th-
century mine building which was
heaved up the mountain to its present
location near the bottom of Pioneer
chair. The food is standard self-service
fare but most reporters prefer it to the
alternatives. The Summit House is cafe-
style – serving chilli, pizza, soup etc.
The Snow Hut is a smaller log building
and usually has an outdoor grill. Caffé
Amante is a coffee house halfway
down the Bonanza chair-lift. There are
more options down at Resort Center.

SCHOOLS AND GUIDES
Thorough, full of enthusiasm
The school offers performance
workshops (Moguls and Beyond,
Dealing with the Diamonds) and Power
Clinics (for strong intermediates) as
well as beginner and private lessons. A
recent reporter who booked two
snowboard group lessons was the only
one on both occasions: 'Great value.'

FACILITIES FOR CHILDREN
Well organised; ideal terrain
There are a number of licensed carers
who operate either at their own
premises or at visitors' lodgings. The
ski school takes children from the age
of three. Book in advance.

STAYING THERE

HOW TO GO
Packaged independence
Park City is the busiest and most
atmospheric of the Utah resorts, and a
good base for visiting the others. We
prefer to stay near Main Street and its
countless restaurants, but outlying
areas such as Kimball Junction are
cheap and convenient (although
soulless) if you have a rental car and
want to visit a different resort each
day.
Hotels There's a wide variety, from
typical chains to individual little B&Bs.
Despite a scathing report last season,
the Yarrow is 'clean and good value',
according to a 2005 reporter.
(((((5 **Park City** (200 2000) Swanky
new all-suite place on outskirts, better
placed for golf than skiing.
(((((4 **Silver King** (649 5500) De luxe
hotel/condo complex at base of the
slopes, with indoor-outdoor pool.
(((((4 **Radisson Inn Park City** (649
5000) Excellent rooms and indoor-
outdoor pool, but out of town.
(((((4 **Washington School Inn** (649
3800) 'Absolutely excellent' historic inn
with 'fantastic service' say reporters. In
a great location near Main Street.
(((((4 **Yarrow** (649 7000) Adequate,
charmless base, a bearable walk from
Main Street. Pool.
((((3 **Best Western Landmark Inn** (649
7300) At Kimball Junction. Pool.
((((3 **Old Miners' Lodge** (645 8068) 100-

THE UTAH INTERCONNECT

*Good skiers should not miss this excellent guided backcountry tour that runs four
days a week from Deer Valley to Snowbird. (Three days a week it runs from
Snowbird, but only as far as Solitude.) When we did it (a few years back, starting
from Park City) we got fresh tracks in knee-deep powder practically all day. After
a warm-up run to weed out weak skiers, you head up to the top chair, go through
a 'closed' gate in the area boundary and ski down a deserted, prettily wooded
valley to Solitude. After taking the lifts to the top of Solitude we did a short
traverse, then down more virgin powder towards Brighton. After more powder
runs and lunch back in Solitude, it was up the lifts and a 30-minute hike up the
Highway to Heaven to north-facing, tree-lined slopes and a great little gully down
into Alta. How much of Alta and Snowbird you get to ski depends on how much
time is left. The price ($150) includes two guides – one leading, another at the
rear – lunch, lift tickets for all the resorts you pass through and transport home.*

ACTIVITIES

Indoor Park City Racquet Club (tennis, racquetball, swimming pool, hot-tub, gym); Silver Mountain Sports Club and Spa (pools, hot-tubs, sauna, steam room, tennis, racquetball, gym); other fitness clubs, spa treatments, museum

Outdoor Ice skating, snowmobiles, dog sledding, sleigh rides, hot-air ballooning, ski jumping, bob-sleigh track, snow-shoeing, snowtubing, winter fly fishing, horse riding

WEBSITES

For links to resort sites, go to our own new site at www.wtss.co.uk

Phone numbers
From distant parts of the US, add the prefix 1 435.
From abroad, add the prefix +1 435.

TOURIST OFFICE

t 649 8111
info@pcski.com
www.parkcitymountain.com
www.parkcityinfo.com

year-old building next to Town lift, restored and furnished with antiques.
② **Chateau Apres Lodge** (649 9372) Close to the slopes: comfortable, faded, cheap.
② **1904 Imperial Inn** (649 1904) Quaint B&B at the top of Main Street.
Self-catering There's a big range available. The Townlift studios near Main Street and Park Avenue condos are both modern and comfortable and the latter have outdoor pool and hot-tubs. Silver Cliff Village is adjacent to the slopes and has spacious units and access to the facilities of the Silver King Hotel. Blue Church Lodge is a well-converted 19th-century Mormon church with luxury condos and rooms.

EATING OUT
Lots of choice
There are over 100 restaurants. Our favourites are Wahso (Asian fusion); 350 Main (new American); and Riverhorse – in a grand, high-ceilinged first-floor room with live music. Zoom is the old Union Pacific train depot, now a trendy restaurant owned by Robert Redford. Chez Betty is small and just may have the best food in town – expensive though. Other reporter favourites include the Grub Steak Restaurant, Cisero's and Grappa (Italian), Wasatch Brew Pub ('lively atmosphere, best value') with an interesting range of beers, Bandits Grill ('good value'). The Claimjumper does 'really juicy steaks and enormous desserts' and the Butchers Chop House has been recommended for 'amazing beef'. There are of course lots of Tex-Mex places; if you like that kind of thing, locals recommend Zona Rosa and El Chubasco. The seafood buffet at Snow Park Lodge, at Deer Valley, is said to be worth the journey.

APRES-SKI
Better than you might think
Although there are still some arcane liquor laws in Utah, provided you're over 21 and can prove it, the laws are never a serious barrier to getting a drink. At the bars and clubs that are more dedicated to drinking (ie don't feature food but do serve spirits or beer stronger than 3.2% alcohol) membership of some kind is required. This may involve one of your party handing over $4 or more – one member can introduce numerous 'guests' – or else there'll be some old guy at the bar already organised to 'sponsor' you (sign you in) for the price of a beer. A membership lasts three weeks, but a reporter points out that the system can be very expensive if you visit different resorts most days and just want a quick beer before hitting the road. Places with tavern licences serve 3.2% beer and don't operate as clubs – but you do still need to be 21.

As the slopes close, Legends and the Brewhouse are the places to head for at the Resort Center. But a 2005 reporter was disappointed – 'Very quiet; by 4.45 everyone had gone home.' In Main Street, the Wasatch Brew Pub makes its own ale. The Claimjumper, JB Mulligans and the scruffy Alamo are lively and there's usually live music and dancing at weekends. Harry O's and Cisero's nightclub are good too. The Monkey Bar has DJs and pole dancing.

OFF THE SLOPES
Should be interesting
There's a factory outlet mall at Kimball Junction. Balloon flights and excursions to Nevada for gambling are popular. Snowmobiling is big around here, and can be good fun out in the backcountry. In January there's Robert Redford's Sundance Film Festival, in February Winterfest is a 10-day celebration of the 2002 Olympics, including concerts and snow sculpture.

There are lots of shops and galleries. The museum and old jail house are worth a visit. Salt Lake City is easily reached by car or bus, and has some good concerts, shopping and Mormon heritage sites. The Capitol Building, open until 8pm, gives good views of the city.

You might like to learn to ski-jump or try the Olympic bob track at the Winter Sports Park down the road.

SNOWBIRD / DEREK SMITH

Snowbird

One of the best spots for powder hounds, linked to Alta

COSTS

① ② ③ ④ ⑤ ⑥

RATINGS

The slopes
Fast lifts	***
Snow	*****
Extent	***
Expert	*****
Intermediate	***
Beginner	**
Convenience	*****
Queues	**
Mountain restaurants	*

The rest
Scenery	***
Resort charm	*
Off-slope	*

NEWS

For 2005/06 a new day lodge, including a cafe and large terrace, is due to open at Gad Valley lift base.

For 2004/05 a super-pipe was built near the Big Emma terrain-park: 114m/375ft long with 6m/18ft walls.

Snowmaking was also increased.

602

+ Quantity and quality of powder snow unrivalled

+ Link to Alta makes one of the largest ski areas in the US

+ Fabulous ungroomed slopes, with steep and not-so-steep options

+ Slopes-at-the-door convenience

− Limited groomed runs for intermediates

− Tiny, claustrophobic resort 'village'

− Stark modern architecture

− Frequent queues for main cable-car

− Mainly slow chair-lifts

− Very quiet at night

There can be few places where nature has combined the steep with the deep better than at Snowbird and next-door Alta, and even fewer places where there are also lifts to give you access. The two resorts' combined area is one of the top powder-pig paradises in the world and one of the US's biggest lift-linked ski areas. So it is a shame that Snowbird's concrete, purpose-built 'base village' is so lacking in charm and ski resort ambience. Snowboarders are banned from Alta's slopes, so cannot take advantage of the link.

THE RESORT

Snowbird lies 40km/25 miles from Salt Lake City in Little Cottonwood Canyon – just before Alta. The setting is rugged and rather Alpine – and both the resort and (particularly) the approach road are prone to avalanches and closure: visitors are sometimes confined indoors for safety. The resort buildings are mainly block-like – but they provide ski-in, ski-out lodging.

The resort area and the slopes are spread along the road on the south side of the narrow canyon. The focal Snowbird Center (lift base/shops/restaurants) is towards the eastern, up-canyon end. All the lodgings and restaurants are within walking distance. The main cable-car station is central and the other main Gad lifts can be reached on snow. There are shuttle-buses, with a service to Alta.

THE MOUNTAINS

Snowbird's link with Alta forms one of the largest ski areas in the US.
Slopes The north-facing slopes rear up from the edge of the resort. Six access lifts are ranged along the valley floor, the main ones being the 125-person cable-car (the Aerial Tram) to Hidden Peak, and the fast Gadzoom quad chair. To the west, in Gad Valley, there are runs ranging from very tough to nice and easy. Mineral Basin, on the back of Hidden Peak, offers 500 acres

of terrain for all abilities, but can be badly affected by sun. One of the two fast quads there forms the link with Alta. The Chickadee nursery slopes are floodlit three times a week.
Terrain-parks There are two terrain-parks, a huge one for experts and one for intermediates. Last season a 114m/375ft long super-pipe was built.
Snow reliability Snowbird and Alta average 500 inches of snowfall a year – twice as much as some Colorado resorts and around 50% more than the nearby Park City area. Snowmaking ensures excellent cover in busy areas.
Experts Snowbird was created for experts; the trail map is liberally sprinkled with double-black-diamonds, and some of the gullies off the Cirque ridge – Silver Fox and Great Scott, for example – are exceptionally steep and frequently neck-deep in powder. Lower down lurk the bump runs, including Mach Schnell – a great run straight down the fall line through trees. There is wonderful ski-anywhere terrain in the bowl beneath the high Little Cloud chair, and the Gad 2 lift opens up attractive tree runs. Fantastic go-anywhere terrain under the High Baldy traverse is controlled by gates – catch the area as the ski patrol opens them after a snowfall and you're in for a real treat. A reporter rates the 'less obvious' challenges from the Baby Thunder chair. Mineral Basin has more expert terrain. Backcountry tours and heli-lifts are available.

Mineral Basin added
some Alpine drama as
well as excellent (but
sunny) slopes served
by fast lifts →

SNOWPIX.COM / CHRIS GILL

KEY FACTS

Resort	2470m
	8,100ft

For Snowbird and
Alta combined area

Slopes	2365-3350m
	7,760-11,000ft
Lifts	25
Pistes	4,700 acres
Green	25%
Blue	37%
Black	38%
Snowmaking	
	125 acres

Snowbird only

Slopes	2365-3350m
	7,760-11,000ft
Lifts	13
Pistes	2,500 acres
Green	27%
Blue	38%
Black	35%
Snowmaking	
	75 acres

WEBSITES

For links to resort
sites, go to our own
new site at
www.wtss.co.uk

Phone numbers
From distant parts of
the US, add the prefix
1 801.
From abroad, add the
prefix +1 801.

TOURIST OFFICE

t 933 2222
info@snowbird.com
www.snowbird.com

Intermediates The winding Chip's Run on the Cirque ridge provides the only comfortable route down from the top. For adventurous intermediates wanting to try powder skiing, the bowl below the Little Cloud lift is a must. There are some challenging runs through the trees off the Gad 2 lift and some nice long cruises in Mineral Basin. But the groomed runs don't add up to a lot.

Beginners There is a good nursery slope next to Cliff Lodge, and the Mountain Learning area part-way up the hill. But progression to longer runs is not easy.

Snowboarding Competent free-riders will have a wild time in Snowbird's powder. Alta does not allow boarders.

Cross-country There are no prepared cross-country trails.

Queues For much of the season serious queues for the Tram are common. The Gadzoom fast quad and the slow, exposed Little Cloud chair form the alternative route to the top.

Mountain restaurants It's the Mid-Gad Lodge self-service cafeteria or back to base. From this season, at least there will be a choice of bases, with a new day lodge at Gad Valley.

Schools and guides The ski school offers a range of lessons and speciality clinics – such as women-only clinics, over-50s lessons and experts-only programmes. Snowbird University is a new camp concept, including telemark and backcountry skills.

Facilities for children The 'kids ski free' programme allows two children (12 and under) to ski for free ($15 a day extra for use of the Tram) with each adult.

STAYING THERE

How to go A few UK tour operators feature Snowbird.

Hotels There are several lodges, and smaller condo blocks. Cliff Lodge is a huge hotel; splendid rooftop pool, but generally depressing. The Lodge at Snowbird was recently renovated.

Eating out Cliff Lodge and Snowbird Center are the focal points. The 'fine dining' Aerie in the Cliff Lodge gets mixed reviews. Readers recommend the Steak Pit in Snowbird Center.

Après-ski Après-ski tends to be a bit muted. The Tram Club and the Keyhole Cantina are lively as the slopes close.

Off the slopes Apart from spas in the various lodges, there's a skating rink and a family tubing hill.

Snowbird

603

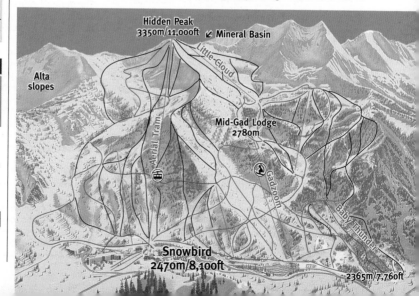

SNOWPIX.COM / CHRIS GILL

Brighton/Solitude

These linked neighbours in the valley next to famous Alta and Snowbird get much the same amount of lovely powder snow. Solitude has come on a lot in recent years, and in some ways is now an attractive destination.

THE RESORTS

Solitude is the obvious place to stay – a smart car-free mini-village with an ice rink in the centre and a choice of condos (some quite luxurious) or the 46-room Inn at Solitude. There are several restaurants, including one doing French gourmet cuisine and a family-friendly Italian. Brighton offers little other than slope-side Brighton Lodge – rooms with breakfast. In either, you're in for a quiet time.

THE MOUNTAINS

The key recent development is that the two resorts now offer a joint lift pass. The total acreage is half that of Alta/Snowbird, but is fair by general US standards. This valley attracts fewer people – experts, in particular – so the powder doesn't get tracked out in

hours, as it does over the hill.

Brighton, at the head of the canyon, has the slicker lift system, with three fast chairs, including one serving the resort's maximum vertical of 530m/1,740ft on Clayton Peak. This and the slightly lower Mt Millicent are almost all expert terrain, but other lifts serve a wide spectrum of runs.

Most (not all) of the slopes immediately above Solitude are easy or intermediate, including a wide area served by the one fast quad. But the top lift accesses lots of steeps in Honeycomb Canyon, on the back of the hill, now with a short quad to bring you back to the front face.

The resorts' boundaries are open, and there are excellent backcountry adventures to be had. The Solitude ski patrol runs guided groups of 10, with all necessary safety kit provided – at $150, including lift pass, good value.

Snowbasin

The 2002 Olympics put Snowbasin on the map. It's a great hill, and it gets great snow (usually). All it needs is a great village – and we don't doubt it will get one. For now, it makes a great day out from Park City, for example.

SNOWPIX.COM / CHRIS GILL

THE RESORT

There is no resort, in the European sense of a village with accommodation. A plush base lodge was built for the 2002 Olympics. Big investment is expected over the next few years, but for now you have to stay elsewhere – in the town of Ogden on the Salt Lake plain, or nearer the mountain in the backwater of Huntsville. The drive from Park City takes less than an hour.

THE MOUNTAIN

Snowbasin's slopes cover a lot of pleasantly varied terrain and its 11 lifts include a fast quad chair and two gondolas, all running bottom to top. A terrain-park made its debut in 2003/04, with features covering about 10 acres, and now there is a super-pipe.

This is a great mountain for experts.

All the lifts serve worthwhile terrain. The downhill course, designed by Bernhard Russi, drops 885m/2,900ft and is already claimed to be a modern classic. Between the race course and the area boundary is a splendid area of off-piste wooded glades and gullies, served by the fast John Paul chair. This is where most experts will want to spend their time. It's good for intermediates, too. The Strawberry gondola accesses mainly long open blue runs but also leads to a lightly wooded steeper slope at the extremity of the area. Middle Bowl is great terrain for the adventurous, with a complex network of blues and blacks. There is a nursery slope, and a few green runs to progress to.

At 400 inches the average snowfall is in the usual Utah class.

There are two smart, recently built self-service mountain restaurants.

This section covers a variety of resorts in different parts of the great Rocky Mountain chain that stretches from Montana and Idaho down through Wyoming and Colorado to New Mexico. Each has its own unique character. Most of the resorts mentioned below get detailed coverage later in this section.

Sun Valley, Idaho, was America's first purpose-built resort, developed in the 1930s by the president of the Union Pacific Railway. It quickly became popular with the Hollywood jet set and has managed to retain its stylish image and ambience; it has one of our favourite luxury hotels.

Also in Idaho, as it happens, is America's latest purpose-built resort (and the first to be built since Beaver Creek) – **Tamarack,** at McCall (two hours north of Boise) on the shores of Cascade Lake, a large reservoir. The resort opened last season with five lifts, including two fast quads serving 700 skiable acres and 850m/2,780ft vertical. They are adding two chairs this summer (one fast) and cutting the rest of the runs. Tamarack gets more snow than Sun Valley (300+ inches) and it still gets a lot of sun. An American reader spent 12 days there this winter and reports: 'Tamarack skis like a mountain that has been open 20 years or more. Great top to bottom fall line cruising with bowls and glades at the top of the lifts. Snowmaking on the lower runs when they need it. Even with only two major lifts in, it skis big. Endless back country either north or south from a long ridge with easy access – and the runs all end at the resort or road.' There is a super-pipe and other terrain features. Lodgings last season comprised 62 high-end chalets, but there are ambitious plans for a 'lively village with three distinct plazas', now under construction.

Jackson Hole in Wyoming is a resort with an impressive snow record and equally impressive steep slopes. Jackson is the nearest there is to a resort with a genuine Wild West cowboy atmosphere. A 90-minute drive (or slower excursion buses) from Jackson over the Teton pass brings you to **Grand Targhee**, which gets even more snow. The slopes are usually blissfully empty, and much easier than at Jackson. The main Fred's Mountain offers 1,500 acres and 610m/2,000ft vertical accessed from a central fast quad. One-third of smaller Peaked Mountain is accessed by a fast quad while the rest – over 1,000 acres – is used for guided snowcat skiing.

A little way north of Jackson, just inside Montana, is **Big Sky** (not to be confused with Big Mountain, away to the north), with one of the biggest verticals in the US(1280m/ 4,200ft). From Big Sky you might visit **Bridger Bowl**, a 90-minute drive away. It boasts broad, steep, lightly wooded slopes which offer wonderful powder descents after a fresh snowfall.

A long way south of all these resorts, **Taos** in New Mexico is the most southerly major resort in America, and because of its isolation it is largely unknown on the international market.

Big Sky

Vast, empty area of slopes – now one of America's biggest

RATINGS

The slopes

Fast lifts	★★★
Snow	★★★★
Extent	★★★
Expert	★★★★
Intermediate	★★★★
Beginner	★★★★
Convenience	★★★★
Queues	★★★★★
Mountain restaurants	★

The rest

Scenery	★★★
Resort charm	★★
Off-slope	★★

KEY FACTS

Resort	2285m
	7,500ft
Slopes	2070-3400m
	6,800-11,150ft
Lifts	17
Pistes	3,600 acres
Green	17%
Blue	25%
Black	58%
Snowmaking	
	350 acres

BIG SKY RESORT

The total vertical is an impressive 1330m/ 4,36oft ↓

606

- ➕ Extensive ski area with runs for all abilities, including great expert runs
- ➕ Excellent snow reliability
- ➕ Big vertical by US standards
- ➕ Few queues, empty slopes

- ➖ Resort village is fairly limited and it can be quiet in the evenings
- ➖ Some slow, old chair-lifts
- ➖ Only one mountain eatery, and that does only fast-food

Big Sky is renowned for its powder, steeps and big vertical, and has blissfully empty gentler slopes and tree skiing, too. The mountain village is not much more than three hotels (including a luxury 5-star), with a few shops, bars, restaurants, and an increasing number of condos and cabins extending out around them.

Keeping up with the bizarre relationship between Big Sky and next-door Moonlight Basin is hard work. But the latest news is good: a joint lift pass, effectively creating one of America's biggest slope areas, totalling over 5,000 acres. (If we seem a bit unclear, it's because the terrain around one lift apparently forms part of both resorts. We did say the relationship was bizarre.)

THE RESORT

Big Sky, which celebrated its 30th anniversary in 2004, is famous for huge snowfalls, big vertical (for North America), and fabulous, deserted slopes. It's a big draw for locals and US visitors, and deserves to be better known internationally.

The resort is set amid the wide open spaces of Montana, one hour's drive from the airport town of Bozeman. At the foot of the slopes is Mountain Village – with three hotels, some slope-side condos and ski shops. There are more bars, shops and restaurants in the Mountain Mall. Some outlying condos and chalets are served by a lift to the slopes, others by free buses, but it's most convenient to stay near the main access lifts.

THE MOUNTAINS

The slopes cover a big area spread over two linked mountains, with long runs for all abilities. There are now four fast quad chairs, but many of the chairs are still old triples and doubles. There are daily free mountain tours.
Slopes Lone Mountain provides the resort's poster shot, with seriously steep, open upper slopes. The Lone Peak chair leads to the Lone Peak Tram – a tiny 15-person cable-car to the top and fabulous 360° views (go up for the view even if you don't fancy the chutes). Lone Mountain's lower slopes are wooded and varied, as are those of Andesite Mountain, which has less vertical, but three of the fast lifts.
Terrain-parks There's a newly-improved terrain-park on Andesite, with rails, boxes, slides and a half-pipe, served by the Ramcharger fast quad. A natural half-pipe features on Lone mountain.
Snow reliability Snowfall averages 400+ inches – more than most resorts in Colorado. Grooming is good, too.
Experts Most of the terrain accessed from the Tram is double-black diamond and some of the steepest stuff requires avalanche safety equipment. If the tram is taking its time to open, take a few runs down the wide open Bowl, off the Lone Peak Triple. More challenges await on the Shedhorn and Challenger chairs; you can also hike to the long, narrow A-Z Chutes from the latter. Check out the gladed runs on Andesite.

NEWS

For 2005/06 Big Sky and Moonlight Basin will offer a joint area lift pass for the two linked areas.

For 2004/05 a fast quad replaced the triple Southern Comfort chair, on Andesite Mountain.

Central reservations
Call 1 800 548 4486 (toll-free within US).
Phone numbers
From distant parts of the US, add the prefix 1 406. From abroad, add the prefix +1 406.

TOURIST OFFICE

t 995 5000
info@bigskyresort.com
www.bigskyresort.com

Intermediates The bulk of the terrain on both mountains is of intermediate difficulty (including lots of easy blacks). There is lots of excellent cruising terrain served by fast quads – Ramcharger and Thunder Wolf on Andesite and Swift Current on Lone Mountain. Several wide, gentle bowls offer a good introduction to off-piste. The Moonlight Basin slopes add a lot more blue/black runs, including some long, top-to-bottom cruises well away from the lifts.

Beginners There's a good nursery area at the base and long greens to progress to, such as Mr K on Lone Mountain, and the runs served by the fast Southern Comfort lift on Andesite.

Snowboarding There's great free-riding and good terrain features.

Cross-country There are 87km/54 miles of trails at Lone Mountain Ranch, and more at West Yellowstone.

Queues The tiny tram attracts serious queues on busy days. Queues are rare otherwise – and the runs are deserted. There are still too many slow lifts.

Mountain restaurants The Dug Out, on Andesite, does fast food and BBQs. Or you can head back to base to eat.

School and guides The ski school receives excellent reviews.

Facilities for children Handprints nursery in the slope-side Snowcrest lodge takes children from age six months ('perfection', says a reporter). Children 10 years and under ski free.

STAYING THERE

Hotels The slope-side Summit (spa baths in the rooms, sculptures in the foyer) is 'hugely impressive'. Huntley Lodge and Buck's T-4 Lodge, 11km/7 miles away, have been recommended

Self-catering The good-value Stillwater condos have been recommended, along with Arrowhead, Beaverhead, Snowcrest Lodge, Big Horn and, way out of town, Powder Ridge Cabins.

Eating out Huntley Lodge has a smart restaurant; The Peaks (in the Summit) and Dante's Inferno are popular. Buses and courtesy cars run to other places.

Après-ski Chet's bar has live music and pool. The Carabiner in the Summit and the Black Bear are also popular.

Off the slopes There's snowmobiling, snow-shoeing, sleigh rides, visiting Yellowstone national park.

Moonlight Basin

If you think Big Sky's slopes are quiet, try Moonlight – when we visited, at times we were outnumbered by hosts and patrollers. The resort continues to expand – a fast quad and 27 new runs opened there last season, with another lift planned so serve the chutes above the tree-line for next season. It has some serious chutes as well as good cruising. Moonlight Lodge has been recommended by a reporter for luxury accommodation and good food.

Big Sky

Lone Mountain
3400m/11,150ft

Big Couloir

The Bowl

Nashville Bowl

New Moonlight Basin terrain

Andesite Mountain
2680m/8,800ft

Southern Comfort

Thunder Wolf

Ramcharger

Swift Current

Moonlight Basin

2070m/6,800ft
Lone Moose Meadows

Mountain Village
2285m/7,500ft

Jackson Hole

Wild West town, exciting slopes and rapidly changing resort village

COSTS

① ② ③ ④ ⑤ ⑥

RATINGS

The slopes

Fast lifts	***
Snow	****
Extent	***
Expert	*****
Intermediate	**
Beginner	***
Convenience	***
Queues	***
Mountain restaurants	*

The rest

Scenery	***
Resort charm	***
Off-slope	***

NEWS

For 2005/06 a new triple chair-lift, Sweetwater, is planned between the upper beginner slopes and the Casper Bowl chair, giving direct access to the intermediate terrain there and to the restaurant at mid-mountain.

Jackson Hole's old cable-car, the Tram, will close at the end of the 2006 summer season – as yet, we don't know what will replace it.

For 2004/05 the Crags terrain, a previously out-of-bounds area adjoining Casper Bowl, was opened.

➕ Some real expert-only terrain and one of the US's biggest verticals

➕ Jackson town has an entertaining Wild West ambience

➕ Unspoiled, remote location with impressive scenery and wildlife

➕ Excellent snow record

➕ Even more snow (and empty slopes) 90 minutes away at Grand Targhee

➕ Plenty to do off the slopes

➕ Airport is only minutes from town

➖ Intermediates wanting groomed runs will find the area very limited

➖ The cable-car serving the top runs generates long queues

➖ Low altitude and sunny orientation mean snow can deteriorate quickly

➖ Town is 15 minutes from the slopes, though the slope-side village has lodgings and is growing quickly

➖ Inadequate mountain restaurants

➖ Getting there from the UK involves two or (more often) three flights

With its wooden sidewalks, country-music saloons and pool halls, tiny Jackson is a determinedly Western town – great fun, if you like that kind of thing. But you don't go to Jackson for the après, you go for the ski.

For those who like steep slopes smothered in deep powder or plastered with big bumps, Jackson Hole is Mecca. Like many American mountains, Jackson has double-diamond steeps that you can't find in Europe except by going off-piste with a guide. What marks it out from the rest is the sheer quantity of terrain that is classified black, and the impressive vertical. With ongoing improvements to the lifts on the gentler lower slopes, the resort may seem to have a broader appeal. Don't be fooled: the beginner slopes are fine, but intermediates wanting to build up confidence or cover some miles should look elsewhere.

Jackson also gets snow in quantities often approaching those found in Utah – in recent seasons it has often been around or above the 500-inch mark. If you get a dump of fresh snow, the place is fabulous. But the combination of modest altitude and south-east orientation means the snow has a limited shelf-life.

The overdue news that the inadequate 40-year-old cable-car is to be scrapped in late 2006 is welcome, despite accompanying PR drivel about its importance as part of 'Wyoming's signature tourism image'. The question is: will they have a replacement up in time for the 2007 winter season?

THE RESORT

The town of Jackson sits at the south-eastern edge of Jackson Hole – a high, flat valley surrounded by mountain ranges, in north-west Wyoming. Jackson gets many more visitors in summer than in winter, thanks to the nearby national parks. To entertain summer tourists the town strives to maintain its Wild West flavour, with traditional-style wooden buildings and sidewalks, and a couple of 'cowboy' saloons. It has lots of clothing and souvenir shops, as well as upmarket galleries appealing to second-home owners. In winter it's half-empty and accommodation prices come down.

The slopes, a 15-minute drive or $3 bus-ride north-east, rise abruptly from the flat valley floor. At the base is Teton Village, with purpose-built lodgings, shops and restaurants, some neo-Alpine but, increasingly, in local style. Teton Village has expanded rapidly over the last few years to become a much more attractive base, with an increased choice of restaurants, bars and hotels – but they are spread over quite an area.

A popular excursion by car or daily bus is over the Teton pass to the smaller resort of Grand Targhee, which gets even more snow (and keeps it better, with gentler, shadier slopes). See Rest of the West introduction.

KEY FACTS

Resort	1925m
	6,310ft

Jackson Hole

Slopes	1925-3185m
	6,310-10,450ft
Lifts	12
Pistes	2,500 acres
Green	10%
Blue	40%
Black	50%
Snowmaking	
	180 acres

Grand Targhee

Slopes	2310-3050m
	7,600-10,000ft
Lifts	5
Pistes	2,000 acres
(plus 1,000 acres	
served by snowcat)	
Green	10%
Blue	70%
Black	20%
Snowmaking	none

JACKSON HOLE RESORT /
WADE MCKOY / FPI

With fresh snow, Jackson is a fabulous place for experts ↓

THE MOUNTAINS

Most of the slopes are below the tree-line, but one of the attractions of the place is that most of the forest is not dense. Trail gradings are accurate: our own small map doesn't distinguish black from double-black-diamond runs, but the distinction matters – 'expert only' tends to mean just that. There are complimentary tours daily.

THE SLOPES
One big mountain, one small one
One big mountain makes Jackson Hole famous – **Rendezvous**. The summit, accessed by a mid-sized cable-car (the Tram) that is entering its last season's service, provides a 1260m/4,130ft vertical – exceptional for the US. It can be incredibly cold and windy at the top of the Tram even when it's warm and calm below.

To the right looking up is **Apres Vous** mountain, with half the vertical and mostly much gentler runs, accessed by the short Teewinot and the longer Apres Vous fast quads.

Between these two peaks is a broad mountainside split by gullies, accessed by the Bridger gondola. This gives speedy access to the Thunder and Sublette quad chairs serving some of the steepest terrain on Rendezvous, and the Casper Bowl triple.

Snow King is a separate area right by Jackson town. There's a good choice of short, steep slopes. Locals use it at lunch-time and in the evenings (it's partly floodlit).

TERRAIN-PARKS
They exist
There's a terrain-park and a half-pipe, and Dick's Ditch is a natural pipe, but you really come to Jackson for the steeps and deeps of the free-riding.

SNOW RELIABILITY
Steep lower slopes can suffer
The claimed average of 460 inches of snow is much more than most Colorado resorts claim. But the base elevation is relatively low for the Rockies, and the slopes are quite sunny – they basically face south-east. If you're unlucky, you may find the steep lower slopes like the Hobacks in poor shape, or even shut. Locals claim that you can expect powder roughly half the time. Don't assume early-season conditions will be good.

LIFT PASSES

Jackson Hole
Covers all lifts in
Jackson Hole

Beginners
No special pass.

Main pass
1 day $67
6 days $372

Senior citizens
Over 65: 6 days $186

Children
Under 22: 6 days
$294
Under 15: 6 days
$186

Notes
Half-day pass
available. Prices may
be cheaper when
booked in advance
through UK tour
operators.

Alternative passes
Grand Targhee (2hr
pass available); Snow
King Mountain

boarding

Jackson Hole is a cult resort for expert snowboarders, as for skiers: the steeps, cliffs and chutes make for a lot of high-adrenalin thrills for competent free-riders. It's not a bad resort for novices, with the beginner slopes served by a high-speed quad. Intermediates not wishing to venture off the groomed runs will find the resort limited. There are some good snowboard shops, including the Hole-in-the-Wall at Teton Village.

FOR EXPERTS
Best for the brave

For the good skier or boarder who wants challenges without the expense of hiring a guide to go off-piste, Jackson is one of the world's best resorts – maybe even the best. Rendezvous mountain offers virtually nothing but black and very black slopes. The routes down the main Rendezvous Bowl are not particularly fearsome; but some of the alternatives are. Go down the East Ridge at least once to stare over the edge of the notorious Corbet's Couloir. The Tram passes right above it, giving a great view of people leaping off the lip. It's the jump-in that's special; the word is that the slope you land on is a mere 50° to the horizontal.

Below Rendezvous Bowl, the wooded flanks of Cheyenne Bowl offer serious challenges, at the extreme end of the single-black-diamond spectrum. If instead you take the ridge run that skirts this bowl to the right, you get to the Hobacks – a huge area of open and lightly wooded slopes, gentler than those higher up, but still black.

Corbet's aside, most of the seriously steep slopes are more easily reached from the slightly lower quad chairs.

From Sublette, you have direct access to the short but seriously steep Alta chutes, and to the less severe Laramie Bowl beside them. Or you can track over to Tensleep Bowl – pausing to inspect Corbet's from below – and on to the less extreme (and less chute-like) Expert Chutes, and the single black Cirque and Headwall areas. Casper Bowl (now with named routes) – accessed through gates only – is recommended for untracked powder. The Crags terrain is a newly opened area of bowls, chutes and glades – but it involves a good half-hour hike to reach it. Thunder chair serves further steep, narrow, north-facing chutes.

Again, the lower part of the mountain here offers lightly wooded single-black slopes.

The gondola serves terrain not without interest for experts. In particular, Moran Woods is a splendid, under-utilised area. And even Apres Vous itself has an area of serious single blacks in Saratoga bowl.

The gates into the backcountry access over 3,000 acres of amazing terrain, which should be explored only with guidance. You can stay out overnight at a backcountry yurt. There are some helicopter operations.

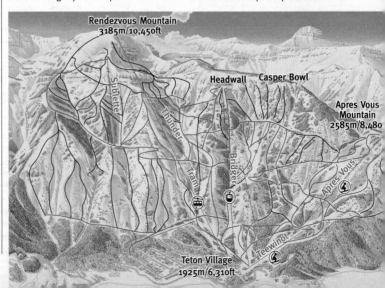

Rendezvous Mountain
3185m/10,450ft

Headwall   Casper Bowl

Apres Vous
Mountain
2585m/8,480

Sublette

Thunder

Tram

Bridger

Apres Vous

Teewinot

Teton Village
1925m/6,310ft

SCHOOLS

Jackson Hole
t 739 2663

Classes
Full day (5½hr) $75
Private lessons
Half day (3hr) $285

CHILDREN

Kids' Ranch
t 739 2691
Wranglers: 8.30-4.30;
ages 6mnth to 2yr;
$100 per day
Rough Riders: 9am-
3.30; ages 3 to 6;
includes skiing; $100
per day

Ski school
Explorers: ages 7 to
14; 9.30-3.30; $100
per day
Team Extreme: ages
12 to 17; 9am-3pm;
$115 per day.

GETTING THERE

Air Jackson 19km/
12 miles (½hr).

FOR INTERMEDIATES
Exciting for some
There are great cruising runs on the
front face of Apres Vous, and top-to-
bottom quite gentle blues from the
gondola. But they don't add up to a
great deal of mileage, and you
shouldn't consider Jackson unless you
want to tackle the blacks. It's then
important to get guidance on
steepness and snow conditions. The
steepest single blacks are steep,
intimidating when mogulled and
fearsome when hard. The daily
grooming map is worth consulting.

FOR BEGINNERS
Fine, up to a point
There are good broad, gentle beginner
slopes. The progression to the blue
Werner run off the Apres Vous chair is
gradual enough and the mid-mountain
blues on the Casper Bowl chair will
now be reachable via the new chair
from the beginner area. But few other
runs will help build confidence.

FOR CROSS-COUNTRY
Lots of possibilities
There are three centres, and one at
Grand Targhee, offering varied trails.
The Spring Creek Nordic Center has
some good beginner terrain and
moonlight tours. The Nordic Center at
Teton has 17km/11 miles of trails and
organises trips into the National Parks.

QUEUES
Always queues for the Tram
The Tram, now entering its last season
in service, is not able to keep up with
demand; there may be queues all day
(10 to 30 minutes) – 'a disgrace',
complains a reporter. Since the
backcountry gates have been opened it
takes only 55 in order to make room
for backpacks. You can access most of
Rendezvous via the Sublette chair. A
2005 early-season reporter was very
critical of the poor information given to
visitors on the slope conditions ('we
were actively misled').

MOUNTAIN RESTAURANTS
Head back to base
There's only one real restaurant on the
mountain – at the base of the Casper
chair-lift; it does a good range of self-
service food, but gets very crowded. A
new restaurant is expected to open at
the top of the gondola for 2006/07.
There are simple snack bars at four
other points on the mountain.

SCHOOLS AND GUIDES
Learn to tackle the steeps
As well as the usual lessons, there are
also special types – steep and deep,
women-only, for example – on certain
dates. You can book Early Tram
lessons and be first on the slopes.
Backcountry guides can be hired –
Rendezvous Ski Tours is 'highly
recommended' by a 2005 reporter who
enjoyed exploring the backcountry
from Teton Pass and in the Teton
National Park.

FACILITIES FOR CHILDREN
Just fine
The area may not seem to be one
ideally suited to children, but in fact
there are enough easy runs and the
'Kids' Ranch' care facilities are good.
There are various classes catering for
ages 3 to 17.

STAYING THERE

HOW TO GO
In town or by the mountain
Teton Village is convenient, while
Jackson has the cowboy atmosphere –
but bear in mind that some of the
hotels are way out of town.
Hotels Because winter is low season,
prices are low.
((((5) Four Seasons Resort (332 3442)
Stylish luxury in Teton Village with a
health club and an exceptional outdoor
pool, set amid landscaped boulders
with waterfalls.
((((5) Amangani Resort (734 7333)
Hedonistic luxury in isolated position
way above the valley.
((((4) Teton Mountain Lodge (734 7111)
Very comfortable ski-in ski-out hotel in
Teton Village. Good indoor and
outdoor pool and fitness centre.
((((4) Alpenhof (733 3242) Tirolean-
style, with varied rooms. Good food.
Pool, sauna, hot-tub.
((((4) Wort (733 2190) Comfortable,
right in the centre of town, above the
lively Silver Dollar Bar. Hot-tub.
((((4) Rusty Parrot Lodge (733 2000) A
stylish place in town, with a rustic feel
and handcrafted furniture. Hot-tub.
((((4) Snake River Lodge & Spa (732
6000) At Teton Village. Smartly
welcoming as well as comfortable and
convenient, with fine spa facilities.
((((4) Spring Creek Ranch (733 8833)
Exclusive retreat between town and
slopes; cross-country on hand. Hot-tub.
((((4) Painted Porch (733 1981)
Gorgeous B&B full of antiques.

ACTIVITIES

Indoor Fitness
centres, swimming,
tennis, library,
concerts, wildlife art
and other museums

Outdoor
Snowmobiles, ice
skating, snow-
shoeing, sleigh rides,
dog-sledding, tubing,
scenic flights, wildlife
tours

WEBSITES

For links to resort
sites, go to our own
new site at
www.wtss.co.uk

Phone numbers
From distant parts of
the US, add the prefix
1 307.
From abroad, add the
prefix +1 307.

TOURIST OFFICES

Jackson Hole
t 733 2292
info@jacksonhole.com
www.jacksonhole.com

Grand Targhee
t 353 2300
info@grandtarghee.
com
www.grandtarghee.
com

(((3 **Jackson Hole Lodge** (733 2992)
Western-style place on fringe of
Jackson town. Comfortable mini-suite
rooms, and free breakfast ('very
good'). Pool, sauna, hot-tubs. Shuttle
to the slopes. Recommended by a
2005 reporter.

(((3 **Snow King Resort** (733 5200) Ski-
in, ski-out hotel and condo complex at
Snow King Mountain.

(((3 **Forty Niner Inn and Suites** (733
7550) Central, good value.
Recommended this year.

(((3 **Parkway Inn** (733 3143) Friendly,
family-run, central in Jackson town; big
rooms, antique furniture, pool, hot-
tubs. Recommended by a reporter.

((2 **Hostel x** (733 3415) Basic, good
value, at Teton Village. Recommended
by a reporter.

((2 **Trapper Inn** (733 2648) Friendly,
good value, a block or two from Town
Square. Hot-tubs.

Self-catering There is lots of choice
around Jackson and at Teton Village.

EATING OUT
A reasonable range of options
Teton Village has pizza, Mexican,
Japanese, a steakhouse and a number
of good hotel restaurants (a recent
reporter enjoyed 'scallops to die for' at
the Alpenhof Bistro). The Mangy Moose
is good value and good fun. In Jackson
town there is more choice. The cool
art-deco Cadillac Grille does good food.
The Blue Lion is small and casually
stylish. The 'saloons' do hearty meals
and good steaks. A reporter praises
Antony's Italian and 'for a treat' the
Rusty Parrot Lodge. Thai Me Up does
'good value, decent food' and the cute
log cabin Sweetwater serves 'Greek-
inspired' food. The Snake River brew-
pub – not to be confused with the
expensive Snake River Grill – serves
'award winning beers and excellent
pasta' and is frequented by the locals.
The Old Yellowstone Garage has

'superb Italian food in an elegant
setting', Nani's (also Italian) is
'surprisingly inexpensive' and
Rendezvous Bistro ('good food and
atmosphere') is very popular. Nikai
Sushi turns into a city-style nightclub
on Friday nights. The Grill at Amangani
has 'a supremely stylish setting,
stunning food and is not nearly as
expensive as expected from a 5-star
establishment'.

APRES-SKI
Amusing saloons
For immediate après-ski at Teton
Village, the Mangy Moose is a big,
happy, noisy place, often with live
music. For a quieter time head for
Dietrich's bar at the Alpenhof.
    In Jackson there are two famous
'saloons'. The Million Dollar Cowboy
Bar features saddles as bar stools and
a stuffed grizzly bear, and is usually
the liveliest place in town, with live
music and dancing some nights. The
Silver Dollar around the corner is more
subdued; there may be ragtime playing
as you count the 2032 silver dollars
inlaid into the counter. The Rancher is
a huge pool-hall. The Shady Lady
saloon sometimes has live music. The
Virginian saloon is much quieter and a
locals' hang-out: 'If you like beer, guns
and ammo, you'll be in good company,'
says one. For a night out of town, join
the locals at the Stagecoach Inn at
Wilson, especially Sundays for church:
'A real western and blue grass swing
night with music from a band that has
not missed a night since 1969.'

OFF THE SLOPES
'Great' outdoor diversions
Yellowstone National Park is 100km/
60 miles to the north. You can tour the
park by snowcat or snowmobile with a
guide; numbers are now restricted in
an attempt to reduce pollution. Views
differ on whether the park is a
knockout or overrated. The National
Elk Refuge, with the largest elk herd in
the US, is next to Jackson and across
the road from the National Museum of
Wildlife Art. Reporters recommend
visiting both – 'You can get really close
to the elk,' says one – and a combined
ticket is available. In town there are
some 40 galleries and museums and a
number of outlets for Indian and
Western arts and crafts. Joining the
Jackson Hole Ski Club ($30) is
recommended – good discounts in
shops, restaurants, lodgings etc.

SUN VALLEY RESORT

Sun Valley

Built in the 1930s, Sun Valley was the US's first luxury, purpose-built winter resort and soon became popular with the stars. For a peaceful, relaxing time, it's hard to beat. For skiing and boarding alone, there are better resorts.

THE RESORT

Sun Valley is based around the old mining village of Ketchum, and its current owner has pumped millions of dollars into the mountain to restore it to state-of-the-art luxury. The town retains its old-world charm and has atmospheric bars, restaurants and shops; you can sometimes find Clint Eastwood in the Pioneer Saloon. The stylish Sun Valley Lodge is one of our favourite ski hotels, and its corridors are lined with photos of film-star guests. Shuttle-buses link the slopes to most accommodation.

THE MOUNTAINS

The slopes of Bald Mountain (known locally as Baldy) are accessed from one of two luxurious base lodge complexes at River Run and Warm Springs. Of the lifts, seven are high-speed quads. The separate Dollar Mountain has good beginner slopes. The resort has an erratic natural snow record, but snowmaking covers over 70% of the runs. There are a few tough slopes for experts, but nothing beyond single-black-diamond pitch. Most of the terrain is ideal for intermediates, with lots of runs at a consistent pitch. There are good blue bowl runs with great views from the top ridge as well as well-groomed cruisers through the trees. Dollar is the place for beginners, with gentle, green runs to progress to. Snowboarding is now allowed, but Sun Valley doesn't have a snowboard culture – it built its first half-pipe a couple of years back. The mountain restaurants and base lodges are way ahead of most US on-slope facilities; Dollar got a new base lodge last year. There are good cross-country facilities.

Short turns

Taos

Set high above an arid New Mexico valley, Taos Ski Valley is the most southerly of North America's major ski areas. It offers some good expert terrain but snowboarders are banned from sampling its slopes.

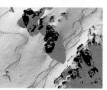

TAOS SKI VALLEY

THE RESORT

Taos Ski Valley, at the foot of the slopes, is tiny. It has around 1,000 beds in a handful of hotels and condos, with little room for expansion and no room for the swimming pools, ice rinks, galleries and boutiques you find in larger places. The Inn at Snakedance, Hotel St Bernard and the Edelweiss all offer good slope-side accommodation. 18 miles down the valley, the traditional adobe town of Taos, with its art and craft galleries and shops, makes an alternative base.

THE MOUNTAINS

When you hit Taos Ski Valley the first thing you will see is Al's Run, a steep mogul field rising sheerly out of the resort. To allay people's fears a prominent sign reads 'Don't panic!

You're looking at 1/30 of Taos Ski Valley. We have many easy runs too.' But it's good skiers who will get the most out of the resort. There are numerous long steep runs through the trees, and many of the best runs require a hike from the top lifts.

There's enough to keep intermediates happy for a few days, especially if they're willing to tackle some of the steeper runs, too. Beginners have their own dedicated area and easy green runs to progress to. And the ski school has an extremely high reputation. Snowfall averages over 300 inches, on a par with some Colorado resorts but not in the premier league; and all the green and blue runs are covered by snowmaking.

There are a couple of basic mountain restaurants but many people head back to base for lunch.

You go to Utah for the deepest snow, to Colorado for the lightest powder and swankiest resorts, to California for the mountains and low prices. You go to New England for ... well, for what? Extreme cold? Rock-hard artificial snow? Mountains too limited to be of interest beyond New Jersey? Yes and no: all of these preconceptions have some basis, but they are an incomplete and unfair picture.

Yes, it can be cold: one of our reporters recorded −27°C, with wind chill producing a perceived −73°C. Early in the season, people wear face masks to prevent frostbite. It can also be warm − another reporter had a whole week of rain that washed away the early-season snow. The thing about New England weather is that it varies. Not as much as in Scotland, maybe, but the locals' favourite saying is: 'If you don't like the weather in New England, wait two minutes.'

New England doesn't usually get much super-light powder or deep snow to play in. But the resorts have big snowmaking installations, designed to ensure a long season and to help the slopes to 'recover' after a thaw or spell of rain. They were the pioneers of snowmaking technology; and 'farming' snow, as they put it, is an art form and a way of life − provided the weather is cold enough. Many of the resorts get impressive amounts of natural snow too − in some seasons.

The mountains are not huge in terms of trail mileage (the largest, Killington, is smaller than all except one of the resorts we feature in western US). But several have verticals of over 800m/2,620ft (on a par with Colorado resorts such as Keystone) and most have over 600m/1,970ft (matching Breckenridge), and are worth considering for a short stay, or even for a week if you like familiar runs. For more novelty, a two- or three-centre trip is the obvious solution. Most resorts suit snowboarders well, often having more than one terrain-park.

You won't lack challenge − most of the double-black-diamond runs are seriously steep. And you won't lack space: most Americans visit over weekends, which means deserted slopes on weekdays − except at peak holiday periods. It also means the resorts are keen to attract long-stay visitors, so UK package prices are low.

But the big weekend and day-trip trade also means that few New England resorts have developed atmospheric resort villages − just a few condos and a hotel, maybe, with places to stay further out geared to car drivers.

New England is easy to get to from Britain − a flight to Boston, then perhaps a three- or four-hour drive to your resort. And there are some pretty towns to visit, with their clapboard houses and big churches. You might also like to consider spending a day or two in Boston − one of America's most charming cities. And you could have a shopping spree at the factory outlet stores that abound in New England.

We cover four of the most popular resorts on the UK market in the chapters that follow − a long chapter on **Killington**, a short one on **Stowe**, and Short Turns entries on **Smugglers' Notch** and **Sunday River**. But there are many other small areas, too. And if you are going for a week or more, we recommend renting a car and visiting a few resorts. In this introduction, we outline the main possibilities.

From Killington (by far the biggest resort), you can go south to a range of smaller resorts. **Okemo** competes with Smugglers' Notch for the family market. Okemo mountain has southern Vermont's biggest vertical (670m/2,200ft) and longest trail (over 7km/4.3 miles). The slopes (610 acres) are largely intermediate or easy − though there are a dozen black runs and a couple of short double-black-diamonds. A few seasons ago the area was expanded considerably by construction of a new fast quad on the next-door mountain, Jackson Gore. The runs here are still being developed − last season two new 'gladed' trails were opened − but there is already a 'beautiful' new base development, including the Jackson Gore Inn − a hotel to complement the many slope-side condos arranged neatly around the base of the main mountain. There's an array of terrain-parks plus a super-pipe and a mini-half-pipe. Snowmaking cover is almost complete, and an American reporter reckons the grooming is 'the best I have seen in the east'. Five of the 18 lifts are fast quads, but only one goes up from the main base and we again have reports of serious queues here at peak times. On-mountain restaurants are better than the US norm, especially if you count the options at Solitude village, a secondary lift base area.

Mount Snow is a one-peak resort, with a long row of lifts on the front face (two fast quads among them) serving easy and intermediate runs of just over 500m/1,640ft vertical. There's a separate area of black runs on the north face – including a couple of short but serious double-blacks – served by a pair of triple chairs. And on the opposite side a small area of intermediate runs above Carinthia base, accessed by a third fast quad. Mount Snow is reputed to have some of the best terrain-parks in the east. Accommodation at the base includes a Grand Summit hotel (it is an American Skiing Company resort).

Stratton offers something like the classic Alpine arrangement of a village at the foot of the lifts: a smart, modern development with a car-free shopping street. The slopes amount to 660+ acres, with a vertical of 610m/2,000ft. They are mostly easy and intermediate, with some blacks and some short double-black pitches, spread widely around the flanks of a single peak, served by modern lifts, including a 12-person gondola (which reportedly produces queues even when other lifts don't) and four fast six-seat chairs. Stratton calls itself the 'snowboarding capital of the east', with no fewer than five terrain-parks. The Pro Power Park has a super-pipe. A couple of reporters have complained that the lift passes here are relatively expensive.

You may find more interest in **Sugarbush**, to the north of Killington, midway between Killington and Stowe, Sugarbush is a fast-developing resort, with one of the physically larger ski areas, its runs spread over broad mountainsides rather than being cut

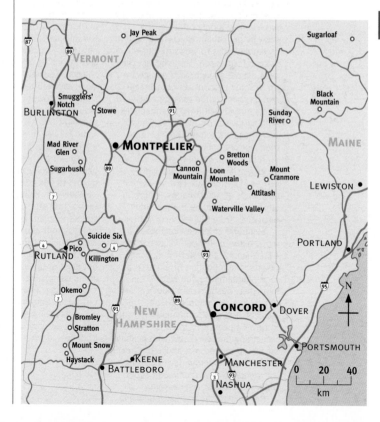

close together. The main sector is an extensive bowl below Lincoln Peak, with lifts up to six points on the rim; a long up-and-over chair-lift accesses the Mt Ellen area – smaller, but with more altitude and more vertical (810m/2,650ft). The easy runs are confined to the lower slopes; higher up, the direct runs are seriously steep. There are terrain-parks in both areas. Five of the 16 lifts are fast – two in each area plus the link lift. Most accommodation is in the historic village of Waitsfield, but a village is developing at the base. The Pitcher Inn, a few minutes away in Warren, is a beautiful recreation of a 19th-century inn, now a Relais & Chateaux place with a dozen individually furnished bedrooms.

Mad River Glen next door is a cult resort with locals, owned for a decade now by a co-operative, with some tough ungroomed terrain, a few well-groomed intermediate trails and old-fashioned lifts – it still has a single-person chair-lift (approaching its 57th year of operation). And snowboarding is still banned.

Further north, near the Canadian border, is **Jay Peak**. It gets crowded at weekends but is quiet in the week. It has Vermont's only cable-car (60 persons per cabin), which takes you to the summit and to views of four US states plus Canada. The only fast chair goes almost as high. Jay Peak gets a lot of snow (350 inches on average) and has some good runs for advanced skiers and adventurous intermediates – notably 100+ acres of glades. There's good beginner terrain too. There are blue cruisers, too, but they don't add up to a lot. Longer-term plans exist for an expansion into the West Bowl – 250 acres of intermediate terrain. There is slope-side accommodation, mainly in condos but including the Jay Hotel, only yards from the cable-car station.

Sugarloaf in Maine already has a much better-developed village at the base than most small New England resorts. The mountain is fair-sized by local standards – 1,400 acres – but a keen piste-basher could ski it out in a day or two. With 860m/2,820ft it claims the biggest continuous vertical in New England, and there is something for everybody, with genuine steeps up around and above the tree line and gentle terrain lower down in the woods. A new 120m/400ft super-pipe was built for last season.

New Hampshire has several small resorts scattered along the Interstate 93 highway. **Bretton Woods** (Director of Skiing a certain Bode Miller) is one of the smaller areas (435 acres, 9 lifts, 460m/1,510ft vertical) on a single mountain face, but it is highly rated, particularly by families, who relish the top-to-bottom easy trails on the main peak, Mt Rosebrook (where, amazingly, there is a proper mountain restaurant). There is a good mix of terrain, with West Mountain consisting mainly of double-diamond slopes. Snowmaking is comprehensive. There's a 150m/500ft half-pipe. For 2004/05 13 new pistes and a new fast quad were added, bringing the fast lift total to four. There are a few places to stay near the base, with the grand old Mount Washington hotel five minutes away. The base area has recently been improved, with the day lodge doubled in size.

Cannon is a ski area and nothing more. Lifts from its two base areas converge on the summit 650m/2,130ft above – a top-to-bottom cable-car, and a pair of fast quad chairs in sequence. This is the state's biggest vertical, but the slope area is very small – 165 acres. The slopes are mainly intermediate; there are quite a few black runs, but no double-blacks. It's a few minutes' drive to hotels and motels in Franconia in one direction and to Lincoln in the other.

Loon Mountain Resort is a small, smart, modern resort just outside the sprawling town of Lincoln. The mountain (275 acres, 640m/2,100ft vertical) is mostly intermediate, though some fall-line runs merit their black grading. There is comprehensive snowmaking. The main lift is a four-person gondola, supported by two fast quads; 10 lifts in total.

Waterville Valley is a compact area (255 acres) with runs dropping either side of a broad, gentle ridge rising 615m/2,020ft above the lift base. There are a couple of short but genuine double-black-diamond mogul fields, but most of the slopes are intermediate. There is 100% snowmaking. The 12 lifts include two fast quads from the base area. The village is a Disneyesque affair a couple of miles away down on the flat valley bottom.

Killington

Good slopes, great après-ski, no village

COSTS

① ② ③ ④ ⑤ ⑥

RATINGS

The slopes

Fast lifts	**
Snow	***
Extent	**
Expert	***
Intermediate	***
Beginner	****
Convenience	*
Queues	****
Mountain restaurants	*

The rest

Scenery	***
Resort charm	*
Off-slope	*

KEY FACTS

Resort	670m
	2,200ft
Slopes	355-1285m
	1,170-4,220ft
Lifts	33
Pistes	1,209 acres
Green	26%
Blue	36%
Black	38%
Snowmaking	
	775 acres

KILLINGTON RESORT

There may not be a village at the base, but there is ski-in ski-out accommodation ↓

+ The biggest mountain in the east, matching some Colorado resorts

+ Lively après-ski, with lots of bar-restaurants offering happy hours and late-night action

+ Excellent nursery slopes

+ Comprehensive and very effective snowmaking

+ Good childcare, although it's not a notably child-oriented resort

− No resort village yet: hotels, condos and restaurants are widely spread, mostly along the five-mile access road – a car is almost a necessity

− Crowds on holidays and weekends

− New England weather – highly changeable, and can be very cold

− The trail network is complex, and there are lots of trail-crossings

− Terminally tedious for anyone who is not a skier or boarder

It's difficult to ignore Killington. It claims to have the largest mountain, the largest number of quad chairs, the largest grooming fleet and longest season in the east, and the world's biggest snowmaking installation. (It tries to be the first resort in America to open, in October, but often shuts again shortly afterwards.) It also claims to have America's longest lift and longest trail (a winding 16km/10 miles) and New England's steepest mogul slope (Outer Limits – average gradient 46%).

These things may matter if your choice of destination is limited to those in the eastern USA. In the general scheme of things, they count for very little. Killington is a minor resort chiefly of interest if you find yourself within driving distance at a time when conditions look good.

THE RESORT

Killington is an extraordinary resort, especially to European eyes. Most of its hotels and restaurants are spread along a five-mile approach road. The nearest thing you'll find to a focus is the occasional set of traffic lights with a cluster of shops, though there is a concentration of buildings along a two-and-a-half mile stretch of the road. The resort caters mainly for weekend visitors who drive in from the east-coast cities. The car is king; but there's also a good free day-time shuttle-bus service around the base areas and lodgings. Beyond this it costs $2.

There are lodgings around the lift base, and plans for something like a village there have been revived, now that the resort's owners have brought in a new partner – development should begin in 2006.

Staying near the start of the access road leaves you well placed for the gondola station on the main highway leading past the resort, and for outings to Pico, a separate little mountain in the same ownership, perhaps one day to be linked to Ram's Head mountain.

THE MOUNTAINS

Runs spread over a series of wooded peaks, all quite close together but giving the resort a basis for claiming to cover six mountains – or seven if you count Pico. An impressive number of runs and lifts are crammed into a modest area. The result is a complex network of runs, and signposting isn't always clear – Skye Peak is particularly confusing – but improvements made at key points across the mountain last

NEWS

Plans for a new
resort village
including lodgings
and shops have been
revived.

For 2005/06 the base
lodges at Ram's
Head and Bear
Mountain are to be
refurbished, following
on from Snowshed
last season.

In 2004/05 the
terrain-parks were
improved greatly and
gained a 130m/430ft
super-pipe. Three
gladed areas (Fusion
Zones) opened on
Bear Mountain.

LIFT PASSES

**Killington Mountain
Pass**
Covers all lifts in the
Killington and Pico
ski areas. Prices
include sales tax.

Beginners
Included in price of
lessons

Main pass
1 day $67
6 days $318

Senior citizens
Over 65: 6 days $206

Children
Under 19: 6 days
$271
Under 13: 6 days
$206
Under 6: free

Notes
Discount if you book
online 14 days in
advance. Special
prices for
combinations of lift
pass, equipment and
lessons.

boarding

A cool resort like Killington has to take boarding seriously, and it does. There are terrain features scattered around the area, with lots of interest for all levels, and parts of the mountain have been reshaped to cut out some of the unpleasant flats on green runs. There are excellent beginner slopes, and plenty of friendly high-speed (ie slow-loading) chair-lifts – and the Perfect Turn Discovery Center caters just for beginners. Several big-name board events are held here, and the terrain-parks just get bigger and better.

season should help make navigation easier. To some extent the terrain on each sector suits a different ability level. But there are also areas where a mixed ability group would be quite happy, and there are easy runs from top to bottom of each peak.

Some runs of all levels are left to form bumps; there is half-and-half grooming on selected trails; and terrain features – ridges etc – are created. There are also Fusion Zones – thinned-out forest areas, not groomed or patrolled, where you pick your own line. They come in blue and single- and double-black-diamond grades. We found them great fun.

THE SLOPES
Complicated
The Killington Base area has chairs radiating to three of the six peaks – **Snowdon**, **Killington** (the high-point of the area) and **Skye** – the last also accessible by gondola starting beside US highway 4. Novices and families head for the other main base area, which has two parts: Snowshed, at the foot of the main beginner slope, served by several parallel chairs; and Rams Head, just across the road up to Killington Base, where there's a Family Center at the foot of the entirely gentle **Rams Head** mountain – the nursery slopes were extended recently.

The two remaining peaks are behind Skye Peak; they can be reached by trails from Killington and Skye, but each also has a lift base accessible by road. **Bear Mountain** is the experts' hill, served by two quad chairs from its mid-mountain base area. The sixth 'peak', **Sunrise**, is a slight blip on the mountainside, with a short triple chair up from the Sunrise Village condos.

TERRAIN-PARKS
Lots of possibilities
There's a good choice, including early and late season parks (plus one at Pico). Bear Mountain is now home to the main park with rails, jumps and

new super-pipe – served by its own rope tow. Timberline on Ram's Head is better suited to intermediates, has a quarter-pipe and trebled in size last season. There's a beginner's mini-park and various other terrain features scattered around the area. Kids now have their own park and pipe classes.

SNOW RELIABILITY
Good if it's cold
Killington has a good snowfall record and a huge snowmaking system – improved again last season as part of a huge investment in upgrades, (although a recent reporter was surprised to find this little used during his peak season visit, despite low temperatures). But even that is no good if temperatures are too high to operate it. Bad weather can ruin a holiday even in mid-season. A reporter who had new powder each night on a March visit went back at the same time the following year to find people skiing in shorts and T-shirts on the few runs that were open. A February visitor told of 'everything from frostbite warnings to pouring rain'. Grooming was also reported to be poor – 'only a couple of trails groomed per peak'.

FOR EXPERTS
Some challenges
The main areas that experts head for are Killington Peak, where there is a handful of genuine double-diamond fall-line runs under the two chair-lifts, and Bear Mountain – though a 2005 reporter did not find them very challenging. Most of the slopes here are single blacks but Outer Limits, under the main quad chair, is a double-diamond, claimed to be 'the steepest mogul slope in the east'. We suspect there are steeper runs at Stowe and Smugglers' Notch. There are two or three worthwhile blacks on Snowdon and Skye, too. Also the Fusion Zones on Skye, Snowdon and now Bear Mountain are well worth seeking out.

SCHOOLS

Perfect Turn
t 1-800-923-9444
Learn to ski clinics
(including lift pass,
equipment and use of
Discovery Centre)
1 day $80
3 days $185

Classes
One 2hr group lesson
$45
Private lessons
$93 for 1hr

WEBSITES

For links to resort
sites, go to our own
new site at
www.wtss.co.uk

FOR INTERMEDIATES
Navigation problems?
There are lots of easy cruising blue
and green runs all over the slopes,
except on Bear Mountain, where the
single blacks present a little more of a
challenge for intermediates. Snowdon
is a splendid area for those who like to
vary their diet, although a reporter
favoured the trails on Skye. There's a
blue-classified Fusion Zone on Rams
Head. Finding your way around the
complicated network of trails may be
tricky, though new signposting should
help. One reporter liked Pico but
complained that the blue run down
was more difficult than some blacks.

FOR BEGINNERS
Splendid
The facilities for complete beginners
are excellent. The Snowshed slope is
one vast nursery slope served by three
chair-lifts and a very slow drag-lift.
Rams Head also has excellent gentle
slopes. The ski school runs a special,
purpose-built Discovery Center just for

first-time skiers and boarders – they
introduce you to the equipment, show
you videos and provide refreshments.

FOR CROSS-COUNTRY
Two main options
Extensive cross-country loops are
available at two specialist 'resorts' –
Mountain Meadows, down on US
Highway 4, and Mountain Top Ski
Touring, just a short drive away
at Chittenden.

QUEUES
Weekend crowds
Killington gets a lot of weekend and
holiday business, but at other times
the slopes and lifts are likely to be
quiet. One holiday visitor found long
lines for the Rams Head chair, the K1
gondola and the Bear Mountain chair.
Overcrowded slopes are more of a
problem than lift queues – the
approaches to Bear Mountain lift base
were singled out by a reporter.

MOUNTAIN RESTAURANTS
Bearable base lodges
The Killington Peak Lodge (in what
was the top station of the old gondola)
is the only real mountain restaurant –
we lack recent reports, but we've
received mixed reports in the past.
There's a warming hut at Northbrook
station on Skye Peak where you can
get soups, and areas are provided if
you wish to bring your own food. Each
of the lift base stations has an eatery –
menus were improved last season, and
Snowshed has a newly refurbished
food court.

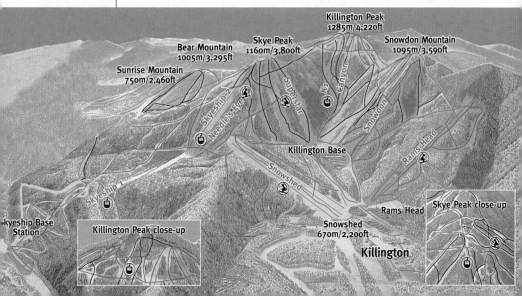

Killington Peak
1285m/4,220ft

Bear Mountain
1005m/3,295ft

Skye Peak
1160m/3,800ft

Snowdon Mountain
1095m/3,590ft

Sunrise Mountain
750m/2,460ft

Skyeship 2

Needle's Eye

Superstar

K1

Canyon

Snowdon

Rams Head

Killington Base

Snowshed

Skyeship 1

Rams Head

Skye Peak close-up

Skyeship Base
Station

Killington Peak close-up

Snowshed
670m/2,200ft

Killington

CHILDREN

t 888-765-7758
**Friendly Penguin Day
Care**
Ages 6wk to 6yr
First Tracks
Ages 2 to 3; 8.30-
4.30; $95 a day;
includes skiing
MiniStars/Lowriders
Ages 4 to 6; 8.30-
3.30; $90 a day;
includes skiing

Ski school
'Superstars' for ages
7 to 12 and
'Snowzone' for ages
13 to 18 ($69 for a
full day)

GETTING THERE

Air Boston 251km/
156 miles (2½hr).

620

ACTIVITIES

Indoor Killington
Grand Resort Hotel
has massage, fitness
centre, outdoor pool,
hot-tub, sauna;
theatre, cinemas,
bowling, at Rutland;
climbing wall at
Snowshed base

Outdoor Ice rink,
snow-shoeing,
snowmobile tours,
sleigh rides

**Central reservations
phone number**
Call 1 800 621 6867
(toll-free from within
the US).

Phone numbers
From distant parts of
the US, add the prefix
1 802.
From abroad, add the
prefix +1 802.

TOURIST OFFICE

t 422 3333
info@killington.com
www.killington.com

NEW ENGLAND

SCHOOLS AND GUIDES
In search of the Perfect Turn

The philosophy of the Perfect Turn
school is to build on your strengths,
and it seems to work for most people.
Beginners start and finish their day in
a dedicated beginners' building with
easy chairs, coffee, videos and help
with choosing and fitting equipment.
Speciality clinics include mogul
weekends and park and pipe classes.

FACILITIES FOR CHILDREN
Fine in practice

There is a Family Center at the Rams
Head base, which takes kids from six
weeks and will introduce them to
skiing from age two years. Classes are
reported to be small.

STAYING THERE

HOW TO GO
Wide choices

There is a wide choice of places to
stay. As well as hotels and condos,
there are a few chalets.
Hotels There are a few places near the
lifts, but most are a drive or bus-ride
away, down Killington Road or on US4.
(((((4) **Cortina Inn** (773 3333) 20
minutes away on US4, near Pico; pool,
'excellent food, poor soundproofing'.
(((((4) **Grand Resort** (422 6888) Swanky
resort-owned place at Snowshed, with
outdoor pool and health club.
(((((4) **Inn of the Six Mountains** (422
4302) Couple of miles down Killington
Road; 'spacious rooms, good pool'.
((((3) **Red Rob Inn** (422 3303) Short
drive from slopes – 'good restaurant, a
cut above the usual motel style'.
((((3) **North Star Lodge** (422 4040) Well
down Killington Road; 'good budget
accommodation'.

EATING OUT
You name it

There are all sorts of restaurants
spread along the Killington Road, from
simple pizza or pasta through to 'fine
dining' places. They get very crowded

at weekends; many don't take
reservations. Many of the places in the
Après-ski section serve food.
   The local menu guide is essential
reading. Claude's Choices, the
'excellent' Grist Mill, Hemingway's,
Charity's, the Cortina Inn and Red Rob
Inn have been recommended. Sugar
and Spice is reported to serve good
breakfasts, as does Ppeppers, which
also has 'good burgers' and desserts.

APRES-SKI
The beast of the east

Killington has a well-deserved
reputation for a vibrant après-ski
scene; many of its short-stay visitors
are clearly intent on making the most
of their few days (or nights) here.
   Although there are bars at the base
lodges, keen après-skiers head down
Killington Road to one of the lively
places scattered along its 8km/5 mile
length. From 3pm it's cheap drinks and
free munchies, then in the early
evening it's serious dining time, and
later on the real action starts (and
admission charges kick in). Most of the
places mentioned here would also rate
a mention in Eating out.
   The train-themed Casey's Caboose
is said to have the best 'wings' in
town. Charity's is another lively bar,
with an interior apparently lifted from a
late-19th-century Parisian brothel. The
Wobbly Barn ('expensive' but 'very
good' food) is a famous live-music
place that rivals Jackson's Mangy
Moose for the position of America's
leading après-ski venue. The Pickel
Barrel caters for a younger crowd, with
theme nights and loud music. The
Outback complex has something for
everyone, from pizzas and free
massages to disco and live bands.

OFF THE SLOPES
Rent a car

If there is a less amusing resort in
which to spend time off the slopes, we
have yet to find it. Make sure you have
a car, as well as a good book.

Stowe

Charming Vermont town some way from its small but serious mountain

RATINGS

The slopes

Fast lifts	**
Snow	***
Extent	*
Expert	***
Intermediate	****
Beginner	****
Convenience	*
Queues	****
Mountain restaurants	**

The rest

Scenery	***
Resort charm	****
Off-slope	*

NEWS

Improvements on Spruce Peak continue. For 2005/06 a fast quad will replace the Big Spruce double chair, improving access to the top runs. This follows replacement of the double chair by a fast quad last season. Snowmaking will be extended to cover all runs on the upper mountain.

There are also plans to construct a new base lodge.

Last season a triple chair was installed for beginners, serving a new green run.

KEY FACTS

Resort	475m
	1,560ft
Slopes	390-1110m
	1,280-3,640ft
Lifts	12
Pistes	485 acres
Green	16%
Blue	59%
Black	25%
Snowmaking	
	354 acres

+ Cute tourist town in classic New England style

+ Some good slopes for all abilities, including serious challenges

+ Few queues

+ Excellent cross-country trails

+ Great children's facilities

– Slopes a bus-ride from town

– Slopes limited in extent, and split into two unlinked sectors

– New England weather – highly changeable, and can be very cold

– Weekend queues

– No après-ski atmosphere

Stowe is one of New England's cutest little towns, its main street lined with dinky clapboard shops and restaurants; you could find no sharper contrast to the other New England resorts we feature. Its mountain, six miles away, is another New England classic: something for everyone, but not much of it.

THE RESORT

Stowe is a picture-postcard New England town – and a popular spot for tourists year-round, with bijou shops and more 3- and 4-diamond hotels and restaurants than any other place in New England except Boston. The slopes of Mount Mansfield, Vermont's snow-capped (though mainly wooded) highest peak, are a 15-minute drive away and much of the accommodation is along the road out to it. There's a good day-time shuttle-bus service but a car is recommended for flexibility (and excursions).

THE MOUNTAIN

There are three sectors, two linked, the third a short shuttle-bus ride away. There are free daily mountain tours.
Slopes The main sector, served by a trio of chair-lifts from Mansfield Base Lodge, is dominated by the famous Front Four – a row of double-black-diamond runs. But there is plenty of easier stuff, too. An eight-seat gondola serves the next sector. The third area, Spruce Peak, has the main nursery area at the bottom. A fast quad heads up to mid-mountain, with another planned to the top for 2005/06, replacing the Big Spruce double chair. The old link with Smugglers' Notch, from the top of this sector over the hill, is now a backcountry route. Night-skiing is offered three times a week.
Terrain-parks Stowe has three terrain-parks and a half-pipe: one is for beginners, the others are best suited to advanced users.

Snow reliability This is helped by snowmaking on practically all the blue (and some black) runs of the main sectors, and on Spruce Peak (due to be fully covered for 2005/06). Grooming is reported to be 'excellent'.
Experts The 'scarily narrow' and seriously steep Front Four and their variants on the top half of the main sector present a real challenge (if they are open) – and there are others nearby. There are various gladed areas.
Intermediates The usual New England reservation applies: the terrain is limited in extent; there's also a severe shortage of ordinary black runs (as opposed to double diamonds). Spruce Peak will now be much more attractive, with two fast quads in place.
Beginners The nursery slopes at Spruce Peak are now excellent. Last season, a short chair-lift and gentle new run were added. There are also

STOWE MOUNTAIN RESORT / DON LANDWEHRLE

It's nice to see an American hill with more forest standing than trails cut out of it ↓

NEW ENGLAND

622

splendid long green runs to progress to in the main sector, down to Toll House base.

Snowboarding Stowe attracts many snowboarders. Beginners learn on special customised boards at the Burton Method Center on Spruce Peak. There's a snowboarder-specific resort web site: www.ridestowe.com

Cross-country There are excellent centres scattered around (including one at the musically famous Trapp Family Lodge) – 150km/93 miles of groomed and 100km/62 miles of backcountry trails form the largest network in the eastern US.

Queues The area is largely queue-free mid-week but we've had reports of 25-minute queues at weekends – the Four Runner quad is mentioned this year. New lifts at Spruce Peak are said to have reduced congestion there.

Mountain restaurants Cliff House, at the top of the gondola, is a lofty room with table-service and good food and views. Next-best is Midway Cafe near the base of the gondola, with a BBQ deck and table-service inside.

Schools and guides We lack recent reports. You can try out the latest equipment, with instruction, at the Stowe Toys Demo Centre. Semi-private lessons are now available (maximum of three in a group).

Facilities for children Facilities are excellent and the nursery takes children from age six weeks to six years.

STAYING THERE

How to go There are hotels in and around Stowe itself and along the road to the slopes, some with Austrian or Scandinavian names and styles.

Hotels 1066 Ye Olde England Inne is recommended (despite the appalling name), as are Stowehof Inn, Green Mountain Inn and the 'pleasant' and welcoming Stowe Inn. The Golden Eagle has 'excellent breakfasts', pool and hot-tub. The smart Inn at the Mountain, at Toll House, is the only slope-side accommodation, with chairlift access to the main sector of slopes.

Self-catering There is a reasonable range of condos available for rent.

Eating out There are restaurants of every kind. The Whip in the Green Mountain Inn, the Shed ('good ribs') and an Italian restaurant, Trattoria La Festa, have all been recommended.

Après-ski Après-ski is muted – Stowe reportedly goes to bed early. The Matterhorn, Shed and Rusty Nail on the access road are popular. There's a good cinema with new releases.

Off the slopes Stowe is a pleasant town in which to spend time off the slopes – at least if you like shopping. The Vermont Ski Museum is 'worth a visit', says a reporter; and a trip to the Burlington shopping mall and a tour (with samples) of Ben & Jerry's ice cream factory just down the road have also been recommended.

SMUGGLERS' NOTCH RESORT

Smugglers' Notch

Smuggs hits the family target squarely, with a constant round of early-evening activities, sympathetic instructors, comprehensive childcare, a generally child-friendly layout and some long, quiet, easy runs.

KEY FACTS

Resort	315m
	1,030ft
Altitude	315-1110m
	1,030-3,640ft
Lifts	8
Pistes	1,000 acres
Green	18%
Blue	54%
Black	28%
Snowmaking	62 %

TOURIST OFFICE

t 644 8851
smuggs@smuggs.com
www.smuggs.com

THE RESORT

Smugglers' Notch is about the nearest thing you'll find in the US to a French-style purpose-built family resort – except that it doesn't look so bad. The resort is entirely focused on the family market, and those not afflicted with children would find the family orientation a bit overpowering. There are lots of comfortable condos on or near the slopes, but no hotels. Après-ski and eating-out options are extremely limited. Off-slope options include a pool and ice rink.

THE MOUNTAINS

Smuggs has varied and satisfying slopes, spread over three hills, with a worthwhile vertical of 800m/2,610ft. Morse is directly above the village, with a separate learning area.

Madonna and Sterling have a separate base area, linked to the village but also reachable by road. Skiing together as a family can be difficult: different levels of ability mean being on different mountains. The lifts are slow but not prone to queues – it's blissfully quiet except at weekends and holidays. There are some challenges at the top of Madonna (genuine double blacks and even one triple) as well as plenty of easy cruising. It's a great area for beginners, with dedicated slopes. Snowboarding is encouraged, with good learning facilities. There are three impressive terrain-parks to suit all abilities and an Olympic-size super-pipe. There are no real mountain restaurants. The ski school (or 'Snow Sport University') has often been voted the best in North America. The childcare and tuition arrangements are of course superb.

Short turns

623

SUNDAY RIVER SKI RESORT

Sunday River

Sunday River was one of the pioneers of snowmaking, and over 90% of its trails are served by it. So the snow should be as good here as anywhere in the east. The terrain is varied but quite limited in extent. There is no village as such.

KEY FACTS

Resort	245m
	800ft
Slopes	245-955m
	800-3,140ft
Lifts	18
Pistes	660 acres
Green	25%
Blue	35%
Black	40%
Snowmaking	
	607 acres

TOURIST OFFICE

t 824 3000
info@sundayriver.com
www.sundayriver.com

THE RESORT

There isn't really a base village yet. At present, mainly condo developments cluster beside the lower slopes at the three main lift bases at the eastern end of the mountain, the dominant feature of which is the Grand Summit hotel. 5km/3 miles away at the western end of the mountain is the Jordan Grand hotel; there are plans for major development here, but not much sign of it happening. Bethel is a small town, a 10-minute drive away; it's a pleasant place with shops, several restaurants and bars as well as lodges and motels.

THE MOUNTAINS

The slopes spread across eight peaks, each basically served by one lift, with links from one to the next. But it's a small area – and many of the runs are

either short or very gentle. You get a satisfying feeling of travel, and the western sector (Aurora, Oz and Jordan Bowl) has far fewer lifts and runs than the eastern end, where most of the lifts as well as most of the beds are concentrated. Only four of the chairs are fast quads, and two of these are on the lower slopes; but queues are not a problem – midweek, the resort is very quiet. 40% of the trails are classified black, and there are challenging narrow, often mogulled double-blacks on White Cap and Barker Mountain, and excellent glade skiing elsewhere. It's good for intermediates, with a series of nice rolling blues (often deserted). There are some easy glades to tempt the bold. South Ridge is a well-organised area for beginners, with good, easy runs to progress to. There are no mountain restaurants. Cross-country is big around here.

Canada

Canada is now more popular with British skiers and snowboarders than the USA. In many ways it combines the best that the US has to offer – good service, a warm welcome, relatively quiet slopes, good lift systems with lots of high-speed lifts, heavy dumps of snow, great grooming and a high standard of accommodation – with more spectacular scenery and lower prices. It also has the advantage that you can get direct flights to its main airports without having to change planes and go through customs part-way through your journey. And last season the charter flights and direct Air Canada and British Airways flights were joined by the budget scheduled airline Zoom, flying from Gatwick and Glasgow.

Last season was an exceptionally poor year for snow in many resorts in western Canada due to abnormally warm weather and a spell of rain during January that hit the resorts nearest to the coast especially badly – closing Vancouver's local hills and many of Whistler's slopes. But the resorts further inland fared better and we had great conditions at both Sunshine Village and Jasper. And in an average year, you can expect much better snow than in the Alps. A few seasons ago we drove from Whistler to Banff, calling in at lots of smaller resorts on the way. The whole trip took two weeks and for eight consecutive days in the middle it did not stop snowing. It made driving from resort to resort tricky, as we stuck to our normal scheme of driving at night after getting in a full day on the slopes. But the skiing was spectacular – day after day of dry, light powder. That's more like a normal winter in western Canada.

Whistler, for example, gets an average of 360 inches of snow and it snows (or rains, at resort level) for half the days in the season. That makes for superb conditions on the upper slopes. Inland at Banff-Lake Louise you might not get quite the same frequency of snow, but it stays in great condition because the air is drier and temperatures are lower. You get a better chance of blue skies there – but also a higher chance of a day or two of very low temperatures (–20°C or less).

So you go to Canada for the skiing or boarding, not the sunbathing. If you prefer long lunches on sun-drenched mountain restaurant terraces, stick to March in the Alps. If you want a good chance of hitting powder, head for western Canada. The east is different: expect snow and extremes of weather more like in New England. The main attraction of Québec for us is the French culture and unique ambience; it also has the advantage of a shorter flight time.

SKI BANFF/ LAKE LOUISE
SCOTT ROWED

← Apologies for the long-lens photography designed to exaggerate the scenic drama (and for the ski suit). But the scenery around Lake Louise really is special

If you really want untracked powder and are feeling flush, there is nothing to beat Canada's amazing heli-skiing and snowcat skiing operations. It is the leading country for both these activities and you can expect run after run in virgin snow. The main difference is that the former is faster paced and more expensive than the latter. You can do it by the day, but the hedonistic option is to book a few days or a week in a luxury lodge, eating gourmet dinners and stepping out of the door each morning straight into the chopper or snowcat.

But if you resist heli-skiing or snowcat heaven, you'll find a holiday in Canada can be reasonably cheap. Package prices start at under £500 for a week to western Canada. And prices for eating and drinking tend to be cheaper than in the US or the Alps.

Both east and west have the disadvantage for young people that laws about buying and consuming alcohol are more strictly enforced than in the UK. The legal age is 18 in Alberta and Québec but 19 in British Columbia; carrying your passport as evidence of age is a good idea even if you are well over the required age. People unable to prove their age may be refused entries to bars and clubs but will usually be allowed in restaurants (though not to drink alcohol).

Another disadvantage is that, as in the USA, lifts close much earlier than in Europe – as early as 3pm in some cases.

INTRAWEST / SCOTT ROWED
From higher up in Panorama they say you can see 1,000 peaks ↘

Western Canada

For international visitors to Canada, the main draw is the west. It has fabulous scenery, good snow and a wonderful sense of the great outdoors. The big names of Whistler, Banff and Lake Louise capture most of the British market but there are lots of worthwhile smaller resorts that more adventurous travellers are now starting to explore. We recommend renting a car and combining two or more of these, with a couple of days on virgin powder served by helicopters or snowcats as well, perhaps. We've done this on several occasions but visiting seven or eight resorts on each trip; it's tiring but rewarding. Take it a bit easier than we do (we're working, of course) and you'll have the holiday of a lifetime.

The three big resorts mentioned above and nine of the smaller ones you're most likely to want to visit for a while get their own write-ups in this section of the book. There are big differences between them, so be sure to read each one. For example, Whistler is the busiest and most developed, Kicking Horse the newest and just starting to be developed. Fernie has great steep powder terrain for experts, Big White great gentle powder terrain to learn how to ski it. Sun Peaks is a fairly new, compact, purpose-built resort with a vaguely Tirolean feel and the second-biggest (to Whistler) ski area in British Columbia. Panorama is a longer-established, purpose-built resort undergoing a renaissance and boasting the second-biggest (to Whistler) vertical in Canada. Banff and Lake Louise are very different bases from which to ski three separate areas, which you need transport to reach.

Jasper, Red Resort and Silver Star are of more limited interest and get shorter write-ups.

There are other resorts in the west, of course. One of the ones we were most surprised by on our 2004 tour of the west was Apex – and that has an extended entry in the Resort index / directory at the back of the book – as does Kimberley.

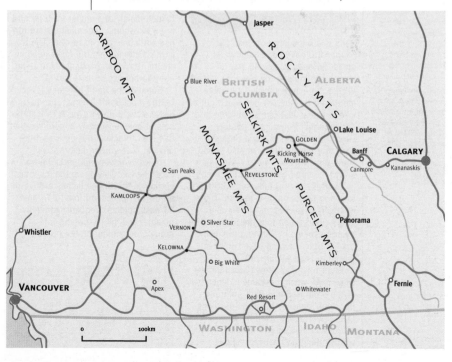

Banff

A winter wonderland with wildlife

COSTS

① ② ③ ④ ⑤ ⑥

RATINGS

The slopes

Fast lifts	★★★
Snow	★★★★
Extent	★★★★
Expert	★★★★
Intermediate	★★★★
Beginner	★★★
Convenience	★
Queues	★★★★
Mountain restaurants	★★★

The rest

Scenery	★★★★
Resort charm	★★★
Off-slope	★★★★★

NEWS

In Sunshine another very steep area called the Wild West on Goat's Eye opened for 2004/05. As with Delirium Dive, you need a companion, avalanche transceiver and shovel to be allowed in. For 2005/06, further rooms are being renovated at the Sunshine Inn.

And in Norquay, the terrain-park is being enlarged for 2005/06, as is the super-pipe. There will also be more snowmaking and 80% of the pistes will be groomed.

628

- ➕ Spectacular high-mountain scenery – quite unlike the Colorado Rockies
- ➕ Some wildlife around the valley
- ➕ Lots of touristy shops
- ➕ Good-value lodging because winter is the area's low season
- ➕ Late season holidays
- ➕ Extensive slopes with excellent snow record at Sunshine, but ...

- ➖ Sunshine is a 20-minute drive away
- ➖ You'll probably want to take in Lake Louise, too – a 45-minute drive
- ➖ Can be very cold; most lifts have no covers and waiting for shuttle-buses can be unpleasant
- ➖ Banff lacks ski resort atmosphere – though it's not an unattractive town
- ➖ Resort can seem over-full of Brits

Huge numbers of British skiers and boarders go to Banff. Price has been a key factor in getting us to make the trip, though costs are now creeping up. Most visitors are delighted with what they find, and are keen to go back.

It's not difficult to see why. The landscape is one of glaciers, jagged peaks and magnificent views, the valleys have wildlife that you'll never see in Europe (though it's much less evident than on our first visit 12 years ago). The slopes have something for everyone, from steep couloirs to gentle cruising. The snow is some of the coldest, driest and most reliable you'll find anywhere in the world, and there's a lot of it (at Sunshine Village, at least). And there are the standard Canadian assets of people who are friendly and welcoming, and low prices for meals and other on-the-spot expenses.

For us, these factors count for more than the drawbacks. But then we, luckily, have never encountered the extremely low temperatures (–35°C is not unknown) that have left some early-season reporters feeling less convinced.

THE RESORT

Banff is a big summer resort that happens to have some nearby ski areas. Norquay is a small area of slopes overlooking the town. Sunshine Village, 20 minutes away, is a bigger mountain; despite the name, it's not a village (it has just one small hotel at mid-mountain) – nor is it notably sunny. Most visitors buy a three-area pass that means they can also spend some time at Lake Louise, 45 minutes away – covered by a separate chapter.

Banff is spectacularly set, with a few towering peaks on its outskirts. There is wildlife to see, especially elk and long-horned sheep (but the town is now trying to keep elk away and the main road to Sunshine and Lake Louise is fenced to keep wildlife off).

Banff town has grown substantially since 1990, when it became independent of the Banff National Park authority. But it still consists basically of a long main street and a small network of side roads built in grid fashion, lined with clothing and souvenir shops

(aimed mainly at summer visitors) and a few ski shops. The buildings are low-rise and some are wood-clad. The town is pleasant enough, but lacks genuine charm; it's a commercial tourist town, not another Aspen or Telluride.

Some of the Banff lodgings (even on the main Banff Avenue) are quite a distance from downtown. A car can be helpful here, especially in cold weather (it's best to splash out on a 4-wheel drive in case you hit heavy snow).

Unless you stay mid-mountain on Sunshine (see Staying up the mountain), getting to the slopes means a drive or a bus-ride. Buses are free to Tri-area lift pass holders, frequent, generally reliable, and 'highly organised' – though, depending on the number of

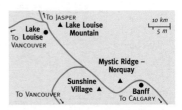

KEY FACTS

Resort	1380m
	4,530ft

Norquay, Sunshine and Lake Louise, covered by the Tri-area pass

Slopes	1630-2730m
	5,350-8,950ft
Lifts	29
Pistes	7,748 acres
Green	23%
Blue	39%
Black	38%
Snowmaking	
	1,900 acres

Norquay only

Slopes	1630-2135m
	5,350-7,000ft
Lifts	5
Pistes	190 acres
Green	20%
Blue	36%
Black	44%
Snowmaking	85%

Sunshine only

Slopes	1660-2730m
	5,440-8,950ft
Lifts	12
Pistes	3,358 acres
Green	22%
Blue	31%
Black	47%
Snowmaking	none

pick ups, they can take twice as long as advertised and it can be a cold wait. One reporter also complained that because skis and boards are piled up in the belly of the bus, her board was 'ruined; scratched beyond recognition'. Another suggests putting your skis/board in a bag. Buses are also arranged to the more distant major resorts of Panorama and Kicking Horse (see separate chapters) and the smaller (and closer) resort of Nakiska, and day-trip heli-skiing and boarding can be organised, too. Banff Airporter does transfers from and to Calgary airport.

THE MOUNTAINS

The Sunshine Village slopes are set right on the Continental Divide and as a result get a lot of snow. Most of the slopes above the village are above the tree line and can be very cold and bleak during a snowfall or cold snap. Although there is a wooded sector served by the second section of the gondola and a couple of chairs, in bad weather you're better off elsewhere. It is great, however, for late-season skiing, which goes on until May.

Norquay is much smaller. But it's worth a visit, especially in bad weather – it has wooded slopes to suit all abilities and the trails can be delightfully quiet.

THE SLOPES
Lots of variety
The main slopes of **Sunshine Village** are not visible from the base station: you ride a two-stage gondola, first to the base of Goat's Eye Mountain, and then on to Sunshine Village itself.

Goat's Eye is served by a fast quad rising 580m/1,900ft. Although there are some blue runs, this is basically a black mountain, with some genuine double-blacks at the extremities (including the new Wild West area that opened last season – which you need

a companion and avalanche safety equipment to ski).

Lifts fan out in all directions from Sunshine Village, with short runs back from Mount Standish and longer ones from Lookout Mountain. Lookout is where the Continental Divide is, with the melting snow flowing in one direction to the Pacific and in the other to the Atlantic. From the top here experts can pass through a gate (you need an avalanche transceiver to get through) and hike up to the extreme terrain of Delirium Dive.

Many people ride the gondola down at the end of the day. But the 2.5km/1.5 mile green run to the bottom is a pretty cruise. If you go down while the lifts are running you can take the Jackrabbit chair to cut out a flat section, but the run gets crowded and is much more enjoyable if you delay your descent a bit. The Canyon trail provides a scenic alternative for more advanced skiers and riders. Though the lower part is marked black diamond, it's not steep – just a bit narrow in places.

The slopes at **Norquay** are served by a row of five parallel lifts and have floodlit trails on Friday nights.

TERRAIN-PARKS
Park – and ride ...
Both Sunshine and Norquay have good half-pipes and terrain-parks offering a vast array of rails and jumps. Norquay has a super-pipe and its park is due to be enlarged for 2005/06; it is floodlit on a Friday night and the area offers a lift ticket for those who want to use only the park and pipe.

SNOW RELIABILITY
Excellent
Sunshine Village claims '100% natural snow', a neat reversal of the usual snowmaking hype. In a poor snow season, some black runs can remain rocky but the blues are usually fine. 'Three times the snow' is another

LIFT PASSES

Tri-area lift pass
Covers all lifts and transport between Banff, Lake Louise, Norquay and Sunshine Village.

Beginners
Lift, lesson and rental package available.

Main pass
3 days C$212
6 days C$424

Senior citizens
Over 65: 6 days
C$379

Children
Under 18: 6 days
C$379
Under 13: 6 days
C$173
Under 6: free pass

Notes
Prices above include taxes. Three-day minimum.

Alternative passes
One-day and half-day passes available for individual areas.

boarding

Boarders will feel at home in Banff and there is some excellent free-riding terrain. 'There are so many natural ledges, jumps and tree gaps to play with that the terrain-park seems almost unnecessary!' said a reporter. But Sunshine also has some flat areas to beware of where scooting or walking is required (such as the green run to the base) and the blue traverse on Goat's Eye is tedious. There are two specialist snowboard shops: Rude Boys and Unlimited Snowboards.

Sunshine slogan – a cryptic reference to the fact that the average snowfall here is 360 to 400 inches (depending on which figures you believe) – as good as anything in Colorado – compared with a modest 140 inches at Lake Louise and 120 inches on Norquay. But we're told the Sunshine figures relate to Lookout, and that Goat's Eye gets less. There is snowmaking on 90% of pistes at Sunshine. So all in all, lack of snow is unlikely to be a problem in a normal season and late-season snow on Sunshine is usually good (we've had great April snow there on our last two visits).

FOR EXPERTS
Pure pleasure
Both areas have satisfying terrain for good skiers and boarders.

Sunshine has plenty of open runs of genuine black steepness above the tree line on Lookout, but Goat's Eye is much more compelling. It has a great, and still expanding, area of expert double-black-diamond trails and chutes, both above and below the tree line. But the slopes are rocky and need good cover, and the top can be windswept.

There are short, not-too-steep black runs on Mount Standish. One more challenging novelty here is a pitch known as the Waterfall run – because you do actually ski down over a snow-covered frozen fall. But a lot of snow is needed to cover the waterfall and prevent it reverting to ice. Also try the Shoulder on Lookout Mountain; it is sheltered, tends to accumulate powder and was deserted when we were there on a busy day last April; stay high to make the traverse out easier.

Real experts will want to get to grips with Delirium Dive on Lookout Mountain's north face and the new Wild West area on Goat's Eye (with some narrow chutes and rock bands). For both, you must have a companion, an avalanche transceiver and a shovel – and a guide is recommended. ('Book in advance' and 'rent your transceiver and shovel in Banff – you can't at Sunshine' advise disappointed reporters.) But a local expert says: 'The patrol neurotically carpet-bombs the entire cirque and closes it upon sighting the first tiny fog-bank, making Delirium the safest off-piste on the planet. The mandatory transceiver routine is pure theatre.'

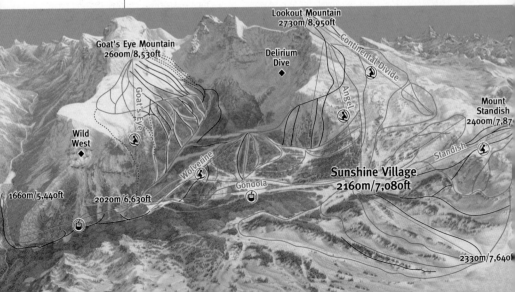

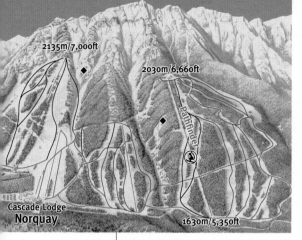

2135m/7,000ft

2030m/6,660ft

Pathfinder

Cascade Lodge
Norquay

1630m/5,350ft

you look there are blues and greens – some of the greens as enjoyable (and pretty much as steep) as the blues.

We particularly like the World Cup Downhill run, from the top of Lookout to the mid-mountain base. The slow Wawa chair gives access to the Wawa Bowl and Tincan Alley. This is a good area for intermediates and offers tree-lined protection from bad weather. There's a delightful wooded area under the second stage of the gondola served by Jackrabbit and Wolverine chairs. The blue runs down Goat's Eye are good cruises too.

The Pathfinder fast quad at Norquay serves a handful of quite challenging tree-lined blues and a couple of sometimes-groomed blacks – great for a snowy day or a 'first day warm-up'.

FOR BEGINNERS
Pretty good terrain
Sunshine has a good area by the mid-mountain base, served by a moving carpet. The long Meadow Park green is a great, long, easy run to progress to.

Norquay has a good small nursery area with a moving carpet and gentle greens served by the Cascade chair.

Banff is not the ideal destination for a mixed party of beginners (who may want to stay in one area) and more experienced friends (who are likely to want to visit other places).

FOR CROSS-COUNTRY
High in quality and quantity
It's a good area for cross-country. There are trails near Banff, around the Bow River, and on the Banff Springs golf course. But the best area is around Lake Louise. Altogether, there are around 80km/50 miles of groomed trails within Banff National Park. Beware of the wildlife though: a few seasons ago a cross-country skier was killed by a mountain lion.

QUEUES
No problem most of the time
Half the visitors come for the day from cities such as Calgary – so it's fairly quiet during the week. But Sunshine can get busy at weekends and public holidays; a 2005 reporter found queues of up to 30 minutes on 27 December and 'gave up at lunchtime'; and there were big queues for Goat's Eye when we were there in early April, though they moved quickly and using the singles line proved a good ploy.

Norquay's two main lifts give only 400m/1,300ft vertical, but both serve black slopes and the North American chair accesses a couple of double-diamond runs that justify their grading.

Heli-skiing is available from bases outside the National Park in British Columbia – roughly two hours' drive.

FOR INTERMEDIATES
Ideal runs
Half the runs on Sunshine are classified as intermediate. Wherever

Banff

SCHOOLS

**ClubSki and
ClubSnowboard**
t 760 7731

Classes
3 days guided tuition
of the three areas
(4½hr per day) C$241
incl. tax.

Private lessons
Half day (3hr) C$352,
incl. tax.

CHILDREN

**Tiny Tigers
(Sunshine)**
t 762 6563
Ages 19mnth to 6yr;
8.30-4.30

Kid's Place (Norquay)
t 760 7709
Ages 19mnth to 6yr;
9.00 to 4.00

Childcare Connection
t 760 4443
Childminding in guest
accommodation

Ski school
Takes ages 6 to 12 (3
days C$241, incl. tax
and lunch).

SUNSHINE VILLAGE

You can stay right at
the heart of the
Sunshine Village ski
area at the Sunshine
Inn (the main building
in this pic) ➔

WEBSITES

For links to resort
sites, go to our own
new site at
www.wtss.co.uk

MOUNTAIN RESTAURANTS
Quite good

Sunshine Village has a choice of eating
places at its mid-mountain base. The
Day Lodge offers three different styles
of food on three floors (table service in
the top-floor Lookout Bistro, with great
views). Mixed reports of the food but
the buffalo stew is recommended. Mad
Trapper's Saloon is a jolly western-
style place in Old Sunshine Lodge,
serving good beer and different food
on its two levels (shame about the
disposable plates though). The
Sunshine Inn hotel has the best food –
table-service snacks in the Chimney
Corner Lounge or a full lunch in the
Eagle's Nest dining room. At the
bottom of Goat's Eye Mountain there's
a temporary tent-like structure called
Goat's Eye Gardens; we've had mixed
reports of the food here.

At the base of Norquay, the big,
stylish, timber-framed Cascade Lodge
is excellent – it has great views and a
table-service restaurant upstairs as well
as a self-service cafeteria.

SCHOOLS AND GUIDES
Some great ideas

Both mountains have their own school.
But recognising that visitors wanting
lessons won't want to be confined to
just one mountain, the resorts have
organised an excellent Club Ski and
Club Snowboard Program – three-day
courses starting on Sundays and
Thursdays that take you to Sunshine,
Norquay and Lake Louise on different
days, offering a mixture of guiding and
instruction and including free video
analysis, a fun race and a group photo.
Reporters rave about it: 'absolutely
brilliant', 'a great way to meet other
people', 'improved more in three days
than in a week anywhere else'. All
abilities are catered for, including
beginners. One reporter recommends
booking a midweek group lesson:

'Normally only one or two people; I did
an excellent Black Diamond class.' We
also have a fat file full of praise for the
free mountain tours by friendly local
volunteer snow hosts.

FACILITIES FOR CHILDREN
Excellent

One reporter who used Sunshine,
Norquay and Lake Louise said: 'I'd
recommend all three.'

STAYING THERE

HOW TO GO
Superb-value packages

A huge amount of accommodation is
on offer – especially hotels and self-
catering, but also a few catered chalets.
Hotels Summer is the peak season
here. Prices are much lower in winter
(though seem to have been creeping
up in the last few years).
((((**Fairmont Banff Springs** (762 2211)
A late 19th-century, castle-style
property, well outside town. It's
virtually a town within itself – it can
sleep 2,000 people, has over 40
shops, several restaurants and bars, a
nightclub and a superb health club and
spa (which costs extra).
((((**Rimrock** (762 3356) Spectacularly
set, out of town, with great views and
a smart health club. Luxurious.
(((**Inns of Banff** (762 4581) About 20
minutes' walk from town, but good for
buses; praised by reporters for large
rooms, comfort, room service and
fitness facilities; 'very large' hot-tub.
(((**Banff Park Lodge** (762 4433) Best-
quality central hotel, with hot-tub,
steam room and indoor pool.
((**Banff Caribou Lodge** (762 5887) On
the main street, slightly out of town. A
variety of wood-clad, individually
designed rooms, sauna and hot-tub
and a good restaurant and bar.
Repeatedly recommended by reporters.
((**Timberline Inn** (762 2281) At foot

GETTING THERE

Air Calgary 122km/
76 miles (1½hr).

ACTIVITIES

Indoor Film theatre,
museums, galleries,
swimming pools (one
with water slides),
gym, squash,
racquetball, weight
training, bowling, hot-
tub, sauna, climbing
wall

Outdoor Swimming in
hot springs, ice rink,
sleigh rides, dog-sled
rides, snowmobiles,
curling, ice hockey,
ice fishing, helicopter
tours, snow-shoeing

Phone numbers
From distant parts of
Canada, add the
prefix 1 403.
From abroad, add the
prefix +1 403.

TOURIST OFFICE

Banff
t 762 4561
info@SkiBig3.com
www.SkiBig3.com

of Norquay and reachable on skis.
Comfortable, good views, hot-tub.
Recently renovated and expanded.
② **Banff King Edward** (762 2202)
Right in the town centre, set above
shops; large rooms and surprisingly
quiet for its position.
② **Banff International** (762 5666)
'Central, saving walking in the
evenings. Excellent, can't fault it,' says
a 2005 reporter.
① **Homestead** (762 4471) Central,
cheap, good-sized rooms, approved of
by two 2005 reporters.
Self-catering Don't expect the choice or
luxury you find in many North
American resorts. But there are some
decent options. The Banff Rocky
Mountain Resort is set in the woods
on the edge of town, with indoor pool,
squash and hot-tubs. Reporters have
also recommended the Douglas Fir
resort for families – though it's 'a bit
out of town'.

EATING OUT
Lots of choice
Banff boasts over 100 restaurants, from
McDonald's to fine dining in the
Fairmont Banff Springs hotel. Many get
crowded and don't take bookings.
Reader recommendations include Earl's
(burgers and ethnic dishes, very
popular and lively), Magpie & Stump
(Mexican, with Wild West decor and
'jars' of ale), Giorgio's (Italian),
Caramba in the Banff Ptarmigan Inn
(Mediterranean, 'well worth the
money'), the Keg ('quality steaks'),
Seoul Country (Korean), Wild Bill's
('the biggest and best burgers in
town', dancing and live entertainment),
Melissa's ('good steaks', 'excellent
choice of beers'), Caboose at the train
station ('best steak', 'superb crab'),
Bumpers ('big slabs of rib'), Grizzly

House ('fondues and fun', 'great
selection of meats'), the Old Spaghetti
Factory ('great for families'), the Maple
Leaf ('best meal I had in Banff'), and
Tommy's Neighbourhood Pub ('very
informal atmosphere and good food in
generous portions'). Sunday brunch at
the Banff Springs hotel is highly
recommended by one reporter.
Designer-cool Saltlik does good game,
steak and fish.

APRES-SKI
Livens up later on
One of the drawbacks of the area is
that tea-time après-ski is limited
because the resort is a drive from the
slopes. But Mad Trapper's Saloon at
the top of the Sunshine gondola is
popular during the close of play happy
hour (with endless free peanuts). They
also do evenings with tobogganing, a
buffet, live music and dancing, followed
by a gondola ride down. In town later,
Wild Bill's has live country and western
music and line dancing. The Rose &
Crown has live music and gets crowded.
The Barbary Coast nightclub is popular.
And Outabounds attracts a young lively
crowd, while Aurora is for more serious
clubbing. The St James Gate Irish pub
has 'great atmosphere, good-value
food and a wide range of beers'.
Melissa's and Saltlik are popular.

OFF THE SLOPES
Lots to do
For those who do not intend to hit the
slopes, Banff has lots to offer: plenty
of wildlife to see, lovely walks (including
ice canyon walks), and you can go
snow-shoeing, dog-sledding, skating
and snowmobiling. There are
'excellent' sightseeing tours, several
interesting museums to visit and
natural hot springs to try although one
reporter said they were a let-down
('you are limited to 20 minutes in a
pool, and it is just that, a pool').
Reporters have enjoyed evenings in
Calgary watching the Flames play ice
hockey ('sit back and enjoy the fights').

STAYING UP THE MOUNTAIN
Worth considering
We loved spending a night on the
slopes of Sunshine Village at the
Sunshine Inn (762 6550), which is at
the later stages of a complete revamp.
Luggage is transported for you in the
gondola while you hit the slopes.
Rooms vary in size. Big outdoor hot-
pool. Sauna. Good restaurant.

Banff

Big White

Big by local standards, white by any standard

COSTS

① ② ③ ④ ⑤ ⑥

RATINGS

The slopes

Fast lifts	***
Snow	*****
Extent	***
Expert	***
Intermediate	****
Beginner	****
Convenience	****
Queues	*****
Mountain restaurants	*

The rest

Scenery	***
Resort charm	**
Off-slope	**

KEY FACTS

Resort	1755m
	5,760ft
Slopes	1510-2320m
	4,950-7,610ft
Lifts	15
Pistes	2,765 acres
Green	18%
Blue	56%
Black	26%
Snowmaking	
	In terrain-park

NEWS

For 2004/05 a two-person chair-lift opened to serve the steep Cliff area, so you don't have to go to the bottom after each run.

A new terrain-park was built above the village, served by a new two-person chair and by Big White's first snowmaking. It includes a half-pipe, super-pipe, boarder-cross and expert and intermediate rail parks and is floodlit at night.

Six new intermediate runs that were due to open in the Gem Lake area for 2004/05 will now open for 2005/06.

634

+ Great for learning to ski powder

+ Extensive, varied slopes, quiet except at weekends and holidays

+ Convenient, purpose-built village with high-quality, good-value condos

+ Very friendly staff; good for families

– Visibility can be poor, especially on the upper mountain, because of snow, cloud or freezing fog

– Few off-slope diversions – and isolated without a car

– Limited après-ski

'It's the snow' says the Big White slogan. And as slogans go, it's spot on. If you want a good chance of skiing powder on reasonably easy slopes, put Big White high on the shortlist. The locals call it 'Big White Out' because the mountain often has a cloud sitting on it while the plains around are bathed in sunshine. So if you want a sun tan (or lively après-ski, or extensive steep bowls and chutes) look elsewhere. If you're an intermediate looking to learn powder and try gladed skiing for the first time, there can be few better places. Consider combining it with another BC resort such as Sun Peaks or Silver Star for variety.

THE RESORT

Big White is a modern, rapidly growing, purpose-built resort 45 minutes from Kelowna airport. The village is rather piecemeal but attractive in wood and stone and much of the accommodation is ski-in/ski-out. Reporters remark on the large number of 'very friendly and happy' Aussie workers. Silver Star resort is under the same ownership and there are weekly day trips by bus.

THE MOUNTAINS

Much of the terrain is heavily wooded. But the trees thin out towards the summits, leading to almost open slopes in the bowls at the top. There's at least one green option from the top of each lift but the one from Gem Lake is narrow and can be tricky and busy.

Slopes Fast chairs run from points below village level to above mid-mountain, serving the main area of wooded beginner and intermediate runs above and beside the village. Slower lifts – a T-bar and four chairs – serve the higher slopes. Quite some way across the mountainside is the Gem Lake fast chair, serving a range of long top-to-bottom runs; with its 710m/2,330ft vertical, this lift is in a different league from the others. 'Snow Hosts' (highly praised by reporters) run twice-daily guided ski tours.

Terrain-parks See News for details of the new park, praised by a 2005 reporter.

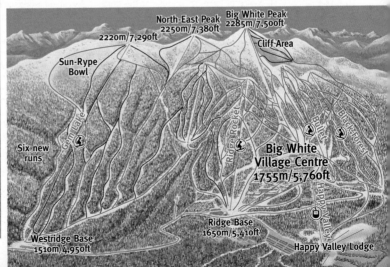

Central reservations
Call 765 8888; toll-free (within Canada) 1 800 663 1772.
Phone numbers
From distant parts of Canada, add the prefix 1 250. From abroad, add +1 250.

TOURIST OFFICE

t 765 3101
bigwhite@bigwhite.com
www.bigwhite.com

Snow reliability Big White has a reputation for great powder; average snowfall is about 300 inches, which is similar to many Colorado resorts. The top of the mountain can suffer from freezing fog, which means the top trees usually stay white all winter; they are known as snow-ghosts and make visibility tricky in a white-out (but are great fun to ski between on clear days).
Experts The Cliff area at the top right of the ski area is of serious double-black pitch; the runs are short but you can ski them repeatedly using the new Cliff chair. The Sun-Rype bowl at the opposite edge of the ski area is more forgiving. There are some long blacks off the Gem Lake chair and several shorter ones off the Powder and Falcon chairs. There are glades to explore and bump runs too.
Intermediates The resort is excellent for cruisers and families, with long blues and greens all over the hill. Good intermediates will enjoy the easier black runs too. In general the runs get steeper from right to left as you look at the mountain. The Black Forest area has some marvellous easy skiing among the trees, while some of the blues off the Gem Lake chair are quite steep, narrow and challenging.
Beginners There's a good dedicated nursery area in the village and lots of long easy runs to progress to.
Snowboarding There's some excellent beginner and free-riding terrain with boarder friendly lifts and few flat areas.
Cross-country Trails total 25km/16 miles.
Queues Queues are pretty rare (except at peak holiday periods when snow elsewhere is poor; '10 to 15 min waits').
Mountain restaurants There aren't any – it's back to the bottom for lunch.
School and guides We receive rave reviews from reporters for both adult and children's lessons.
Facilities for children The excellent Kids' Centre takes children from 18 months. Evening activities are organised.

STAYING THERE

How to go There's an increasing range of packages to Big White.
Hotels The White Crystal Inn was recommended over the Inn at Big White by a recent reporter.
Self-catering Standards are high. We stayed at the Stonebridge condos in 2004 and loved them – big, central, well-furnished, private hot-tub on the balcony. The limited grocery shopping should improve when the grocery store is doubled in size for 2005/06.
Eating out We had good meals in the Copper Kettle in the White Crystal Inn and the Kettle Valley Steakhouse at Happy Valley ('flights' of four different glasses of local wines to try). Reporters also recommend Snowshoe Sam's, Powder Keg, Swiss Bear in the Chateau Big White and Frank's Chinese Laundry.
Après-ski The atmospheric Snowshoe Sam's has a DJ, live entertainment and dancing. Raakel's in the Hopfbrauhaus has live music and dancing.
Off the slopes Happy Valley has ice skating, snowmobiling and snow-shoeing. There are two health spas.

Big White

635

Fernie

Lots of snow and lots of steeps – best with a guide

NEWS

For 2004/05 better access from Currie Bowl to the fast Great Bear chair was introduced, cutting out the need to ski all the way back to the slow Elk chair to change areas (the route is not signposted though, in typical Fernie fashion, and one of our best reporters had to ask a ski patroller the way).

The resort tells us that more glading to thin out the trees and bushes has been done in the last two summers. And the Griz Bar was fitted with a new deck (sponsored by Kokanee) for 2004/05.

➕ Good snow record, with less chance of rain than at Whistler (and less chance of Arctic temperatures than at resorts up in the Rockies)

➕ Great terrain for those who like it steep and deep, with lots for confident intermediates too

➕ Snowcat operations nearby

➕ Some good on-slope accommodation available, but ...

➖ Mountain resort is very limited

➖ Still too many slow, old lifts

➖ After a dump it can take time to make the bowls safe

➖ Little groomed cruising for timid or average intermediates

➖ Poor trail map and on-mountain signposting

➖ No decent mountain restaurants

Fernie has long had cult status among Alberta and British Columbia skiers for its steep gladed slopes and superb natural snow. In the last few years there has been a lot of investment in the development of the village at the foot of the slopes – though it remains small, without many facilities. Some visitors would rather see more investment in the mountain, to replace slow old lifts, cut down hiking and traversing and to hasten reopening after a serious snowfall. We see their point, but most reports we get are dominated by excitement at Fernie's combination of snow and terrain – 'just like Jackson Hole' and 'the hiking and traversing isn't that bad; Fernie's not for expert wimps', to quote two reporters. You'll enjoy Fernie most if you are a good skier or rider wanting adventure.

THE RESORT

Fernie Alpine Resort is set at the lift base a little way up the mountainside from the flat Elk Valley floor and a couple of miles from the little town of Fernie. It has grown from very little in the past few years, but there's still not much there except convenient lodging and a few restaurants, bars and small shops. It is quiet at night.

The town of Fernie is named after William Fernie – a prospector who discovered coal here and triggered a boom in the early 1900s. Much of the town was destroyed by fire in 1908 but some buildings survived. It is primarily a town for locals, not tourists. There are some lively bars, decent places to eat and good outdoor shops. It is down to earth rather than charming and reporters' reactions to it vary: 'I liked the way it felt like real Canada and enjoyed staying in a town with some history,' said one; 'The flipside of being a real town is having a real highway run through it,' said another. Most stress the friendliness of the locals, though a 2005 visitor complained about poor service and being ignored by seasonnaires working in the hire shops and at the Day Lodge.

There are buses between the town and the mountain, which run at half-hourly intervals at peak times and cost C$3 one way (they are free in the evenings and run every half an hour until 2am). Each hotel has specific pick-up times although we have a report that the service is unreliable.

Outings to Kimberley are possible; a coach does the trip every Thursday – the drive takes about 90 minutes. (there's also a helicopter option).

THE MOUNTAINS

Fernie's 2,500 acres pack in a lot of variety, from superb green terrain at the bottom to ungroomed chutes (that will be satisfyingly steep to anyone but the extreme specialist) and huge numbers of steep runs in the trees. A lot of the runs have the rare quality of consistently steep pure fall lines.

THE SLOPES
Bowl after bowl

What you see when you arrive at the lift base is a trio of impressive mogul slopes towering above you. The slow Deer chair approaches the foot of these slopes, but goes no further. You get to them by traversing and hiking

KEY FACTS

Resort	1065m
	3,490ft
Slopes	1065-1925m
	3,490-6,320ft
Lifts	10
Pistes	2,504 acres
Green	30%
Blue	40%
Black	30%
Snowmaking	
	125 acres

Bowl) and it takes quite a while to get back for another go.

There are free tours of the area in groups of different abilities for two hours twice a day, but the hosts can only take you on blue and green runs. For the steeper, deeper stuff you need to hire a guide or join the Steep and Deep tours. Using these services to get your bearings is a good idea. Going with someone who knows the area makes it hugely more enjoyable. We found both signs and trail map dangerously inadequate – see feature panel later in this chapter.

TERRAIN-PARKS
Two to choose from
There's a good half-pipe at the bottom of the mountain, served by the Deer chair, and a terrain-park on the Falling Star trail near the top of the Timber Chair in Siberia Bowl, with berms jumps, rollers, table top, large hip and box and curved rails and boarder-cross features. There are also two kids' rails.

SNOW RELIABILITY
A key part of the appeal
Fernie has an excellent snow record – with an average of 350 inches per year, better than practically all of Colorado. But the altitude is modest – rain is not unknown, and in warmer weather the lower slopes can suffer. Snowmaking has increased in recent years, and now covers most of the base area. Reporters found piste maintenance poor last season, which was a particularly bad one snow-wise for the resort. In earlier years reporters said that, while some runs were well groomed after a snowfall, some blue runs were never groomed at all.

FOR EXPERTS
Wonderful – deep and steep
The combination of heavy snowfalls and abundant steep terrain with the shelter of trees makes this a superb mountain for good skiers. There are

from the main Lizard Bowl, on the right, or you can take a high traverse from Currie Bowl, skirting the boundary. Lizard Bowl is a broad snowfield reached by a series of lifts: the slow Elk quad (which reporters continue to complain about stopping frequently, as they do the Deer chair); the fast Great Bear quad; and finally the short Face Lift, a dreadful rope tow which has been somewhat improved by adding buttons to the handles on the rope. It often doesn't run, because of either too little or too much snow. This is also the main way into Cedar Bowl and to Snake Ridge beyond it. The only lift here is the Haul Back T-bar, which brings you out. You can still traverse into the lower parts of both Lizard and Cedar Bowls when the Face Lift isn't working. There is a mini-bowl between them, served by the Boomerang chair.

The Timber Bowl fast quad chair gives access to Siberia Bowl and the lower part of Timber. But for access to the higher slopes and to Currie Bowl you must take the White Pass quad. A long traverse from the top gets you to the steeper slopes on the flanks of Currie (our favourite area). From there you have to go right to the bottom (unless you head over into Lizard

Fernie

637

boarding

Fernie is a fine place for good boarders (and there are a lot of local experts here). Lots of natural gullies, hits and endless off-piste opportunities – including some adrenalin-pumping tree-runs and knee-deep powder bowls – will keep free-riders of all abilities grinning from ear to ear. And, as one reader commented, 'The only flat sections are at the base and coming out of Falling Star.' The main board shops, Board Stiff and Edge of the World, are in downtown Fernie, the latter with an internet connection and an indoor skate park to use while your board gets tuned. But beginners and faint-hearted intermediates should stay away.

WESTERN CANADA

638

LIFT PASSES

Fernie

Beginners
T-bar only, C$20 a day

Main pass
1 day C$64.20
6 days C$372

Senior citizens
Over 65: 6 days C$295

Children
Under 18: 6 days C$257
Under 13: 6 days C$128
Under 6: free pass

Notes
Prices include taxes. Half-day pass available from 12.30.

about a dozen identifiable faces offering genuine black or double-black slopes, each of them with several alternative ways down. Currie and Timber Bowls both have some serious double-diamonds but mainly have single-diamonds. However, as one of our regular reporters says, 'Most of the single blacks are tough. With some I don't see how you could get anything harder without falling off the mountain ... just like Jackson Hole but without the cliffs.' Even where the trail map shows trees to be sparse, expect them to be close together, and where there aren't any, expect alder bushes unless there's lots of snow. And see our warning in the feature panel below about the trail map and signposting.

There are backcountry routes you can take with guidance (some include an overnight camp) and snowcat operations in other nearby mountains – see feature panel opposite. A regular reporter especially enjoyed exploring Fish Bowl last season, a short hike outside the resort boundary.

FOR INTERMEDIATES
Far from ideal
Although there are intermediate runs both low down and high up, they don't add up to a lot of mileage. Most high runs are not groomed, and one reporter said, 'The blues in all bowls except Timber would be black in most resorts.' Adventurous, strong intermediates willing to give the ungroomed terrain a try will enjoy the area. But if you want miles of groomed cruising, go elsewhere.

FOR BEGINNERS
Excellent
There's a good nursery area served by two lifts (a moving carpet and a drag) and the lower mountain served by the Deer and Elk chairs has lots of wide, smooth trails to gain confidence on. But the green runs from the top of the mountain are usually cat-tracks, which nonetheless have tough parts to them.

FOR CROSS-COUNTRY
Some possibilities
There are 14km/9 miles of trails marked out in the forest adjacent to the resort, and the Fernie golf and country club allows enthusiasts on to their white fairways.

QUEUES
Not usually a problem
Unless there are weekend crowds from Calgary, or heavy snow keeps part of the mountain closed, queues are rare. The slopes are delightfully quiet too. But people do complain about the slow chair-lifts.

THE TRAIL MAP AND ON-MOUNTAIN SIGNPOSTING

We have complained about many poor trail maps and resorts with inadequate on-mountain signposting over the years. But we have rarely come across such a dangerous combination of the two as you get at Fernie. Runs marked on the map just aren't clearly marked on the mountain, especially some of the steeper runs through the trees. For example, when we tried to find the long black Diamond Back run from the top of the White Pass quad, we failed and ended up in tight trees on a slope of triple-diamond steepness – scary. Comments from reporters include: 'You can often find yourself on unexpected terrain, which is fine if you are a competent skier and can handle most things, otherwise it could lead to some unpleasant situations,' 'This is an issue the resort needs to address, especially for timid intermediates, who are going to have a hard time there anyway,' and 'I find the mountain signposting more of a problem than the map.' As one past reporter said, 'It's great to go out with someone who knows where they're going, and to make the most of the area you've almost got to stop worrying about following what's on the map.'

Fine, as long as you know where you are going and how steep the terrain will be. Others would prefer a more helpful map and on-mountain directions.

RIDE THE SNOWCATS – HELI-SKIING AT AN AFFORDABLE PRICE

Good skiers who relish off-piste should consider treating themselves to some cat skiing; there are several operations in this area. Island Lake Lodge (423 3700) does three- or four-day all-inclusive packages in a cosy chalet 10km/6 miles from Fernie, amid 7,000 acres of spectacular bowls and ridges. It has 36 beds, and four snowcats to act as lifts. In a day you might do eight powder runs averaging 500m/1,640ft vertical, taking in all kinds of terrain from gentle open slopes to some very Alpine adventures. We've heard they can be booked solid up to three years in advance. You can do single days without accommodation, but only on a standby basis; we managed this once and loved it, but our second attempt failed. A 2005 reporter praised another operation, Powder Cowboy (422 8754), owned by the people who run Island Lake Lodge. It has two snowcats accessing 6,000 acres 60km/37 miles from Fernie. 'Despite terrible snow at Fernie, they managed to find freshies and made the best of otherwise challenging conditions. It was an awesome day.' We've had mixed reports of Fernie Wilderness Adventures (423 6704); one reader said it was 'excellent'; another 'had a great day' despite mismatched abilities in their group 'leading to frustration all round'; yet another said, 'It's billed as intermediate level but it's not – there's a lot of tree skiing, some steep and tight, and we were always skiing in a big crowd.'

SCHOOLS

Fernie
t 423 4655

Classes
Half day C$58 (incl. taxes)

Private lessons
C$234 (incl. taxes) for 2hr for up to 3 people

CHILDREN

Day care centre
t 423 2430
Newborn to age 6; 8.30 to 4.30; ski lessons available for ages 3 and 4

Ski school
For ages 5 to 12 (C$79, incl. taxes, per day)

MOUNTAIN RESTAURANTS
What mountain restaurants?
Bear's Den at the top of the Elk chair is an open-air fast-food kiosk, not a mountain restaurant, so it's back to base for lunch. The ancient Day Lodge is grim, busy but cheap and serves good soups and sandwiches.

SCHOOLS AND GUIDES
Highly praised
Reporters praise the school. A couple who booked a group snowboarding lesson said, 'There were only the two of us, both novices, and within minutes we were grinning like loons and linking turns.' Of their daughter's class they said, 'Every instructor she had was very friendly and competent and sometimes she was the only one in the group.' Another reporter loved the beer, snacks and video session that you get if you book a ski week. We've also had good reports of the Steep and Deep camps and private lessons. 'First Tracks' gets you up the mountain at 7.45am for two hours, but when we tried it the instructor didn't know which lifts were open and there was a lot of wasted time.

FACILITIES FOR CHILDREN
Good day care centre
There's a day care centre in the Cornerstone Lodge, which a reporter found 'very well run'. There are also 'Kids' Activity Nights' for children aged six to twelve.

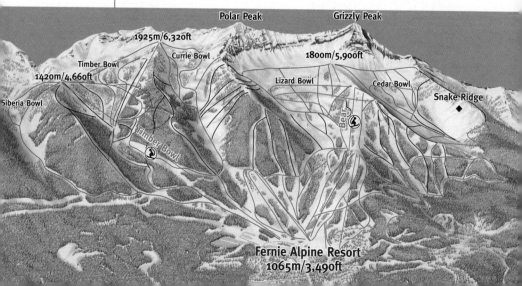

Polar Peak · Grizzly Peak · 1925m/6,320ft · Currie Bowl · Timber Bowl · 1800m/5,900ft · 1420m/4,66oft · Lizard Bowl · Cedar Bowl · Siberia Bowl · Snake Ridge · Timber Bowl · Bear

Fernie Alpine Resort
1065m/3,49oft

GETTING THERE

Air Calgary
322km/200 miles
(3½hr).

ACTIVITIES

Indoor Museum,
galleries, aquatic
centre, saunas,
bowling, fitness
centre, ice skating,
cinema, curling

Outdoor Sleigh rides,
snowmobiling, dog-
sledding, helicopter
rides, snow-shoe
excursions, ice fishing

WEBSITES

For links to resort
sites, go to our own
new site at
www.wtss.co.uk

**Central reservations
phone number**
For all resort
accommodation call
1 800 258 7669
(toll-free from within
Canada).

Phone numbers
From distant parts of
Canada, add the
prefix 1 250.
From abroad, add the
prefix +1 250.

TOURIST OFFICE

t 423 4655
info@skifernie.com
www.skifernie.com

STAYING THERE

HOW TO GO
More packages
Fernie is increasingly easy to find in
tour operator brochures. Unless stated,
accommodation listed is at the resort.
Chalets Some UK tour operators run
chalets. Beavertail Lodge is run along
chalet lines and has received several
rave reviews from reporters: 'The best
chalet I have ever stayed in, with food
equal to a Michelin-starred restaurant.'
Canadian Powder Tours has a chalet
and includes in the price guiding by
the owners, who know the mountain
well: 'Food was excellent. I am a novice
off-piste skier but had a brilliant time.'
Hotels and condos There's a wide
choice, some impressively comfortable.
(((4) **Lizard Creek Lodge** Luxury ski-in,
ski-out condo hotel. Spa, outdoor pool
and hot-tub. We loved it and a 2005
reporter gives it '10 out of 10'.
(((3) **Cornerstone Lodge** Condo hotel.
(((3) **Best Western Fernie Mountain
Lodge** Next to golf course near town.
Recommended by reporters. Pool, hot-
tub, fitness room.
(((3) **Griz Inn Sport Hotel** Condo-hotel
with good facilities. Pool.
((2) **Wolf's Den Mountain Lodge** 'Simple
but comfortable,' say reporters. Indoor
hot-tub, small gym. At base of slope.
((2) **Timberline Lodges** Very comfortable
condos a shuttle-ride from the lifts.
((2) **Cedar Lodge Motel** on road to
town. 'Comfortable and clean, but not
very welcoming,' said reporters.
((2) **Alpine Lodge** B&B recommended
by a reporter.

EATING OUT
Steadily improving
At the base, the Lizard Creek Lodge is
expensive but serves gourmet food (in
small portions). Reporters highly praise
the food at Beavertail Lodge (which
takes outsiders if it's not full): 'worth a

Michelin star' and 'superb food
including wild mushroom soup, parfait
de foie gras, duck confit.' The Wood in
the Hill is recommended although 'it's
on the pricey side for Fernie and there
is limited choice'. We've had very
mixed reports on Kelsey's (part of a
chain). Gabriella's does cheap and
cheerful Italian, and lots of readers
have enjoyed it. The Slope Side Coffee
and Deli in the Cornerstone Lodge has
been recommended.

In Fernie, there are quite a few
options. Reader recommendations
include the Old Elevator (a converted
grain store with 'good grills and pasta'),
Jamochas (a coffee house that does
meals), the Curry Bowl (various Asian
styles), the Royal hotel (Australian
cuisine), Rip'n Richard's Eatery (south-
western food and a lively atmosphere),
the Corner Pocket in the Grand Central
Hotel ('good atmosphere, wide range
of dishes'), Yamagoya ('good sushi')
and Tres Hermanas ('good Tex Mex').

APRES-SKI
Have a beer
The Griz bar has been improved with a
new sun deck and is quite lively when
the lifts close – sometimes with live
bands. During the week, the bars are
pretty quiet later on. In town, the bars
of the Royal hotel are popular with
locals. Other recommendations are the
Park Place Lodge Pub, the bar in the
Grand Central hotel and the Eldorado
Lounge which sometimes has live
bands for later on.

The resort offers BBQ at Bear's Den
twice a week, with a torchlit descent.

OFF THE SLOPES
Get out and about
There is a heritage walking tour of
historic Fernie and the old railroad
station is now the Art Station. You
could take in an ice-hockey game. But
the main diversion is the great outdoors.

Kicking Horse

Powdery adventure high above a fledgling resort village

COSTS

① ② ③ ④ ⑤ ⑥

RATINGS

The slopes
Fast lifts	**
Snow	****
Extent	***
Expert	****
Intermediate	***
Beginner	***
Convenience	*
Queues	*****
Mountain restaurants	**

The rest
Scenery	***
Resort charm	*
Off-slope	*

+ Great terrain for experts and some for adventurous intermediates

+ Big vertical served by a fast lift

+ Splendid mountain-top restaurant

− Resort village still in early stages

− Gondola has no mid-station, so you may have to ski crud lower down

− Few groomed intermediate runs

In 2000/01, a tiny local hill with lifts only on the lower slopes was transformed by a new gondola rising 1150m/3,770ft to the top of high, powdery bowls and chutes. In 2002 came a new quad chair-lift (slow, sadly) serving more high slopes. Now a few lodges have opened to form the first stage of a mountain village at the lift base. The resort suits experts best and makes a good day trip from Banff or Lake Louise for them and adventurous intermediates. But it's a shame there's no gondola mid-station so that you could ski the top half repeatedly without depending on less reliably good snow below.

THE RESORT

Eight miles from the small logging town of Golden, Kicking Horse is in the early stages of development and the first phase of a real resort village was in place last season: three attractive lodges, a couple of restaurants and a ski shop. More lodging and restaurants are planned for 2005/06 and the idea is for the resort to be complete by 2010. Daily round-trip buses run from Banff and Lake Louise – in 2005, they cost C$82 including a lift pass.

Golden is a spread-out place beside the transcontinental highway. It has no real charm or centre – we'd prefer to stay at the mountain.

THE MOUNTAINS

The lower two-thirds of the hill are wooded, with trails cut in the usual style. The upper third is a mix of open and lightly wooded slopes. There's a (securely fenced) grizzly bear sanctuary right by a blue run at mid-mountain.
Slopes The only way up to the top part of the mountain is by the eight-seat gondola to Eagle's Eye. Despite the serious vertical of 1150m/3,770ft, this lift goes up in a single stage. The lack of a mid-station is a real drawback: unless you ride the slow chair to the slightly higher peak of Blue Heaven all the time, you have to make the full descent (and the snow conditions on the lower slopes may be poor). As well as the marked runs, there are literally hundreds of ways down through the bowls, chutes and trees. Two chair-lifts from near the base serve the lower runs that formed the original ski area.
Terrain-park There isn't one.
Snow reliability It gets an average of 275 inches of snow a year; not enough to put it in the very top flight, but not far off. The top part of the mountain usually has light, dry powder; the lower part may have crud and thin cover.
Experts It's advanced skiers and riders who will get the most out of the area.

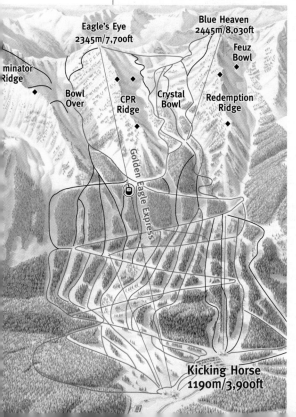

Eagle's Eye
2345m/7,700ft

Blue Heaven
2445m/8,030ft

Feuz Bowl

...minator Ridge

Bowl Over

CPR Ridge

Crystal Bowl

Redemption Ridge

Golden Eagle Express

Kicking Horse
1190m/3,900ft

↑ The base lodge in front of Glacier Lodge, the first condo-hotel

KICKING HORSE RESORT

NEWS

By 2005/06 there should be three small, friendly B&Bs (where we'd choose to stay) and two bigger condo-hotels as well as self-catering lodging – see 'Staying there'. But there are still very few bars and restaurants, and you should expect very quiet evenings.

KEY FACTS

Resort	1190m
	3,900ft
Slopes	1190-2445m
	3,900-8,030ft
Lifts	5
Pistes	2,750 acres
Green	20%
Blue	20%
Black	60%
Snowmaking	None

Central reservations phone number
For resort accommodation call
1 250 439 5400 (toll-free from within Canada).

Phone numbers
From distant parts of Canada, add the prefix 1 250.
From abroad, add the prefix +1 250.

TOURIST OFFICE

t 439 5400
guestservices@kicking horseresort.com
www.kickinghorse resort.com

From CPR ridge, drop off to skier's right through trees or to skier's left through chutes – there are endless options. If it's open you can also hike to Terminator Ridge (often closed due to avalanche danger). The chair to Blue Heaven opens up easier ski-anywhere terrain down into Crystal Bowl. From the top you can also drop down into the steeper but wonderfully wide Feuz Bowl. The lower half of the mountain has fine black runs on cleared trails, some with serious moguls.

Intermediates Adventurous intermediates will have a fine time learning to play in the powder from Blue Heaven down to Crystal Bowl. Most of it is open but you can head off into trees if you want to. The resort is planning to increase its groomed terrain but up till now there has been very little. The only easy, groomed way down the mountain has been a 10km/6 mile winding road called It's a Ten. Piste-bashers and timid intermediates should go elsewhere.

Beginners We can't imagine why a UK-based beginner would come here.

Snowboarding Free-riders will love this powder paradise.

Cross-country There are 12km/7 miles of trails at Dawn Mountain and a 5km/3 mile loop on the golf course.

Queues None of our reporters have experienced any large queues.

Mountain restaurants The Eagle's Eye table-service restaurant at the top of the gondola serves excellent food in stylish log-cabin surroundings and has splendid views. The base lodge is also smartly built with logs and beams and has a small self-service restaurant. A yurt (tent) in Crystal Bowl serves snacks.

Schools and guides Two reporters booked group lessons and each was the only pupil. 'Excellent', they both said. Another joined a free mountain tour and again was the only one. Yet another took an avalanche safety course that 'was worth every penny; a truly memorable day'.

Facilities for children The school teaches children from the age of three.

STAYING THERE

How to go Try the new lodges or condos at the slopes.

Hotels We were very impressed with the 10-room log-built Vagabond Lodge B&B, personally run by the owners. Huge open-plan living room with log fire, rooms with delightfully comfortable-looking beds and nice bathrooms. Steam room and outdoor hot-tub. Copper Horse Lodge next door has bigger rooms, more modern ambiance (leather bedheads, satellite TV in rooms), outdoor hot-tub. The 10-room Highland Lodge is due to open for 2005/06 to include a Scottish Pub (one of the owners is Scottish). The 56-room Glacier Lodge is much less personal than the B&Bs but looked comfortable. The 51-unit Mountaineer Lodge is due to open for 2005/06.

Self-catering The Whispering Pines town homes were 'the most luxurious ski lodgings we've had' said a reporter.

Eating out Options are very limited at the mountain. Corks in the Copper Horse Lodge does 'mountain bistro dining' and takeaway dishes. Kuma is a sushi bar that closed at 7pm last season. Eagle's Eye at the top of the gondola opens some nights and is well worth a visit. A big new restaurant is due to open in Glacier Lodge for 2005/06. In Golden, we enjoyed the cosy Sisters and Beans (pasta, steaks, Asian); the Kicking Horse Grill and the out-of-town Cedar House Cafe are highly rated.

Après-ski Not much at the mountain. The Mad Trapper is the main drinking spot in Golden – a lively pub.

Off the slopes There is snowmobiling, snow-shoeing, ice-climbing and dog-sledding.

Lake Louise

Knockout views from Canada's second-biggest mountain

643

COSTS

① ② ③ ④ ⑤ ⑥

RATINGS

The slopes

Fast lifts	★★★
Snow	★★★
Extent	★★★★
Expert	★★★★
Intermediate	★★★★
Beginner	★★★
Convenience	★
Queues	★★★★
Mountain restaurants	★★

The rest

Scenery	★★★★★
Resort charm	★★★
Off-slope	★★★★

➕ Spectacular high-mountain scenery – the best of any North American resort

➕ Slopes are the largest in the Canadian Rockies

➕ Snowy slopes of Sunshine Village within reach (see Banff chapter)

➕ Lots of wildlife around the valley

➕ Good value for money

➖ Local slopes are a short drive away from the 'village', Banff areas further

➖ Snowfall modest by local standards

➖ Can be very cold and the chair-lifts have no covers, but new gondola should be warmer

➖ 'Village' is just a few hotels and shops, fairly quiet in the evening

➖ Slopes can seem full of Brits

If you care more for scenery than for après-ski action, Lake Louise is worth considering for a holiday. We've seen a few spectacular mountain views, and the view from the Fairmont Chateau Lake Louise hotel of the frozen lake and the Victoria Glacier behind it is as spectacular as they come; it is simply stunning.

Even if you prefer the more animated base of Banff, you'll want to make expeditions to Lake Louise during your holiday. It can't compete with Sunshine Village for quantity of snow, but it's a big and interesting mountain. And from the slopes you get a distant version of that view.

THE RESORT

SNOWPIX.COM / CHRIS GILL

The Lake Louise area has the most spectacular high-mountain scenery of any North American ski resort ↓

Although it's a small place, Lake Louise is a resort of parts. First, there's the lake itself, in a spectacular setting beneath the Victoria Glacier. Tom Wilson, who discovered it in 1882, declared, 'As God is my judge, I never in all my exploration have seen such a matchless scene.' Neither have we. And it can be appreciated from many of the rooms of the vast Fairmont Chateau Lake Louise hotel on the shore. Then there's Lake Louise 'village' – a collection of a few hotels, condos,

petrol station, liquor store and shops, a couple of miles away on a road junction. Finally, a mile or two across the valley is the lift base station. A car helps, especially in cold weather. Buses to the Lake Louise ski area run every half hour, but a lot less frequently to the Banff areas of Sunshine and Norquay. Bus trips to the more distant resorts of Panorama and Kicking Horse and the small resorts of Nakiska and Fortress are possible. Day-trip heli-skiing can also be arranged. Banff Airporter do transfers from and to Calgary airport.

NEWS

For 2004/05 the fast Friendly Giant quad and slow Eagle chair were replaced by the ski area's first gondola, the six-seat Grizzly Express, which takes you from the base to an access point for the Ptarmigan area of the Back Bowls as well as runs on the Front Side.

There are longer-term plans to build a new mountain restaurant close to the top of this new gondola.

KEY FACTS

Resort	1645m
	5,400ft

Sunshine, Norquay and Lake Louise, covered by the Tri-area pass	
Slopes	1630-2730m
	5,350-8,950ft
Lifts	29
Pistes	7,748 acres
Green	23%
Blue	39%
Black	38%
Snowmaking	
	1,900 acres

Lake Louise only	
Slopes	1645-2635m
	5,400-8,650ft
Lifts	12
Pistes	4,200 acres
Green	25%
Blue	45%
Black	30%
Snowmaking	40%

THE MOUNTAINS

The Lake Louise ski area is big, with a mixture of high open slopes, low trails cut through forest and gladed slopes between the two. Reporters are usually full of praise for the free guided tours given by volunteer 'Ski Friends'. There has been some criticism of inconsistent piste grading and lots about cold lifts with no covers.

THE SLOPES
A wide variety

From the base area you have a choice of a fast quad to mid-mountain, followed by a six-pack to the top centre of the **Front Side** (also called the South Face), or the new gondola direct to a slightly lower point on the right side of the Front Side. From both places, as elsewhere, there's a choice of green, blue or black runs (good for a group of mixed abilities who want to keep meeting up). In poor visibility, the gondola is a better option as the tree line goes almost to the top there. Or stay on the lower part of the mountain using the chairs. From mid-mountain on the left, the long Summit drag-lift takes you to the high-point of the area, at the shoulder of Mount Whitehorn – there's a stunning view of peaks and glaciers including Canada's Matterhorn lookalike, Mount Assiniboine.

From here or the top chair you can go over the ridge and into Lake Louise's almost treeless **Back Bowls** – open, predominantly north-facing and mainly steep. From the top of the gondola, the Ptarmigan area of the Back Bowls is more wooded.

From low down in the bowls you can take the Paradise lift back to the top again or continue lower to the separate **Larch** area, served by a fast quad chair. With a lift-served vertical of 375m/1,230ft it's not huge, but it has pretty wooded runs of all grades. From the bottom you can return to the top of the main mountain via the Ptarmigan chair or take a long green path back to the main base area.

Lake Louise is a great mountain for free-riders, with all the challenging terrain in the bowls and glades. The Summit drag-lift is a tricky one to ride (very long and with a difficult start and steep pitches), but it's worth it to access the top Back Bowls and the views. The long green run that goes from the Larch area back to the base is to be avoided – it's really flat. In Banff, two specialist snowboard shops are Rude Boys and Unlimited Snowboards.

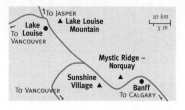

TERRAIN-PARKS
Huge and varied

There's a big park called Showtime, on the lower part of the Front Side, with nine varied rails, nine jumps and a quarter-pipe at the bottom; it was 'rated brilliant' by the 14-year-old nephew of a 2005 reporter. There's also an Olympic-sized super-pipe and a beginner park with a small half-pipe, rollers and banked turns.

SNOW RELIABILITY
Usually OK

Lake Louise gets around 140 inches a year on the Front Side, which by the standards of western Canada is not a lot. But it is usually enough, and there is snowmaking on 40% of the pistes. The north-facing Back Bowls and Larch hold the snow pretty well.

FOR EXPERTS
Widespread pleasure

There are plenty of steep slopes. On the Front Side, as well as a score of marked black-diamond trails in and above the trees, there is the alluring West Bowl, reached from the Summit drag – a wide open expanse of snow outside the area boundary. Because this is National Park territory, you can in theory go anywhere. But outside the boundaries there are no patrols and, of course, no avalanche control. A guide is essential. 'You get a real feel of being in the middle of nowhere. The return through thick woods with small plunges and over-hanging branches is great fun,' says a reporter.

Inside the boundaries, going over to the Back Bowls opens up countless black mogul/powder runs. From the Summit drag, you can drop into (if it is

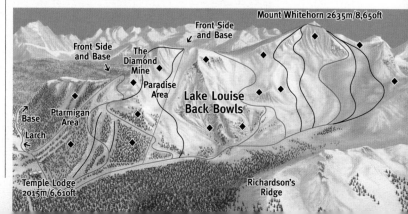

LIFT PASSES

Tri-area lift pass
Covers all lifts and
transport between
Banff, Lake Louise
and Sunshine Village.

Beginners
Lift, lesson and rental
package available.

Main pass
3 days C$212
6 days C$424

Senior citizens
Over 65: 6 days
C$379

Children
Under 18: 6 days
C$379
Under 13: 6 days
C$173
Under 6: free pass

Notes
Prices above include
taxes. Three days
minimum.

Alternative passes
One-day and half-day
passes available for
individual areas.

open) the Whitehorn 2 area directly
behind the peak. This gave our Aussie
editor what she called 'some of the
most exciting in-bounds skiing in North
America' – a row of extreme chutes,
almost 1km/0.5 miles long. You can
also access much tamer, wide open
Back Bowl slopes that take you right
away from all signs of lifts.

The Top of the World six-pack takes
you to the very popular Paradise Bowl,
served by its own triple chair – there
are endless variants here. The seriously
steep slope served by the Ptarmigan
quad chair provided many of the logs
for the newest base lodge, and offers
great gladed terrain as a result. It's a
good place to beat the crowds and
find good snow. The Larch area has
some steep double-diamond stuff in
the trees, and open snowfields at the

top for those with the energy to hike
up. Heli-skiing is available from bases
outside the National Park.

FOR INTERMEDIATES
Some good cruising
Almost half the runs are classified as
intermediate. But from the top of the
Front Side the blue runs down are little
more than paths in places, and there
are only two blue and two green
routes marked in the Back Bowls. Once
you get part way down the Front Side
the blues are much more interesting.
And when groomed, the Men's and
Ladies' Downhill black runs are great
fast cruises on the lower half of the
mountain. Juniper is a wonderful
cruising run in the same area.
Meadowlark is a beautiful tree-lined
run to the base area – to find it from

SCHOOLS

Lake Louise
t 522 1333

**ClubSki and
ClubSnowboard**
t 762 4561

Classes (Lake Louise)
3 days guided tuition
of the three areas
(3hr per day) C$213
incl. tax

Private lessons
Half day (3hr) C$352,
incl. tax

CHILDREN

**Telus Play Station &
Daycare**
t 522 3555
Ages 18 days to 6yr;
8.30 to 4.30

Ski school
Takes ages 5 to 12 (3
days C$245, incl. tax
and lunch)

the Grizzly Express gondola, first follow Eagle Meadows. The Larch area has some short but ideal intermediate runs – and reporters have enjoyed the natural lumps and bumps of the aptly named blue, Rock Garden. The adventurous should also try the blue-classified Boomerang, which starts with a short side-step up from the top of the Summit drag, and some of the ungroomed Back Bowls terrain.

FOR BEGINNERS
Excellent terrain

Louise has a good nursery area near the base, which has attracted praise, served by a short T-bar, which has not. You progress to the gentle, wide Wiwaxy, Pinecone Way and the slightly more difficult Deer Run or Eagle Meadows (all designated 'slow skiing zones'). There are even green slow-skiing zones round the Back Bowls and in the Larch area – worth trying for the views, though some do contain slightly steep pitches. A past reporter lost confidence on these, and found that people still skied fast in the slow areas and that they were quite crowded.

FOR CROSS-COUNTRY
High in quality and quantity

It's a very good area for cross-country, with around 80km/50 miles of groomed trails in the National Park. There are excellent trails in the local area and on Lake Louise itself. And Emerald Lake Lodge 40km/25 miles away has some lovely trails and has been recommended as a place to stay for a peaceful time.

QUEUES
Not unknown

Half of the area's visitors come for the day from nearby cities such as Calgary – so it can have queues at weekends and public holidays, especially for the slow chairs on the back of the mountain.

MOUNTAIN RESTAURANTS
Good base facilities

There's not much choice up the mountain. Temple Lodge, near the bottom of Larch, is built in rustic style with a big terrace. Sawyer's Nook there is the only table-service option on the mountain. 'We were impressed with both food and prices,' said a reporter; it gets busy, so reserve a table. The self-service cafeteria can get very crowded. Whitehorn Lodge, at mid-mountain on the Front Side, is a cafeteria with fine views from its balcony. At the base, the Lodge of the Ten Peaks is a hugely impressive, spacious, airy, modern, log-built affair with various eating, drinking and lounging options including the new Great Bear Room self-service (which they describe as having 'Interactive Lunch Stations'). The neighbouring Whiskeyjack building has another self-service. The Kokanee Kabin has BBQ food.

SCHOOLS AND GUIDES
Generally good reports

'The best teaching we've encountered' is how a reporter described his 'bumps' lesson at Lake Louise. Another reporter enjoyed the lessons, but said she could not get afternoon-only classes. And her five-year-old daughter did not like being put in classes with eight- to ten-year-olds. See the Banff chapter for details on the excellent three-day, three-mountain Club Ski and Club Snowboard Program.

The base area has very gentle slopes, ideal for beginners →

GETTING THERE

Air Calgary
177km/110 miles
(1½hr).

ACTIVITIES

Indoor Mainly hotel-based pools, saunas and hot-tubs, bowling, cinema, museums

Outdoor Ice rinks, walking, ice fishing, swimming in hot springs, sleigh rides, dog-sled rides, snowmobiles, helicopter rides, snow-shoeing

WEBSITES

For links to resort sites, go to our own new site at www.wtss.co.uk

Phone numbers
From distant parts of Canada, add the prefix 1 403.
From abroad, add the prefix +1 403.

TOURIST OFFICE

t 762 4561
info@SkiBig3.com
www.SkiBig3.com

FACILITIES FOR CHILDREN
Varying reports
A reporter who used Lake Louise, Sunshine and Norquay facilities said: 'I'd recommend all three and advise booking in advance at Lake Louise.'

STAYING THERE

HOW TO GO
Good value accommodation
Hotels Summer is the peak season here. Prices are much lower in winter.
◖◖◖4 Fairmont Chateau Lake Louise (522 3511) Isolated position with stunning views over frozen Lake Louise, 500 rooms, lots of shops, groups of Japanese tourists, pool, hot-tub, steam room.
◖◖◖4 Post (522 3989) Small, comfortable Relais & Châteaux place in the village with good restaurant (huge wine list) with pool, hot-tub, sauna, steam. Avoid rooms on railway side.
◖2 Lake Louise Inn (522 3791) Cheaper option in the village, with pool, hot-tub and sauna. 'Comfortable rooms'; 'good food'; 'staff helpful' said a 2005 reporter.
◖2 Deer Lodge (522 3747) Charming old hotel next to the Chateau, good restaurant, rooftop hot-tub.
Self-catering Some is available but local shopping is limited. The Baker Creek Chalets (522 3761) were highly recommended by reporters on their honeymoon ('really romantic').

EATING OUT
Limited choice
We had a delicious dinner at the Post hotel in 2005, with good-value house wine. The Fairview Dining Room at the Chateau is also top notch. The Outpost Pub (part of the Post) does inexpensive pub food. The Station restaurant is in an atmospheric old station building. The bakery/ coffee shop in the village has been praised by reporters and is good for breakfast.

APRES-SKI
Lively at tea time, quiet later
There are several options at the bottom of the slopes. The Lodge of the Ten Peaks has lovely surroundings, an open fire and a relaxed atmosphere. The Kokanee Kabin has live music on spring weekend afternoons. Twice a week there's live music and dancing and a buffet dinner at the mid-mountain Whitehorn Lodge. You ski or ride there as the lifts close and the evening ends with a torchlit descent. It is hugely popular with British visitors.

Later on, things are fairly quiet. But the Glacier Saloon, in Chateau Lake Louise, with traditional Wild West decor, often has live music until late. Explorer's Lounge, in the Lake Louise Inn, has entertainment. The Post's Outpost Pub is worth a look.

OFF THE SLOPES
Beautiful scenery
Lake Louise makes a lovely, peaceful place to stay for someone who does not intend to hit the slopes. The lake itself makes a stunning setting for walks, snow-shoeing, cross-country skiing and ice skating. You can go on ice canyon walks, sleigh rides, dog-sledding, sightseeing tours and visit natural hot springs.

For a more lively day or for shopping you can visit Banff.

Lake Louise is near one end of the Columbia Icefields Parkway, a three-hour drive to Jasper through National Parks, amid stunningly beautiful scenery of high peaks and glaciers – one of the world's most beautiful drives.

STAYING UP THE MOUNTAIN
Try ski touring
Skoki Lodge (522 3555) is 11km/ 7 miles on skis from Temle Lodge. Built in the 1930s, it sleeps 22 in the lodge and cabins and allegedly has 'gourmet food'. Reports welcome.

Lake Louise

647

Panorama

Great views, some challenging runs, a rapidly developing resort

COSTS

① ② ③ ④ ⑤ ⑥

RATINGS

The slopes
Fast lifts	***
Snow	***
Extent	**
Expert	****
Intermediate	***
Beginner	****
Convenience	****
Queues	*****
Mountain restaurants	*

The rest
Scenery	***
Resort charm	**
Off-slope	*

➕ Car-free village with some slope-side accommodation, plus a lower village

➕ Fair-sized area with big vertical drop

➕ Runs are usually deserted

➖ Not many easy cruising runs

➖ Snowfall record not impressive by high local standards

➖ Village quiet with no real focus

Panorama has benefited from a huge investment in the past few years. New slope-side accommodation has been built, along with outdoor hot-pools and a skating rink. And two seasons ago two new quads replaced two T-bars and a slow, queue-prone chair – previously the source of reporters' complaints. The mountain's vertical of 1220m/4,000ft is one of the biggest in North America, and it has some excellent terrain for experts and adventurous intermediates. It's good for beginners too. But timid intermediates may find some of the runs intimidating and prefer to stick to the rather limited lower mountain. And the resort is quiet – a better place for families than singles looking for nightlife.

THE RESORT

Panorama is a small, quiet, purpose-built resort above the lakeside town of Invermere in eastern British Columbia, about two hours' scenic drive south-west of Banff. Accommodation is concentrated mainly in two car-free areas. There are attractive lodges with a hot-pool complex and a skating rink at the foot of the main slopes, and with ski-in ski-out convenience, this is the best place to stay. But a lot of lodging is in a 'lower village' which lacks character or life. This is linked to the 'upper village' and the slopes by a bucket lift that runs until 10pm, but the village lacks a central focus.

The resort runs day trips to Lake Louise and Kicking Horse.

THE MOUNTAIN

The slopes basically follow three ridges, joined at top and bottom. Almost all of the terrain is wooded. Free mountain tours are available twice daily ('Informative and instrumental in our choice of runs for the week,' said a 2005 reporter). Some runs are floodlit Thursday to Sunday evenings.

Slopes From the upper village, a fast quad goes over gentle slopes to mid-mountain. Above this another fast quad serves both intermediate and expert slopes. Then a fixed-grip quad takes you to the summit. From here there is only one blue run (a gentle but narrow cat-track). The other runs are all single- or double-black-diamonds. There are long runs down the two outer ridges as well as the central one. At the top are a couple of black-diamond areas – see 'Experts'.

Terrain-parks There are two: the main Showzone terrain-park, with table tops, spines, rails, fun boxes and a half-pipe, and the Blue Park for beginner freestylers, with scaled-down rails, kickers and fun boxes. They are both floodlit Thursday to Sunday evenings.

Snow reliability Annual snowfall is low by local standards – less than half the Fernie figure. But snowmaking covers 40% of trails and grooming is good.

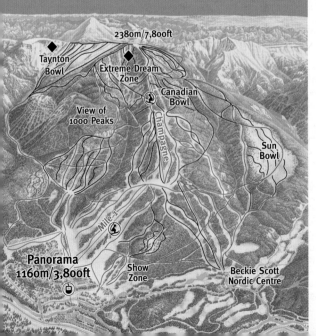

2380m/7,800ft

Taynton Bowl

Extreme Dream Zone

Canadian Bowl

View of 1000 Peaks

Champagne

Sun Bowl

Mile 1

Panorama
1160m/3,800ft

Show Zone

Beckie Scott
Nordic Centre

KEY FACTS

Resort	1160m
	3,800ft
Slopes	1160-2380m
	3,800-7,800ft
Lifts	9
Pistes	2,847 acres
Green	20%
Blue	55%
Black	25%
Snowmaking	40%

Central reservations
1 800 663 2929 (toll-free within Canada).

Phone numbers
From distant parts of Canada, add the prefix 1 250. From abroad, add +1 250.

TOURIST OFFICE

t 342 6941
paninfo@intrawest.com
www.skipanorama.com

WEBSITES

Experts There are genuine black runs scattered all over the mountain, and some expert-only areas. At the very top of the mountain and accessed through a gate is the Extreme Dream Zone – seriously steep trails with cliffs as well as tight trees. Off the back of the summit is the Taynton Bowl area, with challenging but (even though it is marked double-black-diamond on the map) less extreme terrain – hiking over to the far runs can be worth it for fresh tracks. Then there's the local heli-skiing – see Intermediates.

Intermediates For adventurous intermediates the terrain is excellent – there are easy blacks all over the mountain, some of them regularly groomed. The black View of 1000 Peaks has fabulous views but can be a bit tricky in parts. Both this and the blue run from the top are long for North America (up to 3.5km/2 miles). Sun Bowl is a good introduction to a powder bowl and Millennium (black running into blue) is a great roller-coaster. But the less confident may find all this uncomfortably challenging. The blues in the centre of the area such as World Cup Way, Skyline and Rollercoaster are gentler but they don't add up to a lot. RK Heli-Skiing has a base right next to the village and specialises in one-day sessions for first-time heli-skiers – 'an exceptional experience', said a 2005 reporter.

Beginners There are a couple of nursery lifts and a moving carpet serving a quiet and gentle nursery area. Then there are good, longer runs to progress to served by the Mile 1 quad.

Snowboarding There is good steep terrain and tree runs for expert free-riders. The main lifts are all chairs and beginners have several good long green runs to practise on, but the main nursery slopes are served by drag-lifts.

Cross-country There are 30 km/19 miles of trails starting from the Nordic Centre.

Queues The two new quads in 2003/04 seem to have eliminated the only queues on the mountain. And the trails are usually delightfully deserted.

Mountain restaurants There are no real mountain restaurants, just two huts offering basic refreshments. But the Ski Tip day lodge at the base is excellent.

Schools and guides We have mainly had glowing reports of the ski school. 'Universally agreed as superb by all who tried it' and 'massive leap in skiing – felt great' are typical comments.

Facilities for children Wee Wascals is

the childcare centre, taking children from 18 months. Snowbirds is for three- to five-year-olds, and the Adventure Club caters for kids from five to 14. Kid's Nights and a Teen Nightclub are arranged some evenings. Evening babysitters are also available.

STAYING THERE

How to go The better places are the newer ones in the upper village.

Hotels Panorama Springs is right on the slopes with a big outdoor hot-pool and sauna facility. Next door Tamarack and Ski Tip have been recommended. And the 1000 Peaks Lodge and 1000 Peaks Summit units, built around a public skating rink, look good. The Pine Inn is a budget option, which reporters have criticised; Toby Creek, in the lower village, seems better.

Self-catering There are plenty of condo blocks and town homes. The store is inadequate, so stock up in Invermere.

Eating out Eating out options are limited but improving. The new Wildfire Grill, the Earl Grey Lodge and the Heli Plex restaurant (with great views of the mountain) have been recommended by reporters. The ski school organises BBQs at Elkhorn Cabin, followed by a torchlight descent. There's a horse-drawn wagon ride followed by chilli around a campfire, and a shuttle-bus to the restaurants in Invermere leaves at 7.15 and comes back around 9.30.

Après-ski Après-ski revolves around the Crazy Horse Saloon in the Pine Inn, which sometimes has live music, and the Jackpine pub in the Horsethief Lodge. Ski Tip Lodge is popular as the lifts close. The Glacier is the nightclub.

Off the slopes The hot-pool facility, with thermal baths, a swimming pool, slides and sauna, is excellent, but it gets rather taken over by kids. There are snowmobile tours, ice-fishing excursions, snow-shoeing and skating.

Sun Peaks

Attractive new village at the foot of BC's second-biggest ski area

COSTS

① ② ③ ④ ⑤ ⑥

RATINGS

The slopes

Fast lifts	***
Snow	****
Extent	***
Expert	***
Intermediate	****
Beginner	****
Convenience	****
Queues	*****
Mountain restaurants	*

The rest

Scenery	***
Resort charm	***
Off-slope	**

NEWS

For 2004/05 extra chairs were added to the Mt Morrisey Express to double its capacity. The Back in Time ski bridge was built to provide better access from Mt Morrisey to Tod Mountain. A new moving carpet was installed at the tubing hill. And a new ice rink was built.

For 2005/06 a second winch cat will be operating to groom steep runs and snowmaking capacity will be further increased and the Children's Learning Centre will be expanded and a moving carpet installed. An Ice Palace hotel is due to be built completely from snow and ice. It will have themed rooms, an ice bar, ice chapel and ice sculptures.

- Some great terrain for all standards
- Slopes very quiet during the week
- Attractive new slope-side village

- Both ski area and village may be too small for some tastes
- Snow on some of the lower steep terrain can suffer from the sun

Sun Peaks has sprung from the drawing board in the past 12 years and we have been increasingly impressed on each of three successive visits. It now has an almost complete small village and a fair amount of varied terrain. We'd suggest combining it with, say, Whistler, Silver Star or Big White on a multi-centre trip.

THE RESORT

Until 1993 Sun Peaks was known as Tod Mountain, a local hill for the residents of nearby Kamloops. Since then the company that bought it has overseen the development of a small, attractive resort village with low-rise pastel-coloured buildings with a vaguely Tirolean feeling to them. The traffic-free main street is lined with accommodation, restaurants and shops including a smart art gallery, great chocolate shop and good coffee bar.

THE MOUNTAINS

With almost 3,700 acres of skiable terrain, Sun Peaks is the second biggest ski area in British Columbia (Whistler is the biggest). There are free guided tours twice a day and every day at 11am and 1.30 you can ski for free with former Olympic champion and Canada's Female Athlete of the 20th century Nancy Greene (don't miss it – she is great fun!).

Slopes There are three distinct sectors, each served by a high-speed quad. One goes from the centre of the village to mid-mountain on Sun Peaks' original ski hill, Mt Tod. This has mainly black runs but there are easier blues and greens. A tiny snowcat offers day-long backcountry skiing here. Also reached from the village centre, the Sundance area has mainly blue and green cruising runs. Both Sundance and Tod have some great gladed areas (12 of them marked on the trail map). Mt Morrisey is reached by a long green run from the top of Sundance and has a delightful network of easy blue runs with trees left uncut in the trails, making them effectively groomed glade runs.
Terrain-parks There's a park with table-tops, rails and fun-boxes, boarder-cross and half-pipe on Sundance.
Snow reliability Sun Peaks gets an average snowfall of 220 inches a year; not in the top league but better than some. The snow can suffer on the lower part of Mt Tod's south-facing slopes, especially later in the season.

Ski Club of Great Britain host hotel
Shuttle from Whistler – 3 days a week

KEY FACTS

Resort	1255m
	4,120ft
Slopes	1200-2080m
	3,930-6,820ft
Lifts	11
Pistes	3,678 acres
Green	10%
Blue	58%
Black	32%
Snowmaking	
	40 acres

Experts Mt Tod has most of the steep terrain, though some of the blacks on Mt Morrisey are long mogul runs too. You could also try the backcountry snowcat operation.

Intermediates This is great terrain for early intermediates, with the easy groomed glades of Mt Morrisey, lovely swooping blues on Sundance and the long 5 Mile run from Mt Tod. More adventurous intermediates can tackle the easier glades (such as Cahilty) and blacks (such as Peek-A-Boo).

Beginners There are nursery slopes right in the village centre, with long easy greens to progress too.

Snowboarding Boarders can explore the whole mountain. But beware the flat greens to and from Mt Morrisey.

Cross-country There are 40km/25 miles of groomed trails.

Queues Weekdays are usually very quiet; it's only at peak weekends that you might find short queues.

Mountain restaurants The Sunburst Lodge is the only option; its cinnamon buns are highly recommended.

Schools and guides Reporters have been impressed with a multi-day ski school course which included après-ski activities and 'ladies' mornings'.

Facilities for children The playschool takes kids from age 18 months and the ski school from three years.

STAYING THERE

How to go There's a lot of self-catering accommodation as well as hotels.

Hotels Nancy Greene's Cahilty Lodge is a friendly and comfortable ski-in, ski-out base and you get the chance to ski with her and husband Al Raine (former Canadian ski team coach) at 9am most days. The ski-in, ski-out Delta Sun Peaks Resort (outdoor pool and hot-tub) is right in the village centre.

Eating out For a small resort, there's a good choice of restaurants. Macker's Bistro is popular and we had great Thai-style sea bass there. Powder Hounds does good steaks and Servus more sophisticated food.

Après-ski Bottoms, Masa's and Macker's are the main après-ski bars. At weekends MackDaddy's nightclub in The Delta can get lively. There are fondue evenings with torchlit descents, winter bonfires and tobogganing.

Off the slopes There's skating, tubing, snowmobiling, dog-sledding and snow-shoeing.

Sun Peaks

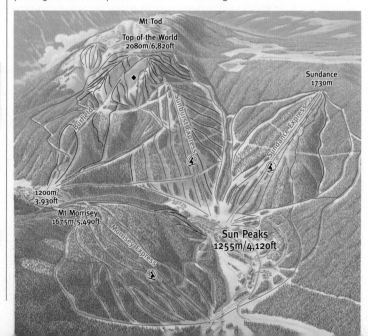

Whistler

North America's biggest mountain with terrain to suit every standard

COSTS

① ② ③ ④ ⑤ ⑥

RATINGS

The slopes

Fast lifts	****
Snow	****
Extent	****
Expert	*****
Intermediate	*****
Beginner	***
Convenience	****
Queues	***
Mountain restaurants	**

The rest

Scenery	***
Resort charm	***
Off-slope	**

KEY FACTS

Resort	675m
	2,210ft
Altitude	650-2285m
	2,140-7,490ft
Lifts	37
Pistes	8,171 acres
Green	18%
Blue	55%
Black	27%
Snowmaking	
	565 acres

652

➕ North America's biggest, both in area and vertical (1610m/5,280ft)

➕ Good slopes for most abilities, with an unrivalled combination of high open bowls and woodland trails

➕ Good snow record (but not in 2004/05)

➕ Almost Alpine scenery, unlike the rounded Rockies of Colorado

➕ Attractive modern villages at the foot of the slopes with car-free centres, one with lively après-ski

➕ Good range of restaurants and bars (though not enough of them)

➖ Proximity to the ocean means a lot of cloudy weather and when it's snowing on the mountain it's often raining at resort level

➖ Two separate mountains are linked only at resort level

➖ Lift queues and crowded runs can be a problem

➖ Mountain restaurants are mostly functional (and overcrowded)

➖ Whistler has become a victim of its own success – attracting more people than it can cope with

Whistler is unlike any other resort in North America. It's bigger, both in terms of vertical drop and skiable area. The town is big too. Combine that with hordes of people pouring in from Vancouver on powder days and weekends and you can get lengthy lift queues and crowded trails – unusual for North America. The facilities in town can get overstretched too, with tables in restaurants difficult to come by. If you want to get away from the crowds, you should go elsewhere.

But a lot of people will put up with the crowds for Whistler's other attractions. There are some fine up-market hotels and a good variety of restaurants. And the mountain is simply the best that North America has to offer. Great open bowls, steeps and deeps, tree-lined intermediate cruising and good beginner slopes. The ski schools are excellent. The lifts are generally fast and efficient. And the snow on the upper half of the mountain is as reliable and powdery as you'll find. But be prepared for rain at resort level and poor snow on the lower slopes.

Whistler will host many events during the 2010 Winter Olympics.

THE RESORT

Whistler Village sits at the foot of its two mountains, Whistler and Blackcomb, a scenic 115km/71 mile drive from Vancouver on Canada's west coast. Whistler started as a locals' ski area in 1966 with a few ramshackle buildings in what is now the revamped Whistler Creek (aka Creekside). Whistler Village, a 10-minute bus-ride away, developed in the late 1970s. And another village spread up the lower slopes of Blackcomb Mountain in the 1980s; this village, a 10-minute walk from Whistler, is now known simply as Upper Village.

The centres of all the villages are traffic-free. The architecture is varied and, for a purpose-built resort, quite tasteful. There are lots of chalet-style apartments on the hillsides. The centres have individually designed wood and concrete buildings, blended together around pedestrian streets and squares. There are no monstrous high-rise blocks – but there are a lot of large five- or six-storey buildings.

Whistler Village has most of the bars, restaurants and shops, and two

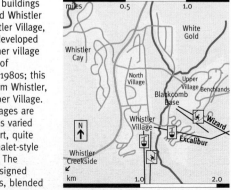

gondolas (one to each mountain). Whistler North, further from the lifts, is newer and has virtually merged with the original village, making a huge car-free area of streets lined with shops, condos and restaurants. Upper Village is smaller and quieter but has also grown rapidly in recent years, the most significant recent addition being a luxurious Four Seasons hotel.

Creekside has been revamped and expanded and it will play an important role in the Olympics, with many of the alpine events finishing here.

There is a free bus between Whistler and Upper Village but, if you're staying near the base of Blackcomb, it's just as quick to walk. Staying further out means paying for buses or taxis – which are not expensive. Some hotels have free shuttle-buses, which you can get to pick you up as well as take you to restaurants and nightlife.

The most convenient place to stay is Whistler Village as you can access either mountain by gondola. Creekside, though convenient for Whistler Mountain, is less so for Blackcomb. Some lodging is an inconvenient walk or bus-ride from the villages and slopes.

Whistler is now getting very busy and some reporters have found the central area around Village Square very noisy in the early hours. Creekside is quieter.

THE MOUNTAINS

The area has acquired a formidable and well-deserved reputation among experts. But both Whistler and Blackcomb also have loads of well-groomed intermediate terrain. Together they have over 200 marked trails, and form the biggest area of slopes, with the longest runs, in North America.

Many reporters enthuse about the mountain host service and the 'go slow' patrol – some find the latter 'over zealous', but crowded slopes, especially on the runs home, mean they're often needed ('They do a good job,' says a 2005 reporter).

But reporters also comment on the early closing times for lifts (3pm until end-January, 3.30 in February and 4pm thereafter). Upper lifts may close earlier.

THE SLOPES
The best in North America
Whistler Mountain is accessed from Whistler Village by a two-stage, 10-person gondola that rises over 1100m/3,610ft to Roundhouse Lodge, the main mid-mountain base. There is an alternative of two consecutive fast quads, which take you slightly lower; they are a good choice when queues for the gondola are long.

Runs back down through the trees fan out from the gondola – cruises to

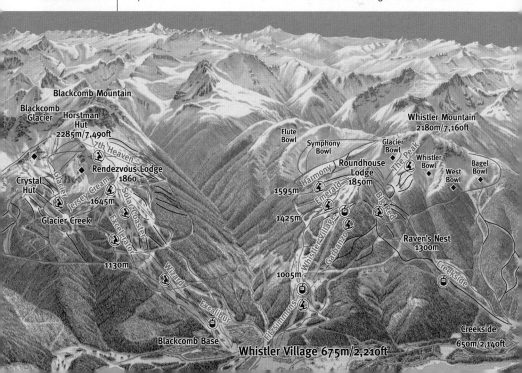

Blackcomb Mountain

Blackcomb Glacier

Horstman Hut 2285m/7,490ft

7th Heaven

Crystal Hut

Rendezvous Lodge 1860

Jersey Cream

Solar Coaster

Glacier Creek

Glacier

1645m

Excelerator

Wizard

1130m

Excalibur

Blackcomb Base

Fitzsimmons

1005m

Whistler Village

Garbanzo

1425m

1595m

Harmony

Emerald

Symphony Bowl

Flute Bowl

Roundhouse Lodge 1850m

Big Red

Glacier Bowl

The Peak

Whistler Mountain 2180m/7,160ft

Whistler Bowl

West Bowl

Bagel Bowl

Raven's Nest 1300m

Creekside

Creekside 650m/2,140ft

Whistler Village 675m/2,210ft

NEWS

For 2004/05 another 700 acres of formerly out-of-bounds terrain in Flute Bowl opened (you have to hike into and out of it). And four new runs (three advanced/ expert trails and an intermediate one) with a vertical descent of over 1500m/4,920ft from the Peak down to Whistler Creekside were due to open, but poor snow conditions curtailed their use.

Creekside was re-launched last season after a four-year face-lift and expansion as a smaller, quieter, family-friendly, traffic-free alternative to the main Whistler Village. A new 5-star Four Seasons hotel opened near the base of Blackcomb.

A new FIS standard super-pipe was built on Blackcomb Mountain and is lit for night jibbing three nights a week. Blackcomb's terrain-park was also upgraded.

For2005/06 upgraded snowmaking on Whistler Mountain is planned.

the Emerald and Big Red fast chairs, longer runs to the gondola mid-station.

From Roundhouse you can see the jewel in Whistler's crown – magnificent above-the-tree-line bowls, served by the fast Peak and Harmony quads. The bowls are mostly go-anywhere terrain for experts but there are groomed trails, so anyone can appreciate the views.

A six-person gondola from Creekside also accesses Whistler Mountain.

Access to **Blackcomb** from Whistler Village is by an eight-seater gondola, followed by a fast quad (which is a bottleneck first thing). From the base of Blackcomb you take two consecutive fast quads up to the main Rendezvous restaurant. From the arrival points you can go left for great cruising terrain and the Glacier Express quad up to the Horstman Glacier area, or right for steeper slopes, the terrain-park or the 7th Heaven chair. The 1610m/5,280ft vertical from the top of 7th Heaven to the base is the largest in North America (and big even by Alpine standards). Or you can go into the glacier area. A T-bar from the Horstman Glacier brings you (with a very short hike) to the Blackcomb Glacier in the next valley – a beautiful run that takes you away from all lifts.

Fresh Tracks is a deal that allows you to ride up Whistler Mountain (at extra cost) from 7.15am, have a buffet breakfast and get to the slopes as they open – very popular with many reporters. A good tip is to hit the slopes first and breakfast after – that way you find the slopes at their quietest.

Free guided tours of each mountain are offered at 11.30am.

TERRAIN-PARKS
For high-fliers and mere mortals
The resort has an array of different-ability parks. Novices can start in the Big Easy Terrain Garden on Blackcomb, with its unthreatening rails, rollers and

hits. Next up in terms of difficulty is the Habitat park on Whistler, which has lots of rails, plus there's a half-pipe at the top of the Emerald chair. The main park on Blackcomb, the Nintendo, next to the Catskinner chair, has slightly bigger hits and rails, fun-boxes, hips, spines and banks. True experts can head into the Highest Level park – to be allowed in you need to wear a helmet, sign a waiver and buy a special pass. There's also an FIS-standard super-pipe on Blackcomb (floodlit three times a week).

SNOW RELIABILITY
Excellent at altitude
Snow conditions at the top are usually excellent – the place gets around 360 inches of snow a year, on average. But because the resort is low and close to the Pacific, the bottom slopes can be wet, icy or unskiable. People may 'download' from the mid-stations due to poor snow, especially in late season. Last season was exceptionally poor for Whistler, when it was plagued by high temperatures and rain (for four days in January there was torrential rain right to the top of the mountain, brought by a freak storm dubbed the 'Pineapple Express'). Reporters also tell us there was a lot of mid-mountain fog and mist later in the season. Hopefully, these conditions won't be repeated.

FOR EXPERTS
Few can rival it
Whistler Mountain's bowls are enough to keep experts happy for weeks. Each has endless variations, with chutes and gullies of varied steepness and width. The biggest challenges are around Glacier, Whistler and West Bowls, with runs such as The Cirque and Doom & Gloom – though you can literally go anywhere in this high, wide area. New for last season was 700 acres of previously out-of-bounds terrain in

LIFT PASSES

Whistler/Blackcomb
Covers all lifts on
both Whistler and
Blackcomb
mountains.

Beginners
Lift, lesson and rental
package available.

Main pass
1 day C$77
6 days C$415

Senior citizens
Over 65: 6 days
C$354

Children
Under 19: 6 days
C$354
Under 13: 6 days
C$219
Under 7: free pass

Notes
Prices include 7%
sales tax.

Flute Bowl, accessed by a 30-minute hike and with another 15-minute hike out.

Blackcomb's slopes are not as extensive as Whistler's, but some are more challenging. From the top of the 7th Heaven lift, traverse to Xhiggy's Meadow, for sunny bowl runs.

If you're feeling brave, go in the opposite direction and drop into the extremely steep chutes down towards Glacier Creek, including the infamous 41° Couloir Extreme, which can have moguls the size of elephants at the top. Or try the also serious, but less frequented, steep bowls reached by hiking up Spanky's Ladder, after taking the Glacier Express lift.

Both mountains have challenging trails through trees. Last season saw the addition of the new 400 acre Peak to Creek area from below Whistler's West Bowl to Creekside (though poor snow conditions curtailed its use).

If all this isn't enough, there's also out-of-bounds backcountry guiding (see Schools and guides), and local heli-skiing available by the day.

FOR INTERMEDIATES
Ideal and extensive terrain
Both mountains are an intermediate's paradise. In good weather, good intermediates will enjoy the less extreme variations in the bowls on both mountains.

One of our favourite intermediate runs is down the Blackcomb Glacier, from the top of the mountain to the bottom of the Excelerator chair over 1000m/3,280ft below. This 5km/3 mile run, away from all lifts, starts with a two-minute walk up from the top of the Showcase T-bar. Don't be put off by the sign that says 'Experts only'. You drop over the ridge into a wide bowl – not too suddenly or you'll get a short, sharp shock in the very steep double-diamond Blowhole. The further you traverse, the shallower the slope.

You are guaranteed good snow on the Horstman Glacier too, and typically gentle runs. The blue runs served by the 7th Heaven chair are 'heavenly on a sunny day', as a reporter put it. Lower down there are lots of perfect cruising runs through the trees – ideal when the weather is bad.

Whistler

655

boarding

Both mountains are excellent for every level of boarder. All the main lifts are chairs and gondolas and terrain ranges from gentle green runs to wide open bowls and heart-stopping cliff drops and chutes. And snowboarders have one advantage over skiers in Whistler – when the snow gets slushy lower down, it's easier and more fun to ride it on a board! There are T-bars on the glacier, but they're not vicious and any discomfort is worth it for the powder. The resort is popular with snowboarders and known for its summer boarding camps. The school runs a lot of specialist classes, including freestyle lessons and women's camps, and Canada's Olympic gold medallist, Ross Rebagliati, is on the team of coaches – he's available on request. The resort regularly hosts big snowboard events, including the 2005 Snowboard World Championships last January. Specialist snowboard shops include Showcase and Katmandu Boards.

On Whistler Mountain, there are
easy blue pistes in Symphony,
Harmony and Glacier bowls. Even early
intermediates should try them, since
there's always an easy way down. The
Saddle run from the top of the Harmony
Express lift is a favourite with many of
our reporters, though it can get busy.
The blue Highway 86 path, which skirts
West Bowl from the top of the Peak
chair, has beautiful views over a steep
valley and across to the rather phallic
Black Tusk mountain. The green Burnt
Stew Trail also has great views.

Lower down the mountain there is a
vast choice of groomed blue runs with
a series of efficient fast chairs to bring
you back up to the top of the gondola.
It's a cruiser's paradise – especially the
aptly named Ego Bowl. A great long
run is the fabulous Dave Murray
Downhill all the way from mid-
mountain to the finish at Creekside.
Although it will be the Olympic men's
downhill course and is marked black
on the map, it's a wonderful fast and
varied cruise when it has been
groomed. There is also the new
groomed blue in the Peak to Creek
area to try if snow is good enough.

FOR BEGINNERS
OK if the sun shines
Whistler has excellent nursery slopes
by the mid-station of the gondola, as
does Blackcomb, down at the base
area. Both have facilities higher up too.

The map has a guide to easy runs,
and slow zones are marked. On
Whistler, after progressing from the
nursery slopes, there are some gentle
first runs from the top of the gondola.
Their downside is other people
speeding past. You can return by
various chairs or continue to the base
area on greens. Check the latter are in
good condition first, and maybe avoid
them at the end of the day, when they
can get very crowded.

On Blackcomb, Green Line runs from
the top of the mountain to the bottom.
The top part is particularly gentle, with
some steeper pitches lower down. As
one reporter said, 'A tentative beginner
in our group found it hard to move
around with confidence because of the
varying steepness of green runs.'

Another reservation is – you
guessed – the weather. Beginners
don't get a lot out of heavy snowfalls,
and might be put off by rain and
unpredictable conditions.

FOR CROSS-COUNTRY
Picturesque but low
There are over 28km/17 miles of cross-
country tracks around Lost Lake,
starting by the river, on the path
between Whistler and Blackcomb. But
it is low altitude here, so conditions
can be unreliable. There's a specialist
school, Cross-Country Connection (905
0071) offering lessons, tours and
rental. Keen cross-country merchants
can catch the train to better areas.

QUEUES
An ever-increasing problem
Whistler has become a victim of its
own success. Even with 15 fast lifts –
more than any other resort in North
America – the mountains are queue-
prone, especially at weekends when
people pour in from Vancouver. There
are noticeboards displaying waiting
times at different lifts, and although
readers generally find them useful
(though one this year found them
'unreliable'), most people would prefer
shorter queues.

Some reporters have signed up with
the ski school just to get lift priority.
Others have visited Vancouver at the
weekend to avoid the crowds.

The routes out of Whistler Village in
the morning can be busy. Creekside is
less of a problem. Some of the chairs
higher up both mountains produce

SCHOOLS

Whistler and Blackcomb
t 604 932 3434

Classes
(Whistler and Blackcomb prices, incl. taxes)
3 days (beginner): C$273

Private lessons
Half day (3hr): C$401

GUIDES

Whistler Guides
t 604 932 3434

CHILDREN

Whistler Kids
t 1 800 766 0449
Ages 3mnth to 48mnth; from 8am; non-skiing; C$105 per day (incl. taxes)

Ski school
Offers Adventure Camps for ages 3 to 12 and **Ride Tribe** programme for ages 13 to 17 (from C$581 incl. taxes for 5 days for 3 to 4 year olds)

long queues – especially Harmony (where even the singles line can take ages). And we had a report of a 45-minute wait for The Peak chair on an early-January Sunday. Visiting outside peak season may not help – we found some lifts, including the gondola to Blackcomb, were kept closed in an early-December visit and readers have reported closed lifts in late season. Crowds on the slopes, especially the runs home, can be annoying too.

MOUNTAIN RESTAURANTS
Overcrowded
The main restaurants sell decent, good-value food but are charmless self-service stops with long queues. They're huge, but not huge enough. 'Seat-seekers' are employed to find spaces, but success is not guaranteed.

Past reporters have stressed the need to lunch early. But even that no longer works – 'avoid 11.15am to 1.45pm' says a 2005 visitor. But late lunches mean little skiing afterwards because the lifts close early; so the answer may be a big breakfast, ski through the day and eat later.

Blackcomb has the Rendezvous, mainly a big (850-seat) self-service place but also home to Christine's, a table-service restaurant – the best on either mountain. Glacier Creek Lodge, at the bottom of the Glacier Express, is a better self-service place ('Try the breakfast croissant,' says a reader). But even this (1,496 seats) gets incredibly crowded. Whistler has the massive (1,740-seat) Roundhouse Lodge; Steeps Grill is its table-service refuge.

Reporters generally prefer the smaller places – but they're still packed unless you time it right, and may be closed early and late season. On Blackcomb, Crystal Hut at the top of the Crystal Ridge chair (great waffles, say reporters) and Horstman Hut at the mountain-top are tiny with great views.

On Whistler, Raven's Nest, at the top of the Creekside gondola, is a small and friendly deli/cafe. The Chic Pea near the top of the Garbanzo chair-lift – 'funky and rustic' but 'noisy' – does pizza and barbecue. The Harmony Hut, at the top of the Harmony chair, specialises in stews and cider. You can of course descend to the base – the table-service Dusty's at Whistler Creek has good sandwiches and soup and doesn't get too crowded. There's also a Snack-Shack on each mountain, if all you fancy is a quick drink and hot-dog.

SCHOOLS AND GUIDES
A great formula
Ski Esprit and Ride Esprit programmes run for three or four days and combine instruction with showing you around the mountains – with the same instructor daily. Many of our reporters have joined these groups (usually small), and all reports are glowing: 'Big improvement in confidence and skill' is typical. 'Tuition very good, 9 out of 10,' says a 2004 reporter. There are specialist clinics and snowboard classes, too. But a 2005 reporter was disappointed that 'it wasn't possible to arrange lessons shorter than three hours' and 'we couldn't sign up for Ski Esprit as a family as our 16-year-old son was classified as too young'.

Extremely Canadian specialises in guiding and coaching adventurous advanced intermediates upwards in Whistler's steep and deep terrain. A lot of its coaches compete in free-ride and skier-cross competitions. We have been with them a few times and they really are great! As a reporter said, 'You end up skiing places that other people don't even know about – we were very impressed.' They run two- and four-day clinics.

Backcountry day trips or overnight touring are available with the Whistler Alpine Guides Bureau.

GETTING THERE
Air Vancouver 115km/71 miles (2hr).

ACTIVITIES
Indoor Sports arena (ice rink, pool, hot-tubs), museum, art galleries, tennis, spa and health clubs, library, cinemas, climbing wall

Outdoor Flightseeing, snow-shoeing, snowmobiling, fishing, dog-sledding, sleigh rides, ziptrek ecotours in the treetops on platforms and boardwalks and using harnesses and wires

Phone numbers
From distant parts of Canada, add the prefix 1 604. From abroad, add the prefix +1 604.

WEBSITES
For links to resort sites, go to our own new site at www.wtss.co.uk

---

FACILITIES FOR CHILDREN
Impressive
Blackcomb's base area has a slow-moving Magic Chair to get children part-way up the mountain. Whistler's gondola mid-station has a splendid kids-only area. A reporter found the staff 'friendly and instilled confidence'.

The Children's Adventure Park on Blackcomb features a Magic Castle, terrain features and 'colourful characters'. A reporter was enthusiastic about 'climb and dine', where children can spend a few fun hours at the Great Wall climbing centre (see Off the slopes), including a meal, while parents go out to eat.

STAYING THERE

HOW TO GO
High quality packages
A lot of British tour operators go to Whistler and some run catered chalets.
Hotels There is a wide range, including a lot of top-end places.
((((5)) **Fairmont Chateau Whistler** (938 8000) Well run and luxurious at the foot of Blackcomb. Excellent spa with pools and tubs. The Gold floor is expensive and especially cosseting.
((((5)) **Westin Resort & Spa** (905 5000) Luxury all-suite hotel at the foot of Whistler mountain next to the lifts.
((((5)) **Four Seasons** (905 3300) Opened last season. Luxury hotel five-minutes walk from Blackcomb base but with ski valet service there. Good fitness and spa facilities.
((((4)) **Pan Pacific** (905 2999) Luxury, all-suite, at Whistler Village base. Pool/sauna/hot-tub.
((((4)) **Lost Lake Lodge** (932 2882) 'Excellent' place: studios and suites, out by the golf course. Pool/hot-tub.
((((4)) **Crystal Lodge** (932 2221) Has been renovated. 'Comfortable, friendly, convenient', in Whistler Village. Pool/sauna/hot-tub.

((((3)) **Glacier Lodge** (932 2882) In Upper Village. 'Big rooms, quiet area, recommended.' Pool/hot-tub.
Self-catering There are plenty of spacious, comfortable condominiums in both chalet and hotel-style blocks.

EATING OUT
High quality and plenty of choice
Reporters are enthusiastic about the range, quality and value of places to eat, but do book well ahead: there simply aren't enough restaurant seats to meet demand. Some cheaper places won't take bookings for small groups, meaning long waits. One reporter 'gave up trying to find a table at Easter weekend and ate in the hotel bar'. Bars serve decent food, too. But if you've got kids, as one reporter found, 'Some places don't allow under-19s in, or even to sit outside, and we had to wait up to two hours elsewhere.'

At the top of the market, Il Caminetto di Umberto in Whistler Village has classy Italian cuisine. The Rimrock Café at Whistler Creek serves 'the best seafood we have ever eaten', says a reporter.

Good mid-market Whistler Village places include Araxi (Italian/Pacific), the Keg ('great value' steak and seafood), Teppan (Japanese), Mongolie (Asian) and Kypriaki Norte ('excellent duck'). We've had mixed reports on Crab Shack (seafood). Reporters also suggest La Bocca (Italian: 'excellent home-made pasta, good value'), the Bearfoot Bistro (European: 'the best gourmet restaurant, with a stellar wine list') and Sushi Village ('The best Japanese I've had outside Tokyo,' says a well-travelled reporter).

In Village North: the good-value Brewhouse (steaks, burgers) has good microbrews and a lively atmosphere, Caramba has 'good Mediterranean food at reasonable prices', and the Tandoori Grill has 'Indian just like at home'. Hy's

TOURIST OFFICE

t 932 3434
wbres@intrawest.com
www.mywhistler.com
www.whistler-
blackcomb.com

WHISTLER RESORT /
BRUCE ROWLES

The spectacular
mountain-top views
are reminiscent of the
Alps rather than
Colorado's rolling hills
↓

Steakhouse has the best steaks ('melt in your mouth'). Sushi-Ya and Quattro (Italian) are good. In Upper Village, Thai One On is 'excellent', and Monk's Grill has 'very good steaks'.

There are plenty of budget places, including the bars mentioned below. Uli's Flipside at Creekside and The Old Spaghetti Factory in Whistler Village have been recommended for pasta.

APRES-SKI
Something for most tastes
Whistler is very lively. Popular at Whistler are the Longhorn, with a huge terrace, and the Garibaldi Lift Company. The Dubh Linn Gate Irish pub has 'great live music and Guinness'. Tapley's seems 'the nearest thing to a locals' bar'. Merlin's is the focus at Blackcomb base, though readers also recommend the Monk's Grill, and Dusty's is the place at Creekside – good beer, loud music.

Later on, Buffalo Bill's is lively and loud and the Amsterdam Café is worth a look. Tommy Africa's, Maxx Fish, the Savage Beagle, Garfinkel's and Moe Joe's are the main clubs. Try the Mallard bar in Chateau Whistler and the Crystal Lodge piano bar for a quieter time.

Bars and clubs are for over-19s only, and readers have found it's advisable to carry age ID. Smoking is generally not allowed in bars, although most have a smoking area outside, sometimes heated. Garfinkel's and the Mallard have inside smoking areas.

OFF THE SLOPES
Not ideal
Whistler is a long way to go if you don't intend to hit the slopes. Meadow Park Sports Centre has a full range of fitness facilities. There are also several luxurious spas. Reporters have recommended walks (or mountain biking last season when there was no snow) around the lake, the Great Wall Underground climbing centre and a shop where you can paint your own pottery. There's an eight-screen cinema in Whistler Village. And Ziptrek Ecotours (935 0001) offers ecological journeys using harnesses, cables and suspension bridges through the forest between Whistler and Blackcomb mountains. You can also do ATV/snowmobile trips and dog-sledding. Excursions to Squamish (famous for its eagles) are easy, as are day trips to Vancouver.

Whistler

659

JASPER PARK LODGE

Jasper

Set in the middle of Jasper National Park, Jasper appeals more to those keen on scenery and wildlife (and cross-country skiing) rather than piste miles. A visit could be combined with a stay in Whistler, Banff or Lake Louise.

KEY FACTS

Resort	1065m
	3,500ft
Slopes	1685-2600m
	5,530-8.530ft
Lifts	9
Pistes	1,675 acres
Green	30%
Blue	30%
Black	40%
Snowmaking	
	10 acres

TOURIST OFFICE

t 780 852 3816
info@skimarmot.com
www.skimarmot.com

THE RESORT

Jasper is a low-key, low-rise little town. The three-hour drive to or from Lake Louise on the Columbia Icefields Parkway past glaciers, frozen waterfalls and lakes is simply stunning.

Most accommodation is out of town or on the outskirts and the local slopes are a 30-minute drive. The Fairmont Jasper Park Lodge (852 3301) has luxurious family-friendly log cabins set 4km/2 miles out of town around a lake.

THE MOUNTAINS

The slopes are very limited in size. A high-speed quad takes you to mid-mountain, with four slow chairs above that. Snowfall is modest by North American standards but last season was a bumper one. There is lots of steep expert terrain that needs good snow to be fun. Keen piste-bashers will cover all the groomed runs in half a day. There are excellent nursery slopes and gentle greens to progress to.

At mid-mountain there are self-service cafe and table-service options and at the base the rebuilt Caribou Chalet is attractive. There are 300km/186 miles of cross-country trails.

RED MOUNTAIN RESORTS INC

Red Resort

A new owner has grand plans for expanding the ski area and building a resort village. But for now Red remains a cult resort for expert skiers who can handle its steep terrain in the trees. If that's your scene, get there quickly.

KEY FACTS

Resort	1185m
	3,890ft
Slopes	1185-2075m
	3,890-6,800ft
Lifts	6
Pistes	1,585 acres
Green	10%
Blue	45%
Black	45%
Snowmaking	none

TOURIST OFFICE

t 250 362 7384
info@redresort.com
www.redresort.com

THE RESORT

Currently there's a smattering of accommodation at the base of the ski hill, but a new owner has plans for a proper village there and to expand the ski area. On our 2004 visit we stayed at the Rams Head Inn (250 362 9577) – a homely B&B with hot-tub a couple of minutes' walk from the lifts (the owner will guide guests around the mountain). Gypsey at Red, an excellent restaurant, is nearby. The sleepy small town of Rossland a couple of miles away has a few hotels and restaurants and the cool Gold Rush bookshop/coffee bar.

THE MOUNTAINS

Red attracts a few experts from afar but you'll mainly find locals on the hill. Its 300 inch average snowfall is up there with many Colorado resorts but not in the super league. There are a few green and blue runs to warm up on (don't believe the 55% statistic they put out), but it's the black and double-black stuff that is the real attraction. The tough stuff is marked on the map but not really on the mountain; and it's mostly in trees, with cliffs and gnarly narrow bits, so you need a guide. There are plenty of friendly local snow hosts who are only too pleased to show you around. The main mountain is Granite, a conical peak with more or less separate faces of blue, black and double-black steepness – all served by a few slow chairs. Next-door Red Mountain itself is half the size and has a double chair. The Paradise Lodge is an on-mountain snackery but most people head back to base for lunch. For 2005/06 cat skiing is planned and for 2004/05 a new terrain-park was built.

Silver Star

This quiet, family-friendly resort has a tiny traffic-free centre resembling a 19th century mining town. There are slopes to suit everyone and it's easy to combine a stay here with one at Big White, which has the same owners.

KEY FACTS

Resort	1610m
	5,280ft
Slopes	1155-1915m
	3,780-6,280ft
Lifts	11
Pistes	3,125 acres
Green	20%
Blue	50%
Black	30%

THE RESORT

Silver Star is a small, recently developed resort built in the style of an 1890s mining town right on the slopes. The centre is a compact car-free area of brightly painted Victorian-style buildings with wooden sidewalks and pseudo gas lights. It's rather Disneyesque but works surprisingly well. Big (also brightly coloured) chalets are dotted in the trees. There are several ski-in ski-out condo-hotels, as well as apartments and large homes to let. New for 2005/06 will be the first phase of Snowbird Lodge, which claims '5-star accommodation', a pool and a hot-tub. Putnam Station does good steaks in a room decorated with railway memorabilia and with a model train running around the walls. Après-ski is quiet; the Vance Creek saloon is the most animated place.

THE MOUNTAINS

The wooded mountain has three main linked faces. The south face around the village has mainly easy intermediate slopes served by a six-pack, which starts below the main village. For 2005/06 it will be joined by the new Silver Woods area of north-east-facing slopes, served by a new high-speed quad. This will add 400 acres of terrain including seven new trails (five intermediate, two advanced and one beginner) and five areas of glades.

But Silver Star's slopes have a Jekyll and Hyde character. While the south face has mainly easy runs, when you get on the back (or north) side you are in a different world – lots of steep black and double-black trails, mostly with big moguls. Easy trails run along three ridges, with the black trails dropping from them to meet the Powder Gulch fast quad. Gowabunga is the steepest challenge but Headwall and Nirvana were quite enough for us.

You can stick to blue alternatives (and one green), too. Because most of the runs here are north-facing, the snow normally keeps in good condition. There's a small atmospheric hut near the top of the chair-lift, serving simple hot food.

We were impressed with the extent of the slopes served by the two existing main fast chairs. But there are also lots of flat areas, including the link with the back side, which make life difficult for snowboarders.

The ski school has a very good reputation and is headed up by one of Canada's top ski instructor trainers (who has also coached the national demonstration team).

Cross-country is very popular here; they claim their 60km/37 miles of groomed trails are 'The Best Nordic Skiing in North America'.

Off the slopes there's a natural ice rink on a lake prettily set around an island and a nearby tubing hill.

TOURIST OFFICE

t 250 542 0224 www.skisilverstar.com

Eastern Canada

NEWS

For 2004/05 the new owner of Le Massif replaced a double chair with a high-speed quad, created six new intermediate and expert runs, widened some existing gladed runs and increased the snowmaking capacity by 90 snow-guns.

At Stoneham, for 2004/05, 80 of the 120 covers were replaced on Lift H (a high speed quad) for better protection again the elements, and for 2005/06 the snowmaking system is to have a major revamp.

Mont-Ste-Anne built a new beginners' half-pipe on the Grande Allée run for 2004/05 and installed new energy-efficient snowmaking. For 2005/06 the South Face is due to have a new Enchanted Forest tree run for kids.

662

For us the main attraction of skiing or riding in eastern Canada is the French culture and language that are predominant in the province of Québec. It really feels like a different country from the rest of Canada – as indeed many of its residents want it to become. It is also only a six-hour flight from the UK, compared with 10 for Canada's west. Tremblant is the main destination resort and is one of the cutest purpose-built resorts we've seen (though it is now in danger of being spoiled by expansion). The other main base is Québec city, which dates from the 17th century and is full of atmosphere and Canadian history. Slopes of the main resorts are small, both in extent and in vertical drop, and the weather can be perishingly cold in early and mid-winter. But at least this means that the extensive snowmaking systems that all the resorts have can be effective for a long season. Be prepared for variable snow conditions and don't go expecting light, dry powder – if that's what you want, head west.

There are lots of ski and snowboard areas in Ontario – Canada's most populated province – but most of them are tiny and cater just for locals. For people heading on holiday for a week or more, eastern Canada really means the province of Québec. Québec and its capital, Québec city, are heavily dominated by the French culture and language. Notices, menus, trail maps and so on are usually printed in both French and English. Many ski area workers are bilingual or just French-speaking. And French cuisine abounds. The Frenchness of it is one of the big attractions for us.

The weather is very variable, rather like New England's – but it can get even colder. Hence the snow, though pretty much guaranteed by snowmaking, can vary enormously in quality. When we were there one April we were slush skiing in Tremblant one

day and rattling along on a rock-hard surface in Mont-Ste-Anne the next. One reporter who visited Mont-Ste-Anne, Stoneham and Le Massif in late January experienced mild temperatures and several perfect blue-sky days.

The main destination resort is **Tremblant** (see separate chapter), about 90 minutes' drive from Montreal. Other areas near here popular with locals include **Mont Blanc** (with only 300m/980ft of vertical, hardly a competitor to the Franco-Italian version) and the **St-Sauveur** valley (five areas, each with around 200m/660ft of vertical and with interchangeable lift passes).

The other main place to stay for easy access to several ski resorts is **Québec city**. Old Québec, at the city's heart, is North America's only walled city and is a World Heritage site. Within the city walls are narrow,

LE MASSIF / MARC ARCHAMBAULT

Ski resorts don't come much closer to sea level – this is Le Massif →

winding streets and 17th and 18th century houses. It is situated right on the banks of the St Lawrence river. In January/February there is a famous two-week carnival, with an ice castle, snow sculptures, dog-sled and canoe races, night parades and grand balls. But most of the winter is low season for Québec city, with good-value rooms available in big hotels. Because of this, the area is popular with British school groups, especially in late season. Non-skiers, or those who like the option to do other activities, won't be bored, whatever time of year they go.

There are several ski and snowboard areas close to Québec city, and a Carte Blanche pass which covers the three main areas: a total of 106 runs, 26 lifts and Canada's largest night skiing area. A car is handy, but there are buses to some areas.

The biggest and most varied area (though easily skied in a day by a good skier) is **Mont-Ste-Anne**, 30 minutes away and with some accommodation of its own. A gondola takes you to the top, and slopes lead down the front (south) and back (north) sides. The views from the front over the ice floes of the St Lawrence are spectacular. There are intermediate cruising runs on both sides and some steep blacks (including World Cup runs) through the trees on the front among its 68km/42 miles of trails. There are some easy top-to-bottom runs and good nursery slopes at the base. In spring you can stop by the Sugar Shack and try fresh maple toffee. The resort has three terrain-parks, a beginners' half-pipe (new last season) and a 600m/1,970ft boarder-cross course. Seventeen trails are floodlit until 10pm seven nights a week (five in January and February). Over 80% of the runs are covered by snowmaking. It also has the largest cross-country centre in Canada, with 223km/139 miles of trails.

Stoneham is the closest resort to Québec city, around 20 minutes away. It also has its own small village with accommodation and an impressive base lodge with bar, restaurant and big wooden deck. Après-ski in the lodge can be lively, and there is often live music. It is a small area, with only around 30km/19 miles of runs spread between three faces and a vertical of 420m/1,380ft. But it is very sheltered in a sunny setting protected from wind. It suits families well, with mainly

intermediate and beginner terrain, and has a special beginner area equipped with a moving carpet. Snowboarders, freestylers and freeskiers are attracted to the area by the resort's impressive terrain-park with 15 rails and 10 table-tops, its 1000m/3,280ft boarder-cross course and its super-pipe. Stoneham also has the biggest night skiing operation in Canada – 16 runs – with two of the three faces lit top to bottom. Some 86% of the area has snowmaking.

Le Massif is around an hour away from Québec city and is a cult area with locals. It is in a UNESCO World Biosphere Reserve and is just metres from the St Lawrence. The views of the ice floes are stunning, and you feel you are heading straight down into them when you are on the pretty, tree-lined trails. The area of slopes, though small, has the largest vertical drop in the east. There are a couple of steep double-black-diamond runs and some good, well-groomed black and blue cruising runs, including a run designed to meet International Ski Federation World Cup standards. They have Québec's longest high-speed quad chair and for 2004/05 another fast chair and six more runs were built – see 'News'. Snowmaking covers 54% of its trails.

Introduction

663

Tremblant

Charming, traffic-free village at the foot of a small area of slopes

COSTS

① ② ③ ④ ⑤ ⑥

RATINGS

The slopes

Fast lifts	****
Snow	****
Extent	*
Expert	**
Intermediate	***
Beginner	****
Convenience	****
Queues	***
Mtn restaurants	**

The rest

Scenery	***
Resort charm	****
Off-slope	***

KEY FACTS

Resort	265m
	8700ft
Slopes	230-875m
	750-2,870ft
Lifts	13
Pistes	628 acres
Green	17%
Blue	33%
Black	50%
Snowmaking	
	885 guns

NEWS

For 2004/05 a new boutique hotel, L'Ermitage du Lac, opened.

+ Charming purpose-built core village
+ Good snow reliability with extensive artificial back-up
+ Some good runs for all abilities

– Limited area for keen piste-bashers
– Can be perishingly cold in midwinter
– Weekend queues and overcrowding
– Rapid expansion planned

Tremblant is eastern Canada's main destination resort and attracts quite a lot of Brits. But for keen piste-bashers the limited slopes don't really do justice to the cute and lively little core village, which has been built in traditional style.

THE RESORT

Tremblant has been transformed in recent years from a day or weekend ski area for locals to being eastern Canada's leading ski resort. Intrawest (which also owns Whistler and several other North American resorts) developed a purpose-built village in the style of old Québec. Buildings in bright, vibrant colours line narrow, cobbled, traffic-free streets and squares, and it has a very French feel to it. Recent expansion on the edge is not so cute.

THE MOUNTAINS

In its small area, Tremblant has a good variety of pleasantly wooded terrain.
Slopes A heated gondola takes you to the top, from where there are good views over the village and a 14km/9 mile lake on the so-called South Side, and over National Park wilderness on the North Side (which is really north-east facing and gets the morning sun). A high-speed quad brings you back and there are two other chairs to play on. The slow Edge lift accesses another summit, serving mainly expert terrain. On the South Side (really south-west facing and so good for the pm sun) you can go right back to town on blue or green runs, or use two high-speed quads to explore the top and bottom halves. The Versant Soleil area is more directly south-facing and has one top-to-bottom blue run, all the rest being black runs and tree runs.
Terrain-parks The excellent 18-acre Gravité terrain-park plus a super-pipe is on the top half of the North Side. There's a mini Gravité park here, too, and a third park on the South Side.
Snow reliability Canada's east coast doesn't get as much snow as the west, but over 75% of the trails are covered by snowmaking. Grooming is excellent.
Experts Half the runs are classified as suitable for advanced skiers and riders. But we found many of the blacks did not deserve their grading. There are steep top-to-bottom bump runs on the North Side and great gladed tree runs off the Edge lift. The Versant Soleil area has more black runs and some tough runs in the trees. However, the gladed runs really need decent, and preferably fresh, snow to be fun.
Intermediates Both North and South Sides have good cruising and we found the North Side less crowded. There are blue-classified runs in the trees as well as on groomed trails.
Beginners The 2-acre beginner area is excellent, and there are long, easy, top-to-bottom green runs to progress to.
Snowboarding The slopes are good for beginners, but better boarders can't count on fresh natural snow to play in. A specialist shop, Adrénaline, runs a

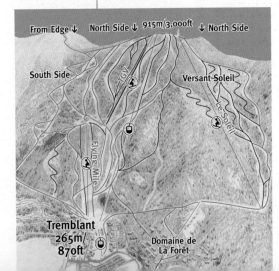

From Edge ↓   North Side ↓ 915m/3,000ft   ↓ North Side

South Side

Versant Soleil

le Soleil

Flying Mile

Tremblant
265m/
870ft

Domaine de
La Forêt

TOURIST OFFICE

t +1 819 681 2000
info_tremblant@
intrawest.com
www.tremblant.ca

Burton learn-to-ride programme.
Cross-country There are around 100km/62 miles of trails, some at the top of the mountain, with great views.
Queues At weekends there can be queues, but they tend to move quickly. We found crowds on the main run back to the village more of a problem.
Mountain restaurants The main Grand Manitou restaurant has good views and decent food but can get crowded. Many people go back to town for lunch.
Schools and guides Reporters praise the school: 'good instructors and both children made progress', 'excellent – a 4-year-old was skiing greens in a week'.
Facilities for children Children from age 1 to 12 can be cared for until 9.30pm.

STAYING THERE

How to go There's no shortage of packages from the UK.
Hotels and condos The luxurious Fairmont Tremblant and the condos in the Place St Bernard, the Tour des Voyagers and the Chouette have been recommended. But the nearest supermarket is a car- or bus-ride away and there can be long waits between buses.
Eating out Try the Forge, Ya'ooo Pizza Bar, Shack, Casey's, Mexicali Rosa's and the Loup Garou at the Fairmont. Plus Minus, Spag & Co, Windigo and Restaurant U were recommended by a 2005 reporter.
Après-ski Octobar Rock is popular with Brits, the Forge is good as the slopes close, the Shack brews its own beer. There is often live music and a good atmosphere in the main square. There are floodlit slopes some nights.
Off the slopes The Aquaclub La Source pool complex resembles a lake set in a forest, but reporters complain it's pricey. For adults only, the 'excellent' Spa Scandinavie offers sauna, steam room, outdoor hot-tubs and waterfalls. You can also go ice-climbing, horse-riding, ice skating, snow-shoeing, tubing, snowmobiling, dog-sledding and swimming – and visit Montreal ('highly recommended').

Spain

666

NEWS

For 2004/05 Sierra Nevada installed a new chair at the new parking area that accesses Borreguiles. Snowmaking was increased to a total of 31km/19 miles (over one-third of the slopes).

At Formigal a six-person gondola was replaced by a fast eight-seat chair. And two six-packs and two quads were also installed. A new area, the Portalet, provides another 75 acres of skiable terrain, with two red, three blue and five green pistes. And 240 new snow-guns have been installed.

At La Molina a new quad has been installed.

TOURIST OFFICES

Sierra Nevada
www.sierranevadaski.com

Formigal
www.formigal.com

Candanchu
www.candanchu.com

Astún
www.astun.com

La Molina
www.lamolina.com

These days it's dangerous to generalise about Spanish resorts – which is why we don't provide the lists of ➕ and ➖ points that we do for other second-division countries. There are now some well-equipped Pyrenean resorts with fine, snow-sure slopes that compare favourably with mid-sized places in the Alps. Two resorts are certainly not downmarket – Sierra Nevada and Baqueira-Beret (see next chapter) are both frequented by the King of Spain. Winter sports are becoming more popular with the prosperous Spanish themselves, and as a result many of the smaller resorts are continually improving.

The general ambience of Spanish resorts is attractive – not unlike that of Italy, with eating, posing and partying taken seriously and late starts to the ski day the norm.

Sierra Nevada (2100m/6,890ft) is in the extreme south of Spain, between Granada (well worth a visit and much quieter than in the summer) and the Costa del Sol, with views from the very top to the Atlas mountains in Morocco.

The hub of the resort is Pradollano, a stylish modern development with shops and a few restaurants and bars set around traffic-free open spaces – likened by one reporter to Whistler. There is a huge but expensive underground car-park here, and parking elsewhere can be difficult.

Most of the accommodation is in older, less smart buildings set along a road winding up the steep hillside. A two-stage chair-lift also goes up the hillside, with red runs back down to the main lift stations at Pradollano. Choose your location with care; the hotel Telecabina is, not surprisingly, ideally placed for the gondolas and is also 'warm, friendly, with good food'.

From Pradollano an old 4-person gondola and a newer 14-person one go up to Borreguiles, at the heart of the 84km/ 52 miles of slopes. Here there are excellent nursery slopes, and lifts going up to the broad upper slopes beneath the peak of Veleta. There are three identifiable sectors, well linked, with a good range of intermediate and easy runs. The snow is well groomed, but it is not a big area, and there is not a lot for experts.

Queues can develop at Pradollano when buses arrive from lower towns, and higher up there are quite a lot of slow old lifts that cause queues at ski school time and after lunch. The chair up the village slope gets the biggest queues of all. Most chairs have singles lines, though. The run back to town at the end of the day can get crowded.

Sierra Nevada's weather can be a problem. The resort's natural snow arrives via completely different weather patterns from those supplying the Alps and the Pyrenees; in 1990, when the Alps were disastrously snowless, Sierra Nevada had the best conditions in Europe. But the much-fêted World Championships in the mid-1990s had to be postponed by a year. The slopes face generally north-west, but some get the full force of the afternoon sun. And when the wind blows, as it does, the slopes close; there are no trees.

A reporter last year liked the 'nice restaurants in the village, but not the cafeteria on the mountain'.

There is a group of worthwhile resorts in the western Pyrenees, between Pau and Huesca.

Formigal is working hard to improve its standing with new chair-lifts, terrain and pistes (see 'News'), but the 68km/ 42 miles of pistes are windswept. When the wind blows, retreat to nearby Panticosa – a charming old village with 34km/21 miles of sheltered pistes. **Candanchu** and nearby **Astún**, with almost 100km/62 miles of pistes between them, are popular on the Spanish market. They offer a wide range of lodging set in some of the Pyrenees' most stunning scenery. Candanchu has some tough runs.

The other resorts of international interest are just east of Andorra. The 50km/31 miles of runs at **La Molina** and its purpose-built satellite Supermolina (1700m/5,580ft) are now linked to those of Masella, over the mountain, via a gondola and six-pack. The whole area, called Alp 2500, now extends over 110km/ 68 miles of mainly intermediate skiing.

Baqueira-Beret

Spain's leading winter resort – fit for their king

COSTS

① ② ③ ④ ⑤ ⑥

RATINGS

The slopes
Fast lifts	**
Snow	***
Extent	**
Expert	***
Intermediate	****
Beginner	**
Convenience	***
Queues	***
Mountain restaurants	**

The rest
Scenery	***
Resort charm	**
Off-slope	*

REPORTS WANTED

Recently we have had few reports on this resort. If you go there, please do send us a report.

BAQUEIRA TOURIST OFFICE

Most of the slopes are above the tree line ↓

➕ Compact modern resort

➕ Reasonable snow reliability

➕ Some good off-piste potential

➕ Lots of good intermediate slopes

➕ Friendly, helpful locals

➖ Drab high-rise blocks dominate the main village

➖ Resort is not cleverly laid out, and suffers from traffic around the lift base station

➖ Few off-slope diversions

Baqueira is in a different league from other resorts in the Spanish Pyrenees – a smart, family-oriented resort with a wide area of north-facing slopes that gives a real feeling of travel. It attracts an almost entirely Spanish clientele (which regularly includes the royal family), so don't count on English being spoken.

THE RESORT

Baqueira was purpose-built in the 1960s and has its fair share of drab, high-rise blocks; these are clustered below the road that runs through to the high pass of Port de la Bonaigua, while the main lift base is just above it. But up the steep hill from the main base are some newer, smaller-scale stone-clad developments. At the very top is an alternative chair-lift into the slopes. The most convenient base is close to the main chair-lift, but the village is small enough for location not to be too much of an issue. There is a lot of accommodation spread down the valley, and a big car park with road-train shuttle up to the lift base.

THE MOUNTAINS

There is an extensive area of long, mainly intermediate, runs, practically all of them on open, treeless slopes and facing roughly west.

Slopes The slopes are split into three distinct but well-connected areas – Baqueira, Beret and Bonaigua. From the base station at Baqueira, a fast quad which you ride without skis (which fit in to slots in the back of the chair in front) takes you up to the nursery slopes at 1800m/5,910ft. Fast chairs go on up to Cap de Baqueira. From here there is a wide variety of long runs, served by chairs and drags – including a long black down to Orri. From several points you can descend into the Bonaigua sector, leading over to the summit of the Bonaigua pass. You can ride a chair from the pass to get to an expanding, recently-opened area of slopes descending to the east of the pass and served by a fast quad.

From the opposite extremity of the Baqueira sector at Orri a triple chair takes you off to the Beret sector, where a series of more-or-less parallel chairs serve mainly blue and red runs. A fast quad and a drag-lift serve a fourth sector across the valley from the Beret slopes, with three blue pistes, a red piste and an itinerary. Beret, Orri and Bonaigua are accessible by road.

Terrain-parks There's a terrain park with half-pipe in the Bonaigua area.

Snow reliability Most of the slopes are above 1800m/5,910ft and there is extensive snowmaking, but afternoon sun is a problem in spring. We've had mixed reports of the grooming.

Experts Experts will find few on-piste challenges, but there are extensive off-

NEWS

The Bonaigua area was expanded for 2004/05 with five new runs – three red, a blue and a black.

A new high-speed quad from near the nursery slopes above Baqueira serves three new blue slopes and gives more direct access to Beret on easy runs.

KEY FACTS

Resort	1500m
	4,920ft
Slopes	1500-2510m
	4,920-8,230ft
Lifts	31
Pistes	104km
	64 miles
Green	7%
Blue	51%
Red	34%
Black	8%
Snowmaking	36km
	22 miles

Phone numbers
From abroad use the prefix +34.

TOURIST OFFICE

t 973 639010
baqueira@baqueira.es
www.baqueira.es

piste opportunities all over the area. And there are four ungroomed itinerary runs including the steep and narrow Escornacrabes, from the top of Cap de Baqueira. Cheap heli-lifts are available.

Intermediates It's excellent, with lots of varied blues and some classic long red runs such as Muntanyo down to Port de la Bonaigua and Mirador above town. Less daring intermediates will enjoy the Beret and Bonaigua areas best.

Beginners There are some good nursery runs above Baqueira but some of the blues you move on to can be a bit tough. Beret (reachable by road) has an excellent nursery slope and gentle blues.

Snowboarding The main nursery slopes are served by drags but experienced free-riders have plenty of chair-served off-piste to play in.

Cross-country There are 7km/4 miles of trails between Orri and Beret.

Queues Weekdays are quiet but at weekends some waits can be 10 minutes. There are some slow old chairs still.

Mountain restaurants Most have good-value food but they are 'lacking in number and variety and many were very smoky,' says a 2005 reporter. You can get table service at Cap del Port, at the Bonaigua pass, at Baqueira 2200 and at Beret.

Schools and guides The school gets good reports – some spoken English.

Ski Miquel organises lessons with British instructors.

Facilities for children The kindergarten takes children from three months but lack of spoken English is a problem. Ski school classes start from age four.

STAYING THERE

How to go There is a reasonable choice of hotels and apartments locally. Ski Miquel has a catered chalet.

Hotels In the main village three have been recommended by reporters – the 4-star Montarto (973 639001) with 'pool and wonderful food' and two 3-stars: the Tuc Blanc (973 644350) with pool, and Val de Ruda (973 645258). The 5-star Rafael La Pleta (973 645550), just above the village, has: 'outstanding rooms and service', 'excellent food'. The Parador (973 640801) down the valley in Arties and the 2-star Husa Vielha (973 640275) further down in Vielha have been recommended.

Eating out The more interesting restaurants are down the valley in Salardu, Arties and Vielha. Reporters have enjoyed the local tapas bars.

Après-ski There are pubs and discos down the valley. Pacha, in the main village, gets going around 1am or 2am.

Off the slopes Pool and spa facilities are available in some hotels. Vielha, 15km/9 miles away, has a sports centre.

Tuc deth Dossau
2510m/8,23oft

2200m

2350m

2100m

Cap de Baqueira
2500m

Port de la Bonaigua
2070m

Beret
1850m

Orri
1850m

1800m

Tuc de Costarjàs
2340m

Cap de Blanhiblar
2240m

1700m

Baqueira
1500m/4,92oft

Finland

COSTS

① ② ③ ④ ⑤ ⑥

NEWS

In Ruka, for 2005/06 a fast six-seat chair is planned to replace several T-bars on Ruka East. The beginners' area on Vuosseli is due to be extended. And this area should get more snowmaking. The terrain-park is being upgraded and the cross-country tracks improved.

There are more plans to replace T-bars with chairs for the 2006/07 season.

For 2004/05 in Levi the Himmeriikki lift was moved to the southern side of the mountain. Its new name is Aurinko. Three new pistes – a red and two blues – were created for it.

More snowmaking and night skiing were introduced, bringing the total pistes for each to 15. The terrain-park now offers kickers, boxes and rails.

The Levitunturi hotel opened its new 1,500-seat Restaurant World with five different restaurants.

In Ylläs for 2004/05 new slopes were created in the woods. A new feel-good centre opened, with gym and spa. The free bus between the hotels and the slopes was reinstated.

➕ Peace, quiet and Lapp charm

➕ Ideal terrain for cross-country and gentle downhilling

➕ Reliable late snow

➕ Jolly outings

➖ Cold

➖ Small ski areas

➖ Quite expensive

➖ Uninspiring food

For skiers with no appetite for the hustle and hassle of Alpine resorts in high season – perhaps especially for families – escape to the white silence of Lapland may be an attractive alternative. Finland has the lion's share of Lapland and has successfully marketed it, not only for day-trip visits to Santa but also for ski holidays to resorts with limited downhill slopes but limitless cross-country. Of the resorts covered here, only Ruka and Iso-Syöte are south of the Arctic Circle.

The Arctic landscape of flat and gently rolling forest punctuated by many lakes and the occasional treeless hill is a paradise for cross-country skiing. Weather permitting, it also offers good beginner and intermediate downhilling, albeit on a small scale.

The resorts usually open a few runs in late November. For two months in midwinter the sun does not rise – at least, not at ground level. Most areas have floodlit runs. The mountains do not open fully until mid-February, when a normal skiing day is possible and Finnish schools have holidays that usually coincide with ours – a busy time. Finland comes into its own at the end of the season, with friendlier temperatures and long daylight hours. Understandably, Easter is extremely popular, and the slopes are crowded.

Conditions are usually hard-packed powder or fresh snow from the start of the season to the end (early May).

The temperature can be extremely variable, yo-yoing between zero and minus 30°C several times in a week. Fine days are the coldest, but usually the best for skiing: it may be 10 to 15 degrees warmer on the slopes than at valley level. 'Mild' days of cloud and wind are much worse, and face masks are widely sold. None of the areas has significant vertical by alpine standards.

The staple Finnish lift is the T-bar. Ruka has some chairs, and Levi has Finland's only gondola. Pistes are wide, uncomplicated and well maintained, with good nursery slopes. The Finns are great boarders and consider their terrain-parks far superior to those in the Alps. Levi and Iso-Syöte have terrain-parks with super-pipe and half-pipe and Ruka built a super-pipe two seasons ago.

The runs are so short that there is no need for mountain restaurants – you are never far from the base, with its shops and self-service restaurant. The ski areas also have shelters or 'kotas' – log-built teepees with an open fire and a smoke hole – where you can eat a snack or grill some food.

Ski school is good, with English widely spoken. All ski areas have indoor playrooms for small children, but they may be closed at weekends.

Excursions are common – husky-sledding, snowmobile safaris, a reindeer sleigh ride and tea with the Lapp drivers in their tent. 'The whole experience is wonderful,' says a typically enthusiastic participant.

Hotels are self-contained resorts, large and practical rather than stylish, typically with a shop, a cafe, a bar with dance floor, and a pool and sauna with outdoor cooling-off area. Hotel supper is typically served no later than seven, sometimes followed by a children's disco or dancing to a live band.

Finns usually prefer to stay in cabins, and tour operators offer the compromise of staying in a cabin but taking half-board at a nearby hotel. Cabins vary, but are mostly spacious and well equipped, with a sauna and heated drying cupboard as standard.

The main resorts are **Levi** and **Ylläs**, respectively 17km/10 miles north and 50km/31 miles west of Kittilä, which has direct charter flights from Britain.

Ylläs mountain has two gateways, of which the major one is Äkäslompolo – a traditional lakeside Lapp settlement, two miles from the lifts. It has a more

WEBSITES

For links to resort sites, go to our own new site at www.wtss.co.uk

Phone numbers
From abroad use the prefix +358 and omit the initial '0' of the phone number.

TOURIST OFFICES

Levi
www.levi.fi

Ylläs
www.yllas.fi

Ruka
www.ruka.fi

Pyhä
www.pyha.fi

Iso-Syöte
www.isosyote.fi

relaxing atmosphere and longer runs than Levi, a purpose-built village of hotels and cabins at the foot of the slopes. Cross-country skiing makes sense of a resort such as Äkäslompolo, which has 320km/200 miles of trails, transforming it from awkward sprawl to doorstep ski resort of limitless scope. From the lift base trails fan out around the mountain, across the frozen lake and away through the endless forest.

Ylläs is the largest downhill ski area in Finland with 463m/1,520ft vertical. Having lifts and pistes on two broad flanks of the mountain gives plenty of scope for skiers just off the nursery slopes. Second- and third-week skiers will rapidly conquer the benign black runs. Ylläs has a welcoming, snow-encrusted restaurant – the highest in the country at 718m/2,360ft.

The Hillankukka log cabins at Äkäslompolo are exceptionally good, but the 10-minute walk to and from meals at the Äkäs hotel (016 553000) is not to be underestimated. A reporter praises the hotel itself – 'beautiful hotel, excellent hydrotherapy pool'.

Levi has 47 slopes served by 26 lifts, including 23 red and five black slopes – one of which hosted a women's World Cup event in 2004. The daughter of a 2005 reporter loved the resort and 'her skiing improved'. Levi has 230km/143 miles of cross-country trails. Its biggest hotel, Levitunturi (016 646301), was rated 'great' by a recent reporter, with 'excellent' facilities – a pool, tennis, and a children's activity centre. Restaurants recommended by reporters are the Steak House, Myllyn Aija ('good value'), Arran and (for a treat) the White Reindeer. Bars that have been recommended are Panimo (a microbrewery), Crazy Reindeer (karaoke), Arran ('more sophisticated').

Ruka lies 80km/50 miles south of the Arctic Circle, 27km/17 miles from Kuusamo airport and only 25km/

15 miles from the Russian border, in a region known for abundant and enduring snow. The ski area, a mixture of open and forest terrain, has 18 lifts (including four chairs), and 28 runs (24 floodlit, 24 with snowmaking, a mogul run and several black runs, none of them steep), and the vertical range is 200m/660ft. The cross-country scope is vast: they advertise 500km/310 miles, of which 40km/25 miles are floodlit.

The atmosphere at the resort and on the slopes is upbeat – with live music in the Wunderbar and sun terraces outside the Piste, very popular in spring. Hotels include the Rukahovi (08 85910), only 50m/160ft from the slopes, and the Royal Ruka (08 868 6000), the resort's flagship property. The best accommodation is in cabins. Good restaurants include Riipinen, which offers capercaillie, bear and boar, Vanha Karhu, and Kalakeidas, an intimate little fish restaurant.

Pyhä, 150km/93 miles north-east of Rovaniemi, has seven lifts (including two chairs) and 10 runs on a mountain, much of which is a National Park. The vertical is only 280m/920ft and there is no steep terrain, but it has good off-piste. The best powder runs are on both sides of a long T-bar on the north slope. The Hotel Pyhätunturi (016 856111) is at mid-mountain.

Iso-Syöte, 150km/93 miles south of the Arctic Circle and 140km/86 miles from Oulu airport, is Finland's southernmost fell region – but it receives the most snow in the country. Catering mainly for families, it suits beginners and intermediates since, of its 12 pistes (covering 20km/12 miles), five are easy and five are intermediate, and there are only two black runs. However, there is a free-ride area among the trees. The runs are short, with the longest 1200m/3900ft and a maximum vertical of less than 200m/660 feet. Seven runs are floodlit at night. There's a terrain-park with boxes and rails plus a super-pipe and quarter pipe, a snow-tubing area and a sledging hill. You can also ski at Pikku-Syöte, a short distance away, which has a handful of short runs, all easy. Cross-country is big here, with 120km/74 miles of trails.

Accommodation is mainly hotels and log cabins, including the Iso-Syöte hotel (0201 476400) at the top of the slopes, with a pool and sauna. You can try snowmobiling, husky safaris, snow-shoeing and reindeer driving.

Norway

671

COSTS

①②③④⑤⑥

+ One of the best places in Europe for serious cross-country skiing

+ The home of telemark – plenty of opportunities to learn and practise

+ Complete freedom from the glitz and ill-mannered lift queues of the Alps

+ Impressive snowboard parks

+ Usually reliable snow conditions throughout a long season

– Very limited downhill areas

– Mountain restaurants that are little more than pit stops

– Booze is prohibitively taxed

– Unremarkable scenery

– Après-ski that is either deadly dull or irritatingly rowdy

– Short daylight hours in midwinter

– Highly changeable weather

– Limited off-slope activities

Norway and its resorts are very different from the Alps, or indeed the Rockies. Some people find the place very much to their taste. For downhillers who dislike the usual ski-resort trappings, and prefer a simpler approach to winter holidays, it could be just the place. For families with young children, in particular, the drawbacks are less pronounced than for others; you'll have no trouble finding junk food to please the kids – the mountain restaurants serve little else.

Speaking for ourselves, any one of the first three – points we've listed above would probably be enough to put us off. Combine these in a single destination – then add in the other non-trivial negative points – and you can count us out.

REPORTS WANTED

We would welcome more reports on Norwegian resorts. If you go there, please do send us a report.

The best reports earn a copy of the next edition, and can lead to free lift passes in future.

See page 10.

There is a traditional friendship between Norway and Britain, and English is widely spoken – universally spoken, in our experience.

For the Norwegians and Swedes, skiing is a weekend rather than a special holiday activity, and not an occasion for extravagance. So at lunchtime they tend to haul sandwiches out of their backpacks as we might while walking the Pennine Way, and in the evening they cook in their apartments. Don't expect a tempting choice of restaurants.

The Norwegians have a problem with alcohol. Walk into an après-ski bar at 5pm on a Saturday and you may find young men already inebriated – not merry, but incoherent. And this is despite – or, some say, because of – prohibitively high taxes on booze. Restaurant prices for wine are ludicrous, and shop prices may be irrelevant – Hemsedal has no liquor store. Our one attempt at self-catering there (well, OK, our one takeaway meal) was an unusually sober affair as a result. Other prices are generally not high by Alpine standards.

Cross-country skiing comes as naturally to Norwegians as walking; and even if you're not very keen, the fact that cross-country is normal, and not a wimp's alternative to 'real' skiing, gives Norway a special appeal. Here, cross-country is both a way of getting about the valleys and a way of exploring the hills. Although you can plod around short valley circuits as you might in an Alpine resort, what distinguishes Norway for the keen cross-country skier is the network of long trails across the gentle uplands, with refuges along the way where backpackers can pause for refreshment or stay overnight. This network of mountain huts offers basic but cheap accommodation which can turn touring into a week-long adventure.

More and more Norwegians are taking to telemarking (a bit like cross-country, with a free-heel binding, but with broader skis) for both downhill and backcountry skiing trips.

Snowboarding is very popular – local youths fill the impressive terrain-parks at weekends.

For downhill skiing, the country isn't nearly so attractive. Despite the fact that it is able to hold downhill races, Norway's Alpine areas are of limited appeal. The most rewarding resort is **Hemsedal**, which we cover in the next chapter.

Just twenty minutes from the centre of Oslo on an extension of the underground system is **Tryvann** (150m/492ft), a small area popular with the locals. The train arrives near the top station (525m/1722ft) on Holmenkollen. The main slopes – with a vertical of 380m/1,250ft – are served by two drags and two chairs, one of them fast. Two drags serve a separate nursery slope. There's a good terrain-park and half-pipe. The whole area has snowmaking, and can offer good conditions even when downtown Oslo has no snow in the streets. The slopes are floodlit until 10pm most evenings – and are busier then than in the day.

The site of the 1994 Olympics, the little lakeside town of **Lillehammer**, is not actually a downhill resort at all. The Olympic slalom events were held 15km/9 miles north at Hafjell (230m/750ft). This is a worthwhile little area with a vertical of 830m/ 2,720ft, 12 lifts, and pistes totalling 33km/20 miles. The downhill and super-G races went to Kvitfjell, about 35km/22 miles further north, developed specially for the purpose. It's steeper but a bit smaller – 19km/12 miles of pistes.

Norway's other internationally known resort is **Geilo** (800m/2,620ft). This is a small, quiet, unspoiled community on the railway line from Bergen, on the coast, to Oslo. It provides all the basics of a resort – a handful of cafes and shops around the railway station, a dozen hotels more widely spread around the wide valley, children's facilities and a sports centre.

Geilo is a superb cross-country resort. As the Bergen-Oslo railway runs through the town it is possible to go for long tours and return by train.

Geilo is very limited for downhillers, but it does claim to have Scandinavia's only super-pipe. The 32km/20miles of piste are spread over two small hills – one, Geilolia (formerly Vestlia), a bus-ride away from Geilo, with a good, informal hotel, a restaurant at its foot and a pizzeria on the mountain. This area was extended last season by a six-pack link to the family beginners' zone, Kikutheisene – which has its own fast quad and new moving carpet. None of the runs is really difficult.

Clearly the best hotel, and one of the attractions of staying in Geilo, is the Dr Holms Hotel (call central reservations on 320 95940) – smartly white-painted outside, beautifully furnished and spacious inside. This is the centre for après-ski, but prices are steep. All the other hotels we have seen can be recommended. The resort is quiet at the end of the day, but the main hotels provide live entertainment.

A long way north of the other resorts is **Oppdal** (550m/1,800ft), with more downhill runs than any of its rivals (55km/34 miles). The total vertical is 790m/2,590ft, but this is misleading – most runs are short.

There are slightly more extensive slopes at **Trysil** (460m/1,510ft), off to the east, on the border with Sweden, and the runs are longer (up to 4km/2 miles and 685m/2,250ft vertical). Well-suited to families, it has a new fast lift to the nursery area and gentle runs to progress to. The runs here are all around the conical Trysilfjellet, some way from Trysil itself – though there is some accommodation at the hill.

In complete contrast to all of these resorts is **Voss** (50m/160ft), a sizeable lakeside town quite close to the sea which 'pleasantly surprised' a recent reporter. A cable-car links the town to the slopes on Hangur and Slettafjell, with a total of 40km/25 miles of pistes – 'excellent' for intermediates, 'good' for beginners and 'no queues'. The ski school is reportedly 'brilliant', with small classes. There are plenty of excursion possibilities, in particular the spectacular Flåm railway.

Hemsedal

The place for Alpine skiing in Norway – though we prefer the Alps

COSTS

① ② ③ ④ ⑤ ⑥

RATINGS

The slopes

Fast lifts	**
Snow	****
Extent	*
Expert	**
Intermediate	****
Beginner	***
Convenience	**
Queues	****
Mountain restaurants	*

The rest

Scenery	**
Resort charm	**
Off-slope	*

NEWS

In 2004/05 an eight-seat chair, Hollvin Express, replaced the old triple between the base and mid-mountain. The beginner and family area was expanded – two new lifts, three slopes and a mini terrain-park for the kids.

For 2005/06 additional features are planned for the children's area, including a slalom course, tobogganing area and moving carpet.

Terrain-park improvements will include a half-pipe for the beginner park on Tinden Mountain. Snowmaking will be increased.

WEBSITES

For links to resort sites, go to our own new site at www.wtss.co.uk

HEMSEDAL TOURIST OFFICE

Some of the lower slopes are genuine blacks →

+ Impressive snow reliability because of northerly location

+ Increasing amounts of convenient slope-side accommodation

+ Extensive cross-country trails compared to the Alps

+ Some quite challenging slopes, and mountains with a slightly Alpine feel

− Not much of a village

− Limited slopes

− Exposed upper mountain prone to closure because of bad weather

− Weekend queues

− One abysmal mountain restaurant

− No liquor store for miles

− Après-ski limited during the week and rowdy at weekends

Hemsedal's craggy terrain is reminiscent of a small-but-serious Alpine resort. Most people not resident in Scandinavia would be better advised to go for the real thing, but if you like the sound of Norway, Hemsedal is the place for downhill skiing. Go after the February school holidays, if possible.

THE RESORT

Hemsedal is both an unspoiled valley and a village, also referred to as Trøym and Sentrum ('Centre'), which amounts to very little – a couple of apartment/hotel buildings, a few shops, a bank and a petrol station (but, note, no liquor store). Though there has been talk of a lift from Trøym to the slopes, for now the lift base is a mile or two away, across the valley.

There are self-catering apartments and houses beside the slopes (more are due for 2005/06) – with a newish development called Skarsnuten linked to the main network by its own lift and red piste – and in a pleasantly woody separate cluster a walkable distance down the hill from the lifts.

A recently improved ski-bus links these points, and others in the valley; but really, the place is geared to weekenders arriving by car or coach.

THE MOUNTAINS

Hemsedal's slopes pack a lot of variety into a small space. They are shaded in midwinter, and can be very cold.

Slopes With no fewer than four fast chairs to play on, you can pack a lot of runs into the day. And there's night skiing until 9pm, Tuesdays to Fridays. The lift pass also covers smaller Solheisen, a few miles up the valley. A small supplement is required to ski at Geilo, an hour away.

Terrain-parks There's an impressive and 'very well maintained' terrain-park and two half-pipes and a second, smaller park for beginners – which is expected to add a half-pipe for 2005/06. Kid's have their own mini-park in the children's area.

Snow reliability The combination of latitude, altitude and orientation makes for impressive snow reliability – and there's extensive snowmaking.

KEY FACTS

Resort	650m
	2,050ft
Slopes	670-1450m
	2,200-4,760ft
Lifts	19
Pistes	42km
	26 miles
Green	33%
Blue	21%
Red	26%
Black	20%
Snowmaking	14km
	9 miles

REPORTS WANTED

Recently we have had few reports on this resort. If you go there, please do send us a report.

The best reports earn a copy of the next edition, and can lead to free lift passes in future.

See page 10.

Phone numbers
From abroad use the prefix +47.

TOURIST OFFICE

t 320 55030
info@hemsedal.com
www.hemsedal.com

Experts There is quite a bit to amuse experts – several black pistes of 450m/1,480ft vertical served by a fast eight-seat chair (or the adjacent 'very steep and very bumpy' T-bar) from the base (one left as a mogul slope) – and wide areas of gentler off-piste terrain served by drags above the tree line.

Intermediates Mileage-hungry piste-bashers will find Hemsedal's runs very limited. There are quite a few red and blue runs to play on, but the difference in difficulty is slight.

Beginners There's a gentle nursery area for absolute beginners. And there are splendid long green runs – but they get a lot of traffic, some of it irresponsibly fast. Some long blues and reds also suit near-beginners.

Snowboarding There is plenty of free-riding terrain, and some pistes are suitable for carving. The parks are popular.

Cross-country By Alpine standards there is lots to do – 130km/80 miles of prepared trails in the valley and forest and (later in the season) 80km/50 miles at altitude. There is a special trail map. Most of the trails are a few miles down the valley at the Gravset centre.

Queues Hemsedal is only a three-hour drive from Oslo, the capital. Good weekend weather fills the car parks, leading to queues for the main access lifts after mid-morning, and possibly for others. But during the week it is quiet. The upper lifts are very exposed, and are easily closed by bad weather, producing crowds lower down.

Mountain restaurants There is one functional self-service mountain restaurant doing dreary fast food, plus two or three kiosks with benches.

Schools and guides Our most recent reporter was greatly impressed: 'Lots of one-to-one, very encouraging.'

Facilities for children The facilities at the lift base are good, with day care for children over three months, free to parents in ski school. The kids' nursery slope is admirably gentle and was expanded last season.

STAYING THERE

How to go Most of the accommodation is in apartments, varying widely in convenience. Catered chalets are available through certain UK operators.

Hotels The best hotel is the Skogstad (320 55000) in central Hemsedal – comfortable, but noisy at weekends. Other hotels along the valley are used by UK tour operators. The hotel Skarsnuten, on the mountain, is stylishly modern (with no smoking).

Self-catering The Alpin apartments, a walk from the lift base, are satisfactory if you don't fill all the beds. The adjacent Tinden ones are quite smart.

Eating out There are half-a-dozen restaurants down in the village.

Après-ski It's minimal in the week, rowdy at weekends and holidays.

Off the slopes Diversions include sleighs, tobogganing and snowmobiling. The hotel Skogstad pool is open to the public.

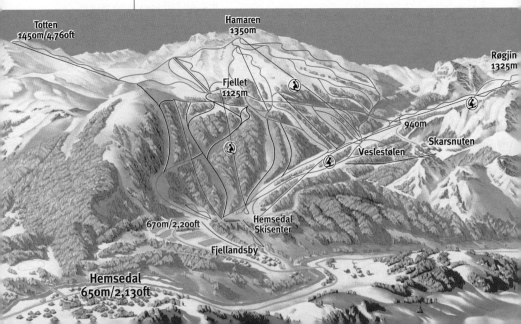

Sweden

COSTS

① ② ③ ④ ⑤ ⑥

NEWS

For 2004/05 a new drag-lift was installed in the nursery area in the Björnrike area of Vemdalen. In the Vemdalsskalet area a new ski square, directly accessible from the slopes, and complete with shops, restaurants and bar has been built.

➕ Snow-sure from December to May

➕ Unspoiled, beautiful landscape

➕ Uncrowded pistes and lifts

➕ Vibrant (but regimented) après-ski

➕ Good range of non-skiing activities

➖ Limited challenging downhill terrain

➖ Small areas by Alpine standards

➖ Lacks the dramatic peaks and vista of the Alps

➖ Short days during the early season

Sweden's landscape of forests and lakes and miles of unspoiled wilderness is entirely different from the Alps' grandeur and traffic-choked roads. Standards of accommodation, food and service are good and the people welcoming, lively and friendly. There are plenty of off-slope activities, but most of the downhill areas are limited in size and challenge. Sweden is likely to appeal most to those who want an all-round winter holiday in a different environment and culture. Don't be put off by the myths that Sweden is expensive, dark and cold – see below.

WEBSITES

For links to resort sites, go to our own new site at www.wtss.co.uk

TOURIST OFFICES

www.visit-sweden.com
Sälen
www.skistar.com
Vemdalen (Björnrike, Vemdalsskalet)
www.skistar.com
Riksgränsen
www.riksgransen.nu
Björkliden
www.bjorkliden.com
Ramundberget
www.ramundberget.se

Holidaying in Sweden is a completely different experience, culturally as well as physically, from a holiday in the Alps. The language is generally incomprehensible to us and, although virtually everyone speaks good English, the menus and signs are often written only in Swedish. The food is delightful, especially if you like fish and venison. And resorts are very family-friendly.

Sweden is is significantly cheaper than neighbouring Norway, but we still have complaints from reporters of beer at £5 a pint, wine at £15 to £20 a bottle and traditional Swedish restaurants being expensive.

One myth about Swedish skiing is that it is dark. It is true that the days are very short in December and early January. But from early February the lifts generally work from 9am to 4.30 and by March it is light until 8.30. Most resorts have some floodlit pistes.

On the down side, downhill slopes are generally limited in both challenge and extent and the lift systems tend to be dominated by T-bars. But there is lots of cross-country and backcountry skiing. Snowboarding is also popular, with parks and pipes in most resorts.

Après-ski is taken very seriously – with live bands from mid- to late-afternoon. But it stops suddenly, dinner is served and then the nightlife starts. There is plenty to do off the slopes: snowmobile safaris, ice fishing, dog-sled rides, ice-climbing, and saunas galore. You can also visit a local Sami village.

The main resort is **Åre** (see separate chapter). **Sälen** is Scandinavia's largest winter sports area – and is made up of four separate sets of slopes totalling 144km/89 miles of piste. Most slopes are very gentle, suiting beginners and early or timid intermediates best. Lindvalen and Högfjället are vaguely linked by a lift and a long cross-country slog. But you need the unreliable bus service to the others.

Vemdalen has two main areas of slopes 18km/11 miles apart by road. **Björnrike** is great for families, beginners and early intermediates, with nine lifts and 15km/9 miles of mainly gentle pistes. It has a terrain-park. There is a hotel right on the slopes, built in modern style. **Vemdalsskalet** has more advanced intermediate terrain, 10 lifts, 13km/8 miles of pistes and a terrain-park. The Högfjällshotell at the base is large, dates from 1936 and prides itself on its lively après-ski.

Riksgränsen, above the Arctic Circle, is an area of jagged mountain peaks and narrow fjords. The season starts in mid-February and ends in June – when you can ski under the midnight sun. There are only six lifts and 21km/13 miles of pistes. But there is some good off-piste and midnight heli-skiing.

Björkliden, also above the Arctic Circle, is famous for its subterranean skiing inside Scandinavia's largest cave system. You need to go with a guide.

Ramundberget is a good, small, quiet family resort with ski-in/ski-out accommodation. It gets large amounts of snow and its 22km/14 miles of pistes are mainly easy or intermediate. There is a special children's area with its own lift. The cross-country is vast, with 300km/186 miles of prepared trails.

675

Åre

Sweden's best slopes, strung out along a frozen lake

COSTS

① ② ③ ④ ⑤ ⑥

RATINGS

The slopes
Fast lifts	**
Snow	***
Extent	**
Expert	**
Intermediate	****
Beginner	****
Convenience	***
Queues	****
Mountain restaurants	***

The rest
Scenery	***
Resort charm	***
Off-slope	***

NEWS

Work continues in the Olympia area on building a new run for the ladies' downhill and super-G events of the Alpine World Ski Championships to be held in Åre in 2007. The Holiday Club opened for 2004/05 in Åre village. It has accommodation, restaurants, spa, sauna, pool, bowling, shops, ski hire centre and concert hall.

676

REPORTS WANTED

Recently we have had few reports on this resort. If you go there, please do send us a report.

The best reports earn a copy of the next edition, and can lead to free lift passes in future.

See page 10.

- **+** Cute little town centre
- **+** Good snow reliability
- **+** Good intermediate and beginner runs
- **+** Extensive cross-country trails
- **+** Excellent children's facilities
- **+** Lively après-ski scene
- **+** Lots of off-slope diversions

- **–** Lots of T-bars
- **–** Exposed upper mountain prone to closure because of bad weather
- **–** High winds detrimental to snow conditions
- **–** Few expert challenges
- **–** High season and weekend queues

Åre has the biggest area of linked slopes in Sweden and some of its most challenging terrain. But it suits beginners, intermediates and families best. It has a dinky little town centre and a long area of slopes set along a frozen lake.

THE RESORT

Åre is a small town made up of old, pretty, coloured wooden buildings and some larger, modern additions. When we were there the main square had a roaring open fire to warm up by. As well as accommodation in town, there is lots spread out along the valley, with a concentration in the Duved area. All the slopes and accommodation are set on the shore of a huge, long lake, frozen in the winter months.

THE MOUNTAINS

The terrain is mainly green and blue tree-lined slopes, with a couple of windswept bowls above the trees.
Slopes There are two main areas (linked by an efficient ski bus). The largest is accessed by a funicular from the centre of town or by a six-pack or cable-car a short climb above it. This takes you to the hub of a network of runs and (mainly) T-bars that stretches for 10km/6 miles from end to end. The cable-car is often shut because it goes to the top of the above-the-tree-line slopes (known as the 'high zone'), which often suffers from howling gales. A gondola also accesses the high zone from a different point. You can get back on-piste right into the town square. A separate area of slopes is above Duved and served by a high-speed chair. There are four floodlit slopes, each open on a different night. A reporter who had suffered altitude problems in the Alps particularly liked the low altitude of the slopes.
Terrain-parks There's a boarder-cross course, a half-pipe and a big terrain-park, plus two parks for novices.
Snow reliability Snow reliability is good from November to May. But high winds can blow fresh snow away. They also mean that artificial snow is often made wet so that it doesn't blow away and it compacts to a hard, icy surface.

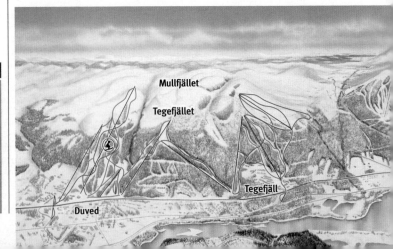

KEY FACTS

Resort	380m
	1,250ft
Slopes	380-1275m
	1,250-4,180ft
Lifts	40
Pistes	97km
	60 miles
Green	12%
Blue	39%
Red	39%
Black	10%
Snowmaking	
	21 pistes

WEBSITES

For links to resort sites, go to our own new site at www.wtss.co.uk

Central reservations phone number
For all resort accommodation call 17700.

Phone numbers
From elsewhere in Sweden add the prefix 0647.
From abroad use the prefix +46 647.

TOURIST OFFICE

t 17720
info@areresort.se
www.skistar.com

Experts Experts will find Åre's slopes limited, especially if the 'high zone' is closed. If it is open, there is a lot of off-piste available, including an 8km/ 5 mile run over the back, accessed by a snowcat service in high season. On the main lower area the steepest (and iciest when we were there) pistes are in the Olympia area. There are also steep black and red runs back to town.

Intermediates The slopes are ideal for most intermediates, with pretty blue runs through the trees. Because they tend to be more sheltered, the blue runs also often have the best snow. You can get a real sense of travelling from hill to hill on the main area.

Beginners There are good facilities, both on the main area and at Duved.

Snowboarding There's good varied terrain for boarders, plus three terrain-parks (see above). But there are a lot of drag-lifts (31 out of a total of 40).

Cross-country There's an amazing 300km/185 miles of cross-country trails, both on prepared tracks and unprepared trails marked with red crosses. Some trails are floodlit.

Queues In high season there can be queues for some lifts, especially in the central area immediately above Åre.

Mountain restaurants There are some good ones. Our favourite was the rustic Buustamons, tucked away in the woods near Rödkulleomradret.

Schools and guides The ski school has a good reputation and reporters agree.

Facilities for children There are special children's areas and under eight-year-olds get free lift passes if wearing helmets. There's a kindergarten that takes children from the age of two.

STAYING THERE

How to go Neilson is the only big UK tour operator to offer packages to Åre.

Hotels The main central hotels are the delightful old Åregarden – 'good breakfast, nice rooms and helpful staff' – and the simpler Diplomat Ski Lodge. The slope-side Park Inn Tott has good spa facilities. The Renen in Duved is popular with families and 'well organised with good meals'. See 'News', too.

Self-catering There are plenty of cabins and apartments; reporters have recommended the ones at Åre Fjällby.

Eating out The Bistro is good and there are plenty of alternatives, but a 2004 reporter found traditional Swedish restaurants expensive.

Après-ski Après-ski is amazingly lively. The Diplomat is packed from 3pm and has live bands. Later on, the Country Club and Bygget also have live bands and there are plenty of bars for a quiet drink. One reporter recommended the concerts held in igloos by the Tannforsen frozen waterfall.

Off the slopes Lots to do, including dog- or reindeer-sled rides, skating, ice fishing, tobogganing, ice-driving, ice-climbing, snowmobiling, paragliding. The new Holiday Club's facilities (see 'News') are open to non-residents.

Åre

Åreskutan 1275m/4,180ft
Tväråvalvet
Lillskutan
Ulládalen
Sadeln
Totthummeln 825m
Förberget 725m
Rödkullen
Åre Björnen
Åre 380m/1,250ft
Åresjön 370m

Bulgaria

678

Bulgaria has traditionally attracted beginners and early intermediates looking for a jolly time on a tight budget. Despite low prices for packages and on the spot, in the past we've found it difficult to recommend the place, because standards were so low. But Bansko, launched on the international scene a couple of seasons ago, has set new standards for Bulgarian resorts, and we have now given the resort its own short chapter, following this one. The long-established resorts of Borovets and Pamporovo are supposedly investing to compete. To judge by reports from readers, they face a struggle to improve not only the infrastructure but also the ambience and the food. There's not a lot they can do about their terrain, and even here Bansko has the edge. What's more, recent visitors have found prices higher than expected – higher than at home, even.

Pamporovo is strictly for beginners and very unadventurous intermediates, with mostly easy runs. Others are likely to find the limited area of short runs inadequate, despite recent expansion. The slopes are pretty and sheltered, with pistes starting at a high point of 1925m/6,320ft and cutting through pine forest. The ski schools are repeatedly praised by reporters – instructors are patient, enthusiastic and speak good English, and class sizes are usually quite small.

The main hotels are in a purpose-built village in an attractively wooded setting slightly away from the slopes – there is a shuttle-bus. The hotel Pamporovo gets the best reports, but the food is reportedly 'very poor'. A new 5-star, the Orlovetz, opens this year. There is a handful of lively bars and discos, but very few restaurants.

Borovets has more to offer intermediates. The resort is a collection of large, modern hotels in a beautiful wooded setting, with bars, restaurants and shops housed within them. There is a small selection of quirkier bars, shops and eating places.

A long gondola rises over 1000m/ 3,280ft to reach both the small, high, easy slopes of Markoudjika and the longer, steepish Yastrebets pistes. The runs are best for good intermediates. There are no challenges for experts. The slopes are not ideal for novices; nursery slopes are overcrowded, and the step from the Markoudjika blue runs to testing reds is a big one.

Queues for the gondola can be bad once novices are ready to go up the mountain. Grooming is erratic and signing poor. The gondola is said to be prone to closure by wind.

Mountain restaurants are mostly basic but serve decent steaks.

Instructors are generally praised by reporters, but classes can be large.

Most reporters stay at the Rila or the Samokov hotels – both huge and impersonal but with 'good, clean rooms'. Meals at the latter seem to have improved of late, but a 2005 visitor to the Rila chose to eat out at Katy's Steak Pub instead. There are lively bars catering well to an '18-30' type crowd. Tour operator reps organise pub crawls, folklore evenings etc. Excursions to the Rila monastery or Sofia by coach are interesting.

Bansko

In a Bulgarian league of its own

COSTS

① ② ③ ④ ⑤ ⑥

RATINGS

The slopes
Fast lifts	****
Snow	***
Extent	*
Expert	**
Intermediate	****
Beginner	**
Convenience	**
Queues	****
Mountain restaurants	***

The rest
Scenery	***
Resort charm	**
Off-slope	*

NEWS

For 2004/05 two further fast quad chairs were put in, extending the slopes and improving access to the Shiligarnika lift base from the top of the gondola at Bunderishka.

Snowmaking and floodlights were provided on the run back to Bansko.

The old town of Bansko has real character and plenty of pubs ↘

- ➕ Bulgaria's best mountain
- ➕ Efficient lifts with few queues
- ➕ Picturesque town at the base
- ➕ Smart new or renovated hotels
- ➕ Low prices
- ➕ Friendly, helpful locals
- ➕ Cheap and very cheerful traditional restaurants all over the town, but ...

- ➖ You may find you want to eat out in those restaurants even if you've bought a half-board package
- ➖ Long gondola ride from the town to the main lift base
- ➖ Limited slopes by Alpine standards
- ➖ Long airport transfers on poor roads
- ➖ Few off-slope diversions

Bansko claims to represent 'the future of Bulgarian mountain resorts'. Let's hope that's how it turns out. This resort, which completed its first season in full operation last winter, has shown us what eastern Europe can offer the skiing world, given a decent level of investment – more than £20 million spent on smart new lifts, snowmaking and even a hands-free lift pass system. Readers are impressed: 'Bansko for us next year,' says one of several highly satisfied reporters – in sharp contrast to reports on the rest of Bulgaria.

THE RESORT

Bansko, set on a flat valley floor circled by spectacular peaks, looks like a giant goods yard on the outskirts – more of an industrial town than a tourist destination. But around the central square the town has a quiet and charming heart, with architecture straight out of Disney's *Beauty And The Beast*. There are few outward signs of commercial tourism here except for hotels, which nestle unobtrusively between homes, shops, restaurants and churches. But a new hub with apartments and hotels is developing near the gondola base.

For visitors, life in the town revolves around the dozens of mehanas (traditional inns) selling traditional Bulgarian food very cheaply and providing entertainment in the shape of live traditional music. There are lots of little shops, well stocked.

THE MOUNTAINS

Until 2003/04, the drag-lifts and pistes in the Pirin National Park were accessible only by army jeeps and minibuses up a tortuous 12km/7 mile road. Now a new eight-seat gondola ferries skiers to the main lift base at Bunderishka. There is a blue piste back to the town, now with snowmaking.
Slopes From Bunderishka two successive fast quad chairs take you up mainly north-facing slopes to the high point of the area. From there you can ski down reds or blues to Shiligarnika, or a red followed by a black (called Alberto Tomba, after the famous Italian racer who opened the revamped ski area) to Bunderishka. New chair-lifts built for the 2004/05 season make it easy to get from Bunderishka to Shiligarnika, and open up some new pistes near Shiligarnika. There are also a few slopes near the

mid-station of the gondola at Chalin Valog. A third area with one red run and one chair above Bunderishka may now be reopened after renovation.

Terrain-parks There's meant to be a half-pipe at mid-mountain and a terrain-park near the top, but one reporter questions their existence.

Snow reliability A claimed 80% of the pistes are covered by snowmaking. Together with good grooming (by Bulgarian standards) and north-facing slopes, this means more reliable snow than the Bulgarian norm.

Experts There are no challenging pistes – the one black ought to be red – but there is some good tree skiing.

Intermediates Good medium-to-difficult reds come straight down the face from the top, and varied blues go round to skiers' right. All in all, there are four or five ways down the 900m/2,95oft vertical of the main area.

Beginners The nursery slopes near the top of the gondola are good, with little through traffic. There are blue runs served by drag-lifts at the top of the mountain and the long ski road back from top to bottom of the gondola is gentle and easy if the snow is good.

Queues Reporters last season found no queues. Alongside all the new chairs there are still some old drag-lifts, which can break down.

Mountain restaurants A fair sprinkling, including some modern ones with outdoor bars. The char-grills they serve are 'delicious and cheap'. The Platoto near the top is reporters' favourite.

Schools and guides The main Ulen school gets good reports this year: 'Excellent tuition, English better than mine,' says a Welsh reporter.

Facilities for children There is a kindergarten at mid-mountain, with a rope tow outside and satellite TV indoors.

STAYING THERE

How to go Several UK operators feature Bansko, and we expect the number to grow.

Hotels There is a growing cluster of new hotels around the gondola station. New for last season were the swanky but traditional-style Grand Arena and the more modern Perun. Refurbished places include the Pirin, near the town square and the Strazhite, near the gondola, both rated 'excellent' by 2005 reporters. All these hotels have pools and some spa/fitness facilities. Sadly the buffet meals in these cheaper places are said to be 'uninspired' at best, and eating out is recommended. Most central hotels run a shuttle-bus service to the gondola.

Eating out Reporters enthuse about the town's scores of authentic mehanas with roaring fires, attentive waiters, real Bulgarian food and good wine.

Après-ski There are lively bars at the gondola base. The bowling alley at the hotel Strazhite is popular. We lack reports on the nightclub, Amnesia.

Off the slopes Excursions to the Rila monastery and trips across the border into Greece are possible.

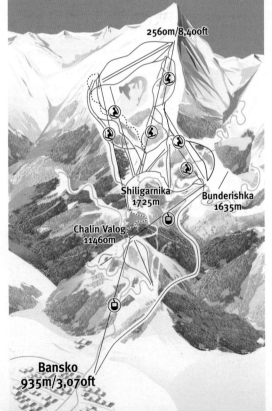

2560m/8,400ft

Shiligarnika
1725m

Bunderishka
1635m

Chalin Valog
1160m

Bansko
935m/3,070ft

Romania

➕ Cheap packages, and extremely low prices on the spot

➕ Interesting excursions and friendly local people

➕ Good tuition from enthusiastic instructors

➖ Primitive facilities – especially mountain restaurants and toilets

➖ Uninspiring food

➖ Very limited slopes – of no interest to anyone other than novices

Like Bulgaria, Romania sells mainly on price. On-the-spot prices, in particular, are very low. Provided you don't have unreasonably high expectations, you'll probably come back from Poiana Brasov content. The real appeal of the place is that it allows complete beginners to try a ski holiday at the absolute minimum cost, and to have a jolly time in the evenings without adding substantially to that cost – rather in the way that Andorra did before it went upmarket.

Reporters have commented on the friendliness of the people, and most recommend exploring beyond the confines of the resorts. Bucharest is 'not to be missed', and there are other worthwhile outings.

Romania's main resort – and now the only one featuring regularly in UK package programmes – is **Poiana Brasov** (1030m/3,380ft). It is a short drive above the city of Brasov in the Carpathian mountains, about 120km/75 miles (on alarmingly rough, slow roads) north-west of the capital and arrival airport, Bucharest.

Poiana Brasov is purpose-built, but not designed for convenience: the hotels are scattered about a pretty, wooded plateau, served by regular buses and cheap taxis. The place has the air of a spacious holiday camp, but one that incorporates some serious-sized hotels – some of them placed right by the lifts.

The slopes are extremely limited – approximately 12km/7 miles of pistes in total. They consist of decent intermediate tree-lined runs of about 750m/2,460ft vertical, roughly following the line of the main cable-car and gondola – both creaky old machines of very limited capacity – plus an open nursery area at the top. There are also some nursery lifts at village level, which are used when snow permits. A black run takes a less direct route down the mountain, which means that on average it is less steep than the red run under the lifts; it has one steepish pitch towards the end. There's a terrain-park and half-pipe. Night skiing is also now available. The resort gets weekend crowds from Brasov and Bucharest, and queues can

681

result, but during the week there are few problems.

A key part of the resort's appeal is the competent, friendly and effective instruction provided.

Hotel standards are higher than you might expect. The linked Bradul (0268 262252) and Sport (0268 262252) hotels are handy for the lower nursery slopes and for one of the cable-cars, and look smart after refurbishment. Guests in both have use of the Sport's sauna/hot-tub/fitness room.

Après-ski revolves around the hotel bars, night clubs and discos – supplemented by carnivorous outings to rustic barns with gypsy music. With cheap beer and very cheap spirits on tap, things can be quite lively. Off-slope facilities are limited; there is a good-sized pool, and bowling. Outings to the bars and restaurants of Brasov are recommended. An excursion to nearby Bran Castle (Count Dracula's home) is also popular.

Slovenia

+ Good value for money
+ Beautiful scenery
+ Good beginners' slopes and lessons

− Limited, easy slopes on the whole
− Mainly antiquated lifts
− Uninspiring food, but improving

Slovenia offers good value for money 'on the sunny side of the Alps'. The main resorts are popular with economy-minded British and Dutch visitors and with visitors from neighbouring Italy and Austria, giving quite a cosmopolitan feel.

Slovenia is a small country bordering Italy to the west and Austria to the north. It was the first state to break away from former Yugoslavia and managed to escape the turmoil that engulfed the Balkans. The economy is improving steadily, and there is a positive feel to the resorts – along with a warm and hospitable welcome.

The main resorts are within two and a half hours' bus-ride of the capital, Ljubljana. The ski areas are generally small, with fairly antiquated lifts but few queues. The mountain restaurants are mainly unappealing, while the ski schools are of a high standard and cheap, with reputedly good English. Hotel star ratings tend to be a trifle generous, but standards of service and hygiene are high. Snow reliability is not particularly good, but some resorts have snowmaking.

Kranjska Gora (810m/2,660ft), not far from the Austrian and the Italian borders, is the best-known resort. The pretty village is dominated by the majestic Julian Alps. The Lek, Kompas and Larix hotels – with pools – are the best placed for slope-side convenience. A reporter enjoyed varied food and 'amazing breakfasts' at the Larix.

There are 30km/20 miles of mainly intermediate slopes, rising up to 1570m/5,150ft. The only challenging slopes are a couple of short runs in the Podkoren area and the World Cup slalom run. For those wanting a change of slopes, trips to Arnoldstein in Austria are available. Snow reliability is not good, despite snowmaking and a northerly exposure. The lift system is rather antiquated (17 of the 22 lifts are T-bars), but at least queues are rare, except at New Year and on local holidays. Mountain restaurants are poor and most people choose to lunch in the village. There are 40km/25 miles of cross-country trails. Although it is family orientated, there is a good selection of bars and discos for Austrian-style après-ski.

Vogel (1535m/5,040ft), in the beautiful **Bohinj** basin, has the best slopes and conditions in the area. The 18km/11 miles of slopes are reached by a cable-car up from the valley. There's a collection of small hotels and restaurants at the base. Pistes of varying difficulty run from the high point at 1800m/5,910ft back into a central bowl with a small beginner area. When conditions permit, there is a long run to the bottom cable-car station. For a change of scene, **Kobla**, with 23km/14 miles of wooded runs, is a short bus-ride away.

Bled, with its beautiful lake and fairly lively nightlife, is an attractive base. Its local slopes are very limited, but free buses run to Vogel (about 20km/12 miles) and Kobla (a bit nearer).

Kanin (980m/3,210ft), offers 15km/9 miles of pistes between 1600m and 2300m (5,250ft and 7,550ft).

Slovenia's second city, **Maribor** (265m/870ft), in the north-east, is 6km/4 miles from its local slopes – the biggest ski area in the country, with 64km/40 miles of runs, 28km/17 miles of cross-country and 21 lifts. There are several atmospheric old inns serving good, Hungarian-influenced food.

Scotland

NEWS

The erratic snowfall that is the bane of Scottish skiing has been particularly in evidence in recent years, creating economic problems for all the resorts and forcing the owner of Glencoe and Glenshee into receivership in 2004. Both resorts changed hands for last season, and both apparently operated. There were excellent conditions for a few weeks last season, in late February and early March.

FURTHER INFORMATION

The VisitScotland brochure, Scottish Snow, has all the information you need to fix up a trip.

t 0131 332 2433
info@visitscotland.com
www.visitscotland.com
www.ski-scotland.com

+ Easy to get to from northern Britain
+ It is possible to experience perfect snow and stirring skiing
+ Decent, cheap accommodation and good-value packages are on offer
+ Mid-week it's rarely crowded
+ Extensive ski-touring possibilities
+ Lots to do off the slopes

- Weather is extremely changeable and sometimes vicious
- Snowfall is erratic, to say the least, and pistes can be closed through lack of snow
- Slopes are limited; runs mainly short
- Queueing can be a problem
- Little ski village ambience and few memorable mountain restaurants

Conditions in Scotland are unpredictable, to say the least. If you live nearby and can go at short notice when things look good, the several ski areas are a tremendous asset. But booking a holiday here as a replacement for your usual week in the Alps is just too risky.

For novices who are really keen to learn, Scotland could make sense, especially if you live nearby. You can book instruction via one of the excellent outdoor centres, many of which also provide accommodation and a wide range of other activities. The ski schools at the resorts themselves are also very good.

Most of the slopes in most of the areas fall around the intermediate level. But all apart from The Lecht offer one or two tough or very tough slopes.

Snowboarding is popular and most of the resorts have some special terrain features, but maintaining these facilities in good nick is problematic. The natural terrain is good for free-riding when the conditions are right.

Cairngorm is the best-known resort, with 16 lifts and 37km/23 miles of runs. Aviemore is the main centre (with a shuttle-bus to the slopes), but you can stay in other villages in the Spey valley. The slopes are accessed by a funicular from the main car park up to Ptarmigan at 1100m/3,610ft.

Nevis Range is the highest Scottish resort and opened in 1989. It has 11 lifts in addition to the long six-seat gondola accessing the slopes, and 35km/22 miles of runs on the north-facing slopes of Aonach Mor – Britain's eighth highest peak. There are many B&Bs and hotels in and around Fort William, 10 minutes away by shuttle.

Glenshee boasts 23 lifts and 40km/25 miles of runs, spread out over three minor parallel valleys. Glenshee remains primarily a venue for day-trippers, though there are hotels, hostels and B&Bs in the area.

Glencoe's more limited slopes (seven lifts, 20km/12 miles of runs) lie just east of moody Glen Coe itself. You have to ride a double chair-lift and a button lift to get to the main slopes, including the nursery area. The isolated Kings House Hotel is 2km/1 mile away.

The Lecht is largely a beginners' area, with 14 lifts and 20km/12 miles of runs on the gentle slopes beside a high road pass with a series of parallel lifts and runs just above the car parks. With a maximum vertical of only 200m/660ft, runs are short. There's extensive snowmaking. And there's a new day lodge at the base. The village of Tomintoul is 10km/6 miles away.

- ✚ Offers skiing and boarding during the European summer
- ✚ In one holiday you can also take in a visit to tropical northern Australia
- ✚ Some of the resorts offer upmarket slope-side accommodation

- ➖ It's a long way from Britain
- ➖ Mountains are rather low, and lift/trail networks are small by Alpine standards
- ➖ Day lift passes are very expensive

Even more than New Zealand, Australia offers resorts that are basically of local interest, but which might amuse people with other reasons to travel there – catching up with those long-lost relatives, say. Skiing among snow-laden gum trees is also a unique experience for northern hemisphere skiers, plus there is often the chance to see kangaroos, emus, echidnas and wombats.

The major resorts are concentrated in the populous south-east corner of the country, between Sydney and Melbourne, with the largest in New South Wales (NSW) – in the National Park centred on Australia's highest mountain, Mt Kosciusko (2230m/ 7,320ft), about six hours' drive from Sydney. Skiing has been going on here since the early 1900s – as in the next-door state of Victoria.

The Australian ski season generally runs from early June to mid-October. Traditionally the big snows rarely arrive before late July. In the last few years it has dumped in June, but August and September are the most reliable months. A major hydroelectric company has started a cloud-seeding programme that some people claim was responsible for the bumper falls enjoyed in recent seasons.

Thredbo, established in 1955, is a relatively upmarket Alpine-style village in NSW. It hosted the only World Cup race event held in Australia, thanks to a vertical of 670m/2,200ft.

Thredbo is rather like a small and quite smart French purpose-built resort – user-friendly, and mostly made up of modern apartments, many new luxury ski-in/ski-out chalets and lodges run by clubs. But there are many more bars than you would find in the French equivalent, and the party atmosphere thrives. The original Austrian flavour is now giving way to modern, casual-elegant bars and restaurants. It's a steep place, with stiff climbs to get around from one part to another. Road access is easy, but it costs A$16 a day just to enter the park.

The slopes, prettily wooded with gum trees, rise up across the valley from the village, served by a regular shuttle-bus through the resort. The runs are many and varied. The dozen lifts include three fast quad chairs, and the trails include Australia's highest (2037m/ 6,680ft) and longest (6km/4 miles). Skiing here isn't cheap – a lift ticket costs $87, the same as Perisher Blue. While the blacks are not difficult – except for one called Funnelweb, after Australia's most poisonous spider – on the higher lifts there are off-piste variants. Thredbo's slopes are now dotted with terrain features.

Heavy investment has produced an abundance of luxury architect-designed apartments, an attractive pedestrian mall with good shopping and some high-class restaurants – Segreto and Sante are top favourites – both on and off the mountain. There is also an impressive sports training complex open to the public, with an Olympic-size pool. The 700m/2,300ft public bob-sleigh track is popular.

On the other side of the mountain range is the large **Perisher Blue** resort complex, with a pass covering 51 lifts – more than anywhere else in Australia – but a vertical of less than 400m/1,310ft. The main area is Perisher/Smiggins, where lifts and runs – practically all easy or intermediate – range over three lightly wooded sectors. The resort is reachable by road, or by the Skitube, a rack railway that tunnels up from Bullocks Flat and goes on to the second area, **Blue Cow/Guthega**, where the slopes offer more challenges.

Perisher Blue is doing its best to

catch up with Thredbo by upgrading hotels and building more facilities. The resort is very spread out and has no central focus, but a pedestrian village is planned. Perisher has more ski-in-ski-out accommodation than Thredbo, although it does appeal more to the masses, with its shopping-mall-style village centre filled with every manner of shop, bar and fast food restaurant. Its main advantage over Thredbo is its snow, thanks to its position further within the mountain ranges and its higher altitude. In 2005 season Perisher Blue introduced a snow-tubing park, and a super-sized terrain-park was built at Blue Cow.

Many on a budget choose to stay in the apartments or hotels in the lakeside town of Jindabyne, a half-hour drive from both Thredbo and Perisher, with a lively youth-oriented nightlife scene. There are also some rather upmarket chalets along the Alpine Way, which leads to Thredbo, the most popular being Lake Crackenback Village next door to the Skitube.

From Perisher, a snowcat can take you on an 8km/5 mile ride to the isolated chalets of Australia's highest resort, **Charlotte Pass** (1760m/5,770ft), with five lifts but only 200m/660ft vertical. People visit the Pass more for its charm than for the skiing. The major hotel is the historic and turreted Kosciusko Chalet, a good spot for romantic weekends. Mt Kosciusko, Australia's highest point, is easily reached on cross-country skis.

If you want to learn to ski among the gum trees at the most affordable price, **Selwyn Snowfields** is your choice. It has 12 lifts, snow tubing and tobogganing and is about an hour from Cooma, near Jindabyne.

In Victoria, resorts are not as high as in NSW but many have good snow since they are set well within the ranges. You're better off flying and coaching to these resorts – most are approached by tricky mountain roads.

Mount Hotham has a justified reputation for good snow. An airport just 20 minutes' drive from the ski field makes it the most accessible resort in Australia, with nine 85-minute flights a week from Sydney alone. There's an emphasis on attracting the professional Sydney crowd, so there are concierges at the airport to arrange everything during your stay. The resort's 13 lifts serve a complete range of runs, with plenty of variety. The longest run is 2.5km/1.5 miles and there is more consistently steep terrain here than at any other area in Australia. A free snowcat service tows skiers out to nearby backcountry slopes. The village is built along the top of a ridge, with the slopes below it. The focus of the village is Mount Hotham Central, with apartments, shops and eateries including a few excellent restaurants and now the new White Mountain Spa. Hotham Heights Chalets is a nest of upscale multi-storey buildings. You can also stay 15 minutes' drive away at Dinner Plain – stunning architect-designed chalets set prettily among gum trees. There are a few restaurants and bars here, many cross-country trails and horse riding.

There is also a six-minute helicopter link from Mount Hotham to another resort nearby (and covered by the same lift pass), **Falls Creek**, that costs all of A$99 return. Falls Creek is the most alpine of Australia's resorts, completely snow-bound in winter (there are snowcats from the car park). There are 18 lifts, though the area is smaller than Mount Hotham's and the runs are mostly intermediate. Falls Creek focuses on providing extensive terrain-park features. Falls Creek also built a lavish spa to rival Mt Hotham's last year, called the Huski, located in an upmarket apartment development.

For some, the big attraction at Falls Creek is being able to access Australia's steepest skiing on the adjacent **Mt McKay** – 365m/1,200ft vertical of true black-diamond terrain. Guided snowcat trips take place twice a day. It's well worth the trip.

The other Victorian resort of note is the isolated peak of **Mt Buller**. Only a two-hour drive from Melbourne, this place is a magnet for old money, which has financed a proper resort village with a luxury hotel, a new pampering spa, Australia's highest cinema complex and even a university campus. Draped around the mountain are 25 lifts – the largest network in Victoria, including 13 chair-lifts. There's a hefty resort entry fee.

Mt Buffalo is worth visiting mainly to stay in the historic Mt Buffalo Chalet, with its dramatic views over the craggy Victorian alps. The Chalet is done up in true 1930s style and offers gourmet dining. The slopes, a short drive away, are in an Alpine basin surrounded by boulders, with five lifts almost purely for beginners.

TOURIST OFFICES

Thredbo
www.thredbo.com.au

Perisher Blue
(for Perisher, Smiggins, Blue Cow, Guthega)
www.perisherblue.com.au

Charlotte Pass
www.charlottepass.com.au

Selwyn Snowfields
www.selwynsnow.com.au

Mount Hotham
www.hotham.com.au

Falls Creek
(for Falls Creek and Mt McKay)
www.fallscreek.com.au

Mt Buller
www.mtbuller.com.au

Mt Buffalo
www.mtbuffalochalet.com.au

+ For Europeans, more interesting than summer skiing on glaciers

+ For Australians, conveniently close, with flights from Sydney

+ Huge areas of off-piste terrain accessible by helicopter on the South Island

+ Some spectacular scenery, as seen in *The Lord of the Rings* movies

– It's a long way from anywhere except Australia

– Limited on-mountain restaurants – though these are being upgraded

– Half-hour-plus drives from accommodation up to the ski areas

– Highly changeable weather

– No trees, so skiing in bad weather is virtually impossible

The number of keen skiers and boarders from New Zealand found kicking around the Alps gives a clue that there must be some decent slopes back home – and indeed there are. The resorts are rather different from those of the Alps or the Rockies – generally, you don't stay near the slopes. The networks of lifts and runs are rather limited, and not enough to tempt Europe-based summer skiers away from Alpine glaciers – unless of course you've got some other reason to visit New Zealand, as many of us have. But the heli-skiing around the Mt Cook region on the South Island is definitely worth writing home about. For Europeans already spending a lot to travel to New Zealand, the extra cost of a day or two's heli-drops around the Methven area is well worth while.

There are resorts on both North Island and South Island. The main concentration on South Island is around the scenic lakeside resort) of Queenstown – see next chapter.

As in the northern hemisphere, the season doesn't really get under way until midwinter – mid or late June; it runs until some time in October. Mount Hutt aims to open first, in mid-May, and disputes the longest-season title with Whakapapa, generally open until mid-November and again in December for Christmas skiing.

Skiing at almost every New Zealand ski resort involves at least a half-hour drive from a nearby town – usually below the snowline – to the ski field itself. Coach transfers from the hotels and towns to the ski fields are generally well organised. The ski field will have a base lodge, usually with a restaurant and a cafeteria, equipment rental and one or two shops, as well as the main lifts. The only on-snow accommodation is in smart apartments at Cardrona on the South Island, and some private lodges at the base of Whakapapa on the North Island.

In what follows, we describe the most prominent resorts (apart from Queenstown and its mountains), but there are other possibilities.

Any of the major resorts is worth a day or two of your time if you're in the area and the conditions are right. But if your credit card is also in good condition, don't miss the heli-skiing; even if you're no expert off-piste, with powder skis it's a doddle, and tremendously satisfying.

Methven Heliski or Wilderness Heliski (03 302 8108) offer the longest and most spectacular runs. Both are operated by the same company, Alpine Guides (based at Mt Cook), but fly to different regions. The cost for about five runs is around NZ$770. There are several other companies operating on South Island. Harris Mountain Heliskiing (03 442 6722), operating out of Queenstown and Wanaka, caters mainly for the large Japanese market, and the three-run days are generally very easy skiing, with long waits between lifts. New last season was Alpine Heliski (03 441 2300), based in Queenstown, started by a breakaway group from the major Queenstown operation, Southern Lakes Heli-Ski (03 442 6222). Both these companies are more amenable to exciting skiing. Try to leave the arrangements loose, to cope with the changeable weather.

An alternative adventure is to fly by plane to ski 10km/6 miles down the

Phone numbers
From abroad use the
prefix +64 and omit
the initial '0' of the
phone number.

KEY FACTS

Whakapapa

Whakapapa	
Altitude	1630-2300m
	5,350-7,550ft
Lifts	14
Pistes	550 hectares
	1,360 acres
Blue	25%
Red	50%
Black	25%
Snowmaking	some

Mount Hutt	
Altitude	1405-2075m
	4,610-6,810ft
Lifts	9
Pistes	365 hectares
	900 acres
Green	25%
Blue	50%
Black	25%
Snowmaking	
	42 hectares
	104 acres

Treble Cone	
Altitude	1200-1860m
	3,940-6,100ft
Lifts	5
Pistes	550 hectares
	1,360 acres
Green	15%
Blue	45%
Black	40%
Snowmaking	
	50 hectares
	125 acres

Cardrona	
Altitude	1670-2060m
	5,480-6,760ft
Lifts	8
Pistes	320 hectares
	791 acres
Green	25%
Blue	55%
Black	20%
Snowmaking	none

length of the Tasman Glacier. For two gentle 10km schusses down the glacier the cost is high – about NZ$700 for the day. The main draw is the immense grandeur of the place, along with the flights over stunning blue ice floes. If you're a good skier, you will find the Clarke Glacier four-run day out of Queenstown more satisfying, though priced at $NZ880.

Snowboarding is very popular in New Zealand, and most of the major resorts have special terrain-parks.

Whakapapa (pronounced Fukapapa) is on the slopes of the active volcano Mt Ruapehu, which has occasionally erupted in recent years, leaving the slopes black with volcanic ash. Until the late 1990s the volcano had not caused havoc since the 1950s, when an eruption carried away a bridge.

Mt Ruapehu is in the middle of the North Island and within four hours' drive of both Auckland and Wellington. Whakapapa, New Zealand's largest ski field, is located on the north-facing slopes, with a vertical of 670m/2,200ft served by 14 lifts including one fast quad. Terrain is typified by large, wide open cruisers plus challenging off-piste. Next to the base lodge is an extensive beginners' area, Happy Valley, with half-a-dozen rope tows, a chair-lift and snowmaking that allows this particular section to open early in the season. The resort's lifts and runs range across craggy terrain made especially interesting because of the twists, turns and drops of the solidified lava on which it sits. There is a mix of deep gullies, superb natural half-pipes

for snowboarders and narrow chutes. There is a handful of mountain restaurants.

Accommodation is mostly 6km/4 miles away at Whakapapa village, with the best middle-of-the-road property being a motel named the Skotel. There is on-snow accommodation at the base. A complete anomaly in this area of rustic lodges is the Chateau, a hotel in the grand style of the 1920s, with overly high ceilings, sweeping drapes over picture windows, a marble foyer and formal dining room with grand piano. It has just undergone major renovations and extensions.

Worth knowing about is the hike to Mt Ruapehu's fizzing Crater Lake. Ask a ski patrol for directions or, better, talk them into taking you on a guided trip. This involves about a half-hour (500m/ 1,640ft) hike up from the top of the highest T-bar, and then a long traverse across a large flat tundra-like area. A few lefts and rights and you are staring into the mouth of a volcano. Awesome views and neighbouring volcanos give this area an other-worldly feel.

On the south-western slope of Mt Ruapehu is **Turoa** – now under the same ownership as Whakapapa. You can ski both on the same ticket, which cost NZ$70 last season, the cheapest deal in NZ skiing. Turoa is a fraction smaller, but with an impressive 722m/2,370ft vertical – the biggest in Australasia. The longest run is 4km/2.5 miles. There's plenty of off-piste scope away from the gentle intermediate runs, plus the chance to ski on the Mangaehuehu Glacier. Accommodation

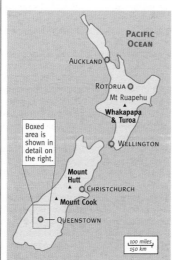

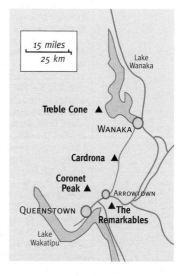

Phone numbers
From abroad use the prefix +64 and omit the initial '0' of the phone number.

TOURIST OFFICES

Whakapapa
t 07 892 3738
info@mtruapehu.com
www.mtruapehu.com

Mount Hutt
t 03 308 5074
service@nzski.com
www.nzski.com

Treble Cone
t 03 443 7443
tcinfo@treblecone.co.nz
www.treblecone.co.nz

Cardrona
t 03 443 7411
info@cardrona.com
www.cardrona.com

Snow Park
t 03 443 9991
info@snowparknz.com

Waiorau Snow Farm
t 03 443 0300
sam@snowfarmnz.com

is 20 minutes away in the funky and lively town of Ohakune, which is well worth a visit.

The South Island has 15 ski areas, including five club fields. **Mt Hutt**, an hour west of Christchurch in the northern part of the island, has a 670m/2,200ft vertical and some of the country's most impressive, consistently steep, wide-open terrain – all within view of the Pacific Ocean. On a clear day you can even see the sandy beaches in the distance beyond the patchwork Canterbury plains – in fact it often snows on the beaches here. The lift system is half the size of Whakapapa's but last season it was totally upgraded and rearranged. The main area is an open bowl with gentle terrain in the centre with the steeper terrain up higher, ringing the skifield.

Mt Hutt has an impressive modern base lodge, including a spacious, welcoming cafe and brasserie with a glorious outdoor terrace, plus a well-stocked rental shop.

Mt Hutt Helicopters (03 302 8401) offers six-run days in the mountains beyond for about NZ$600. The helicopter departs from the heli-pad right in the car park – just wander up to the heli-hut and book in.

There is no accommodation on-mountain – most people stay in the little town of **Methven**, where there are several comfortable up-market B&Bs as well as motels. The very British South Island capital of Christchurch, 90 minutes away, is also an option.

About six hours' drive south of Christchurch is the quiet lakeside town of Wanaka, which is also 90 minutes from Queenstown, and there are two resorts accessible from here.

Treble Cone, 20km/12 miles from Wanaka, has more advanced slopes than any other NZ ski area, plus the advantage of a better lift system, including the first six-pack in the southern hemisphere. In area, the ski-field comes second only to the North Island fields. New last season was another chair-lift, which meant more terrain and nine new trails. Backcountry ski tours were also introduced for the first time, offering powder runs in Treble's back bowls. Back on the ski field, there are two well-maintained intermediate trails, one 3.5km/2 miles, the other 2km/1.2 miles. Both on the main flank and off to the side in Saddle Basin there are long natural half-pipes which are great fun

when snow is good, as well as smooth, wide runs for cruising. Treble Cone is reached by a long and winding dirt track that adds to the excitement, although the new owners are planning to install a gondola from the valley floor. The ski field offers stunning views across Lake Wanaka, with snowcapped Alpine-style peaks in the distance. There's a cosmopolitan cafe at the lift base. An enormous sun deck sharing that view was added in 2004. The food here and at Cardrona is generally better than at other resorts.

Cardrona, 34km/21 miles from Wanaka, is famous for its dry snow and is popular with families due to its superior childcare and teaching facilities. The terrain is noted for its well-groomed, flattering cruisers. But there are some serious if short chutes, and the middle basin, Arcadia, hosts the New Zealand Extreme Skiing Championships. The total vertical is a modest 390m/1,280ft. Millions have been poured into the resort by its family owners over the past few years, resulting in a large base area focused around an odd clock tower. Cardrona is unique in that it has a 1.2km/0.75 mile long terrain-park – the largest in the Southern Hemisphere, with four half-pipes – and right beside it a park for intermediates/learners.

There's a bar and brasserie-style restaurant, a new ski-in/ski-out noodle bar with sun deck overlooking the nursery slopes, large rental facility and a licensed childcare centre, plus 10 modern apartments at the base (but bring all your own supplies). Learners are looked after well, with three moving carpets.

Snow Park – a dedicated terrain-park on the South Island dead opposite Cardrona – is really making waves and attracting the cream of international free-ride skiers and snowboarders during their off-seasons. Snow Park is in its fourth season and provides world-class kickers, table-tops, rails, slides and any other feature worth doing a trick in, on or over.

Nearby, at a height of 1500m/4,920ft, is New Zealand's only cross-country ski area, the **Waiorau Snow Farm**, a beautiful place with 55km/34 miles of what the owners claim are the best prepared trails in the world. There are classic and skating lanes on all trails designed for all levels. Accommodation is in the older-style Snow Farm Alpine Lodge.

Queenstown

Lively base for sampling a range of South Island resorts

RATINGS

The slopes

Fast lifts	**
Snow	**
Extent	*
Experts	***
Intermediates	***
Beginners	***
Convenience	*
Queues	***
Mountain restaurants	*

The rest

Scenery	****
Resort charm	**
Off-slope	*****

➕ For Europeans, more interesting than summer skiing on glaciers

➕ Huge areas of off-piste terrain accessible by helicopters

➕ Lots to do off the slopes, especially for adrenalin junkies

➕ Lively town, with lots going on and good restaurants

➕ Grand views locally, and the spectacular 'fjord' country nearby

➖ Slopes (in two separate areas locally) are a drive from town

➖ Limited lift-served slopes in each area

➖ It's a long way from anywhere except Australia

➖ Highly changeable weather

➖ No trees, so skiing in bad weather is virtually impossible

If you want a single destination in New Zealand – as opposed to visiting a few different mountains on your travels – Queenstown is probably it, especially if you can cope with the cost of a few heli-drops. Although the resorts of North Island are impressive, the Southern Alps are, in the end, more compelling – and their resorts are free of volcanic interruptions. Mount Hutt may be a slightly more impressive area than either of Queenstown's local fields – Coronet Peak and The Remarkables – but it's a rather isolated place. From Queenstown you have a choice of the two local fields plus the option of an outing to Treble Cone – the mountain to visit if you are an advanced-to-expert skier – and Cardrona, perhaps with a few nights in Wanaka.

THE RESORT

Queenstown is a winter-and-summer resort on the shore of Lake Wakatipu. (There is a map of the area in the introductory chapter on New Zealand.) Although the setting is splendid, with views to the peaks of the aptly named Remarkables range beyond the lake, the town itself is no great beauty – it has grown up to meet tourists' needs, and has a very commercial feel. Shopping is good, of course.

In recent years much effort has been put into smartening up the town, with such additions as the classy new Steamer Wharf complex by the lake and lots of lakeside luxury apartments and hotels. It has a lively, relaxed feel, and makes a satisfactory base, with more than 160 licensed bars and cafes, some good restaurants, and lots of touristy clothes shops. There are no less than 173 activity operators in town; it's the base for every kind of adventure activity, offering bungee jumping, jet boating, river surfing, horse-trekking.

There are four lift-served mountains – all small by Alpine standards – that you can get to from Queenstown. The two described here – Coronet Peak and

The Remarkables – are close by (about a 30-minute drive). The others – Treble Cone and Cardrona – are a more serious drive away (at least 90 minutes), near Wanaka – another town in a beautiful lakeside setting with accommodation, but much quieter.

THE MOUNTAINS

At each base area you'll find a mini-resort – a ski school, a ski rental shop, a functional self-service restaurant, but no accommodation except at Cardrona.

All the areas have something for all abilities of skier or boarder, with off-piste opportunities as well as prepared and patrolled trails. They use the American green/blue/ black convention for run classification, not the European blue/red/black.

THE SLOPES
Not the height of convenience
The Remarkables, true to their name, are a dramatic range of craggy peaks visible across the lake from some parts of Queenstown. The slopes are tucked in a bowl right behind the largest visible peak, a 45-minute drive from town. This resort is fine for families and beginners, (though there is limited

KEY FACTS

Resort	310m
	1,020ft

The Remarkables	
Slopes	1580-1935m
	5,180-6,350ft
Lifts	5
Pistes	220 hectares
	545 acres
Green	30%
Blue	40%
Black	30%
Snowmaking	
	25 acres

Coronet Peak	
Slopes	1230-1650m
	4,040-5,410ft
Lifts	6
Pistes	280 hectares
	690 acres
Green	20%
Blue	45%
Black	35%
Snowmaking	
	200 acres

boarding

Boarding is popular in New Zealand, and although the two mountains close to Queenstown don't seem to have quite such a hold on the boarding market as Cardrona (see New Zealand introduction), they have everything you need, including equipment and tuition. You needn't go anywhere near a drag-lift, and there are no flats to worry about except on the lowest green at The Remarkables.

extreme skiing for experts), with the emphasis on taking it easy and enjoying entertainment on the restaurant's sun decks during the week. Children under 10 ski for free at The Remarkables.

Two chairs go up from the base, a fast quad serving easy runs and the Sugar Bowl chair, which accesses mainly long, easy runs plus a couple of black chutes. The terrain parks have transformed the resort and attracted a whole new market of jibbers. The Shadow Basin chair leads to steeper terrain, including three hike-accessed, expert-only chutes that drop down to Lake Alta, and the Homeward Run – a broad, fairly gentle, unprepared slope down to the resort access road, where a shuttle-truck takes you back to the base.

Coronet Peak, about 25 minutes' drive from Queenstown, is a far more satisfying resort, especially for intermediates and above. There is some seriously steep terrain for experts. Again, there are three main chair-lifts, including a fast quad that accesses practically all the runs, and new last season a six-seater that opened up more terrain and improved the resort dramatically. A novice trail

was added a few seasons ago to appeal to beginner skiers and boarders. The main mountainside is a pleasantly varied intermediate slope, full of highly enjoyable rolling terrain that snowboarders adore, though it steepens near the bottom. A fourth lift, a T-bar, serves another mainly intermediate area to one side. There are also drags for beginners. Night skiing runs from July to September on Fridays and Saturdays only. For the 2004 season the resort added 30 new guns on the 1.8km/1.1 mile main trail.

TERRAIN-PARKS
Coronet rules
Coronet Peak has two half-pipes and The Remarkables recently became a competitor in the park market with its super-pipe plus two enormous terrain-parks, new for the 2005 season, one aimed at beginners and the other for intermediate/advanced.

SNOW RELIABILITY
Good overall, but unpredictable
The New Zealand weather is highly variable, so it's difficult to be confident about snow conditions – though the mountains certainly get oodles of snow. The South Island resorts are at

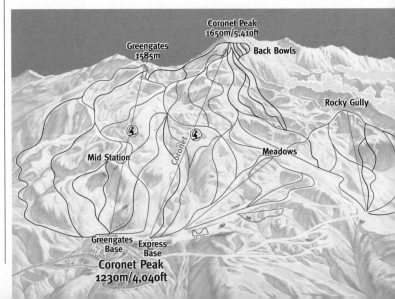

↑ Coronet Peak is a short drive from Queenstown, with a day lodge at the base

FOR BEGINNERS
Excellent
There are gentle slopes at both areas, served by rope tows, and longer green runs served by chairs. And many other diversions if you decide it's a drag.

FOR CROSS-COUNTRY
Limited
There is a short loop around a lake in the middle of The Remarkables area, but the only serious cross-country area is the elevated plateau of Waiorau Snow Farm, near Cardrona.

QUEUES
It depends
Coronet and The Remarkables can suffer a little from high-season crowds – there are certainly enough beds locally to lead to queues at peak times. But these aren't normally a major worry.

MOUNTAIN RESTAURANTS
Er, what mountain restaurants?
Both areas have a simple cafeteria at the base, and Coronet has a brasserie facing the slopes, but nothing up the mountain. The Remarkables cafeteria has a big sunny deck, often visited by the large local mountain parrots, called keas, and entertainment most days.

SCHOOLS AND GUIDES
All the usual classes
The schools are well organised, with a wide range of options, including 'guaranteed' beginner classes.

FACILITIES FOR CHILDREN
Look good
Childcare looked okay to us. At both resorts there is a nursery for children aged from two to five years old. Coronet Peak has a Skiwiland Club for children aged four to six with morning and afternoon sessions. The Remarkables has Skiwiland for four and five year olds, also with morning and afternoon sessions. There's also a wide range of kid's activities on offer each day. The Queenstown nursery can take younger children all day.

STAYING THERE

HOW TO GO
Sheer luxury?
There are lots of big, luxury hotels – all either new or refurbished – built to meet the big summer demand for beds in this popular lakeside resort.

the same sort of latitude as the Alps, but are much more influenced by the ocean; fortunately, their ocean is a lot colder than ours. Coronet tends to receive sleet and/or rain even when it's snowing in The Remarkables. But Coronet Peak has snowmaking on practically all its intermediate terrain, from top to bottom of the mountain.

FOR EXPERTS
Challenges exist
Both areas have quite a choice of genuinely black slopes. Coronet's Back Bowls is a seriously steep experts-only area, and there are other black slopes scattered around the mountain. The main enjoyment comes from venturing off-piste all over the place. The Remarkables' Shadow Basin chair serves some excellent slopes. And The Remarkables' hike-up expert chutes are truly world-class.

FOR INTERMEDIATES
Fine, within limits
There's some very enjoyable intermediate skiing in both areas – appreciably more at Coronet, where there are also easy blacks to go on to. But remember: these are very small areas by Alpine standards.

Hotels Some hotels are quite some way from central Queenstown – inconvenient for après-ski unless there's a shuttle-bus. In town they range from the very simple to the glossily pretentious Millennium (03 441 8888). Aim to get a room with a view across Lake Wakatipu and the mountains – the view is worth the extra dollars. Two of the best places to stay are the Heritage Hotel (03 442 4988) or the Mercure Grand Hotel St Moritz (03 442 4990). New upmarket boutique hotels that come highly recommended are The Dairy Private Luxury Hotel and The Spire.

EATING OUT
Lots of choice
We're told there are now over 160 bars and restaurants – a quite astonishing figure. Restaurants include Chinese, Italian, Malaysian, Japanese – you name it, Queenstown has it. The Boardwalk in the Steamer Wharf complex overlooking the lake is the place to go for seafood, especially the Wai. Breakfast at Joe's Garage is a must. You might see the famous actor Sam Neil, who's a local. A dining experience with a difference is the Bath House, located in a 1911 Victorian bath house right on the lake shore. Solero Vino has delicious Mediterranean food and a rustic bar, and Dux Deluxe (formerly McNeill's) is an excellent brew-pub with a range of tasty beers, housed in a stone cottage. The Bunker does excellent local cuisine such as Bluff oysters and lamb. Gantley's, housed in a historic home a little way out of town, is a classic restaurant with the most expensive wine list in the area. At the other end of the scale, pizza-lovers crowd into The Cow, a cosy barn-like place where you sit on logs around a fire waiting for tables or takeaways. Lone Star offers satisfying American-style food.

APRES-SKI
Lively little town
Queenstown has a good range of bars and clubs that stay open late, with disco or live music. Winnebagos is very lively and has a roof that slides back to the night sky to allow the hot and sweaty dance floor a blast of fresh air and even fresh snow. There's a small upmarket casino in the plush Steamer Wharf, which also holds a classy cigar bar and good duty-free shopping.

OFF THE SLOPES
Scare yourself silly
There are lots of scary things to do – see the feature box. To the west is the spectacularly scenic 'fjord country', and you can go on independent or guided walks. The sightseeing flights by plane or helicopter are to be preferred to the slow bus-ride – weather permitting. A marvellous thing to do is to take the Skyline gondola 400m/1,310ft above Queenstown for the great view; try a spin down the public go-cart track, too. Cruise the lake on an historic steamship or go wine tasting. Arrowtown is interesting for a quick visit – it's a cute, touristy old mining town where you can kit yourself out to go panning for gold. The Winter Festival, in early July, is an annual 'action-packed week of mayhem'.

GET THAT ADRENALIN RUSH

The streets of Queenstown are lined by no less than 173 activity operators offering various artificial thrills. We've sampled just a few.

AJ Hackett's bungee jump at Kawarau Bridge is where this crazy activity got off the ground – you plunge towards the icy river, but are pulled up short by your bungee cord and lowered into an inflatable boat.

The Shotover Jet Boat experience is less demanding. You get chauffeured at high speed along the rocky river in a boat that can get along in very shallow water, execute high-speed 360° turns and pass very close to cliffs and trees.

Fly By Wire, where you swing through a canyon on a cable propelled by a fan engine on your rear, is new and unusual.

The whitewater rafting is genuinely thrilling – and not as uncomfortable as you'd expect, thanks to the full wetsuit, helmet, boots and gloves, and to the exertion involved. The rivers have some exciting rapids. One route even passes through a tunnel excavated in the gold-mining days, after which comes a small but steep waterfall where your souvenir shots are snapped.

Phone numbers
From abroad use the prefix +64 and omit the initial '0' of the phone number.

TOURIST OFFICES
The Remarkables
t 03 442 4615
service@theremarkables.co.nz
www.nzski.com

Coronet Peak
t 03 442 4620
service@coronetpeak.co.nz
www.nzski.com

Reference section

A classified listing of the names, numbers and addresses you are likely to need.

Tour operator directory 695

Most people still prefer the convenience of a package holiday, which is what most of the companies listed are set up to provide. But note that we've also included some operators that offer accommodation without travel arrangements.

Ski business directory 701

Resort directory / index 709

693

TOUR OPERATOR DIRECTORY

This is a list of all the UK-based companies we know of that offer ski holidays – mainly but not exclusively package holidays including travel as well as accommodation. Lists of which operators go where are given in the Resort directory / Index right at the back of the book.

360 Sun and Ski
Family holidays in Les Carroz
Tel 0870 068 3180
info@360sunandski.com
www.360sunandski.co.uk

Absolute Ski
Chalet in Méribel
Tel 01788 822100
holiday@absoluteski.com
www.absoluteski.com

Airtours
Mainstream operator
Tel 0800 916 0623
www.airtours.co.uk

Albus Travel
St Anton specialist
Tel 01449 711952
info@albustravel.com
www.albustravel.com

Alpine Action
Chalets in Les Trois Vallées
Tel 01273 597940
sales@alpineaction.co.uk
www.alpineaction.co.uk

Alpine Answers Select
Tailor-made holidays
Tel 020 8871 4656
select@alpineanswers.co.uk
www.alpineanswers.co.uk

The Alpine Club
Chalet in St-Martin-de-Belleville
Tel 0797 746 5285
info@thealpineclub.co.uk
www.thealpineclub.co.uk

Alpine Events
Corporate ski specialist
Tel 01962 829777
alpine@offsiteevents.com
www.alpineevents.co.uk

Alpine Tours
Group and schools holidays, mainly in Austria and Italy
Tel 01628 826699
sales@alpinetours.co.uk

Alpine Weekends
Weekends in the Alps
Tel 020 8944 9762
info@alpineweekends.com
www.alpineweekends.com

Altitude Holidays
Catered chalet in Les Carroz
Tel 0870 870 7669
info@altitudeholidays.com
www.altitudeholidays.com

AmeriCan Ski
Hotels and apartments in France and North America
Tel 01892 511894
ian@awwt.co.uk
www.awwt.co.uk

American Ski Classics
Holidays in major North American resorts
Tel 020 8392 6660
sales@holidayworld.ltd.uk
www.americanskiclassics.com

Aravis Alpine Retreat
Chalet in St Jean-de-Sixt (La Clusaz)
Tel 020 8878 8760
info@aravis-retreat.com
www.aravis-retreat.com

Balkan Holidays
Holidays in Bulgaria, Slovenia, Romania and Serbia
Tel 0845 130 1114
res@balkanholidays.co.uk
www.balkanholidays.co.uk

Barrelli Ski
Chalets in Champagny, Chamonix and Les Houches
Tel 0870 220 1500
whiplash@barrelliski.co.uk
www.barrelliski.co.uk

Belvedere Chalets
Luxury chalets in Méribel
Tel 01264 738 257
info@belvedereproperties.net
www.belvedereproperties.net

Bigbluemountain.com
Chalet in Morzine
Tel 01797 254000
info@bigbluemountain.com
bigbluemountain.com

Bigfoot Travel
Variety of holidays in Chamonix
Tel 0870 300 5874
sales@bigfoot-travel.co.uk
www.bigfoot-chamonix.com

Bladon Lines
Chalet arm of Inghams
Tel 020 8780 8800
bladonlines@inghams.co.uk
www.inghams.co.uk

Board and Lodge
Catered snowboarding holidays in Chamonix
Tel 020 7419 0722
info@boardnlodge.com
www.boardnlodge.com

Bonne Neige Ski Holidays
Catered chalets in Méribel
Tel 01270 256966
ukoffice@bonne-neige-ski.com
www.bonne-neige-ski.com

Borderline
Specialist in Barèges
Tel 00 33 562 926895
info@borderlinehols.com
www.borderlinehols.com

Canadian Powder Tours
Chalet holidays in Canada
Tel 00 1 250 423 3019
cdnpowder@elkvalley.net
www.canadianpowdertours.com

Canterbury Travel
Holidays in Finland
Tel 01923 457017
reservations@laplandmagic.com
www.laplandmagic.com

Catered Ski Chalets
Catered chalets in Europe and North America
Tel 020 7835 0635
info@catered-ski-chalets.co.uk
www.catered-ski-chalets.co.uk

Chalet Chocolat
Chalet in Morzine
Tel 01872 580814
info@chalet-chocolat.co.uk
www.chalet-chocolat.co.uk

The Chalet Company
Catered chalets in Morzine and Ardent (Avoriaz)
Tel 0871 717 4208 /
00 33 450 79 68 40
moran@thechaletco.com
www.thechaletco.com

www.catered-ski-chalets.co.uk

Catered chalets throughout Europe, USA and Canada
Call the resort experts on 020 7835 0635

The Chalet Group
Chalet holidays in the French Alps and Fernie (Canada)
Tel 01884 256542
katie@chaletgroup.com
www.chaletgroup.com

Chalet Gueret
Luxury chalet in Morzine
Tel 01884 256542
info@chaletgueret.com
www.chaletgueret.com

Chalet Kiana
Chalet in Les Contamines
Tel 00 33 450 915518
chaletkiana@aol.com
www.chaletkiana.com

Chalet Ltd
Chalet in Ste-Foy and apartment in Val-d'Isère
Tel 01291 673898
richard.hawkins@chalet.co.uk
www.chalet.co.uk

Chalet Number One
Chalet in Ste-Foy
Tel 00 33 479 069533
info@chn1.co.uk
www.chn1.co.uk

Les Chalets de St Martin
Catered and self-catered chalets in St-Martin
Tel 00 33 479 089177
les.chalets@virgin.net
www.leschalets.co.uk

Chalet Snowboard
Snowboard holidays in Morzine
Tel 0870 800 4020
info@chaletsnowboard.co.uk
www.chaletsnowboard.co.uk

Chalet World Ski
Chalets in big-name resorts
Tel 01743 231199
sales@chaletworldski.co.uk
www.chaletworldski.co.uk

Challenge Activ
Chalets/apartments in Morzine
Tel 0871 717 4113
info@challenge-activ.com
www.challenge-activ.com

Chamonix.uk.com
Apartments in Chamonix
Tel 028 9042 4662
sales@chamonix.uk.com
www.chamonix.uk.com

Le Chardon Mountain Lodges Val d'Isère
Upmarket chalets in Val-d'Isère
Tel 01738 842800
sales@lechardonvaldisere.com
www.lechardonvaldisere.com

Chez Jay Ski Chalets
Chalet in Villaroger (Les Arcs) and Montchavin (La Plagne)
ski@chezjayski.com
www.chezjayski.com

Classic Ski Limited
Holidays for 'mature' skiers/beginners
Tel 01590 623400
info@classicski.co.uk
www.classicski.co.uk

Club Europe Schools Skiing
Schools trips to Europe
Tel 0800 496 4996
ski@club-europe.co.uk
www.club-europe.co.uk

Club Med
All-inclusive holidays in 'ski villages'
Tel 020 8780 8601
admin@clubmed.com
www.clubmed.com

Club Pavilion
Budget ski holidays
Tel 0870 241 0427
info@conceptholidays.co.uk
www.conceptholidays.co.uk

Collineige
Chamonix valley specialist
Tel 01276 24262
sales@collineige.com
www.collineige.com

Connick Ski
Chalet in Châtel
Tel 00 33 450 732212
nick@connickski.com
www.connickski.com

Contiki Holidays
Coach holidays for 18-35s
Tel 020 8290 6422
travel@contiki.co.uk
www.contiki.com

Cooltip Mountain Holidays
Chalets in Méribel
Tel 01964 563563
ski@cooltip.com
www.cooltip.com

The Corporate Ski Company
Corporate specialists
Tel 020 8542 8555
ski@vantagepoint.co.uk
www.thecorporateskicompany.
co.uk

Crystal
Major mainstream operator
Tel 0870 160 6040
skires@crystalholidays.co.uk
www.crystalski.co.uk

CV Travel
Holidays in upmarket resorts
Tel 0870 0623425
cvski@cvtravel.co.uk
www.cvtravel.co.uk

Descent International
Luxury chalets in Europe
Tel 020 7384 3854
sales@descent.co.uk
www.descent.co.uk

Directski.com
Holidays in Austria, France, Italy and Andorra
Tel 0800 587 0945
sales@directski.com
www.directski.com

Elegant Resorts
Luxury ski holidays
Tel 01244 897333
enquiries@elegantresorts.
co.uk
www.elegantresorts.co.uk

Elevation Holidays
Holidays in the Austrian Alps
Tel 0845 644 3578
info@elevationholidays.com
www.elevationholidays.com

Equity School Ski
School group holidays
Tel 01273 886886
schoolski@equity.co.uk
www.equityschooltravel.co.uk

Equity Ski
All-in holidays
Tel 01273 298298
travel@equity.co.uk
www.equityski.co.uk

Erna Low
Hotel/self-catering holidays in the Alps and N America
Tel 0870 750 6820
info@ernalow.co.uk
www.ernalow.co.uk

Esprit Ski
Families specialist in Europe and North America
Tel 01252 618300
www.esprit-holidays.co.uk

The Family Ski Company
Family holidays in France
Tel 01684 540333
enquiries@familyski.co.uk
www.familyski.co.uk

Ferme de Montagne
Chalet in Les Gets
Tel 00 33 450 753679
enquiries@fermedemontagne.
com
www.fermedemontagne.com

Finlays
Mainly chalets in France
Tel 01573 226611
info@finlayski.com
www.finlayski.com

First Choice Ski
Major mainstream operator
Tel 0870 754 3477
sales@fcski.co.uk
www.firstchoice.co.uk/ski

Flexiski
Flexible breaks in chalets and hotels in Europe
Tel 0870 909 0754
reservations@flexiski.com
www.flexiski.com

Freedom Holidays
Tailor-made holidays to Châtel
Tel 01798 861888
freedomhols@hotmail.com
www.freedomholidays.co.uk

French Freedom Holidays
*Self-catered apartments/
chalets in the French Alps*
Tel 01724 290660
info@french-freedom.co.uk
www.french-freedom.co.uk

French Ski Life
Self-drive holidays to France
Tel 0870 197 6963
enquiries1@frenchlife.co.uk
www.frenchlifeski06.co.uk

Friendship Travel
Holidays for singles 25 to 60
Tel 028 9446 2211
sales@friendshiptravel.com
www.friendshiptravel.com

Frontier Ski
Holidays in Canada and Alaska
Tel 020 8776 8709
info@frontier-travel.co.uk
www.frontier-ski.co.uk

Frozenplanet.co.uk
*Chalets and apartments,
mostly in the Alps*
Tel 07947 331606
contact@frozenplanet.co.uk
www.frozenplanet.co.uk

Haig Ski
*Hotels with guiding in Châtel
and Morzine*
Tel 00 33 450 811947
sales@haigski.com
www.haigski.com

Hannibals
Holidays in Serre-Chevalier
Tel 01233 813105
sales@hannibals.co.uk
www.hannibals.co.uk

Headwater Holidays
Cross-country skiing holidays
Tel 01606 720199
info@headwater.com
www.headwater.com

High Mountain Holidays
Holidays in Chamonix
Tel 01993 775540
info@highmountain.co.uk
www.highmountain.co.uk

Hucksters
Lodges in the French Alps
Tel 01208 821100
info@hucksterslodge.com
www.hucksterslodge.com

Huski
Chalet holidays in Chamonix
Tel 020 7938 4844
ski@huski.com
www.huski.com

Independent Ski Links
*Tailor-made holidays in Europe
and N America*
Tel 01964 533905
info@ski-links.com
www.ski-links.com

Inghams
Major mainstream operator
Tel 020 8780 4433
reservations@inghams.co.uk
www.inghams.co.uk

Inntravel
Cross-country skiing holidays
Tel 01653 617920
winter@inntravel.co.uk
www.inntravel.co.uk

Inspired to Ski
Holidays with tuition in France
Tel 0870 128 8989
sally@inspiredtoski.co.uk
www.inspiredtoski.co.uk

Interhome
*Apartments and chalets in
Europe*
Tel 020 8891 1294
info@interhome.co.uk
www.interhome.co.uk

Interski
Group holidays in Italy
Tel 01623 456333
email@interski.co.uk
www.interski.co.uk

James Orr Heli-ski
*Heli-skiing packages in
Canada*
Tel 01799 516964
james.orr@btinternet.com
www.heliski.co.uk

Jeffersons Private Jet Holidays
Private jet holidays
Tel 0870 850 8181
info@jeffersons.com
www.jeffersons.com

Just Slovenia
Accommodation in Slovenia
Tel 01373 814230
just slovenia@planos.co.uk
www.justslovenia.co.uk

Kaluma Ski
Holidays in the Alps
Tel 0870 442 8044
enquiries@kalumatravel.co.uk
www.kalumatravel.co.uk

Kuoni
Holidays in Switzerland
Tel 01306 747000
switzerland.sales@kuoni.co.uk
www.kuoni.co.uk

Lagrange Holidays
Ski holidays in Europe
Tel 020 7371 6111
info@lagrange-holidays.co.uk
www.lagrange-holidays.co.uk

The Last Resort
*Chalet and apartments in St
Jean-de-Sixt*
Tel 0800 652 3977
info@lastresort.info
www.lastresort.info

Le Ski
*Chalets in Courchevel, Val-
d'Isère and La Tania*
Tel 0870 754 4444
email@leski.com
www.leski.com

Lotus Supertravel
*Upmarket European and North
American holidays*
Tel 020 7962 9933
ski@lotusgroup.co.uk
www.supertravel.co.uk

Made to Measure Holidays
*Wide variety of tailor-made
holidays*
Tel 01243 533333
sales@mtmhols.co.uk
www.mtmhols.co.uk

Mark Warner
*Chalet-hotel holidays in big-
name resorts*
Tel 0870 898 8945
sales@markwarner.co.uk
www.markwarner.co.uk

MasterSki
Christian holidays
Tel 020 8942 9442
holidays@mastersun.co.uk
www.mastersun.co.uk

McNab Snowboarding
*Snowboarding holidays based
around Argentière*
Tel 01546 830243
info@mcnab.co.uk
www.mcnab.co.uk

Meriski
Chalet specialist in Méribel
Tel 01285 648510
enquiries@fourwindsresorts.
com
www.meriski.co.uk

MGS Ski Limited
Apartments in Val-Cenis
Tel 01799 525984
skimajor@aol.com
www.mgsski.com

Momentum Ski
Tailor-made specialists
Tel 020 7371 9111
sales@momentumski.com
www.momentumski.com

Moswin Tours
Small German programme
Tel 08700 625040
germany@moswin.com
www.moswin.com

Mountain Beds
*Tailor-made holidays, mainly
in Verbier*
Tel 020 7924 2650
info@mountainbeds.com
www.mountainbeds.com

Mountain Highs
Chalet specialist in Morzine
Tel 00 33 450 792954
info@mountainhighs.co.uk
www.mountain highs.co.uk

Mountainsun Ltd
*Chalets in Paradiski and Alta
Badia*
Tel 07941 196517
mail@mountainsunltd.com
www.mountainsunltd.com

Mountain Tracks
*Ski safaris in Europe and
North America*
Tel 020 8877 5773
info@mountaintracks.co.uk
www.mountaintracks.co.uk

Neilson
Major mainstream operator
Tel 0870 333 3347
sales@neilson.com
www.neilson.com

Neilson School Groups
*School trips to North America
and Europe*
Tel 0870 333 3620
infoschools@neilson.com
www.skiersworld.com

Optimum Ski
*Chalet in Villaroger, part of
the Les Arcs ski area*
Tel 08702 406198
info@optimumski.com
www.optimumski.com

Tour operator directory

697

698

The Oxford Ski Company
Chalets in France and Switzerland
Tel 0870 787 1785
rupert@oxfordski.com
www.oxfordski.com

Panorama Holidays
Budget-oriented holidays in Europe
Tel 08707 595595
panorama@phg.co.uk
www.panoramaholidays.co.uk

Parklife
Summer boarding camps in Les Deux-Alpes
Tel 0870 800 4020
info@myparklife.com
www.myparklife.com

Peak Leisure
Chalets in France
Tel 0870 760 5610
info@peak-leisure.co.uk
www.peak-leisure.co.uk

Peak Retreats
Holidays to the lesser-known Alpine resorts
Tel 0870 770 0408
bonjour@peakretreats.co.uk
www.peakretreats.co.uk

Peak Ski
Chalets in Verbier
Tel 01442 832629
peakski@which.net
www.peakski.co.uk

PGL Ski Europe
Specialist in school group holidays
Tel 0870 1626622
ski@pgl.co.uk
www.pgl.co.uk

PGL Travel
Holidays for teenagers
Tel 08700 507507
holidays@pgl.co.uk
www.pgl.co.uk

Piste Artiste Ltd
Self-catered chalets in Champéry
reserve@pisteartiste.com
www.pisteartiste.com

Powder Byrne
Small programme of luxury hotel holidays in Europe
Tel 020 8246 5300
enquiries@powderbyrne.co.uk
www.powderbyrne.com

Powder Skiing in North America Limited
Heli-skiing holidays in Canada
Tel 020 7736 8191
info@psna.co.uk

Premiere Neige
Chalets/apartments in Ste-Foy
Tel 0709 2000 300
enquiries@premiere-neige.com
www.premiere-neige.com

Purple Ski
Chalet holidays in Méribel
Tel 01494 488633
michael@purpleski.com
www.purpleski.com

Pyrenees Ski Experience
Catered chalet holidays in the Pyrenees
Tel 00 33 468 041879
sarah.blackmore@tiscali.fr
www.pyrenees-ski-experience.com

Ramblers Holidays
Mostly cross-country holidays
Tel 01707 331133
info@ramblersholidays.co.uk
www.ramblersholidays.co.uk

Re-lax Holidays
Hotel holidays in Switzerland
Tel 020 8360 1185
sarah@re-laxholidays.co.uk
www.re-laxholidays.co.uk

Rocketski
All-in holidays online
Tel 01273 262626
info@rocketski.com
www.rocketski.com

Scott Dunn Latin America
Holidays to South America
Tel 020 8682 5030
latin@scottdunn.com
www.scottdunn.com

Scott Dunn Ski
Upmarket holidays
Tel 020 8682 5050
ski@scottdunn.com
www.scottdunn.com

Silver Ski
Chalet holidays in France
Tel 01622 735544
karen@silverski.co.uk
www.silverski.co.uk

Simon Butler Skiing
Holidays and tuition in Megève
Tel 0870 873 0001
info@simonbutlerskiing.co.uk
www.simonbutlerskiing.co.uk

Simply Ski
Specialist chalet operator in big-name resorts
Tel 020 8541 2209
ski@simply-travel.com
www.simplyski.co.uk

Ski 2
Monterosa specialists
Tel 01962 713330
info@ski-2.com
www.ski-2.com

Ski Activity
Holidays in big-name resorts
Tel 01738 840888
sales@skiactivity.com
www.skiactivity.com

Ski Addiction
Chalets and hotels in Châtel, Chapelle d'Abondance and Monterosa Ski
Tel 01580 819354
sales@skiaddiction.co.uk
www.skiaddiction.co.uk

Ski a la Carte
Luxury chalet in Alpe-d'Huez
Tel 020 8542 5559
info@skialacarte.co.uk
www.skialacarte.co.uk

Ski All America
N and S American holidays
Tel 08701 676 676
sales@skiallamerica.com
www.skiallamerica.com

Skialot
Chalet in Châtel
Tel 020 8363 8326
stuey@skialot.com
www.skialot.com

Ski The American Dream
Major operator to North
America
Tel 0870 350 7547
holidays@skidream.com
www.skidream.com

Ski Amis
Catered chalet and self-catered
holidays in the French Alps
Tel 020 7692 0850
info@skiamis.com
www.skiamis.com

Ski Arrangements
Chalets/apartments in Europe
and North America
Tel 08700 110565
info@skiarrangements.com
www.skiarrangements.com

Ski Balkantours
Holidays in Eastern Europe
Tel 028 9024 6795
mail@balkan.co.uk
www.balkan.co.uk

Ski Barrett-Boyce
Chalet in Megève with tuition
Tel 01737 831184
info@skibb.com
www.skibb.com

Ski Basics
Chalets in Méribel
Tel 01225 444143
sales@skibasics.co.uk
www.skibasics.co.uk

Ski Beat
Chalets in the French Alps
Tel 01243 780405
Ski@skibeat.co.uk
www.skibeat.co.uk

Ski Blanc
Chalet holidays in Méribel
Tel 020 8502 9082
info@skiblanc.co.uk
www.skiblanc.co.uk

Ski Bon
Chalets in Méribel
Tel 01604 247723
sales@skibon.com
www.skibon.com

SkiBound
Schools division of First Choice
Tel 0870 900 3200
sales@skibound.co.uk
www.skibound.co.uk

Ski Chamois
Holidays in Morzine
Tel 01302 369006
sales@skichamois.co.uk
www.skichamois.co.uk

Ski Cuisine
Chalets in Méribel
Tel 01702 589543
info@skicuisine.co.uk
www.skicuisine.co.uk

Ski Deep
Chalets in La Tania and Le
Praz
Tel 01483 722706 /
00 33 660 081905
ferg@skideep.net
www.skideep.net

Ski Etoile
Chalets and hotels in
Montgenèvre
Tel 01588 640442
info@skietoile.co.uk
www.skietoile.co.uk

Ski Expectations
Mainly hotels and chalets in
Europe
Tel 01799 531888
ski.expectations@virgin.net
www.skiexpectations.com

Ski Famille
Family holidays in Les Gets
Tel 0845 644 3764
info@skifamille.co.uk
www.skifamille.co.uk

Ski France
Chalets and catered
apartments in France
Tel 0870 787 3402
ski@skifrance.co.uk
www.skifrance.co.uk

Ski Freshtracks
Holidays for Ski Club of GB
members
Tel 0845 458 0784
holidays@skifreshtracks.co.uk
www.skifreshtracks.co.uk
www.skiclub.co.uk

SkiGower
School trips to Switzerland
Tel 01527 851411
peter@gowstrav.demon.co.uk

Ski Hame
Catered chalets in the Three
Valleys
Tel 01875 320157
powderpigs@skihame.co.uk
www.skihame.co.uk

Ski Hillwood
Austrian, French and Canadian
family holidays
Tel 01923 290700
sales@hillwood-holidays.co.uk
www.hillwood-holidays.co.uk

Ski Hiver
Chalets in Peisey (Paradiski)
Tel 01329 847788
skihiver@wanadoo.fr
www.skihiver.co.uk

Ski Independence
USA and Canada and self-drive
to France and Switzerland
Tel 0845 310 3030
ski@ski-i.com
www.ski-i.com

Ski La Cote
Catered chalet holidays in the
Portes du Soleil
Tel 01482 668357
adrian@ski-la-cote.karoo.co.uk
www.ski-la-cote.karoo.net

Ski Leisure Direction
Mainly self-catering in France
Tel 0870 442 9842
ski@leisuredirection.co.uk
www.leisuredirection.co.uk

Ski Line
Chalet holidays in Europe and
North America
Tel 0870 950 4420
angus@skiline.co.uk
www.skiline.co.uk

Ski Link
Holidays in Courchevel
Tel 0871 218 1754
enquiries@ski-link.com
www.ski-link.co.uk

Ski McNeill
Tailor-made to USA and
European weekends
Tel 0870 600 1359
contact@skimcneill.com
www.skimcneill.com

Ski Miquel
Small but eclectic programme
Tel 01457 821200
ski@miquelhols.co.uk
www.miquelhols.co.uk

Ski Morgins Holidays
Chalet holidays in Morgins
Tel 01568 770681
info@skimorgins.com
www.skimorgins.com

Ski Morzine
Holiday accommodation in
Morzine
Tel 01372 470104
info@skimorzine.com
www.skimorzine.com

Ski 'n' Action
Chalet in Le Praz (Courchevel)
Tel 00 33 (0) 630 855691
info@ski-n-action.com
www.ski-n-action.com

Ski Olympic
Chalet holidays in France
Tel 01302 328820
info@skiolympic.co.uk
www.skiolympic.com

Ski Peak
Specialist in Vaujany
Tel 01428 608070
info@skipeak.com
www.skipeak.com

SkiPlan Travel Service
Schools programme
Tel 01273 774778
sales@topstravel.co.uk

Ski Power
Chalets in the Three Valleys
Tel 01737 823232
info@skipower.co.uk
www.skipower.co.uk

Ski Rosie
Catered chalet in Morgins and
apartments in Châtel
Tel 00 33 450813100
rosie@skirosie.com
www.skirosie.com

Ski Safari
Canadian/US specialist, but
also Chile
Tel 01273 224060
info@skisafari.com
www.skisafari.com

Skisafe Travel
Mainly holidays in Scotland
Tel 0141 812 0925
info@osatravel.co.uk
www.osatravel.co.uk

Ski Scott James
Chalets in Argentière
Tel 01845 501139
jamie@skiscottjames.co.uk
www.skiscottjames.co.uk

Ski Solutions
Tailor-made holidays
Tel 020 7471 7777
alc@skisolutions.com
www.skisolutions.com

Ski St Anton
St Anton specialist
Tel 01276 61072 /0871 666
1259
office@skistanton.net
www.skistanton.net

Ski Supreme
Coach and self-drive holidays
to France
Tel 01355 260547
info@skisupreme.co.uk
www.skisupreme.co.uk

Skitopia
*Holidays to the southern
French Alps*
Tel 01872 272767
hannah@skitopia.com
www.skitopia.com

Ski Tracer
*Holidays to Europe and North
America*
Tel 0870 420 5782
sales@skitracer.com
www.skitracer.com

Ski-Val
Holidays in France and Austria
Tel 0870 746 3030
reservations@skival.co.uk
www.skival.co.uk

Ski Verbier
Specialists in Verbier
Tel 020 7385 8050
info@skiverbier.com
www.skiverbier.com

Ski Weekend
Weekend and ten-day holidays
Tel 0870 060 0615
sales@skiweekend.com
www.skiweekend.com

Ski Weekends & Board Breaks
*3- and 6-day holidays to Les
Trois Vallées*
Tel 0870 4423400
sales@harris-travel.com
www.skiweekends.com

Ski Wild
*Holidays in Europe and North
America; specialise in Austria*
Tel 0870 746 9668
info@skiwild.co.uk
www.skiwild.co.uk

Ski with Julia
*Hotels and catered chalets in
Verbier*
Tel 01386 584478
julia@skijulia.co.uk
www.skijulia.co.uk

Skiworld
*European and North American
programme*
Tel 0870 241 6723
sales@skiworld.ltd.uk
www.skiworld.ltd.uk

Ski Yogi
Holidays in Italy
Tel 01799 531886
ski.expectations@virgin.net
www.skiexpectations.com

Sloping Off
*Schools and group holidays by
coach*
Tel 01273 886888
info@sloping-off.co.uk
www.sloping-off.co.uk

Snowbizz
Holidays in Puy-St-Vincent
Tel 01778 341455
wendy@snowbizz.co.uk
www.snowbizz.co.uk

Snowcoach
Holidays to Austria and France
Tel 01727 866177
info@snowcoach.co.uk
www.snowcoach.co.uk

SnowCrazy
Chalet in La Rosière
Tel 01342 302910
enquiries@snowcrazy.co.uk
www.snowcrazy.co.uk

Snowebb
*Catered chalets in Big
White/Silver Star*
Tel 01797 224861
david@snowebb.com
snowebb.co.uk

Snowfocus
Chalet in Châtel
Tel 01392 479555
action@snowfocus.com
www.snowfocus.com

Snowlife
Catered chalet in La Clusaz
Tel 01534 863630
info@snowlife.co.uk
www.snowlife.co.uk

Snowline
Chalet holidays in France
Tel 08701 123118
ski@snowlineVIP.com
www.snowline.co.uk

Snow Monkey Chalets
Chalets in the Paradiski area
Tel 00 33 626 807767
enquiries@snowmonkey
chalets.co.uk
www.snowmonkeychalets.
co.uk

Snoworks
Holidays with tuition
Tel 0870 1225549
philsmith@snoworks.co.uk
www.snoworks.co.uk

Snowscape
Flexible trips to Austria
Tel 01905 357760
www.snowscape.co.uk

Snowstar Holidays
Catered chalets in Tignes
Tel 0870 068 6611
info@snowstar.co.uk
www.snowstar.co.uk

Solo's
Holidays for singles 25 to 69
Tel 08700 720700
travel@solosholidays.co.uk
www.solosholidays.co.uk

La Source
*Accommodation in Villard-
Reculas (Alpe-d'Huez)*
Tel 01707 655988
lasourcefrance@aol.com
www.lasource.org.uk

Stanford Skiing
Megève specialist
Tel 01603 477471
info@stanfordskiing.co.uk
www.stanfordskiing.co.uk

St Anton Ski Company
Hotels and chalets in St Anton
Tel 00 43 676 495 3438
jonathanstanton@mac.com
www.atlas.co.uk/ski

Susie Ward Alpine Holidays
Flexible holidays to Châtel
Tel 01872 553055
susie@susieward.com
www.susieward.com

Swiss Travel Service
Hotels in Switzerland
Tel 0870 191 7175
swiss@bridge-travel.co.uk
www.swisstravel.co.uk

Switzerland Travel Centre
Specialists in Swiss resorts
Tel 020 7420 4900
sales@stc.co.uk
www.stc.co.uk

Thomson Ski & Snowboarding
Major mainstream operator
Tel 0870 606 1470
info@thomson-ski.com
www.thomson-ski.co.uk

Tops Ski Chalets
*Chalets and hotels in French
resorts*
Tel 01273 774666
sales@topstravel.co.uk
www.topstravel.co.uk

Total
*Chalet holidays in Europe and
Canada*
Tel 08701 633633
www.skitotal.com

Trail Alpine
Chalet in Morzine
Tel 0870 750 6560
info@trailalpine.co.uk
www.trailalpine.co.uk

Trailfinders
North American programme
Tel 0845 050 5900
www.trailfinders.com

**United Vacations Ski Freedom
USA & Canada**
US and Canada programme
Tel 0870 606 1006
uvuk@unitedvacations.com
www.unitedvacations.co.uk

Val d'Isère A La Carte
*Specialists in Val-d'Isère hotels
and self-catering holidays*
Tel 01481 236800
skialacarte@aol.com
www.skivaldisere.co.uk

Vanilla Ski
*Chalet in Seez (near La Rosière
and Les Arcs)*
Tel 01932 860696
sam@vanillaski.com
www.vanillaski.com

VIP
*Chalets in Val d'Isère and
Méribel*
Tel 08701 123119
ski@vip-chalets.com
www.vip-chalets.com

Virgin Snow
Holidays to America
Tel 0870 220 2707
customerrelations@
virginholidays.co.uk
www.virgin.com/Holidays

Waymark Holidays
Cross-country skiing holidays
Tel 01753 516477
enquiries@waymarkholidays.
com
www.waymarkholidays.com

Weekends in Val d'Isère
*Weekends – and not just in
Val d'Isère*
Tel 020 8944 9762
info@alpineweekends.com
www.alpineweekends.com

White Heat Skiing
Swiss specialist with tuition
Tel 0208 989 3281
info@whiteheatski.biz
www.whiteheatski.biz

White Roc
*Weekends and tailor-made
hotel holidays*
Tel 020 7792 1188
snow@whiteroc.co.uk
www.whiteroc.co.uk

Wood Advent Chalet
Chalet in Les Gets
Tel 01984 640920
info@skilesgets.com
www.skilesgets.com

YSE
*Variety of holidays in
Val-d'Isère*
Tel 0845 122 1414
sales@yseski.co.uk
www.yseski.co.uk

SKI BUSINESS DIRECTORY

This is a list of companies and organisations providing goods and services you might find helpful in organising a holiday, grouped under a dozen headings. Tour operators are listed separately, in the previous section, starting on page 695.

AIRLINES

Air Canada
Tel 0871 220 1111
www.aircanada.ca

Air France
Tel 0870 142 4343
www.airfrance.com/uk

Air New Zealand
Tel 0800 028 4149
www.airnewzealand.com

Alitalia
Tel 0870 544 8259
www.alitalia.co.uk

American Airlines
Tel 020 7365 0777
www.aa.com

Austrian Airlines
Tel 0870 124 2625
www.austrianairlines.co.uk

Bmibaby
Tel 0870 264 2229
www.bmibaby.com

British Airways
Flight enquiries:
0870 55 111 55
Tel 0870 850 9850
www.britishairways.com

Continental Airlines
Tel 01293 776464
www.continental.com

Delta Airlines
Tel 0800 414767
www.delta.com

EasyJet
Tel 0870 6 000 000
www.easyjet.com

Flybe
Tel 0871 700 0535
www.flybe.com

Helvetic
www.helvetic.com

Jet2.com
Tel 0871 226 1737
www.jet2.com

KLM
Tel 08705 074074
www.klmuk.co.uk

Lufthansa
Tel 0870 837 7747
www.lufthansa.com

Qantas
Tel 0845 774 7767
www.qantas.com.au

Ryanair
Tel 0871 246 0000
www.ryanair.com

Swiss International Air Lines
Tel 0845 601 0956
www.swiss.com

Thomsonfly
Tel 0870 190 0737
www.thomsonfly.com

United Airlines
Tel 0845 844 4777
www.unitedairlines.co.uk

Virgin Atlantic Airways
Tel 01293 562345
www.virgin-atlantic.com

Zoom Airlines
Flights to Canada
Tel 0870 240 0055
www.flyzoom.com

AIRPORTS

Aberdeen
Tel 0870 040 0006
www.baa.co.uk

Belfast
Tel 028 9448 4848
info.desk@bial.co.uk
www.bial.co.uk

Birmingham
Tel 08707 335511
info@bhx.co.uk
www.bhx.co.uk

Bournemouth
Tel 01202 364000
feedback@bournemouth
airport.co.uk
www.flybournemouth.com

Bristol
Tel 0870 121 2747
feedback@bristolairport.com
www.bristolairport.co.uk

Cardiff
Tel 01446 711111
infodesk@cwl.aero
www.cial.co.uk

Dublin
Tel 00 353 1 814 1111
information@
dublinairport.com
www.dublin-airport.com

Durham Tees Valley
Tel 01325 332811
information@durhamtees
valleyairport.com
www.durhamteesvalleyairport.
com

Edinburgh
Tel 0870 040 0007
www.baa.co.uk

Exeter
Tel 01392 367433
marketing@exeter-
airport.co.uk
www.exeter-airport.co.uk

Glasgow
Tel 0870 040 0008
www.baa.co.uk

Leeds Bradford
Tel 0113 250 9696
www.lbia.co.uk

London Gatwick
Tel 0870 000 2468
www.baa.com

London Heathrow
Tel 0870 000 0123
www.baa.co.uk

London Luton
Tel 01582 405100
info@ltn.aero
www.london-luton.com

London Stansted
Tel 0870 000 0303
www.baa.co.uk

Manchester
Tel 0161 489 3000
www.manchesterairport.co.uk

Newcastle
Tel 0870 122 1488
Callctr@
newcastleinternational.co.uk
www.newcastleairport.com

Nottingham East Midlands
Tel 0871 919 9000
enquiries@
nottinghamema.com
www.eastmidlandsairport.com

Southampton
Tel 0870 040 0009
www.baa.co.uk

AIRPORT TRANSFERS

Airport Transfer Service
Tel 00 33 450 536397
sales@a-t-s.net
www.a-t-s.net

AlpineCab
Tel 00 33 450 731938
info@alpinecab.com
www.alpinecab.com

Flytransfer
Tel 028 9042 4662
info@flytransfer.com
www.flytransfer.com

BREAKDOWN INSURANCE

AA Five Star Europe
Tel 0870 600 0371
customer.services@theAA.com
www.theAA.com

Autohome
Tel 0800 371 280
www.autohome.co.uk

Direct Line Rescue
Tel 0845 246 0940
www.directline.com/rescue

Europ Assistance
Tel 0870 737 5720
customerservices@
europ-assistance.co.uk
www.europ-assistance.co.uk

**Green Flag Motoring
Assistance**
Tel 0800 400 638
european-sales@
greenflag.com
www.greenflag.com

Leisurecare Insurance Services
Tel 01793 750150

Mondial Assistance UK
Tel 0800 777148
enquiries@
mondial-assistance.co.uk
www.mondial-assistance.co.uk

RAC Travel Services
Tel 0800 550055
traveladmin@rac.co.uk
www.rac.co.uk

CAR HIRE

Alamo Rent A Car
Tel 0870 599 4000
international@goalamo.com
www.alamo.com

Avis Rent A Car
Tel 08700 100 287
customer.service@avis.co.uk
www.avis.co.uk

Budget Car and Van Rental
Tel 08701 565656
reservations@budget-uk.com
www.budget-uk.com

Europcar UK
Tel 0870 607 5000
reservationsuk@
mail.europcar.com
www.europcar.co.uk

Hertz UK Ltd
Tel 08708 448844
www.hertz.co.uk

Holiday Autos International
Tel 0870 400 4447
www.holidayautos.com

Suncars
Tel 0870 500 5566
customerservices@
suncars.com
www.suncars.com

CAR WINTER EQUIPMENT

Brindley Chains Ltd
Pewag snowchains
Tel 01925 825555
enquiries@
brindley-chains.co.uk
www.brindley-chains.co.uk

GT Towing Ltd
Ski boxes and snowchains
Tel 01707 287287
sales@gttowing.co.uk
www.gttowing.co.uk

Lakeland Roof Box Centre
Roof boxes, snowchains
Tel 08700 766326
www.roofbox.co.uk

Latchmere Motor Spares
*Snowchains, roof bars, ski
clamps, boxes*
Tel 020 7228 3907

Motor Traveller/Carbox
*Thule racks and boxes; Milz
snowchains*
Tel 01753 833442
info@carbox.freeserve.co.uk
www.carbox.co.uk

RUD Chains Ltd
Snowchains
Tel 01227 276611
sales@rud.co.uk
www.rud.co.uk

skidrive.co.uk
*Thule roof systems, Karrite
boxes, Skandibox, Konig
snowchains*
Tel 01223 323488
skidrive@dapcambridge.co.uk
www.skidrive.co.uk

Snowchains Ltd
*Thule ski boxes, roof bars and
ski racks; Weissenfels
snowchains*
Tel 01732 884408
info@snowchains.co.uk
www.snowchains.co.uk

Spikes Spider
Tel 01706 819365
pparkinson@ndirect.co.uk
www.spikesspider.com

The Roof Box Company
Tel 08700 766326
www.roofbox.co.uk

Thule Ltd
Tel 01275 340404
www.thule.co.uk

CROSS-CHANNEL TRAVEL

Brittany Ferries
Portsmouth–Caen
Tel 08703 665 333
reservations@
brittany-ferries.com
www.brittanyferries.co.uk

Eurotunnel
*Folkestone–Calais/Coquelles
via the Channel Tunnel*
Tel 08705 35 35 35
www.eurotunnel.com

Hoverspeed
Dover–Calais
Tel 0870 240 8070
www.hoverspeed.com

Norfolkline
Dover–Dunkerque
Tel 0870 870 1020
doverpax@norfolkline.com
www.norfolkline.com

P&O Ferries
*Dover–Calais; Portsmouth-Le
Havre; Hull Rotterdam
Zeebrugge*
Tel 08705 20 20 20
customer.services@posl.com
www.poferries.com

SeaFrance
Dover–Calais
Tel 08705 711 711
enquiries@seafrance.com
www.seafrance.com

SpeedFerries
Dover-Boulogne
Tel 0870 220 0570
mail@speedferries.com
www.speedferries.com

Stena Line
Harwich–Hook of Holland
Tel 08705 707070
www.stenaline.co.uk

DRY SKI SLOPES

SOUTH-WEST ENGLAND

Avon Ski Centre
Lyncombe Lodge, Churchill,
North Somerset
Tel 01934 852335
info@highaction.co.uk
www.highaction.co.uk

Christchurch Ski Centre
Matchams Lane, Hurn,
Christchurch, Dorset
Tel 01202 499155
info@christchurch-
skicentre.com
www.newforest-online.co.uk/
christchurch_ski

Exeter and District Ski Club
Clifton Hill Sports Ground,
Belmont Road, Exeter
Tel 01392 211422

**John Nike Leisuresport –
Plymouth**
Plymouth Ski Centre, Alpine
Park, Marsh Mills, Plymouth
Tel 01752 600220
www.jnll.co.uk

Torquay Alpine Ski Club
Barton Hall, Kingskerswell
Road, Torquay, Devon
Tel 01803 313350
info@skitorquay.co.uk
www.skitorquay.co.uk

Warmwell Ski Centre
Warmwell, Dorchester, Dorset
Tel 01305 853245

Yeovil Ski Centre
Addlewell Lane, Nine Springs,
Yeovil, Somerset
Tel 01935 421702

SOUTH-EAST ENGLAND

Alpine Snowsports Aldershot
Gallwey Road, Aldershot,
Hants
Tel 01252 325889
info@alpinesnowsports.co.uk
www.alpinesnowsports.co.uk

Bowles Outdoor Centre
Eridge Green, Tunbridge Wells
Tel 01892 665665
admin@bowles.ac
www.bowles.ac

Bromley Ski Centre
Sandy Lane, St Paul's Cray,
Orpington, Kent
Tel 01689 876812
management@
bromleyski.co.uk
www.c-v-s.co.uk/bromleyski/

Calshot Activities Centre
Calshot Spit, Fawley,
Southampton
Tel 023 8089 2077
calshot.ac@hants.gov.uk
www.hants.gov.uk/calshot

Christ's College Ski Club
Larch Avenue, Guildford,
Surrey
Tel 01483 504988
www.ccski.co.uk

**Folkestone Sports Centre Ski
Slope**
Radnor Park Avenue,
Folkestone, Kent
Tel 01303 850333
www.folkestonesports.ndo.
co.uk/swimski.html

**John Nike Leisuresport –
Bracknell**
Bracknell Ski Centre, Amen
Corner, Bracknell, Berkshire
Tel 01344 789000
www.jnll.com

**John Nike Leisuresport –
Chatham**
Chatham Ski and Snowboard
Centre, Alpine Park, Capstone
Road, Gillingham, Kent
Tel 01634 827979
www.jnll.co.uk

Plas y Brenin
Capel Curig, Conwy
Tel 01690 720214
info@pyb.co.uk
www.pyb.co.uk

Sandown Ski Centre
More Lane, Esher, Surrey
Tel 01372 467132
sandown@
sandownsports.co.uk
www.sandownsports.co.uk

Southampton Alpine Centre
The Sports Centre, Bassett,
Southampton
Tel 023 8079 0970
info@southampton-alpine-
centre.co.uk
www.southampton-alpine-
centre.co.uk

Wycombe Summit
Abbey Barn Lane, High
Wycombe, Bucks
Tel 01494 474711
info@wycombesummit.co.uk
www.wycombesummit.co.uk

MIDDLE ENGLAND

Gloucester Ski and Snowboard Centre
Jarvis International Hotel and
Country Club, Robinswood
Hill, Matson Lane, Gloucester
Tel 08702 400375
www.gloucesterski.com

**John Nike Leisuresport –
Swadlincote**
Swadlincote Ski Centre, Hill
Street, Swadlincote,
Derbyshire
Tel 01283 217200
www.jnll.co.uk

Kidsgrove Ski Centre
Bathpool Park, Kidsgrove,
Stoke-on-Trent
Tel 01782 784908
info@ski-kidsgrove.co.uk
www.ski-kidsgrove.co.uk

Stoke Ski Centre
Festival Park, Stoke-on-Trent
Tel 01782 204159
wilsonpb@postmaster.co.uk
www.stokeskicentre.co.uk

Tallington Ski and Snowboard Centre
Tallington Lakes Leisure Park,
Barholm Road, Tallington,
Stamford, Lincs
Tel 01778 344990
sales@waspdirect.com
www.waspdirect.com

Tamworth Snowdome
Leisure Island, River Drive,
Tamworth, Staffordshire
Tel 08705 000011
info@snowdome.co.uk
www.snowdome.co.uk

Telford Ski Centre
Court Street, Madeley, Telford,
Shropshire
Tel 01952 586862
madeleyskicentre@
telford.gov.uk
www.telford.gov.uk/FreeTime/
Sports/LeisureAndSport
Centres.htm

The Ackers
Golden Hillock Road, Small
Heath, Birmingham
Tel 0121 772 5111
www.ackers-adventure.co.uk

Xscape Snozone
602 Marlborough Gate,
Central Milton Keynes
Tel 0871 222 5670
www.xscape.co.uk

EASTERN ENGLAND

**Brentwood Park Ski and
Snowboard Centre**
Warley Gap, Brentwood, Essex
Tel 01277 211994
info@brentwoodskicentre.
co.uk
www.brentwoodskicentre.
co.uk

Gosling Ski Centre
Stanborough Road, Welwyn
Garden City, Hertfordshire
Tel 01707 331056
info@goslingsports.co.uk
www.goslingsports.co.uk

Hemel Ski Centre
St Albans Hill, Hemel
Hempstead, Herts
Tel 01442 241321
communicate@hemel-ski.co.uk
www.hemel-ski.co.uk

Norfolk Ski Club
Whitlingham Lane, Trowse,
Norwich, Norfolk
Tel 01603 662781
info@norfolkskiclub.co.uk
www.norfolkskiclub.com

Suffolk Ski Centre
Bourne Hill, Wherstead,
Ipswich
Tel 01473 602347
enquiries@suffolkskicentre.
co.uk
www.suffolkskicentre.co.uk

NORTHERN ENGLAND

**Alston Training and Adventure
Centre**
High Plains Lodge, Alston,
Cumbria
Tel 01434 381886
alstontraining@btconnect.com
www.alstontraining.co.uk

**Halifax Ski and Snowboard
Centre**
Ploughcroft Lane, Halifax
Tel 01422 340760
skislope@ridehalifax.co.uk
www.ridehalifax.co.uk

Kendal Ski Club
Canal Head North, Kendal,
Cumbria
Tel 01539 732948
sec@kendalski.co.uk
www.kendalski.co.uk

Pendle Ski Club
Clitheroe Road, Sabden,
Clitheroe, Lancs
Tel 01200 425222
info@pendleskiclub.org.uk
www.pendleskiclub.org.uk

**Runcorn Ski and Snowboard
Centre**
Town Park, Palace Fields,
Runcorn, Cheshire
Tel 01928 701965
info@runcornskicentre.co.uk
www.runcornskicentre.co.uk

Sheffield Ski Village
Vale Road, Parkwood Springs,
Sheffield
Tel 0114 276 9459
www.sheffieldskivillage.co.uk

Ski Rossendale
Haslingden Old Road,
Rawtenstall, Rossendale,
Lancashire
Tel 01706 226457
ski-rossendale@rltrust.co.uk
www.rltrust.co.uk/
 ski_rossendale

**Whickham Thorns Outdoor
Centre**
Market Lane, Dunston
Tel 0191 433 5767
whickhamthorns@
 leisure.gatesheadmbc.gov.uk
www.gateshead.gov.uk/
 leisserv/whickhamthorns.htm

Xscape
Colorado Way,
Glasshoughton, Castleford,
West Yorkshire
Tel 0871 222 5671
enquiriescastleford@
xscape.co.uk
www.xscape.co.uk

WALES

**Cardiff Ski & Snowboard
Centre**
Fairwater Park, Fairwater Rd,
Cardiff
Tel 029 2056 1793
info@skicardiff.com
www.skicardiff.com

Dan-yr-Ogof Ski Slopes
Glyn Tawe, Abercraf, West
Glamorgan
Tel 01639 730284
www.showcaves.co.uk

**John Nike Leisuresport –
Llandudno**
Wyddfyd Road, Great Orme,
Llandudno
Tel 01492 874707
www.jnll.co.uk

Pontypool Ski Centre
Pontypool Leisure Park,
Pontypool, Gwent
Tel 01495 756955

Ski Pembrey
Pembrey Country Park, Burry
Port, Llanelli, Dyfed
Tel 01554 834443

SCOTLAND

Alford Ski Centre
Greystone Road, Alford,
Aberdeenshire
Tel 01975 563024
keith.morris@
aberdeenshire.gov.uk
www.aberdeenshire.gov.uk/
recreation

**Ancrum Outdoor Education
Resource Centre**
10 Ancrum Road, Dundee,
Tayside
Tel 01382 435911
ancrum.centre@
dundeecity.gov.uk
www.ancrum.com

Bearsden Ski & Board
Stockiemuir Road, Bearsden,
Glasgow
Tel 0141 943 1500
info@skibearsden.co.uk
www.skibearsden.co.uk

Firpark Ski Centre
Tillicoultry, Clackmannanshire
Tel 01259 751772
www.clacksweb.org.uk/culture/
sport/

**Glasgow Ski & Snowboard
Centre**
Bellahouston Park, 16
Dumbreck Road, Glasgow
Tel 0141 427 4991
info@ski-glasgow.org
www.ski-glasgow.org

Glenmore Lodge
Scottish National Sports
Centre, Aviemore, Inverness-
shire
Tel 01479 861256
enquiries@
glenmorelodge.org.uk
www.glenmorelodge.org.uk

Loch Insh Watersports and Ski Centre
Loch Insh, Near Aviemore
Tel 01540 651272
enquiries@lochinsh.com
www.lochinsh.com

Midlothian Snowsports Centre
Hillend, Near Edinburgh,
Midlothian
Tel 0131 445 4433
ski@midlothian.gov.uk
ski.midlothian.gov.uk

Neptune Ski and Snowboard Club
The Sports Drome, HMNB
Clyde, Helensburgh
neptune.skiboard@virgin.net

Polmonthill Ski Centre
Polmont, Falkirk
Tel 01324 503835
ski@polmonthill.freeserve.
co.uk

NORTHERN IRELAND

Craigavon Golf and Ski Centre
Turmoyra Lane, Silverwood,
Lurgan, Co Armagh
Tel 028 3832 6606
golf.ski@craigavon.gov.uk
www.craigavon.gov.uk

INSURANCE COMPANIES

Atlas Insurance
Tel 0870 811 1700
sales@travel-insurance.co.uk
www.atlasdirect.net

AUL
Tel 01206 577770
enquiries@aul.co.uk
www.aul.co.uk

Best Ski Insurance
Tel 0870 458 2985
sales@
best-ski-insurance.co.uk
www.best-ski-insurance.co.uk

CGNU
Tel 0800 1050 362
support@norwich-union.co.uk
www.norwichunion.co.uk

Direct Line Travel Insurance
Tel 0845 246 8704
www.directline.com/travel

Direct Travel Insurance
Tel 01903 812345
info@direct-travel.co.uk
www.direct-travel.co.uk

Douglas Cox Tyrie
Tel 01708 385969

Matthew Gerard Travel Insurance Ltd
Tel 01483 730900
sales@mgtis.easynet.co.uk

P J Hayman & Company
Tel 023 9241 9050
travel.insurance@
pjhayman.com
www.pjhayman.com

Preferential
Tel 0870 600 7766
www.preferential.co.uk

Primary Insurance Group
Tel 0870 222 0634
customersupport@
primaryinsurance.co.uk
www.primaryinsurance.co.uk

Select Travel Insurance
Tel 0870 737 0870
select@inter-group.co.uk
www.select-insurance.co.uk

ski-insurance.co.uk
Tel 0870 755 6101
info@ski-insurance.co.uk
www.ski-insurance.co.uk

Skicoverdirect
www.skicoverdirect.co.uk

Skisure.com
Tel 0845 2220020
info@skisure.com
www.skisure.com

Snowcard Insurance Services Ltd
Tel 01327 262805
enquiries@snowcard.co.uk
www.snowcard.co.uk

Sportscover Direct Ltd
Tel 0845 120 6400
contact@sportscover.co.uk
www.sportscover.co.uk

Travel Insurance Direct
Tel 01603 464123
info@insurance.uk.com
www.travelcover.com

WorldCover Direct
Tel 0800 365 121
world.cover@gecapital.com

WorldSki
Tel 0870 043 4122
info@worldski.co.uk
www.worldski.co.uk

Worldwide Travel Insurance Services Ltd
Tel 0870 112 8100
sales@worldwideinsure.com
www.worldwideinsure.com

NATIONAL TOURIST OFFICES

Andorran Embassy
Tel 020 8874 4806

Argentine Embassy
Tel 020 7318 1300
info@turismo.gov.ar
www.turismo.gov.ar

Australian Tourist Commission
Tel 09068 633235
www.australia.com

Austrian National Tourist Office
Tel 0845 101 1818
holiday@austria.info
www.austria.info/uk

Canadian Tourism Commission
Tel 0906 871 5000
visitcanada@dial.pipex.com
www.travelcanada.ca

Chile – Consulate General
Tel 020 7580 1023
cglonduk@
congechileuk.demon.co.uk
www.echileuk.demon.co.uk

Czech Tourism
Tel 020 7631 0427
info-uk@czechtourism.com
www.czechtourism.com

Finnish Tourist Board
Tel 020 7365 2512
finlandinfo.lon@mek.fi
www.finland-tourism.com

French Government Tourist Office
Tel 09068 244123
info.uk@franceguide.com
www.franceguide.com

German National Tourist Office
Tel 020 7317 0908
gntolon@d-z-t.com
www.germany-tourism.co.uk

Italian State Tourist Office
Brochure line: 09065 508925
Tel 020 7408 1254
italy@italiantouristboard.co.uk
www.italiantouristboard.co.uk

Japan National Tourist Organisation
Tel 020 7734 9638
info@jnto.co.uk
www.seejapan.co.uk

Norwegian Tourist Board
Tel 0906 302 2003
infouk@ntr.no
www.visitnorway.com

Romanian Tourist Office
Tel 020 7224 3692
infouk@RomaniaTourism.com
www.romaniatourism.com

Scottish Tourist Board
ski.visitscotland.com

Slovenian Tourist Office
Tel 0870 225 5305
info@slovenian-tourism.co.uk
www.slovenia-tourism.si

Spanish Tourist Office
Tel 020 7486 8077
tourspain@latestinfo.co.uk
www.tourspain.co.uk

Swedish Travel and Tourism Council
Tel 0207 108 6168
info@swetourism.org.uk
www.visit-sweden.com

Switzerland Tourism
Tel 00800 100 200 30
info.uk@myswitzerland.com
www.MySwitzerland.com

Tourism New Zealand
Tel 0906 601 3601
www.newzealand.com

Turkish Tourist Board
Tel 020 7629 7771
info@gototurkey.co.uk
www.gototurkey.co.uk

Visit USA Association
Tel 09069 101020
www.visitusa.org.uk

RAILWAYS

Deutsche Bahn AG
Tel 0870 243 5363
sales@bahn.co.uk
www.deutsche-bahn.co.uk

Eurostar
Tel 08705 186 186
new.comments@
eurostar.co.uk
www.eurostar.com

Rail Europe
Tel 08708 371 371
reservations@raileurope.co.uk
www.raileurope.co.uk

Swiss Federal Railways
Tel 00800 100 200 30
(Switzerland Tourism)
info.uk@switzerland.com
www.rail.ch

RETAILERS

SOUTH-WEST ENGLAND

Christchurch Ski and Leisure Centre
Matchams Lane, Hurn,
Christchurch, Dorset
Tel 01202 499155
www.christchurch-
skicentre.com

Devon Ski Centre
Oak Place, Newton Abbot,
Devon
Tel 01626 351278
www.devonski.co.uk

Kidski
Tel 01202 631222
help@kidski.co.uk
www.kidski.co.uk

Mission Adventure Ltd
1 Bank Lane, Brixham, Devon
Tel 01803 855796
www.missionadventure.co.uk

Noahs Ark
London Road, Chalford,
Stroud, Gloucestershire
Tel 01453 884738
www.noahsark.co.uk

Penrose Outdoors
Town Quay, Truro, Cornwall
Tel 01872 272116
www.penroseoutdoors.co.uk

Skate and Ski
104 High Street, Staple Hill,
Bristol
Tel 0117 970 1356

Snow & Rock
Units 1-3 Shield Retail Centre,
Link Road, Filton, Bristol
Tel 0845 100 1017
www.snowandrock.com

Snow Togs
6 St Michaels Road,
Bournemouth, Dorset
Tel 01202 557690
www.skishops.co.uk

Team Ski
37 High East Street,
Dorchester, Dorset
Tel 01305 268035
www.teamski.co.uk

Westsports
Market House, Marlborough
Rd, Old Town, Swindon
Tel 01793 532588
www.skishops.co.uk

SOUTH-EAST ENGLAND

Activ (Folkestone)
145 Sandgate Road,
Folkestone, Kent
Tel 01303 240110
www.activfolkestone.com

Alpine Room
71-73 Main Road, Danbury,
Essex
Tel 01245 223563
www.alpineroom.co.uk

John Pollock
157 High Road, Loughton,
Essex
Tel 020 8508 6626
www.johnpollock.co.uk

John Pollock
67 High Street, Barnet
Tel 020 8440 3994
www.johnpollock.co.uk

Lang & Hunter
12 Thames Street, Kingston-
upon-Thames, Surrey
Tel 020 8546 5427
www.langandhunter.com

Outdoor Life
3 High Street, Old Town,
Eastbourne, East Sussex
Tel 01323 725372

Snow & Rock
188 Kensington High Street,
London
Tel 0845 100 1011
www.snowandrock.com

Snow & Rock
4 Mercer Street, Covent
Garden, London
Tel 0845 1001018
www.snowandrock.com

Snow & Rock
150 Holborn, Corner of Grays
Inn Road, London
Tel 0845 100 1013
www.snowandrock.com

Snow & Rock
99 Fordwater Road, Chertsey,
Surrey
Tel 0845 100 1016
www.snowandrock.com

Snow & Rock
The Boardwalk, Port Solent,
Portsmouth, Hampshire
Tel 0845 100 1019
www.snowandrock.co.uk

Snow Togs
431 Millbrook Road,
Southampton, Hampshire
Tel 023 8077 3925
www.skishops.co.uk

MIDDLE ENGLAND

Active Outdoor & Ski
77 Castle Quay, Banbury,
Oxfordshire
Tel 01295 273700
www.aosbanbury.com

Beans
86 Sheep Street, Bicester,
Oxfordshire
Tel 01869 246451
www.beansonline.co.uk

BestBuys
Nene Court, 27-31 The
Embankment, Wellingborough,
Northamptonshire
Tel 01933 272699
www.best-buys.co.uk

Force
26 Bakers Lane, Lichfield,
Staffordshire
Tel 01543 411249
www.skiforce.co.uk

Force
Guildhall Shopping Centre,
Stafford
Tel 01785 225737
www.skiforce.co.uk

Fox's
1 London Road, Amersham
Tel 01494 431431
www.foxsoutdoor.co.uk

Lockwoods Ski Shop
125-129 Rugby Road,
Leamington Spa, Warwickshire
Tel 01926 339388
www.lockwoods.com

Mountain Fever
25 Brunswick Street, Hanley,
Stoke-on-Trent
Tel 01782 266137
www.mountainfever.co.uk

Noahs Ark
London Road, Chalford,
Stroud, Gloucestershire
Tel 01453 884738
www.noahsark.co.uk

Snow & Rock
14 Priory Queensway,
Birmingham
Tel 0845 100 1012
www.snowandrock.com

Sporting Triangle
18 West Street, Hereford
Tel 01432 271500
www.sportingtriangle.com

EASTERN ENGLAND

Snow & Rock
Hemel Ski Centre, St Albans
Hill, Hemel Hempstead,
Hertfordshire
Tel 0845 100 1014
www.snowandrock.com

SnowFit
2 Cucumber Lane, Brundall,
Norwich
Tel 01603 716655
www.snowfit.co.uk

Snowsun
Suffolk Ski Centre, Bourne
Hill, Wherstead, Ipswich,
Suffolk
Tel 01473 602601
www.snowsun.com

NORTHERN ENGLAND

BAC Outdoor Leisure
Central Hall, Coronation
Street, Elland, Halifax, West
Yorkshire
Tel 01422 371146
www.bac-e.com

Glide & Slide
5/7 Station Road, Otley
Tel 01943 461136
www.glideslide.co.uk

Sayers
66 High Street, Yarm,
Cleveland
Tel 01642 785423
www.skiwearhire.com

Severn Sports/Boardworx
80 Town Street, Armley,
Leeds, West Yorkshire
Tel 0113 279 1618
www.severnsports.co.uk

Snow & Rock
Sheffield Ski Centre, Vale
Road, Parkwood Springs,
Sheffield
Tel 0845 100 1015
www.snowandrock.com

Snow & Rock
Princess Parkway, Princess
Park, Didsbury, Manchester
Tel 0845 100 1020
www.snowandrock.com

NORTHERN IRELAND

Macski
140 Lisburn Road, Belfast
Tel 028 9066 5525
www.macski.com

REPUBLIC OF IRELAND

The Great Outdoors
Chatham Street, Dublin 2,
Ireland
Tel 00 353 1679 4293
www.greatoutdoors.ie

SKI EMPLOYMENT

Bunac / Gap Canada
Tel 020 7251 3472
enquiries@bunac.org.uk
www.bunac.org

Free Radicals
Tel 07968 183848
enquiries@freeradicals.co.uk
www.freeradicals.co.uk

Just Jobs 4 Students
www.justjobs4students.co.uk

Natives.co.uk
Tel 08700 463377
info@natives.co.uk
www.natives.co.uk

Season Workers
www.seasonworkers.com

Ski Connection
www.skiconnection.co.uk

Voovs
Tel 01707 396511
info@voovs.com
www.voovs.com

SKI/BOARDING ORGANISATIONS

**British Association of
Snowsport Instructors (BASI)**
Tel 01479 861717
basi@basi.org.uk
www.basi.org.uk

**British Ski Club for the
Disabled**
BSCDWeb@hotmail.com
www.bscd.org.uk

British Snowboard Association
Tel 0131 445 2428
info@thebsa.org
www.thebsa.org

English Ski Council
Tel 0121 501 2314
admin@englishski.org
www.englishski.org

Ski Club of Great Britain
Tel 020 8410 2000
skiers@skiclub.co.uk
www.skiclub.co.uk

Snowboard Club UK (SCUK)
www.SnowboardClub.co.uk

Snowsport Scotland
Tel 0131 445 4151
info@snowsportscotland.org
www.snsc.demon.co.uk

Snowsport Wales
Tel 029 2056 1904
admin.snowsportwales@
virgin.net
www.snowsportwales.net

SnowsportGB
Tel 0131 445 7676
info@snowsportgb.com
www.seasonsportgb.com

The Uphill Ski Club
*Ski organisation and ski
school for people with
disabilities*
Tel 01479 861272
info@uphillskiclub.co.uk
www.uphillskiclub.co.uk

SKI TRAVEL AGENTS

Alpine Answers
Tel 020 8871 4656
ski@alpineanswers.co.uk
www.alpineanswers.co.uk

Catered Ski Chalets
Tel 020 7835 0635
info@catered-ski-chalets.co.uk
www.catered-ski-chalets.co.uk

Iglu.com
Tel 020 8542 6658
enquiries@iglu.com
www.iglu.com

Independent Ski Links
Tel 01964 533905
info@ski-links.com
www.ski-links.com

Kwik Ski
Tel 0870 499 3114
ski@kwiktravel.co.uk
www.kwik-ski.co.uk

Ski & Surf
Tel 020 8958 2418
janm@skisurf.com
www.skisurf.com

Ski-direct.co.uk
Tel 08700 171935
www.ski-direct.co.uk

Ski Expectations
Tel 01799 531888
ski.expectations@virgin.net

Ski Line
Tel 0870 950 4420
angus@skiline.co.uk
www.skiline.co.uk

Ski McNeill
Tel 0870 600 1359
contact@skimcneill.com
www.skimcneill.com

Ski Solutions
A La Carte department:
020 7471 7777
Tel 020 7471 7700
www.skisolutions.com

Ski Tracer
Tel 0870 420 5782
sales@skitracer.com
www.skitracer.com

Ski Travel Centre
Tel 0141 649 9696
snow@skitravelcentre.com
www.ski-travel-centre.co.uk

Skiers Travel
Tel 0870 010 0032
sales@skiers-travel.co.uk
www.skiers-travel.co.uk

Skis and Tees
Tel 0870 240 7416
enquiries@skisandtees.co.uk
www.skisandtees.co.uk

Snow Finders
Tel 01858 466888
sales@snowfinders.com
www.snowfinders.com

Snow Line
Tel 0870 050 7025
sales@snow-line.co.uk
www.snow-line.co.uk

Ski business directory

707

RESORT DIRECTORY / INDEX

This is an index to the resort chapters in the book; you'll find page references for about 400 resorts that are described in those chapters. But you'll also find brief descriptions here of another 700 resorts, most of them smaller than those we've covered in full. We also list the companies offering package holidays to each resort. To get in touch with one of these tour operators, look them up in the list starting on page 695.

Key

🛉 Lifts
🛉 Pistes
✉ UK tour operators

49 Degrees North USA
Inland area with best snow in Washington State, including 120-acre bowl reserved for powder weekends.
1195m; slopes 1195–1760m
🛉 5 🛉 780 acres

Abetone Italy
Resort in the exposed Appennines, less than two hours from Florence and Pisa.
1390m; slopes 1390–1900m
🛉 25 🛉 50km
✉ Alpine Tours

Abtenau Austria
Sizeable village in Dachstein-West region near Salzburg, on plain ideal for cross-country.
710m; slopes 710–1260m
🛉 6 🛉 10km

Achenkirch Austria
Unspoilt, low-altitude Tirolean village close to Niederau and Alpbach. Beautiful setting overlooking a lake.
930m; slopes 930–1800m
🛉 7 🛉 25km
✉ Ramblers Holidays, Waymark Holidays

Adelboden 534
✉ Interhome, Kuoni, Swiss Travel Service, Thomson

Les Aillons France
Traditional village near Chambéry. Sheltered slopes.
1000m; slopes 1000–1900m
🛉 22 🛉 40km

Alagna 432
Small resort on the western fringe of Monterosa Ski area.
✉ Alpine Answers, Lotus Supertravel, Mountain Tracks, Ski 2, Ski Freshtracks, Ski Weekend

Alba Italy
Picturesque Trentino village with a small, quiet area; access to the Sella Ronda at Canazei.
1515m; slopes 1515–2440m
🛉 5 🛉 10km

Albiez-Montrond France
Authentic old French village in Maurienne valley with panoramic views. Own easy slopes and close to other ski areas.
1500m; slopes 1500–2200m
🛉 12 🛉 40km
✉ Lagrange Holidays

Alleghe Italy
Dolomite village near Cortina in a pretty lakeside setting close to numerous areas.
980m
🛉 24 🛉 80km
✉ Interhome

Les Allues 304
Rustic village on the road up to Méribel, close to the mid-station of the gondola up from Brides-les-Bains.

Alpbach 118
✉ Crystal, Inghams, Interhome, Made to Measure Holidays

Alpe-d'Huez 224
✉ Airtours, Alpine Answers, Catered Ski Chalets, Chalet World Ski, Club Med, Crystal, Directski.com, Erna Low, First Choice Ski, French Freedom Holidays, French Ski Life, Friendship Travel, Independent Ski Links, Inghams, Interhome, La Source, Lagrange Holidays, Made to Measure Holidays, Mark Warner, Neilson, Ski a la Carte, Ski Arrangements, Ski Expectations, Ski France, Ski Freshtracks, Ski Independence, Ski Leisure Direction, Ski Line, Ski Miquel, Ski Solutions, Ski Supreme, Ski Tracer, Skiworld, Thomson, Tops Ski Chalets and Club Hotels

Alpe-du-Grand-Serre France
Tiny resort near Alpe-d'Huez and Les Deux-Alpes. Good for bad-weather days.
1400m; slopes 1400–2200m
🛉 20 🛉 55km
✉ Sloping Off

Alpendorf 215
Outpost of St Johann im Pongau, at one end of an extensive three-valley lift network leading via Wagrain to Flachau – all part of the Salzburger Sportwelt area.

Alpine Meadows 552
✉ Ski The American Dream

Alps South Korea
Korea's most northerly, snow-reliable resort, about five hours from Seoul. 🛉 5

Alta 591
✉ AmeriCan Ski, Mountain Tracks, Ski All America, Ski Independence, Ski The American Dream

Alta Badia 441

Altenmarkt Austria
Unspoiled village, well placed just off the Salzburg-Villach autobahn for numerous resorts including snow-sure Obertauern and those in the Salzburger Sportwelt.
855m; slopes 855–2130m
🛉 23 🛉 150km
✉ Sloping Off

Alto Campoo Spain
Barren, desolate place with undistinguished slopes, but with magnificent wilderness views.
1650m; slopes 1650–2170m 🛉 11

Alt St Johann Switzerland
Old cross-country village with Alpine slopes connecting into Unterwasser area near Liechtenstein.
900m; slopes 900–2260m
🛉 21 🛉 50km

Alyeska USA
Alaskan area 60km/37 miles from Anchorage, with luxury hotel. 'Spectacular views – a very special place,' enthuses a 2004 visitor.
75m; slopes 75–1200m
🛉 9 🛉 785 acres
✉ Frontier Ski, Ski All America

Aminona 474
Purpose-built resort on the eastern side of the Crans-Montana network.
✉ Lagrange Holidays

Andalo 454
Trentino village not far from Madonna.
✉ Equity Ski, Rocketski, Sloping Off

Andermatt 468
✉ Crystal, Mountain Tracks, Ski Freshtracks, Ski Weekend, Switzerland Travel Centre

Andorra la Vella 98
✉ Lagrange Holidays

Angel Fire USA
Intermediate area near Taos, New Mexico. Height usually ensures good snow.
2620m; slopes 2620–3255m
🛉 5 🛉 455 acres

Les Angles France
Attractive resort with one of the best ski areas in the Pyrenees. Pretty, tree-lined, mostly easy skiing.
1650m; slopes 1650–2400m
🛉 24 🛉 40km
✉ Lagrange Holidays, Pyrenees Ski Experience

Annaberg-Lungötz Austria
Peaceful village in a pretty setting, sharing a sizeable area with Gosau. Close to Filzmoos.
775m; slopes 775–1620m
🛉 33 🛉 65km

Anzère Switzerland
Sympathetically designed modern resort on a sunny balcony near Crans-Montana, suited to leisurely intermediates.
1500m; slopes 1500–2460m
🛉 13 🛉 40km
✉ Interhome, Lagrange Holidays

Aosta Italy
Historic valley town with gondola up to mountain resort of Pila; it's an 18-minute ride to the slopes. Aosta is a real working town with people in suits rather than skiwear. It has good-value accommodation, a lot more bars and restaurants than Pila, and a lovely traffic-free centre. Other resorts in the Aosta valley are within a day trip and covered by the lift pass.
1800m; slopes 1550–2710m
🛉 13 🛉 70km
✉ Crystal

Apex Canada
Small, friendly, rather isolated resort, well worth stopping off here for a night or two on a tour of western BC resorts. Modern, purpose-built slope-side base with some accommodation and a few bars and restaurants. The Sheeprock Lodge is one of the nicest B&Bs we've stayed in – great rooms with big wooden beds (ask for Room 1), comfy sitting room with open fire and panoramic view of slopes, hot-tub, very friendly owners. The slopes suit confident intermediates upwards best. There are some steep, narrow double-black-diamond runs in the trees, wonderful single-diamond Wildside glades, and great cruising blues, which adventurous intermediates will love but more timid ones might freeze on. There are also excellent beginner slopes and runs to progress to. There's a (unique as far as we know) 1km/0.5 mile floodlit ice-skating trail through the woods.
1575m; slopes 1575–2180m
🛉 4 🛉 1112 acres
✉ AmeriCan Ski, Frontier Ski, Ski Safari

Beaulard Italy
Little place just off the road between Sauze d'Oulx and Bardonecchia.
1215m; slopes 1215–2120m
⚡ 6 🚡 20km

Beaver Creek 561
✉ AmeriCan Ski, Crystal, CV Travel, Elegant Resorts, Made to Measure Holidays, Ski Activity, Ski All America, Ski Independence, Ski Line, Ski Safari, Ski The American Dream, Ski Tracer, Ski Wild, Skiworld, United Vacations, Virgin Snow

Beaver Mountain USA
Small Utah area north of Salt Lake City, too far from Park City for a day trip.
2195m; slopes 2195–2680m
⚡ 3 🚡 525 acres

Beitostølen Norway
Small family resort in southern Norway (east of Bergen), with lots of cross-country in the region.
900m
⚡ 9 🚡 25km

Belleayre Mountain USA
State-owned resort near Albany, New York State. Cheap prices but old lifts and short runs.
775m; slopes 775–1015m
⚡ 7 🚡 170 acres

Belle-Plagne 327
High-altitude satellite of La Plagne built in a pleasing neo-Savoyard style.

Ben Lomond Australia
Small intermediate/beginner area in Ben Lomond National Park, Tasmania, 260km/162 miles from Hobart.
1450m; slopes 1460–1570m
⚡ 6 🚡 14ha

Berchtesgaden Germany
Pleasant old town close to Salzburg, known for its Nordic skiing but with several little Alpine areas nearby.
550m
✉ Moswin Tours

Bergün Switzerland
Traditional, quiet, unspoiled, virtually traffic-free little family resort on the rail route between Davos and St Moritz. 5km/3 mile toboggan run.
1375m; slopes 1400–2550m
⚡ 5 🚡 25km

Berthoud Pass 584
Powder heaven on the drive to Winter Park.

Berwang Austria
Unspoiled village nestling in a spacious valley, close to Lermoos.
1335m; slopes 1335–1740m
⚡ 12 🚡 40km

Bessans France
Old cross-country village near Modane. Well placed for touring Maurienne valley resorts such as Val-Cenis.
1710m; slopes 1740–2200m
⚡ 4 🚡 5km

Besse France
Charming old village built out of lava, with purpose-built slope-side satellite Super-Besse. Beautiful extinct-volcano scenery.
1050m; slopes 1300–1850m
⚡ 22 🚡 45km
✉ Lagrange Holidays

Bethel USA
Pleasant, historic town very close to Sunday River, Maine. Attractive alternative to staying in the slope-side resort.

Le Bettex 296
Small base at the gondola mid-station above St-Gervais, with links to the Megève network.

Bettmeralp Switzerland
Central village of the sizeable Aletsch area near Brig, perched high above the Rhône valley, amid spectacular glacial scenery. Reached by cable-cars from the valley.
1955m; slopes 1900–2900m
⚡ 32 🚡 90km

Beuil-les-Launes France
Alpes-Maritimes resort closest to Nice. Shares area with Valberg.
1400m; slopes 1400–2100m
⚡ 26 🚡 90km

Bezau Austria
Virtually no slopes of its own, but the main village lies in low Bregenzerwald region north-west of Lech.
650m; slopes 1210–1650m ⚡ 2
✉ Inntravel

Biberwier Austria
Limited little village with a small area of its own. Best as a quiet base from which to access the Zugspitz area.
1000m; slopes 1000–1790m
⚡ 6 🚡 8km

Bichlbach Austria
Smallest of the Zugspitz villages with very limited slopes of its own. Suitable as an unspoiled base for visiting the rest of the area.
1070m; slopes 1070–1620m
⚡ 3 🚡 7km

Bielmonte Italy
Popular with day-trippers from Milan. Worthwhile on a bad-weather day.
1200m; slopes 1200–1620m
⚡ 13 🚡 20km

Big Mountain USA
At least one of our reporters (who now makes an annual pilgrimage) rates this place, close to the Canadian border and even closer to Montana's Glacier National Park, as simply the best. Big is one thing that BM is not, with a modest base altitude, a middling vertical and a mere dozen lifts. But its 3,000 acres embrace a wide range of slopes that are not only impressively snowy but also blissfully devoid of people. There's easy cruising in dense forest around the base area, and

steeper stuff higher up on 'gladed' slopes – mainly single diamond but with double-diamond runs dotted around. There is accommodation at the base, and more in the small town of Whitefish, a few miles away. Our principal reporter, a man, reckons Ladies' Night at the Great Northern bar is something not to be missed.
1370m; slopes 1370–2135m
⚡ 10 🚡 3000 acres
✉ AmeriCan Ski, Ski Activity, Ski All America, Ski Independence

Big Powderhorn USA
The most 'resort' facilities in south Lake Superior region – and the highest lift capacity too. The area suffers from winds.
370m; slopes 370–560m
⚡ 10 🚡 250 acres

Big Sky 606
✉ AmeriCan Ski, Ski All America, Ski Independence, Ski Safari, Ski The American Dream

Big White 634
✉ AmeriCan Ski, Crystal, Frontier Ski, Independent Ski Links, Made to Measure Holidays, Ski Activity, Ski All America, Ski Freshtracks, Ski Independence, Ski Line, Ski Safari, Ski The American Dream, Snowebb

Bischofshofen Austria
Working town and mountain resort near St Johann in Pongau, with very limited local runs and the main slopes starting nearby at Muhlbach (Hochkönig area).
545m; slopes 545–1000m
⚡ 1 🚡 2km

Bivio Switzerland
Quiet village near St Moritz with easy slopes opened up by a few lifts.
1775m; slopes 1780–2600m
⚡ 4 🚡 40km

Bizau Austria
One of two main areas in the low Bregenzerwald region north-west of Lech.
680m; slopes 680–1700m
⚡ 6 🚡 24km

Björkliden 675

Björnrike 675

Blackcomb 652
Smaller and quieter than neighbouring Whistler, conveniently sited at the bottom of its own mountain.
✉ Frontier Ski

Black Mountain USA
New Hampshire area with lodging in nearby Jackson.
⚡ 4 🚡 143 acres

Blatten Switzerland
Mountainside hamlet above Naters, beside the Rhône near Brig. Small but tall area in stunning glacial scenery, with larger Aletsch area nearby.
1320m; slopes 1320–3100m
⚡ 9 🚡 60km

Bled 682
✉ Balkan Holidays, Crystal, Just Slovenia, Thomson, Waymark Holidays

Blue Cow 684

Blue Mountain Canada
Largest area in Ontario, with glorious views of Lake Huron. High-capacity lift system and 100% snowmaking.
230m; slopes 230–450m
⚡ 15 🚡 275 acres

Blue River Canada
Base of world-famous Mike Wiegele heli-ski operation in Cariboo and Monashee mountains.

Bluewood USA
Particularly remote area even by American north-west standards. Worth a visit if you're in Walla Walla.
1355m; slopes 1355–1725m
⚡ 3 🚡 530 acres

Bogus Basin USA
Sizeable area overlooking Idaho's attractive, interesting capital, Boise.
1760m; slopes 1760–2310m
⚡ 8 🚡 2600 acres

Bohinj 682
✉ Balkan Holidays, Crystal, Just Slovenia, Thomson

Bois-d'Amont France
One of four resorts that make up the Les Rousses area in Jura region.
1050m; slopes 1120–1680m
⚡ 40 🚡 40km
✉ Lagrange Holidays

Bolognola Italy
Tiny area in Macerata region near the Adriatic Riviera.
1070m; slopes 1070–1845m
⚡ 7 🚡 5km

Bolton Valley USA
Resort near Stowe with mostly intermediate slopes.
465m; slopes 465–960m
⚡ 6 🚡 155 acres

Bonneval-sur-Arc France
Unspoiled, remote old village in the Haute Maurienne valley with many of its slopes at high altitude. Pass to neighbouring Val-d'Isère is closed in winter.
1800m; slopes 1800–3000m
⚡ 10 🚡 25km

Bons 280
Rustic, unspoiled old hamlet linked to Les Deux-Alpes' skiing, conveniently placed down the valley for day trips to La Grave, Alpe-d'Huez and Serre-Chevalier.

Boreal USA
Closest area to north Lake Tahoe town, Truckee. Limited slopes, best for novices.
2195m; slopes 2195–2375m
⚡ 9 🚡 380 acres

Bormio 409
✉ Equity Ski, Interhome, Rocketski, Ski Arrangements, Sloping Off

☒ 360 Sun and Ski, Altitude Holidays, AmeriCan Ski, Erna Low, French Ski Life, Lagrange Holidays, Peak Retreats, Ski Independence, Ski Leisure Direction

Caspoggio Italy
Attractive, unspoiled village north-east of Lake Como, with easy slopes (and more at nearby Chiesa).
1100m; slopes 1100–2155m
▟8 ⟈ 22km

Castelrotto Italy
Picturesque village west of Sella Ronda circuit with small sunny Alpine area and good cross-country trails.
1060m

Castel S Angelo Italy
Tiny area in Macerata region near Adriatic Riviera.
805m
▟4 ⟈ 2km

Cauterets 398
☒ Lagrange Holidays

Cavalese Italy
Unspoiled medieval town in Val di Fiemme with pretty slopes at Alpe Cermis.
1000m; slopes 975–2265m
▟9 ⟈ 70km
☒ Alpine Tours, First Choice Ski, Thomson

The Cedars Lebanon
The largest of Lebanon's ski areas, 130km/80 miles inland from Beirut. Good, open slopes with a surprisingly long season.
1850m; slopes 2100–2700m ▟5

Ceillac France
Tight cluster of rustic old buildings near Serre-Chevalier. Not far from the highest village in Europe, St-Veran.
1600m; slopes 1600–2400m

Celerina 499
Quiet, unpretentious village, with links up to St Moritz's Corviglia sector.
☒ Made to Measure Holidays

Cerler Spain
Very limited, purpose-built resort with a compact ski area similar to that of nearby Andorra's Arinsal.
1500m; slopes 1500–2630m
▟16 ⟈ 45km

Le Cernix France
Hamlet near Megève where Les Saisies' slopes link to those of Crest-Voland. Uncrowded retreat.
1250m; slopes 1150–1950m
▟41 ⟈ 80km

Cerrato Lago Italy
Very limited area near the coastal town of La Spezia.
1270m; slopes 1270–1890m
▟5 ⟈ 3km

Cerro Bayo Argentina
Limited area amid stunning scenery 10km/6 miles from La Angostura, and 90km/56 miles from San Carlos de Bariloche.
slopes 1050–1780m
▟12 ⟈ 200ha

Cerro Castor Argentina
The most southern ski runs in the world are on the Martial Glacier, Tierra del Fuego. Lodgings are in Ushuaia, the southernmost city in the world. Also plenty of cross-country skiing on the island.

Cerro Catedral (Bariloche) Argentina
The most developed ski and boarding resort in South America, linked with Lado Bueno and 19 km/12 miles from San Carlos de Bariloche. Luxury lodgings available at the foot of the slopes.
slopes 1040–2050m
▟28 ⟈ 600ha
☒ Scott Dunn Latin America, Ski All America, Snoworks

Cervinia 411
☒ Alpine Answers, Alpine Events, Club Med, Crystal, Elegant Resorts, First Choice Ski, Independent Ski Links, Inghams, Interhome, Momentum Ski, Rocketski, Ski Arrangements, Ski Solutions, Ski Supreme, Ski Tracer, Ski Weekend, Thomson

Cesana Torinese 314
Little Italian village linking the Sauze d'Oulx, Sestriere and Sansicario side of the Milky Way to the Clavière, Montgenèvre side.

Le Châble 505
Small village below Verbier, linked by gondola.

Chacaltaya Bolivia
Highest lift-served ski area in the world and the only ski area in Bolivia. Reached by four-wheel drive vehicle from La Paz 30km/19 miles away. Only open in summer (too cold in winter).
5190m; slopes 5220–5420m
▟1 ⟈ 2km
☒ Scott Dunn Latin America

Chaillol France
Cross-country base on the edge of the beautiful Ecrins National Park, near Gap. Small Alpine area, lots of snowmakers.
1600m; slopes 1450–2000m ▟11

Chamois Italy
Small area above Buisson, a few miles down the road from Valtournenche (near Cervinia) – good for bad-weather days.
1815m; slopes 1815–2270m
▟9 ⟈ 20km

Chamonix 246

Champagny-en-Vanoise 327
Charming village with pretty, south-facing local slopes linking to the La Plagne network.
☒ Barrelli Ski, Erna Low, Independent Ski Links, Lagrange Holidays, Made to Measure Holidays, Ski Independence, Skitopia

Champéry 472
☒ Alpine Answers, Alpine Events, Corporate Ski Company, Made to Measure Holidays,

Piste Artiste Ltd, Ski Weekend, Switzerland Travel Centre, White Roc

Champex Switzerland
Lakeside hamlet tucked away in the trees above Orsières. A nice quiet, unspoiled base from which to visit Verbier's area.
1470m; slopes 1470–2220m
▟4 ⟈ 8km

Champfèr 499
Lakeside hamlet between St Moritz and Silvaplana with speedy access to the Corvatsch lifts.

Champoluc 432
Unspoiled, inexpensive village in the Monterosa Ski area.
☒ Alpine Answers, Catered Ski Chalets, Crystal, CV Travel, Esprit Ski, Momentum Ski, Ski 2, Ski Yogi, Skitopia

Champorcher Italy
Small village south of Aosta valley with tall but narrow ski area, mostly red runs on open slopes, with one black through the trees to the lift base at Chardonney.
1430m; slopes 1430–2500m
▟5 ⟈ 21km

Champoussin 472
Quiet mountainside village with convenient links to the rest of the Champéry slopes.

Chamrousse France
Functional family resort near Grenoble. Sheltered slopes.
1650m; slopes 1400–2255m
▟26 ⟈ 77km
☒ Erna Low, Lagrange Holidays

Chandolin Switzerland
Picturesque, unspoiled village in the Val d'Anniviers off the Valais, with high, easy open slopes (shared with St Luc) served almost entirely by drags. Valley pass also covers Zinal, Grimentz and Vercorin – 220km/137 miles of runs in total.
1935m; slopes 1660–3025m
▟16 ⟈ 75km

Chantemerle 347
One of the main valley villages with direct access to Serre-Chevalier's slopes.

Chapelco Argentina
Small ski area with full infrastructure of services 19km/12 miles from sizeable town of San Martin de Los Andes. Accommodation in hotels 11km/7 miles from the slopes.
slopes 1250–1980m
▟7 ⟈ 140ha
☒ Ski All America

La Chapelle-d'Abondance 256
Unspoiled village 5km/3 miles down the valley from Châtel, with lift access to the Portes du Soleil network.
☒ Ski Addiction, Ski La Cote

Charlotte Pass 684

Château d'Oex Switzerland
Pleasant little valley town that is the main French-speaking component of the shared lift-pass area around Gstaad. Local slopes are pleasant and undemanding but low (La Braye, at the top, is at only 1650m/5,400ft) and not connected to any of the Gstaad sectors – though the local railway makes moving around to other resorts painless. This is where Alpine hot-air ballooning first took off, and it's still a local speciality.
970m; slopes 890–3000m
▟67 ⟈ 250km
☒ Alpine Tours, Crystal, Lagrange Holidays

Châtel 256
☒ Catered Ski Chalets, Chalet Group, Connick Ski, First Choice Ski, Freedom Holidays, Haig Ski, Interhome, Lagrange Holidays, MasterSki, Peak Retreats, Ski Addiction, Ski Arrangements, Ski Independence, Ski Leisure Direction, Ski Line, Ski Rosie, Skialot, Snowfocus, Susie Ward Alpine Holidays, Tops Ski Chalets and Club Hotels

Le Chatelard France
Small resort in remote Parc des Bauges between Lake Annecy and Chambéry.

Cheonmasan South Korea
Purpose-built resort 30km/19 miles north-east of Seoul. ▟7

Chiesa Italy
Attractive beginners' resort in a fairly high plateau of easy runs above the resort.
1000m; slopes 1700–2335m
▟16 ⟈ 50km

Chillán Chile
Ski and spa resort 480km/300 miles south of Santiago. Base village has lodgings or you can stay at Las Trancas a few minutes' drive away.
1650m; slopes 1600–2700m
▟9 ⟈ 35km
☒ Elegant Resorts, Momentum Ski, Scott Dunn Latin America, Ski All America, Ski Safari, Snoworks

Le Chinaillon 261
Modern, chalet-style village at lifts above Le Grand-Bornand.

Chiomonte Italy
Tiny resort on the main road east of Bardonecchia and Sauze d'Oulx. A good half-day trip from either.
745m; slopes 745–2210m
▟6 ⟈ 10km

Chsea Algeria
Largest of Algeria's skiable areas, 135km/84 miles south-east of coastal town of Alger in the Djur Djur mountains.
1860m; slopes 1860–2510m ▟2

Churwalden Switzerland
Hamlet on fringe of Lenzerheide-
Valbella area.
1230m; slopes 1230–2865m
⛷ 35 ⛷ 155km

Claviere 314
Small Italian village linked to
Montgenèvre (in France) and the
rest of the Milky Way ski area.
✉ Crystal, Equity Ski, First
Choice Ski, Rocketski

La Clusaz 261
✉ Aravis Alpine Retreat,
Classic Ski Limited, Crystal,
Interhome, Lagrange Holidays,
Last Resort, Made to Measure
Holidays, Ski Activity, Ski
Arrangements, Ski Leisure
Direction, Ski Supreme, Ski
Weekend, Skitopia, Snowlife

Les Coches 327
Small, purpose-built village,
linked to the La Plagne ski area.
✉ Catered Ski Chalets, Erna
Low, Family Ski Company,
Finlays, French Ski Life,
Independent Ski Links,
Lagrange Holidays,
Mountainsun, Ski
Independence, Ski Leisure
Direction, Ski Line

Cogne Italy
One of Aosta valley's larger
villages. Small area worth a
short visit from nearby Pila.
1530m; slopes 1530–2245m
⛷ 5 ⛷ 8km

Colfosco 441
Small but sprawling village that
makes up part of the Sella
Ronda circuit.

Colle di Tenda Italy
Dour, modern resort that shares
a good area with much nicer
Limone. Not far from Nice.
1400m; slopes 1120–2040m
⛷ 33 ⛷ 80km

Colle Isarco Italy
Brenner Pass area – and the
bargain-shopping town of
Vipiteno is nearby.
1095m; slopes 1095–2720m
⛷ 5 ⛷ 15km

Le Collet-d'Allevard France
Ski area of sizeable summer spa
Allevard-les-Bains in remote
region east of Chambéry-
Grenoble road.
1450m; slopes 1450–2100m
⛷ 13 ⛷ 35km

Collio Italy
Tiny area of short runs in a
remote spot between lakes
Garda and d'Iseo.
840m; slopes 840–1715m ⛷ 14

Les Collons 505
A collection of roadside chalets,
including bars and restaurants,
below purpose-built Thyon
2000.

Combelouvière 390
Quiet hamlet tucked away in the
trees at the foot of Valmorel's
slopes.
✉ Lagrange Holidays

Combloux 296
Quiet, unspoiled alternative to
linked Megève.
✉ Lagrange Holidays

Les Contamines 267
✉ Alpine Answers, Chalet
Kiana, Classic Ski Limited,
Interhome, Lagrange Holidays,
Ski Arrangements, Ski
Expectations, Ski Line

Copper Mountain 568
✉ AmeriCan Ski, American Ski
Classics, Crystal, Equity Ski,
Erna Low, Neilson, Ski All
America, Ski Independence, Ski
Safari, Ski The American
Dream, Skiworld, Thomson,
United Vacations, Virgin Snow

Le Corbier 360
✉ Equity Ski, Erna Low,
Interhome, Lagrange Holidays,
Rocketski, Ski Independence

Coronet Peak 689
428m/1,400ft vertical. Closest
area to Queenstown (20
minutes). Good mix of bowls,
chutes, varied level pistes.
Relies on large snowmaking
facility for good snowcover.
Spectacular views.

Corrençon-en-Vercors France
Charming, rustic village at foot
of Villard-de-Lans ski area. Good
cross-country, too.
1160m; slopes 1160–2170m
⛷ 25 ⛷ 130km

Cortina d'Ampezzo 416
✉ Alpine Answers, Alpine
Events, Corporate Ski Company,
Crystal, CV Travel, Elegant
Resorts, Inghams, Made to
Measure Holidays, Momentum
Ski, Ski Arrangements, Ski
Freshtracks, Ski Solutions, Ski
Tracer, Ski Weekend, Ski Yogi,
Thomson, White Roc

Corvara 441
The most animated Sella Ronda
village, with lots of facilities and
good lift links.
✉ Directski.com, Neilson, Ski
Yogi

Courchevel 269
✉ Airtours, Alpine Answers,
Alpine Events, Alpine
Weekends, Bladon Lines,
Catered Ski Chalets, Chalet
Group, Chalet World Ski,
Corporate Ski Company, Crystal,
Descent International,
Directski.com, Elegant Resorts,
Erna Low, Esprit Ski, Finlays,
First Choice Ski, Flexiski, French
Ski Life, Independent Ski Links,
Inghams, Inspired to Ski,
Jeffersons, Kaluma Ski,
Lagrange Holidays, Le Ski,
Lotus Supertravel, Made to
Measure Holidays, Mark
Warner, Momentum Ski,
Neilson, Oxford Ski Company,
Powder Byrne, Scott Dunn Ski,
Silver Ski, Simply Ski, Ski 'n'
Action, Ski Activity, Ski Amis,
Ski Arrangements, Ski Deep,
Ski Expectations, Ski France,
Ski Independence, Ski Leisure
Direction, Ski Line, Ski Link, Ski

*Olympic, Ski Power, Ski
Solutions, Ski Supreme, Ski
Tracer, Ski-Val, Ski Weekend,
Skiworld, Snoworks, Thomson,
Total, White Roc*

Courmayeur 421
✉ Alpine Answers, Alpine
Events, Alpine Weekends,
Catered Ski Chalets, Corporate
Ski Company, Crystal, First
Choice Ski, Friendship Travel,
Independent Ski Links,
Inghams, Interhome, Interski,
Mark Warner, Momentum Ski,
Neilson, Ski Arrangements, Ski
Expectations, Ski Freshtracks,
Ski Line, Ski Solutions, Ski
Tracer, Ski Weekend, Ski Yogi,
Thomson, White Roc

Cranmore USA
New Hampshire area with
attractive town/resort of North
Conway. Good for families.
150m; slopes 150–515m
⛷ 9 ⛷ 190 acres

Crans-Montana 474
✉ Alpine Answers, Alpine
Events, Corporate Ski Company,
Crystal, Independent Ski Links,
Inghams, Interhome, Jeffersons,
Kuoni, Made to Measure
Holidays, Momentum Ski,
Oxford Ski Company, Ski Line,
Ski Weekend, Swiss Travel
Service, Switzerland Travel
Centre

Crested Butte 589
✉ AmeriCan Ski, Club Med,
Crystal, Ski Activity, Ski
Independence, Ski Safari, Ski
The American Dream, United
Vacations

Crest-Voland France
Attractive, unspoiled traditional
village near Megève and Le
Grand Bornand with wonderfully
uncrowded intermediate slopes
linked to Les Saisies.
1150m; slopes 1230–1650m
⛷ 17 ⛷ 45km
✉ Peak Retreats

Crissolo Italy
Small, remote day-tripper area,
south-west of Turin. Part of the
Monviso ski area.
1320m; slopes 1745–2340m
⛷ 4 ⛷ 20km

La Croix-Fry 261
Couple of hotels on the pass
close to La Clusaz.

Les Crosets 472
Isolated mini-resort, in a prime
position within the Portes du
Soleil circuit, above Champéry.

Crystal Mountain USA
Area in glorious Mt Rainier
National Park, near Seattle.
Good, varied area given good
snow/weather, but it's often wet.
1340m; slopes 1340–2135m
⛷ 10 ⛷ 2300 acres

Cuchara Valley USA
Quiet little family resort in
southern Colorado, some way
from any other ski area.
2800m; slopes 2800–3285m
⛷ 4 ⛷ 250 acres

Cutigliano Italy
Sizeable village near Abetone in
the Appennines. Less than two
hours from Florence and Pisa.
1125m; slopes 1125–1850m
⛷ 9 ⛷ 13km

Cypress Mountain Canada
Vancouver's most challenging
area, 20 minutes from the city
and with 40% for experts. Good
snowfall record but rain is a
problem.
920m; slopes 910–1445m ⛷ 5

Daemyeong Vivaldi Resort
South Korea
One of the less ugly Korean
resorts, 75km/47 miles from
Seoul. ⛷ 12

La Daille 380
Ugly apartment complex at the
entrance to Val-d'Isère.

Daisen Japan
Western Honshu's main area,
four hours from Osaka.
800m; slopes 740–1120m ⛷ 8

Damüls Austria
Scattered but attractive village
in Bregenzerwald area close to
the German and Swiss borders.
1430m; slopes 1430–2010m
⛷ 10 ⛷ 40km

Davos 476
✉ Alpine Answers, Alpine
Events, Alpine Weekends,
Corporate Ski Company, Crystal,
Flexiski, Headwater Holidays,
Independent Ski Links,
Inghams, Interhome, Kuoni,
Made to Measure Holidays,
Momentum Ski, Ski Freshtracks,
Ski Weekend, Swiss Travel
Service, Switzerland Travel
Centre, White Heat Skiing,
White Roc

Deer Mountain USA
South Dakota area close to 'Old
West' town Deadwood and
Mount Rushmore.
1825m; slopes 1825–2085m
⛷ 4 ⛷ 370 acres

Deer Valley 595
✉ AmeriCan Ski, American Ski
Classics, Ski All America, Ski
Independence, Ski Safari, Ski
The American Dream, United
Vacations

Les Deux-Alpes 280
✉ Airtours, AmeriCan Ski,
Catered Ski Chalets, Chalet
World Ski, Club Med, Crystal,
Erna Low, First Choice Ski,
French Ski Life, Independent
Ski Links, Inghams, Interhome,
Lagrange Holidays, Made to
Measure Holidays, Mark
Warner, McNab Snowboarding,
Neilson, Parklife, Peak Retreats,
Ski Arrangements, Ski
Independence, Ski Leisure
Direction, Ski Line, Ski
Solutions, Ski Supreme, Ski
Tracer, Skiworld, Thomson,
Tops Ski Chalets and Club
Hotels

Les Diablerets   Switzerland
Unspoiled but spread-out village towered over by the Diablerets massif, with two areas of local slopes, plus Glacier 3000. A high-speed quad followed by a slow chair lead up to the red runs of the Meilleret area and the link to Villars. A gondola in the centre of town takes you to Isenau, a mix of blues and reds served by drag-lifts. From Isenau there's a red run down to Col du Pillon and the cable-car to and from the glacier. You can also reach the glacier cable-cars by bus from town. On Glacier 3000, you'll find blue runs at over 3000m/9,840ft, stunning views and the long, red Combe d'Audon – a wonderful, usually quiet, run away from all the lifts with sheer cliffs rising up on both sides. The splendid Botta 3000 restaurant with stunning views at the top of the glacier is recommended for lunch. There's an evening toboggan run down from Les Mazots; there's also an ice rink and skate park.
1150m; slopes 1150–3000m
⛷ 46 ⛏ 125km
✉ Crystal, Equity Ski, Interhome, Lagrange Holidays, Momentum Ski, Rocketski, Sloping Off, Solo's, Swiss Travel Service, Switzerland Travel Centre, Thomson

Diamond Peak   **540**
✉ Ski The American Dream

Dienten   **131**
Quiet village east of Saalbach at the heart of large, low-altitude Hochkönig area that spreads impressively over four mountains linking Maria Alm to Mühlbach.

Dinner Plain   Australia
Attractive resort best known for cross-country skiing. Shuttle to Mt Hotham for Alpine slopes. four hours from Melbourne.
1520m; slopes 1490–1520m

Discovery Ski Area   USA
Pleasant area miles from anywhere except Butte, Montana, with largely intermediate slopes but double-black runs on the back of the mountain – and the chance of seriously good snow. Usually deserted. Fairmont Hot Springs (two huge thermal pools) nearby.
2080m; slopes 2080–2485m
⛷ 4 ⛏ 380 acres

Disentis   Switzerland
Unspoiled old village in a pretty setting on the Glacier Express rail route near Andermatt. Scenic area with long runs.
1135m; slopes 1150–2850m
⛷ 10 ⛏ 50km
✉ Interhome

Dobbiaco   Italy
One of several little resorts near the Austrian border; a feasible day out from the Sella Ronda.
1250m; slopes 1250–1610m

⛷ 5 ⛏ 15km
✉ Headwater Holidays, Ramblers Holidays, Waymark Holidays

Dodge Ridge   USA
Novice/leisurely intermediate area north of Yosemite. The pass from Reno is closed in winter, preventing crowds.
2010m; slopes 2010–2500m
⛷ 12 ⛏ 815 acres

Dolonne   **421**
Quiet suburb of Courmayeur – the gondola link is no more, but the off-trail run home is still a classic.

Dorfgastein   **120**
Quieter, friendlier alternative to Bad Gastein and Bad Hofgastein.

Dundret   Sweden
Lapland area 100km/62 miles north of the Arctic Circle with floodlit slopes open in winter when the sun barely rises.
slopes 475–825m
⛷ 7 ⛏ 15km

Durango Mountain Resort 589
✉ AmeriCan Ski, Ski Independence

Eaglecrest   USA
Close to famous Yukon gold rush town Skagway. Family resort famous for its ski school.
365m; slopes 365–790m
⛷ 3 ⛏ 640 acres

Eaux-Bonnes-Gourette France
Most snow-sure resort in the French Pyrenees. Very popular with local families, so best avoided at weekends.
1400m; slopes 1400–2400m
⛷ 23 ⛏ 30km

Eben im Pongau   Austria
Part of Salzburger Sportwelt Amadé area that includes nearby St Johann, Wagrain, Flachau and Zauchensee. Village spoilt by the autobahn passing through it.
855m; slopes 855–2185m
⛷ 100 ⛏ 350km

Ehrwald   Austria
Friendly, relaxed, pretty village with several nicely varied areas, notably the Zugspitz glacier.
1000m; slopes 1000–3000m
⛷ 11 ⛏ 45km

El Colorado/Farellones Chile
One of Chile's best ski areas, 40km/25 miles east of Santiago, and connected to the Valle Nevado ski area. Crowded at weekends.
slopes 2430–3335m
⛷ 18 ⛏ 1000ha

Eldora Mountain   USA
Day-visitor resort with varied terrain (including plenty of steep stuff) close to Denver Boulder (45min by regular scheduled bus). All forest trails, but with some good glade areas. Crowded at weekends, and all the chairs are slow.
2795m; slopes 2805–3230m
⛷ 12 ⛏ 680 acres

Elk Meadows   USA
Area south of Salt Lake City, more than a day trip from Park City.
2775m; slopes 2745–3170m
⛷ 6 ⛏ 1400 acres

Ellmau   **123**
✉ Crystal, Inghams, Interhome, Neilson, Ski Line, Ski Wild, Thomson

Encamp   **98**

Enego   Italy
Limited weekend day-trippers' area near Vicenza and Trento.
1300m; slopes 1300–1445m
⛷ 7 ⛏ 30km

Engelberg   **534**
✉ Alpine Answers, Alpine Events, Corporate Ski Company, Crystal, Independent Ski Links, Inntravel, Interhome, Kuoni, Made to Measure Holidays, Momentum Ski, Ski Freshtracks, Ski Weekend, Swiss Travel Service, Waymark Holidays, White Roc

Entrèves   **421**
Unremarkable cluster of hotels at the base of the lift up to Courmayeur's slopes.

Escaldes   Andorra
Central valley town, effectively part of Andorra la Vella.

Etna   Italy
Scenic, uncrowded, short-season area on the volcano's flank, 20 minutes from Nickolossi.
1800m; slopes 1800–2350m
⛏ 5km

Evolène   Switzerland
Charming rustic village with own little area in unspoiled, attractive setting south of Sion.
1380m; slopes 1300–3330m
⛷ 100 ⛏ 400km

Faak am See   Austria
Limited area, one of five overlooking town of Villach.
560m; slopes 560–800m
⛷ 1 ⛏ 2km

Fai della Paganella   Italy
Trentino village near Madonna that shares its slopes with Andalo.

Fairmont Hot Springs Canada
Major luxury spa complex ideal for a relaxing holiday with some gentle skiing thrown in.
⛷ 2 ⛏ 60 acres

Faistenau   Austria
Cross-country area close to Salzburg and St Wolfgang. Limited Alpine slopes.
785m; slopes 785–1000m
⛷ 5 ⛏ 3km

Falcade   Italy
Trentino village south of the Sella Ronda with lifts up to slopes at San Pellegrino.
1145m; slopes 1145–2170m
⛷ 11 ⛏ 39km
✉ Alpine Tours

Falera   **483**
Small, rustic village, with improved access to big ski area shared by Flims and Laax.

Le Falgoux   France
One of the most beautiful old villages in France, set in the very scenic Volcano National Park. Several ski areas nearby.
930m; slopes 930–1350m

Falkertsee   Austria
Base area rather than a village, with bleak, open slopes in contrast to nearby Badkleinkirchheim.
1690m; slopes 1690–2385m
⛷ 5 ⛏ 15km

Falls Creek   **684**

La Feclaz   France
One of several little resorts in the remote Parc des Bauges.

Fernie   **636**
✉ Alpine Answers, AmeriCan Ski, American Ski Classics, Canadian Powder Tours, Catered Ski Chalets, Chalet Group, Crystal, Frontier Ski, Independent Ski Links, Inghams, Made to Measure Holidays, Mountain Tracks, Neilson, Ski All America, Ski Activity, Ski Arrangements, Ski Independence, Ski Safari, Ski The American Dream, Skitopia, Skiworld, Snoworks, Snoworks, Virgin Snow

Fieberbrunn   **215**
✉ Snowscape, Thomson

Fiesch   Switzerland
Traditional Rhône valley resort close to Brig, with a lift up to Fiescheralp (2220m/7,280ft) at one end of the beautiful Aletsch area extending across the mountainside via Bettmeralp to Riederalp.
1060m; slopes 1900–2900m
⛷ 50 ⛏ 100km

Fiescheralp   Switzerland
Mountain outpost of Fiesch, down in the Rhône valley. At one end of the beautiful Aletsch area extending across the mountainside via Bettmeralp to Riederalp.
2220m; slopes 1900–2900m
⛷ 32 ⛏ 90km

Filzmoos   Austria
Charming, unspoiled, friendly village with leisurely slopes that are ideal for novices. Good snow record for its height. 'Nice resort; just not big enough,' says a 2004 reporter.
1055m; slopes 1055–1645m
⛷ 12 ⛏ 32km
✉ Inghams

Finkenberg   **157**
Between Mayrhofen and Hintertux, with a large area of mainly intermediate skiing.
✉ Crystal

Fiss   **215**
Nicely compact, quiet, traditional village sharing an extensive, sunny area with bigger Serfaus.
✉ Alpine Tours, Interhome

Flachau 215
Quiet, spacious village in a pretty setting at one end of an extensive three-valley lift network linking via Wagrain to Alpendorf. Flachauwinkl, up the valley, is at the centre of another similarly extensive lift system. All these resorts are covered by the Salzburger Sportwelt area. A 2005 visitor comments on the lack of clear signposting.
☒ *Interhome, Made to Measure Holidays*

Flachauwinkl Austria
Tiny ski station beside Tauern autobahn, at the centre of an extensive three-valley lift network linking Kleinarl to Zauchensee. Flachau, down the valley, is at one end of a similarly extensive lift system. All these resorts are covered by the Salzburger Sportwelt ski pass that our figures relate to.
930m; slopes 800–2185m
⛷ 59 ⛷ 200km

Flaine 286
☒ *Alpine Answers, Classic Ski Limited, Crystal, Erna Low, French Freedom Holidays, French Ski Life, Independent Ski Links, Inghams, Lagrange Holidays, Neilson, Ski Arrangements, Ski Freshtracks, Ski Independence, Ski Leisure Direction, Ski Supreme, Ski Weekend, Thomson*

Flims 483
☒ *Alpine Answers, Alpine Events, Corporate Ski Company, Interhome, Made to Measure Holidays, Momentum Ski, Powder Byrne, Ski Freshtracks, Ski Weekend, Swiss Travel Service, Switzerland Travel Centre, White Heat Skiing, White Roc*

Flumet France
Surprisingly large traditional village, the main place from which to ski the sizeable Val d'Arly ski area. Close to better-known Megève.
1000m; slopes 1000–1600m
⛷ 10 ⛷ 40km

Flumserberg Switzerland
Collective name for the villages sharing a varied area an hour south-east of Zürich.
1220m; slopes 1220–2220m
⛷ 42 ⛷ 142km

Folgaria Italy
Largest of several resorts east of Trento. Old lift system.
1165m; slopes 1185–2005m
⛷ 38 ⛷ 70km
☒ *Alpine Tours, Directski.com, Ski Wild, Sloping Off*

Folgarida 430
Small, pleasant Dolomite village, with links to Madonna di Campiglio's extensive area. Life revolves around a handful of hotels close to the gondola.
☒ *Alpine Tours, Equity Ski, Rocketski*

Foncine-le-Haut France
Major cross-country village in the Jura Mountains with extensive trails.
☒ *Lagrange Holidays*

Fonni Gennaragentu Italy
Sardinia's only 'ski area' – and it's tiny.
⛷ 1 ⛷ 5km

Font-Romeu 398
☒ *Headwater Holidays, Lagrange Holidays, Pyrenees Ski Experience, Solo's, Waymark Holidays*

Foppolo Italy
Relatively unattractive but user-friendly village, a short transfer from Bergamo.
1510m; slopes 1610–2160m
⛷ 9 ⛷ 47km
☒ *Equity Ski*

Forca Canapine Italy
Limited area near the Adriatic and Ascoli Piceno. Popular with weekend day-trippers.
1450m; slopes 1450–1690m
⛷ 11 ⛷ 20km

Formazza Italy
Cross-country base with some downhill slopes.
1280m; slopes 1275–1755m
⛷ 8km

Formigal 666
☒ *White Roc*

Le Fornet 380
Rustic, old hamlet 3km/2 miles further down the valley from Val-d'Isère.

Forstau Austria
Secluded hamlet above Radstadt–Schladming road. Very limited area with old lifts, but nice and quiet.
930m; slopes 930–1885m
⛷ 7 ⛷ 14km

La Foux-d'Allos France
Purpose-built resort that shares a good intermediate area with Pra-Loup.
1800m; slopes 1800–2600m
⛷ 52 ⛷ 167km
☒ *Lagrange Holidays*

Frabosa Soprana Italy
One of numerous little areas south of Turin, well placed for combining winter sports with Riviera sightseeing.
850m; slopes 860–1740m
⛷ 7 ⛷ 40km

Frisco 563
Small town based on a Victorian settlement, down the valley from Breckenridge.
☒ *AmeriCan Ski*

Frontignano Italy
Best lift system in the Macerata region, near the Adriatic Riviera.
1340m; slopes 1340–2000m
⛷ 8 ⛷ 10km

Fügen Austria
Unspoiled Zillertal village with limited area best suited to beginners.
550m; slopes 550–2400m
⛷ 19 ⛷ 48km
☒ *Lagrange Holidays, Ski Wild*

Fulpmes 134
☒ *Crystal*

Furano Japan
Small Hokkaido resort, two hours from Sapporo. One of the few Japanese areas to get reasonable powder.
235m; slopes 235–1065m ⛷ 13

Fusch Austria
Cheaper, quiet place to stay when visiting Zell am See. Across a golf course from Kaprun and Schuttdorf.
805m; slopes 805–1050m
⛷ 2 ⛷ 5km

Fuschl am See Austria
Attractive, unspoiled, lakeside village close to St Wolfgang and Salzburg, 30 minutes from its slopes. Best suited to part-time skiers who want to sightsee as well.
670m

Gålå Norway
Base for downhill and cross-country skiing, an hour's drive north of Lillehammer.
930m; slopes 830–1150m
⛷ 7 ⛷ 20km
☒ *Inntravel*

Gallio Italy
One of several low resorts near Vicenza and Trento. Popular with weekend day-trippers.
1100m; slopes 1100–1550m
⛷ 11 ⛷ 50km

Galtür 138
Charming traditional village near Ischgl, in the news in 1998/99 due to a tragic avalanche disaster.
☒ *First Choice Ski, Inghams, Lagrange Holidays, Made to Measure Holidays*

Gambarie d'Aspromonte Italy
Italy's second most southerly ski area (after Mt Etna). On the 'toe' of the Italian 'boot' near Reggio di Calabria.
1310m; slopes 1310–1650m ⛷ 3

Gantschier Austria
No slopes of its own but particularly well placed for visiting all the Montafon areas.
700m

Gargellen 163
Quiet, tiny and secluded village tucked up a side valley in the Montafon area.
☒ *Interhome, Made to Measure Holidays*

Garmisch-Partenkirchen Germany
Twin classic old-fashioned winter sports resorts – unspoiled, traditional Partenkirchen is much the prettier. The ski areas are a bus-ride away, and offer limited challenge for experts and adventurous intermediates (though the long Kandahar black downhill course is excellent); there are good beginners' areas. The lift system is rather antiquated, although the 76-year-old Kreuzeck cable car was replaced by a new lift in

2002/03. A visitor reports that piste maintenance and marking is poor. There are no bars or hotels near the slopes so you return to town for après-ski. There's plenty for non-skiers.
720m; slopes 720–2830m
⛷ 38 ⛷ 71km
☒ *Moswin Tours*

Gaschurn 163
Attractive, unspoiled village with the largest of the pretty Montafon areas, well suited to intermediates.

Gaustablikk Norway
Small snow-sure Alpine area on Mt Gausta in southern Norway with plenty of cross-country.
⛷ 15km
☒ *Waymark Holidays*

Geilo 671
☒ *Crystal, Headwater Holidays, Inntravel, Neilson, Thomson*

Gérardmer France
Sizeable lakeside resort in the northerly Vosges mountains near Strasbourg, with plenty of amenities. Limited downhill slopes nearby include one of almost 4km/2.5 miles. Extensive ski de fond trails in the area.
665m; slopes 750–1150m
⛷ 20 ⛷ 40km
☒ *Lagrange Holidays*

Gerlitzen Alpe Austria
A gondola ride above Villach and with good views. A worthwhile excursion from Badkleinkirchheim.
500m; slopes 1003–1911m
⛷ 14 ⛷ 20km

Gerlos Austria
One of Austria's few inexpensive but fairly snow-sure resorts, now linked to Zell im Zillertal as well as Königsleiten to form a fair-sized intermediate area.
1250m; slopes 1250–2300m
⛷ 44 ⛷ 115km
☒ *Interhome*

Les Gets 292
☒ *Alpine Answers, AmeriCan Ski, Catered Ski Chalets, Chalet Group, Descent International, Ferme de Montagne, First Choice Ski, Haig Ski, Independent Ski Links, Lagrange Holidays, Made to Measure Holidays, Oxford Ski Company, Peak Retreats, Rocketski, Ski Activity, Ski Expectations, Ski Famille, Ski Hillwood, Ski Independence, Ski Tracer, Ski Weekend, Total, Wood Advent Chalet*

La Giettaz 296
Tiny rural village in steep-sided valley between La Clusaz and Megève, now linked by lift and piste to the latter's Jaillet sector.

Gitschtal/Weissbriach Austria
One of many little areas near Hermagor in eastern Austria, close to Italian border.
690m; slopes 690–1400m
⛷ 4 ⛷ 5km

Glaris Switzerland
Hamlet base station for the uncrowded Rinerhorn section of the Davos slopes.
1455m; slopes 1455–2490m
≤ 5 ⟟ 30km

Glencoe 683

Glenshee 683
⊠ Skisafe Travel

Going 123
Small local ski area near Ellmau, linked to the huge Ski Welt area.
⊠ Solo's

Goldegg Austria
Year-round resort famous for its lakeside castle. Limited slopes but Wagrain (Salzburger Sportwelt) and Grossarl (Gastein valley) are nearby.
825m; slopes 825–1250m
⟟ 4 ⟟ 12km

Golden Canada
Small logging town, the place to stay when visiting Kicking Horse resort 15 minutes away. Also the launch pad for Purcell heli-skiing.

Gore Mountain USA
One of the better areas in New York State. Near Lake Placid, sufficiently far north to avoid worst weekend crowds. Intermediate terrain.
455m; slopes 455–1095m
⟟ 9 ⟟ 290 acres

Göriach Austria
Hamlet with trail connecting into one of the longest, most snow-sure cross-country networks in Europe.
1250m

Gortipohl Austria
Traditional village in pretty Montafontal.
920m; slopes 900–2395m
⟟ 62 ⟟ 209km

Gosau Austria
Straggling village with plenty of pretty, if low, runs. Snow-sure Obertauern and Schladming are within reach.
755m; slopes 755–1800m
⟟ 37 ⟟ 80km

Göstling Austria
One of Austria's easternmost resorts, between Salzburg and Vienna. A traditional village in wooded setting.
530m; slopes 530–1880m
⟟ 12 ⟟ 19km

Götzens Austria
Valley village base for Axamer Lizum slopes.
870m ⟟ 1
⊠ Lagrange Holidays

Grächen Switzerland
Charming chalet-village reached by tricky access road off the approach to Zermatt. A small area of open slopes, mainly above the trees and of red-run difficulty, reached by two gondolas – one to Hannigalp (2115m/6,940ft), the main focus of activity with a very impressive

children's nursery area. The village has almost a score of hotels, mostly 3-star; most of the accommodation is in chalets and apartments. The sports centre offers tennis and badminton, as well as a natural ice-rink.
1615m; slopes 1615–2890m
⟟ 13 ⟟ 40km
⊠ Interhome

Le Grand-Bornand 261
⊠ Crystal, French Freedom Holidays, Lagrange Holidays

Grand Targhee 608
Powder skiing paradise an hour from Jackson Hole.
⊠ AmeriCan Ski, Ski Safari

Grangesises Italy
Small satellite of Sestriere, with lifts up to the main slopes.

Grau Roig 104
Mini-resort at foot of Pas de la Casa's only woodland runs, with one smart hotel and abundant day-tripper parking.

La Grave 294
⊠ Alpine Answers, Crystal, Interhome, Lagrange Holidays, Mountain Tracks, Peak Retreats, Ski Arrangements, Ski Freshtracks, Ski Weekend

Great Divide USA
Area near Helena, Montana, best for experts. Mostly bowls; plus near-extreme Rawhide Gulch.
1765m; slopes 1765–2195m
⟟ 6 ⟟ 720 acres

Gresse-en-Vercors France
Resort south of Grenoble. Sheltered slopes worth noting for bad-weather days.
1250m; slopes 1600–1800m
⟟ 16 ⟟ 18km
⊠ Interhome, Lagrange Holidays

Gressoney-la-Trinité 432
Smaller and higher of the two villages in the central valley of the Monterosa Ski area.
⊠ Alpine Answers, Crystal, Momentum Ski, Ski Addiction, Ski Freshtracks, Ski Yogi, Snowworks

Gressoney-St-Jean 432
Larger and lower of the two villages in the central valley of the Monterosa Ski area.
⊠ Alpine Answers

Grimentz Switzerland
Located in the Val d'Anniviers, a side valley near the Valais town of Sierre, this an exceptionally cute, unspoiled mountainside village with high, varied runs including genuine reds and blacks, mostly on open slopes above the mid-mountain nursery area of Bendolla (2100m/6,890ft), which are mostly served by drag-lifts. The valley lift pass also covers St Luc/Chandolin, Vercorin and Zinal – 220km/137 miles of runs in total. Zinal is a short bus-ride up the valley, with a splendid itinerary run back to Grimentz.

Good off-piste terrain, too. Grimentz has half a dozen small hotels, 2- and 3-star – the de Moiry is recommended by a 2004 reporter, who also describes the après-ski as 'very quiet'. There's a public pool and a natural ice-rink.
1570m; slopes 1570–2900m
⟟ 12 ⟟ 50km
⊠ Ski Freshtracks

Grindelwald 485
⊠ Alpine Events, Corporate Ski Company, Crystal, Elegant Resorts, Independent Ski Links, Inghams, Interhome, Kuoni, Made to Measure Holidays, Momentum Ski, Powder Byrne, Ski Freshtracks, Solo's, Swiss Travel Service, Switzerland Travel Centre, Thomson, White Roc

Grossarl 120
Secluded village linked to Dorfgastein in the Gastein valley.

Grosskirchheim Austria
Very limited area near Heiligenblut.
1025m; slopes 1025–1400m

Grouse Mountain Canada
The Vancouver area with the largest lift capacity. Superb city views from mostly easy slopes; night skiing.
880m; slopes 880–1245m
⟟ 11 ⟟ 120 acres

Grünau Austria
Spacious riverside village in a lovely lake-filled part of eastern Austria. Nicely varied area, but very low.
525m; slopes 600–1600m
⟟ 14 ⟟ 40km

Gryon 515
Village below Villars, with which it shares a ski area.

Gstaad 535
⊠ Alpine Answers, Alpine Events, Corporate Ski Company, Headwater Holidays, Interhome, Made to Measure Holidays, Momentum Ski, Ski Weekend, White Roc

Gunstock USA
One of the New Hampshire resorts closest to Boston, popular with families. Primarily easy slopes. Gorgeous Lake Winnisquam views.
275m; slopes 275–700m
⟟ 8 ⟟ 220 acres

Guthega 684
⊠ Crystal

Hafjell Norway
Main ski area for Lillehammer.
⟟ 12 ⟟ 33km
⊠ Crystal

Hakuba Happo One Japan
European-style resort four hours from Tokyo. One of Japan's more challenging areas.
750m; slopes 750–1830m ⟟ 33

Harrachov Czech Republic
Closest resort to Prague, with enough terrain to justify a day trip. No beginner area. A new quad replaced the old chair-lift in 2002/03.
685m; slopes 650–1020m ⟟ 15

Hasliberg Switzerland
Four rustic hamlets on a sunny plateau overlooking Meiringen and Lake Brienz. Two of them are the bottom stations of a varied intermediate area.
1055m; slopes 600–2435m
⟟ 16 ⟟ 60km

Haus 181
Village next to Schladming, with good local slopes connected to the rest of the network.

Haystack 614

Heavenly 542
⊠ AmeriCan Ski, American Ski Classics, Crystal, Equity Ski, Erna Low, Independent Ski Links, Lotus Supertravel, Neilson, Ski Activity, Ski All America, Ski Freshtracks, Ski Independence, Ski Line, Ski Safari, Ski The American Dream, Ski Tracer, Skiworld, Trailfinders, United Vacations, Virgin Snow

Hebalm Austria
One of many small areas in Austria's easternmost ski region near Slovenian border. No major resorts in vicinity.
1350m; slopes 1350–1400m
⟟ 6 ⟟ 11km

Heiligenblut Austria
Picturesque village in beautiful surroundings with mostly high terrain. Its remote position west of Bad Gastein ensures that it remains uncrowded.
1300m; slopes 1300–2910m
⟟ 14 ⟟ 55km

Hemlock Resort Canada
Area 86km/55 miles east of Vancouver towards Sun Peaks. Mostly intermediate terrain and with snowfall of 600 inches a year. Lodging is available at the base area.
1000m; slopes 1000–1375m
⟟ 4 ⟟ 350 acres

Hemsedal 673
⊠ Crystal, Neilson, Thomson

Heremence Switzerland
Quiet village in unspoiled setting south of Sion. Verbier's slopes are a few minutes' drive away at Les Masses.
1250m

Hermagor Austria
Main village base for the Nassfeld ski area in Carinthia.
600m; slopes 610–2000m
⟟ 30 ⟟ 100km

Hintersee Austria
Easy slopes very close to Salzburg. Several long top-to-bottom runs means the size of the area is greatly reduced if the snowline is high.
745m; slopes 750–1470m
⟟ 9 ⟟ 40km

Kals am Grossglockner Austria
Village in a remote valley north of Lienz.
1325m; slopes 1325–2305m
⛟ 7 ⛷ 28km

Kaltenbach Austria
One of the larger, quieter Zillertal areas, with plenty of high-altitude slopes, mostly above the tree line. 'Excellent runs beneath the gondola,' says a 2004 reporter.
560m; slopes 560–2300m
⛟ 18 ⛷ 86km

Kananaskis Canada
Small area near Calgary, nicely set in woods, with slopes at Nakiska and Fortress Mountain.
slopes 1525–2465m
⛟ 12 ⛷ 605 acres
⊠ Frontier Ski

Kandersteg Switzerland
Good cross-country base set amid beautiful scenery near Interlaken.
1175m; slopes 1175–2000m
⛟ 7 ⛷ 13km
⊠ Crystal, Headwater Holidays, Inghams, Inntravel, Kuoni, Swiss Travel Service, Waymark Holidays

Kanin 682

Kappl 138
Small village down-valley from Ischgl and covered by the regional lift pass.

Kaprun 210
Classic Austrian charmer of a village. Extensive sheltered slopes at nearby Zell am See.
⊠ Airtours, Catered Ski Chalets, Crystal, Directski.com, Esprit Ski, First Choice Ski, Neilson, Ski Line, Ski Wild, Thomson

Les Karellis France
Resort with slopes that are more scenic, challenging and snow-sure than those of better-known Valloire, nearby.
1600m; slopes 1600–2550m
⛟ 19 ⛷ 60km

Kastelruth Italy
German name for Castelrotto.
⊠ Inntravel

Kasurila Finland
Siilinjarvi ski area popular with boarders. ⛟ 5

Katschberg Austria
Cute hamlet on the road pass from Styria to Carinthia, now by-passed by Tauern motorway through Katschberg tunnel. Non-trivial area of intermediate slopes, linked to lower St Margarethen; lifts include several fast chairs, one a six-pack.
1140m; slopes 1075–2220m
⛟ 16 ⛷ 60km

Keystone 570
⊠ AmeriCan Ski, American Ski Classics, Crystal, Erna Low, Ski Activity, Ski All America, Ski Independence, Ski Safari, Ski The American Dream, Ski Tracer, Thomson, United Vacations

Kicking Horse 641
⊠ AmeriCan Ski, Canadian Powder Tours, Crystal, Frontier Ski, Made to Measure Holidays, Ski All America, Ski Independence, Ski Safari, Ski The American Dream, Skiworld

Killington 617
⊠ American Ski Classics, Crystal, Equity Ski, Independent Ski Links, Inghams, Ski Activity, Ski All America, Ski Arrangements, Ski Independence, Ski Line, Ski Safari, Ski The American Dream, Solo's, Thomson, Trailfinders, United Vacations, Virgin Snow

Kimberley Canada
This mining town turned twee mock Austro-Bavarian/English Tudor resort is not as tacky as it sounds, and it enjoys a beautiful setting two hours from Banff. Its original base area is not quite at the bottom of the hill, and has a range of lodgings. Below this, a new village is being built, served by a fast quad. Both bases are very limited and quiet, and bars and restaurants are few. Trickle Creek Golf Resort is transformed into Trickle Creek Winter Adventure Park each winter – facilities include a skating rink, cross-country skiing, snow-shoeing and campfires. The town of Kimberley, about five minutes' drive away, is known for its indescribably naff 'Bavarian theme'. But it is reported to have some good restaurants, including the Old Bauernhaus.
Kimberley's terrain offers a mix of blue and black runs (plus the occasional green) and a vertical of 750m/2,460ft. In addition to the lifts up there front there are two other slow chairs. The runs – all in forest of varying density – are spread over two rather featureless hills. There are only a few short double-diamonds, but grading tends to understate difficulty, and many of the single diamonds are quite challenging. When we last visited, using the chair from the new village meant descending a steep, traffic-polished and congested final slope to get back to the lower level. The resort has a reputation for good powder, although it doesn't get huge amounts by the standards of this region. Further expansion is planned.
1230m; slopes 1230–1980m
⛟ 10 ⛷ 1800 acres
⊠ AmeriCan Ski, Frontier Ski, Inghams, Ski Activity, Ski All America, Ski Independence, Ski Safari, Ski The American Dream

Kirchberg 144
Lively little town close to Kitzbühel, with which it shares its slopes.
⊠ Directski.com, First Choice Ski, Interhome, Lagrange Holidays

Kirchdorf 202
Attractive village a bus-ride from St Johann in Tirol.
⊠ Snowcoach, Thomson

Kirkwood 552

Kitzbühel 144
⊠ Airtours, Alpine Answers, Alpine Events, Catered Ski Chalets, Corporate Ski Company, Crystal, Directski.com, Elegant Resorts, First Choice Ski, Independent Ski Links, Inghams, Interhome, Lagrange Holidays, Made to Measure Holidays, Momentum Ski, Neilson, Panorama Holidays, Ski Freshtracks, Ski Line, Ski Solutions, Ski Wild, Snowscape, Thomson

Kleinarl Austria
Secluded traditional village up a pretty side valley from Wagrain, at one end of a three-valley lift network linking it via Flachauwinkl to Zauchensee – all part of the Salzburger Sportwelt ski pass area that our figures relate to.
1015m; slopes 800–2185m
⛟ 59 ⛷ 200km

Klippitztörl Austria
One of many little areas in Austria's easternmost ski region near Slovenian border.
1550m; slopes 1460–1820m
⛟ 6 ⛷ 25km

Klösterle Austria
Valley village at the base of the Sonnenkopf ski area a few km west of the Arlberg pass – and covered by the Arlberg ski pass.
1100m; slopes 1100–2300m
⛟ 10 ⛷ 39km

Klosters 476
Affluent village sharing huge ski area with Davos.
⊠ Alpine Answers, Descent International, Flexiski, Inghams, Kuoni, Made to Measure Holidays, Momentum Ski, Oxford Ski Company, Powder Byrne, Ski Freshtracks, Ski Solutions, Ski Weekend, Swiss Travel Service, Switzerland Travel Centre, White Heat Skiing, White Roc

Kobla 682

Kolsass-Weer Austria
Pair of Inn-side villages with low, inconvenient and limited slopes.
555m; slopes 555–1010m
⛟ 3 ⛷ 14km

Königsleiten Austria
Quiet, high resort sharing fairly snow-sure area with Gerlos, now also linked to Zell im Zillertal to form a fair-sized area.
1600m; slopes 1245–2300m
⛟ 55 ⛷ 155km

Kopaonik Serbia
Modern, sympathetically designed family resort.
1770m; slopes 1110–2015m
⛟ 21 ⛷ 57km
⊠ Balkan Holidays, Crystal, Thomson

Koralpe Austria
Largest and steepest of the gentle little areas in Austria's easternmost ski region near the Slovenian border.
1550m; ⛟ 10 ⛷ 25km

Kössen Austria
Village near St Johann in Tirol with low, limited local slopes.
600m; ⛟ 9 ⛷ 25km

Kötschach-Mauthen Austria
One of many little areas near Hermagor in south Austria, close to the Italian border.
710m; slopes 710–1300m
⛟ 4 ⛷ 7km

Kranjska Gora 682
⊠ Balkan Holidays, Crystal, First Choice Ski, Inghams, Just Slovenia, Solo's, Thomson

Krimml Austria
Sunny area, high enough to have good snow usually. Shares regional pass with Wildkogel resorts (Neukirchen).
1075m; slopes 1640–2040m
⛟ 9 ⛷ 33km

Krispl-Gaissau Austria
Easy slopes very close to Salzburg. Several long top-to-bottom lifts mean the size of the area is greatly reduced if the snowline is high.
925m; slopes 750–1570m
⛟ 11 ⛷ 40km

Kronplatz Italy
Charming Dolomite village with a delightful, sizeable area well covered by snow-guns. Italian name is San Vigilio.
⊠ Momentum Ski

Kühtai 134
⊠ Crystal, Inghams

Kusatsu Kokusai Japan
Attractive spa village with hot springs, three hours from Tokyo. ⛟ 13

Laax 483
Old farming community with a lot of character linked to Flims.
⊠ Alpine Answers

Le Lac Blanc France
Mini-resort about to install the first six-pack in the northerly Vosges mountains near Strasbourg. Extensive ski de fond trails.
830m; slopes 830–1235m
⛟ 9 ⛷ 14km

Ladis Austria
Smaller alternative to Serfaus and Fiss, with lifts that connect into the same varied ski area.
1200m; slopes 1200–2540m
⛟ 42 ⛷ 160km

Le Laisinant 380
Tiny hamlet a short bus-ride down the valley from Val-d'Isère.

and forest trails. A good day trip from Summit County resorts, especially Keystone. Lodgings also available 19km/12 miles east in Georgetown.
3230m; slopes 3230–3870m
⛷ 9 ⛟ 1265 acres

Luchon France
Sizeable village with plenty of amenities, with gondola (8 minutes) to its ski area at purpose-built Superbagnères.
630m; slopes 1440–2260m
⛷ 16 ⛟ 35km
✉ Lagrange Holidays, Ski Leisure Direction

Lurisia Italy
Sizeable spa resort, a good base for visits to surrounding little ski areas and to Nice.
750m; slopes 800–1800m
⛷ 8 ⛟ 35km

Lutsen Mountains USA
Largest ski area in between Vermont and Colorado, with panoramic views of Lake Superior, only 3km/2 miles away. Four small linked hills with 95% snowmaking offer surprisingly good and extensive terrain, with something for everyone. Moose Mountain has the biggest vertical (250m/820ft), with cruisers or bumps top to bottom, great views of the lake, and backcountry glade runs. Small slope-side village. Good cross-country, snow-shoeing and snowmobiling nearby.
80m; slopes 80–335m
⛷ 9 ⛟ 1000 acres

Luz-Ardiden France
Spa village below its ski area. Cauterets and Barèges nearby.
710m; slopes 1730–2450m
⛷ 15 ⛟ 60km

Macugnaga 460
✉ Neilson

Madesimo 460
✉ Inghams

Madonna di Campiglio 430
✉ Crystal, Directski.com, Equity Ski, First Choice Ski, Inghams, Interhome, Rocketski, Ski Arrangements, Ski Freshtracks, Ski Wild, Ski Yogi, Solo's

Mad River Glen 614

La Magdelaine Italy
Close to Cervinia, and good on bad-weather days.
1645m; slopes 1645–1870m
⛷ 4 ⛟ 4km

Maishofen Austria
Cheaper place to stay when visiting equidistant Saalbach and Zell am See.
765m

Malbun Liechtenstein
Quaint user-friendly little family resort, 16km/10 miles from the capital, Vaduz. Limited slopes and short easy runs.
1600m; slopes 1595–2100m
⛷ 6 ⛟ 21km

Malcesine Italy
Large summer resort on Lake Garda with a fair area of slopes, served by a revolving cable-car from the 2002/03 season.
1430m; slopes 1430–1830m
⛷ 8 ⛟ 12km

Malga Ciapela Italy
Resort at the foot of the Marmolada glacier massif, with a link into the Sella Ronda. Cortina is nearby.
1445m; slopes 1445–3270m
⛷ 8 ⛟ 18km

Mallnitz Austria
Village in a pretty valley close to Slovenia, with two varied areas providing a fine mix of wooded and open runs.
1200m; slopes 1300–2650m
⛷ 5 ⛟ 30km

Mammoth Mountain 547
✉ AmeriCan Ski, American Ski Classics, Independent Ski Links, Made to Measure Holidays, Ski Activity, Ski All America, Ski Freshtracks, Ski Independence, Ski Line, Ski Safari, Ski The American Dream, United Vacations, Virgin Snow

Manigod France
Small valley village over the Col de la Croix-Fry from La Clusaz.

Marble Mountain Canada
Area in the Humber Valley near the charming Newfoundland town Corner Brook and Gros Morne National Park. It has one of the east coast's highest snowfall records.
85m; slopes 10–545m
⛷ 5 ⛟ 175 acres
✉ Club Pavilion, Frontier Ski

Maria Alm 131
Charming unspoiled village east of Saalbach at one end of the varied Hochkönig area that spreads impressively over four linked mountains via Hintertal and Dienten to Mühlbach. A 2004 reporter warns of the 'nightmare' link between Hinterthal and Hintermoos.
✉ Elevation Holidays

Mariapfarr Austria
Village at the heart of one of the longest, most snow-reliable cross-country networks in Europe. Sizeable Mauterndorf-St Michael Alpine area and Obertauern area are nearby.
1120m
⛷ 5 ⛟ 30km

Mariazell Austria
Traditional Styria village with an impressive basilica. Limited slopes.
870m; slopes 870–1265m
⛷ 5 ⛟ 11km

Maribor 682

Marilleva 430
Small resort with direct links to Madonna di Campiglio's extensive intermediate slopes.
✉ Alpine Tours, Interhome, Interhome

Le Markstein France
Long-standing small resort in the northerly Vosges mountains near Strasbourg, which has hosted World Cup slalom races. Extensive ski de fond trails.
slopes 770–1270m ⛷ 10

Masella Spain
Pyrenean village linked with slopes of La Molina to form the Alp 2500 area.
1600m; slopes 1600–2535m
⛷ 20 ⛟ 100km

La Massana 98
✉ First Choice Ski

Le Massif 662
✉ Frontier Ski, Ski All America, Ski Safari, Ski The American Dream

Matrei in Osttirol Austria
Large market village south of Felbertauern tunnel. Mostly high slopes.
1000m; slopes 1000–2400m
⛷ 7 ⛟ 33km

Maurienne Valley France
A great curving trench with over 20 winter resorts, ranging from pleasant old valley villages to convenience resorts purpose-built in the 1960s.

Mauterndorf Austria
Village near Obertauern with tremendous snow record.
1120m; slopes 1075–2360m
⛷ 10 ⛟ 35km
✉ Equity Ski, Sloping Off

Maverick Mountain USA
Montana resort with plenty of terrain accessed by few lifts. Cowboy Winter Games venue.
2155m; slopes 2155–2800m
⛷ 2 ⛟ 500 acres

Mayens de Riddes 505
Tiny hamlet next to La Tzoumaz with its links up to Savoleyres and the Verbier network.
✉ Interhome

Mayens-de-Sion 505
Tranquil hamlet off the road up to Les Collons – part of the Verbier area.

Mayrhofen 157
✉ Airtours, Alpine Events, Crystal, Equity Ski, First Choice Ski, Independent Ski Links, Inghams, Interhome, Neilson, Rocketski, Ski Line, Ski Wild, Snowcoach, Snoworks, Thomson

Méaudre France
Small resort near Grenoble with good snowmaking to make up for its low altitude.
1000m; slopes 1000–1600m
⛷ 10 ⛟ 18km

Megève 296
✉ Alpine Answers, Alpine Events, AmeriCan Ski, Classic Ski Limited, Corporate Ski Company, Erna Low, French Ski Life, Interhome, Lagrange Holidays, Made to Measure Holidays, Momentum Ski, Oxford Ski Company, Peak Retreats, Simon Butler Skiing,

Ski Arrangements, Ski Barrett-Boyce, Ski Expectations, Ski Freshtracks, Ski Independence, Ski Leisure Direction, Ski Solutions, Ski Supreme, Ski Weekend, Stanford Skiing, White Roc

Meiringen Switzerland
Varied terrain, a good outing from the nearby Jungfrau resorts or Interlaken. Particularly suitable for beginners. New high-speed gondola in 2003/04.
600m; slopes 600–2435m
⛷ 20 ⛟ 80km

Les Menuires 302
✉ Club Med, Erna Low, Family Ski Company, First Choice Ski, French Freedom Holidays, French Ski Life, Independent Ski Links, Interhome, Lagrange Holidays, Neilson, Ski Arrangements, Ski Independence, Ski Leisure Direction, Ski Olympic, Ski Supreme, Skitopia

Merano Italy
Purpose-built base on a high plateau near Bolzano.
2000m; slopes 2000–2240m
⛷ 18 ⛟ 28km

Méribel 304
✉ Absolute Ski, Airtours, Alpine Action, Alpine Answers, Alpine Events, Belvedere Chalets, Bladon Lines, Bonne Neige Ski Holidays, Catered Ski Chalets, Chalet Group, Chalet World Ski, Club Med, Cooltip Mountain Holidays, Corporate Ski Company, Crystal, Descent International, Directski.com, Elegant Resorts, Erna Low, First Choice Ski, Flexiski, French Freedom Holidays, French Ski Life, Independent Ski Links, Inghams, Inspired to Ski, Interhome, Kaluma Ski, Lagrange Holidays, Lotus Supertravel, Made to Measure Holidays, Mark Warner, Mark Warner, Meriski, Momentum Ski, Mountain Tracks, Neilson, Oxford Ski Company, Purple Ski, Scott Dunn Ski, Silver Ski, Simply Ski, Ski Activity, Ski Amis, Ski Arrangements, Ski Basics, Ski Beat, Ski Blanc, Ski Bon, Ski Cuisine, Ski Expectations, Ski France, Ski Hame, Ski Independence, Ski Leisure Direction, Ski Line, Ski Olympic, Ski Solutions, Ski Supreme, Ski Tracer, Ski Weekend, Skiworld, Snowline, Thomson, Total, VIP, White Roc

Métabief-Mont-d'Or France
Twin villages in the Jura region, not far from Geneva.
900m; slopes 880–1460m
⛷ 22 ⛟ 42km

Methven 686
Nearest town/accommodation to Mt Hutt, and helicopter base for trips to Arrowsmith range – good for intermediates as well as advanced.

Mount Baker USA
Almost on the coast near Seattle, yet one of the top resorts for snow (averages 600 inches a year). Plenty of challenging slopes. Known for spectacular avalanches.
1115m; slopes 1115–1540m
⛷9 ⛷ 1000 acres

Mount Baldy Canada
Tiny area, but a worthwhile excursion from Big White. Gets ultra light snow – great glades/powder chutes.
slopes 1705–2150m
⛷2 ⛷ 150 acres

Mount Baldy USA
Some of the longest and steepest runs in California. Only an hour's drive from Los Angeles so a day-trip is feasible, but 20% snowmaking and antiquated lifts are major drawbacks.
1980m; slopes 1980–2620m
⛷4 ⛷ 400 acres

Mount Baw Baw Australia
Small but entertaining intermediate area in attractive woodland, with great views. Closest area to Melbourne (150km/93 miles).
1450m; slopes 1450–1560m
⛷8 ⛷ 61 acres

Mount Buffalo 684

Mount Buller 684

Mount Dobson New Zealand
Mostly intermediate slopes in a wide, treeless basin near Mt Cook, with good snow-cover. Accommodation in Fairlie, 40 minutes away.
1610m; slopes 1610–2010m
⛷3 ⛷ 990 acres

Mount Hood Meadows USA
One of several sizeable areas amid magnificent Oregon scenery. Impressive snowfall record but snow tends to be wet, and weather damp.
1375m; slopes 1375–2535m
⛷12 ⛷ 2150 acres

Mount Hood Ski Bowl USA
Sizeable area set amid magnificent Oregon scenery. Weather can be damp.
1095m; slopes 1095–1540m
⛷9 ⛷ 960 acres

Mount Hotham 684

Mount Hutt 686

Mount Lemmon USA
Southernmost area in North America, close to famous Old West town Tombstone, Arizona. Reasonable snowfall.
2500m; slopes 2500–2790m
⛷3 ⛷ 70 acres

Mount McKay 684

Mount Pilio Greece
Pleasant slopes cut out of dense forest, only 15km/9 miles from the holiday resort of Portaria above town of Volos. 'Very small and disorganised,' says a reporter.
1500m ⛷3

Mount Rose 540

Mount Snow 614

Mount Spokane USA
Little intermediate area outside Spokane (Washington State).
1160m; slopes 1160–1795m
⛷5 ⛷ 350 acres

Mount St Louis / Moonstone Canada
Premier area in Toronto region, spread over three peaks. Very high-capacity lift system and 100% snowmaking.
⛷13 ⛷ 175

Mount Sunapee USA
Area in New Hampshire closest to Boston; primarily intermediate terrain.
375m; slopes 375–835m
⛷10 ⛷ 230 acres

Mount Vermio Greece
Oldest ski base in Greece. Two areas in central Macedonia 60km/37 miles from Thessaloniki. Barren but interesting slopes.
slopes 1420–2000m ⛷4

Mount Washington Resort Canada
Scenic area on Vancouver Island with lodging in the base village. Impressive snowfall record but rain is a problem.
1110m; slopes 1110–1590m
⛷6 ⛷ 970 acres
✉ *Frontier Ski, Ski Safari*

Mt Falakro Greece
Area two hours' drive from Salonica in northern Greece; almost as big as Parnassos, uncrowded and with good views.
1720m ⛷2

Mount Waterman USA
Small Los Angeles area where children ski free. The lack of much snowmaking is a drawback.
2135m; slopes 2135–2440m
⛷3 ⛷ 210 acres

Mühlbach 131
Village east of Saalbach, a short bus-ride from one end of the Hochkönig area that spreads over four mountains via Dienten to Maria Alm.

Mühltal Austria
Small village halfway between Niederau and Auffach in the Wildschönau. No local skiing of its own.
780m; slopes 830–1900m
⛷29 ⛷ 42km

Muhr Austria
Village by Katschberg tunnel well placed for visiting St Michael, Badkleinkirchheim, Flachau and Obertauern.
1110m

Muju South Korea
Largest area in Korea and with a fair amount of lodging. Though it is the furthest resort from Seoul (some four hours south) it is still overcrowded. ⛷13

Mürren 489
✉ *Alpine Events, Inghams, Kuoni, Made to Measure Holidays, Ski Line, Ski Solutions, Swiss Travel Service, Switzerland Travel Centre*

Mutters Austria
Innsbruck satellite resort, temporarily closed.
830m

Myoko Suginohara Kokusai Japan
A series of small resorts two or three hours from Tokyo, which together make up an area of extensive slopes with longer, wider runs than normal for Japan. ⛷15

Naeba Japan
Fashionable resort with lots of accommodation 2 hours north of Tokyo. Crowded slopes.
900m; slopes 900–1800m ⛷28

Nakiska Canada
Small area of wooded runs between Banff and Calgary, with emphasis on downhill speed. Unreliable snow, but state-of-the-art snowmaking and pancake-flat grooming.
1524m; slopes 1525–2215m
⛷4 ⛷ 230 acres
✉ *Ski The American Dream*

Nasserein 193
Quiet suburb of St Anton, a short bus-ride from the lifts.

Nassfeld Austria
Fair-sized, scenic area – Carinthia's biggest – on the sunny side of the Alps, right on the Italian border. There is accommodation at Nassfeld itself (a mid-mountain base) and at Sonnleiten (the other main mid-mountain base), and more in the valley village of Tröpolach, at the bottom of the access gondola, or in the village of Hermagor, 10km/6 miles to the east. The two-stage Millennium Express gondola takes you up directly to the centre of the slopes at Madritsche (1920m/6,300ft). There are nursery slopes here and at the gondola mid-station. Off to the right is a wide bowl served by two further gondolas beneath Trogkofel. To the left is the higher peak of Gartnerkofel (2195m/7,200ft). Two of the area's three six-packs are on the back of this peak. Most of the slopes are graded red, and the few blues are short. But each of the lifts between Madritsche and Trogkofel accesses a black piste or ski route as well as red runs. There are two terrain-parks (including a novel twin-pipe), and a floodlit piste. There are extensive cross-country trails and a range of other activities.
1500m; slopes 610–2195m
⛷30 ⛷ 110km
✉ *Equity Ski, Ski Line, Ski Wild, Sloping Off*

Nauders 166

Nax Switzerland
Quiet, sunny village in a balcony setting overlooking the Rhône valley. Own little area and only a short drive from Veysonnaz.
1300m

Nendaz 505
Enormous apartment development offering quiet alternative to Verbier.
✉ *Interhome*

Neukirchen Austria
Quiet, pretty beginners' resort with a fairly snow-sure plateau at the top of its mountain.
855m; slopes 855–2150m
⛷14 ⛷ 35km
✉ *Crystal, Sloping Off*

Neustift 134
✉ *Alpine Tours, Catered Ski Chalets, Crystal, Esprit Ski, Interhome, Made to Measure Holidays*

Nevegal Italy
Weekend place near Belluno, south of Cortina.
1030m; slopes 1030–1650m
⛷14 ⛷ 30km

Nevis Range 683
✉ *Skisafe Travel*

Niederau 206
Amorphous chalet-style village in the Wildschönau region.
✉ *Airtours, Directski.com, First Choice Ski, Inghams, Neilson, Panorama Holidays, Thomson*

Niseko Japan
Town on Hohhaido, three hours from Sopporo and with three ski areas close by. Good snow record and powder. ⛷28

Nockberge Innerkrems Austria
Area just south of Katschberg tunnel.
1500m; slopes 1500–2300m
⛷10 ⛷ 33km

Nordic Valley USA
Utah cross-country area close to Salt Lake City. Powder Mountain and Snowbasin are nearby Alpine areas.
⛷3 ⛷ 100 acres

Nordseter Norway
Cluster of hotels in deep forest north of Lillehammer. Some Alpine facilities but best for cross-country.
850m; slopes 1000–1090m
⛷2 ⛷ 2km

Norefjell Norway
Norway's toughest run, a very steep 600m/1,970ft drop. 120km/75 miles north-west of Oslo.
185m; slopes 185–1185m
⛷10 ⛷ 23km

La Norma France
Traffic-free, purpose-built resort near Modane and Val-Cenis, with mostly easy terrain.
1350m; slopes 1350–2750m
⛷ 18 ⛓ 65km
✉ *AmeriCan Ski, Erna Low, Interhome, Lagrange Holidays, Peak Retreats, Ski Leisure Direction*

Norquay 628
Banff's quiet local hill – worth a visit, especially in bad weather.

North Conway USA
Attractive factory-outlet-shopping town in New Hampshire close to Attitash and Cranmore ski areas.
✉ *Virgin Snow*

Northstar-at-Tahoe 553
✉ *AmeriCan Ski, Ski The American Dream, United Vacations*

Nôtre-Dame-de-Bellecombe France
Pleasant village spoiled by the busy Albertville-Megève road. Inexpensive base from which to visit Megève, though it has fair slopes of its own.
1130m; slopes 1130–2070m ⛷ 18
✉ *AmeriCan Ski, Peak Retreats*

Nova Levante Italy
Village close to Bozen/Bolzano with lifts up to small network around Passo di Costalunga.
1180m; slopes 1180–2200m
⛷ 14 ⛓ 20km

Nozawa Onsen Japan
Spa village with good hot springs three hours from Tokyo. The runs are cut out of heavy vegetation.
500m; slopes 500–1650m ⛷ 24

Nub's Nob USA
One of the most sheltered Great Lakes ski areas (many suffer fierce winds). 100% snowmaking; weekend crowds from Detroit. Wooded slopes suitable for all abilities.
275m; slopes 275–405m
⛷ 8 ⛓ 245 acres

Oberau 206
Pretty village, most central of those forming the Wildschönau region – but least convenient for the slopes.
✉ *Inghams*

Obereggen Italy
Tiny resort close to Bozen/Bolzano with modest area of slopes also accessible from Predazzo in Val di Fiemme.
1550m; slopes 1550–2200m
⛷ 6 ⛓ 10km

Obergurgl 168
✉ *Airtours, Alpine Events, Catered Ski Chalets, Crystal, Esprit Ski, First Choice Ski, Independent Ski Links, Inghams, Made to Measure Holidays, Neilson, Ski Expectations, Ski Freshtracks, Ski Solutions, Thomson*

Oberlech 150
Car- and crowd-free family resort alternative to Lech. Snow-sure due to height, snow-pocket position and snow-guns.
✉ *Elegant Resorts, Kaluma Ski*

Oberndorf 202
Quiet hamlet with beginners' area and a chair connecting it to St Johann's undemanding ski area.
✉ *Lagrange Holidays*

Oberperfuss 134
Attractive winter-sports town near the Austrian border with three small areas. Famous ski-jumping hill. The Nordic World Ski Championships is due to be held here in 2005.
815m; slopes 800–2220m
⛷ 31 ⛓ 30km
✉ *Moswin Tours*

Obertauern 173
✉ *Alpine Answers, Directski.com, Inghams, Made to Measure Holidays, Ski Wild, Snowscape, Thomson*

Ochapowace Canada
Main area in Saskatchewan, east of Regina. It doesn't get a huge amount of snow but 75% snowmaking helps.
⛷ 4 ⛓ 100 acres

Oetz Austria
Village at the entrance to the Oetz valley with an easy/intermediate ski area of its own and access to the Sölden, Kuhtai and Niederau areas.
820m; slopes 820–2200m
⛷ 10 ⛓ 25km

Ohau New Zealand
Some of NZ's steepest slopes, with great views of Lake Ohau 9km/6 miles away (where you stay). 320km/200 miles south of Christchurch.
1500m; slopes 1425–1825m
⛷ 3 ⛓ 310 acres

Okemo 614

Oppdal 671

Orcières-Merlette France
High, convenient family resort a few km north-east of Gap, Merlette being the ugly, purpose-built ski station above the village of Orcières (1450m4,760ft). Snow-sure beginner area. Slopes have a good mix of difficulty spread over several mountain flanks, and are currently being expanded – a process due to culminate in 2006/07 with the opening of a cable-car up to almost 3000m/9,840ft on Roche Brune. Most accommodation is in apartments, but there are a few simple hotels. There is an impressive Palais des Sports, with pools, bowling alley and ice-rink.
1850m; slopes 1850–2725m
⛷ 29 ⛓ 85km
✉ *French Ski Life, Lagrange Holidays, Ski France*

Ordino 98
Valley village near La Massana, on the way up to Andorra's best snow at Arcalis.

Orelle France
Village in the Maurienne with access by gondola to Val-Thorens in the Trois Vallées.

Oropa Italy
Little area just off the Aosta–Turin motorway. An easy change of scene from Courmayeur.
1180m; slopes 1200–2390m
⛓ 15km

Les Orres France
Friendly modern resort with great views and varied intermediate terrain, but the snow is unreliable, and it's a long transfer from Lyon.
1550m; slopes 1550–2720m
⛷ 23 ⛓ 62km
✉ *Lagrange Holidays, Rocketski, Skitopia, Sloping Off*

Orsières Switzerland
Traditional, sizeable winter resort near Martigny. Well-positioned base from which to visit Verbier and the Chamonix valley.
900m

Ortisei 441
Charming, lively, old market town in the Italian Dolomites with indirect links to the Sella Ronda.
✉ *Inghams, Interhome*

Oslo Norway
Capital city with cross-country ski trails in its parks. Alpine slopes and lifts in Nordmarka region, just north of city boundaries.
✉ *Directski.com, Headwater Holidays, Neilson*

Otre il Colle Italy
Smallest of many little resorts near Bergamo.
1100m; slopes 1100–2000m
⛷ 7 ⛓ 7km

Oukaimeden Morocco
Slopes 75km/47 miles from Marrakech with a surprisingly long season.
2600m; slopes 2600–3260m
⛷ 8 ⛓ 15km

Ovindoli Italy
One of the smallest areas in L'Aquila region east of Rome, but it has higher slopes than most and one of the better lift systems.
1375m; slopes 1375–2220m
⛷ 9 ⛓ 10km

Ovronnaz Switzerland
Pretty village set on a sunny shelf above the Rhône valley, with a good pool complex. Limited area but Crans-Montana and Anzère are close.
1350m; slopes 1350–2080m
⛷ 10 ⛓ 25km

Owl's Head Canada
Steep mountain rising out of a lake, in a remote spot bordering Vermont, away from weekend crowds.
⛷ 7 ⛓ 90 acres

Oz-en-Oisans 224
Attractive old village with a higher satellite at the base of the lifts into Alpe-d'Huez.
✉ *AmeriCan Ski, Erna Low, Independent Ski Links, Lagrange Holidays, Ski Independence*

Pajarito Mountain USA
Los Alamos area laid out by nuclear scientists. Atomic slopes too – steep, ungroomed. Open Fridays, weekends and holidays. Fun day out from Taos.
2685m; slopes 2685–3170m
⛷ 6 ⛓ 220 acres

Pal 102
Prettily wooded mountain, now linked with slopes of Arinsal.
✉ *Panorama Holidays*

Palandöken Turkey
Varied skiing area, transformed by new lifts and two big hotels, overlooking the Anatolian city of Erzurum.
slopes 2125–3125m ⛷ 7

Pamporovo 678
✉ *Balkan Holidays, Crystal, Directski.com, First Choice Ski, Inghams, Panorama Holidays, Ski Balkantours, Solo's, Thomson*

Panarotta Italy
Smallest of the resorts east of Trento. It is at a higher altitude than nearby Andalo, so it is worth a day out from there.
1500m; slopes 1500–2000m
⛷ 6 ⛓ 7km

Panorama 648
✉ *AmeriCan Ski, Frontier Ski, Inghams, Ski Activity, Ski All America, Ski Independence, Ski Safari, Ski The American Dream*

Panticosa Spain
Charming old Pyrenees spa village near Formigal with sheltered but limited slopes.
1200m; slopes 1200–1900m
⛷ 7 ⛓ 34km
✉ *White Roc*

Paradiski 324

Park City 597
✉ *Alpine Answers, AmeriCan Ski, American Ski Classics, Crystal, Momentum Ski, Ski Activity, Ski All America, Ski Independence, Ski Line, Ski Safari, Ski The American Dream, Skiworld, Thomson, United Vacations*

Parnassos Greece
Biggest and best-organised area in Greece, 180km/110 miles from Athens and with surprisingly good slopes and lifts. 'The Mykonos of winter and very crowded at weekends,' says a reporter.
slopes 1600–2300m
⛷ 10 ⛓ 14km

Parpan   Switzerland
Pretty village linked to the large intermediate area of Lenzerheide.
1510m; slopes 1230–2865m
🚠 35 ⛷ 155km

Partenen   163
Traditional village in a pretty setting at the end of Montafontal. The slopes start at Gaschurn, and there are lots more in the vicinity.

La Parva   Chile
One of Chile's best ski areas, linked with Valle Nevado and El Colorado ski areas. Only 50km/31 miles east of Santiago so it gets crowded at weekends.
2660m; slopes 2660–3630m
🚠 14 ⛷ 38km
✉ Scott Dunn Latin America

Pas de la Casa   104
✉ Airtours, Crystal, Directski.com, First Choice Ski, Independent Ski Links, Inghams, Lagrange Holidays, Neilson, Panorama Holidays, Thomson

Passo di Costalunga   Italy
Dense network of short lifts either side of the road over a pass, close to Val di Fassa, with links up from Nova Levante.

Passo Lanciano   Italy
Closest area to Adriatic. Weekend crowds from nearby Pescara when the snow is good.
1305m; slopes 1305–2000m 🚠 13

Passo Rolle   Italy
Small group of lifts either side of the road over a high pass just north of San Martino di Castrozza.

Passo San Pellegrino   Italy
Trentino area south of the Sella Ronda linked with Falcade.

Passo Tonale   454
✉ Airtours, Alpine Tours, Crystal, Directski.com, Equity Ski, First Choice Ski, Inghams, Neilson, Rocketski, Ski Wild, Sloping Off, Thomson

Pass Thurn   144
Road-side lift base for Kitzbühel's most snow-sure, but unconnected, ski area.

Pebble Creek   USA
Small area on Utah-Jackson Hole route. Blend of open and wooded slopes.
1920m; slopes 1920–2530m
🚠 3 ⛷ 600 acres

Pec Pod Snezku   Czech Republic
Collection of hamlets spread along the valley road leading to the main lifts and the very limited ski area.
770m; slopes 710–1190m
🚠 5 ⛷ 12km

Peisey   233
Small village (often referred to as Peisey-Nancroix) linked to Les Arcs and the Paradiski area.

Peisey-Vallandry   233
Group of small villages linked to Les Arcs and the Paradiski area.
✉ AmeriCan Ski, Club Med, Erna Low, Esprit Ski, French Ski Life, Lagrange Holidays, Ski Beat, Ski Hiver, Ski Leisure Direction, Ski Line, Ski Olympic, Snow Monkey Chalets

Pejo   454
Trentino resort near Madonna.

Perisher/Smiggins   684

Pescasseroli   Italy
One of numerous areas east of Rome in L'Aquila region.
1250m; slopes 1250–1945m
🚠 6 ⛷ 25km

Pescocostanzo   Italy
One of numerous areas east of Rome in L'Aquila region.
1395m; slopes 1395–1900m
🚠 4 ⛷ 25km

Pettneu   193
Snow-sure specialist beginners' resort with an irregular bus link to nearby St Anton.

Petzen   Austria
One of many little areas in Austria's easternmost ski region near the Slovenian border.
600m; slopes 600–1700m
🚠 5 ⛷ 16km

Peyragudes-Peyresourde France
Small Pyrenean resort with its ski area starting high above.
1000m; slopes 1600–2400m
🚠 15 ⛷ 37km
✉ French Ski Life, Lagrange Holidays

Pfunds   Austria
Picturesque valley village with no slopes but quick access to several resorts in Switzerland and Italy, as well as Austria.
970m
✉ Lagrange Holidays

Phoenix Park   South Korea
Golf complex with 12 trails in winter. Two hours (140km/87 miles) from Seoul.
slopes 650–1050m 🚠 9

Piancavallo   Italy
Uninspiring yet curiously trendy purpose-built village, an easy drive from Venice.
1270m; slopes 1270–1830m
🚠 17 ⛷ 45km
✉ Equity Ski, Sloping Off

Piani delle Betulle   Italy
One of several little areas near the east coast of Lake Como.
730m; slopes 730–1850m
🚠 6 ⛷ 10km

Piani di Artavaggio   Italy
Small base complex rather than a village. One of several little areas near Lake Como.
875m; slopes 875–1875m
🚠 7 ⛷ 15km

Piani di Bobbio   Italy
Largest of several tiny resorts above Lake Como.
770m; slopes 770–1855m
🚠 10 ⛷ 20km

Piani di Erna   Italy
Small base development – no village. One of several little areas above Lake Como.
600m; slopes 600–1635m
🚠 5 ⛷ 9km

Piau-Engaly   France
User-friendly St-Lary satellite in one of the best areas in the Pyrenees.
1850m; slopes 1700–2500m
🚠 20 ⛷ 40km
✉ Lagrange Holidays

Piazzatorre   Italy
One of many little areas in the Bergamo region.
870m; slopes 870–2000m
🚠 5 ⛷ 25km

Pichl   181
In Dachstein-Tauern region, close to Schladming.

Pico   617
Low-key little family area (no resort) close to Killington in central Vermont.

Piesendorf   Austria
Cheaper, quiet place to stay when visiting Zell am See. Tucked behind Kaprun near Niedernsill.
780m
🚠 3 ⛷ 3km

Pievepelago   Italy
Much the smallest and most limited of the Appennine ski resorts. Less than two hours from Florence and Pisa.
1115m; slopes 1115–1410m
🚠 7 ⛷ 8km

Pila   461
✉ Crystal, Independent Ski Links, Interhome, Interski, Ski Supreme, Thomson

Pinzolo   454
Trentino resort near Madonna.

Pisoderi   Greece
The longest run in Greece (over 2km), in an unspoiled setting 18km/11 miles from the town of Florina in the north.
1650m 🚠 5

Pitztal   Austria
Long valley with good glacier area at its head, accessed by underground funicular.
1250m; slopes 880–3440m
🚠 19 ⛷ 87km

Pla-d'Adet   France
Limited purpose-built complex at the foot of the St-Lary ski area (the original village is further down the mountain).
1680m; slopes 1420–2450m
🚠 32 ⛷ 80km
✉ Lagrange Holidays

La Plagne   327
✉ Airtours, Alpine Answers, Catered Ski Chalets, Chalet Group, Chalet World Ski, Chez Jay Ski Chalets, Club Med, Crystal, Equity Ski, Erna Low, Esprit Ski, Finlays, First Choice Ski, French Freedom Holidays, French Ski Life, Independent Ski Links, Inghams, Interhome, Lagrange Holidays, Made to

Measure Holidays, Mark Warner, MasterSki, Neilson, Rocketski, Silver Ski, Ski Activity, Ski Amis, Ski Arrangements, Ski Beat, Ski Expectations, Ski France, Ski Freshtracks, Ski Independence, Ski Leisure Direction, Ski Line, Ski Olympic, Ski Solutions, Ski Supreme, Ski Tracer, Skiworld, Snow Monkey Chalets, Thomson

Plan-Peisey   233
Small development above Peisey with cable-car link to Les Arcs and the Paradiski area. For package holidays see Peisey-Vallandry.

Poiana Brasov   681
✉ Balkan Holidays, Inghams, Neilson, Solo's

Pomerelle   USA
Small area in Idaho on the Utah–Sun Valley route.
2430m; slopes 2430–2735m
🚠 3 ⛷ 300 acres

Pontechianale   Italy
Highest, largest area in a remote region south-west of Turin. Day-tripper place.
1600m; slopes 1600–2760m
🚠 8 ⛷ 30km

Ponte di Legno   Italy
Attractive sheltered alternative to bleak, ugly neighbour Passo Tonale. Linked by piste and bus.
1255m; slopes 1255–1920m
🚠 5 ⛷ 15km

Pontresina   499
Small, sedate base linked to nearby St Moritz by road, with extensive cross-country trails.
✉ Made to Measure Holidays

Port-Aïné   Spain
Small but high intermediate area in the Spanish Pyrenees near Andorra. Lifts include a six-pack; eponymous 3-star hotel at base.
1975m; slopes 1650–2440m
🚠 8 ⛷ 44km

Porter Heights   New Zealand
Closest skiing to Christchurch (one hour). Open, sunny bowl offering mostly intermediate skiing – with back bowls for powder.
1340m; slopes 1340–1950m
🚠 5 ⛷ 200 acres

Portes du Soleil   336

Portillo   Chile
Luxury hotel 150km/93 miles north-east of Santiago. Uncrowded snow-sure slopes used for training by US national ski team.
2850m; slopes 2590–3350m
🚠 12 ⛷ 25km
✉ AmeriCan Ski, Crystal, Lotus Supertravel, Momentum Ski, Scott Dunn Latin America, Ski All America, Ski Safari

Powderhorn USA
Area in west Colorado perched on the world's highest flat-top mountain, Grand Mesa. Sensational views. Day trip from Aspen.
2490m; slopes 2490–2975m
⬒4 ⬆ 300 acres

Powder King Canada
Remote resort in British Columbia, between Prince George and Dawson City. As its name suggests, it has great powder. Plenty of lodging.
880m; slopes 880–1520m
⬒3 ⬆ 160 acres

Powder Mountain USA
Massive Utah area sprawled over six ridges, an hour and a quarter's drive from Salt Lake City. An ample 2,800 acres is lift-served, a mix of mainly north-facing slopes with enough green, blue and black runs to satisfy all abilities. You access the rest by snowcat or snowmobile tow, buses and hiking. It is the abundance of intermediate free-ride terrain that makes it special: try the superb black powder runs plunging through trees beneath the Paradise Lift, and the Powder Country area which drains down to the access road. Away from the lifts, Lightning Ridge is great for black run free-riding. A couple of lifts run till 10pm and there's a terrain-park and half-pipe. Hidden Lake Lodge provides good food on the mountain. The spread-out base area is limited, with a couple of eateries, rental shops and one accommodation option. You can also stay in Ogden, 32km/20 miles away.
2100m; slopes 2100–2740m
⬒7 ⬆ 5500 acres

Pozza di Fassa Italy
Pretty Dolomite village with its own slopes, three other small areas close by, and access to the Sella Ronda at Campitello.
1340m; slopes 1340–2155m
⬒6 ⬆ 20km
✉ Crystal

Pragelato Italy
Inexpensive base, a short drive east of Sestriere. Its own area is worth a try for half a day.
1535m; slopes 1535–2700m
⬒6 ⬆ 50km

Prägraten am Grossvenediger
Austria
Traditional mountaineering/ski-touring village in lovely setting south of Felbertauern tunnel. The Alpine ski slopes of Matrei are nearby.
1310m; slopes 1310–1490m
⬒2 ⬆ 30km

Prali Italy
Tiny resort east of Sestriere – a worthwhile half-day trip.
1450m; slopes 1450–2500m
⬒7 ⬆ 25km

Pralognan-la-Vanoise France
Unspoiled traditional village overlooked by spectacular peaks. Champagny (La Plagne) and Courchevel are close by.
1410m; slopes 1410–2355m
⬒14 ⬆ 30km
✉ Erna Low, Lagrange Holidays, Ski Independence

Pra-Loup France
Convenient, purpose-built family resort with an extensive, varied intermediate area linked to La Foux-d'Allos.
1500m; slopes 1500–2600m
⬒32 ⬆ 83km
✉ Equity Ski, French Ski Life, Lagrange Holidays, Rocketski, Ski Leisure Direction

Prati di Tivo Italy
Weekend day-trip place east of Rome and near the town of Teramo. A sizeable resort by southern Italy standards.
1450m; slopes 1450–1800m
⬒6 ⬆ 16km

Prato Nevoso Italy
Purpose-built resort with rather bland slopes. Part of Mondolé ski area with Artesina.
1500m; slopes 1500–1950m
⬒25 ⬆ 90km
✉ Crystal, Equity Ski, Rocketski, Thomson

Prato Selva Italy
Tiny base development (no village) east of Rome near Teramo. Weekend day-trip place.
1370m; slopes 1370–1800m
⬒4 ⬆ 10km

Le Praz 269
The lowest and most attractive of the Courchevel resorts, with direct access to the slopes.

Les Praz 246
Quiet hamlet 4km/2 miles from Chamonix, with convenient lift link to the varied Flégère area.
✉ High Mountain Holidays

Praz-de-Lys France
Little-known snow-pocket area near Lake Geneva that can have good snow when nearby resorts (eg La Clusaz) do not.
1500m; slopes 1200–2000m
⬒23 ⬆ 60km
✉ Directski.com, French Ski Life, Lagrange Holidays

Praz-sur-Arly France
Traditional village in a pretty, wooded setting just down the road from Megève, with its own varied slopes.
1035m; slopes 1035–2000m
⬒14 ⬆ 60km
✉ Lagrange Holidays, Ski France, Ski Leisure Direction

Le Pré 233
Charming, rustic hamlet with lifts up to Arc 2000 and excellent runs back down.

Predazzo Italy
Small, quiet place between Cavalese and the Sella Ronda resorts, with lift into modest area of slopes above Obereggen.
1015m; slopes 995–2205m
⬒8 ⬆ 17km

Premanon France
One of four resorts that make up Les Rousses area in Jura region.
1050m; slopes 1120–1680m ⬒40
✉ Lagrange Holidays

La Presolana Italy
Large summer resort near Bergamo. Several other little areas nearby.
1250m; slopes 1250–1650m
⬒6 ⬆ 15km

Pucón Chile
Ski area on the side of the active Villarrica volcano in southern Chile, 800km/500 miles south of Santiago. Lodgings are at Pucón village, 30 minutes away from the slopes.
1200m; slopes 1200–1800m ⬒9
✉ Snoworks

Puy-St-Vincent 338
✉ Equity Ski, Erna Low, Interhome, Lagrange Holidays, Snowbizz

Pyhä 669
✉ Crystal

Pyrenees, French 398

Pyrenees 2000 France
Tiny resort built in a pleasing manner. Shares a pretty area of short runs with Font-Romeu. Impressive snowmaking.
2000m; slopes 1750–2250m
⬒32 ⬆ 52km
✉ Pyrenees Ski Experience

Québec 662
✉ Crystal, Equity Ski, Waymark Holidays

Queenstown 689

Radium Hot Springs Canada
Summer resort offering an alternative to the purpose-built slope-side resort of Panorama.
slopes 975–2155m
⬒8 ⬆ 300 acres
✉ AmeriCan Ski

Radstadt Austria
Interesting, unspoiled medieval town near Schladming that has its own small area, with the Salzburger Sportwelt slopes accessed from nearby Zauchensee or Flachau.
855m; slopes 855–2185m
⬒100 ⬆ 350km

Rainbow New Zealand
Northernmost ski area on South Island. Wide, treeless area, best for beginners and intermediates. Accommodation at St Arnaud.
1440m; slopes 1440–1760m
⬒5 ⬆ 865 acres

Ramsau am Dachstein Austria
Charming village overlooked by the Dachstein glacier. Renowned for cross-country, it also has Alpine slopes locally, on the glacier and at Schladming. 'Spectacular cable car ride to Hunerkogel,' says a 2004 reporter.
1200m; slopes 1100–2700m
⬒18 ⬆ 30km

Ramundberget 675

Rauris Austria
Old roadside village close to Kaprun and Zell am See, with a long, narrow area that has snow-guns on the lower slopes.
950m; slopes 950–2200m
⬒10 ⬆ 30km
✉ Crystal

Ravascletto Italy
Resort in a pretty wooded setting near Austrian border, with most of its terrain high above on an open plateau.
920m; slopes 920–1735m
⬒12 ⬆ 40km

Reallon France
Traditional-style village, with splendid views from above Lac de Serre-Ponçon.
1560m; slopes 1560–2115m
⬒6 ⬆ 20km

Red Lodge USA
Picturesque Old West Montana town. Ideal for a combined trip with Big Sky or Jackson Hole.
1800m; slopes 2155–2860m
⬒8 ⬆ 1600 acres
✉ AmeriCan Ski

Red Resort 660
✉ AmeriCan Ski, Frontier Ski, Nonstopski, Ski Independence, Ski Safari

Red River USA
New Mexico western town – complete with stetsons and saloons – with intermediate slopes above.
2665m; slopes 2665–3155m
⬒7 ⬆ 290 acres

Reichenfels Austria
One of many small areas in Austria's easternmost ski region near the Slovenian border.
810m; slopes 810–1400m

The Remarkables 689
Three bleak basins with great views of 'remarkable' jagged alps, 45 minutes from Queenstown.

Rencurel-les-Coulumes France
One of seven little resorts just west of Grenoble. Unspoiled, inexpensive place to tour. Villard-de-Lans is the main resort.

Reutte Austria
500-year-old market town with many traditional hotels, and rail links to nearby Lermoos.
855m; slopes 855–1900m
⬒9 ⬆ 19km

Revelstoke   Canada
Town from which you can heli-ski in Monashees or cat-ski locally at a more reasonable cost than most places.
460m
✉ *Canadian Powder Tours, Powder Skiing in North America*

Rhêmes-Notre-Dame   Italy
Unspoiled village in the beautiful Rhêmes valley, south of Aosta. Courmayeur and La Thuile within reach.
🚡 *2* 🎿 *5km*

Riederalp   Switzerland
Pretty, vehicle-free village perched high above the Rhône valley amid the glorious scenery of the Aletsch area. Access by cable-car or gondola from the valley village of Mörel near Brig.
1900m; slopes 1900–2900m
🚡 *32* 🎿 *90km*

Rigi-Kaltbad   Switzerland
Resort on a mountain rising out of Lake Lucerne, with superb all-round views, accessed by the world's first mountain railroad.
1440m; slopes 1195–1795m
🚡 *9* 🎿 *30km*

Riihivuori   Finland
Small area with 'base' at the top of the mountain. 20km/12 miles south of the city of Jyväskylä. 🚡 *5*

Riksgränsen   **675**

Riscone   Italy
Dolomite village sharing a pretty area with San Vigilio. Good snowmaking. Short easy runs.
1200m; slopes 1200–2275m
🚡 *35* 🎿 *40km*

Risoul   **340**
✉ *Catered Ski Chalets, Crystal, First Choice Ski, Interhome, Lagrange Holidays, Ski Arrangements, Ski Independence, Ski Leisure Direction*

Rivisondoli   Italy
Sizeable mountain retreat east of Rome, with one of the better lift systems in the vicinity.
1350m; slopes 1350–2050m
🚡 *7* 🎿 *16km*

Roccaraso   Italy
Largest of the resorts east of Rome – at least when snow-cover is complete.
1280m; slopes 1280–2200m
🚡 *12* 🎿 *56km*

Rohrmoos   **181**
Situated below a small mountain in the Dachstein-Tauern region, next to Schladming.

La Rosière   **343**
✉ *Alpine Answers, Catered Ski Chalets, Chalet Group, Crystal, Erna Low, Esprit Ski, Interhome, Mountain Tracks, Ski Amis, Ski Arrangements, Ski Leisure Direction, Ski Olympic, Ski Supreme, SnowCrazy, Thomson, Vanilla Ski*

Rossland   Canada
Remote little town 5km/3 miles from cult powder paradise Red Mountain.

Rougemont   Switzerland
Cute rustic hamlet just over the French/German language border near Gstaad, with worthwhile local slopes and links to Gstaad's Eggli sector.
991m; slopes 890–3000m
🚡 *67* 🎿 *250km*

Les Rousses   France
Group of four villages – Les Rousses, Premanon, Lamoura and Bois d'Amont – in the Jura mountains, 50km/31 miles from Geneva airport.
1120m; slopes 1120–1680m
🚡 *37* 🎿 *40km*
✉ *Lagrange Holidays*

Ruka   **669**
✉ *Crystal, Inghams, Thomson*

Russbach   Austria
Secluded village tucked up a side valley and linked into the Gosau-Annaberg-Lungotz area. The slopes are spread over a wide area.
815m; slopes 780–1620m
🚡 *33* 🎿 *65km*

Saalbach-Hinterglemm   **175**
✉ *Airtours, Alpine Answers, Board and Lodge, Catered Ski Chalets, Crystal, Directski.com, Equity Ski, First Choice Ski, Inghams, Interhome, Neilson, Panorama Holidays, Rocketski, Ski Wild, Thomson*

Saalfelden   Austria
Town ideally placed for touring eastern Tirol. Extensive lift networks of Maria-Alm and Saalbach are nearby.
745m; slopes 745–1550m
🚡 *3* 🎿 *3km*

Saanen   Switzerland
Cheaper and more convenient alternative to staying in Gstaad – but much less going on.
slopes 950–3000m
🚡 *69* 🎿 *250km*

Saanenmöser   Switzerland
Small village with rail/road links to Gstaad. Scenic and quiet local slopes, with good mountain restaurants (Horneggli and Kübelialp are 2004 recommendations).
1270m; slopes 1270–1995m 🚡 *14*

Saas-Almagell   Switzerland
Compact village up the valley from Saas-Grund, with good cross-country trails and walks, and a limited Alpine area.
1670m 🚡 *6*

Saas-Fee   **493**
✉ *Alpine Answers, Alpine Events, Catered Ski Chalets, Crystal, Erna Low, Esprit Ski, Independent Ski Links, Inghams, Interhome, Kuoni, Made to Measure Holidays, Momentum Ski, Ski Freshtracks, Ski Independence, Ski Line, Ski*

Solutions, Swiss Travel Service, Switzerland Travel Centre, Thomson, Total

Saas-Grund   Switzerland
Sprawling valley village below Saas-Fee, with a separate, small but high Alpine area.
1560m; slopes 1560–3100m
🚡 *7* 🎿 *45km*

Saddleback   USA
Small area between Maine's premier resorts. High slopes by local standards.
695m; slopes 695–1255m
🚡 *5* 🎿 *100 acres*

Sahoro   Japan
Ugly, purpose-built complex on Hokkaido island. A limited area, but one of the most exotic package destinations.
400m; slopes 400–1100m
🚡 *9* 🎿 *15km*
✉ *Club Med*

Les Saisies   France
Traditional-style cross-country venue in a pretty setting, surrounded by varied four-mountain Alpine slopes.
1650m; slopes 1150–2000m
🚡 *24* 🎿 *40km*
✉ *AmeriCan Ski, Classic Ski Limited, Erna Low, French Ski Life, Lagrange Holidays, Peak Retreats, Ski Independence, Ski Leisure Direction*

Sälen   **675**

Salt Lake City   USA
Underrated base from which to ski Utah. 30 minutes from Park City, Deer Valley, The Canyons, Snowbird, Alta, Snowbasin. Cheaper and livelier than the resorts.
✉ *AmeriCan Ski*

Salzburg-Stadt   Austria
A single, long challenging run off the back of Salzburg's local mountain, accessed by a spectacular lift-ride from a suburb of Grodig.
425m

Samedan   Switzerland
Valley town, just down the road from St Moritz.
1720m; slopes 1740–2570m
🚡 *3* 🎿 *7km*

Samnaun   **138**
Shares large ski area with Ischgl.

Samoëns   **345**
✉ *AmeriCan Ski, Chalet Group, French Ski Life, Interhome, Lagrange Holidays, Peak Retreats, Ski Independence*

San Bernardino   Switzerland
Pretty resort south of the road tunnel, close to Madesimo.
1625m; slopes 1600–2595m
🚡 *8* 🎿 *35km*

San Candido   Italy
Resort on the border with Austria on the road to Lienz.
1175m; slopes 1175–1580m
🚡 *4* 🎿 *15km*
✉ *Waymark Holidays*

San Carlos de Bariloche   Argentina
Year-round resort, with five areas nearby.
790m
✉ *Scott Dunn Latin America*

San Cassiano   **441**
Pretty village linked to the Sella Ronda.
✉ *Mountainsun, Powder Byrne*

Sandia Peak   USA
The world's longest lift ride ascends from Albuquerque. Mostly gentle slopes; children ski free.
slopes 2645–3165m
🚡 *7* 🎿 *100km*

San Grée di Viola   Italy
Easternmost of resorts south of Turin, surprisingly close to the Italian Riviera.
1100m; slopes 1100–1800m
🎿 *30km*

San Martin de los Andes   Argentina
Sizeable town with accommodation, 19 km/12 miles from the Chapelco ski area.
✉ *Scott Dunn Latin America*

San Martino di Castrozza   **454**
Trentino village south of Val di Fassa.

San Pellegrino   Italy
Little ski area south of the Sella Ronda, with lifts each side of the pass road and links with the valley village of Falcade.

Sansicario   **436**
Small, stylish, modern resort, well placed in the Milky Way near to Sauze d'Oulx.

San Simone   Italy
Tiny development north of Bergamo, close to unappealing Foppolo area.
2000m; slopes 1105–2300m
🚡 *9* 🎿 *45km*

Santa Caterina   Italy
Pretty, user-friendly village near Bormio, with a snow-sure novice and intermediate area.
1740m; slopes 1740–2725m
🚡 *8* 🎿 *25km*
✉ *Airtours, Equity Ski*

Santa Cristina   **441**
Quiet village on the periphery of the Sella Ronda.
✉ *Neilson*

Santa Fe   USA
One of America's most attractive and interesting towns. Varied slopes – glades, bowls, cruiser pistes, desert views. Great excursion from Taos.
3145m; slopes 3145–3645m
🚡 *6* 🎿 *660 acres*

Santa Maria Maggiore   Italy
Resort south of the Simplon Pass from the Rhône valley, and near Lake Maggiore.
820m; slopes 820–1890m
🚡 *5* 🎿 *10km*

San Vigilio   Italy
Italian name for Kronplatz.
1200m; slopes 1200–2275m
🚡 *33* 🎿 *40km*

San Vito di Cadore Italy
Sizeable, alternative place to
stay to Cortina. Negligible local
slopes, though.
1010m; slopes 1010–1380m
⛷9 ⬆ 12km

Sappada Italy
Isolated resort close to the
Austrian border below Lienz.
1215m; slopes 1215–2050m
⛷17 ⬆ 21km

Sappee Finland
Resort within easy reach of
Helsinki, popular with boarders
and telemarkers. Lake views. ⛷7

Sarnano Italy
Main resort in the Macerata
region near Adriatic Riviera.
Valley village with ski slopes
accessed by lift.
540m
⛷9 ⬆ 11km

Le Sauze France
Fine area near Barcelonnette,
sadly remote from airports.
1400m; slopes 1400–2440m
⛷23 ⬆ 65km

Sauze d'Oulx 436
✉ *Airtours, Crystal, Equity Ski,
First Choice Ski, Independent
Ski Links, Inghams, Interhome,
Neilson, Panorama Holidays,
Ski Arrangements, Ski Tracer,
Thomson*

Savognin Switzerland
Pretty village with a good mid-
sized area; a good base for the
nearby resorts of St Moritz,
Davos/Klosters and Flims.
1200m; slopes 1200–2715m
⛷13 ⬆ 80km

Scheffau 187
Rustic beauty not far from Söll.
✉ *Crystal, Esprit Ski, Ski Line,
Ski Wild, Thomson*

Schia Italy
Very limited area of short runs –
the only ski area near Parma.
1245m; slopes 1245–1415m
⛷7 ⬆ 15km

Schilpario Italy
One of many little areas near
Bergamo.
1125m; slopes 1125–1635m
⛷5 ⬆ 15km

Schladming 181
✉ *Alpine Answers, Crystal,
Equity Ski, Interhome,
Rocketski, Sloping Off*

Schönried Switzerland
A cheaper and quieter resort
alternative to staying in Gstaad.
1230m; slopes 890–3000m
⛷67 ⬆ 250km
✉ *Interhome*

Schoppernau Austria
A scattered farming community,
in Bregenzerwald, north-west of
Lech.
860m; slopes 860–2060m
⛷8 ⬆ 39km

Schröcken Austria
Bregenzerwald area village close
to the German border.
1260m; slopes 1260–2050m
⛷14 ⬆ 60km

Schruns 163
Pleasant little town at the heart
of the Montafon region.
✉ *Interhome*

Schüttdorf 210
Ordinary dormitory satellite of
Zell am See.

Schwarzach im Pongau
Austria
Riverside village with rail links.
There are limited slopes at
Goldegg; Wagrain (Salzburger
Sportwelt) and Grossarl (Gastein
valley) are also nearby.
600m

Schwaz Austria
Valley town beside the Inn with
a lift into varied terrain shared
with the village of Pill and its
mountain outpost, Hochpillberg.
540m; slopes 540–2030m
⛷6 ⬆ 10km

Schweitzer USA
Excellent small family resort in
the Rockies, near Spokane
(Washington state), but long
journey (from UK) a drawback.
Low altitude but snow-sure.
1215m; slopes 1215–1945m
⛷6 ⬆ 2350 acres
✉ *AmeriCan Ski*

Scopello Italy
Low area close to the Aosta
valley, worth considering for a
day trip in bad weather.
slopes 690–1700m
⛷6 ⬆ 35km

Scuol Switzerland
Year-round spa resort close to
Austria and Italy, with an
impressive range of terrain.
1250m; slopes 1250–2785m
⛷15 ⬆ 80km

Searchmont Resort Canada
Ontario area with modern lift
system and 95% snowmaking.
Fine Lake Superior views.
275m; slopes 275–485m
⛷4 ⬆ 65 acres

Sedrun Switzerland
Charming, unspoiled old village
on the Glacier Express rail route
close to Andermatt, with fine
terrain amid glorious scenery.
1440m; slopes 1150–2850m
⛷12 ⬆ 50km

Seefeld 216
✉ *Crystal, Directski.com,
Inghams, Interhome, Thomson,
Waymark Holidays*

Le Seignus-d'Allos France
Close to La Foux-d'Allos (which
shares large area with Pra-Loup)
and has own little area, too.
1400m; slopes 1400–2425m
⛷13 ⬆ 47km

Seis Italy
German name for Siusi.

Sella Nevea Italy
Limited but developing resort in
a beautiful setting on the
Slovenian border. Summer
glacier nearby.
1140m; slopes 1190–1800m
⛷11 ⬆ 8km
✉ *Sloping Off*

Selva/Sella Ronda 441
✉ *Alpine Answers, Bladon
Lines, Catered Ski Chalets,
Crystal, Esprit Ski, First Choice
Ski, Independent Ski Links,
Inghams, Momentum Ski,
Neilson, Ski Arrangements, Ski
Tracer, Ski Yogi, Thomson,
Total*

Selvino Italy
Closest resort to Bergamo.
960m; slopes 960–1400m
⛷9 ⬆ 20km

Selwyn Snowfields 684
Long-established winter sports
resort set in pretty scenery,
100km/62 miles from Vienna,
towards Graz. Mostly
intermediate terrain.
1000m; slopes 1000–1340m
⛷5 ⬆ 14km

Les Sept-Laux France
Ugly, user-friendly family resort
near Grenoble. Pretty slopes for
all grades.
1350m; slopes 1350–2400m
⛷25 ⬆ 100km
✉ *Lagrange Holidays*

Serfaus 217
✉ *Alpine Tours, Interhome,
Made to Measure Holidays*

Serrada Italy
Very limited area near Trento.
slopes 1250–1605m ⛷5
✉ *Equity Ski*

Serre-Chevalier 347
✉ *Airtours, Alpine Answers,
Bladon Lines, Catered Ski
Chalets, Chalet Group, Club
Med, Crystal, Equity Ski, Erna
Low, First Choice Ski, French
Ski Life, Hannibals,
Independent Ski Links,
Inghams, Interhome, Lagrange
Holidays, Neilson, Rocketski,
Ski Arrangements, Ski
Expectations, Ski France, Ski
Freshtracks, Ski Independence,
Ski Leisure Direction, Ski
Miquel, Ski Supreme, Skitopia,
Skiworld, Sloping Off,
Thomson, Tops Ski Chalets and
Club Hotels*

Sesto Italy
Dolomite village on the road to
Cortina, surrounded by pretty
little areas.
1310m; ⛷31 ⬆ 50km

Sestola Italy
Appennine village a short drive
from Pisa and Florence with its
pistes, some way above, almost
completely equipped with
snowmakers.
900m; slopes 1280–1975m
⛷23 ⬆ 50km

Sestriere 450
✉ *Alpine Answers, Crystal,
Equity Ski, First Choice Ski,
Independent Ski Links,
Inghams, Interhome,
Momentum Ski, Neilson,
Rocketski, Ski Arrangements,
Ski Tracer, Ski Weekend,
Thomson*

Sexten Italy
German name for Sesto.

Shames Mountain Canada
Remote spot inland from coastal
town of Prince Rupert and with
impressive snowfall record. Deep
powder.
670m; slopes 670–1195m
⛷3 ⬆ 183 acres

Shawnee Peak USA
Small area near Bethel and
Sunday River renowned for its
night skiing. Spectacular views.
Mostly groomed cruising.
185m; slopes 185–580m
⛷5 ⬆ 225 acres

Shemshak Iran
Most popular of the three
mountain resorts within easy
reach of Tehran (60km/37 miles).
'Plenty of untracked lines and
bumps; lifts get quite busy,'
says a 2004 reporter.
3600m; slopes 2550–3050m ⛷7

Shiga Kogen Japan
Largest area in Japan, the site of
Nagano's 1998 Olympic skiing
events and including 21
individual resorts.
930m; slopes 1220–2300m
⛷73 ⬆ 130km

Showdown USA
Intermediate area in Montana
cut out of forest north of
Bozeman. 50km/30 miles to the
nearest hotel.
2065m; slopes 2065–2490m
⛷4 ⬆ 640 acres

Sierra-at-Tahoe 540
✉ *Ski The American Dream*

Sierra Nevada 666
✉ *Independent Ski Links,
Thomson*

Sierra Summit USA
Sierra Nevada area accessible
only from the west. 100%
snowmaking.
2160m; slopes 2160–2645m
⛷8 ⬆ 250 acres

Silbertal 163
Low secluded village in the
Montafon area, linked to
Schruns. A good base for
touring numerous areas.

Sils Maria 499
Pretty lakeside village, linked to
the St Moritz Corvatsch slopes
via a lift to Furtschellas.
✉ *Interhome*

Silvaplana 499
Pretty lakeside village near St
Moritz, a short drive from the lift
connections.
✉ *Interhome*

Silver Creek USA
Child-oriented resort close to
Winter Park. Low snowfall record
for Colorado.
2490m; slopes 2490–2795m
⛷5 ⬆ 250 acres

Silver Mountain USA
Northern Idaho area near delightful resort town of Coeur d'Alene. Best for experts, but plenty for intermediates too.
1215m; slopes 1215–1915m
⛟ 6 ⛷ 1500 acres

Silver Star 661
⊠ AmeriCan Ski, Frontier Ski, Made to Measure Holidays, Ski Activity, Ski All America, Ski Independence, Ski Line, Ski Safari, Ski The American Dream, Snowebb

Silverthorne USA
Factory outlet town on main road close to Keystone and Breckenridge. Good budget base for skiing those resorts plus Vail and Beaver Creek.
⊠ AmeriCan Ski

Silverton USA
Expert-only area in southern Colorado that used to be heli-ski country. Served by one lift. Avalanche transceiver, shovel and probe compulsory.
3170m; slopes 3170–3750m; ⛟ 1

Sinaia Romania
Depressed and depressing main-road town with a modest area.
795m; slopes 795–2030m
⛟ 10 ⛷ 20km

Sipapu USA
Great little New Mexico area, with mostly tree-lined runs. Snow unreliable, but 70% snowmaking. Nice day out from Taos when conditions are good.
slopes 2500–2765m
⛟ 4 ⛷ 70 acres

Siusi 441
Village west of the Sella Ronda circuit, since 2003 linked to the Alpe di Siusi area above Ortisei by a long, powerful gondola (as well as by road). Seis is the German version of its name.
⊠ Equity Ski, Rocketski

Siviez 505
A quieter and cheaper base for skiing Verbier's Four Valleys circuit.
⊠ Interhome

Sixt-Fer-a-Cheval 286
Traditional village near Samoëns, at foot of a new run down from the Flaine area. Own little area across the valley, too.
⊠ AmeriCan Ski, Lagrange Holidays, Peak Retreats

Sjusjøen Norway
Cluster of hotels in deep forest close to Lillehammer. Some Alpine facilities but better for cross-country.
885m; slopes 1000–1090m
⛟ 2 ⛷ 2km
⊠ Inntravel, Waymark Holidays

Ski Apache USA
Apache-owned area south of Albuquerque noted for groomed steeps. Panoramic views. Nearest lodging in charming Ruidoso.
2925m; slopes 2925–3505m
⛟ 11 ⛷ 750 acres

Ski Cooper USA
Small area close to historic Old West town of Leadville. Good ski/sightseeing day out from nearby Vail, Beaver Creek and Copper Mountain.
slopes 3200–3565m ⛟ 4

Ski Windham USA
Two hours from New York City and second only to Hunter for weekend crowds. Decent slopes by eastern standards.
485m; slopes 485–940m
⛟ 7 ⛷ 230 acres

Smokovec Slovakia
Spa town with small modern centre near Poprad, with three small areas known collectively as High Tatras. Funicular railway and snowmaking facilities.
1480m; slopes 1000–1500m
⛟ 6 ⛷ 4km

Smugglers' Notch 623
⊠ Ski The American Dream, Virgin Snow

Snowbasin 604
⊠ AmeriCan Ski

Snowbird 602
⊠ AmeriCan Ski, American Ski Classics, Ski All America, Ski Independence, Ski The American Dream, Skiworld, United Vacations

Snowbowl (Arizona) USA
One of America's oldest areas, near Flagstaff, Arizona, atop an extinct volcano and with stunning desert views. Good snowfall record.
2805m; slopes 2805–3505m
⛟ 5 ⛷ 135 acres

Snowbowl (Montana) USA
Montana area renowned for powder, outside lively town of Missoula. Intermediate pistes plus 700 acres of extreme slopes. Grizzly Chute is the ultimate challenge.
1520m; slopes 1520–2315m
⛟ 4 ⛷ 1400 acres

Snowmass 572
⊠ Alpine Answers, AmeriCan Ski, Ski All America, Ski Independence, Ski The American Dream, United Vacations

Snow Park 686

Snow Summit USA
San Bernardino National Forest ski area near Palm Springs. Lovely lake views. 100% snowmaking. High-capacity lift system for weekend crowds.
2135m; slopes 2135–2500m
⛟ 12 ⛷ 230 acres

Snow Valley USA
Area quite near Palm Springs. Fine desert views. High-capacity lift system copes with weekend crowds better than nearby Big Bear.
2040m; slopes 2040–2390m
⛟ 11 ⛷ 230 acres

Solda Italy
The other side of the Stelvio Pass from Bormio. Very long airport transfers.
1905m; slopes 1905–2625m
⛟ 19 ⛷ 25km

Sölden 185
⊠ Neilson, Ski Wild, Thomson

Soldeu 106
⊠ Airtours, Club Pavilion, Crystal, Directski.com, First Choice Ski, Independent Ski Links, Inghams, Lagrange Holidays, Neilson, Panorama Holidays, Ski Wild, Thomson

Solitude 604
⊠ AmeriCan Ski, Ski Independence, Ski The American Dream

Söll 187
⊠ Airtours, Catered Ski Chalets, Crystal, Directski.com, First Choice Ski, Independent Ski Links, Inghams, Neilson, Panorama Holidays, Ski Hillwood, Ski Line, Ski Wild, Thomson

Sommand France
Purpose-built base that shares area with Praz-de-Lys.
1420m; slopes 1200–1800m
⛟ 22 ⛷ 50km

Sonnenkopf Austria
Ski area above Klösterle a few km west of the Arlberg pass – and covered by the Arlberg ski pass.
slopes 1100–2300m
⛟ 10 ⛷ 39km

Sorenberg Switzerland
Popular weekend retreat between Berne and Lucerne, with a high proportion of steep, low runs.
1165m; slopes 1165–2350m
⛟ 18 ⛷ 50km

South Lake Tahoe USA
Tacky base for skiing Heavenly, with cheap lodging, traffic and gambling.

Spindleruv Mlyn Czech Republic
Largest Giant Mountains region resort but with few facilities serving several little low areas.
715m; slopes 750–1300m
⛟ 23 ⛷ 25km

Spital am Pyhrn Austria
Small village near Hinterstoder in Upper Austria, a bus-ride from its limited intermediate slopes at Wurzeralm. From the valley station a 3km/2 mile funicular goes up to a mid-mountain col with several restaurants and nursery slopes. Lifts and runs go off from here in several directions over pleasantly wooded intermediate terrain; the blues are good, so transition from the nursery slopes is not easy. On the flat Teichlboden (1370m/4,500ft) beyond the col

there are cross-country loops. The local lift pass also covers the slopes of Höss and Bärenalm at Hinterstoder, a short drive away.
650m; slopes 810–1870m
⛟ 8 ⛷ 14km

Spittal an der Drau Austria
Historic Carinthian town with a limited area starting a lift-ride above it. A good day trip from Bad Kleinkirchheim or from Slovenia.
555m; slopes 1650–2140m
⛟ 12 ⛷ 27km

Spitzingsee Germany
Beautiful small lake (and village) an hour from Munich.
⛟ 18 ⛷ 25km

Sportgastein 120
Mountain village with some of the more interesting skiing in the Badgastein valley.

Squaw Valley 553
⊠ AmeriCan Ski, American Ski Classics, Lotus Supertravel, Ski Activity, Ski All America, Ski Independence, Ski Safari, Ski The American Dream, United Vacations

Stafal 432
Tiny, isolated village, with good access to the Monterosa Ski area.

St Andrä im Lungau Austria
Valley-junction village ideally placed for one of the longest, most snow-sure cross-country networks in Europe. Close to the Tauern pass and to St Michael.
1045m

St Anton 193
⊠ Airtours, Albus Travel, Alpine Answers, Alpine Events, Alpine Weekends, Bladon Lines, Catered Ski Chalets, Chalet World Ski, Corporate Ski Company, Crystal, Directski.com, Elegant Resorts, Esprit Ski, First Choice Ski, Flexiski, Friendship Travel, Independent Ski Links, Inghams, Kaluma Ski, Lotus Supertravel, Made to Measure Holidays, Mark Warner, Momentum Ski, Neilson, Simply Ski, Ski Activity, Ski Expectations, Ski Freshtracks, Ski Line, Ski Solutions, Ski St Anton, Ski Tracer, Ski Wild, Ski-Val, Skiworld, Snoworks, Snowscape, Solo's, St Anton Ski Company, Thomson, Total, White Roc

St Cergue Switzerland
Limited resort in the Jura mountains, less than an hour from Geneva and good for families with young children.
1045m; slopes 1045–1700m
⛟ 9 ⛷ 20km

St Christoph 193
Small village on Arlberg pass above St Anton.
⊠ Alpine Answers, Elegant Resorts, Flexiski, Made to Measure Holidays, Powder Byrne

St-Colomban-des-Villards 360
Small resort in next side valley
to La Toussuire.

Steamboat 574
✉ Alpine Answers, American
Ski Classics, Catered Ski
Chalets, Crystal, Erna Low,
Independent Ski Links, Lotus
Supertravel, Made to Measure
Holidays, Ski Activity, Ski All
America, Ski Independence, Ski
Line, Ski Safari, Ski The
American Dream, Ski Tracer,
Skiworld, Thomson, United
Vacations, Virgin Snow

Ste-Foy-Tarentaise 354
✉ Alpine Answers, Alpine
Weekends, Chalet Group, Chalet
Ltd, Chalet Number One,
Crystal, Erna Low, Independent
Ski Links, Mountain Tracks,
Peak Leisure, Premiere Neige,
Ski Arrangements, Ski
Independence, Ski Leisure
Direction, Ski Weekend,
Weekends in Val d'Isère

Steinach Austria
Pleasant village in picturesque
surroundings, just off the
autobahn near the Brenner Pass.
An easy outing from Innsbruck.
1050m; slopes 1050–2205m
⛷6 🚡 15km

Stevens Pass USA
A day trip from Seattle, and
accommodation 60km/37 miles
away in Bavarian-style town
Leavenworth. Low snowfall and
no snowmakers. Mostly
intermediate slopes,
1235m; slopes 1235–1785m
⛷14 🚡 1125 acres

St-François-Longchamp 390
Sunny, gentle slopes. Linked to
Valmorel.
✉ Erna Low, French Ski Life,
Lagrange Holidays, Peak
Retreats, Ski Independence, Ski
Leisure Direction

St Gallenkirch 163
Smaller, less attractive village
than Gaschurn, with which it
shares a sizeable intermediate
area in the Montafon valley.

St-Gervais 296
Small town sharing its ski area
with Megève and Chamonix.
✉ AmeriCan Ski, Erna Low,
French Ski Life, Interhome,
Lagrange Holidays, Peak
Retreats, Ski France, Ski Leisure
Direction, Snowcoach

St Jakob in Defereggen
Austria
Unspoiled traditional village in a
pretty, sunny valley close to
Lienz and Heiligenblut, and with
a good proportion of high-
altitude slopes.
1400m; slopes 1400–2520m
⛷9 🚡 34km

St Jakob in Haus Austria
Snowy village with its own
slopes. Fieberbrunn, Waidring
and St Johann are nearby.
855m; slopes 855–1500m
⛷8 🚡 16km

St-Jean-d'Arves 360
Small traditional village south of
the Maurienne valley that is now
linked with the slopes of St-
Sorlin-d'Arves, La Toussuire and
Le Corbier, to form Les Sybelles.
✉ AmeriCan Ski, First Choice
Ski, French Ski Life, Peak
Retreats, Ski France, Ski
Independence, Ski Leisure
Direction, Thomson

St Jean d'Aulps France
Small village in Portes du Soleil
area, not part of main circuit but
with its own interesting slopes
consisting of two small areas –
Domaine Chèvrerie and Domaine
Grande Terche.

St-Jean-de-Sixt 261
Traditional hamlet, a cheap base
for La Clusaz and Le Grand-
Bornand (3km/2 miles to both).
✉ Last Resort

St-Jean-Montclar France
Small village at the foot of
thickly forested slopes. Good
day out from nearby Pra-Loup.
1300m; slopes 1300–2500m
⛷18 🚡 50km
✉ Lagrange Holidays

St Johann im Pongau 215
Bustling, lively town with its
own small area. An extensive
three-valley lift network starts
4km/2 miles away at Alpendorf,
linking via Wagrain to Flachau –
all part of the Salzburger
Sportwelt ski pass area.

St Johann in Tirol 202
✉ Crystal, Directski.com, Ski
Line, Ski Wild, Snowscape,
Thomson

St Lary Espiaube 398

St-Lary-Soulan 398
✉ French Ski Life, Lagrange
Holidays, Ski Leisure Direction

St Leonhard in Pitztal Austria
Village beneath a fine glacier in
the Oetz area, accessed by
underground funicular.
1250m; slopes 1735–3440m
⛷12 🚡 40km

St Luc Switzerland
Quiet, unspoiled rustic village in
the Val d'Anniviers on the south
side of the Rhône valley, with
plenty of high, easy slopes
(shared with Chandolin) served
almost entirely by drags. Most
of the slopes are above the
nursery area at Tignousa
(2180m/7,150ft), reached by
funicular – also the site of an
astronomical observatory. Valley
pass also covers Zinal, Grimentz
and Vercorin – 220km/137 miles
of runs in total.
1650m; slopes 1660–3025m
⛷16 🚡 75km
✉ Inntravel

St Margarethen Austria
Valley village near Styria/
Carinthia border, sharing slopes
with higher Katschberg.
1065m; slopes 1075–2210m
⛷14 🚡 70km

St Martin bei Lofer Austria
Traditional cross-country village
in a lovely setting beneath the
impressive Loferer Steinberge
massif. Alpine slopes at Lofer.
635m

St-Martin-de-Belleville 357
✉ Alpine Club, Chalet Group,
Chalets de St Martin, Crystal,
Erna Low, First Choice Ski,
Independent Ski Links, Kaluma
Ski, Ski Independence, Ski
Leisure Direction, Skitopia,
Thomson

St Martin in Tennengebirge
Austria
Highest village in the Dachstein-
West region near Salzburg. It
has limited slopes of its own but
nearby Annaberg has an
interesting area.
1000m; slopes 1000–1350m
⛷5 🚡 4km

St-Maurice-sur-Moselle France
One of several areas near
Strasbourg. No snowmakers.
550m; slopes 900–1250m
⛷8 🚡 24km

St Michael im Lungau Austria
Quiet, unspoiled village in the
Tauern pass snowpocket with an
uncrowded but disjointed
intermediate area. Close to
Obertauern and Wagrain.
1075m; slopes 1075–2360m
⛷25 🚡 105km
✉ Alpine Tours, Equity Ski,
Rocketski

St Moritz 499
✉ Alpine Answers, Alpine
Events, Alpine Weekends, Club
Med, Corporate Ski Company,
Crystal, CV Travel, Elegant
Resorts, Flexiski, Independent
Ski Links, Inghams, Interhome,
Jeffersons, Kuoni, Made to
Measure Holidays, Momentum
Ski, Oxford Ski Company,
Powder Byrne, Ski Line, Ski
Solutions, Ski Weekend, Swiss
Travel Service, Switzerland
Travel Centre, White Heat
Skiing

St-Nicolas-de-Véroce 296
Small hamlet on the northern
fringes of the Megève network.

St-Nicolas-la-Chapelle France
Small village close to larger
Flumet, in the Val d'Arly.
1000m; slopes 1000–1600m
⛷10 🚡 40km

St-Nizier-du-Moucherotte
France
Unspoiled, inexpensive resort
just west of Grenoble with no
lifts of its own. Villard-de-Lans is
the main resort.

Stoneham 662
✉ Frontier Ski, Ski All America,
Ski Safari, Ski The American
Dream

Stoos Switzerland
Small, unspoiled village an hour
from Zürich. Overcrowded at
weekends. Magnificent views of
Lake Lucerne.
1300m; slopes 570–1920m ⛷7

Storlien Sweden
Small family resort amid
magnificent wilderness scenery,
One hour from Trondheim, 30
minutes from Åre.
600m; slopes 600–790m
⛷7 🚡 15km

Stowe 621
✉ American Ski Classics,
Crystal, Erna Low, Ski All
America, Ski Arrangements, Ski
Independence, Ski Line, Ski
Safari, Ski The American
Dream, Trailfinders, United
Vacations, Virgin Snow

St-Pierre-de-Chartreuse
France
Locals' weekend place near
Grenoble. Unreliable snow.
900m; slopes 900–1800m
⛷14 🚡 35km

Stratton 614

Strobl Austria
Close to St Wolfgang in a
beautiful lakeside setting. There
are slopes at nearby St Gilgen
and Postalm.
545m; slopes 545–1510m
⛷8 🚡 12km

St-Sorlin-d'Arves 360
✉ AmeriCan Ski, Crystal, First
Choice Ski, French Ski Life,
Lagrange Holidays, Peak
Retreats, Ski France, Ski
Independence, Ski Leisure
Direction, Thomson

St Stephan Switzerland
Unspoiled old farming village at
the foot of the largest sector of
slopes in the area around
Gstaad.
995m; slopes 950–2155m
⛷69 🚡 250km

Stuben 150
Small, unspoiled village linked
to St Anton.
✉ Alpine Answers

St Veit im Pongau Austria
Spa resort with limited slopes at
Goldegg; Wagrain (Salzburger
Sportwelt) and Grossarl (Gastein
valley) are nearby.
765m

St-Veran France
Said to be the highest 'real'
village in Europe, and full of
charm. Close to Serre-Chevalier
and the Milky Way. Snow-
reliable cross-country skiing.
2040m; slopes 2040–2800m
⛷15 🚡 30km

St Wolfgang Austria
Charming lakeside resort near
Salzburg, some way from any
slopes, best for a relaxing winter
holiday with one or two days on
the slopes.
540m; slopes 665–1350m
⛷9 🚡 17km
✉ Crystal, First Choice Ski,
Inghams, Thomson

Sugarbowl 540

Sugarbush 614
✉ Ski Arrangements

Sugarloaf   **614**
✉ *Equity Ski*

Summit at Snoqualmie   USA
Four areas – Summit East, Summit Central, Summit West and Alpental – with interlinked lifts. Damp weather and wet snow are major drawbacks.
slopes 915–1645m
⛷ 24 ⛷ 2000 acres

Sun Alpina   Japan
Collective name for three ski areas four hours away from Tokyo. ⛷ 20

Sundance   **590**
✉ *AmeriCan Ski, Ski All America, Ski Independence, Ski Safari, Ski The American Dream*

Sunday River   **623**
✉ *American Ski Classics, Crystal, Equity Ski, Ski Independence, Ski Safari, Ski The American Dream, Virgin Snow*

Sunlight Mountain Resort USA
Quiet area near Glenwood Springs. Varied terrain with fine glades and terrain-park. Works well as a half-day ski half-day sightseeing trip from Aspen or Vail.
2405m; slopes 2405–3015m
⛷ 4 ⛷ 460 acres

Sun Peaks   **650**
✉ *AmeriCan Ski, Frontier Ski, Made to Measure Holidays, Ski Activity, Ski All America, Ski Freshtracks, Ski Independence, Ski Line, Ski Safari, Ski The American Dream, Skiworld*

Sunrise Park   USA
Arizona's largest area, operated by Apaches. Slopes are spread over three mountains; best for novices and leisurely intermediates.
2805m; slopes 2805–3500m
⛷ 12 ⛷ 800 acres

Sunshine Village   **628**
One-hotel mountain station with Banff's second-largest ski area on its doorstep.
✉ *Ski The American Dream*

Sun Valley   **613**
✉ *AmeriCan Ski, Ski Activity, Ski All America, Ski Independence, Ski Safari*

Suomu   Finland
A lodge (no village) right on the Arctic Circle with a few slopes but mostly a ski-touring place.
140m; slopes 140–410m ⛷ 3
✉ *Canterbury Travel*

Superbagnères   France
Little more than a particularly French-dominated Club Med; best for a low-cost, low-effort family trip to the Pyrenees. Said to have good off-piste if the snow is good.
1880m; slopes 1440–2260m
⛷ 16 ⛷ 35km
✉ *Lagrange Holidays*

Super-Besse   France
Purpose-built resort amid spectacular extinct-volcano scenery. Shares area with Mont-Dore. Limited village.
1350m; slopes 1300–1850m
⛷ 22 ⛷ 45km
✉ *Lagrange Holidays*

Superdévoluy   France
Purpose-built but friendly family resort, consisting of a few huge apartment blocks, a few km north-west of Gap, with a sizeable intermediate area shared with La Joue-du-Loup.
1500m; slopes 1500–2510m
⛷ 29 ⛷ 100km
✉ *Erna Low, Lagrange Holidays*

Supermolina   Spain
Dreary, purpose-built satellite of Pyrenean resort of La Molina, with a reasonable sized area of its own and linked to the slopes of Masella to form an area called Alp 2500.
1700m; slopes 1600–2535m
⛷ 29 ⛷ 100km

Les Sybelles   **360**

Tahko   Finland
Largest resort in southern Finland. Plenty of intermediate slopes in an attractive, wooded, frozen-lake setting. ⛷ 9

Tahoe City   USA
Small lakeside accommodation base for visiting nearby Alpine Meadows and Squaw Valley.

Talisman Mountain Resort Canada
One of the best areas in the Toronto region, but with a relatively low lift capacity. 100% snowmaking.
235m; slopes 235–420m ⛷ 8

Tamarack   **650**

Tamsweg   Austria
Large cross-country village with rail links in snowy region close to Tauern Pass and St Michael.
1025m

La Tania   **365**
✉ *Airtours, Alpine Action, Alpine Answers, Catered Ski Chalets, Chalet Group, Chalet World Ski, Club Pavilion, Crystal, Erna Low, First Choice Ski, French Freedom Holidays, French Ski Life, Hucksters, Independent Ski Links, Lagrange Holidays, Le Ski, MasterSki, Mountain Tracks, Neilson, Silver Ski, Ski Activity, Ski Amis, Ski Arrangements, Ski Beat, Ski Deep, Ski France, Ski Hame, Ski Independence, Ski Leisure Direction, Ski Line, Ski Power, Ski Solutions, Ski Tracer, Ski Weekends, Snowline, Thomson*

Taos   **613**
✉ *AmeriCan Ski, Ski Activity, Ski Independence, Ski The American Dream*

Tärnaby-Hemavan   Sweden
Twin resorts in north Sweden, with their own airport.
slopes 465–1135m
⛷ 13 ⛷ 44km

El Tarter   **106**
Relatively quiet, convenient alternative to Soldeu, with which it shares its slopes.
✉ *Airtours, Club Pavilion, First Choice Ski, Panorama Holidays*

Tarvisio   Italy
Interesting, animated old town bordering Austria and Slovenia. A major cross-country base with fairly limited Alpine slopes.
750m; slopes 750–1860m
⛷ 12 ⛷ 15km
✉ *Sloping Off*

Täsch   **523**
The final base accessible by road on the way to car-free Zermatt – you take the train the rest of the way.
✉ *Interhome*

Tauplitz   Austria
Traditional village at the foot of an interestingly varied area north of Schladming.
900m; slopes 900–2000m
⛷ 19 ⛷ 40km

Telluride   **576**
✉ *Alpine Answers, AmeriCan Ski, American Ski Classics, Crystal, Lotus Supertravel, Ski All America, Ski Independence, Ski Safari, Ski The American Dream, Skiworld, United Vacations*

Temù   Italy
Sheltered hamlet near Passo Tonale. Worth a visit in bad weather.
1155m; slopes 1155–1955m
⛷ 4 ⛷ 5km

Tengendai   Japan
Tiny area three hours by train and bus from Tokyo. One of Japan's best snow records, including occasional powder. ⛷ 5

Termignon   France
Traditional rustic village with good slopes of its own. A good base for touring Maurienne valley resorts such as Valloire and Val-Cenis.
1300m; slopes 1300–2500m
⛷ 6 ⛷ 35km
✉ *Erna Low, Lagrange Holidays*

Terminillo   Italy
Purpose-built resort 100km/62 miles from Rome with a worthwhile area when its lower runs have snow cover.
1500m; slopes 1500–2210m
⛷ 15 ⛷ 40km

Thollon-les-Mémises   France
Attractive base for a relaxed holiday. Own little area and close to Portes du Soleil.
1000m; slopes 1000–2000m
⛷ 19 ⛷ 50km
✉ *Lagrange Holidays*

Thredbo   **684**

La Thuile   **452**
✉ *Alpine Answers, Crystal, First Choice Ski, Independent Ski Links, Inghams, Interski, Neilson, Ski Arrangements, Thomson*

Thyon 2000   **505**
Extremely limited ski-from-the-door mid-mountain resort above Veysonnaz in the Verbier ski area.

Tignes   **369**
✉ *Airtours, Alpine Answers, Alpine Events, Catered Ski Chalets, Chalet Group, Chalet World Ski, Club Med, Corporate Ski Company, Crystal, Directski.com, Erna Low, Esprit Ski, First Choice Ski, French Ski Life, Hucksters, Independent Ski Links, Inghams, Inspired to Ski, Interhome, Lagrange Holidays, Made to Measure Holidays, Mark Warner, MasterSki, Neilson, Ski Activity, Ski Amis, Ski Arrangements, Ski Expectations, Ski France, Ski Freshtracks, Ski Independence, Ski Leisure Direction, Ski Line, Ski Olympic, Ski Solutions, Ski Supreme, Ski Tracer, Ski Weekend, Ski-Val, Skitopia, Skiworld, Snoworks, Snowstar Holidays, Thomson, Total, White Roc*

Timberline (Palmer Snowfield)   USA
East of Portland, Oregon, and the only lift-served summer skiing in the US: winter snow is maintained by spreading vast amounts of salt to harden it.
slopes 1830–2600m
⛷ 6 ⛷ 2500 acres

Toblach   Italy
German name for Dobbiaco.

Togari   Japan
One of several areas close to the 1998 Olympic site Nagano, 2.5 hours from Tokyo. ⛷ 10

Torgnon   Italy
Small village off the road up to Cervinia, good for bad-weather days. Some good cross-country loops.
1500m; slopes 1500–1965m
⛷ 7 ⛷ 6km

Torgon   Switzerland
Old village in a pretty wooded setting, with a connection to the Portes du Soleil. 'Appalling lifts,' says a recent reporter.
1150m; slopes 975–2275m
⛷ 219 ⛷ 650km
✉ *Interhome*

Le Tour   **246**
Charming, unspoiled hamlet at the head of the Chamonix valley.

La Toussuire   **360**
✉ *Equity Ski, Erna Low, French Ski Life, Interhome, Lagrange Holidays*

Vars 340
Large, convenient purpose-built resort linked to Risoul.
⊠ *Catered Ski Chalets, Crystal, Erna Low, Interhome, Lagrange Holidays, Ski Supreme, Tops Ski Chalets and Club Hotels*

Vasilitsa Greece
Resort in northern Greece, in the Pindos range, offering 'very good intermediate skiing'. according to reports.
1750m ⟂ 2

Vaujany 224
Tiny, rustic village with lift accessing the heart of the Alpe-d'Huez ski area.
⊠ *AmeriCan Ski, Erna Low, Lagrange Holidays, Peak Retreats, Ski Independence, Ski Leisure Direction, Ski Peak*

Vegas Resort USA
Area formerly known as Lee Canyon, cut from forest only 50 minutes' drive from Las Vegas. Height and snowmaking gives fairly reliable snow. Night skiing.
2590m; slopes 2590–2840m
⟂ 3 ⟂ 200 acres

Vemdalen 675
⊠ *Neilson*

Vemdalsskalet 675

Venosc France
Captivating tiny village of cobbled streets, ancient church and craft shops.
⊠ *Peak Retreats*

Vent Austria
High, remote Oztal village known mainly as a touring base, with just enough lift-served skiing to warrant a day trip from nearby Obergurgl.
1900m; slopes 1900–2680m
⟂ 4 ⟂ 15km

Ventron France
Small village near La Bresse in the northerly Vosges mountains near Strasbourg, with more ski de fond than downhill terrain.
630m; slopes 900–1110m
⟂ 8 ⟂ 15km

Verbier 505
⊠ *Alpine Answers, Alpine Events, Alpine Weekends, Bladon Lines, Catered Ski Chalets, Chalet World Ski, Corporate Ski Company, Crystal, Descent International, Elegant Resorts, Erna Low, First Choice Ski, Flexiski, Independent Ski Links, Inghams, Interhome, Jeffersons, Kaluma Ski, Lotus Supertravel, Made to Measure Holidays, Momentum Ski, Mountain Beds, Mountain Tracks, Oxford Ski Company, Peak Ski, Simply Ski, Ski Activity, Ski Expectations, Ski Freshtracks, Ski Independence, Ski Line, Ski Solutions, Ski Tracer, Ski Verbier, Ski Weekend, Ski with Julia, Skiworld, Swiss Travel Service, Thomson, Total, White Roc*

Vercorin Switzerland
Cluster of picture-postcard chalets on a shelf overlooking the Valais, reached by roundabout road or cable-car from near Chalais. Mix of wooded and open intermediate slopes served by a gondola and drags. Valley pass also covers Zinal, Grimentz and St Luc/Chandolin – 220km/137 miles of runs in total. The village has a natural ice rink.
1330m; slopes 1330–2400m
⟂ 9 ⟂ 35km

Verditz Austria
One of several small, mostly mountain-top areas overlooking the town of Villach.
675m; slopes 675–2165m
⟂ 5 ⟂ 17km

Vex Switzerland
Major village in unspoiled, attractive setting south of Sion. Verbier slopes accessed nearby at Mayens-de-l'Ours.
900m

Veysonnaz 505
Little, old village within Verbier's Four Valleys network.

Vic-sur-Cère France
Charming village with fine architecture, beneath Super-Lioran ski area. Beautiful extinct-volcano scenery.
680m; slopes 1250–1850m
⟂ 24 ⟂ 60km
⊠ *Lagrange Holidays*

Viehhofen Austria
Cheaper place to stay when visiting Saalbach. It is 3km/2 miles from the Schönleiten gondola, and there is a run back to the village from the Asitz section.
860m ⟂ 1

Vigo di Fassa Italy
Best base for the Fassa valley, with Sella Ronda access via nearby Campitello.
1430m; slopes 1465–2060m
⟂ 8 ⟂ 25km

La Villa 441
Quiet Sella Ronda village in pretty setting, surrounded by mostly very easy skiing.

Villach-Dobratsch Austria
One of several small, mostly mountain-top areas overlooking the town of Villach.
900m; slopes 980–2165m
⟂ 8 ⟂ 15km
⊠ *Equity Ski*

Villar-d'Arêne France
Tiny area on main road between La Grave and Serre-Chevalier. Empty, immaculately groomed, short easy runs, plus a couple of hotels.
1650m

Villard-de-Lans France
Unspoiled, lively, traditional village west of Grenoble. Snow-sure, thanks to snowmaking.
1050m; slopes 1160–2170m
⟂ 29 ⟂ 130km
⊠ *AmeriCan Ski, Lagrange Holidays*

Villard-Reculas 224
Rustic village on periphery of Alpe-d'Huez ski area, with few local amenities.

Villaroger 233
Rustic hamlet with direct links up to Arc 2000 and excellent runs back down.

Villars 515
⊠ *Alpine Events, Club Med, Corporate Ski Company, Crystal, Erna Low, Inghams, Interhome, Kuoni, Lagrange Holidays, Made to Measure Holidays, Momentum Ski, Ski Independence, Ski Line, Ski Weekend, Swiss Travel Service, Switzerland Travel Centre, Thomson*

Vipiteno Italy
Bargain-shopping town close to Brenner Pass.
960m; slopes 960–2100m
⟂ 12 ⟂ 25km

Virgen Austria
Traditional village in a beautiful valley south of the Felbertauern tunnel. Slopes at Matrei.
1200m

Vitosha Bulgaria
A few widely scattered dour hotels (there's no resort) and a very limited area of slopes. The resort is close to Sofia, allowing short transfers and easy excursions, but leading to crowds at weekends. The slopes are north-facing and have a decent snow record.
1810m; slopes 1515–2290m
⟂ 8 ⟂ 29km

Vogel 682

Vorderlanersbach 126
Small, satellite village of pretty Lanersbach, with access to Mayrhofen ski area.

Voss 671
⊠ *Crystal, Inghams*

Vuokatti Finland
Small mountain in a remarkable setting, surrounded on three sides by lots of little lakes. Good activity base. ⟂ 8

Wagrain 217

Waidring Austria
Quiet valley village north of Kitzbühel, with nursery slopes on the doorstep and a powerful gondola (with big car parks) on the outskirts going up to Steinplatte – an area of mainly gentle open slopes which is also accessible from Germany. Impressive lift system with two six-packs and four quads, but still prone to weekend queues. Slopes face north, and there is extensive snowmaking.
780m; slopes 1230–1860m
⟂ 8 ⟂ 25km
⊠ *Thomson*

Waiorau Snow Farm 686

Wald im Pinzgau Austria
Cross-country village surrounded by Alpine areas – Gerlos, Krimml and Neukirchen – and with Pass Thurn also nearby.
885m
⟂ 55 ⟂ 155km

Wanaka 686
Quiet, diffuse village in beautiful lakeside mountain setting. Two ski areas, each 30 mins away.

Waterville Valley 614

Weinebene Austria
One of many gentle little areas in Austria's easternmost ski region near the Slovenian border. No major resorts in the vicinity.
1560m; slopes 1560–1835m
⟂ 5 ⟂ 12km

Weissbach bei Lofer Austria
Traditional resort between Lofer and Saalfelden. It has no slopes of its own, but it's well placed for touring the Tirol. Kitzbühel, Saalbach, St Johann and Zell am See are nearby.
665m

Weissensee Naggeralm Austria
Little area in eastern Austria and the location of Europe's largest frozen lake, which is used for all kinds of ice sports, including ice-golf.
930m; slopes 930–1400m
⟂ 5 ⟂ 6km

Weisspriach Austria
Hamlet on snowy pass near Obertauern that shares its area with Mauterndorf and St Michael.
1115m; slopes 1115–2050m
⟂ 5 ⟂ 30km

Wengen 518
⊠ *Alpine Events, Club Med, Crystal, Independent Ski Links, Inghams, Kuoni, Made to Measure Holidays, Re-lax Holidays, Ski Freshtracks, Ski Line, Ski Solutions, Swiss Travel Service, Switzerland Travel Centre, Thomson*

MONEY BACK VOUCHER – PART 1

To be sent to
SKI SOLUTIONS, 84 Pembroke Road, London W8 6NX
along with your signed booking form

Name

Address

E-mail address

Daytime phone number

Tour operator (if applicable)

Departure date   Number in party

I have bought a copy of Where to Ski and Snowboard 2006 and claim a refund of the £16.99 cover price. I understand this amount will be deducted from the cost of the holiday I am booking through Ski Solutions. Offer valid for bookings for 2005/06 and 2006/07 seasons holidays made before 30 April 2006.

Signature   Date

MONEY BACK VOUCHER – PART 2

WHERE *to* SKI
AND Snowboard 2006

To be sent to
WHERE TO SKI AND SNOWBOARD,
The Old Forge, Norton St Philip, Bath BA2 7LW

Name

Address

E-mail address

Daytime phone number

Resort(s) to be visited

Departure date   Number in party

I have booked a ski holiday through Ski Solutions and claimed a refund of the £16.99 cover price of Where to Ski and Snowboard 2006.

Signature   Date

Have you booked any other
holiday through Ski Solutions
in the last two seasons?   Yes   No